The
ALLYN & BACON
Handbook
Fourth Edition

▼

LEONARD J. ROSEN
Harvard University, Graduate School of Education

LAURENCE BEHRENS
University of California, Santa Barbara

Allyn & Bacon
Boston   London   Toronto   Sydney   Tokyo   Singapore

▲

Vice President, Humanities: Joseph Opiela
Developmental Editor: Allen Workman
Editorial Assistant: Mary Varney
Executive Marketing Manager: Lisa Kimball
Sr. Editorial Production Administrator: Susan McIntyre
Editorial Production Service: Kathy Smith
Interior Text Designer: Darci Mehall, Aureo Design
Composition Buyer: Linda Cox
Manufacturing Buyer: Megan Cochran
Cover Administrator: Linda Knowles
Electronic Composition: Omegatype Typography, Inc.

Allyn & Bacon
A Pearson Education Company
160 Gould Street
Needham Heights, MA 02494

Internet: www.abacon.com

Between the time web site information is gathered and published, some sites may have closed. Also, the transcription of URLs can result in typographical errors. The publisher would appreciate notification where these occur so that they can be corrected in subsequent editions.

Library of Congress Cataloging-in-Publication Data

Rosen, Leonard J.
        The Allyn & Bacon handbook / Leonard J. Rosen ; Laurence
Behrens. — 4th ed.
        p.   cm.
    ISBN 0-205-29856-7
    1. English language—Rhetoric Handbooks, manuals, etc.   2. English
language—Grammar Handbooks, manuals, etc.   3. Report writing
Handbooks, manuals, etc.   I. Behrens, Laurence.   II. Title.
    PE1408.R677   1999
    808'.042—dc21   99-39238
                                                                          CIP

Printed in the United States of America
10 9 8 7 6 5 4 3 2 1   03 02 01 00 99

Credits appear on page 815, which should be considered an extension of the copyright page.

In Memoriam

E.R.R.

The Allyn & Bacon Handbook— A Reference You'll Never Outgrow

As someone who's been out of college and working in marketing for several years, I don't find it easy to write an introduction for a book about grammar, mechanics, and other such imposing topics. Imagine the pressure of knowing your writing will precede 800 some pages of *do*s and *don't*s about writing—especially when you haven't taken an English class since freshman year.

On the other hand, I'm fortunate to have next to me on the couch a comprehensive, easy-to-understand handbook about writing on any subject, for any purpose and in any situation. In fact, it's the handbook you're holding right now.

Whether you're a college freshman or the president of a large corporation, writing is a skill you will use almost every day of your life. You'll be assigned essays in your freshman composition course. You'll be required to write a thesis to complete your graduate study in psychology. Your boss may ask you to write a marketing proposal for a prospective client. Your twelve-year-old son will ask for your help on his research paper about insects of the rainforest.

The Allyn & Bacon Handbook

It's a grammar reference.

It's a reference on the writing process.

It's a reference on documentation.

It's a reference for all of your classes.

It's a reference for business writing.

Sources such as an encyclopedia or the Internet will provide you with the facts, and a dictionary will give you the words and their definitions. But where do you look for help on putting your thoughts together? On how to write sentences that effectively communicate your ideas? On the right way to construct paragraphs that are clear and concise, and that have an impact on the reader?

Just as you need a dictionary and reference books as part of your permanent library, you also need a handbook. It's something to which you'll refer when you have a question about when to use a semicolon or how to document a source—you know, those pesky questions that you won't find answered in a dictionary.

The more you write, the more you'll learn, and your writing situations will always be changing. *The Allyn & Bacon Handbook* is designed for writers at all levels, so you'll never outgrow it.

How is *The Allyn & Bacon Handbook* specifically geared for use beyond your freshman composition course?

It's a grammar reference. There will be times when you'll want to make sure you're not splicing your commas or putting a quotation mark in the wrong place. Perhaps you can't remember when to use *lay* rather than *lie*. Through features such as "Spotlight on Common Errors," you'll be able to find answers to your questions on grammar and usage both quickly and easily. If you're a nonnative speaker, you'll find Part XII, the *ESL Reference Guide*, particularly useful.

It's a reference on the writing process. Having problems narrowing your topic for your ten-page sociology paper? Can't come up with an appropriate thesis sentence? Refresh your memory by reading Chapters 3 and 4 in Part II, *Writing as a Process*.

It's a reference on documentation. You'll probably have to write several research papers during your college career. Part IX, *Writing the Research Paper*, will help you whether you're taking notes from a book or gathering information on the World Wide Web. Most importantly, you'll have a handy reference that will remind you how to document a journal, a book with two authors, and even a movie or a CD-ROM.

It's a reference for all of your classes. Throughout the text, "Across the Curriculum" boxes will show you writing strategies for a variety of courses in the sciences, social sciences, and humanities. Turn also to Part X, *Writing and Reading in the Disciplines*, for more detailed, discipline-specific information.

It's a reference for business writing. How many résumés do you think get tossed because they are poorly written? Plenty! Before you send out that application, read Chapter 43, *Writing in a Business Environment*, to make sure your résumé ends up in the "interview" pile and not in the trash. Refer to this section throughout your career for reminders on how to write specific types of letters and memos, and to make sure your proposals and reports are on target, as well as error-free.

Take a look at the next two pages and get a feel for the organization of *The Allyn & Bacon Handbook*. It's inherently simple to use, with several ways to find what you need to know. Think of some questions and flip through to find the answers. Once you're familiar with the *The Allyn & Bacon Handbook*, you'll want to hang on to it beyond Freshman Composition. It's more than just a college handbook—it's a reference you'll never outgrow.

Lisa Linard
Webmaster, Allyn & Bacon

■ TO SPOT-CHECK FOR COMMON ERRORS

■ **Check the back endpaper chart.** The nine sections in this chart cover over 90 percent of the most common sentence and punctuation errors you are likely to make. Look in these sections for sentence patterns and word forms close to what you have written. If any of the examples or explanations lead you to suspect an error in your work, follow the references to one of the text chapters.

SPOTLIGHT ON COMMON ERRORS

I. FORMS OF NOUNS AND PRONOUNS See the SPOTLIGHT (page 184), Chapter 8.

Apostrophes can show possession or contraction. Never use an apostrophe with a possessive pronoun.

Faulty Forms	*Revised*
The scarf is *Chris*. It is *her's*.	The scarf is *Chris's*. It is *hers*.
Give the dog *it's* collar.	Give the dog *its* collar.
Its a difficult thing.	*It's* [it is] a difficult thing.

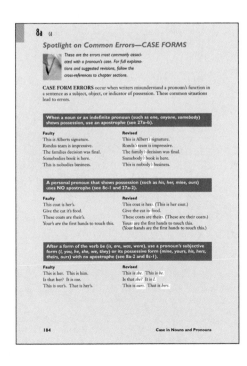

■ **Go to the orange-tinted "spotlight" summary page that matches your situation.** Colored "spotlight" pages in nine chapters give basic recognition patterns and sentences that fit common error situations.

■ **Narrow the search. Find a sentence or situation** that more closely resembles a sentence you have written. *Note* the revision suggested. Do you suspect a possible error? If so, *note* the reference to the chapter section where this revision is explained.

■ **Go to the Handbook section; find a usage guideline and example** that describes the possible error in your work. Challenge your sentence: Does it meet the Handbook's usage guideline? Make a decision about revising your sentence.

■ TO FIND KEY TERMS AND TOPICS

■ Use these information locators:

Front endpapers: The compact contents chart provides an overview of the section and page numbers of the major topics.

Main contents: This detailed listing shows sections and pages for all topics and usage guidelines.

Index: This alphabetical listing shows the page numbers of every key term, word, or topic.

Revision symbols—inside back endpaper: This guide to common instructor markings will help locate discussions of revision topics.

Useful checklists, summaries, and boxes—inside front endpaper: Locates the special panels that provide rapid checklists of basic procedures.

"Spotlight on Common Errors": See page vii.

■ To narrow the search, look for these features on each page:

Tab shows the section-number combination for every topic. A *symbol* next to the tab shows typical instructor markings used to call attention to the topic.

Section number gives chapter and section letter accompanying the *heading* that states or identifies a usage guideline.

Subsection number identifies subtopics.

Explanations describe how or why processes or usage guidelines operate. *Cross-references* lead to related background or definitions found elsewhere in the Handbook. *Bold type* identifies key terms being defined on location or in a cross-reference.

Revision examples are labeled to identify problems and the best revisions. In the nine chapters devoted to the most common errors, additional examples appear beneath the headings as an aid to spotting errors.

Boxed checklists, summaries or "critical decisions" boxes are in shaded panels.

Footer briefly identifies chapter section topics.

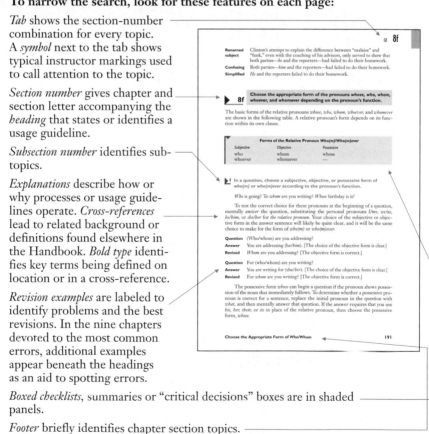

Contents

Preface to the Instructor

Welcome to the Fourth Edition

In its first three editions, *The Allyn & Bacon Handbook* was unique in linking for students the skills of critical thinking, reading, and writing—in the composition classroom and throughout the curriculum. The success of this approach has encouraged us to build further on what has proved most useful. We have continued to strengthen the book's signature features—critical thinking and writing across the curriculum—by adding an extensive section on evaluating Web-based sources and over twenty new panel features to enhance the well-received "Across the Curriculum" and "Critical Decisions" boxes of the third edition. Students will find a new chapter devoted to Internet-based research as well as the latest MLA guidelines for citing electronic sources. Chapter 34 ("Using Electronic Sources") provides the following important information:

- a catalog of resources available on the Internet,
- strategies for formulating good queries,
- strategies for conducting *multiple* searches using different (specialized) search engines and directories,
- criteria for evaluating Internet-based sources, and
- a catalog of excellent general and discipline-specific Web sites.

The fourth edition offers a second new Internet-based chapter on "Writing for the Web," which introduces students to the fundamentals of Web-page design and construction, as well as the rhetorical considerations students should bear in mind when developing Web pages. Also new to this edition is the example argumentative essay in Chapter 6, where the student writer takes an alternate point of view on the topic (Technology and Gender) developed by the essay writer in Chapters 3 and 4. More has been added on writing and developing theses; example essays in Chapters 4 and 36 have been revised to show a deductive arrangement; and a section on writing electronic résumés now appears in the business-writing chapter. Notwithstanding these important changes, the fourth edition retains *The Allyn & Bacon Handbook's* comprehensive core features.

Core Features

Critical thinking   With its opening chapters—"Critical Thinking and Reading" and "Critical Thinking and Writing"—*The Allyn & Bacon Handbook* continues to mark a departure in the world of handbooks. We open with specific strategies for developing critical thinking skills that students can apply immediately to their reading assignments and to the writing that follows from these assignments. This approach, based on a survey of current research in the field, follows our conviction that writing at the college level is most often based on reading. If students want to write well, they must also read well. We develop these points on critical thinking and its relation to the writing process in two key places: in the rhetoric section (Chapters 1–4) and in the research section (Chapters 33–37). The evolving papers in both places show student writers changing their thinking, and their theses, as they work through a real writing process. Chapters 1 and 2 use a refined group of fresh examples (focused on the topic of women and computers) to serve as continuous source readings for demonstrating student thinking and writing skills.

The new reading selections in Chapters 1 and 2 provide occasions for critical thinking, but also serve as background material for the essay developed in Chapters 3 and 4, where the student writer's emerging ideas are sparked by earlier reading.

Writing as a process Chapters 3 through 6 on writing processes are designed to serve both as a quick-reference tool and as a mini-rhetoric, with assignments that call on students to write and revise paragraphs and whole papers. *Revision*, here, is key: the process of writing, discovery, and rediscovery through revision yields an example student paper that undergoes fundamental changes in its thinking—changes that would have been impossible had the writer not worked recursively from invention to multiple drafts through to a final effort. Similarly, the student paper in the research chapters (Part IX, Chapters 33–37) demonstrates how a writer's thinking evolves through reading, writing, and rewriting. Throughout these sections of the text, and in the sections devoted to sentence construction and word choice, we emphasize the role of revision in clarifying meaning and achieving a clean, spare style.

Because we have found that writing improves significantly when students give careful and sustained attention to a paper's governing sentence, we have made our discussion of thesis far more extensive than is commonly found in handbooks.

Writing across the curriculum and argumentation Our comprehensive cross-curricular chapters (38, 39, and 40) orient students to the kinds of thinking, reading, and writing they will be called on to do in their various courses. After a general introduction devoted to characteristic assumptions and questions, each cross-curricular chapter reviews patterns for writing to inform and for making arguments in its discipline area; it reviews typical kinds of reading and audience situations; and it presents types of assignments found in the discipline, a complete student paper, and a listing of specialized reference materials. Two of the student papers in these chapters explore the topic of alcohol (from differing disciplinary perspectives). The third paper is a literary analysis of Kate Chopin's "A Shameful Affair"; the story appears in its entirety in the chapter.

Writing about literature. A guiding assumption of this book is that college-level writing is based to a great extent on reading. Recognizing that for some composition classrooms reading involves literature as a context for writing, Chapter 38 includes material on writing about literature. The chapter retains its unique detail on making arguments throughout the humanities, but it also develops principles for writing about literature by providing specific guidelines and examples, including the story and student paper on Kate Chopin's "A Shameful Affair."

Argumentation in the disciplines. As an outgrowth of this book's pervasive attention to critical thinking and its emphasis on writing and evaluating arguments, Chapters 38–40 provide the only handbook treatment of foundations for making claims in each discipline across the curriculum. Chapter 6, the first in a handbook to offer a Toulmin-based model for constructing arguments, uses basic terminology that composition students can put to use in any discipline. Combined, these chapters offer more depth than any handbook available in constructing claims and arguments across the disciplines.

Our "Across the Curriculum" panels highlight the ways in which writers beyond the composition classroom use strategies discussed in the handbook to advance their written work. Twenty such boxes examine an element of the writer's craft being put to use in a specific disciplinary context—for instance, the use of analogies by a physicist, or the use of subordination and coordination by an economist. To expand our already distinctive discussion of claims and evidence for writing in each of the disciplines, we wanted to demonstrate how the specific, writerly strategies we emphasize in the composition classroom are highly valued when students write in other courses. Finally, student researchers using the cross-curricular chapters will find dozens of discipline-specific Web sites new to this edition.

The research paper   Integrating discussions found elsewhere on critical thinking, the writing process, and writing across the curriculum, this *Handbook's* five chapters on research offer a wealth of practical, direct advice for launching college-level research projects. The research section draws heavily on critical thinking concepts from Chapters 1 and 2 in the use of sources; it incorporates phases of the writing process from Chapters 3–6; it also looks ahead to research assignments in the three major discipline areas (Chapters 38 through 40). The result is a strong treatment on the use and evaluation of sources and their integration into students' writing. In addition, the documentation coverage in Chapter 37 treats four different conventions: the MLA system, the APA system, the footnote style (based on the *Chicago Manual of Style*), and the CBE systems used in the sciences. Also addressed are the most current conventions from the Modern Language Association for citing electronic sources: CD-ROMs and online materials. These sections, with their research paper samples from a variety of discipline areas, provide comprehensive coverage on research.

Forming the backbone of the research chapters is the continuing example of a student paper, entitled "What Do We Want at the Mall?"—an examination of mall culture and the issue of community. In developing the sample paper, student writer Jason Koman discovers that his source materials—some found in the library, some found on the Internet—do not support the argument he is expecting to write. The sources require Jason to rethink his premises, adjust his research question, and conduct additional research before completing his effort. These chapters on research clearly emphasize what we want our students to know: that the process of research is a process of challenging and clarifying one's thinking through a judicious use of source materials. The example paper has been revised for this edition to include more Internet sources; its thesis has been fronted and now appears in the paper's opening paragraphs.

The fourth edition presents an extremely thorough introduction to the Internet and to using Internet resources in research. Based on the work of Rick Branscomb (Salem State College, Massachusetts), Keith Gresham (University of Colorado at Boulder), and Michael Bergman (The WebTools Company), Chapter 34 is designed to help students understand that the Internet is a resource that is as important as the school library. Students receive direct, practical advice for forming effective search queries, launching and revising multiple searches, and evaluating Internet-based sources.

Guidelines and choices in sentence revision   Any experienced writer knows that there is often more than one solution to a common sentence error. Therefore, when appropriate, we discuss alternative solutions and encourage students in their role as writers to make decisions. When usage is a matter of strict convention, we offer firm, clear guidelines for eliminating common errors and understanding key concepts of grammar, usage, and style. We have used student and professional writing from the disciplines as the basis for more than 90 percent of the exercises *and* example sentences. Both exercises *and* examples almost always feature connected discourse from a variety of disciplines—on topics as varied as micro-breweries and Elizabethan stagecraft. To make the book easy to use as a reference tool and visually appealing, we have created numerous boxes that summarize important information, provide useful lists, or apply critical thinking to decisions and choices.

The "Spotlight" system: An alternative way to locate errors   To help students identify remedies for the most common trouble spots in grammar and usage, this handbook has developed the unique "Spotlight on Common Errors." This system offers an alternative for students who may be uncomfortable or unfamiliar with the formal terminology of grammar needed to locate errors in a traditional index. Students can find their way to remedies for common errors using the three parts of the "Spotlight" system:

1. The Spotlight chart on the back endpaper, with its broad view of error patterns, refers students to
2. The color-tinted "Spotlight" summary pages in selected chapters, which provide error recognition and brief remedies, in turn referring students to
3. Chapter sections with detailed explanations and revisions.

A few basic recognition examples are featured in all three elements of the "Spotlight" system. The use of the "Spotlight" system is described on the back endpaper, on the "Spotlight" summary pages, and in the "How to Use This Book" section following the title page.

Comprehensive ESL coverage   Students whose native language is not English have been entering mainstream composition courses in increasing numbers, with varying degrees of prior preparation from specialized English as a Second Language (ESL) courses. As a result, composition instructors have been called on to help international students cope with features of English that have not traditionally caused problems for native speakers. This handbook provides international students with unique help at three levels:

ESL notes in the text: These notes briefly identify troublesome English language features before referring readers to pertinent descriptive units in ESL Chapters 45–47.

Three ESL chapters: The chapters of the ESL section, developed with help from Will Van Dorp of Northern Essex Community College, summarize troublesome features of English language usage in three functional areas: nouns and related structures (Chapter 45); verbs and related structures (Chapter 46); and modifying structures (Chapter 47). Idioms and constructions with prepositions and particles—

especially troublesome forms for international students—are treated in appropriate sections in all three chapters.

Supplements for the Student

For students who need a self-help study workbook and for instructors who want to assign work that parallels the handbook, *The Allyn & Bacon Workbook*, 4th Edition, by Kathleen Shine Cain of Merrimack College, continues to serve as a distinctive source for student supplementary work. With its abridged topical explanations keyed to handbook sections, it offers a set of illustrative examples and an abundance of additional exercises. Most distinctively, these exercises include new readings and assignment materials suited to in-class or self-study work on critical thinking. Exercises also provide extensive supplementary work on the writing process, paragraph structure, sentence construction, punctuation and mechanics, and material on ESL features.

Three self-help supplements are available for students working on computers: first, a new *Interactive Edition*, a CD-ROM that contains the complete book as well as contextualized media links that provide audio and video clips, practice exercises, links to relevant Web sites and a search function; second, *Grammar Coach*, a set of computer-based tutorial exercises; and finally, a Web site with an online study guide, Web links, a message board, and a chat room. For other software materials for students, consult your Allyn & Bacon representative.

Finally, special workbooks are available to prepare students for writing and usage topics in English sections of the CLAST competency tests as given in Florida.

Supplements for the Instructor

The *Instructor's Manual* of the handbook features succinct comments for each chapter to provide instructional help in a wide variety of areas, including ESL, the writing process, teaching with text examples, suggested assignments, and extensive professional references. This material has evolved over three editions with contributions from several individuals, notably Kathleen Shine Cain of Merrimack College.

The ESL Cues in the *Instructor's Manual* promote individualized help for international students, especially if their first language may encounter grammatical interference from linguistic features of English, or if their cultural conventions of writing, rhetoric, and research may differ from those prevailing in American colleges. The "ESL Cues" were developed by Andrew and Gina Macdonald of Loyola University in New Orleans, based on extensive practical experience in both composition and ESL programs.

The *Instructor's Resource Manual* provides background material for both new and experienced instructors. It contains suggested syllabi and exercise sequences, extensive sections on teaching critical thinking and writing across the curriculum, and practical ideas and materials for teaching writing processes, research processes, writing about literature, and argumentation. The manual includes a separate section of "Notes on Teaching Composition to International Students" and also a complete bibliography of key topics in the composition curriculum.

Testing and exercise instruments in computerized form and in booklet form are also available to support the instructor's composition program. Two Diagnostic Tests are keyed to the text; a test analysis for every error item identifies a topic and handbook or workbook section to which students can be referred for specific help. Second, a computerized Exercise Bank contains hundreds of exercise examples keyed to grammar and usage topics in the handbook, providing extra material for students needing practice either independently or in a class or lab setting.

Adopters may also receive copies of *The Allyn & Bacon Sourcebook for College Writers*, 2/e by James C. McDonald, *Teaching College Writing* by Maggy Smith, and *An Introduction to Teaching Composition in an Electronic Environment* by Eric Hoffman and Carol Scheidenhelm.

Acknowledgments

A number of people have helped us with special contributions to key elements of the text and supplements of this edition. Special thanks go to Sarah Lefton for her help in designing and creating Chapter 41, "Writing for the Web." Thanks to Eric Wirth of the Modern Language Association, who patiently answered our questions concerning recent changes in MLA recommended style for researchers. Thanks to Kathleen Shine Cain of Merrimack College for her fine work on the instructor's annotations, and to Professors Andrew and Gina Macdonald of Loyola University for their wisdom and experience in the "ESL Cue" notes based on work with both ESL and composition sections over many years. In the text we are most grateful to H. Eric Branscomb of Salem State College for contributions on electronic resources, and also to Will Van Dorp of Bradford College and Northern Essex Community College, for his apt examples and descriptions on ESL topics in Part XII.

To the many reviewers who took time to critique our work both in the earlier editions and in this revision we give warm thanks. The following reviewers were both generous and realistic in their comments; we are grateful for the force and insight of their arguments, which led us to rethink and improve on countless dimensions of this text. For their reviews of the first edition, many thanks go to Chris Anson, University of Minnesota; Phillip Arrington, Eastern Michigan University; Kathleen Shine Cain, Merrimack College; Barbara Carson, University of Georgia; Thomas Copeland, Youngstown State University; Sallyanne Fitzgerald, University of Missouri, Saint Louis; Dale Gleason, Hutchinson Community College; Stephen Goldman, The University of Kansas; Donna Gorrell, St. Cloud State University; Patricia Graves, Georgia State University; John Hanes, Duquesne University; Kristine Hansen, Brigham Young University; Bruce Herzberg, Bentley College; Vicki Hill, Southern Methodist University; Jeriel Howard, Northeastern Illinois State University; Clayton Hudnall, University of Hartford; David Joliffe, University of Illinois at Chicago; Kate Kiefer, Colorado State University; Nevin Laib, Franklin and Marshall University; Barry Maid, University of Arkansas at Little Rock; Thomas Martinez, Villanova University; Mary McGann, University of Indianapolis; Walter Minot, Gannon University; Jack Oruch, University of Kansas; Twyla Yates Papay, Rollins College; Richard Ramsey, Indiana/Purdue University at Fort Wayne; Annette Rottenberg, University of Massachusetts, Amherst; Mimi Schwartz, Stockton State College; Louise Smith, University of Massachusetts, Boston; Sally Spurgin, Southern Methodist University; Judith Stanford, Rivier College; Barbara Stout, Montgomery College; Ellen Strenski, University of California, Los Angeles; Christopher Thaiss, George Mason University; Michael Vivion, University of Missouri, Kansas City; and Barbara Weaver, Ball State University.

For their reviews of the second edition, thanks to Bruce Appleby, Southern Illinois University; Linda Bensel-Myers, University of Tennessee; Melody Brewer, University of Toledo; Therese Brychta, Truckee Meadow Community College; Christopher Burnham, New Mexico State University; Peter Carino, Indiana State University; Neil Daniel, Texas Christian University; Virginia Draper, Stevenson College; Ray Dumont, University of Massachusetts, Dartmouth; Kathy Evertz, University of Wyoming; Barbara Gaffney, University of New Orleans; Ruth Greenberg, Jefferson Community College; Stephen Hahn, William Paterson College; Kathleen Herndon, Weber State University; Maureen Hoag, Wichita State University; Ralph Jenkins, Temple University; Rodney Keller, Ricks College; Judith Kohl, Dutchess Community College; Douglas Krienke, Sam Houston State University; Wendell Mayo, Indiana University–Purdue University Fort Wayne; Charles Meyer, University of Massachusetts, Boston; Joan Mullin, University of Toledo; Patricia Murray, California State University, Northridge; Richard Nordquist, Armstrong State University; Jon Patton, University of Toledo; Randall Popken, Tarleton State University; Kirk Rasmussen, Utah Valley Community College; Sally Barr Reagan, University of Missouri; David Roberts, Samford University; John Shea, Loyola University; Margot Soven, La Salle University; Ann Taylor, Salem State College; Elizabeth Tentarelli, Merrimack College; and Richard Zbaracki, Iowa State University.

For their reviews of the third edition, thanks to John Clark, Bowling Green State University, as well as Patsy Callaghan, Central Washington University; Michel deBenedictis, Miami Dade Community College; Kathryn Fitzgerald, University of Utah; Nancy Jermark, Hutchinson Community College; Todd Lundberg, Cleveland State University; Kevin Morris, Greenville Technical College; Ruth Morris, Greenville Technical College; Donna Nelson, Bowling Green State University; Carol Scheidenhelm, Northern Illinois University; Nancy Schneider, University of Maine, Augusta; Margaret Shaw, Kent State University; Laura Yowell, Hutchinson Community College; and Trudy Zimmerman, Hutchinson Community College. Reviewers of the fourth edition reminded us that a widely used handbook is always a candidate for improvement. We wish to thank Anne Bliss, University of Colorado; Eric Branscomb, Salem State College; Jane Dugan, Cleveland State University; Rima Gulshan, University of Maryland, Eastern Shore; Julie Hagemann, Purdue Calumet; Bill Lalicker, West Chester University; Roarke Mulligan, Christopher Newport University; Steven Szilagyi, University of Alabama, Huntsville; Marilyn Valentino, Lorain County Community College; Lisa Williams, Jacksonville State University; and Lynn Zimmerman, Kent State University. Most of these reviewers used their experiences with the third edition to make many helpful comments that led directly to important revisions in this new edition.

Many others helped us along the way; their particular contributions are too numerous to list, but we gratefully acknowledge their assistance. From Bentley College, we thank Tim Anderson, Christy Bell, Lindsey Carpenter, Robert Crooks, Nancy Esposito, Barbara Gottfried, Sherman Hayes, Tom Heeney, Richard Kyte, Donald McIntyre, Kathy Meade, and George Radford. We thank other colleagues as well: John Clarke of the University of Vermont, whose work on critical thinking aided the formulating of our pedagogy for the book, and Carol Gibbens of the University of California, Santa Barbara, for suggestions on the reference unit. Thanks also go to Burke Brown, University of Southern Alabama; Eric Godfrey, Ripon College; Clarence Ivie, University of Southern Alabama; John Laucus, University Librarian, Boston University; William Leap, The American University; Larry Renbaum; Carol G. Schneider, Association of American Colleges; Alison Tschopp, Boston University; and Arthur White, Western Michigan University.

As writers we are indeed fortunate to work with an editorial, production, marketing, and sales staff as fine as the team at Allyn & Bacon. Joe Opiela, Vice President and Editor-in-Chief for Humanities, shared and helped to shape our vision for this book. Throughout the manuscript's writing and rewriting, Joe proved himself a tireless advocate and a steady source of helpful ideas. Allen Workman, with his more than twenty years of experience, again showed himself to be one of the industry's premier developmental editors. Susan McIntyre and Kathy Smith shepherded the manuscript through production with an unfailing eye for style and detail.

Major support for this handbook has come from the Allyn & Bacon marketing team: Lisa Kimball, Executive Marketing Manager and John Gilman, Vice President for Sales. Bill Barke, President, and Sandi Kirshner, Senior Vice President of Allyn & Bacon have generously committed the editorial, production, and marketing resources needed to make this a project in which all concerned can take pride. To all we give hearty and warm thanks.

Leonard Rosen, Harvard University, Graduate School of Education
Laurence Behrens, University of California, Santa Barbara

Critical Thinking and Reading

Especially in college, to be successful as a writer you must be an effective reader. This chapter, which begins a book that will serve your reference needs throughout college and beyond, has a twofold purpose: first, to suggest general habits of mind that will prepare you for thinking critically about college-level reading materials, and second, to provide you with *particular* strategies for understanding and beginning to write about sources.[1]

ACTIVE, CRITICAL HABITS OF MIND

Develop habits of mind that prompt you to think critically about what you read. *Critical* in this sense does not mean "negative" but, rather, "active" and "alert."

http://www.sonoma.edu/cthink/
The Center for Critical Thinking, a repository of information about the theory and practice of critical thinking.

Critical habits include being alert to similarities and differences, posing questions, setting issues in broader contexts, and forming and supporting opinions. Developing the habits of a critical thinker will prepare you for working with the source materials on which you will base much of your writing.

1a **Active, critical thinkers search for and question similarities and differences.**

Two or more sources on a particular topic will nearly always present similarities and differences concerning facts, interpretations of facts, value judgments, or policies that the writers think you ought to pursue. With practice, you can approach similarities and differences with questions that will get you thinking critically. Freshman writer Lou Cassetta demonstrates how, using two sources on gender differences in high-tech companies. You will follow Lou and this topic through several chapters as Lou begins thinking about an essay and works through the process of writing to arrive at a finished essay (see 4e). Watch closely how Lou's observation of similarities and differences leads to questions that deepen his investigation into the topic.

[1]We use the terms *source materials, sources,* and *texts* interchangeably to mean any reading selection.

1a

From "Why Women Are So Invisible in Silicon Valley" (1997)

It shouldn't matter if you wear suspenders or a dress, least of all in the world's techno-epicenter, where the only price of admission is supposed to be smarts and hard work. But the numbers say otherwise: Among the Valley's 1,686 major tech companies, only 5.6% are led by women, according to CorpTech, a publisher in Woburn, Mass.

What gives? Is the supposedly wide-open Valley capped by a silicon ceiling? Blatant sex discrimination is rare, say women tech execs, but subtle barriers are encountered routinely. Anita Borg, a senior researcher at Digital Equipment Corp. in Palo Alto, calls it the "invisible-woman syndrome," where women's ideas are discounted or ignored. "You run into subtle sexism every day," she says. "It's like water torture. It wears you down."

But even if sexism were wiped out tomorrow, women still would be underrepresented in tech. The reason: Fewer women than men are pursuing degrees in computer science. In 1984, 37.1% of such bachelor's degrees went to women, according to the National Center for Education Statistics. By 1995, that had shrunk to 28.4%.

For all the gloomy statistics, there are glimmers of change. In the past few years, as new companies surfaced, more female execs took the startup plunge. [. . .] Despite a new crop of female entrepreneurs, women still have a tough time getting venture financing. Companies established or run by women received just 1.6% of the $33.5 billion in venture capital invested in tech from 1991 through to the third quarter of 1996, according to VentureOne Corp. (256)

—Steve Hamm

From "Women of the Valley: Success Stories" (1996)

The media repeat endlessly that there is a glass ceiling keeping women from rising beyond middle management in the business world. If that ceiling is so solid, how to account for the following?

Five years ago prestigious venture capitalists rarely received proposals from women starting high-technology businesses. Today Patricia Cloherty, president of New York City-based venture capital firm Patricof & Co., says that 15% of the new business proposals she gets comes from women. At San Francisco-based venture capital outfit Weiss, Peck and Greer Venture Partners, 5 of the 40 companies in its portfolio have female chief executives. "There are more ladies out there than I have seen in 20 years," says Frank Bosnal, a founding partner at New Enterprise Associates, one of venture capital's hottest houses.

"In the tech industry people don't care how old you are, what color you are or what sex you are." That comes from Christina Jones, who cofounded Austin, Tex.'s Trilogy Development Group [. . .].

Why are so many women making it big in high-techland? Explains [one woman entrepreneur], "There is more mobility [in high-tech companies] because there isn't a man with 20 years' experience in line for the job ahead of you."

The evidence bears her out. Because things change so fast in high-tech businesses, new opportunities open faster there than in older lines of work. "Slow growth inhibits change," declares Donna Dubinsky [of Palm Computing] in response to our question.

—Nina Munk and Suzanne Oliver

As a reader, prepare yourself to find similarities and differences in the articles you read. Here are Lou Cassetta's observations on the selections concerning gender and the high-technology workforce:

Similarities

- Both Munk and Oliver and Hamm discuss the "glass ceiling" phenomenon of female workers stalling out in middle management positions while male workers are promoted to executive suites.
- Both authors look to venture capital financing—the money that investors are willing to produce to fund new technology start-ups—as a key indicator of success for women in high-tech businesses.
- Both authors acknowledge (at least in popular belief) that competence is a quality highly valued in the high-tech industries.

Differences

- Munk and Oliver believe that gender does not matter in the promotion of employees to senior positions in high-tech industries. In the more recent article (by eight months), Hamm makes exactly the opposite point.
- Munk and Oliver suggest that competence is highly valued in Silicon Valley, regardless of an employee's gender. Hamm cites statistics to make the opposite point.
- Munk and Oliver claim that venture capitalists are supporting women-owned businesses in high-tech industries. Hamm makes the opposite point.
- Munk and Oliver suggest that the glass ceiling is shattering. Hamm disagrees.

Spotting similarities or differences in your reading is one way to begin having a conversation with your sources and, more generally, with a given topic. Based on your observations of differences, try posing questions. The more questions you pose and attempt to answer, the better you will know a reading selection.

Question similarities.

If two statements look alike, ask *why*. Are the facts the same? Are the interpretations of facts the same? Have facts been established in the same way? Examine opinions: If two or more authors share the same view, what does this suggest? Is the reasoning or value system underlying these views necessarily the same? Do you share this reasoning or value system? What social conditions might explain the similarities? Other questions are possible. The point is that your awareness of similarity marks a *beginning* point for your thinking. Here's how Lou Cassetta works with the similarities he's noticed:

> The authors base their selections on a shared view of the high-tech workplace as an environment that values hard work and competence more than anything—including gender. Munk and Oliver seem to think that the gender-blind workplace in high-tech industries is a fact. Hamm disagrees—but it is interesting to note that both of their positions rest on the same idea: that high-tech industries are different from other industries when it comes to gender.

Questions:

1. Where and when did the idea of gender equality in high-tech industries originate?
2. In the early years of the computer industry, were there many female engineers?
3. How did female engineers contribute to the industry?

4. Were female engineers given the same respect as their male counterparts?
5. How important a part of the computer culture is the idea of gender equality?

Questions such as these can prompt new inquiry—perhaps even a search for new sources. In Lou's case, these questions helped to focus his emerging paper.

Question differences.

Differences also point to questions. When authors disagree about facts, you should ask *why*. Do methods of determining facts differ? Which presentation of facts seems more authoritative? Examine opinions: when they differ, investigate. What logic and what values underlie differing opinions? If writers disagree over what policies we should follow, ask why. Do their analyses of problems differ? Are their assumptions about correct or ethical behaviors different? Many questions are possible based on differences. Your awareness of differences marks a beginning point for thinking. Here's how Lou Cassetta explores the differences he's noticed:

> You read these selections and have to wonder if the authors are writing about the same industry. One says that venture capitalists are funding women-led start-ups at an unprecedented rate. The other says that venture capitalists are spending next to nothing on women-led businesses. Both authors cite statistics—and both seem convincing, which confuses me.

> *Questions:*
> 1. Is there a glass ceiling, generally, in industry?
> 2. Do women face a glass ceiling in the *computer* industry?
> 3. Do the sexes differ with respect to talent with, or uses for, computers?
> 4. To what degree are venture capitalists funding women-led businesses?
> 5. How accurate is the gender-blind ideal of "competence" in the computer industry?
> 6. What are the trends regarding women's success in the computer industry?

Again, questions prompt new investigation. Lou Cassetta found himself particularly interested in Question 3. He pursued the issue of gender differences, as you will see in his use of two other sources for his paper.

▶ **EXERCISE I**

Every day for a week, read three or more newspapers—your town's local paper(s) and one or more of the following: the *New York Times*, the *Wall Street Journal*, and *USA Today*. Pay special attention to each paper's coverage of a single news event. Read the accounts and observe differences—among the three or between what any of the pieces report and your own experience. Pose questions based on these differences. Finally, outline a plan for potential research based on your questions.

▶ **1b**   Active, critical thinkers challenge and are challenged by sources.

Beyond searching for similarities and differences, try to maintain a generally questioning attitude when you read. Some questions you can direct to a source; others,

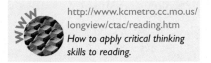
http://www.kcmetro.cc.mo.us/
longview/ctac/reading.htm
*How to apply critical thinking
skills to reading.*

to yourself. In both cases, your goal is to begin exploring the source and the issues it raises. Many readers consider the following guidelines to be useful:

▶1 **Challenge the author: Ask questions of the source.**

Every reading invites specific questions, but the following basic questions can get you started in your effort to read any text critically:

- What central problem, issue, or subject does the text explore? If the text explores a problem, what are the reasons for this problem? What are the effects of this problem?
- What is the most important or the most striking statement the author makes? Why is it important or striking?
- Who is the author, and what are the author's credentials for writing on this topic? What is the author's stake in writing this text? What does the author have to gain?
- How can I use this selection? What can I learn from it?

COMPUTER TIPS

Electronic Democracy at Its Best . . . and Worst

Usenet newsgroups represent perhaps the pinnacle of democracy and free speech. The exchanges in this new medium can be uninhibited, unrestrained, and uncensored. But that free flow of information increases the critical thinking challenge for researchers. Everybody from world-renowned experts in a field to ignorant, malicious crackpots has equal access to the medium, and it may be difficult to tell one group from the other. Be careful when using a Usenet posting as evidence in your writing. If possible, try to verify the information first in another, more reliable source.

▶2 **Challenge yourself: Ask questions of yourself.**

A critical reading points in two directions: to the text(s) you are reading and to *you*. The questions you ask about what you read can prompt you to investigate your experience, values, and opinions. As part of any critical reading, allow the issues that are important to the text to *challenge* you. Question yourself and respond until you know your views about a topic. Pose the following questions to yourself:

- What can I learn from this text? Will this knowledge change me?
- What is my background on this topic? How will my experience affect my reading?
- What is the origin of my views on the topic?

- What new interest, or what new question or observation, does this text spark in me?
- If I turned the topic of this selection into a question on which people voted, how would I vote—and why?

Here are Lou Cassetta's thoughts on his background with gender and technology:

> I've definitely seen differences in the ways men and women talk about technology. Last summer, when I interviewed for the data entry job, I scored points when I could talk shop about the boss's laptop computer. Today, a lot of guys talk about computer power the way they used to talk about cars: power and speed are key. How do women talk about computers?[2]

ACROSS THE CURRICULUM

Being Alert to Differences

Whatever the discipline, faculty and students search for differences, or discrepancies—for information and explanations that are supposed to fit neatly together but do not. Differences lead to questions; questions, to investigations; and investigations (very often), to writing projects. In the opening paragraph of a paper on international relations, policy analyst Gerald Segal observes a contradiction that launches his essay.*

> The twenty-first century is supposed to be the "Pacific Century," but it is also supposed to be the age of information technology. Yet these two strands of the future do not fit together very well. As anyone who has tried to plug in a portable modem in Japan will know, the East Asians are not as technologically advanced as many Americans and Europeans think. Even more important, and despite all their confidence about their economic success, East Asians are becoming seriously worried about their ability to resist the challenges posed by the new technology to their core values and the authority of their states.

A contradiction in two views of the future

Discipline focus: international relations

A difference brings challenges

*Gerald Segal is a senior fellow at the International Institute for Strategic Studies. His article "Asians in Cyberia" appeared in the *Washington Quarterly* 18.3 (1995).

▶ **EXERCISE 2**

Reread the three newspaper articles you selected for Exercise 1. Based on suggestions in the preceding section, pose questions that challenge the underlying assumptions in each piece. Also, use one or two of the pieces as a basis for posing questions that challenge *you*.

[2]Reflecting on this question helped Lou to formulate part of the thesis for his essay.

> **lc**   **Active, critical thinkers set issues in a broader context.**

Whenever possible, identify the issues and questions that are important to a single reading selection and then think large: assume that every particular issue, concern, or problem that you read about exists in a larger context—a larger cluster of related issues, concerns, or problems. This larger context will not always be obvious. Often, you will have to work to discover it. Here is a set of techniques for doing so:

http://www.colostate.edu/
Depts/WritingCenter/
references/reading/
toulmin/page1.htm
A Web site devoted to philosopher Stephen Toulmin's model of critically analyzing texts.

- Begin by identifying one or more issues that you feel are important to a text.
- Assume that each issue is an instance, or example, of something larger. Your job is to speculate on this larger something.
- Write the name of the issue at the top of a page, or on the computer screen. Below this, write a question: "What is this a part of?" Then write a one-paragraph response.
- Reread your response, and briefly state the broader context.
- Use this broader context to stimulate more thought on the reading selection and to generate questions about issues of interest.
- Option: Begin an investigation. Find new reading selections about the issues you've defined.

Lou Cassetta found a textbook from his psychology class that directly addressed several broader issues he had identified concerning gender roles. Here are Lou's notes on these issues:

> Women pursuing careers in computer science, and not advancing, is part of a larger question about the ways women and men pursue jobs, generally, and the ways gender plays a role. The current thinking is that most intellectual abilities are the same between men and women. We see more men or women in certain jobs because of training, not inborn ability. Still, some differences between the sexes exist, and researchers haven't yet defined these completely. For now, differences in learning seem to explain the differences between the sexes.

Here is the paragraph from a psychology text that helped Lou Cassetta set issues in a broader context:

> Researchers are still trying to determine whether basic differences in intelligence exist between males and females and, if so, under what conditions. Biologically based mechanisms may account for some gender-based cognitive differences, but learning is far more potent in establishing and maintaining sex-role stereotypes and gender-specific attitudes.
>
> —LESTER LEFTON, *Psychology*, 6th ed. (Boston: Allyn and Bacon, 1997)

> **EXERCISE 3**

Explore the larger context suggested by the differing news accounts of the three articles that you found for Exercise 1. Create a phrase that summarizes one issue, subject, or problem that you think is important to these accounts. Place that phrase at the top of a page and the question "What is this a part of?" below it. Then write an answer in order to identify a broader context. Based on this broader context, generate an action plan: identify some research activity that could follow from your writing.

> ## 1d Active, critical thinkers will form and support opinions.

Know what you think about what you see and read. Have an opinion and be able to support it. Opinions generally follow from responses to questions such as these:

- Has the author explained things clearly?
- In what ways does this topic confuse me?
- Has the author convinced me of his or her main argument?
- What is my view on this topic?
- Would I recommend this source to others?

Whatever your opinion, be prepared to support it with comments that are based on details about what you have seen or read. Later in this chapter (see 1g), you will learn techniques for reading to evaluate a source; and in Chapter 2 (see 2b), you will learn techniques for writing an evaluation—a type of writing in which you formally present your opinions and give reasons for holding them. It is not practical or necessary for you to develop a formal response (oral or written) to every source you read. Just the same, as a critical and active thinker, you should be able to offer reasons for believing as you do. Here's Lou Cassetta's opinion, based on the articles he's read thus far on the representation of women in the computer industry. This opinion becomes a fundamental part of his first-draft essay:

> What can explain the difficult time women have had in advancing to senior positions in high-tech industries? Munk and Oliver and Hamm take as their starting point that historically, men have advanced more quickly than women. They disagree about the extent of the problem today—but I'm interested in why there was ever a difference in the first place. Clearly, women are as capable as men in math, science, and engineering. So if they're as capable, why don't we (1) see more of them in the computer industry and (2) see more of them in executive positions? The answer must have to do with how men and women relate in the workplace. From my experience, men tend to expect women colleagues to think and act (and even talk) the same way they do. This isn't realistic, and it isn't fair, but it may be necessary in order for women to advance in the workplace.

You and your classmates will agree and disagree about the ideas expressed in a source. You should be able to have an informed discussion about these ideas. You do so by stating and supporting opinions. See Chapter 6 for advice when you want to convert your opinions to a formal argument.

> ### EXERCISE 4

Use the suggestions in the preceding section to develop an opinion based on one or more of the articles you selected for Exercise 1. In writing, state your opinion in a sentence or two. Then, in a brief paragraph, support your opinion by pointing to particular paragraphs or sentences in the news accounts.

COMPONENTS OF A CLOSE, CRITICAL READING

Noticing differences, challenging and being challenged by sources, setting issues in a broader context, and forming and supporting opinions—these habits of mind, so important to thinking critically, do not necessarily lead to formal statements on your part about the materials you encounter. When you read and use source materials as a basis for writing, you *will* need to formalize and systematize your critical thinking skills. A close, critical reading requires that you read to understand, respond, evaluate, and synthesize. These are the tasks that you will find discussed in this section. The forms of writing associated with close reading—summary, evaluation, analysis, and synthesis—are discussed in Chapter 2.

Reading and *rereading*

To read closely and critically, experienced readers often find they must read a text two or more times. We discuss the types of close, critical reading in four sections (1e–1h), but we do *not* mean to suggest that you must read your sources four times in order to understand them thoroughly. Still, you should commit yourself to reading however much is necessary to understand, respond, evaluate, and synthesize.

▶ **le**   **Critical reading (1): Reading to understand**

Every use to which you can put a source is based on your ability to understand it. Without understanding you can do nothing, so understanding must be your first goal as a critical reader.

▶**I**   **Setting goals for reading to understand**

The steps in reading to understand can be summarized as follows:

- *Identify the author's purpose.* This will likely be to inform or to argue.
- *Identify the author's intended audience.* The text will be written with particular readers in mind. Determine whether you are the intended audience.
- *Locate the author's main point.* Every competently written text has a main point that you should be able to express in your own words.
- *Understand the structure of the text.* If the author is arguing, locate the main point and supporting points; if the author is presenting information, locate the main point and identify the stages into which the presentation has been divided.
- *Identify as carefully as possible what you do not understand.*

Read the following selection, which is typical of the reading you might encounter in one of your courses. (This happens to be a source that Lou Cassetta used in writing his essay on gender and the high-tech workforce.) Throughout this chapter, we will add layers of notes to this passage in order to demonstrate strategies for reading to understand, respond, evaluate, and synthesize. The notes you see on the passage here illustrate how you might read to understand. (Lou uses the symbols ♀ and ♂ to indicate women and men, respectively.) Techniques for annotating in this way follow the passage itself.

Technology Perceptions by Gender
By Cornelia Brunner and Dorothy Bennett
From Education Digest, *condensed from* NASSP Bulletin, February 1998

Section I sets up gender differences

1 Many educators have noticed that boys use computers more readily than girls. Some years ago, we at the *Center for Children and Technology,* of the *Education Development Center,* did a series of studies about gender differences around attitudes and approaches to technology.

♂ comfortable ♀ ambivalent re: tech

2 We found, to nobody's surprise, that girls are more ambivalent about technology than boys, who are more positive; that boys are more excited about their experiences with technology, particularly video games, while girls like video (i.e., stories) and tend to get bored when they encounter bad technology experiences. Girls are also less likely than boys to attempt to fix a broken piece of technology, and all the youngsters in this study talked about a male when asked about a "technology nut" they know.

Research question

3 What might account for these differences? As part of our research, we asked architects, engineers, scientists, video editors, film makers, software designers, hardware developers, and students aged 11 to 18 to describe their feelings and fantasies about technology. We found the expert women and men in our sample had very different expectations of and feelings about technology. We came to think of this difference as a feminine and a masculine "voice" in the technological universe.

Section II: Research

Findings

4 Not all the women we studied spoke in a feminine voice, nor did all the men speak in a masculine voice; but the differences we found were clear and dramatic and in keeping with gender differences found over the years in other studies.

Findings

Findings

5 These differences can best be summarized as follows: Feminine fantasies are about small, flexible objects that can be worn or carried easily and that allow women to communicate and connect and to share ideas and stories. Masculine fantasies are about magic wands (or brain implants) that allow men to transcend the limitations of time and space. Gender differences in technology fantasies among students also mirror the differences among the experts.

Implications of research

6 What are some implications of these differences for the use of technology in the classroom? While more formal research is needed, we can speculate based on our collaborative work with many schools.

Section III: Implications

Authors speculate

♀ sees functions ♂ sees machine

7 The feminine attitude toward technology looks right through the machine to its social function, while the masculine view is more focused on the machine itself. One implication of this difference might be that pre-

Critical Thinking and Reading

senting technology as an end in itself—a special subject of study (as in a programming class)—is less likely to appeal to young women than to young men. If the technology is introduced as a means to an end, such as a tool for in-depth research or for making a multimedia presentation, young women are as likely to find it appealing as young men.

8

Emphasize tech as solution

A greater emphasis on exploring whether a new technology solves a social problem, rather than merely speeding up a process or making it more powerful, and on making sure that a new invention does not create a new problem while solving an old one, might make technology more interesting to many young women. The Science, Technology & Society movement among educators, which integrates science and social studies into a curriculum that considers the impact of science and technology on society, addresses these kinds of issues and is likely to make young women feel invited into a discussion of technology.

Humanizing

♀ need role models

Without opportunities to come to terms with their conflicts about technology, young women often feel they are not suited for technological careers because they are not whole-heartedly "for" technology. They need role models of women in high-tech professions who share their concerns about technology but have found ways to cope with their ambivalence. Mentoring programs in which girls can discuss personal and professional matters with women in high-tech professions serve to humanize technology for many young women.

9

Section IV: Humanizing technology

Assignments should reflect ♀ interests

In technology classes, assignments should reflect the interests of girls as well as boys. In one high-school class, students were asked to design a catapult that shoots pellets at targets for points, a crane that lifts a designated load to a specific point in a designated period of time, and a vehicle that goes up a ramp as quickly as possible and defends itself against an opponent on the opposite side. Few of the girls in the class were inspired by these topics.

10

Net can appeal equally to ♀ and ♂ if communication, as well as archives, stressed

The Internet, particularly the World Wide Web, is as likely to appeal to young women as to young men. The ability to communicate with others and to share ideas, stories, news, and advice corresponds to the feminine fantasies we found in our research. The ability to send and receive information instantly from vast resource archives and to publish one's own ideas to the world at large, overcoming limitations of time and space, corresponds to the masculine fantasies. If the Internet is used as a vast database and the student's task becomes primarily one of figuring out efficient search strategies for finding specific information, girls are less likely to be

11

interested than boys. If Internet access is also used to allow students to communicate with each other and with mentors, it will appeal to girls as well.

Pivotal Moment

We are at a pivotal moment in the evolution of technology and education. Technologies can now be easily designed to embrace different ways of knowing, inviting diverse learners to express and develop multiple points of view. Technologies are now capable of richly supporting three ingredients that make for a kind of learning that is inviting to all students, particularly girls: exploration, interpretation, and communication. The power of discovery lies in being able to build one's own meanings, and debate and discuss one's ideas with others. Distributed technologies like the Internet are well suited to support this kind of learning.

As an educational community we should make sure, however, that the feminine perspective on technology is as much part of the conversation as the masculine one. We run the danger of thinking about these new communications tools only as a distance learning technology, that is, as a way to send information from a central archive or expert into the outer reaches, a kind of broadcasting model designed to grant schools access to new sources of information.

This is an excellent use of the technology, of course, even though there is an important difference between the availability of information and real access to it. A lot of primary source materials are available from large archives (such as the Library of Congress) but using them in a meaningful manner in schools—granting students conceptual access, in other words—requires staff development and new ways of thinking about teaching and learning.

The complement to this masculine notion of the power of new communications tools is a more feminine idea in which students and teachers use the technology to produce information and to represent their knowledge as well as to gather information. This, too, requires staff development and new ways of teaching and learning, but it places the emphasis on using the technology to share ideas, collaborate on projects, and communicate point-to-point, from individual class or teacher or student to others, rather than as a broadcast medium to display information.

Margin notes:

Key moment: Tech can be made inclusive

The key idea

Focus on communication

12   Section V: Seize the moment

13

14

15

2 Applying techniques for reading to understand

When you know that you must base later writing on a source you are reading, you should consciously adopt a system for reading to understand. There are many systems you can follow, but each commonly entails reading in three stages.

Preview   Skim the text, reading quickly both to identify the author's purpose and to recall what you know about the topic.

Read   Read with pen in hand, making notes (on separate sheets or on photo-copied pages) about the content and the structure of the text. Stop periodically to monitor your progress.

Review   Skim the text a second time to consolidate your notes: jot down questions and highlight especially important passages.

Following are techniques for taking notes on information important to understanding a source. These same techniques led to notes Lou Cassetta made on the passage by Brunner and Bennett, above.

Preview the text.

- *Read titles, openings, and closings in full.* This preview will give you a sense of topic, audience, purpose, and main point. Read the title, and guess the relationship between the title and text. If you are reading an article or a chapter of a book, read the opening and closing paragraphs in full. If you are reading a book, read the preface along with the first and last chapters.

- *Skim the rest of the text.* A brief look at the text will help you to understand its structure, or layout. When skimming an article, read all headings, along with a few sentences from every second or third paragraph. When skimming a book, review the table of contents, and then read the opening and closing paragraphs of each chapter.

- *Recall what you know about the topic.* A review of your experience with a topic will prepare you to be interested and ready with questions. After skimming, think about the topic: reflect on your experience.

- *Predict what you will learn from reading.* Based on your quick review of the text and your knowledge of the topic, predict what you will learn. Predictions keep you focused on the content and alert to potential difficulties.

Read the text.

Read with a pen or pencil in hand, and make notes that will help you understand.

- *Identify the author's purpose.* The author's purpose will likely be to inform or to argue. Locate passages that illustrate this purpose.

- *Underline important phrases and sentences.* Your underlining or highlighting of important information should work with your notes (see below) so that you can return to the text and spot the author's main topic at a glance.

- *Write notes that summarize your underlining.* You can summarize important points of an explanation or an argument by writing brief phrases in the margins; this will help you to understand as you read and to recall important information as you reread.

- *Identify sections.* A section of a text is a grouping of related paragraphs (see 5a). Sometimes, an author will provide section headings; at other times, you will need to write them. In either case, your awareness of sections will help you understand the structure of a text.

- *Identify difficult passages.* Use a question mark to identify passages that confuse you, and circle unfamiliar words. Unless a particular word is repeated often and seems central to the meaning of a text, postpone using a dictionary until you complete your reading. Frequent interruptions to check the meaning of words will fragment your reading and disrupt your understanding (see 22e).
- *Periodically ask: Am I understanding?* Stop at least once during your reading to ask this question. If you are having trouble, change your plan for reading. For especially difficult selections, divide the text into small sections, and read one section at a sitting. Read until you understand each section, or until you can identify what you do not understand.

Review the text.

After reading and making notes, spend a few minutes consolidating what you have learned. Focus on the content of the passage and its structure. Understand the pattern by which the author has presented ideas and information. These additional minutes of review will crystallize what you have learned and be a real help later on, when you are asked to refer to and *use* the selection, perhaps for an exam or paper.

- *Consolidate information.* Skim the passage, and reread your notes. Clarify them, if necessary, so that they accurately represent the selection. Reread and highlight (with boxes or stars) what you consider to be the author's significant sentences or paragraphs.
- *Organize your questions.* Review the various terms and concepts you have had trouble understanding. Organize your questions concerning vocabulary and content. Use dictionaries; seek out fellow students or an instructor to clarify especially difficult points. Your questions, gathered into one place, such as a journal, will be an excellent place to begin reviewing for an exam.

▶ **EXERCISE 5**

Using the techniques discussed in the preceding section, read to understand (a) an editorial from a newspaper's OP-ED page or (b) any article in which a writer clearly expresses an opinion on a topic of interest to you. On a photocopy of the article, underline what you consider to be important sentences and phrases, and make notes that summarize important ideas and information. Also, identify the different sections of the passage.

▶ **If** Critical reading (2): Reading to respond

Your personal response to a text is the second component of a critical, comprehensive reading. If your responses are to be informed, you must understand what you have read—which is why your first job is to understand. This done, focus on yourself. Aside from the merits of the text (for instance, whether it is well written and accurate), explore your responses. What reactions do particular lines or paragraphs spark in you? The focus here is on you. Soon enough, you will turn your attention to the text (when you evaluate). For the moment, react. Are you intrigued? Disappointed? Angered?

▶ I **Setting goals for reading to respond**

The overall goal of reading to respond is to identify and explore *your* reactions to a text. More specifically, these goals are as follows:

■ Reflect on your experience and associations with the topic of a text. Know what you feel about a text—know your emotional response.
■ Let the text challenge you.
■ Use the text to spark new, imaginative thinking.

Following is a portion of the passage by Brunner and Bennett that you read in 1e-1, along with Lou Cassetta's comments. Reread the passage, this time observing the second layer of notes in blue, which represent Lou Cassetta's response to the passage. Recommended techniques for highlighting in this way follow. You will have a chance to practice these techniques on the passage you chose for Exercise 5.

Technology Perceptions by Gender
By Cornelia Brunner and Dorothy Bennett
From Education Digest, *condensed from NASSP Bulletin, February 1998*

Many educators have noticed that boys use computers more readily than girls. Some years ago, we at the *Center for Children and Technology*, of the *Education Development Center*, did a series of studies about gender differences around attitudes and approaches to technology.   1

Section I sets up gender differences

♂ *comfortable*
♀ *ambivalent*
re: tech

We found, to nobody's surprise, that girls are more ambivalent about technology than boys, who are more positive; that boys are more excited about their experiences with technology, particularly video games, while girls like video (i.e., stories) and tend to get bored when they encounter bad technology experiences. Girls are also less likely than boys to attempt to fix a broken piece of technology, and all the youngsters in this study talked about a male when asked about a "technology nut" they know.   2

Why is no one surprised at gender diffs?

Research question

What might account for these differences? As part of our research, we asked architects, engineers, scientists, video editors, film makers, software designers, hardware developers, and students aged 11 to 18 to describe their feelings and fantasies about technology. We found the expert women and men in our sample had very different expectations of and feelings about technology. We came to think of this difference as a feminine and a masculine "voice" in the technological universe.   3

Section II: Research

Findings

Are the diffs learned? B+B seem to think so.

Not all the women we studied spoke in a feminine voice, nor did all the men speak in a masculine voice; but the differences we found were clear and dramatic and in keeping with gender differences found over the years in other studies.   4

Findings

These differences can best be summarized as follows: Feminine fantasies are about small, flexible objects that can be worn or carried easily and that allow women to   5

Findings communicate and connect and to share ideas and stories. Masculine fantasies are about magic wands (or brain implants) that allow men to transcend the limitations of time and space. Gender differences in technology fantasies among students also mirror the differences among the experts.

Implications of research

What are some implications of these differences for the use of technology in the classroom? While more formal research is needed, we can speculate based on our collaborative work with many schools.   **6**   *Section III: Implications*

Authors speculate

♀ sees function; ♂ sees machine

The feminine attitude toward technology looks right through the machine to its social function, while the masculine view is more focused on the machine itself. One implication of this difference might be that presenting technology as an end in itself—a special subject of study (as in a programming class)—is less likely to appeal to young women than to young men. If the technology is introduced as a means to an end, such as a tool for in-depth research or for making a multimedia presentation, young women are as likely to find it appealing as young men. [. . .]   **7**   *How can we take advantage of the diffs? Crazy to insist ♀ and ♂ alike if they aren't*

♀ need role models

Without opportunities to come to terms with their conflicts about technology, young women often feel they are not suited for technological careers because they are not whole-heartedly "for" technology. They need role models of women in high-tech professions who share their concerns about technology but have found ways to cope with their ambivalence. Mentoring programs in which girls can discuss personal and professional matters with women in high-tech professions serve to humanize technology for many young women. [. . .]   **9**   *Section IV: Humanizing technology*

Good idea in any profession.

Key moment: Tech can be made inclusive

We are at a pivotal moment in the evolution of technology and education. Technologies can now be easily designed to embrace different ways of knowing, inviting diverse learners to express and develop multiple points of view. Technologies are now capable of richly supporting three ingredients that make for a kind of learning that is inviting to all students, particularly girls: exploration, interpretation, and communication. The power of discovery lies in being able to build one's own meanings, and debate and discuss one's ideas with others. Distributed technologies like the Internet are well suited to support this kind of learning.   **12**   *Section V: Seize the moment*

Businesses won't act unless there's $ to be made. But schools can act.

As an educational community we should make sure, however, that the feminine perspective on technology is as much part of the conversation as the masculine one.   **13**

▶2 Applying techniques for reading to respond

You can achieve the goals of reading to respond when you approach a text with a set of questions that continually return your focus to *you* and *your* reactions. Here is a sampling of such questions.

Questions that promote a personal response

- *Which one or two sentences did I respond to most strongly in this text? What was my response?* Explore your reasons for being excited, angry, thoughtful, surprised, or threatened. Keep the focus on you.
- *What is the origin of my views on this topic? Who else shares my views?* Explore where and under what circumstances you learned about the topic. Criticize the views of people who believe as you do. Apply this criticism to yourself. What do you discover?
- *If I turned the topic of this text into a question on which people voted, how would I vote—and why?* Get involved with the text by locating a debate in the text and by taking sides.
- *What new interest, question, or observation does this text spark in me?* Use a text to spark your own thinking. Let the text help you pose new questions or make new observations. Use the text as a basis for speculation.

See 38d for a discussion of a special case of reading to respond: responding to literature.

Many of the techniques just discussed are illustrated in the passage by Brunner and Bennett in 1f-1. Observe the personal nature of Lou Cassetta's notes. Two of Lou's comments clearly represent a point of view: "Why is no one surprised at gender differences?" and "How can we take advantage of the differences?" These comments differ in kind from those that summarize, such as "Woman sees function, man sees machine." Responses, by definition, are personal. They will differ from one reader to the next.

> **EXERCISE 6**
>
> Reread the passage you selected for Exercise 5, this time to respond. Write notes and underline phrases and sentences, based on your response. Use a different color of pen or pencil for your notes this time than you used while reading to understand, so that you can recreate your various layers of reading.

▶ 1g   Critical reading (3): Reading to evaluate

Evaluating a text is the third component of a close, critical reading. When you read to respond, you focus on personal associations with the text. Were you pleased or displeased? Engaged? Angry? A response is focused on you. When you evaluate, you turn systematic attention to the text in order to determine how effectively the author has presented material. Certainly a response can lead to an evaluation, as you reread the text to understand why you reacted as you did. At the end of an evaluation, you should be able to explain the extent to which the author succeeded and the points on which you and the author agree or disagree.

▶ 1   Setting goals for reading to evaluate

You have four goals in reading to evaluate:

- Distinguish between an author's use of facts and an author's use of opinions.
- Distinguish between an author's assumptions (fundamental beliefs about the world) and your own.

- Judge the effectiveness of an explanation.
- Judge the effectiveness of an argument.

Following is part of the passage by Brunner and Bennett that you read in 1e-1, where you saw summary notes, and again in 1f-1, where you saw response notes. Reread the passage, this time observing a third layer of notes in red, Lou Cassetta's evaluation of the passage. Recommended techniques for reading to evaluate follow.

Technology Perceptions by Gender
By Cornelia Brunner and Dorothy Bennett
From Education Digest, *condensed from NASSP Bulletin, February 1998*

Many educators have noticed that boys use computers more readily than girls. Some years ago, we at the *Center for Children and Technology,* of the *Education Development Center,* did a series of studies about gender differences around attitudes and approaches to technology. **1**

Section I sets up gender differences

♂ *comfortable* ♀ *ambivalent re: tech*

We found, to nobody's surprise, that girls are more ambivalent about technology than boys, who are more positive; that boys are more excited about their experiences with technology, particularly video games, while girls like video (i.e., stories) and tend to get bored when they encounter bad technology experiences. Girls are also less likely than boys to attempt to fix a broken piece of technology, and all the youngsters in this study talked about a male when asked about a "technology nut" they know. **2**

Why is no one surprised at gender diffs?

Research question

What might account for these differences? As part of our research, we asked architects, engineers, scientists, video editors, film makers, software designers, hardware developers, and students aged 11 to 18 to describe their feelings and fantasies about technology. We found the expert women and men in our sample had very different expectations of and feelings about technology. We came to think of this difference as a feminine and a masculine "voice" in the technological universe. **3**

Section II: Research

Findings

A fair sample of the population?

Are the diffs learned? B+B seem to think so.

Not all the women we studied spoke in a feminine voice, nor did all the men speak in a masculine voice; but the differences we found were clear and dramatic and in keeping with gender differences found over the years in other studies. **4**

These differences can best be summarized as follows: Feminine fantasies are about small, flexible objects that can be worn or carried easily and that allow women to communicate and connect and to share ideas and stories. Masculine fantasies are about magic wands (or brain implants) that allow men to transcend the limitations of time and space. Gender differences in technology fantasies among students also mirror the differences among the experts. **5**

Findings

Findings

Confirming a stereotype. Any negative cases?

Implications of research

What are some implications of these differences for the use of technology in the classroom? While more **6**

Section III: Implications

Authors speculate

formal research is needed, we can <u>speculate</u> based on our collaborative work with many schools.

♀ sees functions
♂ sees machine

<u>The feminine attitude toward technology looks right through the machine to its social function, while the masculine view is more focused on the machine itself.</u> One implication of this difference might be that presenting technology as an end in itself—a special subject of study (as in a programming class)—is less likely to appeal to young women than to young men. If the technology is introduced as a means to an end, such as a tool for in-depth research or for making a multimedia presentation, young women are as likely to find it appealing as young men. [. . .] **7**

How can we take advantage of the diffs? Crazy to insist ♀ and ♂ alike if they aren't.

♀ need role models

Without opportunities to come to terms with their conflicts about technology, <u>young women</u> often feel they are not suited for technological careers because they are not whole-heartedly "for" technology. They <u>need role models of women in high-tech professions</u> who share their concerns about technology but have found ways to cope with their ambivalence. Mentoring programs in which girls can discuss personal and professional matters with women in high-tech professions serve to humanize technology for many young women. [. . .] **9**

Section IV: Humanizing technology

Good idea in any profession.

Mentors can inspire. B + B believe differences are learned. On what basis do they believe this?

We are at a pivotal moment in the evolution of technology and education. Technologies can now be easily designed to embrace different ways of knowing, inviting diverse learners to express and develop multiple points of view. <u>Technologies are now capable of richly supporting three ingredients that make for a kind of learning that is inviting to all students, particularly girls: exploration, interpretation, and communication.</u> The power of discovery lies in being able to build one's own meanings, and debate and discuss one's ideas with others. Distributed technologies like the Internet are well suited to support this kind of learning. **12**

Key moment: Tech can be made inclusive

Section V: Seize the moment

Businesses won't act unless there's $ to be made. But schools can act.

Demand equal access, but insist on high-quality ed.

<u>As an educational community we should make sure, however, that the feminine perspective on technology is as much part of the conversation as the masculine one.</u> **13**

▶2 Applying techniques for reading to evaluate

When you are reading to evaluate, you want to be alert to an author's use of *facts*, *opinions*, and *definitions*, and his or her *assumed views of the world*. You also want to know if an author's purpose is primarily to inform or to argue, so that you can pose specific questions accordingly.

Distinguish facts from opinions.

Before you can evaluate a statement, you should know whether it is being presented to you as a fact or an opinion. A **fact** is any statement that can be verified.

Nationwide, the cost of college tuition is rising.

New York lies at a more southerly latitude than Paris.

Andrew Johnson was the seventeenth president of the United States.

The construction of the Suez Canal was completed in 1869.

These statements, if challenged, can be established as true or false through appropriate research. As a reader evaluating a selection, you might question the accuracy of a fact or how the fact was shown to be true. You might doubt, for instance, that Paris is a more northerly city than New York. The argument is quickly settled by reference to agreed-upon sources—in the case of Paris, a map.

http://www.gcse.com/
teach/fo.htm
Useful tutorial on distinguishing fact from opinion.

An **opinion** is a statement of interpretation and judgment. Opinions are not true or false in the way that statements of fact are. Opinions are more or less well supported. If a friend says, "That movie was terrible," this is an opinion. If you ask why and your friend responds, "Because I didn't like it," you are faced with a statement that is unsupported and that makes no claim on you for a response. Someone who writes that the majority of U.S. space missions should not have human crews is stating an opinion. Someone who refers to the *Challenger* disaster is referring to a fact, a matter of historical record. Opinions are judgments. If an opinion is supported by an entire essay, then the author is, in effect, demanding a response from you.

Identify the strongly stated opinions in what you read, and then write *comment notes:* in the margin, jot down a brief note summarizing your response to each opinion. Agree or disagree. Later, your notes will help you crystallize your reactions to the selection.

Distinguish your assumptions from those of an author.

An **assumption** is a fundamental belief that shapes people's views. If your friend says that a painting is "beautiful," she is basing that statement, which is an opinion, on another, more fundamental opinion—an assumed view of beauty. Whether or not your friend directly states what qualities make a painting beautiful, she is *assuming* these qualities and is basing her judgment on them. If the basis of her judgment is that the painting is "lifelike," this is an assumption. Perhaps she dislikes abstract paintings, and you like them. If you challenged each other on the point or asked *why*, you both might answer, "I don't know why I think this way. I just do." Sometimes assumptions are based on clearly defined reasons, and other times (as in the painting example) they are based on ill-defined feelings. Either way, the opinions that people have (if they are not direct expressions of assumptions themselves) can be better understood by identifying the underlying assumptions.

Consider two sets of assumptions.

When you read a source, two sets of assumed views about the world come into play: yours and the author's. The extent of your agreement with an author depends largely on the extent to which your assumptions coincide. Therefore, in evaluating a source, you want to understand the author's assumptions concerning the topic at hand, as well as your own. To do so, you must perform two related tasks: identify an author's opinions, and determine whether each opinion is based on some other opinion or assumed view.

Identify direct and indirect assumptions.

Assumptions may be stated directly or indirectly. In either case, your job as a critical reader is to identify and determine the extent to which you agree with them.

Assumption stated directly

#1 A nation is justified in going to war only when hostile forces threaten its borders.

#2 A nation is justified in going to war when hostile forces threaten its interests anywhere in the world.

At times, an author hints at, but does not directly state, an assumed view—as in this example:

Assumption not stated

#3 A conflict 7,000 miles from our border does not in any way threaten this nation, and we are therefore not justified in fighting a war that far from home.

Sentence 3 is based on the assumption expressed in Sentence 1. Suppose you were reading an editorial and came across Sentence 3. In a close, critical reading you would see in this statement an unexpressed assumption about the reasons nations *should* go to war. If you can show that an author's assumed views (whether directly or indirectly expressed) are flawed, then you can argue that all opinions based on them are flawed and should be rejected, or at least challenged.

Distinguish your definitions of terms from those of an author.

Consider this statement: *Machines can explore space as well as, and in some cases better than, humans.* What do the words *as well as* and *better than* mean? If an author defines these words one way and you define them another way, you and the author are sure to disagree. In evaluating a source, identify the words that are important to the author's presentation. If the author does not define these words directly, then state what you believe the author's definitions to be. At times you will need to make educated guesses based on your close reading of the source.

Question sources that explain and sources that argue.

Outside of the literature classroom, you will read sources that are written primarily to inform or to argue. As a critical reader engaged in evaluating a source, determine the author's primary purpose, and pose questions accordingly.

Sources that explain

When a selection asks you to accept an explanation, a description, or a procedure as accurate, pose—and respond to—these questions:

- For whom has the author intended the explanation, description, or procedure? The general public—nonexperts? Someone involved in the same business or process? An observer, such as an evaluator or a supervisor?
- What does the text define and explain? How successful is the presentation, given its intended audience?
- How trustworthy is the author's information? How current is it? If it is not current, are the points being made still applicable, assuming more recent information could be obtained?

- If the author presents a procedure, what is its purpose or outcome? Who would carry out this procedure? When? For what reasons? Does the author present the stages of the procedure?

Sources that argue

When a selection asks you to accept an argument, pose—and respond to—these questions:

- What conclusion am I being asked to accept?
- What reasons and evidence has the author offered for me to accept this conclusion? Are the reasons logical? Is the evidence fair? Has the author acknowledged and responded to other points of view?
- To what extent is the author appealing to logic? To my emotions? To my respect for authorities?[3]

Many of the techniques just discussed are illustrated in the notes made for the sample passage by Brunner and Bennett in 1g-1. The third layer of comments that you see (in red) would prepare a reader for writing a formal evaluation of the passage.

▶ EXERCISE 7

Reread the passage you selected for Exercise 5, this time to evaluate the success of the author's presentation. Write notes and underline phrases and sentences, based on the discussion in the preceding section. Use a different color of pen or pencil for your notes than the ones you used while reading to understand and reading to respond, so that you can recreate your various layers of reading.

▶3 Applying evaluation techniques to Web-based sources[4]

You can find a great deal of current, useful information on the World Wide Web. But as a researcher, you should approach Web-based information and arguments with special caution and questions because people can "publish" on the Web without their materials being scrutinized for accuracy or fairness. Caution is required, as well, because of the distinctive nature of electronic online information.

- Web pages that appear to be informational may in fact be advertisements.
- Search engines tend to retrieve links unrelated to a query.
- Web pages, as well as the hyperlinks that connect one page to another, tend to be unstable and can disappear.

http://refserver.lib.vt.edu/libinst/critTHINK.HTM

An extensive list of sources on applying critical thinking to Internet material.

A highly useful approach to evaluating information on the Web has been provided by Janet E. Alexander and Marsha A. Tate, reference librarians at the Wolfgram Memorial Library at Widener University. In 34c you will find a more extensive discussion of their strategy for evaluating Web-

---

[3]See 6g for a full discussion of evaluating arguments.

[4]This section is taken in large part from the Web site "Evaluating Web Resources" (http://www2.widener.edu/Wolfgram-Memorial-Library/webeval.htm, copyright 1996–1999), which complements the book *Web Wisdom: How to Evaluate and Create Information Quality on the Web* (1999) by Janet Alexander and Marsha Ann Tate.

based sources. We summarize that discussion here. Alexander and Tate categorize Web pages into five major types:

1. Advocacy Web pages attempt to influence public opinion.
2. Business/marketing Web pages seek to generate money.
3. News Web pages try to provide extremely current information.
4. Informational Web pages seek to provide factual information.
5. Personal Web pages vary in purpose, depending on the intentions of the authors.

In addition to posing the basic questions for evaluation developed in this chapter, you can ask the following questions in analyzing the five types of Web sites:

Does the page or its related links help you establish that the information comes from credible sources?

Does the page provide source information that will help you verify facts?

Are the organization's or the individual's biases clearly stated?

Is the page current, and does it provide basic bibliographic information?

How thoroughly and persuasively does the page address its stated topic?

Be an informed, critical consumer of Web sites. Be aware of the kinds of sites you are viewing, and ask questions accordingly.

ILLUSTRATION: EVALUATING A WEB PAGE

Let's consider how some of these criteria apply to a particular Web page. Following is the home page for Women in Technology International (WITI), found at <http://www.witi.com>. WITI is an organization founded to promote the interests and competencies of women in technology and science. Following the home page is the text of a WITI research report found at <http://www.witi.org/Center/Research/page1.html>, which is linked to the home page. The example evaluation is based on the opening paragraphs of the research report.

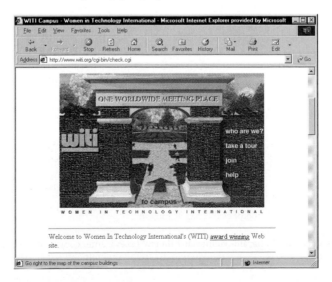

Business Impact
by Women in Science and Technology
A WITI Research Paper

- Women-owned firms will make approximately $50 million in computer-related purchases this year.
- 39% of business influencers, defined as those who are involved in the purchase of computers and related products for their organizations, are women. This is a universe of 9.2 million female business influencers.
- Women-owned businesses now employ 35% more people in the U.S. than the *Fortune* 500 companies employ worldwide.
- Women-owned businesses number 7.7 million, provide jobs for 15.5 million people and generate nearly $1.4 trillion in sales.
- Ten years ago, women made up only 10% of online users. Today it has grown to 43%.

"It's no longer a question, it's a fact—women have major impact as both influencers and purchasers of technology. Those companies committed to hiring women at every level of the organization today will have a significant competitive advantage in the 21st century!"

—CAROLYN LEIGHTON, executive director, Women in
Technology International (WITI)

Evaluation

Using the categories set out by Alexander and Tate, the WITI Web site can be classified as an advocacy site. On this page and linked pages, WITI states its biases clearly as being an organization "dedicated to breaking barriers" that women face in high-tech careers. The page provides phone numbers and e-mail addresses and seems willing to be contacted for follow-up questions. WITI clearly stands by its published work.

The page presents as facts four items of information about the influence of women in technology. The information appears to be legitimate. But given that (1) the sources for this information are not provided and (2) the purpose of WITI is to promote women's interests in technology, these facts—which show the significant influence of women in technology—should be verified in at least one other source. From all indications, fact checking would confirm the WITI information.

As for the conclusion drawn from WITI's facts, readers should be cautious. Will "companies committed to hiring women at every level of the organization today [. . .] have a significant competitive advantage in the 21st century"? If the preceding facts are true, the statement is at best an educated guess. Until the facts were verified, however, a researcher would not want to accept the statement attributed to the executive director of WITI.

▲

▶ **EXERCISE 8**

Evaluate one or more of the following Web sites.[5] Apply the criteria of *authority, accuracy, objectivity, currency,* and *coverage* to each site. (Note: To fully evaluate a site, once you have arrived at a home page you will need to follow some of the links to other pages.)

[5]These sites are taken from a list compiled by Janet E. Alexander and Marsha A. Tate (http://www2.widener.edu/Wolfgram-Memorial-Library/examples.htm, copyright 1996–1999).

- *OncoLink* <http://oncolink.upenn.edu>
- *Smoker's Home Page* <http://www.tezcat.com/~smokers/>
- *Essays on the Anti-Smoking Movement* <http://www.tezcat.com/~smokers/issues1.html>
- *The True but Little Known Facts About Women with Aids, with documentation* <http://147.129.1.10/library/lib2/AIDSFACTS.html>
- *Feline Reactions to Bearded Men* <www.improb.com/airchives/cat.html>
- *Roget's Thesaurus* <http://humanities.uchicago.edu/forms_unrest/ROGET.html>
- *Webster's Revised Unabridged Dictionary*, 1913 Edition <http://humanities.uchicago.edu/forms_unrest/webster.form.html>

1h Critical reading (4): Reading to synthesize

Once you have understood, responded to, and evaluated a single source, you are in a position to link that source with others. By establishing links between one author and others (including yourself), you achieve a synthesis: an *integration* of sources. Synthesis is the fourth and in some ways the most complex component of a close, critical reading: it requires that you read and understand *all* your source materials and that you respond to and evaluate each one.

1 Setting goals for reading to synthesize

You are the organizing force of a synthesis. Without your active involvement with source materials, without your creative and integrating ideas, synthesis is impossible. You have four goals in reading to synthesize:

- Read to understand, respond to, and evaluate multiple sources on a subject, problem, or issue.
- Understand your own views on the subject, problem, or issue. Be able to state these views in a sentence or two.
- Forge relationships among source materials, according to your purpose. In a synthesis, *your* views should predominate. Use the works of various authors to support what you think.
- Generally, try to create a conversation among sources. Be sure that yours is the major voice in the conversation.

2 Applying techniques for reading to synthesize

When you are reading to synthesize, you want to be alert to the ways in which various sources "talk to" each other concerning a particular topic. Seek out relationships among sources. Be sure to consider yourself as a source—and a valuable one.
    Students find the following plan helpful when writing syntheses:

- *Read, respond to, and evaluate multiple sources on a topic.* It is very likely that the authors will have different observations to make. Because you are working with the different sources, you are in a unique position to find relationships among them.

- *Subdivide the topic into parts, and give each part a brief title.* Call the topic that the several authors discuss *X*. What are all the parts, or the subdivisions, of *X* that the authors discuss? List the separate parts, giving each one a brief title.
- *Write cross-references for each part.* For each subdivision of the topic, list *specific* page references to whichever sources discuss that part. This is called *cross-referencing*. Once you have cross-referenced each of the topic's parts, you will have created an index to your reading selections.
- *Summarize each author's information or ideas about each part.* Now that you have generated cross-references that show you which authors discuss which parts of topic *X*, take up one part at a time, and reread all the passages you have cross-referenced. Summarize what each author has written on particular parts of the topic.
- *Forge relationships among reading selections.* Study your notes, and try to link sources. Here are several relationships that you might establish:

Comparison: One author *agrees* with another.

Contrast: One author *disagrees* with another.

Example: Material in one source *illustrates* a statement in another.

Definition: Material from several sources, considered together, may help you *define* or redefine a term.

Cause and effect: Material from one source may allow you to *explain directly* why certain events occur in other sources.

Personal response: You find yourself agreeing or disagreeing with points made in one or more sources. Ask yourself *why*, and then develop an answer by referring to specific passages.

For ways to synthesize details you've observed in a work of literature, see 37d, 2–4.

Cross-reference each part and summarize.

In actual course work, your reading selections will come from different journals, newspapers, and books—and cross-referencing should prove useful. Assume that you have identified parts of your topic and have listed page numbers from your sources that relate to each part. Following the page references, write a brief note summarizing the author's information or ideas. Exercise 9 asks you to do just this.

Forge relationships among your sources.

Based on your close reading of each selection and on your cross-references and notes, you should be able to establish relationships among the readings. Five general questions should get you started:

1. Which authors agree?
2. Which authors disagree?
3. Are there examples in one source of statements or ideas expressed in another source?
4. What definitions can you offer, based on the readings?
5. Do you detect a cause-and-effect relationship in any of the readings?

EXERCISE 9

Lou Cassetta gathered several sources on the topic of gender and technology. Read the excerpts that follow, and you'll find that you can make several connections across sources, linking the facts and ideas presented by one author with those presented by others:

> While we socialize our men to aspire to feats of mastery, we socialize our women to feats of submission. Men are hard; women are soft. Men are meant to conquer nature; women are meant to commune with it. Men are rational, women irrational [. . .]. We have trained our women to opt out of the technological order as much as we have trained our men to opt into it.
>
> —RUTH SCHWARTZ COWAN, "Women and Technology in American Life" (1979)

> Biologically based mechanisms may account for some gender-based cognitive differences, but learning is far more potent in establishing and maintaining sex-role stereotypes and gender-specific attitudes.
>
> —LESTER LEFTON, *Psychology* (6th ed., 1997)

> The media repeat endlessly that there is a glass ceiling keeping women from rising beyond middle management in the business world. If that ceiling is so solid, how to account for the following?
>
> Five years ago prestigious venture capitalists rarely received proposals from women starting high-technology businesses. Today [. . .] 15% of the new business proposals [a prominent New York investor] gets comes from women.
>
> —NINA MUNK and SUZANNE OLIVER, "Women of the Valley: Success Stories" (1996)

> Among the Valley's 1,686 major tech companies, only 5.6% are led by women, according to CorpTech, a publisher in Woburn, Mass.
>
> What gives? Is the supposedly wide-open Valley capped by a silicon ceiling? Blatant sex discrimination is rare, say women tech execs, but subtle barriers are encountered routinely.
>
> —STEVE HAMM, "Why Women Are So Invisible in Silicon Valley" (1997)

> Not all the women we studied spoke in a feminine voice, nor did all the men speak in a masculine voice; but the differences we found were clear and dramatic and in keeping with gender differences found over the years in other studies. [. . .]
>
> The feminine attitude toward technology looks right through the machine to its social function, while the masculine view is more focused on the machine itself.
>
> —CORNELIA BRUNNER and DOROTHY BENNETT, "Technology Perceptions by Gender" (1998)

Based on your reading of the excerpts, make a connection across readings for each of the following categories. Write a brief note on how each author offers a fact or idea about a specific category. Note that each author will not have something to say for each of these categories. Finally, be sure to consider yourself as a source: you should offer a comment about the category as well.

1. Broader perspective on men/women in science and technology

   Cowan:

   Lefton:

   Munk/Oliver:

   Hamm:

   Brunner/Bennett:

   You:

2. The "glass ceiling" in high-tech industries

   Cowan:

   Lefton:

   Munk/Oliver:

   Hamm:

   Brunner/Bennett:

   You:

3. Origins of differences between men and women

   Cowan:

   Lefton:

   Munk/Oliver:

   Hamm:

   Brunner/Bennett:

   You:

CHAPTER 2

Critical Thinking and Writing

Y ou will often be asked to demonstrate your understanding of sources by writing summaries, evaluations, analyses, and syntheses—four forms of writing that are fundamental to college-level work. Each form emphasizes a particular way of thinking about texts,[1] and each is built on particular skills in critical reading.

Forms of writing that build on reading

- **Summary.** Briefly—and neutrally—restate the main points of a text. Summary draws on your skills of reading to understand (see 1e).
- **Evaluation.** Judge the effectiveness of an author's presentation and explain your agreement or disagreement. Evaluation draws on your skills of reading to understand (1e), reading to respond (1f), and reading to evaluate (1g).
- **Analysis.** Apply the clearly defined principles set out by one or more authors to investigate the work of other authors (or to investigate various situations in the world). Analysis draws on your skills of reading to understand (1e), reading to respond (1f), and reading to evaluate (1g).
- **Synthesis.** Gather the work of various authors according to *your* purpose. Synthesis draws on your skills of reading to understand (1e), reading to respond (1f), reading to evaluate (1g), and reading to synthesize (1h).

The cumulative layers of writing

The forms of writing discussed in this chapter are interrelated. You will write summaries as part of writing evaluations, analyses, and syntheses. Before you evaluate an author's presentation, you must demonstrate through summary that you understand the text. When you gather and synthesize multiple texts for a research paper, you will summarize *and* evaluate the texts as you forge relationships among them. When you conduct an analysis, you must have thoroughly understood and evaluated the principles you apply; this calls for written summary and evaluation as part of your analysis.

These forms of academic writing are cumulative: one builds on the next in much the same way that strategies for reading comprehensively do. For clarity of presentation, we discuss summary, evaluation, analysis, and synthesis in separate sections and as separate tasks. In practice—in the texts you read and in the papers you write—you will find that these forms of writing and thinking merge.

---

[1]We use the term *text* interchangeably with *source* to mean any reading selection.

> **2a** Writing a summary

The **summary**—a brief, neutral restatement of a text—is fundamental to working with sources in any academic setting. You will read texts in every course, and before you can comment on them or otherwise put them to use, you must show that you understand the authors on their own terms. Like any piece of writing, a summary calls for you to make decisions and to plan, draft, and revise. While sometimes called for on exams, a summary more typically appears as part of evaluations, analyses, and syntheses. The following three assignments require summaries.

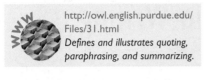

http://owl.english.purdue.edu/Files/31.html
Defines and illustrates quoting, paraphrasing, and summarizing.

Assignments that explicitly call for a summary

Mathematics Read the article "Structuring Mathematical Proofs," by Uri Leron [*The American Mathematical Monthly* 90 (March 1983): 174–185]. In two to four typed pages, summarize the concept of linear proof, giving one good example from the course.

Film studies Summarize Harvey Greenberg's discussion of *The Wizard of Oz*.

Social psychology Write a summary of your textbook's discussion of the "realistic conflict theory." Make sure that you address the theory's explanation of prejudice as an intergroup conflict.

An assignment may not explicitly call for a summary but may require it just the same, as in the following example. In completing this assignment, a student would need to summarize the Mary Shea argument and then respond.

Assignment that implies the need for a summary

Business ethics In "Good Riddance to Corporate America," Mary Shea argues that highly credentialed female MBAs are beginning to quit corporate America because of its "essential emptiness." How convinced are you by Shea's argument?

> **1** Setting goals for writing a summary

The focus of a summary is on a specific text, *not* on your reactions to it. Overall, your goal is to restate the text, as briefly as possible, in your own words. More specifically, you should aim to meet these goals:

- Clearly state the author's purpose in writing (for instance, to inform, explain, argue, justify, defend, contrast, or illustrate).
- Clearly state the author's thesis.
- Clearly state the author's main points in support of this thesis.

> **2** Understanding techniques for writing a summary

Summary begins with reading to understand. In 1e you were advised to make notes as you previewed, read, and reviewed a text.

Students find the following process helpful in preparing for and writing a summary:

- Determine the purpose of the source—for instance, to inform, explain, argue, justify, defend, compare, contrast, or illustrate.

- Summarize the thesis. Based on the notes you have made and the phrases or sentences you have highlighted while reading, restate the author's main point in your own words. In this statement, refer to the author by name; indicate the author's purpose (for example, to argue or inform); and refer to the title.
- Summarize the body of the text.

  STRATEGY 1: Write a one- or two-sentence summary of every paragraph. Summarize points important to supporting the author's thesis. Omit minor points and illustrations. Do not simply translate phrase for phrase from sentences in the text.

  STRATEGY 2: Identify sections (groupings of related paragraphs), and write a two- or three-sentence summary of each section.

- Study your paragraph or section summaries. Determine how the paragraphs or sections work together to support the thesis.
- Write the summary. Join your paragraph or section summaries with your summary of the thesis, emphasizing the relationship between the parts of the text and the thesis.
- Revise for clarity and for style. Quote sparingly. Provide transitions where needed.

COMPUTER TIPS

Use a Scratchpad to Record Your Thoughts

When you're writing or when you're reading online material, it is useful to keep a second file window open for jotting down thoughts, ideas, and questions. If you have a big enough computer screen, you can even keep both windows visible at the same time and just switch between them. Some computers have small notepad utilities that simplify this process. Use this second file to record questions you may have, tangential material you think of, or bibliographic citations and URLs you need to remember. Be sure to save this file each time you enter something, if it doesn't have an auto-save feature. If your computer doesn't keep multiple windows open, embed your comments, questions, and off-topic musings in the text, surrounded by some kind of marker (such as *** or —). Later, when you need these entries or want to delete them, a simple search for the marker will locate each entry.

Techniques for summarizing an especially difficult text

When the topic of a text is completely new to you, or when you are reading a text intended for an audience that has more experience with a topic than you have, reading to understand—and writing a summary—will be especially difficult. In addition to the reading strategies discussed in 1e, try these reading strategies to help you understand and summarize a difficult text:

1. Identify every example in the text and ask, What point is being illustrated here? Make a list of these points. Considered together, they will reveal the author's thesis.

2. Look for repeated terms or phrases. Define them, consulting specialized dictionaries or encyclopedias, if necessary.
3. Read and reread the opening and closing paragraphs of the text. Look for a sentence or two—the thesis—that seems to summarize the whole. "Interrogate" that sentence, following the advice in 3d-4. Link specific parts of the sentence to different parts (or sections) of the text. Understand what you can; identify what you cannot understand—and then take *specific* questions to a fellow student or your instructor.

▶3 Applying techniques for writing summaries

The techniques for writing summaries can now be applied to an example passage found in Chapter 1: Brunner and Bennett's "Technology Perceptions by Gender" (see 1e-1). You may want to reread the selection so that you can better understand the preparations for summary that follow.

Prepare: Make notes for a summary.

These preparatory notes are based on the above plan for writing summaries. The first note concerns Brunner and Bennett's purpose; the second is a clear statement of the thesis—in the writer's own words, not the authors'. Finally, there is a one-sentence summary of each paragraph in the article.

Purpose To argue

Thesis The educational community should help teachers recognize and teach to the interests of girls as well as boys when working with technology in the classroom.

Identify sections

Section 1 (¶s 1–2): Opener: Sets up gender differences
  ¶1: The Center for Children and Technology conducted studies to investigate gender differences in perceptions of technology.
  ¶2: The study found that girls are more "ambivalent" about technology than boys and that boys are confident and excited about technology.

Section 2 (¶s 3–5): Research
  ¶3: The authors surveyed professionals and students about perceptions of technology and found a distinct feminine and masculine "voice" or set of attitudes.
  ¶4: The "clear and dramatic" differences confirmed finds of other studies.
  ¶5: Women and men fantasize about technology differently—with women imagining portable high-tech objects that facilitate communication and men imagining high-tech objects that boost their powers.

Section 3 (¶s 6–8): Implications of research
  ¶6: Based on their work in schools, the authors can speculate on the implications of their research.
  ¶7: Women tend to see technology in terms of its "social function"; men tend to focus on the "machine itself."
  ¶8: Female students might be more attracted to technology if instructors focused on how technologies could solve problems.

Critical Thinking and Writing

Section 4 (¶s 9–11): Humanizing technology

¶9: Technology can be humanized and made more approachable for young women through mentoring programs that show women succeeding as professionals in high-tech jobs.

¶10: Teachers should craft assignments that tap the interests of girls as well as boys.

¶11: The Internet can appeal equally to male and female students *if* communication, as well as the technology's archive capacities, is stressed.

Section 5 (¶s 12–15): Seize the moment/conclusion

¶12: We are at a key moment in history—a moment in which technologies can be made inclusive and inviting to both girls and boys.

¶13: The educational community should help teachers recognize and teach to the interests of girls as well as boys when working with technology in the classroom.

¶14: Regarding the Internet as only an archive (a masculine interest) is useful but limiting. Giving students "conceptual access" to Internet information (a feminine interest) is a goal that will require innovation and effort.

¶15: The authors argue for the "feminine idea" of regarding new technologies as opportunities to create new information and to communicate.

Write the summary.

Join paragraph or section summaries to the thesis, and emphasize the relationship of parts. Revise as needed to ensure a smooth flow of ideas.

> In "Technology Perceptions by Gender," Cornelia Brunner and Dorothy Bennett argue that the educational community should help teachers recognize and teach to the interests of girls as well as boys when working with technology in the classroom. Through research conducted at the Center for Children and Technology, the authors observed a distinct masculine and feminine "voice" with regard to technology. Girls tend to be less sure of themselves than boys with technology. Girls and women tend to focus on the "social function" of technology, while boys and men tend to focus on hardware and on how technology can increase their powers. Given these differences, Brunner and Bennett recommend that classroom teachers emphasize the uses of technologies for solving problems rather than focusing on technical elements such as programming languages and hardware. The authors also recommend that women in technology serve as role models for girls, and that the Internet be presented not merely as a vast archive of files (a masculine interest) but also as an environment that promotes communication and discovery (a feminine interest). Technologies are now powerful enough to accommodate both masculine and feminine learning styles, and educators must work to make sure that both styles are valued and nurtured in the classroom.

▶ **EXERCISE 1**

Working with the article you selected for Exercises 5–7 in Chapter 1, and with the notes you made while reading that selection, write a summary. For specific help in doing so, follow the advice given in this section.

▶ 2b   Writing an evaluation

In an **evaluation** you judge the effectiveness and reliability of a text and discuss the extent to which you agree or disagree with its author. Consider the following assignments, which call for evaluation.

Sociology   Write a review of Christopher Lasch's *Culture of Narcissism.*

History   In "Everyman His Own Historian," Carl L. Becker argues for a definition of history as "the memory of things said and done." Based on your reading in this course, evaluate Becker's definition.

Physics   Write a review of *Surely You're Joking, Mr. Feynman!*

Writing an evaluation formalizes the process of reading to evaluate, which, in turn, depends on reading to understand and to respond (see 1e,f). Evaluation will always entail summary writing (see 2a), since before you can reasonably agree or disagree with an author's work or determine its effectiveness, you must show that you understand and can restate it.

▶1   Setting goals for writing an evaluation

You have two primary goals when writing to evaluate, and both depend on a critical, comprehensive reading: (1) to judge the effectiveness of the author's presentation, focusing for the moment only on the *quality* of the presentation; then (2) to agree and/or disagree with the author and explain your responses.

▶2   Understanding techniques for writing an evaluation

The basic pattern of evaluation is as follows: (1) offer a judgment about the text; (2) refer to a specific passage—summarize, quote, or paraphrase; and (3) explain your judgment in light of the passage referred to. Using these components of evaluation, you will help to establish your authority as someone whose insights a reader can trust.

Prepare: Make notes on the effectiveness of the presentation.

Evaluate the effectiveness and reliability of a presentation according to the author's purpose for writing. If the author is attempting to persuade you, you use one set of criteria, or standards of judgment, to evaluate the text; if the author is informing—providing explanations or presenting procedures or descriptions—you use another set of criteria.

Criteria for texts that inform or persuade

Use the following criteria to judge the effectiveness of any text. Remember to support your evaluation by referring to and discussing a specific passage.

Accuracy   Are the author's facts accurate?

Definitions   Have terms important to the discussion been clearly defined—and if not, has lack of definition confused matters?

Development   Does each part of the presentation seem well developed, satisfying to you in the extent of its treatment? Is each main point adequately illustrated and supported with evidence?

Criteria for texts that inform

When an author writes to inform, you can evaluate the presentation based on any of the preceding criteria, as well as on the ones discussed in this section. Remember to support your evaluation by referring to and discussing a specific passage.

Audience   Is the author writing for a clearly defined audience who will know what to do with the information presented? Is the author consistent in presenting information to one audience?

Clarity   How clear has the author been in defining and explaining? Is information presented in a way that is useful? Will readers be able to understand an explanation or follow a procedure?

Procedure   Has the author presented the stages of a process? Is the reader clear about the purpose of the process—about who does it and why?

Criteria for texts that persuade

When an author writes to persuade, you can evaluate the presentation based on any of the preceding criteria, as well as on the ones that follow. Remember to support your evaluation by referring to and discussing specific passages.

Fairness   If the issue being discussed is controversial, has the author presented opposing points of view? Has the author seriously considered and responded to these points? (See 6e.)

Logic   Has the author adhered to standards of logic? Has the author avoided, for instance, fallacies such as personal attacks and faulty generalization? (See 6g.)

Evidence   Do facts and examples fairly represent the available data on the topic? Are the author's facts and examples current? Has the author included negative examples? (See 6g.)

Authority   Are the experts that the author refers to qualified to speak on the topic? Are the experts neutral? (See 6d-3 and 6g.)[2]

Prepare: Make notes on your agreement and disagreement with the author.

By applying the criteria above, you may decide that a selection is well written. Just the same, you may disagree with the author in part or in whole, or you may agree. In any case, you should examine the reasons for your reactions. For instance, in Lou Cassetta's evaluation of Brunner and Bennett's article "Technology Perceptions by Gender" (2b-3), he acknowledges the usefulness of the statistics that the authors cite, but he warns against compromising the rigorous technical education of engineers.

Whatever your reaction to a text, you should (1) identify an author's views, pointing out particular passages in which these views are apparent; (2) identify your own views; and (3) examine the basis on which you and the author agree or disagree. For the most part, you can explain agreements and disagreements by examining both your assumptions and the author's. Recall from Chapter 1 that an assumption is a fundamental belief that shapes people's opinions. Here is a format for distinguishing your views from the author's. (For an example of note making that follows this format, see 2b-3.)

---

[2]In 6g you will find an extended discussion of evaluating arguments.

Author's view on topic *X:*

Author's assumption:

My view:

My assumption:

Prepare: Organize your notes and gain a general impression.

Once you have prepared for writing an evaluation by making notes, review your material and develop an overall impression of the reading. In writing an evaluation, you will have enough space to review at least two, but probably not more than four or five, aspects of an author's work. Therefore, be selective in the points you choose to evaluate. Review your notes concerning the quality of the presentation and the extent of your agreement with the author; select the points that will best support your overall impression of the reading. As with any piece of formal writing, plan your evaluation carefully. If you are going to discuss three points concerning a selection, do so in a particular order, for good reasons. Readers will expect a logical, well-developed discussion.

Students find these steps helpful in preparing evaluations:

- Introduce the topic and author: one paragraph. One sentence in the introduction should hint at your general impression of the piece.
- Summarize the author's work: one to three paragraphs. If brief, the summary can be joined to the introduction.
- Briefly review the key points in the author's work that you will evaluate: one paragraph.
- Identify key points in the author's presentation; discuss each in detail: three to six paragraphs. If you are evaluating the quality of the author's presentation, state your criteria for evaluation explicitly; if you are agreeing or disagreeing with opinions, try to identify the underlying assumptions (yours and the author's).
- Conclude with your overall assessment of the author's work.

The order of parts in the written evaluation may not match the actual order of writing. You may be unable to write the third section of the evaluation without first having evaluated the author's key points—the next section. The evaluation will take shape over multiple drafts.

3 Applying techniques for writing evaluations

Brunner and Bennett's argument on the need for a more gender-balanced instruction in technology (1e-1) provides an opportunity to demonstrate how you can evaluate a text. The first step of evaluation, neutrally presenting the authors' views in a summary, was developed earlier in this chapter (2a-3). Beyond the summary, your evaluation will address one or both of these questions: How effective and reliable is the authors' presentation? Do I agree with the authors?

How effective and reliable is the authors' presentation?

In 2b-2 you found ten criteria, or standards of judgment, one or more of which you can use to determine the effectiveness and reliability of a source:

accuracy, definitions, development, audience, clarity, procedure, fairness, logic, evidence, and authority. Following is an example of how three of these standards—definitions, authority, and logic—become criteria for evaluating Brunner and Bennett's discussion. This particular evaluation assumes that the authors are arguing.

Definitions Brunner and Bennett clearly define feminine versus masculine "voices" regarding technology. The authors devote three paragraphs to differentiating these voices so that readers can understand the distinctions.

Authority The authors do not share details about their "series of studies" on gender perceptions and technology. But the presentation seems authoritative and trustworthy for several reasons. First, the authors are affiliated with a recognized organization: the Center for Children and Technology of the Education Development Center. Second, the article appears in the *NASSP Bulletin*, a respected journal. Third, Brunner and Bennett make reasonable claims about gender differences. They observed differences, but they were also honest in noting that "[n]ot all the women we studied spoke in a feminine voice, nor did all the men speak in a masculine voice." The selection seems to be an entirely reliable source.

Logic Brunner and Bennett make a clear argument for a new educational policy. Based on research, they report the fact that girls are more ambivalent about technology than boys. They also report as fact a basic distinction of feminine versus masculine voices regarding technology. Technology is generally taught in ways that appeal to masculine interests, so it's not surprising that girls regard technology less positively than boys. The authors argue that if technology were taught in ways that appealed to a "feminine voice," girls would form more positive perceptions about technology, and eventually, more women would choose careers in high-tech fields. The argument is logical, but it addresses only one kind of education—education about the use of already created tools or technologies, such as the Internet. Brunner and Bennett's observations about gender differences (and their recommendations for the classroom) do not apply to the education of engineers, who actually build new technologies. The logic of science, not masculine or feminine perceptions, determines how engineers do their work.

Do I agree with the author?

One of your jobs as an alert reader is to respond (see 1f). When you do so, make notes: point out specific passages that illustrate the author's view, summarize that view, respond, and then explain the assumptions underlying both your view and the author's. In a thoroughly active reading, you would point to many such passages and make notes. When you write a formal evaluation, choose the passages that seem the most interesting to you and that appear to involve the author's main point most directly. Here's an example response to a point made by Brunner and Bennett:

Brunner and Bennett's view Making technology classrooms more welcoming to female students will, over time, help girls to become more confident about technology and will result in more women pursuing careers in high-tech industries.

The authors' assumption	Making technology classrooms more welcoming to female students will have a direct impact on the willingness of girls to take an interest in technology, master technology, and pursue careers in technology.
My view	Gender-neutral classrooms have no necessary connection to the effectiveness of technology instruction in those classrooms.
My assumptions	Technology is based on an application of scientific principles, not gender principles. Gender perceptions have nothing to do with the design of new tools and technologies.

Evaluation of "Technology Perceptions by Gender"

by Cornelia Brunner and Dorothy Bennett

Far fewer women than men run high-tech companies. In industry, generally, there has been a great deal of controversy over the "glass ceiling" that keeps women from advancing to the most senior management positions. Although the trend may be changing with the emergence of more women-led companies, in high-tech industries women continue to have trouble advancing to leadership roles. With scientists and engineers such as Ada Lovelace, Madame Curie, and Grace Hopper, history plainly shows that women are as capable as men in technical and scientific pursuits. Why, then, should we see such gender disparities in the world of high-tech? In "Technology Perceptions by Gender," Cornelia Brunner and Dorothy Bennett suggest that the technical education of girls--or rather, their miseducation--plays a role in keeping women out of the computer industry. Brunner and Bennett argue convincingly that to address these disparities, the educational community should help teachers recognize and teach to the interests of girls as well as boys when working with technology in the classroom.

Through research conducted at the Center for Children and Technology, the authors observed a distinct masculine and feminine "voice" with regard to technology. Girls tend to be less sure of themselves than boys with technology. Girls and women tend to focus on the "social function" of technology, whereas boys and men tend to focus on hardware and on how technology can increase their powers. Given these differences, Brunner and Bennett recommend that classroom teachers emphasize the uses of technologies for solving problems rather than focusing on technical elements such as programming languages and hardware. The authors also recommend that women in technology serve as role models for girls, and that the Internet be presented not merely as a vast archive of files (a masculine interest) but also as an environment that promotes communication and discovery (a feminine interest). Technologies are now powerful enough to accommodate both masculine and feminine learning styles, say the authors, and educators must work to make sure that both styles are valued and nurtured in the classroom.

Summary

Brunner and Bennett's research on gender perceptions about technology clearly shows that the sexes regard technology differently. Their recommendations for increasing girls' confidence with technology make sense and should be implemented, as long as we accept one essential fact about engineering: although new technologies are used in social settings that may (or may not) be gender biased, the actual building of these technologies does not depend in any way on gender and can be advanced only on a strictly scientific basis.

Preview of key points of evaluation

Certainly in classrooms where teachers introduce students to computers, every effort must be made to make girls as well as boys comfortable with technology. To the extent that negative perceptions of computers are learned, teachers have a responsibility to change perceptions. This they can do with lesson plans that show an awareness of Brunner and Bennett's insights. Girls as well as boys can be taught to find computer technology useful and engaging. Teachers must be alert to gender differences and plan accordingly by emphasizing how technology can solve problems, rather than focusing on the raw technological power. Teachers can also emphasize how computers--

Agreement with main argument

especially through the Internet--can help people communicate. Effective instruction will encourage girls as well as boys to discover their abilities through high-tech tools.

While Brunner and Bennett's suggestions are sound and worth following, we should make one distinction clear. These researchers investigated how women and men, and girls and boys, react to and use technology. Gender perceptions take place in a social world. But technology itself--the computer coding written in various programming languages and the design and manufacture of hardware components--exists in a scientific world, not a social one. The lines of code and the floppy drives and the semiconductors that make computers work are neither masculine nor feminine. They are logical, built on scientific principles that engineers manipulate to achieve a single purpose: building things that work. In an effort to equalize gender representation in high-tech industries, there is no room for a "feminization" of the science that makes computers function--not because women aren't welcome but because the science itself is gender neutral. No one cares if an Internet browser or a word processing program works because a woman, as opposed to a man, designed it. Passengers on airplanes don't care if the computers that control the flow of fuel to the engines were programmed by women or men. Our only concern is that the technology does what it is supposed to do.

Qualified agreement: main argument must be clarified

Up to a point, teachers who introduce students to technologies should follow Brunner and Bennett's suggestions, because the classrooms in which highly technical skills are taught are also social environments that can be gender biased. A professor teaching the intricacies of the C++ or Java programming languages may have different expectations for men and women. The male students in the class may create a frat-house atmosphere that makes female students uncomfortable. And the contexts for assignments may

Conclusion: evaluator agrees with author— but with qualifications

be cast in a "masculine voice," such as this one: "Design a catapult that shoots pellets at targets." Brunner and Bennett are right: the classrooms and the assignments that provide the occasions for technology students to build things should engage the imaginations of both boys and girls. At a certain point, though, once an effective assignment has sparked the imaginations of all students, teachers must keep a strictly technical focus that has nothing to do with gender. To do otherwise is to compromise the technology.

The point of research like Brunner and Bennett's is to provide news about the social world in which we live. Our responsibility on hearing such news is to act, and Brunner and Bennett have set a clear agenda that is worth following. We must honor the ways girls and women find technology useful and in so doing encourage them to enter high-tech professions in greater numbers. At the same time, we should recognize the limits of promoting the interests of women in high-tech industries. No amount of gender awareness or forward-thinking classroom strategies will change the fact that technology itself is built on the logic of science.

Works Cited

Brunner, Cornelia, and Dorothy Bennett. "Technology Perceptions by Gender." Education Digest 56.3 (Feb. 1998).

▶ **EXERCISE 2**

Write an evaluation of the article you summarized in Exercise 1. In preparing for your evaluation, take notes both on the author's presentation—for instance, its fairness and use of evidence and logic—and on your response to the author's key points. In writing the evaluation, use the summary you have written, but be aware that you may need to alter it by dividing it into several parts—presenting first a one-paragraph overall summary and then more sharply focused summaries of individual points you wish to evaluate.

> ▶ **2c** Writing an analysis (an application paper)

An **analysis** is an investigation that you conduct by applying a principle or definition to an activity or object in order to see how that activity or object works, what it might mean, or why it might be significant. Analysis enables you to make interpretations. You might analyze, for instance, an event, condition, behavior, painting, novel, play, or television show. As an illustration of the range of ways analysis can be used, read the following assignments from different disciplines. Notice how each asks students to apply a principle or a definition.

Literature Apply principles of Jungian psychology—that is, an archetypal approach to literature—to Hawthorne's "Young Goodman Brown." In your reading of the story, apply Jung's concepts of the *shadow, persona,* and *anima.*

Physics Use Newton's Second Law ($F = ma$) to analyze the acceleration of a fixed pulley, from which two weights hang: m_1 (.45 kg) and m_2 (.90 kg). Having worked the numbers, explain in a paragraph the principle of Newton's law and your method of applying it to solve a problem. Assume that your reader is not comfortable with mathematical explanations: do not use equations in your paragraph.

Finance Using Guilford C. Babcock's "Concept of Sustainable Growth" [*Financial Analysts Journal* 26 (May–June 1998): 108–114], analyze the stock price appreciation of the XYZ Corporation, figures for which are attached.

In these assignments, students are asked to analyze a short story, the acceleration of a pulley, and the stock performance of a corporation. In every discipline, certain principles and definitions play a key role in helping researchers to pose questions from a particular point of view, in order to better understand the activities and objects under study. Teachers will assign analyses to determine the extent to which you have understood principles and definitions important to your coursework. A key test of understanding is *application:* can you apply what you have learned to new situations? By writing an analysis, you show that you can. Analysis builds on skills of reading to understand (1e) and writing summaries (2a).

> ▶ **1** Setting goals for writing the analysis/application paper

An analysis should show readers how an activity or object works, what it might mean, or why it is significant. The specific goals of analysis follow:

- Understand a principle or definition and demonstrate your understanding by using it to study an activity or an object.
- Thoroughly apply this principle or definition to all significant parts of the activity or object under study.
- Create for the reader a sense that your analysis makes the activity or object being studied understandable—if not for the first time, then at least in a new way.

Different analyses lead to different interpretations.

What you discover through analysis depends entirely on which principles you apply to the activity or object under study. One event or text, analyzed according to different principles, will yield different interpretations. For example, over the years many writers have analyzed the L. Frank Baum classic, *The Wizard of Oz*, and the movie based on it. These writers have arrived at different interpretations, according to the different principles or definitions they applied to the story. Consider three specific insights into *The Wizard of Oz*, based on an application of three different principles.

Psychological analysis   At the dawn of adolescence, the very time she should start to distance herself from Aunt Em and Uncle Henry, the surrogate parents who raised her on their Kansas farm, Dorothy Gale experiences a hurtful reawakening of her fear that these loved ones will be rudely ripped from her, especially her Aunt (Em—M for Mother!). [Harvey Greenberg, *The Movies on Your Mind* (New York: Dutton, 1975).]

Political analysis   [*The Wizard of Oz*] was originally written as a political allegory about grass-roots protest. It may seem harder to believe than Emerald City, but the Tin Woodsman is the industrial worker, the Scarecrow [is] the struggling farmer, and the Wizard is the president, who is powerful only as long as he succeeds in deceiving the people. [Peter Dreier, "Oz Was Almost Reality," *Cleveland Plain Dealer* 3 Sept. 1989.]

Literary analysis   The Kansas described by Frank Baum is a depressing place. Everything in it is gray as far as the eye can see: the prairie is gray, and so is the house in which Dorothy lives. As for Auntie Em, "The sun and wind [. . .] had taken the sparkle from her eyes and left them a sober gray; they had taken the red from her cheeks and lips, and they were gray also. She was thin and gaunt, and never smiled now." And "Uncle Henry never laughed. [. . .] He was gray also, from his long beard to his rough boots." The sky? It was "even grayer than usual." [Salman Rushdie, "Out of Kansas," *New Yorker* 11 May 1992.]

Different analytical approaches yield different insights, and no analysis can be ultimately correct. There will be as many different interpretations of *The Wizard of Oz*, for instance, as there are principles of analysis; and each, potentially, has something to teach us. Not every analysis will be equally useful, however. An analysis is useful or authoritative to the extent that a writer (1) clearly defines a principle or definition to be applied; (2) applies this principle or definition thoroughly and systematically; and in so doing (3) reveals new and convincing insights into the activity or object being analyzed.

▶2 Understanding the techniques for writing an analysis/application paper

Prepare: Turn the principle or definition you are using to guide your analysis into a question—and then *probe*.

When preparing to write an analysis, you must be satisfied that you thoroughly understand the definition or principle you will be using. Read and reread the material that will become your analytical tool, and think of this material as a lens through which you will see new elements of the object under analysis. Turn your material into a series of questions that you will direct at the object under analysis.

Before writing your analysis, direct as many questions as possible to the object under study, and make many notes. In your final written piece, you will not

ACROSS THE CURRICULUM

Writing an Analysis

Faculty and students across the curriculum write analyses. Consider two parts of an essay written by a freshman sociology student, Edward Peselman, "The Coming Apart of a Dorm Society." Peselman (1) introduces a principle (how powerful people get their way) that will guide his analysis and (2) applies that principle. You will follow similar organizational steps in writing analyses for courses across the curriculum.

First, Edward introduces a concept:

> According to sociologist Randall Collins, what a powerful person wishes to happen must be achieved by controlling others (61).

Next, Edward applies this concept. He turns it into a question (though the question never appears in the essay itself): How does Collins's observation about power help to explain what happened in my dorm? Edward's *answer* becomes part of the analysis:

> Collins's observation helps define who had how much power in our dormitory's social group. Marc and Eric clearly had the most power. Everyone feared them and agreed to do pretty much what they wanted. Through violent words or threats of violence, they got their way. I was next in line: I wouldn't dare to manipulate Marc or Eric, but the others I could manage through occasional sarcasm. To avoid my quips, Benjamin became very cooperative. Up and down the pecking order, we exercised power through macho taunts, challenges, and biting language.

draw on every note, but only on those that prove most revealing—and you won't be able to tell which notes these are until you actually begin posing questions. Many students find the following guide for writing analyses helpful. (The third point assumes you've made a preliminary analysis and are choosing to incorporate the most revealing insights into your essay.)

- Introduce and summarize the activity or object to be analyzed. Whatever parts of this activity or object you intend to analyze should be mentioned here.
- Introduce and summarize the key definition or principle that will form the basis of your analysis.
- Analyze. Systematically apply elements of this definition or principle to parts of the activity or object under study. Part by part, discuss what you find.
- Conclude by reviewing all the parts you have analyzed. To what extent has your application of the definition or principle helped you to explain how the activity or object works, what it might mean, or why it is significant?

▶ 3　Applying techniques for writing analyses/application papers

The most common error in writing analyses is to present your readers with a summary only. Summary is naturally a *part* of analysis: you will need to summarize the object or activity you are examining and the principle or definition with which you are working, if this is not known to your readers. You must then take the next step and *apply* the principle or definition, using it as an investigative tool.

> **EXERCISE 3**
>
> Choose one of the three lines of analysis presented at the start of 2c-1—approaches to analyzing the classic film *The Wizard of Oz* from a psychological, political, or literary view. Apply one of these analytic schemes to the movie, identifying key elements of the movie that can be explained in terms of the analytic principles offered.

> ## 2d Writing a synthesis

A **synthesis** is a written discussion in which you gather and present source materials according to a well-defined purpose. In the process of writing a synthesis you answer these questions: (1) Which authors have written on my topic? (2) In what ways can I link the work of these authors to one another and to my own thinking? (3) How can I best use the material I've gathered to create a discussion that supports *my* views? The following assignment calls for synthesis:

Sociology   This semester we have read a number of books, articles, and essays on the general topic of marriage: its legal, religious, economic, and social aspects. In a 5-page paper, reflect on these materials, and discuss the extent to which they have helped to clarify or confuse your understanding of this "sacred institution."

The word *synthesis* does not appear in this assignment; nonetheless, the professor is asking students to gather and discuss sources. Note the importance of the writer here. Given multiple sources, a dozen students working on this sociology assignment would produce a dozen different papers; what would distinguish one paper from the next and make each uniquely valuable are the *particular* insights of each student. You are the most important source in any synthesis. However much material you gather into a discussion, your voice should predominate.

No synthesis is possible without a critical, comprehensive reading of sources. The quality of a synthesis is tied directly to the quality of prior reading. You have the best possible chance of producing a meaningful synthesis when you have read sources to understand (1e), respond (1f), evaluate (1g), and synthesize (1h). At one point or another, a synthesis will draw on all your skills of critical reading and writing; synthesis therefore represents some of the most sophisticated and challenging writing you will do in college.

Ensuring that your voice is heard

When writing a synthesis, avoid letting sources dominate a discussion unless you are being asked to write a literature review (see 40c-2—though even in this case your point of view dominates in that you select the articles to be discussed and determine the principles that organize discussion). In its most extreme form, the error of allowing sources to dominate leads to a series of summaries in which the writer, making no attempt at merging sources, disappears. The problem can be avoided if you remember that a synthesis should draw on your insights first, and only then on the insights of others. *A paper organized as a series of summaries of separate sources, introduced by a statement such as "Many authors have discussed topic X," is not a synthesis, because it makes no attempt to merge ideas.*

Do Not Become Invisible in Your Papers

The DANGER signs:

1. Your paragraphs are devoted wholly to the work of the authors you are synthesizing.
2. Virtually every sentence introduces someone else's ideas.
3. The impulse to use the first-person *I* never arises.

Instead of writing a string of paragraphs organized around the work of others, write paragraphs organized around your own statements. In the context of a paper on advertising, for example, a discussion organized as summaries of separate sources would leave you invisible. Generally, a statement such as the one that follows indicates that the writer will never appear:

Several authors have discussed the topic of advertising.

This statement, and the paper likely to be built on it, is *source* based and exhibits all the danger signals mentioned in the preceding box. By contrast, a paper in which the author is present will show an active, interested mind engaged with the reading material and headed in some clear direction, with a purpose:

The topic of advertising is guaranteed to generate debate whenever it is discussed. It is rare to find a person who does not have strong, specific opinions about advertising and its effects on our culture.

This statement is *writer* based. The writer's purpose and direction are made known, and we sense the reading material will not overshadow the writer. If you find source materials monopolizing your work, reexamine your thesis, and make it into a writer-based statement.

▶ 1 Setting goals for writing a synthesis

Your goal in writing a synthesis is to create and participate in a discussion, joining your views on a topic with the views of others. Specifically, you want to do the following:

- Understand your purpose for writing.
- Define your topic and your thesis (see 3d).
- Locate the work of others who have written on this topic, and read to understand, respond, and evaluate.
- Forge relationships among sources; link the thinking of others to your own thinking.
- Create a discussion governed by your views; draw on sources as contributors to a discussion that you design and control.

▶ 2 Understanding techniques for writing a synthesis

In writing a synthesis, you will at some point write partial summaries, evaluations, and analyses. Synthesis draws on these forms and is larger and more ambitious than any one of them. Summary and evaluation treat single sources; analysis is limited to an application of one source (or set of ideas) to a second source; but synthesis merges sources and looks for larger patterns of relationship.

Cross-referencing ideas

A synthesis organized by *ideas* shows that you are intellectually present and involved with the material you have gathered. To organize a paper by ideas, you must first divide the topic into the component parts that the various authors take up in their discussions. These component parts then become the key ideas around which you organize your paper. You can follow this method when your writing is based on library research. Cross-referencing is a necessary step in the process (see 1h-2); once you have identified a component part of a topic and cross-referenced authors' discussions, you are nearly ready to write. In response to Exercise 9 in Chapter 1, you worked on completing a note sheet. If you have not completed this assignment, do so now.

Clarifying relationships among authors

Your cross-referenced notes enable you to lay out and examine what several authors have written about *particular* parts of a topic, in this case gender and technology. Working with what your sources say on a particular point, you can now forge relationships. Sources can be related in a variety of ways, but you will find that patterns emerge, which can be identified by asking several questions:

Which authors agree?

Which authors disagree?

Are there any examples in one source of statements made in another?

Can you offer any definitions?

Are any readings related by cause and effect?

Pose these questions (and others that occur to you) to get a conversation started among the particular parts of the topic you've identified. Ask: If these authors could talk to one another, what would they say—based on what they've written? What would *you* say to each of them? With whom do you agree? Why? Who seems right, or more authoritative? Take notes in response to these questions. When the time comes for writing, you may not use all your notes, but you will be prepared to launch a discussion in which you and your sources participate.

Many students find the following guidelines helpful when synthesizing source materials:

- Read sources on the topic; subdivide the topic into parts, and infer relationships among parts, cross-referencing sources when possible.
- Clarify relationships among authors by posing questions (for example, Which authors agree? Which authors disagree? and so on).
- Write a thesis (see 3d) that ensures your voice is heard and that allows you to develop sections of the paper in which you refer to sources.
- Sketch an outline of your paper (3d-4), organizing your discussion by *idea*, not by summary. Enter the names of authors into your outline, along with notes indicating how these authors will contribute to your discussion.
- Write a draft of your paper and revise, following strategies discussed in Chapter 4.

▶3 **Applying techniques for writing a synthesis**

Since the writer's own views should predominate in a synthesis, no two syntheses, even if based on the same source materials, will be the same. Below is an example of how Lou Cassetta generated a conversation among his sources. In an early stage of note taking, Lou listed his authors and cross-referenced the passages in which the authors commented on a particular point that interested him: the causes of number disparities between women and men in high-tech industries. Here, Lou summarizes each author's position on the point; he states what each would say to at least one other author; and then he responds personally to each author. (Lou is working with source materials from Chapter 1. See excerpts in Exercise 9, page 27.)

The "glass ceiling" in high-tech industries

Cowan
Although she was writing in 1979, before the term *glass ceiling* became popular, Cowan understood and anticipated the problem. Her analysis is that as a society, we have trained women not to be interested in science and technology. It would follow, then, that women who do make it to high-tech jobs would stall out, since the male culture that trained women "to opt out of the technological order" is the same culture in charge of the high-tech businesses.

Lefton
Lefton comments on the socialization of the sexes—on how men and women learn to take on the gender roles they do. He allows some room for inborn differences. Most differences he accounts for through learned behaviors. He would agree for the most part with Cowan.

Munk and Oliver
Munk and Oliver examine the high-tech world and see considerable progress on women breaking the glass ceiling. The number of proposals for women-led high-tech start-ups, they claim, is evidence that more women than ever are breaking through the glass ceiling.

Hamm
Hamm sees the glass as half empty. He reviews the same territory as Munk and Oliver and yet reaches exactly the opposite conclusion: that the glass ceiling, along with the sexism that has put it in place, is preventing women from advancing in their careers in high-tech industries.

Brunner and Bennett
The authors don't address the glass ceiling directly, but given their research showing that female students are not as encouraged in technology classes as male students, they would not be surprised to see unequal treatment in the high-tech workplace.

Cassetta
First, Munk and Oliver and Hamm are writing only eight months apart, and they take opposite sides on the question of the glass ceiling. The reality of gender equality in the high-tech workplace must be complicated if in two respected magazines we see two opposing conclusions in such a short span of time. Women should be advancing more equitably in high-tech industries. Why aren't they? Probably because of male culture.

Once you have narrowed a topic, identified its parts, and assembled sources that discuss these parts, you are in a position (as Lou Cassetta has demonstrated) to get a conversation started among your sources. The next step is to write your synthesis, which will require you to think critically not only about what other writers say on a topic but also about what *you* have to say. Your voice and your insights are crucial elements in a synthesis; they are the elements that distinguish your efforts from those of others writing on the same topic. In Chapter 3, you will follow Lou Cassetta's progress as he draws relationships among sources and, just as important, draws on his own experience to create an effective essay.

▶ **EXERCISE 4**

You have seen Lou Cassetta's efforts to forge relationships among the selections on gender and technology you read in Chapter 1: Munk and Oliver, Hamm, Cowan, Brunner and Bennett, and Lefton. Given that no two readers respond to a passage in quite the same way, take your turn at forging relationships among these sources. Identify two or three parts of the larger topic of gender and technology, which these authors discuss. Then follow Lou Cassetta's lead, and generate a conversation among your sources.

3

Planning, Developing, and Writing a Draft

A writer's thoughts take shape through the very act of writing and rewriting. When you write you are also thinking, and when you revise you are thinking again about your topic. As you become an experienced writer, you will learn to produce a first draft and then revise at least once. The many decision points you will face in the process are discussed in this chapter.

An Overview of the Writing Process

Preparing to write

3a **Discovering your topic, purpose, and audience.** Know your topic and, if necessary, research it. Let your purpose for writing generate and organize ideas. Keep specific readers in mind as you write.

3b **Generating ideas and information.** Use strategies such as freewriting to generate ideas and information for your draft.

3c **Reviewing and categorizing ideas and information.** Review the material you have generated, and group like ideas and information into categories.

3d **Writing a thesis and sketching your paper.** Study your material and write a working thesis, a statement that will give your draft a single, controlling idea. Based on your thesis, sketch your draft.

Writing

3e **Writing a draft.** Write a draft by adopting a strategy suited to your temperament. As you write, expect to depart from your sketch.

Revising

4a **Early revision: Rediscovering your main idea.** Refine your thesis; use it to check that the broad sections of your document, as well as paragraphs, are coherent and logically arranged.

4b **Later revision: Bringing your main idea into focus.** Clarify individual sentences. Check grammar, usage, punctuation, and spelling.

The three stages of writing are, broadly speaking, distinct. Different activities take place in each stage, and the stages unfold more or less in this order: preparing to write, writing, and revising. But the stages also blend into each other. In the

http://dlc.tri-c.cc.oh.us/ wb/write/docs/ process.htm
A hyperlinked map of the steps of the writing process, with a discussion of each.

middle of a first draft, you may pause to revise an important sentence or paragraph, deciding to make one part of your document nearly finished while other parts remain rough or not yet written. In a first draft, you may discover new approaches to your topic and stop to write new lists and make new outlines, activities associated with preparing to write.

Typically, writers loop backward and forward through the three stages of writing—several times for any one document. The process of writing is **recursive**: it bends and it circles, and it is illustrated well with a wheel.

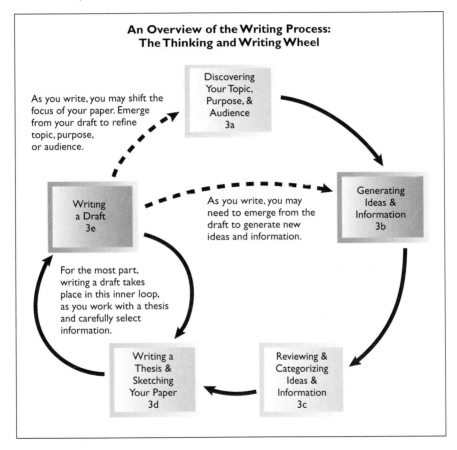

An Overview of the Writing Process: The Thinking and Writing Wheel

Discovering Your Topic, Purpose, & Audience 3a

As you write, you may shift the focus of your paper. Emerge from your draft to refine topic, purpose, or audience.

Writing a Draft 3e

As you write, you may need to emerge from the draft to generate new ideas and information.

Generating Ideas & Information 3b

For the most part, writing a draft takes place in this inner loop, as you work with a thesis and carefully select information.

Writing a Thesis & Sketching Your Paper 3d

Reviewing & Categorizing Ideas & Information 3c

3a Discovering your topic, purpose, and audience

1 Understanding your topic

In both college and business, you can expect to be assigned topics for writing and to define topics for yourself. In either case, you will write most efficiently, and with greatest impact, when you write about what you know (or what you can learn in a

Discovering Your Topic, Purpose, and Audience **51**

reasonably brief time); when you find some way to own your topic; and when you sufficiently narrow your topic so that you can write on it fully within an allotted number of pages.

Know your topic.

Readers respect, and indeed demand, authority in a writer. Knowing your topic will usually require some investigation on your part. The following suggestions may help you to investigate and refine your topic:

Read: If you do not know a topic well, read and gather information: letters, photographs, articles, lecture notes, and so on.

Interview: Locate people who are knowledgeable about the topic, and interview them. Avoid questions that can be answered with basic research. Develop questions that yield information and ideas unique to this source. (See 33g-3 for help on generating questions.)

Reflect: What is your personal commitment to the topic? What experiences have you had that influence your thinking? Issues on which you write may require that you take a stand. Know your position. (See 1b for strategies that can aid reflection.)

Own your topic.

Effective writing is produced by those who understand *and* are committed to a topic. If you are assigned a topic that does not, at first, stimulate you, try these strategies:

- *Stretch the topic to fit your interests.* Redefine the assignment in such a way that it touches on your experience and at the same time is acceptable to your professor.
- *Identify a debate.* Try to understand why the topic is debatable (if it is) and whom the topic affects, as well as the merits and limitations of each side of the debate. Personalize the debate. Take a position.
- *Talk with friends.* Sometimes informal conversations will help you to identify elements of a topic that interest you. Get a conversation going, listen, and participate.

Restrict and define your topic.

Know how long your document is expected to be, and limit your writing accordingly. Avoid the frustration of choosing a broad topic (for example, the issue of privacy on the Internet) for a brief paper or report—a mistake that will guarantee a superficial product. The briefer your document, the more narrowly directed your topic should be. The following guidelines will help you to restrict a topic:

- *Divide the topic into parts.* What are the component parts of this topic? What parts (or subtopics) do I know most about? Can I link subtopics in meaningful ways? In which subtopic am I most interested?
- *Ask a journalist's questions.* To focus on a subtopic that interests you, pose questions: *who, what, where, when, why, how?* A response to one or more of these questions can become the focus of a paper.

ACROS S THE CURRICULUM

Broadening the Context

Across the curriculum, both faculty and students create occasions to think critically by asking: *How are the details of what I'm studying an instance or example of something larger?* Read the opening sentences of an article by media researcher Shelley Stamp Lindsey.* Observe how she takes a particular event, "the fight for female enfranchisement"—or the right to vote—and identifies it as a particular, interesting example of a larger issue.

> *Initial topic is women's suffrage*
>
> [Much more than the vote was at stake in the campaign for women's suffrage. As the fight for female enfranchisement escalated in America during the early teens, the debate grew to encompass issues far beyond the ballot, or even the larger question of gender equality. Competing claims furnished a landscape where new ideals of feminine behavior could be tested—*and contested*—against women's increasing prominence in civic affairs. Indeed, female voting rights engaged a struggle over the very definition of modern womanhood.
>
> *Writer broadens topic to "modern womanhood"*
>
> *Discipline focus: study will be in visual arts*
>
> With the image of femininity at stake, much of the debate was waged in _visual_ terms, in posters, cartoons, pageants, marches, and ultimately on movie screens where conservatives and activists fought over appropriate manifestations of "womanliness."

*Lindsey's article "*Eighty Million Women Want*—? Women's Suffrage, Female Viewers, and the Body Politic" appeared in *Quarterly Review of Film and Video* 16.1 (1995).

EXERCISE I

List three topics with which you are intimately familiar and about which you can write for *public* view. Subdivide each topic into as many parts as you can. Eventually, you will select from these parts a focus for your paper.

EXERCISE 2

Of the topics you have narrowed in Exercise 1, which do you care most about? Write a brief paragraph in which you explain to yourself the *reasons* you are interested in one of these narrowed topics.

2 Identifying your purpose

There are four basic purposes or aims for writing: to *inform*, to *persuade*, to *express*, and to *entertain*. Since you will generally be asked to produce informative and persuasive pieces in college, this book addresses primarily these types of writing.

Informative writing

When writing to *inform*, you explain, define, or describe a topic so that the reader understands its component parts, its method of operation, its uses, and so on. The following assignments call for informative writing:

Literature Cite three examples of metaphor in *Great Expectations*, and explain how each works.

Chemistry Explain the chemical process by which water, when boiled, becomes steam.

Psychology What is "cognitive dissonance," and in what ways does it contribute to the development of personality?

What the reader already knows about the topic will in large part determine the level of language you use and the difficulty of the information that you present. An engineer discussing the flight of planes would use one vocabulary with fellow engineers and another vocabulary with a nontechnical audience. (See 3a-3.)

Persuasive writing

When writing to *persuade*, you attempt to change a reader's views. As with informative writing, the persuasive writer carefully considers the reader's prior knowledge in order to provide the background information needed for understanding. If you knew nothing about international business, you might not be persuaded about the need to master a foreign language in college. The person urging you to learn Japanese would need to inform you, first, of certain facts and trends. As a persuasive writer, you will provide information both to establish understanding and to provide a base for building an argument. (See Chapter 6, which is devoted entirely to argumentation.) The following assignments call for persuasive writing:

Astronomy Given limited government money available for the construction and updating of astronomical observatories, which of the projects discussed this semester deserve continued funding? Argue for your choices based on the types of discoveries you expect the various projects to make in the next five years.

Sociology You have read two theories on emotions: the Cannon-Bard theory and the James-Lange theory. Which seems the more convincing to you? Why?

Marketing Select three ads that describe similar products. Which ad is most effective? Why?

Expressive writing and writing to entertain

Through *expressive* writing you explore your own ideas and emotions. When private, expressive writing can lead you to be more experimental, less guarded, perhaps even more honest than in a paper meant for others. When public, expressive writing will not be a journal entry, but rather an essay in which you reflect on your impressions. In many composition courses, the first part of a semester or an entire semester will be devoted to expressive writing.

The least frequent purpose of academic writing is to *entertain*. Possibly you will write a poem, story, or play in your college career, and certainly you will read forms of writing that are intended to entertain readers. What makes a piece of writing entertaining is subject to debate. It suffices to say here that writing to entertain need not be writing that evokes smiles.

Purposes for writing may overlap: in a single essay, you may inform, persuade, and entertain a reader. But if an essay is to succeed, you should identify a *single*, primary purpose for writing. Otherwise, you risk having a document that tries to do all things but does none well.

▶ **EXERCISE 3**

Return to the writing you produced for Exercises 1 and 2. This will become your topic for a five-page paper. Write a brief paragraph explaining your purpose for this paper. Although purposes may overlap to some extent, decide on one of two primary purposes: to inform *or* persuade your reader. If the topics in Exercises 1 ▶ and 2 left you uninspired, choose a new topic.

COMPUTER TIPS

Compose Alternate Versions

Even if you're a worse-than-average typist, drafting is probably easier on a computer, because it allows you to make changes quickly and easily. Take advantage of this ease by composing multiple versions of sentences and paragraphs, particularly at crucial points in your papers, such as beginnings and endings. Don't be afraid to play with language, to experiment, and to try different phrases and sentence structures. Type each version into your draft, and then simply delete the ones you don't like during revision.

▶**3** **Defining your audience**

You write in order to communicate *with* someone. Whether your intent is primarily to inform or to persuade, you must know your audience, since what you write will depend greatly on who will read your work. Questions that you ask about an audience *before you write a first draft* can help you make decisions concerning your paper's content and level of language.

Writing for an unspecified audience

If your audience is not clearly specified, then regard your instructor as the main reader. Do not think that because he or she is an expert, you are relieved of developing points thoroughly. Many assignments are given to gauge what you know about a topic; in these instances, to omit information intentionally is self-defeating.

Assume that the instructor functions as an expert editor who will review your paper before passing it on to another reader. This second reader is *not* an expert on your topic and must therefore rely fully on your explanation. Assume that this reader is skeptical and neutral regarding your topic. The reader will hear you out, but will probe with questions and will require that you develop general statements with specific illustrations and that you defend any assertions needing support.

Analyze the Needs of Your Audience

Pose these general questions, regardless of your purpose:

- Who is the reader? What is the reader's age, sex, religious background, educational background, and ethnic heritage?
- What is my relationship with the reader?
- What impact on my presentation—on choice of words, level of complexity, and choice of examples—will the reader have?
- Why will the reader be interested in my paper? How can I best spark the reader's interest?

If you are writing to inform, pose these questions as well:

- What does the reader know about the topic's history?
- How well does the reader understand the topic's technical details?
- What does the reader need to know? Want to know?
- What level of language and content will I use in discussing the topic, given the reader's understanding?

If you are writing to persuade, pose both sets of questions above, as well as the following:

- What are the reader's views on the topic? Given what I know about the reader (from the preceding questions), is the reader likely to agree with my view on the topic? To disagree? To be neutral?
- What factors are likely to affect the reader's beliefs about the topic? What special circumstances (work, religious conviction, political views, etc.) should I be aware of that will affect the reader's views?
- How can I shape my argument to encourage the reader's support, given his or her present level of interest, level of understanding, and beliefs?

▶ **EXERCISE 4**

Return to the topic you selected in Exercise 3, where you wrote a paragraph explaining your purpose for a proposed five-page paper. Working with your topic and your purpose (to inform or persuade), answer the questions in the box "Analyze the Needs of Your Audience" three times, once for each of three different audiences: a friend at another school, your parents, and some other audience of your choosing. Select one of these as the audience for your paper.

▶ **4 Analyzing topic, purpose, audience—and the writing occasion**

Each new writing project constitutes a distinct occasion for writing and requires that you consider the relationship of topic, purpose, and audience. Depending on the writing occasion, you will decide on the tone and the register for your project.

Tone is a writer's general attitude toward the reader and the subject. Every paper *will* have, and cannot help but have, a characteristic tone. English offers numerous ways of saying the same thing. For example, the most simple request can be worded to reflect a variety of tones:

| May I have the salt? | Give me that salt! | Salt! |
| Pass the salt. | Pass the salt, please. | |

For every writing occasion, choose words to create a tone that you think is appropriate to your topic, purpose, and audience. Mismatching tone and topic can create problems. Imagine discussing some grim event with a lighthearted, devil-may-care tone. Readers would turn away, and the purpose of communication would be defeated.

Register is the degree of formality in your writing.

- In a **formal register,** you follow all the rules and conventions of writing expected in the professional and academic worlds. Formal writing is precise and concise; it avoids colloquial expressions, and it is thorough in content and tightly structured.
- The **informal register** is common in personal correspondence and journals, and it tends to be conversational. Word choice is freely colloquial and structure need not be as tightly reasoned as in a formal paper. Occasional lapses in grammar, usage, spelling, or punctuation matter little in personal correspondence and not at all in personal journal writing.
- The **popular register** is typical of most general interest magazines. It adheres to all conventions of grammar, usage, spelling, and punctuation; it is also carefully organized. The language, however, is more conversational than that found in formal writing. Heavy emphasis is placed on engaging readers and maintaining their interest. For suggestions on matching tone and register to the writing occasion, see 21e, on the use of formal English.

You can inform or persuade a reader in *any* register or tone, but once chosen, register and tone should be used consistently. The diagram on page 58 suggests the need for a balanced, four-way relationship among the basic elements of the writing occasion.

When Does Your Audience Need to Know More?

Consider these points when deciding whether your audience needs to know more about a key term or person.

- Major personalities referred to in textbooks or in lectures will help constitute the general, shared knowledge of a discipline. In all cases, *refer to people in your papers either by their* last *names or by their first* and *last names.* Do not identify "giants of a field" with explanatory tags like *who was an important inventor in the early part of the twentieth century.*
- Terms that have been defined at length in a textbook or lecture also constitute the general, shared knowledge of a discipline. Once you have understood these terms, use them in your papers—but do not define them. Demonstrate your understanding by using the terms accurately.
- The same people and terms not requiring definition in an academic context may need to be defined in a nonacademic one. Decide what information to include based on a careful audience analysis.

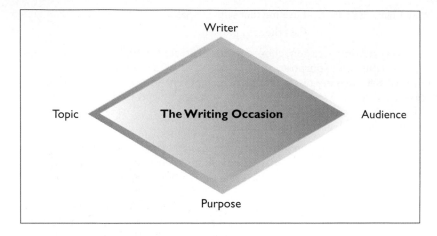

EXERCISE 5

Write a series of three brief letters to a mail-order business. Ask why you have not received the computer software you ordered and paid for. The letters should show a change in tone, moving from a neutral inquiry in the first letter to annoyed concern in the second to controlled anger in the third. In each case, maintain a formal tone. Avoid using colloquial expressions.

EXERCISE 6

Given the audience and the purpose you have chosen for the paper you are planning (see your answers to Exercises 3 and 4), decide on the tone and register you should adopt.

3b   Generating ideas and information

http://www.gsu.edu/~wwweng/rh/
invention.htm
In classical rhetoric, the term for generating ideas and information was "invention."

At times you may stare at a topic you intend to write about and feel as though there is *nothing* to say. When you are feeling frantic, try proven strategies in this section for generating ideas and information. As you review these strategies, bear in mind this "User's Manual":

- No one method will work for all topics.
- Some methods may not suit your style of discovery.
- Some methods work well when combined.
- Move quickly to a new strategy if one does not work.
- Tell your internal critic to take a vacation.

The invention strategies discussed in this section can complement each other; you will generate one type of information using one strategy and other types using others. When you examine *all* the material you have generated, you should find

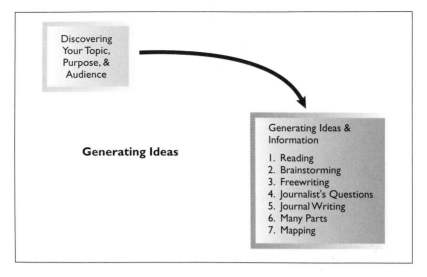

ample opportunities to advance to the next stage of writing. The work of a single student, Lou Cassetta (whose completed paper appears in 4e), illustrates how you might put the various strategies to use.

▶ I   Reading

Most academic writing is based on reading. Early in the writing process, when you are still not precisely sure what your topic will be, reading can be an excellent stimulus. Source materials may present compelling facts or strongly worded opinions with which to agree or disagree. Be alert to your responses and jot them down; they may later become important to your paper. (See Chapter 1 and the discussion of strategies for reading effectively.) If you are writing a paper that will not draw heavily on sources, use your reading mainly as a stimulus. If you are writing a research report, read to generate the information you will then use to write the paper. In this case, realize that you will need to cite sources (see Chapter 37).

At the time Lou Cassetta was preparing to write, he was enrolled in an introductory psychology course. He browsed through the textbook and found that material on gender roles sparked his interest. Lou's tentative topic was "gender roles and technology." Lou made the following notes.

········ILLUSTRATION: LOU CASSETTA'S PAPER

READING

> According to my textbook, society creates most of the behavioral differences between men and women. Nevertheless, research still has not been able to pinpoint any gender-specific intellectual differences. Many women tend to avoid computers, while a great number of men treat computers as an

enjoyable and exciting diversion. In my opinion, women do not
avoid computers because of any inherent genetic instruction,
but it is society that tells them to pay little attention to
technology. Women who do choose to explore technology do not
treat machines the way men do. Their insight in the field of
computers may prove to be very helpful, if they are given the
chance to express themselves.

▲

2 Brainstorming

The object of **brainstorming** is to write quickly and, once finished, to return to
your work with a critical eye. Place your topic at the top of a page, and then list any
related phrase or word that comes to mind. Set a time limit of five or ten minutes,
and list items as quickly as you can. To brainstorm in a small group, a technique that
allows the ideas of one person to build on those of another, write your topic on a
board or sheet of easel paper. (If you have no topic, see "Freewriting," 3b-3.) Sit in
a circle, and ask each member of the group to offer two or three words or phrases
for your list. Work around the circle a second time, asking each member to add another one or two ideas. Finally, open the floor to anyone who can add more ideas.

After you have generated your list, group related items, and set aside items
that do not fit into a grouping. Groupings with the greatest number of items indicate areas that should prove fertile in developing your paper. Save the results of
your brainstorming session for your next step in the planning process: selecting,
organizing, and expanding information.

ILLUSTRATION: LOU CASSETTA'S PAPER

BRAINSTORMING

<u>Men discussing computers</u>
need for speed--men want the newest and fastest machines
jargon--men like to know the buzzwords
knowledge--men like to impress each other with facts and
     figures
learning--find out about the latest information by word of
     mouth
exclusion--only the well versed can "talk shop"
advice--everybody has some to give
bonding--men create close friendships through these
     conversations
opinions--opinions about products often overshadow facts
excess--some men go too far and spend or do too much
women--are not invited to (are not interested in?) these
     conversations

```
future--high hopes for future machines
sharing--helping friends with their own computers
```

Lou grouped his list as follows. The question mark denotes the "leftover" category, which includes items Lou did not know how to group.

```
                    Men discussing computers

    Negatives            Positives            ?

    exclusion            knowledge            need for speed

    opinions             learning             jargon

    excess               advice               future

    women                bonding

                         sharing
```

COMPUTER TIPS

Writing in the Dark

If you're a fairly speedy typist, one interesting use of your computer is to turn off the monitor and just type. You can either freewrite or compose a rough draft in this manner. It removes the fear of making mistakes, the urge to reread at inappropriate times, and the hypnotic effect of your works on the screen. Just type; then turn on the monitor to see what you have. You have no idea how liberating it can be, especially if you're stuck with writer's block.

▶ 3 Freewriting and focused freewriting

Freewriting is a technique to try when you are asked to write but have no topic. Think for a moment about the subject area in which you have been asked to write. Recall lectures or chapters read in textbooks. Choose a broad area of interest, and then start writing for some predetermined amount of time—say, five or ten minutes. Alternately, you can write until you have filled a certain number of pages (typically one or two). As you write, do not stop to puzzle over word choice or punctuation. Do not stop to cross words out because they do not capture your meaning. Push on to the next sentence. Freely change thoughts from one sentence to the next, if this is where your thinking takes you. Once you have reached your time limit or page allotment, read over what you have done. Circle ideas that could become paper topics. To generate ideas about these specific topics, you may then try a more focused strategy for invention: brainstorming, focused freewriting, or any of the other strategies that will be discussed in later sections.

Focused freewriting gives you the benefits of freewriting, but on a *specific* topic. The end result of this strategy is the same as brainstorming, and so the choice of invention strategies is one of style: do you prefer making lists or writing sentences? Begin with a definite topic. Write for five or ten minutes; reread your work;

Generating Ideas and Information **61**

and circle any words, phrases, or sentences that look potentially useful. Draw lines that link circled words, and make notes to explain the linkages. Then clarify these linkages on a separate sheet of paper. The result will be a grouping of items, some in sentence form, that looks like the result of brainstorming. Save your work for the next step in planning: selecting, organizing, and expanding information.

Following is a portion of Lou's focused freewrite on the topic "talking shop."

........**ILLUSTRATION: LOU CASSETTA'S PAPER**

FOCUSED FREEWRITING

I have always talked shop. I have had many conversations about machines and technology. It started with automobiles. I tried to learn as much as I could about cars, and used my knowledge to impress and to bond. Men definitely bond when talking about machines. I often talked to the same people about both cars and computers. It's all the same really. The need for speed--I've got it. Although I've never had the latest or best computer, I always knew the latest developments in the industry. Some people went to the other extreme. They not only knew about the latest developments in the industry, they went out and bought them. I'm glad I'm not rich, or I'd have a lot of outdated computers lying around by now. The industry changes so quickly. That's what makes it so exciting. Exciting for men, at least. Women never chimed in about computers and cars. That's guy talk. It may not be "locker room" profanity, but women count themselves out of it just the same. Computers and cars are "toys for the boys" and women count themselves out at a very early age. It really shouldn't be that way, but men have dominated the computer world so much, that women are not even given a chance to offer their opinions.

Lou organized his freewriting into these categories:

Talking Shop
-male bonding
-cars and computers same
-need for speed

Exciting for Men
-"toys for the boys"
-men have dominated
-women aren't given chance (or aren't interested)

Planning, Developing, and Writing a Draft

▶4 The journalist's questions

You have read or heard of the journalist's questions: *who, what, when, where, why,* and *how.* In answering the questions, you can define, compare, contrast, or investigate cause and effect. Again, the assumption is that by thinking about parts, you will have more to write about than if you focused on a topic as a whole. The journalist's questions can help you to restrict and define a topic (see 3a-1), giving you the option to concentrate, say, on any three parts of the whole: perhaps the *who, what,* and *why* of the topic. Under the topic of mapping (3b-7), you will find Lou Cassetta's notes made in response to four of the journalist's questions.

▶5 Journal writing

You might keep a journal in conjunction with your writing course. A *journal* is a set of private, reflective notes that you keep, in which you describe your reactions to lectures, readings, discussions, films, current events—any topic touching on your course work. A journal borrows from both diary writing and course notebooks.

- As in a diary, your journal entries are private, reflective, and "safe" in the sense that you know no one is looking over your shoulder; thus, you are free to experiment with ideas and to express your thoughts honestly.
- Unlike a diary, a journal focuses on matters relating to your course work and not on matters of your private life, unless such observations tie in with your course work.

Journal writing gives you an opportunity to converse with yourself in your own language about what you have been studying. You pose questions, develop ideas, reflect on readings, speculate and explore, and try to pinpoint confusions. The more you write, the more you clarify what you know and, equally important, what you do not know. The language of your journal entries should reflect your voice: use the words, expressions, and rhythms of vocabulary that you use when you chat with friends.

Punctuation is not important as long as you can reread your journal entries. Periodically review your journal entries, looking for ideas in which you seemed particularly interested. As with freewriting, use these ideas as the basis for a more focused strategy of invention.[1]

▶6 The "many parts" strategy[2]

Another method for generating ideas about a topic is to list its parts. Number the items on your list. Then ask, "What are the uses of Number 1? Number 2? Number 3?" and so on. If *uses of* does not seem to work for the parts in question, try *consequences of:* "What are the consequences of Number 1?" The *many parts* strategy lets you be far more specific and imaginative in thinking about the topic as a whole

---

[1]Discussion of journal writing here is based on Toby Fulwiler, ed., *The Journal Book* (Portsmouth, NH: Boynton/Cook-Heinemann, 1987) 1–7.

[2]This strategy is adapted from John C. Bean and John D. Ramage, *Form and Surprise in Composition: Writing and Thinking across the Curriculum* (New York: Macmillan, 1986) 170–71.

than you might be ordinarily. Once you have responded to your questions about the uses or consequences of some part, you might pursue the one or two most promising responses in a focused freewrite.

········ **ILLUSTRATION: LOU CASSETTA'S PAPER**

THE "MANY PARTS" STRATEGY

```
I. What are the parts of gender roles in computing?
   1. Women are discouraged from using computers.
   2. Men treat computers as an enjoyable hobby.
   3. Women treat computers like tools.

One part, explored:

II. What are the consequences of discouraging women from using
    computers?
    -computers become the domain of men and only men
    -women avoid technology in general
    -women cannot relate to men through discourse on
     technology
    -it is difficult for women to work in the computer
     industry
    -computer industry loses women's insights
```

▲

▶7 Mapping

If you enjoy thinking visually, try **mapping** your ideas. Begin by writing your topic as briefly as possible (a single word is best). Circle the topic, and draw three, four, or five short spokes from the circle. At the end of each spoke, place one of the journalist's questions, making a major branch off the spoke for every answer to a question. Now, working with each answer individually, pose one of the six journalist's questions once again. After you have completed the exercise, you will have a page that places ideas in relation to one another. Notice how the "map" distinguishes between major points and supporting information.

http://braindance.com/
bdimmap1.htm
An in-depth look at the creative, cognitive, and organizational value of mind maps.

▶ **EXERCISE 7**

Generate ideas about three of the following topics, using *two* of the previously mentioned methods of invention for each idea.

river rafting	the symphony	dorm life
a cousin	compulsory draft	space flight

Planning, Developing, and Writing a Draft

.........**ILLUSTRATION: LOU CASSETTA'S PAPER**

MAPPING THE JOURNALIST'S QUESTIONS

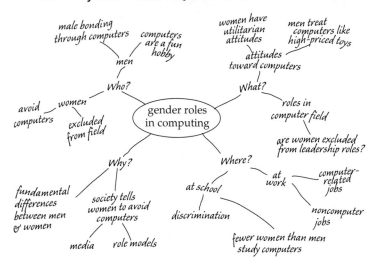

▶ **EXERCISE 8**

If you are preparing a paper as you read this chapter, use any *three* methods of invention to generate ideas about your topic. The end result of your work should be several categories of grouped ideas.

▶ **3c** | **Reviewing and categorizing ideas and information**

Not all of the information you have generated will be equally useful. Therefore, your next task in the writing process is to select those ideas that look most promising. *Promising* in this context is an inexact term, and at this stage of the writing process there is no way to be exact. Until you have completed a first draft, you cannot know for certain the content of your paper. Despite the plans you make when preparing to write, your actual writing is where you will discover much of your content. For this reason, the choices you make about which ideas and information to include in a paper must be based on hunches: informed guesses about what will work.

▶**I** **Reviewing ideas and making meaningful categories**

Make sense of the information you have generated by creating categories. A category is akin to a file drawer into which you place related materials. Your job is to consolidate: take all the ideas and information you have generated; spread your notes out before you; and then take a clean sheet of paper and group ideas. Give each new grouping a general category name. Beneath each category name, list subordinate, or supporting, information.

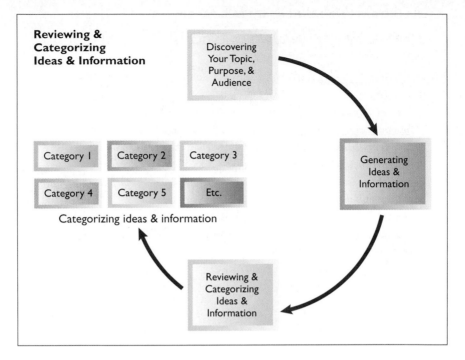

Lou Cassetta generated five categories of information on which he could base a paper. Following is one of those categories, with information consolidated from the results of four different methods for generating information.

........ILLUSTRATION: LOU CASSETTA'S PAPER

SELECTING INFORMATION INTO CATEGORIES

Conflicting attitudes between men and women about computers
-men like to talk about computers--and experience "male bonding"
-women show less interest in talking about computers
-computers represent the traditional technical domain of men
-women excluded from high-level positions in computer field
-fewer women than men study computers
-computer field losing women's contributions and insights

▶2 Organizing information *within* categories

Organize information within categories to clarify your ideas and their relation to one another. First, you will need to identify main, or *general*, points within each category and the subordinate, or *specific*, points supporting them, which is exactly what you will do when writing a paper. Use an informal outline or a tree diagram to organize major and supporting points within a category.

ORGANIZING INFORMATION WITHIN CATEGORIES

Organization by informal outline

<u>Conflicting attitudes between men and women about computers</u>

<u>Major point:</u> Men like to talk about computers--and experience "male bonding"

    <u>Supporting points:</u> (1) Men like to talk about many kinds of technology; (2) I often had long talks about computer hardware with friends

<u>Major point:</u> Many women seem less interested than men in talking about computers

    <u>Supporting points:</u> (1) I rarely have conversations about technology with women; (2) Some women say that computers are a "guy thing"--like cars.

<u>Major point:</u> Women choose not to use computers

    <u>Supporting point:</u> Some computer classes have fewer women than men

Organization by tree diagram

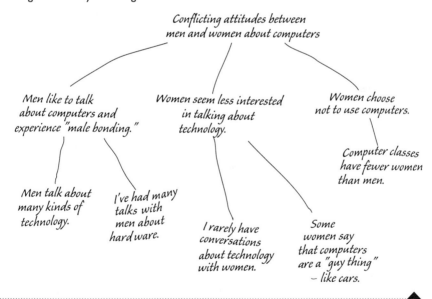

Conflicting attitudes between men and women about computers

Men like to talk about computers and experience "male bonding."

Women seem less interested in talking about technology.

Women choose not to use computers.

Computer classes have fewer women than men.

Men talk about many kinds of technology.

I've had many talks with men about hardware.

I rarely have conversations about technology with women.

Some women say that computers are a "guy thing" – like cars.

▶ 3 Expanding information: Filling in gaps

Organizing material within a category is an excellent technique for revealing which of your main points will need further development once you begin writing a first draft. When Lou Cassetta organized his category on the conflicting attitudes between men and women about computers, he realized that he had neglected to generate enough supporting materials for his point about women who choose *not* to use computers. When Lou asked, "What other examples of women not using computers can I point to?" answers came quickly. An asterisk marks the two additions to the category.

```
Major point: Some women choose not to use computers
    Supporting points: (1) Some computer classes have fewer women
    than men
    *Few women I know would call computers a hobby
    *The Internet is dominated by men and by male "flaming"
```

Look to each of your main points to see how you might add supporting points. You may need to read additional sources to fill in gaps. Developing categories fully at this stage will maximize the information you will have to work with when devising a thesis.

EXERCISE 9

Select the most promising information from your efforts to generate ideas about your topic, as defined in Exercise 8. *Form categories:* consolidate information from all three invention strategies. Write a brief sentence or phrase of definition for each category. *Organize each category* into a main point and supporting points. Finally, *expand information:* fill in gaps, and if you are interested (or if your professor requires it), seek out source material that you can use in your paper. At the conclusion of this exercise, each category should have a main point supported by at least two specific, subordinate points.

3d   Writing a thesis and sketching your paper

A **thesis** is a general statement that you make about your topic, usually in the form of a single sentence, that summarizes the controlling idea of your paper. You cannot produce a fully accurate **final thesis** until you have written a complete draft. When sitting down to a first draft, you will at best have a **working thesis**: a statement that, based on everything you know about your topic, should prove to be a reasonably accurate summary of what you will write.

http://www.indiana.edu/
~wts/wts/thesis.html
An extended look at the process of composing and revising a thesis statement.

A thesis, like any other sentence, has a subject and a predicate. The subject announces the person, place, or thing that the sentence is about. The predicate makes a claim concerning the subject: it states that the subject takes a certain action, exists (or should exist), has a certain value, and so on.

Subject	Predicate
Alex	smiles.
Patricia	opens the door.

What distinguishes the thesis from other sentences is that it invites development and discussion. The sentence *Alex smiles* offers a subject and an action taken by that subject, but once stated, the sentence completes its own meaning. Aside from descriptions of the smile, which might be expressed in a few follow-up sentences, *Alex smiles* invites no further discussion. By contrast, a thesis is more complex: it invites—and requires—follow-up discussion, because its meaning is not yet complete. The job of the essay or research paper is to develop and complete the thesis. Consider these examples:

Subject	Predicate
A largely invisible but rich biological world	can be found in the three inches of grass and topsoil immediately below our feet.
Courses taught over the Internet	should support, but should never replace, courses taught face-to-face in a real classroom.

Each of these sentences has a subject and a predicate, just as the example *Patricia opens the door* has a subject and a predicate. Notice, though, that these latter examples are more complicated: to be understood and accepted, they must be developed. These theses ask the reader to accept as true or desirable a complex statement about how the world works or should work. Readers might be willing to accept these statements as true or desirable, but not on face value.

Informational versus argumentative theses

When a thesis is not likely to spark debate, its development will be purely informational—as, for instance, would be the development about the biological world just under our feet. Following such a thesis, you would expect a good deal of information to follow so that, having finished your reading, you could say, "Yes, there's more life under my feet than I ever realized." There would not be much debate about the thesis, assuming the information presented were trustworthy.

When a thesis can reasonably be expected to spark disagreement, then development will take the form of an argument that provides reasons to encourage agreement. The last example thesis, concerning the proper role of Internet-based courses, is argumentative. Some people might immediately accept the statement; others (for instance, those who have recently earned college degrees having taken all Internet-based courses) might disagree. When the writer expects disagreement, an argument that supports and completes the thesis should follow. (See Chapter 6 for an extended discussion of how to write and support an argumentative thesis.)

Realize that your ideas for a paper and, consequently, for your thesis develop and change as your paper develops. Don't be bound by a single sentence at the beginning of your draft. Your working thesis *will* change. Nonetheless, you must depend on it to get you started.

▶**I Focusing on the subject of your thesis**

As much as possible, you want the subject of your thesis statement to name something that is relatively specific and well defined; you want to name something you can discuss thoroughly within the allotted number of pages. How will you focus your subject?

Build on the fact that you have organized your information into categories. To settle on a subject for your thesis, review your categories, and select from among them your most promising and interesting material. Most likely, you will focus on only a fraction of this material in your actual paper.

Focusing the Subject of a Thesis with Questions

One useful way to limit and focus the subject of your thesis is to pose a journalist's questions: *who, what, when, where,* and *which aspects.*

Subject (too broad): wilderness

Limiting questions: which aspects?

Focused subject: wilderness camping

▶2 Basing your thesis on a relationship you want to clarify

Once you have focused your subject, you must make an assertion about it; that is, you must complete the predicate part of your thesis. If you have generated ideas on your own, you have several pages of notes; if you have conducted research, you have filled out perhaps fifty file cards. You cannot write until you have begun to forge relationships among the ideas and information that you have generated. It is only *in the process* of forging relationships—trying to make logical connections one way, seeing that a certain tactic does not work, trying other tactics, and constantly making adjustments—that sense emerges and you come to know what you think about your material.

In examining the notes you have generated and organized into categories, ask yourself, What new statement can I make that ties all—or part—of my material together? You will express this relationship in the predicate part of your thesis.

▶3 The thesis and your ambitions for a paper

Whether you intend to inform or persuade, the relationship that you assert in your thesis can be more or less ambitious. When the assertion is ambitious, your thesis and the paper that you build from it will be, too. What determines the ambition of a thesis is the complexity of the relationship you establish between the predicate part of the sentence and the subject. In the example theses that follow, the predicates are underlined.

> *Least Ambitious Thesis*
> (1) Wilderness camping <u>poses many challenges.</u>
>   —Challenge #1
>   —Challenge #2, etc.
> (2) Lou Cassetta's thesis:
>   Women <u>are not entering the field of computers in large numbers.</u>
>   —Society tells them that computers are the domain of men.
>   —Men are discriminating against women.

Each thesis requires little more than a summary of the topic's component elements. The writers make no attempt to forge relationships among these elements.

Moderately Ambitious Thesis

(1) Like holding a mirror to your personality, wilderness camping <u>shows you to yourself—for better and worse.</u>
    —Wilderness camping described
    —The camper in the wilderness, described
    —Ways in which the wilderness elicits personal response, positive and negative

(2) Lou Cassetta's thesis:
    Computers <u>have become the domain of men, who have developed a language about computers that excludes women.</u>
    —Society has long defined computing as an activity for men only.
    —Some men have patterned their lives and language around computers.
    —The development of computing as a male activity has caused women to avoid the field of computing.

Each thesis forges a relationship between two previously unrelated elements: between wilderness camping and self-reflection and between the domains of men and the language of computers. The writers will be reasoning with the facts, not merely presenting them in summary form. They will be making connections.

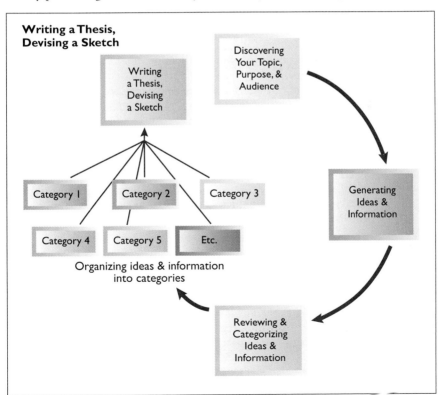

Writing a Thesis, Devising a Sketch

Discovering Your Topic, Purpose, & Audience

Writing a Thesis, Devising a Sketch

Category 1   Category 2   Category 3

Category 4   Category 5   Etc.

Organizing ideas & information into categories

Generating Ideas & Information

Reviewing & Categorizing Ideas & Information

Another Point of View

In Chapter 6, another student writer takes up the same topic as Lou Cassetta: gender roles in the high-tech workplace. Marie Hobahn makes a very different claim about this topic, though she uses some of Lou's same sources, including the example readings (by Munk and Oliver, Hamm, and Brunner and Bennett) in Chapter 1:

> Although women are certainly underrepresented at present in the computer industry, market forces will inevitably bring about a more equitable proportion of women to men.

Following the discussion in 3d-3, we can observe that Marie is being extremely ambitious with her thesis. First, she will clearly be reasoning with the facts she has gathered in order to make a point. Second, with the conjunction *although*, she is introducing a tension into her paper that will engage the interest of readers, who want to know, What are the factors that will change the visibility of women in the computer industry? You will find Marie's essay—presenting another point of view—at 6a.

Most Ambitious Thesis

(1) Wilderness camping <u>teaches that we must preserve what is brutal in Nature, even at the expense of public safety.</u>
—Rigors of wilderness camping
—Potential danger to public
—Paradox: dangers notwithstanding, wilderness must be maintained

(2) Lou Cassetta's thesis:
Since <u>women</u> are as capable as men in technology-related fields, they <u>need to participate in discussing computer technology on the same level as men do to succeed in the field.</u>
—There are some significant differences in attitude between men and women about computers.
—Men have often related to each other through talking about computers, while women have not.
—In dealing with men who now dominate the computer field, women should learn the men's subtleties of language about technology.
—Paradox: If women are as capable as men, why can't they use whatever language suits them?

Each thesis broadens the scope of the paper and creates interest through paradoxical opposites. Each thesis promises a paper that will be argumentative. In addition to making connections where none existed previously, each thesis shows a writer willing to take intellectual risks: that is, the writer is willing to expand the scope of the paper, widening its context in order to take up a broader, more complex, and (if executed well) more important discussion. A fully ambitious thesis will create a paradox, a tension among its parts, by setting opposites against each other.[3]

---

[3]The term *tension*, as it relates to the thesis statement, is borrowed from John C. Beam and John D. Ramage, *Form and Surprise in Composition: Writing and Thinking across the Curriculum* (New York: Macmillan, 1986) 168–69.

In a thesis with tension, you often find the conjunctions *although* and *even if*. The writer's job is to navigate between paradoxical opposites. The reader, sensing tension, wants to know what happens and why.

What sort of paper are you writing?

An ambitious thesis leads to an ambitious paper. Sometimes you will understand the ambition of your paper before you set out to write it; at other times you will not have a clear sense of how "large" a paper you are writing until you get midway or most of the way through a draft and discover or challenge your ideas. In any event, you should know what sort of paper you are writing as you sit down to *revise* your first draft. Reread the draft; see what you have; and determine how ambitious your final draft should be. You will choose your final thesis, and shape your final paper, accordingly.

Generating a Working Thesis

1. Focus and restrict your subject so that you will be able to write specifically on it in the number of pages allotted.
2. Assemble the notes—arranged in categories—that you have generated for your paper.
3. Forge a relationship that clarifies the material you have assembled.
4. Devise a sentence—a working thesis—that links the relationship you have forged with your focused subject.
5. Determine how ambitious you will be with your thesis—and your paper.
6. Let your thesis evolve as you develop and challenge your thoughts on your topic.

EXERCISE 10

Refer to your results from Exercise 9. Given the ideas you generated, write three theses for this topic—each with a different level of ambition.

EXERCISE 11

Classify the following theses as least, moderately, or most ambitious. Explain your classifications:

1. In a national trend that has blurred the line between private and public, several cities and states have agreed to spend public funds to finance the construction of new stadiums.
2. Several cities and states have agreed to spend public funds to finance the construction of new stadiums.
3. In a national trend that has blurred the line between private and public, several cities and states have buckled to the demands of sports teams and agreed to spend public funds to finance the construction of new stadiums.

Writing a Thesis and Sketching Your Paper

▶ **4 Devising a sketch of your paper or developing a formal outline**

Look to your working thesis for clues about the ideas you will need to develop in your essay. For your academic paper to succeed, you must develop all directly stated or implied ideas in the thesis. You may want to regard your thesis as a contract. In the final draft, the contract exists between you and your reader; the thesis promises the reader a discussion of certain material, and the paper delivers on that promise.

CRITICAL DECISIONS

Challenge and be challenged: Quizzing your working thesis to determine major sections of your paper

In writing a thesis, you compress a great deal of information into a single sentence; in writing a paper based on this thesis, you will need to "unpack" and discuss this information. Use the following technique as an aid to unpacking: challenge, or quiz, your thesis with questions (see box on page 75). The technique will lead to a sketch of your paper.

Thesis   *define*   *which fields?*

Since women are as (capable) as men in (technology-related fields,) they need to (participate in discussing computer technology on the same level as men do) (to succeed in the field.)   *Are they not succeeding now?*   *How does each talk*
                                                                Why not, if women are as capable?   *about computers?*

Sketching the paper
—Define which technology-related fields. Define *capability.*
—Examine why women are not prospering in technology-related fields.
—Discuss how men, as opposed to women, talk about computers.
—Discuss men's outlook on computers, and contrast it with women's.
—Explain the paradox: the political reality of the high-tech workplace is that men dominate; even though women are as technically capable as men, they do not advance through corporate management. If the problem is social, the solution should be social as well.

Identifying significant parts of your thesis

Write the working thesis at the top of a page, and circle its significant words. Then ask development questions of, or make comments about, each circled element. If you are thorough in quizzing your thesis, you will identify most of its significant parts. (You may not discover some parts until you write a first draft.) Having identified these significant parts, briefly sketch the paper you intend to write.

Option: Preparing a formal outline of your paper

Many writers feel that a rough sketch (as illustrated in the Critical Decisions box above) is sufficient for beginning the first draft of a paper. Others feel more com-

> **Question or Make Comments about Your Thesis in Order to Identify Major Sections of Your Paper**
>
> ### Questions
>
> how does/will it happen?
> how to describe?
> what are some examples?
> what are the reasons for?
> what is my view?
> compared with what?
> what is the cause?
> any stories to tell?
> how?
> when?
>
> what has prevented/will prevent it
>   from happening?
> who is involved?
> what are the key features?
> what are the reasons against?
> how often?
> possible to classify types or parts?
> what is the effect of this?
> which ones?
>
> ### Comments
>
> define
> review the facts
>
> review the reasoning
> explain the contrast or paradox

fortable with a formal plan of action—an outline with clearly delineated major and minor points. In collaborative writing situations, with different writers responsible for various sections of the project, a formal outline is probably the only way to reach agreement on what each writer will contribute.

A formal outline establishes the major sections and subsections of your paper. The outline shows how each section is supported by points you plan to discuss (see 18e). It also shows how these points are themselves supported. The goal of a formal outline is to make visible the material you plan to use in the paper. Standard outline form is as follows: uppercase roman numerals indicate the most general level of heading in the outline; headings in this level correspond with major sections of your paper. Uppercase letters mark the major points you will use in developing each heading. Arabic numbers mark the supporting points you will use in developing main points. Lowercase letters mark further subordination—support of supporting points. Note that the entries at each level of heading are grammatically parallel (see 18e); that each level of heading has at least two entries; and that only the first letter of an entry is capitalized. A formal outline need not show plans for your introduction or conclusion.

Useful as an outline can be, you will still need to discover the important elements of your paper during the process of writing, and necessarily, your outline or sketch will change as the writing takes shape.

ILLUSTRATION: FORMAL OUTLINE *What is the problem? Are there fewer women in high-tech jobs than men?* *Explain the need to prove themselves.*

Thesis: If the minority of women in the world of computers wish to prove themselves as capable as men, the path is clear and, very likely, painful: women should learn to speak the language of their male counterparts.

Why painful?

Are women as capable?

Why this solution and not others?

I. Problem
   A. Differences, men/women
      re: computers (¶s 2–3)
      1. Men/computers focus
         on power
      2. Women/computers
         focus on use of tool
      3. Example quotation
         a. Men—conquer
         b. Women—solve
   B. Explanation of differences
      (¶ 4)
      1. Biology
      2. Environment
   C. Problem defined (¶ 5)
      1. Male-dominated
         high-tech classrooms
         a. Women abandon
            high-tech majors
         b. More men than women
            w/advanced degrees
      2. Self-perpetuating cycle

II. Solution
   A. Solution proposed (¶ 6)
      1. Thesis: women take on male
         language
      2. Value of talking shop
   B. Other solutions explored (¶ 7)
      1. Sexist solution?
      2. Political realities
      3. Gender gap in high-tech part of
         larger problem
   C. Psychological costs of solution (¶ 8)
      1. Male talk may be damaging
      2. Language learning as a tool
         for success

ILLUSTRATION: FORMAL OUTLINE WITH SENTENCES

Each item of a formal outline can also be written as a sentence, which you may prefer in your efforts to begin writing. The following is one section of the preceding outline, written in sentence form:

   C. There can be no doubt that stereotypes have very real consequences.
      1. Males dominate high-tech classrooms both as teachers and as students.
         a. In coeducational schools, women abandon high-tech majors more frequently than they do in all-women schools.
         b. About three out of four master's degrees in computer science go to men; almost nine out of ten Ph.D.'s in computer science go to men.
      2. Gender stereotyping keeps women out of computer science; in a self-perpetuating cycle, the low numbers of women in the field discourage new generations of women from pursuing degrees.

► EXERCISE 12

Turn to the theses you wrote in Exercise 10. Circle significant words or phrases, pose development questions, and prepare an informal or formal outline of your paper. Then expand your outline into a first draft of your paper (3e).

ACROSS THE CURRICULUM

Organizing Scientific Writing

In *Scientific and Technical Writing: A Manual of Style,** writers are advised to create an "obvious," easily understood organization that is highlighted with clear "guideposts" (such as headings and cross-references). The editors offer the following overview of "typical organizational approaches" found in scientific and technical writing:

- Be sure that a document's organization explains and logically arranges all necessary ideas. Although there is no perfect organization for any technical or scientific document, some organizational methods will be more appropriate than others, depending on the document's audience and purpose.
- Typical organizational approaches include chronological, spatial, climactic, and task-oriented. Some documents may need an organization that combines more than one of these approaches.
- Use chronological organization when time is the organizing principle. It orders information according to when concepts develop, events occur, or actions happen, generally from the earliest to the latest.
- Use spatial organization when placement or geography is the organizing principle. Consider, for instance, describing equipment by parts or components, or presenting product sales figures or health statistics by geographic region.
- Use climactic organization to progress from least to greatest impact, concluding with the most interesting or forceful concepts, ideas, or facts. Brochures, when convincing readers to take action or make a decision, use this organization.
- Use task-oriented organization when readers will use information to do something. Thus, an instruction manual organizes its information into procedures or activities users perform.

*Philip Rubens, ed. (New York: Henry Holt, 1992) 15–16.

 3e Writing a draft

Your working thesis and your sketch or outline are essential for giving you the confidence to begin a first draft. Realize, however, that your final paper will *not* be identical to your original plans. Once begun, writing will lead you to discard and revise some of your original ideas and will lead to new ideas as well.

The object of a first draft is to get ideas down on paper, to explore them, and to establish the shape of your paper. The object is *not* to produce anything that is readable to anyone other than yourself. Finished, readable documents come through revision. If you plan to revise, you will free yourself to write quickly—and imperfectly. Your draft will put you well on the way toward achieving a final product.

Strategies for Drafting

Working yourself through the draft

1. Write *one* section of the paper at a time: write a general statement that supports some part of your thesis, then provide details about the supporting statement. Once you have finished a section, take a break. Then return to write another section, working incrementally in this fashion until you have completed the draft.

   ■ Alternately, write one section of the paper and take a break. Then reread and revise that one section before moving to the next. Continue to work in this fashion, one section at a time, until you complete the draft.

2. Accept *two* drafts, minimum, as the standard for writing any formal paper. In this way, you give yourself permission to write a first draft that is not perfect.

3. If you have prepared adequately for writing, then trust that you will discover what to write *as* you write.

4. Save substantial revisions concerning grammar, punctuation, usage, and spelling for later. In your first draft(s), focus on discovery and content.

▶ I Beating writer's block

Everybody avoids writing at some point or another. Odd as it may seem, this information can be of comfort: if you avoid writing, be assured that avoidance does *not* mean that you have done things poorly or that you do not "have what it takes" to be a competent writer. Avoidance and the anxiety that causes it are natural parts of the writing process. By no means are they ever-present parts, and if you devote sufficient time to preparing yourself to write, you minimize the danger of writer's block. Still, preparing is not the same as writing a draft, and you inevitably face a moment in which you decide to take a step—or not. Think about the feelings you get when you do not want to write. When you are stuck as a writer, what might you be telling yourself? And how might you get unstuck?

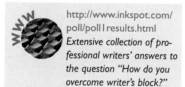

http://www.inkspot.com/poll/poll I results.html
Extensive collection of professional writers' answers to the question "How do you overcome writer's block?"

Stuck   *I cannot get started.* I am afraid of the blank page—or its electronic equivalent, the empty screen. As I try to write, what I *have not* written seems so vast that I cannot start.

Unstuck   *Prepare yourself mentally to write one section of the paper, not the entire paper.* Three-page papers, just like 500-page books, get written one section at a time. When you sit down to write a draft, identify a *section:* a grouping of related paragraphs that you can write in a single sitting.

Stuck   *I want my writing to be perfect.* My early attempts to express anything are messy. I get a sinking feeling when I reread my work and see how much revision is needed. Whenever I cannot think of the right word, I freeze up.

Unstuck	*Accept* two *drafts, minimum, as the standard for writing any formal paper.* When you understand that you will rewrite the first draft of all formal papers or letters, you can give yourself permission to write a first draft quickly and at times imprecisely.
Stuck	*Why advertise my problems?* I worry about grammar, punctuation, and spelling, and I do not want to embarrass myself.
Unstuck	*Use a writer's reference tools.* Many people are nervous about these errors. The fear is real. However, as long as you know how to use standard desk references—a dictionary and a handbook—there is no need to memorize rules of grammar, punctuation, and spelling. Of course, knowing the rules *does* save you time.

▶2 Working with your sketch or outline

Following are three strategies for using your sketch or outline as a basis for writing. None of these strategies is *correct* in the sense that one produces a better draft than the others. All will get you a first draft, and all have advantages and disadvantages. How you choose to use a sketch or outline is a matter of your temperament as a writer.

Adhering closely to your outline

One strategy for writing a draft is to follow closely the sketch or outline you made prior to actual drafting. To make full and frequent use of the detailed outline you have assembled makes a great deal of sense, as long as you are aware that your paper *will* deviate from the outline.

Advantages

By regularly consulting your outline, you will feel that you are making progress toward the completion of your paper.

Disadvantages

A comprehensive outline can so focus your vision that you will not allow yourself to stray and discover the true territory of your paper. The paper planned will be the paper written, for better or worse.

COMPUTER TIPS

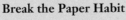

Break the Paper Habit

If you are in the habit of handwriting your first drafts, experiment with writing at the keyboard. There will be times when you need to print out a paper copy of your draft and edit it, but much of your revising, editing, and proofreading can (and should) be done quickly and efficiently on the screen. You may decide that preparing first drafts of one type of writing (for example, academic papers) works well at the keyboard, whereas drafting other types of writing (poetry) does not. Experiment and learn your preferences.

Writing a Draft

Adhering loosely to your outline

You may prefer to use a sketch or outline exclusively as a strategy for preparing; in the actual drafting of the paper, you can abandon your plan in favor of one that you generate *while* writing the draft. Examine your outline, studying its first section carefully, and then begin writing. Set aside the outline, and once writing is under way, create a new outline for each section of the paper you are about to write, based on the material you have just written. As you complete each section, update and adjust your outline.

Advantages

This strategy gives you the best chance of discovering material, since each new section of the paper is based on the writing you have just completed and not on an outline prepared in advance.

Disadvantages

The same freedom that gives you room to be creative can result in paragraphs that do not lead logically from one to the next and whole groupings of paragraphs that drift away from the working thesis.

Combining strategies

You may prefer more freedom than close adherence to a predraft outline allows, but still like more structure than the outline-as-you-go approach provides. If so, borrow from both methods. First, carefully review your predraft outline for each section of the paper before writing it; then write the section *without* further reference to the outline. At the end of each section, compare your work against the outline, and plan to add or delete material as needed. Also look ahead to the next section and revise the outline, if necessary.

How to Write One Section of a Paper

1. **Prepare to write.** Identify your purpose and define your audience; generate and organize your ideas and information; and devise a working thesis.
2. **Identify sections of the paper.** Ask of your thesis, What parts must I develop in order to deliver on the promise of this statement? Your answer of perhaps three or four points will identify the sections you need to write to complete that statement.
3. **Plan to write one section of your paper at a sitting.** If a section is long, divide it into manageable parts, and write one part at a sitting.
4. **Write individual paragraphs.** Each paragraph will be related to others in the section. As you begin a second paragraph, clearly relate it to the first. Relate the third paragraph to the second, and so on until you finish writing the section. Then take a break.
5. **Write other sections, one at a time.** Continue writing, building one section incrementally on the next, until you complete your first draft.

CRITICAL DECISIONS

Overcome obstacles to writing: Identifying and resolving problems in mid-draft

At some point in the writing process you may find yourself unable to steam ahead, one section after the next. You may become aware that your work in one section of the paper is not as good as it is elsewhere, or that after several attempts at writing a section you find the effort too difficult. When you are feeling especially frustrated, stop. Step back from your work, and decide how you will get past this obstacle. Ask, Why am I having trouble? Here are several possibilities:

1. You do not have enough information to write. You have not gathered enough information, or if you have, you may not thoroughly understand it.
2. You do not understand the point you planned to make or its relation to the rest of your paper.
3. The point you planned to make no longer seems relevant or correct, given what you have discovered about your subject while writing.
4. You recognize a gap in the structure of your paper, and you suddenly see the need to expand an existing section or to write an entirely new section.
5. The material in the section seems inappropriate for your audience.
6. You have said everything you need to say in a page, but the assignment calls for six to ten pages.
7. At the moment, you do not have the attention span to write.

Each of these obstacles can frustrate your attempts at writing. You will come of age as a writer the moment you can realize you are having trouble and can then step away to name your problem and find a solution.

▶3 Working collaboratively

Your instructor may ask you to work collaboratively—that is, in a group. The great advantage of creating and writing a document collaboratively is that you can put the power of several minds to work on a task that might prove overwhelming for one person. Both in content and in presentation, however, your group's work should read as though *one* person had written it, even if several people have been involved in the actual writing.

- To minimize rewriting, meet as a group before any writing takes place. Agree on a structure for the overall document, and then assign parts to individuals. Agree on a consistent point of view for the paper.
- At a second meeting after writing has just begun, ask each group member to outline his or her section and to discuss its structure. As a group, think specifically of the ways in which one section will build from and lead to another. Also raise and address any problems encountered thus far in the writing.

Writing a Draft

- At the completion of a first draft, distribute the assembled document to the entire group, and have each member revise for content and consistency of perspective.
- Incorporate all revisions in a single version of the document. *One* member of the group should then take responsibility for rewriting the paper in order to ensure continuity of style and voice.

▶ 3f Student paper: Rough draft

Here is Lou Cassetta's rough draft, preparations for which you have followed throughout Chapters 1 through 3. His instructor's comments appear in the margins and at the end of the draft. You'll see this draft revised a second time in Chapter 4. Lou's thesis is highlighted.

                    The Value of Shop Talk

                        (First Draft)

     When I applied for a job in computer data entry
last summer at one of the world's largest management
consulting firms, I never thought that my experience   *Your bringing*
as a grease monkey would help. Although knowing how   *together of*
to work a gas pump did not make me a better typist,   *opposites--*
                                                          computer data
I learned important communication skills at the gas   *entry &*
station that I used to get the office job. At the gas   *pumping gas--*
station, my co-workers and I always talked about the   *creates interest.*
fastest and most sophisticated automobiles and how   *Good opening.*
much we would like to own them. When I applied for
the data entry position, I impressed my boss by engaging in a conversation about his laptop computer.
Many men are fascinated by the newest and fastest
machines and love to talk about them. I have always
taken part in conversations about these machines, and
for once it paid off.
     Many men treat their computers in the same way
that muscle car enthusiasts treat their hot rods.
Both want the fastest, most powerful machines that
money can buy. Although I am writing this paper on
one of the most antiquated PCs imaginable, it is
money--not desire--that prevents me from purchasing a
fast computer. I can't imagine keeping this dinosaur

---

82   Planning, Developing, and Writing a Draft for much longer, despite the fact that it has served me well for many years. In contrast, Esther Dyson, editor of an influential software-industry news-letter, said that she doesn't "really care about [her computer's] innards, [she] just want[s] it to work" (qtd. in Kantrowitz 50). Oliver Strimpel, executive director of The Computer Museum in Boston, finds this pattern very common among male and female computer owners. "Men tend to be seduced by the technology itself" (qtd. in Kantrowitz 50). Women are more likely to approach new technology in functional terms, as they would a household appliance.

You're moving from individual statements about gender and computers to generalizations. Will these generalizations hold?

Even among women who are technologically so-phisticated, we find differences in fundamental attitudes about technology and its uses. <u>Newsweek</u> writer Barbara Kantrowitz reports the following:

> In one intriguing study by the Center for Children and Technology, a New York think tank, men and women in technical fields were asked to dream up machines of the future. Men typically imagined devices that could help them "conquer the universe," says Jan Hawkins, director of the center. She says women wanted machines that met people's needs, "the perfect mother." [. . .] If everyone approached technology the way women do now, "we wouldn't be pushing envelopes," says Cornelia Bruner, associate director of the center. "Most women, even those who are technologically sophisticated, think of machines as a means to an end." Men think of machines as an extension of their own power. (55)

Good use of block quotation.

What explains the difference? Clearly social conditioning matters. Biology may mix with social training to account for gender differences we see in the sciences and technology. Perhaps women and men in fact differ in intellectual styles and interests. But as psychologist Lester Lefton says, "learning

You've used sources well to document stereotypes.

is far more potent in establishing and maintaining
sex-role stereotypes and gender-specific attitudes"
(347).

There can be no doubt that the stereotypes
have very real consequences. In the classroom, the
presence of men--both as teachers and as fellow
students--is enough to deter women from studying computers. Research has shown that in schools attended
by both sexes, women tend to abandon a major in
science more often than they do in women's colleges
(Healy). Little more than one-third of bachelor's
degrees in computer science are awarded to women.
Fewer women than men pursue this education further:
women earn about 27 percent of master's degrees in
computer science, and a mere 13 percent of Ph.D.'s
(Wylie 3). These effects of gender stereotyping, in
turn, become causes. Each new generation of women that
abandons science and technology sets an unhappy precedent for the next generation. The cycle continues.

If the minority of women in the world of computers wish to prove themselves as capable as men, the
path is clear and, very likely, painful: women should
learn to speak the language of their male counterparts. That women can do the technical work of engineers and scientists is beyond question--millions
have demonstrated their skills. If ability is not the
issue, then social interaction must be. Relatively
few women advance beyond middle management in computer hardware and software companies (Kantrowitz
52). To advance in the computer industry, women will
need to address the social problem. One sure way of
doing this is to show an interest in talking about
computers--that is, in learning the value of "shop
talk."

Ironically, for one who advocates more fairness
for women in the computer field, I find myself
offering what some might call sexist advice: I'm
suggesting that women become more like men, at least
in their speech. But the need to speak the language

*Lou: Challenge
your assumptions!
See note 1 at the
end of your paper.*

*Lou: Consider
alternatives? See
note 2 at the end
of your paper.*

of the dominant group is a political reality. Women could try to revolutionize the computer industry and higher education from the outside--with their own language, spoken in their own corporations and schools. But this approach is not realistic. The problems women face in the computer industry are part of a much larger, society-wide problem of gender discrimination. Fundamental assumptions about the roles men and women play in society change slowly. The quickest way for women to advance in the computer industry will be for women to integrate themselves into existing companies, rise to the top, and then change the rules. They can best do this through channels of communication already present.

Success may come with a high psychological cost, as women talk in ways that perhaps don't interest them. But it is not unfair to expect people, male or female, to learn the language of the computer industry when their jobs involve computers. People use many different types of speech, depending on the occasion. On the job, women can speak the language of computers developed by a male-dominated computer industry. Even as their on-the-job language helps them to break social barriers and advance through corporations, women can drop that language the moment they leave the office each afternoon.

Lou: Another assumption? See note 3 at the end of your paper.

My job last summer was certainly male dominated, with no female programmers. Had a woman with my same skills applied for the data entry job, she may not have been hired unless she was able to impress my boss through a simple conversation about computers. I am sure that there are many women who have lost jobs to men who were better able to impress other males with a knowledge of technology. Very likely the women were just as qualified as the men, but the men, talking shop, appeared to know more about technology. Women can correct this unfair situation. They can begin talking shop.

Student Paper: Rough Draft

Works Cited

Healy, Bernadine. "Quotable: The Astonishing Thing Is That Young Women Pursue Careers in Science and Medicine at All." The Chronicle of Higher Education 25 Mar. 1992: B5.

Kantrowitz, Barbara. "Men, Women and Computers." Newsweek 16 May 1994: 48–55.

Lefton, Lester. Psychology. 6th ed. Boston: Allyn and Bacon, 1997.

Wylie, Margie. "No Place for Women: Internet Is Flawed Model for the Infobahn." Digital Media 4.8 (1995): 3+. Digital Media Online. Nexis. 19 Nov. 1995.

Lou:

You've written a problem-solution essay. You've been clear enough for me to identify and challenge three unexamined assumptions, the first two of which cause problems for your proposed solution.

(1) In asking women to talk like men, you are assuming, through a process you've not yet defined, that "talking shop" will somehow make women equal in the workplace. Why? How? Unless you carefully explain this process and give readers a chance to evaluate, your proposed solution cannot stand.

(2) Does a person's being competent obligate him or her to talk shop? You assume so, and what follows is a belief that those who talk shop will be perceived as competent and will rise in an organization. Have you considered an alternate assumption? I know people (some, computer scientists!) who don't feel compelled to talk shop in order to demonstrate knowledge. This they demonstrate through work well done. Here's a competing view of competence that creates a problem for you. I'm not sure that even men must talk shop in order to succeed.

(3) Please examine your assumption that being able to talk shop—that is, having a technical vocabulary—is the same as being competent in a field. Is it? I could learn buzzwords and "talk shop" with the guys; but surely a high-tech vocabulary alone would not make me computer literate. For example, you talk shop but are not, yet, a computer scientist. Your data entry job, after all, required typing (not computer) skills.

Still, you're onto something useful in this essay. If we begin with the view that there might well be differences between men and women, aside from the physical, then exploring the ways these differences manifest themselves in the computer field seems quite interesting. Please hold to your proposed solution if you believe in it; but you'll need to address my criticisms. You might, on the other hand, want to revise your solution. Or perhaps you'll want to shift away from a problem-solution format altogether and concentrate, instead, on perceived or real gender differences in the computer field. Whatever your decision, let's consider your next draft final.

CHAPTER 4

The Process of Revision

As much as a first draft, revision is an act of creation. In a first draft you work to give a document potential: the writing may be incomplete, but you are working toward an important, controlling idea. In your subsequent drafts, you work to make an earlier draft's potential *real:* you make decisions about content and structure. You revise, and through revision—by adding, altering, or deleting sentences and paragraphs—you clarify your main point for yourself and, on the strength of that, for your reader.

The Process of Revision

Think of revision as occurring in three stages—early, later, and final:

4a **Early revision:** Reread your first draft and rediscover your main idea. What you *intended* to write is not always, or even usually, what you *in fact* have written.

4b **Later revision:** Make all significant parts of your document work together in support of your main idea.

4c **Final revision (editing):** Correct errors at the sentence level that divert attention from your main point.

▶ **4a   Early revision: Rediscovering your main idea**

Successful writing clearly communicates an idea, and it is the process of revision that helps to clarify this idea. You can learn techniques of revision. The key to a successful revision is the commitment to rework drafts until they express your meaning *exactly*. Early revision involves adding, altering, or deleting entire paragraphs with the sole purpose of clarifying your main idea. Commit yourself to real and meaningful revision, and your writing will be good consistently; back away from this commitment, and your efforts will likely falter.

http://www.powa.org/
revifrms.htm
Detailed view of revision from the Paradigm Online Writing Assistant.

Strategies for Early Revision

Pose three questions to get started on early revision. Your goal is to rediscover and clarify what you have written in a first draft.

- What I *intended* to write in my first draft may not be what I have *in fact* written. What is the main idea of this first draft?

  Underline one sentence in your draft in answer to this question; if you cannot find such a sentence, write one.

  Choose a title for your second draft. The title will help you to clarify your main idea.

- Does what I have written in this draft satisfy my original purpose for writing?

  Review the assignment that began your writing project. Restate the purpose of that assignment. To the degree that you have not met the expectation of the assignment, revise.

- Does my writing communicate clearly to my audience?

  Think of your audience. If need be, revise your level of language, your choice of illustrations, and your general treatment of the topic in order to help your audience understand.

▶1   Choosing a revision strategy that suits you

There are as many different strategies for revising a paper as there are for writing one, and the strategy you choose will depend on your temperament:

- Some first-draft writers work on individual paragraphs, revising continually until they achieve their idea for a particular paragraph before they move on.
- Others write and revise one section of their paper at a time, revising a grouping of related paragraphs continually until that grouping functions as a single, seamless unit.
- Still other writers complete an entire first draft and then revise.

The approach to revision advocated here is that a writer make several "passes" over a draft and on each pass revise with a different focus. *First,* revise the largest elements (the sections); *on the next pass,* revise paragraphs within sections; and *on the final pass (or passes),* revise individual sentences within paragraphs.

▶2   Strategies for clarifying and developing your main idea

The overall objective of your first revision is to rediscover your main idea. Has the paper developed your working thesis? If so, fine. Still, what you intended to write may not be what you have written. Now is the time to check.

Reread your first draft with care, looking for some sentence other than your working thesis that more accurately describes what you have written. Often, such a "competing" thesis appears near the end of the draft, the place where you have forced yourself to summarize. If you can find no competing thesis, but are sure that your original working thesis does not fit the paper you have written, modify the existing working thesis, or write a new one. Be prepared to quiz the new thesis as you did before. See the box in 3d-4 to review techniques for doing this.

REVISING THE THESIS

As Lou reread his first draft and reacted to challenges from his instructor, he still did not find a competing thesis. He felt that he'd written a first draft on more or less the topic he intended. As Lou met with his instructor and reviewed comments on the first draft, he realized that he could not support three key assumptions on which the paper rested: that "talking shop" will lead to equality for women in the workplace, that competent workers like to talk shop, and that talking shop is a sign of competence. Lou therefore revised his working thesis:

First-draft thesis

If the minority of women in the world of computers wish to prove themselves as capable as men, the path is clear and, very likely, painful: women should learn to speak the language of their male counterparts.

Second-draft thesis

Two problems, ignorance and fear, have prevented us from making greater strides in the computer industry: too many people accept the stereotype that women are not technologically oriented, and too many people have been intimidated by political correctness into believing that women and men must be exactly alike.

The major shift in Lou's thesis is his move *away* from a proposed solution to the problem of the lack of women in the computer industry. Reread his first thesis, and you will notice that he implies what the problem is but does not state it outright. Lou devotes his first thesis to a proposed solution. In the face of his instructor's comments, though, Lou realized he could not defend his solution. So he scrapped that emphasis and chose a new one: carefully defining the causes of the problems that women face in the computer industry.

▲

Outline the sections of a revised paper.

Recall that a *section* of your paper is a group of related paragraphs (see 5a-1). Based on your revised thesis and on your development questions and comments about that thesis, outline the sections of a revised paper.

REVISING THE OUTLINE

Once Lou revised his thesis, he created an obligation to revise the body of his essay so that sections would develop every element of the new thesis. Compare the outline of the draft Lou has completed with the outline of the draft he intends to write:

Draft 1	*Draft 2*
Introduction (¶1)	Introduction: problem (¶s 1–2)
Problem	Gender stereotyping in computer industry
Differences, men/women re:	Attitudes re: men, women, &
computers (¶s 2–3)	technology (¶s 3–4)
Explanation of differences (¶4)	Women students in computer science
Problem defined (¶5)	(¶5)
Solution	Discredit false differences between
Solution proposed (¶6)	sexes (¶6)
Other solutions explored (¶7)	Political correctness
Psychological costs of solution	Acknowledge real differences (¶7)
(¶8)	Uses: men, women w/computers (¶8)
Conclusion	Differences → better design (¶9)
	Conclusion (¶s 10–11)

Incorporate sections of your first draft into your revised outline.

Study your new outline. Reexamine your first draft to determine how much of it will fit, with or without changes, into your plans for the final paper. Then retrieve your first draft, and cut and paste usable sections of this draft into your final outline. Be sure to reread each sentence of first-draft writing that you move into the second draft. Every sentence must contribute toward developing the meaning of your newly conceived thesis.

Write new sections of the final outline, as needed.

The preceding step will leave you with a partial paper: a detailed outline, some of the sections of which (imported from your first draft) are close to being complete, other sections of which are indicated by a phrase in your outline. You will need to write these sections from scratch. Before beginning a new section of your paper, write a section thesis to help focus your efforts (see 5a-2).

▶ **3 Reconsidering purpose and audience**

Purpose

At some point in the process of revision you will want to reconsider your earliest reasons for writing. You may have been asked to explain, describe, argue, compare, analyze, summarize, define, discuss, illustrate, evaluate, or prove. (See explanations of these and other important word meanings in assignments in 44b.) With your purpose firmly in mind, evaluate your first draft to determine the extent to which you have met that purpose. Alter your revision plans, if necessary, to satisfy your reason for writing.

- Identify the key verb in the assignment, and define that verb with reference to your topic. (See 44b.)

- If you have trouble understanding the purpose, seek out your instructor. Bring your draft to a conference, and explain the direction you've taken.
- Once you identify the parts of a paper that will achieve a stated purpose, incorporate those parts into your plans for a revised draft.

An Overview of the Revision Process

Use the Thinking and Writing Wheel adapted from Chapter 3 to guide you through the revision process:

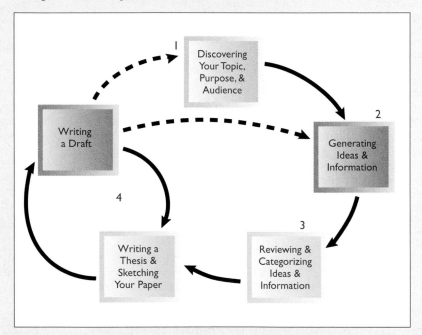

1. While revising, you may need to leave the draft to reconsider your topic, purpose, or audience. You may also need to pursue and develop new ideas.
2. You may need to leave the draft and return to your source materials, searching for additional supporting materials.
3. Fresh materials need to be integrated into a coherent and unified essay.
4. (a) **Early Revision:** If necessary, revise major elements of your draft to clarify your topic, purpose, and audience; to generate new materials; and to incorporate new elements into the revision.
   (b) **Later Revision:** You will probably not need to leave this inner loop for new materials. Concentrate on the ways in which paragraphs work together to support the essay's main idea.
   (c) **Final Revision:** Revise, refining your essay's tone, sentence structure, and word choice.

Audience

Revisit your initial audience analysis (see 3a-3); will your audience be classmates, fellow majors, or an instructor? Take whatever conclusions you reached in your analysis, and use them as a tool for evaluating your first draft. You may find it useful to pose these questions:

- How will this subject appeal to my readers?
- Is the level of difficulty with which I have treated this subject appropriate for my readers?
- Is my choice of language, in both its tone (see 3a-4) and its level of difficulty, appropriate for my readers?
- Are my examples appropriate in interest and complexity for my readers?

Make changes to your revision plans according to your analysis of the first draft.

▶4 Choosing and using a title

Before rewriting your paper, use your revised thesis to devise a title. A title creates a context for your readers; a title alerts readers to your topic and your intentions for treating it. Forcing yourself to devise a title before beginning your major revision will help you to clarify your main idea. A *descriptive* title directly announces the content of a paper and is appropriate for reports and write-ups of experiments: occasions when you are expected to be direct. An *evocative* title is a playful, intriguing, or otherwise indirect attempt to pique a reader's interest. Both descriptive and evocative titles should be brief (no longer than ten words).

▶ EXERCISE I

Following advice offered in this section, revise the first draft of the paper you wrote in response to Exercise 12 in Chapter 3. Your early revision may be a major one, requiring you to rework your thesis and to redefine major sections of the paper.

▶ **4b**   Later revision: Bringing your main idea into focus

Your first major revision of a draft (if you completed Exercise 1) requires the courage to look deep into your paper and make fundamental changes in order to present a single idea clearly. Later revisions will not be dramatic or far-reaching and will require, for the most part, that you understand and are able to systematically apply certain principles of organization. Three principles of organization important to a later revision are unity, coherence, and balance.

▶I Focusing the paper through unity

A paper is unified when the writer discusses only those elements of the subject implied by its thesis. In a unified paper, you discuss only those topics that can be anticipated by someone who reads your thesis.

A unified discussion will not stray from the sentence that organizes and focuses any one of the principal parts of the paper. At each level of the essay, a general statement is used to guide you in assembling specific, supporting parts.

Essay-level unity	The thesis (the most general statement in the essay) governs your choice of sections in a paper.
Section-level unity	Section theses (the second-most-general statements in the essay) govern your choice of paragraphs in a section.
Paragraph-level unity	Topic sentences (the third-most-general statements in the essay) govern your choice of sentences in a paragraph.

A unified section of a paper is a discussion of those topics implied by your section thesis (see 5a-2). Every topic generated by quizzing the thesis will become a *section* of your final paper. You will devote at least one paragraph, and maybe more, to developing each section, or subtopic, of the thesis. In a unified paragraph, you discuss only one topic, the one implied by your topic sentence (see 5c).

COMPUTER TIPS

Don't Delete It—You May Want to Recycle It

Word processors have made the concept of discrete drafts obsolete. When handwriting or typewriting, you can be certain when a draft is finished and another one begins. Composing, revising, and editing on a word processor, however, is usually one long, seamless process. It is wise to save a version of your paper in a separate file (using the "Save As" function) from time to time, especially if you're embarking on some major changes. Later in the process, you may decide to restore a sentence or paragraph that you discarded.

▶ 2 Focusing the paper through coherence

Coherence describes the clarity of the relationship between one unit of meaning and another: between sections of a paper, between paragraphs within sections, and between sentences within paragraphs.

- A *whole paper* is coherent when its sections (groupings of related paragraphs) follow one another in a sensible order.
- A *section* of the paper is coherent when the individual paragraphs that constitute it follow one another in a sensible order.
- A *paragraph* is coherent when the individual sentences in it follow one another in a sensible order.

At every level of a paper, you establish coherence by building logical bridges, or transitions, between thoughts. A **transition** may be a word, a sentence, or a paragraph devoted to building a smooth, logical relationship. In all cases, a transition has a double function: to remind readers of what they have just read and then to forecast for them what they are about to read. Transitional expressions include *additionally; likewise; first, second,* and so on; *afterward; for example; of course; accordingly; however; in conclusion;* and *on the whole.* (See 5d-3 for a detailed discussion of transitions and a more complete list.)

Later Revision: Bringing Your Main Idea into Focus   **93**

Transitions serve to highlight relationships that already exist. If you have trouble finding a word or sentence to serve as an effective transition, reexamine the sentences, paragraphs, or sections that you are trying to link. You may not have arranged them coherently and may need to rearrange them.

As you revise your paper, pause to analyze its sections *in relation* to each other. Rearrange sections, if need be, in order to improve the logical flow of ideas among the largest units of meaning, the paper's sections.

▶3 Focusing the paper through balance

Balance is a principle of development that guides you in expanding, condensing, and cutting material as you revise. First drafts are typically uneven in the amount of attention given to each section of a paper. In revision, one of your jobs is to review the weight (the extent of development) you have given each of the topics you have discussed and to determine how appropriate that weight is to the importance of that particular point. At times, you will need to *expand:* to add material, in which case you will need to return to the notes you made in preparing to write. You may need to generate new information by reflecting on your subject, by conducting

---

ACROSS THE CURRICULUM

Sentence-Level Revision

Computer scientist Linda Cohen revises a brief paragraph on the automation of semiconductor (computer-chip) manufacturing:

First draft: Because technicians introduce particulate matter into the environment, automated equipment and robots are used in the manufacture of semiconductor chips. Oil from the skin, dust, hairs from eyelashes, and even residual smoke from the lungs can contaminate the chips, rendering them worthless.

Revisions: Because technicians introduce ~~particulate matter~~ into the environ- *Human,* *dirt* *cleanroom* ∧ ∧ ∧ ment, ~~automated equipment and robots are used in the manufacture~~ of semiconductor ~~chips.~~ Oil from the skin, dust, hairs from eyelashes, *manufacturing* ∧ and even residual smoke from the lungs can contaminate the chips, rendering them worthless. *For this reason, the process is now automated.* ∧

Final draft: Human technicians introduce dirt into the cleanroom environment of semiconductor manufacturing. Oil from the skin, dust, hairs from eyelashes, and even residual smoke from the lungs can contaminate the chips, rendering them worthless. For this reason, the process is now automated.

---

additional library research, or both. At times you will need to *condense:* to take a lengthy paragraph, for example, and reduce it to two sentences. At other times you will need to *cut:* to delete sentences because they are off the point or because they give too much attention to a subordinate point.

▶ **EXERCISE 2**

Revise your first draft for unity, coherence, and balance following the guidelines discussed in this chapter.

▶ **4c**   Final revision

▶**1   Editing**

Editing is revision at the sentence level: the level at which you attend to style, grammar, punctuation, and word choice. Depending on their preferences, writers will edit (just as they revise) throughout the writing process, from the first draft through to the last. It would be misleading to state flatly that the process of sentence-level rewriting should wait until all issues of unity and coherence are resolved. Still, to the extent that you *can* hold off, save editing until the later drafts, once you are relatively confident that your paper has a final thesis and that the major sections of the paper are in order. In any event, don't allow sentence-level concerns to block your writing process early on—especially since the sentence you are fretting over may not even make it to the final draft.

A suggestion made in the Preface is worth repeating here: take an hour to read the introductions to each of the chapters in the handbook. If such a review is not realistic, then read the introductions to the chapters on sentence errors (see 12–16), effective sentences (see 17–20), and punctuation (see 24-29). Your review will give you a sense of the types of errors to watch for when editing. In addition, you can use the "Spotlight on Common Errors" device in the endpapers and in key chapters of this book. Use the "Spotlight" pages as checklists for uncovering and revising the most common sentence and punctuation errors.

▶**2   Proofreading**

Before you call a paper finished, check for minor errors that may annoy readers and embarrass you. Reread your paper to identify and correct misspelled words; words (often prepositions) omitted from sentences; words that have been doubled; punctuation that you tend to forget; and homonyms (writing *there* instead of *their*). If you have trouble spotting these minor errors in your writing, find a way to disrupt your usual pattern of reading so that the errors will become visible to you.

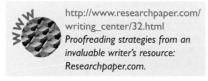
http://www.researchpaper.com/
writing_center/32.html
*Proofreading strategies from an
invaluable writer's resource:
Researchpaper.com.*

■ One technique is to photocopy your work and have a friend read it aloud. You read along and make corrections.

- Another technique is to read each line of your paper in reverse order, from the last word on the line to the first. This approach forces you to focus on one word at a time.
- Besides checking for minor errors, review your writing assignment one last time to make sure you have prepared your manuscript in an appropriate form. (See Appendix A on Manuscript Form and Preparation.)

▶3 Determining when a final draft is *final*

At some point you must stop writing. In the age of word processing, deciding when to stop is not always easy, since you can make that one last correction and have the computer print a new page with relative ease. When changes seem not to improve the product, then you have reached an end to revision and editing. To consider a draft final, make sure your paper has met these standards:

- The paper has a clearly stated main point to communicate.
- It has met all requirements of unity and coherence at the levels of the paper, section, and paragraph.
- It is punctuated correctly and is free of errors in grammar and usage.

Stylistically, you could edit your papers ad infinitum. Stylistic editing can mean the difference between a good work and an excellent one. Eventually, however, you will reach a point at which changes do not improve the quality of your paper. When you reach this point, stop.

▶ **EXERCISE 3**

Edit the draft of the paper you have revised for unity, coherence, and balance. Realize that you may need to make several passes at your draft to put it into final form. Now proofread your final draft.

COMPUTER TIPS

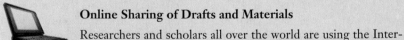

Online Sharing of Drafts and Materials

Researchers and scholars all over the world are using the Internet to share their writing quickly and easily with people at distant locations. If you have trusted friends or colleagues in other classes or even at other schools, you can ask for their feedback via e-mail as you begin to revise a paper. If your particular Internet connection and computer system allow you to send "attached files," then you can compose a brief message and attach the whole word-processed file for the other person to download into his or her own file system. If you cannot easily attach files to your e-mail messages, then just copy your paper, paste it into the body of your message, and then send it as you would any other e-mail message.

The Process of Revision

Another Point of View

In Chapter 6, another student writer takes up the same topic as Lou Cassetta: gender roles in the high-tech workplace. Marie Hobahn uses some of Lou's same sources, including the example readings (by Munk and Oliver, Hamm, and Brunner and Bennett) found in Chapter 1. Here is the first paragraph from Marie's argumentative essay. You will find her completed essay at 6a.

> How well are women doing in the professional world of computing? There's no use denying it: the numbers don't look good. None of the top 50 computer companies boasts a female CEO, even though women make up about a third of the high-tech workforce (DeBare, "High-tech" 1). Women fill less than 30% of programming, engineering, and management jobs at high-tech companies. Companies created or run by women received just 1.6% of the venture capital invested in high-tech firms from 1991 to 1996 (Crain; Hamm). The glass ceiling that keeps women from advancing seems real. According to D. J. Young, a software quality assurance manager at the software firm Intuit, "More women are [. . .] reaching that first level of management, but [. . .] the higher [they] go, the harder it is to get to the next level" (qtd. in DeBare, "Voices" 1). Considering this discouraging news, it might seem a hopeless act of faith to believe that things will get better anytime soon. But that faith would, in fact, be justified. Although women are certainly underrepresented at present in the computer industry, market forces will inevitably bring about a more equitable proportion of women to men.

▶ 4d   Responding to editorial advice from peers or professors

One of your jobs as a writer is to give and receive editorial advice. All writers can benefit from an editor, a person whose fresh perspective can identify trouble spots that escaped the writer's view.

▶ I   Receiving advice

As the writer of a paper that does not yet succeed, be aware that critical comments, provided they come from a responsible source, are being directed at your work and not at you. To the extent possible, disengage your ego from the editorial review, and respond not according to your hurt feelings but according to the substance of the comments directed at your paper.

As a writer, you have the absolute prerogative to accept, to accept partially, or to reject editorial advice. If you truly disagree with your editor, even one who will at some point be grading you, then you should hold your ground and *thoughtfully* explain what you were trying to do in the paper, what you would like to do, and why you cannot accept a particular suggestion for revision. But remember that if the editor is responsible, he or she has the interests of your paper in mind and is making suggestions to improve your effort. These suggestions deserve an honest hearing.

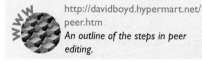

http://davidboyd.hypermart.net/peer.htm
An outline of the steps in peer editing.

Guidelines for Peer Editing

1. Understand your role as an editor. Disinvest your ego, and work to improve the paper according to the author's needs, not your own.

2. Ask the writer to identify elements of the paper to which you should pay special attention.

3. Questions you might consider as you are reading:

   Is the writer helping me to become interested in this topic?

   Do all the parts of this paper seem to be present? Are general points backed up with specific examples?

   Is the writing at the sentence level sharp?

   How much help does the writer need with the nuts and bolts of grammar and punctuation?

4. Begin with the positive. Whether you are writing your editorial comments or are delivering them in conference, begin with the parts of the paper that you liked. If at all possible, find *something* that is worthy of a compliment.

5. Be specific with criticism. When you see room for improvement, identify specific words, sentences, or paragraphs, and state specifically what you think needs changing and why. If possible, build your constructive criticisms on earlier strengths:

   Avoid statements such as "This is vague."

   Strive for statements such as "Your sentences in this section don't have the same vivid detail as your earlier sentences."

6. End your editorial advice with a summary of what you have observed. Then suggest a point-by-point action plan for the writer. That is, advise the writer on specific steps to take that will lead to an improved paper.

2 Giving advice

As an editor, you must allow the writer his or her topic and interest in it. Do not criticize because a topic does not interest you. Also, realize that this is not your paper that you are commenting on. Disinvest your ego from the job so that you do not attempt in your comments to make the paper yours. Realize as well the power of your criticism. Many people feel fragile about their writing, and when you must criticize, be respectful. Most writing has something good in it. Start there, and be specific with your praise. State, "I like this sentence," and say why. Then compare passages that don't work with those that do, and explain the differences you see. Be honest with your criticism.

http://ec.hku.hk/writing_turbocharger/ collaborating/
How to use your computer to peer-edit friends' and classmates' writing, by talking about your work and exchanging drafts, from U. of Hong Kong.

The better you edit other people's work, the more proficient you will become at editing your own. Whatever your editorial skills, you can benefit from the editorial advice of others precisely because they are not you and can therefore offer a fresh perspective. In developing your own guidelines for giving editorial advice, you may want to build on the notes in the box at the top of the page.

The Process of Revision

The process of writing a draft and responding to criticism clarified for Lou Cassetta several problems with his thinking about women and men in the computer industry. In the process of writing, he discovered a *new* thesis—the basis of which you can find in his earliest responses to the sources he read on his topic.

As you will see, Lou Cassetta spent time refining his sentences so that they would read effortlessly. You will find in his essay the paradox evident in all good writing: when sentences are clear and easy to read, they mask the considerable effort that went into making them. Good writing looks to readers as if it took no work at all; the writer knows otherwise.

```
          Gender Differences in the Computer Industry
                         (Final Draft)


     When I applied for a job in computer data entry last summer
at one of the world's largest management consulting firms, I never
thought that my experience as a grease monkey would help. Although
knowing how to work a gas pump did not make me a better typist, I
learned important communication skills at the gas station that I
used to get the office job. At the gas station, my co-workers and I
always talked about the fastest and most sophisticated automobiles
and how much we would like to own them. When I applied for the data
entry position, I impressed my boss by engaging in a conversation
about his laptop computer. Many men are fascinated by the newest
and fastest machines and love to talk about them. I have always
taken part in conversations about these machines, and I don't once
recall having these conversations with women.
     I was grateful for the job, of course. But the way of think-
ing that gave me an advantage exposed a problem--actually, two
problems--that will prevent us from making strides in the computer
industry: too many people accept the stereotype that women are not
technologically oriented, and too many people have been intimidated
by political correctness into believing that women and men must be
exactly alike.
     The signs are everywhere that gender stereotyping has followed
women and men from our general culture into computer culture. Most
industry executives are men, and relatively few women advance be-
yond middle management in computer hardware and software companies
(Kantrowitz 52). The glass ceiling that has blocked advancement of
women in other settings throughout corporate America has blocked
their advancement in the computer industry as well. When promoting
```

sexism in the corporation, industry executives don't openly endorse
the more Neanderthal characterizations of women as natural-born
homemakers. A more subtle sexism exists, which begins with the
patronizing view that while women are of course as smart as men,
it is men, not women, who are more naturally inclined to technology. And thus we should expect to find more men in technologically
intensive fields.

It's an old story, the view that men are good at math and logical thinking and, therefore, naturally excel at computers. In fact,
numerous studies have failed to find any such "natural" superiority
among boys. When differences are observed, they can be traced to
social settings--for instance, to the differing interactions of
teachers with their male and female students (American Association
74). Historian of science Ruth Schwartz Cowan believes that America
has systematically trained its women to avoid technology:

> No country on earth has been so much in the sway of the
> technological order or so proud of its involvement in it.
> Doctors and engineers are central to [American] culture;
> poets and artists live on the fringes.
>
> If practicality and know-how and willingness to get
> your hands dirty down there with the least of them are
> signatures of the true American, then we have been
> systematically training slightly more than half of our
> population to be un-American. I speak, of course, of
> women. [. . .] We have trained our women to opt out of
> the technological order as much as we have trained our
> men to opt into it. (62)

In the years since Cowan made these observations, more women
have entered the computer field. Still, problems persist. Writing
in The Chronicle of Higher Education about America's training of
women for careers in science, Bernadine Healy, director of the
National Institutes of Health, cites a "study by the American
Association for the Advancement of Science [that] found that women
in science classes are subject to more negative treatment than
their male colleagues--by both faculty and other students." Healy
further reports that women are underrepresented in the sciences.
For instance, during the 1992-93 academic year, women earned little
more than one-third of bachelor's degrees in computer science,
compared with their earning 54 percent of all bachelor's degrees
awarded. Fewer women than men pursued this education: women earned
about 27 percent of master's degrees in computer science, as

opposed to earning 54 percent of the master's degrees overall. And
a mere 13 percent of Ph.D.'s in computer science went to women, as
opposed to 38 percent of all doctorates awarded (Wylie 3; United
States 174). Women achieve their share of degrees, but dispropor-
tionately few seek careers in computer science--a trend that is
continuing into the next century.

The number of women in this field is up over the past twenty
years; but almost certainly, gender stereotyping continues to
affect women's career choices. Each new generation of women that
embraces a field such as computer science sets a good precedent
for the next generation. Over time, gender inequalities can be
corrected. The evidence is clear, however, that sexism continues
to infect both academics and, as measured by the lack of senior
executive positions for women, the computer industry. In continuing
the fight against sexism, we must hunt down and discredit false
claims of differences between women and men regarding technology.
The more we do so, the more girls will regard the sciences as simply another career choice for which they are as qualified as boys.

Yet what will we do if we find there are <u>real</u> differences between the sexes regarding technology? It is almost impossible to
believe that men and women are alike in every way, aside from
the physical. Differences are bound to exist, and we would be
as foolish to avoid pursuing them, for fear of being politically
incorrect, as we have been in insisting that women aren't any good
at math and science. We should use real differences positively, as
a source of advancement. One fruitful area for research might be
the ways in which women and men use computers.

Generalizations never apply to all individuals, but impres-
sionistic evidence suggests that men tend to treat their computers
in the same way that muscle car enthusiasts treat their hot rods.
Both want the fastest, most powerful machines that money can buy.
The relationship that women enjoy with computers seems to differ.
Esther Dyson, editor of an influential software-industry newsletter, characterizes the relationship this way: I don't "really
care about its innards, I just want it to work" (qtd. in Kantrowitz
50). Oliver Strimpel, executive director of The Computer Museum
in Boston, finds this pattern very common among male and female
computer owners. "Men tend to be seduced by the technology itself,"
he says, while women are more inclined to look past the technology
and judge a machine's efficiency and overall usefulness (qtd. in
Kantrowitz 50). Cornelia Brunner and Dorothy Bennett of the Center

for Children and Technology make exactly the same point. Based on "a series of studies about gender differences around attitudes and approaches to technology," the researchers observed that "[t]he feminine attitude toward technology looks right through the machine to its social function, while the masculine view is more focused on the machine itself" (57).

These impressions, although unproven, are provocative. If sociologists or anthropologists confirm them (and again, we're not discussing intellectual ability but rather style of interacting with computers), we must be brave enough to admit that, at least in some measures, women and men do differ. Differences are neutral: They do not suggest better or worse, equal or unequal. Well-understood differences between the sexes could provide information with which to better design machines and software. We might look for less "muscular" machines and more intuitive operating systems; we might expect more variety among video games and see perhaps fewer slice-em-up kung fu warriors.

My job last summer was completely dominated by men. Had a woman with my same skills applied for the data entry job, she may not have been hired unless she was able to impress my boss through a conversation about his laptop. Too bad. In a smarter, not to mention more equitable, world, my boss would have interviewed women candidates along with men and found plenty (of both) who were qualified. By asking intelligent questions, he might have discovered that women and men could bring different, equally valid perspectives to bear on the work done in his office. He could have used these perspectives to his company's advantage, improving his product.

We need to get beyond the ignorance and fear that have kept us from making greater strides in the computer industry. These problems diminish our potential; not until we eliminate them will America be putting its full human resources to work in an industry that demands our very best.

Works Cited

American Association of University Women. The AAUW Report: How Schools Shortchange Girls. Washington: AAUW, 1992.
Brunner, Cornelia, and Dorothy Bennett. "Technology Perceptions by Gender." Education Digest 56.3 (Feb. 1998).

Cowan, Ruth Schwartz. "From Virginia Dare to Virginia Slims: Women and Technology in American Life." Technology and Society 20.1 (1979): 51–63.

Healy, Bernadine. "Quotable: The Astonishing Thing Is That Young Women Pursue Careers in Science and Medicine at All." The Chronicle of Higher Education 25 Mar. 1992: B5.

Kantrowitz, Barbara. "Men, Women and Computers." Newsweek 16 May 1994: 48–55.

United States Dept. of Education. Digest of Educational Statistics. Washington: GPO, 1995.

Wylie, Margie. "No Place for Women: Internet Is Flawed Model for the Infobahn." Digital Media 4.8 (1995): 3+. Digital Media Online. Nexis. 19 Nov. 1995.

CHAPTER 5

The Paragraph and the Paper

A **paragraph** is a group of related sentences organized by a single, controlling idea. Marked with an indented first word (typically five spaces from the left margin), a paragraph can be as brief as a sentence or longer than a page. Paragraphs rarely stand alone: they are extended units of thought that, carefully pieced together, build the content of a paper through strategic decisions you make in the writing and revision process. In this chapter you will learn about the characteristics of a well-written paragraph and the relationship of individual paragraphs to larger units of thought.[1]

▶ 5a The relationship of single paragraphs to a whole paper

At times, you may feel that generating a paragraph is easy enough, but that writing an entire essay, paper, or report is beyond your abilities. (How will I *ever* write twenty pages?) In these moments, you need to remember that whole documents are written one paragraph at a time and whole paragraphs, one sentence at a time.

▶ 1 The relationship of paragraphs to sections

Just as sentences are the units that make up individual paragraphs, paragraphs are the units that make up whole letters, essays, and reports. Aside from specialized occasions for writing, such as summaries and short-answer essay exams, you will seldom write a single, isolated paragraph.

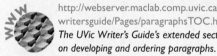
http://webserver.maclab.comp.uvic.ca/
writersguide/Pages/paragraphsTOC.html
*The UVic Writer's Guide's extended section
on developing and ordering paragraphs.*

Usually, any paragraph will be situated in a grouping—a **section**—that constitutes part of the larger document. Except for the beginning of a paper and the end (see 5f), any one paragraph will be involved directly with at least two others: the one immediately preceding and the one that follows. If you can write a group of three related paragraphs in a single sitting, you will be able to piece together an entire paper.

The following paragraphs form a section—one part of a chapter—of Helen Keller's autobiography. At the age of nineteen months, Keller was stricken by a

---

[1]Example paragraphs from various sources are consecutively numbered throughout the chapter for ease of reference.

disease that left her deaf and blind. Not until she was seven, with the arrival of her teacher Anne Sullivan, did Keller discover language. The moment described in these famous paragraphs is one of extraordinary awakening: the realization that things in the world have names. These paragraphs are related; they read as a carefully written section, as if they appeared from the pen of the author all at the same instant. Be assured, however, that Keller wrote this section of her autobiography one paragraph at a time, one sentence at a time. She was twenty-two and a sophomore at Radcliffe College when *My Life Story* was published.

1   The morning after my teacher came she led me into her room and gave me a doll. The little blind children at the Perkins Institution had sent it and Laura Bridgman had dressed it; but I did not know this until afterward. When I had played with it a little while, Miss Sullivan slowly spelled into my hand the word "d-o-l-l." I was at once interested in this finger play and tried to imitate it. When I finally succeeded in making the letters correctly I was flushed with childish pleasure and pride. Running downstairs to my mother I held up my hand and made the letters for doll. I did not know that I was spelling a word or even that words existed; I was simply making my fingers go in monkey-like imitation. In the days that followed I learned to spell in this uncomprehending way a great many words, among them *pin, hat, cup* and a few verbs like *sit, stand* and *walk.* But my teacher had been with me several weeks before I understood that everything has a name.

2   One day, while I was playing with my new doll, Miss Sullivan put my big rag doll into my lap also, spelled "d-o-l-l" and tried to make me understand that "d-o-l-l" applied to both. Earlier in the day we had had a tussle over the words "m-u-g" and "w-a-t-e-r." Miss Sullivan had tried to impress it upon me that "m-u-g" is *mug* and that "w-a-t-e-r" is *water,* but I persisted in confounding the two. In despair she had dropped the subject for the time, only to renew it at the first opportunity. I became impatient at her repeated attempts and, seizing the new doll, I dashed it upon the floor. I was keenly delighted when I felt the fragments of the broken doll at my feet. Neither sorrow nor regret followed my passionate outburst. I had not loved the doll. In the still, dark world in which I lived there was no strong sentiment or tenderness. I felt my teacher sweep the fragments to one side of the hearth, and I had a sense of satisfaction that the cause of my discomfort was removed. She brought me my hat, and I knew I was going out into the warm sunshine. This thought, if a wordless sensation may be called a thought, made me hop and skip with pleasure.

3   We walked down the path to the well-house, attracted by the fragrance of the honeysuckle with which it was covered. Someone was drawing water and my teacher placed my hand under the spout. As the cool stream gushed over one hand she spelled into the other the word *water,* first slowly, then rapidly. I stood still, my whole attention fixed upon the motions of her fingers. Suddenly I felt a misty consciousness as of something forgotten—a thrill of returning thought; and somehow the mystery of language was revealed to me. I knew then that "w-a-t-e-r" meant the wonderful cool something that was flowing over my hand. That living word awakened my soul, gave it light, hope, joy, set it free! There were barriers still, it is true, but barriers that could in time be swept away.

4   I left the well-house eager to learn. Everything had a name, and each name gave birth to a new thought. As we returned to the house every object which I touched seemed to quiver with life. That was because I saw everything with the strange, new sight that had come to me. On entering the door I remembered the doll I had broken. I felt my way to the hearth and picked up the pieces. I

tried vainly to put them together. Then my eyes filled with tears; for I realized what I had done, and for the first time I felt repentance and sorrow.

    I learned a great many new words that day. I do not remember what they all were; but I do know that *mother, father, sister, teacher* were among them—words that were to make the world blossom for me, "like Aaron's rod, with flowers." It would have been difficult to find a happier child than I was as I lay in my crib at the close of that eventful day and lived over the joys it had brought me, and for the first time longed for a new day to come.

                    —HELEN KELLER, *My Life Story*

▶2   The relationship of sections to the whole paper

A **thesis** explicitly states the topic you will address in a paper and either directly or indirectly suggests the points you will make about that topic (see 3d). You will probably devote one section of your paper to discussing each point you wish to develop. For each section of your paper you will write a **section thesis,** a statement that explicitly announces the point you will address in the section and either directly or indirectly suggests what you will discuss relating to this point. You will organize your discussion in paragraphs.

    The section thesis organizing the paragraphs by Helen Keller appears at the end of ¶1: *"But my teacher had been with me several weeks before I understood that everything has a name."* The next four paragraphs focus on and develop various aspects of this statement.

    ¶2 Events leading to the moment of discovery: an account of Sullivan's frustrated attempts to teach Keller.

    ¶3 The moment of discovery: clearly the most famous in the autobiography, Keller realizing the mystery of language.

    ¶4 Consequence 1 of the discovery: objects quivering with life and Keller knowing repentance and sorrow for the first time.

    ¶5 Consequence 2 of the discovery: joy in having learned that everything has a name.

    These five paragraphs form a distinct section of one chapter in Keller's autobiography. The section as a whole is *unified* and *well developed* in that all paragraphs focus on and amply discuss a single controlling idea: the section thesis highlighted previously. Each paragraph is unified and well developed; each focuses on and amply discusses its own, more narrowly defined controlling idea. And because each paragraph builds on the one that precedes it and is positioned according to a clear plan, the whole section is *coherent.* In the same way, every paragraph in the section is itself coherent, since the sentences of each lead from one to the next and establish a clear pattern of relation.

▶   EXERCISE I

Locate an article in a magazine or a chapter of a book (a textbook will do), and divide the article or chapter into its component sections. Analyze the paragraphs in one section as follows: (1) identify the controlling idea, or section thesis; and (2) explain how the section is unified, developed, and coherent.

Unity, Coherence, and Development

■ Each *paragraph* of a paper consists of *sentences* that are
Unified: The sentences are all concerned with a central, controlling idea.
Coherent: The sentences are arranged in a clear order, according to a definite plan.
Well developed: The sentences provide details that explain and illustrate the paragraph's controlling idea.

■ Each *section* of a paper consists of *paragraphs* that are
Unified: The groups of paragraphs are devoted to one controlling idea, a section thesis that develops some part of the thesis.
Coherent: The groups of paragraphs within a section are arranged in a clear order, according to a definite plan.
Well developed: The groups of paragraphs provide details that explain and illustrate the section's controlling idea.

■ Every *paper* consists of *sections* (groups of related paragraphs) that are
Unified: Each section is devoted to developing one part of the thesis, the central, organizing idea of the paper.
Coherent: The sections are arranged in a clear order, according to a definite plan.
Well developed: Each section of the paper provides details important for developing the thesis.

▶ **5b**   The paragraph: Essential features

To develop an idea well, you will need to make sure that the sentences of your paragraphs are unified: sentences in any given paragraph should refer to one organizing idea. The paragraph should also be *well developed:* sentences should explain or defend well the main point of the paragraph. In addition, the paragraph should be *coherent:* sentences of the paragraph should be arranged in a clear order.

The following is an example of a well-written paragraph from a biology text.

> Life on this planet began in water, and today, almost wherever water is found, life is also present. There are one-celled organisms that eke out their entire existence in no more water than that which can cling to a grain of sand. Some species of algae are found only on the melting undersurfaces of polar ice floes. Certain species of bacteria and certain blue-green algae can tolerate the near-boiling water of hot springs. In the desert, plants race through an entire
> 6   life cycle—seed to flower to seed—following a single rainfall. In the jungle, the water cupped in the leaves of a tropical plant forms a microcosm in which a myriad of small organisms are born, spawn, and die. We are interested in whether the soil of Mars and the dense atmosphere surrounding Venus contain water principally because we want to know whether life is there. On our planet, and probably on others where life exists, life and water have been companions since life first began.
> —HELENA CURTIS, "Water"

Examine the qualities that make this grouping of sentences a paragraph, a unit of thought. First, the sentences of Curtis's paragraph are narrowly focused by a single, controlling idea: *water* and its relation to life. Given this focus, the grouping of sentences is unified. Observe as well that Curtis develops her central idea according to a clear plan. In the first six sentences, she associates water with life on earth. Notice how she moves from an extreme presented in one sentence to an opposite extreme presented in the next.

Curtis's next-to-last sentence, about water on Mars or Venus, extends observations made concerning water and life on earth to other planets, and once again she drives home her point, which she repeats by way of summary in the paragraph's last sentence. She has taken care to present eight *unified* sentences that *develop* a central idea and that are arranged in a meaningful, *coherent* order. Thus, Curtis has written a paragraph: a well-developed unit of thought organized around a single idea and arranged according to some definite plan.

▶ **EXERCISE 2**

Choose any numbered paragraph in this chapter, and explain why it can justifiably be called a paragraph. In your explanation, (1) identify the central, organizing idea that unifies the sentences; (2) identify the parts of the paragraph that explain or defend this central idea; and (3) explain how the sentences are organized according to a definite, coherent plan.

▶ **5c** **Writing and revising to achieve paragraph unity**

A unified paragraph will focus on, will develop, and will not stray from the paragraph's central, controlling idea, or **topic sentence.** Recall that a *thesis* announces and controls the content of an entire essay, and that a *section thesis* announces and controls the content of a section. Just so, a *topic sentence* announces and controls the content of sentences in a single paragraph.

Essay-level unity	The thesis (the most general statement in the essay) governs your choice of sections in a paper.
Section-level unity	Section theses (the second-most-general statements in the essay) govern your choice of paragraphs in a section.
Paragraph-level unity	Topic sentences (the third-most-general statements in the essay) govern your choice of sentences in a paragraph.

Within a paragraph, a topic sentence can appear anywhere, provided that you recognize it and can lead up to and away from it with some method in mind.

▶ **1** **Placing the topic sentence at the beginning of a paragraph**

Very often, a topic sentence is placed first in a paragraph. You will want to open your paragraphs this way when your purpose is to inform or persuade a reader and you wish to be as direct as possible, as in the following example:

The college town is an American institution. Throughout the 19th century, it was common practice to locate private colleges in small towns like Amherst in Massachusetts, Middlebury in Vermont and Pomona in California. The idea was

7 that bucolic surroundings would provide the appropriate atmosphere for the pursuit of learning and (not incidentally) remove students from the distractions and temptations of the big city. The influence of the small college on its town was minimal, however, beyond providing a few local residents with service jobs.

—WITOLD RYBCYNSKI, "Big City Amenities"

Witold Rybcynski begins the paragraph with a direct statement: *The college town is an American institution.* Every subsequent sentence focuses on and develops this topic sentence.

▶2 Placing the topic sentence in the middle of a paragraph

When you want to present material on two sides of an issue in your paragraph, consider placing the topic sentence in the middle of the paragraph. Lead up to the topic sentence with supporting material concerning its first part; lead away from the topic sentence with material concerning its second part, as in the following example:

8   A host of simple-minded cliches about Moslems and Islam exists. When the hostage crisis in Iran occurred, most Westerners began to view all Moslems, the followers of Islam, as Arab or Iranian militants seeking to return the world to the 14th century. There is, however, great diversity in Islam, a religion that covers one-seventh of the earth's inhabitable area and includes a sixth of its population. To judge all Moslems as the same is as futile as judging all Christians and Jews in the same way. Most of the world's 800 million Moslems are not fatalistic radicals. Like most Christians and Jews, they, too, devoutly believe in and respect God and seek to live a good life in peace with others.

—JACK SHAHEEN, "In Search of the Arab"

Jack Shaheen's topic sentence is the pivot on which this paragraph turns: *There is, however, great diversity in Islam, a religion that covers one-seventh of the earth's inhabitable area and includes a sixth of its population.* Two sentences lead up to this topic sentence, preparing for it; three sentences follow and develop this topic sentence.

▶3 Placing the topic sentence at the end of a paragraph

When writing an informative or argumentative paper, in specific paragraphs you may want to postpone the topic sentence until the end. You would do this to ensure that readers would consider all the sentences in a paragraph before coming to your main point. The strategy works especially well when you are arguing, as in the following example:

9   It is a fact that many children today are watching a great deal of televised fare that is inappropriate for their age and sophistication level. This concern raises two possible courses of action. If we take the position of technology determinist Neil Postman that "it is pointless to spend time or energy deploring television or even making proposals to improve it," then the only response is to lock the television set up, or do whatever is necessary to keep it away from the innocent eyes of children. But if we believe that television can offer the potential to complement and enliven children's literacy experiences, it is imperative that greater efforts be made to improve both the quality of programming, and children's viewing habits.

—SUSAN B. NEUMAN, "The Myth of the TV Effect"

Writing and Revising to Achieve Paragraph Unity   109

If you place the last sentence of this paragraph first, you see that subsequent sentences support and develop the idea that *greater efforts be made to improve both the quality of programming, and children's viewing habits.* This statement is debatable, a fact that Susan Neuman implicitly acknowledges by presenting two solutions to the opening problem (that children are watching television inappropriate for their age and level of sophistication). She follows with the first solution, which she rejects, and then offers a competing solution, which she endorses. By delaying her paragraph's main idea, Neuman ensures that her audience will have some background on the problem and reason enough to agree with her position.

▶4 Omitting the topic sentence from the paragraph

In narrative and descriptive papers, and much less frequently in informative and persuasive papers, writers will occasionally omit the topic sentence from a paragraph. In a narrative paragraph in which you are telling a story, including the topic sentence may be too heavy-handed and may ruin an otherwise subtle effect. The subject of descriptive writing may be so obvious that including a topic sentence seems redundant. When you decide to omit a topic sentence from a paragraph, take care to write the paragraph as though a topic sentence were present. Focus each sentence on the implied topic and do not include any sentence that strays from that implied topic. Helen Keller does exactly this in ¶2 (page 105). Had she written a topic sentence for this paragraph, it might have read as follows: *The events immediately leading up to my discovery of language showed how thoroughly difficult and insensitive a child I was.*

The following is an example of an informative paragraph with an implied topic sentence:

> Glossy brochures [from colleges to prospective high-school applicants] tend to portray a diverse group of beaming students frolicking happily and thinking deep thoughts on every page. "They're all the same," recalled one college freshman, happy to be finished with the process. Each brochure speaks of "rich diversity" and "academic rigor" and dozens of other high-minded ideals that are often in reality nothing more than hollow catch-phrases. Likewise, any campus can look beautiful through the lens of an admissions office photographer. Just remember, the building that looks so picturesque in the fading twilight could be part of the law school, miles from where the undergraduates study.
>
> —YALE DAILY NEWS STAFF, "The Insider's Guide to the Colleges"

10

The sentence that comes closest to being a topic sentence is the paragraph's final one. Yet even this sentence implies, rather than states directly, the following main idea: *When reviewing glossy college brochures, high-school students should not assume that they are being presented with a fully accurate portrayal of undergraduate life.* Placed at the head of this paragraph, this sentence would function adequately as a topic sentence. The existence and placement of every sentence in the paragraph is governed by this implied sentence, just as if it had been stated directly.

▶ EXERCISE 3

Reread several paragraphs that you have recently written for one of your classes. Choose one paragraph to revise for unity: add, delete, or modify sentences as needed.

EXERCISE 4

Locate the topic sentence of the paragraphs in the section you worked with in Exercise 1. Analyze each paragraph, and be prepared to discuss how every sentence contributes to the paragraph's unity.

▶ **5d**   Writing and revising to achieve paragraph coherence

When your paragraphs are coherent, readers will understand the logic by which you move from one sentence to the next, toward or away from your topic sentence. When writing the first draft of a paper, you may not have a plan to ensure paragraph coherence; you may not even have a clear idea of every paragraph's main point. Revision is the time when you sort these matters out—when you can make certain that each paragraph has a clear purpose and a clear, coherent plan for achieving that purpose.

1 Arranging sentences to achieve coherence

There are standard patterns for arranging paragraphs. The most common are arrangements by space, by time, and by importance. If it occurs to you as you are writing a first draft that one of these patterns lends itself to the particular point you are discussing, then by all means write your paragraph with that pattern in mind. Very often, you will revise paragraphs with one of these patterns in mind.

Arrangement by space

You can help readers visualize what you are describing by arranging a paragraph spatially. Start the reader at a well-defined position with respect to the object being described, and then move him or her from that position to others by taking systematic steps, one at a time, until your description is complete. Your description could proceed from front to back, right to left, top to bottom, outside to inside, and so on.

> By the 17th and 18th centuries, Edinburgh was already overbuilt. Gray stone buildings filled every nook and cranny along the city's maze of roads and alleys. Space was so scarce inside the city walls that doctors, merchants and other professionals conducted their business in the pubs that lined the streets. [. . .] When Edinburgh needed more room to pack in people, the resourceful Scots had to expand upward. It was not uncommon [. . .] for some buildings to go up 12 to 14 stories. The higher floors were reserved for the upper crust of Scottish society. The richer you were, the farther away you lived from the dark, wet and always filthy Edinburgh streets.
>
> —George Homsy, "From Kings to Caddies in Edinburgh"

The spatial organization in this paragraph rests on a principle of upward movement, the need for which was created by overcrowding at the base. The lower stories of buildings are associated with squalor. The upper stories are literally the realm of the upper class.

Arrangement by time

You can arrange a paragraph according to a sequence of events. Start the paragraph with a particular event, and move forward or backward in time in some definite order. Give your readers signals in each sentence that emphasize the forward or backward movement. In these example paragraphs on the rise of homelessness in the 1980s, the writer moves the reader forward in time with a series of phrases and single words, which are highlighted.

12
If the large numbers of the homeless lived in hospitals before they reappeared in subway stations and in public shelters, we need to ask where they were and what they had been doing from 1972 to 1980. Were they living under bridges? Were they waiting out the decade in the basements of deserted buildings?

13
No. The bulk of those who had been psychiatric patients and were released from hospitals during the 1960s and early 1970s had been living in the meantime in low-income housing, many in skid-row hotels or boarding houses. Such housing—commonly known as SRO (single-room occupancy) units—was drastically diminished by the gentrification of our cities that began in 1970. Almost 50 percent of SRO housing was replaced by luxury apartments or by office buildings between 1970 and 1980, and the remaining units have been disappearing at even faster rates. As recently as 1986, after New York City had issued a prohibition against conversion of such housing, a well-known developer hired a demolition team to destroy a building in Times Square that had previously been home to indigent people. The demolition took place in the middle of the night. In order to avoid imprisonment, the developer was allowed to make a philanthropic gift to homeless people as a token of atonement. This incident, bizarre as it appears, reminds us that the profit motive for displacement of the poor is very great in every major city. It also indicates a more realistic explanation for the growth of homelessness during the 1980s.

—JONATHAN KOZOL, "Distancing the Homeless"

Arrangement by importance

Just as you discuss different parts of a thesis at different locations in a paper, you will discuss different parts of a topic sentence at different locations in a paragraph. When revising, be aware of a paragraph's component parts so that you can arrange these parts in the most logical, accessible order. Arrangement is largely determined by where you position the topic sentence. How will your sentences lead up to and away from the topic sentence? You should be aware of two basic patterns: general to specific and specific to general.

General to specific: When the topic sentence begins the paragraph

By far the most common method for arranging sentences in a paragraph is to begin with your topic sentence and follow with specific, supporting details. When beginning a paragraph this way, decide how to order the information that will follow. You might ask, What does this paragraph's topic sentence obligate me to discuss? What are the *parts* of this paragraph, and in what order will I discuss them? In this paragraph, Jerry Dennis explains how birds increase the chances that their fledglings will survive.

There is a simple reason so many birds remain with one mate: the kids. The demands of raising young often take the full attention of two adults. Biologists like to discuss the behavior in economic terms, speaking of parental "invest-

14 ment," and pointing out that it is more profitable for a male bird intent on propagating his own genes to stick with one mate and ensure the survival of a brood than to impregnate many females haphazardly. Once committed to monogamy, a male bird takes the job seriously. He may help build nests, take turns brooding the eggs, gather food, and stand watch. In studies where the male has been removed, the percentages of eggs that hatch and fledglings that survive decline dramatically.

—JERRY DENNIS, "Mates for Life"

Specific to general: When the topic sentence ends the paragraph

When you are writing a description or narration or arguing a point, you may want to delay your topic sentence until the final sentence of a paragraph. Here you reverse the standard arrangement of a paragraph and move from specific details to a general, concluding statement. The goal is to build one sentence on the next so securely that the final sentence strikes the reader as inevitable.

15 Einstein [. . .] wrote: "The most beautiful experience we can have is the mysterious. It is the fundamental emotion which stands at the cradle of all true art and true science." At first, this might seem a strange thought. We are frequently asked to believe that science is the antithesis of mystery. Nothing could be further from the truth. Mystery invites the attention of the curious mind. Unless we perceive the world as mysterious—queer and wonderful—we will never be curious about what makes it tick.

—CHET RAYMO, "To Light the Fire of Science,
Start with Some Fantasy and Wonder"

Raymo begins with a specific quotation from Albert Einstein. He develops the paragraph by exploring Einstein's use of the word *mysterious*. In so doing, he moves from the specific (the quotation) to the general, his larger point, which he locates in the paragraph's final sentence.

▶2 Achieving coherence with cues

When sentences are arranged with care, you need only highlight this arrangement to ensure that readers will move easily through a paragraph. To highlight paragraph coherence, use **cues:** words and phrases that remind readers as they move from sentence to sentence (1) that they continue to read about the same topic and (2) that ideas are unfolding logically. Four types of cues help to highlight sentence-to-sentence connections: pronouns, repetition, parallel structures, and transitions (5d-3). You may want to wait until the revision stage to add cues to a paragraph, when you are better able to discern the paragraph's shape.

Pronouns

The most direct way to remind readers that they continue to examine a certain topic as they move from sentence to sentence is to repeat the most important noun, or the subject, of your topic sentence. To prevent repetition from becoming tiresome, use a pronoun to take the place of this important noun.

Writing and Revising to Achieve Paragraph Coherence   **113**

.... **ILLUSTRATION: PRONOUN SUBSTITUTION**

> The choice of Peter Hall to supply vigorous entrepreneurial leadership was logical. Only twenty-nine, he was already an eminent director. He had earned his credentials with the theatre work he began at Cambridge and continued with the Elizabethan Theatre Company, formed by Oxford and Cambridge students to tour Shakespeare plays. More impressive and attention-getting was his direction of the 1955 premiere at the London Arts Theatre of Samuel Beckett's *Waiting for Godot*, an event that alone would have entered Hall's name into theatre history.
>
> —ROGER CORNISH and VIOLET KETELS,
> *Landmarks of Modern British Drama*

Repetition

While unintentional repetition can make sentences awkward, planned repetition can contribute significantly to a paragraph's coherence. The strategy is to repeat identically or to use a substitute phrase to repeat an important word or words in a paragraph. As with pronoun use, repetition cues readers, reminding them of the paragraph's important information. In the example concerning the word *performance*, combinations of the following four words are repeated eight times: *performance/performer, minstrels, scops, and gleemen*. Skillful use of repetition ties sentences together.

.... **ILLUSTRATION: WORD REPETITION**

> Although the performance practices of the Church held considerable power and influence, the medieval audience was familiar with other types of performance events. The jongleurs and the troubadours of southern France were professional performers who glorified heroic life and courtly love in verse, often singing of love in rather earthy terms. In Anglo-Saxon England, such performers were called scops and gleemen; later, they were known as minstrels. Usually accompanying themselves with a harp, minstrels probably composed such literary texts as *Widsith, Doer's Lament*, and *Beowulf*. Just as important, each of these texts offers a picture of the minstrels' performance work.
>
> —RONALD J. PELIAS, *Performance Studies*

The Paragraph and the Paper

Parallelism

Chapter 18 is devoted entirely to a discussion of **parallelism:** the use of grammatically equivalent words, phrases, and sentences to achieve coherence and balance in your writing. A sentence whose structure parallels that of an earlier sentence has an echo-like effect, linking the content of the second sentence to the content of the first.

ILLUSTRATION: PARALLELISM

STUDENT EXAMPLE: JIM WALKER

All students need to be aware of what some students know by instinct: that you can divert or reduce aggression with a quick apology or with humor. This is what social psychologists call reducing levels of arousal by introducing an incompatible response. Also, the school can implement Peer Mediation where if students feel a physical or emotional threat they can report it and discuss it with other students.

18 Students talk through the issues with each other—and talking, it turns out, is the important thing: getting two sides together to talk rather than using weapons or fists to solve differences. Talking can also show students that disagreements are not worth a trip to the emergency room or worth the legal problems or medical bills— the consequences of violence that movies and rap videos don't usually show. If more students would have used these simple measures at my high school, I'm convinced that at least several fights could have been avoided.

Parallel structures found *within* sentences are:

you can divert or reduce

with a quick apology or with humor

what social psychologists call reducing levels of arousal by introducing

if students feel a physical or emotional threat

they can report it and discuss it

getting two sides together to talk rather than using

disagreements are not worth a trip to the emergency room or worth the legal problems

that movies and rap videos

▶3 Highlighting coherence with transitions

Transitions establish logical relationships between sentences, between paragraphs, and between whole sections of an essay. A transition can be a single word,

CRITICAL DECISIONS

Set issues in a broader context: Revising paragraphs for coherence

As a writer, you probably have too much to do in a first draft to monitor the relationships among sentences and paragraphs or to develop coherence. In a second or third draft, however, you should evaluate your sentences in the broader context of paragraphs, and paragraphs in the broader context of sections.

- **Revise every paragraph within its section.** To revise an individual paragraph, examine it in relation to the ones that come before and after. Develop the habit of including transitional words at the beginning or end of paragraphs to help readers move from one paragraph to the next.

- **Revise every sentence within its paragraph.** Once you are sure of a paragraph's place in your paper, revise for coherence. Use cues—pronouns, parallelism, repetition, and transitions—to help move the reader from one sentence to the next through a paragraph.

a phrase, a sentence, or an entire paragraph. In each case it functions the same way: first, it either directly summarizes the content of a preceding sentence (or paragraph) or it implies that summary. Having established a summary, transitions then move forward into a new sentence (or paragraph), helping the reader anticipate what is to come. For example, when you read the word *however*, you are immediately aware that the material you are about to read will contrast with the material you have just read.

Transitions *within* paragraphs

Transitions act as cues by helping readers to anticipate what is coming *before* they read it. Within a paragraph, transitions tend to be single words or short phrases.

ILLUSTRATION: TRANSITIONS

When we think about addiction to drugs or alcohol we frequently focus on negative aspects, ignoring the pleasures that accompany drinking or drug-taking. And yet the essence of any serious addiction is a pursuit of pleasure, a search for a "high" that normal life does not supply. It is only the inability to function without the addictive substance that is dismaying, the dependence of the organism upon a certain experience and an increasing inability to function normally without it. Thus people will take two or three drinks at the end of the day not merely for the

19

The Paragraph and the Paper

pleasure drinking provides, (but also) because they "don't feel normal" without them.

—MARIE WINN, "The Plug-in Drug"

Transitions *between* paragraphs

Transitions placed between paragraphs help readers move through sections of your paper. If you have done a good job of arranging paragraphs so that the content of one leads logically to the next, the transition will highlight a relationship that already exists by summarizing the previous paragraph and telegraphing something of the content of the paragraph that follows. A transition between paragraphs can be a word or two—*however, for example, similarly*—a phrase, or a sentence.

Student Example: Mike Bergom

20   Machines today are being integrated with all aspects of life, music included. For instance, we have seen the development of the synthesizer, the electric bass, and the electronic wind instrument (a flute-like instrument connected to a computer). These new instruments have slowly begun to infiltrate jazz clubs around the world. Recording techniques have also progressed to technologies such as multitrack digital recording and digital tone modulation and amplification. Jazz has definitely not gone untouched by the pervasive force of technology.

21   And yet several jazz musicians are saying "No!" to technology and are pursuing, with acoustic instruments, what might be called the "roots" of jazz. Trumpeter and jazz historian Wynton Marsalis, saxophonist and band leader Branford Marsalis, and acoustic guitarist Mark Whitfield—these musicians refuse to use the latest technologies in their music. They instead employ traditional instrumentation and jazz formats. On the face of it, this rejection is odd: as a culture, we are quick to demand and accept new technologies. We scramble for faster computers, we insist on cars with dual airbags, we debate which electric toothbrush will keep our smiles brightest. Why, then, do these young musicians, who have grown up in a technological age, refuse what has been designed to help them?

The first part of the transitional sentence that has been highlighted recalls the preceding paragraph with the words *musician* and *technology*, and then sets a strong contrast with the words *And yet* and *"No!"* The second part of this transitional sentence points to the content in the remainder of the paragraph: the jazz musicians who are using acoustic instruments.

Transitions *between* sections

At times, you may want to write a paragraph-length transition between sections of a paper, as in ¶23 of this example:

22   The electronic age has given us an almost magical ability to store, retrieve, and analyze data. Whether you're making travel plans, checking the status of an insurance policy, or changing an assumption in a five-year plan, the computer can provide almost instantaneous answers to questions that only a decade ago might have remained unanswered for a day, a week, or even a month.

23　　But the electronic age has not given us a paperless office. In fact, in a single year computers are said to churn out some 1200 pages of print for every man, woman, and child in the United States. Although they help us manage individual pieces of data, computers have increased our information overload.

24　　In the midst of this overload, at a time when multimedia commands so much attention, it's useful to remember the fundamental power of print. Print is tangible; it has a life of its own. You can read it when you want, at your own pace, and keep it for future reference. And with desktop technology, you can produce more pages faster and cheaper than ever before.

—Ronnie Shushan and Don Wright,
Desktop Publishing by Design

Whatever its length, a transition will establish a clear relationship between sentences, parts of sentences, paragraphs, or entire sections of an essay. Transitions serve to highlight relationships already present by virtue of a writer's having positioned sentences or paragraphs next to one another. If you have difficulty writing a particular transition, rethink the logical connection between paragraphs or sentences. Transitions highlight a logic already present. A rough transition, always a disruption to the smooth flow of ideas, is a sign of faulty logic.

The following box lists the most common transitions, arranged by type of relationship.

Transitional Expressions

To show addition	additionally, again, also, and, as well, besides, equally important, further, furthermore, in addition, moreover
To show similarity	also, in the same way, just as . . . so too, likewise, similarly
To show an exception	but, however, in spite of, on the one hand . . . on the other hand, nevertheless, nonetheless, notwithstanding, in contrast, on the contrary, still, yet
To indicate sequence	first, second, third, . . . next, then, finally
To show time	after, afterwards, at last, before, currently, during, earlier, immediately, later, meanwhile, now, recently, simultaneously, subsequently, then
To provide an example	for example, for instance, namely, specifically, to illustrate
To emphasize a point	even, indeed, in fact, of course, truly
To indicate place	above, adjacent, below, beyond, here, in front, in back, nearby, there
To show cause and effect	accordingly, consequently, hence, so, therefore, thus
To conclude or repeat	finally, in a word, in brief, in conclusion, in the end, on the whole, thus, to conclude, to summarize

---

▶4 Combining techniques to achieve coherence

Experienced writers will often combine the four techniques just discussed to establish coherence within a paragraph. A skillful mix of pronouns, repeated words and phrases, parallel structures, and transitions will help to maintain the focus of a paragraph and will provide multiple cues, or signposts, that help readers find their way from one sentence to the next.

ILLUSTRATION: ACHIEVING COHERENCE

For many people the years after age sixty are filled with excitement. Financially, two-thirds of American workers are covered by pension plans provided by their employers. Socially, most maintain close friendships and stay in touch with family members. Some, however, experience financial problems, while others experience loneliness and isolation because many of their friends and relatives have died or they have lost touch with their families. In the United States, there are now as many people over the age of sixty as there are under the age of seven, yet funding for programs involving the health and psychological well-being of older people is relatively limited.

— LESTER LEFTON, *Psychology*

In this paragraph, Lefton combines techniques for achieving coherence. He sets up parallel sentences with the words *Financially* and *Socially*. He also uses parallelism within sentences—for instance, *as many people over the age of sixty as there are under the age of seven*. As pronoun substitutes for the word *people*, Lefton uses *most, Some, others, their*, and *they*. He uses the transitional words *however* and *yet*. And he keeps the paragraph focused by repeating the word *people*, using several logical subsets of that general term: *workers, family members, friends, relatives*, and *older people*.

▶ EXERCISE 5

Choose any four example paragraphs in this chapter. For each paragraph, identify the techniques that the author uses to establish coherence. Show the use of pronouns, repetition, parallel structures, and transitions. In addition, identify the use of transitions between paragraphs.

EXERCISE 6

Reread a paragraph you have recently written, and circle all words that help to establish coherence. Photocopy your paragraph and then revise it for coherence, using the techniques discussed previously: arrange sentences according to a pattern and then highlight that arrangement with pronouns, repeated words, parallel structures, and transitions. Write a clean copy of the paragraph, and make photocopies of both the original and the revision for class discussion.

> ## 5e   Writing and revising to achieve well-developed paragraphs

One important element of effective writing is the level of detail you can offer in support of a paragraph's topic sentence. To *develop* a paragraph means to devote a block of sentences to a discussion of its core idea. Sentences that develop will explain or illustrate, and will support with reasons or facts. The most common technique is **topical development:** announcing your topic in the opening sentence, dividing that topic into two or three parts (in the case of chronological arrangement, into various *times*), and then developing each part within the paragraph. The various strategies presented here will help you to develop paragraphs that inform and persuade.

Developing Paragraphs: Essential Features

In determining whether a paragraph is well or even adequately developed, you should be able to answer three questions without hesitation:

- **What is the main point of the paragraph?**
- **Why should readers accept this main point?** (That is, what reasons or information have you provided that would convince a reader that your main point is accurate or reasonable?)
- **Why should readers care about the main point of this paragraph?**

When writing the first draft of a paper, you may not stop to think about how you are developing the central idea of every paragraph. There is no need to be this deliberate in first-draft writing. By the second draft, however, you will want to be conscious of fully developing your paragraphs.

Try combining methods of developing a paragraph's core idea, as needed. The same paragraph that shows an example may also show a comparison or contrast. No firm rules constrain you in developing a paragraph. Let your common sense and an interest in helping your reader understand your subject be your guides.

1   Narration and description

Stories that you tell (*narrative*) and events or scenes that you describe (*description*) are two strategies for developing effective paragraphs. Narratives usually involve descriptions; a narrative's main purpose is to recount for readers a story that has a point pertinent to the larger essay. Brief stories are often used as examples. Most often, narratives are sequenced chronologically and occur in an essay either as a single paragraph or as a grouping of paragraphs. The challenge in writing a narrative is to keep readers involved both in the events you are relating and in the people involved in those events. Vivid description helps to maintain this involvement.

> It was a chilly, 60 degree night in southern Arizona last Monday. The moon was full, and Amtrak's 12-car Sunset Limited, bearing 248 passengers and 20 crew members, was doing between 50 and 55 m.p.h. as it approached a gentle curve not too far from the tiny town of Hyder. It was 1:20 A.M., and most of the

passengers on the train, which is especially popular among retirees traveling from Los Angeles to Miami and back, were in bed. Suddenly, they were not so much awakened as catapulted from sleep. Those who kept their wits about them remember a terrible, prolonged shriek of metal against metal. For others, their waking sensation was pain, as they smashed into a wall or a chair or a sink. The Limited's two diesel locomotives had safely crossed a 30-ft.-high trestle over a desert gulch. But the next five cars—a dormitory car for crew members, two sleeping cars for passengers and a dining car—had jumped the rails. One hit the ground below; the other three hung down from the trestle like beads in a giant's necklace.

26

—DAVID VAN BIEMA, "Murder on the Sunset Limited"

▶2 Example

An example is a particular case of a more general point. After topical development, development by example is probably the most common method of supporting the core idea of a paragraph. Examples *show* readers what you mean; if an example is vivid, readers will have a better chance of remembering your general point. The topic sentence of a paragraph may be developed with one extended example or several briefer ones.

> Nervousness [. . .] is absolutely and entirely normal [in a college interview]. The best way to handle it is to admit it, out loud, to the interviewer. Miles Uhrig, director of admission at Tufts University, sometimes relates this true story to his apprehensive applicants: One extremely agitated young applicant sat opposite him for her interview with her legs crossed, wearing loafers on her feet. She swung her top leg back and forth to some inaudible rhythm. The loafer on her top foot flew off her foot, hit him in the head, ricocheted to the desk lamp and broke it. She looked at him in terror, but when their glances met, they both dissolved in laughter. The moral of the story—the person on the other side of the desk is also a human being and wants to put you at ease. So admit to your anxiety and don't swing your foot if you're wearing loafers! (By the way, she was admitted.)

27

> —ANTHONY F. CAPRARO III, "The Interview"

Several transitions are commonly used to introduce examples: *for example, for instance, a case in point, to illustrate.*

▶3 Sequential order/process

A paragraph that presents a process will show carefully sequenced events. The range of possibilities is endless: What is the process by which people fall in love? By which children learn? By which a computer chip is manufactured? These cases, different as they are, require a clear delineation of steps. In paragraphs organized as a process, you may want to use transitions that show sequence in time: *first, second, after, before, once, next, then,* and *finally.*

> The first and simplest type of iron furnace was called a bloomery, in which wrought iron was produced directly from the ore. The ore was heated with charcoal in a small open furnace, usually made of stone and blown upon with bellows. Most of the impurities would burn out, leaving a spongy mass of iron mixed with siliceous slag (iron silicate). This spongy mass was then refined by

28

Writing and Revising to Achieve Well-Developed Paragraphs

hammering, reheating, and hammering some more, until it reached the desired fibrous consistency. During the hammering, the glasslike slag would be evenly distributed throughout the iron mass. This hammered slab of wrought iron, or "bloom," was then ready to forge into some usable object.

—Eliot Wigginton, "Furnaces"

▶4 Definition

Paragraphs of definition are always important. In informative writing, readers can learn the meaning of terms needed for understanding difficult concepts. In essays intended to persuade, writers define terms in order to establish a common language with the reader, an important first step toward gaining the reader's agreement. Once a term is defined, it can be clarified with examples, comparisons, or descriptions.

29 Alzheimer's disease is a slow death of the brain in which the first disturbing symptom is increasing forgetfulness. People with AD can no longer recall recent events or assimilate new information and ideas. They constantly misplace objects and repeat questions that have just been answered. Eventually they develop aphasia (loss of language), agnosia (inability to recognize people and objects), and apraxia (inability to perform everyday actions). They search their minds for words they have always known. They have increasing difficulty in following a conversation; their own talk becomes disjointed and empty, their vocabulary impoverished and their language simplified. Their judgment declines, and they lose the capacity to generalize and classify. They start a routine action and no longer know how to finish it. They cannot find their way even in familiar places, or recall the day of the week or time of year. Cooking, driving, and using tools become too complicated for them. Toward the end they have difficulty in dressing and even using the bathroom and eating.

—Harvard Medical School, "Mental Health Letter"

▶5 Division and classification

Division (also called *analysis*) and classification are closely related operations. A writer who divides a topic into parts to see what it is made of performs an analysis.

COMPUTER TIPS

Use the TAB Key for Paragraph Indentation

One major difference between word processors and typewriters is that the former uses a proportional font: each letter takes up a different amount of space. Typewriters use monospaced fonts: each letter takes up exactly the same amount of space. Starting a paragraph with five taps on the typewriter space bar always gives you exactly the same indentation, but this is not true for a word processor. Depending on the font and size, typographical distinctions (boldface or italics), and the page justification setting, the amount of space taken up by five spaces varies quite a bit. Use the TAB key for paragraph indentations; it's one keystroke, it's absolutely consistent, and the command can be easily deleted.

A *classification* is a grouping of like items. Working with notes, the writer begins with what may appear at first to be bits of unrelated information. Gradually, patterns of similarity emerge that can be expressed as a paragraph that establishes categories for grouping. Most often, the writer devotes a sentence or two to developing each category.

> Archaeological sites are most commonly classified according to the activities that occurred there. Thus, cemeteries and other sepulchers like Tutankhamun's tomb are referred to as ⟨burial sites⟩ A 20,000-year-old Stone Age site in the Dnieper Valley of the Ukraine, with mammoth-bone houses, hearths, and other signs of domestic activity, is a ⟨habitation site⟩ So too are many other sites, such as caves and rockshelters, early Mesoamerican farming villages, and Mesopotamian cities—in all, people lived and carried out greatly diverse activities. ⟨Kill sites⟩ consist of bones of slaughtered game animals and the weapons
> 30 that killed them. They are found in East Africa and on the North American Great Plains. ⟨Quarry sites⟩ are another type of specialist site, where people mined stone or metals to make specific tools. Prized raw materials, such as obsidian, a volcanic glass used for fine knives, were widely traded in prehistoric times and profoundly interest the archaeologist. Then there are such spectacular ⟨religious sites⟩ as the stone circles of Stonehenge in southern England, the Temple of Amun at Karnak, Egypt, and the great ceremonial precincts of lowland Maya centers in Central America at *Tikal,* Copán, and Palenque. ⟨Art sites⟩ are common in southwestern France, southern Africa, and parts of North America, where prehistoric people painted or engraved magnificent displays of art.
> —BRIAN FAGAN, *Archaeology*

▶ 6 Comparison/contrast

To *compare* is to discuss the similarities between people, places, objects, events, or ideas. To *contrast* is to discuss differences. The writer developing a paragraph that uses comparison and contrast conducts an analysis of two or more subjects, studying the parts of each and then discussing the subjects in relation to each other. Specific points of comparison and contrast make the discussion possible.

Paragraphs of comparison and contrast should be put to some definite use in a paper. It is not enough to point out similarities and differences; you should *do* something with this information. You should make a point. Paragraphs developed by comparison and contrast use transition words such as *similarly, also, as well, just so, by contrast, but, however, on the one hand/on the other hand,* and *yet.* When writing your paragraph, consider two common methods of arrangement: by subject or point by point.

In the following paragraph, Stephen Jay Gould organizes his comparative discussion by subject. Note that when a comparative discussion becomes relatively long, you have the option of splitting it into two paragraphs, as Gould does in this example.

> Science works with testable proposals. If [. . .] new information continues to affirm a hypothesis, we may accept it provisionally and gain confidence as further evidence mounts. We can never be completely sure that a hypothesis is right, though we may be able to show with confidence that it is wrong. The best
> 31 scientific hypotheses are also generous and expansive: they suggest extensions and implications that enlighten related, and even far distant, subjects. Simply

consider how the idea of evolution has influenced virtually every intellectual field.

Useless speculation, on the other hand, is restrictive. It generates no testable hypothesis, and offers no way to obtain potentially refuting evidence. Please note that I am not speaking of truth or falsity. The speculation may well be true; still, if it provides, in principle, no material for affirmation or rejection, we can make nothing of it. It must simply stand forever as an intriguing idea. Useless speculation turns in on itself and leads nowhere; good science, containing both seeds for its potential refutation and implications for more and different testable knowledge, reaches out.

—STEPHEN JAY GOULD, "Sex, Drugs, Disasters"

Organizing a Paragraph of Comparison and Contrast

Comparison and contrast is a type of analysis in which parts of two (or more) subjects are discussed in terms of one another. Particular points of comparison and contrast provide the means by which to observe similarities and differences. A comparative analysis is usually arranged in one of two ways.

Arrangement by subject

Topic sentence (may be shifted to other positions in the paragraph)

Introduce Subject A
  Discuss Subject A in terms of the first point
  Discuss Subject A in terms of the second point
Introduce Subject B
  Discuss Subject B in terms of the first point
  Discuss Subject B in terms of the second point
Conclude with a summary of similarities and differences.

Arrangement point by point

Topic sentence (may be shifted to other positions in the paragraph)

Introduce the first point to be compared and contrasted
  Discuss Subject A in terms of this point
  Discuss Subject B in terms of this point
Introduce the second point to be compared and contrasted
  Discuss Subject A in terms of this point
  Discuss Subject B in terms of this point

When comparisons are relatively brief, arrangement by subject works well. When comparisons are longer and more complex, a point-by-point discussion works best.

In the next paragraph, Michele Pelletier uses a point-by-point arrangement to compare and contrast two types of armies of the fifteenth and sixteenth centuries. Pelletier uses her comparisons to make a point: both the mercenary and militia experiences "have found their way into American military history of the past thirty years."

Student Example: Michele Pelletier

33   Armies of volunteers and conscripts are today's versions of the militias and mercenary forces that existed in the 15th and 16th centuries. Militias were armies made up of citizens who were fighting for their home country. Mercenaries were professional soldiers who, better trained than militia men (they were always men), were hired by foreign countries to fight wars. Mercenaries had no cause other than a paycheck: if the country that hired them did not pay, they would quit the battlefield. Mercenaries may have been fickle, but technically they were good fighters. Militia men may not have been as technically proficient as mercenaries, but they had the will to fight. Both of these traditions—fighting for a cause and fighting for money—have found their way into American military history of the past thirty years.

▶ 7 Analogy

An **analogy** is a comparison of two topics that, on first appearance, seem unrelated. An analogy gains force by surprising a reader, by demonstrating that an unlikely comparison is not only likely but in fact is illuminating. Well-chosen analogies can clarify difficult concepts. In the following example, theoretical physicist Stephen Hawking describes the birth of a star, helping nonspecialists to understand difficult concepts through the use of two analogies:

34   A star is formed when a large amount of gas (mostly hydrogen) starts to collapse in on itself due to its gravitational attraction. As it contracts the atoms of the gas collide with each other more and more frequently and at greater and greater speeds—the gas heats up. Eventually, the gas will be so hot that when the hydrogen atoms collide they no longer bounce off each other, but instead coalesce to form helium. The heat released in this reaction, which is like a controlled hydrogen bomb explosion, is what makes the star shine. This additional heat also increases the pressure of the gas until it is sufficient to balance the gravitational attraction, and then the gas stops contracting. It is a bit like a balloon—there is a balance between the pressure of the air inside, which is trying to make the balloon expand, and the tension on the rubber, which is trying to make the balloon smaller. Stars will remain stable like this for a long time, with heat from the nuclear reactions balancing the gravitational attraction.

—Stephen Hawking, *A Brief History of Time*

    The words *like* and *analogous to* often signal the beginning of an analogy. After describing the first of the two topics in the comparison, the writer may follow with an expression such as *just so* or *similarly* and then continue with the second part of the comparison.

▶ 8 Cause and effect

Development by cause and effect shows how an event or condition has come to occur—which requires careful analysis. As discussed elsewhere (see 6d-1), causes are usually complex, and a writer must avoid the temptation to oversimplify. Frequently, therefore, cause-and-effect reasoning is developed over several paragraphs. When you are developing a causal connection, avoid the mistake of suggesting that because one event precedes another in time, the first event causes the second. A causal relationship is not always so clear-cut, a point that James Watts and Alan Davis acknowledge in the following paragraph on the Great Depression of the

1930s. Paragraphs developed by cause and effect frequently use these transition words: *therefore*, *thus*, and *consequently*.

> The depression was precipitated by the stock market crash in October 1929, but the actual cause of the collapse was an unhealthy economy. While the ability of the manufacturing industry to produce consumer goods had increased rapidly, mass purchasing power had remained relatively static. Most laborers, farmers, and white-collar workers, therefore, could not afford to buy the automobiles and refrigerators turned out by factories in the 1920s, because their incomes were too low. At the same time, the federal government increased the problem through economic policies that tended to encourage the very rich to over-save.
>
> —JAMES WATTS and ALAN F. DAVIS,
> *Your Family in Modern American History*

35

▶ **EXERCISE 7**

Return to Exercise 1 (page 106), in which you selected one section of a magazine article or book chapter to study in depth. If you have not done so, complete that exercise, and then for that same block of paragraphs analyze each paragraph and identify its pattern of development.

EXERCISE 8

Reread a paper you have recently written, and select a paragraph to revise so that its topic sentence is thoroughly developed. Use any of the patterns of development presented here so that you are able, without hesitation, to answer the three questions in the box on page 120. Make photocopies of your original paragraph and your revision; plan to address a small group of classmates and explain the choices
▶ you have made in revision.

▶ **5f** Writing and revising paragraphs of introduction and conclusion

The introduction and conclusion to a paper can be understood as a type of transition. Transitions provide logical bridges in a paper: they help readers to move from one sentence to another, one paragraph to another, and one section to another (see 5d-3). At the beginning of a paper, the introduction serves as a transition by moving the reader from the world outside of your paper to the world within. At the end of the paper, the conclusion works in the opposite direction by moving readers from the world of your paper back to their own world—with, you hope, something gained by their effort.

▶ **1 Introductions**

Writing an introduction is often easier once you know what you are introducing; for this reason many writers choose not to work seriously on an introduction until they have finished a draft and can see the overall shape and content of the paper. Other writers need to begin with a carefully written introduction. If this is your preference, remember not to demand perfection of a first draft, especially since the material you will be introducing has yet to be written. Once it is written, your introduction may need to change.

COMPUTER TIPS

Save Frequently

This is probably the most frequently given advice in all guides to writing with computers, and it's certainly the most ignored: **Save your writing frequently.** Everything that you've typed since the last save will be lost if there's a power failure or someone walks by and accidentally kicks the plug out of your computer. How long would it take you to reconstruct and re-type all that material? It takes almost no time or effort to execute the keystroke combination necessary to save: get in the habit of doing it automatically, mindlessly, whenever you stop to think, to reread, to rest, to get up from the computer for any reason.

Newer word-processing software allows you even more options for protecting your work: it saves your work automatically at regular timed intervals, allows you to work with a copy of your document rather than the original, and provides automatic backups. However, with multiple versions of your papers such as copies and backups, you need to be careful when you resume work at your next session: be sure you're using the most current version of your paper.

The introduction as a frame of reference

Introductions establish frames of reference. On completing an introduction, readers know the general topic of your paper; they know the disciplinary perspective from which you will discuss this topic; and they know the standards they will use in evaluating your work. Readers quickly learn from an introduction if you are a laboratory researcher, a field researcher, a theorist, an essayist, a reporter, a student with a general interest, and so on. Each of these possible identities implies for readers different standards of evidence and reasoning by which they will evaluate your work. Consider the paragraph that follows. The introduction, explicitly in the thesis and implicitly in the writer's choice of vocabulary, establishes a frame of reference that alerts readers to the type of language, evidence, and logic that will be used in the subsequent paper. Thus situated, readers are better able to anticipate and evaluate what they will read.

ILLUSTRATION: WRITING IN THE HUMANITIES

STUDENT EXAMPLE: SARIKA CHONDRA

(James Joyce's) "Counterparts" (tells the story) of a man, Farrington, *Language of literary analysis*

who is abused by his boss for not doing his job right. Farrington

spends a long time drinking after work; and when he finally arrives *Evidence: based on close reading of a story*

home, he in turn abuses—he beats—his son Tom. In eleven pages,

36 Joyce tells much more than a story of yet another alcoholic (venting) *Logic: generalization*

Writing and Revising Paragraphs of Introduction and Conclusion   **127**

failures and frustrations) on family members. *In "Counterparts," Far-rington turns to drink in order to gain power—in much the same way his wife and children turn to the Church.*

Drinking and church going related to a need for power

Also comparison/ contrast

By comparison, read the following introduction to a paper written from a sociological perspective. This paragraph introduces a paper you will find in Chapter 39, Writing and Reading in the Social Sciences.

ILLUSTRATION: WRITING IN THE SOCIAL SCIENCES

STUDENT EXAMPLE: KRISTY BELL

Currently, in the United States, there are at least two million women alcoholics (Unterberger, 1989, p. 1150). Americans are largely unaware of the extent of this (debilitating disease) among women and the problems it presents. Numerous women dependent on alcohol remain (invisible largely because friends, family, co-workers,) and the women themselves refuse to acknowledge the problem. *This denial amounts to a virtual conspiracy of silence and greatly complicates the process of (diagnosis) and (treatment).*

Language of sociology

Evidence: based on review of sociological literature

Logic: cause and effect. Will show how denial complicates diagnosis and treatment.

37

The introduction as an invitation to continue reading

Aside from establishing a frame of reference and set of expectations about language, evidence, and logic, an introduction also does—or does not—establish in your reader a desire to *continue* reading. A complete introduction provides background information needed to understand a paper. An especially effective introduction gains the reader's attention and gradually turns that attention toward the writer's thesis and the rest of the paper. Writers typically adopt specialized strategies for introducing their work. In the discussion that follows you will learn several of these strategies, all of which can be developed in one or two paragraphs, at the end of which you will place your thesis. These examples by no means exhaust the possible strategies available to you for opening your papers.

Student Example: Daniel Burke, "Defense of Fraternities"

A revolutionary event took place at Raleigh Tavern in 1776, an event that has added an important dimension to my life at college. In fact, nearly all American undergraduates are affected in some way by the actions of several students from the College of William and Mary on December 5, 1776. The formation of the first Greek-letter fraternity, Phi Beta Kappa, started the American college

38

fraternity-sorority tradition that today can be an important addition to your undergraduate education.

In this example, student writer Daniel Burke provides pertinent historical information that sets a context for the paper. By linking a "revolutionary event" in 1776 to his own life over two hundred years later, Burke captures the reader's interest.

The following example begins with a question, the response to which leads to the author's thesis.

Student Example: Bonnie Michaels, "What's the Good of Government?"

Is government the solution, or is it the problem? Many Americans believe that government plays an essential role in making our lives safer and our society more productive and more fair. But many others believe that government is too powerful and intrusive, and that it stifles personal initiative. Within the government itself, there are deep divisions: conservatives typically argue for "less government" and for "getting government off the backs of Americans"; liberals argue for a "humane government" that defends the interests of the poor and elderly and, generally, of groups that cannot defend themselves. These diametrically opposed viewpoints about the proper role of government have created a productive tension that benefits our country.

39

See 5f-3 for two additional strategies for opening a paper: using a quotation and telling a story.

Strategies for Writing Introductions

1. Announce your topic, using vocabulary that hints at the perspective from which you will be writing. On completing your introduction, readers should be able to anticipate the type of language, evidence, and logic you will use in your paper.
2. If readers lack the background needed to understand your paper, then provide this background. In a paragraph or two, choose and develop a strategy that will both orient readers to your subject and interest them in it: define terms, present a brief history, or review a controversy.
3. If readers know something of your subject, then devote less (or no) time to developing background information and more time to stimulating interest. In a paragraph or two, choose and develop a strategy that will gain the reader's attention: raise a question, quote a source familiar to the reader, tell a story, or begin directly with a statement of the thesis.
4. Once you have provided background information and gained the reader's attention with an opening strategy, gradually turn that attention toward your thesis, which you will position as the last sentence of the introductory paragraph(s).

▶2 Conclusions

At minimum, a conclusion will summarize your work, but often you will want to do more than write a summary. Provided you have written carefully, you have

---

Strategies for Writing Conclusions

1. **Summary.** The simplest conclusion is a summary, a brief restatement of your paper's main points. Avoid conclusions that repeat exactly material presented elsewhere in the paper.

2. **Summary and comment.** More emphatic conclusions build on a summary in one of several ways. These conclusions will:

   set ideas in the paper in a larger context
   call for action (or research)
   speculate or warn
   purposefully confuse or trouble the reader
   raise a question
   quote a familiar or authoritative source
   tell a story

---

earned the right to expand on your paper's thesis in a conclusion: to point the reader back to the larger world and to suggest the significance of your ideas.

A conclusion gives you an opportunity to answer a challenge that all readers raise—*So what? Why should this paper matter to me? What actions should I take?* A well-written conclusion will answer these questions and will leave readers with a trace of

http://leo.stcloudstate.edu/
acadwrite/conclude.html
Strategies for writing conclusions, with many examples.

your thinking as they turn away from your paper and back to their own business.

The example conclusions that follow do not exhaust the strategies for closing your papers; they should, however, give you a taste of the variety of techniques available. Here is a paragraph that presents the simplest possible conclusion: a summary—in this case, of an argument that colleges must cut costs and rethink their educational missions if they are to avoid going bankrupt. This concluding paragraph summarizes the author's key points:

> Already most colleges are looking carefully at ways to cut costs. But this cost-cutting is not examining basic questions about how a college is organized to provide for the advancement of knowledge and student learning. It is time to ask basic questions, to conceptualize fundamentally different ways—less costly
> 40 ways—of providing education. Higher education will have to make hard choices. It will not be able to satisfy every need or respond to every constituent. The colleges that ask, and answer, basic questions about how to educate students in less expensive ways will be the colleges that survive.
> —Daniel S. Cheever, Jr., "Higher and Higher Ed"

A more ambitious conclusion will move beyond a summary and call for involvement on the reader's part. For instance, you might ask the reader to address a puzzling or troubling question, to speculate on the future, or to reflect on the past. In the next example, the reader is given a challenge.

Student Example: Alison Tschopp

The task of shaping children's values, like their diets, is better addressed through ongoing discussions between parents and children than through limit-

ing the right of free speech. There is no need to silence advertisers in order to teach values or protect the innocent and unskeptical. The right to free speech is protected by the Constitution because as a nation we believe that no one person is capable of determining which ideas are true and rational. Like media critic Jean Kilbourne, we may disagree with some of the messages being conveyed
41   through advertising—say, the message that women are attractive only when they are young and thin (44). Like Peggy Charren, we can agree that advertisements can create stresses in a family's life (15). Nevertheless, we must allow all ideas a place in the market place. As Charles O'Neil, an advertiser and a defender of the medium, suggests, "[a]dvertising is only a reflection of society; slaying the messenger will not alter the fact" that potentially damaging or offensive ideas exist (196). If we disagree with the message sent in an ad, it is our responsibility to send children a different message.

▶3 The opening and closing frame

You might consider creating an introductory and concluding frame for your papers. The strategy is to use the same story, quotation, question—any device that comes to mind—as an occasion both to introduce your subject and, when the time is right, to conclude emphatically. Provided the body of a paper is unified, coherent, and well developed, an opening and closing frame will give the paper a pleasing symmetry. In the following example, Rachel L. Jones works with a quotation.

Introduction

42   William Labov, a noted linguist, once said about the use of black English, "It is the goal of most black Americans to acquire full control of the standard language without giving up their own culture." He also suggested that there are certain advantages to having two ways to express one's feelings. I wonder if the good doctor might also consider the goals of those black Americans who have full control of standard English but who are every now and then troubled by that colorful, grammar-to-the-winds patois that is black English. Case in point—me.

Conclusion

43   I would have to disagree with Labov in one respect. My goal is not so much to acquire full control of both standard and black English, but to one day see more black people less dependent on a dialect that excludes them from full participation in the world we live in. I don't think I talk white; I think I talk right.
—RACHEL L. JONES, "What's Wrong with Black English"

See Lou Cassetta's final draft (pages 99–103)—specifically his opening and closing paragraphs—for another "frame" strategy: a story that illustrates a key idea of his essay.

▶ EXERCISE 9

Locate a collection of essays and/or articles: any textbook that is an edited collection of readings will work. Read three articles, and examine the strategies the authors use to introduce and conclude their work. Choose one article to analyze more closely. Examine the strategies for beginning and ending the selection, and relate these strategies to the selection itself. Why has the writer chosen these *particular* strategies? Be prepared to discuss your findings in a small group.

EXERCISE 10

In connection with a paper you are writing, draft *two* opening and *two* closing paragraphs, using different strategies. Set your work aside for a day or two, and then choose which paragraphs appeal to you the most. Be prepared to discuss your choices in a small group.

▶ **5g** Determining paragraph length

If for no other reason than to give readers visual relief, keep paragraphs moderate in length. *Moderate* is a variable and personal term. Perhaps you decide that your paragraphs should average one-third to two-thirds of a typewritten page. If your sentences tend to be brief, your average number of sentences per paragraph may be ten or twelve; if your sentences tend to be long, the average number of sentences per paragraph may drop to six.

Devote your energies to the content of your paragraphs first. Turn to paragraph length in the later stages of revision, when you are relatively satisfied with your work. You should freely divide a long paragraph for reasons of length alone. A new paragraph created because of length does not need its own topic sentence, provided this paragraph is a clear continuation of the one preceding it.

Brief paragraphs of one, two, or three sentences can be useful for establishing transitions between sections of a paper (see ¶23) and, as illustrated in the next example, for creating emphasis.

44   In nation with 40 million handguns—where anyone who wants one can get one—it's time to face a chilling fact. We're way past the point where registration, licensing, safety training, waiting periods, or mandatory sentencing are going to have much effect. Each of these measures may save some lives or help catch a few criminals, but none—by itself or taken together—will stop the vast majority of handgun suicides or murders. A "controlled" handgun kills just as effectively as an "uncontrolled" one.

45   Most control recommendations merely perpetuate the myth that with proper care a handgun can be as safe a tool as any other. Nothing could be further from the truth. A handgun is not a blender.

46   Those advocating a step-by-step process insist that a ban would be too radical and therefore unacceptable to Congress and the public. A hardcore 40 percent of the American public has always endorsed banning handguns. Many will also undoubtedly argue that any control measure—no matter how ill-conceived or ineffective—would be a good first step. But after more than a decade, the other foot hasn't followed.

                         —JOSH SUGARMANN, "The NRA Is Right"

If in revising a first draft you find that your paragraphs are consistently two or three sentences long, consider ways in which you can further develop each paragraph's topic sentence. Unless you are writing in a journalism class or in some other context where consistently brief paragraphs are valued, once again the advice is to maintain a moderate length and only rarely—for clear reasons—use very brief or very long paragraphs.

CHAPTER 6

Writing and Evaluating Arguments

Arguments provide a way of knowing about and participating in the world of academics. The knowledge you learn from textbooks and lectures might seem to be factual and beyond dispute. But, in truth, what we know about the world is the end result of argumentation. In academic circles, researchers experiment, read critically, and administer surveys; and then, observing patterns, they make statements—the validity of which they try to demonstrate to others through arguments. In this chapter you will learn the elements essential to arguing in *any* context. Later, in Chapters 38–40, you will learn how these elements change according to the discipline in which you are writing.[1]

> **6a**   **An overview of argument**

An **argument** is a process of influencing others, of changing minds through reasoned discussion. Arguments consist of three parts: claim, support, and reasoning.

http://www.kcmetro.cc.mo.us/
longview/ctac/flowpt1.htm
*Hypertext flow chart for
evaluating arguments.*

To construct an argument, you engage in a writing process (with phases of discovery, drafting, and revising—see Chapters 3 and 4). You develop a claim, or point you want to argue; then you develop support for accepting this claim. Support consists of two elements:

- Evidence—facts, statistics, examples, and expert opinions that you gather.
- The reasoning by which you connect that evidence to your claim.

The process of constructing an argument is illustrated here, with examples from the example argument that appears immediately after this introduction.

To write an argument, follow these steps:

1. **Make a *claim*.** Choose a subject; then make an assertion about the subject (see 6b). Here is the claim from the sample argument:

   Although women are certainly underrepresented at present in the computer industry, changing cultural and market forces will inevitably bring about a more equitable proportion of women to men.

2. **Gather *evidence*.** Carefully choose facts, statistics, opinions, and examples that support the claim. Group related evidence into clusters (see 6c). Here are the five clusters of evidence that support the claim in the example argument that follows:

   Cluster 1: Interviews show that sexism is not as big a problem as it has been.

   Cluster 2: Female computer professionals are forming mentoring groups.

---

[1]The approach to argument taken here is based on the work of Stephen Toulmin, as developed in *The Uses of Argument* (Cambridge: The University Press, 1958).

Cluster 3: Computing jobs no longer require background in math and science.

Cluster 4: The Web has emerged as a marketplace emphasizing communication.

Cluster 5: Women are buying more high-tech equipment.

3. **Link evidence to the claim** with a clear **line of reasoning.** Evidence by itself does not advance an argument's claim. To advance an argument, provide clear reasoning that shows how and why each item of evidence makes the claim more believable. Choose from three types of reasoning to link evidence and claim:

- *Reasoning with logic:* appeal to the reader's respect for clear, orderly thinking. Types of logic used: generalization, cause, sign, analogy, and parallel case.
- *Reasoning with authority:* appeal to the reader's respect for an expert who says, "I believe this claim to be true (or desirable)."
- *Reasoning with emotion:* move readers to agreement by an appeal to their emotions.

In academic settings, you will most often link evidence to claim by reasoning with logic (see 6d).

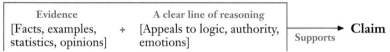

A typical argument will present three or more supports for the claim. The claim in the example argument offers five supports—that is, five items of evidence, each linked to the claim with a specific line of reasoning. In the example argument, the writer uses appeals to logic—but no appeals to authority or emotion:

Evidence	+	**Line of reasoning**
Less sexism is evident.		This is a **sign** that women are facing improved conditions in the computer industry.
Evidence	+	**Line of reasoning**
Female mentoring groups are emerging.		This is a **sign** that women are facing improved conditions in the computer industry.
Evidence	+	**Line of reasoning**
There is a shift in the computer industry away from a reliance on math.		This shift will **cause** a more equitable split of jobs between women and men.
Evidence	+	**Line of reasoning**
The Web has emerged as a marketplace.		This development will **cause** a more equitable split of jobs between women and men.
Evidence	+	**Line of reasoning**
Women have emerged as consumers of high-tech equipment.		This development will **cause** a more equitable split of jobs between women and men.

support *support* *support* *support* *support*

Claim: Although women are certainly underrepresented at present in the computer industry, changing cultural and market forces will inevitably bring about a more equitable proportion of women to men.

4. *Rebut* (argue against) *counterarguments* (see 6e).

Counterargument: Women are not biologically equal to men in technical fields.

Rebuttal: 1. Socialization explains all the differences.
2. There are many examples of superb female engineers.

5. **Decide on a *structure* for your argument.** Will you place your claim at the beginning, middle, or end of the argument? Ask: Why this placement as opposed to another? Determine where you will raise and challenge counterarguments (see 6f).

Outline of the Example Argument

In the example argument that follows, the claim appears at the beginning.

Introduction: Women are not getting senior management jobs in the computer industry.

Claim: Although women are certainly underrepresented at present in the computer industry, changing cultural and market forces will inevitably bring about a more equitable proportion of women to men.

Counterargument and rebuttal: Women are not naturally geared toward math/science.

Supporting claim: Evidence + clear lines of reasoning:
#1 Less sexism evident—sign that times are changing.
#2 Emergence of female mentoring groups—sign that times are changing.
#3 Shift of industry away from reliance on math—will cause changes.
#4 Emergence of Web as a marketplace—will cause changes.
#5 Emergence of women as consumers of high-tech equipment—will cause changes.

Conclusion: Cultural and market forces are changing high-tech business. Signs are already present that changes are taking place. In the future, women *will* have greater access to senior management jobs.

A sample argument

The argument, "Women and Computing: Beyond the Glass Ceiling," uses (with some modification) the classic five-part structure for writing arguments presented on page 160. Marie Hobahn begins her argument by introducing her topic (the difficulty women have with securing senior management positions in the computer industry) and stating her claim. Before moving to directly support her claim, she first raises and rebuts arguments that challenge her own. She then turns to supporting her argument, linking distinct clusters of evidence to her claim with five lines of reasoning, two signs that conditions are improving for women, and three causes that will improve the employment of women in the computer industry.

Women and Computing: Beyond the Glass Ceiling
By Marie Hobahn

How well are women doing in the professional world
of computing? There's no use denying it: the numbers
don't look good. None of the top 50 computer companies
boasts a female CEO, even though women make up about a
third of the high-tech workforce (DeBare, "High-tech" 1).
Women fill less than 30% of programming, engineering, and
management jobs at high-tech companies. Companies created
or run by women received just 1.6% of the venture capital
invested in high tech firms from 1991 to 1996 (Crain;
Hamm). The glass ceiling that keeps women from advancing
seems real. According to D. J. Young, a software quality
assurance manager at the software firm Intuit, "More
women are [. . .] reaching that first level of management, but [. . .] the higher [they] go, the harder it is
to get to the next level" (qtd. in DeBare, "Voices" 1).
Considering this discouraging news, it might seem a hopeless act of faith to believe that things will get better
anytime soon. But that faith would, in fact, be justified. <u>Although women are certainly underrepresented at
present in the computer industry, changing cultural and
market forces will inevitably bring about a more equitable proportion of women to men.</u>

Introduction

*Claim
(argumentative
thesis)*

Let's first establish that there is no biological
reason why women should not be the equal of men in the
world of computing. Arguments like those used by opponents of women in the military--they have smaller, weaker
bodies, and so are unsuited for combat--cannot be used
here. True, some traditionalists will argue that male
superiority in technology is genetic. George Gilder, a
fellow at the Discovery Institute, insists that the dominance of males in mathematics, logic, and physics (not to
mention business and politics) is "not an effect of socialization since they arise in all societies known to
anthropology" ("Women and Computers" 16). Some also argue
that the left hemisphere of the brain, which controls
logic and analytic ability, dominates in men, while the
right hemisphere, which controls emotions, dominates in
women (Bulkeley).

*Counter-
argument*

Writing and Evaluating Arguments

But few accept such arguments today. As Susan Mer-
ritt, dean of the School of Computer Science at Pace Uni-   *Rebuttal*
versity, points out, "The belief that women will have
less affinity for computing is more myth than reality."
Whatever differences exist between men and women in computer aptitude can be attributed to learned behavior. Jo
Sanders, who runs the Gender Equity Program at the City
University of New York, maintains that "looking for the
functional equivalent of a computer gene [to explain why
there are more men in the computer industry than women]
is at best misguided and at worst a cynical attempt to
keep women out of computing" ("Women and Computers" 16).
Up to around the fifth grade, girls and boys demonstrate
equal interest in, and ability with, computers. After
that point, because of subtle (sometimes not-so-subtle)
messages, patterns of reinforcement, and the presence or
absence of role models, boys' interest in technology
rises and girls' drops off (Kantrowitz 51). Then we begin
to see a familiar gender distinction of men being fascinated by power and speed and women being more interested
in utility and communication (Brunner and Bennett 46).
One male writer states:

> When I talk about computers with other men, we
> chat about them the way we do--or used to--
> about cars. We boast about the speed of the
> processors and the size of our hard drives.
> [. . .] On the other hand, I think most women
> are [. . .] more interested in whether the com-
> puter works well enough to do what they want it
> to do. (Nicholson 21)

Despite the effects of socialization, women's
achievements in computing have been numerous and substan-   *Rebuttal*
tial enough to disprove any doubts about female aptitude
for programming. Charles Babbage, the nineteenth-century
mathematician generally credited with inventing the computer, received substantial assistance from Ada Byron
(daughter of the poet). Her plan to calculate Bernoulli
numbers is now generally regarded as the first computer
program. In 1979 the Defense Department named a software
language "Ada" in her honor (Toole). During World War II,
the army assigned the name <u>computers</u> to the women who

An Overview of Argument   137

were calculating trajectories for artillery gunners. Some
of these women were assigned to enable the first modern
computer, ENIAC, to perform these calculations; they
called the process "programming" (Petzinger). Another
woman, Grace Hopper, who was trained as a mathematician
and who rose to the rank of rear admiral in the U.S.
Navy, helped program the UNIVAC, the first large commercial computer (Lee 273). Many other notable women have
participated in historic events in the computer industry,
and some are celebrated and discussed in a growing number
of academic Web sites. (See, for instance, the "ADA
Project" at <http://www.cs.yale.edu/HTML/YALE/CS/
HyPlans/tap/> and "Past Notable Women of Computing" at
<http://www.cs.yale.edu/homes/tap/past-women-cs.html>.)

    Clearly, women in the computer industry have the
ability to excel. Still, the skeptic may wonder on what
basis anyone can predict that the position of women in   *Transition*
the world of computing will significantly improve in the
near future. Based on the marginal opportunities for
women in the computer industry to date, this skepticism
seems fair--but only until one examines changing market
forces and signs of an already improved status for women.

    One sign that the computer industry is becoming a
more hospitable place for women is that increasing num-
bers of women are advancing without encountering sexist   *Argument from*
attitudes. While no one is suggesting that the tradi-   *sign (one sign*
                                                               that conditions
tional male-dominated computer industry is a thing of the   *are improving)*
past, a 1996 survey of twenty female high-tech entrepre-
neurs conducted by Nina Munk and Suzanne Oliver revealed
that none of the respondents felt limited by on-the-job
sexism (105). In early 1998, Computerworld's senior editor for security and network operating systems, Laura
DiDio, interviewed four female information services (IS)
executives. One, Pauline Nist, told DiDio, "The 'woman
thing' is not so important as long as you're technically
competent" (76). The other women agreed so heartily that
DiDio was able to conclude: "These women all had one
thing in common: They [. . .] saw the glass ceiling as
just another obstacle. They paid no attention to it and
kept on going" ("Crashing" 77).

Another sign that women are emerging as a force is the growing presence of mentoring programs in which women computer professionals serve as role models for younger women contemplating careers in the industry. Such programs include PipeLINK, organized by two Rensselaer Polytechnic Institute professors; the "Young Women in Technology" program sponsored by the Idaho Department of Vocational Education; and Jo Sanders's Computer Equity Training Project at the Women's Action Alliance in New York (Holzberg 43-45). Other groups include Girls, Inc., EQUALS, Screenplay, and the Women's Education Equity Act (Koch 23). The presence of these mentors suggests that women have established secure enough footholds in the high-tech workforce to believe that they can actually help others. The mentors understand that a new generation of women will be coming into the high-tech workforce, and they want to ease the way.

Argument from sign (another sign that conditions are improving)

Opportunities are expanding for women, and gains are being made. In the next few years these gains will broaden as three important changes sweep through the computer industry. The first involves a shift in the world of computing away from a strict reliance on math and science and toward areas of strength traditionally associated with women--communications and visual design. Researchers Pamela E. Kramer and Shelia Lehman characterize the old associations of computers with skills in math as "increasingly inaccurate":

Argument from cause (a shift in the industry will help women)

> Metaphors for computer technology are moving
> away from the number-crunching computer [. . .]
> and toward an understanding of computing as
> an interactive process in which the computer
> becomes an intelligent participant in and
> facilitator of individual and group communi-
> cation. This shift reflects the fact that
> creative computing now relies at least as
> much upon language, visual design, problem
> definition, and organizational skills as upon
> quantitative analysis. (170-71)

In other words, computing is moving away from those areas in which men have been socialized to excel and toward

other areas in which women have been socialized to excel.
The fact that computers may be (as one headline writer
suggested) "A Tool for Women, a Toy for Men" (Bulkeley)
should work to boost women's opportunities now that the
personal computer as "toy" is giving way to the personal
computer as "tool."

A second market force that is changing the availability of senior management jobs for women in high-tech
industries is the emergence of the World Wide Web as a
place for information exchange, commerce, and communication. With raw computing power doubling every nine
months, personal computers have not come close to reaching the limits of their potential power and speed. But
however fast the machines become, almost all computer
professionals predict that the future of computing is going to be improved not by raw power but by the Internet
and Web applications. People want to be able to communicate more easily and more systematically, both globally
and on small local networks. Ease of communication and
the design of interfaces to enhance communication will be
key areas of growth. In these areas, socialization works
to favor women (Holzberg).

*Argument from
cause (a second
shift that will
help women)*

The third force that is creating greater opportunities for women in high-tech industries is the emerging
importance of women both as users and as potential consumers of technology. According to a recent note in
Byte, "women may be geekier than you think": In a 1996
survey, 66% of women had purchased a computer in the last
two years ("Geekette"). More than 30% had installed the
PC themselves. A 1997 study by Women in Technology International revealed that women-owned business would
make $50 million in purchases that year ("Women's Buying
Power"). In a change of strategy, advertising agencies
are beginning to depict women in computer ads, and they
are doing so in ways that don't imply that women use computers only for storing recipes (Pope B1). A columnist in
Advertising Age remarks: "I think it would be beneficial
to show girls that their moms have no trouble handling
computers. Calgon could create a commercial of a mother
printing out her daughters' hectic schedules from her

*Argument from
cause (a final
shift that will
help women)*

laptop, then having enough time left over for a relaxing bath" (Crain).

The signs are present that conditions for women in the computing industry are already improving. Cultural   *Conclusion* and market forces will gather momentum and change the face of the computing industry, creating a need for senior managers who understand the changing market and can exploit it. The obvious choice for such managers will be women. And as more women managers take their places in the boardrooms, the messages that get communicated to girls in the schoolroom will be clear: computing is a career for women. Inevitably, more girls will choose high-tech careers. Not immediately, perhaps, but sooner rather than later, the era of male dominance in the world of computing is coming to an end. Here and there "dinosaur" attitudes will persist, but in general there is no future for sexist attitudes and practices in the high-tech workplace.

Works Cited

"ADA Project: Tapping Internet Resources for Women in Computer Science." 20 July 1998. <http://www.cs.yale.edu/HTML/YALE/CS/HyPlans/tap/>.

Brunner, Cornelia, and Dorothy Bennett. "Technology Perceptions by Gender." Education Digest 56.3 (Feb. 1998).

Bulkeley, William M. "A Tool for Women, a Toy for Men." Wall Street Journal 16 Mar. 1996: B1.

Crain, Rance. "Helping Women Embrace Computers." Advertising Age 8 July 1996: 15.

DeBare, Ilana. "High-tech Industry Zipping Along, but Women Often Are Left Behind." Sacramento Bee 1996. 18 July 1998. <http://www.sacbee.com/news/projects/women/wcmain.html>.

---. "Voices: Women in the Computer Industry." Sacramento Bee 1996. 18 July 1998. <http://www.sacbee.com/news/projects/women/wcvoices.html>.

DiDio, Laura. "Crashing the Glass Ceiling." Computerworld 26 Jan. 1998: 73+.

"Geekette Power." <u>Byte</u> Jan. 1997: 26.

Hamm, Steve. "Why Women Are So Invisible in Silicon Valley." <u>Business Week</u> 25 Aug. 1998: 136.

Holzberg, Carol S. "Computer Technology: It's a Girl Thing." <u>Technology & Learning</u> May–June 1997: 42–48.

Kantrowitz, Barbara. "Men, Women & Computers." <u>Newsweek</u> 16 May 1994: 48–55.

Koch, Melissa. "Opening Up Technology to Both Genders." <u>Education Digest</u> Nov. 1994: 18–23.

Kramer, Pamela E., and Sheila Lehman. " 'Mismeasuring Women': A Critique of Research on Computer Ability and Avoidance." <u>Signs: Journal of Women in Culture and Society</u> 16.1 (1990): 158–72.

"Leading Women Visionaries to Converge in the Silicon Valley for Women in Technology International (WITI) 1998 Technology Summit." 20 July 1998. <http://www.witi.com/Center/Offices/Witinews/Summit/060198.html>.

Lee, J. A. N. "Grace Hopper." <u>Annals of the History of Computing</u> 9.3 (1987): 273.

Merritt, Susan. "For Women, a Central Role in Computers." Letter. <u>New York Times</u> 27 July 1986: A26.

Munk, Nina, and Suzanne Oliver. "Women of the Valley." <u>Forbes</u> 30 Dec. 1996: 102–08.

Nicholson, David. "Stereotype Does Not Compute." <u>Washington Post</u> 4 Mar. 1996: Business 15+.

"Past Notable Women of Computing." 20 July 1998. <http://www.cs.yale.edu/homes/tap/past-women-cs.html>.

Petzinger, Thomas. "History of Software Begins with the Work of Some Brainy Women." <u>Wall Street Journal</u> 15 Nov. 1996: B1.

Pope, Kyle. "High-Tech Marketers Try to Attract Women without Causing Offense." <u>Wall Street Journal</u> 17 Mar. 1996: B1+.

Toole, Betty. "Ada Byron, Lady Lovelace (1815–1852)." 30 July 1998. <http://www.cs.yale.edu/homes/tap/Files/ada-bio.html>.

"Women and Computers: Nature or Nurture?" Panel discussion. <u>Los Angeles Times</u> 11 Apr. 1997: Supplement 16+.

"Women's Buying Power." <u>Computerworld</u> 16 June 1997: 41.

ACROSS THE CURRICULUM

Writing Arguments in the Sciences

A teacher of biology and freshman composition at Colgate University, Victoria McMillan explains that the papers and reports you write for science courses are—or should be—arguments, even though the word *argument* may not appear in your assignments:

Although a scientific paper may be descriptive, it is also a well-structured *argument* founded on supporting evidence. Scientific papers provide a forum for presenting one's own findings and conclusions and for arguing for or against competing hypotheses. In more practical terms, they also serve as a principal means by which a particular scientist's ideas and contributions are evaluated by his or her peers.

Academic assignments such as laboratory reports and independent research projects also incorporate the principles of scientific argument. They are excellent practice for writing a "real" scientific paper—which is the reason, of course, they are emphasized in biology courses. They force you not only to think like a scientist, but also to write like one. And most important, they show you that data cannot speak for themselves: you still have to incorporate them into a coherent, meaningful story, a scientific argument, that supports your conclusions.*

Writing Papers in the Biological Sciences. New York: St. Martins, 1988. 1–2.

▶ **6b** **Making a claim (an argumentative thesis)**

A claim is an argument's thesis: a single statement that expresses a paper's subject and the assertion (that is, the argument) you are making about that subject. Every paper that you write in college will have a thesis (an extended discussion of which you will find in 3d. An argumentative paper has an argumentative thesis, or claim, which differs from theses for papers that intend to inform. Consider two example theses. Assume that each introduces a paper and, like any thesis, summarizes in a single statement an entire discussion. Which thesis promises an argument?

> Beginning in the eighteenth century and continuing through to our day, researchers and philosophers have speculated on the possibility that, aside from human beings, there exists other intelligent life in the universe.

> Given the urgent nutritional and health needs of people around the world, governments today are spending obscene amounts of money searching the cosmos for signs of intelligent life.

Although both theses address the same general subject, the search for intelligent life in the universe, clearly the second is the one that promises an argument. An argumentative thesis, or claim, makes a point about which reasonable people can be expected to disagree. An informational thesis, in contrast, is not likely to spark debate. Provided the writer of the first thesis writes a paper that adequately explains how, over the past three centuries, different people have speculated about, or actually searched for, intelligent life in the cosmos, readers will likely accept the information as legitimate and informative.

▶ I Answering one of three questions with your claim

In contrast, the argumentative thesis—the claim—addresses the same topic, the search for intelligent life, and casts it as a debate in which the writer takes a position. Generally, there are three kinds of debates in the context of which you will write arguments and craft individual claims: debates about what is a fact, what is the best policy, and what is valuable. You can confirm that you've written an argumentative claim by making sure it answers a question about fact, policy, or value.

Claims that answer questions of fact

A question of *fact* can take the following forms:

> Does X exist?
>
> Does X lead to Y?
>
> How can we define X?

The answer to any of these questions will be an argumentative claim—as, for instance, the claim of the example argument:

> Although women are certainly underrepresented at present in the computer industry, changing cultural and market forces will inevitably bring about a more equitable proportion of women to men.

This claim is a prediction: it answers a question about a (future) fact. The present fact is that "women are . . . underrepresented in the computer industry." By claiming that this fact will change in the future, the writer obligates herself to an argument: she will need to support her claim.

Once established, a fact can be used in other arguments—for instance, in problem-solution arguments (see the box at 6f). In a problem-solution argument, the writer may need to argue that a problem exists. Then, having established the problem, the writer can proceed with a solution—an argument about policy, about what should be done.

Claims that answer questions of policy

A question of *policy* takes the following form:

> What action should we take?

Politics and social action are major arenas in which arguments about policy occur. These arguments help to determine which legislative actions are taken and how money is spent. The example claim about searching for intelligent life promises an argument about policy:

> Given the urgent nutritional and health needs of people around the world, governments today are spending obscene amounts of money searching the cosmos for signs of intelligent life.

The writer is taking a clear stand that certain policies should *not* be followed. Notice that with the mention of nutritional and health needs, the claim suggests the type of support the writer will use in arguing for the claim.

Writing and Evaluating Arguments

Claims that answer questions of value

A question of *value* takes the following form:

What is *X* worth?

X can be a movie, a book, a college course, a theory, a vacation—any topic on which people might cast an approving or disapproving opinion. Essentially, the writer who enters into an argument about value commits to giving a rating and defending that rating. In the argument itself, the writer is obliged to define the standards by which *X* is being evaluated. Notice how each of these claims about value has embedded in it a term of judgment:

The tickets to professional sports games are overpriced.

Great Expectations is the best novel that Dickens wrote.

Despite some problems, the Internet-based course I took this summer was a success.

Overpriced, best, some problems, and *success* are all terms signaling that an evaluation is about to take place. (See the discussion at 2b, "Writing an evaluation.")

▶2 Defining key words in your claim

Once an argument has been made, it creates a discussion between the writer and readers. The writer is asking readers to agree that the argument's claim is true or desirable. For any discussion, in person or on paper, to succeed, all participants must use key terms in the same way. For a written argument, it is the writer's responsibility to define all key words in the claim so that people are debating the same topic. Consider this claim:

The United States should not support totalitarian regimes.

Unless the term *totalitarian regimes* is clearly defined (and distinguished from, say, *authoritarian regimes*), the argument cannot succeed. Examine your claims. If one or another word requires it, write a paragraph (or more) of definition into your argument. Take special care to define terms when you are sure that readers will disagree with your definitions. At times, entire arguments are needed to define complex terms, such as *honor.* If a key term in your claim is not complicated, a paragraph or even a sentence of definition will do. Then, with terms well defined, argumentation can begin.

Here are the example claims presented in this section. Boldfaced terms need definition. In each case, the writer could not reasonably support the claim without first defining key terms:

Market forces will inevitably bring about **a more equitable proportion** of women to men.

Governments today are spending **obscene amounts** of money searching the cosmos for signs of intelligent life.

The tickets to professional sports games are **overpriced.**

Great Expectations is the **best** novel that Dickens wrote.

Despite some **problems,** the Internet-based course I took this summer was a **success.**

▶ **EXERCISE 1**

In a paragraph, recall an argument that you had recently in which some issue of importance to you was debated. With whom did you argue? What positions did you and the other person (people) argue? What was the outcome? To what extent did your powers of persuasion affect the argument's outcome?

EXERCISE 2

Choose two subjects, and pose questions of fact, policy, and value about them. Of each topic, ask, Does *X* exist? (or Does *X* lead to *Y*? or How can we define *X*?). What should we do with regard to *X*? and What is the value of *X*? Answer these questions with statements that could serve as claims for later arguments. Possible topics: artificial intelligence, posttraumatic stress disorder, ozone holes, and gene splicing.

EXERCISE 3

Circle any terms needing definitions in the following claims made by historian Barbara Tuchman. Choose any two of the terms you have circled, and explain why they need to be defined.

> *Example:* [The(sins) of the United States] in the twentieth century—greed,
> violence, inhumanity—have been profound, with the result that
> the pride and the(self-confidence of the nineteenth century) have
> turned to(dismay and self-disgust.)

The writer assumes that readers have a well-developed historical sense—that they can cite specific examples of this country's "greed, violence, [and] inhumanity" and that they understand the basis of the United States' "self-confidence" in the nineteenth century. If her audience had a less developed understanding of history, Tuchman would need to define these sins and the country's earlier self-confidence. Only then would readers be able to understand her references to "dismay and self-disgust."

1. In the United States we have a society pervaded from top to bottom by contempt for the law.
2. Government—including the agencies of law enforcement—business, labor, students, the military, the poor no less than the rich, outdo each other in breaking the rules and violating the ethics that society has established for its protection.
3. The average citizen, trying to hold a footing in standards of morality and conduct he once believed in, is daily knocked over by incoming waves of venality, vulgarity, irresponsibility, ignorance, ugliness, and trash in all senses of the word.
4. Our government collaborates abroad with the worst enemies of humanity and liberty.

5. It wastes our substance on useless proliferation of military hardware that can never buy security no matter how high the pile.

6. It learns no lesson, employs no wisdom, and corrupts all who succumb to Potomac fever.

ACROSS THE CURRICULUM

Making Claims in Different Subject Areas

Compare how the claims a writer will make change from one discipline area to the next.

In Chapter 38 (Writing and Reading in the Humanities), you learn the following:

To make a claim about literature, find a pattern of meaning in a literary text. Confirm and refine that pattern; state it in a sentence, and you will have your claim. (See 38a-2.)

In Chapter 39 (Writing and Reading in the Social Sciences), you learn this:

Claims in the social sciences will often commit you to observing the actions of individuals or groups and to stating how these actions are significant, both for certain individuals and for the people responding to them. (See 39a-2.)

And in Chapter 40 (Writing and Reading in the Sciences), you learn this:

Scientific arguments often involve two sorts of claims. The first takes the form *X is a problem* or *X is somehow puzzling*. This claim establishes some issue as worthy of investigation, and it is on the basis of this claim that experiments are designed. [. . .] The process continues when you make a second claim that attempts to explain the puzzle. Such a claim takes this form: *X can be explained as follows.* (See 40a-2.)

▶ 6c   Gathering evidence

By definition, an argument requires support. If reasonable people disagree about what is a fact, what should be done, or what is valuable, agreement can be reached only through civil, logical discussion—through arguments. For antagonists in a debate to come to some understanding, each has to offer convincing support for a claim. Support for an argument consists of both evidence and a clear line of reasoning. In this section we consider evidence.

Evidence can be of three types:

- Facts and statistics.
- Opinions of experts (and of others affected by the outcome of the argument).
- Examples that illustrate the point you are making.

Evidence in and of itself does not advance a claim. To do that, you need to link the evidence to the claim, as you will learn to do in the next section. For the moment, concentrate on the types of evidence that you think can provide a basis for good, strong support for your claim. Every argument requires that you carefully examine its claim and ask:

> What combination of facts, opinions, and examples will readers need to see in order to accept my claim as true, probable, or desirable?

To the degree you will need to do research in order to gather evidence for your argument, see Chapters 33 and 34 for assistance. Through research, you will gather relevant facts, opinions, and examples.

CRITICAL DECISIONS

Evaluate the writing occasion: What will convince your readers?

Once you have decided on a claim, turn your attention to gathering evidence. Question your claim vigorously: What will readers need to see in order to accept your view as true, probable, or desirable? Assemble support from the categories available to you:

- **Facts and statistics:** Find sources on your topic. Take notes on any facts or statistics that you think are pertinent. Remember that the facts you gather should accurately represent the available data. The U.S. Government Printing Office publishes volumes of statistics on life in the United States. These are often the source for statistics used in other studies.

- **Expert opinions:** Locate experts by reviewing source materials and checking for people whose work is referred to repeatedly. Also compare bibliographies, and look for names in common. Within a week or so of moderately intensive research, you will identify acknowledged experts on a topic. Quote experts when their language is particularly powerful or succinct; otherwise, summarize or paraphrase.

- **Examples:** Examples give you the opportunity to discuss in real and practical terms the points you wish to make in an argument. When you argue, make your points *through* particular details of a well-chosen example. The details demonstrate your argument, and concrete, understandable terms may be more memorable than your abstract claim. Readers will recall your example and then your point—and you will have communicated effectively.

Organizing your evidence

Having gathered facts, examples, and opinions that will help to advance your claim, organize your evidence into topical clusters. For the example argument (6a) on women in the high-tech workplace, writer Marie Hobahn conducted research and located some fifty pieces of evidence she considered using for her argument. From various sources, she found closely related evidence that she grouped into five categories:

> Less sexism evident.
>
> Emergence of female mentoring groups.

Shift of industry away from reliance on math.

Emergence of Web as a marketplace.

Emergence of women as consumers of high-tech equipment.

Within each category, Marie looked to combine the facts, examples, and expert opinions she had gathered. For instance, in the first category ("Less sexism is evident"), Marie grouped the three related pieces of evidence—facts, survey results of twenty female high-tech entrepreneurs, and expert opinions—from two analysts. These facts and opinions did not, in themselves, support Marie's claim. To develop such support, she needed to link evidence to her claim with a clear line of reasoning (see 6d).

▶ **EXERCISE 4**

Provide paragraph-length examples for two of the following general statements. If you feel that the statement is inaccurate, revise it to your liking. Then provide an example based on your own experience.

1. During the first weeks of their first semester, freshmen are unsure of themselves socially.
2. Assignments at the college level are much more demanding than those in high school.
3. My friend _____ (you provide the name) usually offers sound advice.

EXERCISE 5

With pen in hand, reread the paragraphs you wrote in answer to Exercise 4. Circle your statements of opinion. Underline your statements of fact. Do any patterns emerge? (Instead of working with your own paragraphs, you might switch papers with a classmate.)

▶ **6d** | Developing support for your claim

You must support a claim in order to convince readers that it is true or desirable. Support consists of two elements: the evidence you have gathered (facts, opinions, and examples) and a clear line of reasoning that links the evidence to your claim. Most often in academic settings, your line of reasoning will be based on an appeal to logic. You can use any of five types of logic to connect evidence to a claim:

Generalization You argue that your evidence shows that your claim is true in all (or most) cases.

Causation You argue that your evidence has caused (or will cause) the claim to be true.

Sign You argue that your evidence is a clear sign that the claim is true.

Analogy You argue that a case—a set of circumstances seemingly unrelated to the facts of your case—actually clarifies your case and the claim you are making about it.

Parallel case You produce as evidence a case (B) that is very similar to the facts of your case (A). You argue that the claim you are making about your present case (A) is proven by the circumstances of the other (parallel) case (B).

Using any of these appeals to *logic*, you attempt to convince readers that your claim is reasonable. You can link evidence to your claim with two other sorts of appeals, which you'll learn about in this section: you can appeal to the reader's regard for *authority* and the reader's *emotions*.

▶1 Appealing to logic

An appeal to logic is by far the most common basis for arguing in the academic world. This section demonstrates five of the most common appeals to logic. You can argue from generalization, from causation, from sign, from analogy, or from parallel case.

Argument from generalization

Given several representative examples of a group (of people, animals, paintings, trees, washing machines, whatever), you can infer a general principle or *generalization*—a statement that applies to other examples of that group. In order for a generalization to be fair, you must select an adequate number of examples that are typical of the entire group; you must also acknowledge the presence of examples that apparently disprove the generalization. Arguments from generalization allow you to support claims that answer questions of fact and value.

Sample argument

As litter, plastic is unsightly and deadly. Birds and small animals die after getting stuck in plastic, six-pack beverage rings. Pelicans accidentally hang themselves with discarded plastic fishing line. Turtles choke on plastic bags or starve when their stomachs become clogged with hard-to-excrete, crumbled plastic. Sea lions poke their heads into plastic rings and have their jaws locked permanently shut. Authorities estimate that plastic refuse annually kills up to 2 million birds and at least 100,000 mammals.

—GARY TURBAK, "60 Billion Pounds of Trouble"

Claim	Plastic litter kills animals.
Evidence	Birds, turtles, sea lions, and various mammals have died from plastic litter.
Reasoning	Generalization. Danger to the animals cited can be generalized to other animals that come into contact with plastic litter.

Reason with generalizations to link evidence to claims in arguments about facts and value. (See 6b-1 for distinctions among claims of fact, policy, and value.)

Argument from causation

In an argument from causation, you begin with a fact or facts about some person, object, or condition. (If readers are likely to contest these facts, then you must make an argument to establish your facts before pushing on with an argument from causation.) An argument from *causation* enables you to claim that an action created by that person, object, or condition leads to a specific result or effect:

Sunspots cause the aurora borealis. Dieting causes weight loss. Smoking causes lung cancer. Working in the opposite direction, you can begin with what you presume to be an effect of some prior cause: the swing of a pendulum, inattention among schoolchildren, tornadoes. Of this presumed effect, you ask: "What causes this?" If you are a scientist or social scientist, you might perform an experiment. Establishing a direct causal link is seldom easy, for usually multiple causes will lead to a single condition (think of the inattentive child at school). In arguing causation, therefore, you need to be sensitive to complexity. Arguments of causation allow you to support a claim that answers a question of fact or of policy. Cause-and-effect reasoning also allows you to use a problem-solution structure in your arguments. (See the box at 6f.)

Sample argument

Under primitive agricultural conditions the farmer had few insect problems. Those arose with the intensification of agriculture—the devotion of immense acreages to a single crop. Such a system set the stage for explosive increases in specific insect populations. Single-crop farming does not take advantage of the principles by which nature works; it is agriculture as an engineer might conceive it to be. Nature has introduced great variety into the landscape, but man has displayed a passion for simplifying it. Thus he undoes the built-in checks and balances by which nature holds the species within bounds. One important natural check is a limit on the amount of suitable habitat for each species. Obviously then, an insect that lives on wheat can build up its population to much higher levels on a farm devoted to wheat than on one in which wheat is intermingled with other crops to which the insect is not adapted.

—RACHEL CARSON, *Silent Spring*

Claim	Insect problems arose with the practice of intensive, single-crop farming.
Evidence	The variety of vegetation in natural habitats discourages infestation; natural habitats have "checks and balances."
Reasoning	Cause and effect. By creating one-crop farms and eliminating the checks and balances of natural habitats, farmers caused their own insect problems.

Use cause-and-effect reasoning to link evidence to claims in arguments about facts and policy. (See 6b-1 for distinctions among claims of fact, policy, and value.)

Argument from sign

A sore throat and fever are signs of flu. Black smoke billowing from a window is a sign of fire. Risk taking is a sign of creativity. In an argument from *sign*, two things are correlated; that is, they tend to occur in the presence of one another. When you see one thing, you tend to see the other. A sign is *not* a cause, however. If your big toe aches at the approach of thunderstorms, your aching toe may be a sign of approaching storms, but it surely does not cause them. Economists routinely look to certain indexes (housing starts, for instance) as indicators, or signs, of the economy's health. Housing starts are *correlated with* economic health, often by means of a statistical comparison. If a sign has proven to be a particularly reliable indicator, then you can use it to support a claim that answers a question of fact.

Sample argument

Advertisments are constructed to make women anxious about the moisture content of their skin. In the language of advertising, dry skin is "a sign of a woman who is all dried up and is not sexually responsive—and who may also be sterile. This is because water is connected, in our psyches, with birth. It is also tied to purity, as in baptismal rites when sin is cleansed from a person. All of this suggests that words and images that picture a body of a woman as being dehydrated and losing water have great resonance."

—ARTHUR ASA BERGER, "Sex as Symbol in Fashion Advertising"

Claim   In advertisements, words and images of dehydration resonate for readers and viewers.

Evidence Readers have profound psychological associations with dryness.

Reasoning Sign. Dry skin is a sign of sterility and infertility, deeply resonant themes for men and women.

Reason with signs to link evidence to claims in arguments about facts. (See 6b-1 for distinctions among claims of fact, policy, and value.)

Argument from analogy

An argument from *analogy* sets up a comparison between the topic you are arguing and another topic that initially appears unrelated. While suggestive and at times persuasive, an analogy actually proves nothing. There is always a point at which an analogy will break down, and it is usually a mistake to build an argument on analogy alone. Use analogies as you would seasonings in cooking. As one of several attempts to persuade your reader, an analogy spices your argument and makes it memorable. You can use analogies in support of claims that answer questions of fact, policy, and value.

Sample argument

In closing, we might describe learning with an analogy to a well-orchestrated symphony, aimed to blend both familiar and new sounds. A symphony is the complex interplay of composer, conductor, the repertoire of instruments, and the various dimensions of music. Each instrument is used strategically to interact with other instruments toward a rich construction of themes progressing in phases, with some themes recurring and others driving the movement forward toward a conclusion or resolution. Finally, each symphony stands alone in its meaning, yet has a relationship to the symphonies that came before and those that will come later. Similarly, learning is a complex interaction of the learner, the instructional materials, the repertoire of available learning strategies, and the context, including the teacher. The skilled learner approaches each task strategically toward the goal of constructing meaning. Some strategies focus on understanding the incoming information, others strive to relate the meaning to earlier predictions, and still others work to integrate the new information with prior knowledge.

—BEAU FLY JONES ET AL., "Learning and Thinking"

Claim	Learning involves a complex blend of learner, materials, and context.
Evidence	In a symphony orchestra, meaning (sound) is created through interaction of musicians, conductor, composer, and history.
Reasoning	Analogy. The complex interactions needed to create symphonic music are analogous to the interaction needed to create meaning for a learner.

Reason with analogies to link evidence to claims in arguments about facts, policy, and value. (See 6b-1 for distinctions among claims of fact, policy, and value.)

Argument from parallel case

While an analogy argues a relationship between two apparently unrelated people, objects, conditions, or events, an argument from *parallel case* argues a relationship between directly related people, objects, events, or conditions. The implicit logic is this: the way a situation turned out in a closely related case is the way it will (or should) turn out in this one. Lawyers argue from parallel case whenever they cite a prior criminal or civil case in which the legal question involved is similar to the question involved in a current case. Because the earlier case ended a certain way (with the conviction or acquittal of a defendant, or with a particular monetary award), so too should the present case have this outcome. An argument from parallel case requires that situations presented as parallel be alike in essential ways; if this requirement is not met, the argument loses force. The argument would also be weakened if someone could present a more nearly perfect parallel case than yours. You can use a parallel case in support of claims that answer questions of fact, policy, or value.

Sample argument

By the year 2000, women and minorities will account for 68 per cent of the new workers. Coupled with the fact that, if current trends continue, the United States will face a shortage of scientists and physicians by the end of the century, it is safe to say that sustaining America's scientific and biomedical preeminence depends upon attracting—and retaining—talented women and minorities.

If we are to ensure our country's future competitiveness, we must change the prevailing [male-dominated] culture [of science and technology]—the rules of the game—in our classrooms, boardrooms, laboratories, and faculty lounges. To do so, we must recognize that brains, not brawn, will dominate the next century, and that means more than ever we must tap into the brain power of women. [. . .]

Eighty years ago, when British women were trying to win the right to vote, they played by men's rules: They broke windows in Parliament Square. Many of the women were treated brutally and arrested. Their leader, Emmeline Pankhurst, pointed out that every advance of men's rights has been marked by violence and the destruction of property. She defended the women's actions, saying, "Why should women go to Parliament Square and be battered about and insulted, and most important of all, produce less effect than when they throw stones? We tried it long enough. We submitted for years patiently in insult and assault. Women had their health injured. Women lost their lives. [. . .] After all, is not a woman's life, is not her health, are not her limbs more valuable than panes of glass? There is no doubt of that, but most important of all, does not the breaking of glass produce more effect upon the Government?"

While I am not advocating that American women in science resort to such behaviors—or even to the breaking of test tubes—it is clear that all of us in the scientific community have a lot of breaking to do—especially old rules, self-defeating habits, and glass ceilings.

—BERNADINE HEALY, director of the National Institutes of Health, *The Chronicle of Higher Education*

Claim   To take their rightful place in the scientific community, women must first challenge the male-dominated culture of science.

Evidence   In the early twentieth century, British women who fought to gain entry into the political community (by winning the right to vote) first had to challenge the male-dominated culture of British politics. Women protested at Parliament Square and broke windows.

Reasoning Parallel case. Just as during the early twentieth century women needed to fight to enter British politics, women today need to fight to enter into, and advance in, scientific fields.

Reason with parallel cases to link evidence to claims in arguments about facts, policy, and value. (See 6b-1 for distinctions among claims of fact, policy, and value.)

▶ 2 Appealing to authority

Two types of authority are important in arguments: the authority you bring as a writer and the authority of those who have expert knowledge on the topic that concerns you.

Establishing yourself as an authority

Before readers will agree with a claim you are making in an argument, they need to trust you, the writer. As a maker of arguments, you must therefore work to establish your trustworthiness—your authority to speak and make a claim. *Authority* in this sense is not the same as having expert knowledge; it has to do, rather, with establishing a presence that readers can yield to in a self-respecting way.

How do you establish this trust? Be honest, first of all. The point is so obvious it hardly seems worth making, but readers generally have a good nose for dishonesty. One whiff and they will turn away—for good. Beyond honesty, which is the main thing, strike a reasonable tone (see 21e), and choose a level of language appropriate for the occasion (see 3a-4). Read thoroughly enough on your topic to establish that, although you are not an expert, you do know the important issues and are knowledgeable enough to have an opinion worth considering.

Referring readers to experts

As a writer, you greatly help your cause when you can quote experts on a subject who support your point of view. If you have done research, you will have many sources to choose from. Which should you choose? See the box on page 155 for advice.

Once you have determined to the best of your ability that an expert whom you wish to quote is indeed expert, you must then identify those points in your discussion where appeals to authority will serve you well. You may want to mix appeals to authority with appeals to reason and, perhaps, to emotion. Appeals to authority can be used to support claims that answer questions of fact, policy, and value.

CRITICAL DECISIONS

Challenge what you read: Using authoritative sources

Read critically to determine which sources you can confidently draw on in a paper. Use the following criteria to help you make your decisions:

1. Prefer acknowledged authorities to self-proclaimed ones.
2. Prefer an authority working within his or her field of expertise to one who is reporting conclusions about another subject.
3. Prefer first-hand accounts over those from sources who were separated by time or space from the events reported.
4. Prefer unbiased and disinterested sources over those who can reasonably be suspected of having a motive for influencing the way others see the subject under investigation.
5. Prefer public records to private documents in questionable cases.
6. Prefer accounts that are specific and complete to those that are vague and evasive.
7. Prefer evidence that is credible on its own terms to that which is internally inconsistent or demonstrably false to any known facts.
8. In general, prefer a recently published report to an older one.
9. In general, prefer works by standard publishers to those of unknown or "vanity" presses.
10. In general, prefer authors who themselves follow [standard] report-writing conventions. [. . .]
11. When possible, prefer an authority known to your audience to one they have never heard of.

Source: Thomas E. Gaston and Bret H. Smith, *The Research Paper: A Common-Sense Approach* (Englewood Cliffs, NJ: Prentice Hall, 1988) 31–33.

Sample argument
Leo Marx claims that Melville's "Bartleby the Scrivener" is autobiographical.

Claim   Herman Melville's "Bartleby the Scrivener" is a story about Melville.

Evidence   Leo Marx says so.

Reasoning   Authority. Leo Marx is a respected literary critic who has taught at leading universities; his insights are valuable and are worth examining.

Use appeals to authority to link evidence to claims in arguments about facts, policy, and value. (See 6b-1 for distinctions among claims of fact, policy, and value.)

▶3 Appealing to emotion

Appeals to reason are based on the force of logic; appeals to authority are based on the reader's respect for the opinions of experts. By contrast, appeals to *emotion* are designed to tap the audience's needs and values. Arguments based on appeals to reason and authority may well turn out to be valid, but validity does not guarantee that readers will *endorse* your position. For instance, you might establish with impeccable logic that the physical condition of your community's public schools has deteriorated badly, to the point of affecting the performance of students. While true, your claim may not carry force enough to persuade the town council to vote on a bond issue or to raise money to renovate several buildings. To succeed in your effort or in any appeal to emotion, you must make your readers feel the same urgency to act that you do. The following paragraphs were written as part of a holiday charity drive by a writer and editor for the *New York Times*. Anna Quindlen's purpose in writing was to prompt readers to make a donation. Her argumentative claim (not stated in the example paragraphs) was *People should give what they can afford to the needy*.

Sample argument

There are the ones who are born with acquired immune deficiency syndrome, born to die because their parents used dirty needles. There are the ones who are left in hospitals to lie in the metal cribs, their only stimulation the occasional visit from a nurse. There are those who are freezing, and starving, and those who are beaten and bruised.

A doctor in the neonatal intensive care unit at one city hospital looked around at the incubators one afternoon and wondered aloud about the tubes, the medicines needed to make the premature thrive and the sickly ones bloom. It was not at all uncommon, she said, to find that an infant who had been coaxed from near death to life in the confines of that overly warm room, in one of those little plastic wombs, had turned up two or three years later in the emergency room with cigarette burns, broken bones, or malnutrition.

—ANNA QUINDLEN, "A City's Needy"

Claim   People should give what they can to the needy.

Evidence   There are children in New York suffering terribly, through no fault of their own.

Reasoning   Emotion. The plight of these blameless, helpless children touches the reader, who almost certainly lives in better circumstances. Quindlen moves the reader to pity, and pity may prompt a contribution.

Use appeals to emotion to link evidence to claims in arguments about policy and value. (See 6b-1 for distinctions among claims of fact, policy, and value.)

Making an Emotional Appeal

1. List the needs of your audience with respect to your subject; these needs might be physical, psychological, humanitarian, environmental, or financial.
2. Select the category of needs best suited to your audience, and identify emotional appeals that you think will be persuasive.
3. Place the issue you are arguing in your reader's lap. Get the reader to respond to the issue emotionally.
4. Call on the reader to agree with you on a course of action.

On the basis of an audience analysis (see 3a-3), you can sketch a profile of your readers and consider strategies suited to win their emotional support. Plan your emotional appeal by beginning with a claim that has already been supported by an appeal to reason. In your efforts to raise taxes for school renovation, you could show photographs, produce a list of items in need of repair, and quote expert witnesses who believe that children's learning suffers in deteriorating environments. Having argued by an appeal to reason, you can then plan an emotional appeal.

4 The limits of argument

In the real world, even the best argument may fail to achieve its objective. Some subjects—for example, abortion or capital punishment—are so controversial or so tied to preexisting religious or moral beliefs that many people have long since made up their minds one way or the other and will never change them. Such subjects are so fraught with emotion that logical arguments are ineffective in persuading people to rethink their positions. Sometimes, also, your audience has a vested interest in *not* being persuaded by your arguments. (Perhaps your audience has a financial stake in holding to an opposing position.) When your audience feels significantly threatened by the prospect of your victory, it is futile to insist on the validity of your argument.

EXERCISE 6

Write the outline of an argument, your claim for which should be based on the following scenario:

Imagine yourself a student at a college or university where the board of trustees has voted to institute a curfew on dormitory visitors. After 11 P.M. on weekdays and 1 A.M. on weekends, no student may have a guest in his or her dormitory room. The rule simply put: no overnight guests.

Decide on a claim, and determine whether it answers a question of fact, policy, or value. Plan a discussion in which you argue three ways in support of your claim.

6e Making rebuttals

By definition, arguments are subject to challenge, or to counterarguments. Because reasonable people will disagree, you must be prepared when arguing to acknowledge differences of opinion and to address them—for two reasons. First, by raising a challenge to your own position, you force yourself to see an issue from someone else's perspective. This can be a valuable lesson in that challenges can prompt you to reevaluate and refine your views. In addition, challenges pique a reader's interest. Research shows that when tension (that is, disagreement) exists in an argument, readers maintain interest: they want to know what happens or how the argument is resolved.

Once you acknowledge opposing views, respond with a *rebuttal*, an argument that addresses and rejects these views. If you can, point out the faulty logic on which they are based. If you do not raise objections, your readers inevitably will; better that you raise them on your terms so that you can control the debate.

When arguing, you should be open to accepting the views of others. Readers will appreciate your ability to concede at least some of your opposition's points, and they will take it as a sign of your reasonableness.

CRITICAL DECISIONS

Be alert to differences: Responding to opposing points of view

Expect opposition. When you have located opposing points of view, use the occasion to extend your thinking. Let disagreement enhance the quality of your argument.

■ **The facts are in dispute.** When the facts in an argument are disputed, investigate the validity of your facts and the opposition's.

Check the credibility of sources. Be sure that your sources are reliable. If you discover some dispute about reliability, raise it in your argument, and establish the trustworthiness of your information. If you cannot, abandon questionable sources, and thank your opposition.

If sources (yours and the opposition's) are equally reliable, ask, Through what process were the facts established? Different methods lead to different perceptions of fact. Acknowledge these methods, and state clearly which methods you (or your sources) have relied on.

■ **Expert opinions are in dispute.** Experts *will* disagree. Respond to differences of expert opinion by checking qualifications. These strategies should help:

Strategy 1: To confirm expertise, be sure that an author is referred to in several sources.

Strategy 2: To confirm expertise, locate a book written by the person in question. Locate two reviews, and you will learn something of the author's reputation.

If the experts holding opposing views are reliable, acknowledge the disagreement in your argument, and attempt to explain it.

▶ **6f** | **Preparing to write an argument**

Devising strategies for argument

There are two time-honored strategies for arranging arguments: the problem–solution structure and the classic five-part structure are summarized in boxes in this section. In these structures, each part of the argument may run as one paragraph or as a section consisting of several paragraphs.

Inductive and deductive arrangements

An inductively arranged argument moves from support—particular facts, examples, and opinions—to a claim. A great deal of scientific and technological argument proceeds this way. The writer makes certain observations, finds patterns in those observations, and then makes a claim about those observations.

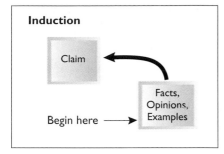

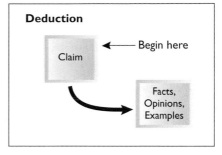

A deductively arranged argument moves from a claim to support—to particular facts, opinions, and examples. A good deal of writing in the humanities, in politics, and in law proceeds this way. The writer begins with a general principle or claim, the truth, likelihood, or desirability of which is then proven.

Writing an Argument: The Problem–Solution Structure

I. There is a serious problem.
   A. The problem exists and is growing.
      (Provide support for this statement.)
   B. The problem is serious.
      (Provide support.)
   C. Current methods cannot cope with the problem.
      (Provide support.)
II. There is a solution to the problem. (Your claim goes here.)
   A. The solution is practical.
      (Provide support.)
   B. The solution is desirable.
      (Provide support.)
   C. We can implement the solution.
      (Provide support.)
   D. Alternate solutions are not as strong as the proposed solution.
      (Review—and reject—competing solutions.)

Source: Adapted from Richard D. Rieke and Malcolm O. Sillars, *Argumentation and the Decision Making Process* (Glenview, IL: Scott, Foresman, 1984) 163.

Regardless of whether you will use an inductive or a deductive arrangement for your argument, realize that in either approach you *begin* writing with identical information: in both cases, you know before you begin writing the draft what your claim, support, and lines of reasoning will be. The decision to move inductively or deductively is a decision about strategy.

You can position the claim in your argument at the beginning, middle, or end of the presentation. In the problem–solution structure, you see that the claim is made only after the writer introduces a problem. Working with the five-part structure, you have more flexibility in positioning your claim. One factor that can help

Preparing to Write an Argument   **159**

Writing an Argument: The Classic Five-Part Structure

1. Introduction: Introduce topic to be argued and establish its importance. Provide background information.
2. Claim: State your claim (your argumentative thesis).
3. Supporting the claim: Construct reasons for accepting the claim.

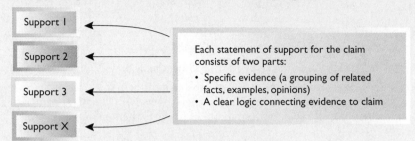

Support 1

Support 2

Support 3

Support X

Each statement of support for the claim consists of two parts:

- Specific evidence (a grouping of related facts, examples, opinions)
- A clear logic connecting evidence to claim

4. Counterargument/rebuttal: Raise arguments against the claim; challenge them.
5. Conclusion: Summarize the argument; remind readers of what you want them to believe or do.

Depending on the writing occasion, you will want to rearrange elements of this typical argumentative structure. For instance, you may want to raise and rebut counterarguments first (as the writer does in the example argument in 6a), or you may want to raise counterarguments immediately after (or before) every support you offer for the claim. You may want to locate the claim at the end of the argument (see 6f). Be flexible. Adapt your approach according to your needs.

---

determine placement is considering the members of your audience and the likelihood of their agreeing with you:

- When an audience is likely to be neutral or supportive, you can make your claim early on with the assurance that you will not alienate readers.
- When an audience is likely to disagree, plan to move your claim toward the end of the presentation, in that way giving yourself space to build consensus with your readers, step by step, until you reach a conclusion.

Readers tend to remember most clearly what they read last. Thus, you may want to present your reasons in support of your claim in the order of least to most emphatic. Conversely, you may want to offer your most emphatic reasons in support of a claim at the very beginning of the argument. In one strong move you might gain the reader's agreement and then cement that agreement with reasons of secondary importance. Any argument can be arranged in a variety of ways. Decisions you make about placing your claim and arranging your points of support will depend on your assessment of the members of your audience and their probable reactions to your views.

▶ **EXERCISE 7**

Return to the argument you outlined in Exercise 6, and introduce in this outline an argument counter to your own. In a paragraph, discuss how you would rebut the counterargument or accept it in part.

Gathering materials for argument

Writing an argument is more a recreation of thinking than an exploration. Exploration—through writing or through talking with friends—comes prior to writing a first draft. Consider writing a *pre*draft: a brief paper, intended for your eyes only, in which you explore the position you want to take in your argument. Whatever your method for doing so, arrive at your views on a topic—your claim—*before* you sit down to write the draft. As you begin, you should understand the support you will present and the lines of reasoning you will use to link that support to your claim. You will flesh out the discussion as you write, but the backbone of your argument should be carefully thought out ahead of time.

Gathering Materials for Your Argument

1. Gather material on your subject. Generate information on your own—see 3b; if necessary, conduct research. See Part IX, on library research.
2. Review your material. Decide what you think about the topic, and in a single sentence answer a question of fact, policy or value. Your one-sentence answer will be the claim of your argument.
3. Understand your audience: What do they know about the topic? What do they need to know? To what sorts of appeals will they respond?
4. Plan out the lines of reasoning you will present to link your evidence with your claim.
5. Identify strong counterarguments, and plan to rebut and neutralize them. Possibly concede some of your opposition's points.
6. Sketch your argument, deciding on placement of your claim and arrangement of your lines of reasoning.
7. Draft your argument, realizing that you will need to backtrack on occasion to get new information or to rethink your strategy. See Chapter 3 on the necessary uncertainties in preparing for and writing a first draft.
8. Revise two or three times. See Chapter 4 for advice.

▶ **EXERCISE 8**

Based on your outline in Exercise 7, write the draft of a five-page argument.

▶ **6g** | Evaluating arguments and avoiding common errors

Whether you are evaluating your own arguments (in an effort to revise them) or someone else's, there are several common errors to watch for. Correct these errors in your own writing, and raise a challenge when you find them in the writing of others.

▶ **1 Defining terms**

Your evaluation of an argument should begin with its claim. Locate the claim, and be sure that all terms are well defined. If they are not, determine whether the lack of definition creates ambiguities in the argument itself. For example, if you define the word *generosity* one way and others define it differently, there is bound to be disagreement. If a word such as *generosity* slips into the claim, very likely informed argument cannot begin until the word is carefully defined. With especially ambiguous words, sometimes whole paragraphs of definition are needed.

▶2 Examining appeals to logic

As you have seen (in 6d), the lines of reasoning that a writer develops—generalization, causation, and so on—establish logical support for a claim. If you as the reader feel that the argument's logic is not valid, then you are entitled to raise a challenge. If the logic is flawed, the validity of the claim may be in doubt. Any of the following seven types of fallacies, or flaws, will undermine an argument's logic. The first four flaws specifically address the lines of reasoning you will use to make arguments: generalization, causation, sign, and analogy.

http://www2.ca.nizkor.org/
features/fallacies/Fallacies
*Detailed descriptions of
forty-two logical fallacies.*

1. *Faulty generalization.* Generalizations may be flawed if they are offered on the basis of insufficient evidence. It would not be valid, for instance, to make the generalization that left-handed people are clumsy because all three lefties of your acquaintance are clumsy. A more academic example: Assume you had administered a survey to students in your dorm. In studying the results you discovered that attitudes toward joining fraternities and sororities were evenly split. Slightly more than 50 percent wanted to join; a bit less than 50 percent did not. It would be a faulty generalization to claim on the basis of this one survey that students on your campus are evenly split on joining fraternities and sororities. In order for your generalization to be accurate, the survey would need to have been administered campus-wide—if not to every student, then at least to a representative cross-section.

2. *Faulty cause and effect.* Two fallacies can lead a writer to infer incorrectly that one event causes another. The first concerns the ordering of events in time. The fact that one event occurs before another does *not* prove that the first event caused the second. (In Latin, this fallacy is known as *post hoc*, a brief form of *post hoc, ergo propter hoc*—"after this, therefore because of this.") If the planets Venus and Jupiter were in rare alignment on the morning of the Mt. St. Helens eruption, it would not be logical to argue that an alignment of two planets caused the volcano to erupt.

    The second flaw in thinking that leads to a faulty claim of causation is the belief that events must have *single* causes. Proving causation is often complicated, for many factors usually contribute to the occurrence of an event. What caused the layoff of production-line workers at the General Motors plant in Framingham, Massachusetts? An answer to this question would involve several issues, including increased competition from foreign auto manufacturers, a downturn in the economy, the cost of modernizing the Framingham assembly line, a need to show stockholders that there were fewer employees on the payroll, and a decision to build more cars out of the country. To claim that *one* of these is the sole cause of the plant shutdown would be to ignore the complexity of the event.

3. *Confusing correlation with causation.* There is a well-known saying among researchers that *correlation does not imply causation*. In one study on creativity, researchers correlated *risk taking* and *a preference for the unconventional* with groups of people classified as creative. It would not be logical to infer from this correlation that creativity *causes* risk taking or that this trait *causes* creativity. The most

that can be said is that the traits are associated or correlated with—they tend to appear in the presence of—creative people. Arguments made with statistical evidence are usually subject to this limitation.

4. *Faulty analogy.* The key components of an analogy must very nearly parallel the issues central to the argument you are making. The wrong analogy not only will *not* clarify, but also will positively confuse. For instance, an attempt to liken the process of writing to climbing a flight of stairs would create some confusion. The analogy suggests that the writing process occurs in clearly delineated steps, when progress in actual writing is seldom so neat. The stages of writing do not progress "step by step" until a final draft is achieved. Analogies should enhance, not obscure, understanding.

5. *Either/or reasoning.* Assume that someone is trying to persuade you that the United States ought to intervene militarily in a certain conflict many thousands of miles from U.S. territory. At one point in the argument you hear this: "Either we demonstrate through force that the United States continues to be a world power or we take a backseat, passive role in world affairs. The choice is clear." Actually, the choice is not at all clear. The person arguing has presented two options and has argued for one. But many possibilities for conducting U.S. foreign policy exist besides going to war or becoming passive. An argument will be flawed when its author preselects two possibilities from among many and then attempts to force a choice.

6. *Personal attacks.* Personal attacks, known in Latin as *ad hominem* arguments, challenge the person presenting a view rather than the view itself. You are entitled to object when you read or hear this type of attack: "The child psychologist on that talk show has no kids, so how can he recommend anything useful to me concerning my children?" Notice that the challenge is directed at the person who is presenting ideas, not at the ideas themselves. It is sidestepping the issue in an argument to dismiss an apparently useful observation by dismissing the person who offers it. At the very least, statements should be evaluated on their merits.

7. *The begged question.* Writers who assume the validity of a point that they should be proving by argument are guilty of begging the question. For instance, the statement "All patriotic Americans should support the president" begs a question of definition: What *is* a patriotic American? The person making this statement assumes a definition that he or she should in fact be arguing.

▶3 Examining evidence

Arguments also can falter when they are not adequately or legitimately supported by facts, examples, statistics, or opinions. Refer to the following guidelines when using evidence.

Facts and examples

1. *Facts and examples should fairly represent the available data.* An example cannot be forced. If you find yourself needing to sift through a great deal of evidence in order to find one confirming fact or example, take your difficulty as a sign, and rethink your point.

2. *Facts and examples should be current.* Facts and examples need to be current, especially when you are arguing about recent events or are drawing information from a field in which information is changing rapidly. If, for example, you are

Evaluating Arguments and Avoiding Common Errors   **163**

arguing a claim about the likelihood of incumbent politicians being reelected, you should find sources that report on the most recent elections. If you are trying to show a trend, your facts and examples should also be drawn from sources going back several years, if not decades.

3. *Facts and examples should be sufficient to establish validity.* A generalization must be based on an adequate number of examples and on representative examples. To establish the existence of a problem concerning college sports, for instance, it would not do to claim that because transcripts were forged for a handful of student-athletes at two schools, a problem exists nationwide.

4. *Negative instances of facts and examples should be acknowledged.* If an argument is to be honest, you should identify facts and examples that constitute evidence *against* your position. Tactically, you are better off being the one to raise the inconvenient example than having someone else do this for you in the context of a challenge.

Statistics

5. *Statistics from reliable and current sources should be used.* Statistics are a numerical compression of information. Assuming that you do not have the expertise to evaluate the procedures by which statistics are generated, you should take certain common-sense precautions when selecting statistical evidence. First, cite statistics from reliable sources. If you have no other way of checking reliability, you can assume that the same source cited in several places is reliable. The U.S. government publishes volumes of statistical information and is considered a reliable source. Just as with facts and examples, statistics should be current when you are arguing about a topic of current interest.

http://www.bates.edu/~ganderso/
biology/resources/statistics.htm
A painless guide to statistics for the non-mathematically inclined.

6. *Comparative statistics should compare items of the same logical class.* If you found statistical information on housing starts in New England in one source and in a second source found information on housing starts in the Southwest, you would naturally want to compare the numbers. The comparison would be valid only if the term *housing starts* was defined clearly in both sources. Lacking a definition, you might plunge ahead and cite the statistics in a paper, not realizing that one figure included apartment buildings in its definition of *housing*, while the other included only single-family homes. Such a comparison would be faulty.

Expert opinions

7. *"Experts" who give opinions should be qualified to do so.* Anyone can speak on a topic, but experts speak with authority by virtue of their experience. Cite the opinions of experts in order to support your claims. Of course, you will want to be sure that your experts are, in fact, expert, and evaluating the quality of what they say can be troublesome when you do not know a great deal about a topic. You can trust a so-called expert if you see that person cited as an authority in several sources. For experts who are not likely to be cited in academic articles or books, use your common sense. (See the box in 6d-2 for more on evaluating expert opinions and choosing authoritative sources.)

8. *Experts should be neutral.* You can disqualify an expert's testimony for possible use in your argument if you find that the expert will profit somehow from the opinions or interpretations offered.

CHAPTER 7

Constructing Sentences

I f you are a lifelong speaker of English, then you are an expert in the language—in its grammar, vocabulary, sentence structures, and the proper relationships among its words. When you speak, people understand. You *know* English, but in all likelihood your knowledge is *implicit:* you can do just fine communicating verbally, and yet you may not know the textbook definition of *participle*, for instance—even though you use participles correctly every day. Knowing the basic vocabulary, structures, and relationships among words will permit you to make sentence-level decisions that will improve your writing.

7a   Understanding sentence parts

The sentence is our basic unit of communication. Each word of a sentence can be classified as a part of speech. As you review definitions of nouns, verbs, and the other parts of speech, remember that these are parts of a whole: meaning in language is built on the *relationship* among words.

1   The basics: Recognizing subjects and predicates

The fundamental relationship in a sentence is the one between a subject and its predicate. Every sentence has a **subject:** a noun or noun-like word group that engages in the main action of the sentence or is described by the sentence. Every sentence has a **predicate:** a verb and other words associated with it that state the action undertaken by a subject or the condition in which the subject exists.

A **simple subject** is the single noun or pronoun that identifies what the sentence is about or produces the action of the sentence. The **simple predicate** is the main sentence verb. You can gain a great deal of confidence from your ability to divide a sentence into its subject and predicate parts. In the sentences that follow, the simple subject is marked "ss" and the simple predicate, "sp."

Subject	Predicate
ss In small doses, alcohol	sp acts as a stimulant.
ss Large doses	sp act as a depressant.
ss Individuals under the influence	sp often become more aggressive.

▶2 **Nouns**

A **noun** (from the Latin *nomen*, or "name") is the part of speech that names a person, place, thing, or idea.[1] Only nouns can be introduced by an **article** or a **determiner**. The **indefinite article** *a* appears before a noun or an adjective describing a noun when these begin with a consonant: *a* book, *a* large book, *a* small egg. Also, words that begin with the letter *u* when it's pronounced *yoo* are preceded by *a*: *a* unit, *a* useful device. The word *an* is placed before a noun beginning with a vowel or unpronounced *h*—as in *hour: an* hour, *an* ant. If an adjective appears before the noun and begins with a consonant, use the article *a*: *a* small ant. The **definite article,** *the*, denotes a specific noun: *the* book. Nouns can also be accompanied by certain classes of words that limit what they refer to. The most common limiting words (and their categories) are *this, that, these, those* (demonstrative); *any, each, some* (indefinite); *one, two, first, second*, etc. (numerical); and *which, that, whose*, etc. (relative).

http://owl.english.purdue.edu/writers/by-topic.html#parts
Handouts on the parts of speech from the Purdue Online Writing Lab.

ESL NOTE The use of articles or of various limiting, quantifying, or determining words indicates whether an English noun names a person or thing that is specific or definite. Nouns that name something generic, nonspecific, or abstract are used without these words or with indefinite limiting words like *some* or *any* (see 45a-2 and 45b).

Classification of Nouns

Proper nouns are capitalized and name particular persons, places, or things:
Sandra Day O'Connor, Chevrolet, "To His Coy Mistress"

Common nouns refer to general persons, places, or things and are not capitalized:
judge, automobile, poem

Count nouns can be counted:
cubes, cups, forks, rocks

Mass nouns cannot be counted:
sugar, water, air, dirt

Concrete nouns name tangible objects:
lips, clock, dollar

Abstract nouns name intangible ideas, emotions, or qualities:
love, eternity, ambition

Animate versus **inanimate nouns** differ according to whether they name something alive:
fox and *weeds* versus *wall* and *honesty*

Collective nouns are singular in form but plural in sense:
crowd, family, group, herd

---

[1]We owe our discussions of the parts of speech to Hulon Willis, *Modern Descriptive English Grammar* (San Francisco: Chandler, 1972).

The use of a plural form or a numerical limiting word often indicates whether an English noun names a person or thing that can be counted—that is, a count noun (versus a mass or noncount noun, which names uncountable quantities or abstractions). See the box on this page and 42a-1.

Nouns change their form to show **number;** they can be made singular or plural: *boy/boys, child/children, herd/herds.* They also undergo limited change in form to show **possession,** but unlike pronouns (see 7a-7), they do this only with the addition of an apostrophe and usually an *s: girl's, children's, herd's.* Finally, nouns can be classified according to categories of meaning that affect the way they are used, as shown in the box on page 166.

Specific uses of nouns are addressed in several places in this text:

Nouns: agreement with verbs 10a
Nouns: as clauses 7e-3
Nouns: as complements 7b
Nouns: as modifiers 11g
Nouns: as objects 7b

Nouns: phrases 7d-2, 3
Nouns: as subjects 7b
Nouns: showing possession 8c, 27a
Nouns with articles and determiners 45b

▶3 Verbs

A **verb,** the main word in the predicate of a sentence, expresses an action, describes an occurrence, or establishes a state of being.

Action   Eleanor *kicked* the ball.
Occurrence   A hush *descended* on the crowd.
State of being Thomas *was* pious.

Classification of Verbs

Transitive verbs transfer action from an actor—the subject of the sentence—to a person, place, or thing receiving that action (see 9d-1).

> *buy, build, kick, kiss, write*
> Wanda *built* a snowman.

Intransitive verbs show action; yet no person, place, or thing is acted on (see 9d-1).

> *fall, laugh, sing, smile*
> Stock prices *fell.*

Linking verbs allow the word or words following the verb to complete the meaning of a subject (see 11d).

> *be (am, is, are, was, were, has/have been), look, remain, sound, seem, taste*
> Harold *seems* happy.

Helping or **auxiliary verbs** help to show the tense and mood of a verb (see 9c and 46d).

> *be (am, is, are, was, were), has, have, had, do, did, will*
> I *am* going. I *will* go. I *have* gone. I *did* go.

Modal auxiliaries such as *might, would, could,* and *must* help a verb to express urgency, obligation, and likelihood (see 9c-1 and 46d).

> I *should* go. I *might* go. I *could* go.

Verbs change form on the basis of their **principal parts.** Building from the **infinitive** or **base form** (often accompanied by **to**), these parts are the **past tense,** the **present participle,** and the **past participle.**

Base form	Past tense	Present participle	Past participle
to escape	escaped	am escaping	escaped
to ring	rang	am ringing	rung

The principal parts of a verb have a major role in showing **tense.** Tense expresses the verb's action in time relative to a present statement.

There are four varieties of verbs in English; each establishes a different relationship among sentence parts, as shown in the box on page 167.

ESL NOTE   To determine whether a word in a sentence is a verb, apply the test sequence described in 12a (on sentence fragments).

See Chapter 9 for a detailed discussion of verbs. The following list provides a brief index to more information on verb use.

Verbs: active and passive
   voices   9g and 43a-1
Verbs: agreement with
   subjects   10a
Verbs: (avoiding) shifts   16a, b
Verbs: linking   11d
Verbs: modal auxiliaries
   9c-1 and 43d

Verbs: mood   9h and 43b-5–6
Verbs: regular and irregular   9a, b
Verbs: strong vs. weak   9g–h, 17b
Verbs: tense   9e, f and 43b-1–4
Verbs: thesis statements   3d-1, 2, 3
Verbs: transitive and intransitive
   9d-1 and 43a-1
Verbs versus verbals   7a-4 and 43e

▶**4   Verbals**

A **verbal** is a verb form that functions in a sentence as an adjective, an adverb, or a noun. There are three types of verbals: gerunds, participles, and infinitives. A **gerund,** the *-ing* form of a verb without its helping verbs, functions as a noun.

Editing is both a skill and an art. [The gerund is the subject of the sentence.]

I am tired of *editing*. [The gerund is an object of a preposition.]

A **participle** is a verb form that modifies nouns and pronouns. Its present and past forms make up two of the verb's principal parts, as shown previously.

The *edited* manuscript was 700 pages. [The past participle modifies the noun *manuscript*.]

The man *editing* your manuscript is Max Perkins. [The present participle modifies the noun *man*.]

An **infinitive,** often preceded by *to,* is the base form of the verb (often called its *dictionary form*). An infinitive can function as a noun, adjective, or adverb.

To edit well requires patience. [The infinitive functions as the noun subject of the sentence.]

The person *to edit* your work is Max Perkins. [The infinitive functions as an adjective.]

He waited *to edit* the manuscript. [The infinitive functions as an adverb.]

The following list is a brief index to other information on verbals.

CRITICAL DECISIONS

Challenge sentences: Checking for key sentence elements

When rereading sentences you have written, check three key relationships:

1. Does the sentence have a subject and a verb? A word grouping that lacks a subject, a verb, or both is considered a fragment. See Chapter 12, on fragments.

   Incomplete   At the beginning of the meeting. [no verb.]

   Revised   At the beginning of the meeting, the treasurer reported on recent news.

2. Does the sentence have a subject and verb that *agree in number*? A subject and verb must both be singular or plural.

   Inconsistent   The treasurer are a dynamic speaker. [The plural verb does not match the singular subject.]

   Revised   The treasurer is a dynamic speaker.

3. Does the sentence have a subject close enough to the verb to ensure clarity? Meaning can be confused if the subject/verb pairing is interrupted with a lengthy modifier. See Chapter 15 for a discussion of misplaced modifiers.

   Interrupted   We because of our dire financial situation have called this meeting.

   Revised   We have called this meeting because of our dire financial situation.

▶5 Adjectives

By modifying or describing a noun or pronoun, an **adjective** provides crucial defining and limiting information in a sentence. It can also provide nonessential but compelling information to help readers see, hear, feel, taste, or smell something named. Adjectives include the present and past participle forms of verbs, such as *fighting* Irish, *baked* potato, and *written* remarks. The single-word adjectives in the following sentences are italicized.

> Climate plays an *important* part in determining the *average* numbers of a species, and *periodical* seasons of *extreme* cold or drought I believe to be the most *effective* of *all* checks.
>
> —CHARLES DARWIN, *On the Origin of Species*

▶6 Adverbs

An **adverb** can modify a verb, an adjective, an adverb, or an entire sentence. Adverbs describe, define, or otherwise limit, generally answering these questions: *when, how,* *where, how often, to what extent,* and *to what degree.* Although many adverbs in English are formed by adding the suffix *-ly* to an adjective, some are not: *after, ahead, already, always, back, behind, here, there, up, down, inside, outside.* **Descriptive adverbs** describe individual words within a sentence.

> The poor *unwittingly* subsidize the rich. [The adverb modifies the verb *subsidize.*]
>
> Poverty *almost* always can be eliminated at a higher cost to the rich. [The adverb modifies the adverb *always.*]
>
> Widespread poverty imposes an *increasingly* severe strain on our social fabric. [The adverb modifies the adjective *severe.*]

Conjunctive adverbs establish adverb-like relationships between whole sentences. These words—*moreover, however, consequently, thus, therefore* and so on—play a special role in linking ideas and sentences. (See 7a-9 and 19a-3.) Chapter 11 provides a detailed discussion of adjectives and adverbs. The following is a brief index to more information on adjectives and adverbs.

Adjectives: and hyphenation 32a	Adjectives: coordinate 25c-2
Adjectives: as subject	Adjectives: phrases as 7d-1, 2, 3
complements 11d	Adjectives: positioning 15a–g
Adjectives: clauses as 7e-2	Adverbs: and hyphenation 32a

▶7 Pronouns

Pronouns substitute for nouns. The word that a pronoun refers to and renames is called its **antecedent.** Like a noun, a pronoun shows **number**—it can be singular or plural. Depending on its function in a sentence, a pronoun will change form—that is, its **case:** it will change from **subjective** to **objective** to **possessive.** The following examples show this change in case for the pronoun *he,* which in each instance is a substitute for the noun *Jake.*

> antecedent   pronoun (subjective)
> Jake reads a magazine. *He* reads a magazine.

> antecedent   pronoun (objective)
> The magazine was given to Jake. The magazine was given to *him.*

> antecedent   pronoun (possessive)
> Jake's subscription is running out. *His* subscription is running out.

There are eight classes of pronouns.

Personal pronouns (*I, me, you, us, his, hers,* etc.) refer to people and things.

> When sugar dissolves in water, the sugar molecules break *their* close connection within the sugar crystal.

Relative pronouns (*who, whose, which, that,* etc.) begin dependent clauses (see 7e) and refer to people and things.

> The presence of the sugar, *which* is now in solution, changes many of the properties of the water.

Demonstrative pronouns (*this, these, that, those*) point to the nouns they replace.

These changes involve the water's density, boiling point, and more.

Interrogative pronouns (*who, which, what, whose,* etc.) form questions.

What does boiling sugar water have to do with coating caramel apples?

Intensive pronouns (*herself, themselves,* and other compounds formed with *-self* or *-selves*) repeat and emphasize a noun or pronoun.

The sugar *itself* can be recovered from the water by the simple act of boiling.

Reflexive pronouns (*herself, themselves,* and other compounds formed with *-self* or *-selves*) rename—reflect back to—a preceding noun or pronoun.

The ease of recovery demonstrates that sugar molecules do not bind *themselves* strongly to water molecules.

Indefinite pronouns (*one, anyone, somebody, nobody, everybody,* etc.) refer to general, or nonspecific, persons or things.

Anyone who has stained a shirt with salad dressing knows that water will not dissolve oil.

Reciprocal pronouns (*one another, each other*) refer to the separate parts of a plural noun.

The many solvents available to chemists complement *one another.*

The following is a brief index to more information on pronouns.

Pronouns: agreement in person
and number 10a, b
Pronouns: case—subjective,
objective, possessive 8a–d

Pronouns: reference to
antecedent 14a–e
Pronouns: relative pronouns 8f, 14e

▶8 Prepositions

A **preposition** links a noun (or word group substituting for a noun) to other words in a sentence—to nouns, pronouns, verbs, or adjectives. *In, at, of, for, on,* and *by,* are all prepositions. Many common prepositions are shown in the following box. Along with the words that follow them, prepositions form **prepositional phrases,** which function as adjectives or adverbs. In the following sentence, an arrow leads from the (three) prepositional phrases to the (three) words modified. Note that the middle prepositional phrase modifies the word *evolution* in the first prepositional phrase.

The theory *of evolution by natural selection* was proposed *in the 1850s.*

ESL NOTE Prepositions occur in a very wide variety of English constructions that are often highly idiomatic. They are often followed by a noun or pronoun in the objective form or case (see 8b-1 and 42c), thus forming a modifying prepositional phrase (see 7d-1).

Understanding Sentence Parts

The following is a brief index to more information on prepositions.

Common Prepositions

Single-word prepositions

about	beyond	off
above	by	on
across	concerning	onto
after	despite	out
against	down	outside
along	during	over
among	except	through
around	for	to
as	from	toward
before	in	under
behind	into	until
below	like	up
beneath	near	with
between	of	

Multiword prepositions

according to	contrary to	on account of
along with	except for	on top of
apart from	in addition to	outside of
as for	in back of	owing to
because of	in case of	with regard to
by means of	in spite of	with respect to

9 Conjunctions

Conjunctions join sentence elements or entire sentences in one of two ways: either by establishing a coordinate or *equal* relationship among joined parts or by establishing a subordinate or *unequal* relationship. (Subordinating conjunctions are discussed in detail in 7e. Coordinating and correlative conjunctions are discussed in Chapter 19.) Briefly, conjunctions are classified in four ways: as coordinating conjunctions, conjunctive adverbs, correlative conjunctions, or subordinating conjunctions.

Coordinating conjunctions join parallel elements from two or more sentences into a single sentence: *and, but, or, nor, for, so, yet.* (For uses of coordinating conjunctions see 10a-2, 3, 19a-1, and 25b.)

> Infants only cry at birth, *but* within a few short years they speak in complete sentences.

Conjunctive adverbs create special logical relationships between the clauses or sentences joined: *however, therefore, thus, consequently*, etc. (For uses of conjunctive adverbs see 13b-4, 19a-3, and 26b.)

> Infants can only cry at birth. Within a few short years, *however*, they can speak in complete sentences.

Correlative conjunctions are pairs of coordinating conjunctions that place extra emphasis on the relationship between the parts of the coordinated construction: *both/and, neither/nor, not only/but also*, etc. (For uses of correlative conjunctions see 10a-3.)

> Three-year-olds *not only* speak in complete sentences *but also* possess vocabularies of hundreds or even thousands of words.

Subordinating conjunctions connect subordinate clauses to main clauses: *when, while, although, because, if, since, whereas*, etc. (For uses of subordinating conjunctions see 7e-1 and 19b-1.)

> *When* children reach the age of three, they can usually carry on complete conversations with their peers and with adults.

▶ 10 Interjections

An **interjection** is an emphatic word or phrase. When it stands alone, it is frequently followed by an exclamation point. As part of a sentence, the interjection is usually set off by commas.

> Oh, they're here.   Never!

▶ 11 Expletives

An **expletive** is a word that fills a slot left in a sentence that has been rearranged. *It* and *there* function as expletives—as filler words without meanings of their own—in the following examples.

Basic sentence	A sad fact is that too few Americans vote.
With expletive	It is a sad fact that too few Americans vote.
Basic sentence	Millions of people are not voting.
With expletive	There are millions of people not voting.

Expletives are used with the verb *be* in sentences with a delayed subject. Sentences with expletives can usually be rearranged back to their basic form. Try to delete expletives from your writing to achieve a spare, concise style (see Chapter 17).

▶ **EXERCISE I**

Place a slash (/) between the subject and predicate parts of the following sentences. Identify the simple subject and simple predicate of each sentence with the abbreviations "ss" and "sp." Circle prepositions.

                ss   sp

    Example: The physics (of) particle behavior / is important (for) designing safe and efficient processing plants.

1. Vega, the hapless hit man of *Pulp Fiction*, brought new life to John Travolta's career.
2. The actor earned his second Oscar nomination for playing Vega.
3. The first, of course, came in 1977 for his breakthrough in *Saturday Night Fever*.
4. Between the poles of these two pictures, Travolta had gone from household name to all-but-employable.
5. But now Travolta is once again at the top of his game.

▶ **7b**   **Understanding basic sentence patterns**

There are five basic sentence patterns in English, from which virtually all of the sentences you read in this and other books are built. Each of the five sentence patterns consists of a subject and a predicate. Depending on the sentence's structure, the predicate may contain a **direct object,** an **indirect object,** or a (subject or object) **complement.** The basic pattern diagrams that follow include definitions of these key terms and concepts.

                     ┌─Predicate─┐

Pattern 1: Subject   verb

          We   *look.*

Subject: a noun or noun-like word group that produces the main action of the sentence or is described by the sentence.

Predicate: a verb, and other words associated with it, that states the action undertaken by the subject or the condition in which the subject exists.

                  ┌──────── Predicate ────────┐

Pattern 2: Subject   verb (tr.)   direct object

          Stories   *excite*   *the imagination.*

Direct object: a noun, or group of words substituting for a noun, that receives the action of a transitive verb (tr.). A direct object answers the question *What or who is acted upon?*

                  ┌──────── Predicate ────────┐

Pattern 3: Subject   verb (tr.) indirect object   direct object

          Stories   *offer*   *us*   *relief.*

Indirect object: a noun, or group of words substituting for a noun, that is indirectly affected by the action of a verb. Indirect objects typically follow transitive verbs such as *buy, bring, do, give, offer, teach, tell, play,* or *write.* The indirect object answers the question *To whom or for whom has the main action of this sentence occurred?*

                                             Constructing Sentences

Pattern 4: Subject | verb (tr.) | direct object | object complement
They | *make* | *us* | *tense.*

Predicate

Object   an adjective or noun that completes the meaning of a direct object by
complement: renaming or describing it. Typically, object complements follow verbs
such as *appoint, call, choose, consider, declare, elect, find, make, select,* or *show.*

Pattern 5: Subject | verb (linking) | subject complement
We | *are* | *readers.*

Predicate

Subject   a noun or adjective that completes the meaning of a subject by re-
complement: naming or describing it. Subject complements follow linking verbs
such as *appear, feel, seem,* and *remain,* as well as all forms of *be.*

▶ **EXERCISE 2**

Working with a topic of your choice, write a paragraph in which you use each of
the five basic sentence patterns.

> *Example:* The curtain finally rose. [Sentence Pattern 1] The set was lavish.
> [Sentence Pattern 5] The actors wore period costumes. [Sentence
> Pattern 2] The set design gave the audience a feast for the eyes.
> [Sentence Pattern 3] The critics declared it an absolute smash.
> [Sentence Pattern 4]

▶ **7c**   **Expanding sentences with single-word modifiers**

Principles of sentence expansion can be found at work in virtually any paragraph
you read. The first technique for expanding sentences is to add modifiers—
descriptive, modifying information. The nouns and verbs in the five basic sentence
patterns can be modified by adjectives and adverbs.

▶**1**   **Modifying nouns and verbs with adjectives and adverbs**

Noun modified   A novel will engage an *active* imagination.
by adjective

Verb modified   I read *thoroughly.*
by adverb

▶**2**   **Positioning modifiers**

The position of an adverb can be shifted in a sentence from beginning to middle
to end. Depending on its location, an adverb will change the meaning of a sentence
or the rhythm. When placing an adverb, take care that it modifies the word you
intend it to modify.

Shifted   I am *only* moving my bed (that is, doing nothing more important
meaning than moving).

I am moving *only* my bed (that is, no other furniture).

Shifted
rhythm *Sometimes,* stories can provide emotional relief.

Stories *sometimes* can provide emotional relief.

Stories can provide emotional relief *sometimes.*

A single-word adjective is often positioned directly before the noun it modifies, although writers make many variations on this pattern. When more than one noun in the sentence could be described by the adjective, take particular care to place the adjective closest to the noun it modifies. See Chapter 15, on editing, to correct misplaced modifiers and 44b for the sequence of adjective modifiers in a typical English sentence.

A *good* story will excite a reader. [*Story* is the word modified.]

A story will excite a *good* reader. [*Reader* is the word modified.]

▶ **EXERCISE 3**

Use single-word adjectives or adverbs to modify the nouns and verbs in the following sentences.

> *Example:* A man walked down a street.
>
> An *old* man walked *slowly* down a *tree-lined* street.

1. College tuition rises. [Sentence Pattern 1]
2. Students hold jobs. [Sentence Pattern 2]
3. The jobs give them wages. [Sentence Pattern 3]
4. Joblessness makes the students tense. [Sentence Pattern 4]
5. The wages are vital. [Sentence Pattern 5]

EXERCISE 4

▶ Take the paragraph you wrote for Exercise 2, and modify its nouns and verbs as you have done in Exercise 3.

▶ **7d** **Modifying and expanding sentences with phrases**

A **phrase** does not express a complete thought, nor can it stand alone as a sentence. Phrases consist of nouns and the words associated with them, or verb forms not functioning as verbs (called *verbals*) and the words associated with them. Phrases function in a sentence as modifiers and as objects, subjects, or complements. As such, they can be integrated into any of the five sentence patterns (see 7b) to add detail.

▶**I** **Adding prepositional phrases**

A preposition, together with its noun, called an *object,* forms a **prepositional phrase,** which functions in a sentence as a modifier.

Adjective Stories can excite the imaginations *of young people.*

Adverb Paul reads *in the evening.*

▶**2 Adding verbals: Infinitive phrases**

A verbal is a verb form functioning not as a verb but instead as a noun, adjective, or adverb. An infinitive—the base form or dictionary form of a verb—often is preceded by the word *to*. Infinitives function as adjectives, adverbs, or nouns, but they behave as verbs in that they can be modified with adverbs and can be followed with direct and indirect objects. Infinitives and the various words associated with them form **infinitive phrases.**

Noun subject	*To read in the evening* is a great pleasure.
Noun object	Some children start *to read at an early age.*
Adjective	Stories offer us a chance *to escape dull routines.*
Adverb	We read *to gain knowledge.*

▶**3 Adding verbals: Gerund and participial phrases**

When appearing without its helping verbs, the *-ing* form of the verb functions as a noun and is called a **gerund.** Without its helping verb, the present or past participle can function as an adjective. A noun or pronoun appearing before a gerund must be written in its possessive form.

Gerund	We did not approve of *Paul's* reading all night. [The gerund phrase functions as the object of the preposition *of.* A noun in the possessive case is used before the gerund.]
Faulty	We did not approve of *him* reading all night. [The pronoun before the gerund does not use the possessive case.]
Revised	We did not approve of *his* reading all night.

▶**4 Adding noun phrases**

A **noun phrase** consists of a noun accompanied by all of its modifying words. A noun phrase can be quite lengthy, but it always functions as a single noun—as the subject of a sentence, as the object of a verb or preposition, or as a complement.

Subject	*Even horror stories with their gruesome endings* can delight readers.
Direct object	A tale of horror will affect *anyone who is at all suggestible.*
Complement	Paul is *someone who likes to read horror stories.* [The phrase is a subject complement.]

▶**5 Adding absolute phrases**

Unlike other phrases, **absolute phrases** consist of a subject and an incomplete predicate. Absolute phrases modify entire sentences, not individual words. When you use an absolute phrase, set it off from your sentence with a comma or pair of commas (see Chapter 25). An absolute phrase is formed by deleting the linking verb *be* from a sentence.

Sentence	His hands were weak with exhaustion.
Absolute phrase	his hands weak with exhaustion
New sentence	His hands weak with exhaustion, Paul lifted the book off its shelf. [The phrase modifies the basic sentence, *Paul lifted. . . .*]

An absolute phrase may also be formed by changing the main verb of a sentence to its *-ing* form, without using an auxiliary.

Sentence   His hands trembled with exhaustion.

Absolute phrase his hands trembling with exhaustion

New sentence   His hands trembling with exhaustion, Paul lifted the book off its shelf.

▶6 Adding appositive phrases

Appositive phrases rename nouns. The word *appositive* describes the positioning of the phrase *in apposition to*, or beside, the noun. Appositives are actually "clipped" sentences—the predicate part (minus the verb) of Sentence Pattern 5.

		Predicate	
Pattern 5: Subject	verb (linking)		subject complement
Paul	*is*		*an old college friend.*

Appositive phrase an old college friend

New sentence   Paul, an old college friend, is an avid reader.

▶ EXERCISE 5

In the sentences that follow, circle all single-word modifiers and underline all modifying phrases.

> *Example:* (Recently,) Stephen W. Hawking published a (popularized) version of his ideas about space and time.

- *Recently* is an adverb and modifies the verb *published.*
- *Popularized* is an adjective and modifies the noun *version.*
- Two prepositional phrases—*of his ideas about space and time*—function as an adjective by modifying the noun *version.*
- The second prepositional phrase, *about space and time*, functions as an adjective by modifying the object of the preceding phrase, *ideas.*

1. On a clear, moonless night, he says, the brightest objects in the sky are the planets nearest Earth.
2. Looking more closely, we can see that the stars near Earth appear to be fixed, but they are not.
3. To measure the distance of a star from Earth, scientists calculate the number of years it takes the star's light to reach us.
4. His calculations having proved it, Sir William Herschel confirmed that our galaxy (the Milky Way) forms a spiral.
5. We now know that our galaxy is only one of some hundred thousand million galaxies.
6. Each of those hundred thousand million galaxies contains a hundred thousand million stars.

▶ **7e** Modifying and expanding sentences with dependent clauses

A **clause** is any grouping of words that has both a subject and a predicate. There are two types of clauses. An **independent** (or **main**) **clause** can stand alone as a sentence. Any sentence fitting one of the five structural patterns reviewed in 7b is an independent clause. A **dependent** (or **subordinate**) **clause** cannot stand alone as a sentence, because it is usually introduced either with a subordinating conjunction (e.g., *while*) or with a relative pronoun (e.g., *who*). There are three types of dependent clauses: adverb, adjective, and noun clauses.

http://www.quiknet.com/
~jukes/sentenc1.htm
http://www.quiknet.com/
~jukes/sentenc2.htm
These two pages provide practice combining sentence parts for more sophistication.

▶ **1** Adding dependent adverb clauses

Dependent **adverb clauses** that modify verbs, adjectives, and other adverbs begin with subordinating conjunctions and answer the question *when, how, where, how often, to what extent,* or *to what degree.* Subordinating conjunctions establish a distinct logical relationship between the clauses joined.

Placed at the head of a clause, a subordinating conjunction makes one sentence grammatically dependent on another. When the subordinating conjunction *if,* for example, is placed at the head of a sentence, it renders that sentence grammatically dependent, unable to stand alone.

Main clause plus subordinating conjunction   *if* + Food is repeatedly frozen and thawed.

Dependent clause   if food is repeatedly frozen and thawed

Although it consists of a subject and predicate, this last grouping of words is no longer a sentence. To make sense, this clause must be set in a dependent relationship with an independent clause.

If food is repeatedly frozen and thawed, it will spoil.

For guidance on punctuating sentences with dependent clauses, see 25a-1.

Subordinating Conjunctions and the Logical Relationships They Establish

To show condition: *if, even if, unless,* and *provided that*
To show contrast: *though, although, even though,* and *as if*
To show cause: *because* and *since*
To show time: *when, whenever, while, as, before, after, since, once,* and *until*
To show place: *where* and *wherever*
To show purpose: *so that, in order that,* and *that*

See 7a-9 for a discussion of conjunctions.

Modifying and Expanding Sentences with Dependent Clauses   **179**

2 Adding dependent adjective clauses

Like adjectives, **adjective clauses** modify nouns. The clauses usually begin with the relative pronoun *which, that, who, whom,* or *whose.* The following examples show an adjective clause modifying the subject of a sentence.

People *who lived through the Depression of the 1930s* remember it well.

A country *that had prospered in the first two decades of the century* now saw massive unemployment and hardship.

For a discussion of when to use which relative pronoun, see 8f.

3 Adding dependent noun clauses

Noun clauses function exactly as single-word nouns do in a sentence: as subjects, objects, complements, and appositives. Noun clauses are introduced with the pronoun *which, whichever, that, who, whoever, whom, whomever,* or *whose* or with the word *how, when, why, where, whether,* or *whatever.*

Subject   *That ozone holes have already caused blindness and skin cancer in grazing animals* suggests the need for immediate legislative action.

Object   Apparently, few inhabitants of populous northern cities are aware of *how the depletion of ozone in the upper atmosphere can harm living organisms—humans included.*

Complement The looming danger that ozone depletion poses is *why researchers have sounded an alarm.*

▶ EXERCISE 6

Combine each of the sentence pairs that follow by using a subordinating conjunction.

> *Example:* Competition in the job market is intense. Job seekers need to approach their task strategically.
>
> *Because* competition in the job market is intense, job seekers need to approach their task strategically.

1. Job seekers tend to deemphasize interpersonal skills. This is a poor strategy in a business climate that seeks those who can communicate effectively and work as team members.
2. Even in a high-tech world, people still have to eat. Many people are studying the culinary arts.
3. Parents are entering the workforce in increasing numbers. The need for child-care workers and preschool workers expands.
4. You should find a job that fulfills you personally. That love will eventually help your career in terms of dollars and cents.
5. A shortage of labor in entry-level construction jobs seems likely in the near future. The construction industry is offering training and making outreach efforts.

▶**I** **Functional definitions**

Sentences are classified by structure and by function. There are four functional types: statements, questions, exclamations, and commands. Statements, called **declarative** sentences, are by far the most common of the four types and make direct assertions about a subject. A question, or **interrogative** sentence, is formed either by inverting a sentence's usual word order (*She did sing./Did she sing?*) or by preceding the sentence with a word such as *who, whom, which, when, where, why,* or *how.* An exclamation, or **exclamatory** sentence, used rarely in academic writing, serves as a direct expression of a speaker's or writer's strong emotion. Commands, or **imperative** sentences, are an expression of an order or urgent wish addressed to a second person.

Declarative	The driver turned on the ignition.
Interrogative	Was the engine flooded?
Exclamatory	What an awful fire! How terrible!
Imperative	Get back! Don't you go near that!

▶**2** **Structural definitions**

There are four structural classes of sentences in English: simple, compound, complex, and compound-complex.

Each of the five basic sentence patterns discussed in 7b qualifies as a **simple sentence:** each has a single subject and a single predicate. The designation "simple" refers to a sentence's structure, not its content. A simple sentence, with all its modifying words and phrases, can be long.

> Vampires play a prominent role in two major works of literary criticism from the first half of this century—Mario Praz's *The Romantic Agony* and D. H. Lawrence's *Studies in Classical American Literature.* [This sentences consists of one subject, *vampires,* and one simple predicate, *play.*]

Compound sentences have two subjects and two predicates. They are created when two independent clauses are joined with a coordinating or correlative conjunction or with a conjunctive adverb. For details on how coordination can be used to create sentence emphasis, see 19a.

> As the Undead, the vampire casts no shadow and has no reflection, but he (or she) manifests prominent canine teeth. [The conjunction *but* joins two independent clauses.]

Complex sentences consist of an independent clause and one or more dependent clauses.

> Stoker's *Dracula* is dignified and still *until* he explodes into ravenous action. [The subordinating conjunction *until* signals a dependent adverb clause.]

Compound-complex sentences consist of at least two independent clauses and one subordinate, dependent clause.

> Anne Rice's vampires seem to regard vampirism amorally, *and* whatever scruples they feel about their predatory nature gradually subside *as* they become increas-

ingly inhuman. [The coordinating conjunction *and* signals a compound sentence, and the subordinating conjunction *as* signals a dependent clause in a complex sentence.]

One way to maintain a reader's interest is to vary sentence types as well as sentence lengths. See Chapter 20 for a series of suggestions for controlling sentence length and rhythm.

▶ **EXERCISE 7**

Use the clauses and phrases provided to build up the core sentence. Add conjunctions when they are necessary to the logic of your expanded sentence.

> *Example:* Athol Fugard is a South African playwright. (a) plays confront difficulties (b) interracial relations (c) his troubled country
>
> Athol Fugard is a South African playwright whose plays confront the difficulties of interracial relations in his troubled country.

1. A common thread connects Fugard's work. (a) respect for humanity (b) search for human dignity (c) struggle to cultivate trust and hope in a demeaning world

2. Fugard's looks reflect his struggles. (a) tenacious (b) weathered

3. Fugard handwrites his plays. (a) in this computer age (b) with a tortoise-shell Parker pen (c) which include *A Lesson from Aloes, The Road to Mecca, "Master Harold" . . . and the Boys,* and *My Children, My Africa,* all successfully produced in America

4. South Africa is changing. (a) for Fugard there are signs (b) the freeing of Nelson Mandela (c) the lifting of the ban on the African National Congress (d) the government's willingness to negotiate

5. Fugard continued writing. (a) during the mid-1960s (b) he staged classic plays with the Serpent players (c) the country's first nonwhite theater troupe

CHAPTER 8

Case in Nouns and Pronouns

The term **case** refers to a noun's or pronoun's change in form, depending on its function in a sentence. Nouns do not change their form when their function changes from subject to object. Especially when revising, you may change a pronoun's function—say, from object to subject. By being alert to how a pronoun's function changes, you will be prepared to make a corresponding change to the pronoun's form. There are eight classes of pronouns. Most troublesome are the **personal pronouns,** which refer to people and things, and these will be the focus of discussion.

http://www.uottawa.ca/
academic/arts/writcent/
hypergrammar/prntrcky.html
*Explanations of some tricky
points of pronoun usage.*

▶ 8a Using pronouns as subjects

▶**I** **Use the subjective case when a pronoun functions as a subject.**

She speaks forcefully. The speaker is *she.*

The executive officers—and only *they*—can meet here.

Subject of an independent clause	In September 1908, Orville Wright began demonstration flights of the Wright brothers' "Signal Corps Flyer" at Fort Meyer, Virginia; *he* invited a young Signal Corps officer, Lieutenant Thomas Selfridge, to be a passenger.
Subject of a dependent clause	When *they* attempted a fourth circuit of the parade grounds, the Flyer's right propeller hit a bracing wire and cracked.
Subject complement	So severely injured were *they* that medics could not revive the unconscious Selfridge.
Appositive that renames a subject	Thomas Selfridge—*he* alone—bears the grim distinction of being the first person to be killed in the crash of a powered airplane.

Pronouns Used as Subjects		
	Singular	*Plural*
1st person	I	we
2nd person	you	you
3rd person	he, she, it	they

Spotlight on Common Errors—CASE FORMS

These are the errors most commonly associated with a pronoun's case. For full explanations and suggested revisions, follow the cross-references to chapter sections.

CASE FORM ERRORS occur when writers misunderstand a pronoun's function in a sentence as a subject, object, or indicator of possession. These common situations lead to errors.

When a noun or an indefinite pronoun (such as *one*, *anyone*, *somebody*) shows possession, use an apostrophe (see 27a–b).

Faulty	**Revised**
This is Alberts signature.	This is Albert's signature.
Rondas team is impressive.	Ronda's team is impressive.
The families decision was final.	The family's decision was final.
Somebodies book is here.	Somebody's book is here.
This is nobodies business.	This is nobody's business.

A personal pronoun that shows possession (such as *his*, *her*, *mine*, *ours*) uses NO apostrophe (see 8c-1 and 27a-2).

Faulty	**Revised**
This coat is her's.	This coat is hers. (This is her coat.)
Give the cat it's food.	Give the cat its food.
These coats are their's.	These coats are theirs. (These are their coats.)
Your's are the first hands to touch this.	Yours are the first hands to touch this. (Your hands are the first hands to touch this.)

After a form of the verb *be* (*is*, *are*, *was*, *were*), use a pronoun's subjective form (*I*, *you*, *he*, *she*, *we*, *they*) or its possessive form (*mine*, *yours*, *his*, *hers*, *theirs*, *ours*) with *no* apostrophe (see 8a-2 and 8c-1).

Faulty	**Revised**
This is her. This is him.	This is *she*. This is *he*.
Is that her? It is me.	Is that *she*? It is *I*.
This is our's. That is her's.	This is *ours*. That is *hers*.

When a personal pronoun (such as *I, me, you, he, she, it*) follows the word *and*, choose the pronoun's form as if the pronoun were alone in the sentence (see 8d and 8b-1).

Faulty	Revised
Sally and me went to the movies.	Sally and *I* went to the movies. [Test: I went to the movies alone.]
She and me went. Her and me went.	She and *I* went. [Test: She went. I went.]
Tom went with Sally and I.	Tom went with Sally and *me*. [Test: Tom went with me.]
It's a secret between you and I.	It's a secret between you and *me*. [Test: It's a secret between me and a friend.]
That's between he and Sally.	That's between *him* and Sally. [Test: That's between him and a friend.]

Use *its* to show possession; use *it's* ONLY for a contraction of *it is* (see 27a-2).

Faulty	Revised
A dog hates it's fleas.	A dog hates *its* fleas.
Its raining.	*It's* raining. (It is raining.)

For a contraction with the verb *be* (*is, are*), use an apostrophe (see 27a-2).

Faulty	Revised
Its a difficult position.	It's a difficult position. (It is a difficult position.)
Their coming home.	They're coming home. (They are coming home.)
There coming home.	They're coming home. (They are coming home.)
Shes home.	She's home. (She is home.)
Your home.	You're home. (You are home.)
Whos there?	Who's there? (Who is there?)

Spotlight on Common Errors—Case Forms

▶2 Use the subjective case for pronouns with the linking verb *be*.

The speaker is *she*.   These are *they*.   It is *I*.

The linking verb *be* in a sentence serves as a grammatical "equals" sign (see 11d); it links the subject of the sentence to a completing or "complement" word that is made identical to the subject. When pronouns are involved in this equation, they too are made identical to the subject and are also used in the subjective form.

Clinton *was* President.   It was *he*, the president, who spoke.

The use of subjective pronoun forms is quite clear in sentences with normal word order (subject + *be* + complement), but writers need to remember that subjective forms are used in the same equation when sentence order is reversed.

In nonstandard or informal usage it is fairly common to hear a linking-verb construction using an objective form: as in "It's me" or "This is her." But in academic English these constructions should be revised using a subjective pronoun that maintains sentence logic and consistency: "It's I" and "This is she." If such a construct sounds stilted, the best remedy is to rewrite, as in "This is Ellen," or "Here she is."

▶ 8b   Using pronouns as objects

▶1 Use the objective form for pronouns functioning as objects.

The governor handed *her* the report. The job appealed to *me*. We enjoyed taking *them* to dinner.

Pronouns functioning as the object of a preposition, as the object or indirect object of a verb, or as the object of a verbal take the objective form.

	Pronouns Used as Objects	
	Singular	*Plural*
1st person	me	us
2nd person	you	you
3rd person	him, her, it	them

Object or indirect object of verb (see 7b)

President Clinton used the word "funk" to describe his perception of the mood of 1990s America; immediately a reporter asked *him* what he meant. [*Him* is the indirect object of *asked*.]

Object of preposition (see 7d-1)

Clinton used the terms "malaise" and "funk," insisting that there was a world of difference between *them*. [*Them* is the object of the preposition *between*.]

Case in Nouns and Pronouns

Appositive that renames the object (see 7d-6)

The president's attempted distinction muddied the waters even more; it became apparent to both parties—*him and the reporters*—that the mistake would become news. [The appositive phrase *him and the reporters* renames and clarifies *both parties*, the object of the preposition *to*. The pronoun in the appositive must also be in the objective case: *him*.]

Object of verbal (see 7a-4)

One reporter, pressing *him* to define his terms, created an embarrassment. [*Him* is the object of the present participle—or verbal—*pressing*.]

▶ **2 Use the objective form for pronouns functioning as the subject of an infinitive.**

Study enabled *us* to reach the goal.

When a pronoun appears between a verb and an infinitive, the pronoun takes the objective form. In this position, the pronoun is called the subject of the infinitive.

With infinitive   Babe Ruth's 60 home runs in 1927 helped *him* to reach a level of stardom unmatched by other athletes of his era. [The objective-form pronoun appears between the verb *helped* and the infinitive *to reach*.]

Babe Ruth's home runs helped *him* reach stardom. [The subject of the infinitive *reach* uses the objective form, *him*.]

▶ 8c   Using nouns and pronouns in the possessive case

Use a possessive noun or pronoun before a noun to indicate ownership of that noun (or noun substitute).

Eleanor Roosevelt gave the Civil Works Administration *her* enthusiastic support for hiring 100,000 women by the end of 1933.

ESL NOTE   Many English nouns are made possessive either with the possessive case form (*a woman's voice*) or with the noun as object of the preposition *of* (*voice of a woman*). With some inanimate nouns the prepositional form is standard, and the possessive case form is seldom used (NOT *a house's color* BUT *color of a house*). See 42c-1.

Possessive Forms of Pronouns

	Singular	Plural
1st person	my, mine	our, ours
2nd person	your, yours	your, yours
3rd person	his, her, hers, its	their, theirs

8c ca

1 Certain possessive pronouns are used as subjects or subject complements to indicate possession.

Yours are the first hands to touch this. These are *theirs*.

The possessive pronouns *mine, ours, yours, his, hers,* and *theirs* are used in place of a noun as subjects or subject complements.

Ours is a country of opportunity for both men and women, Eleanor Roosevelt argued. This opportunity is *ours*. (*mine, yours, his, hers, theirs*)

2 Use a possessive noun or pronoun before a gerund to indicate possession.

The group argued for *Lynette's* getting the new job.

Be careful not to mistake a gerund for a participle, which has the same *-ing* form but functions as an adjective. A participle is often preceded by an objective pronoun.

Participle with objective pronoun	Clinton quickly tried to do damage control. One account describes *him circling* the room, trying to extricate himself from his verbal blunder. [*Him*, an objective pronoun, is modified by the participle *circling*.]
Gerund with possessive pronoun	One account describes *his circling* the room in an attempt to do damage control as the instinctive move of a politician.

The focus in this last sentence is no longer on *him* (on Clinton) but on *circling*—a difference in meaning. Confusion between an *-ing* word's function—as a gerund or as a participle—can lead to errors.

Faulty Hard work resulted in *them* getting government jobs. [*Getting* is mistakenly treated as a participle and is incorrectly preceded by an objective pronoun.]

Revised Hard work resulted in *their* getting government jobs. [*Their* indicates possession of the gerund *getting government jobs*.]

► EXERCISE 1

Based on your analysis of each of the following sentences, fill in the blanks with an appropriate subjective, objective, or possessive pronoun: *I/we, you, he/she/it/they; me/us, you, him/her/it/them; my/mine/our/ours, your/yours, his/her/hers/its/their/theirs.*

> *Example:* _____ changing costumes, mid-performance, amused the audience.
>
> *Changing costumes* is a gerund phrase and takes a possessive pronoun. *His* (or *her*) changing costumes, mid-performance, amused the audience.

1. Delegates to the convention watched _____ changing positions on important issues and deserted the candidacy.
2. Delegates wanted _____ to remain steadier under challenges from contenders.

3. After _____ left the convention, the delegates searched for a restaurant.

4. The newly elected president arrived and said the delegates had worked so effectively that she wanted to give _____ a banquet.

5. "_____ is an organization that recognizes honest effort," the president said.

EXERCISE 2

Complete the sentences that follow by filling in the blanks with pronouns or nouns of the appropriate form.

1. Presenting the newly discovered evidence—the intruder's gloves—to the district attorney, the chief inspector said: "These are _____ ."

2. It is _____ who has won.

3. It is _____ who have won.

4. This is _____ contest.

5. Mark answered the phone and, listening to a person asking for him, said: "Yes, this is _____ ."

▶ **8d** **In a compound construction, use pronouns in the objective or subjective form according to their function in the sentence.**

Sally and *I* went to the movies. Tom went with Sally and *me*.

The coordinating conjunction *and* can create a compound construction—a doubled subject or object. These can sometimes mask how a pronoun functions in a sentence. When you have difficulty choosing between a subjective or objective pronoun in a compound construction, try this test: *Create a simplified sentence by dropping out the compound;* then *try choosing the pronoun.* With the compound gone in the simpler construction, you should be able to tell whether the pronoun operates as a subject or an object.

Compound subject

Pierre and Marie Curie worked collaboratively; together Marie and *he* discovered polonium and radium. [The subjective pronoun forms the second part of a compound subject.]

Confusing Marie and *him* received the Nobel Prize in physics in 1903. [The pronoun subject is mistakenly put in the objective form.]

Simplified Marie received the Nobel Prize; *he* also received it. [In the simplified construction, the need for the subjective pronoun is clear.]

Revised Marie and *he* received the Nobel Prize in 1903.

Compound object

The 1903 Nobel Prize in physics was awarded to Pierre and *her* for their work on radioactivity. [The objective pronoun is the object of a preposition in a compound construction.]

Confusing	An award was presented to Pierre and *she* in 1903, for their work on radioactivity. [In this construction, the pronoun functions as part of the preposition's compound object. Mistakenly, the pronoun is made subjective.]
Simplified	The award was presented to Pierre; it was also presented to *her.*
Revised	An award was presented to Pierre and *her* in 1903.

▶ **8e**   **Pronouns paired with a noun take the same case as the noun.**

▶ **1 For first-person plural pronouns (*we, us*) paired with a noun, use the same case as the noun.**

We first-year students face important challenges.

Transitions can be challenging for *us* first-year students.

The first-person plural pronoun *we* or *us* is sometimes placed before a plural noun to help establish the identity of the noun. Use the subjective-case *we* when the pronoun is paired with a noun subject, and use the objective-case *us* when the pronoun is paired with an object of a verb, verbal, or preposition. To test for the correct pronoun, simplify the sentence and *drop out* the paired noun. In the simpler sentence, you should be able to determine which pronoun case is required.

Nonstandard	*Us* strikers demand compensation. [*Strikers* is the subject of the sentence, and the pronoun paired with it should be the subjective-case *we.*]
Simplified	*We* . . . demand compensation. [The need for the subjective-case *we* is now clear.]
Revised	*We* strikers demand compensation.

Nonstandard	Give *we* strikers a fair share. [*Strikers* in this sentence is the indirect object of the verb *give*, and the pronoun paired with it should be the objective-case *us.*]
Simplified	Give *us* . . . a fair share. [The need for the objective-case *us* is now clear.]
Revised	Give *us* strikers a fair share.

▶ **2 In an appositive, a pronoun's case should match the case of the noun it renames.**

The executive officers—and only *they*—can attend.

Give this report to Linda—*her* and no one else.

Pronouns may occur in an **appositive**—a word or phrase that describes, identifies, or renames a noun in a sentence. If so, the pronoun must take the same case as the noun being renamed. Once again, you can test for pronoun choice by simplifying the sentence: *Drop the noun being renamed out of the sentence.* The simpler sentence that remains will usually reveal what pronoun case is required.

Case in Nouns and Pronouns

Renamed subject	Clinton's attempt to explain the difference between "malaise" and "funk," even with the coaching of his advisors, only served to show that both parties—*he* and the reporters—had failed to do their homework.
Confusing	Both parties—*him* and the reporters—had failed to do their homework.
Simplified	*He* and the reporters failed to do their homework.

▶ **8f** **Choose the appropriate form of the pronouns *whose, who, whom, whoever,* and *whomever* depending on the pronoun's function.**

The basic forms of the relative pronouns *whose, who, whom, whoever,* and *whomever* are shown in the following table. A relative pronoun's form depends on its function within its own clause.

Forms of the Relative Pronoun Who(m)/Who(m)ever		
Subjective	*Objective*	*Possessive*
who	whom	whose
whoever	whomever	—

▶ **I** **In a question, choose a subjective, objective, or possessive form of *who(m)* or *who(m)ever* according to the pronoun's function.**

Who is going? To *whom* are you writing? *Whose* birthday is it?

To test the correct choice for these pronouns at the beginning of a question, mentally *answer* the question, substituting the personal pronouns *I/me, we/us, he/him,* or *she/her* for *the relative pronoun.* Your choice of the subjective or objective form in the answer sentence will likely be quite clear, and it will be the same choice to make for the form of *who(m)* or *who(m)ever.*

Question	(Who/whom) are you addressing?
Answer	You are addressing (he/*him*). [The choice of the objective form is clear.]
Revised	*Whom* are you addressing? [The objective form is correct.]

Question	For (who/whom) are you writing?
Answer	You are writing for (she/*her*). [The choice of the objective form is clear.]
Revised	For *whom* are you writing? [The objective form is correct.]

The possessive form *whose* can begin a question if the pronoun shows possession of the noun that immediately follows. To determine whether a possessive pronoun is correct for a sentence, replace the initial pronoun in the question with *what,* and then mentally answer that question. If the answer requires that you use *his, her, their,* or *its* in place of the relative pronoun, then choose the possessive form, *whose.*

Question What name goes on the envelope? [Is a pronoun in the possessive case— his/her/their/its—needed?]

Possessive *Whose* name goes on the envelope?

▶**2 In a dependent clause, choose the subjective, objective, or possessive form of *who(m)* or *who(m)ever* according to the pronoun's function within the clause.**

Henry Taylor, *who* writes poems, lives in Virginia. Taylor, *whom* critics have praised, has a new book. The poet, *whose* book won a prize, lives quietly.

To choose the correct case for a relative pronoun in a dependent clause, eliminate the main clause temporarily; consider the pronoun's function *only* in the dependent clause. When deciding between the subjective or objective forms, apply the following tests.

Determine whether the relative pronoun functions as the subject of a dependent clause.

If the relative pronoun is followed immediately by a verb, you should probably use the subjective-case *who* or *whoever.* To be sure that the choice of pronouns is correct, substitute the word *I, we, you, he,* or *she* for *who* or *whoever.* Does this yield a legitimate sentence? If so, the choice of the subjective case is correct.

Subjective Your request will be of concern to (whoever/whomever) gets it.

Simplified (Whoever/whomever) gets it. [The pronoun is followed by a verb, *gets,* so the likely choice of pronouns will be *whoever.*]

Revised Your request will be of concern to *whoever* gets it.

Determine whether the relative pronoun functions as an object in the dependent clause.

If the relative pronoun is followed immediately by a noun or by the pronoun *I, we, you, he, she, few, some, many, most, it,* or *they,* you should probably use the objective-case *whom* or *whomever.* To be sure of the choice, consider the dependent clause as if it were a sentence by itself (without the main clause). Rearrange the clause into normal word order, and then substitute the word *him, her,* or *them* for the relative pronoun. If one of these newly substituted pronouns fits into the sentence as an object of a verb, verbal, or preposition, then the choice of the objective-case *whom* or *whomever* is correct.

Objective Please send this to *whomever* it might interest. [The relative pronoun is followed by the pronoun *it,* so the choice of pronoun will likely be objective form. A second test: The objective-case *them,* substituted for *whomever,* yields a rearranged sentence, "It might interest *them.*"]

Determine whether the relative pronoun needs to show possession.

If the relative pronoun beginning a dependent clause needs to show possession, then you should use the possessive-case *whose.* Confirm the choice by substituting the word *his, her, their,* or *its* for the relative pronoun. A sentence should result when the dependent clause is considered by itself.

Possessive   Daly, *whose* theories on urban wildlife have generated heated discussion, believes that we can profit by finding nature in our cities. [The possessive-case *his* yields a sentence: "*His* theories on urban wildlife . . . "]

▶ **8g**   **Choose the case of a pronoun in the second part of a comparison depending on the meaning intended.**

I studied Keats more than *him* (more than I studied Arnold—him).

I studied Keats more than *she* (more than Margo—she—studied Keats).

The words *than* and *as* create a comparison.

Calcutta is more densely populated *than* New York.

The new magneto engines are as efficient *as* traditional combustion engines.

For brevity's sake, writers and speakers often omit the second part of a comparison. Written in their complete form, the preceding examples would read as follows.

Calcutta is more densely populated than New York is densely populated.

The new magneto engines are as efficient as traditional combustion engines are efficient.

A comparison links two complete clauses. The brief form of a comparison is its "clipped" form; the fully expressed comparison, its "complete" form. When you compare people and use pronouns in the second part of your comparison, be sure to express your exact meaning. At times, the pronoun in the second part of a comparison will take the place of a noun functioning as a subject; in this case, use the subjective form: *he, she, we.*

Complete   Some think that Prospero is a more perplexing figure than Hamlet is perplexing. [*Hamlet* functions as a subject in the second part of the comparison. A pronoun replacement for *Hamlet* would take the subjective form.]

Complete   Some think that Prospero is a more perplexing figure than *he* is perplexing.

Clipped   Some think that Prospero is a more perplexing figure than *he.*

At times, the pronoun in the second part of a comparison will take the place of a noun functioning as an object; in this case, use the objective form: *him, her, us.*

Complete   Many critics are more intrigued by Prospero than they are intrigued by Hamlet. [*Hamlet* functions as the object of the preposition *by* in the second part of the comparison. A pronoun replacement for *Hamlet* would take the objective form.]

Complete   Many critics are more intrigued by Prospero than they are intrigued by *him.*

Clipped   Many critics are more intrigued by Prospero than by *him.*

Avoid "clipping" the second part of a comparison unless all its parts are obvious. If you do clip the comparison, mentally recreate the full comparison to

CRITICAL DECISIONS

Challenge your sentences: Applying a test for *who* and *whom*

In a clause the relative pronouns *who* and *whom* take the place of nouns (or pronouns) that function as subjects or objects. Choosing the correct relative pronoun requires that you see that pronoun in relation to the words immediately following. You must examine the broader context of the clause in which the pronoun is located. Two questions should help you to choose between *who* and *whom* correctly.

■ **Is the relative pronoun followed by a verb?**

—"Yes": choose the subjective-case *who* or *whoever.*

A relative pronoun followed by a verb indicates the pronoun occupies the subject position of the clause. To confirm this choice, substitute *I, we, you, he,* or *she* for the pronoun.

Clinton, *who* won by a landslide in the electoral college, did not win as convincingly in the popular vote. [*Who* is followed by a verb, and when it is converted to *he* it yields a sentence: "*He* won by a landslide."]

—"No": choose the objective-case *whom* or *whomever.* See the next test.

■ **Is the relative pronoun followed by a noun or by any of these pronouns: *I, we, you, he, she, few, some, many, most, it, they*?**

—"Yes": choose the objective-case *whom* or *whomever.*

A relative pronoun followed by a noun or one of the listed pronouns indicates that the normal order of the clause (subject-verb-object) has been rearranged, suggesting the need for a pronoun in its objective form. To confirm your choice of *whom* or *whomever,* consider the pronoun and the words immediately following. Rearrange these words, and substitute *him, her,* or *them* for the relative pronoun.

Clinton, *whom* most analysts counted out of the presidential race, surprised supporters and detractors alike. [*Whom* is followed by *most,* and when it is converted to *him* it yields a sentence: "Most analysts counted *him* out."]

determine the function of the noun your pronoun is replacing. When that noun functions as a subject, use pronouns in the subjective form; when that noun functions as an object, use pronouns in the objective form.

 EXERCISE 3

In the following sentences, correct the usage of the italicized pronouns. If a pronoun choice is correct, circle the pronoun.

> *Example:* Anne told me it was Simon's fault; but between you and *I*, she's as much to blame as *him.*
>
> Anne told me it was Simon's fault; but between you and *me*, she's as much to blame as *he*. [Pronouns that follow a preposition must be objective case: thus, <u>between you and me</u>. The second part of

the comparison requires a subjective-case pronoun: <u>She is to blame</u> <u>as much as *he is to blame*.</u>]

1. It was *her* who wanted to leave early.
2. *She* is a better manager than *he*.
3. "*Who* do you want to reach?" asked the operator.
4. *He* is an employee in *whom* the firm has placed great trust.
5. Eric prepared a meal for both *you* and *he*.
6. *You* and *he* have been out of town for two months.
7. Maintaining discipline in the classroom is a problem *us* teachers face.
8. Maintaining discipline in the classroom is a problem facing *us* teachers.
9. *Whoever* drew the shortest straw would be the one to take our complaints to the principal.
10. Beth, *who* drew the shortest straw, cheerfully accepted her unpleasant task.
11. *She* being so willing and pleasant was an inspiration to *us* all.

9

Verbs

Verb forms convey three important messages that are the focus of this chapter: *tense*—an indication of when an action or state of being occurs; *mood*—your judgment as to whether a statement is a fact, a command, or an unreal or hypothetical condition contrary to fact; and *voice*—your emphasis on the actor of a sentence or on the object acted on.

VERB FORMS

 9a Using the principal parts of regular verbs consistently

All verbs other than *be* have two basic forms and three principal parts; these five

http://vweb1.hiway.co.uk/ei/intro.html
The English Institute's Elementary Grammar, with eleven sections on verbs.

forms and parts are the foundation for all the varied uses of verbs. A full dictionary entry may present these forms and parts: base form, present tense (*-s* form), past tense, past participle, and present participle.

The Principal Parts of Regular Verbs

Base form	Present tense (-s form)	Past tense	Past participle	Present participle
share	shares	shared	shared	sharing
start	starts	started	started	starting
climb	climbs	climbed	climbed	climbing

Most verbs in the dictionary are **regular** in that they follow the simple, predictable pattern shown in the box, in which the past tense and past participle are identical. (For regular verbs, only base forms appear in most dictionaries.)

1 Recognizing the forms of regular verbs

Alison *walks* to the theater.   Yesterday, she *walked* there.
She *has walked* often.   She *is walking* there now.

Base form + the -s form = present tense

The **base** (or infinitive) **form** of a verb—often called its **dictionary form**—is the base from which all changes are made. Use the base form of a verb with *no* ending for occasions when the action of a verb is present for plural nouns or for the personal pronouns *I, we, you,* or *they.*

> Alaska's Pacific mountains *create* a region of high peaks, broad valleys, and numerous island fjords.

The *-s form* of a verb (creates, tries, loves) occurs with third-person, singular subjects when an action is in the present. A verb's -s form (add *-s* or *-es* to a verb) is used in three instances: with the personal pronouns *he, she,* or *it;* with any noun that can be replaced by these pronouns; and with a number of indefinite pronouns (such as *something* or *no one*) that are often considered singular.

> Alaska's north slope *consists* of the plateaus and coastal regions north of the Brooks mountain range.

Difficulties with subject–verb agreement occur when a writer is unsure whether to use a verb's base form or -s form in a sentence. For a discussion of subject–verb agreement, see Chapter 10.

Past-tense form

The **past tense** of a verb indicates that an action has been completed in the past. The regular verbs follow a predictable pattern in forming the past tense by taking the suffix *-ed* or *-d.*

> Secretary of State William H. Seward *arranged* for the purchase of Alaska from Russia in 1867.

Irregular verbs follow no such pattern: their base forms change their root spelling to show the past tense (see 9b).

Two participle forms

For regular verbs, the form of the **past participle** is identical to that of the past tense. A verb's past participle is used in three ways: paired with *have,* the past participle functions as a main verb; paired with *be,* the past participle forms a passive construction; and paired with a noun or pronoun, the past participle functions as an adjective.

> The Crimean War *had depleted* [main verb] the tsar's treasury. With the treasury *depleted* [adjective], the tsar needed to raise money. Selling land to fill the treasury *was considered* [passive construction] a devil's bargain by some.

ESL NOTE Both past and present participles have uses as adjective modifiers, usually placed before the nouns or pronouns modified—as in *a confused speaker* or *a confusing speaker.* Note that while the past and present participles from this verb are related in meaning, they work in opposite directions on the word modified (see 44a-1).

Spotlight on Common Errors—VERBS

These are errors most commonly associated with verb use. For full explanations and suggested revisions, follow the cross-references to chapter sections.

TENSE ERRORS: Keep clear the time relationships among two or more verbs in closely linked clauses or sentences.

If you refer to *past events occurring at roughly the same time*, use past-tense verbs (see 9f):

Faulty

Tom *had traveled* where jobs *presented* themselves. [past perfect/past]

Tom *traveled* where jobs *had presented* themselves. [past/past perfect]

[The different tenses wrongly suggest that the events happened at different times.]

Revised

    past event   past event

Tom *traveled* where jobs *presented* themselves. [past/past]

[The sentence refers to events that occurred at the same time.]

If you refer to *past events occurring one before the other*, use the past tense for the more recent event and the past perfect for the earlier event.

Faulty

I *remembered* Mrs. Smith, who *showed* me kindness. [past/past]

[The tenses wrongly suggest that actions occurred at the same time.]

Revised

 later event   earlier event

I *remembered* Mrs. Smith, who *had shown* me kindness. [past/past perfect]

[Mrs. Smith's "showing" occurred before the remembering.]

BUT if a key word (such as *before* or *after*) establishes a clear time relation, then the past perfect form of the verb is not used.

earlier event   later event

I *was* unable to follow current events, *before* Mrs. Smith *showed* me how to read. [past/past]

Avoid abrupt tense shifts between closely linked sentences (see 16b).

Faulty tense shift

The problem started when Fred *forgot* his appointment. Today he *comes* in late again. [past/present]

Revised

The problem started when Fred *forgot* his appointment. Today he *came* in late again. [All action is in the past tense.]

ERRORS OF VERB FORM occur when writers confuse regular verbs with irregular verbs, the moods of verbs, and transitive verbs such as *lay* with intransitive verbs such as *lie*.

Regular/irregular: Know whether a verb is regular or irregular (see 9b).

Faulty	**Revised**
I begun the story.	I *began* the story.
I had drank three full glasses.	I *had drunk* three full glasses.

Mood: When writing about an event that is unreal or hypothetical, use a verb's subjunctive forms. Expressions such as *recommend, suggest,* and *it is important* signal an unreal or hypothetical event (see 9h).

Faulty	**Revised**
I recommend that Sarah builds a playhouse.	I recommend that Sarah *build* a playhouse.

In sentences expressing unreal conditions and beginning with *if,* use *were* in the first part of the sentence and *would* as a helping verb in the second part (see 9h).

Faulty	**Revised**
If it was any colder, the pipes will freeze.	*If it were* any colder, the pipes *would freeze.*

Transitive/intransitive: Use a transitive verb (*set, lay, raise*) to show an action transferred from an actor to an object. Use an intransitive verb (*sit, lie, rise*) to limit action to the subject (see 9d).

Faulty	**Revised**
Sit the books on the table.	*Set* the books on the table. [Transitive]
It hurts only when I set.	It hurts only when I *sit*. [Intransitive]
I think I'll lay down.	I think I'll *lie* down. [Intransitive]
Lie the blanket in the corner.	*Lay* the blanket in the corner. [Transitive]

The forms of *lie* and *lay* are particularly tricky. (See pages 206–207.)

Faulty	**Revised**
Yesterday, I laid down to rest.	Yesterday, I *lay* down to rest.
I had lain the book on the table.	I had *laid* the book on the table.

The **present participle,** the -*ing* form of the verb, has three uses: it functions as a main verb of a sentence and shows continuing action when paired with a form of *be* (*am, are, is, was, were*); it functions as an adjective when paired with a noun or pronoun; or it functions as a noun, in which case it is called a *gerund* (see 7a).

The *decimating* [gerund] of seal herds *was proceeding* [main verb] at an *alarming* [adjective] rate.

ESL NOTE   The role of a gerund in a sentence is determined by the verb being used. Certain verbs pair idiomatically with gerunds, as in *go swimming* or *enjoy swimming* (see 43e-2). Gerunds can be objects of certain prepositions that are idiomatically determined by the preceding verb: *I have reasons for coming* versus *I decided on walking.* Certain other verbs are paired idiomatically with the other verbal noun form, the infinitive (see 43e-2).

▶2   Revising nonstandard verb forms by using standard -*s* and -*ed* forms

Nonstandard	He walk home.
Revised	He walked home.

In rapid conversation, many people skip over -*s* and -*ed* endings. In some dialects the base (or infinitive) form of the verb is used in place of verbs with -*s* and -*ed* endings. Writers of standard academic English, however, need to observe the regular forms.

Nonstandard	She was *ask* to read this assignment. She *like* to stay up late, and she *be* still wide awake.
Revised	She was *asked* to read it. She *likes* to stay up late, and she *is* still wide awake. [Base forms have been replaced by standard verb forms with -*s* and -*ed* endings.]

Rapid speech often skips or "swallows" an -*ed* ending when it forms an "st" sound, as in two common verbal expressions, *used to* (meaning *accustomed to*) and *supposed to* (meaning *expected to*). Writers must be especially careful to supply the standard forms.

Nonstandard	We were *suppose to* be home early, but we are *use to* walking slowly.
Revised	We were *supposed to* be home early, but we are *used to* walking slowly.

The same speech patterns may also swallow final -*ed* endings in common modifiers (adjectives in past participle form) such as *prejudiced* or *iced.* These often need attention in proofreading.

Nonstandard	They were *prejudice* against drinking *ice* tea.
Revised	They were *prejudiced* against drinking *iced* tea.

▶ 9b   Learning the forms of irregular verbs

An irregular verb forms its past tense and past participle by altering the spelling of the base verb, as in *build/built.* A dictionary entry will show you when a verb is irregular.

Be

The most frequently used verb in our language, *be*, is also the only verb with more than five forms. It functions both as the main verb in a sentence and as a frequently used auxiliary verb (see 9c and 7a-3). The eight forms of *be* are shown in the box.

The Principal Parts of be		
Base form	*Present tense*	*Past tense*
(to) be	he, she, it *is* I *am* we, you, they *are*	he, she, it *was* I *was* we, you, they *were*
	Past participle	*Present participle*
	been	*being*

The following box contains the principal parts for a partial list of irregular verbs. Remember that the past participle is the form of the verb used with the auxiliary *have*. Without the auxiliary, it functions as an adjective.

Some Irregular Verb Forms		
Base form	*Past tense*	*Past participle*
bear	bore	borne, born
beat	beat	beaten
become	became	become
begin	began	begun
bend	bent	bent
bind	bound	bound
bite	bit	bit, bitten
bleed	bled	bled
blow	blew	blown
break	broke	broken
bring	brought	brought
build	built	built
burn	burned, burnt	burned, burnt
burst	burst	burst
buy	bought	bought
catch	caught	caught
choose	chose	chosen
cling	clung	clung
come	came	come
cost	cost	cost
cut	cut	cut
dig	dug	dug
dive	dove, dived	dived
do (does)	did	done

(continued)

▼

Some Irregular Verb Forms (continued)

Base form	Past tense	Past participle
draw	drew	drawn
drink	drank	drunk
drive	drove	driven
eat	ate	eaten
fall	fell	fallen
feed	fed	fed
feel	felt	felt
fight	fought	fought
find	found	found
flee	fled	fled
fling	flung	flung
fly	flew	flown
forbid	forbade, forbad	forbidden *or* forbid
forget	forgot	forgot *or* forgotten
freeze	froze	frozen
get	got	got, gotten
give	gave	given
go	went	gone
grow	grew	grown
hang*	hung	hung
have (has)	had	had
hear	heard	heard
hide	hid	hidden
hit	hit	hit
keep	kept	kept
know	knew	known
lead	led	led
leave	left	left
lend	lent	lent
lose	lost	lost
make	made	made
mean	meant	meant
pay	paid	paid
prove	proved	proved *or* proven
read	read	read
ride	rode	ridden
ring	rang	rung
run	ran	run
say	said	said
seek	sought	sought
send	sent	sent

(continued)

Hang as an irregular verb means to *suspend*. When *hang* means to *execute*, it is regular: *hang, hanged, hanged.*

Base form	Past tense	Past participle
see	saw	seen
shake	shook	shaken
shine†	shone	shone
sing	sang	sung
sink	sank	sunk
sleep	slept	slept
speak	spoke	spoken
spend	spent	spent
spring	sprang, sprung	sprung
stand	stood	stood
steal	stole	stolen
stick	stuck	stuck
strive	strove	striven
swear	swore	sworn
swim	swam	swum
swing	swung	swung
take	took	taken
teach	taught	taught
tear	tore	torn
tell	told	told
think	thought	thought
throw	threw	thrown
wake	woke, waked	waked, woken
wear	wore	worn
wind	wound	wound
wring	wrung	wrung
write	wrote	written

†*Shine* as an irregular verb means to *emit light*. When *shine* means to *polish*, it is regular: *shine, shined, shined.*

9c Using auxiliary verbs

An **auxiliary** (or helping) **verb** is combined with the base form of a verb or the present or past participle form to establish tense, mood, and voice in a sentence. This combination of verbs creates a **verb phrase**. The most frequently used auxiliaries are *be, have,* and *do. Be* functions as an auxiliary when it combines with the *-ing* form of a verb to create the progressive tenses (as in I *am going*). *Have* functions as an auxiliary when it combines with the past participle form of a verb to create the perfect tenses (as in I *have gone*). *Do* functions as an auxiliary when it combines with the base form of a verb to form questions, to show emphasis, and to show negation. (*Do* you care? I *do* care. I *don't* care.)

ESL NOTE For illustrations of the varied uses for auxiliary verbs in English, see 46c–d.

Using Auxiliary Verbs   **203**

▶ **1 Use modal auxiliaries to refine meaning.**

The producers *should* agree to this.   They *must* agree.
They *might* agree to these terms.

When paired with the base form of a verb, a **modal auxiliary** expresses urgency, obligation, likelihood, possibility, and so on: *can/could, may, might, must, ought to, should, would.* Unlike the auxiliaries *be, have,* and *do,* most of these modal auxiliaries do not change form. They follow singular or plural subjects in the first, second, or third person. Modal auxiliaries can follow the pronouns *I, we, you, he, she, one, it, they.* Observe how meaning in a sentence changes depending on the choice of modal auxiliary:

I must resign.   I ought to resign.   I would resign.
I could resign.   I can resign.   I might resign.

Modal auxiliaries can combine with other auxiliaries to create complex verbal phrases that require careful use.

I ought to have resigned.   I might have been resigning.

The auxiliaries *will* and *shall* establish the future tense.

When shall I resign?   She will resign then.

Avoid careless of usage when *have* is part of past tenses used with modals.

Rapid speaking sometimes forms contractions with past tenses using common modals such as *could, would, should, must, may, might;* thus, *would have* can become *would've* or *might have* can become *might've.* Such colloquial usages can translate into sounds like "would of" or even "woulda," "might of," or "mighta," leading some into a careless habit of writing *of* when *have* is the form intended.

Careless   She should *of* told me about it; then I might *of* had time to avoid it.

Revised   She should *have* told me about it; then I might *have* had time to avoid it.

ESL NOTE   For illustrations of how modal auxiliaries affect word order and verb constructions, see 46d.

▶ **2 Revise nonstandard auxiliaries by using standard forms of *be.***

Faulty   She going to class.

Revised   She is going to class.

Some dialects form present-tense auxiliary constructions with variations on the base form of *be.* For written academic English, these forms must be revised.

Nonstandard   She *be* singing beautifully. [The base form of *be* is a nonstandard usage here. The -*s* form of the verb is needed.]

Nonstandard   She singing a beautiful melody. [The *be* form has been dropped.]

Revised   She *is* singing a beautiful melody. [The base form of *be* in the auxiliary has been replaced by the standard -*s* form.]

▶ **EXERCISE 1**

Identify the main verb and any auxiliary verb associated with it in the sentences that follow.

>   *Example:* Peru presents many contrasts to a traveler. (The verb is *presents*.)

1. Peru has both modern cities, such as Lima, and ancient ones, such as Cuzco.
2. Anthropologists believe Cuzco to be the oldest continuously inhabited city in the Western Hemisphere.
3. In fact, the city's population is actually growing.
4. Travelers have long admired the city's massive walls.
5. Craftsmen began work on the cathedral in 1659 and finished nearly one hundred years later.
6. The Pizzeria Giorgio Gourmet exemplifies the old and the new.
7. The restaurant serves a thoroughly modern food—pizza; yet the restaurant incorporates into its architecture an Inca-built wall.

EXERCISE 2

In the sentences that follow, use the appropriate form of the irregular verb.

>   *Example:* Over the past five years, nearly every woman in our therapy
>   groups [confess] to a negative body image. [confessed]

>   Most of the women we interviewed had negative body images, not because they [have] _____1_____ homely bodies but because they [see] _____2_____ themselves incorrectly. Their images of their bodies [be] _____3_____ distorted. In the cases of some women, this distortion was so extreme that their bodies [become] _____4_____ caricatures. Many of the women also [feel] _____5_____ to some extent alienated from their own bodies. This estrangement is probably inevitable, given the fact that women have been [teach] _____6_____ to perceive the mind as divorced

▶   from the body.

▶ **9d** | **Using transitive and intransitive verbs**

Action verbs are classified as *transitive* and *intransitive*. A **transitive verb** (marked with the abbreviation **tr.** in the dictionary) transfers an action from a subject to an object; the action of an **intransitive verb** is limited to the subject of a sentence.

▶**1 Distinguish between verbs that take direct objects and those that do not.**

Sharon studied.   Sharon studied her lecture notes.

A large number of verbs regularly take a direct object and are always transitive; others never take an object and are always intransitive.

Transitive   The politician kissed the baby. [The transitive verb *kissed* transfers action from *politician* to *baby*.]

Intransitive   The politician smiled. [An action is performed, but no object is acted on.]

Many verbs can have both a transitive and an intransitive sense. Such "two-way" verbs will take a direct object or not, depending on their use.

Intransitive   She runs every day. [The verb takes no object.]

Transitive   She runs a big business. [The verb has changed meaning and now takes an object.]

ESL NOTE   Note that a transitive verb is the *only* type that can be made passive (see 9g); neither intransitive nor most linking verbs can take a passive form in modern English. For specifics on transitive verbs and passive constructions, see 46a-1.

▶ **2   Avoid confusion between the verbs *sit/set, lie/lay, rise/raise.***

Set the books on the table.
It hurts only when I *sit.*
I think I'll *lie* down for a rest.
Lay the blanket in the corner.

Difficulties in distinguishing between transitive and intransitive verbs lead to misuse of *sit/set, lie/lay,* and *rise/raise.* The forms of these verbs are shown in the box on page 207. Because the meaning of the verbs in each pairing is somewhat similar, the verbs are sometimes used interchangeably in speech. In formal writing, however, careful distinctions should be maintained: the first verb in each pair is intransitive—it takes no object—while the second verb is transitive.

Sit is normally an intransitive verb; its action is limited to the subject.

adverb
You sit *on the bench.*

Set is a transitive verb. It transfers action to an object, which must be present in the sentence.

object   adverb
You set *the papers on the bench.*

Lie is an intransitive verb; its action is limited to the subject.

adverb
I lie *on the couch.*

Lay is a transitive verb. It transfers action to an object, which must be present in the sentence.

object   adverb
I lay *the pillow on the couch.*

Rise is an intransitive verb; its action is limited to the subject.

adverb
I rise *in the morning.*

Raise is a transitive verb. It transfers action to an object, which must be present in the sentence.

object   adverb
I raise *the flag each morning.*

		The Principal Parts of *sit/set, lie/lay,* and *rise/raise*		
Base form	Present tense	Past tense	Past participle	Present participle
sit	sits	sat	sat	sitting
set	sets	set	set	setting
lie	lies	lay	lain	lying
lay	lays	laid	laid	laying
rise	rises	rose	risen	rising
raise	raises	raised	raised	raising

EXERCISE 3

Choose the appropriate form of *sit/set, lie/lay,* or *rise/raise* in these sentences.

> *Example:* A squirrel was (*sit/set*) _____ on a picnic table.
> A squirrel was *sitting* on a picnic table.

1. A man walked by and (*sit/set*) _____ a newspaper on a nearby table.
2. He then (*sit/set*) _____ down and unfolded the paper.
3. From one pocket he produced a tomato, which he (*lie/lay*) _____ on the paper.
4. From another pocket came a salt shaker, which he (*rise/raise*) _____ ceremoniously.
5. The squirrel (*rise/raise*) _____ at the scent of food.

EXERCISE 4

In the following sentences, fill in the blanks with the appropriate form of the verb indicated in parentheses.

> *Example:* The First World War _____ (begin) as an Old World War.
> The First World War *began* as an Old World War.

1. Everything about the war expressed the world that Americans _____ (hope) they had _____ (leave) behind.
2. That Old World _____ (be) a battlefield of national ambitions, religious persecutions, and language barriers.
3. European armies had _____ (fight) over whether a nation's boundary should _____ (be) on one side or the other of a narrow river.
4. Old World monarchs had _____ (transfer) land from one flag to another, _____ (barter) people as if they _____ (be) mere real estate.
5. In the 1800s, the English, French, and German empires _____ (expand) across the globe.

▶ **9e**   Understanding the uses of verb tenses

A verb's **tense** indicates when an action has occurred or when a subject exists in a given state. There are three basic tenses in English: *past, present,* and *future.* Each has a **perfect** form, which indicates a completed action; each has a **progressive** form, which indicates ongoing action; and each has a **perfect progressive** form, which indicates ongoing action that will be completed at some definite time. The time relationships among these tenses are charted in the box on pages 212–213.

▶ **I**   The varied uses of the present tense

> **Present:** I start the engine.
> **Present perfect:** I have started the engine.
> **Present progressive:** I am starting the engine.
> **Present perfect progressive:** I have been starting the engine.

The simple present tense

A verb's base form is the present-tense form for first- and second-person subjects, singular or plural (*I, we, you* play), as well as plural third-person subjects (*they* play). A present-tense verb for a third-person, singular noun or pronoun ends with the suffix -*s* (*he* plays). The **simple present tense** indicates an action taking place in the writer's present time: *You see these words.* But the present tense in combination with other time-specific expressions (such as *after, before, when,* or *next week*) indicates other time references, such as ongoing action or future action (see 9f-1).

> After I *arrive,* they can announce where I *am* staying,
> Before I *depart,* my bags should be packed.
> Tomorrow we *walk* to school.
> Next week, Nelson *dances* in New York.

The historical present tense

The so-called **historical present tense** is used when referring to actions in an already existing work: a book, a report, an essay, a movie, a television show, an article, and so on. Action in an existing work is always present to a reader or viewer.

> In *The Songlines,* Bruce Chatwin *explores* the origins and meanings of Aboriginal "walkabouts" in Australia.
> In *Blade Runner,* Harrison Ford *plays* a world-weary detective whose job it *is* to disable renegade, humanlike robots.

Additionally, the present tense is used to express information that, according to current scientific knowledge or accepted wisdom, is true or likely to be true.

> Evidence *indicates* that Alzheimer's patients *show* a decrease in an important brain transmitter substance.
> Absence *makes* the heart grow fonder.
> She *is* an excellent dentist.

The present tense is also used to indicate a generalized time or a customary, repeated action.

Time *flies.*

Each Tuesday I *walk* to the bakery.

The present perfect tense

The **present perfect tense** is formed with the auxiliary *have* or *has* and the verb's past participle. This tense indicates an action completed at an indefinite past time.

I *have returned* and she *has left.*

The present perfect tense also indicates an action that, although begun at some past time, continues to have an impact in the present.

He *has* recently *given* support to museums.

ESL NOTE   Expressions for duration of time, such as *since* and *for,* require the use of the perfect tense.

Faulty   I *was* here *since* four o'clock and *waited* here *for* many hours. [The simple past is not used with these expressions showing duration of time.]

Revised   I *have been* here *since* four o'clock and *have waited* here for many hours. [The present perfect is used.]

In constructions that indicate a specific past time using phrases or clauses (with *when, after, before, while*), the simple past is required.

Faulty   I *have met* him at eight o'clock and I *have left* after he arrived. [These expressions for a specific past time or event do not use the perfect.]

Revised   I *met* him at eight o'clock, and I *left* after he arrived.

For more information on the use of tenses with time expressions, see 46b-2.

The present progressive tense

The **present progressive tense** is formed with the auxiliary *is, am,* or *are* and the verb's present participle. This tense indicates a present, ongoing action that may continue into the future.

She *is considering* a move to Alaska.

ESL NOTE   Certain verbs, such as *have,* are generally not used in a progressive tense, except with some idioms: *having a good time; having a baby* (see 46b-1).

The present perfect progressive tense

The **present perfect progressive tense** is formed with the auxiliary *has been* or *have been* and the verb's present participle. This tense indicates an action that began in the past, is continuing in the present, and may continue into the future.

She *has been studying* English for a year.

▶2 **The past and future tenses**

PAST TENSES

Past: I started the engine.
> **Past perfect:** I had started the engine.
> **Past progressive:** I was starting the engine.
> **Past perfect progressive:** I had been starting the engine.

The simple past tense

Regular verbs form the **simple past tense** by adding *-d* or *-ed* to the infinitive of the verb; irregular verbs form the past tense in less predictable ways and are best memorized or verified in a dictionary. The simple past tense indicates an action completed at a definite time in the past.

> Mothers *found* themselves unable to give their daughters accurate and positive perceptions about their bodies, since they themselves *were* preoccupied with faulty body images of their own.

The past perfect tense

The **past perfect tense** is formed with the auxiliary *had* and the verb's past participle. This tense indicates a past action that has occurred prior to another action.

> By the time a girl reached puberty, she *had* already *developed* a negative body image.

The past progressive tense

The **past progressive tense** is formed with the auxiliary *was* or *were* and the verb's present participle. This tense indicates an ongoing action conducted—and completed—in the past.

> In the 70s women *were striving* for a thin, boyish figure.

The past perfect progressive tense

The **past perfect progressive tense** is formed with the auxiliary *had been* and the verb's present participle. This tense indicates a past, ongoing action completed prior to some other past action.

> During the three decades preceding the 70s, however, women *had been trying* to project a more full-figured look.

FUTURE TENSES

Future: I will start the engine.
> **Future perfect:** I will have started the engine.
> **Future progressive:** I will be starting the engine.
> **Future perfect progressive:** I will have been starting the engine.

The future tense

The **future tense** consists of the base form of the verb, along with the auxiliary *will* for all nouns and pronouns. This tense indicates an action or state of being that will begin in the future. In very formal writing, the first person *I* and *we* have traditionally taken the auxiliary *shall*; increasingly, this word is reserved for opening (first-person) questions implying obligation: "Shall I?"

> Even if a woman does match the current ideal body image, she still must realize that she *will* not *fit* the mold forever.

ESL NOTE   English has no simple future tense but expresses future events with a variety of constructions, including some uses of the present tense (described above), as well as auxiliaries and such expressions as *going to* or *about to* (see 46b-3).

The future perfect tense

The **future perfect tense** is formed with the verb's past participle and the auxiliary *will have*. This tense indicates an action occurring in the future, prior to some other action.

> By the time many girls reach the age of 16, they *will have spent* hundreds of dollars on such products as reducing aids, diet foods, fitness equipment, and self-help manuals.

The future progressive tense

The **future progressive tense** is formed with the auxiliary *will be* (or *shall be*) and the verb's present participle. This tense indicates an ongoing action in the future.

> Many young women believe that if they do not maintain a standard of physical loveliness, they *will be enduring* loneliness, ostracism, and the contempt of others for the rest of their lives.

The future perfect progressive tense

The **future perfect progressive tense** is formed with the auxiliary *will have been* and the verb's present participle. This tense indicates an ongoing action in the future that will occur before some specified future time.

> By the year 2005, many women born in the early 1960s *will have been dieting* for as long as 30 years.

▶ **9f**   Sequencing verb tenses

Although a sentence will always have a main verb located in its independent clause, it may have other verbs as well: a complex sentence will have a second verb in its dependent clause, and a sentence with an infinitive or participle (verb forms that function as adjectives, adverbs, and nouns) will also have at least two verbs or verb forms. Since every verb shows tense, any sentence with more than one verb may indicate actions that occur at different times. Unless the sequence of these actions is precisely set, confusion will result.

Unclear   Before I *leave*, I *reported* on my plans. [The logic of this sentence suggests that two events (one in each clause) are related, but the time sequencing of the events—one future, the other past—makes the relationship impossible.]

Clear	Before I *leave*, I *will report* on my plans. [The two actions take place in the future, one action earlier than the other.]
Clear	Before I *left*, I *reported* on my plans. [The two actions take place in the past, one action earlier than the other.]

Time Line of Verb Tenses

Past	Present	Future

||||||||||||||||||||||||||||||||||||||| **Simple present** (She *walks* and *eats*; I *walk.*)
Action takes place in the writer's current time.

||||||||||||||||||||||||||||||||||||| **Historical/habitual present** (He *walks*; we *eat* every day.)
Action is customary or general, or action occurs in a text or story.

||||||||||||||||||||||||||||||||||||||| **Present progressive** (She *is walking*; I *am eating.*)
Action is in progress now and may continue into the future.

|||||||||||||||||||||||||||||||||||||||||||||||||||||||||| **Simple present** with time word (He *walks* tomorrow or tonight.)
Action is predicted in the future.

||||||||||||||||||||||||||||||||||||||||||||||||||||||||||| **Present progressive** with future time word (She *is walking* tomorrow or tonight.)
Action is definitely planned for the future.

|||||||||||||||||||||||||||| **Present perfect** (She *has walked*; I *have eaten.*)
Action was completed or was repeated at an indefinite time in the past.

|||||||||||||||||||||||||||||||| **Present perfect** with *since* or *for* + time word (She *has walked for* an hour; he *has* not *eaten since* noon.)
Action began in the past and has continued for a specific duration.

|||||||||||||||||||||||||||||| **Present perfect progressive** often with *since* or *for* + time word (I *have been walking* since morning; he *has been eating* for an hour.)
Action began in the past, is continuing, and may continue into the future.

||||||||||||||||||||||||| **Simple past** (I *walked* yesterday; he *ate* this morning.)
Action began and ended at a specific time in the past.

|||||||||||||||||||| **(X) Past progressive** (She *was walking* until noon; he *was eating* until 7A.M.)
Action was ongoing and was completed in the past.

|||||||||||| **(X) Past perfect** (She *had eaten* before that; we *had walked* out before it ended.)
Action occurred in the past prior to another action.

||||||||||||||||| **(X) Past perfect progressive** (He *had been walking* for days before their return.)
Action was ongoing and was completed prior to an action completed in the past.

Past	Present	Future

IIIIIIIIIIIIIIIIIIIIIIIIIIIIIIIIIIIIIIIIIIIIIIIIIIIIIIIIIIIIIIIIIIIIIIII **Future** Use *shall/will* + base form.
(We *will walk*.)
Action is intended to occur in the future.

IIIIIIIIIIIIIIIIIIIIIIIIIIIIIIIIIIIIIIIIIIIIIIIIIIIIIIIIIIIIIIIIIIII **Predicted future**
Use *be* + *going to* + base. (He *is going to* walk.)
Action is predicted to occur in the future.

IIIIIIIIIIIIIIIIIIIIIIIIIIIIIIIIIIIIIIIIIIIIIIIIIIIIIIIIIIIIIIIII **Future progressive**
Use *shall/will* + *be* + present participle. (She *will be eating* and *walking*.)
Action is expected to be ongoing in the future.

IIIIIIIIIIIIIIIIIIIIIIIIIIIIIIIIIIIIIIIIIIIIIIIIIIIIIIIIIIIIIIIII **(X) Future perfect**
Use *will* + *have* + past participle.
(We *will have eaten* before you do.)
Action is expected to occur prior to some other action in the future.

IIIIIIIIIIIIIIIIIIIIIIIIIIIIIIIIIIIIIIIIIIIIIIIIIIIIIIIIIIIIIIIII **(X) Future perfect progressive**
Use *will* + *have* + *been* + present participle. (I *will have been eating* before you go.)
Action is ongoing and is expected to occur prior to some other action in the future.

(*X* represents a definite time.)

I Sequence the events in complex sentences with care.

Jones *attacked* Representative Kaye, who *had proposed* the amendment.
Jones *has spent* months preparing for the trial that *will begin* next week.

A complex sentence joins an independent clause with a dependent clause, forming a close relationship between events described with two verbs. Look at the logical relationship of time sequence in the two clauses, and check the Time Line of Verb Tenses chart to clarify the time relationships you want to show. Choose verb tenses that clarify that relationship, and make a decision about tenses as shown in the Critical Decisions box on page 214.

ESL NOTE Indirect quotation or reported speech is a common case of tense sequence involving two verbs. A main verb, such as *says*, makes the report while another makes the indirect quotation in a *that . . .* clause—often occurring at a different time from the report: *She says that she will go.* When one event occurs before another, the verb sequence requires careful attention (see 46b-4).

CRITICAL DECISIONS

Challenge your sentences: Maintaining clear time relationships among closely linked verbs

If you refer to *past events occurring at roughly the same time*, use past-tense verbs:

Faulty

Tom *had traveled* where jobs *presented* themselves. [past perfect/past]
[The different tenses wrongly suggest that the events happened at different times.]

Revised

   past event   past event
Tom *traveled* where jobs *presented* themselves. [past/past]

If you refer to *past events occurring one before the other*, use the past tense for the more recent event and the past perfect for the earlier event.

Faulty

I *remembered* Mrs. Smith, who *showed* me kindness. [past/past]
[The tenses wrongly suggest that actions occurred at the same time.]

Revised

   later event   earlier event
I *remembered* Mrs. Smith, who *had shown* me kindness. [past/past perfect]

BUT if a key word (such as *before* or *after*) establishes a clear time relationship, then the past perfect form of the verb is not used.

earlier event   later event
I *was* unable to follow current events *before* Mrs. Smith *showed* me how to read.
[past/past]

2 Choose verb tense in an infinitive phrase based on your choice of verb in the main clause.

Ellen hoped to get rich.   To have voted was critical.

An **infinitive phrase** begins with the word *to* placed before a verb such as *see, want, watch, wish, need, go, like,* and *hope.* A present infinitive shows an action that occurs at the same time as or later than the action of the main verb. In the following sentences, the main verb is underlined.

Many critics rejected Roland Jaffe's film adaptation of *The Scarlet Letter.* After much pre-release publicity, critics <u>arrived</u> *to see* a screen version that took many liberties with Hawthorne's original story. [*To see* shows an action at the same time as *arrived.*]

Purists anticipating the movie evidently <u>expected</u> *to see* a more faithful adaptation. [*To see* shows a possible action in the future, later than *expected.*]

A perfect infinitive is formed by placing the auxiliary *have* between the word *to* and the past participle of the verb. A perfect infinitive phrase shows an action that occurs before the action of the main verb.

> *To have played* the role of Hester Prynne <u>presented</u> actress Demi Moore with an opportunity to portray the wrongness of censoring women who have something powerful to communicate. [The opportunity *presented* to Demi Moore is past; her having *played* the role of Hester occurred earlier than, and created, the opportunity.]

ESL NOTE Certain transitive verbs take an infinitive or infinitive phrase as their object (as in the examples above), while other verbs (such as *enjoy*) take a gerund as object (see 43e-2).

▶3 Choose the verb tense of a participle based on your choice of verb in the main clause.

> *Arriving* early, the speaker <u>had</u> time to relax.
> *Having* thoroughly *studied* the matter, the judge <u>made</u> her decision.
> *Impressed* with the novel, Marie <u>recommended</u> it to friends.

Participles, past and present, function as adjectives in a sentence. A participle in its present (*-ing*) form indicates an action that occurs at the same time as the action of the sentence's main verb. The main verb in each of the following examples is underlined once, and the participial phrase is underlined twice.

> <u>*Starting with a few unmemorable roles in a few forgettable films,*</u> Moore <u>worked</u> in relative obscurity for several years. She quickly built momentum, however, with her work in *Blame It on Rio* and *St. Elmo's Fire.* [Moore's efforts at the beginning of her career occurred at the same time as her working in obscurity. Both actions occur in the past.]

A participle's present perfect form (the past participle preceded by the auxiliary *having*) shows an action that occurs before that of the main verb.

> <u>*Having proven her versatility in such films as*</u> Ghost, A Few Good Men, *and* Disclosure, Moore <u>turned</u> to the role of Hester because she admired that character's courage. [Moore played roles in these earlier movies before she took on the role of Hester in *The Scarlet Letter.*]

A participle in its past form (the base form + *-ed* for regular verbs) shows an action that occurs at the same time as or earlier than the action of the main verb.

> <u>*Hauled from place to place during a childhood that saw her family move 48 times in 13 years,*</u> Moore <u>formed</u> strong, clear, and steady goals for her career and her personal life. [The memory of moving existed for Moore both before and during her efforts to form goals for her career and personal life.]

▶ EXERCISE 5

In each sentence that follows, identify the tense of the italicized verb. Then choose the appropriate tense for subsequent verbs in each sentence.

> *Example:* Personality *is* the unique but stable set of characteristics and behavior that _____ (set) each individual apart from all others.
>
> *is* present tense   *sets* present tense

1. Most people *have accepted* the view that human beings _____ (possess) specific traits that _____ (be) fairly constant over time.

2. You *may be* surprised _____ (learn) that until recently a heated debate _____ (exist) in the behavioral sciences over the definition's accuracy.

3. On one side of this debate *were* scientists who _____ (contend) that people _____ (do) not _____ (possess) lasting traits.

4. According to these researchers (whom we *will term* the "anti-personality" camp), behavior _____ (be) shaped largely by external factors.

5. On the other side of the controversy *were* scientists who _____ (hold), equally strongly, that stable traits _____ (do) exist.

VOICE

▶ 9g   Using the active and passive voices

Voice refers to the emphasis a writer gives to the actor in a sentence or to the object acted upon. Because only transitive verbs (see 9d) transfer action from an actor to an object, these verbs exhibit the active and passive voices. The **active voice** emphasizes the actor of a sentence.

> Brenda scored the winning goal.

> Thomas played the violin.

In each case, an actor, or agent, is *doing* something. In a **passive-voice** sentence, the object acted on is emphasized.

> The winning goal was scored by Brenda.

> The violin was played by Thomas.

The emphasis on the object of a passive-voice sentence is made possible by a rearrangement of words—the movement of the object, which normally follows a verb, to the first position in a sentence. A passive-voice construction also requires use of the verb *be (is, are, was, were, has been, have been)* and the preposition *by.*

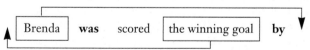

| Brenda | **was** | scored | the winning goal | **by** |

The winning goal was scored by Brenda.

In a further transformation of the active-voice sentence, you can make the original actor/subject disappear altogether by deleting the prepositional phrase.

> The winning goal was scored.

▶ I   Use a strong active voice for clear, direct assertions.

Stronger   A guidance counselor recommended the book.

Weaker   A book was recommended.

In active-voice sentences, people or other agents *do* things. Active-voice sentences attach ownership to actions and help create a direct, lively attitude between the subject and the reader. By contrast, passive-voice sentences are inherently wordy and reliant on the weak verb *be*. Unintended overuse of the passive voice makes prose dull. Unless you have a specific reason for choosing the passive voice (see the following discussion), use the active voice.

You can make a passive-voice sentence active by restoring a subject/verb sequence. Rewording will eliminate both the preposition *by* and the form of *be*. Note that if an actor of a passive-voice sentence is not named, you will need to provide a name.

Passive (weak)	In 1858, Stephen Douglas was challenged to a series of historic debates. [The "challenger" is not named.]
Active (stronger)	In 1858, Abraham Lincoln challenged Stephen Douglas to a series of historic debates.
Passive (weak)	The Senate race was won by Douglas, but a national reputation was established by Lincoln.
Active (stronger)	Douglas won the Senate race, but Lincoln established a national reputation.

ACROSS THE CURRICULUM

Using Active Verbs in Legal Writing

Richard H. Weisberg, professor of law at Benjamin N. Cardozo School of Law (Yeshiva University), advises lawyers to use active-voice verbs in their writing:*

To reinvigorate the active verbal juices flowing through even the most seasoned legal writer, [s/]he must periodically recite five simple sentences.

1. "I love the law."
2. "The law needs good writers."
3. "Good writers seek brevity."
4. "Brevity thrives where strong verbs abound."
5. "I love strong verbs."

"Love" is a strong verb. So is any verb that in appropriate situations ties together the subject of a sentence with the object it is affecting. For example, "John loves Mary" ties together John and Mary through a verb describing as strongly as possible John's action in her regard. Similarly, in a more legalistic mode, "The Price-Anderson waiver of defenses clause benefits the claimants in this action" is a good, active sentence. The verb, "benefits," links the subject to the object. [. . .]

The language redounds with vividly descriptive words of action. When the legal writer finds such a verb and uses it to link [a] subject directly to an object, the sentence is almost inevitably strong.*

*Richard H. Weisberg, *When Lawyers Write* (Boston: Little, Brown, 1987), 61–63.

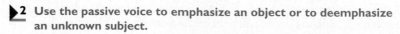

2 Use the passive voice to emphasize an object or to deemphasize an unknown subject.

Object emphasized   The funding goal was reached earlier than expected.

Actor(s) emphasized   We reached the funding goal earlier than expected.

While you should generally prefer the active voice for making direct statements, you will find the passive voice indispensable on two occasions: to emphasize an object and to deemphasize an unknown subject/actor.

Emphasize an object with a passive construction.

When the subject/actor of a sentence is relatively unimportant compared with what is acted on, use the passive voice both to deemphasize the subject/actor and to emphasize the object. The passive voice will shift the subject/actor to a prepositional phrase at a later position in the clause. You may then delete the phrase.

Active	We require twelve molecules of water to provide twelve atoms of oxygen.
Passive (actor retained)	Twelve molecules of water are required by us to provide twelve atoms of oxygen.
Passive (actor deleted)	Twelve molecules of water are required to provide twelve atoms of oxygen.

Deemphasize an unknown subject with the passive voice.

You may deemphasize or delete an *unknown* subject/actor by using the passive voice. Instead of writing an indefinite subject/actor (such as *someone* or *people*) into a sentence, use the passive voice to shift the subject/actor to a prepositional phrase. You may then delete the phrase.

Active	People mastered the use of fire some 400,000 years ago.
Passive (actor retained)	The use of fire was mastered by people some 400,000 years ago.
Passive (actor deleted)	The use of fire was mastered some 400,000 years ago.

▶ **EXERCISE 6**

Change the passive-voice sentences that follow to the active voice, and change active-voice sentences to passive. Invent a subject if need be for the active-voice sentences.

> *Example:* A trillion dollars will be claimed by retirement plans in the next few years. [The passive voice involves the verb *will be claimed*.]
>
> Retirement plans will claim a trillion dollars in the next few years. [The verb *will claim* is expressed in the active voice.]

1. Nearly 18.5 million Americans maintain 401(k) retirement plans.
2. The 401(k) plan is recommended by economists, politicians, and investment advisers as a key to a comfortable retirement.

3. In practice, however, the 401(k) is often mismanaged by the planholder's employer.
4. Some workers have voiced their concerns about the structuring and funds allocation of their 401(k)s.
5. As it turns out, the company executives who choose 401(k) plans for their employees do not investigate alternative, possibly better plans.

MOOD

▶ **9h** Understanding the uses of mood

The **mood** of a verb indicates the writer's judgment as to whether a statement is a fact, a command, or an unreal or hypothetical condition contrary to fact. In the **indicative mood,** a writer states a fact, opinion, or question. Most of our writing and speech is in the indicative mood.

The mayor has held office for eight years. [fact]

The mayor is not especially responsive. [opinion]

Did you vote for the mayor? [question]

In the **imperative mood,** a writer gives a command, the subject of which is "you," the person being addressed. In this book, for example, the imperative addresses readers with specific guidelines for writing or making revisions. An imperative uses the verb in its base form. Often, the subject of a command is omitted, but occasionally it is expressed directly.

Follow me!

Do not touch that switch.

Don't you touch that switch!

By using the **subjunctive mood,** a writer shows that he or she believes an action or situation is unreal or hypothetical. With a subjunctive verb, a writer can also make a recommendation or express a wish or requirement, usually preceded by such a verb construction as *recommend, suggest, insist, it is necessary,* or *it is important.* The **present subjunctive** uses the base form (infinitive) of the verb for all subjects.

I recommend that he *develop* his math skills before applying.

I recommend that they *develop* their skills.

The **past subjunctive** uses the past-tense form of the verb—or, in the case of *be*—the form *were.*

If management *assumed* traveling costs, the team would be happier.

He wished he *were* four inches taller.

ESL NOTE   *If* constructions require a subjunctive verb form only when they express a condition that is considered unreal or hypothetical. Section 46b-5 demonstrates differences between real and unreal conditions with *if* constructions.

▶**I** **Use the subjunctive mood with certain *if* constructions.**

If I owned a dog, I would walk it every day.

When an *if* clause expresses an unreal or hypothetical condition, use the subjunctive mood. In a subjunctive *if* construction, the modal auxiliary *would, could, might,* or *should* is used in the main clause. (See 9c-1 for a discussion of modals.)

Faulty   If Tom was more considerate, he would have called. [Clearly, Tom was not considerate (he did not call), and so the indicative or "factual" mood is at odds with the meaning of the sentence.]

Subjunctive   If Tom *were* more considerate, he would have called.

Subjunctive   If I *were* elected, I might raise taxes.

Note: When an *if* construction is used to establish a cause-and-effect relationship, the writer assumes that the facts presented in a sentence either are true or could very possibly be true; therefore, the writer uses an indicative ("factual") mood with normal subject–verb agreement.

Faulty   If I were late, start without me.

Revised   If I am late, start without me. [The lateness is assumed to be a likely or possible fact.]

▶**2** **Use the subjunctive mood with *as if* and *as though* constructions.**

He dances as though he were weightless.

When an *as if* or *as though* construction sets up a purely hypothetical comparison that attempts to explain or characterize, use the subjunctive mood.

Faulty   She swims as if she *was* part fish. [But since the speaker knows she is not, the indicative ("factual") mood is inconsistent.]

Revised   She swims as if she *were* part fish.

Subjunctive   He writes quickly, as though he *were* running out of time. [The sentence assumes that he is not running out of time.]

▶**3** **Revise to eliminate auxiliary *would* or *could* in subjunctive clauses with *if, as if,* or *as though.***

Clear   If I had listened, I would have avoided the problem.

Confusing   If I would have listened, I would have avoided the problem.

In subjunctive constructions like those shown previously, the modal auxiliary verbs *would, could,* or *should* may appear in the main clause to help indicate that its action is unreal or conditional. The auxiliaries *would* and *could* cannot appear in the *if* clause, however, since this creates a kind of "double conditional"; these auxiliaries must be replaced with the appropriate subjunctive form.

Faulty   If the mate at the wheel *would have* been alerted, the oil spill would have been avoided.

Revised   If the mate at the wheel *had* been alerted, the oil spill would have been avoided.

Faulty   He could have acted as though he *could have* seen the reef.

Revised   He could have acted as though he *had* seen it.

▶**4 Use the subjunctive mood with a *that* construction.**

I think it is important that he arrive early.

Use the subjunctive mood with subordinate *that* constructions expressing a requirement, request, urging, belief, wish, recommendation, or doubt. In each of these constructions, the word *that* may be omitted.

The rules require that we *be* present.

I wish that I *were* a painter.

We recommend that he *accept* the transfer.

ESL NOTE   *That* clauses can occur in a variety of sentences not requiring a subjunctive form. See 46b-6 for rules in constructions involving *wish that*.

▶ **EXERCISE 7**

Use the subjunctive mood, as appropriate, in revising the sentences that follow.

> *Example:* Some experts claim that unmarried couples living together would be happier if they would make finances and spending an explicit topic of discussion and negotiation.
>
> Some experts claim that unmarried couples living together would be happier if they made finances and spending an explicit topic of discussion and negotiation.

1. The couples often wish that there are more precedents to help them decide who pays for what.
2. If each partner communicated his or her expectations to the other, there are fewer squabbles over "your crackers" and "my paper towels."
3. Some experts recommend that each partner keeps a separate bank account but also open a joint checking account to cover household expenses.
4. Experts suggest that each party should be fully informed about the discretionary spending of the other.
5. One specialist, in her book *Financial Planning for Couples*, recommends that the partner with the higher income pays a proportionately higher share of joint household expenses.

10

Agreement

Agreement is a term that describes two significant relationships in a sentence: between a subject and a verb and between a pronoun and an antecedent. These elements occur in pairs and require you to make decisions about every sentence you write. The subject of a sentence must be paired with a verb to make a complete statement. A subject and its verb are either *both* singular or *both* plural.

A pronoun derives meaning from its relation to the noun, or antecedent, that it renames. A pronoun and its antecedent are also either *both* singular or *both* plural.

SUBJECT–VERB AGREEMENT

Subjects and verbs must agree in both number and person. The term **number** indicates whether a noun is singular (denoting one person, place, or thing) or plural (denoting more than one). The term **person** identifies the subject of a sentence as the same person who is speaking (the first person), someone who is spoken to (the second person), or someone or something being spoken about (the third person). Pronouns differ according to person.

	First-person subject	*Second-person subject*	*Third-person subject*
Singular	I	you	he, she, it
Plural	we	you	they

Agreement between a verb and first- or second-person pronoun subject does not vary. The pronouns *I*, *we*, and *you* take verbs *without* the letter *s*.

I walk.   We walk.   You walk.

I scream, you scream, we scream—for ice cream.

Problems of confusion sometimes occur, however, in the forms of agreement for third-person subjects and verbs.

▶ **10a**   Make a third-person subject agree in number with its verb.

The suffix -*s* or -*es*, affixed to a present-tense verb, indicates an assertion about a singular third-person subject (A frog do*es* this.); the suffix -*s* or -*es*, affixed to most nouns or third-person pronouns, indicates a plural (Frog*s* do this.).

Spotlight on Common Errors—AGREEMENT

 These are the errors most commonly associated with agreement between subject and verb or pronoun and antecedent. For full explanations and suggested revisions, follow the cross-references to chapter sections.

AGREEMENT ERRORS occur when the writer loses sight of the close link between the paired subjects and verbs, or between pronouns and the words they refer to (antecedents). Paired items should both be singular (referring to *one* person, place, or thing) or both be plural (referring to *more than one* person, place, or thing).

> **A subject and its verb should both be singular or both be plural (they should agree), whether or not they are interrupted by a word or word group (see 10a-1). Match subject and verb. Disregard interrupting words.**

Faulty	Revised
Some people, when not paying attention, easily *forgets* names.	Some **people**, when not paying attention, easily *forget* names.

> **A sentence with a singular subject needs a singular form of the verb *be* (*am, is, was*); a sentence with a plural subject needs a plural form of the verb *be* (*are, were*) (see 10a-7). To ensure agreement in sentences beginning with the subject, ignore words following the verb *be*.**

Faulty	Revised
The reason for her success *are* her friends.	The **reason** for her success *is* her friends.

When the subject comes after the verb in sentences beginning with *it* or *there*, verb and subject must still agree. Ignore the word *it* or *there*.

Faulty	Revised
There *is* seven hills in Rome.	There *are* **seven hills** in Rome. [The subject, *hills*, needs a plural verb.]

> **When *and* joins words to create a two-part pronoun referent or a two-part subject, the sense is usually plural, and so the matching pronoun or verb must be plural (see 10a-2 and 10b-1). When *or/nor* creates a two-part pronoun referent or a two-part subject, the nearer word determines whether the matching pronoun or verb is singular or plural (see 10a-3 and 10b-2).**

Faulty	Revised
A cat and a dog often *shares* **its** food.	A cat and a dog often *share* **their** food. [The plural pronoun and verb match a two-part referent and subject, *cat and dog*.]

Faulty	Revised
Neither the rats nor the dog *chase* **their** tail.	Neither the rats nor the dog *chases* **its** tail. [The singular pronoun and verb match the nearer singular subject, *dog*.]

The "tradeoff" technique

To remember the basic forms of third-person agreement for most verbs in the present tense, you may find it helpful to visualize something like a balanced tradeoff of -*s* endings between most noun subjects and their verbs: if one ends with an -*s*, then the other does not. Thus if the noun subject is singular and lacks an -*s* or -*es* ending, then the singular verb takes the -*s* ending. If the subject is a plural noun with an -*s* ending, then it takes the -*s*, and the plural verb does not.

Singular   A boy__ hikes.   A girl__ swims.   A kid__ does it.

Plural   The boys hike__.   The girls swim__.   Kids do__ it.

If a noun or pronoun has a plural sense, even if it does not end with an -*s* (for example, *children, oxen, geese, they, these*), then the tradeoff technique still applies. Since the noun or pronoun is plural (just as it would be if it were a word made plural with an -*s* ending), the verb is also plural—that is, the verb now lacks its -*s* ending.

Singular   A child plays.   He plays.   He does it.

Plural   Children play __.   They play __.   They do__ it.

Note: The "tradeoff" technique does not apply when a verb is paired with an auxiliary (or helping) verb (see 9c). Verbs paired like this do *not* use -*s*.

A child will play.	He may play.	He might do it.
Children should play.	They could play.	They must do it.

Revising nonstandard verb and noun forms to observe -*s* and -*es* endings

In rapid conversation people sometimes skip over the -*s* or -*es* endings of verbs that are paired with singular nouns. In some English dialects, the base (or infinitive) form of the verb is used for singular nouns. Standard academic English, however, requires that writers observe subject–verb agreement.

Nonstandard	He read the book.	**Nonstandard**	She do it.
Standard	He reads the book.	**Standard**	She does it.

▶ **I   A subject agrees with its verb regardless of whether any phrase or clause separates them.**

The *purpose* of practicing daily for several hours is to excel.

Often a subject may be followed by a lengthy phrase or clause that comes between it and the verb, confusing the basic pattern of agreement. To clarify the matching of the subject with the verb, mentally strike out or ignore phrases or clauses separating them. Verbs in the following examples are underlined; subjects are italicized.

Downward mobility—a swift plunge down America's social and economic ladders—poses an immediate and pressing problem. [The verb *poses* agrees with its singular subject, *downward mobility*, not with the plural *ladders* in the interrupting phrase.]

One of my friends in a nearby town <u>has</u> heard this. [The prepositional phrases must be ignored to make the singular *one* agree with *has*.]

The words *each* and *every* have a singular sense. When either of these words precedes a compound subject joined by *and*, use a singular verb.

Every city and county in Massachusetts <u>has</u> struggled with the problem of downward mobility.

Exception: When *each* follows a compound subject, the sense is plural, and the plural verb is used.

Boston and New York *each* <u>are</u> launching programs to reeducate workers.

Note: Phrases beginning with *in addition to, along with, as well as, together with*, or *accompanied by* may come between a subject and its verb. Although they add material, these phrases do *not* create a plural subject; they must be mentally stricken out to determine the correct number of the verb.

Faulty   *The anthropologist*, as well as social researchers such as statisticians and demographers, <u>are</u> always looking for indicators of change in status. [The interrupting phrase before the verb gives a false impression of a plural subject.]

Revised   *The anthropologist*, as well as social researchers such as statisticians and demographers, <u>is</u> always looking for indicators of change in status. [The singular subject *anthropologist* agrees with the singular verb.]

▶**2   A compound subject linked by the conjunction *and* is in most cases plural.**

UPS and Federal Express <u>compete</u> with the U.S. postal system.

When a compound subject linked by *and* refers to two or more people, places, or things, it is usually considered plural.

Plural   *Statistical information* and *the analysis based upon it* <u>allow</u> an anthropologist to piece together significant cultural patterns. [The compound subject has a plural sense. Thus the verb, *allow*, is plural.]

Exception: When a compound subject refers to a single person, place, or thing, it is considered singular.

Singular   Whatever culture she studies, *this anthropologist* and *researcher* <u>concerns</u> herself with the relations among husbands, wives, children, kin, and friends. [The compound subject has a singular sense—it refers to one person and can be replaced by the singular pronoun *she*. Thus the verb, *concerns*, is singular.]

▶**3   When parts of a compound subject are linked by the conjunction *or* or *nor*, the verb should agree in number with the nearer part of the subject.**

Neither the crew members nor the *captain* <u>speaks</u> Arabic.

When all parts of the compound subject are the same number, agreement with the verb is fairly straightforward.

Either John or *Maria* <u>sings</u> today.
Either the Smiths or the *Taylors* <u>sing</u> today.

When one part of the compound subject is singular and another plural, there can be confusion; the subject nearer the verb determines the number of the verb. If the nearer subject is singular, the verb is singular.

Singular   According to popular wisdom, either poor habits or *ineptitude* <u>is</u> responsible when an individual fails to succeed in American culture. [The singular subject, *ineptitude*, is nearer to the verb; therefore the verb, *is*, is singular.]

When the subject nearer the verb is plural, the verb is plural.

Plural   Neither the downwardly mobile individual nor the *people* surrounding him <u>realize</u> that losing a job is often due to impersonal economic factors. [The plural subject, *people*, is nearer to the verb; therefore the verb, *realize*, is plural.]

A compound subject is sometimes preceded by a verb in sentences with inverted word order. Here, too, the verb agrees in number with the part of the subject that is nearer to the verb. (See 10a-8.)

There <u>is</u> neither a *dentist* nor doctors in that remote village.

Note: Subject–verb agreement in this situation may appear to be mismatched unless the plural part of the compound subject is placed closest to the verb. Avoid such awkwardness by revising to place the plural part closest to the verb.

▶**4 Most indefinite pronouns have a singular sense and take a singular verb.**

Virtually *everybody* in developed countries <u>travels</u> by bus.
Many who live elsewhere <u>have</u> no choice but to walk.

Indefinite pronouns (such as *any* and *each*) do not have specific antecedents— they rename no particular person, place, or thing and thus raise questions about subject–verb agreement.
The following indefinite pronouns have a singular sense:

another	each one	more	one
any	either	much	other
anybody	every	neither	somebody
anyone	everybody	nobody	someone
anything	everyone	none, no one	something
each	everything	nothing	

Singular   *Much* of the law concerning the admissibility or exclusion of evidence <u>involves</u> standards of truth and fairness.

Singular   Although there was some evidence indicating the guilt of O. J. Simpson, *nothing* <u>was</u> sufficient to prove beyond a reasonable doubt that the accused was guilty.

The indefinite pronouns *both, ones,* and *others* have a plural sense and take a plural verb.

Plural   Some critics of the trial believe that the verdict damaged the American jurisprudence system; *others* <u>argue</u> that the system worked splendidly and proved that tainted evidence has no place in a court of law.

The indefinite pronouns *all, any, more, many, enough, none, some, few,* and *most* have a singular or plural sense, depending on the meaning of a sentence.

Try substituting *he, she, it, we,* or *they* for the indefinite pronoun. The context of a sentence will give you clues about the number of its subject.

Plural   Millions of Americans watched the trial. *Most* <u>were</u> tuned in as if to a soap opera. [*Most* (Americans) has a plural sense. It can be replaced by the pronoun *they,* and thus it takes a plural verb, *were.*]

Singular   Some of the public interest in the trial was sparked by the legal maneuverings of well-paid lawyers. But *most* of the interest <u>was</u> rooted in voyeurism. [*Most* (of the interest) can be replaced by the pronoun *it.* The singular sense, here, creates the need for a singular verb, *was.*]

▶ **5** Collective nouns have a plural or a singular sense, depending on the meaning of a sentence.

At this school, the *faculty* <u>meets</u> as a group with the president.

When a collective noun, such as *audience, band, bunch, crew, crowd, faculty, family, group, staff, team,* and *tribe,* refers to a single unit, the sense of the noun is singular and the noun takes a singular verb. The context of a sentence will give you clues about the number of its subject.

Singular   The *jury* <u>hears</u> all the evidence presented by both the prosecution and the defense. [The *jury* is referred to as a single unit; it has a singular sense and takes a singular verb, *hears.*]

When the collective noun refers to individuals and their separate actions within a group, the sense of the noun is plural and the noun takes a plural verb.

Plural   The *jury* often <u>have</u> diverse reactions to the evidence they hear. [*Jury* in this case emphasizes the actions of individual members; thus it has a plural sense and takes a plural verb, *have.*]

▶ **6** Nouns plural in form but singular in sense take singular verbs.

Economics <u>depends</u> heavily on mathematics.

The nouns *athletics, economics, mathematics, news, physics,* and *politics* all end with the letter -*s,* but they nonetheless denote a single activity.

Note: *Politics* can be considered plural, depending on the sense of a sentence.

News of a layoff <u>causes</u> some people to feel alone and blame themselves.

Politics often <u>comes</u> into play. [*Politics* has a singular sense and takes a singular verb.]

Note: The nouns *pants* and *scissors* are considered singular, but they take a plural verb.

The scissors *are* handy. The pants *need* to be cut and hemmed.

▶7 **A linking verb agrees in number with its subject, not with the subject complement.**

One *reason* for his success <u>is</u> his friends.
His *friends* <u>are</u> one reason for his success.

In a sentence with a linking verb, identify the singular or plural subject when deciding the number of the verb. Disregard any distracting phrase or clause that interrupts the subject and verb; also disregard the subject complement *following* the linking verb.

Singular   The *reason* for Simpson's acquittal <u>was</u> the many mistakes made by the police in gathering evidence. [The singular verb *was* agrees in number with the singular subject, *reason*, not with the plural subject complement, *mistakes*.]

Plural   *The many mistakes made by the police in gathering evidence* <u>were</u> the reason for Simpson's acquittal. [The plural verb, *were*, agrees in number with the plural subject, *mistakes*, not with the singular subject complement, *reason*.]

▶8 **In sentences with inverted word order, a verb should agree in number with its subject.**

Here *is* Michael.   Here *are* Janice and Michael.   There *is* a strategy.

The subject of an English sentence is normally placed before a verb. When this order is rearranged, the subject and verb continue to agree in number. Most errors with rearranged sentences occur with the verb *be*.

Here and *there* as adverbs

When inverted sentences begin with *here* and *there* as adverbs, the verb will agree in number with the subject (which follows the verb), not with the adverb.

Normal   The adviser said, "The Pattersons are here." [The plural subject, *Pattersons*, needs a plural verb.]

Rearranged   The adviser said, "Here *are* the Pattersons."

Singular   The adviser said, "Here *is* David Patterson."

Expletives

The words *it* and *there* often function as **expletives,** words that fill gaps in a sentence when normal word order is reversed (see 7a-11). *There* can never serve as the subject of a sentence. Disregard it when determining whether the sentence has a singular or plural subject.

Plural There <u>were</u> several *factors* that influenced the outcome of the Simpson trial. [*There* is disregarded; the plural subject, *factors*, needs to agree with a plural verb, *were*.]

Singular There <u>was</u> a single *factor*, however, that was most significant—the lack of high-quality evidence. [*There* is disregarded; the singular subject, *factor*, needs to agree with a singular verb, *was*.]

Notice that the expletive *it* is always followed by a singular verb.

Singular It <u>is</u> a very good *idea* to help them.

When an expletive and a verb precede a compound subject with *or/nor*, the verb still agrees in number with the part of the subject that is nearer to the verb.

There <u>is</u> neither a *dentist* nor doctors on the Sioux reservation.

ESL NOTE Some languages do not use *expletives*. In this very common English form, a "dummy subject" or filler word *it* or *there* occupies a position normally filled by the subject, followed by the verb *be* or any linking verb: *There were children inside*. The real subject, *children*, is on the other side of the linking verb "equation" (see 11d). See 7a-11 and 46a-2 for ways to use this construction; see 14e and 17a for ways to avoid wasting words with expletives.

Questions

Inverting a sentence's word order is one method of forming a question. The relocated verb must still agree in number with the subject.

Statement <u>He</u> really *wants* to hold on to that idea.

Question <u>Does</u> he really <u>want</u> to hold on to that idea? [The verb *does want* agrees with the subject *he*.]

Many questions are formed with *wh* words (*what, where, when, why*), with a verb following the *wh* word and a noun following that. The verb and noun should agree in number.

Singular What <u>is</u> *the cost* to him of abandoning it?

Plural What <u>are</u> *the costs* aside from that?

When the verb in a question precedes a compound subject with *or/nor*, make the verb agree in number with the part of the subject that is nearer to the verb.

<u>Have</u> either *nurses* or a doctor been seen entering the hospital area?

▶**9** **The verb of a dependent clause introduced by the pronoun *which, that, who,* or *whom* should agree in number with the pronoun's antecedent.**

In such a dependent clause, both the pronoun subject (*which, that*, etc.) and verb are dependent for their number on an antecedent in the main clause.

The *books, which* <u>are</u> old, <u>are</u> falling apart.

Make a Third-Person Subject Agree in Number with Its Verb   **229**

10 **Phrases and clauses that function as subjects are treated as singular and take singular verbs.**

Often a noun clause or a phrase with a gerund or infinitive will act as the subject of a sentence. Such a construction is always regarded as a singular element in the sentence.

To swim well is the first prerequisite for scuba diving.

That the child is able to cough is a good sign.

11 **Titled works, key words used as terms, and companies are treated as singular in number and take singular verbs.**

Titles of works, names of companies or corporations, underlined or italicized words referred to as words, numbers, and units of money are regarded as singular entities in a sentence and take singular verbs.

Classics is an overused word.   "The Killers" is a Hemingway story.

EXERCISE 1

In the following sentences, determine whether a subject is singular or plural. Choose the correct form in parentheses, and be able to explain your choice.

> *Example:* How (do/does) we get other people to agree with us?
>
> How *do* we get other people to agree with us? [The subject of the sentence is the plural pronoun, *we*. Even though the auxiliary part of the verb, *do*, is placed before the subject to form a question, the full verb (including the auxiliary) and the subject must agree in number.]

1. One reason for making a purchase (is/are) a buyer's emotional needs.
2. There (is/are) no single method that (assure/assures) success in persuading others; still, several methods (seem/seems) helpful.
3. One effective way of getting a "yes" from other people (is/are) to get them to like us.
4. Flattery, an extremely common tactic for gaining compliance, (has/have) a long history.
5. Both flattering people and getting them to talk about themselves (work/works) in surprisingly consistent ways.

PRONOUN–ANTECEDENT AGREEMENT

An **antecedent** is a word—usually a noun, sometimes a pronoun—that is renamed by a pronoun. Pronouns in the following examples are underlined, and antecedents are italicized.

> antecedent   pronoun
> *Van Leeuwenhoek* called the microorganisms that he found everywhere in vast numbers "little animals."

A pronoun's antecedent must be clearly identified in order for the pronoun itself to have a meaningful reference (see Chapter 14 on pronoun reference). A pronoun and antecedent must agree in *number, person,* and *gender.* **Gender** refers to whether a noun or pronoun is feminine, masculine, or neuter.

Mary flies planes. She flies planes. (feminine)
Bob rides trolleys. He rides trolleys. (masculine)
A trolley runs on tracks. It runs on tracks. (neuter)

In most cases, as in the preceding examples, a pronoun is easily matched to its antecedent in terms of person (first, second, or third), number (singular or plural), and gender (masculine or feminine). At times, however, choosing the right pronoun requires careful attention.

▶ 10b | Pronouns and their antecedents should agree in number.

Of the three components that determine pronoun selection, agreement in number causes the most difficulty—for the same reason that subject–verb agreement is sometimes difficult: the *number* of a noun (either as subject or antecedent) is not always clear. The following conventions will help you to determine whether an antecedent is singular or plural.

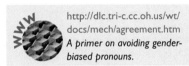

http://dlc.tri-c.cc.oh.us/wt/docs/mech/agreement.htm
A primer on avoiding gender-biased pronouns.

▶ 1 | **A compound antecedent linked by the conjunction *and* is usually plural.**

Watson and Crick were awarded a Nobel Prize for their achievement.

Plural In all early attempts at classification, living things were separated into two major groups—*the plant kingdom* and *the animal kingdom.* These were then subdivided in various ways. [The compound antecedent has a plural sense; therefore, the pronoun renaming it is plural in form.]

Plural In the 4th century B.C., *Aristotle* made a study of the animal kingdom, and *Theophrastus* studied the plant kingdom; their systems for classifying animals and plants began the scientific effort of classifying all living things. [The compound antecedent has a plural sense; therefore, the pronoun renaming it is plural in form.]

Exceptions: When a compound antecedent with parts joined by the conjunction *and* has a singular sense, use a singular pronoun.

Singular *An English naturalist and writer,* Thomas Blythe, used his classification scheme to identify more than 18,000 different types of plants. [The compound antecedent refers to one person—Thomas Blythe; therefore, the pronoun renaming it is singular.]

The words *each* and *every* have a singular sense. When either of these words precedes an antecedent joined by *and,* use a singular pronoun.

Singular Every *visible organism* and *microscopic organism* has its own distinctive, two-word Latin name according to the system designed by Carolus Linnaeus in the early eighteenth century.

Exception: When *each* follows an antecedent joined by *and,* the sense is plural, and the plural pronoun is used.

Plural   Daly and Blythe have *each* made <u>their</u> contribution to our understanding of classification systems.

▶**2 When parts of a compound antecedent are linked by the conjunction *or* or *nor,* a pronoun should agree in number with the nearer part of the antecedent.**

Neither the captain nor the *crew members* understood *their* predicament.

This pattern of agreement with *or* or *nor* follows the same convention as does subject–verb agreement (10a-3).

Singular   Neither the traditional two-kingdom systems nor the recent five-kingdom *system* is complete in <u>its</u> classification of organisms. [The pronoun is nearer to the singular *system* and so agrees in the singular.]

Note: Avoid awkward pronoun use by revising to place the plural part of the compound antecedent nearer to the pronoun.

Revised   Neither the five-kingdom system nor the traditional two-kingdom *systems* are complete in <u>their</u> classifications. [The plural part of the antecedent is revised to fall nearer to the pronoun; the sentence is no longer awkward in its agreement.]

▶**3 Make pronouns agree in number with indefinite pronoun antecedents.**

Each one has <u>her</u> own job.   *Both* have begun <u>their</u> research.

Indefinite pronouns (such as *each, anyone,* and *everyone*) do not refer to particular persons, places, or things. Most often these indefinite pronouns have a singular sense as an antecedent and will be renamed with a singular pronoun. (See the complete list of singular and plural indefinite pronouns in 10a-4.) Writers sometimes forget that the pronouns *anyone* and *everyone* are singular and must agree with a singular pronoun.

Faulty   *Everyone* seems to have <u>their</u> own idea about *each* of the millions of organisms and <u>their</u> purpose.

Revised   *Everyone* seems to have <u>his or her</u> own idea about *each* of the millions of organisms and <u>its</u> purpose. [See 10c for choosing gender-appropriate pronouns.]

When an indefinite pronoun (such as *both* or *others*) functions as an antecedent and has a plural sense, rename it with a plural pronoun.

Plural   Some organisms are readily classified as animal or plant; *others,* most often the simplest single-cell organisms, find <u>themselves</u> classified in different ways, depending on the classification system used.

A few indefinite pronouns (such as *some*, *more*, or *most*) can have a singular or a plural sense, depending on the context of a sentence. Determine the number of an indefinite pronoun antecedent before selecting a pronoun replacement.

Plural   *Some* of the simplest living organisms defy classification, by virtue of <u>their</u> diversity. [*Some* has a plural sense.]

Singular   *Some* of the recent research made possible by microscopes is startling in <u>its</u> findings that certain unicellular organisms, such as the euglena, have both plant-like and animal-like characteristics. [*Some* has a singular sense.]

▶4   Make pronouns agree in number with collective noun antecedents.

A well-informed group, the *faculty* is outspoken in <u>its</u> opinions.
The *faculty* at the gathering shared <u>their</u> thoughts on the issue.

Collective nouns will be singular or plural depending on the meaning of a sentence. When a collective noun such as *audience, band, group,* or *team* refers to a *single unit*, the sense of the noun as an antecedent is singular, and the noun takes a singular pronoun.

Singular   A *group* of similar organisms that interbreed in nature is called a species and is given <u>its</u> own distinct Latin name. [*Group* has a singular sense.]

When a collective noun refers to individuals and their *separate actions* within a group, the sense of the noun as an antecedent is plural, and the noun takes a plural pronoun.

Plural   Human beings are the only *group* of primates who walk on two legs, without the aid of <u>their</u> hands. [*Group* has a plural sense.]

Rename indefinite antecedents with gender-appropriate pronouns.

10c

A lawyer serves *his or her* clients. Lawyers serve *their* clients.

Gender-specific pronoun use can be inaccurate and offensive. To avoid unintentional sexism, use five techniques, either alone or in combination. (For more discussion on gender reference, see 21g.)

Use the constructions *he or she, his or her,* or *him or her* in referring to an indefinite pronoun or noun.

Choose this option when the antecedent of a pronoun must have a singular sense. Realize, however, that some readers object to the *he or she* device as cumbersome.

Awkward   To some extent, *a biologist* must decide for <u>him- or herself</u> which system of classification <u>he or she</u> will use.

Revised   To some extent, *a biologist* must decide which system of classification <u>he or she</u> will use.

Revised   To some extent, *a biologist* must decide which system of classification to use. [The infinitive *to use* avoids the *he or she* difficulty.]

Make a pronoun's antecedent plural, if the accuracy of a sentence will permit a plural antecedent.

Plural To some extent, *biologists* must decide for <u>themselves</u> which system of classification *they* will use.

Use the passive voice to avoid gender-specific pronouns and to deemphasize a subject.

Note, however, that using the passive voice creates its own problems of vague reference. (See 9g-2 and 17b-1.)

Neutral It is every biologist's responsibility to specify which system of classification *is being used.*

Reconstruct the entire statement to avoid pronouns altogether.

Neutral When choosing among competing systems of classification, the biologist makes a choice that greatly affects later work both in the field and in the lab. [*Later work* is left without a limiting, gender-specific modifier.]

Arbitrarily assign gender identity.

Assign a masculine identity to one indefinite antecedent and a feminine identity to another. Maintain these assignments throughout a document.

Alternate gender assignments A *biologist* must decide which system of classification <u>she</u> will use. An *anthropologist* must also choose when selecting the technological attributes <u>he</u> will use in distinguishing ancient objects from one another.

▸ ## EXERCISE 2

Revise the following sentences to ensure agreement between pronouns and antecedents. Eliminate the generic *he*. Place a check before the sentences in which a pronoun agrees in number with its antecedent.

> *Example:* The characters, plots, and settings of Stephen King's stories have haunted readers with its believable eeriness.
>
> The characters, plots, and settings of Stephen King's stories have haunted readers with *their* believable eeriness.

1. In one of these novels, a 1958 Plymouth Fury is a jealous monster who seeks out and destroys the enemies of her male owner.
2. Anyone who considers himself a horror connoisseur has read at least some of the novels of Stephen King.
3. Whenever King's novels are turned into motion pictures, it grosses millions of dollars.
4. In their adaptation of King's short novel *The Body* into the full-length feature film *Stand by Me*, artist and director Rob Reiner created a tender-hearted crowd pleaser, quite unlike other movies made from King's novels.

EXERCISE 3

Revise the following gender-biased sentences so that they do not stereotype males or females or restrict references to males. When you make singular nouns plural, other words in the sentence will change.

> *Example:* The behaviorist theory in psychology assumes that man's response to his environment is similar to the response of other animals.
>
> The behaviorist theory in psychology assumes that humans respond to their environment in the same ways that other animals do.

1. Each operator answers her phone.
2. As part of her job, a nurse prepares injections for her patients.
3. A miner would take a canary below ground to make sure the air was safe for him to breathe.
4. A pilot, today, takes much of his training in flight simulators.
5. Recent research has suggested a relationship between the amount of time a child watches television and his later performance in school.

ACROSS THE CURRICULUM

Using Words Precisely to Avoid Bias in Social Scientific Writing

The Publication Manual of the American Psychological Association, fourth edition, advises writers to choose words precisely when characterizing groups—both to maintain accuracy and to avoid giving offense:*

Precision is a necessity in scientific writing; when you refer to a person or persons, choose words that are accurate, clear, and free from bias. [. . .] For example, using *man* to refer to all human beings is simply not as accurate as the phrase *men and women.* To describe age groups, it is better to give a specific age range ("ages 65–83") instead of a broad category ("over 65"; see Schaie, 1993). When describing racial and ethnic groups, be appropriately specific and sensitive to issues of labeling. For example, instead of describing participants as Asian American or Hispanic American, it may be helpful to describe them by their nation or region of origin (e.g., Chinese Americans, Mexican Americans). If you are discussing sexual orientation, realize that some people interpret *gay* as referring to men and women, whereas others interpret the term as including only men (for clarity, *gay men* and *lesbians* currently are preferred).[. . .]

Part of writing without bias is recognizing that differences should be mentioned only when relevant. Marital status, sexual orientation, racial and ethnic identity, or the fact that a person has a disability should not be mentioned gratuitously.

The Publication Manual of the American Psychological Association, 4th ed. (Washington: APA, 1994) 47–48.

Rename Indefinite Antecedents with Gender-Appropriate Pronouns

▶ **EXERCISE 4**

Revise the following paragraph to ensure agreement between subject and verb and between pronoun and antecedent. Also, revise any sentence in which the generic *he* is used.

The haunted house loom large in American literature and film. Some of the most famous has been Poe's castle in "The Masque of the Red Death," his "house" of Usher, Shirley Jackson's Hill House, the Bates mansion in Hitchcock's *Psycho*, and the suburban home in *The Amityville Horror*. A relatively recent haunted house story, a genre piece in the tradition of horror classics, were King's *The Shining*. Any reader of the book or viewer of the movie was sure to satisfy his need for chills and thrills. As is the case in so many stories of the haunted house, none of the characters are ever
▶ entirely sure where he fits into the house's scheme of things.

CHAPTER

11

Adjectives and Adverbs

Adjectives and adverbs are **modifiers**—descriptive words, phrases, or clauses that enliven sentences with vivid detail. In Chapter 7 you learned how phrases and clauses function as modifiers. But even when dealing with single-word modifiers, as in this chapter, you can see that the effectiveness of modifiers depends on thinking clearly about the two main types: adjectives and adverbs.

▶ **11a** **Distinguishing between adjectives and adverbs**

Some basic distinctions between the use of adjectives and adverbs are summarized in the following box.

Distinguishing Adjectives from Adverbs

An **adjective** modifies a noun or pronoun and answers these questions:

Which: The *latest* news arrived.
What kind: An *insignificant* difference remained.
How many: The *two* sides would resolve their differences.

An **adverb** modifies a verb and answers these questions:

When: *Tomorrow* the temperature will drop.
How: The temperature will drop *sharply*.
How often: Weather patterns change *frequently*.
Where: The weather patterns *here* change frequently.

An **adverb** also modifies adjectives, adverbs, and entire clauses:

Modifying an adjective: An *especially* large group enrolled.
Modifying an adverb: Courses at this school *almost* never get closed.
Modifying a clause: *Consequently*, the registrar closed the course.

When choosing between an adjective and adverb form for a sentence, identify the word being modified, and determine its part of speech. Then follow the conventions presented in this chapter.

▶ **1   Identifying and using adjectives**

An **adjective** modifies a noun or pronoun by answering these questions: **Which?** the *tall* child; **What kind?** the *artistic* child; **How many?** *five* children. Pure adjectives are not derived from other words: *large, small, simple, difficult, thick, thin, cold, hot.* Many adjectives, however, are derived from nouns.

Base noun	Suffix	Adjective
science	-ic	scientific
region	-al	regional
book	-ish	bookish

Adjectives are also derived from verbs.

Base verb	Suffix	Adjective
respect	-ful	respectful
respect	-ed	respected (past participle)
respect	-ing	respecting (present participle)
demonstrate	-ive	demonstrative
hesitate	-ant	hesitant

Writers frequently build up their desired meanings by taking a word and adapting its base form, thereby converting the word into the part of speech needed for a new sentence.

The audience maintained a (respect + ful) silence.

The (region + al) conference was about to begin.

ESL NOTE   The past and present participles formed from the same basic verb are related in meaning. Consider, though, how two forms derived from a transitive verb (such as *confuse*) may work in opposite directions on the word modified: *a confused speaker* experiences confusion, while *a confusing speaker* gives others this experience (see 47a-1).

Placement

A single-word adjective is usually placed before the word it modifies. Occasionally an adjective will appear after a noun or pronoun—usually when the adjective is formed by a phrase or clause.

The speaker was received with *enthusiastic* applause.

The speaker, *bookish* and *hesitant*, approached the podium.

ESL NOTE   In most English sentences, two or more adjectives that accumulate as modifiers before a noun or pronoun are typically given a standard order or sequence. For example, adjectives describing nationality and color are typically placed nearer than others to the noun or pronoun.

Confusing   *a blue Japanese cheerful flower*

Typical   *a cheerful blue Japanese flower*

Section 47f-1–2 describes typical patterns for placement of English adjective modifiers.

COMPUTER TIPS

Beware of Grammar Checkers

Avoid using a grammar checker, no matter how tempted you are by the concept of a software program that will "correct" your grammar mistakes. The technology required to support such a function effectively is still years away. Unfortunately, today's grammar checkers literally make more mistakes than they correct: they might tell you that a certain sentence is a run-on, for example, when it's not; or they might advise you to use a plural verb to agree with a singular subject that happens to be spelled like a plural one. Software programs for desktop computers are simply not powerful enough to capture the complexities of grammar and usage in any language, let alone the sometimes illogical, erratic English language. If your mastery of grammar is already nearly perfect, then grammar software may have some value. You can test your writing decisions against the recommendations of the program and then decide whether your approach is valid. However, remember to proceed cautiously.

▶ 2 Identifying and using adverbs

An **adverb** modifies a verb by answering several questions: **When?** *Yesterday*, the child sang. **How?** The child sang *beautifully*. **How often?** The child sings *regularly*. **Where?** The child sang *here*. Adverbs modify adjectives: The child sang an *extremely* intricate melody. Adverbs can modify other adverbs: The child sings *almost* continuously. Certain adverbs can modify entire sentences: *Consequently*, the child's voice has improved.

Pure adverbs are not derived from other words: *again, almost, always, never, here, there, now, often, seldom, well*. Many adverbs, however, are formed from adjectives. These adverbs may be formed simply by adding the suffix *-ly* to adjectives.

Adjective	*Add -ly*	*Adverb*
beautiful		beautifully
strange		strangely
clever		cleverly
respectful		respectfully

However, an *-ly* ending alone is not sufficient to establish a word as an adverb, since certain adjectives show this ending: a friend*ly* conversation, a love*ly* afternoon. In any standard dictionary look for the abbreviations **adj.** and **adv.**, which will distinguish between the forms of a word.

Thousands of words in our language have both adjective and adverb forms. Consider the noun *grace*, defined by the *American Heritage Dictionary* as "seemingly effortless beauty or charm of movement, form, or proportion." *Graceful* and *gracious* are adjectives, and *graciously, gracefully*, and *gracelessly* are adverbs.

Placement

The location of an adverb may be shifted in a sentence, depending on the rhythm and emphasis a writer wants to achieve. An adverb (as a word, phrase, or clause) can appear in the sentence's beginning, middle, or end.

Formerly, Zimbabwe was known as Rhodesia.

Zimbabwe was *formerly* known as Rhodesia.

Zimbabwe was known as Rhodesia, *formerly.*

A note of caution: Lengthy adverb phrases and clauses should not split sentence elements that occur in pairs, such as a subject and verb or a verb and its object (see 15d). Also, limiting modifiers such as *only, almost,* or *nearly* must be carefully placed close to the word they modify (see 15b).

ESL NOTE While the placement of most English adverbs is flexible, limiting adverbs and others require specific positions in the sentence, as described in 47c-1–2.

▶ **EXERCISE 1**

Identify the single-word adjectives and adverbs in the following sentences; also identify the words being modified.

adj　　　　adj
Example: Every personality has its introverted and extroverted parts.

adv
American culture greatly exaggerates the virtues of extroversion.

1. Our culture prefers the assertive, flexible, and extroverted individual over the introverted, cautious, and inhibited individual.
2. The popular perception is that the introverted personality is uptight, socially isolated, unable to achieve goals, and prone to melancholy.
3. One could argue, however, that since introverted behavior is not rewarded by our culture, introverts should naturally feel underappreciated.
4. Some theorists correctly observe that such individuals have been responsible for much of the artistic, scientific, and scholarly achievement of the human race.
5. Social scientists theorize that in earlier historical epochs, introverts contributed subtly to social stability.

EXERCISE 2

Convert the following nouns and verbs to adjectives and adverbs; convert the adjectives to adverbs. (Use a dictionary for help, if necessary.) Then use each newly converted word in a sentence.

Example: courtesy　　courteous　　courteously
　　　　　　(noun)　　(adjective)　　(adverb)

A courteous driver will signal before turning.

▶　substance　　hope　　　　argue
　reason　　　understand

Use an adverb (not an adjective) to modify verbs as well as verbals.

Adverbs are used to modify verbs even when a direct object stands between the verb and its modifier.

Faulty If you measure an object in Denver *precise*, it will weigh somewhat less than the same object measured in Washington. [The adjective *precise*—following a direct object—is used incorrectly to modify the verb *measured*.]

Revised If you measure an object in Denver *precisely*, it will weigh somewhat less than the same object measured in Washington.

Faulty A *precise* measured object in Denver will weigh somewhat less than the same object measured in Washington. [The adjective *precise* incorrectly modifies the participle *measured*.]

Revised A *precisely* measured object in Denver will weigh somewhat less than the same object measured in Washington.

Faulty An object's weight can be determined by measuring it *careful* against a known weight. [The adjective *careful* incorrectly modifies the gerund *measuring*.]

Revised An object's weight can be determined by measuring it *carefully* against a known weight.

Use an adverb (not an adjective) to modify another adverb or an adjective.

Although informal or nonstandard usage occasionally finds adjectives like *real* or *sure* functioning as adverbs ("a real bad time," "it sure was good"), standard academic usage requires that adverbs modify adjectives and other adverbs.

Nonstandard A *reasonable* accurate scale can measure hundredths of a gram. [The adjective *reasonable* incorrectly modifies the adjective *accurate*.]

Revised A *reasonably* accurate scale can measure hundredths of a gram.

Faulty An object on the Moon weighs *significant* less than it does on Earth. [The adjective *significant* incorrectly modifies the adverb *less*.]

Revised An object on the Moon weighs *significantly* less than it does on Earth.

Use an adjective (not an adverb) after a linking verb to describe a subject.

The following verbs are linking verbs: forms of *be* (*is, are, was, were, has been, have been*), *look, smell, taste, sound, feel, appear, become, grow, remain, seem, turn,* and *stay*. A sentence with a linking verb establishes, in effect, an equation between the first part of the sentence and the second:

A LINKING VERB *B*, *or A* = *B*.

In this construction, the predicate part, *B*, is called the *subject complement*. The function of a **subject complement** is to rename or modify the subject of a sentence, which is a noun. The subject complement may be a noun, pronoun, or adjective—but *not* an adverb. In these examples, the linking verbs are followed by adjectives that describe a subject.

Linking   The dessert looks *delicious.*

The crowd turned *violent.*

The pilots were *thirsty.*

Important exceptions: Several linking verbs, especially those associated with the five senses, can also express action. When they do, they are considered *action* (not linking) *verbs* and are modified by adverbs.

Action   Palmer looked *menacingly* at the batter. [*Looked* is an action verb with an adverb modifier.]

Linking   Palmer looked angry and *menacing.* [*Looked* is now a linking verb meaning "appeared." The adjective *menacing* describes the subject's apparent attitude.]

Action   The storm turned *violently* toward land. [*Turned* is an action verb with an adverb modifier.]

Linking   The storm turned *violent.* [*Turned* is now a linking verb meaning "became." The adjective *violent* is linked as a modifier to *storm.*]

▶ l   Good, well, bad, badly

The words *good* and *well*, along with *bad* and *badly*, are not interchangeable in formal writing (though they tend to be interchangeable in conversation). The common linking verbs associated with well-being, appearance, or feeling—*looks, seems, appears, feels*—can cause special problems. The rules of usage follow.

Good and well

Good is an adjective, used either before a noun or after a linking verb to describe the condition of a subject.

Acceptable   Kyle looks good. [After a linking verb, *good* describes the subject's appearance.]

Kyle is a good dancer. [*Good* modifies the noun *dancer.*]

Nonstandard   Susan drives good. [*Drives* is an action verb and requires an adverb as modifier.]

Revised   Susan drives well.

The word *well* can be used as either an adjective or an adverb. It has limited use as an adjective only after certain linking verbs (*looks, seems, be/am/is/are*) that describe the subject's good health.

Acceptable   Robert looks well. [*Looks* is a linking verb. The sense of this sentence is that Robert seems to be healthy.]

Well functions as an adverb whenever it follows an action verb.

Nonstandard	Janet sings good. [*Sings* is an action verb and requires an adverb as modifier.]
Revised	Janet sings well.

Bad and badly

Bad is an adjective, used before a noun and after a linking verb to describe a subject. Again, the linking verbs that involve appearance or feeling—*looks, seems, appears, feels*—can cause special problems.

Faulty	Marie feels badly. [*Feels* is a linking verb and must tie the subject, *Marie*, to an adjective.]
Revised	Marie feels bad. [As an adjective, *bad* is linked to the subject to describe *Marie* and her mental state.]

Exception: The verb *feels* could possibly be an action verb indicating a sense of touch rather than a linking verb indicating well-being: "The blind reader feels braille letters carefully and well." Only in this limited meaning would the phrases *feels badly* or *feels well* be used properly to show how that sense is operating.

Badly is an adverb, used after an action verb or used to modify an adjective or adverb.

Nonstandard	John cooks bad. [*Cooks* is an action verb and must be modified by an adverb.]
Revised	John cooks badly.

EXERCISE 3

Browse through a dictionary, and locate five words that have both adjective and adverb forms. Write a sentence for the two uses of each word—ten sentences in all. Draw an arrow from each adjective or adverb to the word modified.

> *Example: patient*   The people in the waiting room were patient.
>
> *patiently*   The people waited patiently.

EXERCISE 4

Fill in the blank in each sentence with *good, well, bad,* or *badly*, and draw an arrow from the word chosen to the word modified.

> *Example:* The team's prospects are _____ .
>
> The team's prospects are *good*.

1. Tom has been looking _____ .
2. If he were under a doctor's supervision, he might look _____ .
3. He certainly sleeps _____ .
4. A _____ sleeper can put in eight hours a night.
5. Sleeping _____ can make one feel old in a hurry.

Use an Adjective after a Linking Verb to Describe a Subject   **243**

▶ 11e Using comparative and superlative forms of adjectives and adverbs

Both adjectives and adverbs change form to express comparative relationships. The base form of an adjective or adverb is called its **positive** form. The **comparative** form is used to express a relationship between two elements, and the **superlative** form is used to express a relationship among three or more elements. Most single-syllable adverbs and adjectives, and many two-syllable adjectives, show comparisons with the suffix -*er* and superlatives with -*est*.

	Positive	Comparative	Superlative
Adjective	crazy	crazier	craziest
	crafty	craftier	craftiest
Adverb	near	nearer	nearest
	far	farther	farthest

Adverbs of two or more syllables and adjectives of three or more syllables change to the comparative and superlative forms with the words *more* and *most*. Adjectives and adverbs show downward (or negative) comparisons with the words *less* and *least* placed before the positive form. If you are uncertain of an adjective's or adverb's form, refer to a dictionary.

	Positive	Comparative	Superlative
Adjective	elegant	more/less elegant	most/least elegant
	logical	more/less logical	most/least logical
Adverb	beautifully	more/less beautifully	most/least beautifully
	strangely	more/less strangely	most/least strangely

▶ I Use irregular adjectives and adverbs with care.

A number of adjectives and adverbs are irregular in forming comparatives and superlatives, and they must be memorized. Consult the following box for these basic forms.

Irregular Forms of Comparison			
	Positive	Comparative	Superlative
Adjective	good	better	best
	bad	worse	worst
	little	less	least
	many	more	most
	much	more	most
	some	more	most
Adverb	well (also adj.)	better	best
	badly	worse	worst

Adjectives and Adverbs

▶2 **Express comparative and superlative relationships accurately, completely, and logically.**

Accuracy

Use the comparative form of adverbs and adjectives to show a relationship between two items; use the superlative form when relating three or more items.

Two items	In the winter months, New York is colder than Miami.
Two items	First-year students are often more conscientious about their studies than second-year students.
Multiples	America Online was voted by *PC Magazine* as the "Best Choice" of all online servers.

Completeness

If the elements of a two- or three-way comparison are not being mentioned explicitly in a sentence, be sure to provide enough context so that the comparison makes sense.

Incomplete	Jason is more efficient. [More efficient than whom? More efficient at what?]
Revised	Jason is the more efficient runner. [Two runners are being compared.] or Jason is a more efficient runner than Dylan.

Logic

Certain adjectives have an absolute meaning—they cannot be logically compared. It makes no sense, for instance, to discuss greater or lesser degrees of *perfect* (although in advertising and in conversation, people often try). *Perfect* represents a logical endpoint of comparison, as do the words *unique, first, final, last, absolute, infinite,* and *dead.* Note, though, that a concert performance might be *nearly* perfect or a patient on an operating table *almost* dead. Once *perfection* or *death* is reached, comparisons literally make no sense.

Illogical	The story was submitted in its most final form.
Revised	The story was submitted in its final form. or The story was submitted in nearly final form.

 11f **Avoid double comparisons, double superlatives, and double negatives.**

Double comparisons/superlatives

Adjectives and adverbs show comparative and superlative relationships either with a suffix (*-er/-est*) or with the words *more, most, less,* or *least.* It is redundant and awkward to use the *-er/-est* suffix with *more/most* or *less/least.*

CRITICAL DECISIONS

Be alert to differences: Applying a test for choosing comparative forms—few/fewer/fewest, little/less/least, many, much

When making comparisons, note the differences between elements that can be counted and those that cannot (see 7a-2 and 45a-1). Then choose the appropriate form for your comparison.

■ **For nouns that can be counted, downward comparisons must be made with *few, fewer,* or *fewest*.**

Faulty Frozen yogurt has *less* calories than ice cream. [Since *calories* can be counted, *less* is the wrong comparative term.]

Revised Frozen yogurt has *fewer* calories than ice cream.

■ **For mass nouns, which cannot be counted (see 7a-2), downward comparisons must be made with *little, less,* or *least*.**

Faulty "Drinker's Delight" coffee has *fewer* caffeine than regular coffee. [Since *caffeine* is a mass noun and cannot be counted, *fewer* is the wrong comparative term.]

Revised "Drinker's Delight" coffee has *less* caffeine than regular coffee.

■ **For nouns that can be counted, use the adjective *many*, not *much*.**

Faulty Ice cream has *much* calories. [Since *calories* can be counted, *much* is the incorrect adjective form.]

Revised Ice cream has *many* calories.

Faulty The World Trade Center is more taller than the Chrysler Building.

Revised The World Trade Center is taller than the Chrysler Building.

Faulty That is the least likeliest conclusion to the story.

Revised That is the least likely conclusion to the story.

Double negatives

Double negatives—the presence of two modifiers that say "no" in the same sentence—are redundant and sometimes confusing, though fairly common in nonstandard usage. A clear negation in a sentence should be expressed only once. Combine the negatives *not, never, neither/nor, hardly,* or *scarcely* with *any, anything,* or *anyone*. Do not combine these negatives with the negatives *no, none, nothing,* or *no one*.

Nonstandard I didn't have none.
I didn't have no cash. [These double negatives risk the implication that the speaker in fact has cash.]

Revised I had none.
I didn't have any cash.

Nonstandard I hardly had none.

Revised I hardly had any.

Nonstandard	I never had nothing.
Revised	I never had anything. I had nothing.

▶ 11g   Avoid overusing nouns as modifiers.

A noun can modify another noun and thus function as an adjective. A few examples include *gate* keeper, *toll* booth, *cell* block, *beauty* parlor, *parlor* game, *finger* puppet, and *tax* collector. Noun modifiers provide handy shortcuts, but when two or more nouns are stacked before a third noun to function as adjectives, the result is logically and stylistically disastrous.

Unclear   The textbook Civil War chapter review questions are due tomorrow.

The sentence falters because we are given five seemingly unrelated nouns from which to choose a subject: *textbook*, *Civil War*, *chapter*, *review*, and *questions*. Unstack noun modifiers by moving the subject to the beginning of the sentence and arranging modifying nouns into phrases.

subject   prep. phrase with possessive   prep. phrase
Revised   The review questions from the textbook's chapter on the Civil War are due tomorrow.

ESL NOTE   With noun modifiers, sequence and placement are more critical than with adjectives or adverbs (see 44a-2 on noun modifiers). Some of the conventions for ordering cumulative adjective modifiers may also apply to nouns (see 44f).

▶ EXERCISE 5

Correct the problems with comparative and superlative forms in the following sentences.

> *Example:* Of the three Brontë sisters, Emily was the taller.
> Of the three Brontë sisters, Emily was the tallest. [The superlative is needed to differentiate among three or more people.]

1. Anne Brontë, the younger sister, wrote *Agnes Grey* and *The Tenant of Wildfell Hall.*
2. Charlotte is better known for *Jane Eyre.*
3. Charlotte was the longest-lived of the three sisters.
4. Emily was the stubbornest: though seriously ill, she refused to see a doctor and insisted on performing her usual chores.
5. Emily was the more private of the three authors; she remained an enigma even to her family.

CHAPTER **12**

Sentence Fragments

One important goal of writing is to keep readers focused on clearly stated ideas. Few errors are more disruptive of this goal than the **sentence fragment,** a partial sentence punctuated as if it were a complete sentence. Because it is only a partial sentence, a fragment leaves readers confused, trying to guess at what claims or statements are being made. To be a sentence, a group of words must first have a subject and a predicate (see 7a-1). A sentence fragment may lack either a subject or a predicate—and sometimes both. A fragment may also be a dependent clause (see 7e) that has not been joined to an independent (or main) clause.

http://leo.stcloudstate.edu/ punct/fragmentcauses.html
A succinct bottom-up view of the causes of sentence fragments, from LEO: Literacy Education Online.

Fragment Ellen took her vacation in March. Whereas, Frank took his vacation in June. [The second clause is introduced by a subordinating conjunction and is not a sentence. (See 12a.)]

Revised Ellen took her vacation in March. Frank took his vacation in June.

▶ **12a** **Check for completeness of sentences.**

Avoid writing fragments by checking your sentences for grammatical completeness. There are three tests you can conduct:

1. Locate a verb.
2. Locate the verb's subject.
3. Check for subordinating conjunctions or relative pronouns.

First test: Locate a verb.

A complete sentence must have a verb. To be sure you've written a sentence, find the verb. Note that verb forms ending in *-ing* must be preceded by a form of *be* (for example, *is, are, were, was, has been,* etc.) in order to function as sentence verbs.

Fragment His arguing a long and tiresome case without any sensitivity to his readers. [*Arguing* is not preceded by a form of *be.*]

Revised *He was arguing* a long and tiresome case without any sensitivity to his readers. [*Was arguing* is a verb. The subject of the revised sentence is *he.*]

Spotlight on Common Errors—
SENTENCE CONSTRUCTION AND FRAGMENTS

*These are the errors most commonly associated
with sentence construction and fragments. For full
explanations and suggested revisions, follow the
cross-references to chapter sections.*

FRAGMENT ERRORS arise when writers incorrectly mark a group of words as a sentence. Apply a three-part test to confirm that a grouping of words can stand alone as a sentence (see 12a).

Test 1: Locate a verb: A sentence must have a verb.

Churchill *was* a leader.	A leader of great distinction.	When he *became* prime minister.
[Verb—*was*]	[No verb—this grouping of words cannot be a sentence; it is a FRAGMENT.]	Verb—*became*—BUT this word grouping fails Test 3 below, so it is still a FRAGMENT.]

Revised   Churchill was *a leader of great distinction.*

Note: Be sure the word selected as a verb is not a verbal, which looks like a verb but actually serves as a subject, object, or modifier (see 7a-4).

After *serving* his country in the First World War.

[Verbal: *serving* looks like a verb but is actually an object in the prepositional phrase beginning with *after*. This grouping of words is therefore a FRAGMENT.]

Revised   **After serving his country in the First World War,** he became prime minister.

Test 2: Locate the verb's subject: A sentence must have a subject.

Churchill was a leader.	*When he became prime minister.*
[Subject—*Churchill*]	[Subject—*he*—BUT this word grouping fails Test 3, so it is still a FRAGMENT.]

Test 3: Be sure that words such as *when, while, because* or *who, which, that* do not prevent the word group from being a sentence (see subordinating conjunctions and relative pronouns, 19b-1–2).

Sentence	Churchill *was* a leader.
	[No words prevent the grouping from being a sentence.]

Fragments	*When* he became prime minister.	*Who* became prime minister.

[*When* (a subordinating conjunction) and *who* (a relative pronoun) prevent these word groups from standing alone as sentences.]

Revised   **He became prime minister.**

See 12b–12d for ways to correct fragments once you have identified them.

Be sure that the word you settle on as the sentence verb is not a verbal, a verb form that functions as a subject, object, or modifier (see 7a-4).

Fragment   The calculated, high risk. [*Calculated* functions as a modifier describing *risk.*]

Revised   *Susan calculated* the high risk. [*Calculated* is paired with a subject, *Susan*, to become a verb.]

Verb forms introduced with the infinitive marker *to* never function as sentence verbs; another verb must be added to make a sentence.

Fragment   To appreciate the alternative.

Revised   *Frank failed* to appreciate the alternative. [The verb *failed* has been added along with the subject *Frank.*]

Second test: Locate the verb's subject.

Once you have located a verb, ask *who* or *what* makes its assertion or action, and you will find the subject.

Fragment   Separated visible light into a spectrum of colors. [Who separated?]

Revised   *Isaac Newton* separated visible light into a spectrum of colors. [The new subject, *Isaac Newton*, answers the question.]

Fragment   First attempted an analysis of the short story. [Who attempted?]

Revised   *Edgar Allan Poe* first attempted an analysis of the short story. [The new subject, *Edgar Allan Poe*, answers the question.]

Imperative sentences—commands—often lack a subject; still, they are considered sentences, since the implied subject is understood to be *you.*

Imperative sentence	Understood as
Open the door!	You open the door!
Come here, please.	You come here, please.

ESL NOTE   The subject of a sentence in English, unlike that in many other languages, is expressed directly as a separate word in one location only. Because the subject is not implied in the form of a verb (other than the imperative) or other sentence part, identifying the subject with a specific word is critical to the structure of an English sentence (see 7a-1 and 7b).

Third test: Check for subordinating conjunctions or relative pronouns.

Subordinating conjunctions

after	although	as if	assuming that
because	before	how	if
provided that	since	though	unless
until	whenever	where	while

Be certain that a subject and verb are not preceded by a subordinating conjunction. If a word grouping consists of a subject and predicate, it is a sentence *unless it* contains an opening subordinating conjunction. Eliminate the conjunction, and the clause will stand as a sentence. Combine the dependent clause with another sentence, and the new dependent clause will function as an adverb.

Fragment   Though people may have a personality disorder. [The conjunction *though* makes the clause dependent on another statement.]

Revised   ~~Though~~ People may have a personality disorder. [Dropping the conjunction makes a simple sentence.]

Revised   Though people may have a personality disorder, *they may see their behavior as normal.* [The dependent clause now functions as an adverb.]

Note: A subordinating conjunction cannot be used as a transitional expression at the beginning of a sentence—in the manner of *therefore* or *however.* These words, called *conjunctive adverbs, do* function as transitions (see 13b-4). Observe the differences:

Fragment   Whereas, Allen went to the second session.

Revised   Allen went to the second session.

Revised   However, Allen went to the second session.

The words *though, although,* and *whereas* are *not* interchangeable with *however* or *therefore.*

Relative pronouns

that	which	whichever	who
whoever	whom	whomever	

A relative pronoun signals that the clause is dependent and cannot stand alone as a sentence. If the pronoun is eliminated and a noun is present to function as the subject, the clause will stand as a sentence. If combined with another sentence, the dependent clause will function as an adjective.

Fragment   People who have a personality disorder. [*Who* takes the place of the subject *people*, creating a dependent clause.]

Revised   People ~~who~~ have a personality disorder. [Eliminating *who* leaves a simple sentence.]

Revised   People who have a personality disorder *see their behavior as acceptable.* [*People* is the subject of a verb, *see*, with a *who* clause as adjective modifier.]

Exception: When one of the above-listed relative pronouns introduces a question, it becomes an interrogative (questioning) pronoun. The resulting construction is not considered to be a fragment: *Who has a personality disorder?*

▶ **EXERCISE I**

Use the three-part test to identify fragments and to explain the cause of each fragment. Place a check before complete sentences, and circle the numbers of items that are fragments.

Example: When the author of one study claims that groups moving in unison tend to think alike.

Fragment—fails Test 3 (The word *when* prevents the clause from standing alone as a sentence.)

1. Rhythmic movements help to establish a group bond.
2. Giving the group a certain advantage over the other groups.
3. One reason why armies put so much emphasis on drilling new recruits.
4. Possibly movement in unison represents or fosters identical, in-group thinking.
5. The Nazi parade is a striking example of the connection between lockstep movement and lockstep thinking.

▶ 12b Eliminate fragments: Revise dependent clauses set off as sentences.

A dependent clause functions as a modifier—either as an adverb (see 19b-1) or as an adjective (see 19b-2). A dependent clause that has been set off incorrectly as a sentence can be corrected in one of two ways: by converting the clause to an independent clause or by joining the clause to a new sentence.

▶ 1 Convert the dependent clause to an independent clause.

Fragment   Even though the president attended the meeting.

Clear   The president attended the meeting.

If the dependent clause begins with a subordinating conjunction, delete the conjunction, and you will have an independent clause—a sentence.

Fragment   While Americans keep recycling the same old clichés.

Revised   ~~While~~ Americans keep recycling the same old clichés.

If a dependent clause uses a relative pronoun, eliminate the relative pronoun, replacing it with a noun or personal pronoun, and you will have an independent clause.

Fragment   Many students, who might read more often.

Revised   Many students ~~who~~ might read more often. [The eliminated relative pronoun leaves the noun, *students*, as the subject.]

Revised   ~~Many students~~ *They* might read more often. [The eliminated relative pronoun is replaced by the pronoun, *they*.]

▶ 2 Join the dependent clause to a new sentence.

Fragment   Though the president attended.

Clear   Though the president attended, she did not speak.

The dependent clause introduced by a subordinating conjunction can be made to function as an adverb by joining it to an independent clause. When the dependent clause introduces a sentence, set it off with a comma (see 25a-1). When the clause ends a sentence, do not use a comma (but see 25a-3).

Fragment	If our culture did not perceive and portray reading as an almost anti-social activity.
Revised	*Many students might read more often* if our culture did not portray reading as an almost antisocial activity.

A dependent clause fragment that uses a relative pronoun can be made to function as an adjective (a relative clause) by attaching it to an independent clause.

Fragment	Verdenal Johnson, a president of the Association for the Encouragement of Correct Pronunciation, Spelling and Usage in Public Communications, who has with a felt-tipped marker corrected errors on public signs. [The noun and modifying clause have no verb.]
Revised	Verdenal Johnson, who has with a felt-tipped marker corrected errors on public signs, served as president of the Association for the Encouragement of Correct Pronunciation, Spelling and Usage in Public Communications. [The *who* clause functions as an adjective in a sentence with a new verb, *served*.]

▶ **EXERCISE 2**

Identify fragments in the following paragraph. Combine fragments to make complete sentences.

> *Example:* Even though Anheuser-Busch, Miller, G. Heileman, Coors, and Pabst brew 95 percent of the 200 million barrels of beer produced annually in the United States. These companies are not the only producers of American beer.
>
> Even though Anheuser-Busch, Miller, G. Heileman, Coors, and Pabst brew 95 percent of the 200 million barrels of beer produced annually in the United States, these companies are not the only producers of American beer.

While only eight microbreweries existed in the United States a decade ago. Today seventy microbreweries are brewing more than 65,000 barrels of specialty beers a year. Microbreweries are winning awards for the tastiness of their products. Which has caused the large producers to alter their production and advertising techniques. Because microbrewery beer is often free of additives. It must be sold locally. Local production, distribution, and advertising has become a key to microbrewery success. Which depends on creating the perception among buyers of a freshness and healthfulness not available in mass-market beers. Even though image is important. Quality of the product is what has convinced an increasing number of American beer drinkers to buy from local, smaller breweries.

▶ **12c** **Eliminate fragments: Revise phrases set off as sentences.**

Phrases consist of nouns and the words associated with them or verb forms not functioning as verbs (called *verbals*) and the words associated with them. Phrases function as sentence parts—as modifiers, subjects, objects, and complements—but never as sentences. The various kinds of phrases are defined in 7d. As with

Eliminating Fragments from Your Writing

1. **Revise dependent clauses set off as sentences.**
   Convert the dependent clause to an independent clause.
   Fragment   Although computers may be revolutionizing the world.
   Revised   ~~Although~~ Computers may be revolutionizing the world.

   Join the dependent clause to a new sentence.
   Fragment   Although, computers may be revolutionizing the world.
   Revised   Although computers may be revolutionizing the world, *relatively few people understand how they function.*

2. **Revise phrases set off as sentences.**
   There are various kinds of phrases: verbal, prepositional, absolute, and appositive (see 7d). None can stand alone as a sentence.
   Fragment   After years of drought.
   Revised   ~~After~~ Years of drought *can devastate a national economy.*
   Revised   After years of drought, *a nation's economy can be devastated.*

3. **Revise repeating structures or compound predicates set off as sentences.**
   Repeating elements and compound predicates cannot stand alone. Incorporate such structures into an existing sentence, or add words to construct a new sentence.
   Fragment   College sports has long been conducted as a business. A profitable business. [The repeating element is a fragment.]
   Revised   College sports has long been conducted as a business—a profitable business. [The repeating element has been incorporated into an existing sentence.]

dependent clauses that form fragments, you may either convert phrases to complete sentences by adding words, or you may join phrases to independent clauses.

▶**1**   **Revising verbal phrases**

Participial and gerund phrases (functioning as modifiers or nouns)

Fragment   Crossing out the word *very*.
Revised   Verdenal Johnson ~~crossing~~ crosses out the word *very*. [The phrase is rewritten as a sentence.]
Revised   Crossing out the word *very*, the copyeditor Verdenal Johnson encourages writers to use more specific words—for example, *crimson* for *very red*. [The participial phrase, functioning as an adjective, is joined to an independent clause.]

Infinitive phrases (functioning as nouns)

Fragment   To delete the word *very*.
Revised   Johnson prefers to delete the word *very* when she works as a copyeditor. [The phrase is rewritten as a sentence.]

▶2 Revising prepositional phrases (functioning as modifiers)

Fragment With its emphasis on quick, informal communication.

Revised With its emphasis on quick, informal communication, e-mail invites users to be careless about the rules of grammar and usage. [The phrase is joined to an independent clause.]

▶3 Revising absolute phrases (modifying an entire sentence)

Fragment The need for unhindered movement being a defining quality of the American character.

Revised The need for unhindered movement is a defining quality of the American character. [The phrase is rewritten as a sentence.]

Revised Not surprisingly, the culture of the automobile first arose in the United States, the need for unhindered movement being a defining quality of the American character. [The phrase is joined as a modifier to an independent clause.]

▶4 Revising appositive phrases (renaming or describing other nouns)

Fragment A tendency to drive first and think about environmental consequences later.

Revised Americans have a tendency to drive first and think about environmental consequences later. [The phrase is rewritten as a sentence.]

Revised Annie Pritzker, director of Clean Airways and Highways, says that American drivers suffer from "Auto-mania," a tendency to drive first and think about environmental consequences later. [The phrase renames the final noun in the independent clause.]

▶ EXERCISE 3

Identify the numbered units that are fragments, and correct them. Place a check before any sentence needing no revision.

Example: Whereas, as children mature, they should learn to sort through conflicting messages. [*Whereas* is a subordinating conjunction. The clause that follows is dependent.]

As children mature, they should learn to sort through conflicting messages.

(1) Children receive conflicting messages from a variety of sources. (2) Which cannot be silenced: teachers, books, friends, and television programs. We have, from time to time, experimented in this country with limiting access to potentially damaging or offensive materials (3) such as books and movies. (4) But these experiments have not withstood legal challenges. (5) The courts have decided that Americans have the right to choose what they see or hear and that writers and others have the right to create what they wish. (6) Although, certain extreme instances, like child pornography, are so offensive and damaging to the children being filmed that as a society we *have* said that such products are repugnant. (7) Which is the argument that Charren is making about advertisements directed at children. (8) But

as a society having agreed to limit speech only in the most extreme cases. (9) There is nothing in the making of advertisements that is as purposefully vulgar or hurtful as there is in child pornography. (10) If anything, advertising more closely resembling the language of our everyday speech.

> ## 12d Eliminate fragments: Revise repeating structures or compound predicates set off as sentences.

Fragment As large as the capitol's rotunda

Clear The foyer was large, as large as the capitol's rotunda.

Repetition can be an effective stylistic tool (see 19c-2). Repeated elements, however, are not sentences but sentence parts and should not be punctuated as sentences. Use a comma or dashes to set off repeated elements.

Fragment Children begin for the first time to differentiate themselves from others as they enter adolescence. *As they begin to develop a personal identity.* [The subordinate *as* clause cannot stand alone.]

Revised Children begin for the first time to differentiate themselves from others as they enter adolescence, as they begin to develop a personal identity. [The clause is subordinated.]

Fragment Adolescents want to know they belong in the social order. An order shaped by forces they barely understand. [The phrase and clause need a connection.]

Revised Adolescents want to know they belong in the social order—an order shaped by forces they barely understand. [The structure repeats and expands the term *social order.*]

Compound predicates consist of two sentence verbs (and their associated words) joined with a coordinating conjunction, such as *and* or *but*. The two predicates share the same subject and are part of the same sentence. When one half of the compound predicate is punctuated as a sentence, it becomes a fragment. To correct the fragment, join it to a sentence that contains an appropriate subject, or provide the fragment with its own subject.

Fragment The process of maturation is lifelong. *But is most critical during the adolescent years.* [The last unit has no subject.]

Revised The process of maturation is lifelong. But *the process* is most critical during the adolescent years. [The unit is given its own subject.]

Revised The process of maturation is lifelong but is most critical during the adolescent years. [The phrase is joined to the preceding sentence as a compound predicate.]

> ### EXERCISE 4

Identify which of the following units are fragments. Correct each by writing a new sentence or by joining the fragment to an independent clause.

Example: Messiness in the workplace. How does it affect your productivity? [The first unit lacks a verb.]

How does messiness in the workplace affect your productivity? [The fragment replaces the pronoun *it* and becomes the subject of the question.]

Specialists suggest that setting up a workable system to organize yourself is only a first step. A small one. The most significant organizing principle in life is a wastebasket in every room. And a willingness to use them. A common myth is that highly creative people are "naturally" messier and more chaotic than those who are relatively uncreative. That being organized and artistic are incompatible. A *Wall Street Journal* article reported that people spend an average of six weeks a year looking for things in their offices. Unbelievable!

COMPUTER TIPS

Help Online

Online Writing Labs (OWLs) are beginning to proliferate on the Internet. These resource centers offer writing services ranging from standard handbook information to reviewers who will actually read a draft and offer suggestions. Most provide help with specific questions on composition, research, grammar, and style. The most popular OWL is located at Purdue University: <http://owl.english.purdue.edu>.

▶ 12e Use fragments intentionally on rare occasions.

Whose business was it? No one's.
The speaker made his point. Barely.

Fragments are not suitable for academic writing. In personal essays and in fiction, experienced writers will occasionally use sentence fragments by design. These intentional uses are always carefully fitted to the context of a neighboring sentence, sometimes answering an implied question or completing a parallel structure that has been separated for emphasis. In academic prose, a fragment will probably be regarded as a lapse, not as a stylistic flourish.

Intentional use of fragments

There are fewer and fewer students, I find, who have playful imaginations. Please understand that I am not asking for profound creativity. *Or resourceful inventiveness.* Rather, I should like to see more students whose minds sparkle.
—ARLEN J. HANSEN, "The Imagination Gap"

CHAPTER **13**

Comma Splices and Fused Sentences

S entence grammar is built on the fundamental rule that independent clauses— complete sentences—are the basic units for making a statement. Sentences must be kept distinct from one another. When sentence boundaries are blurred, statements become confused; readers must struggle to decipher which combinations of words might form meaningful units.

To keep your statements distinct and clear, remember: independent clauses must be separated with a period, a semicolon, or a colon, or they must be carefully linked with a conjunction and appropriate punctuation.

Five Ways to Mark the Boundary between Sentences

Mark a sentence boundary with punctuation.

1. Use a period: He laughed. He danced. He sang.
2. Use a semicolon: He laughed; he danced and sang.

Mark a sentence boundary with a conjunction and punctuation.

3. Use a coordinating conjunction: He laughed, and he danced.
4. Use a subordinating conjunction: While he laughed, he danced.
5. Use a conjunctive adverb: He laughed; moreover, he danced.

Sentence boundaries can become blurred in two ways: with comma splices or with fused (run-on) sentences. In the **fused** (or **run-on**) **sentence,** the writer fails to recognize the end of one independent clause and the beginning of the next.

Fused sentence   The blurring of sentence boundaries can create a comprehension problem readers must often stop to decipher which combinations of words form meaningful units. [*Readers* is a new subject of a new independent clause; a period or semicolon should precede it.]

The writer of a **comma splice** recognizes the end of one independent clause and the beginning of the next, but marks the boundary between the two incorrectly— with a comma.

Spotlight on Common Errors—
SENTENCE CONSTRUCTION AND
SENTENCE BOUNDARIES

These are the errors most commonly associated with sentence construction and sentence boundaries. For full explanations and suggested revisions, follow the cross-references to chapter sections.

RECOGNIZING SENTENCE BOUNDARIES: The end of a sentence is usually marked with a period. Not clearly marking the end will result in a FRAGMENT (see 12a), a FUSED SENTENCE (see 13b-1), or a COMMA SPLICE (see 13b-1).

Correct Winston Churchill became a leader. He served his country in the First World War. Churchill was a leader of distinction.

Fused sentences Winston Churchill became a leader he served his country in the First World War Churchill was a leader of distinction.

Comma splices Winston Churchill became a leader, he served his country in the First World War, Churchill was a leader of distinction.

REVISING ERRORS OF SENTENCE CONSTRUCTION: Learn to recognize sentence boundaries (see 12a). Link sentences with these strategies:

Link by combining parts of two sentences into one (see 12c).

Winston Churchill became a leader. Churchill was a leader **of distinction.**

Winston Churchill became a leader of distinction.

Link by using a comma plus one of these conjunctions—*and, but, or, nor* (see coordinating conjunctions, 13b-2, 19a-1).

Winston Churchill served his country in the First World War**, *and*** he became a leader of distinction.

Link by using a semicolon (see 13b-3, 26a–c).

Winston Churchill served his country in the First World War**;** he became a leader of distinction.

Link by using a semicolon (or period) and a word such as *however, consequently,* or *therefore* (see conjunctive adverbs, 13b-4, 19a-3).

Winston Churchill served his country in the First World War**;** *subsequently,* he became a leader of distinction.

Link by using a word such as *when, while,* or *because* (see subordinating conjunctions, 13b-5, 19b).

After he served his country in the First World War**,** Winston Churchill became a leader of distinction.

259

▶ **13a**   **Identify fused sentences and comma splices.**

Fused   In the last election, voter turnout was low turnout should be higher.

Comma splice   In the last election, voter turnout was low, turnout should be higher.

Clear   In the last election, voter turnout was low. Turnout should be higher.

Before submitting a draft of your work to others, read your sentences aloud. When you listen to your writing, you can often catch errors that go undetected when you read silently. Look for long sentences that seem to consist of two or more separate statements, or those that seem so long they force you to stop midway to take a breath. Be on the alert, especially, for the following three circumstances in which fused sentences and comma splices are found.

1. **A sentence of explanation, expansion, or example** is frequently fused to or spliced together with another sentence that is being explained, expanded on, or illustrated. Even if the topics of the two sentences are closely related, the sentences themselves must remain distinct.

   Fused   The Brotherhood was a group of young, enthusiastic painters, poets, and painter-poets their artistic aims varied widely.

   Comma splice   The Brotherhood was a group of young, enthusiastic painters, poets, and painter-poets, their artistic aims varied widely.

   Revised   The Brotherhood was a group of young, enthusiastic painters, poets, and painter-poets. Their artistic aims varied widely.

2. **The pronouns** *he, she, they, it, this,* and *that,* when renaming the subject of a sentence, can signal a comma splice or a fused sentence. Even when the subject named or renamed in adjacent sentences is identical, the sentences themselves must be kept distinct.

   Fused   Dante Gabriel Rossetti was a poet he was also a painter.

   Comma splice   Dante Gabriel Rossetti was a poet, he was also a painter.

   Revised   Dante Gabriel Rossetti was a poet, and he was a painter.

3. **Conjunctive adverbs** (words such as *however, furthermore, thus, therefore,* and *consequently*) **and transitional expressions** (phrases such as *for example* and *on the other hand*) are commonly found in fused or spliced clauses. Conjunctive adverbs and transitions always link complete sentences. Writers must reflect this linkage with appropriate punctuation: a period or semicolon. (For a complete list of conjunctive adverbs, see 19a and 19a-3.)

   Fused sentence   Ninety percent of the Hispanic vote is concentrated in nine states that cast seventy-one percent of all electoral ballots consequently Hispanics have emerged as a nationally influential group of voters.

Comma splice	Ninety percent of the Hispanic vote is concentrated in nine states that cast seventy-one percent of all electoral ballots, consequently, Hispanics have emerged as a nationally influential group of voters.
Revised	Ninety percent of the Hispanic vote is concentrated in nine states that cast seventy-one percent of all electoral ballots. Consequently, Hispanics have emerged as a nationally influential group of voters. [*Consequently* starts a new main clause.]

EXERCISE 1

Use a slash mark (/) to identify the points at which the following sentences are fused or spliced together.

> *Example:* Designers of advertisements for professional medical journals use multiple strategies for convincing their readers sometimes they use shocking visual images.
>
> Designers of advertisements for professional medical journals use multiple strategies for convincing readers **/** sometimes they use shocking visual images.

1. Advertisements for aspirin and other pain relievers are incredibly dull, they are so like one another, so unmemorable that we remember them only because of their sheer frequency.
2. Unlike most other advertising, pain reliever commercials are very modest in their claims, in other words, they promise only partial relief from minor aches and only relatively quickly.
3. One would expect that such commercials would press harder to represent both the intensity of the pain as well as the joy of relief however these advertisements never suggest that the sufferer was ever in acute pain or that the sufferer's relief is now total.
4. Oddly enough, ads for pain relievers claim very little, they are undramatic, uninteresting.
5. The advertisements that physicians and surgeons see in their professional journals do attempt to represent acute pain, the difference may be attributable to the fact that the audience in this case (doctors) is not experiencing pain itself, but rather is treating pain.

13b Correct fused sentences and comma splices in one of five ways.

1 Separate independent clauses with a period (and sometimes a colon).

Comma splice	Cotton was once the lead farm product in Alabama, today poultry has replaced it.
Clear	Cotton was once the lead farm product in Alabama. Today, poultry has replaced it.

Using a period is the most obvious way to repair a fused or spliced construction. Occasionally, writers use a colon between independent clauses when the first sentence is a formal and emphatic introduction to the second sentence.

Fused sentence	Logging is often the first step in deforestation it may be followed by complete clearing of trees and a deliberate shift to unsound land uses.
Comma splice	Logging is often the first step in deforestation, it may be followed by complete clearing of trees and a deliberate shift to unsound land uses.
Revised	Logging is often the first step in deforestation. It may be followed by complete clearing of trees and a deliberate shift to unsound land uses.
Revised	Logging is often the first step in deforestation: it may be followed by complete clearing of trees and a deliberate shift to unsound land uses. [The colon gives the opening clause an emphatic introductory function.]

▶ 2 Link clauses with a comma and a coordinating conjunction.

http://parallel.park.uga.edu/
~sigalas/Commas/2ic.html
Here's an upbeat page with a handy mnemonic device for curing comma splices.

Fused	January may be the coldest month it is a month of great productivity.
Clear	January may be the coldest month, **but** it is a month of great productivity.

Use a comma placed *before* a coordinating conjunction—*and, but, or, nor, for, so,* and *yet*—to link sentences that are closely related in content and that are equally important. (See 19a for a detailed discussion of coordinating conjunctions.)

Fused sentence	Deforestation has a severe environmental impact on soil in heavy tropical rains soil erodes quickly.
Comma splice	Deforestation has a severe environmental impact on soil, in heavy tropical rains soil erodes quickly.
Revised	Deforestation has a severe environmental impact on soil, **for** in heavy tropical rains soil erodes quickly.

▶ 3 Link clauses with a semicolon.

Fused	Wind is one cause of erosion water is another cause.
Comma Splice	Wind is one cause of erosion, water is another cause.
Clear	Wind is one cause of erosion; water is another cause.

Use a semicolon in place of a comma and a coordinating conjunction to link sentences that are closely related and equally important. The semicolon links independent clauses without making the relationship between them explicit. You might choose a semicolon to repair a fused or spliced construction either when the relationship between clauses is crystal clear and a conjunction would be redundant or when you wish to create anticipation—leaving your readers to discover the exact relationship between clauses.

Fused sentence	Experience reinforces the argument that deforestation has not been a path to economic development in most tropical countries it has instead been a costly drain on resources.
Comma splice	Experience reinforces the argument that deforestation has not been a path to economic development, in most tropical countries it has instead been a costly drain on resources.

Revised   Experience reinforces the argument that deforestation has not been a path to economic development; in most tropical countries it has instead been a costly drain on resources.

CRITICAL DECISIONS

Challenge and be challenged: Choosing a method to link independent clauses

A period helps readers focus on and understand one sentence at a time. To show the relationship *between* sentences, consider linking clauses. You have various options for doing so; which option you choose depends on the relationship you want to establish between independent clauses.

- **Use a colon to make one independent clause announce another.** (See 13b-1.)

    Separated   The race was postponed for one reason. The sponsors withdrew their support.

    Linked   The race was postponed for one reason: the sponsors withdrew their support.

- **Use one of three options to maintain equal emphasis between two independent clauses.** (See 13b-2–4 and 19a.)

Coordinating conjunction with a comma

   Separated   Runners had already arrived. They were angry with the postponement.

   Linked   Runners had already arrived, **and** they were angry with the postponement.

Conjunctive adverb with a semicolon or a period

   Separated   The sponsors cited financial worries. They had political concerns as well.

   Linked   The sponsors cited financial worries; **however,** they had political concerns as well.

Semicolon

   Separated   One faction of runners wanted to boycott all future races in that city. Another faction wanted to stage a protest march.

   Linked   One faction of runners wanted to boycott all future races in that city; another faction wanted to stage a protest march.

- **Use a subordinating conjunction to emphasize one independent clause more than the other.** (See 13b-5 and 19b.)

    Separated   The press was embarrassing. The sponsors canceled the race permanently.

    Linked   **Because** the press was embarrassing, the sponsors canceled the race permanently.

Correct Fused Sentences and Comma Splices in One of Five Ways   **263**

4 Link clauses with a semicolon (or period) and a conjunctive adverb.

Comma splice   Joyce Carol Oates is a novelist, essayist, playwright, and poet, she is a distinguished scholar.

Clear   Joyce Carol Oates is a novelist, essayist, playwright, and poet; **moreover,** she is a distinguished scholar.

Use conjunctive adverbs—words such as *however, furthermore, thus, therefore,* and *consequently*—to link closely related, equally important clauses. (See 19a and 19a-3 for a complete list of conjunctive adverbs.) Conjunctive adverbs establish the same relationships—such as addition, contrast, and cause—as do coordinating conjunctions.

Place a period between clauses when you want a full separation of ideas. Place a semicolon between clauses when you want to emphasize the link between ideas. As with most adverbs, a conjunctive adverb can shift its location in a sentence. If placed at the beginning, the conjunctive adverb is followed (usually) by a comma. If placed in the middle, it is usually set off by a pair of commas. And if placed at the end, it is preceded by a comma. Wherever you place the adverb, be sure to use a period or a semicolon between the two clauses you have linked.

Fused sentence   Deforestation is not irreversible once a forest is cleared regeneration takes a lifetime.

Comma splice   Deforestation is not irreversible, once a forest is cleared regeneration takes a lifetime.

Revised   Deforestation is not irreversible; however, once a forest is cleared, regeneration takes a lifetime. [The semicolon emphasizes the link between ideas.]

Revised   Deforestation is not irreversible. However, once a forest is cleared, regeneration takes a lifetime. [The period makes a full separation.]

Revised   Deforestation is not irreversible. Once a forest is cleared, however, regeneration takes a lifetime.

5 Link clauses with a subordinating conjunction or construction.

Comma splice   Hannibal crossed the Alps, he defeated the Romans in the Po Valley.

Clear   **After** Hannibal crossed the Alps, he defeated the Romans in the Po Valley.

Use a subordinating conjunction to join fused or spliced independent clauses. By placing a subordinating conjunction at the beginning of an independent clause, or by using a relative pronoun such as *who, whom, which,* or *that,* you render that clause dependent. The new dependent clause will function as a modifier. Be aware of comma use with these constructions: when the clause begins a sentence, a comma follows it. The dependent clause at the end of a sentence often does not use a comma. (See 19b and 25 for discussions of subordination.)

Fused sentence   International development-assistance agencies have begun to lend help a number of governments are now strengthening their forest-management programs.

Comma splice	International development-assistance agencies have begun to lend help, a number of governments are now strengthening their forest-management programs.
Revised	**Because** international development-assistance agencies have begun to lend help, a number of governments are now strengthening their forest-management programs. [A dependent clause begins the sentence.]
Revised	A number of governments are now strengthening their forest-management programs **because** international development-assistance agencies have begun to lend help. [A dependent clause ends the sentence.]
Revised	A number of governments are now strengthening the forest-management programs **that** have begun to get help from international development-assistance agencies. [A dependent relative clause ends the sentence, creating a different meaning.]

Conjunctions and Punctuation

Coordinating Conjunctions

and   but   so   or   for   nor   yet

Use coordinating conjunctions with punctuation in this pattern:

Independent clause   ,   CONJUNCTION   independent clause.

Fused sentence   Newton developed calculus he discovered laws of gravity.

Comma splice   Newton developed calculus, he discovered laws of gravity.

Revised   Newton developed calculus, and he discovered laws of gravity.

Conjunctive Adverbs

however   furthermore   thus   therefore   consequently

Use conjunctive adverbs with punctuation in these patterns:

Independent clause   ;   CONJUNCTION   ,   independent clause.
Independent clause   .   CONJUNCTION   ,   independent clause.

Revised   Newton developed calculus; moreover, he discovered laws of gravity.

Revised   Newton developed calculus. Moreover, he discovered laws of gravity.

Subordinating Conjunctions

after   although   because   once   since   though   while

Use subordinating conjunctions with punctuation in these patterns:

CONJUNCTION   clause   ,   independent clause
Independent clause   CONJUNCTION   clause.

Revised   After Newton developed calculus, he discovered laws of gravity.

Revised   Newton discovered laws of gravity after he developed calculus.

▶ **EXERCISE 2**

Using any of the strategies discussed in this chapter, correctly punctuate the following word groupings in which you find fused sentences or comma splices. In each case, name the error (or errors) you are correcting.

> *Example:* Genetic engineering has been called the great scientific breakthrough of the century there are still many doubts concerning its potential effects on our environment.
>
> *Fused sentence.* Genetic engineering has been called the great scientific breakthrough of the century. **However,** there are still many doubts concerning its potential effects on our environment.

1. Genetic engineering is the technique by which scientists alter or combine hereditary materials, genes are part of all living material they carry chemical information that determines every organism's characteristics.

2. The movement of creating genetically engineered organisms began in the early 1900s based on the earlier experiments of the Austrian monk Gregor Mendel he laid the foundation for future experiments with his work on cross-breeding in plants.

3. Scientists have discovered the benefits and uses of genetically engineered organisms in agriculture one of the first examples is the ice-minus bacterium created by Steve Lindow and Nicholas Panopoulos.

4. Lindow and Panopoulos realized that a bacterium commonly found in plants produces a protein that helps ice to form causing damaging frost, they removed this unfavorable gene, they prevented ice from forming on greenhouse plants.

5. Researchers hope in 20 to 30 years to create corn and wheat plants that can fix their own nitrogen in this way the plants would not need to be fertilized, this would save anywhere from $3 to $14 billion annually.

6. Geneticists have found beneficial uses of engineered organisms in agriculture, they have also found ways to use these organisms to clean up environmental hazards for instance, Dr. Anandra M. Chakrabarty has engineered an organism that breaks up oil spills.

EXERCISE 3

Correct the fused sentences and comma splices in the following paragraph, making use of all five strategies discussed in this chapter. One consideration governing your choice of corrections should be sentence variety. Vary methods for correcting fused and spliced clauses to avoid repeating sentence structures in consecutive sentences.

> Whatever they may believe about what happens to the soul after death most cultures bury their dead. Given the grim fact of history that corpses can sometimes pile up at an alarming rate, it has not always been easy for managers of cemeteries, in a way cemetery planning is much like urban planning. Streets have to be mapped out and plots need to be sold, often, above-ground structures—mausoleums—have to be designed and executed. A chapel of some sort is usually called for—decorated Gothic or vertical Gothic, above all the cemetery must be landscaped in such a way as to afford comfort to the mourners.

▶

CHAPTER 14

Pronoun Reference

A pronoun substitutes for a noun, allowing you to talk about someone or something without having to repeat its name (see 7a-7). To serve this function, a pronoun must take on meaning from a specific noun; the pronoun must make a clear and unmistakable reference to the noun for which it substitutes—called its **antecedent.** When the reference is not clearly made to a specific noun, the meaning of the whole sentence can become vague or confused.

Unclear   Michelangelo had a complex personality, as did Raphael, though *his* was the more complex. *His* art was not nearly so typical of the High Renaissance, and *he* was frequently irascible—as impatient with the shortcomings of others as with *his* own.

To whom do the pronouns *he* and *his* refer in these sentences? No one can tell. The sentences need to be revised, and the pronouns and antecedents must be placed with care to keep readers moving forward.

Revised   Michelangelo had a complex personality, as did Raphael, though *Michelangelo's* was the more complex. *His* art was not nearly so typical of the High Renaissance, and *he* was frequently irascible—as impatient with the shortcomings of others as with *his* own. [The proper noun replaces an unclear pronoun, providing a reference point for all the pronouns that follow.]

▶ 14a   Make pronouns refer clearly to their antecedents.

Confusing   When Mark and Jay return home, *he* will call.
Clear   When Mark and Jay return home, *Mark* will call.

Revise a sentence whenever a pronoun can refer to more than one antecedent. Use a noun in place of a pronoun, if needed for clarity; or reposition a pronoun so that its antecedent is unmistakable.

Confusing   In 1949, astronomer Gerard Kuiper proposed the existence of a comet-strewn belt girting our solar system, although the same theory had been advanced by British astronomer K. E. Edgewater two years earlier. Astronomer Hal Levin comments that there is much uncertainty as to whether Kuiper knew about *him*. [Does the pronoun *him* refer to Levin or Edgewater?]

Revised	In 1949, astronomer Gerard Kuiper proposed the existence of a comet-strewn belt girting our solar system, although the same theory had been advanced by British astronomer K. E. Edgewater two years earlier. Astronomer Hal Levin comments that there is much uncertainty as to whether Kuiper knew about Edgewater.

Describing a person's speech indirectly can lead to unclear pronoun reference. Occasionally, if you can document what was said, you can convert indirect quotations to direct ones in order to clarify a pronoun's reference. Otherwise, you can restate the sentence carefully to avoid confusion among the nouns.

Confusing	One of the astronomers, showing telescopic photos of the belt to the reporter, said that *he* didn't know whether *he* had discovered the home base of the comets or whether *he* was simply seeing the effects of cosmic rays hitting the lens of the telescope's camera. [Do any of these *hes* refer to the reporter?]
Direct statement	One of the astronomers, showing telescopic photos of the belt to the reporter, said: "I didn't know whether I had discovered the home base of the comets or whether I was simply seeing the effects of cosmic rays hitting the lens of the telescope's camera."
Restatement	One of the astronomers told the reporter that the photos could have been pictures of the home base of our comets or simply an optical effect produced by cosmic rays hitting the lens of the telescope's camera.

ESL NOTE   In a standard English sentence, the subject is not repeated elsewhere in the sentence with an unnecessary pronoun. Pronouns are involved when the subject is renamed in a dependent clause (see 7e-2). Repeated subjects must be avoided in sentences with long dependent clauses separating subjects from verbs (see 14e-1 and 47d-1).

▶ **14b**   **Keep pronouns close to their antecedents.**

Confusing	The *statement* that Dr. Parker made and that she issued as a formal warning infuriated the mayor, who knew *it* would alarm the public.
Clear	Issued as a formal warning, Dr. Parker's *statement* alarmed the public, and *it* infuriated the mayor.

Even when pronoun choice is correct, too many words between a pronoun and its antecedent can confuse readers. If, in a long sentence or in adjacent sentences, several nouns appear between a pronoun and its proper antecedent, these nouns will incorrectly claim the reader's attention as the word renamed by the pronoun.

Confusing	*Prehistoric peoples* used many organic substances, which survive at relatively few archaeological sites. Bone and antler were commonly used, especially in Europe some fifteen thousand years ago. *They* relied heavily on plant fibers and baskets for their material culture. [The pronoun *they* must refer to *prehistoric peoples*, since only people can *rely*, but the intervening nouns distract from this reference.]

Spotlight on Common Errors—
PRONOUN REFERENCE

These are the errors most commonly associated with pronoun reference. For full explanations and suggested revisions, follow the cross-references to chapter sections.

PRONOUN REFERENCE ERRORS arise when a sentence leaves readers unable to link a pronoun with an *antecedent*—a specific noun that the pronoun refers to and renames (see 7a-7). If the identity of this antecedent is unclear, readers may miss the reference and become confused. Four error patterns lead to problems with pronoun reference.

> **A pronoun should refer clearly to a single noun. When the pronoun can refer to either of two (or more) nouns within a sentence or between sentences, revise sentences for clarity (see 14a).**

Within a sentence

Faulty	Revised
When Mark and Jay return home, *he* will call. [To whom does *he* refer?]	When Mark and Jay return home, *Mark* will call.

Between sentences

Faulty	Revised
The conversation between Clara and Nancy lasted two hours. At the end, *she* was exhausted. [Which one is *she*?]	The conversation between Clara and Nancy lasted two hours. At the end, *Clara* was exhausted.

> **A pronoun should be located close to the noun it renames. When a pronoun is too far from its antecedent, revise the sentence to narrow the distance and clarify meaning (see 14b).**

Within a sentence

Faulty	Revised
The statement that Dr. Parker made about a city water fountain and that she issued as a formal warning infuriated the mayor, who knew *it* would alarm the public. [Does *it* clearly refer to the faraway *statement* and not to something else?]	Issued as a formal warning, Dr. Parker's *statement* about a city water fountain alarmed the public, and *it* infuriated the mayor. [Less distance between the pronoun and antecedent makes the reference clear.]

(continued)

Between sentences

Faulty

Major oil spills have fouled coastlines in Alaska, France, and England and have caused severe ecological damage. *Some* could almost certainly be avoided. [Does *some* refer to faraway *spills* or to *coastlines?*]

Revised

Major oil spills have fouled coastlines in Alaska, France, and England and have caused severe ecological damage. *Some spills* could almost certainly be avoided. [*Spills* is added to clear up the reference.]

> **The pronouns *this* and *that* should refer to specific words. When either is used as a one-word summary of a preceding sentence, revise to clarify the reference between sentences by adding an additional word or phrase of summary (see 14c-3).**

Faulty

The purpose of the conference was to explore the links between lung cancer and secondhand smoke. *This* was firmly established. [What was established?]

Revised

The purpose of the conference was to explore the links between lung cancer and secondhand smoke. *This connection* was firmly established. [A summary word added makes the reference clear.]

> **Once you establish a pattern of first-person (*I/we*), second-person (*you*), or third-person pronouns (*he/she/it/they*) in a sentence or paragraph (see 8a, 8b), keep references to your subject *consistent*. Prevent confusion by avoiding shifts and revising sentences for consistency (see 16a-1).**

Within a sentence

Faulty

Students generally fare better when *you* are given instruction on taking lecture notes. [Confusion arises between third-person *students* and second-person *you*. Who is the subject?]

Revised

Students generally fare better when *they* are given instruction on taking lecture notes.[Consistent third person] OR
As a student, *you* will generally fare better when you are given instruction on taking lecture notes.

Between sentences

Faulty

Students fare better when given instruction on basic skills. *You* can improve *your* notetaking after getting help with the techniques. [Have *students* suddenly become *you?*]

Revised

Students fare better when given instruction on basic skills. *They* can improve *their* notetaking after getting help with the techniques.

Closer antecedent	*Prehistoric peoples* used many organic substances, which survive at relatively few archaeological sites. *They commonly used* bone and antler, especially in Europe some fifteen thousand years ago. *They* also relied heavily on plant fibers and baskets for their material culture.
Pronoun replaced	*Prehistoric peoples* used many organic substances, which survive at relatively few archaeological sites. Bone and antler were commonly used, especially in Europe some fifteen thousand years ago. *The desert peoples of western North America* relied heavily on plant fibers and baskets for their material culture.

The relative pronouns *who*, *which*, and *that*, when introducing a modifying adjective clause, should be placed close to the nouns they modify (see 19b-2).

Confusing	Prehistoric peoples used many organic substances difficult to find at archaeological sites, which included bone and antler. [Does *which* refer to *sites* or *substances*?]
Closer antecedent	Prehistoric peoples used many organic substances, including bone and antler, which survive at relatively few archaeological sites.

▶ **EXERCISE 1**

Rewrite the sentences that follow so that pronouns are replaced or are close to and refer clearly to the nouns they rename. Place a check beside the sentences that need no revision.

> *Example:* When Bob talks with Joe by phone, he can hardly get a word in edgewise because he expects a more delayed response from him.
>
> When Bob talks with Joe by phone, Bob can hardly get a word in edgewise because he expects a more delayed response from Joe. [The pronouns are replaced with nouns.]

1. The ritual of greeting varies from one culture to another; for example, Americans ask, "How are you?" whereas Filipinos ask, "Where are you going?"—a question that seems prying to them.
2. Professor Deborah Tannen claims that while conducting research in a corporate environment, she found many women who rightly perceived themselves as highly successful; these women felt that their coworkers shared this perception but that higher-level management did not recognize it.
3. The men whom Tannen interviewed often told her that if she hadn't been promoted, it was because she didn't deserve it.

▶ **14c**   **State a pronoun's antecedent clearly.**

To be clear, a pronoun's antecedent should be stated directly, either in the sentence in which the pronoun appears or in an immediately preceding sentence. If the antecedent is merely implied, the pronoun's meaning will be weak or imprecise, and the reader will probably be confused.

▶**1** Make a pronoun refer to a specific noun antecedent, not to a modifier that may imply the antecedent.

Confusing	From *animated* films such as *Fantasia* in 1940 to *Mulan* in 1998, Disney studios have raised *it* to an art form.
Clear	From films such as *Fantasia* in 1940 to *Mulan* in 1998, Disney studios have raised *animation* to an art form.

Although an adjective may imply the antecedent of a pronoun, an adjective is not identical to, and thus cannot serve as, that antecedent. Revise sentences so that a *noun* provides the reference for a pronoun.

Confusing	Two glass rods will repel each other when they are electrified. *It* is created from a buildup of positive and negative charges in the rods. [What does *it* refer to?]
Noun antecedent	Two glass rods will repel each other when they carry *electricity*. *It* is created from a buildup of positive and negative charges in the rods.
	OR
	Two glass rods will repel each other when they are electrified. *Electricity* is created from a buildup of positive and negative charges in the rods.

▶**2** Make a pronoun refer to a noun, not to the possessive form of a noun.

Confusing	*Sally's* case is in trouble. Does *she* know that?
Clear	*Sally* is in trouble with this case. Does *she* know that?

Although the possessive form of a noun may imply the noun as the intended antecedent of a pronoun, this form is not identical to, and thus is not clear enough to serve as, that antecedent. Revise sentences so that a *noun* provides the reference for a pronoun. Alternately, change the pronoun so that it, too, is in the possessive form.

Confusing	The *Greeks'* knowledge of magnetic forces was evident before 600 B.C. *They* observed how certain minerals, such as lodestone, have the ability to attract pieces of iron.
Noun antecedent	The *Greeks* had knowledge of magnetic forces before 600 B.C. *They* observed how certain minerals, such as lodestone, have the ability to attract pieces of iron. [The possessive form—*Greeks'*—is eliminated to provide an antecedent for the pronoun *they*.]
Pronoun replaced	The *Greeks'* knowledge of magnetic forces was evident before 600 B.C. *Their scientists* observed how certain minerals, such as lodestone, have the ability to attract pieces of iron.

▶**3** Give the pronouns *that, this, which,* and *it* precise reference.

Confusing	The paper proposed to link cancer and secondary smoke. *This* was established.
Clear	The paper proposed to link cancer and secondary smoke. *This connection* was established.

The pronouns *that, this, which,* and *it* should refer to specific nouns. Avoid having them make vague reference to the overall sense of a preceding sentence.

Confusing	Magnets have two poles—called north and south poles—and these poles obey the same kind of rule as electric charges: like poles repel each other, and unlike poles attract each other. *This* was not well understood until the twentieth century. [What, exactly, does *this* refer to?]
Antecedent provided	Magnets have two poles—called north and south poles—and these poles obey the same kind of rule as electric charges: like poles repel each other, and unlike poles attract each other. *This phenomenon* was not well understood until the twentieth century.
Confusing	Knowledge of atomic structure was advanced in the late nineteenth century by British scientist J. J. Thomson, *which* established that one component of the atom, electrons, are negatively charged. [The pronoun *which* does not refer to a particular noun.]
Antecedent provided	Knowledge of atomic structure was advanced in the late nineteenth century by British scientist J. J. Thomson, *who* established that one component of the atom, electrons, are negatively charged.

▶4 Avoid indefinite antecedents for the pronouns *it, they,* and *you.*

Nonstandard	*It* will rain tomorrow.
Standard	*We* are expecting rain tomorrow.

Expressions such as "you know," "they say," and "it figures" are common in speech and informal writing. The pronouns in these expressions do not refer to particular people—or, in the case of *it,* to a particular object. These pronouns are said to have *indefinite* reference. In academic writing, pronouns should refer to specific antecedents. *You* should be used either to address the reader directly or for a direct quotation; *it* and *they* should refer to particular things, ideas, or people.

Nonstandard	Today, *they say* that an atom has a nucleus with neutrons and protons.
Standard	Today, *physicists believe* that an atom has a nucleus with neutrons and protons.
Nonstandard	Because physicists work with abstract models and mathematical languages, *you* must almost take what physicists say as an item of faith.
Standard	Because physicists work with abstract models and mathematical languages, *nonscientists* must almost take what physicists say as an item of faith.

How to Revise Unclear Pronoun Reference

1. Provide a clear, nearby antecedent.
2. Replace the pronoun with a noun and thereby eliminate the problem of ambiguous reference.
3. Totally recast the sentence to avoid the problem of ambiguous reference.

5 Avoid using a pronoun to refer to the title of a paper in the paper's first sentence.

A pronoun should have a reference in the sentence in which it appears or in an immediately preceding sentence. A title, while directly related to a paper or essay, does not occur *within* the paper or essay and thus cannot function appropriately as an antecedent.

A title	"Eliot's Desert Images in *The Waste Land*"
A first sentence	They are plentiful, and their cumulative effect is to leave readers thirsty—in both body and soul.
First sentence revised	Desert images in T. S. Eliot's *The Waste Land* are plentiful, and their cumulative effect is to leave readers thirsty—in both body and soul.

▶ 14d   Avoid mixing uses of the pronoun *it.*

The word *it* functions both as a pronoun and as an expletive (see 7a-11)—that is, as a space filler in a rearranged sentence.

As an expletive	*It* is clear that the committee is resisting the initiative. [The clause *that the committee is resisting the initiative* functions as the subject.]
As a pronoun	Although the committee voted, *it* [that is, the committee] showed no leadership.

Avoid using the word *it* as both an expletive and a pronoun in the same sentence.

Confusing	*It* is clear that *it* is shirking *its* responsibilities.
Weak	*It* is clear that the committee is shirking *its* responsibilities.
Clear	Clearly, the committee is shirking *its* responsibilities.

▶ 14e   Use the relative pronouns *who, which,* and *that* appropriately.

▶1   Selecting relative pronouns

Relative pronouns (see 7e-2) introduce dependent clauses that usually function as adjectives. The pronouns *who, which,* and *that* rename and refer to the nouns they follow. The pronoun *who* can refer to people, divinities, or personified animals.

> The most highly respected baseball player in the year 1911 was Ty Cobb, *who* had joined the Detroit Tigers in 1905.

That refers to animals, things, or people (when not referring to a *specific* person, in which case the pronoun *who* is used).

> For decades, Cobb held a record *that* remained unbreakable—until Pete Rose stroked his 4,192nd career hit in 1985.

Which refers to animals and things.

> His career, *which* lasted 24 years, was marked by extraordinary statistics—for example, a batting average of .367, 2,244 runs, and 892 stolen bases.

ESL NOTE   Avoid repeating the subject of a sentence with an unnecessary pronoun, especially when a long dependent clause separates a subject from its verb (see 47d-1).

Avoid   The taller *man*, who ran away quickly, *he* recognized me. [An unnecessary pronoun repeats the subject.]

Revised   The taller man, who ran away quickly, recognized me.

CRITICAL DECISIONS

Be alert to differences: Applying a test for choosing *who*, *which*, or *that*—with or without commas

Writers can be unsure of themselves when choosing relative pronouns (*who*, *which*, and *that*) and when using commas with relative clauses. Relative pronouns begin relative clauses, and these function in a sentence as if they were adjectives: they modify nouns. You can apply three tests for deciding which pronoun to use and whether or not to use commas.

Identify the noun being modified.

■ **Is this a proper noun—the name of a *specific* person (George), place (Baltimore), or thing (Levis)?** If yes, then use the pronoun *who*, *whom*, or *whose* (for a person) or *which* (for a place or thing) *with* commas. The noun does not need the modifying clause to specify its meaning. This clause is *nonessential*.

My friend George, *who* is constantly angry, has developed a stress disorder.

The Levis, which fit me well, were on sale.

■ **Is the noun being modified a common noun—an unspecified person (people), place (city), or thing (pants)?** If yes, then it is quite likely that the modifying information of the clause is essential for specifying the noun's identity. Use *who*, *whom*, or *whose* (for a person) and *which* or *that* (for a place or thing) *without* commas. The modifying clause is *essential*.

People *who* are constantly angry often develop stress disorders.

The pants *that* fit me best were on sale.

■ **Is the identity of the common noun being modified made clear and specific to the reader in the context of the paragraph?** If yes, then treat the common noun in the same way that you would a proper noun: use a relative clause, with commas.

Over a year ago, I met the woman *who* is seated at that table in the corner.

The woman, *whose* name I can't remember, is a friend of Joan's.

[In the first sentence, the relative clause *who is seated at that table in the corner* is needed to identify which woman, presumably in a roomful of people. In the second sentence, the reader knows who is being referred to, so the relative clause in that sentence (*whose name I can't remember*) is nonessential and takes commas.]

Use the Relative Pronouns *Who*, *Which*, and *That* Appropriately   **275**

2 Using relative pronouns in essential and nonessential clauses

Essential	People who are constantly angry become stressed.
Nonessential	Jim, who is constantly angry, has become stressed.

Use either *that* or *which*, depending on whether a clause begun by one of these words is essential or nonessential to the meaning of the noun being modified. Use *that* or *which* (with *no* commas around the dependent clause) to denote an **essential** (or restrictive) **modifier**—a word, phrase, or clause that provides information crucial for identifying a noun.

> As a young man, Gabriel García Márquez advocated many left-wing proposals for reform *that* were not in the end accepted.

> As a young man, Gabriel García Márquez advocated many left-wing proposals for reform *which* were not in the end accepted.

As the noun being modified becomes more specific (when it becomes a proper noun, for instance, that identifies a *particular* person, place, or thing), then a modifying clause is no longer essential, since the core information of the noun is already established. Use *which* (*with* commas around the dependent clause) to denote a **nonessential** (or nonrestrictive) **modifier.**

> Norman, Oklahoma, *which* has been dubbed the "Storm-chasing capital of the U.S.," is the home of the National Severe Storm Laboratory. [Because the location is specifically identified, any modifying information is nonessential.]

Use *who* to denote either an essential or a nonessential modifier.

Essential	As recently as the 1970s, meteorologists *who* conducted storm chases were viewed as irresponsible by many of their colleagues. [Because there are many meteorologists and none is named, the information in the modifying clause is essential.]
Nonessential	Eric Rasmussen, who is a meteorologist on staff at the laboratory, makes the decision whether or not to send his "storm-chasing troopers" on a mission to study, measure, and photograph emergent twisters. [Because a *particular* meteorologist is named, the modifying clause is nonessential.]

See 25d for a full discussion of essential and nonessential modifiers with commas.

3 Avoid a confusing overuse of *which* or *that*.

Writers who pile up too many modifying clauses using *which* or *that* may need to rethink sentences to clarify the main statement as distinct from the modifying clauses.

Confusing fragment	Norman, Oklahoma, *which* has been dubbed the "Storm-chasing capital of the U.S.," *which* is the home of the National Severe Storm Laboratory.
Revised	Norman, Oklahoma, *which* is the home of the National Severe Storm Laboratory, has been dubbed the "Storm-chasing capital of the U.S."
Revised	Norman, Oklahoma, *which* has been dubbed the "Storm-chasing capital of the U.S.," is the home of the National Severe Storm Laboratory.

EXERCISE 2

Revise the following sentences so that pronouns refer clearly to their antecedents. Place a check beside the sentences that need no revision.

> *Example:* "Tornado Alley" gets its name from what is essentially a fight within the atmosphere that occurs seasonally over the Midwest. This is due to the collision of a cold current of air from the Rockies with warm, moist air drifting north from the Gulf of Mexico.
>
> "Tornado Alley" gets its name from what is essentially a fight within the atmosphere that occurs seasonally over the Midwest. *This struggle* is due to the collision of a cold current of air from the Rockies with warm, moist air drifting north from the Gulf of Mexico.

1. Though storm experts generally understand the preconditions of severe storms, they are unsure of specific details—which is a problem for the millions who reside in Tornado Alley.
2. These have killed about 18,000 people over the course of the past 200 years.
3. It can contain winds of 200 miles per hour, or even higher.
4. The updraft of a tornado generally narrows, causing it to spin even faster. This can cause severe damage during the peak of the storm.
5. This tendency to spin (called *vorticity*) is a quality of the air itself which can interact with the updraft of a thunderstorm; it can spawn a tornado.

EXERCISE 3

The pronouns *this, that, these, which,* and *it* are often used ambiguously, especially when they refer to ideas, situations, or circumstances not previously identified or clearly explained. In the following sequence of sentences, avoid vagueness by rewriting sentences to provide clear references. Use information from adjoining sentences to provide references.

> *Example:* Archaeology offers a unique approach to studying long-term change in human societies. This has characterized the study of humankind in North America.
>
> Archaeology offers a unique approach to studying long-term change in human societies. *This approach* has characterized the study of humankind in North America.

1. Unfortunately, archaeologists have only recently undertaken it in the context of the European Contact Period.
2. In the past they somewhat rigidly saw it as the ending point of prehistory, when Native Americans came into the orbit of Western civilization.
3. This was apparent especially because archaeologists tended to be preoccupied with the classification of discrete periods in the past, rather than with the processes of cultural change.
4. These were given names such as Paleo-Indian, Archaic, Woodland, and so on.
5. In short, these narrowly constrained the interests of archaeologists.
6. Now they are taking a closer look at the phenomenon of European Contact as a part of long-term developments in that society.

CHAPTER **15**

Misplaced and Dangling Modifiers

A modifier can be a single word: a *sporty* car; a phrase: Joanne drove *a car with racing stripes*; or a dependent clause: *After she gained confidence driving a sporty car,* Joanne took up racing. As you write, you will need to make decisions about where to place modifiers within your sentences. In order to function most effectively, a modifier should be placed directly next to the word it modifies. If this placement disrupts meaning, then the modifier should be placed *as close as possible* to the word it modifies. These two principles inform the discussion that follows.

 http://www.osu-okmulgee.edu/
faculty/carsten/nisod/
For a lighthearted look at the problems incorrect modifiers can cause, check out the Misplaced Modifiers, Misplaced Modifiers II, and Dangling Modifiers sections on this page.

MISPLACED MODIFIERS

▶ **15a** **Position modifiers so that they refer clearly to the words they should modify.**

Confusing   A truck rumbled down the street, gray with dirt.

Clear   A dirty, gray truck rumbled down the street. A truck rumbled down the gray, dirty street.

Readers expect a modifier to be linked clearly with the word the writer intended it to modify. When this link is broken, readers become confused or frustrated.

Confusing   This chair was designed for weekend athletes with extra padding.

Revised   This chair with extra padding was designed for weekend athletes.

Here is a more complicated example of a sentence made confusing by a misplaced modifier.

Confusing   The behavior of a chemical compound in the laboratory that is put together is similar to the behavior of an identical compound obtained from plants and animals growing in nature.

Key elements in the sentence do not seem to fit: Does *in a laboratory* modify *compound* or *behavior?* Is it the *laboratory* that is *put together?* The writer has misplaced the modifier *in the laboratory.* When the prepositional phrase is repositioned, the sentence becomes clear.

Revised   The behavior of a chemical compound that is put together *in the laboratory* is similar to the behavior of an identical compound obtained from plants and animals growing in nature.

If a phrase or clause beginning a sentence functions as an adjective modifier, then the first words after the modifier—that is, the first words of the independent clause—should include the noun being modified.

Confusing   A small Green Mountain town, Calvin Coolidge was born in Plymouth, Vermont. [Who or what is a *Green Mountain town?*]

Revised   Calvin Coolidge was born in Plymouth, Vermont, a small Green Mountain town. [*Green Mountain town* is now positioned next to what it modifies: *Plymouth, Vermont.*]

ESL NOTE   In most English sentences, two or more adjectives that accumulate as modifiers before a noun or pronoun are typically given a standard order or sequence. Section 47f-1–2 describes typical patterns for placement of English adjective modifiers.

ACROSS THE CURRICULUM

Using Modifiers

Modifiers are fundamental sentence elements, and writers use them in every discipline area. In the following example, historian Simon Schama uses modifiers of varying length and positionings to create rich detail in his discussion of Henry David Thoreau.*

Returning to the cabin in the woods by Walden Pond, a catch of fish tied to his pole, Henry David Thoreau was seized with an overwhelming urge to eat raw woodchuck. It was not that he was particularly hungry. And he already knew the taste of woodchuck, at least cooked woodchuck, for he had killed and eaten an animal that had been complacently dining off his bean field. It was simply the force of wildness he suddenly felt possessing his body like an ancient rage.

Modifying clause
the force of wildness *he suddenly felt possessing his body*

Modifying phrases
Returning to the cabin in the woods by Walden Pond, a catch of fish tied to his pole, Henry David Thoreau

he already knew the taste of woodchuck, *at least cooked woodchuck,*

possessing his body *like an ancient rage*

Modifying words
overwhelming urge   *raw* woodchuck   *particularly* hungry   *already* knew

complacently dining   his *bean* field   *suddenly* felt   an *ancient* rage

*The passage is excerpted from Simon Schama, *Landscape and Memory* (New York: Knopf, 1995) 571.

Spotlight on Common Errors—MODIFIERS

Four errors are most commonly associated with modifiers. For full explanations and suggested revisions, follow the cross-references to chapter sections.

MODIFIER ERRORS arise under two conditions: when the word being modified is too far from the modifier (a misplaced modifier) and when the word being modified is implied but does not appear in the sentence (a dangling modifier). Both errors will confuse readers.

Position a modifier near the word it modifies (see 15a).

Faulty

A truck rumbled down the street, gray with dirt. [What is gray and dirty?]

Revised

A **dirty, gray** truck rumbled down the street.

A truck rumbled down the **gray, dirty** street.

Make a modifier refer clearly to one word (see 15c).

Faulty

The supervisor who was conducting the interview thoughtfully posed a final question. [Was this a thoughtful interview or thoughtful question?]

Revised

The supervisor who was conducting the interview posed a final, **thoughtful question.**

The supervisor, who was conducting a **thoughtful interview,** posed a final question.

Reposition a modifier that splits sentence elements (see 15d–15g).

Faulty

Vigorous exercise—complemented by a varied diet that includes nuts, grains, vegetables, and fruits—is one key to fitness. [The "key to fitness" is unclear.]

The agent signed, with her client seated beside her, the contract. [What is "signed" is unclear.]

Revised

Vigorous exercise, **one key to fitness,** should be complemented by a varied diet that includes nuts, grains, vegetables, and fruits.

With her client seated beside her, the agent **signed the contract.**

Make introductory phrases refer clearly to a *specific* word in the independent clause (see 15h-1–2).

Faulty

After considering his difficulty in the interview, the application was withdrawn. [Who withdrew the application?]

Revised

After considering his difficulty in the interview, **the candidate withdrew** his application.

▶ **EXERCISE 1**

Reorganize or rewrite the following sentences so that the misplaced modifier is correctly placed. (You may need to add a word or two in some sentences and provide something specific for the modifier to describe.) Place a check mark beside any sentence in which modifiers are used clearly.

> *Example:* Turning to black subculture as an alternative to homogenized mainstream culture, black slang and music became increasingly common among American teenagers after 1950.
>
> Turning to black subculture as an alternative to homogenized mainstream culture, American teenagers after 1950 began using black slang and listening to black music. [The sentence is given a new subject, *American teenagers*, that can be modified by the introductory phrase.]

1. Black rhythm and blues, with its typical twelve-bar structure, among white teenagers became rock 'n' roll's most common format.
2. Organized by a disc jockey in Cleveland, Ohio, two-thirds of the audience for a stage show featuring black rhythm and blues acts in 1953 were white.
3. Strung down the center of the theater, black and white members of the audience were separated by a rope that was often gone by the end of the performance.
4. Combining elements of black rhythm and blues and white country western music, American teenagers found rock 'n' roll attractive.

▶ **15b** Position limiting modifiers with care.

> The children trusted only him.
> Only the children trusted him.

In conversation, **limiting modifiers**—words such as *only, almost, just, nearly, even,* and *simply*—are often shifted within a sentence with little concern for their effect on meaning. When written, however, a limiting modifier is taken literally to restrict the meaning of the word placed directly after it.

> *Nearly* 90 percent of the 200 people who served in presidential cabinets from 1897 to 1973 belonged to the social or business elite.
>
> Ninety percent of the *nearly* 200 people who served in presidential cabinets from 1897 to 1973 belonged to the social or business elite.

Placement of the limiting modifier *nearly* fundamentally alters the meaning of these sentences.

▶ **EXERCISE 2**

Use the limiting modifier in parentheses to rewrite each sentence two ways, giving each version a different meaning.

> *Example:* Acquiring a copy of one's own medical records is very difficult because medical records are the property of physicians and health-care facilities. (usually)

Acquiring a copy of one's own medical records is *usually* very difficult because medical records are the property of physicians and health-care facilities.

Acquiring a copy of one's own medical records is very difficult because medical records are *usually* the property of physicians and health-care facilities.

1. One study indicated that one-quarter to one-third of patient health records contain errors. (only)

2. For many years the Medical Information Bureau was known for being uncooperative with patients who desperately needed access to their records. (even)

3. Massachusetts patients have a right to see any medical document retained by a hospital supported or licensed by the state. (even)

4. Through the "patient advocate" of his or her hospital, any patient can obtain any personal health information. (almost)

▶ 15c   Reposition modifiers that describe two elements simultaneously.

Confusing   The supervisor conducting the interview thoughtfully posed a final question.

Clear   The supervisor conducting the interview posed a final, thoughtful question.

A **squinting modifier** appears to modify two words in the sentence—the word preceding it and the word following it. To convey a clear meaning, the modifier must be repositioned so it can describe only a *single* word.

Confusing   The official being questioned aggressively shut the door. [What does *aggressively* describe—how the official was being questioned or how the official shut the door?]

Revised   The official, who was being questioned aggressively, shut the door. [A clause is set off to become a nonessential modifier of *official*.]

Revised   The official who was being questioned shut the door aggressively. [*Aggressively* is moved to an unambiguous position and modifies *shut*.]

▶ EXERCISE 3

The following sentences are made awkward by squinting modifiers. Revise each sentence twice so that the modifier describes a different word in each revision.

Example: Sitting in the hot summer sun often accelerates the skin's aging process.

Sitting *often* in the hot summer sun accelerates the skin's aging process. [*Often* modifies *sitting*—the sense being that one must sit in the sun many times to accelerate the skin's aging.]

Often, sitting in the hot summer sun accelerates the skin's aging process. [The sense here is that sitting in the sun even once or a few times can accelerate the aging of the skin.]

1. Going to the movies sometimes makes me wish I were an actress.
2. The equation that Steven thought he had analyzed thoroughly confused him on the exam.
3. The father reprimanding his son angrily pushed the shopping cart down the supermarket aisle.
4. The suspect being questioned thoroughly believed his constitutional rights were being violated.
▶ 5. Taking long walks frequently helps me to relax.

CRITICAL DECISIONS

Challenge sentences: Questioning your placement of modifiers

Modifiers provide much of the interest in a sentence; but when misused, they confuse readers. Pose three questions to know precisely *which* word in a sentence you are modifying.

■ **What modifiers am I using in this sentence?** You should be able to recognize modifiers when you write them. Single words, phrases, and clauses can function as modifiers.

Modifying word (see 7c)

Adverb　The artist succeeded *brilliantly.*

Modifying phrase (see 7d)

Adjective　The painting, *displayed on a dark wall*, glowed.

Modifying clause (see 7e)

Adverb　*After the gallery closed that evening*, the staff celebrated.

■ **What word is being modified? (See 15a–c.)**

The artist made a *deliberate* effort.　　The artist succeeded *brilliantly.*
[The noun *effort* is being modified.]　　[The verb *succeeded* is being modified.]

Confusing　Several patrons who returned repeatedly called the young artist "a wonder." [The single-word modifier *repeatedly* seems to modify two words, *returned* and *called.*]

■ **Does the modifying word, phrase, or clause clearly refer to this word? (See 15a–c, 15h.)**

Clear　On returning, several patrons repeatedly *called* the young artist "a wonder." [The modifier *repeatedly* now clearly modifies the verb *called.*]

> **15d** | **Reposition a lengthy modifier that splits a subject and its verb.**

Confusing   One key to fitness—which should be complemented by a varied diet that includes nuts, grains, vegetables, and fruit—is exercise.

Clear   One key to fitness is vigorous exercise; another is a varied diet that includes nuts, grains, vegetables, and fruit.

Lengthy modifiers disrupt the link between subject and verb and should be repositioned to keep that link clear.

Confusing   Stagnant blue-collar wages, *which (after adjusting for inflation) have not risen for 20 years, despite the fact that corporate profits have skyrocketed,* is one reason why workers are angry and increasingly pro-union.

Revised   Despite the fact that corporate profits have skyrocketed, blue-collar wages have remained stagnant over the past 20 years *(after adjusting for inflation)—which is one reason for increasing anger and pro-union sympathies among workers.* [Modifying elements have been shifted to the beginning and the end of the sentence; the core sentence is no longer interrupted.]

Revised   *Despite the fact that corporate profits have skyrocketed,* blue-collar wages have remained stagnant over the past 20 years (after adjusting for inflation). This lack of progress is one reason for increasing anger and pro-union sympathies among workers. [The final modifying element has been revised and is now a separate sentence.]

EXERCISE 4

Reposition modifiers in rearranged, rephrased, or divided sentences to establish clear links between subjects and verbs. Try rewriting sentences in more than one way.

Example: "Hypermusic," a product of both musical instrument and computer, which blends the sounds produced by traditional instruments with simple-to-operate computer interfaces, thus allowing the player, whether musically trained or not, to sound like a virtuoso, is the brainchild of Tod Machover of MIT.

"Hypermusic," a product of both musical instrument and computer, blends the sounds produced by traditional instruments with simple-to-operate computer interfaces. The brainchild of Tod Machover of MIT, this new technology allows the player, whether musically trained or not, to sound like a virtuoso.

1. Hyperinstruments, which perform the chores of playing a musical instrument with the virtuosity of the most accomplished musician, allow the player to control the tempo and volume of the performance.
2. Machover, the child of a musician and a computer graphics specialist, who had thus been exposed to music and computers from childhood, eventually abandoned traditional instruments for electronic ones.
3. Machover, insisting that the average music lover is neglected while an elite corps of musicians receives all the serious attention, a system that deprives the average player of the joy of performance, favors democratizing music.

> **15e** **Reposition a modifier that splits a verb and its object or a verb and its complement.**

Confusing	The agent signed, with her client seated beside her, the contract.
Clear	With her client seated beside her, the agent signed the contract.

A lengthy adverb phrase or clause can create an awkward sentence if it splits a verb and its object or a verb and its complement. Reposition these adverbs by placing them at the beginning or the end of a sentence.

Awkward A number of presidents have emphasized *in foreign disputes* nonintervention. [The verb and object are split.]

Revised A number of presidents have emphasized nonintervention *in foreign disputes.*

Awkward Millard Fillmore became, *after serving eight years as a U.S. representative from New York*, the elected vice president in 1848. [The verb and complement are split.]

Revised *After serving eight years as a U.S. representative from New York*, Millard Fillmore was elected vice president in 1848.

Note that one- or two-word adverbial modifiers commonly appear before a direct object or complement.

Clear Zachary Taylor became *in 1848* the twelfth president.

However, when a modifier (or a combination of modifiers) places too great a distance between a verb and its object or complement, the modifier should be repositioned.

Awkward Millard Fillmore became, *on the death of Taylor in 1850*, the thirteenth president of the United States.

Revised Millard Fillmore became the thirteenth president of the United States *on the death of Taylor in 1850.*

> **EXERCISE 5**

Reposition modifiers in order to restore clear links between verbs and objects or complements in these sentences.

Example: One of Machover's strangest inventions, the "hypercello," seamlessly blends, by programming the computer to "sense" the cellist's tiniest arm movements, musician and instrument.

One of Machover's strangest inventions, the "hypercello," seamlessly blends musician and instrument by programming the computer to "sense" the cellist's tiniest arm movements.

1. The experience of listening to a hypercello performance is, since one can't tell where the player leaves off and the computer takes over, a strange one.

2. Machover is planning, given his emphasis on making musical performance available to the nonprofessional, an interactive event called *Brain Opera*.

3. Attendees at *Brain Opera* will learn to play, even though they may never have picked up a musical instrument in their lives, hyperinstruments.

4. The audience of *Brain Opera* will perform, after they have learned to play the easier types of hyperinstruments, followed by taking part in sessions involving increasingly complex music games, their very own opera.

5. One wonders what standards critics will use to judge *Brain Opera*, which is eccentric, visionary, and radical, a success.

> **15f** **Reposition a modifier that splits the parts of an infinitive.**

Confusing Her wish to boldly and decisively break the record won many supporters.

Clear Her wish to break the record, boldly and decisively, won many supporters.

An **infinitive** is the dictionary or **base** form of a verb: *go, walk, see.* In a sentence, the infinitive form is often immediately preceded by the word *to: to go, to walk, to see.* Because the base word of the infinitive is a verb, the words that modify infinitives are adverbs. In conversation, emphasis on a short adverbial modifier sometimes interrupts the two parts of an infinitive: *"Please try to quickly move up."* Such an interruption in long or complex written sentences can be disruptive to the intended meaning.

Move an adverb to a position before or after an infinitive, or rewrite the sentence and eliminate the infinitive.

Split Many managers are unable *to* with difficult employees *establish* a moderate and reasonable tone.

Revised Many managers are unable *to establish* a moderate and reasonable tone with difficult employees.

Split One of a manager's responsibilities is *to* successfully *manage* conflict.

Revised One of a manager's responsibilities is *to manage* conflict successfully.

Occasionally, a sentence with a split infinitive will sound more natural than a sentence rewritten to avoid the split. This will be the case when the object of the infinitive is a long phrase or clause and the adverbial modifier is short.

Split Some managers like to *regularly* interview a variety of workers from different departments so that potential problems can be identified and averted.

Avoiding the split may become somewhat awkward.

No split Some managers like to interview *regularly* a variety of workers from different departments so that potential problems can be identified and averted.

No split Some managers like *regularly* to interview a variety of workers from different departments so that potential problems can be identified and averted.

Some readers do not accept split infinitives, no matter what the circumstances of a sentence. The safe course for a writer is to avoid the split by eliminating the infinitive or changing the modifier.

Modifier *On a regular basis,* some managers like to interview a variety of workers
changed from different departments so that potential problems can be identified and averted.

> **15g** | Reposition a lengthy modifier that splits a verb phrase.

Confusing The search for fairy tale origins has for over two centuries fascinated scholars.

Clear The search for fairy tale origins has fascinated scholars for over two centuries.

A *verb phrase* consists of a main verb and its auxiliary or helping verb. Like an infinitive, a verb phrase is a grammatical unit. Unlike infinitives, verb phrases are commonly split with brief modifiers.

In developed countries, the commitment to children as a natural resource *has* long *been linked* to huge investments in education and health care.

The sense of a verb phrase is disrupted when the phrase is split by a lengthy modifying phrase or clause. Repair the split by relocating the modifier.

Confusing Despite severe economic limitations, many third-world countries *have* in efforts to improve the health, well-being, and education of children *invested* large sums.

Revised Despite severe economic limitations, many third-world countries *have invested* large sums in efforts to improve the health, well-being, and education of children.

> ### EXERCISE 6

In the following sentences, reposition modifiers in order to repair split infinitives and restore clear links between auxiliary and main verbs.

> *Example:* In one of Machover's music games, "Sonic Simon Says," players must try to, whatever their initial reservations, imitate simple melody patterns invented by the computer.
>
> In one of Machover's music games, "Sonic Simon Says," players must try to imitate simple melody patterns invented by the computer, whatever their initial reservations.

1. To effectively play a musical instrument in most cases requires years of patient practice, but Machover's hyperinstruments may change all of that.
2. In another one of Machover's music games, "wild orchestration," players can, as music is being performed by the hyperorchestra, change the instrumentation of a given musical piece.
3. Enormous speakers will, as audience members come and go, blast the continuously evolving *Brain Opera* throughout the auditorium.

4. Machover's hyperinstruments make it possible for anyone to, musically creative or not, conduct an orchestra or play like a musical prodigy.

5. There are already some instruments on the market that allow players to, whether they are interested in composing or simply jamming with a favorite artist, live out the fantasy of playing like a pro.

DANGLING MODIFIERS

▶ **15h**   **Identify and revise dangling modifiers.**

Confusing	After considering these issues, the decision was postponed.
Clear	After considering these issues, the candidate postponed his decision.

A modifier is said to "dangle" when the word it modifies is not clearly visible in the same sentence. Correct the error by rewriting the sentence, making sure to include the word modified.

▶ **1**   **Give introductory clauses or phrases a specific word to modify.**

First-draft sentences beginning with long introductory phrases or clauses often contain dangling modifiers. Revision involves asking what the opening clause or phrase modifies and rewriting the sentence to provide an answer.

Dangling	Dominated though they are by a few artists who repeatedly get the best roles, millions of people flock to the cinemas. [Who or what are dominated? If the *millions* are not, the main clause lacks a visible word to be modified.]
Revised	Dominated though they are by a few artists who repeatedly get the best roles, *movies* continue to attract millions of people. [With a rewritten main clause, the opening clause is immediately followed by a noun it can modify.]
Dangling	After appearing in *The Maltese Falcon*, it was clear that Warner Brothers had a box-office star. [Who appeared in the film?]
Revised	After appearing in *The Maltese Falcon*, <u>Humphrey Bogart</u> became Warner Brothers' box-office star.

▶ **2**   **Rewrite passive constructions to provide active subjects.**

Often a modifying phrase that begins a sentence will dangle because the independent clause is written in the passive voice (see 9g). Missing from this passive-voice sentence is the original subject, which would have been modified by the introductory phrase or clause. Correct the dangling modifier by rewriting the independent clause in the active voice.

Dangling	With his weary, sardonic style and his cigarettes lipped loosely, the persona of the private detective was etched into the American psyche. [The persona of the private detective was etched *by whom?*]
Revised with active voice	With his weary, sardonic style and his cigarettes lipped loosely, <u>Bogart</u> etched the persona of the private detective into the American psyche.

▶ ## EXERCISE 7

Repair the dangling modifiers that follow by restoring the word modified to each sentence. (You will find this word in parentheses.) Place a check in front of any sentence in which modifiers are used correctly.

> *Example:* Having conquered an area stretching from the southern border of Colombia to central Chile, civilian and military rule was maintained for two hundred years before the Spanish discovery of America. (the Incas)
>
> Having conquered an area stretching from the southern border of Colombia to central Chile, the Incas maintained civilian and military rule for two hundred years before the Spanish discovery of America.

1. Centering on the city of Cuzco in the Peruvian Andes, the coastal and mountain regions of Ecuador, Peru, and Bolivia were included. (the empire)

2. As the only true empire existing in the New World at the time of Columbus, wealth both in precious metals and in astronomical information had been assembled. (the Inca empire)

3. Knitting together the two disparate areas of Peru, mountain and desert, an economic and social synthesis was achieved. (the Incas)

4. Growing and weaving cotton and planting such domesticated crops as corn, squash, and beans, Peru had been settled dating from before 3000 B.C. (the Incas)

CHAPTER **16**

Shifts and Mixed Constructions

onsistency is an essential quality of language, allowing us to learn vocabulary and sentence structure. We expect that within sentences writers will adhere to certain patterns or conventions. When these patterns are violated, clear communication suffers.

SHIFTS

Aside from the content it communicates, a sentence expresses other important information: person, number, tense, mood, voice, and tone. Once writers make a decision about these matters, they should follow that decision conscientiously within any one sentence. To do otherwise will confuse readers.

▶ 16a   Revise shifts in person and number.

The term **person** identifies whether the speaker of a sentence is the person speaking (the first person), the person spoken to (the second person), or the person spoken about (the third person). **Number** denotes whether a person or thing is singular or plural (see 7a-2 and 7a-7).

▶ I   Revise shifts in person by keeping all references to a subject consistent.

A shift from one person form to another obscures a subject's identity, changing the reference by which the subject is known. Shifts in person often occur when a writer switches from the second person (*you*) to the first person (*I, we*) or to the third person (*he, she, it*). You can avoid this difficulty by recognizing the first-, second-, or third-person orientation of your sentences and by maintaining consistency.

Inconsistent	A person who is a nonsmoker can develop lung troubles when you live with smokers.
Third person	A person who is a nonsmoker can develop lung troubles when he or she lives with smokers.
Second person	If you are a nonsmoker, you can develop lung troubles if you live with smokers.

2 Revise shifts in number by maintaining consistent singular or plural forms.

Pronouns should agree in number with the nouns they replace. You can avoid shifting number and confusing readers by maintaining a clear plural or singular sense in all significant words throughout a sentence.

Inconsistent   They had the best time of their life.
Revised   They had the best time of their lives.

Any significant words related to a subject or object should match its number.

Inconsistent   The seven candidates for the judgeship have a liberal record.
Revised   The seven candidates for the judgeship have liberal records.

When, in an effort to avoid sexist language, you change the number of a subject from singular to plural, be sure to change the number of subsequent pronouns that refer to the subject (see 10c).

Sexist reference   Any candidate should file his papers by noon on December 1.
Revised but no agreement   Any candidate should file their papers by noon on December 1.
Revised   Any candidates should file their papers by noon on December 1.

▶ **EXERCISE 1**

Correct shifts in person and number in the following sentences.

> *Example:* During the ninth and tenth centuries, some members in the Catholic Church's hierarchy suggested that by using elements of stage drama, we could enhance the appeal of public worship.
>
> During the ninth and tenth centuries, some members in the Catholic Church's hierarchy suggested that by using elements of stage drama, *the Church* could enhance the appeal of public worship.

1. A typical monastic community would usually confine their dramatic activities to Christmas, Easter, and perhaps one or two saints' days.
2. Although we can locate a number of saints' plays in the early drama of Western Europe, you can't find them all collected in one place.
3. Until the nineteenth century, comedy was inappropriate to serious religious dramas; they saw it as almost blasphemous.
4. The villainous characters in medieval drama are usually comic but not lovable; he is insensitive, even cruel.

▶ **16b**   Revise shifts in tense, mood, and voice.

Tense, mood, and *voice* denote important characteristics of main sentence verbs: when the action of the verb occurs, what a writer's attitude toward that action is, and whether the *doer* or *receiver* of the action is emphasized. When these characteristics are treated inconsistently, readers can be confused.

▶1 Revise shifts in tense by observing the appropriate sequence of verb tenses.

A verb's **tense** shows when an action has occurred or when a subject exists in a certain state of being (see 9e and 9f). The tenses are marked by verb endings and auxiliary verbs: He walk*ed* home. He *was* walk*ing* home.

Tenses are often changed within sentences in regular and consistent patterns. Shifts in tense that disrupt these patterns strike readers as illogical, especially when the shifts alter the logic or time sequencing within or between sentences.

Inconsistent	The road climbed from the Montezuma Castle National Monument, and the vegetation changes from desert scrub to scrub pines and finally to thick forests of ponderosa pine.
Consistent	The road climbed from the Montezuma Castle National Monument, and the vegetation *changed* from desert scrub to scrub pines and finally to thick forests of ponderosa pine. [The past tense is used consistently.]

The "historical present tense" is often used in academic writing to refer to material in books or articles or to action in a film (see 9e-1).

Inconsistent	In her article, Karen Wright referred to Marshall McLuhan's global village and asks rhetorically, "Who today would quarrel with McLuhan's prophecy?" [The reference to Wright's work should either be past or "historically" present, but not both.]
Consistent	In her article, Karen Wright refers to Marshall McLuhan's global village and asks rhetorically, "Who today would quarrel with McLuhan's prophecy?"

Occasionally, a shift of tense in one sentence will be needed to establish a proper sequence of events.

Acceptable	After he *had read* of experiments in electricity, Nathaniel Hawthorne *observed* that the world *was becoming* "a great nerve." [The tenses change from past perfect to past to past progressive. See Chapter 9 for a full discussion of tenses.]

▶2 Revise for shifts in mood.

A verb's **mood** indicates whether a writer judges a statement to be a fact, a command, or an occurrence contrary to fact (see 9h). Sentences in the **indicative mood,** by far the most common, are presented as fact. In the **imperative mood,** writers express commands—addressing them usually to an implicitly understood "you." In the **subjunctive mood,** writers express doubt or a condition contrary to fact (see 9h-1–4). When mood shifts in a sentence, readers cannot be sure of a writer's intended judgment about the information presented. You can avoid confusion by choosing a mood (most often the indicative) and using it consistently.

Inconsistent	If he were more experienced, he will be able to help us. [The sentence shifts from the "doubtful" subjunctive to the "factual" indicative, leaving readers unsure about what is intended.]
Consistent subjunctive	If he were more experienced, he would be able to help us.

3 Revise for shifts in voice.

A **transitive verb**—one that transfers action from a subject to an object—can be expressed in the active or passive voice. Both the active and passive voices have their uses (see 9g-1–2). However, if writers shift from one voice to the other in a single sentence, both emphasizing and deemphasizing a subject (or *doer* of an action), then readers will be confused. Avoid the difficulty by choosing an active *or* a passive voice in any one sentence.

Inconsistent	Columbus arrived in the New World, and it was believed he had found the coast of Asia. [The shift from active voice to passive leaves doubt about who believed this.]
Consistent	Columbus arrived in the New World and believed he had found the coast of Asia.

EXERCISE 2

Correct the shifts in tense, voice, and mood in the following sentences.

> *Example:* Sports metaphors are popular in modern speech; they appeared most often in the language of advertising, business, and politics.
>
> Sports metaphors are popular in modern speech; they *appear* most often in the language of advertising, business, and politics.

1. Business has always been attracted by the language of football, for example, and it often will have invoked terms such as *team player*, *game plan*, and *optioned out*.
2. The connection is far from accidental in that both areas celebrated aggression.
3. If there were any doubt left about the connection between sports and business, recent surveys show that companies pay extravagant sums in order to rent private viewing suites at sports complexes.
4. Politicians will routinely use sports talk, and they use these figures of speech to curry favor with sports-minded voters.
5. Politicians and businesspeople use sports analogies, and complex ethical issues are often transformed into simple matters of strategy.

16c Revise for shifts in tone.

Tone refers to the writer's attitude toward the subject or the audience. Without doubt, tone is a difficult element to revise, since so much determines it: choice and quality of description, verb selection, sentence structure, and sentence mood and voice. See 3a-4 and the box in 21e for more on matching the tone of a paper to your occasion for writing.

In papers that you prepare for your courses, your tone should be characterized by writing that is precise, logical, and formal, though not stuffy or filled with jargon (see 21e). Abrupt shifts from any established basic tone in a paper will be disconcerting to readers.

Disconcerting   In his famous painting *Persistence of Memory*, Salvador Dalí creates his most haunting allegory of empty space in which time is deader than a doornail. [The final slang expression creates an informal tone inconsistent with a formal analysis.]

Consistent   In his famous painting *Persistence of Memory*, Salvador Dalí creates his most haunting allegory of empty space in which time is at an end. [A more formal expression is consistent with the analysis.]

▶ **EXERCISE 3**

Correct any shifts in tone in the following sentences so that the sentences are consistent.

   Example: Can you name a person who is always in a hurry, is extremely competitive, and blows his stack frequently?

   Can you name a person who is always in a hurry, is extremely competitive, and is often angry?

1. In contrast, can you think of someone who is so low-key that he's a couch potato, not very competitive, and easygoing in relations with others?
2. You now have in mind two *homo sapiens* who could be described as showing Type A and Type B behavior patterns.
3. Type A individuals get frazzled by stress more easily and tend to suffer more coronary problems than Type Bs.
4. Type Bs have the patience of the blessed saints and perform well under high levels of stress and on tasks involving complex judgments and accuracy.
5. Who would make the better executive, the better spouse, the better party animal?

▶ **16d   Maintain consistent use of direct or indirect discourse.**

Direct discourse reproduces exactly, with quotation marks, spoken or written language. **Indirect discourse** approximately reproduces the language of others, capturing its sense, though not its precise expression (see 28a-1).

Direct   Lawrence asked, "Is that the telephone ringing?"
Indirect   Lawrence asked whether the telephone was ringing.

Mixing discourse in one sentence can disorient a reader by raising doubts about what a speaker has actually said. You can avoid the problem by making a conscious choice to refer to another's speech either directly or indirectly.

CRITICAL DECISIONS

Challenge your sentences: Distinguishing between direct and indirect discourse

Reported speech, or indirect discourse, is very different from directly quoted speech, which gives the exact verb tense of the original. Most often, reported speech has occurred sometime before the time of the main verb reporting it. An indirect quotation therefore requires changes in verb tense and pronouns.

The following table shows the patterns for changing verb tenses, verb forms, and modal auxiliaries in reported speech or indirect discourse.

Direct Speech	*Reported Speech*
Tenses:	
present	→ **past**
Ellie said, "I like horses."	Ellie said [that] she liked horses.
past	→ **past perfect**
Ellie said, "I rode the horse."	Ellie said [that] she had ridden the horse.
present progressive	→ **past progressive**
Ellie said, "I'm going riding."	Ellie said [that] she was going riding.
present perfect	→ **past perfect**
Ellie said, "I have ridden there."	Ellie said [that] she had ridden there.
past progressive	→ **past perfect progressive**
She said, "I was out riding."	She said [that] she had been out riding.
***past perfect**	→ **past perfect**
She said, "I had ridden there."	She said [that] she had ridden there.
Auxiliary verbs:	
can	→ **could**
She said, "I can show him."	She said [that] she could show him.
will	→ **would**
She said, "I will ride again."	She said [that] she would ride again.
***could**	→ **could**
She said, "I could ride."	She said [that] she could ride.
***would**	→ **would**
She said, "I would go."	She said [that] she would go.

*These verbs do not change form as they undergo tense shifts.

▶ **EXERCISE 4**

Correct the shifts in discourse in the following sentences by making direct quotations indirect.

> *Example:* As a boy in his teens, Albert Einstein asked how our view of the world would change if "I rode on a beam of light."
>
> As a boy in his teens, Albert Einstein asked how our view of the world would change if we rode on beams of light.

1. The great physicist Niels Bohr nailed a horseshoe on a wall in his cottage because "I understand it brings you luck whether you believe or not."
2. The mystery writer Agatha Christie believed that being married to an archaeologist, a man whose business it was to excavate antiquities, was a stroke of great good luck, because as she got older "he shows more interest in me."
3. In a feverish letter from a battlefield in Italy, Napoleon wrote Josephine that he had received her letters and that "do you have any idea, darling, what you are doing, writing to me in those terms?"

MIXED CONSTRUCTIONS

A **mixed construction** occurs when a sentence takes a reader in one direction by beginning with a certain grammatical pattern and then concludes as if the sentence had begun differently. The resulting mix of incompatible sentence parts invariably confuses readers.

▶ **16e**   Establish clear, grammatical relations between sentence parts.

Mixed constructions are common in speech. We can compensate for grammatically inconsistent thoughts in speech with gestures or intonation, and listeners usually understand. More so than listeners, readers are likely to be sensitive to, and confused by, mixed constructions. Proofread carefully to identify and correct mixed constructions, which tend to occur in predictable patterns.

"The fact that"

The expression "the fact that" and words immediately associated with it result in a mixed construction when writers forget that the expression begins a noun clause that functions as a subject or object. Writers see the subject and verb of the clause and mistakenly conclude that they have written a sentence.

Mixed   The fact that design elements are as important to a play's success as actors. [Even though *are* is a verb and *design elements* functions as a noun, this string of words is not a sentence. It is a noun clause that could take the place of a noun in another sentence, as below.]

Revised   The fact that design elements are as important to a play's success as actors is often overlooked by beginning students of theater. [The noun clause beginning with *The fact that* and ending with *actors* functions as the subject of the sentence.]

Revised   Design elements are as important to a play's success as actors. [Deleting the words *the fact that* converts the dependent noun clause to an independent clause. The main verb is *are*.]

An adverb clause

Adverb clauses begin with subordinating conjunctions—words such as *when, because*, and *although* (see the box in 19a). A mixed construction occurs when the final word of an introductory adverb clause also serves as the subject (or a word modifying the subject) of an independent clause.

Mixed	When a set is successful design pleases actors and theatergoers alike. [The last word of the adverb clause, *successful*, is also used to modify the subject, *design*.]
Revised	When a set is successful, the design pleases actors and theatergoers alike. [The adverb clause ends with *successful;* the independent clause begins with *the.*]
Revised	A successfully designed set pleases actors and theatergoers alike.

A prepositional phrase

A prepositional phrase consists of a preposition (*by, of, in,* etc.) and a noun—the object of the preposition (see 7d-1). A noun functioning as the object of a prepositional phrase cannot simultaneously function as the subject of an independent clause.

Mixed	By creating a functional set design can help the audience believe the "place" on the stage is real. [The words *creating a functional set design* operate both as part of the prepositional phrase beginning with *by* and as the subject of the independent clause.]
Revised	Creating a functional set design can help the audience view the stage as a believable other world. [*Creating a functional set design* functions as the subject of the independent clause. The preposition *by* is deleted.]
Revised	By creating a functional set design, a designer can help the audience view the stage as a believable other world. [The prepositional phrase remains, and a new subject, *a designer,* is added.]

 16f | **Establish consistent relations between subjects and predicates.**

A second type of mixed construction occurs when the predicate part of a sentence does not logically complete its subject. The error is known as **faulty predication** and most often involves a form of the verb *be*, a linking verb that connects the subject complement in the predicate part of the sentence with the subject. You are familiar with the sentence pattern *A is B: The child is happy* (see 7b, Pattern 5). In this sentence, the verb functions as an equals sign. If the subject complement, *B*, is logically inconsistent with the subject, *A*, then the predicate is faulty and the sentence will confuse readers.

Inconsistent	The resolving power of an electron microscope is keenly aware of life invisible to the human eye. [Can a microscope's power be keenly aware?]
Revised	The resolving power of an electron microscope helps us to be keenly aware of life invisible to the human eye. [Now it is people (*us*) who have been made aware.]
Revised	Aided by the resolving power of the electron microscope, we have grown keenly aware of life invisible to the human eye.

Faulty predication occurs in three other constructions involving the verb *be* and the sentence pattern *A is B* or *A = B*. If in writing a definition you begin the subject complement (*B*) with the words *when, if,* or *where,* or if in giving a reason you begin the subject complement with *because,* you may create a mixed construction.

Faulty   Electron illumination is if beams of electrons instead of light are used in a microscope. [In this sentence pattern, the subject (*electron illumination*) must be renamed by a noun or described by an adjective.]

Faulty   Electron illumination is when beams of electrons instead of light are used in a microscope. [In this sentence pattern, the subject (*electron illumination*) must be renamed by a noun or described by an adjective.]

Faulty   The reason electron microscopes have become essential to research is because their resolving power is roughly 500,000 times greater than the power of the human eye. [In this sentence pattern, the subject (*reason*) must be renamed by a noun or described by an adjective.]

The sentence pattern of *subject/linking verb/subject complement* requires an adjective or a noun to serve as subject complement. The words *when, where, if,* and *because* begin adverb clauses and, thus, do not fit grammatically into the pattern. Revise a faulty predicate by changing the adverb clause to a noun clause or by changing the verb and reordering the sentence. Usually a revision requires adding and deleting words.

Revised   Electron microscopes have become essential because their resolving power is roughly 500,000 times greater than the power of the human eye.

Verbs other than *be* can assert actions or states that are not logically consistent with a subject. Wherever you find faulty predication, correct it.

Faulty   The rate of Native American enrollment in institutions of higher learning sees an improvement in the last ten years. [A *rate* cannot see.]

Revised   The rate of Native American enrollment in institutions of higher learning has increased in the last ten years.

Revised   Over the last ten years, educators have seen an increase in the rate of Native American enrollment in institutions of higher learning.

▶ **EXERCISE 5**

Revise the sentences that follow in two ways, making each consistent in grammar or meaning. Place a check beside any sentence that needs no revision.

> *Example:* By implanting cats with microchip bar codes could resolve Novato, California's problem with strays.
>
> Implanting cats with microchip bar codes could resolve Novato, California's problem with strays.
>
> By implanting cats with microchip bar codes, the town of Novato, California, tried to resolve its problem with strays.

1. The fact that strays were overrunning the town and creating a health problem and a nuisance.

2. When minute, pellet-sized bar codes became available and created a radical alternative to neutering or destroying strays.

3. With the bar code implants, runaway cats could be identified and quickly returned to pet owners instead of being destroyed.
4. One sign of trouble was when animal rights groups protested the "indignity" of the solution and when comedians asked, "Are people next?"
5. Advanced, miniaturized technology used for instant identification breathes fear into those who vigilantly protect against invasions of privacy.

INCOMPLETE OR ILLOGICAL SENTENCES

An **incomplete sentence,** as its name implies, is one that lacks certain important elements. A fragment (see Chapter 12), the most extreme case of an incomplete sentence, has no subject or predicate. In less extreme cases, a sentence may lack a word or two, which you can identify and correct with careful proofreading.

▶ 16g   Edit elliptical constructions to avoid confusion.

Both in speech and in writing, we omit certain words in order to streamline communication. These "clipped" or shortened sentences are called **elliptical constructions,** and when used with care, they can be concise and economical. But elliptical constructions may confuse readers if a writer omits words that are vital to sentence structure.

▶1 Use *that* when necessary to signal sentence relationships.

You can omit *that* and create an elliptical construction if the omission does not confuse readers.

The problem (that) town planners of Novato, California, tried to correct by mandating microchip implants for cats paled by comparison to the bad press they received for mandating a Brave New World for pets.

If the omission of *that* alters the relationship among words in a sentence, then restore *that* to the sentence.

Unclear   Thoughtful people honestly fear an implant of miniature ID tags in cats is a precursor to implants in humans. [The wording incorrectly points to *an implant* as the object of *fear*.]

Clear   Thoughtful people honestly fear *that* an implant of miniature ID tags in cats is a precursor to implants in humans. [The word *that* now indicates that an entire noun clause will serve as the object of *fear*.]

ESL NOTE   *That* clauses can occur in a variety of sentences. Notice that the noun clauses retain their structure even when the specific word *that* is omitted. For special rules in constructions involving *wish that*, see 46b-6.

Indirect quotation or reported speech is a very common special case of tense sequence involving two verbs in a *that* clause (see 46b-4).

▶2 **Provide all the words needed for parallel constructions.**

Elliptical constructions are found in sentences where words, phrases, or clauses are joined by the conjunction *and* or are otherwise made parallel. Grammatically, an omission is legitimate when a word or words are repeated *exactly* in all compound parts of the sentence, as in the following examples. Words that could be omitted are placed in parentheses. (See the discussion of parallelism at 18a–b.)

Parallel   According to one widely accepted theory, humans possess sensory (memory), short-term (memory), and long-term memory. [A word is omitted.]

Parallel   Information moves from short- (term memory) to long-term memory when we think about its meaning or (when we think) about its relationship to other information already in long-term memory. [A clause is omitted.]

An incomplete sentence results when words omitted in one part of an elliptical construction do not match identically the words appearing in another part.

Not parallel   Sensory and short-term memory *last* seconds or minutes, while long-term memory years or decades.

Parallel   Sensory and short-term memory *last* seconds or minutes, while long-term memory *lasts* years or decades.

The omitted word, *lasts*, is not identical to the word in the first part of the parallel structure, *last*. One verb completes a singular subject and the other, a plural subject.

▶3 **Use the necessary prepositions with verbs in parallel constructions.**

Elliptical constructions also result from the omission of a preposition that functions idiomatically as part of a complete verb phrase: believe *in*, check *in*, handed *in*, hope *in*, hope *for*; looked *up*, tried *on*, turned *on*. When these expressions are doubled by the conjunction *and*, and you wish to omit the second preposition, be sure this preposition is identical to the one remaining in the sentence. (See 18a-2 and 18a-3 on parallel constructions.) In the following example, the doubled preposition is *on*: "relied *on*" and "ultimately thrived *on*."

In 1914, Henry Ford opened an auto manufacturing plant that relied and ultimately thrived on principles of assembly-line production.

To be omitted from a parallel construction, a preposition must be identical to the one left remaining in the sentence. If the prepositions are not identical, then *both* must appear in the sentence so that the full sense of each idiomatic expression is retained.

Faulty   Henry Ford believed and relied *on* the assembly line as a means to revolutionize American industry.

Revised   Henry Ford believed *in* and relied *on* the assembly line as a means to revolutionize American industry.

▶ **16h**   Make comparisons consistent, complete, and clear.

Writers have many occasions to devote sentences, paragraphs, and even entire essays to writing comparisons and contrasts. To make comparisons effective, you should compare logically consistent elements and state comparisons completely and clearly. (In Chapter 11 you will find more on comparative forms of adjectives and adverbs.)

▶ **I** Keep the elements of a comparison logically related.

The elements you compare in a sentence must in fact be comparable—of the same logical class.

Illogical   Modern atomic theory provides for fewer types of atoms than Democritus, the ancient Greek philosopher who conceived the idea of atoms. [Atoms are being compared with Democritus, a person. The comparison must be made logical.]

Logical   Modern atomic theory provides for fewer types of atoms than did Democritus, the ancient Greek philosopher who conceived the idea of atoms.

▶ **2** Complete all elements of a comparison.

Comparisons must be made fully, so that readers understand which elements in a sentence are being compared.

Incomplete   Democritus believed there existed an infinite variety of atoms, each of which possessed unique characteristics—so that, for instance, atoms of water were smoother. [Smoother than what?]

Complete   Democritus believed there existed an infinite variety of atoms, each of which possessed unique characteristics—so that, for instance, atoms of water were smoother than atoms of fire.

Incomplete   The ideas of Democritus were based more on speculation. [More on speculation than on what?]

Complete   The ideas of Democritus were based more on speculation than on the hard evidence of experimentation.

▶ **3** Make sure comparisons are clear and unambiguous.

Comparisons that invite alternate interpretations must be revised so that only one interpretation is possible.

Unclear   Scientists today express more respect for Democritus than his contemporaries. [Two interpretations: (1) Democritus's contemporaries had little respect for him; (2) scientists respect the work of Democritus more than they respect the work of his contemporaries.]

Clear   Scientists today express more respect for Democritus than they do for his contemporaries.

Clear   Scientists today express more respect for Democritus than his contemporaries did.

▶ **EXERCISE 6**

Revise the sentences that follow to eliminate problems with mixed constructions. Place a check beside any sentence that needs no revision.

   Example: We have a special reverence and fascination *with* fire.

   We have a special reverence *for* and fascination *with* fire.

1. Since ancient times, fire has been regarded more as a transforming element than sheer destructive power.
2. Medieval alchemists believed in fire resided magical properties.
3. In legend, Prometheus's gift of fire made humans better, and for this Prometheus was punished.
4. Although humans have used fire for about 400,000 years, not all people have known how to *make* fire.

CHAPTER **17**

Being Clear, Concise, and Direct

R evising sentences for clarity and directness means more than making a correct, complete expression. Revision at this level means making choices about wording that will help your audience to clearly understand your ideas. Your knowledge of an audience's readiness and level of understanding will strongly influence your choices.

▶ **17a** Revise to eliminate wordiness.

There are many kinds of wordiness, including the use of empty words and phrases (see 21b-3, 21e-4, 21h-2); passive-voice constructions (see 9g); and buzzwords,

http://webster.commnet.edu/
hp/pages/darling/grammar/
concise.htm
*An extended list of suggestions for
making your writing clearer and
more concise, followed by a self-test.*

redundancy, and unnecessary repetition. When you are revising a first draft, search out wordiness and eliminate it. Try to avoid saying things two different ways or with two words when one will do. Eliminating extra words is a reliable way to give your message direct impact; padded wording never makes writing sound more authoritative. If used as filler to meet the length requirement of an assignment, padded writing will backfire by obscuring your message to readers, causing them to be confused and annoyed.

▶**1** Combine sentences that repeat material.

When writing a first-draft paragraph, you are apt to string together sentences that repeat material. When revising your work, combine sentences to eliminate wordiness and to sharpen focus.

Wordy The high *cost* of multimedia presentations is due to the combined *cost* of studio shoots and *expensive* video compression. The *costs* of graphic design and programmers are also high. [The word *cost* and its equivalents appear four times.]

Combined Studio shoots, video compression, graphic design, and programmers' work all contribute to the high cost of multimedia presentations.

▶**2** Eliminate wordiness from clauses and phrases.

Eliminate wordiness by eliminating relative pronouns and by reducing adjective clauses to phrases or single words.

303

Complex	Josephine Baker, *who was* the first black woman to become an international star, was born poor in St. Louis in 1906. [The clause creates some interruption in this complex sentence.]
Concise	Josephine Baker, the first black woman to become an international star, was born poor in St. Louis in 1906.
Complex	Many were drawn by her vitality, *which was* infectious.
Concise	Many were drawn by her infectious vitality. [A simple sentence is created.]
Option	Her vitality was infectious; many were drawn by it. [Simple independent clauses are created.]

Wordiness can also be eliminated by shortening phrases. When possible, reduce a phrase to a one-word modifier (see 7c).

Wordy	*Recent revivals of* Baker's French films have included *rereleases of subtitled versions of Zou-Zou* and *Princess Tam-Tam.*
Concise	*Recently* Baker's French films *Zou-Zou* and *Princess Tam-Tam* have been *rereleased with subtitles.* [The phrases are reduced to simpler modifiers.]

Keep alert: avoid losing necessary content in revision

Writers seeking to eliminate wordiness need to challenge themselves to keep an eye on expressions and concepts that convey their key ideas. With too much zeal in cutting wordiness, you could lose more than you gain, as might easily happen in the example sentence above if excess trimming had eliminated the ideas of "recently," "French [. . .] with subtitles," or "rereleased"—all key elements in the original statement.

▶3 **Revise sentences that begin with** *it is, there is, there are,* **and** *there were.*

Expletive constructions (*it is, there is, there are, there were*) fill blanks in a sentence when a writer inverts normal word order (see 7a-11, 14d). Expletives are almost always unnecessary and should be replaced with direct, active verbs whenever possible.

Wordy	*There were many reasons why* Josephine Baker was more successful in Europe than in America. [The expletive is unnecessary here.]
Direct	Josephine Baker was more successful in Europe than in America for many reasons.
Wordy	*It is* because Europeans in the 1920s were interested in anything African *that* they so readily responded to Baker's outrageous style. [The expletive is indirect; it also sets up an unnecessary *that* clause.]
Direct	Because Europeans in the 1920s were interested in anything African, they readily responded to Baker's outrageous style.

▶4 **Eliminate buzzwords.**

Buzzwords are vague, often abstract expressions that sound as if they mean something but are only "buzzing" or adding noise to your sentence, without contributing anything of substance (see 21c–d). Buzzwords can be nouns: *area, aspect, case, character, element, factor, field, kind, sort, type, thing, nature, scope, situation, quality.* Buzzwords can be adjectives, especially those with broad meanings: *nice, good, interesting, bad, important, fine, weird, significant, central, major.* Buzzwords can be adverbs: *basically, really, quite, very, definitely, actually, completely, literally, hopefully, absolutely.* Eliminate buzzwords. When appropriate, replace them with more precise expressions.

Wordy	*Those types of major* disciplinary problems are *really quite* difficult to solve. [None of these buzzwords has any meaning.]
Concise	Disciplinary problems are difficult to solve.
Wordy	*Basically,* she was *definitely* a *nice* person.
Concise	She was friendly. [*Kind, thoughtful, outgoing,* or any other, more precise adjective could replace the vague *nice.*]

▶ **5 Eliminate redundant writing.**

Occasional, intentional repetition can be a powerful technique for achieving emphasis (see 19c-2). Writers may not realize they are repeating themselves, however, and the result for readers is usually a tedious sentence. When you spot unintended repetition in your own writing, eliminate it.

Redundant	James English believes that a lottery, *jackpot* mentality has undermined the will of Americans to succeed through hard work.
Revised	James English believes that a lottery mentality has undermined the will of Americans to succeed through hard work.
Redundant	Historically, immigrants *who came to this country* arrived in America expecting to work long hours; even if they did not benefit directly *from their 70-hour weeks,* they believed their children would.
Revised	Historically, immigrants arrived in America expecting to work long hours; even if they did not benefit directly from their efforts, they believed their children would.

Redundant phrases

A **redundant phrase** repeats a message unnecessarily. Redundant phrases include *small in size, few in number, continue to remain, green in color, free gift, extra gratuity, repeat again, combine together, add to each other,* and *final end.* Make your sentences concise by omitting one part of a redundant phrase.

Redundant	Today, the earlier belief in the value of hard work seems like naive *innocence.*
Concise	Today, the earlier belief in the value of hard work seems naive.
Redundant	The quickest route to expendable *extra* income in the 90s is to hit the lottery.
Concise	The quickest route to expendable income in the 90s is to hit the lottery.

Revise to Eliminate Wordiness

6 Eliminate long-winded phrases.

Long-winded phrases such as *at this point in time* do not enhance the meaning or elegance of a sentence. Such expressions are tempting because they come to mind ready-made and seem to add formality, sophistication, and authority to your writing. But do not be fooled. Using such phrases muddies your sentences, making you sound either pretentious or inexperienced. Eliminate these phrases and strive for simple, clear, direct expression.

Wordy   *In the final analysis*, hard work is hard and *in a very real sense* explains why some people would rather bet on the lottery than work a 60-hour week.

Revised   The demands of working hard may explain why some people would rather bet on the lottery than work a 60-hour week.

Avoiding Wordy Expressions

Wordy	*Direct*
at this moment (point) in time	now, today
at the present time	now, today
due to the fact that	because
in order to utilize	to use
in view of the fact that	because
for the purpose of	for
in the event that	if
until such time as	until
is an example of	is
would seem to be	is
the point I am trying to make*	____
in a very real sense*	____
in fact, as a matter of fact*	____

*These expressions are fillers and should be eliminated.

EXERCISE I

Revise these sentences to eliminate wordiness by combining repeated material, reducing phrases and adjective clauses, and avoiding expletives.

> *Example:* What type of consumer do you want to advertise to? Specifying the target or consumer that you want to reach with your product is the main step in advertising.
>
> Effective advertising targets specific consumers.

1. When defining the purpose of advertising some experts admit that it is a manipulation of the public while others insist that advertising promotes the general well-being of its audience.
2. Advertising is one of the most eye-catching methods of selling a product. This is because advertising is a medium of information.
3. There are many consumers who are drawn to a product because the advertising campaign has been effectively utilized.

4. There are many qualities which an advertisement must have to lure the public to buy its product. The advertisement must be believable, convincing, informative, and persuasive. With these qualities in the ads, they will be the first ones to sell.

5. Like I mentioned before, it is not only women who are being portrayed sexually. Men are used in many advertisements also.

6. There exists a built-in sexual overtone in almost every commercial and advertisement around.

7. Advertising is one of several communications forces which performs its role when it moves the consumer through successive levels. These levels include unawareness, awareness, comprehension, conviction, and action.

EXERCISE 2

Revise the following sentences to eliminate wordiness.

> *Example:* Early forms of advertisements were messages to inform the consumers of the benefits and the availability of a product.
>
> Originally, advertisements informed consumers of a product's benefits and availability.

1. The producer must communicate with the product's possible customers in a way that is quite personal and quite appealing to the customer.

2. By identifying the product you start to narrow down the range of people you want to buy the product.

3. Advertising is a complex, but not mysterious, business.

4. To summarize a successful advertiser in today's world in one word, it would have to be opportunistic.

5. From campaign to campaign there are many different objectives and goals ads are trying to accomplish.

6. It used to be that women were mainly portrayed in the kitchen or in other places in the home.

7. We find advertising on television, on the radio, in newspapers and magazines, and in the phone book, just to name a few places.

▶ 17b   Use strong verbs.

A verb is like an engine. Strong verbs move sentences forward and precisely inform readers about the action a subject is taking or the condition or state in which the subject exists. One way to improve a draft is to circle all your verbs, revising as needed to ensure that each verb makes a crisp, direct statement.

▶ 1   Give preference to verbs in the active voice.

Sentences with verbs in the active voice emphasize the actor of a sentence rather than the object that is acted on (see 9g).

Active	A cancer patient using the Internet can access volumes of cyberspace-stored medical information about the nature and prognosis of his or her disease.
Passive	Volumes of cyberspace-stored medical information about the nature and prognosis of his or her disease can be accessed by a cancer patient using the Internet.
Passive	Volumes of cyberspace-stored medical information about the nature and prognosis of one's disease can be accessed on the Internet. [The actor is not named.]

Unless a writer intends to focus on the object of the action, leaving the actor secondary or unnamed, the active voice is the strongest way to make a direct statement. When the actor needs to be named, a passive-voice sentence is wordier and thus weaker than an active-voice sentence.

Passive	This widespread availability of medical information is not viewed favorably in all quarters. [The passive voice obscures the identity of those who hold negative views.]
Active	Some doctors view the widespread availability of medical information unfavorably.
Passive	It is feared that the sheer volume, combined with the uncensored nature of Internet material, will mislead and/or confuse patients. [The passive voice conceals the identity of those who are in doubt.]
Active	Some physicians fear that the sheer volume combined with the uncensored nature of Internet material will mislead and/or confuse patients.

CRITICAL DECISIONS

Broaden the context: Understanding the need to be clear, concise, and direct

I have made this letter longer than usual, only because
I have not had time to make it shorter.
—Blaise Pascal

Over three hundred years ago, the French mathematician and philosopher Blaise Pascal knew what writers know today: writing concisely is a challenge that takes time. The time spent in revising for clarity, conciseness, and directness is well spent—both for you and your readers.

Be clear, concise, and direct for yourself.
Writing becomes clearer as you revise to eliminate wordiness and to increase your use of active verbs. Revise for clarity, conciseness, and directness in order to be confident and satisfied that you have produced your best work.

Be clear, concise, and direct for your readers.
Revising for clarity, conciseness, and directness also has practical benefits. Readers can more clearly understand the points you want to make. Rather than wasting time trying to understand your meaning, they can respond directly to your points.

ACROSS THE CURRICULUM

Using Strong Verbs

Writers in all disciplines have good reason to use strong verbs, which heighten a reader's interest by establishing clear and vigorous relationships between the actors of a sentence and what is acted on. Unless you have good reason to deemphasize this relationship (see 9g-2), choose strong verbs when writing, regardless of discipline area. Observe, for instance, the use of verbs in this introduction to a scientific article on the analysis of DNA fragments from mummified humans.* (We have boldfaced the verbs.)

> Using sensitive techniques of molecular biology, we **have investigated** the possibility of recovering and analyzing genetic materials (deoxyribonucleic acid, DNA) from mummified human tissue and bone from selected archaeological sites in Greenland. Simple extraction procedures of both skin and bone samples **yielded** DNA material in purified form. Using human specific probes, we **demonstrated** that a minor, but distinct, portion of the purified DNA material was of human origin. Further analysis **showed** the remaining portion of the isolated DNA to consist mainly of DNA of fungal origin. The finding of DNA of human origin in mummified skin and bone samples, in particular, **opens up** the possibility for detailed anthropological genetic studies.

In each of the five sentences excerpted here, the authors use a strong verb in the main clause. Cumulatively, these verb choices send a message to the reader: that the authors feel excitement for their work and think it significant. Readers may not register this message directly; still, the verb choices communicate enthusiasm and confidence, a message readers are certain to receive. Whatever the discipline area in which you find yourself writing, prefer strong, active verbs.

*The passage is excerpted from Ingolf Thuesen and Jan Engberg, "Recovery and Analysis of Human Genetic Material from Mummified Tissue and Bone," *Journal of Archaeological Science* 17 (1990): 679. A longer excerpt of this article appears in Chapter 40.

2 **Use forms of *be* and *have* as main verbs only when no alternatives exist.**

The verb *be* is essential in forming certain tenses, such as a progressive tense.

> The ability to retrieve medical information so readily *is fostering* in many patients an urge to question the kind of care they are receiving.

In a sentence of definition, *be* functions as an equal sign.

> The National Cancer Institute, the National Institutes of Health, and the University of Pennsylvania Medical Center *are* three institutions with Web sites on the Internet that patients can consult to answer the most common questions.

Beyond these uses, *be* is a weak verb. Even weaker are the forms *seems to be* (or *seems that*) and *appears to be* (or *appears that*), which lack the courage to make a direct statement. When possible, replace these with strong, active-voice verbs.

Weak	Many health-care professionals *are of the opinion* that health information on the Internet is not the appropriate vehicle by which to teach people about serious health issues.
Stronger	Many health-care professionals *claim* that health information on the Internet is not the appropriate vehicle by which to teach people about serious health issues. [The stronger verb makes a more active sentence.]

The verb *have* functions as an auxiliary in forming the perfect tenses. This verb tends to make a weak and indirect statement when used alone as the main verb of a sentence. Replace forms of *have* with strong, active-voice verbs.

Weak	The easy accessibility of medical information *has* the effect of getting patients more involved in planning their treatment programs. [The verb produces a vague statement.]
Stronger	The easy accessibility of medical information *enables* patients to become more involved in planning their treatment programs. [The new verb is more direct and has a specific meaning.]

▶**3 Revise nouns derived from verbs.**

A noun can be formed from a verb by adding a suffix: dismiss/dismiss*al*, repent/repent*ance*, devote/devot*ion*, develop/develop*ment*. Often these constructions (sometimes called *nominalizations*) result in a weak, wordy sentence, since the noun form replaces what was originally an active verb and requires the presence of a second verb. When possible, restore the original verb form of a noun derived from a verb.

Wordy	Many patients *made the discovery* that communication with other patients via the Internet *was helpful* in providing emotional support to everyone. [The writer could replace *discovery* and *helpful* with stronger forms of the verbs.]
Direct	Many patients *discovered* that communicating with other patients via the Internet *helped* everyone emotionally. [The verbs are more direct and so, too, is the sentence.]
Wordy	The Internet is capable of acting as a tool for the dissemination of health information.
Direct	The Internet can disseminate health information.

▶ **EXERCISE 3**

Revise these sentences for clarity and directness by changing passive verbs to active verbs, replacing weak verbs with strong verbs, and converting nouns made from verbs back into verbs.

> *Example:* Both positive and negative reactions to a product should be expected.
>
> Consumers should expect both positive and negative reactions to products.

1. Advertising has always been generally understood as a form of communication between the buyer and the seller.
2. The aim of advertising is to give exposure of a certain product to a targeted audience.

3. Without catalogue viewership the product may be forgotten because the consumer will not have the ability to view it again.

4. There is a discussion of effective marketing in Thomas R. Forrest's article which is entitled "Such a Handsome Face: Advertising Male Cosmetics."

5. It has been noticed that in today's society a man's appearance is thought to be an important factor in his success.

6. There are several aspects of advertising that are seen to be essential to the successful marketing of a product.

7. Five questions should be asked before the implementation of a successful advertising campaign.

8. The association of a product with something that is desirable increases its visibility.

EXERCISE 4

Revise the following first draft of a student paper. Use all the techniques described in this and related chapters to achieve conciseness, clarity, and directness.

Advertising can be displayed in many different ways. One major way that advertisers try to sell their products is through the use of sexism. Sexism is portrayed in the majority of ads lately and it appears to be only getting worse.

It is now over twenty years after the feminist movement and sexism is as big of a problem as ever. Usually in the advertising industry it is the female that is used in the ad that portrays sexism: however, male sexism is found also. The latest problem occurred when Miller Beer tried to hook spring-break college bound kids with an ad insert for campus newspapers about annual trips to Florida that are often taken by college students. The ad included sketches of women in bikinis with hints of ways for these college kids to "pick up women." This ad insert drew a lot of attention from college students, mainly females that were outraged over it. There were even threats to boycott the product. However there were no results because the National Advertising Review Board has not issued guidelines on the use of women in ads since 1978. Also, there are very few agencies that have particular rules or regulations on sexism in ads. This could be due to the fact that the top managements are mostly male.

Everyone knows that sexism is used in advertisements all over the place but the question is, are they avoidable? Many advertising executives say no because they feel that advertisers have to address themselves to such a huge chunk of people that they are never going to be able to make everyone happy. This is why sexism and stereotyping in advertising is such a big problem today.

18

Maintaining Sentence Parallelism

In writing, **parallelism** involves matching a sentence's structure to its content. When two or more ideas are parallel (that is, closely related or comparable), a writer can emphasize similarities as well as differences by creating parallel grammatical forms.

Parallel structures help sentences to cohere by establishing clear relationships among sentence parts. Through their closely matched word elements, parallel structures present ideas in a logical comparison or contrast. Parallelism in writing thus draws on your skills in creating a logical analogy, a comparison, or a parallel argument (see 6d-1). To use parallelism effectively, you must become consciously logical and systematic about how you present parallel ideas.

> ▶ **18a** **Use parallel words, phrases, and clauses with coordinating conjunctions.**

Whenever you use a coordinating conjunction (*and, but, for, or, nor, so, yet*), the words, phrases, or clauses joined form a *pair* or a *series* (a list of three or more related items) and become *compound* elements: compound subjects, objects, verbs,

 http://webserver.maclab.comp.uvic.ca/
writersguide/pages/SentParallel.html
A concise one-page overview of parallelism from the UVic Writers Guide.

modifiers, and clauses. For sentence parts to be parallel in structure, the compound elements must share an equivalent, but not necessarily identical, grammatical form. If in one part of a parallel structure a verb is modified by a prepositional phrase, then a corresponding verb in the second part of the sentence should also be modified by a prepositional phrase—*but* that phrase need not begin with the same preposition.

 1 Using parallel words

Not parallel	The candidate was a visionary but insisting on realism.
Parallel	The candidate was <u>visionary</u> *but* <u>realistic</u>.

Words that appear in a pair or a series are related in content and should be parallel in form.

Not parallel   Psychologist Howard Gardner identifies specific and a variety of types of intelligence, rather than one monolithic "IQ" score.

Determine the parallel elements.

   Gardner identifies Slot 1 and Slot 2 types of intelligence, rather than one monolithic "IQ" score.

   Gardner identifies *specific* and Slot 2 types of intelligence, rather than one monolithic "IQ" score.

In this sentence the adjective *specific* completes Slot 1, and the noun *variety* completes Slot 2. In order for the sentence to be parallel, both slots must show the same part of speech. In this case, the words should be adjectives, since both are being used to modify the noun *types*.

Revise so that parallel elements have equivalent grammatical form.

Parallel   Psychologist Howard Gardner identifies *specific* and *varied* types of intelligence, rather than one monolithic "IQ" score. [Two adjectives are now comparable in grammatical structure.]

If the elements that should be logically parallel shift their function in a sentence, they may well shift their part of speech. In the following sentence, the parallel words are nouns—acting as a subject.

Parallel   *Mathematics* and *art* are two of Gardner's seven types of intelligence. [The parallel terms are nouns.]

If these parallel words needed to modify the word *intelligence* in a second sentence, then the nouns would be changed to their adjective form:

Parallel   *Mathematical* and *artistic* intelligence are two of Gardner's seven types. [The parallel terms are adjectives.]

In parallel constructions, idiomatic terms must be expressed completely (see also 16g-3).

Not parallel   White people were called "Flop Ears" by some Indians who were both aghast and entertained *by* the way white parents grabbed their children by the ears to discipline them.

Determine the parallel elements.

   who were both Slot 1 and Slot 2 the way white parents grabbed their children by the ears to discipline them.

The preposition *at* is necessary for completing the first verb phrase, since the idiom is *aghast at*, not *aghast by*.

Revise so that parallel elements have equivalent grammatical form.

Parallel   White people were called "Flop Ears" by some Indians who were both aghast *at* and entertained *by* the way white parents grabbed their children by the ears to discipline them. [Each parallel item now has its proper idiomatic preposition.]

Spotlight on Common Errors—PARALLELISM

 These are the errors most commonly associated with parallelism. For full explanations and suggested revisions, follow the cross-references to chapter sections.

FAULTY PARALLELISM occurs when writers compare or contrast sentence parts without using similarly constructed wordings. In the examples that follow, parallel structures are highlighted.

Conjunctions suggest comparisons and require parallel structures.

Conjunctions such as *and* and *but* require parallel structures (see coordinating conjunctions, 18a).

Faulty	Revised
The candidate was a visionary but insisting on realism. [The verb forms *was a visionary* and *insisting* are not parallel.]	The candidate was **visionary** but **realistic.** [Similarly worded adjectives are linked by the conjunction *but*.]
The candidate attended meetings, spoke at rallies, and she shook thousands of hands. [The candidate's three activities are not parallel.]	The candidate **attended meetings, spoke at rallies, and shook thousands of hands.** [The candidate's three activities are similarly worded.]

Paired conjunctions such as *either/or* and *both/and* require parallel structures (see correlative conjunctions, 18b).

Faulty	Revised
Depending on your tolerance for adventure, traveling without a map can either be exciting or you can be frustrated. [The words that describe *traveling—exciting* and *you can be frustrated*—are not parallel.]	Depending on your tolerance for adventure, traveling without a map can either be **exciting** or **frustrating.** [Similarly worded adjectives are joined by the paired conjunctions *either/or*.]

Faulty	Revised
Explorers can be both afraid of the unknown and, when they encounter something new, they want to understand it. [The verb forms *can be afraid* and *want to understand* are not parallel.]	Explorers can be both **afraid of the unknown** and **curious about it.** [Similarly worded adjectives and phrases are joined by the paired conjunctions *both/and*.]

Direct comparisons and contrasts require parallel structures (see 18c).

Faulty

The staff approved the first request for funding, not the second presenter requesting funds. [The objects *request* and *presenter* are not parallel.]

Revised

The staff approved the first request for funding, not the second. [The requests being contrasted share similar wording.]

Faulty

The old American frontier was frequently lawless, and so too anyone who surfs the Internet must grow accustomed to life without a central, regulating authority. [The compared items are not parallel.]

Revised

The Internet, no less than the old American frontier, is a lawless place that lacks a central, regulating authority. [Compared items, the *Internet* and the *frontier*, are similarly worded; both are now completed with the second part of the sentence: *is a lawless place.*]

Lists require parallel structures (see 18e).

Faulty

Make sure you pack the following in your kit:
—an alcohol solution that will
  cleanse wounds
—bandages
—Remove splinters with a tweezers.
—matches
[Items in the list are not parallel.]

Revised

Make sure you pack the following in your kit:
—alcohol
—bandages
—tweezers
—matches
[Items in the list are similarly worded.]

2 Using parallel phrases

Not parallel	The judge had an ability to listen to conflicting testimony and deciding on probable guilt.
Parallel	The judge had an ability <u>to listen to conflicting testimony</u> *and* <u>to decide on probable guilt.</u>

To echo the idea expressed in a phrase in one part of a sentence, use a phrase with the same grammatical structure in another part.

Not parallel	Unstable technologies and searching for development funds have prompted some schools to cancel their online courses.

Determine the parallel elements.

    __Slot 1__ and __Slot 2__ have prompted
    Unstable technologies and *searching for development funds* have prompted

Slot 1 is completed with a noun and modifier; slot 2 is not parallel since it is completed with a gerund (*ing*) phrase.

Revise so the elements have equivalent grammatical form.

Parallel	*Unstable technologies* and *money shortages* have prompted some schools to cancel their online courses.

Both slots are now completed with a noun (*technologies, shortages*) and a modifier (*unstable, money*). Note that the sentence can also be made parallel by completing both slots with gerund phrases:

Parallel	The dual problems of *coping with unstable technologies* and *searching for development funds* have prompted some schools to cancel their online courses.

This revision converts the gerund phrases used as subjects to gerund phrases used as objects of the preposition *of.* The two slots in the sentence are parallel: both consist of a gerund followed by a prepositional phrase.

3 Using parallel clauses

Not parallel	Before the storm's end but after the worst was over, the captain radioed the Coast Guard.
Parallel	<u>Before the storm had ended</u> *but* <u>after the worst was over,</u> the captain radioed the Coast Guard.

A *clause* is a grouping of words that has a complete subject and predicate. Both independent clauses (that is, sentences) and dependent clauses can be set in parallel, provided they are parallel in content.

In order to maintain parallel structure in sentences that have a pair or series of dependent relative clauses, you will need to repeat the relative pronouns *who, whom, which,* and *what.*

Not parallel   Archimedes was the celebrated mathematician of antiquity *who*
(dependent   invented the Archimedes' screw, *who* explained the theory of the lever,
clauses)   and *he* defended his native Syracuse against the Romans with great
               mechanical skill.

Determine the parallel elements.

Archimedes was the celebrated mathematician of antiquity   Slot 1 ,   Slot 2 , and   Slot 3 .

Archimedes was the celebrated mathematician of antiquity *who invented the Archimedes' screw*,   Slot 2 , and   Slot 3 .

Slot 1 is completed with a relative clause beginning with the relative pronoun *who*. Slots 2 and 3 must have the same structure: each slot must be completed with a clause that begins with the word *who* (but see the variation immediately following).

Revise so that parallel elements have equivalent grammatical form.

Parallel   Archimedes was the celebrated mathematician of antiquity *who* invented the
            Archimedes' screw, *who* explained the theory of the lever, and *who* defended
            his native Syracuse against the Romans with great mechanical skill.

Variation: Brief words that begin a series (for example, a relative pronoun such as *who*, a preposition such as *by* or *in*, and the infinitive *to*) may be written once at the beginning of the first item in the series and then omitted from all remaining items.

Parallel   Archimedes was the celebrated mathematician of antiquity *who* invented the
            Archimedes' screw, explained the theory of the lever, and defended his na-
            tive Syracuse against the Romans with great mechanical skill.

A caution: If one of these introductory words appears in more than one part of the series but not in *all* parts, the parallelism will be faulty.

Not parallel   I want *to* go home, wash up, and *to* eat.

Parallel   I want *to* go home, *to* wash up, and *to* eat.
            I want *to* go home, wash up, and eat.

 18b   **Use parallelism with correlative conjunctions: *either/or,*** **neither/nor, both/and, not only/but also.**

Not parallel   Explorers can be both afraid of the unknown and, when they
                encounter something new, they want to understand it.

Parallel   Explorers can be *both* <u>afraid of the unknown</u> *and* <u>curious
            about it</u>.

Whenever you join parts of a sentence with pairs of words called *correlative conjunctions* (*either/or, neither/nor, both/and, not only/but also*), you must use the same

ACROSS THE CURRICULUM

Parallelism

Making sentence elements parallel is, perhaps, the single most successful strategy you can adopt for giving your sentences a professional polish. You will find writers in all disciplines using parallel structures to make their presentations concise, rhythmically balanced, and logical—as author Harold Livesay demonstrates in this excerpt from his biography of Andrew Carnegie. In three sentences, Livesay employs three sets of parallel structures.* Whatever the subject area, expect to encounter numerous examples of parallelism in your reading; and attempt, when possible, to employ parallelism in your writing.

> Carnegie's twelve years' experience on the Pennsylvania Railroad shaped his subsequent career. On the railroad he assimilated the managerial skills, grasped the economic principles, and cemented the personal relationships that enabled him to become successively manager, capitalist, and entrepreneur. His most spectacular achievement—building Carnegie Steel into the world's largest steel producer—rested primarily on his successful transfer of the railroads' managerial methods to the manufacturing sector of the economy.

Parallel structure   On the railroad he _A_, _B_, and _C_.

On the railroad he _assimilated_ the managerial skills, _grasped_ the economic principles, and _cemented_ the personal relationships

Parallel structure   that enabled him to become successively _A_, _B_, and _C_.

that enabled him to become successively manager, capitalist, and entrepreneur.

Parallel structure   rested primarily on his successful transfer of _A_ to _B_.

rested primarily on his successful transfer of the railroads' managerial methods to the manufacturing sector of the economy.

*This passage is excerpted from Harold Livesay, _Andrew Carnegie and the Rise of Big Business_ (Boston: Little, Brown, 1975) 29.

grammatical form in both parts. Once again, think of the conjunction as creating parallel slots in the sentence. Whatever grammatical structure is used to complete the first slot must be used to complete the second.

Not parallel   After defeating Custer at Little Bighorn, Crazy Horse managed both to stay ahead of the army and _escape_.

Determine the parallel elements.

managed both ___Slot 1___ and ___Slot 2___ .

managed both _to stay ahead of the army_ and ___Slot 2___ .

Slot 2 must take the same form as Slot 1. Each must be a verb in its infinitive form: _to_ _____.

Revise so that parallel elements have equivalent grammatical form.

Parallel   After defeating Custer at Little Bighorn, Crazy Horse managed both *to stay* ahead of the army and *to escape.*

Variation: By slightly modifying the sentence—by moving the word *to* outside of the parallel structure created by the correlative conjunction— you can eliminate the word *to* in both of the sentence's parallel slots.

managed *to* both   Slot 1   and   Slot 2 .

managed *to* both *stay ahead of the army* and   Slot 2 .

Parallel   After defeating Custer at Little Bighorn, Crazy Horse managed *to* both *stay ahead of the army* and *escape.*

> ## 18c Use parallelism in sentences with compared and contrasted elements.

Not parallel   The staff approved the first request for funding, not the second presenter who requested funds.

Parallel   The staff approved <u>the first request for funding</u>, *not* <u>the second request</u>.

When words, phrases, or clauses are compared or contrasted in a single sentence, their logical and grammatical structures must be parallel (see 16h). Expressions that set up comparisons and contrasts include *rather than, as opposed to, on the other hand, not, like, unlike,* and *just as/so too.*

Not parallel   The word *mensch,* derived from Yiddish, describes an assertive, affectionate man, while a *schnook* (also derived from Yiddish) is being spineless and sneaky. [The phrase *is being spineless and sneaky* is not parallel with the phrase *describes an assertive, affectionate man.*]

Determine the parallel elements.

The word *mensch,* derived from Yiddish,   Slot 1 , while a *schnook* (also derived from Yiddish) Slot 2 .

The word *mensch,* derived from Yiddish, *describes an assertive, affectionate man,* while a *schnook* (also derived from Yiddish) Slot 2 .

Slot 1 consists of a present-tense verb and a noun that is modified by two adjectives; Slot 2 begins with a verb in the present progressive tense (*is being*), which is followed by two adjectives. Slot 2 should take the same basic form as Slot 1.

Revise so that parallel elements have equivalent grammatical form.

Parallel   The word *mensch,* derived from Yiddish, *describes an assertive, affectionate man,* while a *schnook* (also derived from Yiddish) *describes someone who is spineless and sneaky.* [The adjectives in Slot 2, *spineless and sneaky,* appear in a relative clause and modify the noun *someone.*]

▶ **EXERCISE I**

The following sentences contain coordinating or correlative conjunctions, or elements of comparison and contrast. Revise each to correct the faulty parallel structure.

> *Example:* Native Americans have one of the highest unemployment rates in the nation, the lowest educational attainment of any U.S. minority group, and they fare worst in the area of health.
>
> Native Americans have one of the highest unemployment rates in the nation, the lowest educational attainment of any U.S. minority group, and *the worst record of health care.* [Each slot in the series now begins with an adjective in its superlative form: *highest, lowest, worst.* Each adjective is followed by a noun and each noun by a prepositional phrase.]

1. Designating Asian Americans as the "model minority" is problematic not only because the term obscures the diversity of the group but they are represented in only a small percentage of top-ranking positions in the United States.
2. Some sociologists say that racism is rooted in a preference for one's "own kind" rather than social causes.
3. Conflict theorists feel that racism results from competition for scarce resources and an unequal distribution of power and racial tension increases during periods of economic decline.
4. Corporate managers do not tend to wield the political power of professionals such as lawyers and doctors, nor workers whom they supervise.
5. Either the percentage of the elderly living below the poverty line has decreased or to underestimate the number of elderly living in poverty is prevalent.

▶ **18d** **Use parallelism among sentences to enhance paragraph coherence.**

Like many other towns on the Great Plains, Nicodemus, Kansas, *was founded* in the 1870s. *Unlike any other* that still survives, *it was founded* by black homesteaders.

Because parallel grammatical structures highlight parallel ideas among sentence parts, parallelism is an excellent device for organizing sentence content. But parallelism can also help to relate the parts of an *entire paragraph* by highlighting the logic by which a writer moves from one sentence to the next. Parallel structures bind a paragraph's sentences into a coherent unit.

Parallel sentences within a paragraph

A house divided against itself cannot stand. I believe this government cannot endure, permanently half slave and half free. I do not expect the Union to be dissolved. I do not expect the house to fall. But I do expect it will cease to be divided. It will become all one thing, or all the other.
—ABRAHAM LINCOLN, 1858

In this famous passage, Lincoln uses parallel structures to show relationships not only among single words or phrases but also among whole sentences. Elements of the first sentence (*house, divided*) are repeated near the end of the paragraph.

Lincoln repeats the phrase *I do not expect* twice and then produces a parallel contrast with *But I do expect* in a third repetition. The final two sentences repeat *it will* with different verbs. The last sentence sets up a parallel opposition governed by *all*. These parallel repetitions of words, phrases, and structures help to make the paragraph coherent by highlighting relationships among sentences. Such relationships could be mapped in parallel "slot" diagrams similar to those used for sentences. Parallel structures also give the paragraph an emphatic, memorable rhythm.

▶ 18e   Use parallel entries when writing lists or outlines.

A list or outline divides a single large subject into equal or coordinate elements. A grocery list is the simplest example: *grocery* is the subject, and all the subdivisions appear as nouns (*steak, cheese, turnips, ketchup*). However, lists or outlines may also be written in phrases or clauses. When preparing a paper or taking notes from a book, keep the elements of lists and outlines in equivalent grammatical form. Like parallel elements in a sentence, parallel elements in a list or outline highlight the logical similarities that underlie parallel content.

▶ I   Making lists

A *list* is a displayed series of items that are logically similar or comparable and are expressed in grammatically parallel form. A list that is not parallel can be very confusing.

Not parallel

Those attending should be prepared to address these issues:
- morale of workers
- Why do we need so much overtime?
- getting more efficient
- We need better sales tools.

A list or outline can be a helpful way to organize your thoughts. To keep the logic of similar or comparable ideas in line, all items of a list should be expressed in equivalent grammatical form. The preceding example shows a list with four forms: a noun phrase, a question, a verb in its -*ing* form, and a sentence. Choosing any one of these forms as a standard for the list would make the list parallel.

Parallel

Those attending should be prepared to address these issues:
- morale of workers
- necessity of overtime
- need for efficiency
- need for better sales tools

Parallel

Those attending should be prepared to address these issues:
- improving worker morale
- reducing the need for overtime
- improving efficiency
- reevaluating sales tools

18e //

▶2 Making outlines

An **outline** is essentially a logically parallel list with further subdivisions and subsections under individual items in the list. To make an outline that will help you write a paper or take summarizing notes from a book, follow the guidelines shown in 3d-4. You should keep elements that are at the same level of generality in the outline parallel in form.

Not parallel

Chapter Title: Jefferson Takes Power [clause]
  A. The man and his policies [compound nouns]
  B. Buying Louisiana [-*ing* form of a verb]
  C. Jefferson, Marshall, and the courts [compound nouns]
  D. There's trouble on the seas [clause]

In this outline, the subdivisions within the chapter are written three different ways: as an independent clause, as a noun or noun phrase, and as a verb in its -*ing* form. You need to choose *one* of these grammatical structures to make a logically parallel outline. Any choice can be correct, but one may be preferable for your purposes. Often a compromise choice is to outline entries as nouns or noun phrases.

Parallel, with a subdivision

Chapter Title: Jefferson in Power
  A. The man and his policies
  B. The Louisiana Purchase
  C. Jefferson, Marshall, and the courts
  D. Trouble on the seas
    1. The benefits of neutrality
    2. The dangers of neutrality

As you expand the outline in greater detail and add subdivisions, once again present each entry of a subdivision in parallel form. Within each subdivision, list all parallel items at the same level of generality. If you wanted to subdivide items in the outline to a still more particular level of detail, you would once again make the listed elements of the next subdivision parallel in form.

▶ EXERCISE 2

Outline the major sections of any chapter in one of your textbooks, using the author's subheadings or your own. Then choose one section to outline in detail. Make parallel entries in your outline for every paragraph in that section, maintaining a consistent grammatical form.

EXERCISE 3

Repeat Exercise 2, using a paper you have recently written. Once you have outlined your paper, use the outline as a tool for evaluating the coherence of your work. Based on your outline, what observations can you make about the structure ▶ of your paper?

19 —

Building Emphasis with Coordination and Subordination

To emphasize a thought, a writer assigns special weight or importance to particular words in a sentence and to particular sentences in a paragraph. You are in the best position to make decisions about emphasis once you have written a draft and have your main points clearly in mind. Then you can manipulate words, phrases, and clauses to create the effects that will make your writing memorable.

Emphatic writing uses specific, concrete images (21c, d); is concise and direct (Chapter 17); employs parallelism (Chapter 18); and is varied (Chapter 20). Your writing can improve immensely if you apply the techniques discussed here; but remember that no amount of emphasis can salvage sentences that are seriously flawed in content, grammar, usage, or punctuation.

COORDINATION

▶ **19a**   **Use coordinate structures to emphasize equal ideas.**

One important and very common technique for both creating emphasis and eliminating wordiness is **coordination,** combining sentence elements by the use of coordinating and correlative conjunctions and conjunctive adverbs. Elements in a coordinate relationship share equal grammatical status and equal emphasis.

▶ **1**   **Give equal emphasis to elements with coordinating conjunctions.**

The **coordinating conjunctions** *and, but, or, nor, so, for, yet* offer an efficient way of joining parallel elements from two or more sentences into a single sentence. The following sentences are parallel in content.

> A market allows sellers of goods to interact with buyers.

> A market allows sellers of services to interact with buyers.

By using the coordinating conjunction *or,* you can create a compound sentence in which each independent clause has equal grammatical status.

CRITICAL DECISIONS

Challenge sentences: Knowing when to coordinate sentence elements

Coordination links sentences and sentence parts. The following sentences can be joined in various ways to establish coordinate relationships.

(1) A complete suit of armor consisted of some 200 metal plates. (2) The armor of the fifteenth century offered protection from cross bows. (3) Armor offered protection from swords. (4) Armor offered protection from early muskets. (5) A suit of armor weighed 60 pounds. (6) A suit of armor would quickly exhaust the soldier it was meant to protect.

Why choose coordinate relationships?

Coordinating Conjunctions and the Relationships They Establish

To show addition: *and*   **To show contrast:** *but, yet*
To show choice: *or, nor*   **To show cause:** *for*
To show consequences: *so*

Link sentences and emphasize specific words.

The armor of the fifteenth century offered protection from cross bows, swords, *and* early muskets.

Link sentences and emphasize specific phrases.

A complete suit of armor consisted of some 200 metal plates *and* weighed 60 pounds.

Link and give equal emphasis to whole sentences.

The armor of the fifteenth century offered protection from cross bows, swords, and early muskets; *but* the armor would quickly exhaust the soldier it was meant to protect.

Conjunctive Adverbs and the Relationships They Establish

To show contrast: *however, nevertheless, nonetheless,* and *still*
To show cause and effect: *accordingly, consequently, thus,* and *therefore*
To show addition: *also, besides, furthermore,* and *moreover*
To show time: *afterward, subsequently,* and *then*
To show emphasis: *indeed*
To show condition: *otherwise*

Use conjunctive adverbs to link and give equal emphasis to two sentences. Conjunctive adverbs can be shifted from the beginning to either the middle or the end of the second sentence (which is not possible with coordinating conjunctions—see 19a-3).

The armor of the fifteenth century offered protection from cross bows, swords, *and* early muskets; *however,* the armor would quickly exhaust the soldier it was meant to protect.

A market allows sellers of goods to interact with buyers, *or* a market allows sellers of services to interact with buyers.

If words are repeated in coordinate clauses, you can economize by coordinating sentence *parts*, in this case the objects of two prepositional phrases. In the following sentence, *goods* and *services* receive equal emphasis.

Combined   A market allows sellers of goods *or* services to interact with buyers. [The object of the preposition has been doubled with a coordinating conjunction.]

Coordinating conjunctions express specific logical relationships between the elements they join. *Or* and *nor* suggest choice, one positive and the other negative. *And* joins elements by addition. *But* and *yet* join elements by contrast. *For* suggests a cause of an occurrence. *So* suggests a result of some action. *For* and *so*, when used as coordinating conjunctions, join entire independent clauses. All other coordinating conjunctions may join sentence elements and entire sentences. Coordinating conjunctions must be used with appropriate punctuation to show that two ideas share the same emphasis.

To establish equality between words

Darwin was a pioneer in biology *and* a thinker with an exceptionally fertile mind.

To establish equality between phrases

Darwin theorized that evolutionary changes proceed not in jumps *but* in leaps.

To establish equality between clauses

Darwin's theory of natural selection was his most daring, *for* it dealt with the mechanism of evolutionary change.

▶**2 Give equal emphasis to elements by using correlative conjunctions.**

Correlative conjunctions are pairs of coordinating conjunctions that emphasize the relationship between the parts of the coordinated construction. The following are the common correlative conjunctions:

either/or	*both/and*	*not only/but*
neither/nor	*whether/or*	*not only/but also*

The first word of the correlative is placed before the first element to be joined, and the second word of the correlative is placed before the second element.

Both supply *and* demand are theoretical constructs, not fixed laws.

▶**3 Use conjunctive adverbs to give balanced emphasis to sentence elements.**

Conjunctive adverbs, also called *adverbial conjunctions*, create compound sentences in which the independent clauses that are joined share a logically balanced emphasis. The following conjunctions (as well as others—see the Critical Decisions box on page 324) provide logical linkages between sentences: *however, otherwise, indeed, nevertheless, afterward,* and *still.* (See 7a-9 and especially 13b-4 for uses of conjunctive adverbs.)

Use Coordinate Structures to Emphasize Equal Ideas   **325**

ACROSS THE CURRICULUM

Emphasis through Coordination

Coordination is a fundamental tool of sentence construction that gives writers in all discipline areas a means of controlling emphasis. Observe how economist Milton Friedman uses coordination to give elements equal weight.*

In a free-enterprise, private property system, a corporate executive is an employee of the owners of the business. He has direct responsibility to his employers. That responsibility is to conduct the business in accordance with their desires, which generally will be to make as much money as possible while conforming to the basic rules of the society, both those embodied in law and those embodied in ethical custom. Of course, in some cases his employers may have a different objective. A group of persons might establish [. . .] for example, a hospital or a school. The manager of such a corporation will not have money profit as his objective but the rendering of certain services.

Coordinate words

_A_, _B_ system
free-enterprise, private property system (comma replaces _and_)
for example, _A_ or _B_
for example, a hospital or a school

Coordinate phrases

both those in _A_ and those in _B_
both those embodied in law and those embodied in ethical custom
will not have _A_ but _B_
will not have money profit as his objective but the rendering of certain services

*The passage is excerpted from Milton Friedman, "The Social Responsibility of Business Is to Increase Its Profits," _New York Times Magazine_ 13 Sept. 1970.

Linked sentences

As the price of a good or service increases, the quantity of the good or service demanded is expected to decrease. _Moreover_, as the price of a good or service decreases, the quantity of the good or service demanded is expected to increase.

Conjunctive adverbs, like most adverbs, can be moved around in a sentence.

We almost take for granted that rain will replenish whatever amount of water we may use up. Water, _however_, is no longer the infinitely renewable resource that we once thought it was.

In the second sentence, the conjunctive adverb may be moved.

However, water is no longer the infinitely renewable resource that we once thought it was.

Note: Because conjunctive adverbs have the force of transitional elements, they are usually set off in a sentence with commas. It is virtually automatic that with the use of a conjunctive adverb one of the joined independent clauses will contain a comma, as in all the preceding examples. (See 13b-4 for avoiding comma splices when using conjunctive adverbs.)

▶**4 Revise sentences that use illogical or excessive coordination.**

Problems with coordination arise when writers use conjunctions aimlessly, stringing unrelated elements together without regard for an equal or balanced relationship of ideas in the joined elements.

Faulty coordination

Two elements linked by a conjunction show faulty coordination when they are not logically related. Revise or reorganize sentences to establish groupings that make sense, using coordination for elements of closely related importance.

Faulty	As a species, spiders can be found in all sorts of habitats, such as the tundra environment of mountain peaks, the deepest crevices of caves, bog-like environments, or even the most scorching deserts, and spiders are not particularly adaptable to new habitats. [The writer coordinates these sentences improperly: clearly, the writer intends a contrast.]
Revised	As a species, spiders can be found in all sorts of habitats, such as the tundra environment of mountain peaks, the deepest crevices of caves, bog-like environments, or even the most scorching deserts; but a given spider will not be particularly adaptable to a new habitat.

Excessive coordination

Readers look to a writer for signals about logical relationships among ideas, as well as for what is important in a paragraph. If a writer has aimlessly used coordinating conjunctions to join every statement to the next, readers will see no real connections among the ideas; no single idea will stand out. In reviewing first-draft writing, study your use of coordinating and correlative conjunctions and of conjunctive adverbs. Coordinate structures should be retained only when you have deliberately equated main ideas.

Faulty	Because the young princess Marie Antoinette of Austria was to be handed over by the Austrian government to the care of the French monarchy, she had to cross the national boundary line all alone, and she had to remove all her articles of Viennese clothing and replace them with French-made ones, and she could retain no trinket or jewelry, no matter what its sentimental value might have been.
Revised	Because the young princess Marie Antoinette of Austria was to be handed over by the Austrian government to the care of the French monarchy, she had to cross the national boundary line all alone. Next, she had to remove all her articles of Viennese clothing and replace them with French-made ones. She could retain no trinket or jewelry, no matter what its sentimental value might have been.

▶ **EXERCISE 1**

Combine the following sets of sentences so that whole sentences or parts of sentences show equal emphasis. Use coordinating conjunctions, correlative conjunctions, or conjunctive adverbs.

> *Example:* Ostriches grow from egg to 150-pound bird in nine months. A young python of five pounds requires ten to twenty years to reach 120 pounds.
>
> Ostriches grow from egg to 150-pound bird in nine months, but a young python of five pounds requires ten to twenty years to reach 120 pounds.

1. Why living things evolve is only partly understood. How living things evolve is only partly understood.
2. Monkeys, apes, and man are all good manipulators of hand-eye coordination. No mammal can rival the chameleon for eye-tongue coordination.
3. Snake anatomy contains the most clever feeding apparatus. Snake anatomy also contains the most intricately efficient feeding apparatus.
4. The snake opens its jaws. It begins to engulf the monkey. It is not hurried. It is deliberate. It is precise.
5. The Nunamiu Eskimo believe that wolves know where they are going when they set out to hunt caribou. They believe that wolves learn from ravens where caribou might be. They believe certain wolves in a pack never kill. Others, they believe, specialize in killing small game.
6. When the wolves come together, they make squeaking noises. They encircle each other. They rub and push one another. They poke their noses into each other's neck fur. They back away to stretch. They chase each other. They stand quietly together. Then they are gone down a vague trail.
7. Mexico still has a small population of wolves. Large populations remain in Alaska and Canada.

EXERCISE 2

Rewrite the sentences in the following paragraph by using coordinating conjunctions, correlative conjunctions, or conjunctive adverbs along with appropriate punctuation. Remember that you want to show equality between ideas or parts of ideas. Be sure that the revised paragraph is cohesive and coherent.

> The smallest living creatures known are viroids. Each is composed of fewer than 10,000 atoms. They can cause several different diseases in plants. They have probably most recently developed from more complex organisms rather than less complicated ones. They are so simple in structure. One wonders how they could be alive at all. They survive because they are parasites. They take over much larger cells and force that cell to begin making more viroids like themselves.

EXERCISE 3

Rewrite the following sets of sentences to correct problems of faulty coordination.

1. Plants adapted to cold climates can conduct photosynthesis at temperatures far below those of their warmer-weather compatriots, and some evergreens still maintain the process at 0°C, and some algae that inhabit hot water

springs can do likewise at 75°C, and yet most plants photosynthesize best between 10° and 35°C.

2. Many arthropods are definitely "dressed to kill." The scorpion sports sharp jaws, strong pincers, and it packs a nasty sting, but it is outclassed by the black widow spider, and her bite can be lethal if untreated, and yet centipedes will attack and paralyze prey twice their size with a bite.

SUBORDINATION

 19b   Use subordinate structures to emphasize a main idea.

Writers use **subordination** within sentences to give more emphasis to one idea than to another. The basic idea always appears in an **independent clause,** a core statement that can stand alone as a sentence in itself. To state another idea closely linked to that core statement, writers add a **dependent clause,** which cannot stand by itself. A dependent clause begins with a subordinating conjunction, such as *if*, *although*, or *because* (see the Critical Decisions box in 19b-1 for a complete list), or with a relative pronoun: *who, which,* or *that.* A sentence with both dependent and independent clauses is known as a **complex sentence.** (For more information on dependent clauses, see 7e.)

▌1 **Use subordinating conjunctions to form dependent adverb clauses.**

A subordinating conjunction placed at the beginning of an independent clause (a complete sentence) renders that clause *dependent.* Once dependent, this clause can be joined to an independent clause and will function like an adverb. In this new complex sentence, the independent clause will receive the primary emphasis, with the dependent clause closely linked to it in a subordinate relationship. To create a dependent adverb clause, begin with two sentences that you think could be combined.

Married women could not leave the home for the twelve-hour work days required in the mills.

Married women lost their ability to earn income.

When you place a subordinating conjunction at the head of the dependent clause, the clause will function like an adverb in the new complex sentence.

Because married women could not leave the home for the twelve-hour work days required in the mills,

Join the now dependent clause to the independent clause.

Because married women could not leave the home for the twelve-hour work days required in the mills, they lost their ability to earn income.

Emphasis and logical sequence determine the placement of a dependent adverb clause.

At the beginning

When the Triangle Shirtwaist Factory fire broke out in a rag bin on a quiet Saturday afternoon in 1911, it spread extraordinarily quickly due to the mass of tissue paper and bits of material that littered the workroom floor.

CRITICAL DECISIONS

Challenge sentences: Knowing when to subordinate sentence elements

Subordination links whole sentences. The following sentences can be joined to establish subordinate relationships.

> A suit of armor weighed 60 pounds.
>
> A suit of armor would quickly exhaust the soldier it was meant to protect.

Why choose subordinate relationships?

Subordinating Conjunctions and the Relationships They Establish

To show condition: *if, even if, unless, provided that, whether,* and *as though*

To show contrast: *though, although, even though, as if, rather than, than,* and *even if*

To show cause: *because, since, how, so,* and *why*

To show time: *when, whenever, while, as, before, after, since, once,* and *until*

To show place: *where* and *wherever*

To show purpose: *so that, in order that,* and *that*

Subordinating conjunctions link whole clauses but, in the process, give one clause greater emphasis. Use a subordinating conjunction when you want one of the two sentences you are linking to modify (that is, to describe or to comment on) the other.

> Because it weighed 60 pounds, a suit of armor would quickly exhaust the soldier it was meant to protect.

Designate one sentence as subordinate by placing a conjunction at its head; thereafter, the sentence is referred to as a *dependent clause* (in this example, *Because it weighed 60 pounds*). Emphasis in a sentence linked with subordination is given to the *independent clause* (in this example, to the clause beginning with *a suit of armor* and ending with *protect*). See the discussion on relative pronouns (14e, 19b-2, 25d-1–2), which also begin dependent clauses.

In the middle

The fire, though it claimed 146 lives, did result in the addition of 30 new ordinances to the New York City fire code.

At the end

The terrorized, virtually all-female workforce was hampered in its efforts to leave because management had purposefully designed narrow escape passages in an effort to spot and catch pilferers.

▶ **2** Use *that, which,* and *who* to form dependent adjective clauses.

A dependent **adjective clause** modifies a noun in an independent clause. Adjective clauses are introduced by relative pronouns that rename and refer to the nouns they follow. The pronoun *who* can refer to people or to personified divinities or animals. *That* refers to people, animals, or things. *Which* refers to animals and things. To create a dependent adjective clause, begin with two sentences that you think could be combined.

> Transylvania qualifies as one of the most fought-over regions in all of Europe.

> Transylvania witnessed the bloody clashes of Bulgarians, Magyars, Huns, and other eastern tribes between the fourth and twelfth centuries.

Substitute a relative pronoun for the subject of the dependent clause, the clause that will function like an adjective in the new complex sentence.

> which witnessed the bloody clashes of Bulgarians, Magyars, Huns, and other eastern tribes between the fourth and twelfth centuries,

Join the now dependent clause to the independent clause.

> Transylvania, which witnessed the bloody clashes of Bulgarians, Magyars, Huns, and other eastern tribes between the fourth and twelfth centuries, qualifies as one of the most fought-over regions in all of Europe.

▶3 Use subordination accurately to avoid confusion.

Three errors are commonly associated with subordination: inappropriate and ambiguous use of subordinating conjunctions, illogical subordination, and excessive subordination.

Inappropriate and ambiguous use of subordinating conjunctions

The subordinating conjunction *as* is used to denote both time and comparison.

> As human beings became more advanced technologically, they learned to domesticate animals and plants rather than to forage and hunt.

As is occasionally used to indicate cause: *Mary didn't arrive this morning, *as* she missed her plane.* This usage is apt to confuse readers, who may expect *as* to indicate time or comparison. When you wish to establish cause and effect, use the subordinating conjunction *because*.

Confusing   *As* the plough is used as a wedge to divide the soil, it is the most powerful invention in all agriculture.

Revised   *Because* the plough is used as a wedge to divide the soil, it is the most powerful invention in all agriculture.

The preposition *like* is used as a subordinating conjunction in informal speech. In formal writing, use the subordinating conjunction *as* in place of *like* when a conjunction is needed.

Nonstandard   American agriculture did not have the plough and the wheel *like* Middle Eastern agriculture did.

Revised   American agriculture did not have the plough and the wheel *as* Middle Eastern agriculture did.

Illogical subordination

The problem of illogical subordination arises when a dependent clause does not establish a clear, logical relationship with an independent clause. To correct the problem, reexamine the clauses in question, and select a more accurate subordinating conjunction or, if the sentences warrant, a coordinating conjunction.

Faulty   *Although* she was agitated at being shut up in a matchbox for so long, the female scorpion seized the first opportunity to escape.

The subordinating conjunction *although* fails to establish a clear, logical relationship between the dependent and independent clauses. The content of the dependent clause gives no reason for the scorpion's wanting to escape.

Revised   *Because* she was agitated at being shut up in a matchbox for so long, the female scorpion seized the first opportunity to escape.

Excessive subordination

As with coordination, a writer may overuse subordination. When all or most parts of a long sentence are subordinate in structure, readers may have trouble identifying points of particular importance. In your review of a first draft, study your use of subordinating conjunctions and relative pronouns. Retain subordinate structures when you have deliberately made the ideas of one clause dependent on another. Choose some other sentence structure when the clauses you are relating do not exist in a dependent/independent relationship.

Faulty   The manatee, which is a very tame beast but extremely unattractive with its dull gray skin, has a hippopotamus-like head and virtually no neck, so that one wonders how the creature could ever have been mistaken for the lovely creature that is supposed to be the mermaid, although there are those who claim that if the animal is seen from sufficiently far away as it sits on the rocks, the lines of its head could convey the impression of flowing hair.

Revised   The manatee, which is a very tame beast but extremely unattractive with its dull gray skin, has a hippopotamus-like head and virtually no neck. One wonders how the creature could ever have been mistaken for the lovely creature that is supposed to be the mermaid. There are those who claim that if the animal is seen from sufficiently far away as it sits on the rocks, the lines of its head could convey the impression of flowing hair.

▶ **EXERCISE 4**

Revise each pair of sentences that follow by creating a complex sentence with one dependent clause and one independent clause. Place the dependent clause in whatever position you think will best demonstrate the relationship of that clause to the main idea.

> *Example:*   The Viennese naturalist Konrad Lorenz took a degree in medicine. Later, Konrad Lorenz became director of the Max Planck Institute for behavioral physiology.
>
> After he took a degree in medicine, the Viennese naturalist Konrad Lorenz became director of the Max Planck Institute for behavioral physiology. [A dependent adverb clause is joined to an independent clause to form a complex sentence.]

1. Social animals such as crows will attack or "mob" a nocturnal predator. The nocturnal predator sometimes appears during the day.

2. A fox is followed through the woods by a loudly screaming jay. The fox's hunting is spoiled.

3. Poisonous or foul-tasting animals have chosen the "warning" colors of red, white, and black. Predators associate these with unpleasant experiences.
4. Scent marks of cats act like railway signals. The scent marks prevent collision between two cats.
5. The surroundings become stranger and more intimidating to the animal. The readiness to fight decreases proportionately.

OTHER DEVICES FOR ACHIEVING EMPHASIS

▶ **19c** **Use special techniques to achieve emphasis.**

Coordination and subordination are fundamental to the structure of so many sentences that often they go unnoticed as devices for directing a reader's attention. Not so subtle are special stylistic techniques such as repetition and contrast, which writers use to achieve highly visible and at times dramatic prose. Precisely because they are so visible, you should mix these techniques both with subordination and coordination and with less emphatic simple sentences in a paragraph.

▶ **I** **Punctuate, capitalize, and highlight to emphasize words.**

Punctuation, capitalization, and highlighting work *with* sentence content to create emphasis. *Capitalizing* a word, especially if it is not a proper name and hence is usually not begun with an uppercase letter, is one sure way to create emphasis. Capitalizing all the letters of a word, as in FIRE, will attract even more attention. So, of course, will **boldfacing** a word. In academic writing, strictly limit your use of these techniques and depend, instead, on the wording of your sentences to create emphasis. Occasionally, however, you might use uppercase letters for effect.

> There does not seem to be any point in my knowing for the rest of my life that, during 1964, 720 tons of soot fell on every square mile of New York City, yet there it is in my notebook, labeled "FACT."

Used sparingly, an exclamation point adds emphasis and will help a reader to share a writer's amazement, enthusiasm—or, in some cases, contempt (see 24c). Ending a sentence with a *colon* sets for your reader an expectation that important, closely related information will follow. The words after a colon are emphasized (see 29a). A *dash*, which you will show on a typewriter or computer as a double hyphen (--), creates a pause in a sentence and the expectation that some significant comment will follow. Used sparingly, a dash is an excellent tool for emphasis. Overused, it creates a choppy effect and will annoy readers (see 29b).

Information set within *parentheses* will be viewed by readers as an aside—interesting, useful, but ultimately nonessential information. Parentheses give material special attention, but of a curious sort: parenthetical material limits its own emphasis and says in effect, pay attention, but not *too much*. Thus, material set off in parentheses is simultaneously emphasized and deemphasized (see 29c).

2 Repeat words, phrases, and clauses to emphasize ideas.

Intentional repetition is a powerful technique for creating emphasis. With repetition, words echo for a reader. Whatever is repeated, if it is repeated well, will be remembered. When using repetition, maintain parallel structure (see Chapter 18) and avoid overuse. It is both more emphatic and less wordy to write

> A market allows sellers of goods or services to interact with buyers.

instead of

> A market allows sellers of goods to interact with buyers. A market allows sellers of services to interact with buyers.

Using repetition to triple sentence elements is more dramatic than doubling and will give a sentence an arresting, memorable rhythm. Think of Caesar's "I came, I saw, I conquered"; or the phrasing in the Declaration of Independence: "Life, Liberty and the pursuit of Happiness"; or Lincoln's lines at Gettysburg: "government of the people, by the people, for the people." (In each case, note the parallel structures.) One repetition too many can ruin a sentence, however, transforming a dramatic rhythm into a boring catalogue: *On arriving home, I folded the laundry, cooked dinner, read the paper, bathed my kids, finished the taxes, and went to sleep.*

Generally, try not to follow one sentence that has a repeated structure with a second sentence of a similar structure. Too much repetition within either a sentence or a paragraph will create an unpleasant, overly balanced effect.

One special case of repetition concerns the *appositive phrase*, used to rename a noun. Although an appositive does not exactly repeat a word, in content the appositive is a technique based on repetition. In the following example, the phrase *a symbolic embodiment of its territorial status* renames (that is, repeats) the noun *flag*.

> Today each nation flies its own flag, a symbolic embodiment of its territorial status.

3 Use contrasts to emphasize ideas.

Contrast, otherwise known as *antithesis* or *opposition*, creates emphasis by setting one element in a sentence off against another, in the process emphasizing both. When using this technique, be sure that the elements you set in contrast have parallel structures.

> Requiring more skill to use and initially more unwieldy to master than the dictionary, *Roget's College Thesaurus* is, nonetheless, a valuable and time-saving aid for the struggling writer.

> If you apply to a college that won't promise to lock in its tuition rates, make sure to check the terms of your financial aid package; if you don't, you may find that after the freshman year your grants have been transformed into loans.

4 Use specialized sentences to create emphasis.

Sentence length is variable and depends both on a writer's preferences and on an audience's needs; still, readers do not expect a steady diet of four- or five-word sentences. Nor do they expect one-sentence paragraphs. Purposefully violating these (and other) expectations regarding the sentence can create emphasis (see 20a and 20b).

The brief sentence

An especially brief sentence located anywhere in a paragraph will call attention to itself. The following paragraph concludes emphatically with a four-word sentence.

> If you apply to a college that won't promise to lock in its tuition rates, make sure to check the terms of your financial aid package; if you don't, you may find that after the freshman year your grants have been transformed into loans. That can be disastrous.

The one-sentence paragraph

Because it is so rare, a one-sentence paragraph calls attention to itself. Often these emphatic paragraphs begin or conclude an essay. In the following example, the one-sentence paragraph appears mid-essay and is both preceded and followed by long paragraphs.

> Not only are fruit seeds dispersed in the coyote's scat, the seeds' pericarp dissolves in his digestive tract, increasing the chance of germination by 85 percent.
>   A coyote's breath is rumored to be so rank that he can stun his prey with it.
>   Most people may never see a coyote—especially if they go looking for one—but everyone can hear them at night. They're most vocal from December to February, during the mating season.[. . .]

The periodic sentence

Most sentences can be classified as *cumulative*. They begin with a subject and gather both force and detail from beginning to end. The advantage of a cumulative sentence is that it directly and emphatically announces its business by beginning with its subject.

Cumulative sentence   Most people may never see a coyote—especially if they go looking for one—but everyone can hear them at night.

A *periodic* sentence delays the subject and verb in an effort to pique the reader's interest. Information placed at the head of the sentence draws readers in, creating a desire to find out what happens. Emphasis is given to the final part of the sentence, where the readers' need to know is satisfied.

Periodic sentence   Washing machines, garbage disposals, lawn mowers, furnaces, TV sets, tape recorders, slide projectors—all are in league with the automobile to take their turn at breaking down whenever life threatens to flow smoothly for their enemies.

▶ **EXERCISE 5**

Read the sentences that follow, and underline the emphatic elements. Label the specific techniques the writer uses: coordination, subordination, punctuation, capitalization, repetition, contrast, or sentence length. Write your analysis in paragraph form.

> In books I've read since I was young I've searched for heroines who could serve as ideals, as models, as possibilities—some reflecting the secret self that dwelled inside me, others pointing to whole new ways that a woman (if only she dared!) might try to be. The person that I am today was shaped by Nancy Drew; by Jo March, Jane Eyre and Heathcliff's soul

mate Cathy; and by other fictional females whose attractiveness or character or audacity for a time were the standards by which I measured myself.

I return to some of these books to see if I still understand the powerful
hold that these heroines once had on me. I still understand.

—JUDITH VIORST

EXERCISE 6

Use the various techniques you have learned in this chapter to combine the short,
choppy sentences that follow, rewording them to make an engaging paragraph.

There are self-regulated devices in the body. One of these can provide
long-term immunity from diseases such as mumps or measles. This same
device somehow also causes the AIDS virus, if present, to infect the immune cells. This discovery was made by researchers. They work at Virginia
Commonwealth University in Richmond. They found that the HIV virus
can get coated with antibodies. Even so, the virus will attack the surrounding T-cells (immune cells).

CHAPTER 20

Controlling Length and Rhythm

Good writing has much to do with timing: how long a sentence takes to read and what rhythmic effects are encountered along the way. Considerations of length and rhythm alone will not make a sentence memorable. But any significant content, once established, can be expressed with a more or less effective style, and effective style has a great deal to do with sentence length and rhythm (as well as conciseness, parallelism, and emphasis—see Chapters 17, 18, and 19). As a writer, you will constantly be making decisions that affect the length and rhythm of your sentences.

▶ 20a   Monitoring sentence length

▶ 1   Track the length of your sentences.

Common sense dictates that when a sentence gets so long that readers forget important sentence parts (for instance, the subject), the length should be revised.

Track the length of your sentences, especially in the late stages of revision, once you are certain of a paper's content. If you want to vary sentence length, you must be aware of the average length of your sentences. The information in the box on the next page will help you make that determination.

As you begin tracking sentence length, following a technique such as the one suggested here will not be necessary for long. Soon you will develop a writer's intuition about sentence length and will begin to make changes subconsciously.

▶ 2   Vary sentence length and alternate the length of consecutive sentences.

Regardless of average sentence length, good writers will (1) write sentences in a paragraph that vary from their average and (2) avoid placing two or more very short or very long sentences consecutively (see 19c-4).

The paragraph below was written by a student, Jenafer Trahar. At twenty words, Trahar's average sentence length is slightly less than that of other stylistically strong writers. She is careful both to vary length and to alternate lengths in consecutive sentences.

(1) One major problem with the commercialization of college sports is the exploitation of student-athletes, many of whom come to school on athletic scholarships. (2) Frequently, student-athletes don't deserve to be admitted to

a school. (3) Many colleges routinely lower admissions requirements for their ball players, and some schools will even waive requirements for that exceptional athlete, who without his sports abilities might not have had a place on a college campus. (4) Most kids not interested in academics would normally shun a college education. (5) But for gifted athletes, college appears to be a road that leads to the pros. (6) Or so they think. (7) According to Richard Lapchick of the Center for the Study of Sport in Society, twelve thousand high school athletes participate in sports in any one year, but only one will subsequently play for a professional team.

—JENAFER TRAHAR

Analysis of sentence length

(20 word avg.)
1. 24 words (average)
2. 11 words (short)
3. 36 words (long)
4. 12 words (short)
5. 15 words (average)
6. 4 words (short)
7. 36 words (long)
    $138 \div 7 \approx 20$

Trahar's sentence lengths are varied: three short, two long, two average.
- No short sentences are placed consecutively.
- No long sentences are placed consecutively.
- No sentences of average length are placed consecutively.

Notice that Trahar varies sentence lengths in the paragraph, and at no point does she write consecutive sentences of the same length. Trahar regularly alternates short sentences with long or average-length ones.

Tracking Sentence Length

Any given sentence in a paragraph is long or short in relation to the *average* number of words per sentence in that paragraph. A simple process of counting and dividing will reveal your average sentence length.

1. Number the sentences in a paragraph and write those numbers in a column on a piece of paper.
2. Count and record the number of words in each sentence.
3. Add the word counts for step 2 to obtain the total number of words in the paragraph.
4. Divide the number of words in the paragraph (step 3) by the number of sentences in the paragraph (step 1): this number is your average sentence length for the paragraph.

Consider a sentence to be *average* in length if it has *five words more or less* than your average. Consider a sentence *long* if it has six or more words more than your average and *short* if it has six or fewer words less than your average.

5. Return to the listing you made in step 2, and designate each sentence of your paragraph as *average* length, *short*, or *long*. (These designations apply to your writing only.)

CRITICAL DECISIONS

Challenge sentences: Varying sentence length and alternating the length of consecutive sentences

No precise formula exists for determining how many long or short sentences should be used in a paragraph. But you may find these general principles helpful as you make decisions about how to revise:

- Determine the average length of sentences in a paragraph.
- Plan to vary from that average by using short and long sentences.
- Use short sentences to break up strings of longer ones.
- Avoid placing short sentences consecutively unless you are doing so for specific stylistic effect.
- Avoid placing more than two or three long sentences consecutively.
- Avoid placing more than three or four sentences of average length consecutively.

EXERCISE 1

Choose three paragraphs you have written recently and analyze them for sentence length. Follow the steps laid out in the preceding box. On finishing your analysis, you should have figured your average sentence length for each paragraph and designated each sentence in the paragraph as *short*, *average*, or *long*. Write a brief paragraph in which you summarize your findings.

20b Strategies for varying sentence length

The techniques discussed here for manipulating sentence length will be helpful *only* if you are working with sentences that are already concise and direct. Sentence length can always be reduced by eliminating wordiness, and revising for conciseness should be your first strategy in managing sentence length. See Chapter 17 for advice.

1 Control the use of coordination.

Coordination is the use of coordinating and correlative conjunctions and of conjunctive adverbs to compound sentence elements. Coordination is the principal means by which parts of two or more sentences are joined into a single sentence (see 19a). In its favor, coordination reduces the overall length of a paragraph by allowing a writer to combine sentence parts (or entire sentences) and eliminate redundancy.

> Between 12,000 and 10,000 B.C., the massive icecap began to recede. The sea level rose as the enormous quantities of ice melted. At the same time, huge land masses such as Britain and Scandinavia, once ice-covered, began to reappear.

Strategies for Varying Sentence Length **339**

The cost of combining sentences with coordination is that the length of the revised sentence will increase:

> Between 12,000 and 10,000 B.C., the massive icecap which had covered huge land masses such as Britain and Scandinavia began to recede, and the enormous quantities of melting ice caused the sea level to rise.

If you decided that the combined sentence made possible by coordination was too long, you could break the combined sentence in two:

> Between 12,000 and 10,000 B.C., the massive icecap which had covered huge land masses such as Britain and Scandinavia began to recede. The enormous quantities of melting ice caused the sea level to rise.

COMPUTER TIPS

Limited Use for a Grammar/Style Checker

You should avoid relying on grammar checkers to evaluate and correct your usage. However, a grammar/style checker can help you identify with a high degree of accuracy style problems such as sexist language, repeated words, overly long or overly short sentences, clichés, and the use of passive voice. Of course, once you have found the problem, you still have to be the judge of what action to take.

▶**2 Control the use of modifying phrases and clauses.**

One way of controlling sentence length is to control the extent to which you use modifying phrases and clauses (see 7d, e). If you determine that a sentence is too long in relation to its neighbors, you can reduce sentence length by converting a modifying clause into a phrase.

> *When a city is threatened with water shortages,* drastic actions become necessary.
>
> *In times of drought,* drastic actions become necessary. [The dependent clause is shortened to two prepositional phrases.]

Move modifying phrases from one sentence to another.

If you determine that a sentence is too long in relation to its neighbors, you may be able to strip a sentence of a modifier, which you can then move to an adjacent sentence (where it may have a new function).

> In Los Angeles, *a city that has suffered through severe droughts,* engineers have considered building desalination plants.
>
> In Los Angeles, engineers have considered building desalination plants. Recently, *that city has suffered through severe droughts,* and municipal leaders are now ready to consider long-term solutions to a persistent problem. [The appositive phrase is converted to a subject and predicate in the new sentence.]

Substitute a single-word modifier for a phrase- or clause-length modifier.

If you determine that a sentence is too long in relation to its neighbors, you may be able to convert phrases or clauses to single-word adjectives or adverbs. In the

---

following example, an important detail (about towing icebergs) is lost in the conversion and would need to be added to some other sentence; still, the desired result, a briefer sentence, is achieved.

The melting of ice, *which would be towed south from the Arctic Ocean*, is one solution that would supply millions of gallons of fresh water.

The melting of *arctic* ice is one solution that would supply millions of gallons of fresh water.

▶**3 Control the use of phrases and clauses used as nouns.**

Sentences can be combined by converting the key words of one sentence into a phrase or clause that then functions as a noun (as a subject, object, or complement) in a second sentence. The disadvantage of the revision is that the newly combined sentence tends to be long.

The English during the Tudor period drank ale in place of water.

It was a widespread custom.

Combined   *To drink ale with one's breakfast*, rather than water, was a widespread custom in Tudor England. [The infinitive phrase functions as the subject.]

If you determine that a sentence is too long in relation to its neighbors, try to identify a phrase or clause functioning as a noun. Revise the sentence, possibly moving the noun phrase or clause into its own sentence.

Sentence with   *The fact that much of the water was polluted* was one main
a noun clause   reason the Tudor English substituted ale for water.

Revision   Much of the water in Tudor England was polluted. This condition prompted many to substitute ale for water.

ESL NOTE   Noun clauses in English have several uses. Notice the special rules in constructions involving *wish that* (see 46b-6). Indirect quotation or reported speech is a very common special use involving *that* clauses. Section 46b-6 describes the tense sequences encountered in reported speech.

▶ **EXERCISE 2**

Use any of the strategies discussed thus far in the chapter to combine the following sentences. Vary sentence length and alternate the length of consecutive sentences.

I have been teaching English literature in a university. I have also been studying literature. I have been doing these things for twenty-five years. Certain questions stick in one's mind in this job; actually, they do in any job. They persist not only because people keep asking them. Such questions stick in one's mind because they are inspired by the very fact of being in a university. First one might ask what is the benefit of studying literature. Then one might ask whether literature helps us think more clearly, or whether it helps us feel more sensitively, or whether literature helps us live a better life than we could if we did not have it.

▶ **EXERCISE 3**

Follow the instructions in Exercise 2 and revise the three paragraphs that you analyzed for sentence length in Exercise 1. Revise to vary sentence length and to alternate the length of consecutive sentences.

▶ **20c** | Strategies for controlling sentence rhythm

▶ **1** Use modifying phrases and clauses to alter sentence rhythm.

Varying sentence openings is the most direct way of varying the rhythm of a sentence. Sentences consist of a subject, followed by a verb and then an object (if the
verb is transitive) or a complement (if the verb is linking). Any of these important
elements can be modified, and it is primarily through placement of modifiers that
sentences change rhythm. When you want to alter sentence rhythm, revise sentence structure by changing the extent and location of your modifiers.

ACROSS THE CURRICULUM

Controlling Sentence Length and Rhythm

You will find writers in all discipline areas who vary sentence length
and rhythm to achieve an effective style. In the following passage,
psychologist David Shapiro attempts to define, in part, "rigid thinking." Observe how Shapiro varies sentence length, controls sentence
rhythm with phrases and clauses, and uses different sentence types.*

What exactly is meant by rigidity of thinking? Consider as a commonplace
example the sort of thinking one encounters in a discussion with a compulsive, rigid person, the kind of person we also call "dogmatic" or "opinion-
ated." Even casual conversation with such a person is often very frustrating,
and it is so for a particular reason. It is not simply that one meets with unex-
pected opposition. On the contrary, such discussion is typically frustrating
just because one experiences neither real disagreement nor agreement. Instead, there is no meeting of minds at all, and the impression is simply of not
being heard, of not receiving any but perfunctory attention.

Sentence types: question, command, direct statement

Sentence structures: simple, compound, complex

Sentence length (based on an average length of 18 words): short, long,
average, short, average, long

Purposeful repetition:
"a compulsive, rigid person, the kind of person we also call"
"the impression is simply of not being heard, of not receiving"

*The passage is excerpted from David Shapiro, *Neurotic Styles* (New York: Basic, 1965) 24.

Modifiers concentrated at the *beginning* of a sentence:

> *Providing a sense of solidarity for the community,* the National Puerto Rican Forum voiced the concerns of its members and lobbied for new laws.

Modifiers concentrated in the *middle* of a sentence:

> The Forum, *the first such organization on the mainland USA,* was established by members of the Puerto Rican community in New York City.

Modifiers concentrated at the *end* of a sentence:

> The Forum and similar organizations have lobbied for laws *that outlaw discriminatory practices against Puerto Ricans in such matters as housing, employment, voting rights, and education.*

Sentence rhythm is also related to length. A brief sentence with relatively few modifiers offers a strong rhythmical contrast to longer, heavily modified sentences.

> The Commonwealth of Puerto Rico was created in 1952.

Vary the position of phrases.

Phrases that function as adverbs may, like adverbs, be moved around in a sentence. Because such movement can change meaning as well as sentence rhythm, beware of altering the meaning of your sentences when revising for style.

> I reached our new home *on Monday,* wondering whether the movers would arrive.

Shifted rhythm	*On Monday,* I reached our new home, wondering whether the movers would arrive.
Shifted meaning	I reached our new home, wondering whether the movers would arrive *on Monday.* [The timing of the movers' arrival has now become the issue.]

A phrase that functions as an adjective should be placed as close as possible to the noun it modifies to avoid confusion and faulty reference.

Faulty	Zebulon Pike ventured west to the Rockies, *an explorer of the Mississippi.*
Revised	Zebulon Pike, *an explorer of the Mississippi,* ventured west to the Rockies.
Shifted rhythm	*An explorer of the Mississippi,* Zebulon Pike ventured west to the Rockies.

Vary the position of clauses.

Like single-word adverbs and phrases functioning as adverbs, adverb clauses can be moved around in a sentence. An adverb clause that begins a sentence can be shifted to the interior or to the end of the sentence. The placement of the clause determines its punctuation.

> *After so many white settlers had come from England,* it was not surprising that the English language, English customs, and English ways of government dominated America.

> It was not surprising, *after so many white settlers had come from England,* that the English language, English customs, and English ways of government dominated America.

It was not surprising that the English language, English customs, and English ways of government dominated America *after so many white settlers had come from England.*

Place a dependent clause that functions as an adjective next to the word it modifies. Neglecting to do so may confuse readers. (See Chapter 15 on revising to correct misplaced modifiers.)

Faulty	The Great Pyramid at Giza has a base area of 13 acres which was built in the fourth dynasty for the pharaoh Khufu.
Revised	The Great Pyramid at Giza, which was built in the fourth dynasty for the pharaoh Khufu, has a base area of 13 acres.
Shifted rhythm	Built in the fourth dynasty for the pharaoh Khufu, the Great Pyramid at Giza has a base area of 13 acres. [The relative clause has been shortened to a phrase beginning with "built."]

Vary the position of transitions.

Transitions (see 5d-3) can be moved around in a sentence; when their position changes, sentence rhythm changes. Brief transitions include *for instance, for example, on the one hand, on the other hand, in addition*, and *additionally.* Conjunctive adverbs also serve as transitions: *however, moreover, consequently*, and *therefore.*

Advertising is an ancient art. *For example,* some early advertisements appear about three thousand B.C. as stenciled inscriptions on bricks made by the Babylonians.

Advertising is an ancient art. Some early advertisements, *for example,* appear about three thousand B.C. as stenciled inscriptions on bricks made by the Babylonians.

▶**2 Revise individual sentences with a disruptive rhythm.**

As with the length of a sentence, the rhythm of a sentence should be evaluated both on its own terms and in relation to neighboring sentences. A sentence that starts and stops a reader repeatedly has a disruptive rhythm and should be revised.

Disruptive rhythm	Francisco Goya's *Los Caprichos*, a series of eighty etchings, published in 1799, described by the author as a criticism of "human errors and vices," and now considered as one of his finest works, was a commercial failure.

Because its erratic, bumpy rhythm interferes with understanding, this sentence needs revision. Revision in this case might lead to two sentences:

Revised	Francisco Goya's *Los Caprichos*, a series of eighty etchings, was published in 1799. Described by the author as a criticism of "human errors and vices," it is now considered as one of his finest works even though, with only 27 sets having been sold, it was a commercial failure.

▶**3 Vary sentence types.**

Sentences are classified by structure and function. There are four functional types of sentences (7f-1): the direct statement, the question, the exclamation, and the

Varying Sentence Rhythm

Vary sentence structures and rhythms to make your writing stylistically strong. You may find the following general principles helpful.

- Use phrases, clauses, and transitions to vary sentence beginnings.
- Consciously shift the location of phrase- and clause-length modifiers in a paragraph: locate modifiers at the beginning of some sentences, in the middle of others, and at the end of others.
- Use short sentences to break up strings of long sentences.
- Limit your concentration of phrase- and clause-length modifiers to one and possibly two locations in a sentence. Heavily modifying a sentence at the beginning, middle, *and* end will create a burden stylistically.
- Vary sentence types.

command. For the most part, academic writing is restricted to statements and questions. The occasional question posed, aside from its contribution to content, will introduce a unique rhythm into a paragraph.

Vary the structure of sentences.

There are four structural types of sentences: simple, compound, complex, and compound-complex. (See 7f-2.) Writing that is strong stylistically tends to mix all four types. As an illustration of a student's effective use of sentence variety, consider again the paragraph by Jenafer Trahar in 20a-2. Here are the types of sentences she used:

(Structural) type of sentence	*Sentence opens with*
1. complex	noun phrase functioning as the subject
2. simple	single-word modifier
3. compound-complex	subject
4. simple	subject
5. simple	coordinating conjunction and modifying phrase
6. simple	coordinating conjunction
7. compound	modifying phrase

The preceding analysis may look technical, but peel away the numbers and structural descriptions and you have a paragraph that succeeds in both content and style. While her sentences are declarative (typical of academic writing), Trahar makes use of all four structural sentence types: simple, compound, complex, and compound-complex. What is more, she nicely varies the openings of her sentences.

Jenafer Trahar's paragraph is stylistically sophisticated. Every technique she has used to gain that sophistication has been discussed in this chapter, and you can apply these same techniques to your own writing. When revising for style, you may want to consult other chapters in this section on matters of conciseness (17), parallelism (18), and emphasis (19).

▶ **EXERCISE 4**

Revise the following paragraph to eliminate the choppiness created by too many short sentences. In your revision, use all the techniques you have learned in this chapter for varying sentence length and rhythm.

The term "derelicts" in naval usage refers to abandoned ships. Derelicts are rarely seen anymore. They were more frequently sighted in the days of the tall-masted sailing ships. At one time they were considered dangerous. In the days before radar, a passing ship could encounter a derelict with absolutely no warning. For example, in 1906, the *St. Louis* had a near-collision with the derelict *Dunmore*. Some derelicts managed to remain afloat for several months. The *Fanny Wolston* stayed afloat for at least 1408 days. Derelicts are to the sea what ghost towns are to the Old West. They become ghostly entities. They were floating haunted houses. The wreck inspires pity. The derelict evokes awe.

EXERCISE 5

Read the paragraph that follows, and analyze the component sentences for length and rhythm. Structure your analysis like the analysis of Jenafer Trahar's paragraph in 20a-2. Be sure to include a paragraph that summarizes your observations.

For the past twenty-five years I have been teaching and studying English literature in a university. As in any other job, certain questions stick in one's mind, not because people keep asking them but because they're the questions inspired by the very fact of being in such a place. What good is the study of literature? Does it help us think more clearly, or feel more sensitively, or live a better life than we could without it?

—NORTHROP FRYE

EXERCISE 6

Reexamine the three paragraphs that you revised for sentence length in Exercise 3. Revise these paragraphs a final time for sentence rhythm, using the techniques you have learned in this chapter.

21

Choosing the Right Word

Your purpose as a writer and your intended audience profoundly affect your **diction**—your choice of words. Like the overall tone of a document, diction can be high or low, formal or informal, or any register between (see 3a-4). The English language usually gives you choices in selecting words. Readers have a certain attention span and a certain radar; they know when writers are invested in their work—when, for instance, writers have taken time to state a thought precisely or to render a description vividly. A document that shows little concern for word choice will quickly lose its readers.

▶ 21a   Understanding denotation and connotation

Your first concern in selecting a word is to be sure that its **denotation,** or dictionary meaning, is appropriate for the sentence at hand. A careless writer might, for instance, state that in performing their jobs diplomats should know when to *precede*. Is this the intended meaning (when to go first), or did the writer mean that diplomats should know when to *proceed* (when to go forward)? Although these words look similar and sound nearly the same, their denotations are very different. Once you are satisfied that you are using a word correctly according to its denotation, consider its **connotations**—its implications, associations, and nuances of meaning. Consider these sentences:

His speech was *brief.*

His speech was *concise.*

His speech was *curt.*

His speech was *abbreviated.*

Brief, concise, curt, and *abbreviated:* these adjectives suggest brevity—but only the word *brief* has this single meaning, with no other associations. The word *brief* suggests nothing about the content of what is said, aside from its duration. Of the four adjectives, *curt* suggests a brief remark, but one made with a degree of rudeness. *Abbreviated* suggests that the speaker has more to say, but is being purposely brief. And *concise* suggests mental rigor and discipline, directed at making one's statements as brief and accurate as possible. Your choice among these words with their different connotations will make a difference in how readers react to your writing.

> ▶ **EXERCISE 1**
>
> Given the following set of words, state which word in each set you would prefer someone to use in describing you. Why? Choose one set of words and, in a paragraph, discuss what you understand to be the differences in connotation among the words. Use a dictionary, if necessary.
>
> 1. thrifty, economical, provident, frugal
> 2. reserved, inhibited, restrained, aloof
> 3. strange, bizarre, eccentric, peculiar, weird
> 4. lively, alert, enthusiastic, pert, spirited, sprightly
> ▶ 5. sentimental, emotional, maudlin, mushy

▶ 21b Revising awkward diction

At times you may find the abbreviation *AWK* in the margins of your papers, with a line leading to a phrase or to a particular word. *Awkward diction*, or word choice, momentarily stops an audience from reading by calling attention to a word that is somehow not quite right for a sentence. You can minimize awkward writing by guarding against four common errors: inappropriate connotation, inappropriate idiom, straining to sound learned, and unintentional euphony (rhyming, etc.).

▶ 1 Choosing words with an appropriate connotation

Frequently, *awkward diction* means that a word's connotation is inappropriate. The sentence in which the word appears is grammatical; the word in question is the right part of speech; but the word's meaning seems only partially correct for the sentence.

Awkward The professor urged *abstinence* in times of emotional stress. [Does the writer mean to suggest the avoidance of alcohol only? The sentence seems to suggest something else.]

If you look at a dictionary's usage entry for *abstinence*, you will see that there are synonyms for this word with nearly the same denotation but which might have a less awkward and limited connotation.

Revised The professor urged *sobriety* in times of emotional stress.

Revised The professor urged emotional *restraint*. [The revisions do not limit the advice to avoiding alcohol.]

▶ 2 Following standard English idioms

An **idiom** is a grouping of words, one of which is usually a preposition, whose meaning may or may not be apparent based solely on simple dictionary definitions. Moreover, the grammar of idioms—particularly the choice of prepositions used with them—is a matter of customary usage and is often difficult to explain.

Not Idiomatic I ran *into* an old letter.

Idiomatic I ran *across* an old letter.

Native speakers of English know intuitively that "running *across* an old letter" is a legitimate phrase, while "running *into* an old letter" is not. To avoid awkwardness, memorize idioms or do not use them at all. You can refer to the detailed listings in a dictionary to find some idioms; for others, you must listen carefully to the patterns of common usage. The box below shows some common idiomatic expressions in English.

▶**3 Writing directly rather than straining to sound learned**

In an effort to sound learned, some students will use words that do not exist in any dialect of English.

Awkward The character's grief and *upsetion* were extreme. [The word does not exist.]

Awkward *Disconcern* is common among the employees at that factory. [*Disinterest, indifference,* or *unconcern* could be used.]

At times, students straining at sophistication will choose lengthy, complicated phrasings when simpler ones will do; they will favor pretentious language because they believe this is the way learned people express themselves. The following sentence is *not* erudite.

Awkward The eccentricities of the characters could not fail to endear them to this reader.

Revised I found the eccentric characters appealing.

Some Common Idioms in American English

We *arrived at* a conclusion.
We *arrived in* time.
We *arrived on* time.
We *brought in* the cake.
We *brought up* the rear of the parade.
Except for my close friends, no one knows of my plan.
Don't call, *except in* emergencies.
I often *get into* jams.
Get up the courage to raise your hand.
I *got in* just under the deadline.
Good friends will *make up* after they argue.
How did you *make out* in your interview?
We'll *take out* the trash later.
Next week, the Red Sox *take on* the Orioles.
The senate will *take up* the issue tomorrow.
A large crowd *turned out.*
At midnight, we will *turn in.*
The request was *turned down.*

▶4 **Listening for unintentional euphony**

A sentence in an essay or report can be awkward when a writer unintentionally creates rhymes or alliterations (words that begin with the same consonant sound) that distract the reader from a sentence's meaning.

Awkward   Particularly in poetry, euphony is put to literary ends. [The rhymes and alliterations distract from the meaning.]

Simplified   In a poem, euphony is used for literary ends.

The surest way to avoid unintentional rhymes or alliterations is to listen for them as you read your work aloud. Reading aloud forces you to slow down and hear what you have written.

▶ **2l c**   **Using general and specific language**

Successful writers combine the general and the specific. The writer who concentrates on details and will not generalize gives the impression of being unable to see "the big picture." Conversely, the writer who makes nothing but general claims will leave readers restless for specific details that would support these claims. Read the following sets of sentences.

> Genetically engineered organisms can be of great benefit to agriculture. Scientists have discovered or are working on organisms that can make plants frost and herbicide resistant and can help plants produce their own nitrogen.

> Scientists have discovered the benefits and uses of genetically engineered organisms in agriculture. One important example is the ice-minus bacterium created by Steve Lindow and Nicholas Panopoulos. Realizing a bacterium commonly found in plants produces a protein that helps ice to form, these scientists removed the unfavorable gene and thereby prevented ice from forming on greenhouse plants. Others have manipulated genetic materials to create tobacco that kills attacking insects and to produce plants that resist herbicides. Geneticists hope in 20 to 40 years to produce plants such as corn and other grains that "fix" their own nitrogen—that will be able to extract nitrogen from the atmosphere without relying on nitrifying bacteria. If such a plant could be created, U.S. farmers would save $3 to $4 billion annually in fertilizer costs and could save one third of all crops lost each year to pests.

In the first paragraph, the writer makes a claim and supports it with three general examples, each of which is named quickly and left undeveloped. In the second example, the writer makes the same claim; but this time, details are provided that give readers specific information about genetically engineered organisms. These details establish the writer's authority and provide reasons for accepting the writer's claim. Effective writers combine general claims and specific, supporting details.

▶ **EXERCISE 2**

Create three lists, the first item of each being a very general word, the next item somewhat less general, the next still less general, and so on. The completed list, top to bottom, will proceed from general to specific.

Example: nation, state, county, city, neighborhood, street, house

EXERCISE 3

Choose a topic that you know well (sports, music, art, etc.) and write a general sentence about it. Then, in support of that sentence, write two additional sentences rich in specific detail.

> *Example:* Topic—Cooking an omelette
>
> General sentence:
> Making omelettes is a delicate operation.
>
> Specific sentences:
> Use a well-seasoned omelette pan—cast iron, well greased, clean but never thoroughly scrubbed.
>
> Scramble the eggs with a splash of water (not milk), blending lightly so as not to toughen the cooked eggs.

▶ 21d Using abstract and concrete language

Abstract words are broad. They name categories or ideas, such as *patriotism, evil,* and *friendship.* **Concrete** expressions (a *throbbing* headache, a *lemon-scented* perfume) provide details that give readers a chance to see, hear, and touch—and in this way to understand how an idea or category is made real. Just as with general and specific language, you should seek a balance between the abstract and concrete.

Balance is the key in all disciplines. See, for example, the balanced use of abstract and concrete terms in the following paragraph on biological inheritance.

> Among all the symbols in biology, perhaps the most widely used and most ancient are the hand mirror of Venus ($♀$) and the shield and spear of Mars ($♂$), the biologists' shorthand for male and female. Ideas about the nature of biological inheritance—the role of male and female—are even older than these famous symbols. Very early, men must have noticed that certain characteristics—hair color, for example, a large nose, or a small chin—were passed from parent to offspring. And throughout history, the concept of biological inheritance has been an important factor in the social organizations of men, determining the distribution of wealth, power, land, and royal privileges.
>
> —HELENA CURTIS

Notice that the abstract term *symbol* is given two more concrete examples: the hand mirror of Venus and the shield and spear of Mars. The abstract term *characteristics* is given concrete examples: *hair color, a large nose, a small chin.* And the abstract phrasing *social organizations of men* is given more concrete examples: *power, wealth, land, social privileges.* Of these last examples, though, one can imagine more concrete cases (*what kinds of privileges?*); but Curtis does not provide these. She *does* weave the abstract with the concrete (even if some of these examples could be made more concrete).

▶ EXERCISE 4

Take an abstract word such as *honesty, truth, friendship,* or *chaos,* and, in two or three sentences, link that word with a specific person, place, or event. Then provide concrete, descriptive details that help give meaning to the abstraction.

Using Abstract and Concrete Language

▶ 21 e   Using formal English as an academic standard

Academic writing is expected to conform to standards of **formal English**—that is, the English described in this handbook. There are many standards, or dialects, of English in this country, all of which are rich with expressive possibilities. The diction of formal English is not better than the diction of other dialects; it *is*, however, the only widely accepted standard for communicating among the many groups of English speakers.

Academic writing avoids language that by virtue of its private references limits a reader's understanding or limits the audience. Slang, jargon, and regional or ethnic dialect language are examples of writing specific to particular groups. When you address an audience *beyond* the group, slang, jargon, dialect, and regionalisms restrict what that audience can understand.

▶ I   Revise most slang expressions into standard English.

Slang is the comfortable, in-group language of neighborhood friends, coworkers, teammates, or of any group to which we feel we belong. Assume for the moment you do not windsurf, and you happen to overhear a conversation between windsurfers in which someone says that she was *dialed in* or *completely powered*. What do these words mean? To someone not involved with the sport, nothing specific. Slang can be descriptive and precise for those who understand; it can just as readily be confusing and annoying to those who do not. In some cases, slang may mislead: the same expression can have different meanings for different groups. For example, *turbo charged* has distinctly different meanings for computer aficionados and for race-car enthusiasts. In the interest of writing accessibly to as many people as possible, avoid slang expressions in academic papers.

▶ 2   Replace regionalisms and dialect expressions with standard academic English.

Regionalisms are expressions specific to certain areas of the country. Depending on where you were born, you will use the word *tonic, soda, cola*, or *pop* to describe what you drink with your *sub, hoagie, grinder, po-boy*, or *hero*. Words that have a clear and vivid reference in some areas of the country may lack meaning in others or have an unrelated meaning. For instance, *muss* means "to make messy" in some places and "to fight" in others. *Bad* means "good" in some places and "bad" in others.

Dialect expressions are specific to certain social or ethnic groups, as well as regional groups, within a country. Like regionalisms, dialects can use a specialized vocabulary and sometimes a distinctive grammatical system. Especially with respect to verbs (see Chapter 9), regional and ethnic dialect usage may regularly differ from standard English in omitting auxiliary verb forms. ("I done everything I can" or "It taken him all day" omit the standard auxiliary *have, had*, or *has*. "They be doing all right" replaces the standard *are* with the infinitive or base form *be*.) These are grammatically consistent and correct usages within the dialects they represent, but they address their language to a specific and restricted group rather than to a general audience. Like slang, regionalisms and dialect usages are appropriate for the audience that understands them; however, for general audiences in academic writing, they should be avoided.

CRITICAL DECISIONS

Set issues in a broader context: Choosing the right tone and register for your papers

Choosing an appropriate tone requires that you carefully analyze the writing occasion—the topic, your purpose, and your audience—and that you then make decisions about your document's content, diction, and style.

Formal
- *Likely audience*—specialists or knowledgeable nonspecialists.
- *Content*—choose content that goes beyond introductory material.
- *Diction*—use technical language whenever needed for precision.
- *Style*—adhere to all the rules and conventions expected of writing in the subject area. Use complicated sentences if needed for precision.

Popular or informal
- *Likely audience*—nonspecialists interested in the subject area.
- *Content*—similar to that of a formal presentation, but avoid examples or explanations that require specialized understanding. Emphasize content that will keep readers engaged.
- *Diction*—avoid specialized terms whenever possible.
- *Style*—adhere to all conventions of grammar, usage, and spelling. Use some slang or colloquial language, but keep it to a minimum.

3 Reduce colloquial language to maintain clarity and a consistent level of academic discourse.

Colloquial language is informal, conversational language. Colloquialisms do not pose barriers to understanding in the same way that slang, jargon, and regionalisms do; virtually all long-time speakers of English will understand expressions like *tough break*, *nitty-gritty*, and *it's a cinch*. In formal English, however, colloquialisms are rewritten or "translated" to maintain precision and to keep the overall tone of a document consistent. A few translations follow.

Colloquial	*Formal*
it's a cinch	it is certain
tough break	unfortunate
got licked	was beaten

Some colloquial expressions are also worn-out figures of speech whose meanings have become vague or obscure (see 21f-3).

4 Revise to restrict the use of jargon.

Jargon is the in-group language of professionals, who may use acronyms (abbreviations of lengthy terms) and other linguistic devices to take shortcuts when speaking with colleagues. When writers in an engineering environment refer to RISC architecture, they mean machines designed to allow for **R**educed **I**nstruction **S**et **C**omputing. RISC is an easy-to-use acronym, and it is efficient—as long as one engineer is writing or speaking to another. (If the in-group that uses these

ACROSS THE CURRICULUM

Word Choice and Audience

In discussing a specialized topic, writers in any discipline should understand their audience's comfort with specialized language. An audience of experts will understand technical terms; an audience of nonexperts will not. And so you will find writers across the curriculum carefully controlling their word choice depending on an audience's needs. Observe, below, how paleontologist and evolutionary biologist Stephen Jay Gould shifts his vocabulary from technical to nontechnical.* To readers of the specialized journal *Evolution*, Gould (and co-author David Woodruff) use technical language to report on the shell of the snail *Cerion:*

> *Cerion* possesses an ideal shell for biometrical work. [. . .] It reaches a definitive adult size with a change in direction of coiling and secretion of a thickened apertural lip; hence, ontogenic and static variation are not confounded. (1026)

To readers of his *Hen's Teeth and Horse's Toes: Further Reflections in Natural History*, written for the general public, Gould avoids technical terms:

> In personal research on the West Indian land snail *Cerion*, my colleague David Woodruff and I find the same two morphologies again and again in all the northern islands of the Bahamas. Ribby, white, or solid-colored, thick and roughly rectangular shells inhabit rocky coasts at the edges of banks where islands drop abruptly into deep seas. Smooth, mottled, thinner, and barrel-shaped shells inhabit calmer and lower coasts at the interior edges of banks, where islands cede to miles of shallow water. (143)

In both cases, Gould's word choice is precise and concise. He chooses the *level* of his language, however, based on the needs of his audience, just as you should. The observation holds for all discipline areas: know your audience; choose your language accordingly.

*The first passage is from Stephen Jay Gould and David Woodruff, "Fifty Years of Interspecific Hybridization: Genetics and Morphometrics of a Controlled Experiment on the Land Snail *Cerion* in the Florida Keys," *Evolution* 41 (1987): 1026. The second passage is from Stephen Jay Gould, *Hen's Teeth and Horse's Toes* (New York: Norton, 1983), 143.

expressions is a prestigious one, the use of jargon can become a form of false or pretentious writing—see 21h-2.) The moment communication is directed outside the professional group, a writer must take care to define terms. Consider this highly technical, in-group language among biologists:

> *Writing directed to an in-group audience*
> Clostridia are ubiquitous, versatile, anaerobic flagellated microorganisms that generally form spores. As a group, they will ferment almost anything organic except plastics—sugars, amino acids and proteins, polyalcohols, organic acids, purines, collagen, and cellulose.
> —LYNN MARGULIS and KATHLENE V. SCHWARTZ

By contrast, in this next passage biologists are addressing a general student population, only a fraction of whom are biology majors.

Writing directed to a general audience

Historically, biology has been considered a "soft" science whose subject was more complex and "laws" less rigorous than disciplines such as chemistry and physics. This soft status, however, has been rapidly changing since the medical discovery of the role of microorganisms in disease, Darwin's theory of evolution by natural selection, Mendel's description of the rules by which traits are inherited, and the understanding of the way DNA both duplicates itself and determines the details for the manufacture of proteins that comprise all living things.

—Dorian Sagan and Lynn Margulis

When you become part of a group, academic or otherwise, you will be expected and will find it convenient to use in-group language. You will need to interpret that language for outsiders, of course; but even within the group, if you can communicate precisely without using jargon, do so.

▶ **EXERCISE 5**

Think of a group—social, geographic, or professional—to which you belong and which you know well. Write a paragraph on some subject using in-group language: slang, jargon, or regionalisms. When finished, translate your paragraph into formal English, rewriting in-group expressions so that the paragraph can be read and understood by a general audience.

▶ **21f** Using figures of speech with care

Similes, analogies, and *metaphors* are **figures of speech,** carefully controlled comparisons that clarify or intensify meaning. Perhaps your spirit *soars* when you read this line of poetry: "Come live with me and be my love." The figurative use of *soar* creates an image of birds in flight, of elevation and clear vision. Literally speaking, birds and planes soar; spirits do not. English allows for the pairing of unlikely, even totally opposite images to help readers feel and see as writers do. In academic writing, figurative language is used across disciplines, though in some disciplines more freely than in others.

▶**1** Use similes, analogies, and metaphors.

A **simile** is a figure of speech in which two different things—one usually familiar, the other not—are explicitly compared. The properties of the thing known help to define what is unknown. Similes make comparison very explicit, often using the word *like* or *as* to set up the comparison.

Plastic is the new protector; we wrap the already plastic tumblers of hotels in more plastic, and seal the toilet seats *like* state secrets after irradiating them with ultraviolet light.

—Lewis Thomas
Physician, researcher

The wind whistled in the street and the music ghosted from the piano *as* leaves over a headstone and you could imagine you were in the presence of genius.

—Bruce Chatwin
Traveler, writer

A particle of spin 2 is *like* a double-headed arrow: it looks the same if one turns it round half a revolution (180 degrees).

—STEPHEN HAWKING
Physicist

As with a simile, the purpose of an **analogy** is to make an explicit comparison that explains an unknown in terms of something known. Analogies most often use direct comparison to clarify a process or a difficult concept.

Just as a trained mechanic can listen to a ping in a car's engine and then diagnose and correct a problem, so too an experienced writer can reread an awkward sentence and know exactly where it goes wrong and what must be done to correct it.

Extended analogies can be developed over a paragraph or several paragraphs. They usually begin and end with certain *cues*, or words that signal a reader that an analogy is about to be offered or concluded. Words that mark a transition to an analogy are *consider*, *by analogy*, and *just as*. The transition from analogy back to a main discussion is achieved with expressions such as *similarly*, *just so*, *so too*, and *in the same way*. (See 6d-1 for use of analogies in building an argument.)

Just as with a simile and an analogy, a **metaphor** illustrates or intensifies something relatively unknown by comparison with something familiar. In the case of metaphor, however, the comparison is implicit: in the expression *hand of time*, for instance, the abstract term *time* is given a physical attribute. *Like* and *as* or other signals of explicit comparison are not used in metaphors.

In the mirror of his own death, each man would discover his individuality.

—PHILIPPE ARIÈS
Historian

The metaphor suggests that contemplating death allows people to see themselves in revealing ways.

Metaphors are not restricted to poetry or academic writing; they are used everywhere in our daily speech when an abstract or unknown idea, thing, or activity is spoken of in terms associated with something else. When we say "round up everybody," we implicitly compare the activity to a cattle roundup. When we say "Walk the thin line between good and bad," we compare a moral dilemma to a tightrope act. By speaking of people who have been "jerked around" or "left hanging," we compare their general situation to those physical activities. At times, such metaphorical comparisons, if not well matched to the situation, can create more confusion for the reader than clarity.

▶**2 Revise mixed metaphors.**

Metaphors need to match elements that can be compared logically (even if not explicitly). Keep your language focused on a single metaphorical image throughout a sentence. Otherwise, you risk a **mixed metaphor,** which will stop your readers for a hearty laugh—at your expense. You would not, for instance, want to be the author of this.

Mixed metaphor	This story weaves a web that herds characters and readers into the same camp. [The comparison mixes spiderwebs with cattle round-ups.]
Consistent	This story weaves a web that tangles characters and readers alike.

3 Replace worn-out metaphors (clichés) with fresh figures.

In a famous essay, "Politics and the English Language," writer George Orwell warns against the *worn-out metaphor.*

> A newly invented metaphor assists thought by evoking a visual image, while on the other hand a metaphor which is technically "dead" (e.g., *iron resolution*) has in effect reverted to being an ordinary word and can generally be used without loss of vividness. But in between these two classes there is a huge dump of worn-out metaphors which have lost all evocative power and are merely used because they save people the trouble of inventing phrases for themselves.

Orwell proceeds to offer his list of worn-out metaphors, also called **clichés.** These include *play into the hands of, no axe to grind, swan song,* and *hotbed.* These trite expressions, current when Orwell's essay was written in 1945, are with us still. Modern-day expressions that can be added to this list of clichés include *the game of life, counting chickens before they hatch, water over the dam* or *under the bridge,* and *burning bridges.* Work to create your own metaphors; keep them vivid; and keep them consistent.

 http://www.mtholyoke.edu/acad/intrel/orwell46.htm
The complete text of Orwell's famous essay—a must-read for everyone who aspires to clear and concise writing.

▶ **EXERCISE 6**

In a few sentences, use figurative language to describe the approach of a thunderstorm, the effect of a sunny morning on your mood, or the feeling of just having finished the last exam of a long and difficult semester.

▶ **21g** Eliminating biased, dehumanizing language

Language is a tool; just as tools can be used for building, they can also be used to dismantle. You have heard and seen the words that insensitive people use to denigrate whole groups. Equally repugnant is language used to stereotype. Any language that explicitly or subtly characterizes an individual in terms of a group is potentially offensive. Writers must take care to avoid stereotyping.

Sexism in diction

English has no gender-neutral pronoun in the third-person singular. Consider this sentence: *A doctor should wash _____ hands before examining a patient.* English demands that we choose the possessive pronoun *his* or *her* to complete this thought. Until recently, the designated "neutral" pronoun was usually masculine (*his*), but changing times have made this usage offensive. Women, along with men, are physicians, engineers, attorneys, construction workers, accountants, realtors, etc. Men, along with women, are elementary school teachers, nurses, cooks, tailors, receptionists, and secretaries. Gender-offensive language can also be found in such expressions as chair*man,* *man*kind, *man*power, *mother*ing, etc. Reread late drafts of your writing to identify potentially gender-offensive language. Unless the context of a paragraph clearly calls for a gender-specific reference, follow the suggestions given in the box to avoid offending your readers. Also see 10c for avoiding gender-offensive pronoun use.

Some Potentially Offensive Gender-Specific Nouns

Avoid: stewardess (and generally nouns ending with *-ess*)
Use: flight attendant

Avoid: chairman
Use: chair or chairperson

Avoid: woman driver; male nurse
Use: woman who was driving; driver; nurse; man on the nursing station

Avoid: mankind
Use: people; humanity; humankind

Avoid: workmen; manpower
Use: workers; work force; personnel

Avoid: the girl in the office
Use: the woman; the manager; the typist

Avoid: mothering
Use: parenting, nurturing

---

1   Rewrite gender-stereotyping nouns as neutral nouns.

Sexist   A cover letter, along with a résumé, should be sent to the *chairman* of the department. [The male suffix may be taken to imply that the writer expects this person to be male.]

Neutral   A cover letter, along with a résumé, should be sent to the department *chair.*

Sexist   *Man's* need to compete may be instinctive. [A generic male noun or pronoun referring to all of humanity is unacceptable.]

Neutral   *The human* need to compete may be instinctive.

2   Balance references to the sexes.

Sexist   The *men* and *girls* in the office contributed generously to the Christmas Fund. [A reference singling out females as children in an adult setting is demeaning.]

Neutral   The *men* and *women* in the office contributed generously to the Christmas Fund. [In a school setting the reference might be to *boys* and *girls.*]

3   Make balanced use of plural and gender-specific pronouns.

See the Critical Decisions box in 10c for five strategies that will help you to correct gender problems with pronoun use.

Sexist   A doctor should wash *his* hands before examining a patient. [Here the generic male pronoun implies that the writer expects most doctors to be male.]

Neutral   *Doctors* should wash *their* hands before examining patients. [The plural strategy is used; see 10c.]

▶ **EXERCISE 7**

Identify gender-offensive language in the following paragraph. Rewrite sentences in whatever way you feel is needed to make the gender references neutral.

> The elementary school teacher, especially at the early grades, has her hands full with helping children adjust to a formal learning environment. Not all of the girls and young men in her class will understand that school is not, primarily, a place for play. Learning, of course, should be fun; but the elementary school teacher must be sure that her students appreciate the distinctions between playground play and intellectual play. By the later grades, a teacher will want his students to understand that serious intellectual play is the business of school. Women and boys in high school must appreciate that ideas should be celebrated with, not hidden from, classmates.

▶ **21h** | **Avoiding euphemistic and pretentious language**

Sometimes writers betray an anxious, condescending, or self-inflated attitude through their word choices. These attitudes may arise from a variety of motives, but the result is almost always a loss of clear expression.

▶ **I** **Restrict the use of euphemisms.**

The **euphemism** is a polite rewording of a term that the writer feels will offend readers. Instead of *dead* or *died*, you will find *passed on, passed away, mortally wounded*. You may also find these clichés: *kicked the bucket, bit the dust*, and so on. If you are concerned about using expressions that might offend readers, create a context within a sentence or paragraph that may soften a potentially harsh word choice.

Euphemism   No one wanted to tell the child that his dog had gone to the Great Beyond.

Revised   Breaking the news to the child that his dog had died was very painful.

In nonacademic writing, use discretion in selecting a euphemism. Debate with yourself your use of language and then make your choice.

▶ **2** **Eliminate pretentious language.**

Pretentious language is unnecessarily ornate and puffed-up with its own importance; it suggests a writer's concern more with image than with clear communication. See 17a-2, 4, and 6 on eliminating wordiness. Pretentious writers will often choose the windy version of everyday expressions that seem too common.

Pretentious	*Direct*
It appears to me that	I believe
In the final analysis	In conclusion
The individual who	The person who
utilize	use
demonstrate	show
functionality	function

In specialized areas of study, you will find that writers need technical terms to communicate precisely. Writing that requires specialized terms is very different from pretentious writing that is calculated to bolster a writer's ego. In your own work, you can distinguish between a legitimate technical term and a pretentious one by being both concise and precise.

Adhering to these two principles—the one helping you to cut wordiness and the other helping you to maintain precision—should make you aware of pretentious language, which can *always* be cut from a sentence.

Pretentious language	Cross-cultural treatises give every indication that all cultures establish relatively distinct gender differentiation.
Direct language	Studies from around the world show that all cultures establish clear roles for men and women.
Specialized language (no revision needed)	Index futures differ from other futures contracts in that they are not based on any underlying commodity or financial instrument that can be delivered; therefore, there is no cash market associated with them.

This passage on "index futures" comes from a book on investing. Students of finance would understand, or would be expected to understand, the terms *index futures, futures contracts, commodity, financial instrument,* and *cash market.* None of the words in this legitimately technical passage is calculated to bolster the writer's ego, as was the case in the preceding example.

Distinguishing Pretentious Language from Legitimate Technical Language

Bear in mind two principles when attempting to eliminate pretentious language:

- **Be concise:** Use as few words as possible to communicate clearly. Delete whole sentences or reduce them to phrases that you incorporate into other sentences; reduce phrases to single words; choose briefer words over longer ones. (See 17a for a full discussion of conciseness.)
- **Be precise:** Make sure your sentences communicate your *exact* meaning. If you need to add clarifying words, add as few words as possible. Use technical language for precision only when no other language will do.

▶ **EXERCISE 8**

In the sentences that follow, identify and revise what you feel are examples of pretentious writing. Find other samples of writing, perhaps from a current newspaper, and conduct a similar analysis.

> In the final analysis, the one unending truth that we must as a nation uphold is mutual respect. Mutual respect, a tolerance for difference, is premised on the notion that we ought to expect from others the same considerations that we believe we ourselves are due. Setting aside, for the moment, high-minded rationales for respecting one another—the Judeo-Christian tradition, for instance, that we ought to love one another—we can observe that for very practical reasons mutual respect serves our own ends.

CHAPTER 22

Dictionaries and Vocabulary

A living language is continually evolving; it is always shifting and changing; it is flexible and yet precise. English is just such a language. Two thousand years ago nobody spoke English; it did not exist. Today, on the eve of the twenty-first century, it is the first truly global language, more widely spoken and written than any language has ever been. English originally spread through British imperialism to such countries as the United States, Canada, Australia, New Zealand, India, and various African and Caribbean nations. But the demise of the British Empire in no way signaled the demise of English as an international language.

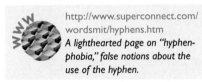

http://www.superconnect.com/
wordsmit/hyphens.htm
A lighthearted page on "hyphen-phobia," false notions about the use of the hyphen.

Rather, as the novelist Salman Rushdie notes, "English, no longer an *English* language, now grows from many roots; and those whom it once colonized are carving out large territories within the language for themselves. The Empire is striking back." At the same time, the cultural dominance of American English, the international language of multinational corporations, science and technology, rock music, Hollywood films, television, and mass consumerism continues to further the dissemination of English worldwide.[1]

USING DICTIONARIES

The emergence of English as a constantly changing global language raises the question of what constitutes "English" and/or the various Englishes. It is the job, indeed often the life work, of the editors and compilers of dictionaries to help readers understand the most current usages of words in the language. The dictionary will tell you what forms and meanings have become widely used or are in restricted use. On the basis of this information, you must decide which forms and meanings are most precisely suited to your purpose. In the next sections you will find descriptions of what is included in a typical dictionary entry, followed by descriptions of abridged and unabridged dictionaries.

[1]This introduction is based on Robert McCrum, William Cran, and Robert MacNeil, *The Story of English* (New York: Elisabeth Sifton Books/Viking, 1986) 19–48.

Dictionaries give us far more than a list of words and their meanings. They not only define a given word, but also provide a brief description of its etymology, spelling, division, as well as pronunciation, and related words and forms. Here is a typical set of entries:

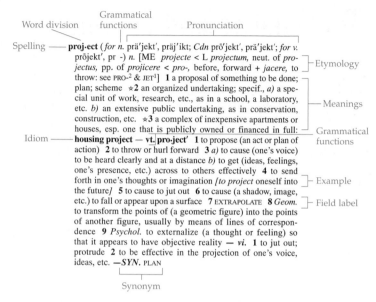

Word division

Grammatical functions

Pronunciation

Spelling —— **proj·ect** (*for n.* prä′jekt′, präj′ikt; *Cdn* prō′jekt′, prä′jekt′; *for v.* prōjekt′, pr -) *n.* [ME *projecte* < L *projectum,* neut. of *projectus,* pp. of *projicere* < *pro-,* before, forward + *jacere,* to throw: see PRO-[2] & JET[1]] **1** a proposal of something to be done; plan; scheme ⋆**2** an organized undertaking; specif., *a)* a special unit of work, research, etc., as in a school, a laboratory, etc. *b)* an extensive public undertaking, as in conservation, construction, etc. ⋆**3** a complex of inexpensive apartments or houses, esp. one that is publicly owned or financed in full: **housing project** — **vt.** **pro·ject′** **1** to propose (an act or plan of action) **2** to throw or hurl forward **3** *a)* to cause (one's voice) to be heard clearly and at a distance *b)* to get (ideas, feelings, one's presence, etc.) across to others effectively **4** to send forth in one's thoughts or imagination *[to project* oneself into the future*]* **5** to cause to jut out **6** to cause (a shadow, image, etc.) to fall or appear upon a surface **7** EXTRAPOLATE **8** *Geom.* to transform the points of (a geometric figure) into the points of another figure, usually by means of lines of correspondence **9** *Psychol.* to externalize (a thought or feeling) so that it appears to have objective reality — *vi.* **1** to jut out; protrude **2** to be effective in the projection of one's voice, ideas, etc. —*SYN.* PLAN

Etymology

Meanings

Grammatical functions

Idiom

Example

Field label

Synonym

▶ **I   Understanding standard entry information in dictionaries**

Most dictionary entries include more information on words than many people expect. In a typical entry you can find:

- *Spelling* (including variations, especially British versus American spellings— see Chapter 23 for more on rules of spelling)
- *Word division* indicating syllabication and where a word should be divided, if necessary
- *Pronunciation* (including variations)
- *Grammatical functions* (parts of speech)
- *Grammatical forms* (plurals, principal parts of irregular verbs, other irregular forms)
- *Etymology* (a given word's history/derivation)
- *Meanings* (arranged according to either currency or frequency of use, or earliest to most recent use)
- *Examples* of the word in context
- *Related words, synonyms* and *antonyms*
- *Usage labels* (see 22a-2)
- *Field labels* (for words that have discipline-specific meanings)
- *Idioms* that include the word

2 Usage labels

Usage refers to how, where, and when a word has been used in speech and writing. When preparing papers in an academic or business setting, use formal English as a standard (see 21e): words not otherwise labeled as nonstandard. When you see the label *slang* assigned to the entry *prof,* for instance, the dictionary is indicating that in standard, formal English usage that word is not accepted. Aware of this *restriction* on the word, you would probably decide not to use it in formal writing. There are other categories of restricted usage, and these are generally listed and explained in the front matter of most dictionaries:

- *Colloquial:* used conversationally and in informal writing
- *Slang:* in-group, informal language; not standard
- *Obsolete:* not currently used (but may be found in earlier writing)
- *Archaic:* not commonly used; more common in earlier writing
- *Dialect:* restricted geographically or to social or ethnic groups; used only in certain places with certain groups
- *Poetic, literary:* used in literature rather than everyday speech

---

COMPUTER TIPS

Thesauri

Electronic thesauri—both the kind that comes with your word processor and the ones available on the World Wide Web—are subject to the same limitations as printed thesauri. Use them as references only. Never replace a word you've written with a word suggested by a thesaurus unless you're absolutely sure of both its denotations and its connotations.

▶ **EXERCISE I**

Consult your dictionary to answer the following questions about grammatical function.

1. Which of the following nouns can be used as verbs: *process, counsel, dialogue, hamper, instance?*
2. How do you make these nouns plural: *annals, humanity, armor, accountancy, deer, analysis, medium, sister-in-law, knife?*
3. What are the principal parts of these verbs: *hang, begin, break, forbid, rise, set?*
4. What are the comparative and superlative forms of these adverbs and adjectives: *unique, bad, mere, initial, playful?*

EXERCISE 2

Using two different dictionaries, list and comment on the usage restrictions that are recorded for the following words:

1. get-up   3. hipster   5. hit
2. whither   4. maverick   6. max

Because the English language is constantly changing and is used in so many environments around the world, no dictionary can ever claim to be the final authority on every possible current meaning or correct usage for the words it lists. A dictionary's authority rests mainly on its attempt to be reasonably comprehensive and linguistically accurate in recording the most frequently used meanings of a word. Dictionaries further try to be as balanced as possible in recording the kind of usage and the restrictions on usage that have been observed for each meaning. In addition, dictionaries record a time dimension for changes in meaning: some list the earliest meanings on record first, moving on to the more recent; others reverse the sequence to start with contemporary meanings. All dictionaries record the basic categories of information shown in the previous section.

▶ **1   Comparing abridged dictionaries**

The most convenient and commonly used dictionaries in households, businesses, and schools are called "abridged"—or shortened. They do not try to be as exhaustive or complete as the "unabridged" dictionaries (described in 22b-2). An abridged dictionary tries to give as much information as possible in one portable volume. You will find that several dictionaries claim the name *Webster's*, after the early American lexicographer Noah Webster. Since his name is in the public domain and is not copyrighted, it appears in the titles of a number of dictionaries with varying characteristics. The following list includes only some of the more widely used abridged dictionaries.[2]

> *The American Heritage Dictionary*, 3rd ed. (Houghton Mifflin, 1992) includes about 200,000 entries. It differs from most other dictionaries in that it presents the most contemporary meaning of a word first, rather than proceeding historically. Guidance to good usage is provided by extensive usage-context indicators and "Usage Notes" which reflect the opinions of a panel of usage experts. The dictionary contains many photographs, illustrations, and maps. Foreign words and the names of mythological and legendary figures appear in the regular listings, while biographical and geographical entries and abbreviations are listed in the back.
>
> *The Concise Oxford Dictionary of Current English*, 9th ed. (Oxford University Press, 1995) is the briefest of the abridged dictionaries listed here. It is based on the work for the unabridged *Oxford English Dictionary* (see 22b-2) and includes current usage and illustrative quotations, scientific and technical terms, many colloquial and slang expressions, and both British and American spellings.

---

[2]The descriptions of abridged, unabridged, and discipline-specific dictionaries that follow are adapted from entries in Eugene Sheehy, *Guide to Reference Books*, 10th ed. (Chicago: American Library Association, 1986); Diane Wheeler Strauss, *Handbook of Business Information: A Guide for Librarians, Students, and Researchers* (Englewood, CO: Libraries Unlimited, Inc., 1988); and Bohdan Wynar, *ARBA Guide to Subject Encyclopedias and Dictionaries* (Littleton, CO: Libraries Unlimited, 1986).

Merriam Webster's Collegiate Dictionary, 10th ed. (G. & C. Merriam, 1998) is based on *Webster's Third New International Dictionary of the English Language* (see 22b-2) and includes some 215,000 entries emphasizing "standard language." Labels indicating usage occur less frequently than in other desk dictionaries. Entries give full etymologies followed by definitions in chronological order, with the most recent meaning listed last. It includes extensive notes on synonyms and illustrative quotations. Foreign words and phrases, biographical and geographical names, and a manual of style are listed separately as back matter.

EXERCISE 3

Look up the following words in one of the abridged dictionaries listed above. How many different meanings does each word have? From observing older meanings versus the more current meanings, how would you describe the overall shifts in meaning that some words have undergone over time?

1. double 3. conductor 5. cross
2. foul   4. weird   6. funky

2 Comparing unabridged dictionaries

The compilers of unabridged dictionaries attempt to be exhaustive both in recounting the history of a word and in describing its various usages. For quick reference—to check spelling, meaning, or commonplace usage, an abridged dictionary will serve you well. But when you are puzzled by or otherwise curious about a word and its history (for instance, if you want to know the route by which the word *farm* has made its way into the language), you will want to consult an unabridged dictionary where the principle for compiling an entry is *thoroughness.*

The second edition of *The Oxford English Dictionary* (Oxford: Clarendon Press), prepared by J. A. Simpson and E. S. C. Weiner, was published in 1989 and includes the text of the first edition, the *Supplement* (1972–1986), and almost 5,000 new entries for a total of more than 500,000 words. It is the great dictionary of the English language, arranged chronologically to show the history of every word from the date of its entry into the language to its most recent usage, supported by almost two million quotations from the works of more than 5,000 authors since 1150. The *O.E.D.* is an invaluable source for scholars.

The Random House Webster's Unabridged Dictionary (Random House, 1997) is considerably briefer than the other unabridged dictionaries listed here, though it is particularly current and includes extensive usage notes. The back matter includes several foreign word lists and an atlas with colored maps.

Webster's Third New International Dictionary of the English Language (G. & C. Merriam, 1993) includes about 450,000 entries, with special attention to new scientific and technical terms. The third edition of 1986 emphasizes the language as currently used (though entries are arranged chronologically, with the earliest uses first), with a descriptive approach to usage, construction, and punctuation. Many obsolete and rare words have been dropped. Although the third edition is widely used as a descriptive standard, some scholars prefer the more prescriptive approach of the second edition of 1959. Most college students will find that the third edition meets their needs and is convenient to use.

▶ **EXERCISE 4**

Choose two of the words you looked up in Exercise 3 and compare what you found with the entry for the same word in an unabridged dictionary, preferably *The Oxford English Dictionary.* Briefly characterize the history of each word, explaining how its meaning has shifted over time.

▶ 22c   Using specialized dictionaries of English

Abridged and unabridged dictionaries of the English language can provide you with a wealth of general information about language. However, there will be times when you will need to consult a specialized dictionary which focuses on a specific kind of word or language information, such as slang, etymologies, synonyms, antonyms, and accepted usage. The following are some particularly useful specialized dictionaries.

▶ I   Dictionaries of usage

When your questions regarding the usage of a word are not adequately addressed in a standard dictionary, consult one of the following dictionaries of usage:

> *A Dictionary of Contemporary American Usage,* ed. Bergen Evans and Cornelia Evans
>
> *Dictionary of Modern English Usage,* ed. H. W. Fowler
>
> *Dictionary of American-English Usage,* ed. Margaret Nicholson
>
> *Modern American Usage,* ed. Jacques Barzun

▶ 2   Dictionaries of synonyms

Dictionaries that present synonyms of words can be a great help for writers wanting to expand vocabulary. A caution, though: while synonyms have approximately the same denotation, their connotations (or nuances of meaning) differ. Before using a synonym, be sure that you thoroughly understand its connotation (see also 22e-3).

> *Webster's Dictionary of Synonyms*
>
> *The New Roget's Thesaurus of the English Language in Dictionary Form*

▶ 3   Other specialized dictionaries

The dictionaries listed here are specialized sources for the historical and social dimensions of word use.

Dictionaries of origins/etymologies

The information on word origins in basic dictionaries can be pursued in more detail in the following specialized references.

> *Dictionary of Word and Phrase Origins,* ed. William Morris and Mary Morris
>
> *The Oxford Dictionary of English Etymology,* ed. C. T. Onions
>
> *Origins: A Short Etymological Dictionary of Modern English,* ed. Eric Partridge

Dictionaries of slang and idioms

Many terms omitted or given only brief notice in basic dictionaries are described in great detail in slang dictionaries.

> *The New Dictionary of American Slang*, ed. Robert Chapman
>
> *Dictionary of Slang and Unconventional English*, ed. Eric Partridge
>
> *Dictionary of American Slang*, ed. Harold Wentworth and Stuart Berg Flexner

Dictionaries of regionalism or foreign terms

The *Dictionary of American Regional English*, compiled by linguist Frederic Cassidy, is the standard work on regional and dialect expressions in America.

> *Dictionary of Foreign Phrases and Abbreviations*, ed. Kevin Guinagh. 3rd ed.
>
> *Dictionary of Foreign Terms*, ed. Mario Pei and Savatore Ramondino
>
> *Harper Dictionary of Foreign Terms*, ed. C. O. Sylvester Mawson and Charles Berlitz. 3rd ed.

▶ **EXERCISE 5**

Look up the following words in a dictionary of usage and a dictionary of origins. Based on information you find out about the meanings, origins, and uses of each word from these specialized sources, characterize the kind of writing or the kind of audience for which each term seems most appropriate.

1. awesome   3. celebrate   5. ere
2. mews   4. groovy   6. flunk

BUILDING VOCABULARY

You will need a good vocabulary to understand discussions in texts and to follow lectures. As you move from discipline to discipline, vocabularies will change: you will, in effect, learn new languages. This section offers strategies for building your vocabulary.

▶ **22d**   Learning root words, prefixes, and suffixes

Where applicable, the editors of college dictionaries will place in square brackets [ ] abbreviations of languages from which words are derived. Some of the abbreviations (and their spelled out versions) include: *F*, French; *Gk*, Greek; *LL*, Late Latin; *L*, Latin; *Heb*, Hebrew; *ME*, Middle English; *Dan*, Danish; *D*, Dutch; *G*, German; *LG*, Low German; *Flem*, Flemish; *Ital*, Italian; *OW*, Old Welsh; *Span*, Spanish; *Skt*, Sanskrit; and *OPer*, Old Persian. There are more than 100 languages from which the half-million words of English are derived. Modern words are often variants of earlier forms that have snaked their way through history, changing outward appearances for different peoples at different times—though retaining a recognizable core or root. The study of the history of words is called **etymology.** In the square brackets of dictionary entries you will usually find either the abbreviation **fr.** or the symbol <, meaning *derived from.*

Once a word enters the language, its core or *root* is often used as the basis of other words that are formed with *prefixes* and *suffixes*—letters coming before, or after, the root. When you can recognize root words, prefixes, and suffixes, often you will be able to understand the meaning of a new word without checking a dictionary.

▶ **EXERCISE 6**

Using two unabridged dictionaries, research the etymology of a word. In four or five sentences, trace the word's use over time.

▶ **1** Becoming familiar with root words

A root anchors a plant or tree in the ground and provides a structural and nutritional base from which it can grow. The **root** of a word anchors it in language, providing a base from which meaning is built. When you encounter an unfamiliar word, try identifying its root; with help from the context of the surrounding sentence, you can often infer an appropriate definition. Consider the following sentence:

Beautiful and *beauteous* are paronymous words.

You have come upon an unfamiliar word, *paronymous*. You might say: "This reminds me of another word—*anonymous*." Immediately, you sense that the similar sounding words share a root: *nymous*. You know that *anonymous* means "having an unknown name." It is not so tremendous a leap to conclude that the root *nymous* means *name*. Now you examine the sentence once more and make an educated guess, or inference. What do the words *beautiful* and *beauteous* have to do with *names*? The words themselves tell you—that they are built on a single name: *beauty*. If you guessed that *paronymous* means "derived from the same word (or root)," you would be correct.

Whether you know a root word or make an educated guess about its meaning, your analysis will aid reading comprehension and, in the process, will improve your vocabulary. Many of the root words in English come from Latin and Greek. The following box contains a small sample of root words.

Common Root Words

Root	Definition	Example
acus [Latin]	needle	acute, acumen
basis [Greek]	step, base	base, basis, basement, basic
bio- [Greek]	life	biography, biology, bionic
cognoscere [Latin]	to know	recognize, cognizant, cognition
ego [Latin]	I	ego, egocentric, egotistical
fleure [Latin]	flow	flow, fluid, effluence
grandis [Latin]	large	grandiose, aggrandize
graphein [Greek]	to write	graph, graphic
hydro [Greek]	water	hydraulic, dehydrate

Root	Definition	Example
hypnos [Greek]	sleep	hypnosis, hypnotic
jur, jus [Latin]	law	jury, justice
lumen [Latin]	light	illuminate, luminary
manu- [Latin]	hand	manage, management, manual, manipulate
mare [Latin]	sea	marine, marinate, marina, marinara
matr- [Latin]	mother	maternal, matrilineal
pathos [Greek]	suffering	empathy, sympathy
patr- [Latin]	father	paternal, patriarch
polis [Greek]	city	metropolis, police
primus [Latin]	first	primitive, prime, primary
psych [Greek]	soul	psychological, psyche
scrib, script [Latin]	to write	describe, manuscript
sentire [Latin]	to feel	sentiment, sentimental, sentient, sense, sensitive
sol [Latin]	sun	solstice, solar, solarium
solvere [Latin]	to release	solve, resolve, solution, dissolve, solvent
tele [Greek]	distant	telegraph, telemetry
therm [Greek]	heat	thermal, thermos
truncus [Latin]	trunk	trunk, trench, trenchant
veritas [Latin]	truth	verity, verify, veritable
vocare [Latin]	to call	vocal, vocation, avocation

▶2 Recognizing prefixes

A **prefix**—letters joined to the beginning of a root word to qualify or add to its meaning—illustrates its own definition: the root *fix* comes from the Latin *fixus*, meaning "to fasten"; *pre* is a prefix, also from Latin, meaning "before." The prefix joined to a root creates a new word, the meaning of which is "to place before." Recognizing prefixes can help you isolate root words. The prefix and the root, considered together, will allow you to infer a meaning. Prefixes can indicate number, size, status, negation, and relations in time and space. The following are some frequently used prefixes.

Prefixes indicating number

Prefix	Meaning	Example
uni-	one	unison, unicellular
bi-	two	bimonthly, bicentennial, bifocal
tri-	three	triangle, triumvirate
multi-	many, multiple	multiply, multifaceted
omni-	all, universally	omnivorous, omniscient
poly-	many, several	polytechnic, polygon

Learning Root Words, Prefixes, and Suffixes

Prefixes indicating size

Prefix	Meaning	Example
micro-	very small	microscopic, microcosm
macro-	very large	macroeconomics
mega-	great	megalomania, megalith

Prefixes indicating status or condition

Prefix	Meaning	Example
hyper-	beyond, super	hyperactive, hypercritical
neo-	new	neonate, neophyte
para-	akin to	parachute, paramilitary
pseudo-	false	pseudoscience, pseudonym
quasi-	in some sense	quasi-official, quasi-public

Prefixes indicating negation

Prefix	Meaning	Example
anti-	against	antibiotic, antidote, anticlimax
counter-	contrary	counterintuitive, counterfeit
dis-	to do the opposite	disable, dislodge, disagree
mal-	bad, abnormal, inadequate	maladjusted, malformed, malcontent, malapropism
mis-	bad, wrong	misinform, mislead, misnomer
non-	not, reverse of	noncompliance, nonalcoholic, nonconformist, nonessential

Prefixes indicating spatial relations

Prefix	Meaning	Example
circum-	around	circumspect, circumscribe
inter-	between	intercede, intercept
intra-	within	intravenous, intramural
intro-	inside	introvert, intrude

Prefixes indicating relations of time

Prefix	Meaning	Example
ante-	before	antecedent, anterior
paleo-	ancient	Paleolithic, paleography
post-	after	postdate, postwar, posterior
proto-	first	protohuman, prototype

▶ 3 Analyzing suffixes

A **suffix**—letters joined to the end of a word or a root—will change a word's grammatical function. Observe how with suffixes a writer can give a verb the forms of a noun, adjective, and adverb.

Dictionaries and Vocabulary

Verb	impress
Noun	impression
Adjective	impressive
Adverb	impressively

The following are some frequently used suffixes.

Noun-forming suffixes

Verb	+	*Suffix*	*(Meaning)*	=	*Noun*
betray		-al	(process of)		betrayal
participate		-ant	(one who)		participant
play		-er	(one who)		player
construct		-ion	(process of)		construction
conduct		-or	(one who)		conductor

Noun	+	*Suffix*	*(Meaning)*	=	*Noun*
parson		-age	(house of)		parsonage
king		-dom	(office, realm)		kingdom
sister		-hood	(state, condition of)		sisterhood
strategy		-ist	(one who)		strategist
Armenia		-n	(belonging to)		Armenian
master		-y	(quality)		mastery

Adjective	+	*Suffix*	*(Meaning)*	=	*Noun*
pure		-ity	(state, quality of)		purity
gentle		-ness	(quality of, degree)		gentleness
active		-ism	(act, practice of)		activism

Verb-forming suffixes

Noun	+	*Suffix*	*(Meaning)*	=	*Verb*
substance		-ate	(cause to become)		substantiate
code		-ify	(cause to become)		codify
serial		-ize	(cause to become)		serialize

Adjective	+	*Suffix*	*(Meaning)*	=	*Verb*
sharp		-en	(cause to become)		sharpen

Adjective-forming suffixes

Noun	+	*Suffix*	*(Meaning)*	=	*Adjective*
region		-al	(of, relating to)		regional
claim		-ant	(performing, being)		claimant
substance		-ial	(of, relating to)		substantial
response		-ible	(capable of, fit for)		responsible
history		-ic	(form of, being)		historic
Kurd		-ish	(of, relating to)		Kurdish
response		-ive	(tends toward)		responsive

Verb	+	*Suffix*	*(Meaning)*	=	*Adjective*
credit		-able	(capable of)		creditable
abort		-ive	(tends toward)		abortive

Learning Root Words, Prefixes, and Suffixes

▶ **EXERCISE 7**

Identify and initially define, without using a dictionary, the roots, prefixes, and suffixes of the following sets of words. Then check your definitions against dictionary entries.

1. photometry
   photogenic
   photograph
   photoelectric
2. excise
   concise
   precise
   incisive
3. conduce
   reduce
   deduce
   ▶ produce

4. optometrist
   optician
   ophthalmologist
   optical
5. discourse
   recourse
6. diverge
   converge
7. convert
   pervert
   revert

8. tenable
   tenacious
   retain
9. memoir
   remember
10. remorse
    morsel

▶ **22e** **Strategies for building a vocabulary**

▶**I Use contextual clues and dictionaries.**

In college, you will spend a great deal of your time reading, and reading provides the best opportunities for expanding your vocabulary. When a new word resists your analysis of root and affix (prefix or suffix), reach for a dictionary or let the context of a sentence provide clues to meaning. Contextual clues will often let you read a passage and infer fairly accurate definitions of new words—accurate enough to give you the sense of a passage. Indeed, using a dictionary to look up *every* new word in the name of thoroughness can so fragment a reading that you will frustrate—not aid—your attempts to understand. Focus first on the ideas of an entire passage; circle or otherwise highlight new words, especially repeated words. Then, if the context has not revealed the meaning, reach for your dictionary.

In the passage that follows, possibly unfamiliar vocabulary is set in italics. Do not stop at these words. Note them, but then complete your reading of these paragraphs from an astronomy text by George O. Abell:

> Let us once again compare the *propagation* of light to the propagation of ocean waves. While an ocean wave travels forward, the water itself is *displaced* only in a *vertical* direction. A stick of wood floating in the water merely bobs up and down as the waves move along the surface of the water. Waves that propagate with this kind of motion are called *transverse* waves.
>
> Light also *propagates* with a transverse wave motion, and travels with its highest possible speed through a *perfect vacuum*. In this respect light differs markedly from sound, which is a physical vibration of matter. Sound does not travel at all through a vacuum. The *displacements* of the matter that carry a sound *impulse* are in a *longitudinal* direction, that is, in the direction of the propagation, rather than at right angles to it.

▶ **EXERCISE 8**

Based on context alone, make an educated guess about the italicized words in the paragraphs on light and sound waves. Write down the definition you would give each word. Then look up each word in an unabridged dictionary. How do your definitions compare?

▶**2 Collect words—and use them.**

If a word is mentioned more than twice, you should know its formal definition since its repeated use indicates that the word is important. Look the word up if you are not sure of its meaning. When attempting to *increase* your vocabulary, proceed slowly when putting newly discovered words to use in your own writing and speech. As an aid to vocabulary building, you may want to create a file of new words, as described in the box on the next page.

▶**3 Use the thesaurus with care.**

A thesaurus (literally from the Greek word meaning "treasure") is a reference tool that lists the synonyms of words and, frequently, their antonyms. Because the thesaurus is found in many computerized word processing programs, its use has become dangerously easy. If you find yourself turning to a thesaurus merely to dress up your writing with significant-sounding language, spare yourself the trouble. Unfortunately, sentences like the one that follows are too often written in a transparent effort to impress—and the effect can be unintentionally comical.

Pretentious   The *penultimate* chapter of this novel left me *rhapsodic.*

This sentence shares many of the problems associated with pretentious diction (see 21h-2). It also suggests how the *diction* (the level) of the two italicized words chosen from the thesaurus is likely to contrast sharply with the diction that characterizes the rest of a paper. Often, the sense of the word (its denotation or connotation) may be slightly off the mark—not precisely what the meaning of the sentence requires (see 21a). In either case, a sentence with such "treasures" usually stands out as awkward (see 21b). A more restrained choice of words would produce a better sentence.

Revised   I was overwhelmed by the next to last chapter of this novel.

By no means should you ignore the thesaurus; it is, in fact, a treasury of language. But when you find a word, make sure you are comfortable with it—that it is *your* word—before appropriating it for use in a paper.

▶**4 Build discipline-appropriate vocabularies.**

Each discipline has a vocabulary that insiders, or professionals, use when addressing one another; one of your jobs as you move from class to class will be to recognize important words and add them to discipline-specific vocabularies that you will develop. The longer you study in a discipline, and especially if you should major in it, the larger and more versatile your specific vocabulary will be. Discipline-specific

CRITICAL DECISIONS

Challenge yourself: Expanding your vocabulary

You can expand your vocabulary. As you read or while you are in class, jot down unfamiliar words. Collect them as follows.

■ Make a set of flash cards with a new word and the sentence in which it appears on one side of each card; place the definition on the other side.

■ Review the cards regularly. Categorize them by discipline or by part of speech. Practice changing the vocabulary word's part of speech with suffixes.

■ Expand entries in your file when you find a previously filed word used in a new context.

■ Consciously work one or two new words into each paper that you write, especially when the new words allow you to be precise in ways you could not otherwise be.

vocabularies consist of two types of words: those that are unique to the discipline and those that are found elsewhere, though with different meanings. For example, the word *gravity* occurs in contexts outside of the physics classroom. In a newspaper article or essay you might find *gravity* used to suggest great seriousness: *The gravity of the accusations caused Mr. Jones to hire a famous attorney.* Present-day physicists use the word *gravity* in an altogether different sense.

Discipline-specific vocabularies also consist of words unique to a particular field of study. The sheer volume of these words makes it impossible to review them here; suffice it to say that as you see new terms repeated in texts or hear them recurring in the speech of your professors, you should note these words and learn their definitions. As you move from introductory courses in a subject to upper-level courses, the new terms will become more familiar.

▶ **EXERCISE 9**

Take an informal survey to see if you can identify five words or phrases unique to a particular group of people. Listen to fraternity or sorority members on campus addressing members of their own houses; listen closely in a locker room to members of a team with which you have practiced; or sit in on a campus club meeting or a session of the student government. List the five words or phrases; then define each expression and illustrate its community-specific use in a sentence.

EXERCISE 10

Review your notes and text for one course and identify five words or phrases particular to that subject. The words or phrases might well occur in contexts beyond the course but should have a course-specific meaning. List the words or phrases; then define each expression and illustrate its discipline-specific use in a sentence.

CHAPTER

23

Spelling

English is an eclectic language derived from several different sources, including Old German, Scandinavian, and Norman French, as well as Latin and Greek. With such a mixed vocabulary, it is remarkable how closely most English spellings are associated with the sounds of words. Nevertheless, many words that look or sound alike may in fact derive from different sources, and thus be spelled or pronounced differently. With practice in writing and reading, you will find that certain basic patterns emerge that connect spelling to word sounds. Spelling can be mastered by learning a few rules and the exceptions to those rules. Spelling "demons" can be overcome by recognizing the words you most commonly misspell and remembering devices for memorizing their correct spelling.

▶ 23a Overcoming spelling/pronunciation misconnections

Long-time speakers and readers of English have learned basic connections between sounds and letter combinations that help them spell a large number of words. How-

http://www.qconline.com/
myword/perfectc.html
A lighthearted look at the shortcomings of computer spell-checkers.

ever, for historical reasons certain combinations of letters are not always pronounced in the same way (for example: thought, bough, through, drought, etc.). In addition, regional and dialect variations in pronunciation may drop or vary the pronunciation of certain endings of auxiliary verbs. It is safer to try

to keep a visual image of a word in your mind, rather than to rely on what you hear to help you to spell a word correctly.

▶ I Recognizing homonyms and commonly confused words

http://www.earlham.edu/
~peters/writing/
homofone.htm
An English homophone (or homonym) dictionary.

One of the most common causes of spelling confusion is **homonyms**—words that sound alike, or are pronounced almost alike, but that have different spellings and meanings. The following box lists the most commonly confused homonyms and near homonyms.

Commonly Confused Homonyms and Near Homonyms

accept [to receive]
except [to leave out]

advice [recommendation]
advise [to recommend]

affect [to have an influence on]
effect [result; to make happen]

all ready [prepared]
already [by this time]

bare [naked]
bear [to carry, endure; an animal]

board [piece of wood]
bored [uninterested]

brake [stop, device for stopping]
break [to smash, destroy]

buy [purchase]
by [next to, through]

capital [city seat of government]
capitol [legislative or government
building]

cite [quote, refer to]
sight [vision, something seen]
site [place, locale]

complement [something that completes]
compliment [praise]

conscience [moral sense, sense of
right/wrong]
conscious [aware]

discreet [respectfully reserved]
discrete [distinct, separate]

dominant [controlling, powerful]
dominate [to control]

elicit [to draw out]
illicit [illegal]

eminent [distinguished]
immanent [inborn, inherent]
imminent [expected momentarily]

fair [just; light-complexioned; lovely]
fare [fee for transportation; meal]

gorilla [ape]
guerilla [unconventional soldier]

heard [past tense of *to hear*]
herd [group of animals]

hole [opening]
whole [entire, complete]

its [possessive form of *it*]
it's [contraction of *it is*]

lead [guide; heavy metal]
led [past tense of *to lead*]

lessen [decrease]
lesson [something learned]

loose [not tight, unfastened]
lose [misplace, fail to win]

moral [object-lesson, knowing right
from wrong]
morale [outlook, attitude]

passed [past tense of *to pass*]
past [after; beyond; a time gone by]

patience [forbearance]
patients [those under medical care]

peace [absence of war]
piece [part or portion of something]

personal [private, pertaining to an
individual]
personnel [employees]

plain [simple, clear, unadorned; flat land]
plane [carpenter's tool, flat surface,
airplane]

presence [attendance, being at hand]
presents [gifts; gives]

principal [most important; school
administrator]
principle [fundamental truth, law,
conviction]

scene [setting, play segment]
seen [past participle of *to see*]

shore [coastline]
sure [certain]

stationary [standing still]
stationery [writing paper]

straight [unbending]
strait [narrow waterway]

than [besides; as compared with]
then [at that time; therefore]

their [possessive form of *they*]
there [opposite of *here*]
they're [contraction of *they are*]

threw [past tense of *to throw*]
through [by means of, finished]
thorough [complete]

to [toward]
too [also, in addition to]
two [number following *one*]

weak [feeble]
week [seven days]

weather [climatic conditions]
whether [which of two]

whose [possessive form of *who*]
who's [contraction of *who is*]

your [possessive form of *you*]
you're [contraction of *you are*]
yore [the far past]

▶ **EXERCISE 1**

From each pair or trio of words in parentheses, circle the correct homonym. Then make up sentences using each of the other word[s] correctly.

1. Funeral etiquette in some cultures dictates that you should pay (your/ you're) respects to the deceased by making (sure/shore) to spend a few quiet moments at the (beer/bier).
2. (There/they're/their) child (threw/through) a rock at (hour/our) child.
3. With the release of the (imminent/eminent) physicist's groundbreaking discovery, the presentation of the Nobel prize seemed (immanent/imminent).
4. If (your/you're) harboring any (illusion/allusion) about becoming a concert pianist someday, (your/you're) bound to be disappointed.
5. The technical staff is devising a method by which the (devise/device) can be installed by even nontechnical personnel.

▶ **2   Recognizing words with more than one form**

A subgroup of homonyms that many people find particularly troublesome consists of words that sometimes appear as one word and other times appear as two words.

We *always* work hard, in *all ways*.

By the time everyone was *all ready* to go, it was *already* too late to catch the early show.

It *may be* a question of etiquette, but *maybe* it's not.

Everyday attitudes are not always appropriate *every day*.

Walking *in to* the theater, he accidentally bumped *into* the usher.

Once we were *all together*, we were *altogether* convinced the reunion had been a wonderful idea.

Unlike *always/all ways* and *already/all ready*, *all right* and *a lot* do not vary: they can be written only as two words.

Faulty   It's *alright* with me if Sally comes along.
Revised   It's *all right* with me if Sally comes along.

Faulty   James has *alot* of homework to do tonight.
Revised   James has *a lot* of homework to do tonight.

▶ **3   Memorizing words with silent letters or syllables**

Many words contain silent letters, such as the *k* and the *w* in *know* or the *b* in dum*b*, or letters that are not pronounced in everyday speech, such as the first *r* in

http://webster.commnet.edu/HP/ pages/darling/grammar/notorious.htm *"Notorious Confusables": over 400 often confused words, defined and illustrated correctly in sentences that can be read aloud on your computer.*

February. The simplest way to remember the spelling of these words is to commit them to memory, mentally pronouncing the silent letters as you do so. Following is a list of frequently used words whose mispronunciation in everyday speech often leads to misspelling.

ai*s*le	Feb*r*uary	para*d*igm
can*d*idate	for*ei*gn	*p*neumonia
clim*b*	gover*n*ment	privi*l*ege
condem*n*	int*e*rest	prob*a*bly

COMPUTER TIPS

Spelling Checkers

Spelling checkers are wonderful inventions. They are quick, accurate, and sharper than your own eye at catching mistakes. But use them wisely. First, wait until the end of your writing process. Spell-checking a rough draft or even an intermediate draft filled with words that you may delete later is a waste of time. Also, remember the limitations of spelling checkers: they will catch only words not in their built-in dictionaries. Because *there, their,* and *they're* are all spelled correctly, the spelling checker will not tell you if you've chosen the wrong one. When a correction is suggested, make sure you choose the correct one (consult a dictionary if you need to). If you've written *alot* and your spelling checker offers to substitute *allot,* be careful not to change your intended meaning. Finally, if your word processor has an ongoing spelling checking feature, consider turning it off. Few things are more damaging to the flow of your thoughts than being interrupted by a beep, a warning that you've misspelled a word, or the silent substitution of an incorrect word.

▶4 Distinguishing between noun and verb forms of the same word

Many spelling problems occur when noun and verb forms of a word have different spellings.

Verb	*Noun*
advise	advice
describe	description
enter	entrance
marry	marriage

▶5 Distinguishing American from British and Canadian spellings

The endings of various words differ depending on whether the American version or the British version of the word is being used. Though each is correct, when in America, do as the Americans do. Above all, you should be consistent. If you are not sure what the correct version of the word is, consult your dictionary, making sure you know whether the dictionary "prefers" British or American variations.

American	*British*
-or (humor, color)	-our (humour, colour)
-ment (judgment)	-ement (judgement)

American	British
-tion (connection)	-xion (connexion)
-ize (criticize, realize)	-ise (criticise, realise)
-er (center, theater)	-re (centre, theatre)
-led (traveled)	-lled (travelled)

Other American/British variations include gray/grey and check/cheque.

▶ **23b** Learn basic spelling rules for *ie/ei*.

Despite the troublesome aspects of English spelling detailed previously, there are a number of general rules that greatly simplify the task of spelling words correctly.

The *i* before *e* rule you learned in grammar school still holds true: "*i* before *e* except after *c*, or when pronounced *ay*, as in n*ei*ghbor."

i before e

achieve	experience
belief/believe	field
brief	fiend/friend

Except after c

ceiling	receipt/receive
conceit	deceit/deceive
conceive	perceive

ei pronounced ay

beige	neighbor
eight(h)	heinous
freight	vein

Exceptions

ancient	foreign
height	seize
either	weird

Finally, if the *ie* is not pronounced as a unit, the rule does not apply: science, conscientious, atheist.

▶ EXERCISE 2

Insert *ie* or *ei* in the following words. If necessary, use a dictionary to confirm your choice.

forf ___ t	s ___ zure	p ___ rce
financ ___ r	f ___ nt	pat ___ nce
consc ___ nce	h ___ ress	counterf ___ t
defic ___ nt	sl ___ ght	r ___ fy

> **23c** **Learn rules for using prefixes.**

Prefixes are placed at the beginnings of words to qualify or add to their meaning. The addition of a prefix never affects the spelling of the root word: do not drop a letter from or add a letter to the original word.

un	+	usual	=	unusual
mis	+	statement	=	misstatement
under	+	rate	=	underrate
dis	+	service	=	disservice
anti	+	thesis	=	antithesis
de	+	emphasize	=	deemphasize

The following are also used as prefixes: *en, in, ante, inter, pre, per, pro,* and *over.*

> **23d** **Learn rules for using suffixes.**

A **suffix** is an ending added to a word in order to change the word's function. For example, suffixes can change a present-tense verb to a past-tense verb (help, help*ed*); make an adjective an adverb (silent, silent*ly*); make a verb a noun (excite, excite*ment*); or change a noun to an adjective (force, forc*ible*). Spelling difficulties often arise when the root word must be changed before the suffix is added.

> **1** **Learn rules for keeping or dropping a final e.**

Many words end with a silent *e* (hav*e*, mat*e*, rais*e*, confin*e*, procur*e*). When adding a suffix to these words, you can use the following rules.

The basic rule: If the suffix begins with a vowel, drop the final silent e.

accuse	+	ation	=	accusation		sedate	+	ive	=	sedative
inquire	+	ing	=	inquiring		cube	+	ism	=	cubism
debate	+	able	=	debatable		pore	+	ous	=	porous

Exceptions

The silent *e* is sometimes retained before a suffix that begins with a vowel in order to distinguish homonyms (dyeing/dying); to prevent mispronunciation (*mileage,* not milage); and especially, to keep the sound of *c* or *g* soft.

courage	+	ous	=	courageous		embrace	+	able	=	embraceable
outrage	+	ous	=	outrageous		notice	+	able	=	noticeable

Rule: If the suffix begins with a consonant, keep the final silent e.

manage	+	ment	=	management		acute	+	ness	=	acuteness
sedate	+	ly	=	sedately		force	+	ful	=	forceful
blame	+	less	=	blameless						

Exceptions

When the final silent *e* is preceded by another vowel, the *e* is dropped (*argument,* not arguement; *truly,* not truely).

Other exceptions include:

judge + ment = judgment   awe + ful = awful
acknowledge + ment = acknowledgment   whole + ly = wholly

> **EXERCISE 3**

Combine the following words and suffixes, retaining or dropping the final *e* as needed. Check your choices in the dictionary to make sure they are correct.

1. investigate + ive   6. service + able
2. malice + ious   7. complete + ly
3. due + ly   8. mistake + en
4. trace + able   9. grieve + ance
5. singe + ing   10. binge + ing

> **2 Learn rules for keeping or dropping a final y.**

When suffixes are added to words that end in a final *y*, use the following rules.

Rule: When the letter immediately before the y is a consonant, change the y to i and then add the suffix.

beauty + ful = beautiful   comply + ant = compliant
breezy + er = breezier   busy + ness = business
worry + some = worrisome   study + ous = studious

Exceptions

Keep the final *y* when the suffix to be added is *-ing*.

study + ing = studying   comply + ing = complying

Keep the final *y* for some one-syllable root words.

shy + er = shyer   wry + ly = wryly

Keep the final *y* when the *y* is the ending of a proper name.

Janey/Janeys   Bobby/Bobbylike

Keep the final *y* when it is preceded by a vowel, and then add the suffix.

journey + ing = journeying   buoy + ant = buoyant
deploy + ment = deployment   play + ful = playful
spray + ed = sprayed   coy + ly = coyly

> **EXERCISE 4**

Combine the following root words and suffixes, changing the *y* to *i* when necessary.

1. supply + er   6. convey + ance
2. stultify + ing   7. cry + er
3. testy + er   8. Kennedy + s
4. rarefy + ed   9. plenty + ful
5. joy + ousness   10. day + ly

Learn Rules for Using Suffixes   381

▶**3** **Learn rules for adding -ally.**

Rule: Add -ally to make an adverb out of an adjective that ends with ic.

terrific   + ally = terrifically
caustic   + ally = caustically
fantastic + ally = fantastically
emphatic + ally = emphatically
music   + ally = musically

> *Exception*
> public + ly = publicly

▶**4** **Learn the rule for adding -ly.**

Rule: Add -ly to make an adverb out of an adjective that does not end with ic.

hesitant + ly = hesitantly   fastidious   + ly = fastidiously
helpful   + ly = helpfully   conscientious + ly = conscientiously
fortunate + ly = fortunately

▶**5** **Learn the rule for adding -cede, -ceed, and -sede.**

Words that sound like *seed* are almost always spelled *-cede*.

intercede   concede   precede
accede   recede   secede

> *Exceptions*
> Only supersede uses *-sede*.
> Only exceed, proceed, and succeed use *-ceed*.

▶**6** **Learn rules for adding -able or -ible.**

These endings sound the same, but there is an easy way to remember which to use.

Rule: If the root word is an independent word, use the suffix -able. If the root is not an independent word, use the suffix -ible.

comfort + able = comfortable   audible
advise + able = advisable   plausible
agree   + able = agreeable   compatible

> *Exceptions*
> culpable, probable, resistible

▶**7** **Learn rules for doubling the final consonant.**

A word that ends in a consonant sometimes doubles the final consonant when a suffix is added.

Rule: Double the final consonant when a one-syllable word ends in a consonant preceded by a single vowel.

flip + ant = fli*pp*ant   slip + er   = sli*pp*er
flat + en = fla*tt*en   split + ing = spli*tt*ing

Rule: Double the final consonant when adding a suffix to a two-syllable word if a single vowel precedes the final consonant and if the final syllable is accented once the suffix is added.

control + er   = contro*ll*er
concur + ence = concu*rr*ence
commit + ing   = commi*tt*ing

Rule: Do not double the final consonant when it is preceded by two or more vowels, or by another consonant.

sustain + ing = sustaining
comport + ed   = comported
insist   + ent = insistent

Rule: Do not double the final consonant if the suffix begins with a consonant.

commit + ment = commitment
fat   + ness = fatness

Rule: Do not double the final consonant if the word is *not* accented on the last syllable, or if the accent shifts from the last to the first syllable when the suffix is added.

beckon + ing   = beckoning
prefer + ence = preference

▶ **EXERCISE 5**

Add the correct suffix to the following roots, changing the roots as necessary. Consult a dictionary as needed.

1. benefit   + ed
2. realistic + (-ly or -ally?)
3. contempt + (-able or -ible?)
4. parallel   + ing
5. proceed   + ure
6. reverse   + (-able or -ible?)
7. allot   + ment
8. occur   + ence
9. room   + mate
10. control   + (-able or -ible?)

▶ **23e** **Learn rules for forming plurals.**

There are several standard rules for making words plural.

▶ **I Learn the basic rule for adding -s/-es.**

Adding -s

For most words, simply add -s.

gum/gums   automobile/automobiles
season/seasons   investment/investments

Adding -es

For words ending in -s, -sh, -ss, -ch, -x, or -z, add -es.

bus/buses   watch/watches
bush/bushes   tax/taxes
mistress/mistresses   buzz/buzzes

For words ending in -o, add -es if the o is preceded by a consonant.

tomato/tomatoes   hero/heroes
potato/potatoes   veto/vetoes

> *Exceptions*
> pro/pros, piano/pianos, solo/solos
> soprano/sopranos

Add -s if the final o is preceded by a vowel.

patio/patios   zoo/zoos

▶ **2 Learn the rule for plurals of words ending in -f or -fe.**

To form the plural of some nouns ending in -f or -fe, change the ending to -ve before adding the -s.

half/halves   leaf/leaves
elf/elves   yourself/yourselves

> *Exceptions*
> scarf/scarfs/scarves   proof/proofs
> belief/beliefs   motif/motifs
> hoof/hoofs/hooves

▶ **3 Learn the rule for plurals of words ending in -y.**

For words that end in a consonant followed by -y, change the y to i before adding -es to form the plural.

amenity/amenities   enemy/enemies
raspberry/raspberries   mystery/mysteries

> *Exceptions*
> proper names such as McGinty/McGintys; Mary/Marys

For words ending in a vowel followed by -y, add -s.

monkey/monkeys   delay/delays
alloy/alloys   buy/buys

CRITICAL DECISIONS

Challenge yourself: Improving your spelling

In addition to learning the spelling rules detailed in this chapter, there are several ways to improve your spelling skills.

- Memorize commonly misspelled words.
- Keep track of the words that give you trouble. See if you can discern a pattern, and memorize the relevant rule.
- Use the dictionary. Check words whose spelling you are not sure of, and add them to your personal list of difficult-to-spell words. If you are not sure of the first few letters of a word, look up a synonym of that word to see if the word you need is listed as part of the definition.
- Pay attention when you read: your mind will retain a visual impression of a word that will help you remember how it is spelled.
- You may also develop mnemonic devices—techniques to improve memory— for particularly troublesome words. For instance, you might use the *-er* at the end of pap*er* and lett*er* as a reminder that station*er*y means writing pap*er*, while station*a*ry means st*a*nding still.
- Edit and proofread carefully, paying particular attention to how the words look on the page. You will find as you train yourself that you will begin to recognize spelling errors, and that you actually know the correct spelling but have made an old mistake in haste or carelessness.
- On word processors, use a spell-checker, but realize that this computer aid will only identify misspelled words: if you have used an incorrect homonym, but have spelled it correctly, the spell-checker will not highlight the word.

▶4 Learn the rule for plurals of compound words.

When compound nouns are written as one word, add an *-s* ending as you would to make any other plural.

snowball/snowballs   mailbox/mailboxes
breakthrough/breakthroughs

When compound nouns are hyphenated or written as two words, the most important part of the compound word (usually a noun that is modified) is made plural.

sister-in-law/sister*s*-in-law   head of state/head*s* of state
nurse-midwife/nurse-midwive*s*   city planner/city planner*s*

▶5 Learn the irregular plurals.

Some words change internally to form plurals.

woman/women   goose/geese
mouse/mice   tooth/teeth

Some Latin and Greek words form plurals by changing their final *-um*, *-on*, or *-us* to *-a* or *-i*.

curricul*um*/curricul*a*   criteri*on*/criteri*a*
syllab*us*/syllab*i*   medi*um*/medi*a*
dat*um*/dat*a*   stimul*us*/stimul*i*
alumn*us*/alumn*i*

For some words, the singular and the plural forms are the same.

deer/deer   sheep/sheep   fish/fish
species/species   moose/moose
elk/elk   rice/rice

▶ **EXERCISE 6**

Make the following words plural. Check your answers in the dictionary.

1. calf
2. memorandum
3. torch
4. chief
5. kilowatt-hour
6. knife
7. editor-in-chief
8. heresy
9. gas
10. ego

CHAPTER 24

End Punctuation

The ending of one sentence and the beginning of the next is a crucial boundary for readers. Sentences provide the primary medium for delivering isolatable, comprehensible chunks of information, and readers are highly sensitive to signals that show when they come to a full stop. When sentence boundaries are blurred, readers have trouble grouping a writer's words into meaningful segments. The end-of-sentence boundary in English is marked in three ways: with a period, a question mark, or an exclamation point.

THE PERIOD

▶ 24a   Using the period

The **period** is our workhorse mark of punctuation, the one used most often for noting a full stop—the end of a sentence.

▶ 1   Placing a period to mark the end of a statement or a mild command

It is conventional to end statements or mild commands with a period.

> For quite some time after the *Titanic*'s collision with the iceberg, the people on board did not believe themselves to be in danger.
> After all, the *Titanic* was supposed to be unsinkable.
> "Women and children must get into the lifeboats."

A restatement of a question asked by someone else is called an **indirect question.** Since it is really a statement, it does not take a question mark.

Direct Question	Many of the women who were being urged to board the life rafts asked, "Is this truly necessary?"
Statement	Many of the women who were being urged to board the life rafts asked whether this measure was truly necessary.

▶ 2   Placing periods in relation to end quotation marks and parentheses

A period is always placed inside a quotation mark that ends a sentence.

The rule was, at least on the port side of the ship, "Women and children only."

When a parenthesis ends a sentence, place a period outside the end parenthesis if the parenthetical remark is not a complete sentence (see 29c). If the parenthetical remark is a separate complete sentence, enclose it entirely in parentheses and punctuate it as a sentence—with its own period.

Faulty   There was, in fact, enough room on the life rafts for first and second-class women and children, but no allowance had been made for steerage passengers (that is, economy class—the cheapest fare.).

Revised   There was, in fact, enough room on the life rafts for first and second-class women and children, but no allowance had been made for steerage passengers (that is, economy class—the cheapest fare).

Revised   There was, in fact, enough room on the life rafts for first and second-class women and children, but no allowance had been made for steerage passengers. (Steerage was defined as economy class, the cheapest fare.)

▶3 Using a period with abbreviations

The following are considered abbreviations that conventionally end with a period:

Mr.   Mrs.   Ms. (even though this is not an abbreviation)
apt.   Ave.   St.   Dr.   Eccles.   mgr.

When an abbreviation ends a sentence, use a single period.

Faulty   The lawyers addressed their questions to Susan Turner, Esq..
Revised   The lawyers addressed their questions to Susan Turner, Esq.

When an abbreviation falls in the middle of a sentence, punctuate as if the word abbreviated were spelled out.

Faulty   The award envelope was presented to Susan Turner, Esq. who opened it calmly.

Revised   The award envelope was presented to Susan Turner, Esq., who opened it calmly.

See 31a–e for a full discussion of abbreviations.

Use no periods with acronyms or certain long abbreviations.

A number of abbreviations do not take periods—most often *acronyms* (NATO for North Atlantic Treaty Organization), the names of large organizations (IBM for International Business Machines), or government agencies (FTC for Federal Trade Commission). To be sure about the proper abbreviation of a word or organizational name, see the box at 31c and consult a standard dictionary for general purposes or specialized dictionaries when you are writing in a particular discipline. The following are some typical abbreviations:

ABC   CNN   AT&T   USA   ABM   FAA

▶ **EXERCISE I**

Add, delete, or reposition periods in these sentences as needed.

> *Example:* Organ transplants have increased since the development of immunosuppressive drugs such as cyclosporin
>
> Organ transplants have increased since the development of immunosuppressive drugs such as cyclosporin.

1. According to one expert, "roughly 5,000 patients are waiting at any given moment for replacement livers. Ten thousand wait for kidneys." (Thomas)
2. Modern transplant techniques have created a rush for human organs and have given rise to what is ghoulishly called the "meat market"
3. "The ethical dilemmas raised by organ transplants are enormous," says Dr. Philip Wier (an ethicist at the Longwood Institute.)
4. Some poor people, faced with the prospect of starving, sell off their kidneys (This practice is the subject of intense debate in some state legislatures)

THE QUESTION MARK

▶ **24b**   Using the question mark

▶ **I**   **Using a question mark after a direct question**

Why do children develop so little when they are isolated from others?

Why is the crime rate higher in the city than the country, in impoverished areas more than other areas? Why do more males than females, more young people than older people, commit crimes?

Note: An indirect question restates a question put by someone else. The indirect question does not take a question mark.

Sociologists Eshleman and Cashion have asked why children develop so little when they are isolated from others.

Requests, worded as questions, are often followed by periods.

Would you pour another glass of wine.

Questions in a series inside a sentence will take question marks if each denotes a separate question.

When an automobile manufacturer knowingly sells a car that meets government safety standards but is defective, what are the manufacturer's legal responsibilities? moral responsibilities? financial responsibilities? [Note that these three "clipped" questions—these incomplete sentences—do not require capitalization.]

When the sense of the questions in a series is not completed until the final question, use one question mark—at the end of the sentence.

Will the agent be submitting the manuscript to one publishing house, two houses, or more?

▶2 Using a question mark after a quoted question within a statement

Placing the question mark *inside* the end quotation mark

When the question mark applies directly to the quoted material, place it inside the quotation mark.

> In a dream, Abraham Lincoln remembered a stranger asking, "Why are you so common looking?"

Place the question mark inside the end quotation mark when the mark applies to *both* the quoted material *and* the sentence as a whole.

> Don't you find it insulting that a person would comment directly to a president, "Why are you so common looking?"

See 28a-7 for more on quotations with questions.

Placing the question mark *outside* the end quotation mark

When the sentence as a whole forms a question but the quoted material does not, place the question mark outside the quotation.

> Was it Lincoln who observed, "The Lord prefers common-looking people; that's the reason he makes so many of them"?

Note: Do *not* combine a question mark with a period, a comma, or an exclamation point.

Faulty   "Are you going with him?!" asked Joan.

Revised   "Are you going with him?" asked Joan.

Revised   "Are you going with him!" shouted Joan.

▶3 Using a question mark within parentheses to indicate that the accuracy of information is in doubt even after extensive research

The question mark can be used to indicate dates or numerical references known to be inexact. The following are equivalent in meaning:

> Geoffrey Chaucer was born in 1340 (?).

> Chaucer was born about 1340.

> Chaucer was born c. 1340. (The c. is an abbreviation for *circa*, meaning "around.")

Note: Do *not* use the question mark in parentheses to make wry comments in your sentences.

Faulty   We found the play a stimulating (?) experience.

Revised   Martin fell asleep in the play's first act, and I persuaded him to leave at intermission.

See 29c for more on parentheses.

▶ **EXERCISE 2**

Add or delete question marks as needed. If necessary, reword sentences.

> *Example:* The candidates' forum provided an illuminating (?) hour of political debate.
>
> The candidates' forum failed to provide an illuminating debate.

1. Many people are quick to complain about the quality of political discourse in American politics, so why is it that more thoughtful people aren't running for elected office.

2. When we find that it is polling information, not philosophical conviction, that shapes the public remarks of political figures, is it any wonder that Americans turn cynical, refuse to vote, bemoan the absence of leadership.

3. Political scientists ask why Americans have one of the lowest voter turnouts among democratic nations?

4. Was it Marie Thompson who asked, "Why do we have so much difficulty rising to the challenge of our democratic traditions"?

5. Thompson reaches no firm answers when she concludes, "If the framers of the Constitution assumed an educated, caring citizenry, then we must wonder aloud—have we failed to meet the challenges laid down 200 years ago"?

THE EXCLAMATION POINT

▶ **24c** Using the exclamation point

In spoken conversation, exclamations are used freely, especially in moments of high passion. For some informal occasions, writers may be tempted to create with exclamation points what their tone of voice cannot show on paper. In academic writing, however, it is far more convincing to create emphasis by the force of your words, as opposed to the force of your punctuation.

▶ **1** Using the exclamation point—sparingly—to mark an emphatic statement or command

Overused exclamation points create a none-too-flattering portrait of a writer who is highly excitable and not too credible. Save the exclamation point to call special attention to a unique, memorable sentence, the content of which creates its own emphasis. The exclamation point will highlight the emphasis already present.

> Enterprising archaeologists visit their dentists regularly, if only to obtain supplies of worn-out dental instruments, which make first-rate fine digging tools!
>
> Please! Let me do it myself! [The use of exclamation points with this emphatic exclamation and command is appropriate for duplicating spoken dialogue.]

2 **Marking mild exclamations with periods or commas**

Please, let me do it myself.

Note: Do not combine an exclamation point with a period, comma, or question mark.

Faulty   "Leave this room**!,**" demanded the judge.

Revised   "Leave this room**!**" demanded the judge.

Faulty   "Can't you give us some privacy**?!**" he snarled.

Revised   "Can't you give us some privacy**!**" he snarled.

EXERCISE 3

Read the following paragraphs on the subject of getting fired from a job and provide periods, question marks, and exclamation points as needed.

Many people who have lost their jobs report that the loss profoundly undermines their self-esteem They blame themselves They ask themselves "How can I be lovable, worthy, and competent if I have lost my job" Having to file an unemployment claim only serves to deepen their sense of shame

Even well-intentioned former coworkers are no source of comfort The newly unemployed often find that even the most sympathetic colleagues tend to abandon them These coworkers are terrified that the same thing might happen to them (in a climate of downsizing this fear is certainly justified) Others tell the victim that this loss is "the best thing that could ever happen to you" From the fired person's point of view, such people are merely trying to alleviate their own discomfort "They say that so that they won't have to worry about me" one woman commented The loss of one's job can cause a person to become cynical and suspicious

25

Commas

One important purpose of punctuation is to help readers identify clusters of related words, both between and within sentences. By far the most common mark used to distinguish one sentence from another is the period. *Within* sentences, the most common mark is the **comma**, and it is used primarily as a signal that some element, some word or cluster of related words, is being set off from a main sentence for a reason.

  http://www.researchpaper.com/ writing_center/3.html *Using Commas: a hypertext guide from Researchpaper.com.*

In this chapter you will find rules and guidelines for helping you make intelligent choices about comma use. Much of the logic of punctuating with commas is tied to the logic of a sentence's structure. See especially Chapters 13, 15, and 19, as well as Chapter 7.

▶ 25a Using commas with introductory and concluding expressions

▶ I **Place a comma after a modifying phrase or clause that begins a sentence.**

Yesterday, the faucet stopped working.
Once the weather turned cold, the faucet stopped working.

A sentence may begin with an opening phrase or clause that is neither the subject nor a simple modifier of the subject. If such an introductory element is longer than a few words, set it off from the main part of the sentence with a comma. The comma will signal the reader that the sentence's subject is being delayed.

According to landscape architect Robert Gibbs, urban shopping centers could learn a lot from suburban malls.

Because Gibbs possesses a commercial shrewdness, he is able to spot the flaws (from a commercial standpoint) in the most elegant street designs.

Option: The comma after an introductory word or brief phrase is optional.

In fact a great many considerations are involved in the overlap of the physical and psychological environments for shopping.

When an introductory element consists of two or more phrases, a comma is required.

> As a commercial space with a retailing bias, the mall should have a design that does not let the shopper become distracted from buying.

Note: An opening verbal phrase or clause is set off with a comma if it is used as a modifier; an opening verbal used as a subject is *not* set off.

Modifier In creating a shopping environment that is too beautiful, commercial designers are failing to serve the needs of the merchants.

Subject Creating a shopping environment that is too beautiful fails to serve the needs of the merchants.

▶2 **Place a comma after a transitional word, phrase, or clause that begins a sentence.**

> Actually, we've had this problem for years.

A transition is a logical bridge between sentences or paragraphs. As an introductory element, it is set off with a comma.

> Once division of labor by sex arose, it must have produced several immediate benefits for the early hominids. *First of all,* nutrition would have improved owing to a balanced diet of meat and plant foods. *Second,* each male or female would have become expert in only part of the skills needed for subsistence and would have increased his or her efficiency accordingly.

When a transitional element is moved to the interior of a sentence, set it off with a *pair* of commas. At the end of a sentence, the transitional element is set off with a single comma.

> Lipid molecules, *of course,* and molecules that dissolve easily in lipids can pass through cell membranes with ease.
> Lipid molecules and molecules that dissolve easily in lipids can pass through cell membranes with ease, *to cite two examples.*

▶3 **Use a comma (or commas) to set off a modifying element that ends or interrupts a sentence *if* the modifier establishes a qualification, contrast, or exception.**

> The ships return to port at all hours, often at night.
> The storm warning was broadcast on the A channel, not the B channel.

A qualification
> The literary form *short story* is usually defined as a brief fictional prose narrative, *often involving one connected episode.*

A contrast
> The U.S. government located a lucrative project for an atomic accelerator in Texas, *not Massachusetts.*

An exception

The children of the rich are the group most likely to go to private preparatory schools and elite colleges, *regardless of their grades.*

When phrases or clauses of contrast, qualification, and exception occur in the middle of a sentence, set them off with a *pair* of commas.

The government chose Texas, *not Massachusetts,* as the site of a lucrative project for an atomic accelerator.

All seas, *except in the areas of circumpolar ice,* are navigable.

If a phrase or clause does *not* establish a qualification, contrast, or exception, do *not* use a comma to separate it from the sentence.

The faucet stopped working once the weather turned cold.

▶ **EXERCISE 1**

The following sentences contain transitional expressions and modifying words or phrases. Rewrite each sentence so that the transition or modifier will come at the *beginning* of the sentence **or** at the *end.* Use commas as needed.

> *Example:* Some of the Balkan nations of southeastern and south central Europe in 1912 declared war on the waning Ottoman Empire.
>
> In 1912, some of the Balkan nations of southeastern and south central Europe declared war on the waning Ottoman Empire.

1. Bulgaria attacked Serbia and Greece in 1913 in a second war over boundaries.
2. Bulgaria was carved up as a result of the 1913 war by its former Balkan allies and Turkey.
3. The assassination of the Archduke Ferdinand of Austria the following year brought on the First World War.
4. A sprawling new nation, Yugoslavia, was formed after the Austro-Hungarian Empire collapsed.
5. The aspirations of Croats and other minorities in Yugoslavia were suppressed under the tenuous domination of the Serbs.
6. The collapse of the Ottoman Empire at the same time left many ethnic Turks subject to their longtime foes the Bulgarians.
7. A million Armenians were slaughtered at the same time as a result of attempts at forging a new Turkish state in Anatolia.
8. Undermined by corrupt and meddling monarchs and by ethnic passions, parliamentary governments of southeastern Europe rose and fell.
9. The fall of Communist regimes in eastern Europe today has led to a resurgence of ethnic fighting.
10. "Ethnic cleansing" reminiscent of Nazi atrocities has annihilated whole villages.

Spotlight on Common Errors—COMMA USE

These are clues to the errors most commonly associated with comma use. For full explanations and suggested revisions, follow the cross-references to chapter sections.

COMMA ERRORS arise when the use—or absence—of commas leaves readers unable to differentiate between a main sentence and the parts being set off. Five error patterns account for most of the difficulty with comma use.

Use a comma to set off introductory words or word groupings from the main part of the sentence (see 25a).

Faulty	Revised
Yesterday the faucet stopped working.	Yesterday, the faucet stopped working.

Faulty	Revised
Once the weather turned cold the faucet stopped working.	Once the weather turned cold, the faucet stopped working.

Do *not* use a comma to set off concluding words or word groupings from a main sentence (but see 25a-3 for exceptions).

Faulty	Revised
The faucet stopped working, yesterday.	The faucet stopped working yesterday.

Faulty	Revised
The faucet stopped working, once the weather turned cold.	The faucet stopped working once the weather turned cold.

Place a comma before the word *and, but, or, for,* or *so* when it joins two sentences (see 25b).

Faulty	Revised
The faucet stopped working *and* the sink leaks.	The faucet stopped working, *and* the sink leaks.

Faulty	Revised
I'll fix them myself *or* I can call a plumber.	I'll fix them myself, *or* I can call a plumber.

BUT use no comma if one key word, usually the subject, keeps the second grouping of words from being considered a sentence.

Faulty
I'll fix them myself, or call a plumber.

Revised
I'll fix them myself or call a plumber.

Use a comma to separate three or more items in a series (see 25c-1).

Faulty
I'll need a washer a valve and a wrench.

Revised
I'll need a washer, a valve, and a wrench.
or
I'll need a washer, a valve and a wrench.

Use a *pair* of commas to set off from a sentence any word or word group that adds nonessential information (see 25d).

Faulty
Ahorn Hardware which is just around the corner will have the materials I need.

Revised
Ahorn Hardware, which is just around the corner, will have the materials I need.

[Since a specific hardware store is named and its identity is clear, the added information is nonessential and is set off with a pair of commas.]

BUT use *no* commas if a word or word group adds essential information needed for identifying some other word in the sentence.

Faulty
The hardware store, which is just around the corner, will have the materials I need.

Revised
The hardware store which is just around the corner will have the materials I need.

[Since the added information is essential for identifying *which* hardware store (perhaps there is more than one store in the area), no commas are used. Note that in the case of essential information, many writers insist on using *that* to introduce the information.]

The hardware store that is just around the corner will have the materials I need.

25b Using a comma before a coordinating conjunction to join two independent clauses

The faucet stopped working, and the sink leaks.
We can fix the problems ourselves, or we can call a plumber.

One of the principal ways to join two independent clauses is to link them with a comma and a coordinating conjunction: *and, but, or, nor, so* (see 19a-1).

The changes in *Homo erectus* are substantial over a million years, *but* they seem gradual by comparison with those that went before.

A computer's data and addressing information are stored in flip-flops within the various memory registers, *or* they take the form of an electrical signal that is moving through wires from one register to another.

Options: You have several options for linking independent clauses: (1) you can separate the clauses and form two distinct sentences—see 24a; (2) you can use a semicolon to link the clauses within one sentence—see 26a–b (and the Critical Decisions box there); (3) you can make one clause subordinate to another—see 19b (and the Critical Decisions box in 19a).

Note: When a coordinating conjunction joins two independent clauses, and when one or both of these clauses has internal punctuation, to prevent misreading change the comma appearing before the conjunction to a semicolon.

Several thousand years ago, probably some lines of Neanderthal man and woman died out; but it seems likely that a line in the Middle East went directly to us, *Homo sapiens.*

25c Using commas between items in a series

One major function of the comma is to signal a brief pause that separates items in a series—a string of related elements.

1 Place a comma between items in a series.

We'll need a washer, a valve, and a wrench.

Items joined in a series should be parallel (see Chapter 18). Items can be single words, phrases, or clauses.

Words A Central Processing Unit contains a large number of special-purpose registers for storing *instructions, addresses,* and *data.*

Phrases Booms and busts have plagued economic activity since the onset of industrialization, *sporadically ejecting many workers from their jobs, pushing many businesses into bankruptcy,* and *leaving many politicians out in the cold.*

Option: Some writers prefer to omit the final comma in a series—the comma placed before the coordinating conjunction *and.* The choice is yours. Whatever your preference, be consistent.

Commas

Option Exercise appears *to reduce the desire to smoke, to lessen any tendency toward obesity* and *to help in managing stress.*

Note: When at least one item in a series contains a comma, use a semicolon to separate items and prevent misreading (see Chapter 26). For the same reason, use semicolons to separate long independent clauses in a series.

> I believe that the sun is about ninety-three million miles from the earth; that it is a hot globe many times bigger than the earth; and that, owing to the earth's rotation, it rises every morning and will continue to do so for an indefinite time in the future.

▶2 **Place a comma between two or more coordinate adjectives in a series, if no coordinating conjunction joins them.**

Getting under the sink can be a tricky, messy job.

A series of adjectives will often appear as a parallel sequence: the *playful, amusing* poet; an *intelligent, engaging* speaker. When the order of the adjectives can be reversed without affecting the meaning of the noun being modified, the adjectives are called **coordinate adjectives.** Coordinate adjectives can be linked by a comma or by a coordinating conjunction.

Series with commas

> The stomach is a thick-walled, muscular sac that can expand to hold more than 2 liters of food or liquid.

Series with *and*

> The stomach is a thick-walled *and* muscular sac that can expand to hold more than 2 liters of food or liquid.

Series with commas

> The left hemisphere of the brain thinks sequential, analytical thoughts and is also the center of language.

Series with *and*

> The left hemisphere thinks sequential *and* analytical thoughts and is also the center of language.

Note: The presence of two adjectives beside one another does not necessarily mean that they are coordinate. In the phrase "the wise old lady," the adjectives could not be reversed in sequence or joined by *and;* the adjective *wise* describes *old lady,* not *lady* alone. The same analysis holds for the phrase "the ugly green car." *Green car* is the element being modified by *ugly.* Only coordinate adjectives modifying the same noun are separated by commas.

▶ **EXERCISE 2**

Combine the following sentences with the conjunction indicated in brackets, and decide whether you need to use a comma. Recall that unless a conjunction joins independent clauses, no comma is needed.

Using Commas between Items in a Series **399**

Example: Anthropologists are currently investigating whether early hominids (proto-humans) ate meat. [and] Did they obtain meat by hunting or scavenging?

Anthropologists are currently investigating whether early hominids (proto-humans) ate meat and whether they obtained it by hunting or scavenging.

1. Proto-humans did not walk as well on two feet as we do. [but] They were better than we are at climbing trees and suspending themselves from branches.
2. Ancestors of present-day leopards were contemporary with early hominids. [and] Ancestors of present-day leopards shared the same habitats as early hominids.
3. Leopards cannot defend their kills from scavenging by lions. [so] They store their kills in trees.
4. Archaeologist John Cavallo thinks that early tree-climbing hominids may have fed off leopard kills stashed in trees. [since] Leopards don't guard the carcasses of their kills.

EXERCISE 3

In each sentence, place a comma as needed between items in a series.

Example: Native American societies were based on close ties of kin and on notions of community mutual obligation and reciprocity.

Native American societies were based on close ties of kin and on notions of community, mutual obligation, and reciprocity.

1. They possessed complex religious beliefs symbolic world views radically different from those of Europeans and cultural values Europeans did not understand.
2. Like other native populations "discovered" after them, Native Americans were exploited decimated by exotic diseases robbed of their lands and ultimately stripped of their traditional cultures.
3. Survivors became serfs slaves or subordinate and often tangential elements in the new social order.
4. Therefore, for centuries Native Americans continued to resist Catholic missionaries explorers and settlers from all over Europe.

▶ ## 25d Using commas to set off nonessential elements

▶ I **Identify essential (restrictive) elements that need no commas.**

The hardware store which is just around the corner will have the materials I need.

When a modifier provides information that is necessary for identifying a word, then the modifier is said to be **essential** (or **restrictive**), and it appears in its sentence *without* commas.

The world-renowned architect *commissioned to design a synagogue for the Beth Shalom congregation in Elkins Park, Pennsylvania* produced an architectural masterpiece.

There have been many famous architects. This sentence refers to the *one* architect hired by this congregation. Without the modifying phrase *commissioned to design a synagogue for the Beth Shalom congregation in Elkins Park, Pennsylvania*, the subject of this sentence, *the world-renowned architect*, could not be conclusively identified. Therefore, the modifying expression is essential, and no commas are used to set apart the phrase from the sentence in which it appears.

http://www.wisc.edu/writetest/Handbook/Commas.html #definitions

Punctuating restrictive and nonrestrictive modifiers: Definitions of nonrestrictive and restrictive modifiers with sample pairs of sentences and self-test sentences and answers.

An essential modifier can also be a single word (or single name).

The world-renowned architect *Frank Lloyd Wright* was born in 1869.

Without the name *Frank Lloyd Wright*, we would not know which world-renowned architect was born in 1869.

An essential modifier can also be a clause.

The cyclotron is an instrument *that accelerates charged particles to very high speeds.*

The noun modified—*instrument*—could be *any* instrument, and the clause that follows provides information essential to the definition of *which* or *what kind* of instrument.

▶**2** **Use a pair of commas to set off nonessential (nonrestrictive) elements.**

Ahorn Hardware, which is just around the corner, will have the materials I need.

If a word being modified is clearly defined (as, for instance, a person with a specific name is clearly defined), then the modifying element—though it might add interesting and useful information—is nonessential. When the modifier is not essential for defining a word, use commas to set the modifier apart from the sentence in which it appears.

Nonessential   Frank Lloyd Wright, *possibly the finest American architect of the twentieth century,* died in 1959.

The subject of the sentence has already been defined adequately by his name, *Frank Lloyd Wright*. The writer uses the modifying phrase not as a matter of definition but as an occasion to add nonessential information. The meaning of a sentence will change according to whether modifying elements are punctuated as essential or nonessential. The two pairs of sentences that follow are worded identically. Punctuation gives them different meanings.

Essential   The students *who have band practice after school* cannot attend the game.
Nonessential   The students, *who have band practice after school,* cannot attend the game.

The essential modifier precisely defines *which* students will not be able to attend the game—only those who have band practice. The meaning of this first sentence, then, is that some students *will* be able to attend—those who do *not* have band practice. The nonessential modifier communicates that *all* of the students have band practice and that none can attend.

Punctuating Modifying Clauses with *Who, Which,* and *That*

The relative pronouns *who, which,* and *that* begin modifying clauses that can interrupt or end sentences.

WHO

Who can begin a clause that is essential to defining the word modified.

> Formal organizations designate managers *who help administrative units meet their specific goals.*

Who can also begin a nonessential clause. Note the presence of commas in this sentence.

> Frank Smith, *who is an administrative manager,* helps his administrative unit meet its goals.

WHICH

Similarly, *which* can begin an essential or a nonessential modifying clause.

> Two sites *which flourished in the dim yet documented past* are Saxon London and medieval Winchester. [essential]

> Some historical archaeologists excavate sites like Saxon London or medieval Winchester, *which flourished in the dim yet documented past.* [nonessential]

THAT

That always denotes an essential clause. Do not use commas to set off a modifying clause beginning with *that.*

> Two sites *that flourished in the dim yet documented past* are Saxon London and medieval Winchester. [essential]

▶ **3 Use commas to set off parenthetical or repeating elements.**

The reasons she gave, all three of them, were convincing.

By definition, a parenthetical remark is not essential to the meaning of a sentence. The remark sometimes illuminates the sentence but by no means provides crucial information. Set off parenthetical expressions as you would any nonessential element.

> Lizzie Borden, *despite the weight of evidence against her,* was acquitted of the murder of her father and her stepmother.

Options: You have the choice of setting off parenthetical elements by using commas, parentheses, or dashes. Any of these options is correct, so base your decision on the level of emphasis you wish to give the parenthetical element. Dashes call the most attention to the element and parentheses the least attention.

CRITICAL DECISIONS

Form, and support, opinions: Distinguishing essential from nonessential information within a sentence

Comma placement often depends on a decision you make about whether certain qualifying (or additional) information is or is not essential to the meaning of a particular word in a sentence.

A Test to Determine Whether Qualifying Information Is Essential or Nonessential

1. Identify the single word in the sentence being qualified by a word group.
2. Identify the qualifying word group.
3. Drop the qualifying word group from the sentence.
4. Ask of the single word from #1, above: Do I understand which one or who?

   a. If you can give a single answer to this question, the qualifying information is nonessential. Set the information off from the sentence with a pair of commas.

   The train arrived early in Baltimore, the birthplace of Babe Ruth.

   b. If you cannot give a specific answer to the question, the qualifying information is essential. Include the information in the main sentence with no commas.

   The cities that have antiquated water systems need to modernize quickly or risk endangering public health.

Repeating elements

Repetition can both add useful information to a sentence and create pleasing sentence rhythms. By definition, a repeating element is nonessential, so the logic of setting off nonessential elements with commas applies. Set off a repeating element with a *pair* of commas if the element appears in the middle of a sentence. (You may also use a pair of dashes.) Use a comma or a dash and a period if the element concludes the sentence.

> The police investigation, *a bungled affair from start to finish,* overlooked crucial evidence and even managed to lose notes taken at the scene of the crime.

> Archaeologists working underwater have exactly the same intellectual goals as their dry-land colleagues—*to recover, reconstruct, and interpret the past.*

> These bare facts have become so familiar, *so essential in the conduct of an interlocking world society,* that they are usually taken for granted.

Appositives

One class of repeating element is called an **appositive phrase,** the function of which is to rename a noun. The phrase is called *appositive* because it is placed in *apposition* to—that is, *side by side* with—the noun it repeats. In the first example, the

Using Commas to Set Off Nonessential Elements

appositive *a bungled affair from start to finish* renames the subject of the sentence, *investigation.* The sentence could be rewritten and repunctuated as follows:

> *A bungled affair from start to finish,* the police investigation of the Borden case overlooked crucial evidence and even managed to lose notes taken at the scene of the crime.

Exception: When a nonessential appositive phrase consists of a series of items separated by commas, set it off from a sentence with a pair of dashes—not commas—to prevent misreading.

Confusing	Motion sickness, nausea, dizziness, and sleepiness, is a dangerous and common malady among astronauts.
Revised	Motion sickness—nausea, dizziness, and sleepiness—is a dangerous and common malady among astronauts.

▶ **EXERCISE 4**

Combine the following pairs of sentences. Use commas to set off nonessential modifiers and omit commas when modifiers are essential.

> *Example:* A number of Hollywood films have depicted historical events. Such films were painstakingly researched.
>
> A number of Hollywood films that have depicted historical events were painstakingly researched.

1. Film by its very nature is better able than prose to present the event in all its intensity.
   Even the most sober historians are willing to admit that fact.

2. In some instances the film has turned out to be more historically accurate than the original historical account.
   Vivien Leigh's portrayal of a spirited Scarlett O'Hara is now considered to be a fairly accurate interpretation of the not-so-helpless Southern belle.

3. Of course there have been plenty of instances of mistakes in historical representation.
   A film might carefully reproduce the material culture of an era but skew the facts of the event.

4. Viewers are more comfortable if the film ratifies their personal biases.
   Hollywood history films tend to reflect the biases of their viewers, especially in political matters.

5. *Bonnie and Clyde* transformed a vapid Bonnie Parker into an aggressive moll.
   Anne of the Thousand Days transformed an ambitious and strong-willed Anne Boleyn into a lovesick, awestruck girl.

6. *A Man for All Seasons* presented a gentle, principled man.
   The historical Thomas More wrote that the execution of heretics was "lawful, necessary and well done."

7. *Bonnie and Clyde* and *Anne of the Thousand Days* were made only two years apart.
   These two films illustrate the rise of the generation gap of the 1960s.

▶ **25e** **Using commas to acknowledge conventions of quoting, naming, and various forms of separation**

▶**1** **Use a comma to introduce or to complete a quotation.**

Tom said, "I'll be back in two hours."

Commas set a quotation apart from the words that introduce or conclude the quotation. Commas (and periods) are placed *inside* end quotation marks.

The prizefighter Rocky Graziano once said, "I had to leave fourth grade because of pneumonia—not because I had it but because I couldn't spell it."

Early in his career, Winston Churchill sported a mustache. At a fancy dinner, he argued with a woman who snapped, "Young man—I care for neither your politics nor your mustache."

"Madam," responded Churchill, "you are unlikely to come into contact with either."

(For more on using commas with quotations, see Chapter 28.)

▶**2** **Use a comma to set off expressions of direct address. If the expression interrupts a sentence, set the word off with a *pair* of commas.**

"Ed, did you bring your computer?"
"Our business, Ed, is to sell shoes."

You will most often encounter expressions of direct address when writing dialogue or when quoting speakers addressing their audiences.

"You, Sir, have the sense of a baboon."
"Paul, run to the exit."
"Run to the exit, Paul."
"My fellow citizens, I come before you with a heavy heart."
"I come before you, my fellow citizens, with a heavy heart."

▶**3** **Use a comma to mark the omission of words in a balanced sentence.**

The first train will arrive at 2 o'clock; the second, at 3 o'clock.

Sentences are balanced when identical clause constructions are doubled or tripled in a series. So that repeating words in the clauses do not become tedious to a reader, omit these words and note the omission with a comma.

Some southern novelists attribute the character of their fiction to the South's losing the Civil War; others, to the region's special blending of climate and race; and still others, to the salubrious powers of mint juleps.

In this example, the comma and the word *others* substitute for *some southern novelists attribute the character of their fiction.*

▶**4** **Place a comma between paired "more/less" constructions.**

The less you smoke, the longer you'll live.

Some constructions involve a paired comparison of "more" of one element contrasted against "more" or "less" of another. Separate these elements with a comma to maintain a clear relationship between them.

The more wires a database contains, the greater the number of bits it can move at a time.

The more some people get, the less they are willing to give.

▶5 Use a comma to set off tag questions that conclude a sentence.

This is the right house, isn't it?

A **tag question,** a brief question "tagged on" to a statement addressed to someone, should be set off from that statement. Tags are used for a variety of purposes, at times to suggest indecision or hesitancy.

You slipped into the office and read that letter, didn't you?

I have reached the only possible conclusion, haven't I?

▶6 Use a comma to set off yes/no remarks and mild exclamations.

"Yes, I'll call him right away."

"Oh well, I can put it off for another day."

▶7 Use commas according to convention in names, titles, dates, numbers, and addresses.

Commas with names and titles

Place a comma directly after a name if it is followed by a title.

Mr. Joe Smith, Executive Editor

Ms. Ann Jacobs, Senior Vice President

Lucy Turner, Ph.D.

Mr. Frank Reynolds, Esq.

Set off a title in commas when writing a sentence.

Mr. Joe Smith, Executive Editor, signed for the package.

Lucy Turner, Ph.D., delivered the commencement address.

Mr. Robert Jones, Sr., attended the ceremony.

Commas with dates

Place a comma between the day of the month and year. If your reference is to a particular month in a year and no date is mentioned, do not use a comma.

January 7, 1998   but   January 1998

When a date is written out, as in an invitation, use the following convention:
the seventh of January, 1998

No commas are used in the military convention for writing dates.

7 January 1998

If you include a day of the week when writing a date, use the following convention:

The package will be delivered on Wednesday, January 7, 1998.

Commas with numbers

Place a comma to denote thousands, millions, and so forth.

543   5,430   54,300   543,000   5,430,000   5,430,000,000

Some writers place no comma in four-digit numbers that are multiples of fifty.

2550   1600   but   1,625

Do *not* use commas when writing phone numbers, addresses, page numbers, or years.

Commas with addresses

When writing an address, place a comma between a city (or county) and state.

Baltimore, Maryland   Baltimore County, Maryland

Place no comma between a state and zip code.

Baltimore, Maryland 21215

When writing an address into a sentence, use commas to set off elements that would otherwise be placed on separate lines of the address. Set off the name of a state with a comma if no zip code follows it.

Mr. Abe Stein, Senior Engineer
Stein Engineering
1243 Slade Avenue
Bedford, Massachusetts 01730

The control boards were shipped to Mr. Abe Stein, Senior Engineer, Stein Engineering, 1243 Slade Avenue, Bedford, Massachusetts 01730.

The office in Bedford, Massachusetts, was not easy to find.

▶**8 Use commas to prevent misreading.**

Confusing   To get through a tunnel will need to be dug.

Revised   To get through, a tunnel will need to be dug.

Although no rule calls for it, a comma may be needed to prevent misreading. Misreading can occur when numbers are placed together.

Confusing   Down by twenty six members of the squad suddenly woke up.

Revised   Down by twenty, six members of the squad suddenly woke up.

Misreading can occur when words that are often used as auxiliary verbs (e.g., *will, should,* forms of *be, do*) function as main verbs and occur before other verbs.

Confusing   Those who do know exactly what must be done.

Revised   Those who do, know exactly what must be done.

Conventions of Quoting, Naming, and Various Forms of Separation

Misreading can occur when a word that functions both as a preposition and as a modifier (e.g., *after, before, along, around, beneath, through*) is used as a modifier and is followed by a noun.

Confusing	Moments after the room began to tilt.
Revised	Moments after, the room began to tilt.

Misreading can occur when identical words are placed together.

Confusing	To speak speak into the microphone and press the button.
Revised	To speak, speak into the microphone and press the button.

▶ **EXERCISE 5**

Decide whether commas are needed to clarify meaning in these sentences. Then make up three sentences of your own in which adding a comma will prevent misreading.

1. If you can come join us.
2. The doctor dressed and performed an emergency appendectomy.
3. The doctor dressed and sutured the wound.
4. From beneath the supports began to weaken.
5. By twos twenty children walked down the aisle.

▶ **25f** Editing to avoid misuse or overuse of commas

▶**1** Eliminate the comma splice.

Confusing	She climbed the ladder, she slid down the slide.
Revised	She climbed the ladder. She slid down the slide.
	She climbed the ladder, **and** she slid down the slide.

The most frequent comma blunder, the **comma splice,** occurs when a writer joins independent clauses with a comma.

Faulty	Christopher Columbus is considered a master navigator today, he died in neglect.

To revise a comma splice, see the following box and Chapter 13.

Four Ways to Avoid Comma Splices

1. Separate the two clauses with a period.
   Christopher Columbus is considered a master navigator today. He died in neglect.
2. Join the two clauses with a coordinating conjunction and a comma.
   Christopher Columbus is considered a master navigator today, but he died in neglect.

3. Join the two clauses with a conjunctive adverb and the appropriate punctuation.

Christopher Columbus is considered a master navigator today; nevertheless, he died in neglect.

4. Join the two clauses by making one subordinate to the other.

Although Christopher Columbus is considered a master navigator today, he died in neglect.

2 Eliminate commas misused to set off essential (restrictive) elements.

Confusing   Athletes, who use steroids, invite disaster. [The sense is that *all* athletes use steroids, which is not true.]

Revised   Athletes who use steroids invite disaster. [Only those athletes who use steroids invite disaster.]

As noted in 25d-1, commas are not used with essential elements. The presence of commas can alter the meaning of otherwise identical sentences. Therefore, be sure of your meaning as you decide to punctuate (or not) a modifying element.

Essential   The students who signed the petition are eligible. [The *who* clause is essential and restricts the meaning of students to those who signed the petition.]

Nonessential   The students, who signed the petition, are eligible. [The presence of commas signals that the *who* clause is nonessential. The sense of the sentence is that *all* the students signed the petition and are eligible.]

3 Eliminate commas that are misused in a series.

Confusing   For tomorrow, memorize the poem, and the song.

Revised   For tomorrow, memorize the poem and the song.

A comma is not placed before a coordinating conjunction if it connects only two elements in a series.

Faulty   You cannot learn much about prices, and the amount of goods traded from demand curves alone.

Revised   You cannot learn much about prices and the amount of goods traded from demand curves alone.

A comma is *not* used after a second coordinate adjective.

Faulty   One reason individuals engage in various efforts at self-improvement is that they can imagine alternate, improved, selves.

Revised   One reason individuals engage in various efforts at self-improvement is that they can imagine alternate, improved selves.

A comma is not placed before the first item in a series or after the last item, unless the comma is required because of a specific rule.

Editing to Avoid Misuse or Overuse of Commas   **409**

Faulty   A Central Processing Unit (CPU) is designed with a fixed repertoire of instructions for carrying out a range of tests involving, data manipulation, logical decision making, and control of the computer. [The comma should be eliminated before the first item in this series.]

Revised   A Central Processing Unit (CPU) is designed with a fixed repertoire of instructions for carrying out a range of tests involving data manipulation, logical decision making, and control of the computer.

▶4 Eliminate commas that split paired sentence elements.

Confusing   The police assisted, the emergency crew.

Revised   The police assisted the emergency crew.

A comma is not placed between a subject and verb—even if the subject is lengthy.

Faulty   What has sometimes been dramatically termed "the clash of civilizations," is merely the difference in the interpretation given by different societies to the same acts. [The noun clause subject should not be split from its verb *is*.]

Revised   What has sometimes been dramatically termed "the clash of civilizations" is merely the difference in the interpretation given by different societies to the same acts.

A comma is not placed between a verb and its object or complement, nor between a preposition and its object.

Faulty   One culture may organize, its social relations around rites of physical initiation. [The comma should not come between the verb and its object.]

Revised   One culture may organize its social relations around rites of physical initiation.

Faulty   The principle of mutual respect among, neighboring peoples requires flexibility and tolerance. [The comma should not come between the preposition and its object.]

Revised   The principle of mutual respect among neighboring peoples requires flexibility and tolerance.

▶5 Eliminate misuse of commas with quotations.

Confusing   "Is anyone home?," he asked.

Revised   "Is anyone home?" he asked.

A comma is not used after a quotation that ends with a question mark or an exclamation point.

Faulty   "Get out!," cried the shopkeeper.
Revised   "Get out!" cried the shopkeeper.

Faulty   "Is this the way home?," asked Arthur.
Revised   "Is this the way home?" asked Arthur.

A comma is not used to set apart words quoted (or italicized) for emphasis.

Faulty   The list of, "exemplary," citizens the Governor referred to includes two convicted felons.

Revised   The list of "exemplary" citizens the Governor referred to includes two convicted felons.

▶ **EXERCISE 6**

Supply the commas for this dialogue between a young child and her nurse, adapted from Amy Tan's *The Joy Luck Club*.

I tugged Amah's sleeve and asked "Who is the Moon Lady?"
"Chang-o" replied Amah "who lives on the moon and today is the only day you can see her and have a secret wish fulfilled."
"What is a secret wish?" I asked her.
"It is what you want but cannot ask" said Amah.
"Then how will the Moon Lady know my wish?" I wanted to know.
"Because she is not an ordinary person" Amah explained.

EXERCISE 7

Correct the misuse of commas in the sentences that follow (from a parody of an anthropological study). Place a check before the sentences in which commas are used correctly.

Example: The daily body ritual, performed by the Nacirema people includes a mouth-rite.

The daily body ritual performed by the Nacirema people includes a mouth-rite.

1. Despite the fact that these people are so punctilious about the care of the mouth, this rite involves, a practice which strikes the uninitiated stranger as revolting.
2. It was reported to me that the ritual consists of inserting a small bundle of hog hairs into the mouth, along with certain magical powders, and then moving the bundle in a highly formalized series of gestures.
3. In addition to the private mouth-rite, the people seek out a holy-mouth-man once, or twice a year.
4. These practitioners have an impressive set of paraphernalia, consisting of a variety of, augers, awls, probes, and prods.
5. The use of these objects in the exorcism of the evils of the mouth involves, almost unbelievable ritual torture of the client.
6. The holy-mouth-man opens the client's mouth and using the above-mentioned tools enlarges any holes which decay may have created in the teeth.
7. Magical materials are put into, these holes.
8. If there are no naturally occurring holes in the teeth, large sections of one or more teeth are gouged out so that the supernatural substance, can be applied.
9. In the client's view, the purpose of these ministrations is to arrest decay, and to draw friends.

10. The extremely sacred and traditional character of the rite is evident in the fact that the natives return to the holy-mouth-men year after year, despite the fact that their teeth continue to decay.

EXERCISE 8

Correct the misuse of commas in the following paragraph. In making your corrections, you may need to add or delete words. You should feel free to combine sentences.

> *Example:* The humidity level which was extremely high made the air feel as if it were 117 degrees.
>
> The humidity level, which was extremely high, made the air feel as if it were 117 degrees.

It's no illusion that the earth has been getting hotter lately. For example the 1980s witnessed the hottest years since meteorological records began to be kept in the nineteenth century, in fact, the 1990s which so far have been a continuation of the same trend promise to remain just as warm and maybe even warmer. As one scientific observer put it "Planet Earth is running a fever." The killer heat wave, that claimed 566 lives in Chicago in July 1995, could have been a freak event but climatologists don't think so. They fear that the big heat wave of 1995 is actually a harbinger of more serious weather disturbances to come.

CHAPTER 26

Semicolons

The main function of a **semicolon** is to separate elements. As its name suggests, the semicolon serves to make only a "semi" or partial separation that maintains a relationship between independent elements. In its primary use, a semicolon can mark the end of one complete statement and the beginning of another. So can a period or a comma with a coordinating conjunction, of course. But whereas a period is chosen to make a full stop, a semicolon denotes a writer's decision to make a partial break. This chapter shows you the situations in which such a partial break is appropriate and gives you the tools for making such decisions as you write or revise your sentences.

http://www.csc.calpoly.edu/ ~ebrunner/GrammatiCat/Punctuate/ SemiColon.html
The semicolon: sophisticated punctuation. Contains a section called "Inspiration" with a number of samples of exemplary uses of the semicolon by professional writers.

> **26a** **Use a semicolon, not a comma, to join independent clauses that are intended to be closely related.**

Secretariat won the race; Lucky Stars finished second.

Joining independent clauses with a semicolon is one of four basic ways to establish a relationship between clauses, ranging from full separation to subordination of one clause to another. (See the Critical Decisions box on page 415.) Never use a comma to join independent clauses. (See Chapter 13 on comma splices.)

Faulty In 1852 Mt. Everest was definitively identified as the highest mountain in the world, shortly thereafter it was named in honor of Sir George Everest, an early British Survey General of India.

Revised In 1852 Mt. Everest was definitively identified as the highest mountain in the world; shortly thereafter it was named in honor of Sir George Everest, an early British Survey General of India.

Use semicolons to join closely related independent clauses, not to string unconnected statements together.

Semicolons can be overused. By themselves, they are not enough to make close connections from a series of statements that are simply added together.

Overused	In 1852 Mt. Everest was definitively identified as the highest mountain in the world; at the time it was believed to be 29,002 feet; we now know that its actual altitude is 29,028 feet.
Revised	Mt. Everest, definitively identified in 1852 as the highest mountain in the world, was believed at the time to be 29,002 feet; we now know that its actual altitude is 29,028 feet.

> ## 26b Use a semicolon, not a comma, to join two independent clauses that are closely linked by a conjunctive adverb.

I had planned to call London; however, the circuits were busy.
Eric arrived late the first day; thereafter, he was on time.

A conjunctive adverb is often used to establish a close connection between independent clauses. (See 19a and the Critical Decisions box on page 415.) With conjunctive adverbs, use a semicolon (or a period) between the clauses, never a comma. (Refer to Chapter 13.)

Faulty	Historical researchers cannot control the events they want to recreate, indeed, they often cannot find enough documentation to learn all the facts of an occurrence. [The comma after *recreate* makes a comma splice; a comma cannot be used to join independent clauses.]
Revised	Historical researchers cannot control the events they want to recreate; indeed, they often cannot find enough documentation to learn all the facts of an occurrence. [Here the conjunctive adverb creates a very close link between clauses.]

Note: When independent clauses are closely connected with a conjunctive adverb, the semicolon always falls between the clauses, no matter where the conjunctive adverb is located.

Option	If chlorophyll is extracted from plant cells and exposed to light, it does momentarily absorb light energy; *however,* this energy is almost immediately reradiated as light.
Option	If chlorophyll is extracted from plant cells and exposed to light, it does momentarily absorb light energy; this energy is almost immediately reradiated as light, *however.* [The semicolon falls between the independent clauses, even if the adverb is moved to the end of the sentence.]

Note: The use of a conjunctive adverb does not necessarily mean that there must be a semicolon between clauses. If you feel that the business of the first clause is finished, or that you do not need a sense of anticipation for the next clause, you can always make a full break between clauses with a period.

Option	If chlorophyll is extracted from plant cells and exposed to light, it does momentarily absorb light energy. This energy, however, is almost immediately reradiated as light, usually of a different wavelength. [Here the writer intends for the period to mark a sharp boundary between clauses.]

CRITICAL DECISIONS

Challenge and be challenged: Using a period to separate sentences versus a semicolon or comma (with a conjunction) to link sentences

As a writer, you can use punctuation to communicate degrees of linkage between sentences. In making decisions, pose these questions.

Why separate sentences with a period?

Use a period to show a full separation between sentences.

> Dante Alighieri was banished from Florence in 1302. He wrote the *Divine Comedy* in exile.

Why link sentences with a semicolon?

Use a semicolon, alone, to join sentences balanced in content and structure. Also use a semicolon to suggest that the second sentence completes the content of the first. The semicolon suggests a link but leaves it to the reader to infer how sentences are related.

Balanced sentence   Agriculture is one part of the biological revolution; the domestication of animals is the other.

Suggested link   Five major books and many articles have been written on the Bayeux tapestry; each shows just how much the trained observer can draw from pictorial evidence.

Why link sentences with a conjunctive adverb and a semicolon or period?

Use a semicolon with a conjunctive adverb (*however, therefore*, etc.) to emphasize one of the following relationships: addition, consequence, contrast, cause and effect, time, emphasis, or condition. With the semicolon and conjunctive adverb, linkage between sentences is closer than with a semicolon alone. The relationship between sentences is made clear by the conjunctive adverb.

> Patients in need of organs have begun advertising for them; **however,** the American Medical Association discourages the practice.

Use a period between sentences to force a pause and then to stress the conjunctive adverb.

> Patients in need of organs have begun advertising for them. **However,** the American Medical Association discourages the practice.

Why link sentences with a comma and a coordinating conjunction?

Use a comma and a coordinating conjunction to join sentences in a coordinate relationship that shows addition, choice, consequence, contrast, or cause (see 19a). Since two sentences are fully merged into one following this strategy, linkage is complete.

> Robotics has increased efficiency in the automobile industry, **but** it has put thousands of assembly-line employees out of work.

26c
Join independent clauses with a semicolon before a coordinating conjunction when one or both clauses contain a comma or other internal punctuation.

After the Shuttle landed, Perkins tried calling the President; but he didn't get through.

Short or uncomplicated independent clauses joined by coordinating conjunctions do not normally use a semicolon. However, internal commas or complicated subordinations within one of the independent clauses can create confusion and misreading; in such cases the clauses need stronger separation with a semicolon before the coordinating conjunction.

Agnosognosia, a normally temporary condition that often afflicts right-hemisphere stroke victims, manifests itself as the patient's denial of the physical existence of the paralyzed limb; and it is for this reason that neuroscientists are studying agnosognosia for clues about how the brain constructs reality.

26d
Use a semicolon to separate items in a series when each item is long or when one or more items contain a comma.

I sent the letters to Baltimore, Maryland; Portland, Oregon; and Dallas, Texas.

Short or uncomplicated items in a series are normally separated only by commas (see Chapter 25). However, when the units to be separated are further subdivided with internal punctuation or are made up of complex clauses, it is necessary to provide stronger separation with a semicolon.

One neuroscientist, Vilayanur Ramachandran, is particularly interested in the functions and malfunctions of the brain and has investigated the neural wiring of vision; the riddle of agnosognosia; and, through research into the "phantom limb" phenomenon experienced by amputees, the ways in which the brain reconfigures itself during learning.

26e
Place semicolons *outside* of end quotation marks.

We read "Ode to the West Wind"; we then discussed the poem in detail.

A semicolon that separates independent clauses and other major elements is not part of a direct quotation.

One neurologist remarks that "we are used to thinking of our bodies as our selves"; in other words, unlike agnosogniacs, we "own" our body parts and have no trouble with expressing that ownership.

26f Edit to avoid common errors.

I Use a comma, not a semicolon, after an introductory subordinate clause.

Use semicolons to link independent clauses; never use them to link subordinate to independent clauses (see Chapter 19).

Faulty When a writer begins a new project; the blank page can present a barrier.

Revised When a writer begins a new project, the blank page can present a barrier.

2 Use a colon, not a semicolon, to introduce a list.

Faulty The writing process consists of three stages; planning, drafting, and revision.

Revised The writing process consists of three stages: planning, drafting, and revision.

EXERCISE I

Join the following pairs of sentences with a semicolon, with a semicolon and conjunctive adverb, or with a period and conjunctive adverb. Explain your decision.

> *Example:* Politics and social realism have not been the hallmarks of the film industry in Hollywood.
>
> Yet there was a time when liberal, conservative, and radical organizations made films for a mass audience aimed at politicizing millions of viewers.
>
> Politics and social realism have not been the hallmarks of the film industry in Hollywood; yet there was a time when liberal, conservative, and radical organizations made films for a mass audience aimed at politicizing millions of viewers.

The sentences are closely enough related in meaning to warrant their being joined into a single, compound sentence. For this reason, the semicolon is appropriate. The conjunction *yet* is kept to establish the contrasting relationship between clauses. Without the conjunction this relationship might not be obvious to a reader.

1. During the early years of the twentieth century, leisure assumed an increasingly important role in everyday life.
   Amusement parks, professional baseball games, nickelodeons, and dance halls attracted a wide array of people anxious to spend their hard-earned cash.
2. Of all these new cultural endeavors, films were the most important.
   Even the poorest worker could afford to take his family to the local movie theater.
3. Cinemas took root in urban working-class and immigrant neighborhoods.
   They then spread to middle-class districts of cities and into small communities throughout the country.

4. As early as 1910 the appeal of movies was so great that nearly one-third of the nation flocked to the cinema each week.

Ten years later, weekly attendance equaled fifty percent of the nation's population.

5. As is true today, early films were primarily aimed at entertaining audiences.

But then, entertainment did not always come in the form of escapist fantasies.

6. Many of the issues that dominated Progressive-era politics were portrayed on the screen.

While most of these films were produced by studios and independent companies, a significant number were made by what we might call today "special-interest groups."

7. The modest cost of making one- or two-reel films allowed many organizations to make movies to advance their causes.

Moreover, exhibitors' need to fill their daily bills with new films meant these films would be seen by millions.

EXERCISE 2

In very long sentences semicolons are used in place of commas to prevent misreading. Combine, repunctuate, or otherwise revise the following sentences by using semicolons.

Example: The traditional view of the diffusion of Indo-European languages over wide areas holds that as nomadic mounted warriors conquered indigenous peoples, they imposed their own proto-Indo-European language, *which,* in turn, evolved in local areas into the various languages we know today.

But many scholars have become dissatisfied with this explanation.

The traditional view of the diffusion of Indo-European languages over wide areas holds that as nomadic mounted warriors conquered indigenous peoples, they imposed their own proto-Indo-European language; *this language,* in turn, evolved in local areas into the various languages we know today. But many scholars have become dissatisfied with this explanation.

1. Linguists divide the languages of Europe into families: the Romance languages include French, Italian, Spanish, Portuguese, and Romanian.

The Slavonic languages include Russian, Polish, Czech, Slovak, Serbo-Croat, and Bulgarian. The Germanic languages include German, Norwegian, Danish, and Swedish.

2. Many archaeologists accept a theory of "Kurgan invasions" as an explanation of the spread of Indo-European languages.

But others dispute it because the archaeological evidence is not convincing, the core words, which resemble each other from place to place, may have changed meaning over time, and the hordes of mounted warriors would have had no obvious reason for moving west at the end of the Neolithic period.

3. There are four models of how language change might occur according to a process-based view: initial colonization, by which an uninhabited territory becomes populated, linguistic divergence arising from separation or isolation, which some think explains the development of the Romance languages in Europe, linguistic convergence, whereby languages initially quite different become increasingly similar to each other, and, finally, linguistic replacement, whereby indigenous languages are gradually replaced by the language of people coming from the outside.

EXERCISE 3

Correct the misuse of semicolons and, if necessary, the wording in the following sentences. Place a check by any sentence in which a semicolon is used correctly.

> *Example:* Until the period of the Enlightenment, most Christians believed that an entity called the Devil existed; that he was not just a metaphor for evil but rather was evil incarnate.
>
> Until the period of the Enlightenment, most Christians believed that an entity called the Devil existed **and** that he was not just a metaphor for evil but rather was evil incarnate.

1. Some sociologists have argued that belief in a literal devil is a matter of social class; a Princeton professor explains: "If you see Cadillacs in the church parking lot, you won't hear Satan preached inside;" but "if you see a lot of pickup trucks, you will."

2. Late twentieth-century American culture; however, is by and large devoid of a sense of an actual Devil.

3. Our preference is to explain the existence of evil in scientific or pseudo-scientific terms; serial murderers, terrorists, and bloodthirsty dictators are explained as psychopaths or sociopaths; evil is not perceived as punishment for our sins but rather as arbitrary and meaningless.

4. One cultural critic regards this loss of a sense of pure, radical evil as regrettable, he sees the disappearance of Satan as a "tragedy of the imagination."

CHAPTER 27

Apostrophes

The **apostrophe** (') is used to show possession, mark the omission of letters or numbers, and mark plural forms. In speech, keeping these matters straight poses no problem. In writing, however, the three uses of the apostrophe very nearly overlap with certain words, creating confusion for the reader. This chapter provides guidelines that will help you to make informed decisions about apostrophe use.

http://www.ex.ac.uk/~SEGLea/psy6002/
apostrophes.html
A one-page guide to the English apostrophe, claiming that "No one born since about 1950 seems to be able to use the apostrophe correctly."

▶27a Using apostrophes to show possession with single nouns

▶1 For most nouns and for indefinite pronouns, add an apostrophe and the letter *s* to indicate possession.

Bill**'s** braces	the government**'s** solution
history**'s** verdict	somebody**'s** cat
Susan**'s** basketball	everyone**'s** business

For singular nouns ending with the letter *s*, *show possession by adding an apostrophe and s* if this new construction is not difficult to pronounce.

Ellis**'s** Diner   hostess**'s** menu   Orson Welles**'s** movie

Note: The possessive construction formed with *'s* may be difficult to read if it is followed by a word beginning with an *s* or *z* sound. If this is the case, you have the option of dropping the *s* after the apostrophe.

Acceptable   Ellis**'** zipper   *or*   Ellis**'s** zipper

Whichever convention you adopt, be consistent.

▶2 Eliminate apostrophes that are misused or confused with possessive pronouns.

Personal pronouns have their own possessive case forms (see Chapter 8); they *never* use apostrophes to show possession.

Possession with Personal Pronouns

its	the book's binding	*its* binding
whose	Who owns the book?	*Whose* book is this?
your	the book owned by you	*your* book
yours	the book owned by you	The book is *yours*.
their	a book owned by Bob and Sue	*their* book
theirs	a book owned by Bob and Sue	The book is *theirs*.
her	a book owned by Sue	*her* book
hers	a book owned by Sue	The book is *hers*.
our	a book owned by us	*our* book
ours	a book owned by us	The book is *ours*.
his	a book owned by Bob	*his* book
his	a book owned by Bob	The book is *his*.

Distinguish personal pronouns in their possessive form from personal pronouns that are contractions.

For readers, the most annoying possible mixup with apostrophes occurs when personal pronouns meant to show possession are confused with personal pronouns that are contractions formed with the verb *be*, as shown here. (See the guidelines for making contractions in 27c.)

 http://www.bus.orst.edu/tools/Writing/apostrop.htm
A page on the "rogue apostrophe," an apostrophe that appears where it doesn't belong.

Personal Pronouns: Contractions Formed with Be

it's	*It is* doubtful he'll arrive.	*It's* doubtful he'll arrive.
who's	*Who is* planning to attend?	*Who's* planning to attend?
you're	*You are* mistaken.	*You're* mistaken.
there's	*There is* little to do.	*There's* little to do.
they're	*They are* home.	*They're* home.

Edit to eliminate apostrophes from personal pronouns that are meant to show possession, not contraction.

Faulty   You're order has arrived.

Revised   Your order has arrived.

▶3 For a plural noun ending with s, add only an apostrophe to indicate possession. For a plural noun not ending with s, add an apostrophe and the letter s.

bricklayers**'** union	teachers**'** strike
dancers**'** rehearsal	men**'s** locker
children**'s** games	cattle**'s** watering hole

▶ EXERCISE I

Read the following sentences. As needed, use an apostrophe or an apostrophe and the letter *s* to make possessive each noun or pronoun in parentheses.

Example: With Windows 98, even the simple task of switching your computer off is serious business—you have to follow the (System) commands for shutdown.

With Windows 98, even the simple task of switching your computer off is serious business—you have to follow the System**'s** commands for shutdown.

1. In fact, you can't hit that off switch until Windows 98 tells you that (its) safe to do so.
2. If you make it a habit to close each window once you've finished with it, you'll find that (you're) work space is maximized.
3. The (Welcome window) function is to provide you with a new Windows 98 tip each time you start a new session.
4. In Windows 98, a (file name) length can be as long as you want to make it.
5. Older (systems) file names had to be kept to an 8-character length (with a 3-character extension).
6. That long file name option sounds like a real advantage until you realize that if the particular program you are using still follows the 8-character rule, your (files) names are not going to be any longer; Windows 98 can't override your program.
7. On the other hand, the 8-character parameter challenges the (user) creativity—how else would you end up with a file name like "taxoops," a file that is actually a letter to the Internal Revenue Service.
8. Software developers, canny souls that they are, know that Windows 98 is not the cure-all for all computer ills and that awful things—like crashes—are still going to happen; (CyberMedia) software package, *First Aid for Windows*, promises to doctor your ailing system.
9. *(First Aid for Windows)* packaging even features the familiar Red Cross logo.
10. With PC healthcare systems readily available, the "DUMMIES" user need worry no more about a (device-driver) incompatibility.
11. The user doesn't have to wait for what seems like hours, waiting for the technical support (staff) advice.

▶ 27b   Using apostrophes to show possession with multiple nouns

Multiple nouns showing possession can be tricky to punctuate, since the apostrophe and the letter *s* will indicate who—and how many people—own what, either separately or together. Because establishing possession is so important (especially in our culture), take care when using the apostrophe with multiple nouns. Punctuate so that your sentences express your exact meaning.

 To indicate possession when a cluster of words functions as a single noun, add an apostrophe and the letter *s* to the last word.

Executive Vice President**'s** role	Chief Executive Officer**'s** salary
brother-in-law**'s** car	Acting Superintendent**'s** car

Apostrophes

CRITICAL DECISIONS

Be alert to differences: Testing your placement of apostrophes with nouns and with indefinite pronouns

The personal pronouns *his, hers, ours, its, yours,* and *theirs* **never** use apostrophes. By contrast, nouns and indefinite pronouns (such as *somebody, other,* and *no one*) do use apostrophes to show possession. Nouns and indefinite pronouns also form plurals with the suffix *-s.* Apply the following tests to determine whether or not you should be using an apostrophe and *s* (*'s*) or the suffix *-s,* with no apostrophe.

Is the noun or indefinite pronoun followed by a noun? If so, then you probably intend to show possession. Use the possessive form *'s.*

noun
government*'s* <u>policy</u>

noun
family*'s* <u>holiday</u>

noun
hospital*'s* <u>program</u>

noun
other*'s* <u>comment</u>

Is a noun or indefinite pronoun followed by a verb or a modifying phrase or clause? If so, then you probably intend to make the noun or indefinite pronoun plural. Use the suffix *-s,* with *no* apostrophe.

modifying phrase
government*s* <u>in that part of the world</u>

modifying phrase
famil*ies* <u>having two or more children</u>

modifying clause
hospital*s* <u>that have large staffs</u>

verb
other*s* <u>believe</u>

But if an omitted word is involved, you may need a possessive form.

Eric's friends attend Central High. Frank*'s* attend Northern.

[In the second sentence, the omitted noun *friends* is clearly intended as the subject of the sentence. The *'s* is needed to show whose friends—*Frank's.*]

▶2 **To indicate possession of an object owned jointly, add an apostrophe and the letter *s* to the last noun (or pronoun) named.**

Smith and Thompson**'s** interview notes are meticulous. [The notes belong jointly to, they were gathered jointly by, Smith and Thompson.]
Mary and Bill**'s** car needs a muffler. [The car belongs jointly to Mary and Bill.]

▶3 **To indicate individual possession by two or more people, add an apostrophe and the letter *s* to each person named.**

Judy**'s** and Rob**'s** interview notes are meticulous. [The reference is to two sets of notes, one belonging to Judy and the other to Rob.]

Using Apostrophes to Show Possession with Multiple Nouns **423**

▶ **27c** **Using apostrophes in contractions to mark the omission of letters and numbers**

When you join or compress words into a contraction, you omit letters to indicate a more rapid, informal pace of pronunciation. The omission *must* be marked in writing with an apostrophe. Similarly, when you omit numbers in a date, use an apostrophe. Because many readers consider contractions an informality, you may want to avoid using them in academic writing. When in doubt about the appropriateness of contractions and the register they indicate in a particular document, check with the professor who will be reading your work.

▶**I** **Use an apostrophe to indicate the omission of letters in a contraction.**

can't = can not   won't = will not   you've = you have

▶**2** **Use an apostrophe to indicate the omission of numbers in a date.**

the '60s   the '80s   the '90s

▶**3** **Eliminate apostrophes from verbs in their -s form.**

The -*s* ending used in regular verb formation does *not* involve the omission of any letters (see 9a). Any apostrophe that creeps into such verb endings should be eliminated.

Faulty   He walk's with a limp.   A cat eat's mice.
Revised He wal**ks** with a limp.   A cat ea**ts** mice.

▶ **EXERCISE 2**

Correct the use of apostrophes in the following sentences by adding or deleting apostrophes as needed. Place a check by the sentences in which apostrophes are used correctly.

> *Example:* Rough weather sailing can be exciting, but only if you're crew is well prepared for it.
>
> Rough weather sailing can be exciting, but only if your crew is well prepared for it.

1. Bad weather inevitably puts you're crew's lives in danger.
2. Obviously their likely to be wetter and colder; foul weather gear should be available and distributed *before* the first splash lands in the cockpit.
3. Its equally important to take precautions to prevent risk of injury to limbs and body.
4. Those who normally lead a sedentary life are much more liable to injuries than those whose muscles are well exercised to withstand rubs, bumps, and twists.
5. Inadequate footwear, or none at all if you're feet are not hardened to such treatment, can lead to real pain if a toe is stubbed against a deck bolt or stanchion.

6. Make sure you have a working man-overboard pole—you're attention to safety could save someone's life.

7. Bad weather is particularly tiring and can result in seasickness; keep a watch to see whose becoming sick.

8. Seasickness and exhaustion combined can lead to a state of not caring what happens next to your boat and crew.

9. An exhausted sailor huddled in a wave- and windswept cockpit, peering into the murk, can easily come to see Poseidon, whose lashing the waves to fury out of spite.

10. Perhaps the easiest precaution to avoid problems in raw weather is to bring a crew whose not afraid of the tense environment faced while sailing in rough seas.

▶ 27d   Using apostrophes to mark plural forms

As readers, we expect the letter *s* or letters *es* placed at the end of a word to show that the word is plural. Yet if we were to follow that convention with letters or symbols, we would quickly create a puzzle of pronunciation: *How many les in Lilliputian?* We avoid the confusion by adopting a different convention to form the plurals of letters, symbols, and so on.

▶ **1 Use an apostrophe and the letter *s* to indicate the plural of a letter, number, or word referred to as a word.**

The letter, number, or word made plural should be underlined if typewritten or set in italics if typeset. Do *not* underline or italicize the apostrophe or the letter *s*.

Standard for Typewriter Usage

Mind your p's and q's.

How many 5's in sixty?

The frequent in's and with's reduced the effectiveness of his presentation.

Standard for Typeset Usage
Mind your *p*'s and *q*'s.
How many *5*'s in sixty?
The frequent *in*'s and *with*'s reduced the effectiveness of his presentation.

Exception: When forming the plural of a proper noun (e.g., someone's name), omit the apostrophe but retain the letter *s*.

Standard for Typewriter Usage

At the convention I met three Franks and two Maudes.

Using Apostrophes to Mark Plural Forms   **425**

Standard for Typeset Usage
At the convention I met three *Frank***s** and two *Maude***s**.

Using an apostrophe in this case would mistakenly suggest possession and thus confuse a reader.

▶**2 Use an apostrophe and the letter *s* to indicate the plural of a symbol, an abbreviation with periods, and years expressed in decades.**

Do *not* underline or italicize the symbol, the abbreviation, or the decade.

Joel is too fond of using &**'s** in his writing.

With all the M.D.**'s** at this conference, I feel safe.

Computer-assisted software engineering will be important in the 1990**'s**.

Option: Some writers omit the apostrophe before the letter *s* when forming the plural of decades, abbreviations without periods, and symbols.

1900**s**   or   1900**'s**

IBM**s**   or   IBM**'s**

%**s**   or   %**'s**

Whichever convention you adopt, be consistent.

▶**3 Eliminate any apostrophes misused to form regular plurals of nouns.**

For a regular noun, an apostrophe is never used to create a plural form; rather, the apostrophe indicates possession (see 7a-2).

Possessive   the cat**'s** meow   that idea**'s** beginning

Faulty plural   Cat**'s** eat meat.   Idea**'s** begin in thought.

Revised plural   Cat**s** eat.   Idea**s** begin.

▶ **EXERCISE 3**

Follow the instructions in parentheses after each sentence to clarify possession.

> *Example:* The *governor office personnel* have formed some close friendships. (Use apostrophes to indicate that the people who have become friends work in the office of the governor.)
>
> The governor's office personnel have formed some close friendships.

1. Isabelle Locke works at the State House as the *governor Press Secretary*. (Use apostrophes to indicate that the Press Secretary for the governor is Isabelle Locke.)

2. *Mrs. Locke and her husband Ted house* is replete with pictures of government officials posing with the Locke family. (Use apostrophes to indicate that Mrs. Locke and Ted own their house together.)

3. The governor lives around the corner, in the *Governor Mansion*. (Use apostrophes to indicate that the governor lives in the mansion.)

4. *Isabelle Locke and the governor homes* are decorated similarly, both in a colonial style. (Use apostrophes to indicate that two different homes are being referred to.)

5. Often they'll have dinner together, cooked by *Isabelle and the governor husbands*. (Use apostrophes to indicate that the two husbands cook together.)

EXERCISE 4

Decide whether an apostrophe is needed to form plurals for the following letters, numbers, or words.

Example: b

b's (or *b*'s if typeset)

1.   2. 42   3. 7   4. j   5. d   6. Karen

EXERCISE 5

Read the following paragraph about Donald Duck. Provide apostrophes and rewrite words as needed.

Theirs one basic product never stocked in Disneys store: parents. Disneys is a universe of uncles and grand-uncles, nephews and cousins. The male-female relationships existence is found only in eternal fiancés. Donald Duck and Daisy relationship, like Mickey Mouse and Minnie relationship, is never consummated or even legitimized through the all-American institution of marriage. More troubling, though, is the origin of all of the nephews and uncles in the Disney Comics worlds. Huey, Dewey, and Louie Uncle Donald is never known to have a sister or sister-in-law. In fact, most of Donald relatives are unmarried and unattached males, like Scrooge McDuck. Donalds own parents are never mentioned, although Grandma Duck purports to be the widowed ancestor of the Duck family (again no husband-wife relationship). Donald and Mickey girlfriends, Daisy and Minnie, are often accompanied by nieces of their own. Since these women are not very susceptible to men or matrimonial bonds, Disneys "families" are necessarily and perpetually composed of bachelors accompanied by nephews, who come and go. A quick look at Walt Disneys own biography demonstrates a possible reason for his comics anti-love, anti-marriage sentiments: Disneys mother is rarely mentioned, and his wifes role in his life was minimal at best. As for the future of the Magic Kingdoms demographic increases, it is predictable that they will be the result of extrasexual factors.

28

Quotation Marks

Quoting the words of others is a necessary, essential fact of academic life, both for professors and for students. For the sake of both accuracy and fairness, your quotations must be managed precisely. (See 35f on quoting sources in research.) If you quote to help make a point, you must do so accurately since readers count on you for a faithful transcription of what another has written. (See Chapter 37 for conventions on citing sources in various disciplines.) This chapter will discuss the conventions for quoting. See 35f-4 for advice on smoothly incorporating quoted language into your work.

▶ 28a   Quoting prose

▶ 1   **Use double quotation marks (" ") to set off a short direct quotation from the rest of a sentence.**

Short quotations—those that span four or fewer lines of your manuscript—may be incorporated into your writing by running them in with your sentences as part of your normal paragraphing. When quoting a

http://owl.english.purdue.edu/Files/14.html
A page on quotation marks, from the Purdue University Online Writing Lab.

source, reproduce exactly the wording and punctuation of the quoted material. For the most part, when you enclose the material in quotation marks, you will do so to indicate **direct discourse,** the exact re-creation of words spoken or written by another person. Direct discourse places another person's language directly before readers as if you (the writer) were not present.

Direct   According to Bernadine Healy, Director of the National Institutes of Health, "By the year 2000, women and minorities will account for 68 percent of the new workers."

Eric asked, "Can I borrow the car?"

Indirect discourse occurs when you quote the words of someone inexactly, and from a distance.

Indirect   Eric asked if he could borrow the car.

Indirect discourse inserts your voice into the quotation. You mediate the quotation, or create the frame through which your readers perceive it.

Altering a quotation: **Quotation marks** denote the *exact* reproduction of words written or spoken by someone else. Changes that you make to quoted material (such as words omitted or added) must be announced as such—either with brackets or ellipses (see 29d and e).

▶**2** Use single quotation marks (' ') to set off quoted material or the titles of short works within a quotation enclosed by double (" ") marks.

The use of single quotation marks can be shown by a comparison of original passages with quotations.

Original passages

> The "business" of school for first-grade students is to learn the distinction between intellectual play and playground play.

> In preparation for class next week, read the first two chapters of our "In Flight" manual.

Quotations

> As educator Monica Landau says, "The 'business' of school for first-grade students is to learn the distinction between intellectual play and playground play."

> The class coordinator said that for next week we should "read the first two chapters of our 'In Flight' manual."

If you find it necessary to quote material within single quotation marks, use double marks once again.

> Historian Beth Bailey cites popular magazines as one source of information. "In *Mademoiselle's* 1938 college issue," writes Bailey, "a Smith college senior advised incoming freshmen to 'cultivate an image of popularity' if they wanted dates. 'During your first term,' the senior wrote, 'get "home talent" to ply you with letters, invitations, and telegrams.' "

COMPUTER TIPS

Smart Quotes

Most word processors offer you a set of fancy typesetter's quotation marks and apostrophes. These smart quotes or curly quotes (" " and ' ') are different from the inch and foot marks (" and ') available on typewriters. For material that will ultimately be submitted in print, use the typesetter's quotes, which look more attractive on the page. However, if the material is to be e-mailed, or published on the World Wide Web, use the old-style typewriter marks, because the curly quotes use nonstandard characters that are interpreted differently by different computers. For example, if you type *a baker's dozen* in your e-mail message, it may appear on your reader's computer as *a bakerUs dozen*. Most good word-processing programs allow you to turn the curly quotes on or off, and some even allow you to convert the quotes in a piece of text from curly to typewriter style.

▶3 **Use commas to enclose explanatory remarks that lie outside the quotation.**

A comma is placed after an explanatory remark that introduces a quotation.

> According to Bailey, "Competition was the key term in the formula–remove it and there was no rating, dating, or popularity."

When a remark interrupts a quotation, a pair of commas or a comma and a period should be used. The conventions for punctuation are as follows: the first comma enclosing an explanatory remark notes the (temporary) ending of the quoted material and is placed inside the quotation. If the sentence continues past the explanatory comment, a second comma is placed before the quotation is reintroduced. If the sentence ends with an explanatory remark, a period is placed after that remark. In this case, when the quotation is resumed in a new sentence, the first letter of the quotation is capitalized.

> "Rating, dating, popularity, competition," writes Bailey, "were catch-words hammered home, reinforced from all sides until they seemed a natural vocabulary."

> "You had to rate in order to date, to date in order to rate," she adds. "By successfully maintaining the cycle, you became popular."

Note: When the word *that* introduces a direct quotation, or when an introductory remark has the sense of a "that" construction but the word itself is omitted, do not use a comma to separate the introduction from the quoted material. In addition, do not capitalize the first letter of the quotation.

Faulty   Bailey discovered that, "The Massachusetts *Collegian* (the Massachusetts State College student newspaper) ran an editorial against using the library for 'datemaking.' "

Revised   Bailey discovered that "the Massachusetts *Collegian* (the Massachusetts State College student newspaper) ran an editorial against using the library for 'datemaking.' "

▶4 **Display—that is, set off from text—lengthy quotations. Quotation marks are *not* used to enclose a displayed quotation.**

Quotations of five or more lines are too long to run in with sentences in a paragraph. Instead they are displayed in a block format in a narrower indentation, without being enclosed by quotation marks.

> In his remarks, Bill Bradley spoke on the impressive economic growth of East Asia:

> > East Asia is quickly becoming the richest, most populous, most dynamic area on earth. Over the last quarter century, the East Asian economies grew at an average real growth rate of 6 percent annually while the economies of the United States and the countries of the European Community grew at 3 percent. East Asia's share of gross world product has more than doubled during the last twenty years, rising from 8 percent to 20 percent.

Manuscript form

Double space the displayed quotation and indent ten spaces from the left margin. Punctuate material as in the original text. Quotation marks inside a displayed quotation remain double (" ") marks. If one paragraph is being displayed, do not indent the first word of the paragraph. If multiple paragraphs are being displayed, indent the first word of each paragraph three additional spaces (that is, thirteen spaces from the left). However, if you are quoting multiple paragraphs and the first sentence quoted does not begin a paragraph in the original source, then do not indent the first paragraph in your paper.

A displayed quotation is best introduced with a full sentence, ending with a colon. The colon provides a visual cue to the reader that a long quotation follows.

5 Place periods and commas inside the end quotation mark.

"The big question is whether this kind of growth is sustainable," says Bradley.

He adds, "Because American trade deficits must shrink in the years ahead, Asian nations can no longer count as heavily on expanding exports to the United States to fuel their growth."

Exception: When a pair of parentheses enclosing some comment or page reference appears between the end of the quotation and the end of the sentence, use quotation marks to note the end of the quoted text, place the parentheses, and then close with a period.

Confusing He adds, "Because American trade deficits must shrink in the years ahead, Asian nations can no longer count as heavily on expanding exports to the United States to fuel their growth. (1)"

Revised He adds, "Because American trade deficits must shrink in the years ahead, Asian nations can no longer count as heavily on expanding exports to the United States to fuel their growth" (1).

6 Place colons, semicolons, and footnotes outside end quotation marks.

Colon Bradley directly asserts that "the futures of Asia and the United States are inextricably intertwined": Asian countries profited by U.S. growth in the 1980s, and the U.S. must profit by Asian growth in the '90s and beyond.

Semicolon Bradley believes that the United States must look to the East with the intention of forming a "strong, lasting partnership"; moreover, he states that we must do so without the condescension that has for so long characterized our relations with countries like Japan and South Korea.

Footnote Bradley believes that the United States must look to the East with the intention of forming a "strong, lasting partnership."[4]

7 Place question marks and exclamation points inside or outside end quotation marks, depending on meaning.

Place a question mark or exclamation point *inside* the end quotation marks when it applies to the quoted material only or when it applies to both the quoted material and the sentence as a whole. Place the mark *outside* the end quotation mark when the sentence as a whole forms a question or exclamatory remark but the quoted material does not.

Mark applies to quoted material only

Naturalist José Márcio Ayres began his field work on the ukaris monkey of the upper Amazon with this question: "How do these primates survive almost exclusively on the pulp and seeds of fruit, when the forests in which they live are flooded much of the year?"

Mark applies both to quoted material and to sentence as whole

How can we, sitting comfortably in living rooms and libraries, appreciate the rigors of field research when even Ayres remarks, "Is the relative protection of the ukaris habitat at all surprising in light of the enormous swarms of mosquitoes one encounters in all seasons and at all hours of the day?"

Mark applies to sentence as a whole but not to quotation

Bachelor ukaris looking for mates behave as badly as hooligans at a soccer match. Ayres reports that fights are frequent and that "after all this trouble, copulation may last less than two minutes"!

▶8 **Place dashes inside quotations only when they are part of the quoted material.**

Part of quoted material

Would-be competitors such as "brocket deer, peccaries, agoutis, armadillos, and pacas—mammals common in upland habitats—" do not inhabit the ukaris forest, most likely because of the Amazon's annual flooding. This is one reason the ukaris has survived.

Separate from quoted material

Once the flood waters recede, each afternoon the ukaris descend from the upper canopy of trees—"where the temperature is uncomfortably high"—to forage for seedlings, which they dig up and eat.

▶ **EXERCISE I**

Use double quotation marks (" ") and single quotation marks (' ') to punctuate the sentences that follow. Words to be quoted are underlined.

> *Example:* According to Carla Fernandez, <u>One third of all offenders are in prison because of property offenses such as larceny, car theft, and burglary.</u>
>
> According to Carla Fernandez, "One third of all offenders are in prison because of property offenses such as larceny, car theft, and burglary."

1. Half of the prison population has been incarcerated for <u>violent crimes such as assault, homicide, and rape.</u>

2. The remaining 20 percent of offenders have been convicted of <u>offenses against public order,</u> such as drug dealing.

3. In a speech on March 2, 1992, New York corrections official Stuart Koman voiced a widely held view: <u>Overcrowded prisons not only do not rehabilitate offenders, they teach offenders to reject the law-abiding life. One individual who has spent 13 of his 25 years behind bars said to me that "I learned my techniques in jail. You know, the tools of my trade."</u>

4. As sociologist Lauren Rose concludes, <u>Efforts to reform prisons and to</u> <u>make them real</u> *penitentiaries*—institutions of penitence—<u>have failed</u> (Jacobs 341).

5. <u>One dilemma that we now face,</u> according to Rolf Hanson, <u>is to understand</u> <u>whether we want incarceration to correct criminal behavior or to punish it.</u>

CRITICAL DECISIONS

Set issues in a broader context: Knowing when and how much to quote

Knowing when to quote is something of an art, and you should see 35f for guidance. The examples in this box draw on the following passage about shopping malls by the noted anthropologist Richard Stein (*The New American Bazaar*).

When they are successful, shopping malls in American cities fulfill the same function as *bazaars* did in the cities of antiquity. The bazaars of the ancient and medieval worlds were social organisms—if we mean by this term self-contained, self-regulating systems in which individual human lives are less important (and less interesting) than the interaction of hundreds, and sometimes thousands, of lives.

■ **How much to quote**

Quote other writers when you find their discussions to be particularly lively, dramatic, or incisive or especially helpful in bolstering your credibility (see 35f). In general, quote as little as possible so that you keep readers focused on *your* discussion.

■ **Quote a word or a phrase, if this will do.**

Anthropologist Richard Stein refers to the American shopping mall as a "social organism."

■ **Quote a sentence, if needed.**

Stein sees in shopping malls a modern spin on an ancient institution: "When they are successful, shopping malls in American cities fulfill the same function as *bazaars* did in the cities of antiquity."

■ **Infrequently quote a long passage as a "block."**

Long quotations of five or more lines are set off as a block (see 28a-4). Limit your use of block quotations, which tempt writers to avoid the hard work of selecting for quotation *only* the words or sentences especially pertinent to a discussion. If you decide that a long quotation is needed, introduce the quotation with a full sentence and a colon. The following might introduce the passage previously quoted from *The New American Bazaar.*

Various commentators have claimed that shopping malls serve a social function. Anthropologist Richard Stein compares the mall to the bazaar in cities of old:

▶ **28b** Quoting poetry, dialogue, and other material

▶ **1** **Run-in brief quotations of poetry with your sentences. Indicate line breaks in the poem with a slash (/). Quote longer passages in displayed form.**

A full quotation of or a lengthy quotation from a poem is normally made in displayed form (see 28a-4).

> In "My Heart Leaps Up," William Wordsworth meditates on the importance of our enduring connection to nature:
>
> > My heart leaps up when I behold
> >   A rainbow in the sky:
> > So was it when my life began;
> > So is it now I am a man;
> > So be it when I shall grow old,
> >   Or let me die!
> > The child is father of the Man;
> > And I could wish my days to be
> > Bound each to each by natural piety.

If you omit a line or lines of a displayed poem, show the omission with an ellipsis: a line of bracketed, spaced periods of approximately the same length as other lines in the poem.

> > My heart leaps up when I behold
> >   A rainbow in the sky:
> > So was it when my life began;
> > [. . . . .]
> > The child is father of the Man;
> > And I could wish my days to be
> > Bound each to each by natural piety.

When quoting a brief extract—four lines or fewer—you can run the lines into the sentences of a paragraph, using the guidelines for quoting prose (see 28a); however, line divisions are shown with a slash (/) with one space before and one space after. Note that omitted lines are indicated with a bracketed ellipsis—the same convention used when altering quoted prose. (See 29e.)

> In "My Heart Leaps Up," William Wordsworth meditates on the importance of our enduring connection to nature: "My heart leaps up when I behold / A rainbow in the sky: / So was it when my life began; / So is it now I am a man [. . .]."

▶ **2** **Use quotation marks to quote or write dialogue.**

When quoting or writing dialogue, change paragraphs to note each change of speaker. Explanatory comments between parts of the quotation are enclosed with two commas. The first, signaling the (temporary) ending of the quoted material, is placed *inside* the end quotation mark. The second comma, signaling the end of the explanatory remark, is placed before the quotation mark that opens the next part of the quotation. When the quotation resumes, its first letter may be capitalized only if a new sentence has been started (in which case the comma concluding the explanatory material is changed to a period).

"Nobody sees you any more, Helen," Nat began. "Where've you disappeared to?"

"Oh, I've been around," she said, trying to hide a slight tremble in her voice. "And you?"

"Is somebody there where you're talking that you sound so restrained?"

"That's right."

"I thought so. So let me make it quick and clean. Helen, it's been a long time. I want to see you. What do you say if we take in a play this Saturday night? I can stop off for tickets on my way uptown tomorrow."

—Bernard Malamud, *The Assistant*

In a speech of two or more paragraphs, begin each new paragraph with opening quotation marks to signal your reader that the speech continues. Use closing quotation marks *only* at the end of the final paragraph to signal that the speech has concluded.

▶ **3 Indicate the titles of brief works with quotation marks: chapters of books, short stories, poems, songs, sections from newspapers, essays, etc.[1]**

I read the "Focus Section" of the *Boston Sunday Globe* every week.

"The Dead" is, perhaps, Joyce's most famous short story.

"Coulomb's law" is the first chapter in volume two of Gartenhaus's text, *Physics: Basic Principles.*

Manuscript form

When placed on the title page of a paper you are submitting to an instructor or peers, the title of your work should *not* be put in quotation marks. Only when you are quoting a title (yours or anyone else's) *in* a paper do you use quotation marks. However, if a title itself contains a title—a reference to some other work, you must quote appropriately. If the title of your own paper included a reference to a poem, the title would look like this:

Loneliness in Stephen Crane's "The Black Riders"

This same title, referred to *in* a sentence:

In his essay "Loneliness in Stephen Crane's 'The Black Riders,' " Marcus Trudeau argues that Crane's universe is unknowable and indifferent—but not, necessarily, hostile.

When a title is included in any other quoted material, double quotation marks (" ") change to single marks (' ').

▶ **4 Use quotation marks occasionally to emphasize words or to note invented words.**

An uncommon usage of a standard term or a new term that has been invented for a special circumstance can be highlighted with quotation marks. Once you have

---

[1]The titles of longer works—books, newspapers, magazines, long poems—are underlined in typewritten text and italicized in typeset text. (See Chapter 37.)

emphasized a word with quotation marks, you need not use the marks again with that word.

> We can designate as "low interactive" any software title that does not challenge learners to think. Low-interactive titles may be gorgeous to look at, but looking—not thinking—is what they invite learners to do.

Words that will be defined in a sentence, or words that are referred to as words, are usually italicized, though they are sometimes set in quotations. Definitions themselves, especially if they provide a translation of a word or phrase in another language, are placed in quotation marks.

> The meaning of the Latin injunction *carpe diem* is "seize the day."
>
> The name of the Greek Titan Prometheus means "forethought."

▶ 28c   Eliminating misused or overused quotation marks

▶1 Eliminate phrases using quotation marks to note slang or colloquial expressions.

If your use of slang is appropriate for and important (as slang) in your paper, then no quotation marks are needed. If, on the other hand, you are uncomfortable with slang or colloquial expressions and choose to show your discomfort by using quotation marks, then find another, more formal way to express the same thoughts.

Overused Kate promised she would "walk that extra mile" for Mark. [The quotation marks do not excuse the use of a cliché here.]

Revised Kate promised to help Mark in any way she could.

▶2 Eliminate phrases using quotation marks to make ironic comments.

Express your thoughts as directly as possible through word choice.

Misused Dean Langley called to express his "appreciation" for all I had done.

Revised Dean Langley called to complain about the accusations of bias I raised with reporters.

▶3 Eliminate quotation marks used to emphasize technical terms.

Assume your readers will note technical terms as such and will refer to a dictionary if needed.

Misused "Electromagnetism" is a branch of physics.

Revised Electromagnetism is a branch of physics.

▶4 Eliminate quotation marks that are overused to note commonly accepted nicknames.

Overused "Ted" Kennedy is a powerful senator.

Revised Ted Kennedy is a powerful senator.

Reserve your use of quotation marks for unusual nicknames, which often appear in parentheses after a first name. Once you have emphasized a name with quotation marks, you need not use the marks again with that name.

Ralph ("The Hammer") Schwartz worked forty years as a longshoreman in San Francisco and was fond of saying, "Don't end your life face down at the bottom of a bird cage."

EXERCISE 2

Correct the use of quotation marks to emphasize specific words in the following paragraph. Two of the eight expressions in quotation marks are emphasized correctly.

> We can designate as "high interactive" any software that requires direct, active engagement on the part of the learner. "High-interactive" titles must not only look good, they must present learners with real "puzzles" to solve. "Real" in this sense means "thinking" problems that are not solved by mere computation (which on-screen calculators can manage) or by quick reference to a passage of text (which basic "search" engines can easily do); "real" problems are ones that invite unique, learner-specific answers to problems that at first may seem unsolvable. The computer screen will not "give away" the answers. No: for a problem to be real, the learner, not the teacher, must solve it.

EXERCISE 3

Following is a passage on Columbus by naval historian J.H. Parry. Quote from the paragraph, as instructed here.

1. Introduce a quotation with the word *that*.
2. Introduce a quotation with a phrase and a comma. End the quotation with a page reference (which you will invent), noted in parentheses.
3. Introduce a quotation with a sentence and a colon.
4. Interrupt a quotation with the phrase "Parry states."
5. Follow a quotation with an explanatory remark.

> Columbus was not concerned with theory for its own sake, but with promoting a practical proposal. He did not study the available authorities in order to draw conclusions; he began with the conviction—how formed, we cannot tell—that an expedition to Asia by a westward route was practicable and that he was the man destined to lead it. He then combed the authorities known to him, and selected from them any assertion which supported his case. The practicability of the voyage—assuming that no major land mass barred the way—depended partly on the pattern of winds and currents likely to be encountered, but mainly on the distance to be covered. Columbus had to show that the westward distance from Europe to Asia was within the operating range of the available ships. We can trace, from what is known of his reading, from his own later writings, and from a biography written by his son Hernando, how he set about it.

29

Other Marks

This chapter reviews the conventions for using colons, dashes, parentheses, brackets, ellipses, and slashes. Of these marks, the first three are the most frequently used. The colon, the dash, and parentheses are important marks for the writer concerned with style. They significantly alter and thereby vary the rhythm of sentence structures. Brackets and ellipses are marks you will need to know when incorporating quotations into your papers.

THE COLON

▶ 29a Using the colon

The **colon** is the mark of punctuation generally used to make an announcement. In formal writing, the colon follows only a *complete* independent clause and introduces a word, phrase, sentence, or group of sentences (as in a quotation). For readers, the colon gives an important cue about the relationship of one part of your text to another: the sentence before the colon leads directly to the word or words after, in the fashion of an announcement.

▶1 Edit to eliminate colons misused within independent clauses.

In formal writing, a colon must always follow a complete statement or independent clause. The mark must never be used as a break inside an independent clause.

Faulty   For someone who is depressed, the best two things in life are: eating and sleeping.

Revised   For someone who is depressed, the best two things in life are eating and sleeping.

Revised   For someone who is depressed, only two things in life matter: eating and sleeping.

▶2 Use a colon to announce an important statement or question.

You create emphasis in a paragraph when you write one sentence to introduce another. Greater emphasis is created when you conclude that introduction with a colon.

How can it be that 25 years of feminist social change have made so little impression on preschool culture? Molly, now 6 and well aware that women can be doctors, has one theory: children's entertainment is made mostly by men.

—KATHA POLLITT

▶3 Use a colon to introduce a list or a quotation.

If at the conclusion of an independent clause you want to introduce a list or a quotation, do so with a colon.

A list

According to Cooley, the looking-glass self has three components: how we think our behavior appears to others, how we think others judge our behavior, and how we feel about their judgments.

A quotation

A New England soldier wrote to his wife on the eve of the First Battle of Bull Run: "I know how great a debt we owe to those who went before us through the Revolution. And I am willing, perfectly willing, to lay down all my joys in this life, to help maintain this government, and to pay that debt."

A colon can introduce either a list or a quotation that is set off and indented.

A New England soldier wrote to his wife on the eve of the First Battle of Bull Run:

I know how great a debt we owe to those who went before us through the Revolution. And I am willing, perfectly willing, to lay down all my joys in this life, to help maintain this government, and to pay that debt.

Chip designers use increased packing density of transistors in one of two ways:

1. They increase the complexity of the computers they can fabricate.
2. They keep the complexity of the computer at the same level and pack the whole computer into fewer chips.

Note: Both when lists and quotations are run in with sentences and when they are set off, the expression *as follows* or some variant often precedes the colon. If this expression is tagged onto a complete sentence, it is preceded by a comma.

There are three reasons to reject the theory of spontaneous generation, as follows:

▶4 Use a colon to set off an appositive phrase, summary, or explanation.

Appositive Food sharing, in which individuals provision other members of a group, is extremely rare in mammals. In addition to bats, only a few species are known to display such behavior: wild dogs, hyenas, chimpanzees, and human beings.

Summary A number of recent studies reveal that female vampire bats cluster together during the day but at night reassort themselves, creating a fluid social organization that is maintained for many years: vampire bats are remarkably social.

Using the Colon

Explanation

When Calais surrendered, King Edward (of England) threatened to put the city to the sword, then offered the people a bargain: he would spare the city if six of the chief burghers would give themselves up unconditionally.

▶**5** **Use a colon to distinguish chapter from verse in Biblical citations, hours from minutes, and titles from subtitles or subsidiary material.**

Biblical citation

It is an irony that almost none of the literature of the people who gave us the alphabet has been preserved. Fragments of Phoenician poetry have survived in the Psalms, where the mountains are described as "a fountain that makes the gardens fertile, a well of living water" (Song of Songs 4:15).

Hours from minutes

8:15 A.M.   12:01 P.M.

Titles from subtitles or subsidiary material

The New American Bazaar: Shopping Malls and the Anthropology of Urban Life

▶**6** **Use a colon after the salutation in a formal letter, and in bibliographic citations.**

Dear Ms. King:
Dear Dr. Hart:
Bikai, Patricia. "The Phoenicians." *Archaeology* Mar./Apr. 1990: 30.

▶ **EXERCISE 1**

Correct the use of colons in these sentences. Add or delete colons as needed.

> *Example:* Increasingly, grade-school Little League coaches of baseball, soccer, and football are confronting an uncomfortable problem rabid parents.
>
> Increasingly, grade-school Little League coaches of baseball, soccer, and football are confronting an uncomfortable problem: rabid parents.

1. Youth soccer games provide an illustration: teenagers serving as referees: have been confronted in the most obnoxious way by parents snarling their disapproval at missed calls.
2. Adult coaches are used to parents whose egos interfere with their ability to watch a game: Young referees can be taught strategies to neutralize obnoxious parents. But no amount of preparation can avert the most serious damage caused by rabid parents the crushed ego of an 8-year-old whose father screams, "You're such a wimp!"
3. Communities around the country have begun to print pamphlets with titles like this "Helping Your Child to Enjoy Recreational Sports A Guide."

EXERCISE 2

Write brief sentences, as instructed.

1. Write a sentence with a colon that introduces a list.
2. Write a sentence with a colon that announces an emphatic statement.
3. Write a sentence with a colon that sets off an appositive phrase, summary, or explanation.

THE DASH

29b Using dashes for emphasis

On the typewritten page, the dash is written as two hyphens (--). The space between these hyphens closes when the dash is typeset (—).

1 Use dashes to set off nonessential elements.

Use dashes to set off brief modifiers, lengthy modifiers, and appositives. In contrast to pairs of commas and parentheses, dashes emphasize the nonessential element set off in a sentence (see 25d). If dashes are the most emphatic interrupting marks and parentheses the least emphatic, commas offer a third, middling choice—neither emphatic nor fully parenthetical.

Brief modifiers in mid-sentence

Seven to thirty percent of vampire bats in a cluster fail to obtain a sufficient blood meal on any given night. By soliciting regurgitated blood from a roost-mate, a bat can fend off starvation—at least for one more night—and so have another chance to find a meal. [The phrase acts as an adverb, modifying *fend off*.]

Lengthy modifiers

Within the past ten years, a new generation of investigators—armed with fresh insights from sociobiology and behavioral ecology—have learned much about social organization in the birds of paradise. [The phrase acts as an adjective, modifying *investigators*.]

Appositives

We study history to understand the present. Yet sometimes the present can help us to clarify the past. So it is with a San-speaking people known as the !Kung—a group of what were once called African Bushmen. [The appositive phrase renames the noun *!Kung*.]

Note: Use dashes to set off appositives that contain commas. Recall that a nonessential appositive phrase can also be set off from a sentence by a pair of commas

29b

CRITICAL DECISIONS

Challenge your sentences: Deciding when to use dashes

On seeing the dash, readers pause; then they speed up to read the words you have emphasized. Then they pause once more before returning to the main part of your sentence:

Effective Zoologist Uwe Schmidt discovered that shortly after birth, vampire bat pups are given regurgitated blood—in addition to milk—by their mothers.

Use the single dash to set off elements at the beginning or end of a sentence and a pair of dashes to set off elements in the middle. When elements are set off at the end of a sentence or in the middle, you have the choice of using commas or parentheses instead of dashes. Whatever punctuation you use, take care to word the element you set off so that it fits smoothly into the structure of your sentence. For instance, in the following sentence the nonessential element would be awkward.

Awkward Zoologist Uwe Schmidt discovered that shortly after birth, vampire bat pups are given regurgitated blood—they drink milk too—by their mothers.

Better Bat pups are given regurgitated blood—in addition to milk—by their mothers.

(see 25d-3). When the appositive is formed by a series, the items of which are already separated by commas, dashes prevent misreading.

Confusing Since the turn of the century, the percentage of information workers, bankers, insurance agents, lawyers, science journalists, has gone from a trickle to a flood.

Revised Since the turn of the century, the percentage of information workers—bankers, insurance agents, lawyers, science journalists—has gone from a trickle to a flood.

▶ **2 Use dashes to set off a significant repeating structure or an emphatic concluding element.**

Repeating structure

To me the vitality of the bird of paradise's mating display was—and continues to be—one of nature's most thrilling sights. [The verb is repeated.]

Emphatic concluding remark

Once disposed of in the landfill, garbage is supposed to remain buried for eternity. So it was in Collier County, Florida—until we found several good reasons to dig it up again. [The dash sets off a sharply contrasting element, in this case a subordinate clause that functions as an adverb.]

Use dashes—with care. [This brief qualifying tag, a prepositional phrase, functions as an adverb.]

▶3 Use a dash to set off an introductory series from a summary or explanatory remark.

Strategic spots on the Boston Common are occupied by regiments of lunch-hour workers, and the Common is still the preferred site for political rallies. Pocket change, ball-point pens, campaign buttons—humanity's imprint continues to be recorded on the grassy slopes of the Boston Common. [This sentence structure, which begins with a series, is relatively rare.]

COMPUTER TIPS

Em Dash and En Dash

You probably already know that the dash is different from the hyphen. On a typewriter, to indicate a dash, you typed two hyphens with no spaces between, before, or after--like this. In addition, there are *two different* dashes that professional typesetters use, and most newer computers can generate both. One is called the "en dash," because it's the width of a capital N; the other is called the "em dash," because it's wider—roughly the width of a capital M. The en dash is used to indicate a span of some sort: 9:30–10:45. It's not a hyphen. It is customarily preceded and followed by very small spaces, but not full spaces. The em dash is used to indicate a break in thought or a parenthetical comment—like this—and it's neither preceded nor followed by spaces. Find out how to type in these special dashes on your particular computer.

▶4 Use a dash to express an interruption in dialogue.

A dash used in dialogue shows interruption—speakers interrupting themselves or being interrupted by others. The dash used in dialogue also shows a change of thought or an uncompleted thought, a change in tone, or a pause.

Adam studied his brother's face until Charles looked away. "Are you mad at something?" Adam asked.

"What should I be mad at?"

"It just sounded— "

"I've got nothing to be mad at. Come on, I'll get you something to eat."

—John Steinbeck

▶5 Use a dash to set off an attribution (by name), following an epigram.

At blows that never fall you falter,
And what you never lose, you must forever mourn.

—Goethe

Dashes used in this fashion often follow epigrams—succinct, provocative quotations placed at the beginning of a paper as a vehicle for the introduction. Typically, the writer opens such a paper with a direct reference to the epigram and its author: "In these lines from *Faust*, the main character laments his limited human powers."

▶ **EXERCISE 3**

Add a dash or a pair of dashes to the following sentences.

> *Example:* Many innovations the Chinese slipper, the Perrault godmother with her midnight injunction and her ability to change pumpkin into coach became incorporated in later versions of "Cinderella."
>
> Many innovations—the Chinese slipper, the Perrault godmother with her midnight injunction and her ability to change pumpkin into coach—became incorporated in later versions of "Cinderella."

1. The chapbooks of the eighteenth century and nineteenth century, crudely printed tiny paperbacks, were the source of most children's reading in the early days of our country. Originally, these were books imported from Europe. But slowly American publishing grew. In the latter part of the nineteenth century one firm stood out McLoughlin Brothers.

2. Golden Press's *Walt Disney's Cinderella* set the new pattern for America's Cinderella. This book's text is coy and condescending. (Sample: "And her best friends of all were guess who the mice!")

3. There is also an easy-reading version published by Random House, *Walt Disney's Cinderella*. This Cinderella commits the further heresy of cursing her luck. "How I did wish to go to the ball," she says. "But it is no use. Wishes never come true."

    But in fairy tales wishes have a habit of happening *wishes accompanied by the proper action*, bad wishes as well as good.

EXERCISE 4

Write brief sentences, as instructed.

1. Write a sentence with a nonessential series placed mid-sentence, set off by a pair of dashes.

2. Write a sentence in which a nonessential element is set off at the end by a dash.

3. Write a sentence in which a dash or pair of dashes sets off a significant re-peating structure or emphatic statement.

PARENTHESES

▶ **29c** Using parentheses to set off nonessential information

Parentheses ( ) are used to enclose and set off nonessential dates, words, phrases, or whole sentences that provide examples, comments, and other supporting in-formation. The remark enclosed by parentheses is the ultimate nonessential mod-ifier; it presents the reader with an aside, an interesting but by no means crucial bit of information. To give nonessential remarks more emphasis, use commas or dashes. (See also the Critical Decisions box in 25d-3.)

▶1 Use parentheses to set off nonessential information: examples, comments, appositives.

Examples

The ground beetle *Pterostichus pinguedineus* vanished from Iowa 15,300 years ago, but today it survives in Alaska, in the Yukon, and in a series of isolated alpine refuges in the northern Appalachians (for example, the peak of Mt. Washington in New Hampshire**)**.

Comments—explanatory or editorial

Beetles **(**especially those species that scavenge or that prey on other arthropods**)** are rapid colonizers and are among the first organisms to invade terrain opened up to them by changing climates.

Appositives

The information content of a slice of pizza (advertising, legal expenses, and so on**)** accounts for a larger percentage of its cost than the edible content does, according to Henry Kelley and Andrew W. Wyckoff of the Congressional Office of Technology Assessment.

▶2 Use parentheses to set off dates, translations of non-English words, and acronyms.

Dates

Thomas Aquinas **(**b. 1225 or 1226, d. 1274**)** is regarded as the greatest of scholastic philosophers.

Translations

The look on the faces of the Efe tribesmen made it clear that they could think of nothing worse than to have a *muzungu* (foreigner) living with them for even a day.

Acronyms

Lucy Suchman, staff anthropologist of Xerox's Palo Alto Research Center **(**better known as PARC**)**, watches workers in an airline operations room at San Jose International Airport to learn how they extract particular information from a chaotic assortment of radio, telephone, text, and video feeds. **[**Typically, an acronym is placed in parentheses directly after the first mention of a term or title subsequently referred to by its acronym.**]**

http://www.mtnds.com/af/
Acronym Finder: A searchable database containing 84,000 common acronyms and abbreviations about all subjects.

▶3 Use parentheses to set off numbers or letters that mark items in a series, when the series is run in with a sentence.

Interactive learning is student-centered two ways: **(1)** students set the pace of their own learning, calling on hypertext help to clarify concepts and information; and **(2)** students set the depth of their own learning, exploring those materials that particularly engage their interest.

When the series appears in list form, omit the parentheses:

Interactive learning is student-centered two ways:

1. Students set the pace of their own learning, calling on hypertext help to clarify concepts and information.
2. Students set the depth of their own learning, exploring those materials that particularly engage their interest.

4 Punctuate parentheses according to convention.

Words enclosed by parentheses should be punctuated according to standard practice. When a parenthetical remark forms a sentence, the remark should begin with an uppercase letter and end with an appropriate mark (period, question mark, or exclamation point) placed *inside* the end parenthesis. In all other cases, end punctuation should be placed outside the end parenthesis, and punctuation that would normally be placed directly after a word should be placed directly after the parenthetical remark.

Faulty   Like other nomads, the Bakhtiari think of themselves as a family, the sons of a single founding-father. (as did the ancient Jews)

Revised   Like other nomads, the Bakhtiari think of themselves as a family, the sons of a single founding-father (as did the ancient Jews).

Faulty   According to J. Bronowski, the Bakhtiari "think of themselves as a family, the sons of a single founding-father." (60)

Revised   According to J. Bronowski, the Bakhtiari "think of themselves as a family, the sons of a single founding-father" (60).

EXERCISE 5

Add parentheses to the following sentences to enclose nonessential information.

Example: Nearly all twin-lens reflex cameras and a few single-lens reflex SLR cameras are designed to accommodate roll film somewhat wider than 35 millimeters.

Nearly all twin-lens reflex cameras and a few single-lens reflex (SLR) cameras are designed to accommodate roll film somewhat wider than 35 millimeters.

1. Because of their size and the "look-down" viewing systems, twin-lens reflexes are not good for quick action candid shooting. An SLR is best in these situations.
2. The look-down viewing system is better for carefully composed photographs in a studio or home, for example when time is not of the essence.
3. For my money, the Canon AE-1 originally designed in 1971 remains one of the best and most flexible workhorse cameras that an amateur photographer could want.
4. I still cannot understand why any amateur photographer would want anything besides a good, reliable, single-lens reflex camera usually referred to as an SLR.

BRACKETS

Use brackets [ ] to clarify or insert comments into quoted material. Throughout this section the following passage will be altered to demonstrate the various uses of brackets. For an extended discussion of using quotations in a research paper, see 35f. Specifically, see 35f-3 for more on using brackets.

> Elephant sounds include barks, snorts, trumpets, roars, growls, and rumbles. The rumbles are the key to our story, for although elephants can hear them well, human beings cannot. Many are below our range of hearing, in what is known as infrasound.
>
> The universe is full of infrasound: It is generated by earthquakes, wind, thunder, volcanoes, and ocean storms—massive movements of earth, air, fire, and water. But very low frequency sound has not been thought to play much of a role in animals' lives. Intense infrasonic calls have been recorded from finback whales, but whether the calls are used in communication is not known.
>
> Why would elephants use infrasound? It turns out that sound at the lowest frequency of elephant rumbles (14 to 35 hertz) has remarkable properties—it is little affected by passage through forests and grasslands. Does infrasound, then, let elephants communicate over long distances?

▶**1 Use brackets to insert your own words into quoted material.**

Recall that quotation marks denote an *exact* reproduction of someone else's writing or speech. When you alter the wording of a quotation either by adding or deleting words, you must indicate as much with appropriate use of punctuation.

Brackets to clarify a reference

When quoting a sentence with a pronoun that refers to a word in another, non-quoted sentence, use brackets to insert a clarifying reference into the quotation. Delete the pronoun and add bracketed information; or, if wording permits (as in this example), simply add the bracketed reference.

> According to Katherine Payne, "Many [elephant rumbles] are below our range of hearing, in what is known as infrasound."

Brackets to weave quoted language into your sentences

You should attempt to make the fit between quoted language and your language seamless. To do this, you will sometimes need to alter a quotation if its structure, point of view, pronoun choices, or verb forms differ from those of the sentence into which you are incorporating the quotation. Show any changes to quoted text in brackets. Directly substituting one or two clarifying words (or letters) for the author's original language requires no use of ellipses to show an omission. (See 29e.) Readers will infer that you've made a substitution.

> The human ear can discern a wide band of sounds, but there are animals we can't hear without special equipment. Elephants emit inaudible (that is, to humans), very low-frequency rumbles called infrasound. At frequencies of 14 to 35 hertz, elephant rumbles have "remarkable properties—[they are] little affected by passage through forests and grasslands" (Payne 67).

The bracketed verb and pronoun have been changed from their original singular form to plural in order to agree in number with the plural *elephant rumbles*. The original subject of the quoted sentence was singular (*sound*). Quoting without brackets would have resulted in an awkward construction: *Elephant rumbles have* "*remarkable properties—it is.*"

Brackets to show your awareness of an error in the quoted passage

When you quote a sentence that contains an obvious error, you are still obliged to reproduce exactly the wording of the original source. To show your awareness of the error and to show readers that the error is the quoted author's, not yours, place the bracketed word *sic* (Latin, meaning "thus") after the error.

> "Intense infrasonic calls have been recorded from finback whales, but weather [sic] the calls are used in communication is not known."

Brackets to note emphasis

You may wish to underline or italicize quoted words. To show readers that the emphasis is yours and not the quoted author's, add the bracketed expression *emphasis added*, *italics added*, or *italics mine*.

> "The universe is *full* of infrasound: It is generated by earthquakes, wind, thunder, volcanoes, and ocean storms—massive movements of earth, air, fire, and water [italics mine]."

 2 Use brackets to distinguish parentheses inserted within parentheses.

> Katherine Payne reports that "sound at the lowest frequency of elephant rumbles (14 to 35 hertz [cycles per second]) has remarkable properties—it is little affected by passage through forests and grasslands."

ELLIPSES

▶ 29e Using an ellipsis to indicate a break in continuity

Just as you will sometimes add words in order to incorporate quotations into your sentences, you will also need to omit words. The overall rule to bear in mind when you alter a quotation is to present quoted material in a way that is faithful to the meaning and sentence structure of the original. If your omission of words risks confusing an author's meaning or misrepresenting the author's sentence structure in any way, use a bracketed ellipsis—three spaced periods set in brackets [. . .]—to indicate that you have altered the original. The spaced periods show that you have omitted either words or entire sentences; brackets indicate that *you* have made the omission and that the spaced periods were not set by the author to indicate a pause.[1]

---

[1]The addition of brackets to the use of three spaced periods is new to the *MLA Style Manual and Guide to Scholarly Publishing*, 2nd edition (1998) and to the *MLA Handbook for Writers of Research Papers*, 5th edition (1999). In earlier editions, MLA editors had recommended the use of spaced periods only.

The following passage will be altered to demonstrate several uses of ellipses. For an extended discussion of using quotations in a research paper, see 35f, especially 35f-3 on the ellipsis. Also, see 28b-1 for using an ellipsis with poetry.

> First, for Americans, the human cost of the Civil War was by far the most devastating in our history. The 620,000 Union and Confederate soldiers who lost their lives almost equaled the 680,000 American soldiers who died in all the other wars this country has fought combined. When we add the unknown but probably substantial number of civilian deaths—from disease, malnutrition, exposure, or injury—among the hundreds of thousands of refugees in the Confederacy, the toll of the Civil War may exceed war deaths in all the rest of American history.

▶1 Know when *not* to use ellipses.

Do *not* use ellipses to note words omitted from the beginning of a sentence if it is obvious that you are quoting a fragment of the original. In the following example, three words are omitted.

Faulty   James McPherson observes that "[. . .] the human cost of the Civil War was by far the most devastating in our history."

Revised   James McPherson observes that "the human cost of the Civil War was by far the most devastating in our history."

Revised (quotation with paranthetical reference)

James McPherson observes that "the human cost of the Civil War was by far the most devastating in our history" (42).

Do *not* use an ellipsis if the passage you quote ends with a period and ends your sentence as well. Readers take for granted that the quoted sentence exists in a paragraph in which other sentences follow.

Faulty   One scholar believes that "the toll of the Civil War may exceed war deaths in all the rest of American history. [. . .]"

Revised   One scholar believes that "the toll of the Civil War may exceed war deaths in all the rest of American history."

Revised (quotation with paranthetical reference)

One scholar believes that "the toll of the Civil War may exceed war deaths in all the rest of American history" (McPherson 42).

▶2 Use an ellipsis to indicate words omitted from the middle of a sentence.

According to James McPherson, "When we add the unknown but probably substantial number of civilian deaths [. . .] among the hundreds of thousands of refugees in the Confederacy, the toll of the Civil War may exceed war deaths in all the rest of American history."

Quotation with a parenthetical reference

According to James McPherson, "When we add the unknown but probably substantial number of civilian deaths [. . .] among the hundreds of thousands of refugees in the Confederacy, the toll of the Civil War may exceed war deaths in all the rest of American history" (42).

Using an Ellipsis to Indicate a Break in Continuity

▶**3** Use an ellipsis to indicate words omitted from the end of a sentence.

When you omit words from the end of a quoted sentence, skip one space after the last quoted word, follow with the bracketed ellipsis, and conclude with a final period. In the example that follows, the bracketed ellipsis shows that the writer has altered the sentence structure of the original.

> Official mortality figures for the Civil War do not include the "probably substantial number of civilian deaths—from disease, malnutrition, exposure, or injury **[. . .].**"

Quotation with a parenthetical reference

> Official mortality figures for the Civil War do not include the "probably substantial number of civilian deaths—from disease, malnutrition, exposure, or injury **[. . .]**" (McPherson 42**).**

When the altered quotation appears in the middle of your sentence, skip one space after the last quoted word, follow with the bracketed ellipsis, and continue with your own sentence.

> Official mortality figures for the Civil War do not include the "probably substantial number of civilian deaths—from disease, malnutrition, exposure, or injury **[. . .]**" (McPherson 42**),** which is one reason historians think that the Civil War may be the costliest, in terms of human lives, in American history.

▶**4** Use an ellipsis to indicate the omission of whole sentences or parts of sentences.

The following passage will be altered to show the use of ellipsis.

> The successful capitalist was a man who could accurately estimate a firm's potential profits. The investors who survived were the ones who knew how to take "risks" in such a way that there was no actual risk at all. They profited through interest and dividends and through the increased value of their holdings, which multiplied as the national economy grew. Under Tom Scott's tutelage, Carnegie learned to collect interest rather than pay it, and he became a shrewd judge of the growth potential of investment opportunities.
>
> —HAROLD C. LIVESAY, *Andrew Carnegie and the Rise of Big Business*

When omitting an entire sentence (or sentences), place the bracketed ellipsis at the spot of the omission. Observe the placement of the sentence-ending period *before* the bracketed ellipsis:

> As Carnegie's biographer points out, "The investors who survived were the ones who knew how to take 'risks' in such a way that there was no actual risk at all. **[. . .]** Under Tom Scott's tutelage, Carnegie learned to collect interest rather than pay it, and he became a shrewd judge of the growth potential of investment opportunities" (Livesay 48).

When omitting the end of one sentence through to the end of another sentence, follow the convention at 29e-3. Observe the placement of the sentence-ending period *after* the end of the bracketed ellipsis.

> According to Livesay, "The investors who survived were the ones who knew how to take 'risks' **[. . .].** Under Tom Scott's tutelage, Carnegie learned to

collect interest rather than pay it, and he became a shrewd judge of the growth potential of investment opportunities" (48).

When omitting the end of one sentence through to the middle of another sentence, place the author's punctuation mark (if any) after the last word of the initially quoted sentence, follow with a bracketed ellipsis, and continue with the remainder of the quotation.

> Writing about the railway boom of the mid 1800s, Carnegie's biographer observes, "The investors who survived [. . .] profited through interest and dividends and through the increased value of their holdings, which multiplied as the national economy grew" (Livesay 48).

▶5 **Use an ellipsis to show a pause or interruption.**

When *you* are writing dialogue or prose—that is, when you are *not* quoting a source, you can use an ellipsis (with *no* brackets) to indicate a brief pause or delay. Within a sentence, use three spaced periods. Between sentences, end the first sentence with a period and then set the ellipsis—four spaced periods in all.

> *In dialogue that you write*
> "No," I said. I wanted to leave. "I . . . I need to get some air."

> *In prose that you write*
> When I left the seminary, I walked long and thought hard about what a former student of divinity might do. . . . My shoes wore out, my brain wore thin. I was stumped and not a little nervous about the course my life would take.

THE SLASH

▶ **29f**   Using the slash

▶1 **Use slashes to separate the lines of poetry run in with the text of a sentence.**

Retain all punctuation when quoting poetry. Leave a space before and after the slash when indicating line breaks.

> The narrator of William Blake's "The Tyger" is struck with wonder: "Tyger! Tyger! burning bright / In the forests of the night. / What immortal hand or eye, / Could frame thy fearful symmetry?"

▶2 **Use slashes to show choice.**

Use slashes, occasionally, to show alternatives, as with the expressions *and/or* and *either/or.* With this use, do not leave spaces before or after the slash.

> *Either/Or* is the title of a philosophical work by Kierkegaard.
> The Unsung Hero/Best Sport award was given to Abbey King.

If your meaning is not compromised, avoid using the slash; instead, write out alternatives in your sentence.

Send a telegram and/or call to let us know you're well.

The sense, here, is that there are three options: send a telegram, call, *or* send a telegram *and* call. If two options are intended, then the sentence should be rewritten one of two ways.

Send a telegram and call to let us know you're well.

Send a telegram or call to let us know you're well.

▶3 Use a slash in writing fractions or formulas to note division.

The February 1988 index of job opportunities (as measured by the number of help wanted advertisements) would be as follows:

$(47,230/38,510) \times 100 = 122.6$

1/2   5/8   20 1/4

▶ EXERCISE 6

Construct sentences, as directed, in which you quote from the following passage by Sigmund Freud.

(1) As to the origin of the sense of guilt, the analyst has different views from other psychologists; but even he does not find it easy to give an account of it. (2) To begin with, if we ask how a person comes to have a sense of guilt, we arrive at an answer which cannot be disputed: a person feels guilty (devout people would say "sinful") when he has done something which he knows to be "bad." (3) But then we notice how little this answer tells us. (4) Perhaps, after some hesitation, we shall add that even when a person has not actually *done* the bad thing but has only recognized in himself an *intention* to do it, he may regard himself as guilty; and the question then arises of why the intention is regarded as equal to the deed. (5) Both cases, however, presuppose that one had already recognized that what is bad is reprehensible, is something that must not be carried out. (6) How is this judgement arrived at?

Example: Quote sentence 1, but delete the phrase "As to the origin of the sense of guilt."

According to Sigmund Freud, "the analyst has different views from other psychologists; but even he does not find it easy to give an account of it."

1. Quote sentence 2, beginning with "a person feels." Delete the parenthetical note.

2. Quote sentence 4 but delete the end of the sentence, beginning with "and the question."

3. Quote sentence 1 and use a bracketed reference to clarify the second use of the pronoun *it.*

▶ 4. Quote sentence 5 and show your awareness of the spelling error.

CHAPTER 30

Capitals and Italics

Capitals and italics are primarily graphic devices that give readers cues on how to read: where to look for the beginning of a new thought, which words in a sentence are emphasized, which words form titles or proper names, and so on. Capitals and italics are also very useful for special designations that can only be shown in writing.

CAPITALS

Before the late nineteenth century, printers manually composed words by placing molded letters in type holders, taking letters from individual compartments, or type cases, set on a nearby wall. Letters used most often (vowels, for instance) were kept on the wall's lower cases, within easy reach. Letters used less often (capital letters, for instance) were kept in a slightly less convenient location in upper cases. In spite of innovations that have made manual typesetting obsolete, we still retain the printer's original designations, upper and lower case, when referring to the appearance of type on a page. Readers depend on capital (uppercase) letters, in contrast to lowercase letters, as cues to help recognize when sentences begin and when a noun refers to a particular person, place, or thing.

▶ **30a**   Capitalize the first letter of the first word in every sentence.

The most basic use of capitals is to signal the start of sentences.

> When a box of mixed-grain-and-nut cereal is shaken, large particles always rise to the top—for the same reason that, over time, stones will rise to the top of a garden lot or field.

▶ **I**   Reproduce capitalization in a quoted passage.

Capitalize the first word of quoted material when you introduce a quotation with a brief explanatory phrase.

> According to archaeologist Douglas Wilson, "Most of what archaeologists have to work with is ancient trash."

> "Most of what archaeologists have to work with is ancient trash," according to archaeologist Douglas Wilson.

Do not capitalize the first word of a quotation run into the structure of your sentence. When you change capitalization in a quoted text, indicate the change with brackets.

> Wilson says that archaeologists who dig through modern trash must come "[e]quipped with rubber gloves, masks, and booster shots."

▶**2** **Capitalize the first word in a parenthetical statement if the remark is a sentence.**

> Once a sleepy suburban town whose workers commuted to Chicago every morning, Naperville, Illinois has acquired its own employment base. (It has become an "urban village," a "technoburb.")

If the parenthetical remark forms a sentence but is placed inside another sentence (this is a relatively rare occurrence), *do not* capitalize the first word after the parenthesis and *do not* use a period. However, do use a question mark or exclamation point if the parenthetical remark requires it.

> Naperville grew robustly (the population nearly quadrupled!), as Amoco and companies large and small erected what Governor James R. Thompson would later term "The Illinois Research and Development Corridor."

▶**3** **In a series of complete statements or questions, capitalize the first word of each item.**

When a series is formed by phrases or incomplete questions, capitalization of the first word is optional.

Capitals	What causes air sickness? Is it inner-ear disturbance? Is it brain waves?
Optional	Air Force scientists want to know what causes motion sickness. Is it inner-ear disturbance? brain wave anomalies? disorienting visual signals?
Optional	Air Force scientists want to know what causes motion sickness. Is it inner-ear disturbance? Brain wave anomalies? Disorienting visual signals?

In a series of phrases run in with a sentence, the phrases are *not* capitalized.

> The program for low-input sustainable agriculture that has emerged from a recent federal study has three objectives: (1) to reduce reliance on fertilizer, pesticide, and other purchased resources to farms; (2) to increase farm profits and agricultural productivity; and (3) to conserve energy and natural resources.

In a displayed series, capitalization of the first word is optional.

Optional	The program for low-input sustainable agriculture that has emerged from a recent federal study has three objectives:

> 1. To reduce reliance on fertilizer, pesticide, and other purchased resources to farms.
> 2. To increase farm profits and agricultural productivity.
> 3. To conserve energy and natural resources.

The word *to* could also be in lowercase letters in each number of the displayed series.

ACROSS THE CURRICULUM

The Importance of Grammar, Style, and Usage in Chemistry

In its *Style Guide** for authors and editors, the American Chemical Society makes it clear that the "seemingly trivial elements" of language such as grammar, style, and usage are crucially important for writers:

Many authors ask why we have a style for seemingly trivial elements like capitalization, hyphenation, abbreviations, and so on. Why can't each author do it his or her own way? A consistent style provides unity and coherence to the journal or book and makes communication clear and unequivocal; thus it saves readers time and effort by not allowing a variety of styles for the same thing to distract them from the content. If readers must pause, even for a moment, to think about matters of style, it will take a lot longer to read the article.

**The ACS Style Guide: A Manual for Authors and Editors* (Washington: ACS, 1986), 11.

4 Capitalizing the first word of a sentence following a colon is optional.

Optional   The program has two aims: The first is to conserve energy.
Optional   The program has two aims: the first is to conserve energy.

 30b **Capitalize words of significance in a title.**

Capitalize all words of significance in the titles of books, journals, magazines, articles, and art works. *Do not* capitalize articles (*a, an, the*) or conjunctions and prepositions that have four or fewer letters, except at the title's beginning. *Do* capitalize the first and last words of the title (even if they are articles, conjunctions, or prepositions), along with any word following a colon or semicolon.

Pride and Prejudice   *Great Expectations*
The Sound and the Fury   *The Joy Luck Club*
Much Ado About Nothing   *West with the Night*
"The Phoenicians: Rich and Glorious Traders of the Levant"

Do not capitalize the word *the* if it is not part of a title or proper name.

the Eiffel Tower   *The Economist*
the Mediterranean Sea   *The Brothers Karamazov*

The first word of a hyphenated word in a title is capitalized. The second word is also capitalized, unless it is very short.

"The Selling of an Ex-President"   *Engine Tune-ups Made Simple*
"Belly-down in a Cave: A Spelunker's Weekend"

Capitalize Words of Significance in a Title   **455**

> **30c** Capitalize the first word in every line of poetry.

Lines of poetry are conventionally marked by initial capitals. The interjection *O*, restricted for the most part to poetry, is always capitalized. The word *oh* is capitalized only when it begins a sentence.

> Break, break, break,
>   On thy cold gray stones, O Sea!
> And I would that my tongue could utter
>   The thoughts that arise in me.
>
> —TENNYSON, from *"Break, Break, Break"*

Note: Very often in contemporary poetry the initial capital is *not* used. When quoting such poets, retain the capitalization of the original.

> **30d** Capitalize proper nouns—people, places, objects; proper adjectives; and ranks of distinction.

Capitalizing the first letter of a noun helps to establish its identity. In general, capitalize any noun that refers to a *particular* person, place, object, or being that has been given an individual, or proper, name.

> **1** Capitalize names of people or groups of people.

Names of people are capitalized, as are titles showing family relationships *if* the title is part of the person's name.

Tom Hanks	Martha Washington
Aunt Millie	Uncle Ralph

Names of family relations—brother, aunt, grandmother—are not capitalized if not used as part of a particular person's proper name.

> He phoned his grandmother, Bess Truman.
>
> I saw my favorite aunt, Janet, on a trip to Chicago.

Names of political groups and of formal organizations are capitalized.

Democrats	the Left
Republicans	the Right
Communists	Socialists

> **2** Capitalize religions, religious titles and names, and nationalities.

Religions, their followers, and their sacred beings and sacred documents are capitalized.

Judaism	Jew	the Bible
Catholicism	Catholic	the New Testament
Islam	Muslim	the Koran
God	Allah	Buddha

Nations and nationalities are capitalized.

America	Americans	Native Americans
Liberia	Liberians	Hispanic Americans
Czech Republic	Czechs	

Note: The terms *black* and *white*, when designating race, are usually written in lowercase, though some writers prefer to capitalize them (by analogy with other formal racial designations such as Mongolian and Polynesian).

▶3 **Capitalize places, regions designated by points on the compass, and languages.**

Places and addresses

Cascades	Asia
Idaho	England
Joe's Diner	Philadelphia
Main Street	Elm Boulevard

Note: Capitalize common nouns such as *main* or *center* when they are part of an address.

Names of regions and compass points designating the names of regions

Appalachia	the frozen Northwest
the Great Lakes	the Sun Belt
the sunny South	Mid-Atlantic

Note: A compass point is capitalized only when it functions as a noun and serves as the name of a particular area of the country. As a direction, a compass point is not capitalized.

No capital   I'll be driving northeast for the first part of the trip. [The word *northeast* in this sentence is a modifier and indicates a direction, not a region.]

We made a course to the northeast, but soon turned to the north. [These are compass points, not the names of regions.]

Capital   I'll be vacationing in the Northeast this year. [The word *Northeast* is the name of an area of the country.]

Names of languages

| English | Arabic | Swahili |
| Spanish | Greek | Italian |

▶4 **Capitalize adjectives formed from proper nouns. Capitalize titles of distinction that are part of proper names.**

Proper adjectives formed from proper nouns

| English tea | French perfume |
| Cartesian coordinates | Balinese dancer |

Note: Both *Oriental* and *oriental* are considered correct, though the capitalized form is more common. Both *Biblical* and *biblical* are considered correct.

Do not capitalize the name of an academic discipline or group of disciplines unless it is derived from a proper noun:

humanities	social science
English	French

Titles of distinction

Capitalize a title of distinction when no words separate it from a proper noun. Do not capitalize most title designations if they are followed by the preposition *of.*

Governor Ventura	Jesse Ventura, governor of Minnesota
Mayor Edward G. Rendell	Edward G. Rendell, mayor of Philadelphia

Note: When titles of the highest distinction are proper names for a specific office—President, Prime Minister—they often remain capitalized, even if followed by a preposition and even if not paired with a specific name.

Jacques Chirac, President of France
Alisa Billings, Vice-President of Citizens Bank

The President arrived at 2 o'clock.
The Secretary of State flew to Geneva.

The Prime Minister's role is to lead both party and government.
A prime minister may do as she pleases. [A specific office is not being named.]

Capitalize titles and abbreviations of titles when they follow a comma—as in an address or closing to a letter.

Martha Brand, Ph.D.	Fred Barnes, Sr.
Sally Roth, M.D.	David Burns, Executive Vice-President

▶**5 Capitalize the names of days, months, holidays, and historical events or periods.**

Monday	New Year's Day
Saturday	Columbus Day
December	Revolutionary War
January	Paleozoic Era
Christmas	Middle Ages

Note: When written out, centuries and decades are not capitalized.

the nineteenth century	the fifties	the twenty-third century

Seasons are capitalized only when they are personified.

spring semester	Spring's gentle breath [The season is personified.]

▶**6 Capitalize particular objects and name-brand products.**

Mount Washington	USS *Hornet*
Jefferson Memorial	Sam Rayburn Building
Aswan Dam	
Bic pen	Toyota Camry
Whopper	Apple computer
Sony television	

▶7 Use capitals with certain abbreviations, prefixes, or compound nouns.

Capitalize abbreviations only when the words abbreviated are themselves capitalized.

Mister James Wolf	Mr. James Wolf
Apartment 6	Apt. 6
1234 Rockwood Avenue	1234 Rockwood Ave.
Silver Spring, Maryland	Silver Spring, MD

Capitalize acronyms and abbreviations of companies, agencies, and treaties.

FAA (Federal Aviation Administration)
ABM Treaty (Anti-Ballistic Missile Treaty)
DEC (Digital Equipment Corporation)

The prefixes *ex*, *un*, and *post* are capitalized only when they begin a sentence or are part of a proper name or title.

a post-Vietnam event	the Post-Vietnam Syndrome
an un-American attitude	the Un-American Activities Committee

Capitalize a number or the first word in a compound number that is part of a name or title.

Third Avenue
the Seventy-Second Preakness

▶ **EXERCISE 1**

Correct the capitalization in these sentences. As needed, change lowercase letters to uppercase and change uppercase to lowercase.

New orleans, the louisiana city associated with the pre-lenten celebration of mardi gras, has also been the site of an even more unusual quasi-Religious festival. This one takes place on november 1, which in the church's calendar is the feast of all saints, otherwise known as all saints' day. The custom of this day in new orleans is the Washing of the Tombs. Since the city was built on the Bayou, the land is quite swampy. Thus most of the City's dead have, over the years, been buried in above-ground vaults. On all saints' day these vaults are cleaned, whitewashed, and decorated with flowers and wreaths. The favored flower is the Chrysanthemum. Despite all of the work going on, the atmosphere has been described as quite festive. Vendors do quite well peddling food, balloons, and even miniature skeletons.

ITALICS

A word set in italics calls attention to itself. On the typewritten (or handwritten) page, words that you would italicize are underlined. Italics have three principal uses: they give emphasis; they mark the plural forms of letters and numbers; and they denote titles of long works and certain names.

http://ec.uvsc.edu/owl/handouts/
quotes.htm
Handout on when to use italics/underlining and when to use quotation marks, from Utah Valley State College's Online Writing Lab.

> ## 30e Underline or italicize words if they need a specific emphasis.

Words that you underline or set in italics are given particular emphasis. As a stylistic tool, italicizing will work well only if you do not overuse it.

> Cultural relativity does *not* mean that a behavior appropriate in one place is appropriate everywhere.

Italicized words can be useful to create emphasis and change meaning in sentences, especially when writing attempts to duplicate the emphasis of speech.

> "*You're* going to the movies with him?" [Why you and not Susan?]
> "You're going to the movies with *him*?" [Why would you go with him?]
> "You're going to the *movies* with him?" [Why aren't you going to the theater?]

Note: The best way to create emphasis in your writing is not to simulate emotion with punctuation or with typeface, but to make your point with words. Italics should be saved for rare occasions and for a specific purpose. Overuse devalues the emphasis of italics and makes your writing appear overexcited and unconvincing.

Overused	The Phoenicians were *masters* of the sea and with the cities they founded, like Tyre and Carthage, they became commercial *giants*. But Rome *envied* the Phoenician wealth. The angry prophet Isaiah called the Phoenicians *sinners*, and the heroic poet Homer thought they were *sly*. Ultimately, these many hatreds *crushed* the Phoenicians.
Reworded	During the hundreds of years that they dominated the seas, the Phoenicians made enemies, the sort of enemies that are inevitable when you are commercially successful. Homer's heroic poems described the Phoenicians as slippery and as swindlers. Isaiah called Tyre a whore. The Romans depicted the Carthaginians as treacherous. In the end, the Phoenicians and Carthaginians lost to those enemies and were completely crushed, militarily and culturally.

> ## 30f Underline or italicize words, letters, and numbers to be defined or identified.

> ### 1 Use italics for words to be defined.

Words to be defined in a sentence are usually underlined or set in italics. Occasionally, such a word is set in quotation marks.

Option	The *operating system* runs a computer as a sort of master organizer that can accept commands whenever no specific program is running.
Option	The remarkable permanence of color in certain statues at the Acropolis is due, partly, to the technique of "encaustic," in which pigment is mixed with wax and applied to the surface while hot.

> ### 2 Use italics for expressions recognized as foreign.

Underline or italicize foreign expressions that have not yet been assimilated into English but whose meanings are generally understood. The following is a brief sampling of such words.

amore [Italian]
enfant terrible [French]
e pluribus unum [Latin]
goyim [Hebrew]
pâté [French]

Doppelgänger [German]
esprit de corps [French]
hombre [Spanish]
post hoc [Latin]

No underlines or italics are used with foreign expressions that have been assimilated into English. The following is a brief sampling of such words.

alter ego [Latin]
ex post facto [Latin]
hoi polloi [Greek]
guru [Sanskrit]
kibitz [Yiddish]
maestro [Italian]

blitz [German]
fait accompli [French]
fellah [Arabic]
kayak [Eskimo]
machete [Spanish]
memorabilia [Latin]

▶**3** **Use italics to designate words, numerals, or letters referred to as such.**

Underline or italicize words when you are calling attention to them as words.

Many writers have trouble differentiating the uses of *lie* and *lay*.

The word *the* is not capitalized in a title, unless it is the first word of the title or follows a colon or semicolon.

Italicize letters and most numerals when they are referred to as letters or numerals.

She crosses the *t* in *top*.

Shall I write a *1* or a *2*?

The combination of italics (or underlining) and an apostrophe with the letter *s* is used to make numbers and letters plural.

Cross your *t*'s and dot your *i*'s.

We saw *1*'s on the scoreboard each inning—a good sign.

▶**30g** **Use underlining or italics for titles of book-length works separately published or broadcast, as well as for individually named transport craft.**

▶**1** **Use italics for books, long poems, and plays.**

Love in the Ruins [novel]
A Discovery of the Sea [book]
Antigone [play]
The Rime of the Ancient Mariner [long poem]

The Joy Luck Club [novel]
Twelfth Night [play]
The Odyssey [long poem]

The titles of sacred documents (and their parts) as well as legal or public documents are frequently capitalized (see 30d) but are not set in italics.

the Bible
the Magna Carta
the Koran

the New Testament
the Bill of Rights
Book of Exodus

Use Underlining or Italics for Titles

▶2 Use italics for newspapers, magazines, and periodicals.

the *Boston Globe*   the *New York Times*
Brookline *Citizen*   *Time*
the *Georgia Review*   *Archaeology*

With newspapers, do not capitalize, underline, or set in italics the word *the*, even if it is part of the newspaper's title. Italicize or underline the name of a city or town only if it is part of the newspaper's title. Titles of particular selections in a newspaper, magazine, or journal are set in quotation marks.

▶3 Use italics for works of visual art, long musical works, movies, and broadcast shows.

Rodin's *The Thinker*   *The Last Judgment*
Van Gogh's *The Starry Night* the *Burghers of Calais*
Mozart's *The Magic Flute*   the *German Requiem*

Note: Underline or set in italics the article *the* only when it is part of a title.

Movies and television or radio shows are italicized.

As the World Turns   *A Prairie Home Companion*
Late Show with David Letterman *All Things Considered*
Life Is Beautiful   *Star Wars: Episode 1 The Phantom Menace*

▶4 Use italics for individually named transport craft: Ships, trains, aircraft, and spacecraft.

USS *Hornet* (a ship)   *Atlantis* (a spacecraft)
HMS *Bounty* (a ship)   the *Montrealer* (a train)
Apollo X (a spacecraft) *Spirit of St. Louis* (an airplane)

Do not underline or italicize USS or HMS in a ship's name.

▶ EXERCISE 2

Correct the use of italics in these sentences. Circle words that should not be italicized. Underline words that should be italicized. Place a check beside any sentence in which italics are used correctly.

> **Example:** The most important tool of the navigator is an ⟨accurate⟩ ⟨current⟩ ⟨chart,⟩ without which it is virtually impossible to navigate successfully.

1. Navigation is the art of staying *out* of trouble.
2. You can keep your charts as current as possible by subscribing to Local Notices to Mariners, a weekly publication of the U.S. Coast Guard.
3. The key to successful navigation is to navigate *continuously,* that is, *always* be able to determine the position of your boat on the chart.
4. *Landmarks* (smokestacks, water towers, buildings, piers, *etc.*) and *aids to navigation* (beacons, lighthouses, buoys) help relate what you see from your boat to items found on the chart.
5. Aids to navigation are installed and maintained by the Coast Guard *specifically* to help you relate your surroundings to the appropriate symbols on the chart.
6. A *beacon* will be denoted on the chart by a triangle and the letters *Bn.*

CHAPTER **31**

Abbreviations and Numbers

The root word of *abbreviation* is the Latin *breviare*, from which come the familiar *brief*, *briefing*, and *brevity*. We use an **abbreviation**—the shortened form of a word followed (for the most part) by a period—only in restricted circumstances, as discussed below. Writers working in an unfamiliar discipline should consult the standard manuals of reference, style, and documentation for guidance in using abbreviations and numbers in the field. Many such reference works are listed in Chapter 37, Documenting Research, with conventions shown in Chapters 38–40 on writing in each of the major discipline areas.

ABBREVIATIONS

▶ **31a** Abbreviating titles of rank both before and after proper names

The following titles of address are usually abbreviated before a proper name.

Mr. Mrs. Ms. Dr.

Though not an abbreviation, *Ms.* is usually followed by a period.

Abbreviations for titles of rank or honor are usually reserved for the most formal references and addresses in connection with a person's full name and title. Mention of a person's title or rank in a less formal context does not call for an abbreviation. Typically, the abbreviations *Gen., Lt., Sen., Rep.,* and *Hon.* precede a full name—first and last.

Faulty	Gen. Eisenhower	Sen. Kennedy
Revised	General Eisenhower	Senator Kennedy
Revised	Gen. Dwight D. Eisenhower	Sen. Ted Kennedy

The following abbreviated titles or designations of honor are placed *after* a formal address or listing of a person's full name.

B.A.	M.A.	M.S.	Ph.D.	C.P.A.
Jr.	Sr.	M.D.	Esq.	

Place a comma after the surname, then follow with the abbreviation. If more than one abbreviation is used, place a comma between abbreviations.

Lawrence Swift Jr., M.D.

Abbreviations of medical, professional, or academic titles are *not* combined with the abbreviations *Mr.*, *Mrs.*, or *Ms.*

Faulty	Ms. Joan Warren, M.D.	Ms. Mindy Lubber, Ed.D.
Revised	Dr. Joan Warren	Mindy Lubber, Ed.D.
	or Joan Warren, M.D.	*or* Dr. Mindy Lubber

Other than for direct reference to academic titles such as *Ph.D.* (Doctor of Philosophy), *M.A.* (Master of Arts), and *M.S.* (Master of Science), do not use free-standing abbreviated titles that have not been paired with a proper name in a sentence.

Acceptable	Jane Thompson earned her Ph.D. in biochemistry. [A degree is referred to separately.]

Faulty	Marie Lew is an M.D. [The degree should either be referred to separately or attached to the person's title.]
Revised	Marie Lew is a physician.
Revised	Marie Lew was awarded an M.D. degree from Harvard.

Faulty	John Kraft is a C.P.A.
Revised	John Kraft is a certified public accountant.
Revised	John passed the C.P.A. examination yesterday.

▶ 31b Abbreviating specific dates and numbers

With certain historical or archaeological dates, abbreviations are often used to indicate whether the event occurred in the last two thousand years.

Ancient times (prior to two thousand years ago)

B.C.   (before the birth of Christ)

B.C.E. (before the common era)

Both abbreviations follow the date.

Modern times (within the last two thousand years)

C.E.   (of the common era)

A.D.   (*Anno Domini*, "in the year of the Lord," an abbreviation that precedes the date)

Augustus, the first Roman Emperor, lived from 63 B.C. (*or* B.C.E.) to A.D. 14 (*or* C.E.).

When the context of a paragraph makes clear that the event occurred in the last two thousand years—suppose you are writing on the Industrial Revolution—it would be redundant, even insulting, to write "A.D. 1820."

Clock time, indicated as prior to noon or after, uses abbreviations in capitals or in lowercase.

5:44 P.M. (or p.m.)

5:44 A.M. (or a.m.)

When typeset, A.M./P.M. often appear in a smaller type size as capital letters: 5:44 P.M.

When numbers are referred to as specific items (such as numbers in arithmetic operations or as units of currency or measure), they are used with standard abbreviations.

No. 23 or no. 23   2 + 3 = 5
$23.01   99 bbl. [barrels]
54%

Abbreviations for time, numbers, units, or money should be used only with reference to specific dates or amounts.

Numerical concepts must be fully written out as part of a sentence, not given shortened treatment with abbreviations, unless they are attached to specific years, times, currencies, units, or items.

Faulty   We'll see you in the A.M.

Revised   We'll see you in the morning.

Faulty   Let's wait until the nos. are in before we make a decision.

Revised   Let's wait until the numbers are in before we make a decision.

Faulty   This happened in the B.C. era.

Revised   This happened almost three thousand years ago.

Faulty   Please tell me the % of dropouts for the year.

Revised   Please tell me the percentage of dropouts for the year.

 31c   **Using acronyms, uppercase abbreviations, and corporate abbreviations**

An **acronym** is the uppercase, pronounceable abbreviation of a proper noun—a person, organization, government agency, or country. Periods are not used with acronyms. If there is any chance that a reader might not be familiar with an acronym or abbreviation, spell it out on first mention, showing the acronym in parentheses.

Medical researchers are struggling to understand the virus that causes Acquired Immune Deficiency Syndrome (AIDS).

The following are some familiar acronyms.

NATO   North Atlantic Treaty Organization

MADD   Mothers Against Drunk Driving

NASA   National Aeronautics and Space Administration

NOW   National Organization for Women

Helping Readers to Understand Acronyms

Unless an acronym or uppercase abbreviation is common knowledge, courtesy obligates you to write out the full word, term, or organizational name at its first mention. Then, in a parenthetical remark, you give the abbreviation. In subsequent references to the person, word, or organization, use the abbreviation—as is illustrated in the beginning of this article from the journal *Archaeology*.

> To the end of the Early Intermediate Period (EIP), the appearance of stunning, elaborately decorated ceramics [. . .] suggests that tribal leaders possessed and exchanged prestige items as a way of consolidating their claims to political power.

In lengthy documents where you will be using many uppercase abbreviations and acronyms, consider creating a glossary in addition to defining abbreviations the first time you use them. The glossary, which is placed at the end of the paper as an appendix, provides one convenient place to make identifications.

Other uppercase abbreviations use the initial letters of familiar persons or groups to form well-known "call letter" designations conventionally used in writing.

JFK   John Fitzgerald Kennedy
SEC   Securities and Exchange Commission
ISBN   International Standard Book Number
NAACP   National Association for the Advancement of Colored People
MVP   Most Valuable Player
VFW   Veterans of Foreign Wars
USA (or U.S.A.)   United States of America

Abbreviations used by companies and organizations vary according to the usage of the organization. When referring directly to a specific organization, use its own preferred abbreviations for words such as *Incorporated (Inc.), Limited (Ltd.), Private Corporation (P.C.),* and *Brothers (Bros.).* Some companies will abbreviate the name of a city or state or the words *Apartment (Apt.), Post Office (P.O.) Box, Avenue (Ave.), Street (St.),* and *Boulevard (Blvd.)* in their formal return addresses; others will not. In a sentence that does not refer directly to a specific corporation, do not abbreviate such terms, but spell out all the pronounceable words.

Faulty   I mailed it to a corp. out on the blvd.
Revised   I mailed it to a corporation on the boulevard.
    I mailed it to The Impax Corp., Zero Wilshire Blvd.

▶ **31d**   Using abbreviations for parenthetical references

From Latin, the traditional language of international scholarship, we have inherited conventional expressions used in research to make brief references or explanations. These are conventionally used in footnotes, documentation, and sometimes in parenthetical comments. All of these Latin expressions should be replaced in a main sentence by their English equivalents.

e.g. (*exempli gratia*)	for example
et al. (*et alii*)	and others
i.e. (*id est*)	that is
N.B. (*nota bene*)	note well
viz. (*videlicet*)	namely
cf. (*confer*)	compare
c. or ca. (*circa*)	about
etc. (*et cetera*)	and such things; and so on

The extremely vague abbreviation *etc.* should be avoided unless a specific and obvious sequence is being indicated, as in *They proceeded by even numbers (2, 4, 6, 8, etc.).* Even here the phrase *and so on* is preferable. When used in parenthetical or bibliographical comments, these Latin abbreviations are not underlined or italicized since they are commonplace in English. Typically, these expressions introduce a parenthetical remark in an informal aside.

Informal   A growing portion of our National Income is composed of government transfer payments (e.g., welfare payments).

Formal   A growing portion of our National Income is composed of government transfer payments (for example, welfare payments).

Bibliographical abbreviations are commonly used in documentation to provide short forms of reference citations, but they should not be used in sentences of a paragraph. The following are some of the most frequently used abbreviations.

p.	page	Jan.	January
pp.	pages	Feb.	February
ed./eds.	editor(s)	Mar.	March
f./ff.	the following (pages)	Apr.	April
n.d.	no date (for a publication lacking a date)	Aug.	August
		Sep./Sept.	September
ch./chs.	chapter(s)	Oct.	October
ms./mss.	manuscript(s)	Nov.	November
col./cols.	column(s)	Dec.	December
vol./vols.	volume(s)		

Each discipline has specific conventions for abbreviations in documentation. For example, the months May, June, and July are not abbreviated in MLA style; other conventions are discussed in Chapter 37.

ACROSS THE CURRICULUM

Writing in the Disciplines

Conventions differ in the disciplines about when and how much writers should use abbreviations—and about which abbreviations are common knowledge and need not be defined. Across disciplines,

(continued)

> **Writing in the Disciplines** *(continued)*
>
> abbreviations are avoided in titles. For specific abbreviations lying beyond common knowledge, writers follow the convention of defining the abbreviation on first use. As a demonstration, a sketch of conventions for abbreviating in some of the science disciplines is provided here. For detailed information about conventions in a specific discipline, see the style manuals recommended in 38f, 39e, and 40e, or consult your professor.
>
> ■ In scientific writing, courtesy dictates that writers define words that are later abbreviated.
>
> Some 800 species of bats live in diverse habitats and vary greatly in behavior and physical characteristics. Their biosonar pulses also differ, even among species within the same genus. Nevertheless, these pulses can be classified into three types: constant frequency (CF), frequency modulated (FM), and combined (CF-FM).
>
> ■ Units of measure are generally abbreviated when they are paired with specific numbers. When not thus paired, the units are written out.
>
> In the next stage, 14 g were added. Several grams of the material were sent away for testing.
>
> ■ Abbreviations of measurements in scientific writing need not be defined on first use.
>
> ■ Symbol abbreviations are standardized, and you will find lists of accepted abbreviations in the *CBE Style Manual* published by the Council of Biology Editors. Generally, the use of abbreviations in titles is not accepted in science writing. Limited abbreviations—without definition—are accepted in tables.

▶ **31e** **Revise to eliminate all but conventional abbreviations from sentences.**

In sentences, no abbreviations are used for the names of days or months, units of measure, courses of instruction, geographical names, and page/chapter/volume references. These abbreviations are reserved for specific uses in charts and data presentations that require abbreviated treatment in each discipline.

Faulty   Come see me on the first Mon. in Aug.
Revised Come see me on the first Monday in August.

Faulty   He weighed 25 lbs.
Revised He weighed 25 pounds.

Exception: Abbreviations of standard, lengthy phrases denoting measurement are common in formal writing: miles per hour (mph or m.p.h.) and revolutions per minute (rpm or r.p.m.).

Faulty   We enrolled in bio. and soc. next semester.
Revised We enrolled in biology and sociology next semester.

Faulty	NYC is a haven for writers.
Revised	New York City is a haven for writers.
Faulty	The reference can be found in Vol. 6, sec. 5, p. 1. [These abbreviations are used in bibliographies and documentation only.]
Revised	The reference can be found in Volume 6, section 5, page 1.

▶ **EXERCISE 1**

Correct the use of abbreviations in these sentences. When appropriate, write out abbreviations.

> *Example:* You can create your own home pg. on the World Wide Web—just consult the appropriate chap. in a self-help manual.
>
> You can create your own home page on the World Wide Web—just consult the appropriate chapter in a self-help manual.

1. The World Wide Web was developed mostly at the European Laboratory for Particle Physics, near Geneva, Switz.
2. The Web project was really a spin-off of Apple Comp. Corp.'s HyperCard program.
3. Netscape, which some users claim is the most popular Web browser, has versions for both Windows and Mac. users.
4. Even if you don't have access to a Web browser, you can type in an e-mail address that will do the job; for example, you can tap into the system at Univ. of Kansas.
5. Best of all, you don't have to be a pHd. To figure out how to do some exciting Web browsing.

NUMBERS

31f Write out numbers that begin sentences and numbers that can be expressed in one or two words.

One to ninety-nine

nineteen	seventy-six
twenty-six	ninety-nine

Fractions

five-eighths	three-fourths
two and three-quarters	seven-sixteenths

Large round numbers

twenty-one thousand	fifteen hundred

Decades and centuries

the sixties	or	the '60s
the twenty-first century	or	the 21st century

Numbers that begin sentences should be written out.

Faulty   57 percent of those attending the meeting fell asleep.

Revised   Fifty-seven percent of those attending the meeting fell asleep.

Revised   Of those attending the meeting, 57 percent fell asleep.

When it is awkward to begin a sentence by writing out a long number, rearrange the sentence.

Awkward   Forty-two thousand eight hundred forty-seven was the paid attendance at last night's game.

Revised   The paid attendance at last night's game was 42,847.

▶ **31g**   **Use figures in sentences according to convention.**

Numbers longer than two words

1,345   2,455,421

Units of measure

Rates of speed	*Temperature*	*Length*
60 mph	32° F	17.6 nanometers
33 rpm	0° C	24¼ in.

Weight	*Money*	
34 grams	$.02 2¢	
21 pounds	$20.00	
	$1,500,000 $1.5 million	

Amounts of money that can be written in two or three words can be spelled out.

two cents
twenty dollars
one and a half million dollars

Scores, statistics, ratios

The game ended with the score 2–1.

In the past presidential election, less than 50 percent of the eligible population voted.

The odds against winning the weekly lottery are worse than 1,000,000 to 1.

A mean score of 72 can be expected on the exam.

Addresses

Apartment 6	2nd Avenue
231 Park Avenue	East 53rd Street
New York, New York 10021	

Telephone numbers

301-555-1212

Volume, page, and line references

Volume 6	act 1 scene 4 line 16
page 81	pages 120–133

Military units

the 41st Tactical Squadron	the 6th Fleet

Dates

70 B.C.	A.D. 70
from 1991 to 1992	1991–1992
1991–92	

Time

Write out numbers when using the expression *o'clock*.

10:00 a.m.	but	ten o'clock in the morning
10:02 p.m.	but	two minutes past ten in the evening

▶ **31h** | **Edit to eliminate numbers and figures mixed together in one sentence, unless these have different references.**

Faulty   A spacecraft orbiting Earth travels at seventeen thousand miles per hour; but because of the craft's distance from the planet, the images of continents and oceans seen through its window appear to be moving not much faster than images seen through the windshield of a car traveling 60 mph.

Revised   A spacecraft orbiting Earth travels at 17,000 mph; but because of the craft's distance from the planet, the images of continents and oceans seen through its window appear to be moving not much faster than images seen through the windshield of a car traveling 60 mph.

Acceptable   For two months before its closing, the U-Trust Savings and Loan advertised wildly fluctuating interest rates in an effort to secure new cash: 9 percent one month and 15 percent the next. [Both numbers referring to advertised rates are presented as figures; the numbers *two* and *one*, referring to measures of time, are written out.]

▶ **EXERCISE 2**

Correct the use of numbers in these sentences. Write out numbers in some cases; use figures in others.

    Example: On August thirty-first, 1995, Bass PLC sold its distribution network to Tradeteam.

                  On August 31, 1995, Bass PLC sold its distribution network to Tradeteam.

---

1. An enterprising British brewery has decided to try out home delivery on its customers with the claim that at least 24 cans of beer will be on the customer's doorstep within forty-eight hours once the order has been placed.

2. 3 cities have been targeted for the service so far—London, Nottingham, and Birmingham.

3. Customers must order a minimum of one crate (24 cans), and they can expect to pay 17.99 pounds with a delivery charge of 1.99£ added on.

4. The service will be tested for 3 months and then evaluated for profitability and consumer satisfaction.

5. Nottingham and Birmingham beer drinkers don't have much of a choice of brands—only one is available—but Londoners can choose from among 8 premium beers.

32

Hyphens

A small but important mark, the **hyphen** (-) has two uses: to join compound words and to divide words at the end of lines. You will find advice on word divisions in any dictionary, where each entry is broken into syllables. If you write on a computer, your word-processing software will probably suggest word divisions. As for compounds, these will require more discernment on your part, for relocating a simple hyphen can alter meanings entirely.

▶ 32a Using hyphens to make compound words

Compound words are created when two or more words are brought together to create a distinctive meaning and to function grammatically as a single word. Many compounds occur together so often that they have become one word, formed without a hyphen.

    sandbox   outline   casework   aircraft

Many words appearing in pairs remain separate. Two-word compounds may become one word over time, so consult a current dictionary when you are uncertain about spelling.

    sand toys   out loud   case study   air conditioning

Use a hyphen to link words when a compound expression would otherwise confuse a reader, even if only momentarily.

Confusing   Helen's razor sharp wit rarely failed her. [Helen's *razor* is not the subject; Helen's *wit* is.]

Clear   Helen's razor-sharp wit rarely failed her. [With the hyphen, meaning is clear.]

Small as they are, hyphens make a difference. Each of the following sentences has a distinct meaning.

    The cross reference helped me to understand the passage.

    The cross-reference helped me to understand the passage.

The first sentence concerns a literary reference to a *cross;* the second, a note that refers readers to some other page in an article or text. The conventions for forming compounds with hyphens are as follows.

▶1 Form compound adjectives with a hyphen to prevent misreading when they precede the noun being modified.

The following hyphenations make compound or multiple-word modifiers out of words that might otherwise be misread.

low-interest loan   state-of-the-art technology   hoped-for success

Note that when a **compound adjective** is positioned *after* the noun it modifies, it does not need hyphenation. Placed after a noun, the first word of the adjective does not compete for the reader's attention as the subject or object in the sentence.

Helen's wit was razor sharp.

A compound modifier is not hyphenated when its first word ends with the distinctive suffix of a modifier.

Helen's impressively sharp wit rarely failed her.

Because of its ending, the first word in this compound modifier is not misread. In this case, the *-ly* suffix marks *impressive* as an adverb, and the reader knows that

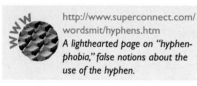

impressively will not function as the subject. Thus, the suffix in effect instructs the reader to move forward in search of the sentence's first noun—*wit*, which is in fact the subject. Because there is no possibility of misreading, no hyphen is used. The same analysis holds when the first word of the compound is a modifier ending with a comparative or superlative suffix *-er* or *-est* form (see 11e). In the following examples, the reader knows that *least* and *sweetest* are modifiers because of their endings.

The least expensive item in that store cost more than I could afford.

The sweetest sounding voice in the choir belonged to a child of ten. [*By contrast:* The sweet-sounding voice belonged to a child of ten.]

▶2 Form compound nouns and verbs with a hyphen to prevent misreading.

Use a hyphen with **compound nouns** and **compound verbs** when the first word of the compound invites the reader to regard that word, alone, as a noun or verb. Hyphenated nouns and verbs are marked as such in a dictionary.

cross-reference (n)   cross-examine (v)   runner-up (n)   shrink-wrap (v)

Hyphenating the compound forms makes reading the following sentence easier.

Confusing   The runner up staged a protest. [What is intended: *runner-up* or *up-staged?*]

Revised   The runner-up staged a protest.

▶3 Use hanging hyphens in a series of compound adjectives.

Hang—that is, suspend—hyphens after the first word of compound adjectives placed in a parallel series. In this usage, observe that the second word of the compound as well as the noun being modified is mentioned *once*.

The eighth-, ninth-, and tenth-grade classes went on the trip. [The second word of the compound, *grade*, and the noun modified, *classes*, are mentioned once.]

▶4 Follow conventions in hyphenating numbers, letters, and units.

Hyphenate fractions and the numbers twenty-one through ninety-nine.

Place a hyphen between the numerator and denominator of a fraction, unless one of these (or both) is already hyphenated.

one-fourth	seven-thousandths	seven one-thousandths
forty-six	seventy-one	

Hyphenate figures and letters joined with words to form nouns or modifiers.

4-minute mile   B-rated   U-turn

Hyphenate units of measure.

light-year   kilowatt-hour

▶5 Hyphenate compounds formed by prefixes or suffixes according to convention.

Use a hyphen with the prefixes *ex*, *quasi*, and *self*, with the suffix *elect*, and with most uses of *vice*. (Consult a dictionary for specifics.)

ex-President   quasi-serious   self-doubt

Use a hyphen with the prefixes *pro*, *anti*, and *pre* only when they are joined with proper nouns.

No hyphen	*Hyphen with proper noun*
prochoice	pro-Democracy
antimagnetic	anti-Maoist

But use a hyphen with a prefix or suffix that doubles a vowel or that triples a consonant.

No hyphen	*Hyphen with doubled or tripled letters*
antiseptic	anti-intellectual
childlike	bell-like

▶6 Hyphenate to avoid misreading.

re-form (to form an object—such as a clay figure—again)

reform (to overhaul and update a system)

▶ 32b   Using hyphens to divide a word at the end of a line

To the extent possible, avoid dividing words at the end of a line. When you must divide words, do so only at syllable breaks (as indicated in a dictionary). Even when given suggestions for hyphenation by word-processing software, you often face a choice concerning hyphenation that could make a difference in clarity. The following conventions improve comprehension.

Divide compound words at the hyphen marking the compound.

When hyphens join compound words, it is unnecessary and confusing to divide the word at any place other than the compound. (See the discussion on writing compounds in 32a.)

Unnecessary	The mouthparts of many insects are exquisitely adapted to the nectaries (*nectar-hold-ing* organs) of special flowers.
Clearer	The mouthparts of many insects are exquisitely adapted to the nectaries (*nectar-holding* organs) of special flowers.

Divide words at a prefix or suffix.

Hundreds of words are formed in English by adding prefixes and suffixes to root words (see 22d-2, 3). Divide these words, when possible, between prefix and root word or between suffix and root word. Thus, *un-necessary* would be preferable to *unnec-essary*.

A number of prefixes—such as *pro*, *anti*, *quasi*, *vice*, and *ex*—require the use of a hyphen. Divide these words at the hyphen.

Awkward	In the election of 1848, the "Free-Soil" party nominated Charles Francis Adams for *Vice-Presi-dent*.
Revised	In the election of 1848, the "Free-Soil" party nominated Charles Francis Adams for *Vice-President*.

Eliminate hyphenations that hang a single letter at the beginning or end of a line.

To avoid misleading your readers, you would not divide these words: *e-nough* or *tast-y*.

Confusing	Inflation creates fractures in the implicit and explicit *a-greements* that bind people together.
Revised	Inflation creates fractures in the implicit and explicit *agree-ments* that bind people together.

Eliminate misleading hyphenations.

The first syllable of a word is sometimes itself a word (for instance, *break-fast*, *arch-angel*, *in-stall*, *match-less*). Confusion results when the first syllable, left hyphenated at the end of a line, fits a sentence's content and suggests one meaning while the full, undivided word suggests another.

Single-syllable words are never hyphenated.

To prevent misleading the reader, you would not, for example, divide any of these words: *ceased*, *doubt*, *friend*, *freeze*, *though*.

Abbreviations, contractions, or multiple-digit numbers are not hyphenated.

Abbreviations (*apt., IBM, NATO*) and contractions (*can't, won't, they're*) are already shortened forms. To shorten them further by a word division will confuse your readers. A multiple-digit number divided at the end of a line is also confusing.

▶ **EXERCISE 1**

Use hyphens in the sentences that follow to form compound adjectives; to mark prefixes or suffixes; to note fractions, numbers less than one hundred, or words formed with figures; and to prevent misreading. Place a check beside any sentence in which hyphens are used correctly.

> *Example:* Following WWII, Pepsi Cola Company succeeded in recruiting Alfred N. Steele, a tough talking, two fisted, pin-striped warrior with a unique grasp of the mood of the fifties.
>
> Following WWII, Pepsi-Cola Company succeeded in recruiting Alfred N. Steele, a tough-talking, two-fisted, pin-striped warrior with a unique grasp of the mood of the fifties.

1. Steele was uniquely qualified to lead the Pepsi Cola Company when it began to falter because of its outdated marketing campaign; he had been educated at the world's greatest soft drink institution—the Coca-Cola Company.

2. Beginning his career running a circus, he moved into advertising and then jumped to a vice presidency at Coca Cola.

3. Subsequently, Steele accepted the more lucrative offer from Pepsi-Cola, though in his first quarter at the company it lost $100,000 as Coca-Cola pulverized the entire industry with a 67% stranglehold on the soft drink market.

4. Coca Cola was the darling of the ever expanding middle class, while Pepsi was a favorite of the downtrodden who couldn't afford to sacrifice Pepsi's extra ounces for Coke's prestige.

5. Thus, Steele set his sights on getting Pepsi into America's living rooms, and to that end redesigned Pepsi's standard 12 ounce bottle.

CHAPTER 33

Understanding the Research Process

Research begins with a question, with a need to *know*. You will enjoy your work as a researcher more if you can manage to take an assignment from your teacher and make it your own by formulating a question that you, personally, want to answer. Then, you will spend your time locating and examining sources because you are truly interested in your topic, not simply because you are fulfilling an assignment.

This is the first of five chapters devoted to research. This chapter provides the basic strategies for posing the questions that launch research and for seeking information, both inside and outside the library, that will help you to answer your questions in the form of a research paper. Chapter 34 gives you the necessary background for conducting electronic searches. Chapter 35 discusses the ways you will actually *use* the source materials you find: by taking notes, summarizing, paraphrasing, and quoting. Chapter 36 provides guidance on arranging materials and writing your paper. And Chapter 37 acquaints you with the process of documenting sources—acknowledging in your papers that you have drawn on the work of others.

http://www.researchpaper.com/
Researchpaper.com
One of the best Internet resources for help with research papers. Check out the Idea Directory and Discussion Area for help getting started.

▶ 33a Making your research worthwhile

▶ 1 Personal interest justifies effort.

The process of conducting research takes time. If you are like most students, you are busy; so for a research project to be worthwhile, you're going to have to justify it as a reasonable investment of time and effort. What will make the investment worthwhile? In a word, *interest*. Any efforts you make at the beginning and through the early stages of the process to become truly interested in your work will pay handsome dividends.

Motivation is easy to talk about in theory. In practice, generating personal interest in a research topic may be more difficult. Let's assume that you have been given an assignment on shopping malls, the topic of the student research paper

Generating Personal Interest in a Topic

With a bit of effort, you can discover enthusiasm for many topics, even those that you do not choose yourself.

- **If you find the topic interesting:** If you are drawn to the topic, so much the better. Divide it into several well-defined parts. Ask: Which part do I want to learn more about? Use your answer to locate general sources. Then read.

- **If you are repelled by an assigned topic:** Try to understand your negative response. Negative reactions, as well as positive ones, can lead to an effective paper. Again, divide the topic into well-defined parts. Ask: What information could help me to understand my reaction? Use your answer to locate general sources. Then read.

- **If the topic leaves you feeling neutral:** At the beginning stages, you may not know enough about a topic to be interested. When you learn even a little about the topic, you may discover possibilities. So go to a general source—an encyclopedia or an introductory book—or try a general index (for example, the *Readers' Guide to Periodical Literature*) to locate two or three promising articles to read.

    1. Based on your reading, identify as many angles of approach to the topic as you can. Discovering an approach you never considered may spark your interest.
    2. Generate as many questions as you can, based on what you read. Perhaps one will become your research focus.
    3. Read in "hyper-alert" mode. Actively respond to multiple points in the article. Perhaps one response will become your research focus.

you'll see developed throughout this section of the book. You've gone to malls. People arrive, shop, and go home. What's to know? Why write about *this* topic?

Such a response is legitimate; but given that a teacher expects you to write a research paper, you will have work to do, and you may as well enjoy it by finding something interesting about which to write. To generate interest where none (or little) exists, try the strategies listed in the box.

▶2 Personal interest improves writing.

Your effectiveness as a writer is directly related to your motivation. Motivated research and writing is actually *better* and more insightful than unmotivated efforts. Evaluating individual sources and, especially, synthesizing multiple sources requires determined effort and creativity.

- Motivated writers work hard with their sources, staying with each one long enough to form a definite, critical response.
- Motivated writers return to a library or make an additional call to locate promising sources.

- Motivated writers are willing to tinker with the various ways in which sources might be related. These relationships can provide original insights for the final paper.

The investment of personal interest pays two types of dividends: you enjoy and actively learn from the process of research, and you produce higher quality work.

CRITICAL DECISIONS

Think actively: Adopting strategies to motivate yourself as a researcher

The best research is conducted by those who are fully interested in their topic. Interest will motivate you to look for sources, find connections among them, and evaluate in ways that will eventually lead to your research question. Interest and motivation are clearly functions of critical thinking, as discussed in Chapter 1:

- Read actively: Be alert to similarities and differences. See 1a.
- Challenge yourself and your sources. See 1b.
- Place particular events or ideas in a broader context. See 1c.
- Evaluate what you read. See 1g.

▶**3 Using essay writing as a foundation for research writing**

The process of writing a research paper is similar to that of writing an essay. Both require that you think critically, not only about the sources you read but also about the positions you take as you develop your ideas.

In Chapter 3, you will find a diagram that models the writing process (see 3a-1). This illustration shows writing and thinking as circular, recursive activities. *Recursive* means looping back on itself. That is, while the writing process has identifiable stages, you will *not* work through these stages in a straight-line fashion. You will devote time to each of the following stages, but not necessarily in this order and not necessarily one stage at a time. You will

- define your purpose and audience;
- generate ideas and organize information;
- write a draft; and
- revise the draft.

A personal commitment to your topic will motivate you not only to challenge your sources but also to challenge yourself. Student researcher Jason Koman initially asked, What *is* a shopping mall? His initial answer: Malls are our modern equivalent of the medieval market. As he learned through research, and as you will see demonstrated in his paper, this is only partially true. As Jason read further on his topic and allowed the sources to challenge his initial ideas, he came to a new, revised question: *What do we want at the mall?* In response to this revised question, Jason completed his research and wrote a successful paper.

Your original ideas are essential.

Writing a research paper involves a process of drafting and revision, in much the same way that writing an essay does—but with a difference: in research writing, you not only have the process itself to help clarify your thinking, but also you have source materials, which will help you test the soundness of your ideas as they evolve. Writing a research paper is *not* a process of locating a certain number of sources and then stitching them together mechanically. The process requires original, active thinking. The successful paper must be based on an original idea: *your* idea.

For more information on the process of writing, see Chapter 3. For an in-depth look at revising and rethinking, see Chapter 4.

▶ **EXERCISE 1**

Interview two of your instructors. Ask what kinds of research they do and why their research interests them personally. Ask what, if any, "burning questions" have directed their research. Why do these questions burn for them? Take notes during the interviews. Then review these notes and write three paragraphs: two paragraphs devoted to summarizing the interviews; and one paragraph in which you make observations about the research your instructors do and their personal relationships to that research.

▶ **33b**	Determining the scope of your paper and identifying a research question

▶ **1 Determining the scope of your paper**

Try to avoid two frustrating experiences: squeezing a great deal of research into a paper, only to feel that you've treated the material superficially and, conversely, trying to pump extra material into a paper for which the topic seems too slight. To avoid these problems, you will need to understand several factors that affect the scope of your work: assignment, audience, topic, and intended level of detail.

■ Your *assignment* helps to set the scope of your project: specific tasks, length, and number and variety of sources expected. In 44b, you will find a list of key verbs associated with essay questions. These same verbs—such as *compare*, *discuss*, and *justify*—will be found in typical research assignments, so you should be aware of them and their definitions.

■ Your *audience* will determine key elements of your paper, ranging from tone, to vocabulary, to structure. Who is your audience? Will you be writing for specialists or nonspecialists? For college students or readers of the OP-ED page? Are your readers likely to agree with you or not? See 3a-3 for specific questions to help you analyze your audience and its needs and to make subsequent decisions in your paper.

■ Your *topic*, and the ways in which you can divide it into subtopics, will also help to define the scope of your paper. Almost immediately on beginning your research, you will learn enough about your topic to define several component parts. In your research paper, you will need to decide how many parts to work with. Your decisions will affect the scope of your paper.

■ Your *intended level of detail* for the paper will also affect the scope of your work and your selection of topics (or subtopics). A single topic can be discussed in minute detail, at great length, or briefly in a quick overview. Be clear about the level of detail you will be bringing to your paper, or to specific sections of the paper.

▶2 Identifying your key research question

As you continue to read about your topic, you will sift through your questions and eventually arrive at one that interests you most—the question that you will answer by conducting still more research. The advantage of working with a question, as

 http://courses.ncsu.edu/classes/ hi482001/step2.htm
Hypertext guide to Forming a Research Question, specifically for History courses, but applicable to any field.

opposed to a thesis, at this point, is that you are acknowledging that you still have to discover the answer(s), rather than just find evidence to support a prematurely established conclusion. How can you tell if your research question is a good one? Consider the advice in the following box:

CRITICAL DECISIONS

Challenge your motivation for writing: Do you have a good research question?

Devise a question that you, personally, **need** to answer to ensure that your research project will be interesting to you. As you reflect on what you think will be your main research question, consider the following:

1. Have any of your sources answered the question completely and, in your view, comprehensively?

   ■ If *no*, then your question is a good one—your research efforts will provide an answer that does not yet exist.

   ■ If your sources *have* completely and comprehensively answered your research question, try to find some aspect of the question that is *not* yet answered, to ensure that your efforts are original.

2. Does your question linger with you? Do you find yourself thinking about this question at odd times—on the way to the mailbox or the cafeteria?

   ■ If *yes*, then stay with your question: it has engaged you. Frequently, it is in these "off" hours, when you are not formally working, that important insights occur.

   ■ If *no*, then reexamine your question. Make sure it fascinates you sufficiently to continue letting it guide your research.

3. Does investigating your question give you opportunities to make connections from one source to another—connections that the sources themselves don't seem to be making?

 ■ If *yes*, then stay with your question: it is prompting efforts of *synthesis*—you are piecing elements of a puzzle together, which is what researchers do.

 ■ If *no*, then reexamine your question. Make sure the question encourages you to forge connections.

▶**3** **Understanding strategies for writing arguments in different disciplines**

Writing a research paper in one discipline or another involves arguing and using evidence in ways that are appropriate to that discipline. Your success in these papers depends on the extent to which you can demonstrate that you think like a researcher in a particular discipline. Are you asking questions and providing evidence like a sociologist or a biologist? like a historian or an engineer? Conventions for constructing arguments, that is, responding to questions, change from one discipline to the next, and you should be aware of these conventions while writing your research papers. Discussions in this book will help: see Chapters 38, 39, and 40 for details on writing arguments in the humanities, the social sciences, and the sciences. Look for these key distinctions across disciplines:

Social science: Writers in business and in the social sciences (as described in 39a), often try to present significant social or economic patterns and to make arguments as to why those patterns are significant.

Humanities: As you will see in 38a, writers in the humanities make statements of interpretation about texts in all their variety, including stories, dramas, movies, sacred literature, correspondence, personal or government records, and the work of others (in the humanities). Textual materials become evidence in interpretive arguments; the goal is to persuade others that interpretations are valid.

Science: As you will see in 40a-2, writers in the sciences often make arguments that involve two claims. The first: *X is a problem*, or *X is puzzling*. The second claim takes this form: *X can be explained as follows*.

Writers and researchers in each of these broad discipline areas pose distinctive types of questions. Familiarize yourself with these questions and use them in your research.

▶ **EXERCISE 2**

Working with roommates, classmates, or friends, generate a collection of assignments from different disciplines that call for writing. Examine the wording of these assignments with care, and answer these questions: What are the key verbs in each assignment? How do these verbs set an action plan for the writer? Does the role of the writer as originator of ideas change from one assignment to the next? What is discipline-specific about the assignment: its topic? method of analysis? presentation of findings?

Perhaps you have selected a broad subject, which you may have already begun to restrict and focus. Or you may have started with a question and have begun to follow it up with additional questions. Here, we consider ways of further focusing your work and of searching for information sources about your topic (see 3a-1). Specifically, we will consider (1) how to keep an ongoing research log of your ideas; (2) how to develop a search strategy for preliminary reading; and (3) how to develop a search strategy for more focused reading, leading toward the development of your working thesis.

▶ **1 Keep a research log.**

Many students find it valuable to keep track of their ideas in a research log. They write down their initial questions in this log and update it as often as possible. The log becomes a running record of all their inspirations, false starts, dead ends, second thoughts, breakthroughs, self-criticisms, and plans.

One technique that is particularly useful at the outset of a project is called *nonstop writing*. Nonstop writing (sometimes called *brainstorming* or *freewriting*) requires you to put pen to paper, consider your topic, and write down anything that occurs to you. Generate as many ideas as you possibly can within ten or fifteen minutes. At the end of the session, you may have some useful ideas to pursue. Here, for example, are some initial ideas generated by brief brainstorming sessions about shopping malls.

> shopping malls—building these huge places, the bucks, the hype in the community, hanging out, going to buy, being part of the excitement. How similar is it to what people used to do—hundreds of years ago? Could be very much the same. Go to market, see the people, buy the goods. Is the mall the old market, updated?

Even though these ideas are in crude form, you can see a paper beginning to take shape here. As you proceed with your research, keep your log updated. You will want to do this not just to preserve a record of your research (often valuable in itself), but also to allow you to return to initially discarded ideas, which, at a later stage in the paper, may assume new relevance or importance.

Researchers use a log for other purposes, as well.

1. To jot down *sources* and possible sources—not only library sources, but also names and phone numbers of people to interview.
2. To freewrite their *reactions* to the material they are reading and to the people they are interviewing; these reactions may later find their way into the finished paper.
3. To jot down *questions* that occur to them in the process of research, which they intend to pursue later. (For example, when were the first malls built—in the United States, in Europe? What came before the mall? Markets have been around for a long time. What were the first ones like?)
4. To try out and revise ideas for *theses* as their research progresses.

Avoid using your log for actually taking notes on your sources; it is best to do this on notecards or on your computer, so that you can freely rearrange notes as you prepare to write your first draft.

Generating Ideas for Your Paper

The following are three additional strategies for generating ideas. Each will help you consider ways in which to divide a broad topic into smaller, more manageable parts. You will probably be more specific and imaginative in thinking about *parts* of a topic than you will be in thinking about the topic as a whole.

■ **Reading:** Read general works that survey your topic. The survey will suggest subdivisions.

■ **Web browsing:** Browsing the Web can be an excellent springboard to ideas. You might check, first, with one of the general subject directories, such as Yahoo! <http://www.yahoo.com> to see how the editors create categories and subcategories of information, in the process providing an overview of an entire subject area. You will be linked to Web documents, which can also spark ideas.

■ **Brainstorming:** Place your topic at the top of a page and, working for five or ten minutes continuously, list any related phrases or words that come to mind. After generating your list, group related items. Groups with the greatest number of items indicate areas that should prove fertile in developing your paper.

■ **Listing attributes:** In a numbered list, jot down all of the attributes, or features, that a broad topic possesses. Then ask of every item on your list: What are its uses? What are its consequences?

▶2 Talk with your instructor or with other authorities.

Before starting your research, do not neglect another important resource: your instructor. Schedule a conference or visit your instructor during office hours. Your conference may turn into a kind of verbal freewriting session, with several unresolved questions remaining at the end of the session—one of which may become the focus of your paper.

You have now focused on one or more research questions; you have done some preliminary reading and perhaps have talked to one or two authorities on the subject; and you have begun generating some written ideas. At this point, you have followed the basic writing process by focusing on a topic (3a-1) and have given some thought to your purpose and audience (3a-2, 3).

Remember that having selected a research question, you are under no obligation to zealously guard it against all changes. Quite possibly, you will need to adjust your focus—and therefore your key question—as your research and your thinking on a subject develop.

▶ EXERCISE 3

Choose a subject and develop some ideas about it, using one or more of the strategies discussed in this section. Read at least two relevant sources, and then develop a research question for a paper on the subject.

> **33d** Developing a strategy for preliminary research

▶ 1 Beginning systematic research

Effective search strategies often begin with the most general reference sources: encyclopedias, bibliographic listings, biographical works, and dictionaries. These

http://encyclopedia.com/
A free searchable site with more than 17,000 articles from the Columbia Concise Electronic Encyclopedia.

general sources are designed for people who want to familiarize themselves relatively quickly with the basic information about a particular subject. Authors of general sources assume that their readers have little or no prior knowledge of the subjects covered and of the specialized terminology used in the field. By design, they review a subject in less depth than do specialized sources. So you'll want to read the more general sources relatively early in your search.

Consult librarians as a resource.

Librarians have made it their career to know how to find information quickly and efficiently. This does not mean that they will do your research for you. It means

http://www.s9.com/biography/
This searchable free online biographical dictionary includes more than 27,000 biographies.

they will be happy to direct you to the tools with which to do your own research. Frequently, the key to getting the information you need is simply knowing where to look. The next sections will provide some assistance in this area. Your

reference librarian will be able not only to supplement our list of sources (see 33-f), but also to tell you which ones are best for your purposes.

▶ 2 Refining your thinking with systematic research

Systematic reading can help you to refine your thinking about a topic. New sources can lead you to a revised research question. Again, Jason Koman's experience provides a good illustration.

A bit too early in the process, Jason settled on his research question: *What is a mall?* Before consulting most of the sources that he would end up using in his paper, he hazarded an answer: *The shopping mall is our modern equivalent of the ancient marketplace.* As Jason continued to read, he found his answer to be premature and his question to be limiting. Further reading in detailed sources revealed that the modern mall is *not* an exact equivalent of the ancient markets, in at least one crucial respect. This key difference, Jason realized, could provide the final focus for his paper. He determined to focus on similarities and differences in the context of a newly refined question: *What do we want at the mall?* This new question enabled him to explore people's motivations for gathering in marketplaces—both modern and ancient.

▶ 3 Bringing your research to an end

You should recognize that any diagram of the search strategy or of the focusing procedure makes these processes look neater than they generally are. In practice,

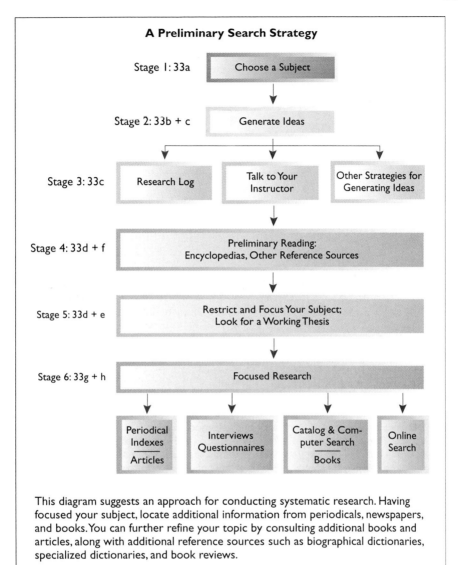

A Preliminary Search Strategy

Stage 1: 33a → Choose a Subject

Stage 2: 33b + c → Generate Ideas

Stage 3: 33c → Research Log | Talk to Your Instructor | Other Strategies for Generating Ideas

Stage 4: 33d + f → Preliminary Reading: Encyclopedias, Other Reference Sources

Stage 5: 33d + e → Restrict and Focus Your Subject; Look for a Working Thesis

Stage 6: 33g + h → Focused Research

Periodical Indexes — Articles | Interviews Questionnaires | Catalog & Computer Search — Books | Online Search

This diagram suggests an approach for conducting systematic research. Having focused your subject, locate additional information from periodicals, newspapers, and books. You can further refine your topic by consulting additional books and articles, along with additional reference sources such as biographical dictionaries, specialized dictionaries, and book reviews.

they are often considerably less systematic, because writing is such a recursive process—as shown in 3a-1 and 3d-3. It is crucial to keep in mind the kinds of resources and procedures that are available to you, and—given the constraints on your time—to use as many as you can.

As you proceed, you will discover that research is to some extent a self-generating process. That is, one source will lead you—through references in the text, citations, and bibliographic entries—to others. Authors will refer to other studies on the subject; and frequently, they will indicate which ones they believe are

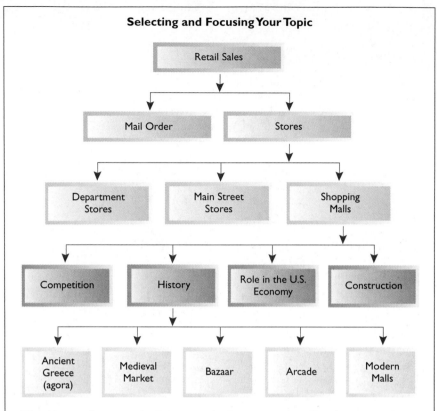

Selecting and Focusing Your Topic

Retail Sales

Mail Order — Stores

Department Stores — Main Street Stores — Shopping Malls

Competition — History — Role in the U.S. Economy — Construction

Ancient Greece (agora) — Medieval Market — Bazaar — Arcade — Modern Malls

This diagram illustrates the focusing and selection process of student researcher Jason Koman. Selection and focusing brings Jason to his initial topic of shopping malls. He quickly sees the need to restrict the topic still more. Guided by additional reading, he identifies four elements of interest: competition, history, role in the U.S. economy, and construction. Any of these areas would provide an appropriate scope for an eight- to ten-page paper. Jason chooses history as his focus.

the most important, and why. At some point you will realize that you have already looked at most of the key research on the subject. This is the point at which you can be reasonably assured that the research stage of your project is nearing its end.

▶ **EXERCISE 4**

Working with your topic, begin preliminary research. Start keeping a research log. Read one or two general reference sources; from these, try restricting the focus of your topic. As you do so, identify several sources that more specifically address your research needs. Having read one or more of these sources, can you refine your research question? Check on your success in focusing your topic by creating a diagram similar to the one above.

33e Devising a working thesis

1 Answering your research question

During your preliminary reading you began to focus on a *research question*. Jason Koman's question was: What do people want when they go to a shopping mall? As you continue to read about your subject, you should begin to develop your own ideas about it. Answer your research question, at least provisionally, and you will have a *working thesis* (see 3d): the clearest, most succinct statement thus far of your paper's main idea.

This thesis is *provisional:* it is subject to change as you come across new material and as your thinking about the subject develops. For now, however, this working thesis is the main idea that shapes your thinking. The working thesis will also influence the focused reading of your subsequent research since, by defining relevant areas and eliminating irrelevant ones, it narrows the scope of your search for supporting evidence.

For the sake of convenience, let's examine four working theses. Here are four discipline areas, and four narrowed topics:

For a paper in the *humanities,* the topic is nineteenth century literature about the potential excesses of science, for example, in *Frankenstein* and *Dr. Jekyll and Mr. Hyde.*

For a paper in *business,* the issue is who owns the information contained in genetic algorithms.

For a paper in the *social sciences,* the topic is social and ethical issues in technological intervention in human reproduction.

For a paper in *science,* the topic is whether genetically altered food products are safe.

2 Taking a stand: The working thesis as a statement to be proven

So far, these are only *topics*—not theses. To develop a working thesis from each

http://www.indiana.edu/~wts/wts/thesis.html
An extended look at the process of composing and revising a thesis statement.

of these topics, you will need to make a *statement* about the topic (after surveying a good deal of source material). Here are four statements that can be used as working theses:

Humanities: Frankenstein was perhaps the first in a long line of books to exploit people's nervousness about scientific progress.

Business: Companies employing genetic engineers try to be diligent about patenting their discoveries.

Social Science: Safeguards need to be strengthened to protect infertile couples being promised "miracle cures" from the latest expensive medical procedure.

Science: Biotechnology promises to improve the *quantity* of food, but quantity will mean little unless we can guarantee the safety of genetically altered foods.

Note that while each thesis requires that the writer support his or her opinion, the first two theses tend to be *informative,* whereas the second two tend to be *argumentative.* That is, in each of the first two cases, the thesis itself is not a particularly controversial one; it is not a proposition that normally generates strong emotions. In the latter two cases, however, the writer will argue one side of a fairly controversial issue. These are issues on which it is sometimes difficult to get people to change their minds, even after considering the evidence, because they have strong underlying feelings about them. As you write the thesis, understand whether you are writing an informative or argumentative research paper. If you are writing an argument, consult Chapter 6 for guidance.

▶ **EXERCISE 5**

Based on your preliminary reading in general sources (Exercise 4), develop two working thesis statements about your topic: an *informative thesis* and an *argumentative thesis.* Make sure that each thesis takes the form of a *statement* about the topic.

▶ **33f** Doing preliminary research and reading

If you follow the strategy for preliminary research presented earlier, you will begin your research efforts with a systematic review of general sources. In this section, we will review some of the most useful general sources. Note: While all of the sources mentioned here have a print format, many (such as the major encyclopedias) are migrating to the World Wide Web. Check with your librarian to see if your school has access to these Web-based resources.

▶ **I** Encyclopedias, bibliographies, dictionaries

Encyclopedias

A general encyclopedia is a comprehensive, often multivolume work that covers events, subjects, people, and places across the spectrum of human knowledge. The articles, usually written by specialists, offer a broad overview of the subjects covered. From an encyclopedia you may discover a particular aspect of the subject that interests you and see how that aspect relates to the subject in general. Encyclopedia entries on major subjects frequently include bibliographies.

Keep in mind that encyclopedias—particularly general encyclopedias—are frequently not considered legitimate sources of information for college-level papers. Thus, while you may want to use an encyclopedia article to familiarize yourself with the subject matter of the field and to locate specific topics within that field, you probably should not use it as a major source, or indeed, for anything other than background information.

One disadvantage of encyclopedias is that since new editions are published only once every several years, they frequently do not include the most up-to-date information on a subject. Naturally, this is of more concern in some areas than others: if you are writing on the American Revolution, you are on safer ground consulting an encyclopedia than if you are writing on whether doctors consider alcoholism a disease. Still, the nature of scholarship is that *any* subject—including the American Revolution—is open to reinterpretation and the discovery of new knowledge, so use encyclopedias with due caution.

Following are some of the most frequently used general encyclopedias:

American Academic Encyclopedia
Collier's Encyclopedia
Columbia Encyclopedia
Encyclopedia Americana
Encyclopædia Britannica

COMPUTER TIPS

The Library without Books

More and more, libraries are beginning to resemble computer labs rather than book repositories. Many of the indexes you may be used to consulting such as the *Readers' Guide to Periodical Literature* and many others, are now available electronically through your library's online subscription, the Internet, or CD-ROM. Often these electronic resources do more than find titles and brief descriptions of articles and other sources of information; they also allow you to retrieve the full text of the article. Ask your reference librarian for a listing of these electronic resources, and for instructions on how to access them and print out articles.

Biographical sources

Frequently, you have to look up information on particular people. Note that some biographical sources are classified according to whether the person is living or dead. The following are some of the most common biographical sources:

For persons still living

> *American Men and Women of Science*
> *Contemporary Authors: A Biographical Guide to Current Authors and Their Works*
> *Current Biography*
> *Directory of American Scholars*
> *International Who's Who*

For persons living or dead

> *American Novelists Since World War II*
> *American Poets Since World War II*
> *Biography Almanac*
> *Contemporary American Composers: A Biographical Dictionary*
> *McGraw-Hill Encyclopedia of World Biography*
> *National Academy of Sciences, Biographical Memoirs*
> *Webster's Biographical Dictionary*

Dictionaries

Dictionaries enable you to look up the meaning of particular terms. As with encyclopedias, dictionaries may be either general or specialized in scope. Some of the more common dictionaries are listed in 22b-1.

▶2 **Other print sources of information**

In addition to encyclopedias, biographical sources, and dictionaries, you may find the following sources useful.

Guides to the literature enable you to locate and use reference sources within particular disciplines. Here are five examples:

Business Information Sources
Guide to Historical Literature
How and Where to Look It Up: A Guide to Standard Sources of Information
Reference Books: A Brief Guide
Sources of Information in the Social Sciences

Handbooks provide facts and lists of data for particular disciplines. Here are several examples:

The Allyn & Bacon Handbook (covers grammar and style)
Gallup Poll: Public Opinion
Handbook of Basic Economic Statistics
Handbook of Chemistry and Physics
Statistical Abstract of the United States

Almanacs also provide facts and lists of data, but are generally issued annually:

Almanac of American Politics
Congressional Quarterly Almanac
Dow Jones Irwin Business Almanac
Information Please Almanac (general)
The World Almanac (general)

Yearbooks, issued annually, update data already published in encyclopedias and other reference sources:

Americana Annual
Britannica Book of the Year
Statesman's Yearbook

Atlases and gazetteers provide maps and other geographical data:

National Atlas of the United States of America
Times Atlas of the World

Citation indexes indicate when and where a given work has been cited *after* its initial publication; these are useful for tracing the influence of a particular work:

Humanities Citation Index
Science Citation Index
Social Science Citation Index

Book review indexes provide access to book reviews; these are useful for evaluating the scope, quality, and reliability of a particular source:

Book Review Digest (includes excerpts from reviews)

Book Review Index

Government publications are numerous and frequently offer recent and authoritative information in a particular field:

American Statistics Index

Congressional Information Service

The Congressional Record

Government Manual

Guide to U.S. Government Publications

Information U.S.A.

Monthly Catalogue of U.S. Government Publications

http://www.access.gpo.gov/
su_docs/dpos/adpos400.html
The Catalog of U.S. Government Publications: a search and retrieval service that provides bibliographic records of U.S. Government information resources.

Consult your librarian for information on guides to the literature, almanacs, and other reference guides relevant to your subject.

Library of Congress Subject Headings

If you are making a systematic search to refine your subject, you should probably check the *Library of Congress Subject Headings*. This set of volumes indicates how the subjects listed according to the Library of Congress System are broken down. For example, drug abuse is broken down into such subtopics as "religious aspects," "social aspects," and "treatment." You can use the *Library of Congress Subject Headings* as you would use encyclopedia entries or the *Bibliographic Index* below. First, you can survey the main aspects of that subject. Second, you can select a particular aspect that interests you. Third, you can focus your subject search (in both the book and periodical indexes) on the particular aspect or subtopic that interests you, since these subtopics indicate the headings to look under in these indexes.

Bibliographic Index

Although we will cover periodical indexes later (see 33g-2), it is appropriate to mention here the *Bibliographic Index* is an excellent research tool both for browsing through some of the subtopics of a subject and for directing you to additional sources. The *Bibliographic Index* is an annual bibliography of bibliographies (that is, a bibliography that lists other bibliographies), arranged by subject. Shown below, for example, is the listing under "Shopping centers" in the 1993 *Bibliographic Index*.

Each of these listings represents a bibliography that appears in another source—a book, a pamphlet, or an article. In most cases, the bibliography appears as a source of additional readings at the conclusion of the book, the chapter, or the article. In some cases, however, the bibliography stands by itself as an independent publication. If you browse through a few successive years of listings on a subject, you will probably discover some topics that interest you, as well as a source of readings on that topic.

Main heading —— **Shopping centers**

Entry under
other main ——
heading

See also

—— Retail trade

Design

O'Neill, M. J. and Jasper, C. R. An evaluation of models
of consumer spatial behavior using the environment-
behavior paradigm. *Environ Behav* 24:438–40 Jl '92

Title of
periodical

Subheading ——————————— **Design and construction**

Volume: page
number(s)

Goss, J. The "magic of the mall": an analysis of form,
function, and meaning in the contemporary retail
built environment. *Ann Assoc Am Geogr* 83:44–7 Mr
'93

Date of
periodical

Great Britain

Location

Author ———————— Brown, Stephen. Retail location; a micro-scale perspective. Avebury 1992 p242–310

Publisher
and date

▶3 General electronic sources

There are two types of electronic database resources: CD-ROM disks and online
material. Most periodical indexes that are available in print (such as *Readers' Guide*
and *Humanities Index*) are also available on CD-ROM. Since a CD can store several years' worth of indexes, a CD search takes less time and effort than a search
through several bound volumes. Many general reference print materials, such as
The Oxford English Dictionary and various encyclopedias, are currently available on
CD-ROM—a format that allows users to make rapid cross-references and searches.

One important index is InfoTrac (originally on CD but migrating to the
Web), which provides access to articles in over 1,000 business, technological, and
general-interest periodicals, as well as the *New York Times* and the *Wall Street Journal*. Some specialized reference works on CD-ROM can be particularly interesting and rich in resources, depending on your research topic; a renowned example

COMPUTER TIPS

Bookmarks

One of the most convenient time savers for using the Internet is
the "bookmark," a record of a URL that you'd like to remember.
URLs are often complex and unwieldy, so to copy them down and later type
them in again by hand invites mistakes. Instead, let your Web browser keep a list
of them for you. In the course of your research, when you access a Web page
from which you use information or one that you think you may need to access
again, add a bookmark to your list. Then, when you need to return to the page,
all you have to do is click on that bookmark. Most browsers let you examine your
bookmarks, so your list can function as a readily accessible record of the URLs
you'll need for your bibliography.

is the *Perseus* CD-ROM program from Harvard University Press, a large compendium of material on the classical world, including social, archaeological, literary, and linguistic material from classics scholarship.

Consult your librarian, who will have a listing of CD-ROMs and Internet resources that you can use in your research. See Chapter 34 for a detailed discussion on searching electronic sources.

Using General Sources

- Use *encyclopedias* to get a broad overview of a particular subject.
- Use *biographical sources* to look up information about persons living or dead.
- Use *general dictionaries* to look up the meaning of particular terms.
- Use *guides to the literature* to locate reference sources in particular disciplines.
- Use *handbooks* to look up facts and lists of data for particular disciplines.
- Use *almanacs* to look up annually updated facts and lists of data.
- Use *yearbooks* to find updates of data already published in encyclopedias and other reference sources.
- Use *atlases* and *gazetteers* to find maps and other geographical data.
- Use *citation indexes* to trace references to a given work after its initial publication.
- Use *book review indexes* to look up book reviews.
- Use *government publications* to look up recent and authoritative information in a given field.
- Use *bibliographic sources* to locate books and articles on a particular subject.
- Use *electronic sources* to locate large databases and current information.

EXERCISE 6

Use your working thesis to guide your access to one or more of the reference materials listed in this section. Keep a record of the sources used (keep full bibliographic information, including electronic access information if you browse the Internet or use an online service). Take notes on each source.

▶ 33g   Focused research: Print sources and interviews

If you have looked through a number of general sources, you have probably also developed a working thesis. At this point, you have some basic knowledge about your subject and some tentative ideas about it. But there are limits to your knowledge—which correspond to the limits of the kinds of sources you have relied on so far. You need more specific information to pursue your thesis.

▶ 1   Looking for specific sources

General sources are not intended to provide in-depth knowledge, nor can they explore more than a few of the often numerous aspects of a subject. Refer back to the diagram on page 488. If you were researching the subject of retail sales, your general sources might be sufficient to get you to the fourth level of the diagram, but the sources' inherent limitations would prevent them from taking you any further. For information about the kind of topics on the fifth level—details on the markets of ancient Greece and medieval Europe, bazaars, arcades, and malls—you would need to do more focused reading. You need a strategy for locating information in articles and books, either online or in the library, or via interviews.

▶2 Finding print materials in libraries

The following overview of available sources will help you focus on the ones that best address your working thesis. This overview will start with articles in order to emphasize the fact that periodical indexes are often preferable to the library catalog (formerly called the card catalog) as a first step in conducting focused research. Note that the search process for most print sources involves searching by author, title, and subject. For good *subject* topics, refer back to the *Library of Congress Subject Headings*, described in 33f-2.

General periodical indexes: Magazines

Periodicals are magazines and newspapers published at regular intervals—quarterly, monthly, daily. Periodical articles often contain information available from no other source and are generally more up-to-date than books published during the same period. You are probably familiar with the *Readers' Guide to Periodical Literature* as a means of locating magazine articles, but there are numerous other periodical reference guides.

For example, consider *Ulrich's International Periodicals Directory*. This is not a periodical index, but rather a subject guide to periodicals; that is, it directs you to periodicals on a given subject. To find out more about the nature or scope of a particular magazine, check *Katz's Magazines for Libraries*. This reference tool lists the most commonly used magazines and offers basic descriptive and evaluative information about each.

Like encyclopedias, periodical indexes are of two types: *general* and *specialized*. The most commonly used general periodical index is, of course, the *Readers' Guide to Periodical Literature*, which indexes magazines of general interest such as *Time, Newsweek, U.S. News and World Report, The New Republic, Sports Illustrated, Commonweal*. Here, for example, is a *Readers' Guide* entry for "shopping" and "shopping centers." The first entry is from the print volume; the one that follows is from the *Readers' Guide* CD-ROM database.

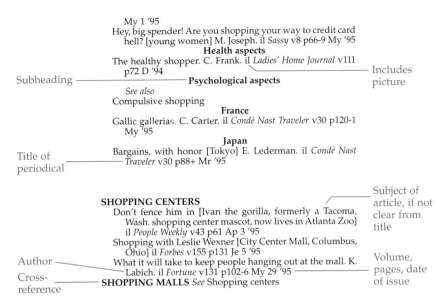

My 1 '95

Hey, big spender! Are you shopping your way to credit card hell? [young women] M. Joseph. il *Sassy* v8 p66-9 My '95

Health aspects

The healthy shopper. C. Frank. il *Ladies' Home Journal* v111 p72 D '94 — Includes picture

Subheading —— **Psychological aspects**

See also

Compulsive shopping

France

Gallic gallerias. C. Carter. il *Condé Nast Traveler* v30 p120-1 My '95

Japan

Title of —— Bargains, with honor [Tokyo] E. Lederman. il *Condé Nast Traveler* v30 p88+ Mr '95
periodical

Subject of article, if not clear from title

SHOPPING CENTERS

Don't fence him in [Ivan the gorilla, formerly a Tacoma, Wash. shopping center mascot, now lives in Atlanta Zoo] il *People Weekly* v43 p61 Ap 3 '95

Shopping with Leslie Wexner [City Center Mall, Columbus, Ohio] il *Forbes* v155 p131 Je 5 '95

Author —— What it will take to keep people hanging out at the mall. K. Labich. il *Fortune* v131 p102-6 My 29 '95 ——

Cross- —— **SHOPPING MALLS** *See* Shopping centers
reference

Volume, pages, date of issue

If you had located the last entry on an electronic search, the screen or print-out would look like this:

```
READERS' GUIDE TO PERIODICAL LIT          Data Coverage: 1/85 thru 11/30/95
              Line   1 of    8 Lines                              READY
áááááááááááááááááááááááááááááááááááááááááááááááááááááááááááááááááááááááááááááá
Multiple subject search (Wilsearch) PRINT MODE      4 of 73 Entries
áááááááááááááááááááááááááááááááááááááááááááááááááááááááááááááááááááááááááááááá
 #4
      AUTHOR:  Labich, Kenneth
       TITLE:  What it will take to keep people hanging out at the mall
      SOURCE:  Fortune  (ISSN:0015-8259) v 131 p 102-6 May 29 '95
    CONTAINS:  illustration(s)
 SUBJECTS COVERED:
 Shopping centers
```

Another useful general periodical index is the *Essay and General Literature Index*, which indexes (by subject, author, and sometimes by title) articles and essays that have been collected into books. The index is especially useful in that it gives you access to material that might not otherwise have surfaced in your search. These articles and essays generally would be classified under the humanities, but some deal with social science issues as well.

General periodical indexes: Newspapers

Most libraries have back issues of important newspapers on microfilm. The *New York Times Index* may be used to retrieve articles in the *Times* as far back as 1913. There are also indexes for the *San Francisco Chronicle*, the *Los Angeles Times*, and the *Wall Street Journal* (an important source of business news). The *Newspaper Index* lists articles from the *Chicago Tribune*, the *New Orleans Times-Picayune*, the *Los*

Angeles Times, and the *Washington Post.* You can print out "hard copies" (from microfilm) of articles you need. If you're looking for articles in newspapers other than these, check dates of stories in the *New York Times Index,* or see whether the newspaper has a search service.

Following is a sample entry on "shopping centers" from the *New York Times Index.* Notice that the entry refers readers to "Retail Stores and Trade," the heading under which most of the articles on shopping centers appear.

Entries under
other headings

SHOPPING CENTERS. See also
Airports, O 2
Food, F 2
Real Estate, Ja 19
Retail Stores and Trade, Ja 5,20,26,28,29, F 3,5,9,16,23, Mr
1,3,5,15,18,22,25,27,29, Ap 1,5,9,12,20,21,26, My 3,10,15,
24,29, Je 14,19,21,28, Jl 5, 12,26,30, Ag 2,9,18,20,21,30 S
13,27,30, O 18,23,25, N 8,15,24,25,27, D 7,10,13

Listed under "Retail Stores and Trade" are the entries noted above for August 18–30, 1992:

Relevant
stories are listed
in chronological
order

GE Capital Corp unit buys 47 shopping centers from
Resolution Trust Corp for $71 million in cash; shopping
centers are in nine states (S), Ag 18,D,4:1
J C Penney Co, GTE Spacenet and Capital Cities/ABC Inc
say they are working on formation of joint venture to provide
audio, video and data communication services to retailers in
shopping malls around country; venture is called Advanced
Retail Communications (S), Ag 20,D,4:4

Date of story,
section no.,
page no., column no.

Addis & Dey's, last of big downtown department stores,
Syracuse, NY, is set to close despite efforts of city's leaders
to rebuild downtown area and store's rent-free use of city-
owned building; closure is symbol of inability of large
downtown stores to compete with suburban malls; photos
(M), Ag 21,B,1:2
Topics of The Times column notes that while New York
does not have glorious leaves of New England's autumn, city
does have indoor 'autumn,' in its freezingly air-conditioned
department stores, Ag 26,A,20:2

Major stories
in boldface

**Article on gigantic new Mall of America in Bloomington,
Minnesota;** 4.2-million-square-foot complex includes
specialty stores catering to every demographic group, as well
as giant movie theater, numerous eateries and Camp Snoopy,
world's largest indoor amusement park; photos; developer
Nader Ghermezian also built Canada's West Edmonton Mall,
still world's largest with 5.2 million square feet (M), Ag
30,IX,5:1

Description
of story

Staten Island Mall begins $50-million expansion that in-
cludes renovation and addition of new stores; rendering (S),
Ag 30,X,1:1

The library catalog

Almost certainly, your library's catalog has been converted to electronic form, allowing you to search for items far more quickly than you could when they were filed on cards. You can search the catalog by *author,* by *title,* or by *subject.* (A typical keyboard command might be "f a Morrison, Toni" (for *find* items by the *author* Toni Morrison). Many library catalog terminals also allow access to magazine and newspaper databases such as MAGS and NEWS. In some cases, you can view (or print out) abstracts or even complete texts of particular items that you locate in such indexes. Electronic catalogs are much more current than print indexes, since they are updated far more frequently. In addition, electronic magazine and newspaper catalogs generally allow you to search more publications at once than their print counterparts, and they almost always cover a greater period of time—usually several years. The disadvantage is that electronic databases generally don't include information more than ten years old. Thus you would still have to rely largely on print indexes for information about—for example—the Watergate scandal of the 1970s.

Browsing through some of the subject entries is a good way of locating books on your topic; but before you do this, you should have at least begun to narrow your subject. Otherwise, you could be overwhelmed with the sheer number of books available. (There may be several hundred books on various aspects of shopping centers.)

http://www.ipl.org/
The Internet Public Library is the first public library of the Internet.

The convenience of electronic catalog searching should not blind you to the old-fashioned advantages and pleasures of going into the stacks and browsing among the shelves in your area of interest. Browsing is not an efficient or comprehensive substitute for methodical catalog searching: some important books may be checked out or shelved in another area. But opening promising titles and examining the contents may reveal valuable sources that you might otherwise have overlooked. Here are two catalog entries for the same book—one from a computer display, the other from a card catalog.

Computer display

```
AUTHOR        Kowinski, William Severini.
TITLE         The malling of America: an inside look
              at the great consumer paradise / William
              Severini Kowinski.
EDITION       1st ed.
IMPRINT       New York : W. Morrow, c 1985
DESCRIPT      415 p. : ill. ; 25 cm.
NOTE          Includes index.
ISN/MUSIC#    0688041809.
SUBJECT       Shopping malls -- United States.

LOCATION         CALL NO.              STATUS
1>Mugar           HF5430.3.K68 1985
```

The computer display reproduces the information on a card in the card catalog. The display will (often) list the status of the source: checked in, checked out, or on reserve.

Catalog (author) card

```
HF
5430.3      Kowinski, William Severini.
K68         The malling of America: an inside
1985        look at the great consumer paradise /
            William Severini Kowinski. -- 1st ed.
            -- New York: W. Morrow, c 1985.
            415 p.: ill.; 25 cm.
            Includes index.
            ISBN 0-688-04180-9

            1. Shopping malls -- United States.
            I. Title
MBNU                    NEDDuc86-114508r872
```

Accurately note the call number (on this card HF 5430.3 K68 1985) and consult a library map before going to retrieve the source.

Book Review Digest

An invaluable source for determining the quality of books is the *Book Review Digest*. This publication, collected into annual volumes, indexes many of the most important books published during a given year by author, title, and subject. More important, it provides lists of reviews of those books, as well as brief excerpts from some of the reviews. Thus, you can use the *Book Review Digest* to quickly determine not only the scope of a given book (each entry leads off with an objective summary) but also how well that book has been received by reviewers. If the reviews are almost uniformly good, that book will be a good source of information. If they are almost uniformly bad, stay away. If the reviews are mixed, proceed with caution.

Trade bibliographies and bibliographies of books

For books too recent to have been acquired by your library or that the library does not have, you may wish to consult *Books in Print* and *Paperbound Books in Print*. These volumes, organized by author, title, and subject, are available in some libraries and in most bookstores. For books that your library does not have, but that may be in other libraries, consult the *Cumulative Book Index* and the *National Union Catalog*.

▶ **EXERCISE 7**

Researching either the topic you have been working on or some other topic, locate at least five books and ten articles on the subject. Provide complete bibliographic information for these sources (see 35b). Locate several reviews of at least one of the books, and summarize the main responses in a paragraph.

Focused Reading for Print Material

- To locate articles in general-interest magazines, use the *Readers' Guide to Periodical Literature*, the *Readers' Guide CD-ROM Index, InfoTrac*, or another database index.
- To locate articles in newspapers, use the *New York Times Index* or other indexes for particular newspapers.
- To identify periodicals specializing in a given subject, use *Ulrich's International Periodicals Directory*.
- To determine the scope of a particular magazine, use *Katz's Magazines for Libraries*.
- To locate books and government publications, use the *library catalog*.
- To determine how a given subject is subclassified in the library catalog, use the *Library of Congress Subject Headings Index*.
- To locate reviews of books, see the *Book Review Digest*.

▶ 3 Finding material through interviews and surveys

Although you will probably conduct most of your research in the college library, remember that professional researchers do most of their work *outside* the library—in the field, in labs, in courthouses, and in government and private archives. Consider the possibilities of conducting original research for your own paper, by interviewing knowledgeable people and devising and sending out questionnaires. (Many subjects have been extensively discussed by experts on television news programs, talk shows, and documentaries. It may be possible to borrow videocassettes or to obtain printed transcripts of such programs.)

Interviews

Interviews allow you to conduct primary research and to acquire valuable information unavailable in print sources. By recounting the experiences, ideas, and quotations of people who have direct knowledge of a particular subject, you add considerable authority and immediacy to your paper. You can conduct three types of interviews: (1) by phone, (2) by e-mail, or (3) in person.

Those you select to interview may include businesspeople, government officials, doctors, professors, community activists, or your own grandparents. If you would like to talk to a business executive or a government official but do not have a particular individual in mind, call the public relations office (in a business) or the public information office (in a government agency) and ask for the names of possible interviewees. Then, call the individual and try to schedule an appointment. Even busy people can usually find some time to give an interview; many will be glad to talk to someone about their experiences. But if you are turned down, as sometimes happens, try someone else.

It is important to prepare adequately for your interview. Devise most of your questions in advance; you can improvise with other questions during the interview, according to the turns it takes. Avoid *leading* questions that presume certain conclusions or answers:

> Why do you think that American workers are lazier today than they were a generation ago?

> What do you think of the fact that the present administration wants to burden small businesses with added health-care costs?

Instead, ask *neutral* questions that allow the interviewee to express his or her own observations:

> What changes, if any, have you noticed in the work habits of your present employees from those who worked here in the 1960s?

> To what extent has government funding of genetic research changed during the present administration?

Also avoid *dead-end* questions that require yes/no answers or *forced choice* questions that impose a simplistic choice on the interviewee:

> Do you think that this was an important experiment? (dead end)

> What should take priority, in your view: jobs or the environment? (forced choice)

Instead, ask *open-ended* questions that allow the interviewee to develop her or his thoughts at some length:

> In what way was this an important experiment for you?

> How do you think it is possible to deal with the seemingly conflicting needs of jobs and the environment?

> What were your impressions of Robert Kennedy when you met him?

Factual questions can be useful for eliciting specific information:

> When did your restaurant begin offering a salad bar?

> How many parade permits has the city denied during the past year?

Ask follow-up questions when appropriate, and be prepared to lead your respondent through promising, though unplanned, lines of inquiry. Throughout the interview show your interest in what your respondent is saying. On the other hand, keep in mind that your own reactions may unintentionally create cues that affect your subject's responses. Your subject, for instance, may begin to tell you what he or she thinks you want to hear (even if it is not quite accurate), based on how you have previously reacted. For this reason, trained interviewers try not to specifically respond to the interviewee's answers.

Surveys

Surveys are useful when you want to measure behavior or attitudes of a fairly large, identifiable group of people—provided that both the group and the measurements are carefully specified. An identifiable group could be freshmen on your campus, Democrats in town, Asian Americans in a three-block area, or autoworkers in two factories; measuring attitudes or behavior could mean obtaining records and comparing the frequency of responses made to specific and carefully worded questions. On the basis of measured comparisons among the responses to questions, a researcher might venture some broad claims about patterns of response as

Checklist for Interviews

- Determine what kind of information you need from the person, based on the requirements of your paper and its thesis.
- Make an appointment, telling the person what your paper is about and how long the interview will take.
- Become knowledgeable about the subject so that you can ask informed questions. If the person has written a relevant article or book, read it.
- Prepare most of your questions in advance.
- Take pen, pencil, and a hardback notebook to the interview. If you take a tape recorder, ask the person's permission to record the interview. Even if you do record the conversation, take notes on especially important comments.
- At the end of the interview, thank the person for his or her time. Promise to send a copy of the finished paper. Soon afterward, send a follow-up thank you note.

indicators of attitudes or behaviors within the population measured (it is not safe to generalize beyond the group actually measured without rigorous statistical procedures). Such generalizations are usually made in quantitative terms: "Fewer than two-thirds of the respondents said they feel threatened by the possibility of contracting AIDS."

To get honest answers to your questions, it is essential to guarantee your respondents' anonymity. Most frequently, questions and answers to surveys are written, though occasionally they may be oral (as when, for example, you ask students entering the library for their attitudes on American military activities in the Middle East). When devising questions for a survey, some of the same considerations apply as for interviews. For example, do not ask *loaded* questions that lead the respondent toward a particular answer ("Do you think that the money the university is spending to upgrade the president's residence would be better spent to reduce class size?"). For surveys, short-answer questions are better than open-ended questions, which are difficult to compare precisely or to quantify. It is relatively easy to quantify yes/no responses or responses on a five-point scale ("How concerned do you feel about the threat of AIDS? 5—extremely concerned; 4—very concerned; 3—moderately concerned; 2—somewhat concerned; 1—unconcerned").

CHAPTER 34

Using Electronic Resources

As you are probably well aware, the Internet holds a universe of searchable information that can enrich your research papers. On the Internet you can—

- Find up-to-the-minute information on your topic.
- Locate pertinent charts, tables, graphs, and pictures for your papers.
- Participate in discussion groups in which experts exchange information.
- Identify and contact experts and conduct virtual interviews.
- Post questions on bulletin boards and in discussion groups with a reasonable expectation that experts will respond.

While you can find a wealth of information online, Internet-based research is a *supplement* to, and does not replace, print-based research. Only a fraction of the world's printed resources—our books, newspapers, and periodicals—are available electronically. Unlike print libraries, the Internet is a decentralized, often chaotic environment in which to work. The search strategies that you use in libraries to locate sources must be adapted when you begin searching online. Finally, unlike the books and journal articles you find in your college library, resources on the Internet are not necessarily edited for fairness or accuracy—and you must take special care before using online sources in your papers. Good researchers develop the habit of evaluating the legitimacy of *all* sources; this obligation is especially important when working with online sources.

Online research, then, differs from print-based research, requiring that you adjust both your research technique and your perspective on what you will find. As you will see, the strategies discussed in this chapter for launching your Internet searches build on techniques discussed in Chapter 33. The following general process of finding online resources will be familiar to you if you have searched for information in print-based libraries:

1. Begin by investigating broad topics.
2. Scan numerous sites, some of which will strike you as immediately promising.
3. Browse these sites and pursue links to other, related sites.
4. Narrow your search and locate Web pages on your specific topic.
5. Along the way, collect pertinent material—in this case not by photocopying articles or checking books out from the library, but by downloading computer files or taking notes electronically. (Some online material is archived onto CD-ROMs and is often conveniently available in CD form in libraries.)

Commercial and Professional Information Services beyond the Internet

Libraries often subscribe to professional and commercial information services that archive in searchable form vast numbers of magazine and newspaper articles, journal articles, abstracts, monographs, and books or sections of books. These commercial services charge a fee for accessing their archives, but as a member of a college community you can (usually) gain access for free. Check in your school library's periodical room to determine which subscription databases are available. Here are a few of the more heavily used, commercial databases:

- Lexis–Nexis: locates news or government publications.
- InfoTrac: locates full-text newspaper and journal articles.
- DIALOG: provides access to more than 300 million items in over 400 separate databases in the humanities, the social sciences, the natural sciences, and business.
- PsychINFO: references items in journals of psychology.
- ERIC: references items in educational journals and reports.
- Arts and Humanities Search: references items in arts and humanities journals.
- WILSONLINE: provides electronic access to the printed indexes published by H. W. Wilson Co., including *Readers' Guide to Periodical Literature*, *Education Index*, and *Social Science Index*.

If your school library subscribes, a computer in the reference area will provide these resources, as well as other sources of information stored in databases and on CDs.

▶ 34a Finding the right online resources

In this section you will find definitions and tips on accessing the basic online resources: e-mail, Usenet discussion groups (or "newsgroups"), discussion lists (or "listservs"), synchronous communication (MOOs), anonymous ftp, and the World Wide Web. As with any information you locate in a search, you will need to assess the reliability of materials found online. You will find a note on reliability for each of the resources discussed here.

http://www.fau.edu/netiquette/netiquette.html

The Netiquette Home Page at Florida Atlantic University, from Arlene H. Rinaldi, who insists she's not Miss Manners of the Internet.

▶ I E-mail

Definition. If you've used the Internet at all, it has probably been with e-mail—sending and receiving messages to and from friends and family. But e-mail can benefit you as a researcher as well. More and more authorities (university and private researchers, journalists, government officials) have and regularly use e-mail.

Many (not all, of course) would welcome an inquiry from a student and would respond with an informed and authoritative reply. Don't overlook the research potential of e-mail. Through e-mail you can do the following:

- Conduct interviews.
- Exchange computer files that are not available to the general Internet user (text, graphics, charts, statistics, and so forth) with people who have such information to share.
- Read the current draft of a new project or an old unpublished conference paper that the scholar would be willing to share with you.

Reliability. Judge the reliability of an e-mail source as you would that of any person you've interviewed. When referring to this source in your paper, provide some background context. Who is this person? What is his or her area of expertise? Why is he or she qualified to speak on your topic? If possible, use an attributive phrase to establish the credibility of your source *in* the paper.

Access. How do you find e-mail addresses of people with whom you would like to correspond?

- Simply ask them. Note that some universities and businesses maintain e-mail phone books.
- You will find that the e-mail addresses of people who contribute to newsgroups and discussion lists are included in the headers of the messages they send. Save one or two messages and you will have their addresses.
- Keep your own list of e-mail addresses of people with whom you may wish to correspond.
- If you don't know the e-mail address of someone you'd like to contact, try one of these directory assistance services:

  Bigfoot   http://www.bigfoot.com
  WhoWhere   http://www.whowhere.com

▶2 Usenet discussion groups or "newsgroups"

Definition. The easiest way to visualize a newsgroup is to think of a standard cork bulletin board hanging on a wall. Anyone can walk by and tack up a message, and anyone else can come by and read the message, respond to it, or put up a new message. Newsgroups on the Internet are electronic versions of that cork bulletin board. Anyone with an Internet account can use a newsreader to follow a continuing discussion, read the current messages, and "post" a reply or a new message. Newsgroups can provide an excellent forum for trying out your ideas on others before you commit to these ideas in your paper.

Reliability. Because they are a radically democratic forum in which everyone—the unknowing and the expert—can offer an opinion, newsgroups vary in reliability. Use material gathered from this resource with caution. If you want to refer to a newsgroup posting in a paper, first try to confirm from other sources the reliability of that information. You may also want to interview the person who posted the message by e-mail.

Access. If your school subscribes to a newsfeed, a central computer where all the messages are stored and fed to other providers, you will have access to a newsreader of some kind and you will be able to choose which newsgroups to follow (remember, there are well over 10,000). Newsgroup addresses read hierarchically, much like domain names, in a series of units separated by dots (see the box on page 517). For example, the newsgroup address "rec.music.bluenote.blues" is read as follows:

Its type is "recreation."

Its subtype is "music."

Its particular category is "bluenote."

Its topic is "blues."

That is, "rec.music.bluenote.blues" is a discussion group about blues music. When you join in on the conversation of a newsgroup, you will be able to read and reply to messages, just as you can with e-mail. Remember that in newsgroup posts, what you write is public.

▶3 Discussion lists or "listservs"

Definition. Academic discussion lists are similar to newsgroups, with one significant difference: you must actively subscribe to the list, and then you receive the messages directly as individual e-mail messages. The mailing of the discussions is essentially managed by automated computer programs that receive all incoming messages and immediately forward them to everyone who subscribes to the list; one of the most common of these automated programs is called "Listserv."

Reliability. Lists usually stick to their stated topics; although theoretically anyone can subscribe to any discussion list, usually contributors are serious about their commitment to the topic. They tend to be knowledgeable—though, as with any source, you will want to verify information before citing it as credible. The mere appearance of information on a discussion list does not ensure its reliability.

Access. To find a listing of currently active academic listservs, use your WWW browser to access the URL http://www.liszt.com (see 34a-5 for accessing WWW sites). If you find a list to which you would like to subscribe, address an e-mail message *to the listserv* (the machine that manages the list), not to the list itself. The machine will ignore the "subject" line of the e-mail box and read only the message, which must contain the following information:

- Type the word "subscribe". Don't use the quotation marks. Simply type the word as the first word in an e-mail message.
- Next, type the name of the list to which you want to subscribe.
- Finally, type your first name, followed by your last name.

The message must contain absolutely nothing else. (Added words can confuse the machine.) For example, if your name were Mary Rose, you would send the basic message "subscribe deos-l Mary Rose" (again, no quotation marks) to the listserv's address to subscribe to the Distance Education list. After you have subscribed, you will receive further instructions about using the list and posting to it.

Communicating away from "real time"

A listserv is an *asynchronous* means of communication. That is, the discussion that occurs in this environment does not occur in real time—as spoken conversations do in person or by phone. On a newsgroup or listserv, one participant may post a comment on Monday; a second participant may post a response on Wednesday; and other responses may follow. All responses following the initial posting are called a "thread," and on a given listserv several threaded discussions may occur simultaneously. Asynchronous communication lacks the immediacy of face-to-face conversation, of course, but it also fosters an extended exchange of ideas in which points, counterpoints, and counter-counterpoints blossom over time. Moreover, asynchronous communication fosters this exchange of ideas among participants who live in different time zones and who maintain different schedules. Note that some newsgroup or listserv discussions—for instance, those used as virtual discussion areas for distance learning classes—are password protected and are not open to the general public.

http://tile.net/listserv/
To find listservs on your chosen topics, check out this searchable listing of e-mail discussion groups.

▶4 Synchronous communication

Definition. E-mail, newsgroups, and listservs are technologies that operate in asynchronous time: that is, a person reading your message is not reading it *as* you compose it and does not respond immediately, as he or she would to something you said in a telephone conversation. The telephone is a synchronous technology: you speak, and your listener hears and responds.

On the computer, you can enjoy real-time, synchronous communications with others in several ways: by participating in a chat room via an online service such as America Online; through software programs such as Microsoft's NetMeeting; or by connecting to a server (a host computer somewhere on the Internet) and entering a text-based virtual world called a MOO. MOO is an abbreviation for **M**ultiuser dimension, **O**bject **O**riented—a more accessible version of an earlier shared virtual space called a MUD, which stands for **M**ulti**u**ser **D**imension. These virtual spaces permit those who have logged on to them to have text-based conversations in real time. In the early years, hundreds of participants from around the world would log on to the same server to play extended games (Dungeons and Dragons, for instance) in the same virtual space. Unlike chat rooms in which virtual participants converse (via the keyboard) in a single location, MOO environments offer multiple "rooms" in the environment that participants enter and in which they engage in one or another adventure, according to the rules of the game.

Educators have been quick to realize the potential of real-time, multiuser, virtual environments. A brick-and-mortar classroom, after all, is a real-time, multiuser environment. Conducting classes virtually makes a great deal of sense when, for reasons of geography or economics, it is impossible for people to meet face to face. Increasingly, MOOs are used as meeting places for virtual conferences in which participants enter into different discussions in different rooms. In a MOO space, classes comprising students from around town or around the world can meet in real time and discuss the day's lessons. You may take a composition course in a MOO:

- ■ Meet as a class to critique a paper.
- ■ Meet group mates virtually in a MOO (or private chat room), instead of meeting face to face in the library.

- Arrange to conduct a real-time interview by inviting an expert to log on to a MOO environment.
- Log on to a MOO-based writing lab in Pittsburgh, Pennsylvania, to get some real-time help on a paper you are working on in Madison, Wisconsin.

A particular advantage of the MOO is its written record: because all exchange is typed, you can record whatever people have communicated that is of interest. This capability is especially helpful when conducting interviews or peer critiques.

Reliability. MOOs can be more or less academic in the discussions you find taking place in them; the reliability of MOO-based information as source material for a paper will therefore vary considerably. Let common sense be your guide. If you use a MOO space to conduct a synchronous interview with an expert source, then you will regard the resulting information with the same authority as you would had it been recorded in a face-to-face interview. Bring the same standards to bear on sources located in MOOs that you would to information found in class discussions, interviews, and so on. In all cases, you will want to verify that sources have the background needed to speak with authority.

Access. You can connect to MOOs in either of two ways. First, using software available at your school, you can link to the server (or host computer) on which the MOO exists. In this type of connection, exchanges will be entirely text-based. Very likely, your school's computer help desk will have a document that can get you started with a hookup for MOOs.

http://139.182.93.107/ MOOcentral/
MOOcentral, an introduction to educational, professional, and experimental MOOs, from Jeffrey R. Galin.

A more recent development is the presence of MOOs on the World Wide Web, an environment that gives MOOs the capability to relay real-time sound and graphics. To gain access to a Web-based MOO, you need a browser. Then, you can get onto any of several general search engines, type MOO as the query, and receive an ample listing of possibilities. For starters, you might try these sites, which provide links to numerous MOOs:

Educational MOOs and MUDs	http://www.daedalus.com/net/moolist.html
The Lost Library of MOO	http://lucien.berkeley.edu/moo.html
A Nice Big List of MOOs	http://members.tripod.com/adm/popup/roadmap.shtml
Rachel's Super MOO List	http://moolist.yeehaw.com/list.html

A note on MOO etiquette: When you log on to a MOO, be aware that it is a social world whose participants see what you have typed as you type it. Therefore, you should bring the same sense of respect and decency to MOOs that you do to face-to-face gatherings.

5 World Wide Web

Definition. Currently the most popular way of browsing and searching the Internet is via the World Wide Web. Its popularity derives both from its hypertext interface (clicking on the screen brings you to a new page of information) and its ability to display color and graphics. In addition, the Web has subsumed all previous Internet modes. Here are some key terms worth knowing:

- *Webservers:* specially configured computers, worldwide, on which information for the WWW is stored.
- *Web page or home page* (or simply page): individual documents on the WWW.
- *Web site or site:* a collection of pages.
- *URL:* the acronym (for Uniform Resource Locator) that designates particular characters used to locate a Web site. The URL is a Web site's "http://" address.
- *Hypertext:* links from information on one Web page to related information on another Web page—perhaps located on another Web server in a different school, country, or continent. Hypertext links are usually underlined in blue. If you see something on a Web page that you'd like to explore further and it's underlined in blue, click your mouse or press the appropriate key—and you're there.
- *Browsing:* linking from one Web document to another, following your interests. Software such as Netscape or Microsoft Explorer are used as browsing tools, or "browsers."
- *Downloading:* Some links on a Web page may not be hypertext links but, rather, links that prompt you to download a file—that is, to transfer a file from the Web server (the machine on which the Web page resides) to your computer. Click on the link and the browser will display a message box asking if you would like to save the file.
- *Search engines.* The Web has many different search engines, but all work on the keyword search principle. You type a word or phrase into the search engine's subject box and the engine scans the Internet for Web pages that have your word(s) listed as a keyword by the creator of the page. Some engines search entire Web pages for occurrences of your word(s). Different engines follow various protocols and specialize in finding particular types of information on the Web. So it is best, when searching for information, to conduct several searches using different engines. The next section, 34b, offers extensive guidance on using Internet search engines to find what you want online.

Reliability. The quality and reliability of information you find on the Web will vary considerably. Individuals, commercial operations, and organizations create their own Web sites. So, while you may find research reports and government documents and online medical journals, you may also find unsubstantiated opinion, self-serving advertisements, and propaganda. Judge your materials carefully—and see section 34c for extensive guidance on evaluating Web-based sources.

Access. Most likely, you will gain access to the Web through a browser such as Netscape Navigator or Microsoft Internet Explorer. You will move from document to document on the Web by following hypertext links. If the trail you follow begins to seem fruitless, you can back out of it by clicking the mouse on the "back" key (the left-pointing arrow near the top of the screen) in your browser. With enough backward steps like this, eventually you'll return to where you began, for a fresh start. (You can also click on "home" or "search" to start your search over.)

▶6 Anonymous FTP

Definition. "FTP" stands for "File Transfer Protocol." It's the standard method for transferring files (text documents, graphics, computer software) over the Internet. Normally, if you find a file you want to transfer to your own computer for viewing, you need to be able to access the computer where the information resides, in which case you would theoretically need an account on that computer and a password. However, many computer systems worldwide have been made partially accessible on the Web to "anonymous" users, people who don't have accounts. Hence, anonymous FTP provides a means for you to retrieve files from computers to which you normally would not have access. Knowing how to use FTP enables you to exchange or distribute lengthy documents for collaborative projects. It also permits you to store Internet files on your own computer so that you can access them more easily as you write.

http://www.shiva.com/prod/
techinfo/fyi/fyi24.txt
Most modern web browsers will perform anonymous FTP for you, but if you ever need to do it by hand, this document provides information for the novice Internet user about using File Transfer Protocol (FTP).

Reliability. Information gathered through anonymous FTP is usually as reliable as print information in a library. Often it will consist of government documents, research reports, statistical tabulations of data, and so on. You may actually access visual and graphical information: pictures from the Hubble Space Telescope are available from NASA by anonymous FTP, for example.

Access. There are several ways of transferring files, but the easiest is to use your Web browser. Both Netscape and Microsoft Internet Explorer use FTP by downloading a file when you click a link on a Web page. Links can be set up not only to take you from one page to another, but also to start a file transfer.

▶ EXERCISE 1

Working with the topic you have been researching in Chapter 33, use two of the following Internet resources to locate online materials that might prove useful in writing your research paper: e-mail, Usenet discussion groups or newsgroups, discussion lists or listservs, synchronous communication, or anonymous FTP.

EXERCISE 2

Use both of the online directory assistance programs mentioned in 34a-1 ("Bigfoot" and "WhoWhere") to locate your name and e-mail address and that of a friend who is attending another school. How useful do you find these services? Next, identify *one* expert on the topic of your research whom you would consider interviewing, if you had his or her e-mail address. (Select your candidate from one of the articles or books you identified in Chapter 33.) Find the expert's contact information. Compose a *brief* e-mail note, introducing yourself and your project. Send the note to the expert and ask for an interview—either by phone or e-mail.
▶ If the interview is granted, consult the advice at 33g-3.

There is no electronic card catalog for the Web, no Dewey Decimal or Library of Congress system by which each document added to the Web is assigned to its appropriate subcategory of knowledge and given a distinct retrieval code. The most frustrating aspect of the Internet for those seeking information is the difficulty of locating the information they're looking for. Typically, people will type in a query to one of the search services and then find themselves deluged with possible sites.

For example, a search in July, 1998, for "black holes" on AltaVista, one of the most popular search engines, yielded 2,621,748 "hits." A search on HotBot yielded a more manageable, but still impractical 78,484 sites. In fact, the first of these 78,484 sites was for "The Capitalist Pig," a company that designs Web pages for businesses, and which has nothing to do with black holes, but whose opening paragraph is addressed to potential clients trying to navigate their Web browsers around "black holes of pages that just won't load." Why was such a useless response returned for this query? The search engine was looking only for the text string "black holes"; it found such a string at the beginning of the document and, having no judgment of its own, had no way of knowing that the site in which it appeared had nothing to do with astronomy or astrophysics.

As an online researcher, *you* must provide the judgment that search engines lack. The way you express this judgment is to construct a precise query—the single most important key to a successful search. Good queries yield good results; poor queries yield poor results. This section will help you to devise good, focused search queries.

▶ **1   Determine the type of information you need; choose appropriate search tools.**

When conducting online searches, approach your task not as a single search but as a *series of related* searches—each focusing on *different* sources of information. The type of information you need in any particular search will determine the type of tools you use. For instance, if you are looking for a very current topic in the news, you would choose to work with search engines such as NewsBot or TotalNews that search news sites on the Web. Using a general search engine such as AltaVista, which searches the entire Web (non-news sites included), would not be productive. You should realize that the information you need may not be freely available on the Web. Assuming your school has access, you might want to check your library's

---

[1]Section 34b is based on our adaptations of two excellent sources on conducting Internet searches. The first is Keith Gresham's "Surfing with a Purpose" from the September/October 1998 issue of *Educom Review*, which provides our overall strategy for conducting Internet research. Gresham is an instruction librarian at the University of Colorado at Boulder. The second source for this section is "Guide to Effective Searching of the Internet," a tutorial on keyword searching prepared in 1998 by Michael Bergman of The Web Tools Company at <www.theWebtools.com>. Suggestions for Web links were provided by Prentiss Riddle, Web Master for Rice University. Visit and launch searches from the Rice University Internet Page at <www.riceinfo.rice.edu/Internet> to get updated advice on the best Internet search tools as they become available.

A Process for Conducting Research on the Internet

We recommend the search process devised by instruction librarian Keith Gresham (University of Colorado at Boulder). The section that follows this summary box is organized around Gresham's four-step process:

1. **Determine the type of information you need; choose appropriate search tools.** Do you need news? Government reports? Industry statistics? Journal articles? Magazines? Choose carefully among general search engines, specialty search engines, and subject directories.
2. **Create a list of search terms.** Search terms are those specific words or phrases that best describe the major concepts of your topic.
3. **Construct a search statement and conduct your search.** Depending on the search tool you are using, search by individual key words, by exact phrases, or by Boolean search expressions.
4. **Evaluate search results and revise the query (if needed).** Even carefully constructed searches retrieve irrelevant results or result lists with thousands of hits. If you don't locate useful information within the first fifteen retrieved sites, revise the query. Construct new search statements using different combinations of search words or phrases.

reference room for Internet-based subscription services such as Lexis–Nexis. However, if you are turning to the Web as a resource, be aware that Web search tools are classified into two types: subject directories and search engines.

Subject directories

Directories classify Web pages into types, according to a subject breakdown. For example, *Yahoo*, the most well-known directory, classifies Web sites into categories such as Arts and Humanities, Business and Economy, Education, Government, Health, News and Media, Reference, and Science. Each category is divided into subcategories: for example, Science includes sites on Astronomy, Biology, and Oceanography. Oceanography is further subdivided into sites such as Coral Reefs, Marine Biology, and Meteorology. The subdividing continues (for example, "seagrasses" is a subdivision of Marine Biology) until there are no more subclassifications, at which point Yahoo provides hyperlinks to one or more relevant sites. Here are the URLs for several popular directories:

Argus Clearinghouse	http://www.clearinghouse.net
Internet Public Library	http://ipl.sils.umich.edu/index.text.html
LookSmart	http://looksmart.com/
About.com	http://www.about.com/
WWW Virtual Library	http://conbio.rice.edu/vl/database/ (for browsing) http://www.vlib.org/ (for general subject directory)
Yahoo	http://www.yahoo.com/

Carriage Returns, Linefeeds, and Formatting Problems

Each major type of computer system used in schools, businesses, and on the Internet—Unix, MS-DOS and Windows, and Macintosh—has a different method for breaking lines on the screen and for printing. As a result, what looks like perfectly formed text on one machine may wind up looking like a series of short, choppy little lines or perhaps like a long line trailing off the screen. When you retrieve text from the Internet, be prepared for such short or long lines, added spaces, and other strange formatting problems which will persist as you cut and paste text into your paper. Take time to reformat as you work, using your delete function and format menu. If necessary, delete multiple spaces with your word processor's search-and-replace function.

Search engines

Search engines index words and terms in Web pages and feature "spiders" or "robots" to retrieve documents containing these terms. AltaVista, Excite, Hotbot, and WebCrawler are some of the more popular search engines. The number of keywords queried by search engines is virtually unlimited, as opposed to the finite number of classifications used by directories (Yahoo has about 1,400). If a Web page's topic doesn't easily fall into one of the pre-established classifications, it may not be accessible through the directory. But the relatively smaller number of sites located through a directory may be an advantage in researching topics that are easily classifiable by the directory. The search for "black holes" in Yahoo, for example, yielded a very manageable 65 sites—in contrast to the thousands, or even millions of sites returned by the search engines.

Many search services are hybrids: Yahoo allows users to search by keywords, and Excite has some features associated with directories. Here are URLs for some of the most highly used general search engines.

General search engines

AltaVista	http://www.altavista.digital.com/
Excite	http://www.excite.com/
Hotbot	http://www.hotbot.com/
Infoseek	http://www.infoseek.com/
Lycos	http://www.lycos.com/
Northern Light	http://www.nlsearch.com/
WebCrawler	http://Webcrawler.com/WebCrawler/WebQuery.html

Launching keyword searches in subject directories such as LookSmart will typically yield fewer sites than using the same keyword in a search engine such as AltaVista. As a rule of thumb, remember: use *several* search services—a variety of search engines and subject directories—in any given search to assure that you don't miss important sites and sources of information.

Depending on your need for specific types of information, you may want to use more specialized search engines, as follows.

Searching to access multiple WWW indexes

Dogpile	http://www.dogpile.com/
MetaCrawler	http://www.metacrawler.com/
MetaFind	http://metafind.com/
Savvy Search	http://www.cs.colostate.edu/~dreiling/smartform.html

Searching for news

http://www.askjeeves.com/
This unique meta-search engine allows you to enter your query in plain English in the form of a question.

When you are searching a topic of current interest in the news (as opposed to more static topics such as the Great Depression), consider using search engines that query news sources, exclusively. The following tools will help you to search a variety of news sources.

CNN	http://www.cnn.com/
Ecola Newsstand	http://www.ecola.com/
NewsBot	http://www.newsbot.com/
NewsIndex	http://www.newsindex.com/
TotalNews	http://totalnews.com/

And you may want to register at the *New York Times* site <http://www.nytimes.com/> for free access to the last year's *Times* online.

Searching mailing lists and Usenet news groups

Browse Usenet Archive	http://www.reference.com/cgi-bin/pn/go?choice=browse_newsgroups
Browse Usenet Groups with FeedMe	http://www.feedme.org/
DejaNews	http://www.dejanews.com/
Liszt Directory of E-Mail Discussion Groups	http://www.liszt.com/
Newsgroups Info Center	http://sunsite.unc.edu/usenet-i/search.html
Scholarly and Professional E-Conferences	http://n2h2.com/KOVACS/Sindex.html
WWW forums	http://www.forumone.com/

Searching for people

Anywho Reverse Telephone Search	http://www.anywho.com/telq.html
Bigfoot	http://www.bigfoot.com/
Finger (by Internet Site)	http://www.cs.indiana.edu/finger/gateway
Personal Web Pages	http://www.utexas.edu/world/personal/

Student Home Pages	http://www.student.net/homepages
Switchboard	http://www.switchboard.com/bin/cgiqa.dll
WhoWhere?	http://www.whowhere.lycos.com/
Yahoo! People Search	http://people.yahoo.com/

Plan for multiple Internet searches.

Take advantage of the numerous search engines and search directories available to help you locate the information you need on the Internet. (See the earlier part of this section for a listing and brief description of these resources.) Given the Internet's vast, unwieldy structure, it is certain that no single search tool will locate all the materials available. If you get into the habit of conducting *multiple* searches whenever you set out to find information, you increase the likelihood of locating useful materials.[2]

Use general search engines.

AltaVista	http://www.altavista.com
HotBot	http://www.hotbot.com
Northern Light	http://www.nlsearch.com

General search engines cast the largest possible net over the Internet, searching through the largest databases available of Web sites. The retrieval lists for the general search engines tend to be large—unless you can limit the search by date or topic.

Use general search engines to find specialized sites.

Use the same general search engines, as above, but use the advanced search features to limit the retrieval list by specifying narrower searches. As part of the advanced search features of various engines, you can specify the domain (for instance, ".gov" or ".mil") that you wish to search, the dates, and types of publications. For more on domain names, see the box on page 517 .

Use specialized news search engines.

NewsBot	http://www.newsbot.com
NewsIndex	http://www.newsindex.com
TotalNews	http://www.totalnews.com

A specialized set of search engines will exclusively search news outlets for matches with your topic. These engines are particularly useful when you are searching topics of a rapidly changeable nature.

Use subject directories.

| Yahoo! | http://www.yahoo.com |
| LookSmart | http://www.looksmart.com |

[2]This discussion is based on the work of Keith Gresham, Instruction Librarian at University of Colorado at Boulder. Material is adapted from his article, "Surfing with a Purpose," in *Educom Review* 33.5 (Sept/Oct 1998): 22–29.

The largest subject directories index tens of thousands of Web sites. If you can find your topic in the directory structure, you will likely discover useful information that you may not have found using any of the standard search engines.

Use engines that search discussion lists.

DejaNews   http://www.dejanews.com
ForumOne   http://www.forumone.com

If you are searching a topic that is likely to generate an ongoing Internet discussion, use one of these search engines to locate the discussion. You can join the discussion list and monitor the conversation about this topic (if the discussion is current), or you can access an archived discussion of your topic. Either way, the text of the discussion is available for you to copy and paste it into a word processor.

The Internet Domain Name System

Accuracy in typing an Internet address is essential: a missed period or transposed letters will frustrate your efforts. To appreciate *why* this is so, read about the Domain Name System.

The naming system

The Domain Name System allows for each computer on the Internet to have its own address, much like the post office's system of states, cities, streets, and house numbers allows each building to have its own unique address. Internet addresses are composed of units separated by the symbol "." (pronounced "dot"). The Internet address "www.gsfc.nasa.gov" is read as follows:

- The abbreviation "gov" means this Internet site is located at a government agency;
- The particular agency is "nasa";
- The particular computer where the Internet service resides is named "gsfc"; and
- The service provided is particular to the World Wide Web ("www").

The major domain names are as follows:

com—companies and commercial sites
edu—educational institutions
gov—government organizations
mil—military organizations
net—Internet service providers and users
org—nonprofit institutions

▶ EXERCISE 3

Determine the type of online information you need to complement the print-based research that you began in Chapter 33. Using the information in this section, choose appropriate research tools—general search engines, specialized search engines, or subject directories. Plan (but do not yet begin) to conduct multiple Internet searches. Identify the tools you will be using.

34b

▶2 Create a list of search terms

The key to getting good results from Web searches and not wasting effort sifting through irrelevant sources is to formulate precise queries. Even the most accurate queries are unlikely to yield a significant number of usable documents, and poorly conceived ones are going to yield considerably worse results. Queries are poorly conceived when they are overly vague or when they employ an insufficient number of keywords. Most users submit an average of 1.5 keywords in their queries—not enough to produce fruitful results. This section will help you to select keywords, which you can then combine in various ways into a search statement (step 3, below).

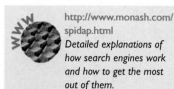

http://www.monash.com/
spidap.html
Detailed explanations of how search engines work and how to get the most out of them.

We'll dramatize the process of formulating queries by presenting a scenario. One spring day, Jan, an office worker in downtown Minneapolis, notices that the fingers of her right hand feel strained when she bends them, and that her wrist is stiff. Later that day, at home, she applies ice but finds that her wrist and fingers still hurt. She decides to do some investigating on the Web.

An Index to Keywords

To select keywords

1. Ask the five Ws and generate a list.
2. Strip out prepositions, articles, etc.
3. Classify the words remaining: nouns, actions, modifiers.
4. Focus on a noun: a person, place, or thing.
5. Narrow the search with a modifier to create a phrase.
6. Find synonyms.
7. Find the right level of generality.

Ask the five Ws.

A good way to begin formulating an accurate query is to jot down the *who, what, where, when, how,* and *why.* Considering her mystery ailment, Jan jots down the following:

- Who/What?—sore fingers, stiff wrist, injury, an accident
- Where?—at workplace, on-the-job pain
- When?—during typing
- How?—when I bend, painful fingers and wrist
- Why?—related to work at a keyboard? typing? safety?

Strip out prepositions, articles, and so on.

The next step is to break down the query by identifying key words. Note that common words such as *and, about, the, of, an, in, as, if, not, is, it* are ignored by search

---

34b

▷2 Create a list of search terms

The key to getting good results from Web searches and not wasting effort sifting through irrelevant sources is to formulate precise queries. Even the most accurate queries are unlikely to yield a significant number of usable documents, and poorly conceived ones are going to yield considerably worse results. Queries are poorly conceived when they are overly vague or when they employ an insufficient number of keywords. Most users submit an average of 1.5 keywords in their queries—not enough to produce fruitful results. This section will help you to select keywords, which you can then combine in various ways into a search statement (step 3, below).

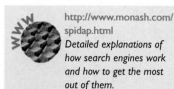

http://www.monash.com/
spidap.html
Detailed explanations of how search engines work and how to get the most out of them.

We'll dramatize the process of formulating queries by presenting a scenario. One spring day, Jan, an office worker in downtown Minneapolis, notices that the fingers of her right hand feel strained when she bends them, and that her wrist is stiff. Later that day, at home, she applies ice but finds that her wrist and fingers still hurt. She decides to do some investigating on the Web.

An Index to Keywords

To select keywords

1. Ask the five Ws and generate a list.
2. Strip out prepositions, articles, etc.
3. Classify the words remaining: nouns, actions, modifiers.
4. Focus on a noun: a person, place, or thing.
5. Narrow the search with a modifier to create a phrase.
6. Find synonyms.
7. Find the right level of generality.

Ask the five Ws.

A good way to begin formulating an accurate query is to jot down the *who, what, where, when, how,* and *why.* Considering her mystery ailment, Jan jots down the following:

- Who/What?—sore fingers, stiff wrist, injury, an accident
- Where?—at workplace, on-the-job pain
- When?—during typing
- How?—when I bend, painful fingers and wrist
- Why?—related to work at a keyboard? typing? safety?

Strip out prepositions, articles, and so on.

The next step is to break down the query by identifying key words. Note that common words such as *and, about, the, of, an, in, as, if, not, is, it* are ignored by search

518   **Using Electronic Resources**

engines since they appear so frequently in connection with any subject. Eliminating such words leaves

sore	job	keyboard	injury
fingers	office	workplace	safety
stiff	typing	bend	accident
wrist	painful	pain	

Classify words.

Now let's further classify these terms by arranging them into three categories: *nouns (persons/places/things)*, *actions*, and *modifiers*.

Person/Place/Thing		Actions	Modifiers
fingers	office	typing	stiff
wrist	job	bend	sore
workplace	pain		painful
injuries	keyboard		
accident	safety		

Focus on a noun: a person, place, or thing.

The most important terms in your query should be *objects*—that is, tangible "things." The thing (or person or place) you want to learn more about becomes the center of your search: your subject. Recall that much of the Internet is searched and classified by comprehensive subject directories such as Yahoo! and the Mining Company. As they scan the Web, the editors of those directories look for subjects that can be classified in categories and subcategories. Search engines will search the entire Web for documents, document summaries, or document titles; every search will be based on a subject—a person, place, or thing—against which the engine will be computing matches. By narrowing in on a subject yourself and focusing on a noun (a person, place, or thing), you will align your search needs with the logic of the search tools on the Web.

In the example search, there are ten potentially useful keywords:

fingers, office, wrist, job, workplace,
pain, injuries, keyboard, accident, safety

But selecting a single keyword, while necessary for conducting a useful search, will not (in most cases) be sufficient for getting the results you want. Very often such one-word searches yield an unmanageably large return list. For instance, conducting an AltaVista search on "injuries" yielded 849,750 hits; a Hotbot search on "wrist" generated 27,680 hits. To conduct a successful search, you need to qualify your search term; the way to do this is to refer back to your list of classified words and search for another word (or two) that can qualify your keyword. That is, you will need to choose a modifier.

Narrow the search with a modifier to create a phrase.

When you begin to qualify and make more precise your search terms by combining them in meaningful ways, Internet searches become more useful. For instance, narrowing "injuries" by including the modifier "workplace" yields the new search term "workplace injuries." Narrowing the keyword "wrist" by converting it to a modifier that qualifies the noun "pain" yields the new search term "wrist pain." Focusing the keywords in these ways had impressive results:

AltaVista search on "injuries": 849,750 hits

AltaVista search on "workplace injuries": 2,704 hits

HotBot search on "wrist": 27,680

HotBot search on "wrist pain": 9,834

Narrowing a search by using a modifier can help in two ways:

1. The narrowed search may directly yield the information you want.
2. The narrowed search may yield information that enables you to focus the search still further, bringing you that much closer to the information you want.

To illustrate: the first returned hit on the HotBot search of "wrist pain" listed a Web site for a product that relieved wrist pain—particularly "carpal tunnel syndrome" and "repetitive stress injuries." As it turned out for Jan, who was doing research on her wrist ailment, she suffered from what she suspected was carpal tunnel syndrome. A search on that term brought her to a wealth of pertinent information.

Using quotation marks: You may want to make sure that a search engine regards the words you have entered as an exact phrase or text string, rather than as individual words. For example, assume that Jan wanted a search engine to search for all occurrences of the word "workplace" when it appeared directly before the word "safety." She did *not* want the search to return all documents with only one of these words or even both of them—if they did not occur together in the desired sequence. You can instruct a search engine to treat words as an exact phrase by enclosing the words within quotation marks. Thus, you would type **"workplace injuries"** into the query box and click "Go" or "Submit." (Note that not all search engines recognize quotation marks as a means of defining phrases.)

Use the results of the five W exercise (see above) to generate two- or three-word phrases that can function as the starting point for your Internet searches. Typically, one of these words will be a noun—a person, place, or thing; and one of these words will be a modifier that limits, or focuses, the noun. Working from her list of individual words, Jan generated several useful search phrases:

workplace injuries

workplace accidents

job safety

typing injuries

work-related pain

Find synonyms.

Spend a few moments thinking of synonyms for your keywords. If you're having trouble thinking of synonyms, use a thesaurus (available on most Word processors—check under "tools," where you'll also find Spell checkers). Synonyms allow a search engine a greater chance to identify sources related to your query. In constructing a search relating to her stiff fingers and wrist, Jan settled on the synonym "occupation" and "occupational" for "job" and "work." She settled on the synonym "accident" for "injury"—not an exact synonym but an approximation she thought might yield more results.

Find the right level of generality.

One key to effective searching on the Internet is to search at the level of generality that will yield useful results. Recall our earlier discussion of directories, when we saw how Yahoo subdivides one of the disciplinary areas of **science** as follows:

> **Science**
>> **oceanography**
>>> **marine biology**
>>>> **seagrasses**

Clearly, keywords at too high a level—the level of *science*—will yield too many documents in an Internet search. Conversely, keywords at too low a level of generality—*seagrasses*—may yield too few documents, should your topic include other aspects of marine biology. If you choose too specific a keyword, the search engine you are using may return a prompt like the following one, from the Anywho Reverse Telephone Search (an engine you may want to use in locating a particular person <http://www.anywho.com/telq.html>): "Providing *more* information on the query form will *not* make your search successful. Instead, you should broaden your search by providing *less* information on the query form."

If you are using a keyword or phrase and the search returns too many or too few documents, shift your level of generality up or down, accordingly. When you are overwhelmed with hits in the tens of thousands, shift the level of generality *down* by experimenting with different modifiers that will limit the keyword. When you have the opposite problem—*no* hits—broaden the search term. For help in developing a sense of generality and specificity of search terms, go to Yahoo! or another subject directory (see the recommended list, above) and work yourself up and down the directory structures.

▶ **EXERCISE 4**

Use the suggestions in this section to create a list of search terms for your topic. Ask the five Ws and generate a list; strip out prepositions; classify the words as nouns, actions, or modifiers; focus on nouns; narrow the focus with a modifier to create a phrase; find synonyms and the right level of generality. At the completion of this exercise, you should have generated a list of search terms.

▶

▶3 Construct the search statement and conduct your search.

You have devoted effort to identifying keywords or key phrases for your search. Now, depending on the search engine you use, you can refine these words and phrases further in an effort to improve your search results. The search engines themselves are increasingly providing a "refine" function—sometimes called "advanced" search tools or "power" searches. The refine function allows you to narrow searches by date, type of publication, and type of Web site—for instance, you might instruct the engine to search only organizations, government, or military sites. Refining your searches is easy: locate the advanced feature set and fill in (or, in some cases, click to check) a box. At the Excite search engine, once you type in a keyword and launch a search, the engine will prompt you to refine the search by offering additional terms that you can check off to include in your search.

Beyond using these "refine" functions that are built into the various search engines, you can refine your queries in two additional ways: use "wildcards" on word stems and use Boolean connectors between keyword terms.

Use "wildcards" on word stems.

You want to be able to select relevant documents containing *work*, but you also want to select documents containing *workplace*. To avoid having to use two similar keywords for the same concept (since it's best to limit the number of keyword terms to about three), you can "truncate" (cut off) the keyword to its stem—in this case *work*. Adding an asterisk to the stem produces *work**. Your search engine can now look for documents containing variants of the keyword—including variant spellings. For instance, some sources spell "carpal" (in carpal tunnel syndrome) as "carpel." Instructing the engine to search for *carp** would locate Web pages with variant spellings of the keyword. But note that the wildcard strategy, if not used carefully, will sometimes yield unintended and unwanted results: for example, a search on *carp** will retrieve documents about fish. Using *cit** in a query to search for documents containing *city* and *cities* will also select documents containing *citadel, citation, cite, citizen, citizenship, citric,* and *citronella*.

Constructing *multiple* internet searches.

Remember this important tip for effective Internet searching: Once you have settled on a topic, search the Internet *multiple* times, using different search tools. Here are two Web sites on carpal tunnel syndrome, found in different searches using different search tools:

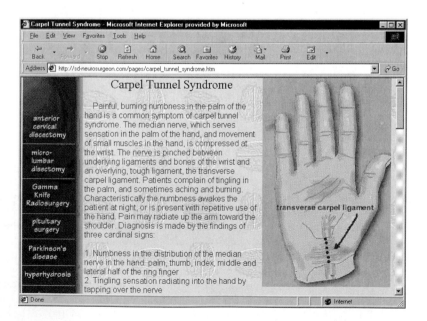

Using Electronic Resources

A general search of the Web using the AltaVista search engine located a site on types of surgical relief for painful conditions—carpal tunnel syndrome being one. Besides defining the condition, this page has an illustration showing the ligament that causes the condition.

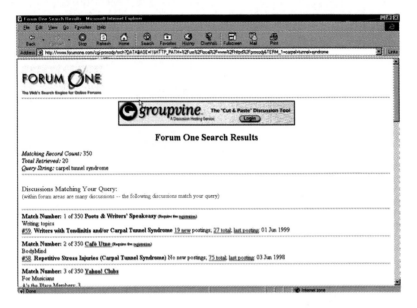

ForumOne is an engine that searches forums and discussion lists. This resource located over 300 discussions in which people with carpal tunnel syndrome, or those wanting to learn more about the condition, can post messages.

Use Boolean connectors between keyword terms

One of the most effective ways to narrow your search is to use Boolean connectors between keywords. (The name comes from George Boole, a nineteenth century mathematician and logician, who developed Boolean algebra.) Such terms are called *operators* and the way they are used to connect keywords is called *syntax*.

http://www.exo.net/uce/
uce6_boolean.html
A basic introduction to Boolean logic.

Note that the "refine" or "advanced" features of several search engines seamlessly incorporate Boolean logic into the search query, eliminating the need to master Boolean terminology. Still, Boolean logic underlies most search functions, so it's a good idea to be familiar with the terms. Note also that not all search engines support the full range of Boolean operators, though almost all recognize **AND, OR,** and **AND NOT** in queries. The main Boolean operators are listed in the box on page 524.

Using the keywords and phrases you have generated and, given the capabilities of the search engines you are using, conduct your search*es*. Notice the plural form of the term. The consistent message of this chapter is that you approach your task of finding information on the Internet not as a single search but as a series of related searches—with each focusing on *different* sources of information, using different search tools.

Using Boolean Logic

- **AND**   Terms on both sides of this operator must be present somewhere in the document to be scored as a result. **AND** may be used more than once in a query to narrow a search: thus, using **London AND "Big Ben" AND "Buckingham Palace" AND Trafalgar** would yield only documents containing all four terms.
- **OR**   Terms on EITHER side of this operator are sufficient to be scored as a result. **OR** means that the document may contain either term, but not necessarily both. In most cases, then, **OR** will yield too many results. It is mainly useful at the introductory stages of a search.
- **AND NOT**   Documents containing the term that occurs AFTER this operator are rejected from the results set. (For instance, you might search on "Queen Elizabeth AND NOT ship.") **AND NOT** is a means of weeding out irrelevant documents. *Note:* Only one instance of an unwanted term is sufficient to eliminate a document from consideration.
- **NEAR**   Similar to AND, only both terms have to occur within a specified word distance from one another to be scored as a result. You might search on "Diana NEAR Wales" or "Diana NEAR Charles."
- **BEFORE**   Similar to NEAR, only the first (left-hand) term before this operator has to occur within a specified word distance *before* the term on the right side of this operator in order for the source document to be scored as a result
- **AFTER**   Similar to NEAR, only the first (left-hand) term before this operator has to occur within a specified word distance *after* the term on the right side of this operator in order for the source document to be scored as a result.

See 34b-2 on using quotation marks with a search string to search for an exact sequence of words.

▶ ### EXERCISE 5

Using the Internet tools that you identified in Exercise 3, conduct *multiple* searches on your topic. If your search tools allow, consider refining the search by date, Boolean operators (see the box in this section), or domain name. (For example, you might limit certain searches to URLs that end with "edu" or "gov".) Experiment with search terms, using different phrases to generalize or limit the search. Revise your search query if you do not locate useful information in the first fifteen retrieved sites. Switch to a different search tool if, after five revisions, you
▶ do not locate useful information.

▶4 **Evaluate search results and revise the query if needed.**

Even carefully constructed searches retrieve irrelevant results or results lists with thousands of hits. *If you don't locate useful information within the first fifteen retrieved sites,* revise the query. Construct new search statements using different combinations of search words or phrases that move up and down the level of generality that you would expect to find, for instance, in a subject directory. An example: if you are overwhelmed with the retrieval list of a keyword search on "computers," refine the keyword with a modifier and try "laptop computers." If that search is similarly overwhelming, add the word "reviews" to the keyword and search on "laptop computer reviews." Soon enough, you will reduce the list of retrieved Web sites to a manageable number. Each new combination of keywords will retrieve different results. *If after five revisions of your keyword you still aren't finding useful information, consider switching to a different search tool.* Then begin the search process again.

To illustrate this process of revision, consider the following example: Using the Northern Light search engine, you could search on "repetitive stress injury" and have 11,365 documents retrieved—far too many "hits" to sort through in any meaningful, systematic way. Northern Light offers a "Power Search" feature that allows the researcher to limit the query. By directing the search engine to look for matches between specific dates (1/1/97 to 12/20/98), and specifying that the engine search only government documents (with a URL ending in ".gov"), you could narrow the retrieval list to 504 items.

The fourth item in the retrieval list in the Northern Light search was a site from the federal government's Occupational Safety and Health Administration (OSHA). This Web site is published by a credible source (an agency of the federal government) and opens with a definition of ergonomics that would prove very useful in a paper on repetitive stress disorders. Here is that Web page:

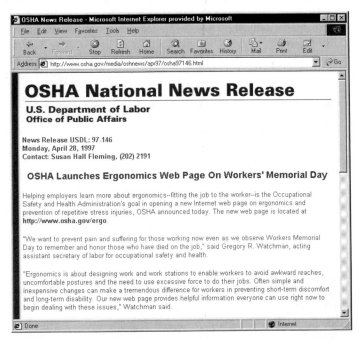

As this example illustrates, you should expect to revise your Internet searches. Very likely, useful information on your topic resides somewhere on the Internet, waiting for you to discover it. But the process of discovery typically takes several attempts with any given tool, such as Northern Light or Excite. Recall from 34b-1 that you do well to launch *multiple* searches on your topic, using different tools. With each tool, expect to be somewhat overwhelmed with the initial retrieval list. Use the tool's "refine" or "advanced search" feature to fine-tune the search. More reliably, you can fine-tune a search using the techniques discussed in 34b-2 and 34b-3.

▶ 34c Evaluating Internet sources

How do you assess the accuracy, reliability, and overall quality of information you find on the Web? In general, the same criteria that apply to print information (see 1g 1–2) also apply to Web-based information. Most major print journals, magazines, and newspapers have Web sites that post current and archived articles, and evaluating articles on these sites presents the same challenges as evaluating a printed article. However, a good deal of information on the Internet presents an additional set of challenges for evaluation primarily because anyone can "publish" on the Web.

Writers can't get an article into print unless a publisher reviews the piece and thinks that there's a wide enough market for this material to justify the cost of publication. And reputable publishers employ editors to check, or at least to question, what is written in order to avoid responsibility for obvious misstatements of fact, inflammatory or potentially libelous statements, or just plain bad writing. No such barriers exist on the Internet. The Web is truly a democratic institution, which is one of its main strengths. The drawback for readers is that anyone with an ax to grind, anyone who imagines his or her words are worth broadcasting to the world, can do so with relatively little effort and expense, and with no outside review.

Moreover, self-published Internet authors may post their sites anonymously— perhaps to begin a conversation about a sensitive topic, perhaps to sidestep responsibility for views expressed. Academic research is premised on the reader's ability to check facts and verify methods. Thus, when you encounter anonymously published Web sites, you face the task not only of determining the accuracy and fairness of the material, but also of inferring clues about the author's credibility. Students who refer to such sites in their research run the risk of using sources that are not valid. You should, therefore, avoid quoting from anonymously published sites unless you are instructed to view them as part of your coursework.

▶1 Evaluating Web pages

You will find a great deal of value on the Web. But as a researcher you should approach Web-based sources with caution—both for the above-mentioned reasons and because of the distinctive nature of electronic information on the Internet: Web search engines frequently retrieve irrelevant or questionable pages. Subsidiary pages may also be retrieved out of context, that is, apart from their "home" pages. Web pages that appear to be informational may actually be "infomercials" for products or services. Web pages may not be regularly updated, and may become outdated. Page hyperlinks may be outdated or inactive. Hyperlinks in otherwise reliable Web pages may lead to pages of doubtful reliability or accuracy at other sites. Web pages are inherently unstable; they can change or even disappear without warning. And outdated browser software, or software without necessary "add-ons" or "plug-ins," may not allow you to view certain Web pages accurately.

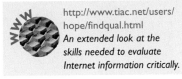

http://www.tiac.net/users/ hope/findqual.html
An extended look at the skills needed to evaluate Internet information critically.

A highly useful approach to evaluating information on the Web has been provided by Jan Alexander and Marsha Tate, reference librarians at the Wolfgram Memorial Library at Widener University. Alexander and Tate categorize Web pages into five major types. Following their explanation of these types, you will find questions to pose of each.

- **Advocacy Web Page:** "one sponsored by an organization attempting to influence public opinion (that is, one trying to sell ideas). The URL address of the page frequently ends in .org (organization)."[3] *Examples:* National Abortion and Reproductive Rights Action League <www.naral.org>, The National Right to Life Committee <www.nrlc.org>, the Democratic Party <www.democrats.org>, the Republican Party <www.rnc.org>.
  —What is the site advocating? Is the advocacy reasonable in tone?
  —What does the organization have to gain through its advocacy?
  —How does the organization characterize its opponents?

- **Business/Marketing Web Page:** "one sponsored by a commercial enterprise (usually it is a page trying to promote or sell products). The URL address of the page frequently ends in .com (commercial)." *Examples:* Adobe Systems, Inc. <www.adobe.com>, Coca Cola Co. <www.cocacola.com>, Oxyfresh <www.oxyfresh.com>.
  —Is advertising clearly differentiated from content?
  —How does the commercial sponsor profit from the content on the site?
  —Is the validity of the information compromised by commerce?

- **News Web Page:** "one whose primary purpose is to provide extremely current information. The URL address of the page usually ends in .com (commercial)." *Examples: USA Today* <www.usatoday.com>, *Washington Post* <www.washingtonpost.com>, CNN <www.cnn.com>.
  —Could you verify the news on the site from a print source?
  —Are sources of information clearly listed so that you can verify them?
  —How current is the page? When was it last revised?
  —Are editorial opinions clearly distinguished from news items?

- **Informational Web Page:** "one whose purpose is to provide factual information. The URL address frequently ends in .edu or .gov, as many of these pages are sponsored by educational institutions or government agencies." *Examples:* U.S. Census Bureau <www.census.gov/>, dictionaries <work.ucsd.edu:5141/cgi-bin/http_Webster>, Health and Human Services (HHS) <www.cdc.gov/nchswww/releases/96news/96news/nrsmoke.htm>, Buddhist Studies <www.ciolek.com/WWWVL-Buddhism.html>.

[3]This section is taken in large part from the Web site "Evaluating Web Resources," (http://www2.widener.edu/Wolfgram-Memorial-Library/webeval.htm, copyright 1996–1999) which complements the book *Web Wisdom: How to Evaluate and Create Information Quality on the Web* (1999) by Janet Alexander and Marsha Ann Tate.

—How current is the information? When was it last revised?

—Can you verify the information?

—How reputable are the sources of information?

- **Personal Web Page:** "one published by an individual who may or may not be affiliated with a larger institution. Although the URL address of the page may have a variety of endings (e.g., .com, .edu, etc.) a tilde (~) is frequently embedded somewhere in the URL."

—Does the individual have any obvious biases?

—Is the site free of obvious errors in grammar, punctuation, and usage?

—On the basis of what experience does the individual publish on the Web?

The first step in evaluating a Web site is to understand its type, and to then pose appropriate questions—some of which have been suggested above. You will find a more complete set of questions in Chapter 1, which is devoted to critical thinking.

2 Evaluating Usenet postings

Usenet postings present the greatest challenge to your critical evaluation skills because of the amount of "noise" you have to filter through to get information. Usually, Usenet posters are just average people expressing their opinions—informed, misinformed; rational, biased; thoughtful, off-the-cuff. Occasionally there will be a posting by experts in a particular field who have substantial information to offer, but this is not common. Ultimately, recognizing misleading, inaccurate, or useless postings is a matter of skill, experience, and taste (different people will place more or less trust in the posting of an enthusiastic Rush Limbaugh supporter, for example), but here are some guidelines that may help as you gain experience in the Usenet world:

1. Consider your first impulse if the posting you're reading appears to contradict what you believe, what you've seen and heard firsthand, or what most other posters in the group are saying. Start with your gut feeling.
2. What are the motivations, biases, and outright prejudices of the poster?
3. This is the hardest part: if you agree with the poster, or most other authorities you've read appear to agree, put yourself in the position of someone who disagrees with you. How would that person react to this particular posting?
4. Try to verify with a second source any information you get from Usenet. How much of what a poster writes is verifiable fact, how much is well-considered opinion, and how much is just mindless ranting and raving?
5. Does the poster use inflammatory or blatantly prejudiced language?
6. Who is the poster? What do you know about him or her? A poster who signs herself as an employee of the Environmental Protection Agency has at least a head start on authority and believability compared with one who signs himself as a member of "Free Americans to Eliminate Government."

EXERCISE 6

Working with the criteria set out in this section, evaluate the usefulness of any three of the Web sites (or other online destinations) you found in Exercises 3 through 5. Be sure to classify each Web page as an Advocacy page, a Business/Marketing page, a News page, or an Information page. Distinguish Web pages from Usenet postings. Pose questions for evaluation appropriate to the types of materials you have gathered.

EXERCISE 7

Evaluate one or more of the following sites.[4] Apply the criteria of *authority, accuracy, objectivity, currency,* and *coverage* to this site. Note: to fully evaluate a site, once you have arrived at a home page, you will need to follow some of the links to other pages.

The "Alternative" White House	http://www.whitehouse.net
The Official White House	http://www.whitehouse.gov
Chips Ahoy	http://www.chipsahoy.com
Joe Boxer	http://www.joeboxer.com
The National Anti-Vivisection Society	http://www.nvas.org
American Smoker's Alliance	http://www.smokers.org
The Minuteman Press Online	http://www.afn.org/~mpress/
ITI Information Center	http://www.itimiami.com
HHS News	http://www.cdc.gov/nchswww/releases/96news/96news/nrsmoke.htm
Philadelphia Online	http://www.phillynews.com
Timothy Burke's Home Page	http://www.swarthmore.edu/SocSci/tburke1

▶34d   URLs for researchers

Below is a list of URLs for sites that are of special interest to writers and researchers in all disciplines. Given the changing nature of the Internet, by the time this book is printed, some of these sites may either have changed or vanished. Visit each site before entering it in your bookmark list. See section *e* in Chapters 38–40 for discipline-specific Web resources in the humanities, social sciences, and sciences.

▶1   General research sites

Berkeley Digital Library	http://sunsite.berkeley.edu/
The Best Information on the Net (Librarians of St. Ambrose University)	http://www.sau.edu/CWIS/Internet/Wild/index.htm
Blue Web'n Online ("a library of Blue Ribbon learning sites on the Web")	http://www.kn.pacbell.com/wired/bluewebn/#table

[4]These sites are taken from a list compiled by Janet Alexander and Marsha Ann Tate (http://www2.widener.edu/Wolfgram-Memorial-Library/examples.htm, copyright 1996–1999).

Complete Reference to Usenet Newsgroups	http://www.tile.net/tile/news/index.html
Ecola Newstand	http://www.ecola.com
ERIC Clearinghouse on Information and Technology	http://ericir.syr.edu
The Internet Public Library	http://www.ipl.org/
Internet Subject Guides (University of Alberta)	http://www.ualberta.ca/~slis/guides/guides.html
Libweb: Library Servers via WWW	http://sunsite.Berkeley.EDU/Libweb/
Listserv Lists Search	http://tile.net/listserv/
Needle in a CyberStack: The InfoFinder	http://home.revealed.net/~albee/index.html
Study Web (70,000 Research Quality Web sites, all disciplines)	http://www.studyweb.com/
Supreme Court Decisions	http://www.law.cornell.edu/supct/
The Universal Library (Carnegie Mellon University)	http://www.ul.cs.cmu.edu/first.htm
University of California InfoMine	http://lib-www.ucr.edu/
Vincent Voice Library (Michigan State University)	http://web.msu.edu/vincent/
WebGems: A Guide to Substantive Web Resources (all disciplines)	http://www.fpsol.com/gems/webgems.html
Webliography (Louisiana State University)	http://www.lib.lsu.edu/hum/lit.html
WWWVirtual Library (All disciplines)	http://vlib.stanford.edu/Overview.html

▶2 Desktop references

Acronym and Abbreviation List   <http://www.ucc.ie/info/net/acronyms/>
Searchable list of acronyms; also reversible to search for acronym from a
keyword.

The Alternative Dictionaries   <http://www.notam.uio.no/~hcholm/altlang/>
Dictionary of slang and expressions you most likely won't find in a normal
dictionary; all entries are submitted by users.

CIA World Factbook   <http://www.odci.gov/cia/publications/95fact/
index.html> Every hard fact about every country in the world.

Computing Dictionary   <http://wombat.doc.ic.ac.uk/> Dictionary of computing terms; often technical.

Hypertext Webster Interface   <http://c.gp.cs.cmu.edu:5103/prog/webster>
A searchable dictionary.

Quotations page <http://www.starlingtech.com/quotes/> Enables searches for quotations by keyword.

Roget's Thesaurus <http://humanities/uchicago.edu/forms_unrest/ROGET.html> An online searchable version of the venerable book of synonyms.

Scholes Library Electronic Reference Desk <http://scholes.alfred.edu/Ref.html> An index of "ready reference" sources.

▶3 Writing help

Allyn and Bacon's Compsite <http://www.abacon.com/compsite/> An interactive meeting place for teachers and students to share resources and work on projects.

Critique Partner Connections <http://www.geocities.com/TheTropics/8977/> A place to find a writing partner for help by e-mail.

Dakota State University Online Writing Lab (OWL) <http://www.dsu.edu/departments/liberal/cola/OWL/> An online writing lab that provides writing help via e-mail.

An Elementary Grammar <http://www.hiway.co.uk/~ei/intro.html> Twenty-two sections of moderately technical discussions of grammatical topics from The English Institute.

Elements of Style <http://www.cc.columbia.edu/acis/bartleby/strunk/> Will Strunk's 1918 classic.

English Grammar FAQ As Posted to alt.usage.english <http://www.lsa.umich.edu/ling/jlawler/aue/> Answers to common grammar questions from linguist John Lawler.

English as a Second Language <http://www.lang.uiuc.edu/r-115/esl/> Bills itself as the starting point for learning English as a second language online. Includes visual and auditory resources, as well as a 24-hour help center.

The "It's" vs. "Its" page <http://www.rain.org/~gshapiro/its.html> The difference between the two homophones.

The King's English <http://www.columbia.edu/acis/bartleby/fowler/> Full text of H. W. Fowler's 1908 classic on English, Victorian style.

Non-Sexist Language <http://mickey.la.psu.edu/~chayton/eng202b/nonsex.htm> Tips for avoiding sexist language, based on National Council of Teachers of English guidelines.

Purdue On-Line Writing Lab <http://owl.english.purdue.edu/> An extensive source of online help for writers, including professional help to specific questions by e-mail. Links to other OWLs worldwide.

University of Michigan OWL <http://www.lsa.umich.edu/ecb/OWL/owl.html> Receive advice about your writing via e-mail, link to other writing resources, or, if you're in Ann Arbor, make an appointment for a face-to-face tutoring session.

The Word Detective <http://www.word-detective.com/> Online version of the newspaper column answering questions about words.

35

Using Sources

This chapter will offer you strategies for using sources with care. To keep matters in perspective, realize that you will present sources in a paper for one reason only: to support and advance your original thinking. Without your guiding, independent purpose, a research paper has no reason for existing. Clearly, a paper that stitches together the words and ideas of others, but that is guided by no original effort, cannot be called research.

> ### 35a Finding sources for authoritative opinions, facts, and examples

How convinced are you by the following?

> Critics of the modern shopping mall make the argument that marketplaces have traditionally been spaces of business as well as community; malls today are places of business, only.

The writer asks us to accept a statement as true. Should we believe it? If we know relatively little or nothing about a topic, how are we to judge the accuracy of statements made about it? Read the following expanded version of the example sentence.

> Critics of the modern shopping mall make the argument that marketplaces have traditionally been spaces of business as well as community; malls today are places of business, only; and American shoppers are the poorer for it. Industry specialists heartily agree—at least with the second point: "Malls are designed to maximize profits," says the Chairman of the Environmental Subcommittee for the International Council of Shopping Centers. "They were not built as a replacement for Main Street. If intimacy encourages sales, there will be intimacy" (Marks). One mall executive makes the point with particular bluntness: "We don't want the mall to be a community in any real sense because we'll attract people we don't want to. People who are not here to shop but are coming for some other purpose. It would upset our tenants who want to make money" (qtd. in Lewis 123). [See the citations for Marks and Lewis in "Works Cited," 36h.]

With the sources added for support, the statement is more convincing than the original, sourceless version. Carefully used sources can provide authoritative opinions, facts, and examples that will advance the ideas of your research papers.

1 Authoritative opinions

When linking the words of experts to your own words, you shift the basis on which you ask readers to accept key statements. Without authoritative support, you ask readers to take you at your word—which some may be willing to do. But skeptical readers will want proof. By offering authoritative opinions, you ask readers to accept your view because experts also believe it to be true. Student writer Jason Koman illustrates this strategy in the example on shopping malls above (see Jason's paper on shopping malls in Chapter 36).

2 Facts

Certain statements about the world exist in the category of things that are demonstrably true or false. Either the aurora borealis is caused by sunspots or it is not; either London is a more northerly city than New York or it is not. When you make statements such as these, readers want assurance that the statements are accurate. You can provide this assurance by turning to sources for factual support.

3 Examples

Turn to sources for examples that clarify and support your points. Indeed, it is often *through* a well-chosen example, which your source materials can provide, that readers remember your point. Consider this paragraph from a discussion of nervousness during college interviews. The writer, Anthony Capraro, III, directs a college counseling service:

> **Nervousness** [. . .] is absolutely and entirely normal. The best way to handle it is to admit it, out loud, to the interviewer. Miles Uhrig, director of admission at Tufts University, sometimes relates this true story to his apprehensive applicants: One extremely agitated young applicant sat opposite him for her interview with her legs crossed, wearing loafers on her feet. She swung her top leg back and forth to some inaudible rhythm. The loafer on her top foot flew off her foot, hit him in the head, ricocheted to the desk lamp and broke it. She looked at him in terror, but when their glances met, they both dissolved in laughter. The moral of the story—the person on the other side of the desk is also a human being and wants to put you at ease. So admit to your anxiety and don't swing your foot if you're wearing loafers! (By the way, she was admitted.)[1]

A well-chosen example can etch the point you want to make in your reader's mind.

▶ 35b Classifying sources: Primary and secondary

When attempting to determine the value and quality of a source, keep in mind the distinction between *primary* and *secondary* sources. Primary sources are written by people who have *direct* knowledge of the events or issues under discussion: they

[1]Anthony F. Capraro, III, "The Interview." *Barron's Profiles of American Colleges*, 19th ed. (Hauppauge, New York: Barron's Educational Series, 1992) 12.

were participants in or observers of those events. Examples of primary sources are letters, diaries, autobiographies, oral histories, historical records or documents, and works of literature. Here is a primary source—an announcement for a Fourth of July celebration in 1871 on the Kansas frontier:

> A great 4th of July at Douglas, 1871, everybody is invited to come and bring filled baskets and buckets. There will be a prominent speaker present, who will tell of the big future in store for southern Kansas. Grand fire works at night! Eighteen dollars worth of sky rockets and other brilliant blazes will illuminate the night! There will also be a bunch of Osage Indians and cowboys to help make the program interesting. After the fire works there will be a big platform dance, with music by the Hatfield Brothers.
>
> —qtd. in JOANNA L. STRATTON, *Pioneer Women: Voices from the Kansas Frontier* (New York: Touchstone, 1981) 135

Authors of secondary sources have *indirect* knowledge, only. They rely on primary or other secondary sources for their information. Examples of secondary sources include biographies, textbooks, historical surveys, and literary criticism. A historian studying nineteenth century Wild West shows in America and Europe might use the Independence Day announcement as a source. Working with the question "How would 'a bunch of Osage Indians and cowboys [. . .] help make the program interesting'?" the historian might investigate what attitudes are revealed about Native Americans in this and similar announcements from the era. If you were writing a research paper on Wild West shows of the nineteenth century, your reference to the historical study would be to a secondary source. The original announcement would remain a primary source.

Can a source be both primary and secondary?

A source can be considered both primary and secondary, depending on how it is used. Consider the historical study of Wild West shows—for your purposes a secondary source, assuming you were writing a paper on this topic. Now imagine a second writer (Writer B) who has begun a research project on the ways in which historians gather evidence. The same historical study of Wild West shows would become for Writer B a *primary* source. Writer B's interest would not concern the shows themselves but rather the ways in which evidence was used and a story was told. Presumably, in Writer B's project, other historical accounts would be treated as primary sources. In certain contexts, then, a secondary source can be approached as a primary source. How that source is used determines the classification.

Advantages and disadvantages of primary and secondary sources

Primary sources are not necessarily superior (or inferior) to secondary sources, but it is good to recognize the strengths and limitations of each.

Primary sources

- provide facts and viewpoints that are not generally available from other sources;
- often have immediacy and drama; but
- may be colored by the bias of the authors, who want to inflate their own importance or to justify questionable decisions.

Secondary sources

- may offer a broader perspective, with their distance from original events;
- tend to be less affected by intense passions of the moment than those who participated in those events; but
- may write with a strong, interpretive bias that you will need to evaluate carefully.

Source by source, you will need to make your decisions on reliability, determining whether you consider the material to be primary or secondary.

▶ 35c   Reading sources critically

Your ability to write a research paper depends on your being able to use sources with care. And your ability to use sources, the subject of this chapter, depends *entirely* on your being able to read well. Because effective reading is a foundational skill on which the success of all research rests, you should turn to Chapter 1 if you are not fully comfortable with the prospect of reading to understand, respond, and forge relationships. Careful, strategic reading is a skill you can teach yourself; once learned, it will serve you well.

Consider how the strategies for critical reading described in Chapter 1 might help as you work with source materials for your research papers.

▶1   Reading to understand and respond

Your main goal during this stage is to familiarize yourself with your sources and to determine their *relevance* for your research project.

- *Understand.* Preview the source by skimming its contents. Read the table of contents, the introduction or preface, the conclusion, headings, and selected topics.
- *Respond.* Read your source carefully enough to *react* and to *ask questions.* Check the credentials of the author and the critical reception of his or her work. Does the author's background or professional affiliation suggest to you the point of view he or she will take? Identify the author's stance on the subject: Is she or he pro, con, or neutral? relatively detached or passionately involved (or something in-between)? Is the tone angry, cynical, witty, solemn, or earnest? Does the author have a personal stake in the issue under discussion? If so, how might this affect your acceptance of her or his arguments?

Highlight important questions, particularly those most relevant to your research question, and make notes in the margins. Take notes, looking for important quotations that you might be able to use in the paper. Identify arguments and the positions of people involved. Finally, be alert to *differences* and *similarities* among sources. After critical reading and additional research, you will probably want to discuss such differences.

▶2 Reading to evaluate and synthesize

Your goal during this stage of critical reading is to clearly assess each source and to consider your sources together, so that you can begin to find patterns of meaning that emerge. As you continue to read with your research question in mind, you will begin to develop a thesis for your paper.

■ *Evaluate.* Determine the *reliability* of your sources. This involves attempting to separate fact from opinion in the source; identifying and assessing the author's assumptions; and evaluating both the evidence offered by the author in support of his or her argument and the logic by which the conclusions are reached (see 6h).

Consider the source. Reading to evaluate also involves considering the source of publication for an article or book. Was the article published in a popular magazine (intended for a general audience) or an academic or professional journal (intended for a specialized audience)? Articles in journals will probably be more difficult to read, but will tend to carry more authority and credibility. Is the book or pamphlet published by a commercial or academic publisher, or by a publisher with a special interest (a chemical company, for example, or a nonprofit agency such as the pro-environmental Earth First! or the American Civil Liberties Union)? Special-interest publications should not necessarily be discounted, but you should consider the source and be aware of potential biases. For more specific advice, see the box in 6d-2, "Appealing to Authority."

■ *Synthesize.* Determine how the evidence from one source is related to evidence from other sources. You must compare what you find in your sources, evaluate the information and assumptions in each, and form your own ideas about the most important relationships among them. The skills for doing this are demonstrated in detail in Chapters 1 and 2 (see 1h and 2d). Your discussion will require cross-references among sources, noting where one author refers to ideas discussed by any others. When possible, establish a relationship among them through comparing, contrasting, defining concepts or examples, or making connections by process or cause and effect. In this way you *synthesize* the sources to let them support your answers to the research question and your argument for the paper's provisional thesis.

▶3 Evaluating electronic sources

In 34b–34c, you will find an extensive discussion on locating, accessing, and evaluating the reliability of electronic sources. When you draw on these sources, be very careful to assess their validity and credibility, keeping the following considerations in mind:

■ Reliability of evidence varies considerably across electronic sources, so judge each source on its merits—as you would any source.
■ Sources gained through anonymous FTP tend to have the same status as print information in the library.
■ Information gained from newsgroups and Web pages can be helpful but also unreliable. Any person or organization can create and post documents

on the Internet. The material you find may have been produced for an expressly commercial, political, racial, or religious motive. Carefully consider each source.

▶35d Creating a working bibliography

Your **working bibliography** is a list of all of the sources you locate in preparing your paper. This includes books, articles, entries from biographical sources, handbooks, almanacs, electronic sources, and the various other kinds of sources cited in 34f–g and Chapter 35. The bibliography should also include sources you locate in indexes that you intend to check later. Your working bibliography differs from your **final bibliography** in that it is more comprehensive: the final bibliography consists only of those sources that you actually use in writing the paper.

It is absolutely essential that you prepare your working bibliography *at the same time* that you are compiling and consulting your sources. That way you can be sure to have accurate and complete information when the time comes to return to your sources to obtain more information or to double-check information, and to compile your final bibliography. It is enormously frustrating to be typing your list of references (quite possibly, the night before your paper is due!) and to suddenly realize that your notes do not contain all the information you need.

Making bibliographic notes

We recommend that you compile a working bibliography on 3" × 5" index cards or by computer record. What you take notes on is less important than your ability to quickly and effortlessly alphabetize entries or to arrange them in any other order (such as by topic and subtopic order, or by sources you have already examined and ones you have not) that is most useful to you during the research and writing process. As you consult each new source, carefully record key information:

1. full name of author (last name first)
2. title (and subtitle)
3. publication information:
   a. place of publication
   b. name of publisher
   c. date of publication
4. inclusive page numbers

In case you have to relocate the source later, indicate the library call number (in the upper right-hand corner) and the name and date of the index where you located the source (at the bottom). It is also a good idea to include a brief annotation (either below the publication information or on the back of the card), in which you describe the contents of that source or the author's main idea, and indicate your reaction to the source and how you might use it in your paper. By surveying your annotations as you proceed with your research, you will quickly be able to see how much you have already found on your subject and what else you still need to look up. Your annotations may also prevent you from wasting time looking up the same sources twice. Finally, you should assign a code number to each bibliographic entry. Then, when you are taking notes on the source, you can simply put that code number in the upper right-hand corner of the note, rather than recopying the complete bibliographic information.

Using your records to create a final bibliography

When the time comes to prepare your final bibliography, you can simply arrange the cards for the sources you used in alphabetical order and type up the pertinent information as a list. If your records are on a computer, you may use "sort" (for database) or "Find" and "cut and paste" functions to alphabetize the entries. Here's a sample bibliography record for a book:

---

⑤ *Geist, Johann F. Arcades: The History of a Building Type.*   *NA*
Trans. Jane O. Newman and John H. Smith.   *6218*
Cambridge: MIT, 1983.   *.G4313x*
                                                             1983

First chapter, 3–58: "The Architectural History of the Arcade." Markets, bazaars, arcades—design features and their social significance.

Here is a sample bibliography record for an article:

---

⑧ *Lewis, George H. "Community Through Exclusion and Illusion: The Creation of Social Worlds in an American Shopping Mall." Journal of Popular Culture 24.2 (1990): 121–36.*

Investigates what sorts of communities, if any, exist in the mall; based conclusions on observations at Mall of New England. Aside from teenagers and elders, no communities exist.

Creating an annotated bibliography

Some instructors may ask for an **annotated bibliography** as an intermediate step between your working bibliography notes and the final bibliography. In effect, an annotated bibliography is a fully annotated working bibliography in manuscript form; it records the same information demonstrated above in card form, presenting it in alphabetical sequence on manuscript sheets for your review and for suggestions from collaborators, peers, or your instructor.

A note on photocopying: Most periodicals and reference books can't be checked out of the library. Therefore, you may find yourself photocopying articles or book chapters. Remember to photocopy or record all pertinent bibliographic data. You will find it handy to photocopy the title page of a book or a periodical's contents page (or whichever page has dates, volume numbers, and other publication information). Two additional reminders may save you hours of retracing your steps late in the writing process:

- Check to see that you've photocopied *all* relevant words on each page. (You'll save yourself the frustration of discovering at a later time that the machine has missed the first five letters of each line.)
- For books that have endnotes, photocopy the corresponding notes at the end of the chapter or end of the book. This way, you won't have to find the source again if you have to track down a reference.

▶ **EXERCISE 1**

Compile a working bibliography—both books and articles—of twenty to twenty-five items for one of the subjects you have been researching for Chapter 33. Or if you prefer, research a new subject. Record key information (as indicated above) on 3" x 5" cards or in your electronic database (if the latter, you will need a printout). Include content annotations for at least five items.

▶ **35e**   Taking notes: Summarizing and paraphrasing

Use your computer's notetaking software or 4" x 6" cards for taking notes. Again, any system will work as long as you are able to (1) clearly identify the source from which the note is taken and (2) sort through and rearrange notes with ease.

Researchers use various formats for recording their notes, but the following elements are most important:

1. a *code number* corresponding to the code number on your bibliography record *or* the bibliographic reference itself;
2. a *topic* or *subtopic* label (these enable you to easily arrange and rearrange your records in topical order);
3. the *note* itself; and
4. a *page reference.*

Do not attempt to include too much information in a single note record. For example, do not summarize an entire article or chapter in one record, particularly if you are likely to use information from a single record in several places throughout your paper. By limiting each note to a single point or illustration, you make it easier to arrange the records according to your outline, and to rearrange them later if your outline changes. A sample note for *Arcades: The History of a Building Type,* by Johann Geist, appears on page 540. (For comparison's sake, it is placed directly after the bibliography record for that source.)

> ⑤   *Geist, Johann F. <u>Arcades: The History of a Building Type</u>.*   NA
>   *Trans. Jane O. Newman and John H. Smith.*   6218
>   *Cambridge: MIT, 1983.*   .G4313x
>   1983
>
> *First chapter, 3–58: "The Architectural History of the Arcade." Markets, bazaars, arcades—design features and their <u>social</u> significance.*

> <u>Design features of arcades</u>   ⑤
>
> *Physical features of the arcade isolate shoppers from outside world and keep them moving along. Arcades built with skylights, and no windows, so rooms—lit from above—could be otherwise totally enclosed. The effect: to avoid distractions from outside + keep shoppers' minds and eyes on the merchandise. (20)*

There are three methods of notetaking: *summarizing, paraphrasing,* and *quoting.* These methods can be used either individually or in combination with one another.

▶ I   Summarizing sources

A *summary* is a relatively brief, objective account, in your own words, of the main idea in a source passage. You summarize a passage when you want to extract the main ideas and use them as background material in your own paper. For details on the process of writing summaries, see 2a. Here is a section of an article by David Guterson, which Jason Koman refers to in his research paper on malls:

> There is, of course, nothing naturally abhorrent in the human impulse to dwell in marketplaces or the urge to buy, sell, and trade. Rural Americans traditionally looked forward to the excitement and sensuality of market day; Native Americans traveled long distances to barter and trade at sprawling, festive encampments. In Persian bazaars and in the ancient Greek agoras the very soul of the community was preserved and could be seen, felt, heard, and smelled as it might be nowhere else. All over the planet the humblest of people have always gone to market with hope in their hearts and in expectation of something beyond mere goods—seeking a place where humanity is temporarily in ascendance, a palette for the senses, one another.
>
>   —DAVID GUTERSON, "Enclosed. Encyclopedic.
>   Endured.: One Week at the Mall of America."
>   *Harper's* Aug. 1993: 51

Here is a sample summary of this source:

> David Guterson claims that marketplaces have traditionally been places of business as well as social centers. People throughout the ages, from the ancient Greeks to rural Americans, have gone to market in search of goods or profit; but they have also gone for something more: to see, and be part of, the vibrant center of community life (51).

▶2 Paraphrasing sources

A paraphrase is a restatement, in your own words, of a passage of text. Paraphrases are sometimes the same length as the source passage, sometimes shorter. In certain cases, particularly if the source passage is written in densely constructed or jargon-laden prose—the paraphrase may even be longer than the original.

You paraphrase a passage when you want to preserve all (or virtually all) the points of the original, major and minor, and when—perhaps for the sake of clarity—you want to communicate the ideas in your own words. Keep in mind that only an *occasional* word (but not whole phrases) from the original source appears in the paraphrase, and that the paraphrase's sentence structure does not reflect that of the source. The following paragraph appears in an article written by a sociologist who has studied shopping malls. Jason Koman refers to this article in his paper.

Original passage:

What emerged from the initial observations and interviews, then, was a picture of mall shoppers as a *collectivity*, located in one enclosed space, but utilizing the mall primarily for their own self-defined and rational economic transactions. They may well shop with a friend, or the family may come to the mall, but they are *not* there for the face to face primary interactive relations that are the core of community.

> —GEORGE H. LEWIS, "Community Through Exclusion and Illusion: The Creation of Social Worlds in an American Shopping Mall." *Journal of Popular Culture* 24.2 (1990): 125

Paraphrase:

Lewis observes that while mallgoers can be said to form a collection of people under one roof, they do not constitute a community: they do not search out the types of interpersonal contacts on which communities are built. Even if they go shopping with a friend or family member, they remain isolated consumers during their time at the mall, looking to buy what they need at prices they can afford (125).

This paraphrase is as long as Lewis's original passage, with roughly the same level of detail. Significantly, the paraphrase eliminates the original's difficult, sociological language: the writer can now take advantage of Lewis's insights, but in a way that does not disrupt the tone of the research paper.

▶ EXERCISE 2

Write a 250–400 word summary of one of the sources you have located for your working bibliography (Exercise 1). Then write a paraphrase of several sentences from a section of text in the same source.

> ## 35f Quoting sources

You may decide to quote from a passage when the author's language is particularly well chosen, lively, dramatic, or incisive, and when you think you could not possibly express the same idea so effectively. Or you may decide to quote when you want to bolster the credibility of your argument with the reputation of your source. By the same token, you may occasionally decide to discredit an opposing argument by quoting a discredited or notorious source.

> ### 1 Avoiding overquoting

Knowing how much to quote is an art in itself. If you underquote, your paper may come across as dry. If you overquote, your paper may come across as an anthology of other people's statements ("a cut-and-paste job"), rather than an original work. Some instructors have developed rules of thumb on quoting. One such rule is that for a ten-page paper, there should be no more than two extended quotations (i.e., indented quotations of more than 100 words); and each page should contain no more than two short quotations. If this rule of thumb makes sense to you (or to your instructor), adopt it; otherwise, modify it to whatever extent you think reasonable.

> ### 2 Deciding how to quote

When you quote a source, you need to record the author's wording *exactly;* the conventions for altering quotations with ellipses and with bracketed words (that you provide) are discussed below and in 29e.

In researching his paper on shopping malls, Jason Koman discovered several helpful books on arcades from which he learned that the arcade, both in design as well as in social and psychological impact on the consumer, was the predecessor of the mall. Here is a passage from Margaret MacKeith, *The History and Conservation of Shopping Arcades* (London: Mansell, 1986) 16. The "success" mentioned in the first sentence refers to the commercial success of the first arcades.

> Once the success of such a venture had been established others quickly followed. These were sited where a growing population coincided with a shortage of shops, availability of land, finance and an entrepreneur. The absence of any one of these factors could prejudice commercial success. The pattern of the development of the arcade in Britain shows a move from the South to the North. First the capital, then the major port and the fashionable holiday resorts were overtaken by the expanding industrial cities. Only two arcades were built in London between 1818 and 1879, and perhaps this was due in part to a parallel and equally diverting means of shopping which went under the name of "bazaar." This despite some contemporary Parisian examples is essentially an English development. The term was chosen not to suggest an exotic environment but to alert the shopper to the extraordinary variety of goods for sale. The segregation of crafts into individual premises and thence into whole streets such as Butcher's Row or Mercer's Street, was a mediaeval method of trade protection which had no relevance by the mid-nineteenth century.

What you consider to be quotable depends on the purpose of your research. Jason Koman read this section of MacKeith's book to investigate the ways in which the modern mall was descended from the arcade of the nineteenth century. For his purposes, the following quotation was most useful:

<u>Determining location for arcades</u>

"These were sited where a growing population coincided with a shortage of shops, availability of land, finance and an entrepreneur." (16)

Sometimes you may wish to quote a passage that has itself been quoted by the source author. Generally, you should try to locate the original author when you want to quote. However, this won't always be practical: the original source may not be available at your library or may not be available at all (if the original source was quoted from an unpublished interview or from a lecture). The following passage appears in George Lewis's article on shopping malls. We reprint his footnote to explain why Jason Koman had to quote the source *through* Lewis:

> [T]he high turnover, volume of persons, and transiency that is a designed part of most malls works *against* the development and emergence of community within their walls.
>
> This is understood by mall managers and developers. As one put it: "Having the *perception* of community feeling does not mean that it actually exists. It is not the same thing. Perception is not necessarily reality."[11] So the important thing, from a marketing perspective, is to create the warm *illusion* of community, while at the same time quietly stacking the deck against its actual development. "We don't want the mall to be a community in any real sense because we'll attract people we don't want to. People who are not here to shop but are coming for some other purpose. It would upset our tenants who want to make money. We don't want anything to upset our tenants."

[11]Interview with mall marketing director, 1986.

If you decided to use only the quotation by the marketing director (and not Lewis or Lewis's commentary), your notecard would appear as follows. (The single quotation marks *within* double quotation marks show a quotation within a quotation.)

<u>Community as an illusion in the mall</u>
[Note #8]

Mall marketing director (no name given), interviewed by Lewis in 1986:
"'We don't want the mall to be a community in any real sense because we'll attract people we don't want to. People who are not here to shop but are coming for some other purpose. It would upset our tenants who want to make money. We don't want anything to upset our tenants.'" (qtd. in Lewis 123)

These are the *exact* words from the original. The student writer has added nothing, omitted nothing, and changed nothing.

▶3 Using brackets and ellipses in quotations

Sometimes for the sake of clarity, conciseness, or smoothness of sentence structure, you will need to make additions, omissions, or changes to quotations. For example, suppose you wanted to quote a passage beginning with the following sentence: "In 1979, one week after receiving a 13.3% pay raise, she received a call from the company president." To clarify the pronoun *she*, you would need to replace it with the name of the person in question enclosed in a pair of brackets: "In 1979, one week after receiving a 13.3% pay raise, [Virginia Rulon-Miller] received a call from the company president." (See 29d.)

Note that when using brackets, you do not need to use the ellipsis to indicate that the pronoun (*she*) has been omitted; brackets surrounding proper nouns imply that one word (or set of words) has replaced another. For more on altering quotations with ellipses and brackets, see Chapters 28 and 29, especially 29d–e.

Sometimes you need to change a capital letter to a lowercase one in order to smoothly integrate the quotation into your own sentence. For example, suppose you want to quote the following sentence: "Privacy today matters to employees at all levels, from shop-floor workers to presidents." You could smoothly integrate this quotation into your own sentence by altering the capitalization, as follows.

> The new reality, as John Hoerr points out, is that "[p]rivacy today matters to employees at all levels, from shop-floor workers to presidents."

▶4 Smoothly integrating quotations into your sentences

Using attributive phrases to introduce quotations

Whether or not you alter quotations by means of ellipses or brackets, you should strive to integrate them smoothly into your own sentences. Use attributive phrases (phrases that attribute, or point to the origin of, the quoted source). Here is a quotation from Jason Koman's interview with Richard Marks, the Chairman of the Environmental Subcommittee for the International Council of Shopping Centers.

> Malls are designed to maximize profits. They were not built as a replacement for Main Street. If intimacy encourages sales, there will be intimacy.

The quotation can be integrated in the text of a paper in any of several ways.

1. According to the Chairman of the Environmental Subcommittee for the International Council of Shopping Centers, "Malls are designed to maximize profits. They were not built as a replacement for Main Street. If intimacy encourages sales, there will be intimacy" (Marks).[2]
2. "Malls are designed to maximize profits," according to Richard Marks.
3. "If intimacy encourages sales," says Richard Marks, "there will be intimacy."

---

[2]Because the source of the quotation is an unpublished interview, *not* a published article or book, there are no page references set in the parenthetical citation. Most sources do have page references associated with them, however, and the parenthetical citation form for them is as follows: "Malls offer no community" (Jones 8). For an extended discussion of citation form, see Chapter 37.

4. Richard Marks, Chairman of the Environmental Subcommittee for the International Council of Shopping Centers, is perfectly candid: "Malls are designed to maximize profits."
5. "Malls are designed to maximize profits," says the Chairman of the Environmental Subcommittee for the International Council of Shopping Centers. "They were not built as a replacement for Main Street" (Marks).
6. According to Richard Marks, malls "were not built as a replacement for Main Street."

An attributive remark ("According to ___") can be shifted around in a sentence from beginning to end. Place a comma after the remark when it introduces a sentence; place a comma before the remark when it ends a sentence; place a *pair* of commas around the remark when it interrupts the quoted sentence. In the fourth example, a sentence (not a phrase) introduces the quotation, so a colon is the appropriate punctuation (to avoid a comma splice or a run-on).

Using statements with present-tense verbs to introduce quotations

Notice that in example 4 above, the quotation is introduced by a sentence. In examples 3 and 5, the quotation is woven into the structure of a sentence. In these cases, the convention is to use a main sentence verb in the *present* tense (see 9e-1). Even though your source has already been written (and so technically, the author has already declar*ed* or stat*ed* or conclud*ed*), when quoting sources you should use the present tense (declares, states, concludes). This convention applies even if you are discussing a literary work; thus you would say that Hamlet ponder*s*: "To be or not to be." The only exception to the use of the present tense would be if you were reporting the historical progress of some development or debate and you wished to emphasize that certain things were said at a particular point in time.

Verbs That Help You Attribute Quotations

Attributive phrases use verbs in the present tense. To vary attributive phrases, you might consider verbs such as these:

adds	defends	points out
agrees	denies	rejects
argues	derides	relates
asks	disagrees	reports
asserts	disputes	responds
believes	emphasizes	reveals
claims	explains	says
comments	finds	sees
compares	holds	shows
concedes	illustrates	speculates
concludes	implies	states
condemns	insists	suggests
considers	maintains	thinks
contends	notes	warns
declares	observes	writes

("The Senator assert*ed*: 'I do not intend to dignify these scurrilous charges by responding to them.' ")

▶5 Using block quotations

You should integrate most quotations into your own text, using quotation marks. If a quotation runs longer than four lines, however, you should set it apart from the text by indenting it ten spaces from the left margin. Quotation marks are not required around block quotations. Block quotations should be double spaced, like the rest of the text (see 28a).

The following box reviews the discussion on summarizing, paraphrasing, and quoting sources.

When to Summarize, Paraphrase, or Quote a Source

Summarize
- to present the main points from a relatively long passage
- to condense information essential to your discussion

Paraphrase
- to clarify complex ideas in a short passage
- to clarify difficult language in a short passage

Quote
- when the language of the source is particularly important or effective
- when you want to enhance your credibility by drawing on the words of an authority on the subject

---

▶ 35g Weaving summaries, paraphrases, and quotations into your paragraphs

To complete the integration of source materials into your paper, devote your attention to the paragraph level, where ideas are developed *across* sentences. The following approach can help you to integrate summaries, paraphrases, and quotations into the overall scheme of your paper. You will want to vary the approach, but here are the basics:

Sources and Cycles of Development

- Introduce your idea into a paragraph before you introduce a source. Working with your paragraph's idea, create a context into which you can fit the source.
- Having created the context, steer the reader directly to your source using an attributive phrase or a sentence with a present-tense verb.
- Quote, summarize, or paraphrase the source.
- *Use* the source by commenting on it, responding to it, or explaining its significance.

When you apply these principles to individual paragraphs, you create what can be called a "cycle of development" for using source materials. A full cycle will ensure that your reader is properly prepared for the source and that the source will advance your paragraph's idea, which originates with you, without overwhelming that idea. The important concept is that your idea comes first; then you follow with, and integrate, your sources. These principles are illustrated below, using labeled paragraphs from drafts of Jason Koman's research paper.

Cycle of development with a quotation

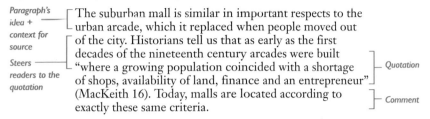

Paragraph's idea + context for source

Steers readers to the quotation

The suburban mall is similar in important respects to the urban arcade, which it replaced when people moved out of the city. Historians tell us that as early as the first decades of the nineteenth century arcades were built "where a growing population coincided with a shortage of shops, availability of land, finance and an entrepreneur" (MacKeith 16). Today, malls are located according to exactly these same criteria.

Quotation

Comment

Cycle of development with a paraphrase

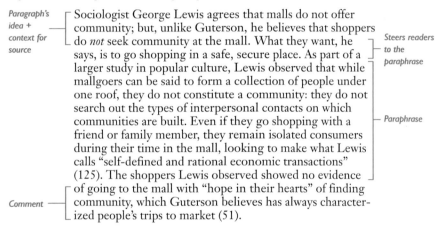

Paragraph's idea + context for source

Sociologist George Lewis agrees that malls do not offer community; but, unlike Guterson, he believes that shoppers do *not* seek community at the mall. What they want, he says, is to go shopping in a safe, secure place. As part of a larger study in popular culture, Lewis observed that while mallgoers can be said to form a collection of people under one roof, they do not constitute a community: they do not search out the types of interpersonal contacts on which communities are built. Even if they go shopping with a friend or family member, they remain isolated consumers during their time in the mall, looking to make what Lewis calls "self-defined and rational economic transactions" (125). The shoppers Lewis observed showed no evidence of going to the mall with "hope in their hearts" of finding community, which Guterson believes has always characterized people's trips to market (51).

Steers readers to the paraphrase

Paraphrase

Comment

Cycle of development with a summary

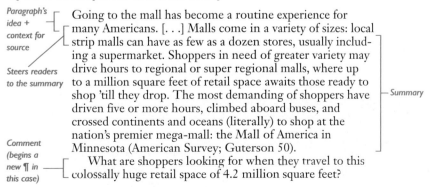

Paragraph's idea + context for source

Steers readers to the summary

Going to the mall has become a routine experience for many Americans. [. . .] Malls come in a variety of sizes: local strip malls can have as few as a dozen stores, usually including a supermarket. Shoppers in need of greater variety may drive hours to regional or super regional malls, where up to a million square feet of retail space awaits those ready to shop 'till they drop. The most demanding of shoppers have driven five or more hours, climbed aboard buses, and crossed continents and oceans (literally) to shop at the nation's premier mega-mall: the Mall of America in Minnesota (American Survey; Guterson 50).

Summary

Comment (begins a new ¶ in this case)

What are shoppers looking for when they travel to this colossally huge retail space of 4.2 million square feet?

▶ **EXERCISE 3**

The following passage appears in the book *Taking Laughter Seriously* by John Morreall. Read the paragraph and then follow the directions below, which ask you to work with the text in various ways. For activities 3–5, create a context in which quoting from Morreall's paragraph makes sense. Pretend you are writing a paper on laughter and that your quotations would fit into that paper.

> (1) When the person with a sense of humor laughs in the face of his own failure, he is showing that his perspective transcends the particular situation he's in, and that he does not have an egocentric, overly precious view of his own endeavors. (2) This is not to say that he lacks self-esteem—quite the contrary. (3) It is because he feels good about himself at a fundamental level that this or that setback is not threatening to him. (4) The person without real self-esteem, on the other hand, who is unsure of his own worth, tends to invest his whole sense of himself in each of his projects. (5) Whether he fails or succeeds, he is not likely to see things in an objective way; because his ego rides on each of the goals he sets for himself, any failure will constitute personal defeat and any success personal triumph. (6) He simply cannot afford to laugh at himself, whatever happens. (7) So having a sense of humor about oneself is psychologically healthy. (8) As A. Penjon so nicely said, it "frees us from vanity, on the one hand, and from pessimism on the other by keeping us larger than what we do, and greater than what can happen to us."

Assume for your answers to the following activities that a "Works Cited" list exists that includes a full entry for Morreall's book. When you quote from Morreall, you should provide a parenthetical citation, the format of which you will find explained in 37a-1. (The above paragraph appears on page 106 of *Taking Laughter Seriously*.)

> Morreall, John. *Taking Laughter Seriously*. Albany: State University of New York, 1983.

1. Write a summary of this passage: limit, 50 words.
2. Write a paraphrase of this passage: limit 140 words.
3. Write a sentence in which you quote any phrase from Morreall's paragraph.
4. Write a sentence in which you quote from the beginning of one of Morreall's sentences and from the end of the same sentence—omitting the middle. Remember to communicate to readers that you've altered Morreall's original language.
5. Quote A. Penjon. Note that the sentence you are quoting appears in a book by Morreall. (See 37a on in-text citations for "Material quoted in your source.")

▶

▶ **35h**   Avoiding plagiarism

Plagiarism is an unpleasant subject, but one that must be confronted in any discussion of research papers. In its most blatant form, **plagiarism** is an act of conscious deception: an attempt to pass off the ideas or the words of another as your own. To take an extreme example, a student who buys a research paper from a commercial "paper mill" or borrows a paper written by someone else and turns it in for academic credit is guilty of the worst kind of plagiarism. Only slightly less guilty is the student who copies into his paper passages of text from his sources without giving credit or using quotation marks.

The penalties for plagiarism can be severe—including a failing grade in the course or even a suspension from school. Graduate students guilty of plagiarism have been dropped from advanced degree programs. Even professionals no longer in school can see their reputations damaged or destroyed by charges of plagiarism. During the 1988 presidential campaign, a Democratic candidate was forced to drop out of the race when it was revealed that some of the material in his campaign speeches was copied from a speech by a prominent British politician.

Much plagiarism is unintentional; but unintentional or not, the effect of plagiarizing is the same, so you'll want to avoid the problem. Here are two general rules to help you avoid unintentional plagiarism:

1. Whenever you *quote* the exact words of others, place these words within quotation marks and properly cite the source.
2. Whenever you *paraphrase* or *summarize* the ideas of others, do not use whole phrases, or many of the same words, or sentence structures similar to the original. You must identify the source of the paraphrased or summarized material. You are obligated to credit your source even if you change the wording of the original statement or alter the sentence structure.

Determining what is common knowledge

The only exception to the second rule stated above is if the information summarized or paraphrased is considered common knowledge. For example, you need not cite the source of the information that General Lee commanded the Confederate forces during the Civil War, or the fact that Mars is the fourth planet from the sun, or the fact that Ernest Hemingway wrote *The Sun Also Rises*. If, on the other hand, you are summarizing one particular theory of why Lee's forces faced almost certain defeat, or the geological composition of the Martian surface, or how the critical assessment of Hemingway's *The Sun Also Rises* has shifted over the years, then you are obliged to cite the sources of your information or ideas, whether or not you quote them directly.

The key issue underlying the question of common knowledge is the likelihood of readers mistakenly thinking that a certain idea or item of information originated with you when, in fact, it did not. If there is *any* chance of such a mistake occurring, you should cite the source.

Your decision regarding what to consider common knowledge depends, partly, on audience. Suppose you are writing on a technical subject, computer software, for an audience of engineers. There's a great deal of technical information you might find in your sources, perhaps about computer languages, that you might reasonably decide would be common knowledge for readers who are specialists. They would clearly know that the information in question did *not* originate with you. Writing on the same topic for nonspecialists, however, you would want to cite the source of that same information, given the likelihood that your technically less sophisticated readers could reasonably mistake the information as yours.

The obligation is yours, then, *with every new research project*, to anticipate what your audience knows and what assumptions they will make about your knowledge. Let a spirit of honesty and fairness guide you, and you will make the right decisions. Jason Koman wrestled with the common knowledge issue in his paper. See paragraphs B and C of the paper, along with their facing-page treatments (36h).

▶2 Identifying blatant plagiarism of a source

We will use the sample passage below to illustrate what can happen when source ideas undergo several possible levels of intentional or unintentional plagiarism in the student examples that follow. The passage is from Steven F. Bloom's "Empty Bottles, Empty Dreams: O'Neill's Use of Drinking and Alcoholism in *Long Day's Journey into Night*," which appears in *Critical Essays on Eugene O'Neill*, edited by James J. Martine (Boston: G. K. Hall, 1984).

> In *Long Day's Journey into Night*, O'Neill captures his vision of the human condition in the figure of the alcoholic who is constantly and repeatedly faced with the disappointment of his hopes to escape or transcend present reality. As the effects of heavy drinking and alcoholism increase, the alcoholic, in his attempt to attain euphoric forgetfulness, is repeatedly confronted with the painful realities of dissipation, despondency, self-destruction, and ultimately, death. This is the life of an alcoholic, and for O'Neill, this is the life of modern man.

Here is a plagiarized student version of this passage. Plagiarized phrases are underlined:

> *Long Day's Journey into Night* shows O'Neill's <u>vision of the human condition in the figure of the alcoholic who is constantly faced with the disappointment of his hopes to escape</u>. <u>As the effects of heavy drinking and alcoholism increase, the alcoholic, in his attempt to attain forgetfulness, is repeatedly confronted with the painful realities of dissipation</u>, semidestruction, <u>and, ultimately, death. This is the life of an alcoholic, and for O'Neill, this is the life of modern man.</u>

This is the most blatant form that plagiarism can take. The student has copied the passage almost word for word and has made no attempt to identify the source of either the words or the ideas. Even if the author *were* credited, the student's failure to use quotation marks around quoted material would render this version unacceptable.

▶3 Avoiding unintentional plagiarism of a source

At times, the well-intentioned writer may attempt to put the ideas of others into his or her own words but may produce an effort that still too closely resembles the original and, still would constitute plagiarism. Remember, for the material to be your own, you must follow basic procedures:

- The language should be your own—with rare exceptions for a quoted word or a brief, exactly quoted phrase.
- The sentence structures should be your own. Do not reproduce the author's sentences, substituting words for the author's original wording.

■ The sequence of ideas that you present (with attribution) from the original source should be your own.

The following paragraph illustrates a failed attempt to make legitimate use of the source on Eugene O'Neil. Plagiarized phrases are underlined.

> The figure of the disappointed alcoholic who <u>hopes to escape reality</u> represents <u>the human condition in</u> *Long Day's Journey into Night.* Trying to forget his problems, the alcoholic, while drinking more and more, <u>is confronted with the realities of his self-destructive</u> condition, <u>and, ultimately, with death.</u> <u>For Eugene O'Neill,</u> the life of the alcoholic represents <u>the life of modern man.</u>

In this version, the writer's attempt to put the ideas of Steven Bloom into his own words still too closely resembles the original in sentence structure, the sequence of ideas, and the use of key phrases. For example, Bloom's "confronted with the painful realities of dissipation" becomes "confronted with the realities of his self-destructive condition." The writer's very slight reworking of Bloom's original would still count as plagiarism even if Bloom were given proper credit in a parenthetical citation—that is, even had the first sentence begun "According to Steven F. Bloom." The student may not have intended to plagiarize—he may, in fact, believe this to be an acceptable rendition—but it would still be considered plagiarism.

▶4 Making legitimate use of a source

The following use of the source passage is entirely acceptable:

> According to Steven F. Bloom, alcoholism in *Long Day's Journey into Night* is a metaphor for the human condition. The alcoholic drinks to forget his disappointments and to escape reality, but the more he drinks, the more he is faced with his own mortality. "This is the life of an alcoholic," asserts Bloom, "and for O'Neill, this is the life of modern man" (177).

The student has carefully attributed both the paraphrased idea (in the first part of the passage) and the quotation (in the second part) to the source author, Steven Bloom. The student has also taken special care to phrase the idea in her own language.

Of course, you cannot avoid keeping *some* key terms: obviously, if you are going to paraphrase the ideas in this passage, you will need to use words and phrases such as "alcoholic," "heavy drinking," "the human condition," and so on. However, what you say *about* these terms should be said in your own words.

It is crucial that you give your readers no cause to believe that you are guilty either of intentional or unintentional plagiarism. When you are summarizing or paraphrasing a particular passage, you must do more than change a few words. You must fully and accurately cite your source, by means of parenthetical citations or by means of attributive phrases, such as "According to Bloom, ..."

▶5 Quoting accurately

When you do quote material directly, be certain that you quote it accurately. For example, consider a student quotation of the preceding passage (which follows the student's introduction).

Long Day's Journey into Night is O'Neill's "vision of the human condition," according to Steven F. Bloom:

> As the effects of his heavy drinking and alcoholism increase, the alcoholic, attempting to achieve forgetfulness, is repeatedly confronted with all the painful realities of dissipation, self-destruction, and death. This is the life of an alcoholic for O'Neill and it is also the life of modern man.

At first glance, this quotation may seem to be accurate. But it is not. The student has *omitted* some words that were in the source passage (in the first sentence, "euphoric" and "despondency"; in the second sentence, "and"); has *changed* other words (in the first sentence, "attempting to achieve," instead of "in his attempt to attain"; in the second, "it," instead of "this"); has *added* some words that were not in the original (in the first sentence, "all"; in the second sentence, "also"); and has also omitted punctuation (in the second sentence, the comma after "O'Neill").

These changes may seem trivial and may not seem to essentially change the meaning of the passage, but once you place a passage within quotation marks (or indent it if it is a block quotation), you are obligated to copy it *exactly*. Deleted material should be indicated by a bracketed ellipsis [. . .] (see 29e); your own insertions should be indicated by brackets [ ] (see 29d). Otherwise, the material within your quotation marks must be word for word, punctuation mark for punctuation mark, *identical* to the original.

With a spirit of honesty and careful attention to accuracy, you will avoid problems with unintentional plagiarism. Develop the habit of proofreading your papers when they are all but final. Compare your typed copy of all quotations, paraphrases, and summaries with your original notes and with photocopies of sources (if you have these). Then enjoy the accomplishment of having used your sources well to advance the ideas of your paper.

▶ **EXERCISE 4**

Paraphrase a short passage from one of the sources you have located during your research. Then write a short paragraph explaining what you have done to eliminate all possibility of inadvertent plagiarism in your paraphrase.

CHAPTER 36

Writing the Research Paper

The material in this chapter parallels that in Chapters 3 and 4 on planning, writing, and revising the essay. Because the *process* of writing a research paper is in many (but not all) respects similar to that of writing an essay, the discussion of process here will be brief and cross-referenced with earlier sections of the book.

▶ 36a Refining the thesis

As you complete your research and prepare to write a paper, you probably have more information than you can possibly absorb. How will you get from the many notes you've taken—on notecards or, perhaps, on computer—to a finished paper? Here is where you must do your work as a critical thinker, synthesizing your sources in ways that advance the single idea at the heart of your paper. At this point in the process, you should be working with a question that interests you, one that motivates you to sift through all your notes in search of a satisfying answer. If you care about your work, the writing and the research will come more easily. With your question in mind, you will work with source materials until you formulate a satisfying answer—a thesis, which will be the core idea of your paper.

In 33e you saw the usefulness of devising a working thesis. *Working*, here, means preliminary. A working thesis offers a provisional idea with which to begin sifting through your notes; with this idea, you can begin to look at new materials in a more focused way. The discussion here will follow the progress of student writer Jason Koman as he works through the process of writing a research paper. After looking through his materials, Jason came up with the following:

Initial working thesis

America's shopping malls are the modern equivalents of ancient marketplaces.

Listen to your sources: Revise your question and working thesis, if need be.

Sometimes, your sources will in effect "give" you the paper you intended to write from the moment you began your research. At other times, your sources will show that the question you're investigating is more complicated than you imagined. In this case, the sources will suggest that you revise both your question and your provisional answer to that question.

This is what happened to Jason Koman. His initial question—in what ways do malls resemble ancient marketplaces—assumed that he would find similarities only. As he progressed in his notetaking, he began to gather information on types

553

Characteristics of a Working Thesis

- The subject of the thesis is *narrow* enough in scope that you can write a detailed paper without being constrained by the page limits of the assignment (3d-1).
- The predicate of the working thesis communicates a relationship you want to clarify about your subject, based on your understanding of the information you have generated (3d-2).
- The main statement of your thesis may involve one or more (but not many more) of the following relationships: sequential order, definition, classification, comparison, contrast, generalization, or causation.
- The thesis clearly suggests the patterns of development you will be pursuing in your paper. (The types of paragraphs you write in your paper will be directly tied to the relationships you develop in your thesis (3d-2, 3).)
- The thesis will clearly communicate your intellectual ambitions for the paper (3d-3).

of marketplaces throughout history: the agora of Greece, the markets of medieval Europe, the bazaars of Islamic countries. The research only partially confirmed the validity of both his question and his working thesis. True, the modern mall reproduced *some* of the functions of the ancient markets—notably, commerce. But his sources were telling him quite directly that the mall differed in an essential respect from older marketplaces: while older markets were places where people gathered in communities, malls are commercial spaces only. People do not go to malls to forge community ties. Moreover, Jason found a word repeated across various sources: *illusion.* Malls presented shoppers with an illusion of community and intimacy. Jason's sources did not give him the paper he expected to write. He continued to work, staying with his original idea of relating malls to older marketplaces, but he refined his thesis to respond to his revised research question: "What do shoppers want at the mall?" Jason answered as follows:

Refined working thesis

> Shoppers in the old markets were able to forge community ties and buy merchandise; shoppers today find merchandise only and, at best, just the illusion of community.

A refined working thesis, reflecting as it does your response to at least several of the sources you've collected, is more sophisticated than an initial working thesis. A refined thesis moves you closer to developing a plan for your paper and writing a first draft.

▶ 36b   Developing a plan

Keeping your refined working thesis in mind, once again review all the notes you have taken, this time consolidating them into categories that will help you create a plan for your first draft.

Organize your notes into groups

If you have been supplying headings for your notecards or computerized records, your task will be considerably easier. Stack the cards, or electronically move your records, into clusters. Jason Koman devised several categories, including "Community in Old-World Markets," "Community in Malls," "Arcades—Design Features," and "Malls—Design Features."

If you have not already written headings on your notecards or computer records, write them as you review your notes with your refined working thesis in mind. There are at least two ways to do this. You can write headings on your notecards, group notes according to headings, and then use these groupings to construct an outline for your first draft. Or you can sketch a first draft by converting sections of the outline as your headings, and then turning to your notes to organize them in a way that fits your outline. Either way (or if you devise some other way), your goal by this point is to have a refined working thesis, a sketch of your first draft, and notes to draw on as you write each section of this draft.

Outlines

Outlines and sketches for a paper come in all shapes and sizes (see 3d-4). A sketch may be a logically arranged map of key topics and their relationships. If your instructor asks for an *informal outline*, it will generally have only two levels: topics and subtopics. For example:

The medieval marketplace
—social functions
—economic functions

Formal outlines have several levels (3d-4). The most common type employs a combination of Roman and Arabic numerals and letters.

I. Major topic
  A. Subtopic
    1. Minor subtopic
      a. sub-subtopic (or illustration)
        (a) illustration, example, explanation
        (b) illustration, example, explanation
    2. Minor subtopic
  B. Subtopic
II. Major topic

For more information on how to write outlines, see 3d-4 and 18e; for a discussion on how to work from outlines as you write a first draft, see 3e-2.

Make room for changes

No matter how much care you take in assembling an outline or map of the paper *before* you write, it will inevitably change, to a greater or lesser extent, as you write the draft. Don't be discouraged by these changes. They are part of the writing process. With each successive draft beyond the first, your changes will tend to point you in a single direction: to a final thesis and a completed paper.

Developing a Plan

► **36c**   Drawing on your sources to support *your* idea

Sources in a research paper exist to help you to advance a thesis that *you* have defined. One purpose of research is for you to make connections across sources where few or no clear connections currently exist. These connections, and what you have to say about them, are what will make your paper original. No matter how many sources you use, focus on the ways that *you* synthesize them; focus on the points *you* want to make.

Three ways of treating sources

As discussed in Chapter 35, there are three ways of dealing with source materials: summary, paraphrase, and quotation. Avoid writing a paper that stitches these methods together and leaves no room for you. You can do this by continually asking yourself: What is my overall point? How does this particular source serve the purpose of my paper by advancing that point? If you can keep the focus on your ideas and your connections across sources, then you will avoid letting your sources overwhelm you.

Filling in gaps

After you have developed your outline and arranged notecards to correspond to the outline, you will probably discover that in some areas you have more information than you need, while in other areas you do not have enough. In the latter case, go back to the library to fill in the gaps or take another look at material you have already gathered. In the former case (too much information), you will have to make some hard decisions. After accumulating so much material, you may be tempted to use it *all*. Resist that temptation.

If you provide *too* much information, you risk inundating your reader and drowning out your unique point of view in the paper. Both problems can defeat communication. Your job is to sift through source materials, select from among them those elements that will advance your idea, and incorporate them into your paper. Balance is the key: you want to establish key relationships but not overwhelm your reader.

► **36d**   Determining your voice

How do you want to come across to your readers? As a student investigating a topic that *fascinates* you? As an authority speaking to specialists? As an authority speaking to nonspecialists? As a critic writing for a magazine? The option you select determines the *voice, tone,* and *register* of your writing. (See 3a-4 and 21e.)

Deciding on tone: Formal vs. informal

Consider, for example, the voice of a passage written by Johann Geist, an architect and historian. Jason Koman quotes this passage in his research paper (see 36h, "Works Cited"):

The arcade [. . .] arose at the beginning of high capitalism. The overproduction caused by technological advances made it imperative for the manufacturers of luxury goods to discover new methods of distribution, faster turnover, and easier promotion.

The voice of this passage is serious, academic, systematic, dry, impersonal, and authoritative. The author makes little attempt to entertain his readers. But entertainment is not his purpose. Though the material is dry and the vocabulary is elevated, the passage is clear and precise. Koman uses it in his paper at a key moment to make an important point about arcades.

Now consider an informal tone from a feature newspaper story, titled "It's a Mall, Mall World," by Kim Ode (see 36h, "Works Cited"):

The Friday night promenade is picking up in Maplewood Mall. Competitors in the BubbleYum Super Blow-Out Contest line up before a man holding giant cardboard calipers to their distended efforts. The elementary sounds of the kid Karaoke contest drift in from the Food Court.

Becoming sensitive to differences in tone

The difference in voice between passages could hardly be greater. Ode's voice is snappy, hip, intelligent, and colloquial. While Ode clearly has a point to make, the language is lively and not at all academic. By using expressions such as "is picking up," Ode directs this piece to a nonacademic audience, while Geist directs his to an academic one. Each author's voice is appropriate for the intended purpose and audience.

When writing your paper, choose a tone that is appropriate both for your attitudes toward your paper and for *your* audience (see 3a-4). Think of your readers as intelligent people who are interested in the issue on which you are writing, but who still expect to be engaged, as well as informed. A good academic paper should be like one side of an intelligent conversation—a conversation in which both participants take pleasure. (See 3a-4 for more on determining your own voice.)

▶36e Writing a draft

Sections 3b–e and 5a provide detailed discussions of strategies that will help you to write a first draft. You will need a method for working (or not working) from your outline, for writing a group of related paragraphs at a single sitting, and for recognizing and responding to obstacles as they arise.

You are finally ready to write:

- You have conducted systematic research on a subject in which you are interested;
- You have accumulated a stack of notes, in which you have summarized, paraphrased, and quoted relevant material;
- You have developed and revised a thesis; and
- You have prepared a careful sketch or an outline, on the basis of which you have organized your notes.

In short, you have become something of an expert on the subject. There is no reason to be anxious at this point. You are not writing the final draft; you are

---

COMPUTER TIPS

Cut, Don't Delete

In freewriting, in early exploratory drafts, and in other initial stages of writing, you may find it useful not to delete information at first. If you've typed a paragraph that you decide you probably don't need, don't be hasty—you *may* need it later. Instead, use your word processor's *cut* function to remove the text. Unlike deleted text, cut text remains in your computer's memory in case you want it back. A word of caution: in nearly all word processors, only one chunk of cut text at a time can stay in memory. Cutting a second chunk of text automatically deletes the first chunk from memory forever. So before you cut a second chunk of text, use your computer's *paste* function to place the first one in some permanent location—perhaps at the very end of your paper or in another "notepad" file. Once your revisions are nearly finished and you're sure of the information you need, then you can delete material you haven't used.

---

simply preparing a rough draft that will be seen by no one but yourself (and possibly some friends whose advice you trust). You will have plenty of opportunity to revise the rough draft.

Writing a skeleton draft and incorporating sources

To avoid overreliance on sources, as well as to clarify the main lines of a paper's argument, some researchers write their first drafts referring only to their outlines—and not to their source notes. As they write, they mark the places where source material (in summarized, paraphrased, or quoted form) will later be inserted. Drafts written in such a manner are simply skeletons or scaffolds. But by examining the skeleton, you can see whether the logic of your paper is sound. Does the argument make sense to you? Does one part logically follow from another? It should, even without the material from your notes. Remember your purpose and your audience: tell readers, as if you were having a conversation, what they should know about your subject and why you believe as you do.

At some point you will turn to your notes and consider how sources can help advance your ideas. Here are some considerations:

- Try arranging source notes in the order in which you intend to use them, but avoid simply transcribing your notes onto your rough draft.
- If you think you have made your point, move on, and skip any additional, unused notes on the topic or subtopic.
- Once you have completed a draft, you can revisit your notes and decide to substitute particularly effective unused notes for less effective ones used in the draft.

To avoid having to transcribe lengthy quotations or notes onto your draft, consider taping or stapling these notes (or photocopies of the quotations) directly onto the appropriate spots on the draft. When you do incorporate sources, remember to transfer bibliographic codes and page numbers, so that later you can enter the correct citations.

Starting in the middle

Many writers skip the introduction on the rough draft and get right into the body of the paper, believing that they are in a better position to draft the introduction later—when they know exactly what they are introducing. If you believe that you must begin at the beginning and work systematically all the way through, then do that. Whichever approach you take (and neither one is inherently preferable), remember that this is only a *rough* draft; nothing at this stage is final.

▶ 36f Revising and editing

In 4a–d, you will find a discussion on revising and editing. Keep in mind that revision literally means "re-seeing." You should not consider revision simply a matter of fixing punctuation and spelling errors and improving a word or phrase here and there. Revision is, rather, a matter of looking at the whole paper from top to bottom and trying to determine whether you have presented material effectively.

http://www.researchpaper.com/
writing_center/111.html
Covers the priorities in revising: Begin with the higher order concerns, the aspects of writing most responsible for the quality of the paper.

Some writers think of revision as a twofold process: *Macro revision* concerns the essay as a whole (its purpose, its voice, its structure), including its larger component units—the section and the paragraph. *Micro revision* concerns sentence structure, grammar, punctuation, and mechanics.

Others consider revision to be a four-stage process, in which writers revise (1) the essay as a whole; (2) individual paragraphs; (3) individual sentences; and (4) individual words.

These strategies are means to the same goal: ensuring that you consider *every* component of your essay, from largest to smallest, as you work to improve it.

Arriving at a final thesis

Before writing a draft, you start with a rough working thesis, which provides enough focus to help you sift through the materials you've gathered. More thinking about your sources may require you to refine your thesis. The act of writing a draft will help you to refine and focus still more. Ask yourself these questions as you reread your work:

- What is the main question of this research project?
- Is the question suitably complex for the subject I've defined?
- Is my answer to this question—my thesis—clear?
- Have I stated my thesis clearly in the draft?

Revising and Editing

Responding to these questions, and making corresponding adjustments in your paper, will help to guide your revision. These questions helped Jason Koman devise a final thesis.

Final thesis

The modern mall is a place intended for business, and it evolved from single-minded, business-like institutions that totally transformed the ancient ways of buying and selling.

Jason's earlier thesis concentrated only on the fact that shoppers do not go to malls in search of community. Through the process of writing and revising, Jason decided to concentrate, as well, on what shoppers *do* want. Jason found that the act of writing helped his paper to become clear as well as more ambitious. In the final draft of his essay, you will see that this single addition to the thesis contributes directly to the overall structure of the paper. Jason organizes sections of the paper in the following manner. First, he poses the question, "What do we want at the mall?" Then, drawing on sources, he offers three conflicting answers. Finally, he uses these differences to propel himself *and* the reader into a historical review of marketplaces. He uses this review to help answer his initial question.

Working with feedback from readers and peer editors

When revising your paper, get as much feedback as possible from others. It is difficult even for professional writers to get perspective on what they have written immediately after they have written it. You are likely to be too close to the subject, too committed to your outline or to particular words to be very objective at this point. Show your draft to a friend or classmate whose judgment you trust and to your instructor. Obtain reactions on everything from the essay as a whole to the details of word choice.

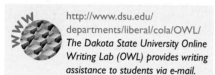

http://www.dsu.edu/departments/liberal/cola/OWL/
The Dakota State University Online Writing Lab (OWL) provides writing assistance to students via e-mail.

▶ 36g Understanding the elements of documentation

Writers can use several systems of documentation to credit their sources (see Chapter 37). The system used depends on the discipline in which they are writing—social sciences, humanities, science and technology, or business—or on the preferences of the audience.

Documenting sources is a two-part process:

1. Cite the source *in your paper* to identify it and give credit immediately after its use. This is called an *in-text* citation.
2. Cite the source *at the end of your paper*, in the form of a list of references that readers can pursue in more detail.

For three of the four documentation systems reviewed in Chapter 37—MLA, APA, and CBE—in-text citations are usually placed within parentheses. For the

CMS—footnote and endnote—system, you make in-text citations with a small superscript numeral, and references are listed in notes.

All information and ideas should be documented—not just the sources that you quote directly. Summaries or paraphrases also require acknowledgment. The only exception to this rule is that *common knowledge*—as determined in part by the nature of your audience's level of expertise—need not be documented. (See 35h-1 for a discussion of what counts as common knowledge; and see paragraphs B and C in the sample paper.) For detailed information on documentation styles, see Chapter 37.

Use Documentation to Give Fair Credit and to Assist Your Reader

Why go to the trouble of documenting your sources?

■ *To give credit where it is due.* Ethics demands that the originators of ideas and information be credited.

■ *To allow readers to gauge the accuracy and reliability of your work.* Any research paper will stand or fall according to how well (how perceptively, accurately, or selectively) you use sources.

■ *To avoid charges of plagiarism.* You certainly do not want to give your readers the impression that you are claiming credit for ideas or words that are not yours.

■ *To allow interested readers to follow up on a point.* Readers will sometimes want to pursue a point you have raised by going to your sources. Therefore, give readers the clearest possible directions for where to look.

▶ 36h A sample research paper: "What Do We Want at the Mall?"

The following research paper (pages 562–574) demonstrates the process of research and writing discussed in these chapters. The student writer, Jason Koman, chose to direct his efforts toward answering a key research question: "What do Americans want at the mall?" This key research question (see 33b-2) led to a working thesis (see 33e-1) and then to a refined thesis (see 36a), but Jason retained the question as the focal point for the paper. Jason describes his motivation for this project as follows:

> My friends and I have always gone to the mall to shop or spend time. Everybody ends up at the mall at some point. Some people (like my grandmother) love to shop. Some old people just sit. Kids hang out. I was interested in why people go to the mall. The whole question of the shopping mall's history and what a mall is—and is not—fascinated me.

Koman's paper conforms to Modern Language Association (MLA) documentation style.

COVER-PAGE FORMAT

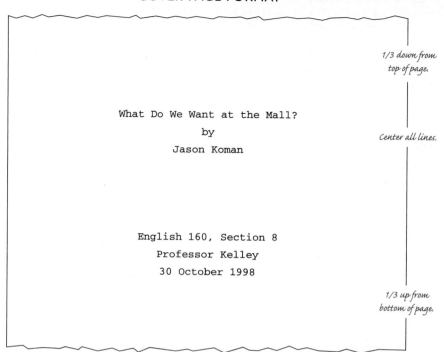

What Do We Want at the Mall?

by

Jason Koman

1/3 down from top of page.

Center all lines.

English 160, Section 8

Professor Kelley

30 October 1998

1/3 up from bottom of page.

FIRST-PAGE FORMAT FOR A PAPER WITH *NO* COVER PAGE

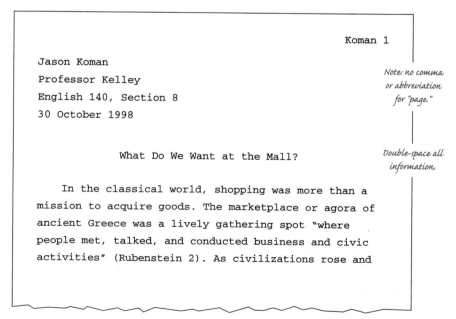

Koman 1

Jason Koman

Professor Kelley

English 140, Section 8

30 October 1998

Note: no comma or abbreviation for "page."

What Do We Want at the Mall?

Double-space all information.

In the classical world, shopping was more than a mission to acquire goods. The marketplace or agora of ancient Greece was a lively gathering spot "where people met, talked, and conducted business and civic activities" (Rubenstein 2). As civilizations rose and

Writing the Research Paper

Koman i

Note the lower-case Roman numeral.

Outline

<u>Thesis statement:</u> The modern mall is a place intended strictly for business, and it evolved from single-minded, business-like institutions that totally transformed the ancient ways of buying and selling.

Begin outline with the thesis.

    Introduction: In ancient times, shopping was a community-building activity. For over 2,000 years, markets were the means by which people in agricultural-based economies socialized.

  I. History: The changes we see in shopping patterns today started 200 years ago.

Place the outline immediately after the cover page.

    A. Ancient marketplaces and bazaars were economic <u>and</u> social centers.

      1. The agora of ancient Greece was a place of business, commerce, and government.

      2. The bazaars of the Orient were social as well as economic centers.

Papers with no cover page do not have an outline.

    B. The revolutionary change began in the late 18th century with the Industrial Revolution. Country dwellers moved to the cities.

      1. The new industries gave rise to a middle class with expendable income.

      2. Shops stayed open all week.

      3. Shopping on market days no longer was the main way of socializing.

Outline highlights unity and coherence.

    C. Indoor shopping areas called arcades arose at the start of the 19th century.

      1. Arcades grew in population centers.

      2. Arcades encouraged people to shop, not socialize.

      3. The arcade was a privately owned space that appeared to be public.

Outline uses parallel elements: all phrases or all sentences.

II. Malls today: the modern shopping mall serves
an exclusively economic function, like the
arcade.

Major sections:
I, II, III

   A. Modern malls descend from the arcades of
   the 19th century.

      1. Malls are located according to the same
      criteria that arcades were, but now in
      suburbs.

      2. Many malls have been built.

   B. Despite many activities in malls, shoppers
   do not look for community but for a safe
   place to shop.

Subsections:
A, B, C

   C. The rise of online shopping will further
   isolate individual shoppers, continuing
   the trend begun during the Industrial
   Revolution.

III. Social critics and developers debate the
value of shopping mall culture.

   A. David Guterson and others lament the rise
   of pure commercialism in the shopping
   experience.

      1. Guterson criticizes the Mall of America.

      2. Others critique shopping mall culture.

Supporting
points: 1, 2, 3

   B. Specialists in the shopping mall industry
   are not nearly so negative.

      1. They believe the function of the mall
      is to make money, nothing else.

      2. Many shoppers want an economic exchange,
      only.

      3. Store owners want an economic exchange,
      only.

Papers that do
not outline easily
may have logic
problems.

Conclusion: Guterson's desire for an older type
of marketplace is not appropriate for the modern
era. Times have changed. Even though online
shopping may give rise to virtual communities
of shoppers who chat with one another, shopping
malls today serve an economic, not social,
function.

FIRST PAGE FORMAT FOR A PAPER *WITH* A COVER PAGE

1

What Do We Want at the Mall?

Introduction

In the classical world, shopping was more than a
mission to acquire goods. The marketplace or agora
of ancient Greece was a lively gathering spot "where
people met, talked, and conducted business and civic
activities" (Rubenstein 2). As civilizations rose and
fell, these multiple functions remained important.
In fact, for over 2,000 years, both the markets of
the West and the bazaars of the East were the primary
means by which people living in agrarian economies
socialized and conducted business (Guterson 51). With
the Industrial Revolution, however, the character of
the marketplace underwent a radical change, and its
social functions faded into oblivion. Although the
malls of today, with their food courts, arcades,
shops, and theaters, may seem deceptively like the
bustling marketplaces of old, they are not. The modern mall is a place intended strictly for business,
and it evolved from single-minded, business like
institutions that totally transformed the ancient
ways of buying and selling.

Section I: History

*Information from
sources is cited;
refers to "Works
Cited" list.*

Thesis

The ancient agora of Greece, the medieval markets of Europe, and the bazaars of the Orient, from
which the mall is descended, did in fact serve important social functions. As early as the sixth century
BC, the Greek market, or agora, offered a wide variety of goods in one convenient location. Significantly, historians describe the space in terms of its
commercial <u>and</u> its social function: "As [Greek] commerce and government expanded, the agora became the
focus of business, the market-place, as well as the
place of assembly" (Rubenstein 2).

The economic and community functions of the agora
extended forward in time, both to the marketplaces
of Europe and to the bazaars of the Orient. In the
medieval towns of Europe, market days were held once

Koman 2

each week. Since "nearly everybody lived in the
country and earned their living in some way from the
land" (Harrison 10), a trip to market became a much-
anticipated social event as well as an opportunity to
buy or barter. Bazaars also had a double function,
social and economic. Medieval Islamic cities consisted of separate "familial clans, each with its own
housing units" that faced inward, to courtyards
(Geist 5). The only shared community space in these
cities was the collection of buildings that included
a bazaar, as well as a mosque and school (Geist 5).
From the fifth century BC through the eighteenth century AD, markets and bazaars served important social
as well as economic functions.

Note: no comma between author and page number.

The revolutionary change in our marketplaces began in the late eighteenth century, when the Industrial Revolution triggered massive migrations from the
countryside to the cities--a direct reversal of older
population patterns ("Industrial"). The new industries
in which these new city dwellers labored created
wealth, and for the first time in history a whole
class of people could afford luxuries. With a rising
urban middle class came shops that remained open practically every day of the week. A trip to market was no
longer a difficult, dangerous outing over poorly maintained roads. Nor--in the city--was it the principal
means by which people expected to meet others. Whereas
farmers could see dozens of faces only once a week, on
market day, city dwellers could walk into the street
and see hundreds of new faces whenever they chose.
Under these new conditions, the need to combine social
interaction with the activity of purchasing goods
gradually became less compelling.

A

In the early years of the nineteenth century, a
new type of marketplace arose: the arcade, precursor
to the modern mall (Jacobs 1-2; Kowinski 119). Historians tell us that these arcades were built "where a
growing population coincided with a shortage of shops,

B

Paragraph A (Reference to an alphabetized or single-page source): When referring to an alphabetized source (in this case an encyclopedia entry) or to a one-page source, there is no need to cite a page number. Readers will find the information in the "Works Cited" list.

Paragraph B (A reference to two sources in a single citation): When you want to refer to two sources in a single citation, place a semicolon between the citations and treat them as you would any citation. Note that you can refer to two *page numbers* in a *single* source: (Geist 4, 17). In this case, use a comma between page numbers.

Paragraph B (Citing the origin of an idea, if it is not yours): The double in-text citation to Jacobs and Kowinski is important, for Koman is here acknowledging that an idea in his paper was not his but one found in a pair of sources. For his argument to succeed, Koman needs to convince readers that the mall is the direct descendant of the arcade. Koman wants help in making this point clear; even though he does not quote or paraphrase Jacobs or Kowinski, he is careful to locate the authority for this idea in their books. Here are brief excerpts from those books.

From Jacobs

> A forerunner of the enclosed shopping mall was the development and expansion of arcades in the 19th century. These were built as a way to deal with the increasingly hostile public environments of urban centers. Enclosed shopping centers of this kind were preceded by the agora of Athens, Roman forums and oriental bazaars (Gruen, 1973). (1–2)

From Kowinski

> The solution [to the weather problem facing the builders of Southdale, which would be the first mall] was, of course, complete enclosure. Gruen [the project's architect] saw it immediately and went to the Dayton-Hudson hierarchy [the developers] with his proposal. He told them about the covered pedestrian arcades in Europe, especially the Galleria Vittorio Emanuele in Milan, Italy, with its arcades rising four stories to a glass barrel vault and a central glass cupola 160 feet high. (119)

Relying on these sources enabled Koman to feel confident about a key claim in his essay: that the arcade was the direct predecessor of the mall. For an example of information that Koman found in several sources but decided not to cite (because he felt the information was common knowledge), see the facing-page note at paragraph C.

Koman 3

availability of land, finance and an entrepreneur" (MacKeith 16). Like the modern mall, the arcade presented an illusion of outdoor space in an indoor space, with pedestrian walkways that wound through rows of store fronts and that encouraged shoppers to make purchases, not to stop and talk (Geist 4, 17). Though the arcade was privately owned, it presented the illusion of being a public place, and it became a destination for people in search of safe, essentially solitary, activity. Indeed, this new venue fundamentally changed the relationship between those who bought and sold--and, significantly, between buyers themselves (Gumpert and Drucker 188). The <u>single</u> purpose of the new marketplace, the arcade, was to exchange goods for money. The historic role that <u>community</u> played in the marketplace was abandoned.

The modern mall descends directly from the arcades of the nineteenth century. Like arcades, malls are located in growing population centers, which in post-World War II America has meant the suburbs. The nation's first completely enclosed mall, the Southdale Center, was built in Edina, Minnesota (a suburb of Minneapolis) in 1956. Over the next forty years, developers added 40,000 more shopping centers to the American retail landscape (International 15). In each case, like the arcades of the last century, the shopping centers have been situated according to consumer need and with one purpose in mind: to promote buying, not socializing.

Section II: Malls today

C

Although the variety of food, merchandise, and entertainment in most malls offers a greater range of possibilities for activity than did the old arcades, sociologist George Lewis observes that the activity modern shoppers seek has nothing to do with community. What they want, he says, is to go shopping in a safe, secure place. As part of a larger study in popular culture, Lewis observed that while mallgoers can be said to form a collection of people under one roof, they do not constitute a community: they do not

D

Paragraph C (Common knowledge): The entire question of what information and ideas count as common knowledge and what should be attributed to a source is complicated. Partly, the issue depends on audience. A great deal of technical information could be considered common knowledge, if you were addressing an expert audience. For an audience of nonspecialists, who might think that the information you're presenting originates with you, cite the source.

Consider the case of Southdale Center, America's first mall, which Jason Koman refers to in paragraph C. Jason decided that Southdale's status as "first" should be considered common knowledge. Identical information identifying Southdale as first appeared in three sources, none of which cited their information. Jason believed that this fact of mall history, even though unknown to his audience, could justifiably be considered common knowledge. By contrast, see paragraph B, where Jason attributes a key idea in his paper to two sources.

Paragraph D (Paraphrase): In an early draft, Koman quoted a long passage from George Lewis and on rereading the draft decided that the material had too many specialized terms. Jason therefore decided to write a paraphrase, keeping Lewis's main points but casting them in more commonplace language. At the very end of the paraphrase, Koman retains one brief phrase from the original. This gives readers a feel for Lewis's language. Note that the paraphrase is roughly the same length as the original.

Original passage

What emerged from the initial observations and interviews, then, was a picture of mall shoppers as a *collectivity*, located in one enclosed space, but utilizing the mall primarily for their own self-defined and rational economic transactions. They may well shop with a friend, or the family may come to the mall, but they are *not* there for the face to face primary interactive relations that are the core of community. (125)

Paraphrase

Lewis observed that while mallgoers can be said to form a collection of people under one roof, they do not constitute a community: they do not search out the types of interpersonal contacts on which communities are built. Even if they go shopping with a friend or family member, they remain isolated consumers during their time in the mall, looking to make what Lewis calls "self-defined and rational economic transactions" (125).

search out the types of interpersonal contacts on
which communities are built. Even those who shop
with a friend or family member remain isolated consumers during their time in the mall, writes Lewis,
looking to make what he calls "self-defined and rational economic transactions" (125). Much the same
could be said of arcade shoppers one hundred years
ago (Geist 35).

Recent technological developments promise even
greater isolation for shoppers, as we conduct business from a distance via the Internet. According to
a recent study, "consumers will spend $26 billion
online in 2002," some $21 billion more than the on-
line dollars spent in 1998 (Deck). This explosion in
virtual shopping will keep increasing numbers of
people at home, threatening (eventually) to create a
marketplace in which shoppers don't even <u>see</u> one another. Not only would community be stripped out of
the shopping experience as has already happened with
the rise of arcades and malls; but direct contact
with other human beings would be stripped out as
well. This move to disembodied shopping on the Internet represents the purest form of the commercial
emphasis on shopping that began during the
Industrial Revolution.

Beginning with the Industrial Revolution, then,
changing economies transformed the marketplaces of
old from social and economic centers into economic
centers only--a shift that has given rise to a debate
between social critics and retail developers. Essayist David Guterson laments the failure to establish a
sense of community in our malls. Along with others
(Gumpert and Drucker 188-89; Ode), he believes that
shoppers secretly want, but won't openly ask for, a
connection with other humans in an isolating world.
Having spent a week at the Mall of America in 1993,
he reports on the disorienting experience of "[g]et-
ting lost, feeling lost, and being lost" (50). Malls,

*Current statistic
from an
authoratative
Web source.*

*Section III:
Debate*

*With source
author's name
in sentence,
citation omits
name.*

*Quotation
altered with
brackets.*

he says, take our money without returning even the hint of intimacy and community:

> Here we are free to wander endlessly and to furtively watch our fellow wanderers, thousands upon thousands of milling strangers who have come with the intent of losing themselves in the mall's grand, stimulating design. [. . .] The mall exploits our acquisitive instincts without honoring our communal requirements, our eternal desire for discourse and intimacy. (50)

Quotation altered with ellipses.

Page reference set outside block quote.

Emphasizing business to the exclusion of community, Guterson argues, has trivialized the act of shopping. A Canadian Broadcasting Corporation video, "Temples of Mammon," makes much the same point, arguing that malls are a "controlled retail environment [. . .] that [have] changed our values and even the course of our lives. Shopping malls have eliminated the concept of neighborhood shopping" (Temples). These cultural changes are now being debated in university-level courses with titles like "Geographies of Consumption" (Crang).

Web sources without pagination get no page reference.

Industry specialists view the change in shopping environments from a different perspective. "Malls are designed to maximize profits," says the Chairman of the Environmental Subcommittee for the International Council of Shopping Centers. "They were not built as a replacement for Main Street. If intimacy encourages sales, there will be intimacy" (Marks). One mall executive makes the point with particular bluntness: "We don't want the mall to be a community. [. . .] It would upset our tenants who want to make money" (qtd. in Lewis 123).

Personal interview gets no page reference.

One source quoted in another.

Transforming the mall into a community, as Guterson and others would have us do, might also upset shoppers, who are used to thinking of shopping centers as places simply to make purchases and then to go home--a perfectly reasonable expectation for those

Conclusion

who are unfamiliar with the richness of ancient marketplaces. Guterson's desire for an older type of
market that encourages direct contact and intimacy is
understandable. But that desire is appropriate for an
era that no longer exists--and that has not existed
for two hundred years.

Projecting into the future, the arrival of online shopping would seem to promise even more gloom
for the critics of shopping malls. But the critics
may not want to abandon all hope. Taking advantage of
our digital times and working with high-tech tools,
young people may be creating shopping-based communities of their own: <u>virtual</u> communities. If we were to
log on to the Internet site of "Downtown Anywhere," a
massive complex of online stores, we would find an
invitation to help build a virtual city that even
Guterson might like to visit. One of the largest of
these enterprises, Galaxy Mall, bills itself as "the
future of online shopping" (Galaxy). More conventional malls, still housed in physical structures,
take care to establish their presence on the Web
(Westfield; Mall of America). Conceivably, the hundreds of thousands of teenagers and adults who now
"chat" with their peers in the thousands of virtual
communities across cyberspace will urge these malls
to institute forums where they can share experiences
as they shop.

Still, we should be realistic about the pros-
pects for such communities. The virtual mall developers who would control chat rooms would have one
purpose only in sponsoring them: to sell more products. If (to paraphrase the industry analyst quoted
earlier) online intimacy encourages sales, there
will be intimacy. Tragic or not, and for historical
reasons that can be clearly traced, the desire for
<u>profit</u>, not community, lives at the heart of the mod-
ern mall.

Works Cited

Crang, Mike. "Geographies of Consumption." Course
    Description. 21 Oct. 1996. 9 Oct. 1998
    <http://www.gold.ac.uk/~soa01ds/crang.htm>.

Deck, Stewart. "Study Sees Growth in Online Shopping."
    CNN Interactive. Computing Storypage with
    IDG.net. 25 May 1998. 10 Oct. 1998
    <http://cnn.com/TECH/computing/9805/25/
    shopping.idg/>.

Downtown Anywhere. "Welcome to Front Street!" 18 May
    1997. 24 Sept. 1998 <www.awa.com/index.html>.

Galaxy Enterprises, Inc. "Access Galaxy Mall." 5 Aug.
    1998 <www.galaxymall.com>.

Geist, Johann F. Arcades: The History of a Building
    Type. Trans. Jane O. Newman and John H. Smith.
    Cambridge: MIT, 1983.

Gumpert, Gary, and Susan J. Drucker. "From the Agora
    to the Electronic Shopping Mall." Critical Stud-
    ies in Mass Communication 9 (1992): 186-200.

Guterson, David. "Enclosed. Encyclopedic. Endured.:
    One Week at the Mall of America." Harper's Aug.
    1993: 49-56.

Harrison, Molly. People and Shopping: A Social Back-
    ground. London: Ernest Benn, 1975.

"Industrial Revolution." Concise Columbia Encyclopedia.
    CD-ROM. Redmond: Microsoft, 1994.

International Council of Shopping Centers. Scope of
    the Shopping Center Industry in the United
    States. New York: ICSC, 1995.

Jacobs, Jerry. The Mall: An Attempted Escape from
    Everyday Life. Prospect Heights, IL: Waveland,
    1984.

Kowinski, William Severini. The Malling of America:
    An Inside Look at the Great Consumer Paradise.
    New York: William Morrow, 1985.

Reference List: See Chapter 37 for details.

Electronic sources: Web

Book entry

Magazine entry

Electronic source: CD-ROM

Koman 8

Lewis, George H. "Community Through Exclusion and
Illusion: The Creation of Social Worlds in an   *Journal entry*
American Shopping Mall, <u>Journal of Popular
Culture</u> 24.2 (1990): 121–36.

MacKeith, Margaret. <u>The History and Conservation of
Shopping Arcades</u>. London: Mansell, 1986.

Mall of America. Home page. 9 Oct. 1998 <http://
www.mallofamerica.com/index.htm>.

Marks, Richard. International Council of Shopping   *Interview*
Centers. Personal interview. 26 Jan. 1996.

Ode, Kim. "It's a Mall, Mall World." <u>Star Tribune</u>
2 Aug. 1992: 6sm. Nexis. 24 Jan. 1996.

Rubenstein, Harvey M. <u>Pedestrian Malls, Streetscapes,
and Urban Spaces</u>. New York: Wiley, 1992.

<u>Temples of Mammon</u>. Videocassette V547. Man Alive. Cana-
dian Broadcasting Corporation. 1987. Abstract.   *Abstract*
3 Oct. 1998 <http://info.wlu.ca/~wwwav/
WLUCollection/T/v547.htm>.

Westfield Shopping Town. "Montgomery Mall." 7 Aug.
1998 <http://www.themontgomerymall.com>.

CHAPTER 37

Documenting Research

A ny time you use material derived from specific sources, whether quoted passages or summaries or paraphrases of fact, opinion, explanation, or idea, you are ethically obligated to let your reader know who deserves the credit. Further, you must tell your readers precisely where the material came from so that they can locate it for themselves. Often readers will want to trace the facts on which a conclusion is based, or to verify that a passage was quoted or paraphrased accurately. Sometimes readers will simply want to follow up and learn more about your subject.

There are basically two ways for a writer to show a "paper trail" to sources. The most widely used format today is the parenthetical reference, also called an *in-text citation.* This is a telegraphic, short-hand approach to identifying the source of a statement or quotation. It assumes that a complete list of references appears at the end of the paper. Each entry in the list of references includes three essential elements: authorship, full title of the work, and publication information. In the references, entries are arranged, punctuated, and typed to conform to the bibliographic style requirements of the particular discipline or of the instructor. With this list in place, the writer is able to supply the briefest of references—a page number or an author's name—in parentheses right in the text, knowing that the reader will be able to locate the rest of the reference information easily in the list of references. The second method for showing a paper trail is the footnote style—which is less often used today than the parenthetical system.

For more detailed information on the conventions of style in the humanities, social sciences, business disciplines, and sciences, refer to these style manuals:

- Gibaldi, Joseph. *MLA Style Manual and Guide to Scholarly Publishing.* 2nd ed. New York: MLA, 1998 and Gibaldi, Joseph. *MLA Handbook for Writers of Research Papers.* 5th ed. New York: MLA, 1999.

- *Publication Manual* (of the American Psychological Association). 4th ed. Washington, DC: APA, 1994.

- *Chicago Manual of Style.* 14th ed. Chicago: University of Chicago Press, 1993.

- *Scientific Style and Format: The CBE Manual for Authors, Editors, and Publishers.* 6th ed. New York: Cambridge University Press, 1994.

- Li, Xia, and Nancy B. Crane. *Electronic Styles: An Expanded Guide to Citing Electronic Information.* Westport: Meckler, 1996.

An Overview of the Four Documentation Systems Presented in This Chapter

▶ **37a**   **Using the MLA system of documentation**

The Modern Language Association (MLA) publishes a style guide that is widely used for citations and references in the humanities. This section gives detailed examples of how the MLA system of parenthetical references provides in-text citation.

In addition, a later section (37c) will show how to use the Chicago Manual of Style (CMS) system of documentation (formerly used in MLA publications), where complete information on each source is given every time a source is cited.

In a research paper, either of these systems of source citation is followed at the end by a list of references. In the MLA system, the list of references is called "Works Cited." Keep in mind that the complete information provided in the list of references will be the basis of your in-text citations. The parenthetical form provides minimal information and sends the reader to the list of references to find the rest. By contrast, the footnote or endnote system virtually duplicates the information in the list of references but uses a slightly different arrangement of the elements in the entry. Following is an index to this section on the MLA system of documentation.

▶ I Making in-text citations in the MLA format

When you make a parenthetical in-text citation, you assume that your reader will look to the list of "Works Cited" for complete references. The list of references at the end of your paper will provide three essential pieces of information for each of your sources: author, title, and facts of publication. Within your paper, a parenthetical citation may point to a source considered as a whole or to a specific page location in a source. Here is an example of an MLA in-text citation referring to a story as a whole.

```
In "Escapes," the title story of one contemporary author's book
of short stories, the narrator's alcoholic mother makes a public
spectacle of herself (Williams).
```

The next example refers to a specific page in the story. In the MLA system, no punctuation is placed between a writer's last name and a page reference.

```
In "Escapes," a story about an alcoholic household, a key moment
occurs when the child sees her mother suddenly appear on stage at
the magic show (Williams 11).
```

Here is how the references to the Williams story would appear as described in the list of references or "Works Cited."

```
Williams, Joy. "Escapes." Escapes: Stories. New York: Vintage,
    1990. 1-14.
```

Deciding when to insert a source citation and what information to include is often a judgment call rather than the execution of a mechanical system. Use common sense. Where feasible, incorporate citations smoothly into the text. Introduce the parenthetical reference at a pause in your sentence, at the end if possible. Place it as close to the documented point as possible, making sure that the reader can tell exactly which point is being documented. When the in-text reference is incorporated into a sentence of your own, always place the parenthetical reference *before* any enclosing or end punctuation.

```
In Central Africa in the 1930s, a young girl who comes to town
drinks beer with her date because that's what everyone does
(Lessing 105).
```

```
In a realistic portrayal of Central African city life in the 1930s
(Lessing), young people gather daily to drink.
```

When a quotation from a work is incorporated into a sentence of your own, the parenthetical reference *follows* the quotation marks, yet precedes the enclosing or end punctuation.

```
At the popular Sports Club, Lessing's heroine finds the "ubiquitous
glass mugs of golden beer" (135).
```

Exception: When your quotation ends with a question mark or exclamation point, keep these punctuation marks inside the end quotation marks, then give the parenthetical reference, and end with a period.

```
Martha's new attempts at sophistication in town prompted her to
retort, "Children are a nuisance, aren't they?" (Lessing 115).
```

Using the MLA System of Documentation **579**

COMPUTER TIPS

Citation Format Software

Software programs such as Daedalus, Inc.'s *BiblioCite* and others now on the market allow you to plug in standard bibliographic information (author's name, title, and so on) to generate a perfectly formatted "Works Cited" or "References" page. If you have access to such software, use it. Following the conventions of standard bibliographic formats is the kind of tedious organizational task at which computers excel. Be sure to check, however, to be sure that your program is set up to comply with the latest formats for Internet sources. If not, then be prepared to do some manual editing to update your citations.

Naming an author in the text

When you want to emphasize the author of a source you are citing, incorporate that author's name into your sentence. Unless you are referring to a particular place in that source, no parenthetical reference is necessary in the text.

```
Biographer Paul Mariani understands Berryman's alcoholism as one
form of his drive toward self-destruction.
```

Naming an author in the parenthetical reference

When you want to emphasize information in a source but not especially the author, omit the author's name in the sentence and place it in the parenthetical reference.

```
Biographers have documented alcohol-related upheavals in John
Berryman's life. Aware, for example, that Dylan Thomas was in an
alcohol-induced coma, dying, Berryman himself drank to escape his
pain (Mariani 273).
```

When you are referring to a particular place in your source and have already incorporated the author's name into your sentence, place only the page number in parentheses.

```
Biographer Paul Mariani describes how Berryman, knowing that his
friend Dylan Thomas was dying in an alcohol-induced coma, himself
began drinking to escape his pain (273).
```

Documenting a block quotation

For block quotations, set the parenthetical reference—with or without an author's name—*outside* of the end punctuation mark.

The story graphically portrays the behavior of Central African young people gathering daily to drink:

> Perry sat stiffly in a shallow chair which looked as if
> it would splay out under the weight of his big body
> [. . .] while from time to time--at those moments when
> laughter was jerked out of him by Stella--he threw back
> his head with a sudden dismayed movement, and flung half
> a glass of liquor down his throat. (Lessing 163)

A work by two or three authors

If your source has two or three authors, name them all, either in your text or in a parenthetical reference. Use last names, in the order they are given in the source, connected by *and*.

Critics have addressed the question of whether literary artists discover new truths (Wellek and Warren 33-36).

One theory claims that the alcoholic wants to "drink his environment in" (Perls, Hefferline, and Goodman 193-94).

A work by four or more authors

For a work with four or more authors, name all the authors, or use the following abbreviated format with *et al.* to signify "and others."

Some researchers trace the causes of alcohol dependence to "flawed family structures" (Stein, Lubber, Koman, and Kelly 318).

Some researchers trace the causes of alcohol dependence to "flawed family structures" (Stein et al. 318).

Stein and his coeditors trace the causes of alcohol dependence to "flawed family structures" (318).

Reference to two or more sources with the same authorship

When you are referring to two or more sources written by the same author, include in your in-text citation a shortened form of each title so that references to each text will be clear. The following example discusses how author Joy Williams portrays the drinking scene in her fiction. Note that a comma appears between the author's name and the shortened title.

She shows drinking at parties as a way of life in such stories as "Escapes" and "White Like Midnight." Thus it is a matter of course that Joan pours herself a drink while people talk about whether or not they want to survive nuclear war (Williams, "White" 129).

Distinguishing two authors with the same last name

Use one or more initials to supplement references to authors with the same last name.

```
It is no coincidence that a new translation of Euripides' The
Bacchae should appear in the United States (C. K. Williams) at a
time when fiction writers portray the use of alcohol as a means of
escape from mundane existence (J. Williams).
```

Two or more sources in a single reference

Particularly in an introductory summary, you may want to group together a number of works that cover one or more aspects of your research topic. Separate one source from another by a semicolon.

```
Studies that confront the alcoholism of literary figures directly
are on the increase (Mariani; Dardis; Gilmore).
```

A corporate author

A work may be issued by an organization or government agency with no author named. Cite the work as if the name given is the author's. Since the name of a corporate author is often long, try incorporating it into your text rather than using a parenthetical note. In this example the corporate author of the book is Alcoholics Anonymous. The book will be listed alphabetically under "Alcoholics" in Works Cited.

```
Among publications that discuss how to help young people cope with
family problems, Al-Anon Faces Alcoholism, put out by Alcoholics
Anonymous, has been reissued frequently since 1974 (117-24).
```

A multivolume work

When citing a page reference to a multivolume work, specify the volume by an arabic numeral followed by a colon, a space, and the page number. The Trevelyan history is in four volumes.

```
Drunkenness was such a problem in the first decades of the
eighteenth century that it was termed "the acknowledged national
vice of Englishmen of all classes" (Trevelyan 3: 46).
```

A literary work

Well-known literary works, particularly older ones now in the public domain, may appear in numerous editions. When referring to such a work or a part of one, give information for the work itself rather than for the particular edition you are using, unless you are highlighting a special feature or contribution of the edition.

For a play, supply act, scene, and line number in arabic numerals, unless your instructor specifies using Roman numerals for act and scene (II. iv. 118–19). In the following example, the title of the literary work includes numerals referring to the first of two plays that Shakespeare wrote about Henry IV, known as parts 1 and 2.

```
Shakespeare's Falstaff bellows, "Give me a cup of sack, rogue. Is
there no virtue extant?" (1 Henry IV 2.4.118-19).
```

To cite a modern editor's contribution to the publication of a literary work, adjust the emphasis of your reference. The abbreviation *n* stands for *note*.

```
Without the editor's footnote in the Riverside Shakespeare ex-
plaining that lime was sometimes used as an additive to make wine
sparkle, modern readers would be unlikely to understand Falstaff's
ranting: "[Y]et a coward is worse than a cup of sack with lime in
it. A villainous coward!" (1 Henry IV 2.4.125-26n).
```

Material quoted in your source

Often you will want to quote and cite material that you are reading at second hand—in a work by an intermediate author. Quote the original material and refer to the place where you found it.

```
Psychoanalyst Otto Fenichel included alcoholics within a general
grouping of addictive personalities, all of whom use addictive sub-
stances "to satisfy the archaic oral longing, a need for security,
and a need for the maintenance of self-esteem simultaneously" (qtd.
in Roebuck and Kessler 86).
```

An anonymous work

A work with no acknowledged author will be alphabetized in a list of references by the first word of its title. Therefore cite the anonymous work in the same way in your parenthetical reference. The title in this example is *The Hidden Alcoholic in Your Midst*.

```
People who do not suffer from addiction often can be thoughtless
and insensitive to the problems of those around them. That is the
message of an emotional and thought-provoking pamphlet (Hidden),
whose author writes anonymously about the pain of keeping his
alcoholism secret.
```

Page locations for electronic sources

You will find that some electronic sources and documents from the Internet have page numbers; others have paragraph numbers; many have neither. Since you need to provide specific information to show readers where to locate and examine sources, you can follow these general guidelines—an extension of those developed by the Modern Language Association for print sources. Examples are hypothetical.

- Begin the parenthetical citation by referring to the author or title of the source, as you would with any other in-text citation (provided these are not previously mentioned in your sentence).

- Refer to a page number in the electronic source, if provided.

> Leading scientists have called for a moratorium on the release of genetically engineered organisms into the environment (Weiss 12).

- If the electronic source has no page numbers, refer to paragraph numbers (if provided). If your citation begins with the author's name or a title, place a comma and follow with the abbreviation *par.* or *pars.*, and indicate the paragraph(s) used.

> Hardy reports that many geneticists object to the idea of a moratorium and have formed their own lobbying groups to fight such moves (par. 14).

- If no pagination or paragraph numbering is provided, you can use abbreviations like those used for classic literary works to refer to a structural division within the source: "pt." for part; "sec." for section; "ch." for chapter; "vol." for volume.

> In the absence of agreement within the scientific community, Norman Stein, director of Genetics Watch, has called for a "sensible government policy" (qtd. in Lubber sec. 5).

- If the electronic source provides no pagination, no paragraph numbering, and no internal structural divisions, cite the source by name only. At the Works Cited page, readers will see that the electronic source was not paginated.

> Scientists prefer to govern themselves; historically, the threat of government intervention has prompted voluntary restraints from scientific organizations (Wesley).

- Finally, when you are citing a one-page electronic source or an electronic source in which entries are arranged alphabetically (such as a CD-based or online encyclopedia), no in-text reference to a page or paragraph is needed. The following reference is to a "Works Cited" list that names an anonymously written article in an online encyclopedia.

> For centuries, farmers have manipulated "genetic materials to achieve desired changes in plants and animals" ("Genetic Engineering").

Following MLA parenthetical style, these in-text citations of electronic sources refer readers to detailed entries in the Works Cited list. See 37a-3 for guidelines on creating these detailed entries.

▶2 Preparing a list of references in the MLA format

In research papers following MLA format, the list of references is called "Works Cited" when it includes those sources you have referred to in your paper. Be aware that some instructors request a more comprehensive list of references—one that includes every source you consulted in preparing the paper. That list would be titled "Bibliography."

The examples in this section show how entries in the "Works Cited" list consist of three elements essential for a list of references: authorship, full title of the work, and publication information. In addition, if the work is taken from an electronic (online) source, consult 37a-3. The basic format for each entry requires the first line to start at the left margin, with each subsequent line to be indented five typed spaces from the left margin.

Not every possible variation is represented here. In formatting a complicated entry for your own list, you may need to combine features from two or more of the examples.

The MLA "Works Cited" list begins on a new page, after the last page of your paper, and continues the pagination of your paper. Entries in the list are alphabetized by the author's last name. An anonymous work is alphabetized by the first word in its title (but disregard *A, An,* and *The*).

Listing books in the MLA "Works Cited" format

The MLA "Works Cited" list presents book references in the following order:

1. *Author's name:* Put the last name first, followed by a comma and the first name (and middle name or initial) and a period. Omit the author's titles and degrees, whether one that precedes a name (Dr.) or one that follows (Ph.D.). Leave two typed spaces after the period.

2. *Title of the book:* Underline the complete title. If there is a subtitle, separate it from the main title by a colon and one typed space. Capitalize all important words, including the first word of any subtitle. The complete title is followed by a period and two typed spaces.

3. *Publication information:* Name the city of publication, followed by a colon and one typed space; the name of the publisher followed by a comma; the date of publication followed by a period. This information appears on the title page of the book and the copyright page, on the reverse side of the title page.

If the city of publication is not well known, add the name of the state, abbreviated as in the zip code system. Shorten the name of the publisher in a way that is recognizable. "G. P. Putnam's Sons" is shortened to "Putnam's." For university presses use "UP" as in the example "U of Georgia P." Many large publishing companies issue books under imprints that represent particular groups of books. Give the imprint name first, followed by a hyphen and the name of the publisher: Bullseye-Knopf.

Any additional information about the book goes between author and title or between title and publication data. Observe details of how to organize, abbreviate, and punctuate this information in the examples below.

A book with one author

The basic format for a single-author book is as follows:

Mariani, Paul. <u>Dream Song: The Life of John Berryman</u>. New York:
    Morrow, 1990.

A book with two or three authors

For a book with two or three authors, follow the order of the names on the title page. Notice that first and last name are reversed only for the lead author. Notice also the use of a comma after the first author.

Roebuck, Julian B., and Raymond G. Kessler. <u>The Etiology of</u>
    <u>Alcoholism: Constitutional, Psychological and Sociological</u>
    <u>Approaches</u>. Springfield: Thomas, 1972.

A book with four or more authors

As in the example under in-text citations (see 37a-1), you may choose to name all the authors or to use the abbreviated format with *et al.*

Stein, Norman, Mindy Lubber, Stuart L. Koman, and Kathy Kelly.
    <u>Family Therapy: A Systems Approach</u>. Boston: Allyn, 1990.
Stein, Norman, et al. <u>Family Therapy: A Systems Approach</u>. Boston:
    Allyn, 1990.

A book that has been reprinted or reissued

In the following entry, the date 1951 is the original publication date of the book, which was reprinted in 1965.

Perls, Frederick, Ralph F. Hefferline, and Paul Goodman. <u>Gestalt</u>
    <u>Therapy: Excitement and Growth in the Human Personality</u>. 1951.
    New York: Delta-Dell, 1965.

A dictionary or encyclopedia

If an article in a reference work is signed (usually by initials), include the name of the author, which is spelled out elsewhere in the reference work (usually at the beginning). The first example is unsigned. The second article is signed (F.G.H.T.).

"Alcoholics Anonymous." <u>Encyclopaedia Britannica: Micropaedia</u>.
    1991 ed.
Tate, Francis G. H. "Rum." <u>Encyclopaedia Britannica</u>. 1950 ed.

A selection from an edited book or anthology

For a selection from an edited work, name the author of the selection and enclose the selection title in quotation marks. Underline the title of the book containing the selection, and name its editor(s). Give the page numbers for the selection at the end of your entry.

Davies, Phil. "Does Treatment Work? A Sociological Perspective."
The Misuse of Alcohol. Ed. Nick Heather et al. New York: New
York UP, 1985. 158-77.

When a selection has been reprinted from another source, include that information too, as in the following example. State the facts of original publication first, then describe the book in which it has been reprinted.

Bendiner, Emil. "The Bowery Man on the Couch." The Bowery Man. New
York: Nelson, 1961. Rpt. in Man Alone: Alienation in Modern
Society. Ed. Eric Josephson and Mary Josephson. New York:
Dell, 1962. 401-10.

Two or more works by the same author(s)

When you cite two or more works by the same author(s), you should write the author's full name only once, at first mention, in the reference list. In subsequent entries immediately following, substitute three hyphens and a period in place of the author's name.

Heilbroner, Robert L. The Future as History. New York: Harper
Torchbooks-Harper, 1960.
---. An Inquiry into the Human Prospect. New York: Norton, 1974.

A translation

When a work has been translated, acknowledge the translator's name after giving the title.

Kufner, Heinrich, and Wilhelm Feuerlein. In-Patient Treatment for
Alcoholism: A Multi-Centre Evaluation Study. Trans. F. K. H.
Wagstaff. Berlin: Springer, 1989.

A corporate author

If authorship is not individual but corporate, treat the name of the organization as you would the author. This listing would be alphabetized under "National Center."

National Center for Alcohol Education. The Community Health Nurse
and Alcohol-Related Problems: Instructor's Curriculum Planning
Guide. Rockville: National Institute on Alcohol Abuse and Alcoholism, 1978.

Signaling publication information that is unknown

If a document fails to state place or date of publication or the name of the publisher, indicate this lack of information in your entry by using the appropriate abbreviation.

Missing, Andrew. Things I Forgot or Never Knew. N.p.: n.p., n.d.

In the above example, the first *n.p.* stands for "no place of publication." The second *n.p.* means "no publisher given," and *n.d.* stands for "no date."

An edition subsequent to the first

Books of continuing importance may be revised substantially before reissue. Cite the edition you have consulted just after giving the title.

Scrignar, C. B. <u>Post-Traumatic Stress Disorder: Diagnosis, Treat-</u>
    <u>ment, and Legal Issues</u>. 2nd ed. New Orleans: Bruno, 1988.

A book in a series

If the book you are citing is one in a series, include the series name (no quotation marks or underline) followed by the series number and a period before the publication information. You need not give the name of the series editor.

Schuckit, Marc A., ed. <u>Alcohol Patterns and Problems</u>. Series in
    Psychological Epidemiology 5. New Brunswick: Rutgers UP, 1985.

An introduction, preface, foreword, or afterword

When citing an introductory or concluding essay by a "guest author" or commentator, begin with the name of that author. Give the type of piece—Introduction, Preface—without quotation marks or underline. Name the author of the book after giving the book title. At the end of the listing, give the page numbers for the essay you are citing. If the author of the separate essay is also the author of the complete work, repeat that author's last name, preceded by *By*, after the book title.

Fromm, Erich. Foreword. <u>Summerhill: A Radical Approach to Child</u>
    <u>Rearing</u>. By A. S. Neill. New York: Hart, 1960. ix-xiv.

In the following book, the editors also wrote the introduction to their anthology.

Josephson, Eric, and Mary Josephson. Introduction. <u>Man Alone:</u>
    <u>Alienation in Modern Society</u>. Ed. Josephson and Josephson.
    New York: Dell, 1962. 9-53.

An unpublished dissertation or essay

An unpublished dissertation, even of book length, has its title in quotation marks. Label it as a dissertation in your entry. Naming the university and year will provide the necessary publication facts.

Reiskin, Helen R. "Patterns of Alcohol Usage in a Help-Seeking
    University Population." Diss. Boston U, 1980.

Listing periodicals in the MLA "Works Cited" format

A *periodical* is any publication that appears regularly over time. A periodical can be a daily or weekly newspaper, a magazine, or a scholarly or professional journal. As with listings for books, a bibliographical listing for a periodical article includes information about authorship, title, and facts of publication. Authorship is treated just as for books, with the author's first and last names reversed. Citation of a title differs in that the title of an article is always enclosed in quotation marks rather than underlined; the title of the periodical in which it appears is always underlined. Notice that the articles *a*, *an*, and *the*, which often begin the name of a periodical, are omitted from the bibliographical listing.

The facts of publication are the trickiest of the three elements because of the wide variation in how periodicals are dated, paginated, and published. For journals, for example, the publication information generally consists of journal title, the volume number, the year of publication, and the page numbering for the article cited. For newspapers, the listing includes name of the newspaper, full date of publication, and full page numbering by both section and page number(s) if necessary. The following examples show details of how to list different types of periodicals. With the exception of May, June, and July, you should abbreviate the names of months in each "Works Cited" entry (see 31d).

A journal with continuous pagination through the annual volume

A continuously paginated journal is one that numbers pages consecutively throughout all the issues in a volume instead of beginning with page 1 in each issue. After the author's name (reversed and followed by a period and two typed spaces), give the name of the article in quotation marks. Give the title of the journal, underlined and followed by two typed spaces. Give the volume number, in arabic numerals. After a typed space, give the year, in parentheses, followed by a colon. After one more space, give the page number(s) for the article, including the first and last pages on which it appears.

```
Kling, William. "Measurement of Ethanol Consumed in Distilled
     Spirits." Journal of Studies on Alcohol 50 (1989): 456-60.
```

In a continuously paginated journal, the issue number within the volume and the month of publication are not included in the bibliographical listing.

A journal paginated by issue

```
Latessa, Edward J., and Susan Goodman. "Alcoholic Offenders: Inten-
     sive Probation Program Shows Promise." Corrections Today 51.3
     (1989): 38-39+.
```

This journal numbers the pages in each issue separately, so it is important to identify which issue in volume 51 has this article beginning on page 38. The plus sign following a page number indicates that the article continues beyond the last-named page, but after intervening pages.

A monthly magazine

This kind of periodical is identified by month and year of issue. Even if the magazine indicates a volume number, omit it from your listing.

```
Waggoner, Glen. "Gin as Tonic." Esquire Feb. 1990: 30.
```

Some magazines vary in their publication schedule. *Restaurant Business* publishes once a month or bimonthly. Include the full date of publication in your listing. Give the day first, followed by an abbreviation for the month.

```
Whelan, Elizabeth M. "Alcohol and Health." Restaurant Business 20
     Mar. 1989: 66+.
```

A daily newspaper

In the following examples, you see that the name of the newspaper is underlined. Any introductory article (*a, an,* and *the*) is omitted. The complete date of publication is given—day, month (abbreviated), year. Specify the edition if one appears on the masthead, since even in one day an article may be located differently in different editions. Precede the page number(s) by a colon and one typed space. If the paper has sections designated by letter (A, B, C), include the section before the page number.

If the article is unsigned, begin your entry with the title, as in the second example ("Alcohol Can Worsen Ills of Aging").

```
Welch, Patrick. "Kids and Booze: It's 10 O'Clock--Do You Know How
     Drunk Your Kids Are?" Washington Post 31 Dec. 1989: C1.
```

The following entry illustrates the importance of including the particular edition of a newspaper.

```
"Alcohol Can Worsen Ills of Aging, Study Says." New York Times 13
     June 1989, natl. ed.: 89.
"Alcohol Can Worsen Ills of Aging, Study Says." New York Times 13
     June 1989, late ed.: C5.
```

A weekly magazine or newspaper

An unsigned article listing would include title, name of the publication, complete date, and page number(s). Even if you know a volume or issue number, omit it.

```
"A Direct Approach to Alcoholism." Science News 9 Jan. 1988: 25.
```

A signed editorial, letter to the editor, review

For these entries, first give the name of the author. If the piece has a title, put it within quotation marks. Then name the category of the piece—Letter, Rev. of (for Review), Editorial—without quotation marks or underline. If the reference is to a review, give the name of the work being reviewed with underline or quotation marks as appropriate.

```
Fraser, Kennedy. Rev. of Stones of His House: A Biography of Paul
     Scott, by Hilary Spurling. New Yorker 13 May 1991: 103-10.
James, Albert. Letter. Boston Globe 14 Jan. 1992: 61.
Stein, Norman. "Traveling for Work." Editorial. Baltimore Sun 12
     Dec. 1991: 82.
```

Listing other sources in the MLA "Works Cited" format

An abstract of an article

Libraries contain many volumes of abstracts of recent articles in many disciplines. If you are referring to an abstract you have read rather than to the complete article, list it as follows.

Corcoran, K. J., and M. D. Carney. "Alcohol Consumption and Looking
    for Alternatives to Drinking in College Students." <u>Journal of</u>
    <u>Cognitive Psychotherapy</u> 3 (1989): 69–78. Abstract. <u>Excerpta</u>
    <u>Medica</u> 60 (1989): item 4136.

A government publication

Often, a government publication will have group authorship. Be sure to name the agency or committee responsible for writing a document.

United States. Cong. Senate. Subcommittee to Investigate Juvenile
    Delinquency of the Committee on the Judiciary. <u>Juvenile</u>
    <u>Alcohol Abuse: Hearing</u>. 95th Cong., 2nd sess. Washington:
    GPO, 1978.

An unpublished interview

A listing for an unpublished interview begins with the name of the person interviewed. If the interview is untitled, label it as such, without quotation marks or underlining. Name the person doing the interviewing only if that information is relevant. An interview by telephone or e-mail can be noted as part of the interview citation.

Bishop, Robert R. Personal interview. 5 Nov. 1987.

Bly, Robert. Telephone interview. 10 Dec. 1993.

An unpublished letter

Treat an unpublished letter much as you would an unpublished interview. Designate the recipient of the letter. If you as the writer of the paper were the recipient, refer to yourself as "the author."

Bishop, Robert R. Letter to the author. 8 June 1964.

If a letter is housed in a library collection or archive, provide full archival information.

Bishop, Robert R. Letter to Jonathan Morton. 8 June 1964. Carol K.
    Morton papers. Smith College, Northampton.

A film or videotape

Underline the title, and then name the medium, the distributor, and the year. Supply any information that you think is useful about the performers, director, producer, or physical characteristics of the film or tape.

Alcoholism: The Pit of Despair. Videocassette. Gordon Jump. AIMS
    Media, 1983. VHS. 20 min.

A television or radio program

If the program you are citing is a single episode with its own title, supply the title in quotation marks. State the name and role of the foremost participant(s). Underline the title of the program, identify the producer and list the station on which it first appeared, the city, and the date.

"Voices of Memory." Li-Young Lee, Gerald Stern, and Bill Moyers.
    The Power of the Word with Bill Moyers. Exec. prod. Judith
    Davidson Moyers and Bill Moyers. Public Affairs TV. WNET, New
    York. 13 June 1989.

An interview that is broadcast, taped, or published

Treat a published interview as you would any print source. A broadcast or taped interview can be treated as a broadcast program.

"The Broken Cord." Interview with Louise Erdrich and Michael
    Dorris. Dir. and prod. Catherine Tatge. A World of Ideas with
    Bill Moyers. Exec. prod. Judith Davidson Moyers and Bill
    Moyers. Public Affairs TV. WNET, New York. 27 May 1990.

A live performance, lecture

Identify the "who, what, and where" of a live performance. If the "what" is more important than the "who," as in a performance of an opera, give the name of the work before the name of the performers or director. In the following example, the name of the speaker, a cofounder of AA, comes first.

Wilson, Bill. "Alcoholics Anonymous: Beginnings and Growth."
    Presented to the NYC Medical Society. New York, 8 Apr. 1958.

A work of art

Underline the title of a work of art referred to, and tell the location of the work. The name of the museum or collection is separated from the name of the city by a comma.

Manet, Edouard. The Absinthe Drinker. Ny Carlsberg Glyptotek,
    Copenhagen.

Computer software

Like a printed book, computer software has authorship, a title, and a publication history. Include this in any bibliographical listing, along with relevant information for your reader about the software and any hardware it requires. Underline the title of the program. Identify the title as computer software. In the example, the name of the author and the location of the company would be added if they were known.

<u>TrueSync Information Manager</u>. Computer software. Starfish Software,
    1997.

A separately issued map, chart, or graph

Even a freestanding map or poster generally tells something about who published it, where, and when. Give the title, underlined, and any identifying information available. Use the abbreviation *n.d.* any time a date is lacking in publication
information.

<u>Roads in France</u>. Map. Paris: National Tourist Information Agency,
    n.d.

▶3 Listing electronic sources in the MLA "Works Cited" format

Electronic source materials are available to writers in a variety of delivery systems;
the Modern Language Association (MLA) documentation style varies slightly,
depending on whether the material is delivered via the Internet or a CD-ROM
(or diskette). The guidelines here are based on
the 1998 *MLA Style Manual and Guide to Scholarly Publishing* and the 1999 *MLA Handbook for
Writers of Research Papers*, 5th ed. As electronic
media evolve, conventions for listing digital
sources in a "Works Cited" list will also change.
Whatever formats may emerge, researchers will always need to give clear, consistent, and specific directions for locating every source used in a paper.

http://www.mla.org/set_stl.htm
*Although the complete MLA Style
Manual is not online, the guidelines for documenting electronic
sources are online.*

Online sources

The MLA offers some general notes regarding publication dates, uniform resource locators (URLs), and page numbering:

- **Publication dates:** Because the content of Web-based sources may change
  from one user's access to another's, provide readers with at least *two* dates in
  your citation, if possible—the date the Web document was created or last
  modified (often located at the bottom of the Web page) and your date of
  access. If the Web document is a digitized version of an earlier print edition,
  you can cite that date as well.

- **Uniform Resource Locators:** The MLA recommends including URLs
  when citing Web-based sources. When fitting a lengthy URL into a citation, break the URL at the end of a line *only* after a forward slash. Do not
  add a hyphen at the line break (as readers could mistake the hyphen for part
  of the electronic address). Enclose the URL in angle brackets, as in this
  example: <http://www.studentadvantage.com>.

- **Page numbering:** Web pages (or paragraphs within Web pages) may or
  may not be numbered. When they are provided, record paragraph or page
  numbering in order to help readers locate information. Use the following
  models as a guide in creating citations for online sources. Cite as much of
  the requested information as is available.

A scholarly project

Underlined Title of Project. Database editor. Specifics on elec-
    tronic publication, including date of creation or revision,
    versions, organizations. Date of access <URL>.
The Life and Works of Herman Melville. Ed. J. Madden. 10 Apr.
    1997. Multiverse. 3 June 1998 <http://www.melville.org/
    melville.htm>.

A short work within a scholarly project

Last name, First name. "Title of Short Work." Specifics on print
    information if any. Underlined Title of Project. Database
    editor. Specifics on electronic publication, including date of
    creation or revision, versions, organizations. Date of access
    <URL>.
O'Brien, Fitz-James. "Our Young Authors--Melville." Putnum's
    Monthly Magazine Feb. 1853. The Life and Works of Herman
    Melville. Ed. J. Madden. 10 Apr. 1997. Multiverse. 3 June
    1998 <http://www.melville.org/obrien.htm>.

An online book published independently

Last name, First name. Title of Work. Editor or translator if any.
    Specifics on print information if any. Specifics on electronic
    publication, including date of creation or revision, versions,
    organizations. Date of access <URL>.
Twain, Mark. The Adventures of Tom Sawyer. Ed. Internet Wiretap.
    1993. 15 Jan. 1998 <http://www.cs.cmu.edu/People/rgs/
    sawyr-table.html>.

An online book within a scholarly project

Last name, First name. Title of Work. Editor or translator if any.
    Specifics on print information if any. Underlined Title of
    Scholarly Project. Editor of Project. Specifics on electronic
    publication, including date of creation or revision, versions,
    organizations. Date of access <URL>.
DuBois, W. E. B. The Souls of Black Folk. Chicago: A. C. McClurg,
    1903. Project Bartleby. Apr. 1995. Columbia U. 12 May 1998
    <http://www.columbia.edu/acis/bartleby/dubois/100.html>.

Personal or professional site

Last Name, First name of creator. Title of Site. Institutional
    affiliation of site. Date of access <URL>.[1]

Hylton, Jeremy. <u>Shakespeare Resources on the Internet</u>. MIT. 14
    Oct. 1998 <http://the-tech.mit.edu/Shakespeare/other.html>.

Reuben, Paul P. <u>Chapter 3: Early Nineteenth Century: Romanticism:</u>
    <u>Herman Melville (1819-1891)</u>. PAL: Perspectives in American
    Literature--A Research and Reference Guide. 3 June 1998
    <http://www.csustan.edu/english/reuben/pal/chap3/
    melville.html>.

Q-Corp. Home page. 5 Feb. 1998 <http://www.qcorp.com>.

An article in a scholarly journal

Last name, First name. "Title of Work." <u>Name of Periodical</u> Print
    information such as volume and issue number (Year of publica-
    tion): Number of paragraphs or pages if given. Date of access
    <URL>.[2]

Badt, Karin Luisa. "The Roots of the Body in Toni Morrison: A
    Matter of 'Ancient Properties.'" <u>African American Review</u> 29.4
    (1995): 11 pp. 5 Mar. 1998 <http://thunder.northernlight.com/
    cgi-bin/pdserv?cbrecid=LW19970923040189466&cb=0>.

An article in a magazine

Connolly, Brian. "Puzzling Pastimes." <u>IntellectualCapital.com</u> 28
    May 1998. 2 Aug. 1998 <http://www.intellectualcapital.com/
    issues/98/0528/iccyberrep.asp>.

Gray, Paul. "Paradise Found." <u>Time</u> 19 Jan. 1998. 5 Feb. 1998
    <http://www.pathfinder.com/time/magazine/1998/dom/980119/
    cover1.html>.

An article in a newspaper

Meyers, Laura. "Britain Backs U.S. on Iraq." <u>Los Angeles Times</u> 3
    June 1998. 17 June 1998 <http://www.latimes.com/HOME/NEWS/
    AUTOAP/tCB00V0294.1.html>.

An unsigned editorial

"Flirting with Disaster." Editorial. <u>New York Times on the Web</u> 3
    June 1998. 18 July 1998 <http://www.nytimes.com/yr/mo/day/
    editorial/03wed3.html>.

---

[1]If the personal or professional site has no title, write "Home page" (no underline or quotation marks).

[2]Use the abbreviation "pp." for pages and "pars." for paragraphs. If no paragraph or page numbers are given for the article, use a period instead of a colon after the year of publication and follow with the date of access.

A signed editorial

Klayman, Larry. "No Special Treatment." Editorial. <u>USA Today</u> 3 June
    1998. 3 June 1998 <http://www.usatoday.com/news/comment/
    ncoppf.htm>.

A letter to the editor

Fletcher, Anthony Q. Letter. <u>New York Times on the Web</u> 3 June 1998.
    3 June 1998 <http://www.nytimes.com/yr/mo/day/letters/
    lfletc.html>.

A review

Lipschutz, Neal. "Buchanan's Anti-Trade Tirade." Rev. of <u>The Great
    Betrayal</u>, by Patrick Buchanan. <u>IntellectualCapital.com</u> 3.21
    (1998): 2 pp. 28 Aug. 1998 <http://www.intellectualcapital.com/
    bibliotech/rev-052898.asp>.

Electronic mail

Chadima, Steve. "Re: Business as Poker." E-mail to Leonard J.
    Rosen. 14 Aug. 1998.

Online postings

You may want to cite a contribution to an e-mail discussion list or a posting
to an online news group or listserv. Generally, follow this format:

Last name, First name. "Title of Posting from Subject Line."
    Online posting. Date of electronic posting. Name of online
    group. Date of access <URL or, if none, e-mail address of
    group's moderator>.
Nostroni, Eric. "Collaborative Learning in a Networked
    Environment." Online posting. 8 Sept. 1997. Electronic Forum.
    9 Nov. 1997 <eforum@cgu.edu>.
Rand, Marc. "Watching the Humans Watching Whales." Online
    posting. 26 May 1998. AnimalRights News. 29 May 1998
    <news:rec.animals>.
Tuttle, AnneMarie. "Waltzing toward the Millennium." Online
    posting. 14 Sept. 1998. The Millennium Project Conference.
    4 Oct. 1998 <http://www.ryu.org/mem~tuttle/waltz.html>.

Synchronous communications: MOOs, MUDs, IRC

Richardson, Lea. Online debate. "The Politics of Recycling."
    16 Aug. 1997. EnviroMOO. 16 Aug. 1997 <telnet://
    enviro.moo.greenearth.org:42557>.

Computer software

<u>Q-Notes for Windows 95</u>. Vers. 1.0.1A. 15 Nov. 1997. Brookline:

    Q-Corp, Inc. 1997.

Online service

    You may locate and use source materials from an online service, such as America Online (AOL), EBSCO, or Lexis-Nexis. If you do so, and the service provides a URL for the source, follow the format above for citing online sources. When you access a source through a keyword or a path and no URL is provided, use the following format—recording as much information as is provided:

Author's Last name, First name. "Name of article" Underlined title

    of source in which the article appears. Version or date of

    creation including page numbers. Name of Online Service. Date

    of access. Keyword or Path (no italics, followed by a colon):

    Write the keyword, followed by a period, or the pathway

    (separating items with a semicolon).

Fenwick, Ben. "Oklahoma Twister Survivors Face Long Recovery."

    <u>Reuters</u>. 9 May 1999. America Online. 10 May 1999. Path: News;

    U.S. and World.

Hunter, James. "Odysseus." <u>Encyclopedia Mythica</u>. 1999. America

    Online. 10 May 1999. Keyword: Mythica.

    If you are citing material found on a premium search service such as UMI's ProQuest Direct or Lexis-Nexis, present as much of the following information as is available: begin with information from the print edition—author, title, publication date and page(s). Follow with the name of the database, underlined; the name of the search service; the abbreviated name of the library and its location (with state, if needed for clarification); date of access; and URL of the service.

Targett, Simon. "Oxford to Offer Degree Courses over Internet."

    <u>Financial Times</u> 20 July 1998: 1. Proquest Direct. Bentley

    Coll. Lib., Waltham, MA. 20 May 1999 <http://proquest.umi.com/

    pqdweb>.

CD-ROMs and diskettes

CD-ROMs and diskettes issued as a single publication (analogous to the publication of a book)

    As when citing an online source, cite as much of the recommended information as is pertinent and available. Follow this general format:

Last name, First name. "Title of Article." <u>Title of Specific</u>

    <u>Collection</u>. Editor of collection if given. Publication

information for printed text if given. <u>Title of CD-ROM or Diskette</u>. Publication medium—i.e., CD-ROM or Diskette. Edition or version number if given. Place of publication: Name of publisher, year of publication.

Chin, Jeffrey. "The Role of Impermanence in American Dating Ritual." <u>Sociological Review of Dating and Marriage: 1990–1998</u>. Ed. Ellen Markham. <u>Dating and Marriage: A Cross-Disciplinary Approach</u>. CD-ROM. Rel.1.2. Newton, MA: Westhill Wired, 1999.

"Industrial Revolution." <u>Concise Columbia Encyclopedia</u>. CD-ROM. Redmond: Microsoft, 1994.

Miller, Arthur. <u>The Crucible</u>. CD-ROM. New York: Penguin, 1994.

Pirsig, Robert M. <u>Zen and the Art of Motorcycle Maintenance</u> and <u>Lila: An Inquiry into Morals</u>. Diskette. New York: Voyager, 1992.

CD-ROMs and diskettes updated periodically (analogous to the publication of a magazine or journal)

Last name, First name. "Title of Article." Publication information for printed text if given. <u>Title of CD-ROM or Diskette</u>. Publication medium--i.e., CD-ROM or Diskette. Name of publisher. Month and year of electronic publication.

Bureau of the Census. "Exports to Germany, East: Merchandise Trade-Exports by Country." <u>National Trade Statistics</u> (1995): 85–96. <u>National Trade Databank</u>. CD-ROM. U.S. Bur. of Census. Aug. 1995.

Gillette. "Gillette Co.: Balance Sheet, 12/31/93–9/30/95." <u>Compact Disclosure</u>. CD-ROM. Digital Library Systems, Inc. Oct. 1995.

▶ 37b   Using the APA system of documentation

The American Psychological Association's *Publication Manual* has set documentation style for psychologists. Writers in other fields, especially those in which researchers report their work fairly frequently in periodicals and edited collections of essays, also use the APA system of documentation. Whichever style of documentation you use in a given research paper, use only one; do not mix features of APA and MLA (or any other format) in a single paper.

APA documentation is similar to the MLA system in coupling a brief in-text citation, given in parentheses, with a complete listing of information about the source at the end of the paper. In the APA system this list of references is called "References." In the in-text citation itself, APA style differs by including the date of the work cited. The publication date is often important for a reader to have immediately at hand in psychology and related fields, where researchers may publish frequently, often modifying conclusions reached in prior publications. Date of publication also serves to distinguish readily among publications for authors who have written numerous titles. Following is an index to this section on the APA system of documentation.

▶ 1 Making in-text citations in the APA format

For every fact, opinion, or idea from another source that you quote, summarize, or otherwise use, you must give credit. You must also give just enough information so that your reader can locate the source. Whether in the text itself or in a parenthetical note, APA documentation calls for you to name the author and give the date of publication for every work you refer to. When you have quoted from a work, you must also give the page or page numbers (preceded by *p.* or *pp.*, in APA format). When you summarize or paraphrase, as well, it is often helpful to supply exact location of the source material by page number as part of the parenthetical reference. Supply the page number(s) immediately following a quotation or paraphrase, even if the sentence is not at a pause point.

In the sample paragraphs that follow, you will find variations on using APA in-text citation. Notice that, wherever possible, reference information is incorporated directly into the text and parentheses are used as a supplement to information in the text. Supply the parenthetical date of publication immediately after an author's name in the text. If you refer to a source a second time within a paragraph, you need not repeat the information if the reference is clear. If there is any confusion about which work is being cited, however, supply the clarifying information. The full reference should be provided the next time the source is cited in a new paragraph.

Dardis's study (1989) examines four twentieth-century American writers--three of them Nobel Prize winners--who were alcoholics. Dardis acknowledged (p. 3) that American painters too include a high percentage of addicted drinkers. Among poets, he concludes (p. 5) that the percentage is not so high as among prose writers.

However, even a casual reading of a recent biography of poet John Berryman (Mariani, 1990) reveals a creative and personal life dominated by alcohol. Indeed, "so regular had [Berryman's] hospital stays [for alcoholism] become [. . .] that no one came to visit him anymore" (Mariani, p. 413). Berryman himself had no illusions about the destructive power of alcohol. About his friend Dylan Thomas he could write, "Dylan murdered himself w. liquor, tho it took years" (qtd. in Mariani, p. 274). Robert Lowell and Edna St. Vincent Millay were also prominent American poets who had problems with alcohol (Dardis, 1989, p. 3).

A work by two authors

To join the names of two authors of a work, use *and* in text but use the ampersand (&) in a parenthetical reference. Notice how the parenthetical information immediately follows the point to which it applies.

```
Roebuck and Kessler (1972) summarized the earlier research
(pp. 21-41).
```

```
A summary of prior research on the genetic basis of alcoholism
(Roebuck & Kessler, 1972, pp. 21-41) is our starting point.
```

Two or more works by the same author

If the work of the same author has appeared in different years, distinguish references to each separate work by year of publication. If, however, you refer to two or more works published by the same author(s) within a single year, you must list the works in alphabetical order by title in the list of references, and assign each one an order by lowercase letter. Thus,

```
(Holden, 1989a)
```

could represent Caroline Holden's article "Alcohol and Creativity," while

```
(Holden, 1989b)
```

would refer to the same author's "Creativity and Craving," published in the same year.

A work by three to five authors

Use names of all authors in the first reference, but subsequently give only the first of the names followed by *et al.* Use the *et al.* format for six or more authors.

```
Perls, Hefferline, and Goodman (1965) did not focus on the addic-
tive personality. Like other approaches to the study of the mind
in the '50s and '60s, Gestalt psychology (Perls et al.) spoke of
addiction only in passing.
```

A work by a corporate author

Give a corporate author's whole name in a parenthetical reference. If the name can be readily abbreviated, supply the abbreviation in brackets in the first reference. Subsequently, use the abbreviation alone.

```
Al-Anon Faces Alcoholism (Alcoholics Anonymous [AA], 1974) has been
reissued many times since its initial publication.
```

```
One of the books most widely read by American teenagers (AA, 1974)
deals with alcoholism in the family.
```

Distinguishing two authors with the same last name

Distinguish authors with the same last name by including first and middle initials in each citation.

(J. Williams, 1990)

(C. K. Williams, 1991)

Two or more sources in a single reference

Separate multiple sources in one citation by a semicolon. List authors alphabetically within the parentheses.

We need to view the alcoholic in twentieth-century America from many perspectives (Bendiner, 1962; Dardis, 1989; Waggoner, 1990) in order to understand how people with ordinary lives as well as people with vast creative talent can appear to behave identically.

▶**2 Preparing a list of references in the APA format**

In research papers following the APA system, the list of references (which is alphabetized) is called "References." Within an entry, the date is separated from the other facts of publication. The APA list of references includes only those works referred to in your paper.

Listing books in the APA format

Leave two typed spaces to separate items in an entry. Double-space the list throughout. Start each entry at the left margin; if the entry runs beyond one line, indent subsequent lines five spaces. (Note that these formatting instructions are for preparing student papers for an APA reference to be read in its final form. If you are preparing a paper for a journal for publication, refer to the APA manual for guidelines.) The following order of presentation is used:

1. Author's name(s): Put the last name first, followed by a comma. Use first—and middle—initial instead of spelling out a first or middle name.
2. Date: Give the year of publication in parentheses followed by a period. If your list includes more than one title by an author in any one year, distinguish those titles by adding a lowercase letter (a, b, etc.) to the year of publication (as in 1989a and 1989b).
3. Title of the book: Underline the complete book title. Capitalize only the first word in a title or subtitle, in addition to proper names.
4. Publication information: Name the city of publication, followed by a colon. Give the full name of the publisher, but without the "Co." or other business designation.

Dardis, T. (1989). <u>The thirsty muse: Alcohol and the American writer.</u> New York: Ticknor & Fields.

A book with two authors

Invert both names; separate them by a comma. Use the ampersand (&).

Roebuck, J. B., & Kessler, R. G. (1972). <u>The etiology of alcoholism: Constitutional, psychological and sociological approaches.</u> Springfield, IL: Charles C. Thomas.

A book with three or more authors

List *all* authors, treating each author's name as in the case of two authors. Use the ampersand before naming the last. (This book was first published in 1951, then reissued without change.)

Perls, R., Hefferline, R. F., & Goodman, P. (1951/1965). Gestalt
    psychology: Excitement and growth in the human personality.
    New York: Delta-Dell.

A selection from an edited book or anthology

Underline the title of the book. The selection title is not underlined or enclosed in quotation marks. (In APA style, spell out the name of a university press.)

Davies, P. (1985). Does treatment work? A sociological perspective.
    In N. Heather (Ed.), The misuse of alcohol (pp. 158-177). New
    York: New York University Press.

A corporate author

Alphabetize the entry in the references list by the first significant word in the name, which is given in normal order.

National Center for Alcohol Education. (1978). The community health
    nurse and alcohol-related problems: Instructor's curriculum
    planning guide. Rockville, MD: National Institute on Alcohol
    Abuse and Alcoholism.

An edition subsequent to the first

Indicate the edition in parentheses, following the book title.

Scrignar, C. B. (1988). Post-traumatic stress disorder: Diagnosis,
    treatment, and legal issues (2nd ed.). New Orleans: Bruno.

A dissertation

In contrast with MLA style, the title of an unpublished dissertation or thesis is underlined.

Reiskin, H. R. (1980). Patterns of alcohol usage in a help-seeking
    university population. Unpublished doctoral dissertation,
    Boston University.

If you are referring to the abstract of the dissertation, the style of the entry differs because the abstract itself appears in a volume (volume number underlined).

Reiskin, H. R. (1980). Patterns of alcohol usage in a help-seeking
    university population. Dissertation Abstracts International,
    40, 6447A.

Listing periodicals in the APA format

A journal with continuous pagination through the annual volume

The entry for a journal begins with the author's last name and initial(s), inverted, followed by the year of publication in parentheses. The title of the article has neither quotation marks nor underline. Only the first word of the title and subtitle are capitalized, along with proper nouns. The volume number, which follows the underlined title of the journal, is also underlined. Use the abbreviation *p.* or *pp.* when referring to page numbers in a magazine or newspaper. Use no abbreviations when referring to the page numbers of a journal.

Kling, W. (1989). Measurement of ethanol consumed in distilled
    spirits. Journal of Studies on Alcohol, 50, 456-460.

A journal paginated by issue

In this example, the issue number within volume 51 is given in parentheses. Give all page numbers when the article is not printed continuously.

Latessa, E. J., & Goodman, S. (1989). Alcoholic offenders: Inten-
    sive probation program shows promise. Corrections Today,
    51(3), 38-39, 45.

A monthly magazine

Invert the year and month of a monthly magazine. Write the name of the month in full. (For newspapers use the abbreviations *p.* and *pp.*)

Waggoner, G. (1990, February). Gin as tonic. Esquire, 30.

A weekly magazine

If the article is signed, begin with the author's name. Otherwise, begin with the article's title. (You would alphabetize the following entry under *d.*)

A direct approach to alcoholism. (1988, January 9). Science News,
    25.

A daily newspaper

Welch, P. (1989, December 31). Kids and booze: It's 10 o'clock--Do
    you know how drunk your kids are? The Washington Post, p. C1.

A review or letter to the editor

Treat the title of the review or letter as the title of an article, without quotation. Use brackets to show that the article is a review or letter. If the review is untitled, place the bracketed information immediately after the date.

Fraser, K. (1991, May 13). The bottle and inspiration [Review of
    the book Stones of his house: A biography of Paul Scott]. The
    New Yorker, 103-110.

Two or more works by the same author in the same year

If you refer to two or more works published by the same author(s) within a single year, list the works in alphabetical order by title in the list of references, and assign each one an order by lowercase letter.

Chen, J. S., & Amsel, A. (1980a). Learned persistence at 11-12
    days but not at 10-11 days in infant rats. Developmental
    Psychobiology, 13, 481-492.

Chen, J. S., & Amsel, A. (1980b). Retention under changed-reward
    conditions of persistence learned by infant rats. Developmen-
    tal Psychobiology, 13, 469-480.

Listing other sources in the APA format

An abstract of an article

Show where the abstract may be found, at the end of the entry.

Corcoran, K. J., & Carney, M. D. (1989). Alcohol consumption
    and looking for alternatives to drinking in college students.
    Journal of Cognitive Psychotherapy, 3, 69-78. (From Excerpta
    Medica, 1989, 60, Abstract No. 1322)

A government publication

U.S. Senate Judiciary Subcommittee. (Hearing, 95th Congress, 2nd
    sess.). (1978). Juvenile Alcohol Abuse. Washington, DC: U.S.
    Government Printing Office.

A film or videotape

For nonprint media, identify the medium in brackets just after the title.

Jump, G. (Producer). (1983). Alcoholism: The pit of despair
    [Videocassette, VHS and Beta]. New York: AIMS Media.

A television or radio program

Erdrich, L., & Dorris, M. (Interviewees). (1990, May 27). The
    broken cord. A world of ideas with Bill Moyers [Television
    program]. New York: Public Affairs TV. WNET.

An information service

Weaver, D. (1988). Software for substance abuse education: A criti-
    cal review of products (Report No. NREL-RR-88-6). Portland,
    OR: Northwest Regional Educational Lab. (ERIC Document Repro-
    duction Service No. ED 303 702)

Computer software

Begin your reference to a computer program with the name of the author or other primary contributor, if known.

```
Cohen, L. S. (1989). Alcohol testing: Self-help [Computer program].
    Baltimore, MD: Boxford Enterprises.
```

Listing electronic sources in the APA format

Conventions for citing electronic sources in APA format begin with the same information on author, date, and title as citations for print sources. Then follow with a reference to the electronic source, making a distinction between Web-based sources and CD-ROM sources.

For information found on a CD-ROM, follow the initial information—author, date, title—with the listing *CD-ROM* placed in brackets as the medium of electronic transmission.

Reference to a work on CD-ROM

```
NCTE. (1987). On writing centers [CD-ROM]. Urbana: ERIC Clearing-
    house for Resolutions on the Teaching of Composition. Silver
    Platter.
```

Reference to part of a work on CD-ROM

```
Peterson, C. L. (1995). Further lifting of the veil: Gender, class,
    and labor in Frances E. W. Harper's Iola Leroy. In New essays
    in feminist criticism [CD-ROM]. Silver Platter.
```

Reference to an Internet source

The APA has not updated its 1994 *Publication Manual* to reflect current scholarly practice regarding the citing of sources found on the Internet. Instead of announcing a standard, APA has elected to let a standard emerge from the scholarly community—which means that, for the moment, anyway, no firm standard exists. Still, the expectation remains that every citation provide clear pointers to a particular source. A Web site being monitored by the APA—Web Extension to American Psychological Association Style (WEAPAS) <http://www.beadsland.com/weapas/>—offers a clear and sensible format for citing Internet sources. The format is as follows:

http://www.apa.org/journals/webref.html
The most recent statement of the APA on how to cite documents retrieved from the World Wide Web.

Begin the entry with bibliographic information just as for a print source: author, date, title. Follow immediately with bracketed information that lists the type of online material you are citing. For a serial publication (for example, a journal), write *Online serial* in brackets. For documents published as a Web page but not as part of an online journal or a Web-based version of a newspaper, write *WWW document* in brackets. Place a period after this bracket and write *URL*. Follow immediately with the URL of the document you have retrieved. Do not enclose the URL in brackets and do not follow the URL with any punctuation. In this presentation of the APA style for citing electronic sources, note that you do *not* list the date you accessed an electronic source (as you do in MLA format). Note that the Tent and Li citation examples, below, appear on the WEAPAS Web site.

Online book

Landow, G. (1997). Hypertext 2.0: The convergence of
    contemporary critical theory and technology [Online].
    URL http://www.stg.brown.edu/projects/hypertext/landow/
    ht/contents.html

Article in an edited online work

Keegan, J. (1999). Normandy: The invasion conceived, 1941-43. In
    Encyclopedia Britannica [Online]. URL http://normandy.eb.com/
    normandy/week1/buildup.html

World Wide Web document

Dice, R. (1998, June 15). Web Database Crash course--Lesson 1
    [WWW document]. URL http://www.hotwired.com/webmonkey/98/24/
    index0a.html?tw=frontdoor
Li, X., & Crane, N. (1996a, May 20). Bibliographic formats
    for citing electronic information [WWW document]. URL
    http://www.uvm.edu/~ncrane/estyles

Online newspaper

McDowell, R. (1999, April 21). Colorado students struggle to
    understand rampage. The Boston Globe [Online newspaper].
    URL http://www.globe.com/news/daily/21/school.htm

Online magazine article

Dubow, C. (1999, April 21). Turning acorns into trees. Forbes
    [Online magazine]. URL http://www.forbes.com/tool/html/99/
    apr/0421/feat.htm

Online article in a journal paginated by issue

Tent, J. (1995, February 13). Citing e-texts summary.
    Linguist list, 6(210) [Online serial]. URL http://
    www.lam.man.deakin.edu.au/citation.txt

Abstract of an online article in a journal with continuous pagination

Jacobs, D. R., Hisashi, A., Mulder, I., Kromhout, D., Menotti,
    A., Nissinen, A., & Blackburn, H. (12 April 1999). Cigarette
    smoking and mortality risk: Twenty-five year follow-up of

```
    the seven countries study. Archives of internal medicine,
    159, 733-740. Abstract [Online serial]. URL http://
    www.medstudents.com.br/jornal/index.htm
```

For more information on citing electronic sources using APA style, see Li and Crane (1996), *Electronic Styles: An Expanded Guide to Citing Electronic Information.* Li and Crane advise a slightly different format—one that ends with the date of access. (See the Web site associated with their *Guide* in the Li citation, above.) Check with your instructor to determine his or her preference regarding date of access.

▶ 37c   Using the CMS style of documentation

The parenthetical reference mode of in-text citation is neat and easy to use. The physical and biological sciences, as well as many social sciences, have used it for decades. However, in many of the humanities (including history, philosophy, and art history), in some social sciences (including economics, communication, and political science), as well as in most business-related disciplines, many writers have long preferred the system of endnotes or footnotes developed in *The Chicago Manual of Style*, fourteenth edition, and the closely related system that is offered as an alternate system in the *MLA Handbook for Writers*, fifth edition. (The MLA footnote/endnote system differs from CMS in some details of punctuation and spacing as noted below.) To use footnotes or endnotes, signal a citation in the text by a raised numeral (superscript) at the appropriate point, preferably after a comma or period. The citation information signaled with this numeral is placed in a separate note numbered to match the one in the text. Both CMS and MLA systems prefer citation information to be collected as *endnotes* at the end of your paper, though some publications continue to use *footnotes* placed at the bottom of pages where in-text citations are signaled.

Place endnotes in double-spaced form at the end of your paper on a separate page, with the heading "Notes" appearing before any listed Bibliography. Indent the start of each note five spaces, and continue the note on subsequent lines with a return to the left margin. The number preceding each endnote should be the same size and alignment as its text (not a superscript), followed by a period and a space. Here is an endnote or footnote in the recommended CMS format (the MLA format omits the comma before page numbers):

```
    3. Paul Mariani, Dream Song: The Life of John Berryman (New
York: Morrow, 1990), 45-49.
```

If footnotes are used, they are placed at the bottom of a page, four line spaces below the text, in single-space format, with a double space to separate footnotes on the same page. While CMS recommends numbering footnotes in the same manner as endnotes, the old MLA style and other traditional formats specify that they be numbered with superscript numerals like those in the text. Many word processing programs are able to handle these formatting conventions automatically, along with the placement of footnotes at the bottoms of pages. A citation note in the CMS style contains essentially the same information—author, title, publication facts—as an entry in a list of references in the MLA "Works Cited" format. There are differences in order and punctuation, and the note, unlike an entry in "Works Cited," concludes with a page reference. A note need not tell the span of pages of a source article when that information appears in a bibliography included at the end of the paper.

The Chicago Manual of Style advises the use of italics for the titles of books and journals. In this discussion, you will find books and journals underlined. If you are working with a computer and can show italics, you may choose to do so.

Here is an index to this section on CMS style:

▶ **1   Making the first and subsequent references in CMS notes**

The first time you cite a source in a CMS paper, you will give complete information about it. If you refer to that source again, you need give only the briefest identification. Usually, this is the author's name and a page reference.

In the following sample paragraph, the first CMS note refers to an entire book. The second note cites a particular passage in a review, and refers to that page only. The third note refers to a work already cited in note 2.

> Alcohol has played a destructive, painful role in the lives of numerous twentieth-century writers. Among poets, Dylan Thomas is often the first who comes to mind as a victim of alcoholism. John Berryman, too, suffered from this affliction.[1] Among novelists who battled alcohol was the great British writer Paul Scott, author of the masterpiece The Raj Quartet. A reviewer of a new biography of

Scott faults the biographer for not understanding fully the effect of alcoholism on Scott and his wife and daughters.[2] Scott's own mother, out of a kind of bravado, encouraged Paul to drink gin at the age of six.[3]

1. Paul Mariani, <u>Dream Song: The Life of John Berryman</u> (New York: Morrow, 1990).

2. Kennedy Fraser, review of <u>Stones of His House: A Life of Paul Scott</u>, by Hilary Spurling, <u>New Yorker</u>, 13 May 1991, 110.

3. Fraser, 108.

Compare the format of these CMS footnotes with their corresponding entries in the MLA "Works Cited" list.

Fraser, Kennedy. Rev. of <u>Stones of His House: A Biography of Paul Scott</u>, by Hilary Spurling. <u>New Yorker</u> 13 May 1991: 103–10.

Mariani, Paul. <u>Dream Song: The Life of John Berryman</u>. New York: Morrow, 1990.

▶2 Following the CMS note style

Citing books in the CMS note style

A book with two or three authors

1. Julian B. Roebuck and Raymond G. Kessler, <u>The Etiology of Alcoholism: Constitutional, Psychological and Sociological Approaches</u> (Springfield, IL: Thomas, 1972), 72.

A book with four or more authors
Name each author, or use the *et al.* format.

2. Norman Stein et al., <u>Family Therapy: A Systems Approach</u> (Boston: Allyn, 1990), 312.

A corporate author

3. National Center for Alcohol Education, <u>The Community Health Nurse and Alcohol-Related Problems: Instructor's Curriculum Planning Guide</u> (Rockville: National Institute on Alcohol Abuse and Alcoholism, 1978), 45–49.

A multivolume work

4. G. M. Trevelyan, <u>Illustrated English Social History</u> (Harmondsworth: Pelican-Penguin, 1964), 3:46.

Two sources cited in one note

     5. Joy Williams, <u>Escapes</u> (New York: Vintage, 1990), 57–62; C. K. Williams, <u>The Bacchae of Euripides: A New Version</u> (New York: Farrar, 1990), 15.

An edition subsequent to the first

     6. C. B. Scrignar, <u>Post-Traumatic Stress Disorder: Diagnosis, Treatment, and Legal Issues</u>, 2nd ed. (New Orleans: Bruno, 1988), 23–28.

A selection in an edited book or anthology

     7. Emil Bendiner, "The Bowery Man on the Couch," in <u>Man Alone: Alienation in Modern Society</u>, ed. Eric Josephson and Mary Josephson (New York: Dell, 1962), 408.

An introduction, preface, foreword, or afterword

     8. Erich Fromm, foreword to <u>Summerhill: A Radical Approach to Child Rearing</u>, by A. S. Neill (New York: Hart, 1960), xii.

Citing periodicals and other sources in the CMS note style

A journal with continuous pagination through the annual volume

     9. William Kling, "Measurement of Ethanol Consumed in Distilled Spirits," <u>Journal of Studies on Alcohol</u> 50 (1989): 456.

A monthly magazine

     10. Glen Waggoner, "Gin as Tonic," <u>Esquire</u>, February 1990, 30.

A weekly magazine

     11. "A Direct Approach to Alcoholism," <u>Science News</u>, 9 January 1988, 25.

A daily newspaper

     12. "Alcohol Can Worsen Ills of Aging, Study Says," <u>New York Times</u>, 13 June 1989, late edition, p. C5.

A dissertation abstract

     13. Helen R. Reiskin, "Pattern of Alcohol Usage in a Help-Seeking University Population" (Ph.D. diss., Boston University, 1980), abstract in <u>Dissertation Abstracts International</u> 41 (1983): 6447A.

Computer software

    14. <u>Alcohol and Pregnancy: Protecting the Unborn Child</u>
Ver. 2.1, Student Awareness Software, Cambridge, MA.

A government document

    15. United States Senate Judiciary Subcommittee, <u>Juvenile Alcohol Abuse: Hearing</u>, 95th Cong., 2nd sess. (Washington, DC: GPO, 1978), 3.

Internet sources

    16. Laura Meyers, "Britain Backs U.S. on Iraq," <u>Los Angeles Times</u>, <http://www.latimes.com/HOME/NEWS/AUTOAP/tCB00V0294.1.html>, 17 June 1998.

http://www.msoe.edu/gen_st/style/stylguid.html
Since The Chicago Manual of Style *has not been revised since 1993, citation of electronic sources is inadequate. This guide is based on* The Chicago Manual of Style *with extensions to cover electronic sources.*

For further guidance on citing Internet sources in CMS format, consult "A Brief Citation Guide for Internet Sources in History and the Humanities," which you can find at <http://www.h-net.msu.edu/~africa/citation.html>. The site is maintained by Melvin Page (Professor of History at East Tennessee State University) and has been endorsed by H-Net (Humanities and Social Sciences Online).

▶ 37d   Using the CBE systems of documentation

The Council of Biology Editors (CBE) systems of documentation are standard for the biological sciences and, with minor or minimal adaptations, are also used in many of the other sciences. See *Scientific Style and Format: The CBE Manual for Authors, Editors, and Publishers*, 6th ed., 1994. You will find many similarities between the CBE styles of documentation and the APA style, which was derived from the conventions used in scientific writing. As in APA and MLA styles, any in-text references to a source are provided in shortened form in parentheses. For complete bibliographic information, readers expect to consult the list of references at the end of the document. Following is an index to this section on the CBE systems for documentation.

▶ I   Making in-text citations in the CBE formats

The *CBE Manual for Authors, Editors, and Publishers* presents three formats for citing a source in the text of an article. Your choice of format will depend on the discipline in which you are writing. Whatever format you choose, remain consistent within any one document.

The name-year system

The CBE convention that most closely resembles the APA conventions is the name-year system. In this system a writer provides in parentheses the name of an author and the year in which that author's work was published. Note that, in contrast to the APA system, no comma appears between the author's name and the year of publication.

```
Slicing and aeration of quiescent storage tissues induces a rapid
metabolic activation and a development of the membrane systems in
the wounded tissue (Kahl 1974).
```

If an author's name is mentioned in a sentence, then only the year of publication is set in parentheses.

```
Jacobsen et al. found that a marked transition in respiratory sub-
strate occurs in sliced potato tissue that exhibits the phenomenon
of wound respiration (1974).
```

If your paper cites two or more works published by the same author in the same year, assign a letter designation (a, b, etc.) to inform the reader of precisely which piece you have cited. This form of citation applies both to journal articles and to books.

```
Chen and Amsel (1980a) obtained intermittent reinforcement effects
in rats as young as eleven days of age. Under the same conditions,
they observed that the effects of intermittent reinforcement on
perseverance are long lived (Chen and Amsel 1980b).
```

When citing a work by an organization or government agency with no author named, use the corporate or organizational name in place of a reference to an individual author. Provide the year of publication following the name as indicated previously.

Style guides in the sciences caution that the "use of nouns formed from verbs and ending in -tion produces unnecessarily long sentences and dull prose" (CBE Style Manual Committee 1983).

The citation-sequence system

The briefest form of parenthetical citation is the citation-sequence system, a convention in which only an Arabic numeral appears in parentheses to identify a source of information. There are two variations on the citation-sequence system. With references *in order of first mention*, you assign a reference number to a source in the order of its appearance in your paper. With references *in alphabetized order*, you assign each source a reference number that identifies it in the alphabetized list of references at the end of the paper.

If possible, use superscripts—a raised number slightly smaller than the regular text—to make your number citation. The second example, below, shows the citation-sequence system with superscripts. If your word processor or typewriter does not permit the use of superscripts, set each citation number in parentheses. Place the parenthetical number immediately following the word, phrase, or sentence to which it refers, as in this first example:

Citation for a reference list in order of first mention

According to Kahl et al., slicing and aeration of quiescent storage tissues induces a rapid metabolic activation and a development of the membrane systems in the wounded tissue (1). Jacobson et al. found that a marked transition in respiratory substrate occurs in sliced potato tissue that exhibits the phenomenon of wound respiration (2).

Citation for a reference list in alphabetical order

According to Kahl et al., slicing and aeration of quiescent storage tissues induces a rapid metabolic activation and a development of the membrane systems in the wounded tissue.[2] Jacobson et al. found that a marked transition in respiratory substrate occurs in sliced potato tissue that exhibits the phenomenon of wound respiration.[1]

▶2 Preparing a list of references using CBE systems

In the sciences the list of references appearing at the end of the paper is often called "Cited References." If you adopt the name-year system for in-text citation (see

37d-1), the entries in your list of references are alphabetized, much as with the APA system, rather than numbered.

If you adopt one of the citation-sequence systems for in-text citation (see 37d-1), you will either number entries alphabetically or in order of appearance in the paper. A numbered entry, beginning with the numeral, starts at the left margin. Place a period after the number, skip two spaces, and list the author's last name followed by the rest of the entry. For the spacing of the second or subsequent lines of a numbered entry, align the second line directly beneath the first letter of the author's last name. For style guides in the specific sciences, see 40e. The following are some of the basic formats for listing sources in the CBE systems.

Listing books in the CBE format

In preparing a list of references in the CBE format, leave two typed spaces between each item in an entry. Sequence the items in an entry as follows:

- *Number:* If you are using the citation-sequence system, assign a number to the entry.
- *Author's name:* Put the last name first, followed by a space and the initials of the first and middle names. Leave no space between initials. After the initial(s), place a period. For a book with two or more authors, place a comma after the initial(s) of each co-author. Do *not* use an ampersand (&) or the word *and* between authors.
- *Title of book:* Do not use underlining or italics. Capitalize the first letter of the first word only. End the title with a period. If the work is a revised edition, abbreviate the edition: 2nd ed., 3rd ed., 4th ed., and so on.
- *Publication information:* Name the city of publication (and state, if needed to clarify). Place a colon and give the abbreviated name of the publisher. Place a semicolon, and give the year of publication followed by a period. Provide number of pages in the book, followed by the letter *p* and a period.

If you refer to more than one work published by the same author(s) in the same year, list the works in order of earliest to latest. Assign the lower-case letter *a* to the earliest work, *b* to the next earliest work, and so on. If you refer to more than one work published by the same author in different years, list the earliest work first.

In CBE, the format of entries for books in "Cited References" changes slightly depending on whether you are using the citation-sequence system or the name-year system.

A book by individual author or multiple authors

Citation-sequence system

Entries are listed in the order of their citation in the paper.

1. Goodwin TW, Mercer EI. Introduction to plant biochemistry. Elmsford, NY: Pergamon; 1972. 643 p.

2. Beevers H. Respiratory metabolism in plants. Evanston, IL: Row, Peterson; 1961. 935 p.

Name-year system

Notice that these *un*numbered entries are alphabetized and the date follows the author's name.

Beevers H. 1961. Respiratory metabolism in plants. Evanston, IL: Row, Peterson. 935 p.

Goodwin TW, Mercer EI. 1972. Introduction to plant biochemistry. Elmsford, NY: Pergamon. 643 p.

A book by corporate authors

Citation-sequence system

3. CBE Style Manual Committee. Scientific style and format: the CBE manual for authors, editors, and publishers. 6th ed. New York: Cambridge Univ Pr; 1994. 825 p.

Name-year system

CBE Style Manual Committee. 1994. Scientific style and format: the CBE manual for authors, editors, and publishers. 6th ed. New York: Cambridge Univ Pr. 825 p.

A book by compilers or editors

Citation-sequence system

4. Smith KC, editor. Light and plant development. New York: Plenum; 1977. 726 p.

Name-year system

Smith KC, editor. 1977. Light and plant development. New York: Plenum. 726 p.

A dissertation or thesis

Citation-sequence system

5. Reiskin HR. Patterns of alcohol usage in a help-seeking university population [dissertation]. Boston: Boston University; 1980. 216 p. Available from: Boston: Boston Univ Pr.

Name-year system

Reiskin HR. 1980. Patterns of alcohol usage in a help-seeking university population [dissertation]. Boston: Boston University. 216 p. Available from: Boston: Boston Univ Pr.

Option: The five numbered entries in the "Cited References" page are formatted for a paper following the citation-sequence system, with entries listed in the order in which they are first cited in the text of the paper. A variation on the citation-sequence system: number citations in a paper can refer to alphabetized entries in the "Cited References" page, in which case these five references would be numbered—but alphabetized.

Listing periodicals in CBE format

Leave two typed spaces between each item in an entry. Sequence the items as follows:

- *Number:* Assign a number to the entry if you are using a citation-sequence system.
- *Author's name:* Put the last name first, followed by a space and the initials of the first and middle names. Leave no space between initials. After the initial(s), place a period. For an article with two or more authors, place a comma after the initials of each co-author. Do *not* use an ampersand (&) or the word *and* between authors.
- *Title of the article:* Do not use underlining or quotation marks. Capitalize the first letter of the first word only.
- *Journal name:* Abbreviate the name, unless it is a single-word name (such as *Nature*); do not underline. *The Journal of Molecular Evolution* would be abbreviated as J. Mol. Evol.
- *Publication information:* Format depends on whether you are using the citation-sequence system or the name-year system.

Journals

Citation-sequence system

Follow this format, observing spacing conventions.

```
Author(s). Article title. Journal title year;volume
number:inclusive pages.
```

6. Coleman RA, Pratt LH. Phytochrome: immunological assay of synthesis and destruction in plants. Planta 1974;119:221–231.

Name-year system

Follow this format, observing spacing conventions. Notice the placement of the year.

```
Author(s). Year. Article title. Journal title volume:inclusive
pages.
```

```
Coleman RA, Pratt LH. 1974. Phytochrome: immunological assay
of synthesis and destruction in plants. Planta 119:221–231.
```

Newspaper and magazine articles

Citation-sequence system

Follow this model (as quoted from *Scientific Style and Format*, 658). Observe space conventions.

Author(s). Article title. Newspaper title and date of publication;section designator:page number(column number).

7. Welch P. Kids and booze: it's 10 o'clock--do you know how drunk
   your kids are? Washington Post 1989 Dec 21;Sect C:1(col 3).

   Author(s). Article title. Magazine title and date of publica-
   tion:page numbers.

8. Waggoner G. Gin as tonic. Esquire 1990 Feb:30.

Newspaper and magazine articles

Name-year system

Follow this model (as quoted from *Scientific Style and Format*, 658). Observe
space conventions.

Author(s). Date of publication. Article title. Newspaper
title;section designator:page number(column number).

Welch P. 1989 Dec 21. Kids and booze: it's 10 o'clock--do you
know how drunk your kids are? Washington Post;Sect C:1(col 3).

Author(s). Date of publication. Article title. Magazine
title:page numbers.

Waggoner G. 1990 Feb. Gin as tonic. Esquire:30.

Listing electronic sources in the CBE Format

When citing sources from the Internet or other electronic media, the CBE recommends listing access location (URLs) and date accessed. Follow the formats above
for books, journals, and newspapers. After the journal, magazine, newspaper, or
book title, place brackets and list the type of electronic medium—for instance, *serial online*. Then conclude the entry with the following information.

Write *Available from* (no italics, followed by a colon). Provide the electronic
citation (or URL).

Write *Accessed* (no italics, not followed by colon). Provide year abbreviated
month day, followed by a period.

Citation-sequence

9. McDowell R. Colorado students struggle to understand rampage.
   Boston Globe [newspaper online]. 1999 Apr 21. Available from:
   http://www.globe.com/news/daily/21/school.htm Accessed 1999
   Apr 23.

Name-year

McDowell R. 1999 Ap 21. Colorado students struggle to understand rampage. Boston Globe [newspaper online]. Available from:
http://www.globe.com/news/daily/21/school.htm Accessed 1999
Apr 23.

CHAPTER **38**

Writing and Reading in the Humanities

T he *humanities*—traditionally considered as the disciplines of literature, history, and philosophy—address many puzzles of life and human nature, frequently by posing "large," difficult questions to which there are seldom definite answers. Those who study the humanities ask in distinctive ways such questions as these: Who are we? What are our responsibilities to ourselves? To others? What is a *good* life? How do we know what we know? Difficult questions lend themselves to difficult and varied answers, and answers in the humanities change from one culture to the next and from one generation to the next. Even within generations and cultures, answers vary. Ask two philosophers *how do we know what we know?* and you will likely get different responses. The same would hold if you approached two historians about the causes of the Civil War or two critics about the literary merit of Kate Chopin's novel *The Awakening*. Indeed, historians, philosophers, and literary critics may fiercely debate among themselves exactly which "large" questions should be asked and how one should go about investigating them.

Still, whatever their specific character, the large questions remain. Philosophers from Plato in ancient times to Richard Rorty today have continued to ask what it means to be an educated human. Two thousand years ago Homer's *Odyssey* told of a Mediterranean hero's search for identity and fulfillment, while James Joyce set his *Ulysses* on the same theme in modern-day Dublin. Thucydides in ancient Greece and Barbara Tuchman today have asked the historian's questions of how we as humans can interpret the events of the past. Such quests for meaning require readers and writers to judge evidence, to develop responsible opinions, to interpret events, and above all to appreciate the value of multiple perspectives.

Students of humanities are concerned with discovering or recreating relationships among (1) the world as it has been observed by or commented on by someone; (2) a *text* that somehow reflects the facts about or the observer's impressions of that world; and (3) an audience—a reader, listener, or viewer. Texts provide the occasion to learn how others have investigated the large questions and to investigate these questions ourselves. A text could be a novel, a philosophical treatise, a letter, a film, a symphony, a song, a poem, a sculpture, or a painting—any creation that records one person's response to or accounting of what is seen and that, later, can be read, viewed, or listened to by someone else.

In this formulation, history is the discipline in which readers question texts to learn what is revealed about a past event and what about that event might be pertinent to the present. Philosophy is the discipline in which readers study the articles and books (the *texts*) of those who, with rigorous and careful reasoning, have reflected on ideas important to understanding human nature. Literature is the discipline in which readers read a work of drama, poetry, or fiction to gain entry into an imaginative world and to learn how this text and its world is constructed, how it might reflect circumstances of the author's experience, and how it might comment on and force questions about the *reader's* experience. For the historian, philosopher, and student of literature, texts are the point of entry into the three-way relationship of text, creator/author, and audience. For a student in the humanities there is always the relationship; there is always the implicit understanding that texts are important and that as we read, view, listen to, and write about them, we create meaning ourselves. In the humanities, we *create* new texts as we study older ones. We carry on a tradition of raising and investigating difficult questions and, through our efforts, seek to grow more aware of who we are and what we have done (Frankel 8–9).[1]

▶ 38a   Writing in the humanities

▶ I   Expressing and informing in the humanities

Students in the humanities write for many purposes, two of which are to inform and to express. Expressive writing, often beginning as a personal response to an individual text, discusses questions such as these: What do I feel when reading this material? Why do I feel this way? How am I changed in response to this text? How can I account for differences I have observed between this text and others, or between this text and my own experience? Readers may find themselves so involved with a text that they want to respond in writing. You might consider keeping a reading journal in which you record responses to texts and, based on your entries, develop ideas for papers. Much of what is best about writing in the humanities begins as a personal response.

All writing in literature, history, and philosophy courses is, at least in part, informative. Working as an historian, you may need to sift through documents in order to establish a *sequence* to events on which to base a narrative—perhaps the story of how your grandparents came to this country. As a student of literature, you may *compare* and *contrast* works of the same author, responding to assignments such as this: *Choose two of Hawthorne's short stories and discuss his treatment of the origins and consequences of sin.* In a philosophy course, you might be asked to *classify* discussions on a topic, such as education, according to the types of arguments authors are making. In informing readers, you will often *define* and illustrate a term by referring to specific passages in a text.

---

[1]In-text citations in this chapter refer to the Works Cited list at the end of the book.

▶2 Making arguments

Frequently in the humanities, you will use informative writing to make arguments. The purpose of making arguments in literature, history, and philosophy is to *interpret* texts and to *defend* interpretations as reasonable.[2] No one will expect your arguments to end all discussion of a question, but as in any discipline, your arguments should be compelling and well supported. The purpose of reading stories, of retelling the past, or of puzzling through large questions is not to arrive at agreement (as in the sciences), but to deepen individual perception and to realize that we are part of a larger human community. The goal of an argument in the humanities is reached when readers can make this or a similar acknowledgment: "I understand your point of view, and I find it reasonable." You should therefore not expect to read—or write—a single, correct interpretation of a play. History professors will urge you to reject single, apparently definitive versions of the past. Philosophy professors will urge you to reject the notion that any one answer to the question *What is a good life?* could satisfy all people.

Consensus is not the goal of arguments in the humanities. But this is not to say that all arguments are equally valid. Arguments must be supported and well reasoned. They can be plainly wrong and they can be irresponsible, as when someone insists: "Since discussions in this course are based on personal opinions, my opinion is as good as anyone else's." Not true. One interpretation, argued well, can be clearly superior to and more compelling than another. In each of the humanities this is so, notwithstanding the fact that students of literature, history, and philosophy pose different questions and examine texts using different methods. As a student of literature, you might investigate living conditions during the Great Depression by reading novels such as *The Grapes of Wrath*. In a history class, you might work with oral accounts such as the one compiled by Studs Terkel in *Hard Times: An Oral History of the Great Depression*. In a philosophy course, you might read and debate discussions of a society's obligations to its poor. You would in every case be arguing for an interpretation, and in every case your argument would be more or less convincing, in light of the conventions for arguing in that discipline. You can help yourself focus on the purpose of argumentation in your humanities classes by posing these questions:

- What sorts of questions will I investigate in this course?
- How do the texts I study help to focus my attention on these questions?
- How do students in this discipline make claims about a text? How do they support these claims?

Claims and evidence

In making a *claim* in the humanities, a writer usually interprets a text. That is, the writer attempts to explain how the text is meaningful—how, for instance, a poem's

[2]This discussion is based directly on the work of Stephen Toulmin, Richard Rieke, and Allan Janik in *Introduction to Reasoning* (New York: Macmillan, 1979). See Chapter 12, their "Introduction" to fields of argument, 195–202; and Chapter 15, "Arguing about the Arts," 265–82. For a related discussion, see Richard D. Rieke and Malcolm O. Sillars, *Argumentation and the Decision Making Process*, 2nd ed. (Glenview: Scott, Foresman 1984).

images direct the reader's attention to certain themes, how an essay confirms or contradicts our understanding of a particular problem, how the content of a letter or diary suggests a revised understanding of some historical event. One much-relied-on process for making and supporting claims in the humanities goes something like this: during the process of reading, you begin to see a pattern emerge—you notice certain details and forge a link between them. (See the discussion of "thesis" at 3d and of "argumentative thesis" at 6b.) At first the pattern may not be well defined; but as you read and reread, the pattern becomes increasingly clear until you can express it as a formal claim. Your claim becomes the basis of an argument that says, in effect: here is one way in which this text is meaningful. You then provide *evidence* for your claim by pointing readers to the same passages in the text that helped you to detect a pattern, explaining why these passages are significant and how they confirm the reasonableness of your claim. The process of claim and support, then, looks like this:

1. Read a text and discover in it certain patterns that help to make the text meaningful (see 38d for hints on detecting patterns in literary works).
2. Reread and confirm that the pattern exists, and then make a claim: a formal statement in which you interpret some element of the text, its relationship to the reader, or its relationship to the writer and the times in which it was written.
3. Refer to the text as evidence for your claim.
4. Comment on or discuss these references (optional).

Consider the following examples of how claims are made and supported in major areas of the humanities.

A literary study. In a paragraph from an essay entitled "The Greatness of *Huckleberry Finn*," the literary critic Lionel Trilling claims that Huck Finn is a character who sympathizes with the misfortunes of others. As you read the paragraph, you will be watching Trilling make his claim *after* he had discovered it for himself. Trilling is persuasive, and you might find yourself thinking "This isn't an interpretation; it's a fact." But Trilling *is* interpreting the novel, and he is trying to convince you that his interpretation is both accurate and useful:

> [Huckleberry Finn's] sympathy is quick and immediate. When the circus audience laughs at the supposedly drunken man who tries to ride the horse, Huck is only miserable: "It wasn't funny to me . . . ; I was all of a tremble to see his danger." When he imprisons the intending murderers on the wrecked steamboat, his first thought is of how to get someone to rescue them, for he considers "how dreadful it was, even for murderers, to be in such a fix. I says to myself, there ain't no telling but I might come to be a murderer myself yet, and then how would I like it?" But his sympathy is never sentimental. When at last he knows that the murderers are beyond help, he has no inclination to false pathos. "I felt a little bit heavy-hearted about the gang, but not much, for I reckoned that if they could stand it I could." His will is genuinely good and therefore he has no need to torture himself with guilty second thoughts.[3]

---

[3]While Trilling's use of ellipses does not conform to current MLA style (see 29e) in that he does not mark his omission of quoted text with a bracket, his use does conform with conventions for altering quotations at the time this passage was written.

Notice that Trilling makes two related claims in this paragraph: first, that Huck's "sympathy is quick and immediate," and second, that this "sympathy is never sentimental." He refers the reader to specific passages that support his claims and, after a final quoted passage, makes a comment: "His [Huck's] will is genuinely good and therefore he has no need to torture himself with guilty second thoughts." With this comment, Trilling cements the relationship between the claims he has made and the evidence he has offered. He has made an *argument*. Be assured that Trilling's awareness of Huck's sympathies did not always exist. There must have been some point before which Trilling simply did not think about Huck's "quick and immediate" sympathy. We can assume that Trilling has read the novel many times; we can imagine that on one rereading he began to see a pattern emerging in various passages. We can further imagine that on noticing this pattern, Trilling was able to confirm and refine it by *re*reading various passages. At this point, he was prepared to write: to convert the pattern he had detected (then confirmed) into a claim, which he then used as the basis for an argument.

In one brief paragraph, Lionel Trilling demonstrates the cycle of claim, reference, and comment that is basic to writing about literature. *To make a claim about literature, first find a pattern of meaning in a text. Confirm and refine that pattern and then make a claim. To support this claim, return to the text and discuss specific passages.* An analysis of a literary text is built by linking many such cycles according to an overall plan or thesis. (See 38d for more on writing about literature.)

An historical study. The historian Joanna Stratton supports a claim in the following passage by referring to a source (information from a letter or journal) but does not comment on the source in the same way Trilling does for a literary text. In her book on pioneer women of the American Frontier, Stratton worked with interviews, letters, and journals that her great-grandmother had collected in the 1920s.

> For the most part, the cavelike dugout provided cramped and primitive quarters for the pioneering family. Damp and dark year round, it was practically impossible to keep clean, for dirt from the roof and the walls sifted onto everything. Although its thick earthen walls did afford warm insulation from the cold and strong protection from the wind, in rain the dugout became practically uninhabitable.
>
> "Father made a dugout and covered it with willows and grass," wrote one settler, "and when it rained, the water came through the roof and ran in the door. After the storms, we carried the water out with buckets, then waded around in the mud until it dried up. Then to keep us nerved up, sometimes the bull snakes would get in the roof and now and then one would lose his hold and fall down on the bed, then off on the floor. Mother would grab the hoe and there was something doing and after the fight was over Mr. Bull Snake was dragged outside. Of course there had to be something to keep us from getting discouraged."
>
> —JOANNA L. STRATTON, *Pioneer Women*

Often in an historical account the writer wants to maintain focus on the narrative or story, and so withholds immediate comment on a source quotation except in footnotes or in specialized analysis. *To make a claim in history, writers make interpretations of available records from the past and try to reconstruct them into a meaningful pattern.*

Sometimes the presentation of a claim in historical writing may seem not to be an interpretation at all:

[I]n the rain the dugout became practically uninhabitable.

This claim reads as a fact, but actually it is a generalization Joanna Stratton has reached based on available evidence, one example of which she provides with a supporting quotation. Other historians examining the same or different evidence might reach a different conclusion. The importance of an historian's interpretations becomes obvious when you read the conflicting accounts of the events immediately before and after Lincoln's assassination. If these conflicting accounts were based on eyewitness testimony, you would realize that historians must interpret evidence as well as gather it. While Lincoln *was* shot at Ford's Theatre on April 14, 1865, the precise circumstances of and reason for the shooting are subject to historical debate—or interpretation.

A philosophical study. The philosopher Ludwig Wittgenstein makes a claim in the following passage without reference to any written text, but rather to the meaning that is attached to a word and to the patterns of human activity that can be observed in connection with that word. In the process, Wittgenstein himself created a philosophical text, one that later became the subject of interpretation and claim by other philosophers. In this passage, Wittgenstein examines the difficulty of defining the word "game." He does so in the larger context of discussing the complexities of defining "language." Just as "family resemblances" describes the relationship between various games, so too does this term describe what is common to various languages—that is, there is no single feature but rather an array of features.

Consider for example the proceedings that we call "games." I mean board-games, card-games, ball-games, Olympic games, and so on. What is common to them all?—Don't say: "There *must* be something common, or they would not be called 'games'"—but *look and see* whether there is anything common to all.—For if you look at them you will not see something that is common to *all*, but similarities, relationships, and a whole series of them at that. To repeat: don't think, but look!—Look for example at board-games, with their multifarious relationships. Now pass to card-games; here you find many correspondences with the first group, but many common features drop out, and others appear. When we pass next to ball-games, much that is common is retained, but much is lost.—Are they all "amusing"? Compare chess with noughts and crosses. Or is there always winning and losing, or competition between players? Think of patience. In ball games there is winning and losing; but when a child throws his ball at the wall and catches it again, this feature has disappeared. Look at the parts played by skill and luck; and at the difference between skill in chess and skill in tennis. Think now of games like ring-a-ring-a-roses; here is the element of amusement, but how many other characteristic features have disappeared! And we can go through the many, many other groups of games in the same way; can see how similarities crop up and disappear.

And the result of this examination is: we see a complicated network of similarities overlapping and criss-crossing: sometimes overall similarities, sometimes similarities of detail.

I can think of no better expression to characterize these similarities than "family resemblances"; for the various resemblances between members of a family: build, features, colour of eyes, gait, temperament, etc. etc. overlap and criss-cross in the same way.—And I shall say: "games" form a family.

—LUDWIG WITTGENSTEIN, *Philosophical Investigations*

This passage has generated enormous discussion on the meaning and significance of "family resemblances." For example, some might argue that "amusement" is common to all games and might proceed to define that concept. As a student of philosophy, you will sometimes generate your own evidence for arguments; but more often, you will refer to and build on the work of the philosophers you are studying. Learning to make claims in philosophy can be especially demanding for those with little experience in the discipline. In literature and history, sources and what one writes about them are connected in concrete ways to a story, imagined or actually lived. Philosophy has no elements of story as such. *To support a claim in philosophy, you will focus on ideas and their relation to other ideas.* (Wittgenstein discusses specific games in order to develop his idea of "family resemblance.") Arguments, consequently, can become quite abstract.

The three examples of claims made by Trilling, Stratton, and Wittgenstein do not begin to represent the variety of claims you will encounter in your study of literature, history, and philosophy. These examples are meant to suggest that variety; they suggest, as well, a common concern in the humanities: interpretation. As you read and study in your courses, try to identify the specific types of claims that are made and the methods of evidence used to support them. To aid this process, pose these questions: What sorts of claims (interpretations) do people make in this subject? In what ways do writers use sources (books, films, works of art, or pieces of music) to support their claims?

▶ 38b Reading in the humanities

When you read a poem, a story, a letter, or an autobiography, you are working with a **primary source.** Of the preceding examples, only the one by Wittgenstein is a primary source. The writings of Trilling and Stratton are examples of **secondary sources,** the work of scholars who themselves have interpreted particular poems, stories, or letters. If you were writing a paper on *Huckleberry Finn*, you might refer to Trilling's interpretations. In doing so, you would need to read with care in order to understand and evaluate his ideas and to distinguish them from your own. In deciding whether to cite Trilling in your paper, you might ask: What point is he making? How well does he make it? Is his observation well grounded in the text that he quotes? On what basis do I agree or disagree with him?

A given source or text in the humanities can be studied from several perspectives within a discipline or across disciplines. Some writers look at a work as a whole, in a broad context of events or ideas surrounding it; others look closely at individual parts of the source, analyzing it independently of its original surroundings. For example, consider how differently Benjamin Franklin's *Autobiography* is studied in the following examples: as a literary expression, as political philosophy, or as an historical event.

Literary critic Joseph Fichtelberg (Fordham University) sees in the *Autobiography* a conscious effort by Franklin to sift through his life's work and beliefs in order to present himself as an "exemplar" to the world, a model of American virtue. The following constitutes one segment of Fichtelberg's argument, which appeared in the journal *Early American Literature*. Numbers in parentheses are page references to sources noted below:

That the correspondent—the reader—is crucial to Franklin's self-conception is evident throughout the *Autobiography*. Part One, readers have often noted, appears to be a fatherly homily to an ambitious young man. "Now imagining it may be equally agreeable to you to know the Circumstances of *my* Life," Franklin begins, alluding to his spectacular success, "I sit down to write them for you" (I). But as Governor of New Jersey in 1771, William Franklin was successful in his own right, hardly in need of counsel, and, at forty-four, hardly a young man. Rather, Franklin seems to be writing for the "Posterity" he addresses several lines later, indeed, for all American readers, who may find his narrative "suitable to their own Situations, & therefore fit to be imitated" (I). Hence his character, as Mitchell Breitwieser notes, would "liv[e] on in the person of the emulating reader, and [. . .] gai[n] a wider circulation than it otherwise would have" (265, 270). As he announces his intention to recount the "conducing Means"—the process—by which he achieves eminence, so Franklin's prose emphasizes the reader's own immersion in that process. The fourth sentence in this introductory paragraph (a revision, incidentally, of an earlier draft) is resonantly ungrammatical:

Having emerg'd from the Poverty & Obscurity in which I was born & bred, to a State of Affluence & some Degree of Reputation in the World, and having gone so far thro' Life with a considerable Share of Felicity, the conducing Means I made Use of, which with the Blessing of God, so well succeeded, my Posterity may like to know, as they may find some of them suitable to their own Situations, & therefore fit to be imitated. (I)

As Tatham notes, the two dangling participial phrases[4] shift the emphasis from the grammatical subject to "my Posterity," as if "future Americans in general" had taken Franklin's course to affluence and were now eager to understand the "Means," the particular process of their ascent (228).

WORKS CITED [BY FICHTELBERG]

Breitwieser, Mitchell. *Cotton Mather and Benjamin Franklin: The Price of Representative Personality*. Cambridge: Cambridge UP, 1984.
Franklin, Benjamin. *The Autobiography of Benjamin Franklin: A Genetic Text*. Ed. J. A. Leo Lemay and P. M. Zall. Knoxville: U of Tennessee P, 1981.
Tatham, Campbell. "Benjamin Franklin, Cotton Mather, and the Outward State." *Early American Literature* 6 (Winter 1971–72): 223–33.

This analysis focuses on Franklin's *Autobiography* as a work of literature. Joseph Fichtelberg is interested in the relationship between Franklin and the readers he presumably had in mind when composing the *Autobiography*. Fichtelberg begins

[4]Fichtelberg assumes readers will follow the reference here to the following phrases: "Having emerg'd [. . .] in the World, and having gone so far [. . .] so well succeeded." The obvious grammatical subject of these phrases is "I"—Franklin is the one who emerged from poverty and who went through life with such success. In the *Autobiography*, however, Franklin dangles these phrases (see 15h) and places "my Posterity" where the grammatical subject, "I," should occur. Both Fichtelberg and the writer he cites (Tatham) find this significant.

with a claim that the reader is crucial to the way Franklin thinks of and presents himself in the *Autobiography*. As evidence for this claim, Fichtelberg quotes from the obvious *primary* source, and he refers to *secondary* sources, the work of two literary critics also interested in Franklin. These references, it should be added, place Fichtelberg's own investigation in a tradition of literary criticism. Writers in *every* discipline similarly refer to the work of others in that discipline to benefit from previous research and to become members of a scholarly community. What identifies Fichtelberg's writing as specifically *literary* criticism is not only his references to secondary sources who are themselves literary critics but also his method of arguing: he relies on a cycle of claim and text-based support that is common to literary studies (see 38a-2). Most important, Fichtelberg assumes that the *Autobiography* is a work of literature. He wants to investigate the role that readers played in the creation of a text.

Philosopher Ralph Ketchem approaches the *Autobiography* with an entirely different set of concerns. He sees in Franklin's work an expression of the author's philosophy on the power of individual initiative in politics:

> As a public philosopher, Franklin assumed that the traditional personal values have political relevance. He shared the Aristotelian belief that government exists for the sake of the good life and that its powers can be used to that end. A good citizen, guided by the virtues Franklin encouraged in *Poor Richard's Almanack* and in his *Autobiography*, would undertake civic improvement and participate disinterestedly in government. In an expanding country filled with opportunity, Franklin saw individual initiative as the essential engine of progress, but he did not hesitate to seek whatever seemed required for the public good through government. His confidence in the virtue of the citizens of the United States caused him to favor government by consent, but he was not a simple democrat who believed majority will should be omnipotent. He accepted democracy because he thought it would yield good government; if it did not, he readily rejected it.

Ketchem shows how the *Autobiography* was part of Franklin's overall ambition to promote the role of the individual and of personal values as a force in political life. He supports his claims by focusing on Franklin's ideas about individual values in relation to other ideas about the role of government.

Still another viewpoint, from Franklin's biographer Carl Van Doren, looks at how parts of the *Autobiography* were written and read in their own time and afterward. While literary or philosophical analysts see the work as a self-contained expression of current or ongoing American ideas, the historian looks at the concrete events of the work's arrival and reception.

> The two copies went off to England and France to set in train the complex textual history of this simple book: of which three parts appeared first in French, and of which the earliest English editions were retranslations from the French, and of which [the author's son] Temple Franklin published as authorized in 1818, the copy sent to Le Veillard instead of Franklin's original, which was not published entire, as Franklin wrote it, till 1868. At some time after the copies [of the original manuscript] were made, Franklin, in the six painful months left to him, wrote the fragmentary fourth part and then broke off. It seems likely that he himself had made the revisions which in the copy tamed the original. He could no longer trust his taste and could now and then prefer round academic phrases to his own natural sharp, homely ones. He had lived too long, and put off writing too late, to be able to do justice to himself in a book. His greatest

years would have to stay unwritten. He might truly have reflected that this was not altogether the loss it seemed. Plenty of other men could find materials for the story of his latest years. Only he had known about his obscure youth, which could never again be obscure. (767–68)

Van Doren's claims and interpretations try to establish how and where the work came into existence, and the extent to which it reflected Franklin's public versus private personality. The argument follows the pattern of interpreting records to reconstruct a meaningful pattern of events for Franklin's life.

Fichtelberg, Ketchem, and Van Doren interpret a single text differently, according to their separate disciplinary perspectives. Each makes a claim—a statement that expresses the pattern of meaning each author had found in the work he was examining.

Fichtelberg   That the correspondent—the reader—is crucial to Franklin's self-conception is evident throughout the *Autobiography*.

Ketchem   As a public philosopher, Franklin assumed that the traditional personal values have political relevance.

Van Doren   [The *Autobiography* has a] complex textual history.

If all three writers were literary critics, philosophers, or historians, they might just as likely offer different interpretations, since each of the humanities has its subdisciplines or subfields, each of which in turn is guided by a unique perspective. (For examples of this variety in literary studies, see 38d-4.) The more experienced you become in any of these disciplines, the more you will differentiate among perspectives *within* disciplines. *Perspective* determines how you will read, what questions you will pursue, and what interpretations you will make—both between and within disciplines.

▶ 38c   Types of writing assignments in the humanities

The writing assignments that you will most often encounter in your humanities courses—close analyses of texts, research papers, and book reviews—have in a gen-

http://humanitas.ucsb.edu/shuttle/general.html
An extensive listing of general humanities resources from the Voice of the Shuttle website.

eral way been addressed in Chapter 2, "Critical Thinking and Writing." The discussion here will introduce the special requirements of these assignments in the humanities and will refer you to pertinent sections in Chapter 2.

▶ 1   The analysis

An **analysis** is an investigation that you conduct by applying a principle or definition to an activity or to an object in order to see how that activity or object works, what it might mean, or why it might be significant. As a writer, your job is to identify and discuss particular parts, or features, of the text that you feel are especially meaningful. In analyzing a short story or novel, for instance, you might focus on characters, themes, plot, or structure. You might analyze a poem for its rhymes, meter, or symbols (see 38d). These features, which are mutually reinforcing, give literary texts their meaning—though the meaning of a work will never be a simple sum of its analyzed parts. Good literature invites and can sustain multiple analyses without ever being "explained away."

Historical events similarly invite a variety of analyses. As one teacher of history has put it, "[H]istorians like to argue [for differing interpretations of events]. In fact, they disagree to a greater or lesser extent in their views of personalities and events in every major period in United States History, from Captain John Smith to William Westmoreland, from the American Revolution to the computer revolution" (O'Reilly 281). Historians present conflicting interpretations in order to understand as fully as possible the causes of events. These causes are usually complex and resist (as mature works of literature resist) a single, definitive explanation.

As a student of literature, philosophy, and history, you will use features specific to these disciplines in conducting your analyses. You have seen previously (in 38b) that one text can be analyzed as a work of literature, philosophy, or history, depending on a writer's perspective. Perspective determines the way in which a writer divides a text into analyzable parts. The more you study in a discipline, the more you will learn which features of a text are important to that discipline and, hence, which are worth analyzing.

The following general pattern serves as a model for writing an analysis, regardless of discipline. Placement of one or more of these elements in a paper may vary according to discipline; but when writing an analysis you can expect to touch on the following:

- Introduce the work being analyzed and the interpretation you will make (your claim).
- Introduce the features you will use to analyze the text. Your choice of features will depend on the discipline in which you are writing.
- Conduct your analysis by discussing one feature of a text (or idea) at a time. For literary texts, quote specific passages and *comment* on the ways the passage supports your interpretation (see 38a-2).
- Conclude by summing up the evidence for your interpretation. Show how the features you have discussed separately reinforce one another in creating the effect or quality you have argued for.

Section 2c discussed analysis as an investigation conducted by systematically applying a set of *principles*. In introductory courses to literature, this set of principles will be general if you are interpreting a poem or story according to standard features such as *theme*. (Other standard features are suggested in 38d-4.) In advanced literature courses, and also in philosophy and history courses, you may be asked to analyze a text or some situation by applying a much-discussed theory. In a philosophy course, for example, you might be asked to apply Wittgenstein's notion of "family resemblances" to some activity other than games. In this instance, your professor would be asking that you analyze a situation, based on principles laid out in a specific source.

2 The book review

You may be asked to read and review a book for your courses, both inside and outside of the humanities. The purpose of a review is to make a judgment about the worth of a text and to communicate and justify that judgment to a reader. See 2b for an extended discussion on preparing and writing a review (which in 2b is called an *evaluation*). Before writing to evaluate you should *read* to evaluate. That is, you should understand what an author has written so that you can summarize main points; you should distinguish an author's facts from opinions; and you should distinguish your assumptions from those of the author. Your overall assessment of a book will rest largely on the extent to which you and the author share assumptions about the subject being discussed.

▶3 The research paper

A research paper calls on you to investigate some topic, using both primary and secondary sources. Often, a research paper in the humanities is an analysis (see 38c-1) that you set in a broader context. In writing an analysis, you typically read and interpret a single text—in the paper that follows, it is a short story ("A Shameful Affair") by Kate Chopin. Broadening your effort into a research paper, you would analyze the story and also draw on available scholarship as an aid to your analysis. Research will also help provide a context for your thesis. By reviewing the literature on your topic, you tap into the conversation that has taken place concerning it. Aware of what others have written, you can add your voice (through your paper) and contribute to the conversation.

For her paper on "A Shameful Affair," Brandy Brooks turned to the work of two Chopin scholars, Joyce Dyer and Martin Simpson. In a research paper, you remain responsible for developing and supporting an interpretation. You draw on sources, as needed, to help make your points.

Gathering sources on a topic and using them judiciously, according to a plan, is the activity central to writing a research paper. In 2d you will find a discussion on writing a synthesis based on multiple sources. To write an effective research paper in the humanities, you must be able to read multiple sources on a topic, understand the main points of each, and then link these points to one another and to your own guiding interpretation, or thesis. In short, you must read source materials effectively. (See Chapter 1, "Critical Thinking and Reading.") If you are uncertain of your ability to draw on and refer to multiple sources, also see Chapters 33, 34, and 35 on the research process. In Chapter 37, you will find a discussion on how to cite sources when writing a paper. In the humanities, you will generally follow the MLA form for documenting sources.

▶38d Writing about literature[5]

To write knowledgeably about a literary work—about a poem, a play, a short story, or a novel—you need to understand, generally, how arguments are made in the humanities. In 38a-2 you saw that arguments in the humanities depend on a cycle of

---

[5]In this discussion, the term *literature* refers to works of art *in writing:* poems, plays, and fiction. The expression "review of the literature," common in the humanities, social sciences, and sciences, refers to a writer's presentation of prior research on a topic. Such a presentation is usually meant to set a broader context for a paper and to demonstrate the need for additional research.

claim, reference to a text, and comment. In that same discussion and in 38b you found examples of such arguments about literary texts (about *Huckleberry Finn* and Franklin's *Autobiography*). The cases illustrated a cycle of claim, reference, and comment. If you have not already done so, read these sections of the chapter. The discussion here assumes your familiarity with the terms *claim*, *text*, *refer/reference*, and *comment*.

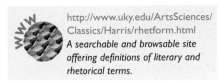

http://www.uky.edu/ArtsSciences/Classics/Harris/rhetform.html
A searchable and browsable site offering definitions of literary and rhetorical terms.

First reading: Respond

> On a *first* reading, respond to the text.

Personal response is fundamental to the critical reading of *any* text. See Chapter 1 for a discussion of critical reading, generally, and of the importance of responding. Pose these questions to a text: *What can I learn from this selection? What is my background on the subject that this selection concerns? What is the origin of my views on the topics of this text? What new interest, or what new question or observation, does this text spark in me?* These questions, which you can ask of any text, can be refined somewhat when applied to literary texts.

Developing a personal response requires that you read a text closely, in such a way that you are alert to details that make the text meaningful. At the risk of stating the obvious, you should prepare for a close reading by finding a block of uninterrupted time when you are feeling alert and able to concentrate on what you read. Realize that close reading involves *multiple* readings. Expect that you will read a full text twice and selected parts of the text three or more times. On your first reading, disregard for the moment the paper you intend to write and read to be engaged, even moved. Read for the same reasons people have read or listened to stories and poetry or watched dramas for centuries: to be fascinated, to learn something of other lives, to wonder, and to question. Writing about literature is premised on the belief that the text you are examining *is* worthy of your extended reflection. If you have not thought about what you have read, if you have not responded to it personally, you can hardly expect to write about it with conviction.[6]

[6]Which specific features of a text merit our calling it *literature* is a matter of some controversy. There is the traditional "canon," the body of works that for generations scholars (and an obedient public) have regarded as important texts in Western culture: Shakespeare, Keats, Brontë, Shelly, Melville, and many more. But a difficulty arises: Given that authors are forever creating new texts, why are some texts added to the canon, the "important" list worthy of study, while other texts are excluded? Applied historically, this same question has caused a revolution in literary studies: What makes Shakespeare, Shelley, and the others canonical—that is, examples of what we call literature? Why were *they* included in the canon and not more women writers, more minorities, or more representatives of less industrial nations? Who made, and who makes, decisions about what texts are to be called literature? What assumptions about art and culture guide these decision makers, and might not different assumptions lead us to create a different canon? These explosive questions may well become guiding concerns in one of your literature courses. Suffice it to say that what counts as "literature" is under intense scrutiny at the moment.

Questions to prompt a personal response on a first reading

- What do I feel when reading this material? Why do I feel this way?
- Does this text make me *want* to read? Why or why not?
- What about this text is worth reading a second time?
- How am I challenged by or changed in response to this text?
- With what questions does this text leave me?
- What differences do I see between the author's observations of the world and my own? How can I explain these differences?

Personal responses based on these and related questions can make you want to know more about what you have read. For instance, if on completing a story, drama, or poem you find yourself *moved, offended, challenged, saddened, confused, needled,* or *intrigued,* you will have an immediate and even pressing reason to return for a second reading. And it is the second reading in which you will discover the patterns that will enable you to write a worthwhile paper. Sometimes, you may need to brainstorm after a first reading in order to understand your particular response to a text (see 3b-2). What follows is a demonstration of such a brainstorming session. Brandy Brooks, whose paper you will read in 38e, spent five minutes writing out her responses to "A Shameful Affair," a short story by Kate Chopin. Read Chopin's story here, along with Brooks's marginal notes from her first reading:

"A Shameful Affair"
Kate Chopin

Kate Chopin (1851–1904) is a much-admired nineteenth-century American writer known widely for her novel *The Awakening* (1899) and for two collections of short stories, *Bayou Folk* (1894) and *A Night in Arcadie* (1897). Chopin began her career as a published writer when she was thirty-eight years old, after her husband died and she was left to care for six children.

1   Mildred Orme, seated in the snuggest corner of the big front porch of the Kraummer farmhouse, was as content as a girl need hope to be.

2   This was no such farm as one reads about in humorous fiction. Here were swelling acres where the undulating wheat gleamed in the sun like a golden sea. For silver there was the Meramec—or, better, it was pure crystal, for here and there one might look clean through it down to where the pebbles lay like green and yellow gems. Along the river's edge trees were growing to the very water, and in it, sweeping it when they were willows.

Beautiful. I can see the river.

3   The house itself was big and broad, as country houses should be. The master was big and broad, too. The mistress was small and thin, and it was always she who went out at noon to pull the great clanging bell that called the farmhands in to dinner.

4   From her agreeable corner where she lounged with her Browning or her Ibsen, Mildred watched the woman do this every day. Yet when the clumsy farmhands all came tramping up the steps and crossed the porch in going to their meal that was served within, she never looked at them. Why should she? Farmhands are not so very nice to look at, and she was nothing of an anthropologist. But once when the half dozen men came along, a paper which she had laid carelessly upon the railing was blown across their path. One of

them picked it up, and when he had mounted the steps restored it to her. He was young, and brown, of course, as the sun had made him. He had nice blue eyes. His fair hair was dishevelled. His shoulders were broad and square and his limbs strong and clean. A not unpicturesque figure in the rough attire that bared his throat to view and gave perfect freedom to his every motion.

The young man gets M's attention, and mine.

5   Mildred did not make these several observations in the half second that she looked at him in courteous acknowledgment. It took her as many days to note them all. For she singled him out each time that he passed her, meaning to give him a condescending little smile, as she knew how. But he never looked at her. To be sure, clever young women of twenty who are handsome, besides, who have refused their half dozen offers and are settling down to the conviction that life is a tedious affair, are not going to care a straw whether farmhands look at them or not. And Mildred did not care, and the thing would not have occupied her a moment if Satan had not intervened, in offering the employment which natural conditions had failed to supply. It was summer time; she was idle; she was piqued, and that was the beginning of the shameful affair.

6   "Who are these men, Mrs. Kraummer, that work for you? Where do you pick them up?"

7   "Oh, ve picks 'em up everywhere. Some is neighbors, some is tramps, and so."

8   "And that broad-shouldered young fellow—is he a neighbor? The one who handed me my paper the other day—you remember?"

9   "Gott, no! you might yust as vell say he was a tramp. Abet he vorks like a steam ingine."

10   "Well, he's an extremely disagreeable-looking man. I should think you'd be afraid to have him about, not knowing him."

11   "Vat you vant to be 'fraid for?" laughed the little woman. "He don't talk no more un ven he vas deef und dumb. I didn't t'ought you vas sooch a baby."

12   "But, Mrs. Kraummer, I don't want you to think I'm a baby, as you say, a coward, as you mean. Ask the man if he will drive me to church tomorrow. You see, I'm not so very much afraid of him," she added with a smile.

13   The answer which this unmannerly farmhand returned to Mildred's request was simply a refusal. He could not drive her to church because he was going fishing.

14   "Aber," offered good Mrs. Kraummer, "Hans Platzfeldt vill drive you to church, oder verever you vants. He vas a goot boy vat you can trust, dat Hans."

15   "Oh, thank him very much. But I find I have so many letters to write tomorrow, and it promises to be hot, too. I shan't care to go to church after all."

16   She could have cried for vexation. Snubbed by a farmhand! a tramp, perhaps. She, Mildred Orme, who ought really to have been with the rest of the family at Narragansett—who had come to seek in this retired spot the repose that would enable her to follow exalted lines of thought. She marveled at the problematic nature of farmhands.

17   After sending her the uncivil message already recorded, and as he passed beneath the porch where she sat, he did look at her finally, in a way to make her positively gasp at the sudden effrontery of the man.

18   But the inexplicable look stayed with her. She could not banish it.

II

19   It was not so very hot after all, the next day, when Mildred walked down the long narrow footpath that led through the bending wheat to the river. High above her waist reached the yellow grain. Mildred's brown eyes filled with a reflected golden light as they caught the glint of it, as she heard the trill that it answered to the gentle breeze. Anyone who has walked through the wheat in midsummer-time knows that sound.

Again I can see this. M into the wheat.

20   In the woods it was sweet and solemn and cool. And there beside the river was the wretch who had annoyed her, first, with his indifference, then with the sudden boldness of his glance.

21   "Are you fishing?" she asked politely and with kindly dignity, which she supposed would define her position toward him. The inquiry lacked not pertinence, seeing that he sat motionless, with a pole in his hand and his eyes fixed on a cork that bobbed aimlessly on the water.

22   "Yes, madam," was his brief reply.

23   "It won't disturb you if I stand here a moment, to see what success you will have?"

24   "No, madam."

25   She stood very still, holding tight to the book she had brought with her. Her straw hat had slipped disreputably to one side, over the wavy bronze-brown bang that half covered her forehead. Her cheeks were ripe with color that the sun had coaxed there; so were her lips.

26   All the other farmhands had gone forth in Sunday attire. Perhaps this one had none better than these working clothes that he wore. A feminine commiseration swept her at the thought. He spoke never a word. She wondered how many hours he could sit there, so patiently waiting for fish to come to his hook. For her part, the situation began to pall, and she wanted to change it at last.

27   "Let me try a moment, please? I have an idea."

28   "Yes, madam."

29   "The man is surely an idiot, with his monosyllables," she commented inwardly. But she remembered that monosyllables belong to a boor's equipment.

30   She laid her book carefully down and took the pole gingerly that he came to place in her hands. Then it was his turn to stand back and look respectfully and silently on at the absorbing performance.

31   "Oh!" cried the girl, suddenly, seized with excitement upon seeing the line dragged deep in the water.

32   "Wait, wait! Not yet."

33   He sprang to her side. With his eyes eagerly fastened on the tense line, he grasped the pole to prevent her drawing it, as her in-

tention seemed to be. That is, he meant to grasp the pole, but instead, his brown hand came down upon Mildred's white one.

34 He started violently at finding himself so close to a bronze-brown tangle that almost swept his chin—to a hot cheek only a few inches away from his shoulder, to a pair of young, dark eyes that gleamed for an instant unconscious things into his own.

35 Then, why ever it happened, or how ever it happened, his arms were holding Mildred and he kissed her lips. She did not know if it was ten times or only once.

The moment!
Kiss

36 She looked around—her face milk white—to see him disappear with rapid strides through the path that had brought her there. Then she was alone.

37 Only the birds had seen, and she could count on their discretion. She was not wildly indignant, as many would have been. Shame stunned her. But through it she gropingly wondered if she should tell the Kraummers that her chaste lips had been rifled of their innocence. Publish her own confusion? No! Once in her room she would give calm thought to the situation, and determine then how to act. The secret must remain her own: a hateful burden to bear alone until she could forget it.

III

38 And because she feared not to forget it, Mildred wept that night. All day long a hideous truth had been thrusting itself upon her that made her ask herself if she could be mad. She feared it. Else why was that kiss the most delicious thing she had known in her twenty years of life? The sting of it had never left her lips since it was pressed into them. The sweet trouble of it banished sleep from her pillow.

39 But Mildred would not bend the outward conditions of her life to serve any shameful whim that chanced to visit her soul, like an ugly dream. She would avoid nothing. She would go and come as always.

40 In the morning she found in her chair upon the porch the book she had left by the river. A fresh indignity! But she came and went as she intended to, and sat as usual upon the porch amid her familiar surroundings. When the Offender passed her by she knew it, though her eyes were never lifted. Are there only sight and sound to tell such things? She discerned it by a wave that swept her with confusion and she knew not what besides.

41 She watched him furtively, one day, when he talked with Farmer Kraummer out in the open. When he walked away she remained like one who has drunk much wine. Then unhesitatingly she turned and began her preparations to leave the Kraummer farmhouse.

42 When the afternoon was far spent they brought letters to her. One of them read like this:

43 "My Mildred, deary! I am only now at Narragansett, and so broke up not to find you. So you are down at the Kraummer farm, on the Iron Mountains. Well! What do you think of that delicious crank, Fred Evelyn? For a man must be a crank who does such things. Only fancy! Last year he chose to drive an engine back and forth across the plains. This year he tills the soil with laborers. Next

year it will be something else as insane—because he likes to live more lives than one kind, and other Quixotic reasons. We are great chums. He writes me he's grown as strong as an ox. But he hasn't mentioned that you are there. I know you don't get on with him, for he isn't a bit intellectual—detests Ibsen and abuses Tolstoi. He doesn't read 'in books'—says they are spectacles for the short-sighted to look at life through. Don't snub him, dear, or be too hard on him; he has a heart of gold, if he is the first crank in America."

44   Mildred tried to think—to feel the intelligence which this letter brought to her would take somewhat of the sting from the shame that tortured her. But it did not. She knew that it could not.

45   In the gathering twilight she walked through the wheat that was heavy and fragrant with dew. The path was very long and very narrow. When she was midway she saw the Offender coming toward her. What could she do? Turn and run, as a little child might? Spring into the wheat, as some frightened four footed creature would? There was nothing but to pass him with the dignity which the occasion clearly demanded.

46   But he did not let her pass. He stood squarely in the pathway before her, hat in hand, a perturbed look upon his face.

47   "Miss Orme," he said, "I have wanted to say to you, every hour of the past week, that I am the most consummate hound that walks the earth."

(He's no farmhand.)

48   She made no protest. Her whole bearing seemed to indicate that her opinion coincided with his own.

49   "If you have a father, or brother, or any one, in short, to whom you may say such things—"

50   "I think you aggravate the offense, sir by speaking of it. I shall ask you never to mention it again. I want to forget that it ever happened. Will you kindly let me by."

51   "Oh," he ventured eagerly, "you want to forget it! Then, maybe, since you are willing to forget, you will be generous enough to forgive the offender some day?"

52   "Some day," she repeated, almost inaudibly, looking seemingly through him, but not at him—"some day—perhaps; when I shall have forgiven myself."

53   He stood motionless, watching her slim, straight figure lessening by degrees as she walked slowly away from him. He was wondering what she meant. Then a sudden, quick wave came beating into his brown throat and staining it crimson, when he guessed what it might be.

Why crimson?

Brandy Brooks wrote for several minutes on completing "A Shameful Affair." Here is her response:

```
I'm impressed by how vivid the images are involving colors in this
story. In any passage where Chopin uses color to describe a scene
or a character, the mental picture that I developed was bright
and clear. It seems like Chopin's color descriptions act as a
highlighter to focus me on an event or passage and signal its
```

importance. Her use of color adds drama and evokes emotion--like when Mildred's walking through the wheat. That's a beautiful spot, and Chopin for the first time lets us see Mildred.

▶**2 Second reading: Analyze the text—find patterns of meaning in it based on your response.**

> Ask *why* and *how* of your personal response, and you will have a specific, guiding question to lead you through a second reading. your goal with this question is to understand your response by finding a pattern that makes the text meaningful.

In Chapter 2, you will find an extended discussion on the ways in which thoughtful writing is based on a close, critical reading of a text. Certainly, thoughtful writing about literature is based on your reading of the literary work. *Response* is the first component of this reading; *analysis,* based on that response, is the second. See 2c for a general discussion on writing analyses. The principles established there apply to this discussion as well.

You can approach a second reading of a text by working with the response that most interested you in your first reading. Convert that response into a pointed question by asking *Why? How? What are some examples?* Guided by this question, return to the text and analyze it (see 2c-2). If your analysis succeeds, it will yield insights into how the text works, how you think it achieves its meaning in one particular way (with respect to your question). As you read a second time, make notes in the margin wherever you feel the text provides details that can help you answer your guiding question. These notes, considered in light of your question, can suggest a pattern that makes the text meaningful. You can write a successful paper by presenting this same pattern to your reader.

Following is an illustration of a second reading—selected paragraphs from the section of "A Shameful Affair" in which Mildred walks through the wheat field in search of Fred Evelyn. The excerpt is accompanied by Brandy Brooks's margin notes. The question she used to guide her second reading was as follows: *How does Chopin use colors in this story to communicate Mildred's emotions and her growing awareness?* Note how the question builds directly on the response she made in her five-minute brainstorming session, in which her main concern was with color. Observe how she uses her question to tease out details in the story that will, subsequently, provide her with material for a paper. If you have trouble deciding on a question to guide your second reading, reflect again on your response to the text. See also 38d-4 for a discussion of how you can pose specific questions based on one or another theory of literary criticism.

19   It was not so very hot after all, the next day, when Mildred walked down the long narrow footpath that led through the bending wheat to the river. High above her waist reached the yellow grain. Mildred's brown eyes filled with a reflected golden light as

M in the wheat—a setting filled w/ Nature's color.

they caught the glint of it, as she heard the trill that it answered to the gentle breeze. Anyone who has walked through the wheat in midsummer-time knows that sound.

20   In the woods it was sweet and solemn and cool. And there beside the river was the wretch who had annoyed her, first, with his indifference, then with the sudden boldness of his glance.

21   "Are you fishing?" she asked politely and with kindly dignity, which she supposed would define her position toward him. The inquiry lacked not pertinence, seeing that he sat motionless, with a pole in his hand and his eyes fixed on a cork that bobbed aimlessly on the water.

22   "Yes, madam," was his brief reply.

23   "It won't disturb you if I stand here a moment, to see what success you will have?"

24   "No, madam."

25   She stood very still, holding tight to the book she had brought with her. Her straw hat had slipped disreputably to one side, <u>over the wavy bronze-brown bang</u> that half covered her forehead. <u>Her cheeks were ripe with color</u> that the sun had coaxed there; <u>so were her lips</u>.

Now M has color—hair, cheeks, lips. She's part of Nature!

26   All the other farmhands had gone forth in Sunday attire. Perhaps this one had none better than these working clothes that he wore. A feminine commiseration swept her at the thought. He spoke never a word. She wondered how many hours he could sit there, so patiently waiting for fish to come to his hook. For her part, the situation began to pall, and she wanted to change it at last.

27   "Let me try a moment, please? I have an idea."

28   "Yes, madam."

29   "The man is surely an idiot, with his monosyllables," she commented inwardly. But she remembered that monosyllables belong to a boor's equipment.

30   She laid her book carefully down and took the pole gingerly that he came to place in her hands. Then it was his turn to stand back and look respectfully and silently on at the absorbing performance.

31   "Oh!" cried the girl, suddenly, seized with excitement upon seeing the line dragged deep in the water.

32   "Wait, wait! Not yet."

33   He sprang to her side. With his eyes eagerly fastened on the tense line, he grasped the pole to prevent her drawing it, as her intention seemed to be. That is, he meant to grasp the pole, but instead, <u>his brown hand came down upon Mildred's white one.</u>

A touch— the moment, & described in colors.

34   He started violently at finding himself so close to a <u>bronze-brown tangle</u> that almost swept his chin—to a hot cheek only a few inches away from his shoulder, to a pair of young, <u>dark eyes that gleamed</u> for an instant unconscious things into his own.

35   Then, why ever it happened, or how ever it happened, his arms were holding Mildred and he kissed her lips. She did not know if it was ten times or only once.

36   She looked around—<u>her face milk white</u>—to see him disappear with rapid strides through the path that had brought her there. Then she was alone.

Color drains out of M's face.

► 3 Construct a pattern of meaning: Making claims and providing evidence

> Refine the pattern you have found and make a claim. Locate passages in the text that support this claim.

Based on your first and second readings of a text, you are ready to make a claim: to state for your readers the pattern you have found and your reasons for believing this pattern is worth your time pursuing and your reader's time considering. With her first and second readings of Chopin's "A Shameful Affair," in mind, Brandy Brooks developed this claim:

```
In "A Shameful Affair," Kate Chopin communicates Mildred Orme's
sexual awakening through descriptions of a farm and, particularly,
through the colors one finds there.
```

Brooks has found a pattern that helps make Chopin's story meaningful to her, and she formally expresses this pattern as a claim. That Brooks found this pattern and not another should not suggest that other patterns do not exist. Many do. "A Shameful Affair" is a story rich with meaning and, like any literary work, lends itself to countless interpretations. The point to remember is that whatever pattern a student of literature finds in a text, she or he is obliged to show readers why, given all the patterns that *could* be found, this one is reasonable and worth the reader's consideration. A writer demonstrates the worthiness of a pattern, or claim, by repeatedly referring the reader to the text—a primary source, and when pertinent, to secondary sources. (See 38a and b.) Again, you have seen in examples in this chapter (38a-2) how claims in the humanities in general, and claims about literary texts in particular, are supported. Often, before planning an argument in support of a claim, the writer will prepare a sketch. Here's how Brooks planned to support the claim above, based on both her reading of the text and her reading of two secondary sources.

```
Intro
    Chopin: sexual awakening, symbolism, importance of location
    Claim
Plot summary
1st demonstration of color being important--farm setting
    Reference to Joyce Dyer--symbolism of farm, nature
2nd demo of color--intro of Fred Evelyn
3rd demo of color--Mildred into the wheat, to see Fred
4th demo of color--but color not used (after kiss)
5th demo of color--reintroduced at key point, the end
Conclusion
    Reference to Martin Simpson
```

When you read the paper in 38e, you will see that Brooks used this sketch as a guide to selecting passages in "A Shameful Affair" and in secondary sources that helped her to support her claim about Chopin's use of color. You will find on reading the paper that Brooks adheres closely to her sketch; that her sketch is built directly from the notes she made in her second reading; and that her second reading followed directly from the question that evolved from her first, personal response to the story.

Writing about Poetry

In analyzing and writing about a poem, approach the text as a *literary* text, in the manner discussed in this chapter. Given that most poetry is brief (compared to the length of short fiction and, of course, the length of novels and dramatic works), you have the luxury of being able to read and reread the poem.

- Read the poem several times and respond.
- Continue to read the poem, looking for a pattern of meaning.
- Express the pattern as a claim; cite lines of the poem to support your claim.

See the example essay in 38e for an illustration on how you might make and support a claim about a poem. Follow the convention illustrated in that paper for introducing lines of poetry: summarize the point you are making about the poem and then prepare readers for a quotation. Using present-tense verbs, familiarize the reader with a specific part of the poem. Then quote, as in this example:

> Stephen Crane's bleak view of the human condition is expressed in lyric 42 of his series "The Black Riders." Walking in a desert, his narrator cries: " 'Ah, God, take me from this place!' "

See 28b-1 for conventions on quoting lines of poetry—on when, for example, to set quoted lines off as a block and when to run the lines together, separating them with a slash. Use parenthetical citations with poetry as you would with other literary works. (Observe the parenthetical references to "A Shameful Affair" in the example paper.)

Plot summaries

Brooks's planned use of the plot summary should be noted here because it is a feature common to so many papers written about literature. A **plot summary** is a brief description of characters and events that provides readers, some of whom may be unfamiliar with the story, context enough to follow a discussion. Plot summaries are written in the historical present tense. Consider these sentences from Brooks's paper (present-tense verbs are underlined):

```
Mildred Orme is a 20-year-old sophisticated beauty who seeks simple
country life for a summer of quiet reading and reflection. [. . .]

Mildred sees the farm hands every day as she sits reading on the
Kraummer's porch.
```

Variations from the present tense may be needed from time to time to clarify sequences of events; but plot summaries are written predominantly in the present tense because the events of a text are always present to a reader—the same actions occur in the same order in the text no matter how many times that text is read. Remember that the purpose of the plot summary is to allow the writer to refer to a text and in this way support a claim. Typically, the writer's observation about the text immediately follows the plot summary, sometimes in the same sentence:

As of yet, Mildred's chosen farmhand is without a name; but like the retouched color rose in a black and white photograph, this young man stands apart from the farmhands that cross Mildred's path, none of whom have been described in terms of color.

The clause beginning "but like the retouched color rose" is not part of Brooks's summary but is one of her observations about the story that supports her claim and follows from her guiding question (*How does Chopin use colors in this story to communicate Mildred's emotions and her growing awareness?*). To ensure that readers can follow her discussion, Brooks summarizes portions of "A Shameful Affair" throughout her paper so that her observations will have a specific reference and will make sense to her readers.

▶4 Literary criticism: More formal readings of texts

What counts as a detail worth noting in a poem, story, or play? What counts as a pattern of details worth discovering? Answers depend on the questions a reader poses. You will see (in 38d-5) that Brandy Brooks observed details of "A Shameful Affair" and fit them together in a pattern based on a question built from her *personal response* to the story. There are other, more formal questions that can be put to a literary text, and these are based on the philosophies of various "schools" of literary criticism, each of which regards texts differently and, based on its approach, poses distinctive questions.

Scholars who write professionally about and teach poetry, plays, and fiction are called *literary critics;* and critics affiliate themselves with one of several approaches to literature. Some critics read *Moby Dick*, for instance, and ask: What is the psychological basis of the relationship between Ishmael and Queequeg? Some read the novel with this question: What echoes can we find of Melville's years at sea? Some look at the public's initial reaction to the novel (they disliked it) and ask: Why and when did this work come to be regarded as an American classic? The possible angles from which to study a literary work are many; and each angle suggests its own set of questions, its own set of problems worth investigating, and its own rules about what counts as acceptable evidence in support of an argument. Fundamentally, readers find in a text what they look for: pose one question, and you will focus on the relationship between Ishmael and Queequeg; pose another, and you will concern yourself with the readers' changing responses to *Moby Dick* over the years.

The questions that guide your reading, then, are of paramount importance. People who make a profession of literary studies insist that their questions be based on sound, carefully thought through philosophical principles. From one school to the next, these principles differ. Differences notwithstanding, all literary critics believe in the abiding value of literature, and believe that we can learn about ourselves and others by reading it. All critics and all teachers of literature accept as a general model of argumentation the cycle of claim, reference to a text, and comment.

It is impossible to say that one approach to a literary text is ultimately correct. There are *many* approaches, and each can show us patterns of meaning in a text that make the text more understandable. If you major in literature, and especially if you go on to graduate school, you will learn about schools of literary criticism. For the moment, even without the benefit of a literary critic's carefully prepared questions (some of which will be presented below), you can gain lasting insights into a poem, play, or work of fiction by finding in it a pattern based on your own personal responses.

Posing more formal questions for a second reading

You may find yourself writing papers for literature courses in which you approach the study of literature according to the viewpoints of various schools of literary criticism. Without naming these schools here and introducing you to complicated terminologies and methods, following are some additional questions you might pose to a text. These questions assume that you have already completed a first close reading.

- What circumstances of the author's life does the text reflect?
- In what ways does the text exist in a relationship with other texts by the same author and with other texts from the same time period?
- How might the text shift its meaning from one reader to the next? from one audience to the next, over time?
- What is the reader's role in making this text meaningful?
- How does the text reflect certain cultural assumptions (about gender or culture, for instance) in the author's and the readers' times?
- What psychological motives underlie the characters' actions?
- What are the economic or power relationships among the characters?

When you want to maintain your focus on a poem, play, or work of fiction itself (as opposed to considering the readers' responses or various influences on the author), then you can pose the following questions, arranged by category. These questions are often appropriate for introductory survey courses in literature.

- **Characterization**   Who are the main characters? What are their qualities? Is each character equally important? Equally well developed?
- **Language**   What devices, such as rhyme (identical sounds), meter (carefully controlled rhythms), and pauses does the author use to create special emphasis? How does the author use metaphors and choose words to create visual images? In what ways are these images tied to the meaning of the text?
- **Narrator, Point of View**   Who is speaking? What is the narrator's personality and how does this affect the telling? Is the narrator omniscient in

the sense that he or she can read into the thoughts of every character? If not, how is the narrator's vision limited?

- **Plot**   How does the writer sequence events so as to maintain the reader's attention? Which actions are central? How are other, subsidiary actions linked to the central ones? What patterning to the plot do you see? Are there ways in which the plot's structure and theme are related?

- **Structure**   In what ways can you (or does the author) divide the whole poem or story into component parts—according to theme? plot? setting? stanza? How are these parts related?

- **Setting**   Where does the story take place? How significant is the setting to the meaning of the text?

- **Symbolism**   Are any symbols operating, any objects that (like a flag) create for readers emotional, political, religious, or other associations? If so, how do these symbols function in the poem, story, or play?

- **Theme**   What large issues does this text raise? Through which characters, events, or specific lines are the questions raised? To what extent does the text answer these questions?

▶**5 Write the paper: Synthesize the details you have assembled.**

> Demonstrate the reasonableness of your claim by making observations about the text; if appropriate, refer to secondary sources and the observations of others. Synthesize these observations into a coherent argument.

The goal of a paper in a literature course is to show that your interpretation, the pattern of meaning you have found, is reasonable and can help others understand the text. Your observations about the text and, if you use them, the observations of others, are the details that you will *synthesize* into a coherent argument. See 2d for a discussion on writing syntheses. The principles reviewed there apply here.

▶**38e**   **Sample student paper: "The Role of Color in Kate Chopin's 'A Shameful Affair' "**

In the following paper, Brandy Brooks examines the ways in which Kate Chopin uses colors and descriptions of nature to suggest the sexual awakening of the character Mildred Orme. Throughout the paper, you will find Brooks following the pattern of claim and support common in literary criticism: Brooks makes a claim, refers to a passage, and then comments on the passage in order to cement its relationship to the claim. She carefully develops an interpretation of the story and, when she finds the need, draws on secondary sources.

$\uparrow$ 1/2"

Brooks 1

↕ 1"

Brandy H. M. Brooks

Dr. Glenn Adelson

English 16

25 October 1998 □ *Double space*

The Role of Color in Kate Chopin's

Indent
5 spaces
"A Shameful Affair" *1"*

← → Kate Chopin is a writer of self-discoveries--

1" of characters who awaken to desires buried deep

← → within and only dimly understood (if understood at

all). In leading the reader through a character's

discovery, Chopin often prefers powerful descriptive

images to explicit speeches or action. The setting

in which a character finds herself, for instance,

can reflect or influence her development of self-

awareness. In "A Shameful Affair," Chopin communi- *The thesis*

cates Mildred Orme's sexual awakening through

descriptions of a farm and, particularly, through

the colors one finds there.

Mildred Orme is a twenty-year-old sophisticated

beauty who seeks simple country life for a summer

of quiet reading and reflection. With the rest of

her family vacationing at Narragansett Bay, Mildred *Plot summary*

arrives at Kraummer's farm as a mature young woman *(present tense)*

who's temporarily free of her parents' restrictions

and fully aware that she's placed herself in the

company of strong, young men. Mildred sees the

farmhands every day as she sits reading on the

Kraummer's porch. While at first "she never look[s]

at them" (632), one day one of the men returns

a slip of paper blown from her side by a gust of

wind.[1] She notices him. And "that," writes Chopin,

is "the beginning of the shameful affair" (633).

At the farm, Mildred finds herself immersed in

a rich, fertile natural world that distracts her

↑ 1"

---

[1] Page references are to "A Shameful Affair" as reprinted in *The Allyn & Bacon Handbook*, on pages 632–36.

1" 1/2"

1"

from the "exalted lines of thought" (633) she had
intended to pursue during her visit. The pull of
nature is strong and sensual:

> *Indent 10 spaces*
> Here were swelling acres where the undu-
> lating wheat gleamed in the sun like a
> golden sea. For silver there was the
> Meramec--or, better, it was pure crystal,
> for here and there one might look clean
> through it down to where the pebbles lay
> like green and yellow gems. Along the
> river's edge trees were growing to the
> very water, and in it, sweeping it when
> they were willows. (632)

1st demonstration of color in the story

1"

These colors are bright and gleaming. There is a
"golden sea," a river described as "silver" or
"pure crystal," and pebbles that sparkle like gem-
stones. With her use of color, Chopin draws our
attention to the farm and its natural setting, to
its physical beauty as a place into which Mildred,
ready for sexual awakening, has stepped. According
to critic Joyce Dyer, the farm is a symbol "of
natural growth and fertility [. . .] that will
help us understand the force that drives Mildred
toward Fred Evelyn" (448).

Reference to a secondary source in support of the thesis

Chopin continues to control the use of color
when introducing Mildred's young man. We learn that
Fred "was young, and brown"; "[h]e had nice blue
eyes. His fair hair was dishevelled" (633). As of
yet, Mildred's chosen farmhand is without a name;
but like the retouched color rose in a black and
white photograph, this young man stands apart from
the farmhands that cross Mildred's path, none of
whom have been described in terms of color. Chopin
gives to Fred the "brown" of the earth and the
"blue" of the sky, making him as much a part of
the natural ripeness of the Kraummer farm as the
"swelling acres" of wheat (632).

2nd demonstration of color in the story

1"

Brooks 3

Indirectly, through Mrs. Kraummer, Mildred asks
Fred to drive her to church the next day--Sunday.
Fred won't because he has plans to go fishing. The
refusal stings Mildred. On Sunday she abandons her
plans for church and decides, instead, on a walk.
And where should she go but to the river. For reasons Mildred does not yet understand but that
nonetheless compel her, she must be near Fred Evelyn. The scene into which she plunges is rich with
the colors of ripe, fertile nature:

Sentences of
plot summary
(present tense)

> High above her waist reached the yellow
> grain. Mildred's brown eyes filled with a
> reflected golden light as they caught the
> glint of it, as she heard the trill that
> it answered to the gentle breeze. (634)

3rd
demonstration
of color in the
story

And Mildred herself takes on color as she works her
way toward the river, drawing closer to the man she
unconsciously desires:

> Her straw hat had slipped disreputably to
> one side, over the wavy bronze-brown bang
> that half covered her forehead. Her cheeks
> were ripe with color that the sun had
> coaxed there; so were her lips. (634)

Mildred's "brown eyes" reflect "golden light";
her "bronze-brown bang" covers her forehead; her
cheeks and lips are "ripe" with color. She, the
wheat fields, the stream, and Fred Evelyn are all
<u>alive</u> with natural energy, as communicated by Chopin
through the use of color. Without ever stating explicitly that Mildred is on the threshold of discovering her sexuality, Chopin prepares us for the
moment.

Sentences of
plot summary
(present tense)

At the river, Fred Evelyn is fishing. Mildred
asks if she can try--and promptly catches a fish. In
the excitement that follows, Fred's "brown hand
[comes] down upon Mildred's white one" (635). The
contrast of colors increases our tension: after the

long build-up, two people (two colors), touch. What
will happen? Fred cannot restrain himself, so close
is he "to a bronze-brown tangle that almost swept
his chin [. . .] to a pair of young, dark eyes that
gleamed for an instant unconscious things into his
own" (635). Without thinking, he reaches for Mildred
and kisses her lips.

    Just as Chopin uses color in this story to
prepare us for her character's fulfillment of
sexual desire, she uses the <u>absence</u> of color to
suggest the dampening effect of society on that
desire. Immediately after the kiss, color drains
from Mildred's once-ripe cheeks. She turns, "her
face milk white" (635), to watch Fred run back to
the farm. Confusion sweeps over her: she stares
blankly, with shock and shame. She cries that
night, wanting to forget the kiss but unable to--
and is frightened that it was "the most delicious
thing she had known in her twenty years of life"
(635).

*4th
demonstration
of color; this
time, color
not used*

    During and following this emotional ordeal,
Chopin stops using color in the story. All the
luscious ripeness of nature is gone while Mildred
struggles with the social consequences of her act.
Color returns when she meets Fred a final time in
the wheat field. Before this meeting, we gain a
crucial piece of information: in a letter from her
family, Mildred learns that Fred belongs to her same
social class. He has come to do farm work in an
effort "to live more lives than one kind" (636).
Suddenly, he is no longer a rough farmhand to whom
she was drawn physically, but an adventurer and
a potential partner--someone who might gain the
approval of her parents. Her next meeting with him,
the last of the story, promises a final drama: not
only might they discuss their kiss, they might
discuss their future.

But the young woman and man awkwardly stammer their words. Fred apologizes (in language very unlike that of a farmhand): "I have wanted to say [. . .] that I am the most consummate hound that walks the earth" (636). Responding to a request that she forgive him, Mildred says: "[S]ome day--perhaps; when I shall have forgiven myself" (636). Fred ponders her meaning. "Then a sudden, quick wave came beating into his brown throat and staining it crimson, when he guessed what it might be" (636).

Final demonstration of color in the story

Color--the blood-red color of animal life-- returns at precisely the moment a physical, natural connection between the young woman and man once again becomes possible. Through her use of color in the final moment of the story, Chopin pulls us away from social worries about kissing and thrusts us back into nature, into the world of "undulating wheat." Mildred's "some day" suggests that she may not simply wish to forget Fred. The moment he understands this, color floods him. Where color is present in this story, sexual fulfillment is possible.

Conclusion

Biographer Joseph Rosenblum has written that Chopin explores "the mental landscapes of her heroines and [. . .] the power of sexual passion at a time when even male American authors generally shunned this subject" (2). These explorations, which he calls "revolutionary" for late 19th century America, are clearly at work in "A Shameful Affair," in which Chopin uses vivid description to trace the path of Mildred Orme's sexual awakening. In a few brief pages, we watch her "drawn out of the world of sheltered social convention and into a natural world that is rich with sensuous physical surroundings" (Simpson 59). Chopin carefully, and subtly, uses color to heighten the drama of each moment in which Mildred grows in sexual awareness.

Reference to a secondary source in support of the thesis

‡ 1/2"   1"
↕ 1/2"
Brooks 6 ←

↓
1"
Works Cited

1"
← →Chopin, Kate. "A Shameful Affair." The Awakening and

Indent   Other Stories. Ed. Lewis Leary. New York: Holt,
5 spaces   1970. 31-37.

Dyer, Joyce. "Symbolic Setting in Kate Chopin's 'A
        Shameful Affair.'" Southern Studies: An Inter-
        disciplinary Journal of the South 20 (1981):
        447-52.

Rosenblum, Joseph. "Kate Chopin." Cyclopedia of
        World Authors. Salem Press: 1 Jan. 1989.
        Northern Light. 21 Oct. 1998
        <http://secure.northernlight.com/cgi-bin/
        pdserv?cbrecid=DG19980107100012343&inid=
        fiolPnxna0x0C3sSBGoIWgteUUEBGBU%253D#doc>.

Simpson, Martin. "Chopin's 'A Shameful Affair.'" The
        Explicator 45.1 (1986): 59-60.

▶ 38f   Reference materials in the humanities

Style guides

The following sources offer discipline-specific guidance for writing in the humanities.

Barnet, Sylvan. *A Short Guide to Writing About Literature.* 8th ed. Glenview: Scott, 1999.

Blanshard, Brand. *On Philosophical Style.* Bloomington: Indiana UP, 1969.

Daniels, Robert V. *Studying History: How and Why.* 3rd ed. Englewood Cliffs, NJ: Prentice, 1981.

Specialized references

The following specialized references will help you to assemble information in a particular discipline or field within a discipline.

Encyclopedias provide general information useful when beginning a search.

Cassell's Encyclopedia of World Literature rev. ed.
Encyclopedia of American History
Encyclopedia of Art
Encyclopedia of Bioethics
Encyclopedia of Dance and Ballet
Encyclopedia of Philosophy
Encyclopedia of Religion and Ethics

Encyclopedia of World Art

An Encyclopedia of World History: Ancient, Medieval, and Modern

International Encyclopedia of Film

International Standard Bible Encyclopedia

The New College Encyclopedia of Music

Oxford Companion to Art

Oxford Companion to Film

Oxford Companion to Canadian Literature (there are also *Oxford Companion* volumes for Classical, English, French, German, and Spanish Literature)

Oxford Companion to Music

Penguin Companion to American Literature (there are also *Penguin Companion* volumes for English, European, Classical, Oriental, and African Literature)

Princeton Encyclopedia of Poetry and Poetics

Dictionaries provide definitions for technical terms.

A Handbook to Literature

Concise Oxford Dictionary of Ballet

Dictionary of American History

Dictionary of Films

Dictionary of Philosophy

Harvard Dictionary of Music

Interpreter's Dictionary of the Bible

McGraw-Hill Dictionary of Art

New Grove Dictionary of Music and Musicians

Periodical indexes list articles published in a particular discipline over a particular period. *Abstracts*, which summarize the sources listed and involve a considerable amount of work to compile, tend to be more selective than indexes.

Abstracts of English Studies

America: History and Life

Art Index

Arts and Humanities Citation Index

British Humanities Index

Cambridge Bibliography of English Literature and New Cambridge Bibliography of English Literature

Essay and General Literature Index

Film Literature Index

Historical Abstracts

Humanities Index

Index to Book Reviews in the Humanities

International Index of Film Periodicals

MLA International Bibliography of Books and Articles on Modern Languages and Literatures

Music Index

New York Times Film Reviews

Philosopher's Index One: Periodicals
Religion Index
Year's Work in English Studies

Humanities resources on the World Wide Web

General Sites

American Communications Association Humanities Gateway
http://www.uark.edu/depts/comminfo/www/books.html

American Studies Web
http://www.georgetown.edu/crossroads/asw

Arts and Humanities Data Service (gateway to history and literature archives)
http://ahds.ac.uk/

Biographies
http://www.biography.com/find/find.html

Chorus: New Media in the Arts and Humanities
http://www-writing.berkeley.edu/chorus/

Creative Impulse: The Artists' View of History and Western Civilization
http://history.evansville.net/

H-Net: Humanities and Social Sciences Online (University of Michigan)
http://h-net2.msu.edu/

Humanist Discussion Group (Princeton University)
http://www.princeton.edu/~mccarty/humanist/humanist.html

Institute for Advanced Technology in the Humanities (University of Virginia)
http://jefferson.village.virginia.edu/home.html

Modern Language Association Online
http://www.mla.org/

Oxford University Humanities Gateway
http://users.ox.ac.uk/~humbul/

Scholarly Sites (in the Humanities)
http://www.wam.umd.edu/~mlhall/scholarly.html

University of California at Santa Barbara Humanities gateway
http://humanitas.ucsb.edu/shuttle/general.html#metapages

Voice of Shuttle Highlights (access to humanities Web links)
http://humanitas.ucsb.edu/shuttle/hilights.html#general

Worldwide Arts Resources (Museums, etc.)
http://wwar.world-arts-resources.com

Literature

Alex database (University of California, Berkeley)
http://sunsite.berkeley.edu/alex/

Film and Folklore Links
http://www.hsu.edu/faculty/beggsm/advcomp/links.html

Literary Resources on the Internet (University of Pennsylvania)
http://www.english.upenn.edu/~jlynch/Lit/

Malaspina College Great Books Home Page
http://www.mala.bc.ca/~mcneil/template.htx

The On-Line Books Page (7,000 books online)
http://www.cs.cmu.edu/books.html

Shakespeare Glossary
http://english-server.hss.cmu.edu/langs/shakespeare-glossary.txt

University of Pennsylvania Gateway to Sources on Comparative
Literature and Theory
http://ccat.sas.upenn.edu/Complit/Eclat/

The Western Canon
http://www.geocities.com/Athens/Acropolis/6681/index.html

History

British Broadcasting Corporation History site
http://www.bbc.co.uk/education/modern/

History Gateway (Kansas State)
http://history.cc.ukans.edu/history/WWW_history_main.html

History Gateway (Mississippi State)
http://www.msstate.edu/Archives/History/index.html

History Time Line
http://www.smokylake.com/Christy/ultimate.htm

Media History Project
http://www.mediahistory.com

U.S. Civil War Center
http://www.cwc.lsu.edu/civlink.htm

Virginia Antiquities Home Page
http://www.apva.org/

Philosophy and Religion

The Bible Online
http://www-writing.berkeley.edu/chorus/bible/index.html
http://etext.virginia.edu/kjv.browse.html

Business Ethics on the Web
http://www.hsu.edu/faculty/beggsm/advcomp/links.html

The Holy Qur'an
http://www.utexas.edu/students/amso/quran_html

The Internet Encyclopedia of Philosophy
http://www.utm.edu/research/iep/

Medical Humanities (New York School of Medicine)
http://endeavor.med.nyu.edu/lit-med/

Philosophy and Religion (Georgetown University American Studies page)
http://www.georgetown.edu/crossroads/asw/philos.html#philo

Philosophy Sites
http://scout18.cs.wisc.edu/sosig_mirror/roads/cgi/
browse.pl?section=philos&area=World

Religion Resources Online
http://www.utoronto.ca/stmikes/theobook.htm

CHAPTER **39**

Writing and Reading in the Social Sciences

erbert Spencer, a nineteenth-century pioneer of social science, observed, "Socially, as well as individually, organization is indispensable to growth" (59).[1] Today, the inheritors of that view—psychologists, sociologists, economists, political scientists, and anthropologists—attempt to discover patterns in human behavior that illuminate the ways in which we behave as members of groups: as members of family or community groups; as members of racial, ethnic, or religious groups; and as members of political or economic groups.

The belief that behavior is patterned suggests that a person's actions in his or her social setting are not random but instead are purposeful—whether or not the actor explicitly understands this. Social scientists do not claim that human behavior can be known absolutely—that, for instance, given enough information we can plot a person's future. They speak, rather, in terms of how and why a person or group is likely to behave in one set of circumstances or another. Social science is not mathematically precise in the manner of the natural sciences, and yet it is similar to those disciplines in the way that claims are based on what can be observed. Social scientists share the following broad theories:

- Human behavior is patterned, rule-governed behavior that can be described and explained.
- Individuals exist in a complex array of social systems, large and small. Individuals within systems interact; systems themselves interact and are dynamic, evolving entities.
- Individuals and social systems evolve—they change over time. Present behaviors can be traced to prior causes.

At any given moment, each of us exists in a broad constellation of systems: economic, political, cultural, psychological, and familial. The fabric of our lives is so complex that, in order to speak meaningfully and in detail about how we interact, social scientists carve up the social world according to the separate systems that

---

[1]In-text citations refer to the Works Cited list at the end of the book.

constitute it. But no one of the social sciences is dominant: each contributes a partial understanding to what we know of human society.[2]

▶ 39a Writing in the social sciences

▶1 Writing to inform

Before significance can be found in social behavior, behavior must be accurately described and, when appropriate, objectively measured. A great deal of what social scientists do when they write is to *inform* readers with precise descriptions. Consider, for instance, an anthropologist's account of ritual drug-taking among the Yanomamo Indians of Venezuela and Brazil.

> Another useful plant provided by the jungle is the *ebene* tree. The inner bark of this tree is used in the manufacture of one kind of hallucinogenic drug. The bark is scraped from the trunk after the exterior layer of bark is removed, or is scraped from the inside of the bark surface itself. This material, which is fairly moist, is then mixed with wood ashes and kneaded between the palms of the hands. Additional moisture is provided by spitting periodically into the pliable wad of drug. When the drug has been thoroughly mixed with saliva and ashes, it is placed on a hot piece of broken clay pot and the moisture driven out with heat. It is ground into a powder as it dries, the flat side of a stone axe serving as the grinding pestle. The dried, green powder, no more than several tablespoons full, is then swept onto a leaf with a stiff feather. The men then gather around the leaf containing the drug, usually in the late afternoon, and take it by blowing the powder into each other's nostrils.

As in other disciplines, informative writing in the social sciences is built on recognizable patterns, one such pattern being a *process* by which some activity takes place. Napoleon Chagnon's account of the process by which a hallucinogenic drug is prepared is precise and authoritative—in a word, informative. Similarly informative accounts can be found in any of the disciplines in the social sciences. A psychologist, for instance, might *compare* and *contrast* the different motivations people have for joining groups. In the course of this discussion, the psychologist might *classify* types of people according to their need for group identity. Such a discussion might begin or end with an attempt to *define* the term *group*. All of the techniques discussed in Chapter 3 for informing writers are put to use in social science writing.

▶2 Making arguments

When social scientists report their findings in journals, they make arguments. Achieving general agreement about the causes of human behavior may be a distant goal of researchers, but achieving this goal is unlikely inasmuch as the subjects that social scientists study—humans—are willful beings whose behavior is deter-

---

[2]To the extent that historical inquiry is based on an interpretation of texts, history is regarded as one of the humanities. Many historians, though, consider themselves to be social scientists in that they use procedures such as statistical analysis to find meaningful patterns in the past. In this book, history is discussed as one of the humanities. See Chapter 38.

mined by numerous, overlapping causes. Researchers acknowledge the complexity of human behavior by avoiding cause-and-effect explanations. They prefer, instead, to express findings in terms of their *probability* of being correct—in terms of their "significance level." A level of .05, for instance, signifies that there is a less than 5 out of 100 possibility that the researcher's findings occurred by chance.

Arguments are the means by which knowledge is built in the social sciences. Various subdisciplines within each discipline carry on these arguments, and each one frames questions differently, uses distinctive methods, and subscribes to different theories. For instance, the discipline of anthropology is broadly understood as the study of humankind in its physical and cultural setting. There are two broad divisions of anthropology: physical anthropology and cultural anthropology. Physical anthropologists study humans as a biological species that evolved in certain environments from earlier forms (such as *Australopithecus*) to its present form (*Homo sapiens*). Cultural anthropologists investigate the artifacts of civilization in an effort to understand how various peoples have organized their lives socially, economically, technologically, or linguistically. Ethnographers, ethnologists, geographers, linguists, archaeologists, and other specialists in the discipline can all be termed anthropologists in that they share basic assumptions—for instance, about the value of studying the physical and/or cultural development of humankind. Nonetheless, both within and between subfields of anthropology, researchers will disagree on how to study human culture or biology. As a student in one of the social sciences, you will learn to read, think, and write in the context of arguments made in a particular field. The more courses you take in a discipline, the more you will learn how to produce arguments and to think like researchers in that discipline.

Claims and evidence

A *claim* is an arguable statement that a writer is obliged to support with evidence. *Claims in the social sciences will often commit you to observing the actions of individuals or groups and to stating how these actions are significant, both for certain individuals and for the people responding to them* (Braybrooke 11). The variety of human behavior is, of course, vast, and researchers have developed methods for gathering data both in controlled laboratory settings and in field settings. The interview and the survey are two widely used techniques that allow researchers to observe aspects of behavior that remain largely invisible such as attitudes, beliefs, and desires. Researchers carefully develop questionnaires, trying not to skew responses by the way questions are framed. If successfully developed and administered, questionnaires yield information about behavior that can be quantified and grouped into categories. These categories, in turn, can be analyzed statistically so that logical and reliable comparisons or contrasts can be drawn. Statistics can then be used as *evidence* in social scientific arguments to show whether a proposed connection between behaviors is significant.

The logic by which social scientists argue and connect evidence to claims (see 3d and 6d-1) will also depend on the method of investigation. Following is a sketch of two social scientific arguments, excerpts of which you will read in 39b-1. You will see in each the interplay of method of observation, type of evidence, and logic that connects evidence to a claim.

Study 1: "Factors Influencing the Willingness to Taste Unusual Foods"

Purpose   Psychologist Laura P. Otis investigates the factors that influence a person's willingness to taste unusual foods.

Method   Laboratory experiment—Otis showed students at a Canadian university various unusual foods (e.g., octopus), which they were led to believe they might eat. At various points during the experiment, subjects responded to questionnaires.

Evidence   Statistical, based on frequency of responses to a questionnaire.

Logic   An argument from correlation or sign (see 6d-1); one pattern of responses is shown to be closely associated with another pattern—one pattern indicates the presence of another.

Claim   The older a person is, the more likely it is that he or she will experiment with unusual foods. Food preference is generally unrelated to an individual's willingness to engage in novel or risky activities.

Study 2:   "The Story of Edward: The Everyday Geography of Elderly Single Room Occupancy Hotel Tenants"

Purpose   Ethnographer Paul A. Rollinson "seeks to provide a rich description of the everyday geography of an often overlooked population in contemporary urban America: elderly tenants of Single Room Occupancy Hotels" (188).

Method   Participant observation—Rollinson spends extended periods of time visiting run-down hotels in a section of Chicago where elderly tenants rent rooms. He tape records his conversations with tenants and forms a close and trusting relationship with one such man, 62-year-old Edward.

Evidence   Personal observations

Logic   An argument from generalization (see 6d-1); the observations made are shown to form a pattern. The observer suggests that this pattern may form a general principle describing conditions for other individuals in similar circumstances.

Claim   "The problems faced by elderly tenants of SRO hotels are numerous and often life-threatening. Their treasured independence is encumbered by their poverty-level incomes, their wide range of chronic disabilities, and their inappropriate housing environments." [The generalization of this particular field study extends only to elderly tenants in SRO hotels. While still a generalization, the claim is kept relatively narrow. As you will see, Rollinson is seeking to inform with his discussion as much as to argue.]

These two studies, excerpts of which follow, represent two distinct strains of social scientific research—one quantitative (a researcher's number-based analysis of experiments in a laboratory setting) and the other qualitative (a researcher's perceptions of life lived in its natural social setting). Social scientists have developed methods for investigating human behavior and, accordingly, many types of evidence are used in a variety of arguments. You can help orient yourself to your courses in the social sciences by understanding the special characteristics of arguments. Pose these questions in each of your courses:

■ What questions about human behavior are studied in this discipline?

- What methods of investigation do researchers in this discipline use to study these questions?
- How are claims that researchers make related to methods of investigation?
- In this discipline, what types of information count as evidence in support of a claim?

Expect a variety of answers to these questions, even when you ask them of a single discipline. Given the many subspecialties in the social sciences, you are likely to find researchers using several methods to investigate a particular question. For instance, sociologists wanting to clarify the relationship between violence on television and the activities of children might set up several studies. One might be a lab experiment in which a group of children, closely monitored for their reactions, watch violent and nonviolent programs; a second study might take researchers into the field to videotape children watching television programs at home; a third study might collect, analyze, and draw conclusions about the state of published research on television violence and behavior of children (Rieke and Sillars 245–46). Each of these studies would properly be described as "sociological," but each would have its own distinct method and would, accordingly, lead to different claims and different sorts of evidence offered in support of these claims.

▶ 39b Reading in the social sciences

The sources you read in the social sciences will represent the variety of investigations carried out by researchers. Aside from textbooks and other general surveys of the disciplines, you will read reports of carefully controlled laboratory experiments as well as field and case studies. These two broad categories of source types parallel two major strategies for generating information in the social sciences: quantitative (number-based) and qualitative (observation-based) research.

▶ 1 Experimental (quantitative) reports

One method that social scientists have developed for studying human behavior is to conduct controlled experiments in a laboratory. Experimental researchers seek evidence for their claims by making careful observations and measurements in a lab. Based on statistical evidence (often questionnaire responses represented numerically), researchers are able to argue that the relationships they claim exist among various behaviors in fact *do* exist and are very likely not due to chance. Equally important can be the finding that no relationship exists between variables. For example, in the following report of a laboratory experiment, psychologist Laura Otis makes the claim displayed previously in Study #1 (39a-2).

Otis began her study with a specific question about human behavior: "Why do some people apparently prefer to eat novel or unusual foods?" Her report represents a particular instance of a social scientist observing the actions of individuals and stating how these actions are significant. Note that whenever Otis makes a direct statement concerning preferences for food, she reviews the literature— that is, she reviews previous research and theories—and thereby situates herself in a tradition of experimental research. Her opening section and the Methods section are reproduced entirely. Most of her highly technical Results and Discussion section has been omitted (as well as her References section), although it is in this technical discussion that Otis conducts her statistical analysis, which she then uses as evidence in support of her claims.

Factors Influencing the Willingness to Taste Unusual Foods

LAURA P. OTIS
York University

Summary.—Factors associated with willingness to taste 12 unusual foods were examined among 42 mature university students in a realistic taste testing situation. Low or nonsignificant correlations were found between subjects' willingness to taste the different foods and their scores on personality measures of sensation seeking as well as their ratings of familiarity with each food. Unexpectedly, age was a significant factor, with the older subjects being somewhat more willing to taste the unusual foods. Only a scale of items dealing specifically with food habits was highly correlated with subjects' willingness to try the unusual foods. The results suggest that food adventurousness is best accounted for by highly specific attitudes about food rather than general personality measures.

Context-setting introduction.

Both humans and animals have strong preferences for familiar rather than novel foods (Barnett, 1956; Domjan, 1977; Hall & Hall, 1939; Hill, 1978; Maslow, 1933, 1937; Meiselman & Waterman, 1978; Peryam, 1963; Pliner, 1982; Rozin, 1976). Typically, the animal research on this topic has been interpreted in terms of the "learned safety" hypothesis (Kalat & Rozin, 1973) while research with humans has been interpreted in terms of the "familiarity breeds liking" hypothesis (Zajonc, 1968).

Review of the literature— of existing research and theories on the topic.

However, neither hypothesis is sufficient to explain the full range of human selection of food. For example, why do some people apparently prefer to eat novel or unusual foods? One possibility is that the desire for novelty in food is a consequence of the negative effects of monotony (Balintfy, Duffy, & Sinha, 1974; Brickman & D'Amato, 1975; Kamen & Peryam, 1961; Siegel & Pilgrim, 1958). Further, it may be that preference for unfamiliar food is a reflection of some personality trait which predisposes some people toward novelty or sensation seeking. In fact, the item "I like to try new foods that I have never tasted before" is included in Zuckerman's Sensation Seeking Scale (Zuckerman, Kolin, Price, & Zoob, 1964) on the assumption that trying new foods reflects a general preference for engaging in risky and exciting kinds of activities.

All statements supported with references to social science literature.

Only a very few studies have actually investigated the relationship between sensation seeking and food preferences. Kish and Donnenwerth (1972) found a significant, although very modest relationship between sensation seeking and preference for sour, crunchy, and spicy foods. Similarly, Brown, Ruder, Ruder, and Young (1974) report a low but significant correlation between scores on the Change Seeker Index and preference for spicy food. But Rozin and Schiller (1980) conclude that sensation seeking is not related to preference for hot chili pepper. The only other evidence of a relationship between sensation seeking and food preference is provided by Back and Glasgow (1981) who noted that self-proclaimed gourmets scored significantly higher than vegetarians on measures of the General Sensation Seeking Scale and the Experience Seeking subscale of the Sensation Seeking Scale.

It is difficult to draw any clear conclusions regarding the relationship between sensation seeking and food preferences from the existing literature. An obvious omission in the research to date is that no study has looked specifically at the relationship between sensation seeking and preference for *novel* foods. The purpose of the present study was to look specifically at the relationship between personality measures of sensation seeking and preference for unfamiliar and unusual foods. Also, since most previous studies used only verbal measures of acceptance of food, the present study employed a realistic food-choice situation. Finally, the Neary-Zuckerman Sensation Seeking and Anxiety State Scale (Zuckerman, 1979) was included to assess the contribution of situational reactions to preference for unusual foods.

Gaps in existing research leave room for additional research.

Present study designed to address gaps in existing research.

METHOD

Subjects

The subjects were 42 students enrolled in a summer session Introductory Psychology class at Glendon College, York University, Toronto. Their ages ranged from 17 to 50 yr., with a mean age of 30 yr. Many of the subjects were public school teachers.

Questionnaire described— research results to be based on data obtained from questionnaire.

Materials and Procedures

As part of a special class exercise, students were given a brief introduction to the present study which was described as research about attitudes towards foods. Questionnaires were distributed and students were asked to fill in the first two sections of the questionnaire. Section one, entitled "General Interest and Preference Survey" was made up of three subscales of Zuckerman's Sensation Seeking Scale (Form V), the Experience Seeking subscale, the Boredom Susceptibility subscale, and the Thrill and Adventure Seeking subscale (Zuckerman, 1979). The second section, entitled "Food Preference Survey" was made up of 13 items dealing specifically with attitudes towards trying new foods. These items were developed and pretested in an earlier pilot study. The survey included statements such as "I consider myself an adventurous eater," "I don't like eating unusual food because it might upset my stomach," and "I often try new brands of food on the chance of finding something different or better." Each statement was answered on a five-point scale going from 1 (not at all) to 5 (very much) according to how much each statement reflected the respondent's own eating habits.

Physical setting of experiment.

While these sections of the questionnaire were being completed, the food display table in the front of the room was set up. Bite-size pieces of 12 different foods (octopus, hearts of palm, seaweed, soya bean milk, blood sausage, Chinese sweet rice cake, pickled watermelon rind, raw fish, quail egg, star fruit, sheep milk cheese, and black beans) were placed on separate paper plates. Each plate was clearly labeled and the product container or intact fresh example of the product was placed beside the food sample plate. When students had finished the Sensation Seeking Scale and the Food Preference Survey they were instructed to leave their seats and walk around the display table where they were to look at but not yet taste the different foods. Students were led to believe that they would be tasting some of the samples at a later time. They were asked not to talk or communicate their feelings about the foods in any way. Students then returned to their seats and completed the third section of the questionnaire, the Sensation Seeking and Anxiety State Scale. The last section of the questionnaire asked students for three kinds of food evaluation. First, they actually ate and then rated the appearance, taste, and preference for an unfamiliar Japanese snack food. Next, they indicated their willingness to try each of the 12 different food items. These two evaluations were made on a five-point scale going from 1 (not at all) to 5 (very much). They then rated their familiarity with each of the 12 foods on a five-point scale from 1 ("I have never heard of it or seen it before") to 5 ("I have tasted it often"). Finally, students were asked to indicate their age, sex, and whether or not they followed any special diet. At the end of the study, students were given a complete explanation of the purpose of the research and were told that they would not be required actually to eat any of the food samples. Of the 42 participants in the study, 32 indicated at this point that they fully believed that they would be expected to taste some of the food items.

RESULTS AND DISCUSSION

Various statistical tests conducted (discussion omitted here).

The data are discussed in terms of the relationship between each of the main predictor variables (familiarity, trait and state measures of Sensation Seeking, the Food Preference Survey, and age) and the subjects' willingness to taste the unusual foods. A multiple regression analysis showing the relative contribution of each of these factors is also described.

[• • •]

Conclusions

Conclusion, based on statistical evidence, is presented and set in context of existing research.

In exploring a number of factors associated with food adventurousness, several surprises were found. An expected positive relationship between familiarity and food adventurousness was not confirmed. On the other hand, an unanticipated positive relationship between food adventurousness and age was noted. Consistent with previous research, personality measures did not appear to play a very significant role in individual food selections. In conclusion, this study suggests that willingness to taste unusual foods is best predicted by specific attitudes about food and is largely unrelated to preferences for engaging in other kinds of novel or risky activities.

▶2 Field (qualitative) studies

Quite different from experimental research, which takes place in the controlled conditions of a laboratory and generates quantifiable data, field studies situate researchers among people in a community in order to observe life as it is lived in its natural social context. The result is a *qualitative* study built on an observer's descriptions and interpretations of behavior. Based on observations, the field worker writes reports and discusses the possible general significance of the behavior he or she has seen, offering what in many cases is a fascinating glimpse into exotic cultures both foreign and local.

Following are excerpts from a field study of an elderly population living in Single Room Occupancy (SRO) hotels in Chicago. You will notice that author Paul Rollinson bases his claims either on prior participant-observer research or on his own observations. Rollinson maintains a distance from his subject that allows him an analytical stance, yet at the same time he is able to enter into the lives of the population he has observed. His report is qualitative, based on personal observations that he then interprets in the context of scholarly work in his discipline. (The References section has been omitted here.) As testament to the impact field studies can have on a researcher, Rollinson dedicates his article to the principal subject of his study, Edward, who (says Rollinson) "taught me infinitely more valuable lessons than my formal academic training."

The Story of Edward

The Everyday Geography of Elderly Single Room Occupancy (SRO) Hotel Tenants

PAUL A. ROLLINSON

This article seeks to provide a rich description of the everyday geography of an often overlooked population in contemporary urban America: elderly tenants of Single Room Occupancy (SRO) hotels. The term SRO is a recent one, originally coined to describe apartment dwellings that had been subdivided into single rooms in New York City (Shapiro 1966). SRO's have also been described as "flophouses" and "fleabag hotels" (Eckert 1979). These buildings, originally designated as transient facilities, have evolved into largely permanent residences for the single poor of all ages. Today, SRO hotels, which are typically located in dilapidated and deteriorating inner city areas, have been characterized as the nation's least desirable housing (Kasinitz 1984).

[• • •]

The problem to be studied is defined and set in context of existing research.

The scope of the problem facing the elderly living in these SRO hotels throughout the nation is great; at least 400,000 are estimated to live in such accommodations (Eckert 1983). Previous ethnographic studies have brought attention to the unique socio-demographic characteristics of this population. Elderly tenants of SRO's are overwhelmingly single males (Eckert 1980; Mackelman 1961; Stephens 1976) who exist in a state of poverty (Tissue 1971). They are not newcomers to the inner city (Erickson and Eckert 1977; Lally et al. 1979), and Shapiro (1971), Siegal (1978), and Sokolovsky et al. (1978) have all found evidence to suggest the presence of considerable ties among elderly SRO tenants. However, little attention has been paid to this population's involvement in the built environment, their geographical movement, the places that are vital to these men and women, and the barriers that constrain them (Stutz 1976).

Purpose of present research.

It is the purpose of this description to pay attention to the elderly tenants' involvement in the built environment within a framework of the geography of everyday experience, defined as "the sum total of a person's first-hand involvements with the geographical world in which he or she typically lives" (Seamon 1979, 15–16). The primary focus of this framework is on understanding and conveying the everyday geographical experience in a "lived" form with as little a priori structuring as possible (Reinharz and Rowles 1988). SRO hotels have, in the past, been portrayed romantically as allowing this population to live independent lives (Eckert 1979; Stephens 1976). In reality, the findings of this exploration suggest that these hotels offer anything but independence. The elderly men and women in this study were caught in an environment that exacerbated their isolation and withdrawal from society. In this research, I portray this unique and vulnerable elderly population's everyday geography.

Framework (or point of view) from which observations will be made.

METHODS

Method of observation set in context of a tradition of observation.

The methodology I used aligns itself with a lengthy tradition of participant-observation studies in exploratory social science research (Clark 1965; Gans 1962; Hill 1986; Jackson 1980; Ley 1974; Rowles 1978; Suttles 1968; Whyte 1943; Zorbaugh 1929).

[• • •]

The Everyday Geography of Edward

This is the story of Edward, an elderly SRO tenant. I compare Edward to the other elderly tenants in the study, briefly describe his life history, how he viewed the SRO hotel and the neighborhood environment, and I discuss his everyday geography and concerns about the future. I met Edward in the lobby of one of the four hotels in August of 1985. Initially, he simply agreed to answer some of my questions. Later, he invited me to his room and subsequently to spend time with him traveling around the neighborhood.

Edward was similar to the majority of the elderly SRO tenant population I saw. The elderly SRO tenant population in the study had a mean age of 70 years, was predominantly white (92%), and male (58%). Edward was a 62-year-old white male. Overall, the elderly tenants had a low educational attainment; almost three-quarters (73%) had achieved education levels of high school or lower. Edward, in contrast, had completed two years of college. Elderly SRO tenants were extremely poor; Edward's yearly income ($4,620 in 1986) was even less than the mean of the elderly tenants in the study ($5,559) and well below the mean poverty level ($5,360). Accompanying his low income was a higher than average rent burden of 69% (compared to the already high mean of 46% for all those I interviewed), which exacerbated the tenuousness of Edward's already critical financial status. Nationally, the accepted normal rent-to-income ratio was 30%. Like 62% of his fellow elderly tenants, Edward received most of his income from Social Security. He was fortunate in that he had some savings to rely upon in times of financial need, as only 10% of all the elderly tenants interviewed had any savings.

[• • •]

Conclusions

The elderly tenants of SRO hotels had few resources or alternatives, and they lived there out of necessity. The SRO hotel environments were largely unsuited to the needs of this population. These hotels were deteriorating, dirty, and dangerous. In the winter, the heating systems were nonfunctional for days at a time. In the summer, the hotels were unbearably hot. The rooms, bathrooms, hallways, and elevators were not designed to accommodate the functionally impaired elderly tenants. It is very important to remember that the hotels in this study represented the least dilapidated and more conscientiously managed of the hotels, both in the study neighborhood and in the city of Chicago. The elderly tenants were overlooked by social scientists, social service providers, and planners because the majority were trapped inside their hotels and not visible to the wider society. This isolation should not be confused with independence. [. . .]

The problems faced by elderly tenants of SRO hotels are numerous and often life-threatening. Their treasured independence is encumbered by their poverty-level incomes, their wide range of chronic disabilities, and their inappropriate housing environments. Their desire to make choices and remain independent is all-important to these men and women. Their residence in the SRO hotels was not a genuine choice. Policymakers and social service agencies must strive to create a genuine choice for these men and women and they must also honor the right of this population to choose their unique and independent life-style. Given the fact that this elderly population had few resources and alternatives, the current and rapid decline in the SRO housing stock poses a serious threat to their ability to secure shelter. SRO hotels were inappropriate to the needs of the elderly tenants, but they did provide shelter at a time when homelessness was on the rise throughout the nation. Tenants of SRO hotels are labelled both deviant and undesirable, as "bums" or "derelicts." These men and women suffer greatly as a result of these inaccurate labels and they are consequently left in isolation, and the hotels are allowed to be removed from the housing stock. Edward noted: "[To] whoever is out there I'd like to say that one day you are going to be old. You will never know what it's like until it happens. A lot of us thought that there would always be someone to look out for us. It's a shock to us all to be in this situation."

▶ 39c   Types of writing assignments in the social sciences

The assignments you will most often be given in your social sciences courses have in a general way been addressed in Chapter 2, "Critical Thinking and Writing," as well as in other chapters. The discussion here will introduce the special requirements of assignments in the social sciences and will provide references to other sections of the book.

▶ I   The lab report (quantitative research)

Experimental researchers in the social sciences have patterned their writing of lab reports on those done in the sciences. Section 40c-1 discusses the general requirements of each section of the standard lab report: introduction, methods, results, and discussion. In the social sciences, you will encounter more variability than in the sciences in titling the various sections of a research report.

The opening

Depending on the conventions in a discipline (check with your instructor), a paper's first section may be titled "Introduction," "Theoretical Background," or "Previous Work," or may appear with no heading at all, as is the case of the example report you read by Laura Otis in 39b. Whatever you call your introduction, make sure it orients your reader to the perspective from which you are conducting research and that it situates your thesis, or claim, in relation to the claims of other scholars. You will need to review the literature on your topic to suggest gaps in existing research and to provide a rationale for your own study. This can be done by reviewing the history of the question you are investigating and by citing pertinent sources.

Methods

This section describes how you conducted your study. In the social sciences, the Methods section is divided into subsections as needed to provide a full and accurate accounting of an experiment. Standard subsections include "Subjects," "Measures," "Apparatus," "Procedures," and "Design." In the Methods section,

39c

Manuscript Form for Research Reports in the Social Sciences

- A research paper should have a (unnumbered) title page. One-third of the way down the page, center your title. Do *not* place it in quotation marks. Center a line below the title and then center your name: first name, middle initial, last name. Below your name, center the name of the department in which you are taking the course. On the next line, center the name of your college or university. On the next line, center the address of your college or university (Solomon 19, 31).
- Place the abstract on a separate numbered page following the title page. (The abstract is the first numbered page of the report.) Center the word Abstract, skip a line, and begin, writing the abstract as a single paragraph.
- The heading, Method, is given its own line and is centered. Skip a line to begin the first subsection, Subjects. Each subheading—such as Subjects, Measures, Apparatus, Procedure, and Design—is given its own line, is underlined, and is placed flush to the left margin.
- Each table or figure should be numbered and titled and placed on its own page at the end of the report, after the Reference list. (In a published article, tables and figures appear in the body of the report.) When referring in your report to a particular table or figure, capitalize the *T* and *F*.
- Observe APA (American Psychological Association) citation form. (See 37b, and see 37a and 37d for citation forms in the humanities and sciences, respectively.)

the researcher discusses any instruments that were used, such as questionnaires, in generating data for the experiment.

Results

This section presents the data generated by your research. If you have used surveys in your research, you will probably compress your results numerically and run one or more statistical programs, the results of which will provide the evidence for whatever claims you are making.

Discussion

This section calls a reader's attention to significant patterns that emerge from your statistical analysis. Your discussion will interpret your results for the reader and lead to a statement of your claims. The discussion will often end with a note on the significance of your research and, if appropriate, suggestions for future research.

▶2 The field report and case study (qualitative research)

Many inquiries in the social sciences do not lend themselves to statistical analysis but rather to observations of social interactions in the communities where they occur. Researchers who conduct qualitative research go into the "field," a closely defined area of study that may be as exotic as the Trobriand Islands or as commonplace as an urban pool hall. The investigator, informed by a particular disciplinary point of view, collects data by directly observing and in many cases participating in social life. Then the researcher sifts through notes and conducts an analysis (see 2c). At the beginning of research, an observer or participant-observer may purposely try *not* to make predictions, as quantitative researchers do, so as to approach the novel social environment with as few preconceived ideas as possible (Richlin-Klonsky and Strenski 90–91; Rollinson 189). One outcome of field research is the field report, which provides a rich and detailed description of the behaviors observed as well as an analysis that discusses the possible significance of those behaviors. In Paul Rollinson's "Story of Edward," you read a field report—which is also called an *ethnography.*

A set of field observations may be put to other uses. When they concern a "relatively short, self-contained episode or segment of a person's life," field notes

http://www.nova.edu/ssss/ QR/QR2–3/presenting.html
An introduction to presenting the results of qualitative research.

may be used in a *case study*, a focused narrative account that becomes the occasion for an analysis (Bromley 1). The case may provide the basis for making a recommendation: for example, concerning the placement of a drunk driver in a rehabilitation program (as opposed to jail) or concerning the placement of a child in an appropriate class. You will find case studies used as the basis of recommendations in most disciplines, but especially in the social sciences and the business and medical professions. You may also be given cases to analyze. In this instance, your professor will present a snapshot narrative of some behavior in its social context: perhaps observations of a child in a daycare setting or observations about employee morale at a business. Your job will be to sort through the information presented just as if you had made and recorded the observations yourself. Then you select the most important information to include in your case analysis, based on a theoretical approach recently read or reviewed in class.

If you go into the field to conduct research, you will keep a notebook or journal in which to record observations. Your professor will review particular methods for observing and making field notes. One challenge of writing your report will involve choosing and organizing the particular observations you want to discuss. The following categories of information often appear in case or field reports, and the categories can be useful for notetaking. (In brief reports, the researcher may not write on each of these categories.)

- An introduction that sets the question or problem you have studied in a context of prior research and that establishes your question or problem as *worthy* of research
- Information on the subjects studied and the environment in which you observed them
- Your theoretical perspective
- Your method of making observations
- Your analysis of significant behaviors
- Your conclusions

3 The library research paper

Just as in other disciplines, your library research paper in the social sciences should be guided by a central "burning" question. (See 33a-1 and, generally, Chapter 33,

"Understanding the Research Process.") You will base your library research on secondary sources of the sort you found illustrated in 39b. Depending on your topic, you will read journal articles and books that are both qualitative and quantitative in their method. As you choose a topic, be aware that you will need to narrow it so that you can reasonably manage your discussion in an allotted number of pages. Also, be aware that instructors will want you to use sources to support a thesis, or claim, of your own design. In a research paper, you will read sources and relate them to each other and to your thesis. As you synthesize material, try to arrange your discussion by *topic* or *idea*, not by source (see 2d). If you need help in conducting your library research, consult Chapters 33, 34, and 35 on writing research papers. For suggestions of discipline-specific sources you might turn to when conducting library research, see 39e. And for the conventions of documenting sources in the social sciences, see 37b.

> ## 39d Sample student paper: "Women Alcoholics: A Conspiracy of Silence"

The following library research paper, written by a student for her sociology class, investigates why women alcoholics in this country are largely an unrecognized population. Kristy Bell read several sources in order to support her thesis that the denial surrounding the problems of women alcoholics "amounts to a virtual conspiracy of silence and greatly complicates the process of diagnosis and treatment." Notice that Bell organizes her material by *idea*, not by source—one clear indication of which is her use of headings in the paper. Each heading develops one part of her thesis. Notice as well her use of the American Psychological Association's (APA's) format for documenting sources.

Women Alcoholics: A Conspiracy of Silence

Kristy Bell
Behavioral Sciences Department
Bentley College
Waltham, Massachusetts
November 4, 1998

Information centered on title page

Bell 1

Currently, in the United States, there are an estimated seven million women alcoholics (Introducing, 1997). Americans are largely unaware of the extent of this debilitating disease among women and the problems it presents. Numerous women dependent on alcohol remain invisible largely because friends, family, coworkers, and the women themselves refuse to acknowledge the problem. This denial amounts to a virtual conspiracy of silence and greatly complicates the process of diagnosis and treatment.

Silence: The Denial of Family, Friends and Employers

Although the extent of the problem of alcoholism among women is slowly being recognized, a tremendous stigma still accompanies the disease for women. The general public remains very uncomfortable in discussing the topic. A primary reason that women alcoholics remain invisible is that they are so well protected. Family and friends, even if aware of the seriousness of the addiction, suffer pain and embarrassment and generally protect their loved one rather than suggesting that she seek professional counseling. By not confronting the issue, family and friends hope the problem will correct itself. According to Turnbull (1988), "The initial response of those close to the alcoholic woman is usually to deny the problem right along with her" (p. 366). Spouses, friends, relatives and even employers tend to protect the alcoholic rather than help her initiate treatment. "A husband will nervously protect his wife's illness from friends and neighbors" (Sandmaier, 1980, p. 8). Family and friends experience a great deal of guilt and responsibility that, in turn, causes them to deny or hide the problem (Grasso, 1990, p. 32).

Introduction: women alcoholics will be studied in their social context.

Thesis

Denial by others.

Claims supported by references to social science literature.

APA format for documenting sources.

Bell 2

The needs of women dependent on alcohol are also ignored by employers, who are unable to confront the problem, in part, due to their having no prior experience with alcoholic women. The conspiracy of silence thus extends to the workplace. Employers tend generally to dodge confrontation by simply firing the alcoholic woman on an unrelated charge rather than steering her to an employee assistance program (Sandmaier, 1980, p. 131).

Silence: Self-Denial Among Women Alcoholics

Women not only fail to seek treatment because they are ignored and abandoned, but also because they deny the extent of the problem themselves. *Denial by alcoholic, herself.* Sandmaier (1980) believes that in "responding to survey questions, women may be more likely than men to minimize alcohol-related problems because of more intense guilt and shame" (p. 73). Thus, statistics published concerning women's dependence upon alcohol understate the extent of the problem. Once again, guilt and pain can be directly related to unfamiliarity with the issue--this time the woman alcoholic's own awareness that alcoholism among women is a debilitating and growing problem. Women alcoholics suffer from the same feelings of guilt and embarrassment felt by family members and friends. Obviously, these feelings are incredibly more intense in the actual alcoholic and tend to force the woman to be driven underground by her drinking problem. Unterberger (1989) observes that "[m]ore often than men, female alcoholics turn their anger on themselves rather than others, with anxiety and guilt being the result" (p. 1150). Specialists in the field of alcoholism believe that there is an inherent trait among women to

Bell 3

ignore the value of their own lives. Unfortunately,
a woman today is rarely taught nor is she able to
properly take care of herself first (Grasso, p. 40).
As soon as she marries, in most cases, she is expected to "take care" of her husband. With the arrival of children she is required to take care of
them. Often, if parents are aged, she will feel responsible for their well-being. Grasso firmly believes that women not only ignore and deny their
problem, but never really think enough about themselves to realize that they are in trouble with
and becoming very dependent on alcohol. This lack
of a healthy self-concept can be devastating. According to the National Center on Addiction and
Substance Abuse at Columbia University ("Alcohol,"
1996), "women who lack a personally fulfilling and
socially accepted role in life are at much higher
risk for alcoholism than women who are happily
employed, whether inside or outside the home, or
both."

Examination of reasons alcoholic women deny their problems.

Difficulties in Treatment and Diagnosis

Many women avoid treatment because of concern
for the well-being of their children. A rehabilitation program including hospital care cannot be
considered because the woman is unable to be ab-
sent from home for an extended period. Feelings of
obligation to a husband and children are extremely
powerful for a woman, especially one whose emotions
are intensified by alcohol. Turnbull (1988) believes that "child-care services need to be provided to allow women to seek and remain in
treatment" (p. 369). Treatment would be considerably easier and progress much more quickly if the
woman was confident that her children would receive
proper care.

New heading signals development of second part of thesis.

Date continues to be cited in this reference since Turnbull has written two articles that are referred to in this paper.

Bell 4

Professionals in the field of social work are not yet experienced enough to recognize alcoholism by its preliminary characteristics. Because female alcoholism has never really been a well-defined problem, health specialists do not have the experience needed to detect it when a woman approaches them with an alcohol-related problem. Frequently, the alcoholic woman is dismissed as being "just depressed" or under stress (Turnbull, 1989, p. 291). Moreover, she is not likely to announce the problem directly:

Social work professionals need help in detecting alcoholism among women.

> An alcoholic woman is unlikely to come into her doctor's office announcing her drinking problem, but she is apt to seek medical attention for a wide range of problems commonly associated with alcohol abuse, including depression, anxiety, stomach trouble, and injuries from alcohol-related accidents or physical abuse. (Sandmaier, p. 207)

Extended block quotation

On numerous occasions, many alcoholic women have had personal contacts with health professionals during which opportunities for intervention went unobserved or ignored (Turnbull, 1988, p. 369).

When alcoholism is detected, it would help for treatment programs to be more sensitive to the needs of women, who may find themselves outnumbered and alone in predominantly male support groups. Natalie Ayers, founder of the Minnesota branch of the national support group, Women for Sobriety, observes that a one-treatment-fits-all approach to alcoholism is not realistic. "[W]omen drink for different reasons than men do," she argues-- primarily the need to mask feelings of powerlessness and inadequacy (as opposed to drinking to seek power, as men tend to do). Ayers believes that women therefore "need a whole different kind of recovery" ("Women for Sobriety," 1998, p. 19).

Bell 5

To this end, women-only groups have formed to make treatment a more inviting prospect.

Conclusion

    Society is now realizing that there is and has been a definite alcohol problem among women. The problem now lies in learning to recognize the symptoms and help women to seek treatment. Many believe that women should be screened routinely at the onset of any kind of treatment program. This would allow for identification of alcohol problems much earlier and would facilitate treatment before problems grow out of control. Social workers, as well, should include screening for drinking problems in all female clients. Some specialists believe that routine screening for substance abuse should become a mandatory part of all gynecological examinations as well as job orientations (Turnbull, 1988, pp. 366-68).

    As the recognition of alcoholism among women grows, changes are being initiated to help make these women more visible to themselves, to health care professionals, and to society at large. "Public education programs must be strengthened to counter the fear of social stigma that inhibits women from seeking treatment" (Turnbull, 1988, p. 369). The public must be made aware of the severity of the problem of alcoholism.

Conclusion: the paper has established that a problem exists.

Two solutions explored.

Self-perception of women alcoholics encouraged.

Bell 6

References

Alcohol. (1996, June). The National Center on
        Addiction and Substance Abuse at Columbia
        University [WWW document]. URL http://
        www.casacolumbia.org/pubs/jun96/alc1.htm

Grasso, A. (1990). Special treatment needs of the
        chemically dependent woman. Syracuse: Crouse-
        Irving Memorial School of Nursing.

Introducing women for sobriety. (1997, May) [WWW
        document]. URL http://www.mediapulse.com/
        wfs/wfs_history.html

Sandmaier, M. (1980). The invisible alcoholics. New
        York: McGraw-Hill.

Turnbull, J. (1988). Primary and secondary alco-
        holic women. Social Casework: The Journal of
        Contemporary Social Casework, 36, 290-298.

Turnbull, J. (1989). Treatment issues for alcoholic
        women. Social Casework: The Journal of Contem-
        porary Social Casework, 47, 364-370.

Unterberger, G. (1989, December 6). Twelve steps
        for women alcoholics. The Christian Century,
        pp. 1150-1152.

Women for sobriety addresses concerns of recovering
        alcoholics. (1998, February 19). Women's
        Health Weekly, p. 19 [Online serial]. URL
        http://www.newsfile.com/protect/nwhic/
        1998020933325.HTM

▶ 39e   Reference materials in the social sciences

Style guides

The following sources offer general or discipline-specific guidance for writing in the social sciences.

Bart, Pauline, and Linda Frankel. *The Student Sociologist's Handbook.* 4th ed. New York: Random House, 1986.

Becker, Howard S., with a chapter written by Pamela Richards. *Writing for Social Scientists: How to Start and Finish Your Thesis, Book, or Article.* Chicago: University of Chicago Press, 1986.

Cuba, Lee J. *A Short Guide to Writing About Social Science.* Glenview: Scott, Foresman, 1996.

Jolley, Janina M., Peter A. Keller, and J. Dennis Murray. *How to Write Psychology Papers: A Student's Survival Guide for Psychology and Related Fields.* Sarasota: Professional Resource Exchange, 1993.

McCloskey, Donald. *The Writing of Economics.* New York: Macmillan, 1987.

Publication Manual of the American Psychological Association. 4th ed. Washington: American Psychological Association, 1994.

Richlin-Klonsky, Judith, and Ellen Strenski, coordinators and eds. *A Guide to Writing Sociology Papers.* New York: St. Martin's, 1994.

Specialized references

The following specialized references will help you to assemble information in a particular discipline or field within a discipline.

Encyclopedias provide general information useful when beginning a search.

Editorial Research Reports (current events)
Encyclopedia of Crime and Justice
Encyclopedia of Education
Encyclopedia of Human Behavior
Encyclopedia of Psychology
Encyclopedia of Social Work
Encyclopedia of Sociology
Guide to American Law
International Encyclopedia of Higher Education
International Encyclopedia of Psychiatry, Psychology, Psychoanalysis and Neurology
International Encyclopedia of the Social Sciences

Dictionaries provide definitions of technical terms.

Black's Law Dictionary
Dictionary of the Social Sciences
McGraw-Hill Dictionary of Modern Economics: A Handbook of Terms and Organizations
The Encyclopedic Dictionary of Psychology
The Prentice-Hall Dictionary of Business, Finance and Law

Periodical indexes and abstracts list articles published in a particular discipline over a particular period. *Abstracts,* which summarize the sources listed and involve a considerable amount of work to compile, tend to be more selective than indexes.

Abstracts in Anthropology
Current Index to Journals in Education (CIJE)
Education Index
Key to Economic Science
Psychological Abstracts

Public Affairs Information Service (PAIS)
Social Sciences Citation Index
Social Science Index
Social Work Research and Abstracts
Sociological Abstracts
Women's Studies Abstracts

Social Sciences Resources on the World Wide Web

General Sites

General Sociological Links
http://www.trinity.edu/~mkearl/resource.html

Information Resources for Social Sciences (University of California, Santa Barbara)
http://www.library.ucsb.edu/subj/social.html

National Center on Addiction and Substance Abuse
http://www.casacolumbia.org

Social Science Gateway
http://sosig.esrc.bris.ac.uk/

Social Science Information Gateway
http://scout.cs.wisc.edu/scout/mirrors/sosig/

Social Sciences Data Center (University of Virginia)
http://www.helsinki.fi/WebEc/aboutweb.html

Sociological Research Online
http://www.socresonline.org.uk/socresonline/welcome.html

Sociological Subject Areas (University of Amsterdam)
http://www.pscw.uva.nl/sociosite/TOPICS/index.html

Suicide Information and Education Center
http://www.siec.ca/

University of California's GPO Gate—access to U.S. government information
http://www.gpo.ucop.edu/

Anthropology

Anthropology Page, Voice of the Shuttle (University of California, Santa Barbara)
http://humanitas.ucsb.edu/shuttle/anthro.html

Anthropology Web Sites (University of California, Santa Barbara)
http://www.anth.ucsb.edu/netinfo.html

Human Languages Page
http://www.june29.com/HLP/

Economics

Economics and Business
http://www.library.ucsb.edu/subj/economic.html

Economics WebEc
http://www.helsinki.fi/WebEc/aboutweb.html

Education

AskERIC
http://www.askeric.org/

The Chronicle of Higher Education
http://chronicle.com

Information Resources for Education
http://www.library.ucsb.edu/subj/educatio.html

United States Department of Education Databases
http://www.ed.gov/databases/ERIC_Digests/index/

United States Department of Education, Topics from A to Z
http://www.ed.gov/topicsaz.html

Yahoo! Education
http://www.yahoo.com/Education/Organizations/

Yahoo! Education (News and Media)
http://www.yahoo.com/Education/News_and_Media/

Political Science

Federal Government Resources (Legislative Branch)
http://www.lib.umich.edu/libhome/Documents.center/fedlegis.html#cdd

General Political Science Web Sites (University of California, Santa Barbara)
http://www.library.uscb.edu/subj/politica.html

Information Resources for Sociology (University of California, Santa Barbara)
http://www.library.ucsb.edu/subj/sociolog.html

Political Science Resources on the Web (University of Michigan)
http://www.lib.umich.edu/libhome/Documents.center/polisci.html

Thomas (Bills before Congress)
http://Thomas.loc.gov

Richard Kimber's Political Science Resources
http://www.psr.keele.ac.uk/

Yahoo! Politics
http://www.yahoo.com/government/politics

Psychology

American Psychoanalytic Association
http://apsa.org/

American Psychological Association
http://www.apa.org/

Classics in the History of Psychology
http://www.yorku.ca/dept/psych/classics/

Cognitive and Psychological Sciences on the Internet
http://www-psych.stanford.edu/cogsci/

Electronic Journals in Psychology (Armin Gunther)
http://www.psywww.com/resource/journals.htm

Electronic Journals in Psychology (Hanover College)
http://psych.hanover.edu/Krantz/journal.html

FreudNet (Abraham Brill Library at the New York Psychoanalytic Institute)
http://plaza.interport.net/nypsan/

Information Resources for Psychology (University of California, Santa Barbara)
http://www.library.ucsb.edu/subj/psych.html

JungWeb
http://www-psych.stanford.edu/cogsci/

PsychJournal Search (an index to 1450 electronic journals in psychology)
http://www.cmhc.com/journals/

Psychology Virtual Library (WWW Virtual Library)
http://www-psych.stanford.edu/cogsci/

Psych Web
http://www.psywww.com/

Yahoo! Psychology
http://www.yahoo.com/Social_Science/Psychology/

Sociology

American Sociological Association
http://www.asanet.org/

Demography and Population Studies (WWW Virtual Library)
http://coombs.anu.edu.au/ResFacilities/DemographyPage.html

Inter-University Consortium for Political and Social Research
http://www.icpsr.umich.edu/

Research Resources for Social Scientists
http://www.socsciresearch.com/

Selected Internet Resources in Sociology (University of Illinois at
Urbana-Champaign)
http://www.library.uiuc.edu/edx/elecsoc.htm

Substance Abuse and Mental Health Data Archive
http://www.icspr.umich.edu/SAMHDA/

Yahoo! Sociology
http://www.yahoo.com/Social_Science/Sociology/

CHAPTER 40

Writing and Reading
in the Sciences

Scientists work systematically to investigate the world of nature—at scales so small that they are invisible to the naked eye and at scales so vast that they are equally invisible. A scientist's investigations are always built on observable, verifiable information, known as *empirical evidence*. Scientific investigations often begin with questions such as these:

- What kinds of things are there in the world of nature?
- What are these things composed of, and how does this makeup affect their behavior or operation?
- How did all these things come to be structured as they are?
- What are the characteristic functions of each natural thing and/or its parts? (Toulmin, Rieke, and Janik 231)[1]

At one point or another, we have all asked these questions and speculated on answers. Scientists do more than speculate. They devise experiments in order to gather information and, on the basis of carefully stated predictions, or **hypotheses,** they conduct analyses and offer explanations. All scientists share two fundamental assumptions about the world and the way it works: that "things and events in the universe occur in consistent patterns that are comprehensible through careful, systematic study" and that "[k]nowledge gained from studying one part of the universe is applicable to other parts" (American Association 25). On the strength of these assumptions, scientists pose questions and conduct experiments in which they observe and measure. Then they make claims (usually) of fact or definition, about *whether* a thing exists and, if it does, *what* it is or *why* it occurs. Questions that cannot be answered by an appeal to observable, quantifiable fact may be important and necessary to ask (for example, "What makes *Moby Dick* a great novel?" or "What are a society's responsibilities to its poor?"), but these are not matters for scientific investigation.

---

[1]In-text citations in this chapter refer to the Works Cited list at the end of the book.

▶ I   Writing to inform

A major function of scientific writing is to *inform;* and scientists try to be precise in their descriptions of the world, writing, when possible, with *mathematical* or *quantifiable* precision. A researcher would report the temperature of water as 4°C, not as "near freezing"—an inexact expression, the meaning of which would change depending on the observer. Precise measurements taken from a thermometer or some other standard laboratory instrument help readers of scientific literature to know exactly what has been observed or what procedures have been followed so that, if necessary, experiments can be repeated.

As in other disciplines, informative writing in science is built on recognizable patterns. One of the ways in which a scientist may inform is by writing a precise *description*—for example, of experimental methods and materials or of observations made in the lab or field. A description may involve presenting a *sequence* of events—perhaps the sequence by which volcanic islands are born. Presenting information can also take the form of a *comparison and contrast*—for example, between the organization of the human brain and that of a computer. Scientists also *classify* the objects they study. When entomologists report on newly discovered insects, they identify each discovery with respect to a known species of insect. If no closely related species exists, researchers may attempt to *define* a new one.

When contributors bring different specialties to a project, researchers very often work and write collaboratively. Look in any journal and you will find a number of multiauthored articles. The great advantage of working collaboratively is that researchers can put the power of several minds to work on a particular problem. The challenge in writing collaboratively is to make a final report read as though *one* person had written it, even if several people have had a hand in its creation. If you are part of a group assigned to write a paper, be sure to meet with group members before any writing takes place. Agree on a structure for the document and then assign parts to individual group members. (See 3e for details on how to manage the logistics of collaborative writing.)

▶ 2   Arguing in the sciences

A scientist's efforts to inform readers are very often part of a larger attempt to *persuade.* In every discipline arguments are built on claims, evidence, and the logical relationships that connect them. But the characteristics of these elements change from one discipline to the next and also *within* disciplines as theoretical perspectives change.[2] Geneticists working on techniques of tissue analysis argue differently from astronomers. Each discipline uses different methods and different tools

---

[2]This discussion is based directly on the work of Stephen Toulmin, Richard Rieke, and Allan Janik in *Introduction to Reasoning* (New York: Macmillan, 1979). See Chapter 12, their "Introduction" to fields to argument, 195–202; and Chapter 14, "Argumentation in Science," 229–63. For a related discussion, see Richard D. Rieke and Malcolm O. Sillars, *Argumentation and the Decision Making Process,* 2nd ed. (Glenview: Scott, Foresman, 1984).

of investigation. Each asks different questions and finds meaning in different sorts of information. Within any one discipline you will find that multiple perspectives give rise to competing communities or schools of thought. Within any one scientific community the purpose of argument will be to achieve agreement about the way in which some part of the universe works.

The process of scientific inquiry generally goes like this: once investigators make their observations in a laboratory or in a natural setting, they report their findings to colleagues in articles written for scientific and technical journals. The scientific community will not accept these reports as dependable until independent researchers can recreate experiments and observe similar findings. As scientists around the world try to replicate the experiments and confirm results, a conversation—an argument—develops in which researchers might publish a challenge or addition to the original findings. In this way, a body of literature—of writing on a particular topic—grows.

As in other disciplines, debates in science can grow heated—for instance, when one person attempts to demonstrate why a particular theory is flawed and should be replaced. Revolutions in scientific thinking may upend whole schools of thought and threaten careers of those who have built reputations on outmoded theories. At any one moment, agreement (if it exists) is provisional and will last only until some new challenge is put to conventional thinking—perhaps by a researcher who has observed some new fact that cannot be explained by existing knowledge. As an undergraduate student in the sciences, you will be introduced to scientific thinking and to the ways in which scientists argue. In each of your science classes, try to identify the purposes of argumentation. Pose these questions:

- In this area of science, what are the particular issues on which researchers seek to gain agreement?
- What questions do researchers pose and why are these questions useful?

Claims

Scientific arguments often involve two sorts of claims. The first takes the form *X is a problem* or *X is somehow puzzling*. This claim establishes some issue as worthy of investigation, and it is on the basis of this claim (which must be supported) that experiments are designed. Recognizing what counts as a problem or a puzzle requires both experience and creativity. Assume it is early October. One evening the temperature drops and you have the first hard frost of the season. The following day you notice that most of the flowers and vegetables in your garden have wilted—but one particular grouping of flowers (your mums) and one vegetable (your turnips) seem as healthy as ever. You and your neighbor both notice this fact. Your neighbor passes it by with a shrug, but you wonder *why*. You have noticed a *difference*, an anomaly (see 1a). If you were scientifically inclined, you might begin an investigation into why a certain plant or flower is frost resistant.

Recognizing a difference or anomaly often begins the process of scientific investigation. The process continues when you make a second claim that attempts to explain the anomaly. Such a claim takes this form: *X can be explained as follows*. If in a book on horticulture you did not find an answer to your puzzle about frost heartiness, you might conduct a study in which you examined the leaf and root structures of the various plants in your garden. Based on your research you might

Tense in Scientific Writing

There is one special convention of writing scientific papers that is very sticky. It has to do with *tense*, and it is important because proper usage derives from scientific ethics.

When a scientific paper has been validly published in a primary journal, it thereby becomes knowledge. Therefore, whenever you quote previously published work, ethics requires you to treat that work with respect. You do this by using the *present* tense. It is correct to say "Streptomycin inhibits the growth of *M. tuberculosis* (13)."

Your own present work must be referred to in the *past* tense. Your work is not presumed to be established knowledge until *after* it has been published. If you determined that the optimal growth temperature for *Streptomyces everycolor* was 37°C, you should say "*S. everycolor* grew best at 37°C." If you are citing previous work, possibly your own, it is then correct to say "*S. everycolor* grows best at 37°C."

In the typical paper, you will normally go back and forth between the past and present tenses. Most of the Abstract should be in the past tense, because you are referring to your own present results. Likewise, the Materials and Methods and the Results sections should be in the past tense, as you describe what you did and what you found. On the other hand, most of the Introduction and much of the Discussion should be in the present tense, because these sections usually emphasize previously established knowledge.

Source: Robert Day, *How to Write and Publish a Scientific Paper,* 3rd ed. (Phoenix: Oryx Press, 1988) 158–59.

develop an educated guess, or hypothesis, to explain why certain plants are frost resistant. To test your hypothesis you might design an experiment in which you exposed several plants to varying temperatures. Based on your results, you might claim that frost resistance in plants depends on two or three specific factors. Generally, when you are reading or writing in the sciences, these questions will help you to clarify how arguments are made:

- What is the question being investigated? What problem or anomaly is said to exist?
- What explanation is offered in response to this problem or anomaly?

Logic and evidence

As in any discipline, writers in science use various principles of logic to examine raw data and to select *particular* information as significant. The variety of logical principles that scientists have available to them in trying to make sense of their research is vast and complex, and if you major in a science it will be the purpose of your entire undergraduate career to train you to understand which principles of logic are appropriately applied in which circumstances. For purposes of demonstration, observe the application of one common logical principle—concerning *types*. Watch how certain kinds of evidence are assembled on the basis of this logic.

Investigations begin with a puzzle or anomaly.

All the flowers and vegetables in my garden—except for mums and turnips—have wilted after the first hard frost. Why weren't these harmed?

A variety of information is available.

This is an above-ground garden, 3 feet deep, 5 feet wide, and 10 feet long. The garden gets full morning sun but is largely shaded each afternoon. I grow tomatoes, beans, peas, cucumbers, turnips, table flowers, geraniums, mums, and morning glories. The soil tests slightly acidic, and it is well fertilized. Turnips are my sweetest crop, high in sugar. All the plants except the turnips grow above ground. The mums differ from the other above-ground plants in that their crown is located below ground. I water the garden twice daily, morning and evening.

The investigator applies a logical principle as an aid to sifting through the available information.

A frost-resistant plant is a type of plant that exhibits two or three of these features: (1) The plant is high in sugar content; solutions high in sugar resist freezing. (2) The cell walls of the leaves are thick and fibrous and are not easily punctured by ice crystals. (3) The crown—the portion of the plant from which the above-ground plant grows—is located below ground and is not harmed until the temperature drops to 25°F.

The investigator uses the principle to distinguish meaningful information—potential evidence—from meaningless information.

Based on the principle above, I see that mums exhibit features 2 and 3, while turnips exhibit features 1 and 3.

Working with an inference and carefully selected evidence, a writer can support a claim (or conclusion).

Of all the *types* of plants in my garden, only mums and turnips can be classified as frost resistant in that only they exhibit two of the three features characteristic of frost-resistant plants.

Each different logical pattern an investigator might use prompts him or her to look for a certain patterning among available information. You can better understand the workings of a science by identifying the varieties of logical principles researchers use in making arguments. As a student reading or writing in a scientific discipline, pose these questions:

- What logical principles are used in this discipline to make meaningful, supportable connections between observed facts and claims?
- What observable, measurable evidence can help to support a scientific claim?

40b

Scientists work with written sources all the time. Accurate written records of experiments are essential in the process of reaching consensus about questions of scientific interest. As a student of science, you will read journal articles and textbooks, and you will do well to establish a strategy for reading both. First of all, adopt the general strategies suggested in Chapter 1 of this book, especially in 1e, "Reading to understand."

Journal articles

Journal articles are written by researchers for colleagues, not for students, and you can expect the language, concepts, and methodologies in journals to be challenging. The use of equations and sophisticated statistical techniques in a study's results section may leave you baffled. But you can still develop a general, useful understanding of an article (if not a critical response to the author's research methodology) by reading as follows. Read the article's Abstract, the Introduction, and the Discussion—in this order. If these sections prove interesting, then read the middle sections (the Materials and Methods, and the Results), which will probably contain the article's most technical elements. As you read, pose these questions:

- What is the purpose of this study?
- What is the researcher's perspective—for instance, biologist, chemist, or electrical engineer—and how does this influence the study?
- What is the researcher's claim or conclusion?
- What seems significant about this research?

The following Abstract, Introduction, and Discussion are sections of a scientific report on mummified human tissue. The authors employ a sophisticated DNA analysis in their study—techniques far too complicated for anyone but specialists to follow. But by reading selected sections of the article, any persistent reader can gain a good sense of how the study develops and why the authors think their work is significant. Written by Ingolf Thuesen and Jan Engberg, "Recovery and Analysis of Human Genetic Material from Mummified Tissue and Bone" appeared in the *Journal of Archaeological Science* 17 (1990): 679–89.

ABSTRACT

Using sensitive techniques of molecular biology, we have been able to demonstrate the presence of genomic material of human origin in samples of mummified human tissue and bone from selected archaeological sites in Greenland. This result has far-reaching consequences for both evolutionary and archaeological studies of past human populations.

INTRODUCTION

Using sensitive techniques of molecular biology, we have investigated the possibility of recovering and analyzing genetic materials (deoxyribonucleic acid, DNA) from mummified human tissue and bone from selected archaeological sites in Greenland. Simple extraction procedures of both skin and bone samples yielded DNA material in purified form. Using human specific probes, we demonstrated that a minor, but distinct, portion of the purified DNA material was of human origin. Further analysis showed the remaining portion of the isolated

DNA to consist mainly of DNA of fungal origin. The findings of DNA of human origin in mummified skin and bone samples, in particular, opens up the possibility for detailed anthropological genetic studies.

DISCUSSION

Recovery and analysis of ancient tissue and bone of human origin has long been intensively investigated. With the rapid advances within molecular biology in recent years, we have seen the first successful extraction of DNA from archaeological and anthropological materials (Higuchi *et al.* 1984; Pääbo 1985*a, b;* Doran *et al.* 1986). The perspective arising from those results and results of the reported work are indeed fascinating. The potential in establishing libraries of ancient DNA is obvious and prepares the road not only for the study of biological evolution (Thomas *et al.* 1989), but also for research into human cultural history.

Within the archaeological discipline the information that may be recovered from survived fragments of DNA may concern inherited diseases, ethnic or racial associations and even sex and lineage. With the successful extraction of DNA from bones, we are also stabilizing and expanding the interpretative basis of the method. Bones are much more abundant in museum magazines and excavations than soft tissue fragments whether from artificially or naturally mummified bodies. According to our results bones are not contaminated in the same way as is skin tissue. An example of future research topics generated by the present project would be a search for the Eskimo–Norseman ethnic relationship and/or the occurrence of inherited diseases, based on successful extraction of DNA from bone material, which is abundantly available in the collections.

Despite being a time-consuming task, the extraction and identification of relevant fragments of ancient DNA should be a challenge for many anthropologists or evolutionists. In particular, after the appearance of the PCR technique, this task no longer seems out of reach (Pääbo and Wilson, 1988). The study of ancient DNA has already been suggested as a subdiscipline to paleoanthropology (Perizonius *et al.* 1989). As a curiosity we may mention, that during our work, which has also involved other mummified tissues such as Danish bog people, Nubian cemetery samples (natural mummification) and artificially mummified Egyptians, the project was nicknamed GAP, Genetic Archaeology Project.

The lengthy and highly technical Materials and Methods section, and Results section (omitted here) are detailed, and other molecular biologists could repeat the authors' DNA analysis. As a student in an introductory course, surely replication will not be your purpose for reading journal articles. Read for other reasons: to see issues important to certain scientists raised and addressed from a particular perspective; to see the process of scientific inquiry at work; and to share in a researcher's excitement.

Textbooks

In introductory courses your reading will be primarily in textbooks, where the writing is directed to students and should, therefore, be more accessible than the writing in journal articles. In the sciences, textbooks play a special role in synthesizing available knowledge in an area and presenting it, with explanations, to students. The material in texts will grow increasingly technical as you move from introductory to specialized courses. Read your texts in science courses closely (see 1e), monitoring your progress frequently to ensure that you understand the material. Highlight any concepts or terms that confuse you, and seek clarification from classmates or a professor.

40c Types of writing assignments in the sciences

As an undergraduate, you will most often be assigned two kinds of writing: a report of a laboratory experiment and a literature review. The purpose of writing in both cases will be to introduce you to methods of scientific thinking and ways that scientists argue.

1 The lab report

A laboratory experiment represents a distinct (empirical) strategy for learning about the world. Experimental researchers agree on this basic premise: that research must be *replicable*—that is, repeatable. Knowledge gained through experiment is based on what can be *observed*; and what is observed, if it is going to be accepted universally as a fact, must be observed by others: hence the need for *reporting on* and *writing* original research. Reports of experimental research usually consist of four parts: Introduction, Methods, Results, and Discussion. Even when scientific papers do not follow this structure, they will mirror its problem-solution approach. Robert A. Day, author of a highly readable and authoritative guide to writing scientific papers, characterizes the logic of the four-part form this way:

> What question (problem) was studied? The answer is the Introduction. How was the problem studied? The answer is the Methods. What were the findings? The answer is the Results. What do these findings mean? The answer is the Discussion. (7)

Introduction

The Introduction of a scientific paper should clearly define the problem(s) or state the hypothesis you are investigating, as well as the point of view from which you will be investigating it. Establishing your point of view will help readers to anticipate the type of experiment you will be reporting on, as well as your conclusions. Your Introduction should also state clearly your reasons for investigating a particular subject. This is common practice in journal articles, where researchers will cite pertinent literature in order to set their current project in a context. In referring to prior work in which the same or similar problems or processes have been reported, you will cite sources. (See 37d for the conventions on citing and documenting sources in the sciences.) These references will help you to establish a context as well as a need for the present experiment.

Materials and methods

The Methods section of the lab report is given slightly different names in different discipline areas: Experimental Details, Experimental Methods, Experimental Section, or Materials and Methods (American Chemical Society [ACS] 6); and Methods and Materials (CBE 590). Whatever heading your instructor prefers, it is in the Materials and Methods section that you provide readers with the basis on which to reproduce your experimental study. Unless you have some reason for not doing so, describe your experimental methods chronologically. When reporting on the Materials and Methods of *field studies* (investigations carried out beyond the strictly controlled environment of the lab), describe precisely *where* you conducted

Keeping a Laboratory Notebook

The notebook should reflect a daily record of work. It is best to make entries explaining the results expected from each stage of the investigation. Entries should be in chronological order, and so thorough and comprehensive that they can be understood by the corroborating witnesses. Each page should be signed by the inventor or researcher below the last entry, and by one or preferably two witnesses. Full names should be used and the signatures dated.

[• • •]

1. Use a *bound* notebook, if possible.
2. If a loose leaf notebook is preferred, the pages should be numbered in advance and a record kept of the numbered pages given to each laboratory worker. The point is to rebut any inference that a worker may have inserted a page at a later date.[1]
3. Do not remove any pages or any part of a page. Pages missing from a notebook will seriously weaken a case in the Patent Office, or in cases that go to court for litigation.
4. Record all entries directly and legibly in solvent-resistant black ink.
5. Define the problem or objective concisely. Make entries consistently as the work is performed.
6. All original work, including simple arithmetical calculations, should be performed in the notebook. If you make a mistake, recalculate—**do not erase.**
7. Never use correction fluid or paste-overs of any kind. If you decide to correct an error, place a single line through the mistake, sign and date the correction, and give a reason for the error. Take care the underlying type can still be read. However, even the practice of drawing a line through numbers entered in error is discouraged in many companies. Instead, workers are asked simply to make a new entry, correcting the error when possible.
8. Do not leave blank spaces on any page. Instead, either draw diagonal lines or a cross through any portion of the page you don't use.
9. Date and sign what you have written on the day of entry. In addition, have each notebook page read, signed, and dated by a qualified witness—someone who is not directly involved in the work performed, but who understands the purpose of the experiment and the results obtained.
10. Extra materials such as graphs and charts should be inserted, signed, and witnessed in the same way as other entries.
11. All apparatus should be identified. Schematic sketches should be included.
12. Head each entry with a title. If you are continuing on the next page, say so at the bottom of the page before you continue.

These rules have received a popular formulation as, "Record it. Date it. Sign it. Have it witnessed."

[1] 1976 Patent Institute. "A Continuing Seminar of New Developments in Law and Practice," College of Business Administration, Fairleigh Dickinson University, Madison, NJ.

Source: Anne Eisenberg, "Keeping a Laboratory Notebook," *Journal of Chemical Education* 59 (1982): 1045–46.

your study, *what* you chose to study, the *instruments* you used to conduct the study, and the *methods of analysis* you employed.

As you set up and conduct your experiment, keep detailed records that will allow you to report precisely on your work when the time comes for writing. Both student and professional experimenters keep a *lab notebook* for this purpose. Even though you may be tempted to make quick, shorthand entries, write in precise and complete sentences that will allow you to retrace your steps. The notebook should be complete, containing the information necessary to write your lab report.

Results

The Results section of your paper should precisely set out the data you have accumulated in your research. The statements you make in this section will provide the basis on which you state conclusions in the Discussion section to follow; your presentation of results, therefore, must be both clear and logically ordered. (Instructors will usually review in class what constitutes clear and logical ordering of results in their disciplines.) As in the Materials and Methods section, when your discussion of results is lengthy, use subheadings to organize the presentation.

Discussion

The purpose of the Discussion section in your report is to interpret experimental findings and to discuss their implications. In the Discussion, your main task is to address the *So what?* question. Readers should know, clearly, what you have accomplished (or failed to accomplish) and why this is significant. Directly address the question or problem that prompted the experimental study, and state the extent to which your data adequately answer the initial question(s). If you believe your research findings are significant, say so and give your reasons. If appropriate, suggest directions for future study. As in the Introduction, set your experimental findings in a context by relating them to the findings of other experiments. When your results differ from those you expected or from results reported by others, explain the difference.

The Abstract

The Abstract is the *briefest possible* summary of an article (see 2a). In some journals, articles conclude with a Summary (marked as such). It is more common to find the

http://www.utoronto.ca/hswriting/abstract.htm
Hypertext guide to writing an abstract from the University of Toronto.

Abstract appearing at the beginning. An article published in a scientific journal will usually have the complete text of its Abstract reproduced on an electronic database. Researchers scanning the database will read the Abstract to determine whether an article is related to their own work and, thus, worth retrieving in its entirety. Abstracts must therefore be concise and self-contained. Typically, they include the following:

- The subject of the paper, its purpose and objectives
- The experiment's materials and methods, including the names of specific organisms, drugs, and compounds
- Experimental results and their significance

Most often, the Abstract excludes the following:

- References to literature cited in the paper
- Any reference to equations, figures, or tables (AIP 5; CBE 20)

When writing the Abstract of your lab report, consider devoting one sentence of summary to each of the major headings (Introduction, Materials and Methods, Results, and Discussion). If necessary, follow your four-sentence Abstract with a concluding sentence.

Title page and manuscript form

Every research report should have a precise, descriptive title. The title, along with the Abstract, will be read first, so if you want to pique interest, this is the place to begin. Check with your instructor about the form your lab report should take. All text—including the Abstract, footnotes, and the reference list—should be double spaced. Generally, all pages of a manuscript are numbered consecutively, *beginning* with the title page. The Abstract page follows, then the body of your report. Each major heading—Introduction, Materials and Methods, Results, and Discussion— should be centered on its own line. (Some instructors will want to see each major section begin on a new page.) Subheadings should be placed flush to the left margin; after each, skip one line and begin your text. Place the reference list at the end of the report and follow with your tables and figures if you do not incorporate them into the text of your paper.

2 The Literature Review

The Literature Review, a prominent and important form of writing in science, synthesizes current knowledge on a topic. Unlike a term paper, which draws on a limited number of sources in order to support a thesis, a Literature Review covers and brings coherence to the range of studies on a topic. A review may also evaluate articles, advising readers pressed for time about which articles merit attention. While every experimental report begins with a review of pertinent literature, only the Literature Review makes this discussion its main business.

Instructors assigning review papers will not ask that you conduct an exhaustive search of literature on a topic. Your search should be limited in such a way that it will both introduce you to a topic and acquaint you with scientific ways of thinking. Your topic should not be so broad that you overwhelm yourself with vast amounts of reading material. For general advice on the skills necessary for conducting a Literature Review, see "Reading to evaluate" (1g), "Reading to synthesize" (1h), and "Writing a synthesis" (2d). (These same principles apply to writing Literature Reviews in the social sciences and the humanities. In both discipline areas, scholars periodically write articles in which they bring their colleagues up to date on research concerning one topic.)

Writing the paper

Writing a Literature Review in the sciences involves several steps. Once you have a topic in mind, you will need to read widely so as to learn enough that you can

Types of Writing Assignments in the Sciences   **687**

ask a pointed question and can begin to conduct more focused library research. Reading scholarly review articles is an excellent place to begin, since by definition they survey a great many potential sources for you and, better still, point out themes and raise questions that you can take up in your own review. Review articles are published for most of the sciences. Locate them by searching for the word *review* in the various publications that abstract and index journal articles, such as *Microbiological Abstracts, Chemical Abstracts, Engineering Index Annual, Physics Abstracts,* and *Science Abstracts.*

If you are unfamiliar with the process of conducting research, then before attempting a Literature Review you might skim Chapter 33, where you will find general strategies for writing a research paper. A Literature Review, like any good synthesis or research paper, is usually organized by *ideas*, not by sources. In Literature Reviews, you will not find a simple listing of summaries: these are the substance of annotated bibliographies, which are themselves useful tools to researchers. The review should represent your best effort at inferring themes, problems, trends, and so on. When referring to sources, use the citation form appropriate to your discipline. See 37d for information on citing and documenting sources in the sciences.

▶ **40d** **Sample student paper: "Comparison of Two Strains of Wine-Producing Yeasts"**

Following is a lab report on the fermentation of wine. The microbiological processes involved in wine production have been known for nearly 150 years, and the student writing this report has added no new knowledge to our understanding of how wine is made. But creating new knowledge was not the purpose of the assignment. Clarence S. Ivie met his professor's objectives by successfully planning and carrying out an experiment, by making careful observations, and by thinking and writing like a biologist.

Here are several features you might look for when reading Clarence Ivie's paper.

- The writer assumes an audience of experts, and it is clear that the occasion for writing is formal. Ivie does not define scientific terms—he assumes his readers will understand all references. (This same observation accounts for the difficulty you might have in reading the paper.)
- The writer demonstrates the logic of a scientific investigation. Ivie bases claims on measurable observations—with an important exception at the end of the paper, in which he makes what he calls "subjective observations" of the two wines he is comparing. In the context of a laboratory experiment, Ivie is careful to distinguish subjective impressions from objective measurements. He follows a standard format for reporting lab results.
- The writer uses graphs and a table to show the relationship among three different sets of information. For those who can read graphs and tables (the assumed reader *can*), these are useful tools for communicating experimental results.
- In sections of the paper where technical language is not needed, the writer avoids such language. See especially the Introduction (the first paragraph) and the Discussion.

Comparison of Two Strains of
Wine-Producing Yeasts

Clarence S. Ivie III

Microbiology 314
Department of Biological Sciences
University of South Alabama
Mobile, Alabama 36688
Professor Burke Brown
4 March 1999

1

Comparison of Two Strains of Wine-Producing Yeasts

The purpose of this experiment was to determine which strain of yeast produced the most favorable wine. Wine yeast, Saccharomyces cerevisiæ var. ellipsoideus and Fleischmann's baker's yeast, Saccharomyces cerevisiæ, were used to make two samples of wine. The wines were then compared with one another to determine which yeast created the best wine based on smell, taste, and alcohol content. The results of the experiment indicated that the wine yeast produced a better wine.

The abstract consists of one-sentence summaries of the report's major sections.

Fermentation is a process whereby a strain of yeast metabolizes sugar to produce alcohol. Wine is most commonly produced from grape juice by the process of fermentation. Grapes are crushed to acquire the juice. Sugar is then added to the grape juice. The grape juice, or must, is then inoculated with yeast and allowed to ferment, a process that takes around fourteen days. The end product is an alcoholic beverage that has been valued for thousands of years. Archeological records hint at wine production as early as 10,000 years ago and show clear evidence of "viniculture" 5,000 years ago in Mesopotamia (2). Throughout the history of wine making, people have constantly made attempts at improving the quality of the product (4). Today, vintners practice several types of fermentation in order to change the character and quality of their wines. Techniques include carbonic maceration, whole berry fermentation, malolactic fermentation, native yeast fermentation, and barrel fermentation (3). Vintners must carefully control the conditions under which wine is produced. One component that is extremely important is the type

In some disciplines, "Introduction," as a heading, is omitted from the lab report.

The introduction sets the study in a larger context and establishes the research perspective: microbiology.

Ivie 2

of yeast used in the fermentation process. The present experiment was undertaken to observe the fermentation process and to judge which of two strains of yeast produced the best wine, as determined on the basis of smell, taste, and alcohol content.

Materials and Methods

Two 1.9L bottles were used in this experiment. Each bottle contained 1.7L of grape juice. Two hundred thirty (230) grams of table sugar was added to each bottle of grape juice. Bottle #1 was then inoculated with one package of Saccharomyces var. ellipsoideus. Bottle #2 was inoculated with one package of Fleischmann's baker's yeast. The mixtures were then shaken to dissolve their contents. Initial measurements were immediately taken, including: pH, specific gravity, and temperature. Subjective observations, such as the mixture's color, were also made. A pH meter was used to measure pH, a hydrometer was used to measure specific gravity, and a thermometer was used to measure temperature. After the initial measurements were taken, both bottles were then sealed and allowed to ferment. Periodically CO_2 gas production rates were measured for each experimental wine fermentation procedure. This was done by measuring the volume of displacement, due to the gas production. As the wine continued to ferment, these measurements were made daily throughout the 20-day duration of the experiment. On the eighteenth day of the experiment, both bottles were inoculated with a bisulphite to stop the fermentation process.

The author provides exact information so that readers can replicate the study.

Results

After the fermentation process was halted, the specific gravity changes of bottles 1 and 2 were compared. The specific gravities of both wine experiments decreased, but the most substantial decrease

The author provides a specific criterion, or test, by which to analyze the two samples.

occurred in bottle #1. These results indicated that the wine yeast metabolized the sugar more efficiently than the Fleischmann's baker's yeast (Fig. 1).

   The results of the pH change, in each case, fluctuated daily. There was, however, an overall increase in both samples.

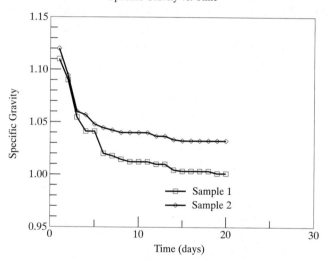

Specific Gravity vs. Time

The graph is given a title; its elements are clearly labeled; its information is self-contained.

Fig. 1. Comparison of specific gravity versus time between Saccharomyces var. ellipsoideus, the wine yeast, and Saccharomyces cerevisiæ, the baker's yeast.

   The temperatures of both samples remained more or less constant at 22.5 degrees Celsius throughout the entire fermentation process.

   The gas production measurements showed that the wine yeast produced more carbon dioxide than the baker's yeast. Gas production is directly related to yeast growth. Because of this fact, it was not a surprise to find that the graph of the gas production rate of the yeast was quite similar to a typical growth curve (Fig. 2).

The author provides three additional criteria by which to analyze the samples.

Ivie 4

Gas Production

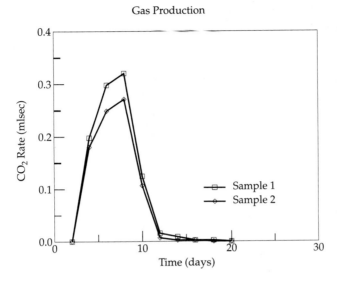

Fig. 2. Comparison of CO_2 production between Saccharomyces var. ellipsoideus and Saccharomyces cerevisiæ.

To calculate the % alcohol content of wine, data from table 1 was used in the following equation (1):
% alc. = (Initial % potential alc.) - (Final % potential alc.)

The wine produced from Saccharomyces var. ellipsoideus was 14.9% alcoholic, while the wine produced from Saccharomyces cerevisiæ was only 12.3% alcoholic.

<u>Subjective observations of smell and taste favored the wine yeast</u>. The wine made from the baker's yeast smelled like bread and tasted bitter. The wine made from the wine yeast smelled like wine and tasted sweet.

Discussion

Wine is the product of yeast fermentation. The purpose of this experiment was to determine which type of yeast produced the best wine. The basis by

Ivie 5

Table 1. Relations between specific
gravities and % potential alcohol

Specific Gravity	% Potential Alcohol
1.000	0
1.010	0.9
1.020	2.3
1.030	3.7
1.040	5.1
1.050	6.5
1.090	7.8
1.080	10.6
1.090	12.0
1.100	13.4
1.110	14.9
1.120	16.3
1.130	17.7

The information in the table is clearly displayed and is self-contained. The table provides the standards by which alcohol percentages are determined in the experiment.

which the wines made in the experiment were judged
included taste, smell, and alcohol content. It was
clearly evident that the wine yeast created a more
pleasant smelling and tasting wine than did the
baker's yeast. The wine produced by the baker's
yeast had a harshly overpowering smell which re-
sembled the smell of bread. Its taste was extremely
bitter. Overall, on the basis of taste and smell,
the baker's yeast created an undesirable wine
while the wine yeast created a pleasant smelling
and more desirable tasting wine. On the basis of
alcohol content, it is clearly seen from the results of this experiment that the wine yeast produced a more alcoholic wine than the baker's

The discussion does more than merely repeat results: it reviews the purpose of the experiment, sets the results in relation to the purpose, and succinctly states a conclusion.

Ivie 6

yeast. The wine yeast proved to be more efficient in the metabolism of sugar than the baker's yeast. Evidence of this is seen in the specific gravity measurements. The wine yeast also achieved a greater rate of fermentation as seen in the gas production measurement. From this experiment, it can be concluded that the use of wine yeast, Sac-charomyces var. ellipsoideus, is far more advanta-geous than the use of baker's yeast in making wine.

Each of the author's claims is supported by evidence gathered during the experiment.

Ivie 7

Cited References

1. Case J, Johnson L. Laboratory experiments in microbiology. Reading, MA: Benjamin/Cummings; 1984.

2. Fermentation of wine. Collier's encyclopedia (Collier Newfield); 1998. Available from http://secure.northernlight.com/ cgi-bin/pdserv?cbrecid=ZZ19971121030170096& inid=YDRTRQMcEUZ5DHsdDWAPVAZX#doc Accessed 21 Oct 1998.

3. Fermentation procedures. Available from http://www.WineKey.com Accessed 3 Oct 1998.

4. Prescott A, Harley J, Klein P. Microbiology. Dubuque, IA: Wm. C. Brown; 1990.

5. Stryer M, Lubert A. Biochemistry. New York: W. H. Freeman; 1988.

▶ **40e**   **Reference materials in the sciences**

Style guides

A source of excellent general advice for writing papers in the sciences is Robert Day's *How to Write and Publish a Scientific Paper*, 3rd ed. (Phoenix: Oryx Press, 1988). For discipline-specific advice on writing, consult the following works:

    AIP [American Institute of Physics] Style Manual. 4th ed. New York: AIP, 1990.

Scientific Style and Format: The CBE Manual for Authors, Editors, and Publishers. 6th ed. Cambridge, UK: Cambridge University Press, 1994.

Dodd, Janet S., et al. *The ACS [American Chemical Society] Style Guide: A Manual for Authors and Editors.* Washington: ACS, 1986.

Michaelson, Herbert B. *How to Write and Publish Engineering Papers and Reports.* 2nd ed. Philadelphia: ISI Press, 1986.

Specialized references

The following specialized references will help you to assemble information in a particular discipline or field within the discipline.

Encyclopedias provide general information useful when beginning a search.

Cambridge Encyclopedia of Astronomy
Encyclopedia of Biological Sciences
Encyclopedia of Chemistry
Encyclopedia of Computer Science and Engineering
Encyclopedia of Computer Science and Technology
Encyclopedia of Earth Sciences
Encyclopedia of Physics
Grzimek's Animal Life Encyclopedia
Grzimek's Encyclopedia of Ecology
Harper's Encyclopedia of Science
Larousse Encyclopedia of Astronomy
McGraw-Hill Encyclopedia of Environmental Science
McGraw-Hill Yearbook of Science and Technology
Stein and Day International Medical Encyclopedia
Universal Encyclopedia of Mathematics
Van Nostrand's Scientific Encyclopedia

Dictionaries provide definitions of technical terms.

Computer Dictionary and Handbook
Condensed Chemical Dictionary
Dictionary of Biology
Dorland's Medical Dictionary
Illustrated Stedman's Medical Dictionary
McGraw-Hill Dictionary of Scientific and Technical Terms

Periodical indexes list articles published in a particular discipline over a particular period. *Abstracts,* which summarize the sources listed and involve a considerable amount of work to compile, tend to be more selective than indexes.

Applied Science and Technology Index
Biological Abstracts
Biological and Agricultural Index
Cumulative Index to Nursing and Allied Health Literature

Current Abstracts of Chemistry and Index Chemicus
Engineering Index
General Science Index
Index Medicus
Index to Scientific and Technical Proceedings
Science Citation Index

Computerized periodical indexes are available for many specialized areas and may be faster than leafing through years of bound periodicals. Access to these databases may be expensive.

Science and Technology Databases
Agricola (agriculture)
Biosis Previews (biology, botany)
CA Search (chemistry)
Compendix (engineering)
NTIS (National Technical Information Search)
ORBIT (science and technology)
SciSearch
SPIN (physics)

Science Resources on the World Wide Web

General Sites

Cornell Math and Science Gateway
http://www.tc.cornell.edu/Edu/MathSciGateway/

Ecola Newsstand Science (Electronic Magazines)
http://www.ecola.com/news/magazine/science/

Electronic Journals in the Sciences (and other disciplines)
http://ejournals.cic.net/toc.Topic.html

Information Resources for the Sciences (University of California, Santa Barbara)
http://www.library.ucsb.edu/subj/sciences.html

National Science Foundation
http://www.nsf.gov/

UniScience Science News Online (Weekly news updates and searchable archive)
http://unisci.com/

Yahoo! Science
http://dir.yahoo.com/Science/

Astronomy

AstroWeb
http://www.cv.nrao.edu/fits/www/astronomy.html

Earth from Space: An Astronaut's Views of the Home Planet
http://earth.jsc.nasa.gov/

Indexes and Gateways to Astronomical Resources on the Internet Sciences (University of California, Santa Barbara)
http://www.library.ucsb.edu/subj/astronom.html

Biology

Biodiversity and Biological Collections Web Server
http://biodiversity.uno.edu

Entomology
http://www.ColoState.edu/Depts/Entomology/ent.html

The Genome Database
http://gdbwww.gdb.org

Human Body Image Browser
http://www.vis.colostate.edu/cgi-bin/gva/gvaview

Indexes and Gateways to Biology and Aquatic Science Sources on the Internet
Sciences (University of California, Santa Barbara)
http://www.library.ucsb.edu/subj/astronom.html

Chemistry

Chemical Information Resource Shelf
http://www.umsl.edu/divisions/artscience/chemistry/books/welcome.html

Information Resources for Chemistry (University of California, Santa Barbara)
http://www.library.ucsb.edu/subj/chemistr.html

ChemWeb
http://chemweb.com/home/home.exe

Science Hypermedia, Inc.
http://www.scimedia.com

Environmental Studies

Environmental Protection Agency
http://www.epa.gov/

Geologylink
http://www.geologylink.com/hot/

Marine Watch
http://www.marinewatch.com/

United States Department of the Interior
http://www.doi.gov/

The Weather Processor
http://wxp.atms.purdue.edu/

Physics

Albert Einstein: Images and Impact
http://www.aip.org/history/einstein/

European Laboratory for Particle Physics
http://www.cern.ch/

The Galileo Project
http://es.rice.edu/ES/humsoc/Galileo/

Physics resources (WWWVirtual Library)
http://www.fisk.edu/vl/Physics/Overview.html

CHAPTER 41

Writing for the Web

T he World Wide Web is a radically democratic publishing forum. Anyone—from individual students like you, to non-profit organizations, to corporations, to state and national governments—can create and post Web sites, spreading points of view and information across town and across continents. The Web site you develop for a course may be viewed not only by your fellow students but, potentially, by a world of computer users in search of the information you might have. The opportunities for exposure are immense: recently a college student in Texas, working from his dorm room, created a Web site on computer security and found himself invited to be a special "expert" guest for a radio show in California. This chapter will introduce you to the basic elements of Web publishing so that you can take the first steps necessary to post your work.

▶ 41a Planning and writing a document for the Web

In one key respect, Web-based documents differ fundamentally from print-based documents: in the print world, both you and your audience assume that an essay, letter, or report will make sense only if read linearly—that is, from start to finish in the order you (as writer) have laid out. You can make no such assumption about the ways in which computer users read a Web page. Given the development of

http://info.med.yale.edu/caim/
manual/contents.html
*The Yale Web Style Guide—
the king of online web design
guides.*

hyperlinks that enable readers to jump from a document on one Web page to related topics on others at the click of a mouse, some readers may follow links that you embed into a document *as* they read. Others may skim the entire Web page as you have designed it and then circle back to

follow links of interest. Readers will likely not work through long Web documents, from start to finish, without taking detours (if these are offered). As you might expect, the nonlinear behavior of readers on the Web involves changes for writers on the Web. Bear these suggestions in mind as you prepare to post documents on the Web:

1. *Anticipate multiple audiences.* Even though you may post a document that you believe only your classmates or teacher might read, other people may find your work as the result of a link from an unrelated site. You should therefore provide readers with a context for your work: pages on the site should be linked to your

home page, and the home page should offer links to course and university information.

2. *Prepare brief units of thought.* The unit of thought in an essay is, at its briefest, a paragraph. Although in print-based documents, related paragraphs are often strung together to form sections, you cannot assume in a document embedded with hypertext links that readers will read multiple paragraphs in the order you've presented. Therefore, keep "thought units" brief—a paragraph or two at most—and link to other thought units, providing readers with multiple paths for inquiry.

3. *Anticipate a nonlinear development of ideas.* Readers *will* jump between sections of a page and, if you provide links, off your site to other pages, so the organization of your page must make sense in whatever order readers choose.

4. *Make navigation easy.* People may skim a Web-based essay to search for facts, find relevant articles, or gain a quick overview, so be sure to provide a site map that will facilitate navigating to the various parts of your document.

5. *Design your documents.* Many people find lengthy text difficult to read onscreen and will print out an essay for offline reading. Design your Web-based documents for legibility, both on the screen and on the printed page. Also, design your documents with the awareness that browsers and computers may display Web pages differently. Try to anticipate your audience and the types of computers they will be using.

A print document can serve as the core of a Web-based document, as is illustrated in this chapter's example pages from Marie Hobahn's Web-based essay on women and computing (the print version of which you will find in Chapter 6). Be aware, though, that in writing for the Web you should anticipate that readers will work through documents in multiple ways, of which the linear or start to finish method is only one. The structure of a print-based document reworked for the Web will likely change radically, due to the Web's hyperlinked environment. Do not assume that your efforts to publish on the Web will be successful if you simply export word-processing files in HTML format. The process of *designing* and *building* a Web site is considerably more complex than HTML coding and requires that you rethink and restructure the essay as well as reimagine your readers and their needs.

Regardless of the length of "thought unit" you are presenting—a paragraph or two in a Web essay and possibly several paragraphs (or sections) in a print essay—your writing should conform to basic principles of unity and coherence: sentences grouped together into paragraphs should develop the same point and should be sequenced clearly. Writing for both the Web and print should be free of errors in grammar, punctuation, and usage. When preparing materials for the Web, consult the chapters of this handbook, just as you would when writing a print-based essay.

▶ **EXERCISE I**

Take a print essay you have written and break it into "thought units"—that is, sections, or groupings of related paragraphs. Working with index cards, give each section of the paper a title and place these titles on separate cards. Also place the thesis

| of your paper on its own card. Finally, arrange the cards in the order in which the paper is written. (In Exercise 3, you will compare the organization of your print-based essay to an essay that you will restructure for the Web.)

▶1 Content planning

As the author of an essay, you are the content expert: whether you have prepared the document for the Web or for print, you have done the research and the writing. Being the content expert, you can work with an Internet designer (or take on that role yourself) to identify items that will serve as hyperlinks to other Web pages. You will probably develop an altogether different organizational plan for your Web-based essay, breaking with the structure you used for print and the expectation that the document must be read more or less linearly. Anticipating multiple navigation paths through your site, you can create brief, interconnected but independent "thought units" of text and images.

You can link citations in an essay to their sources wherever possible, adding links not only in the formal bibliography but also within the text of the essay whenever the work is cited. You can also incorporate anecdotes and other materials not included in the print-based version of the essay. You might allocate a separate Web page for each such element and then link to it where appropriate, using an icon within the essay text.

▶2 Site maps

Like professional Web developers who have collected and understood the content of a Web site, you will collect your information and materials and then begin planning your Web site with a site map. A Web site consists of many, sometimes dozens (or more) individual Web pages. The site map is a logistical illustration of all of the pages in a site, the content that is contained on each page, and where links exist. On page 702 you'll find an illustration of a site map created by student Marie Hobahn as she prepared to make a Web-based version of her essay, "Women and Computing: Beyond the Glass Ceiling," which you will find in Chapter 6. (See page 705 for the first page of her Web-based version of the essay.)

This site map restructures for the Web the print essay that Marie Hobahn wrote for a composition class. In recasting her work, Marie understood that her readers might want to enter her argument at several points; thus, from a home page that includes her introduction and thesis, Marie creates links that will take readers to all the major "thought units" of her essay. Also, each thought unit is linked to others, so that readers may navigate to different parts of the essay as they please. Marie intends for users to enter the site through the home page (unless they have bookmarked a page within the site) and then progress into the major content areas.

Site maps can be as useful as you allow them to be. Some site maps consist of pencil scrawling on a single sheet of paper, while others are the size of conference-room tables and contain color-coded areas, elaborate illustrations, and hundreds of link-arrows marching back and forth. The more detailed the map, the clearer

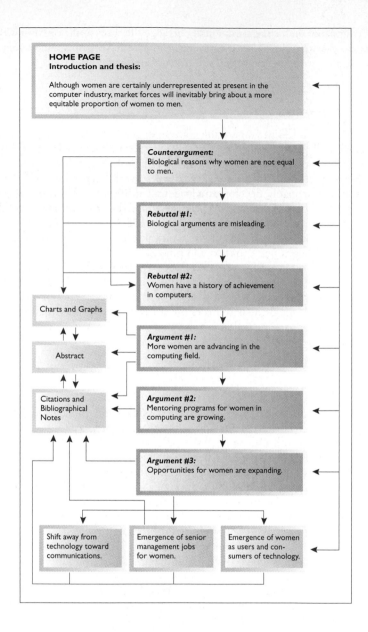

HOME PAGE
Introduction and thesis:

Although women are certainly underrepresented at present in the computer industry, market forces will inevitably bring about a more equitable proportion of women to men.

Counterargument:
Biological reasons why women are not equal to men.

Rebuttal #1:
Biological arguments are misleading.

Rebuttal #2:
Women have a history of achievement in computers.

Charts and Graphs

Argument #1:
More women are advancing in the computing field.

Abstract

Citations and Bibliographical Notes

Argument #2:
Mentoring programs for women in computing are growing.

Argument #3:
Opportunities for women are expanding.

Shift away from technology toward communications.

Emergence of senior management jobs for women.

Emergence of women as users and consumers of technology.

the Web site's content and structure will be. Regardless of how complex or simple the site map, creating it is the most important step in building a Web site. Developers who make haste will *always* regret their decision to omit drawing out the structure of their projects on paper before actually building the site. As Web links proliferate on a site, the potential for confusion is great. A clear plan—a map— early in the process will minimize confusion later. The low-tech pencil and paper still offer the most efficient means of planning a site.

Writing for the Web

The (Messy) Process of Web-Page Design and Production

Every page of a well-designed Web site is built on sketches, maps, and mega-bytes of digital revisions. Much as the essay-writing process benefits from thoughtful outlining of ideas and multiple revisions, the process of Web-page design and construction involves a good deal of planning and a commitment to iterative design.

Iterative design is the process of creating a rough estimate of what something (in this case, a Web page) ought to be, presenting the work to others for critique, revising based on feedback, and re-presenting—to revise again and again until a finished, polished product is created. Like the iterative process of writing an essay, iterative design for the Web developer is a messy process: typically, Web sites are built up and partially torn down, only to be rebuilt and repeatedly torn down during the production of a single page. Constant refinement (along with continual updating of site maps and storyboards) improves the end product. When building your Web pages, expect that a messy process will gradually give way to clarity and a clean design.

EXERCISE 2

Compare Marie Hobahn's site map for her Web-based essay with her print-based essay, which you will find at the beginning of Chapter 6. Observe closely how she dissects the print essay into briefer elements or thought units, which then become separate Web pages in the site she is planning.

EXERCISE 3

Working with the sections of your print-based essay, which you defined in Exercise 1, take two sections of the essay and create briefer thought units, each a paragraph or so in length. Give each paragraph a title, and place these titles on separate index cards. Again, place the thesis on its own card. Using Marie Hobahn's site map as a guide, try drawing links (you might use lengths of string) between the thesis and paragraphs, and between paragraphs themselves. How many ways, other than start-to-finish, can you think of for a reader to navigate through these parts of your essay?

3 Storyboards

It isn't unusual to walk into an Internet development office and find dozens of sketches (sometimes on yellow "stickies" for ease of rearrangement) taped on the wall. Moveable paper sketches give developers the opportunity to grab Web-page elements and change their location (relative to other elements) until the whole vision of the Web site makes sense. (See the box above about the process of Web-page production and see Chapters 3 and 4 for more on the process of creation and revision.) This technique of manipulating Web page elements, called "storyboarding," is used by moviemakers to plan out scenes before filming begins. You can think of a user's trip through your Web site just as you would an audience member's viewing of a movie, only for the Web experience, each user's trip will differ since the user can select different viewing paths. Still, both moviemakers and Web designers use paper and pencil (and, sometimes, software) to sketch a job before beginning it.

In the Web developer's office you will find elaborate sketches for all pages in a project, with each sketch indicating what photographs will be used, what illustrations will be needed, and where links will be. (Recall from Chapters 3 and 4 that essay writers also must locate where they will place important elements such as statistics, supporting arguments, and examples.) Creating detailed sketches early in the process helps designers anticipate the amount of content—text *and* images—that can realistically fit on a page. (See the discussion of images at 42c. If an image is central to your plan for a particular Web page, then you should integrate this image into your site map and storyboard very early in the process.)

The amount of content you should place on a single Web page is a function of your audience's interests, abilities and, significantly, the type of Internet connection they have. If you're designing a site for children, you might want to limit each page to a few sentences and one large picture. If you're designing a site for users likely to have slow Internet connections, you should probably keep your images small, since artwork files are large and take a long time to download.

Remember: Web developers continually revise their site maps and storyboards. As they make changes in one, they make corresponding changes to the other. The process of developing a Web page is marked by the continual revision and the intertwining of the site map and storyboard.

As you sketch the individual pages of your Web site, bear in mind the kinds of users likely to be attracted to your project and plan the site accordingly. If you are posting an essay on the Web, your audience will probably consist of fellow students, teacher(s), and possibly researchers using Web browsers to search on a topic. Consider adding these elements to increase the usefulness of your site:

- For readers who may want to contact you, provide an e-mail address.
- For those who may come to your work unfamiliar with the assignment or the academic context in which you are working, consider providing course information and an abstract. Provide researchers with a summary of key data that they can save for their own presentations.

The principle to bear in mind as you are creating a storyboard for your Web site is to design with readers in mind. Here's the first page of Marie Hobahn's Web-based essay, which incorporates these reader-friendly elements. Note: the following example page from Marie Hobahn's essay is shown *out* of a browser window so that the entire page is viewable. On a computer monitor, the reader would need to use the scroll bar to see the full page as presented here:

HOME PAGE: Women and Computing: Beyond the Glass Ceiling

For Comp 101 @ New York University

By Marie Hobahn (marie.hobahn@nyu.edu)

Introduction and Thesis

How well are women doing in the professional world of computing? There's no use denying it: the numbers don't look good. None of the top 50 computer companies boasts a female CEO, even though women make up about a third of the high-tech workforce (DeBare, "High-tech" 1). Women fill less than 30% of programming, engineering, and management jobs at high-tech companies. Companies created or run by women received just 1.6% of the venture capital invested in high-tech firms from 1991 to 1996 (Crain; Hamm). The glass ceiling that keeps women from advancing seems real. According to D. J. Young, a software quality assurance manager at the software firm Intuit, "More women are [. . .] reaching that first level of management, but [. . .] the higher [they] go, the harder it is to get to the next level" (qtd. in DeBare, "Voices" 1). Considering this discouraging news, it might seem a hopeless act of faith to believe that things will get better anytime soon. But that faith would, in fact, be justified. Although women are certainly underrepresented at present in the computer industry, cultural and market forces will inevitably bring about a more equitable proportion of women to men.

Home Page: Introduction and Thesis
Counterargument: Biological reasons why women are not equal to men.
  Rebuttal #1: Biological arguments are misleading.
  Rebuttal #2: Women have a history of achievement in computers.
Argument #1: More women are advancing in the computer field.
Argument #2: Mentoring programs for women are growing.
Argument #3: Opportunities for women are expanding.
  A: Shift away from technology towards communications.
  B: Emergence of senior management jobs for women.
  C: Emergence of women as users and consumers of technology.
Charts and Graphs
Abstract

▶4 Production

To create a Web file, you need to learn a bit about HTML, **H**yper**T**ext **M**arkup Language. The word *language* may sound formidable and lead you to believe that

http://www.ncsa.uiuc.edu/
General/Internet/WWW/
HTMLPrimerP1.html
Though it's easiest to create your pages with a Web page editor, this Beginner's Guide to HTML from NCSA may help with fine-tuning your pages.

only Web developers can learn it, but, in truth, HTML is not truly a programming language. Complete beginners can usually make their first Web page within twenty minutes. HTML is a *markup* language. The basic process of creating a Web page involves taking a page of text that you want to present online and adding to it a few lines of code, or instructions to the computer on how to "read" your text. (Recall that the text you mark up using HTML is not likely to be a simple export of a document's word-processing file into HTML format. The text that you code in HTML should be written and especially structured with Web readers in mind.)

The world's simplest Web page looks like this:

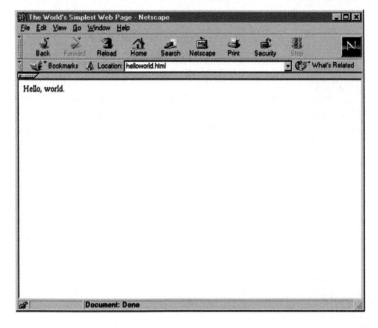

Here is the HTML coding that makes this page viewable as a Web document. Note that instructions to the browser, or code, are enclosed in angle brackets, called tags:

```
<HTML>
<HEAD>
<TITLE>Hello, world.</TITLE>
</HEAD>
```

```
<BODY>
Hello, world.
</BODY>
</HTML>
```

Included in this sample HTML page are basic elements that every Web page must contain in order to work properly. HTML code instructs browsers on how to interpret and display information. Content without proper tagging will not be displayed when a browser opens that page. Let's examine each HTML tag involved in the creation of the example Web page:

- **<HTML>** This tag announces to the browser that the content that follows is formatted in HTML and that instructions for screen display will follow in angle brackets.
- **<HEAD>** This tag announces that key, global information will follow about the Web page, for example, the document's title, author, subject matter, and date of publication. The forward slash character (/) marks the ending for all tagged elements that occur in pairs, such as </HEAD>, </TITLE>, </BODY>, and </HTML>. Information within the <HEAD> tags will not appear in the browser page itself, but will be indexed by search engines.
- **<TITLE>** All text between the opening tag <TITLE> and the closing tag </TITLE> will be regarded as the title of the document, which will appear at the top of the browser window when the page loads.
- **<BODY>** This tag opens the body of the document. All text and graphics following this tag will appear on the Web page, provided these elements are followed by the ending tag </BODY>. The entire document is completed with the ending tag </HTML>. In the example Web page, the only information between the opening and closing <BODY> tags is the text "Hello world!"
- **Some miscellaneous tags:**
  - **</B>** and **</B>** Everything between these tags will appear as **bold type.**
  - **</I>** and **</I>** Everything between these tags will appear as *italicized type.*
  - **<U>** and **</U>** Everything between these tags will appear as <u>underlined type.</u>
  - **<P>** This tag (no closing tag required) makes a paragraph break.
  - **
** This tag (no closing tag required) creates a line break.
  - **<FONT SIZE=+1>** and **</FONT>** placed around words make them one size larger than other type on the page. Likewise, **<FONT SIZE=-1>** and **</FONT>** make words one size smaller than other words. Unfortunately, you can't precisely control the size of any words appearing on a Web page because users can specify their preferred font size on their own computers.

Rather than learning HTML coding, you can create your Web pages using one of several commercially available HTML programs that make creating HTML much easier than coding by hand. Word processing programs such as Microsoft Word allow writers to save documents in HTML format. More advanced programs for Web developers include "HomeSite" (PC only), "Dreamweaver" (Mac and PC), "Cyberstudio" (Mac only), and "BBBEdit" (Mac only).

```
<HTML>
<HEAD>
<TITLE>Women and Computing: Beyond the Glass Ceiling</TITLE>
</HEAD>
<BODY>
<CENTER><H2>Women and Computing: Beyond the Glass Ceiling</H2>
By <A HREF="http://students.nyu.edu/~marie_hobahn/index.html">Marie
Hobahn</A> (<A
HREF="mailto:marie.hobahn@nyu.edu">marie.hobahn@nyu.edu</A>)
<P>
<CENTER><TABLE WIDTH=500><TR><TD><B>Argument #3:
Opportunities for Women Are Expanding</B><BR>
      <FONT
SIZE="+1">O</FONT>pportunities are expanding for women, and gains are
being made.  In the next few years
these gains will broaden as three important changes sweep through the
computer industry. <P>
A. <A HREF="essay_a.html">Shift away from technology towards
communications</A><BR>
B. <A HREF="essay_b.html">Emergence of senior management jobs for
women</A><BR>
C. <A HREF="essay_c.html">Emergence of women as users and consumers of
technology</A><BR>
 </TD></TR></TABLE></CENTER>
<P>
<IMG SRC="nav_3.jpg" WIDTH=340 HEIGHT=176
BORDER="0"></CENTER>
</BODY>
</HTML>
```

Source code for one page from Marie Hobahn's Web-based essay.

In these programs (to take a simple example), you click on a "bold" button, as you would in a word processor, and the program inserts the correct HTML tags. Again, when converting word-processing files into HTML format, you should consider the significant ways your print document might change when presented in a hyperlinked, Web environment. Recall, for instance, that Web-based "thought units" tend to be briefer than thought units of print-based writing (see page 700).

▶ **EXERCISE 4**

Take one paragraph, or thought unit, from the print essay with which you have been working in Exercises 1 and 3, and develop HTML coding for it as if you were going to post the Web site. Use the HTML tags reviewed in this section, and simply skip coding any elements not reviewed in this chapter.

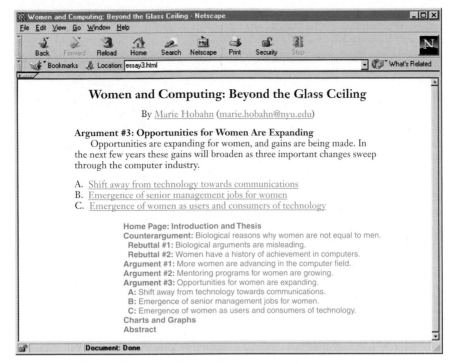

A page from Marie Hobahn's Web-based essay.

▶5 Hyperlinks

Readers will move from one page in your Web site to related pages by means of hyperlinks. You add links to a page by using HTML tags, as in this example:

> This is a sample sentence from a Web page. When users click **<A HREF="page2.html">here</A>**, they will go to another Web page.

Here is how this tagged example text would look on a Web page:

> This is a sample sentence from a Web page. When users click <u>here</u>, they will go to another Web page.

The underlined <u>here</u> is now a hyperlink. In HTML coding, the tag <A HREF="page2.html"> tells the browser that all text until the closing tag </A> is a hyperlink. Anchored words appear as a link in the browser (typically underlined in blue), and clicking on the link will take the user to another HTML page, called "page2.html," which has been placed after the equal sign (=) in the hypertext reference. To make the link work, you'll need to create two HTML pages: "page1.html," on which the link is featured, and "page2.html," the page to which the link is attached.

There are two other kinds of hyperlinks. The jump link enables the user to skip down a page, for instance, to a footnote at the bottom of a page. The last type of link brings a user to another site entirely on the World Wide Web. As a Web author, you can link elements on your pages to any site in the world, from the Library of Congress to your nephew's kindergarten site. And those sites can link to your page, too. Every site on the Web has a URL (Uniform Resource Locator); if you can find it, you can link to it.

The best way to learn HTML coding is to look at other people's code. Find a page on the Web that you like, and select the View Source (sometimes this will read View Document Source or View Frame Source) command from your browser's View menu. The HTML code that is the skeleton for this page will appear. You can print out the code and study it. The technique is free and it's fast, and you may learn an ingenious way to create special effects that the HTML books don't mention.

▶ **EXERCISE 5**

Return to the HTML code you developed for Exercise 4 and embed (in the coding) a hypertext link, following the suggestions in this section.

▶ **41b**   Images, page design, and launching on the Web

One of the exciting developments that awaits your publishing efforts on the Web is the relative ease with which you can design a graphical look for your pages. To lend your site a unique appearance, you will be able to choose background and text colors, images, font sizes, and navigational devices.

▶ **I   Images**

An all-text Web page will probably look bland to readers. When possible, try including an image related to your content. To the extent you are able to do so, you will need to plan the presentation of your content with images in mind. Note that it is only for ease of presentation, that you find discussions of writing for the Web in one section of this chapter and a discussion of images in another. Working Web developers bear both of these elements in mind as they plan and build their sites.

Most computer stores sell CD-ROM collections of thousands of clip-art images that you can use royalty free. Of course, images are also available wherever you find them on the Web (but see the note on citing sources, below). And you will find a multitude of Web sites that specialize in stock photography. Here are four:

http://www.digitalstock.com/

http://www.picturequest.com/

http://www.corbis.com/

http://www.photostogo.com/

Once at a site that specializes in images, you can search on keywords (for instance, "Chrysler building") and find dozens of possible images. You can usually download complementary versions for free—small, low-resolution files for mock-ups—or pay a fee for a larger, higher-quality file.

Once you select an appropriate work of art, photo, chart, or graph, you will need to position it on the page you are designing. As you might expect from the discussion of coding text, above, special tags exist to mark images in the source code of a Web page. For instance, if you wanted to place your image on a Web-based résumé (see 43e), you would code the image as follows:

<IMG SRC = "myimage.gif" height=200 width=300 border=0 align=left>

This instruction places an image called "myimage.gif" on the page and aligns it to the left. IMG is short for "image" and alerts the browser to the existence of the image and its source (SRC) in a file called "myimage.gif." Almost all of the images you see on the Web are either GIF (pronounced "jiff" or "giff") or JPG (pronounced jay-peg) files. Most illustrations are GIFs and most photographs are JPGs. Since Web pages are stored on computers that don't understand the difference between image files and other files, you have to name them explicitly, as in "myimage.gif."

Every aspect of visual presentation, down to the finest detail, is controlled by the presence of HTML tags. For instance, the file "myimage.gif" won't have a border when viewed in a browser because of the instruction "border=0." If an HTML coder had written "border=5," you would see a fat, 5 pixel-wide black border around the image.

Many Web developers scan photographs and illustrations into their computers and include these on the Web. Others create new art in programs such as Photoshop or Illustrator. You can take either of these approaches, or work with art you find on the Web. Since every element you find on the Web is in digital format, you can easily make perfect copies of anything you see.

Remember to cite sources: An image on the Web is likely to be the property of the person who made the page, unless that material is clearly labeled as available for anyone's use. Even if you are making a practice page that will not be published, you should credit your source, at least (see 37a-3); and, depending on your intended use, you may need to secure written permission from the copyright holder before reproducing the image (or text) on your Web page.

Saving images

To save an image from a Web page, right-click on your computer's mouse (click and hold your mouse over the image if you're using a Macintosh). Select the Save Image menu item; save the image (and give it a file name); and then use the <IMG SRC> tag to include it in your own Web page. With experience, you'll develop a sense of what makes one image's file size larger than another's. (You can check an image's file size by right-clicking to view its "Properties" on a PC, or selecting "Get Info" on a Macintosh.) The smaller your images, the quicker your page will load.

When working with images, remember your users and their modem speeds. It's a good habit to "weigh" your pages for file size. If the total weight of a page is more than 30K, chances are that most home users with 28.8 modems will be frustrated by waiting for your page to download. Then again, if you're building a site targeted at technically oriented people, you can assume that they'll be viewing your site on a fast connection and up-to-date hardware. Remember: your Web page may be displayed differently on different computers and Web browsers. Images that you manipulate on a PC, working with Internet Explorer, may look quite different displayed on a Mac or with Netscape.

▶2   **Page design**

In laying out pages for the Web, you should be aware of both design principles in general (see 42a–c) and the constraints that technology places on you. Often, and unfortunately, your vision of a Web page is rendered impossible due to some limitation of the browsers or monitors people will use in viewing the page. Thus, it is important, early on, to understand the technical limitations within which you will work and to design with these limitations in mind.

Not everyone with an Internet connection has the same computer and monitor that you have. Some people have huge monitors capable of displaying high resolution graphics, while others have small screens that can only display half a page at a time. Some people view Web sites on very fast office connections, downloading fancy animations quickly, while others dial up on 28.8 modems and must wait for long periods of time to view a simple page. This variability in hardware means that you cannot predict what an experience of your page will be like for each user. Still, there are several design principles to follow that will give your Web pages the highest probability of being viewed in the way you intend them to be, by the widest possible audience.

1. Use high contrast between type and background colors. It's hard to read pink type on a yellow background. Dark text on a light background is a standard design that has dominated the print world for hundreds of years, for good reason.
2. Don't use background images if you expect anyone to read the text on your page. Such imagery might work on an art-oriented site, or on an introductory page to an entire Web site but keep your core content on a solid (preferably light) background. Before finalizing your Web site, check your use of background colors on different computers (PC and Mac) and with different browsers (Internet Explorer and Netscape).
3. Text is often easier to read when formatted into narrow columns, a layout that allows the eye to skip down the screen easily.
4. Use animation judiciously—to explain a concept or just to make your user smile. Free GIF animation software is downloadable from the Web and is easy to use. Two good programs are "GifBuilder" for Macintosh and "Animagic GIF" for PC. You'll find them at popular shareware sites such as <http://www.shareware.com>.
5. Use the power of images as navigational aids. Many users find it easier to navigate from graphic representations on a Web site than from hotlinked words or phrases. An example: If you're building a travel Web site, why not use a clickable image of the world as a way of navigating through the Web site? You'll need to build an "image map" that instructs the browser what page to load if a user clicks on a certain part of the image. There are dozens of free image-mapping

software programs. For Macintosh, you might try "Web Map"; for PCs, try "Live Image" or "CoffeeCup Image Mapper." All of these are available from popular shareware sites such as <http://www.shareware.com>.

6. Let your users talk back to you. They'll let you know if a feature isn't working, if they find an idea interesting, or if they would change something on the site. Include your e-mail address (if you're comfortable doing so) with the "mailto" tag:

<A HREF=<u>mailto:marie@nyu.edu</u>>email me!</A>

Also consider placing a survey on your site using HTML forms. These can include areas for people to type in comments and to answer multiple-choice questions. You'll need the assistance of a programmer, but you can compile fascinating information this way.

▶3 Launching

Now that you have built your own site, you are ready to post it on the Web. Web pages live on a server, a computer specially designed to hold thousands of HTML files, images, and other materials that comprise Web sites. These computers are connected to the Internet, where any browser can find the HTML files and request pages. A server earns its name by delivering (serving) Web pages, on demand, to browsers. A demand for a Web page must be phrased in HyperText Transfer Protocol, otherwise known as http. This is the language your Web browser speaks and the language that you use when specifying a Web address (or URL), such as <http://www.mypage.com>.

Many universities maintain servers on which students can post Web sites. When preparing a Web site for a course, ask your instructor if his or her department has space (server memory) allocated for the course. If so, you will want to know how much space you will be allowed. If you have only a small allotment, you will need to work with relatively few images, which consume precious server space.

If your university has not provided you with server space, you can rent your own space from an Internet Service Provider (ISP). There are thousands of ISPs around the world, and you can search for an inexpensive one on the Web. As an alternative, you might consider posting your pages on a free Web site hosting service such as Geocities.com, Tripod.com, or theglobe.com. Each of these services allows you to establish a Web presence for free; but, being commercial sites, they will insert advertising into your pages.

Not all servers can support advanced Web applications. If your Web sites contain elements such as java applets (programs that enhance your browser's functions), animations, video, or sound, you will need to locate space on a server that will support these file types. Simple pages, like the ones described in this discussion, require minimal server support.

Regardless of how complex your Web site may be, when you're ready to make your HTML files and images available on the Web, you'll need to transfer them from your computer onto the server. You'll do this with File Transfer Protocol. Your instructor or a technical support person at your Internet Service Provider will show you how to use an FTP program to move files from one computer to another, and where to put them. The process is usually straightforward. Many FTP programs look just like your computer's file system. You simply drag and drop files from one folder to another. Depending on the server arrangements

Images, Page Design, and Launching on the Web   **713**

you make, the FTP destination folder might exist on another computer (your Web server) halfway across the world.

A note for advanced Web developers

The information in this chapter offers a general overview of Web publishing. For a more complete introduction and tips on creating Web pages with advanced features, consult the following books and Web pages:

Books

Designing Web Graphics 3 by Linda Weinman is a good resource for graphics design and production for the Web. The book contains many examples and useful techniques.

HTML 4 for the World Wide Web: Visual QuickStart Guide by Elizabeth Castro and Nancy Davis is a good HTML self-help book with easy-to-follow lessons.

Learning Perl, 2nd Edition by Randal L. Schwartz, Tom Christiansen and Larry Wall is the definitive book for starting to program in CGI with Perl. The book is practical and easy to read.

Webmaster in a Nutshell: A Desktop Quick Reference by Stephen Spainhour and Valerie Quercia covers HTML thoroughly and many other technologies such as Javascript, and CGI. It is an indispensable reference work.

Web sites

Builder.com <http://www.builder.com> has a comprehensive magazine format with broad coverage and discussions of new technologies.

Developer.com <http://www.developer.com> is a magazine style site with downloadable scripts and Q&A.

Project Cool <http://www.projectcool.com/developer> is a friendly HTML reference site with tips and examples for many new technologies. The site covers multimedia issues as well (e.g. audio production).

Webmonkey <http://www.webmonkey.com> offers tips on Web design and construction with a fun attitude.

World Wide Web Consortium <http://w3c.org> is a "command center" for the Web, where you will find official HTML specifications.

CHAPTER 42

The Visual Design of Documents

Your goal in writing is to communicate a particular content. If your content is clear, readers will understand—and your efforts will have succeeded. Everything you have read in this book encourages you to communicate clearly, through words. Here we consider how document design—the use of art, graphics, typeface, and format—can make your content more accessible to readers. A single principle underlies this discussion:

> Every design element in a document should help readers to understand the content.

Without content, you have no reason for writing. Therefore, understand your content first. Articulate it as clearly as you can, with words; then look to the ways effective design can help you to deliver that content.

▶ 42a Design elements and the audiences for your documents

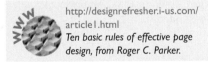
http://designrefresher.i-us.com/
article1.html
Ten basic rules of effective page design, from Roger C. Parker.

When you write for traditional academic audiences—papers for your college courses, for instance—look for design conventions in Appendix A, "Manuscript Form" and also in the example student papers for the humanities, social sciences, and sciences in Chapters 38, 39, and 40. There you will find discussions and illustrations of basic visual elements of academic writing:

- Titles—to focus attention on your topic and argument
- Headings—to provide summary organizers for sections of a paper
- Displayed (or "block") quotations—to emphasize key words of others
- Graphs, charts—to synthesize often complex data into visual form

Design elements for nonacademic audiences

When you address readers in the world of business, government, or technical fields beyond academic settings, it is especially important to make the unity and coherence of your writing accessible, and a well-planned design can help. The following types of documents will benefit from carefully designed visual elements:

- Presentation pieces intending to educate, technically train, or persuade business or government audiences. This text is an example of one kind of instruction and presentation material.
- Special reports, especially proposals in the science and business worlds, which need to emphasize clear and persuasive problem-solution structures. The science research paper in 40d develops some of the conventions common in this type of presentation.
- Promotional, public relations, and marketing pieces designed to attract and persuade specific audiences.
- Newsletters and public information bulletins in print and on electronic media.

Readers of these types of documents have many demands on their time. They will first skim articles and reports to determine if there is anything of use to them; only then will they read sections (if not an entire piece) slowly and carefully. You must therefore try to focus the attention of these readers, capturing their interest so that they will give your document consideration. You can focus attention by using techniques found in conventional, academic writing (titles, headings, block quotations, and graphs and charts). You can also focus attention in more visually exciting ways.

- Emphatic type—to highlight key words and phrases
- Art and photos—to express information, mood, and ideas
- Layout and use of white space—to ensure a balanced, open look

The magazines you read, along with advertisements, promotional materials, newspapers, and electronic communications (Web pages, for instance), can provide visually stimulating and sophisticated examples, many of them prepared by specialists well-versed in type design, art, and layout. This chapter can help you look for basic ways to ensure that visual interest and clarity are part of your writing; you also can consult a number of books for detailed help on document design for business and technical communication. Some recent books include K. W. Houp et al., *Reporting Technical Information*, 9th edition, 1998; M. J. Killingsworth, *Information in Action: A Guide to Technical Communication*, 2nd edition, 1999; or P. W. Agnew et al., *Multimedia in the Classroom*, 1996 (all Boston: Allyn & Bacon).

▶ 42b Effective headings and typography emphasize content.

Begin with clear, concise writing. Well-chosen typography will improve readability and reduce confusion. Clearly worded, brief headings will communicate the logic of your document's organization. The combination of clear typeface and carefully worded headings will bring a visual coherence to your work that suggests coherent ideas.

Typeface

A type "face" is the name given to the distinctive design and shape of a family of lettering used for text. A face or design usually includes several "fonts," or lettering of different sizes and styles, including italics or boldface. As a general principle, the fewer the typefaces in one document, the better.

Assigning different typefaces to specific functions

Sometimes, when you need to distinguish one kind of text function from another, a distinctive typeface can be assigned for each function, adding coherence as well as visual interest to a document. As a second principle, when you introduce a different typeface, assign each face a single function.

The typography of this textbook illustrates the point. Notice that the book has only three typefaces or designs (though it uses different fonts and type sizes); each clearly signals that a different category of information is being presented.

You are now reading the regular typeface used for the text. When you read the color-printed headings, you see a slightly different, thicker font used only for these emphatic headlines. When student writing is shown, as in the papers for Chapters 38 to 40, you see the student text in a very different face (called Courier, seen in typewriters or in e-mail) to show a distinctive kind of writing.

Word processing typefaces

If you write with a word processor, you will likely have many choices of typefaces. Your most basic consideration, for anything simpler that an advertising brochure, is whether to use a typeface that features "serif" lettering, or "sans serif" lettering. Serif lettering, as used throughout this book, is the family of typefaces most commonly seen in North America for basic text. If you closely observe the two samples below, you will notice an important difference. The text sample on the left features fine horizontal lines, called "serifs," at the top and bottom of each vertical stroke in the lettering. But the sample on the right, lacking these horizontal serifs, has a plainer look and (using the French term for "without") is called a "sans serif" or sometimes "gothic" family of lettering.

This is serif lettering.   This is sans serif lettering.

For most North American readers the difference is more than stylistic; the serifs are thought to act like a horizontal ruler, leading the eye smoothly across a long line of type on a page. For this reason serif type is commonly considered effective for lengthy documents featuring long lines of text. Sans serif, with its clean, emphatic appearance, is often considered useful for headings or brief messages presented in short lines.

Type size

Your word processor will be able to vary emphasis and readability by expanding or contracting type sizes. These sizes are commonly designated with numbers from as low as 6 or 8 "points" (a typesetter's unit of measure) to 10, 11, or 12, commonly seen for basic text in books or magazines, up to point sizes as large as the 30-, 40-, or even 50-point headings seen in advertising.

If you vary type size in your document, again bear in mind the principle of orderliness. Assign specific type sizes to specific functions. Relative to the size of the standard type size you are using in your document, you may want to assign section headings a larger size and chapter titles an even larger size, while footnotes and index entries might receive a smaller size. You can see several varieties of type sizes in this book, each for a distinct purpose.

Formatting the margins

If you work with a word processor, another decision you need to make for basic text is how to treat the margins. It is standard to see the left margin in straight alignment for documents other than advertising brochures, where centering or right-alignment of type is sometimes used. The left-aligned convention helps the eye begin each line at the same place on the page.

For the right margin you need to decide whether or not to "justify"—that is, to align letters on both left and right exactly in a vertical line. Right-justified margins are common in professionally prepared documents and are possible with most word processors, often without complex hyphenation for line breaks. (Hyphenation, available on many word processors, is often avoided because it slows scrolling and processing.) Unless the software is very sophisticated, right-justified documents without hyphenation may create uneven spacing, or "holes" on the page, making reading erratic and difficult. To avoid this, and to help readers follow individual lines more smoothly without hyphenation, many professional documents prefer to show the typewriter's standard "ragged right" format, with which most readers are quite comfortable.

Highlighting with boldface, italics, and boxes

Again, the principle of restraint holds: less is usually more. If you want boldfaced, italicized, or boxed words and phrases to receive special emphasis, then use these tools sparingly. Maintain a "base" of plain text that contrasts clearly with any emphatic type, and try to establish a convention for its use. For instance, you could reserve boldfaced words for headings; you could reserve italics for words that are being defined; you could draw a box around material that you consider crucially important. Overuse of these tools will quickly diminish their effectiveness and disorient your readers with a cluttered document.

In this text, italicized words are used only to emphasize important terms, to identify key words in examples, and for conventional usage in titles. Boldface type is restricted to terms that are included in the glossary; boxed information appears only with the stepwise procedures in 38d and the one key principle in this chapter:

> Every design element in a document should help readers to understand the content.

Overall format and heading structure

A coherent overall plan

Plan an overall structure for your document in such a way that its internal logic, and its key points, are quickly communicated to anyone who takes a few minutes to scan the pages. To communicate structure and idea, divide your content into well-connected chunks of varying sizes: major units, sections, subsections, paragraphs. Communicate these chunks of material with format elements such as these:

- Table of contents—For longer, formal presentations, a listing of titles or topics can provide a map and overview of your document's plan. Schematic overviews or charts can also be used—as on the endpapers of this book.
- Unit or chapter titles—Units that begin on new pages will focus attention on the main elements of your presentation.
- Unit or chapter openings—Brief overviewing paragraphs can set out the unit's plan—as typified by the opening of Chapter 29 in this book.
- Section titles—Headings at different levels of emphasis can focus the reader's attention on broad ideas and specifics. (See the next section.)
- Unit summaries—When clearly marked and located at the end of a unit, or possibly at the opening of a chapter and called an "abstract" (see 39b or 40b, c), summary restatements can distill key points.

When you choose format elements for your document, be consistent in structure, heading scheme, and typeface. Readers will understand these visual elements and will come to depend on them as cues to your content.

Headings

Headings—words or brief phrases or sentences—announce the content of your presentation. An effective scheme for headings will communicate your overall idea to readers who scan a long document, but a clear scheme is also important for newsletters, brochures, or Web pages. By assigning a particular typestyle and heading structure to each element of your document, you can enhance its clarity, interest, and visual coherence.

The wording of headings should forecast the main issues or thesis ideas to come in each section. Frame your headings with enough white space to give the full visual emphasis you desire. Here is a checklist of questions to help you to plan a heading scheme:

- How many levels of heads will you use? Consult your outline and try to reduce the number of hierarchical levels to a simple scheme.
- Will you number the heads? Avoid numbering except in complex reference or technical works where numbered heads make it easy to cross-reference, as in this book.
- What typographical emphasis will you give the hierarchy of headings? For each level, make a consistent scheme for distinctive treatment of size, typeface, boldface, italics, or color, with all headings made distinct from your text.
- Will you use color in headings or in type? If so, keep the color scheme simple. Too many colors used unsystematically may confuse readers and make your scheme harder to follow.
- In addition to heads, will you use software to make "headers" or "footers"—brief identifying phrases that appear at the top or bottom of pages, usually on the line with page numbers? If yes, use these as brief locating labels, not

as a way to convey detailed information. Will headers and footers be different on the left and right pages? If so, it is common for the left header or footer to give a brief version of the unit or chapter heading, and for the right side to give a label for lesser sections or subsections.

A warning: When your final document is laid out in pages, survey it to make sure that headings at the bottom of a page are not left alone ("widowed"), but have at least two or three lines of text following. If need be, break pages to run a short page and push the lone heading to the top of a new page.

Itemized lists

Lists, outlines, and bullet points are effective visual tools for concentrating the reader's attention on the content you deem important. A list of brief items can compress ideas and connect them in a series that forecasts a direction or a pattern you want readers to see. Many examples of listed and bulleted items appear in this chapter, but lists are a frequent feature of newsletters, brochures, and Web pages. For lists and bullet points, bear these considerations in mind:

- List items that you can express in a sentence or two.
- Use a bullet (•), a dash (—), or an asterisk (*) for briefer material that you can express in one or two indented lines.
- Keep listed and bulleted items grammatically parallel. The rules of parallelism for outlining apply especially to lists, and often to a series of headings as well. (See 18e-1, 2.)
- Indent the listed numbers or bullet points to set them off from your text.
- Use bullet points if the order of items is unimportant; otherwise, use numbers.
- For the left margins of lists, either use the list format on your word processor, or else the "hanging indent" form, with second and subsequent lines indented back from the initial word, number, or bullet, and aligned as in this example.

If your list or your bullet points run longer than seven or eight items, consider regrouping material and presenting two lists or sets of bullet points, each with its own heading. As with other formatting elements, it is important to make a consistent plan for functional use of itemized or bulleted lists, avoiding visual confusion from inconsistency or overuse.

Using white space

Too much text on a page tires readers' eyes as they scan the page looking for important information. Some experts on page design (especially for documents intended for nonacademic audiences) suggest that writers devote no more than 60 percent of a page to text. The remainder of the page should consist of graphical elements and white space. The use of white space on a page creates a frame for information you have already highlighted with type styles, and thus doubly emphasizes it. For examples of white space strategically used, see the following sections of this book: 40d, a scientific report with graphs; 43b, a business letter; 43f, a memorandum.

▶ 42c   Graphic material in reports, presentations, or proposals

The documents you write are intended to convey a meaning and to leave a message with readers. Along with creative, functional, and simple use of headings and typography, graphics can add considerable interest to a document. Quite aside from the visual variety graphics contribute to a document, flowcharts, tables, charts, graphs, photographs, and art can actually be "worth a thousand words" as the clearest and most compact way of delivering information. As with your use of headings and typography to focus a reader's attention, you should strive in your use of graphics for a simple, consistent, and clean design framed by plenty of white space.

Graphic elements and their functions

Ideally, your use of graphics will complement—but not repeat—the material you've already written. To achieve an effective visual balance in your documents, plan the document's layout in advance. Understand in broad terms the balance you want to achieve between text and graphics. When you do incorporate graphical elements, refer in your text to these elements at the earliest opportunity. Try to not wait until your reader has completed reading your text to present related graphics. Consider using these graphical forms for the following specific purposes:

TO review, preview, emphasize, or prioritize	USE a flowchart, table list, outline list
TO orient readers in terms of space or sequences	USE a chart, diagram, map, photo views
TO show flow of functions or actions	USE a flowchart, diagram, photo
TO add emphasis to key relationships	USE a bar graph, pie chart, simple table
TO analyze or summarize key data	USE a complex graph, table, diagram
TO illustrate original data and sources	USE a facsimile recreating your source
TO help motivate	USE a photo, image, drawing, cartoon

For a detailed look at how to organize and present the types of graphical materials just mentioned, see the following recent texts: K. W. Houp et al., *Reporting Technical Information*, 9th edition, 1998, Chapter 10, "Graphical Elements" and M. J. Killingsworth, *Information in Action: A Guide to Technical Communication*, 2nd edition, Chapter 6, "Developing Purposeful Graphics," 1999 (both Boston: Allyn & Bacon).

Tables, charts, graphs

Tables present data that usually shows a relationship between at least two sets of varying quantities, listed in columns. To show a table's relationships clearly, each set of quantities in each column or section of data is labeled, as shown in the example at the end of the paper in 40d. The often dense, complex data in tables needs simple, direct labels. Any qualifying or complex elements should be explained in footnotes.

Tables are the best vehicle for displaying large blocks of dense quantitative data. When you need a vivid display of critical changes or patterns of relationships in the table, a graph is the next option. The student paper in 40d shows similar data displayed both in tabular and graphed form. Using software packages, you can convert tabular data into line, bar, or circle graphs.

Consider the following examples showing similar material displayed in a line graph, a bar graph, and a circle graph. All three graphs compress a great deal of numerical information into a readily understood visual format. While the graphs show similar material relating to Medicare/Medicaid finances, each type offers a different emphasis and different options for the presentation best suited to your data and the points you wish to emphasize.

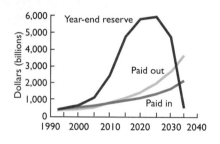

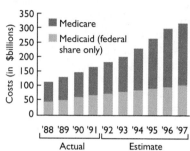

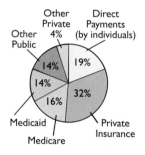

Note that in all three presentations there is a brief label, similar to those for tables, that identifies the significance of the quantities in each dimension of the graph. In constructing line or bar graphs, it is very important to plan the proportions you attach to the vertical and horizontal scale of quantities being displayed. If either dimension appears too short or too long, readers are likely to challenge the relationship you are showing between the graphed quantities, especially if the graph looks steeper or flatter than seems warranted by the data.

A line graph can show complex relationships, trends, and changes over space or time—in this case money paid into and out from federal Medicaid/Medicare funds, with surpluses and projected deficits shown. The scales on both axes of the graph are proportionally chosen to represent the abruptness of change.

When your message consists of simpler, less dense information, consider converting line graphs to bar graphs or pie charts. A bar graph emphasizes sim-

The Visual Design of Documents

ple contrastive relationships among distinct units being compared, rather than the continuous trend relationships of line graphs. A pie chart is good for showing proportional parts of a whole entity—especially percentages.

Diagrams and images

Use diagrams, photographs, and images to help readers focus on your content and to amplify its meaning. For example, this book's "Thinking and Writing Wheel" graphic in Chapter 3 (see particularly 3a and 3b), is a schematic diagram that complements the text in those sections, giving readers a conceptual "map" and overview of a complex process. Use graphical elements with care, positioning them where you think they will best enhance the reader's understanding of your content.

Writers working on computers now have thousands of images available for use from clip-art programs. Here are three much-used examples:

Clip-art images can sometimes direct a reader's attention effectively and thus have a place in document design. But take care to match clip-art images with your content. Do not decorate documents with images that can't be justified on the basis of content.

▶ 42d Designing newsletters

You may find yourself working in organizations that produce pamphlets, brochures, newsletters, or their electronic cousin—Web pages. For all of these formats, the basic principles from preceding sections for typography, headings, organizing schemes, and graphic elements are even more important than for reports and technical documents. If your job description calls for you to produce these types of documents, the success of which depends heavily on good visual design, then you should consult a specialized book such as J. J. Yopp and K. C. McAdams, *Reaching Audiences: A Guide to Media Writing* (Boston: Allyn & Bacon, 1999).

Newsletters

Organizations of all sorts use newsletters to disseminate information both internally, to employees, and externally, to the public. The newsletter is often presented in an 8-1/2 × 11 inch format that takes advantage of the various design tools discussed in this chapter. One distinctive feature is the newsletter's newspaper-like column width for text, which you see in the example on page 724 from the Massachusetts Cultural Council, a state agency for the arts. Notice the use of type style and size, headers, a box, white space, ruled lines of varying thickness, and clip-art images to achieve unity, balance, and proportion. Attractively designed, this first page of the newsletter invites readers to continue reading inside.

MASSACHUSETTS CULTURAL COUNCIL

cultural education e✗*change*

The Newsletter of the Education Department Vol. 2, No. 2   Winter 1997

Bringing Multicultural Programming into the Classroom

*P*arents, teachers, and community members explore a classroom that has been transformed into an East African rainforest. Colorfully costumed students answer questions about the impact of the rainforest on its inhabitants. Another room has become a Moroccan market featuring North African crafts. In another room, students share writings based on West African myths, poetry, and legends.

For five weeks sixth-graders at Marblehead Middle School have studied Africa, as part of their year-long World Cultures curriculum. Artists-in-residence De Ama Battle and Jafar Manselle have incorporated dance, music, and folklore into the curriculum, creating a program so successful that it is now a permanent unit of study.

Implementing in-depth multicultural programming is a challenging but rewarding process, and successful programs are the result of substantive collaboration among teachers, parents, administrators, and the community. By working closely with local artists and cultural organizations, schools can develop programs that probe into the heart of various cultures and integrate meaningful learning into their curricula.

Questioning Finds Similarities

A first step is realizing that it is impossible to know everything about any culture.

"Learning about cultures is a process of discovery, not a mastery of 'knowable things'," said Gail Matthews-Denatle, a member of the National Task Force on Folk Arts in Education. "In effective programs, children learn to be 'questioners.' A spirit of inquiry allows us to see people as individuals as well as part of a community."

Teaching that each student has his/her own culture can be equally important.

"Culture is the way a group of people survive," says Motoko, an artist specializing in folktales from Japan.

> "Learning about cultures is a process of discovery, not a mastery of 'knowable things'."

"It's a product of people's ingenuity. Therefore no culture is exotic. Teaching should focus on similarities in human experience."

Motoko achieves this by relating Japanese festivals to students' experiences. For example, after learning about a festival in which parents celebrate children reaching ages 3, 5, and 7, students answer questions such as: At age 3, what were your favorite games? Who did you learn them from? Students learn about Japanese culture while exploring their own lives and discovering similarities.

Plan Ahead, Follow Through

Multicultural programming involves research, planning, and commitment. Eshu Bumpus, an African and African American folklorist, suggests that teachers begin by defining terms. What is culture? What is multiculturalism? It is important to remember that different communities exist within cultures; they can be "multicultural." For example, Native American cultural practices vary by region and tribe.

Artists-in-residence significantly enhance multicultural programming, though the most successful programs require commitment year-round.

"Consider doing curriculum development with the artist," said Battle, founder of the Art of Black Dance and Music. "Plan with the artists before the program begins and be willing to do research and follow up."

In Marblehead, teachers set aside planning time to review resources and exchange ideas. Teacher involvement is critical to an artist's presentation in the classroom.

During the residency, teachers learned dances alongside the students, and helped them rehearse for performances.

Continued on P.4

Important Dates

April 1, 1997
Event & Residency Grant Deadline for Fall 1997 Programs

April 25, 1997
Education Partnership Planning Grants Deadline

43

Writing in a Business Environment

In a business environment, much is accomplished—meetings are attended, information is shared, agendas are set, arguments are settled—based on writing alone. When you enter this environment by writing a letter or memo, you must understand that people are not obligated to answer you (rude as this might seem). Businesspeople have many demands placed on them simultaneously. When reading, they must know a writer's purpose and they must be given a motivation for continuing to read. Lacking either of these qualities, a document will not represent itself as *important* enough to merit attention, and the reader will simply turn to more pressing concerns.

You will significantly improve your chances of readers acting on your letters and memos if you begin by appreciating the constraints on their time. Think of your readers as busy people inclined to help if your writing is direct, concise, and clearly organized. A *direct* letter or memo will state in its opening sentence your purpose for writing. A *concise* letter or memo will state your exact needs in as few words as possible. A *well-organized* letter or memo will present only the information that is pertinent to your main point, in a sequence that is readily understood.

The writing process in a business environment

Direct, concise, and clearly organized writing takes time, of course, and is seldom the effort of a single draft. Writing a document in a business setting involves a process, just as your writing a research paper in an academic setting involves a process. It may seem counterintuitive, but you will spend less time writing a letter twice (producing both rough and revised drafts) than you will trying to do a creditable job in a single draft. Generally, you will do well to follow the advice in Chapters 3 and 4 on planning, developing, drafting, and revising a paper. For every document that you write, aside from the simplest two- or three-line notes, you should prepare to write, write a draft, and then revise.

Standard formats

Use unlined, white bond paper (8½ × 11 inches) or letterhead stationery for your business correspondence. Prepare your letter on a typewriter or word processor, and print on one side of the page only. Format your letter according to one of three conventions: full block, block, and semi-block—terms describing the ways in which you indent information. The six basic elements of a letter—return address, inside address and date, salutation, body, closing, and abbreviated matter—begin at the left margin in the *full block* format. Displayed information such as lists begins five spaces from the left margin. In the *block* format, the return address and the closing are aligned just beyond the middle of the page, while the inside address, salutation, new paragraphs, and abbreviated matter each begin at the left margin. (See the "Letter of Inquiry" in 43b for an example of block format.) The *semi-block* format is similar to the block format except that each new paragraph is indented five spaces from the left margin and any displayed information is indented ten spaces. (See the "Letter of Application" in 43d for an example of a semi-block format.)

Standard spacing

Maintain a one-inch margin at the top, bottom, and sides of the page. Single-space the document for all but very brief letters (two to five lines), the body of which you should double-space. Skip one or two lines between the return address and the inside address; one line between the inside address and the salutation (which is followed by a colon); one line between the salutation and opening paragraph; one line between paragraphs; one line between your final paragraph and your complimentary closing (which is followed by a comma); four lines between your closing and typewritten name; and one line between your typewritten name and any abbreviated matter.

Standard information

Return address and date

Unless you are writing on letterhead stationery (on which your return address is preprinted), type as a block of information your return address—street address on one line; city, state, and zip code on the next; the date on a third line. If you are writing on letterhead, type the date only, centered one or two lines below the letterhead's final line.

Inside address

Provide as a block of information the full name and address of the person to whom you are writing. Be sure to spell all names—personal, company, and address—correctly. Use abbreviations only if the company abbreviates words in its own name or address.

Salutation

Begin your letter with a formal greeting, traditionally *Dear* _____: Unless another title applies, such as *Dr.* or *Senator*, address a man as *Mr.* and a woman as *Miss* or

Mrs.—or as *Ms.* if you or the person addressed prefer this. When in doubt about a woman's marital status or preferences in a salutation, use *Ms.* If you are not writing to a specific person, avoid the gender-specific and potentially insulting *Dear Sirs.* Many readers find the generic *Dear Sir or Madam* and *To whom it may concern* to be equivocal, and you may want to open instead with the company name, *Dear Acme Printing*, or with a specific department name or position title: *Dear Personnel Department* or *Dear Personnel Manager.* See the discussion at 31a for the conventions on abbreviating titles in a salutation or an address.

Body of the letter

Develop your letter in paragraph form. State your purpose clearly in the opening paragraph. Avoid giving your letter a visually dense impression. When your content lends itself to displayed treatment (if, for instance, you are presenting a list), indent the information. You may want to use bullets, numbers, or hyphens. (See, for example, the "Letter of Inquiry" in 43b.)

Closing

Close with some complimentary expression such as *Yours truly, Sincerely,* or *Sincerely yours.* Capitalize the first word only of this closing remark and follow the remark with a comma. Allow four blank lines for your signature, then type your name and, below that, any title that applies.

Abbreviated matter

Several abbreviations may follow at the lefthand margin, one line below your closing. If someone else has typed your letter, indicate this as follows: the typist should capitalize your initials, place a slash, then place the typist's initials in lowercase—*LR/hb.* If you are enclosing any material with your letter, type *Enclosure* or *Enc.* If you care to itemize this information, place a colon and align items as in the example letter in 43d. If you are sending copies of the letter to other readers (known as a *secondary audience*), write *cc:* (for *carbon copy*) and list the names of the recipients of the copies, as in the example letter in 43f.

The second page

Begin your letter's second page with identifying information so that if the first and second pages are separated the reader will easily be able to match them again. The blocked information should consist of your name, the date, and the page number presented in a block at the upper lefthand corner of the page.

```
Jon Lipman
January 7, 1999
Page 2

and in the event of your coming to Worcester, I would be
happy to set up an interview with you here. Perhaps the
week of May 17 would be convenient, since I will be trav-
eling to eastern Massachusetts.
```

Standard Formats, Spacing, and Information in a Business Letter   727

Envelope

Single-space all information. If you are not using an envelope with a preprinted return address, type your return address at the upper lefthand corner. Center between the right- and lefthand sides the name and address of the person to whom you are writing. Vertically, type the address just below center.

```
Jon Lipman
231 Gray Street
Worcester, Massachusetts 01610


                    Ms. Hannah Marks
                    Equipment Design, Inc.
                    1254 Glenn Avenue
                    Arlington, Massachusetts 02174
```

▶ 43b Letters of inquiry

A letter of inquiry (see page 729) is based on a question you want answered. Presumably, you have done enough research to have identified a person knowledgeable in the area concerning you. Do not ask for too much information or for very general information that you could readily find in a library. Avoid giving your reader the impression that you are asking him or her for basic information that you should have managed to locate yourself. If you are inquiring about price or product information, simply ask for a brochure.

■ Begin the letter with a sentence that identifies your need. State who you are, what your general project is (if the information is pertinent), and the reason for your writing.

■ Follow with a sentence devoted to how you have learned of the reader or the reader's company and how this person or company could be of help to you.

■ Pose a few *specific* questions. Frame these questions in such a way that you demonstrate you have done background research.

■ State any time constraints you may have. Do not expect your reader to respond any sooner than two or three weeks.

■ Close with a brief statement of appreciation. If you feel it would expedite matters, you might include a self-addressed, stamped envelope.

BLOCK FORMAT

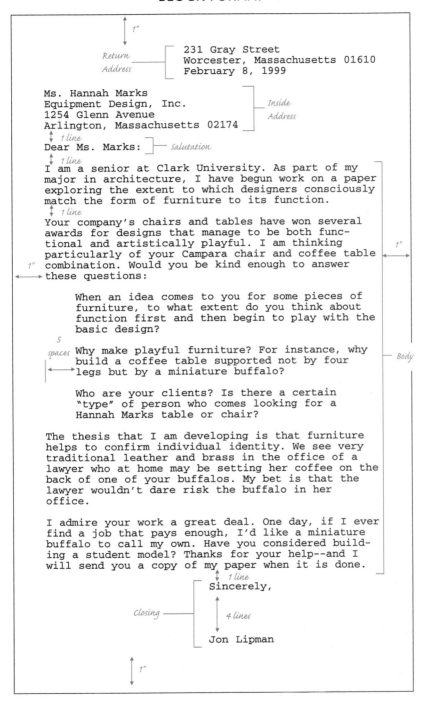

Return Address
231 Gray Street
Worcester, Massachusetts 01610
February 8, 1999

1"

Ms. Hannah Marks
Equipment Design, Inc.
1254 Glenn Avenue
Arlington, Massachusetts 02174

Inside Address

1 line
Dear Ms. Marks: *Salutation*

1 line
I am a senior at Clark University. As part of my
major in architecture, I have begun work on a paper
exploring the extent to which designers consciously
match the form of furniture to its function.

1 line
Your company's chairs and tables have won several
awards for designs that manage to be both functional and artistically playful. I am thinking
particularly of your Campara chair and coffee table
combination. Would you be kind enough to answer
these questions:

1"

> When an idea comes to you for some pieces of
> furniture, to what extent do you think about
> function first and then begin to play with the
> basic design?

5 spaces
> Why make playful furniture? For instance, why
> build a coffee table supported not by four
> legs but by a miniature buffalo?

Body

> Who are your clients? Is there a certain
> "type" of person who comes looking for a
> Hannah Marks table or chair?

The thesis that I am developing is that furniture
helps to confirm individual identity. We see very
traditional leather and brass in the office of a
lawyer who at home may be setting her coffee on the
back of one of your buffalos. My bet is that the
lawyer wouldn't dare risk the buffalo in her
office.

I admire your work a great deal. One day, if I ever
find a job that pays enough, I'd like a miniature
buffalo to call my own. Have you considered building a student model? Thanks for your help--and I
will send you a copy of my paper when it is done.

1 line
Sincerely,

Closing

4 lines

Jon Lipman

1"

43c Letters of complaint

When you have a problem that you want remedied, write a letter of complaint. No matter how irate you may be, keep a civil but firm tone and do not threaten. If the time comes to take follow-up action, write a second letter in which you repeat your complaint and state your intentions. Your letter of complaint should be clear on the following points:

- Present the problem.
- State when and where you bought the product in question (if this is a consumer complaint). Provide an exact model number. If this is a complaint about poor service or ill treatment, state when and where you encountered the unacceptable behavior.
- Describe precisely the product failure or the way in which a behavior was unsatisfactory.
- Summarize the expectations you had when you bought the product or when you engaged someone's services. State succinctly how your expectations were violated and how you were inconvenienced (or worse).
- State exactly how you want the problem resolved.

43d Letters of application

Whether you are applying for summertime work or for a full-time job after graduation, your first move probably will be to write a letter of application in which you ask for an interview. A successful letter of application will pique a prospective employer's interest by achieving a delicate balance. On the one hand you will present yourself as a bright, dependable, and resourceful person while on the other you will avoid sounding like an unabashed self-promoter. Your goal is to show a humble and earnest confidence. As you gather thoughts for writing, think of the employer as someone in need of a person who can be counted on for dependable and steady work, for creative thinking, and for an ability to function amiably as a member of a team. Avoid presenting yourself merely as someone who has a particular set of skills. You are more than this. Skills grow dated as new technologies become available. You want to suggest that your ability to learn and to adapt will never grow dated.

- Keep your letter of application to one typewritten page.
- Open by stating which job you are applying for and where you learned of the job.
- Review your specific skills and work experience that make you well suited for the job.
- Review your more general qualities (in relation to work experience, if appropriate) that make you well suited for the job.
- Express your desire for an interview and note any constraints on your time: exams, jobs, and other commitments. Avoid statements like "you can contact me at _____." You will provide your address and phone number on your résumé.
- Close with a word of appreciation.

SEMI-BLOCK FORMAT

231 Gray Street
Worcester, Massachusetts 01610
March 30, 1999

Ms. Hannah Marks
Equipment Design, Inc.
1254 Glenn Avenue
Arlington, Massachusetts 02174

Dear Ms. Marks:

5 spaces

I would like to apply for the marketing position you advertised in Architectural Digest. As you know from our previous correspondence, I am an architecture major with an interest in furniture design. As part of my course work I took a minor in marketing, with the hope of finding a job similar to the one you have listed.

For the past two summers I have apprenticed myself to a cabinet maker in Berkshire County, Massachusetts. Mr. Hiram Stains is 70 years old and a master at working with cherry and walnut. While I love working in a shop, and have built most of the furniture in my own apartment (see the photographic enclosures), I realize that a craftsman's life is a bit too solitary for me. Ideally, I would like to combine in one job my woodworking skills, my degree in architecture, and my desire to interact with people.

Your job offers precisely this opportunity. I respect your work immensely and am sure I could represent Equipment Design with enthusiasm. Over time, if my suggestions were welcomed, I might also be able to contribute in terms of design ideas.

I would very much like to arrange an interview. Final exams are scheduled for the last week of April. I'll be preparing the week before that, so I'm available for an interview anytime aside from that two-week block. Thank you for your interest, and I hope to hear from you soon.

Sincerely,

Jon Lipman

Jon Lipman

enc.: photographs
      writing sample

Align itemized enclosures

When you have written a second draft of your letter, seek out editorial advice from those who have had experience applying for jobs and particularly from those who have been in a position of reading letters of application and setting up interviews. Here are a few questions you can put to your readers: What sort of person does this letter describe? Am I emphasizing my skills and abilities in the right way? How do you feel about the tone of this letter? Am I direct and confident without being pushy? Based on editorial feedback, revise. Proofread two or three times so that your final document is direct, concise, well organized, and letter-perfect with respect to grammar, usage, and punctuation. Write your letter in a block or semi-block format (see page 731) on bond paper that has a good, substantial feel to it. Use paper with at least a twenty-five percent cotton fiber content, which you will find at any stationery store. Use an envelope of matching bond paper.

▶ 43e   Résumés

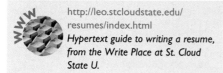

http://leo.stcloudstate.edu/
resumes/index.html
*Hypertext guide to writing a resume,
from the Write Place at St. Cloud
State U.*

A résumé (see page 734) highlights information that you think employers will find useful in considering you for a job. Typically, résumés are written in a clipped form. Although word groups are punctuated as sentences, they are, strictly speaking, fragments. For instance, instead of writing "I supervised fund-raising activities" you would write "Supervised fund-raising activities." Keep these fragments parallel. Keep all verbs in either the present or the past tense; begin all fragments with either verbs or nouns.

Not parallel   Supervised fund-raising activities. Speaker at three area meetings on the "Entrepreneurial Side of the Art World." [The first fragment begins with a verb; the second begins with a noun.]

Parallel   Supervised fund-raising activities. Spoke at three area meetings on the "Entrepreneurial Side of the Art World." [Both fragments begin with a verb in the past tense.]

A résumé works in tandem with your job application. The letter of application establishes a direct communication between you and your prospective employer. Written in your voice, the letter will suggest intangible elements such as your habits of mind and traits of character that make you an attractive candidate. The résumé, by contrast, works as a summary sheet or catalog of your educational and work experience. The tone of the résumé is neutral and fact-oriented. The basic components are these:

- Your name, address, and telephone number—each centered on a separate line at the top of the page.

Provide headings, as follows:

- *Position Desired* or *Objective.* State the specific job you want.
- *Education.* Provide your pertinent college (and graduate school) experience. List degrees earned (or to be earned); major; classes taken, if perti-

nent; and your grade point average, if you are comfortable sharing this information.

- *Work Experience.* List your jobs, including titles, chronologically, beginning with your most recent job.
- *Related Activities.* List any clubs, volunteer positions, or activities that you feel are indicative of your general interests and character.
- *References.* Provide names and addresses if you expect the employer to contact references directly. If you are keeping references on file at a campus office, state that your references are available upon request.

Jon Lipman
231 Gray Street
Worcester, Massachusetts 01610
508-555-8212

Objective: Marketing position in an arts-related
                company

Education: Clark University, Worcester,
                Massachusetts
                Bachelor of Arts in Architecture, May
                1999
                Minor in Marketing, May 1999
                Grade point average (to date) 3.3/4.0

Work   September 1998-present: Directed mar-
Experience: keting campaign for campus-based artists'
                collective and supervised fund raising.
                Spoke at three area meetings on the
                "Entrepreneurial Side of the Art World."
                Generated community interest in the work
                of campus artists by organizing a fair
                and a direct mail program.

                May 1998-August 1998: Studied cabinet
                making with Hiram Stains, master cabinet-
                maker in Berkshire County, Massachusetts.
                Prepared wood for joining, learned dove-
                tail technique, and applied design prin-
                ciples learned in school to cabinet
                construction.

                September 1997-April 1998: Organized
                artists' collective on campus and
                developed marketing plan.

                May 1997-August 1997: Studied cabinet
                making with Hiram Stains. Learned tool
                use and maintenance.

Related   Supervised set design for theater
Activities: productions on campus. Donated services
                as carpenter to local shelter for the
                homeless. Designed and built virtually
                all furniture in my apartment.

References: Mr. Hiram Stains
                Route 16
                Richmond, Massachusetts 01201

                Ms. Amanda Lopez
                Center Street Shelter
                Worcester, Massachusetts 01610

                Dr. Edward Bing
                Department of Architecture
                Clark University
                Worcester, Massachusetts 01610

ON-LINE RÉSUMÉ

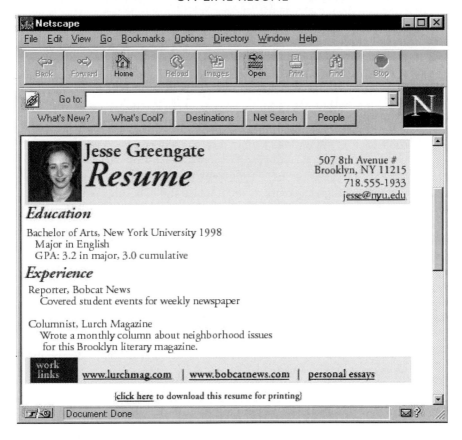

Principles for Writing an Online Résumé

Increasingly, job applicants are creating résumés for view on the World Wide Web, where the résumé is one hyperlink on the applicant's Home page. While the goal of any résumé is to introduce the applicant in a favorable light, Web-based résumés differ from traditional paper résumés in important ways. Most of these differences, you'll find, will work to your advantage. Some tips:

1. Adhere to basic strategies and design principles for creating Web sites. See Chapter 41 for advice.
2. Include links to your work. Whether you have posted writing samples or other efforts online, here is a superb opportunity to showcase your work. Add hyperlinks within the body of your résumé, or create a special links area.
3. Because readers may not have the patience to click through multiple pages on the Web, try to keep your key information—contact information, education, and work experience—well organized and on one page.
4. Place the most important items of your résumé in the topmost 300 pixels of the screen—the area that every Web user should be able to read without scrolling down the page. It is the area of highest impact.

5. Include an e-mail link on the page (if you are comfortable doing so). A reason not to do so: anyone who finds your page, including advertisers, can use your e-mail address.
6. Incorporate relevant graphics into your résumé: showcase projects (such as artwork) with scanned photographs or images from a digital camera.
7. Give your page an informative title, such as "Marie Hobahn's Résumé," so that users who bookmark it will recognize that this is your résumé.
8. Include the date that you have most recently updated the page. Users will want to know that your résumé is current.
9. **The Scannable Résumé:** Provide a non-Web version of your résumé in downloadable form for readers who want to print the résumé or scan it into a résumé database. (You might, at an employer's request, attach a scannable résumé to an e-mail message.) Prepare a résumé for scanning as follows:

   - Eliminate design elements: avoid boldface and italics; remove photos and hyperlinks; remove boxes, underlining, and tab spaces; run text flush to the left margin.
   - Use a standard type face (such as Times Roman), with a 12-point font.
   - Use standard résumé headings, including Education, Work experience, References.
   - Separate categories of information with one line of white space.
   - Add a "keywords" section (after your contact information) with nouns that represent your achievements: for example, biology major, student representative, field hockey player, hospice volunteer, dean's list member. Make sure to use the individual keywords throughout the résumé, so that database search engines will produce your name when a prospective employer searches on a particular keyword.
   - See the example scannable résumé on page 737.

SCANNABLE RÉSUMÉ

```
Jon Lipman
231 Gray Street
Worcester, Massachusetts 01610
Phone: (508) 555-8212
E-mail: jonl@clark.edu


Keywords: architecture, marketing, fund raising, wood
working, speaker, project organizer, leader, set design


Objective
Marketing position in an arts-related company


Education
Clark University, Worcester Massachusetts
B.A. in Architecture, May 1999
Minor in Marketing, May 1999
Grade point average: 3.3/4.0


Work Experience
September 1998-present: Directed marketing campaign for
campus-based artists' collective and supervised fund rais-
ing. Spoke at three area meetings on the "Entrepreneurial
Side of the Art World." Generated community interest in the
work of campus artists by organizing a fair and a direct
mail campaign.
```

▶ **43f** Memoranda

Memoranda, or memos, are internal documents written from one employee to another in the same company. The reasons for writing memos are many: you may want to announce a meeting, summarize your understanding of a meeting, set a schedule, request information, define and resolve a problem, argue for funding, build consensus, and so on. Because they are written "in-house," memos tend to be less formal in tone than business letters; still, they must be every bit as direct, concise, and well organized, or readers will ignore them. When writing a memo longer than a few lines, follow the process discussed earlier of preparing to write, writing, and revising. A memo will differ from a business letter in the following ways:

- The memo has no return address, no inside address, and no salutation. Instead, the memo begins with this information:
  (Date)
  To:
  From:
  Subject:
- The memo follows a full block format, with all information placed flush to the left margin.
- The memo is often divided into headings that separate the document into readily distinguished parts.
- Portions of the memo are often displayed—that is, set off and indented when there are lists or other information lending itself to such treatment.
- Some companies highlight the information about distribution of memo copies to others, either placing the *cc:* line under the *To:* line or adding a subsection titled *Distribution:* with the opening section.

If your memo is three-quarters of a page or longer, consider highlighting its organization with headings, as in the example memo on page 739. Headings work in tandem with the memo's subject line and first sentence to give readers the ability to scan the memo and quickly—within thirty seconds—understand your message. Once again, realize that your readers are busy; they will appreciate any attempt to make their job of reading easier.

February 14, 1999

TO: Linda Cohen

FROM: Matthew Franks

SUBJECT: Brochure production schedule

Thanks for helping to resolve the production schedule for our new brochure. Please review the following production and distribution dates. By return
memo, confirm that you will commit your department
to meeting this schedule.

Production dates

Feb. 19	1999	First draft of brochure copy
March 1	1999	First draft of design plans
March 8	1999	Second draft of brochure copy and design
March 15	1999	Review of final draft and design
March 17	1999	Brochure to printer

Distribution dates

April 4	1999	First printing of 10,000 in our warehouse
April 11	1999	Mailing to Zone 1
April 14	1999	Mailing to Zone 2
April 17	1999	Mailing to Zones 3 and 4

Please let me hear from you by this Friday. If I
haven't, I'll assume your agreement and commitment.
It looks as though we'll have a good brochure this
year. Thanks for all your help.

cc: Amy Hanson

CHAPTER

44

Writing Essay Exams

Increasingly, professors across the curriculum are using essay exams to test student mastery of important concepts and relationships. A carefully conceived exam will challenge you not only to recall and organize what you know of a subject but also to extend and apply your knowledge. Essay exams will require of you numerous responses; but the one response to *avoid* is the so-called information dump in which at first glimpse of a topic you begin pouring onto the page *everything* you have ever read or heard about it. A good answer to an essay exam question requires that you be selective in choosing the information you discuss. What you say about that information and what relationships you make with it are critical. As is often the case with good writing, less tends to be more—provided that you adopt and follow a strategy.

▶ 44a   A strategy for taking essay exams

Prepare

Ideally, you will have read your textbooks and assigned articles with care *as* they were assigned during the period prior to the exam. If you have read closely, or "critically" (see 1e–1h), your preparation for an exam will amount to a *review* of material you have already thought carefully about. Skim assigned materials and pay close attention to notes you have made in the margins or have recorded in a reading log. Take new notes based on your original notes: highlight important concepts from each assignment. Then reorganize your notes according to key ideas that you think serve as themes or focus points for your course. List each idea separately, and beneath each, list any reading that in some way comments on or provides information about that idea. In an American literature course this idea might be "nature as a character" or "innocence lost." In a sociology course the idea might be "social constructions of identity." Turn next to your class notes (you may want to do this *before* reviewing your reading assignments), and add information and comments to your lists of key ideas. Study these lists. Develop statements about each idea that you could, if asked, support with references to specific information. Try to anticipate your instructor's questions.

http://owl.english.purdue.edu/FILES/119.html
Overview, with discussion and examples, of techniques for writing an essay exam, from the Purdue Online Writing Lab.

Read the entire exam before beginning to write.

Allot yourself a certain number of minutes to answer each essay question, allowing extra time for the more complex questions. As you write, monitor your use of time.

Adopt a discipline-appropriate perspective.

Essay exams are designed in part to see how well you understand particular ways of thinking in a discipline. If you are writing a mid-term exam in chemistry, for instance, appreciate that your professor will expect you to discuss material from a chemist's perspective. That is, you will need to demonstrate not only that you know your information but also that you can *do* things with it: namely, think and reach conclusions in discipline-appropriate ways.

Adapt the writing process according to the time allotted for a question.

Assuming that you have thirty minutes to answer an essay question, spend at least five minutes of this allotted time in plotting an answer.

- Locate the assignment's key verb and identify your specific tasks in writing. (See the box on page 742.)
- Given these tasks, list information you can draw on in developing your answer.
- Examine the information you have listed and develop a thesis (see 3d), a statement that directly answers the question and that demonstrates your understanding and application of some key concept associated with the essay topic.
- Sketch an outline of your answer. In taking an essay exam, you have little or no time for writing to discover. Know before you write what major points you will develop in support of your thesis and in what order.

Spend twenty minutes of your allotted time on writing your answer. When you begin writing, be conscious of making clear, logical connections between sentences and paragraphs. Well-chosen transitions (see 5d-3) not only will help your instructor follow your discussion but also will help you to project your ideas forward and to continue writing. As you do in formal papers, develop your essay in sections, with each section organized by a section thesis (see 5a). Develop each section of your essay by discussing *specific* information.

Save five minutes to reread your work and ensure that its logic is clear and that you address the exam question from a discipline-appropriate point of view. Given the time constraints of the essay exam format, instructors understand that you will not submit a polished draft. Nevertheless, they will expect writing that faces the question and that is coherent, unified, and grammatical. Again, avoid an information dump. Select information with care and write with a strategy.

▶ 44b The importance of verbs in an essay question

In reading an essay assignment, you will need to identify a specific topic and purpose for writing. Often, you can identify exactly what an instructor expects by locating a key verb in the assignment such as *illustrate*, *discuss*, or *compare*. Following is a guide to students on "Important Word Meanings" in assignments. Developed by the History Department at UCLA, this guide was intended to help students develop effective responses to essay questions. The guide will serve you well in any of your courses.

Important Word Meanings

Good answers to essay questions depend in part upon a clear understanding of the meanings of the important directive words. These are the words such as *explain*, *compare*, *contrast*, and *justify*, which indicate the way in which the material is to be presented. Background knowledge of the subject matter is essential. But mere evidence of this knowledge is not enough. If you are asked to *compare* the British and American secondary school systems, you will get little or no credit if you merely *describe* them. If you are asked to *criticize* the present electoral system, you are not answering the question if you merely *explain* how it operates. A paper is satisfactory only if it answers directly the question that was asked.

The words that follow are frequently used in essay examinations:

summarize sum up; give the main points briefly. *Summarize the ways in which man preserves food.*

evaluate give the good points and the bad ones; appraise; give an opinion regarding the value of; talk over the advantages and limitations. *Evaluate the contributions of teaching machines.*

contrast bring out the points of difference. *Contrast the novels of Jane Austen and William Makepeace Thackeray.*

explain make clear; interpret; make plain; tell "how" to do; tell the meaning of. *Explain how man can, at times, trigger a full-scale rainstorm.*

describe give an account of; tell about; give a word picture of. *Describe the Pyramids of Giza.*

define give the meaning of a word or concept; place it in the class to which it belongs and set it off from other items in the same class. *Define the term "archetype."*

compare bring out points of similarity and points of difference. *Compare the legislative branches of the state government and the national government.*

discuss talk over; consider from various points of view; present the different sides of. *Discuss the use of pesticides in controlling mosquitoes.*

criticize state your opinion of the correctness or merits of an item or issue; criticism may approve or disapprove. *Criticize the increasing use of alcohol.*

justify show good reasons for; give your evidence; present facts to support your position. *Justify the American entry into World War II.*

trace follow the course of; follow the trail of; give a description of progress. *Trace the development of television in school instruction.*

interpret make plain; give the meaning of; give your thinking about; translate. *Interpret the poetic line, "The sound of a cobweb snapping is the noise of my life."*

prove establish the truth of something by giving factual evidence or logical reasons. *Prove that in a full-employment economy, a society can get more of one product only by giving up another product.*

illustrate use a word picture, a diagram, a chart, or a concrete example to clarify a point. *Illustrate the use of catapults in the amphibious warfare of Alexander.*

Source: Andrew Moss and Carol Holder, *Improving Student Writing: A Guide for Faculty in All Disciplines* (Dubuque, IA: Kendall/Hunt, 1988) 17–18.

45

Using English Nouns, Pronouns, and Articles

T he next three chapters are designed to supplement the rest of the *Handbook*. They provide basic information on structural and idiomatic features of the English language that students from an English as a Second Language (ESL) background may need for reference.

These chapters assume that ESL students are now working in a basic English composition course alongside native speakers, and that they have already completed a college-level course of instruction (or its equivalent) in using English as a Second Language. The role of this material is not to provide primary ESL instruction but to give students help in three ways: (1) to identify key topics and problems that persistently cause difficulties for ESL students from many different backgrounds; (2) to propose standard usage guidelines and remedies for such problems (with the assistance of exercises); and (3) to refer ESL students to sections of Chapters 1–44 that will give particular help with difficult language and usage issues in English. Students should also notice that Chapters 7–33 have been furnished with topical "ESL Note" references, which briefly describe key issues and refer readers to pertinent sections of these supplementary chapters.

The following chapters cover topics in the three functional areas of English language usage: Chapter 45—nouns and noun-related structures (including articles and determiners); Chapter 46—verbs, verbals, and related structures (including particles with phrasal verbs); and Chapter 47—usage for modifiers and modifying structures. Prepositions—perhaps the most troublesome feature of English—are treated in connection with the structures that determine them in each chapter of this part. (Prepositions determined by nouns are discussed in 45c; those determined by phrasal verbs are discussed in 46f; and those governed by adjectives are discussed in 47b.)

▶ 45a Using the different classes of English nouns

English nouns name things, abstractions, or people that are considered either countable or not countable in English. English also distinguishes whether a noun names a person or thing that is specific, or something that is generic.

1 Identifying and using count nouns

In English, **count nouns** name things or people that are considered countable. They identify one of many possible individuals or things in the category named. Count nouns have three important characteristics.

■ Singular count nouns can be preceded by *one*, or by *a/an*—the indefinite articles that convey the meaning "one (of many)."

one car   a rowboat   a truck   an ambulance

Singular count nouns can also be preceded by demonstrative pronouns (*this, that*), by possessive pronouns (*my, your, their*), and often by the definite article (*the*).

■ Plural count nouns can be preceded by expressions of quantity (*two, three, some, many, a few*) and can use a plural form.

two cars   some rowboats   many trucks   a few ambulances

■ A count noun used as a singular or plural subject must agree with a singular or plural verb form.

This *car stops* quickly. [A singular subject and verb agree.]

Other *cars stop* slowly. [A plural subject and verb agree.]

(See 10a for guidelines on subject–verb agreement.)

2 Forming plurals with count nouns

Plural count nouns are either regular or irregular. Regular nouns form the plural with *-s* or *-es*. Irregular plural forms—such as *man/men, tooth/teeth, wolf/wolves, medium/media*—follow the models shown in 23e. (See rules for plural forms in 10a and in the spelling sections in 23e-1, 3, and 5.)

3 Identifying and using noncount (mass) nouns

In English, **noncount (mass) nouns** name things that are being considered as a whole, undivided group of items not being counted. Noncount (mass) nouns name various kinds of individuals or things that are considered as group categories in English, such as these:

abstractions: courage, grammar

fields of activity: chemistry, tennis

natural phenomena: weather, dew, rain

whole groups of objects: rice, sand, oxygen, wood, oil

Objects that are considered too numerous or shapeless to count are often treated as noncount nouns, as with the word *rock* in this sentence.

We mined dense rock in this mountain.

As such objects become individually identifiable, the same word may be used as a count noun.

Four *rocks* fell across the road.

Some nouns name things that can be considered either countable or noncountable in English, depending on whether they name something specific or something generic.

| Countable (and specific) | A *chicken* or two ran off. |
| | A *straw* or two flew up. |

| Noncountable (and generic) | *Chicken* should be cooked well. |
| | *Straw* can be very dry. |

Nouns that name generalized or generic things often occur in noncountable form, but may also occur in singular form in scientific usage (see 45a-5).

Three characteristics distinguish noncount (mass) nouns:

- Noncount nouns never use the indefinite article *a/an* (or *one*). (Articles are discussed in detail in 45b.)
- Noncount nouns are never used in a plural form.
- Noncount nouns always take singular verbs. (See 10a for guidelines on subject–verb agreement.)

4 Using expressions of quantity with count and noncount nouns

Expressions of quantity—such as *many, few, much, little, some,* and *plenty*—are typically used to modify nouns. Some expressions are used to quantify count nouns; some are used with noncount nouns; and others are used with both kinds of nouns.

Count nouns	Noncount nouns	Both count and noncount nouns
many potatoes	*much* rice	*lots of* potatoes and rice
few potatoes	*little* rice	*plenty of* potatoes and rice
		some, any potatoes and rice

When the context is very clear, these expressions can also be used alone as pronouns.

Do you have *any* potatoes or rice?

I have *plenty* if you need *some.*

5 Using nouns in specific and generic senses

English nouns show differences in usage between nouns that name specific things or people and nouns that name generalized or generic things.

| A definite noun | The whale migrated thousands of miles. |
| | The whales migrated thousands of miles. [When a noun names something very specific, either singular or plural, it is preceded by the **definite article** (or by demonstrative pronouns *this/that*).] |

| An indefinite noun | A whale surfaced nearby; then several whales surfaced. [When a noun names something indefinite but countable, the **indefinite article** is used.] |

| Generic usage | Whales are migratory animals. |
| | A whale is a migratory animal. [When the reference is to a general group, nouns often use either the **plural with no article** or the **singular with an indefinite article**.] |

| Scientific usage | The whale is a migratory animal. |
| | Whales are migratory animals. [A generic noun may also be singular or plural with a definite article (see 45b-2).] |

Using the Different Classes of English Nouns

6 Distinguishing pronouns in specific and indefinite or generic uses

Most pronouns, including personal pronouns, rename and refer to a noun located elsewhere that names a specific individual or thing. However, indefinite pronouns, such as *some, any, one, someone,* or *anyone,* may refer to a noun in an indefinite or generic sense.

Personal pronoun Where are my pencils? I need *them.* [Meaning: I need specific pencils that are mine.]

Indefinite pronoun Where are my pencils? I need *some.* [Meaning: I need generic, indefinable pencils; I will use any I can find.]

(The list in 7a-7 gives terms that describe various classes of pronouns.)

▶ **45b** Using articles with nouns

Articles are the most important class of words used in English to show whether nouns are being used as count or noncount nouns, or as specific or generic nouns. There are three articles in English: *a, an,* and *the. Some,* the indefinite pronoun, is occasionally used as if it were an indefinite article.

1 Nouns sometimes take the indefinite articles *a* and *an.*

The indefinite articles *a* and *an* are grammatically the same. They are singular indefinite articles that mean "one (of many)," and they are used only with singular count nouns. Pronunciation determines which to use. *A* precedes a noun beginning with a consonant or a consonant sound (a bottle, a hotel, a youth, a user, a xylophone). *An* precedes a noun beginning with a vowel or vowel sound (an egg, an hour, an undertaker).

http://leo.stcloudstate.edu/grammar/useartic.html
The Use and Nonuse of Articles, from LEO: Literacy Education Online.

A is sometimes used with the quantifiers *little* and *few.* Note the differences in the following examples.

Example	*Meaning*
a little, a few	a small amount of something
a few onions	
a little oil	
little, few	a less-than-expected amount of something
few onions	
little oil	

A and *an* are rarely used with proper nouns, which usually identify a unique individual rather than one of many. The indefinite article occasionally appears with a proper noun in a hypothetical statement about one of many possible persons or things in the category named, as in this sentence.

Dr. King dreamed of *an America* where children of all colors would grow up in harmony. [We may dream of more than one possible "America."]

▶**2 Nouns sometimes take the definite article *the*.**

Use *the* with specific singular and plural count nouns and with noncount nouns.

Specific nouns

> I need *the tool* and *the rivets*. [one singular and one plural noun]
>
> I need *the equipment*. [a noncount noun]
>
> | I need *the tool* on *the top shelf.* | [Note the modifiers, |
> | I need *the tools* that are painted orange. | clauses, and phrases that |
> | I need *the smallest tool* on *that shelf.* | make the nouns specific.] |

Generic nouns

> I need tools for that work. [In this case, no article is used.]

(For varieties of usage with generic nouns, see 45a-5.)

Use *the* in a context where a noun has previously been mentioned, or where the writer and the reader both know the particular thing or person being referred to.

> I saw a giraffe at the zoo. *The giraffe* was eating leaves from a tree.
>
> I stopped at an intersection. When *the light* turned green, I started to leave. [The sentence assumes the existence of a particular traffic light at the intersection.]

Other uses of the definite article

- Use *the* with items that are to be designated as one of a kind (*the* sun, *the* moon, *the* first, *the* second, *the* last).

- Use *the* with official names of countries when it is needed to give specific meaning to nouns such as *union, kingdom, state(s), republic, duchy*, and so on (*the* United States, *the* Republic of Cyprus, *the* Hashemite Kingdom of Jordan). No article is needed with certain other countries (Cyprus, Jordan, Japan, El Salvador).

- Use *the* when a noun identifies institutions or generic activities *other than sports*, and in certain usages for generic groups (see 45a-5).
  We called *the* newspapers, *the* radio, and *the* news services.
  Sergei plays *the* piano, *the* flute, and *the* guitar.
  The whales are migratory animals. *The* birds have feathers.
  Without an article Nadia plays basketball, hockey, and volleyball.

- Use *the* with names of oceans, seas, rivers, and deserts.
  the Pacific   *the* Amazon   *the* Himalayas   *the* Sahara
  Without an article Lake Michigan   Mt. Fuji

- Use *the* to give specific meaning to expressions using the noun *language*, but not for the proper name of a language by itself.
  He studied the Sanskrit language, not the Urdu language.
  Without an article He studied Sanskrit, not Urdu.

- Use *the* with names of colleges and universities containing *of*.
  He studied at *the* University *of* Michigan.
  Without an article (typically) He studied at Michigan State University.

▶**3** Nouns sometimes take no article.

Typically no article is needed with names of unique individuals, because they do not need to be made specific and they are not usually counted as one among many. In addition, nouns naming generalized persons or things in a generic usage commonly use no article: *Managers often work long hours. Whales are migratory animals.* (See 45a-5.)

Some situations in which no article is used are shown in 45b-2. Here are some others.

- Use no article with proper names of continents, states, cities, and streets, and with religious place names.

  Europe   Alaska   New York   Main Street   heaven   hell

- Use no article with titles of officials when accompanied by personal names; the title effectively becomes part of the proper noun.

  President Truman   King Juan Carlos   Emperor Napoleon

- Use no article with fields of study.

  Ali studied literature.   Juan studied engineering.

- Use no article with names of diseases.

  He has cancer.   AIDS is a very serious disease.

- Use no article with names of magazines and periodicals, unless the article is part of the formal title.

  Life   Popular Science   Sports Illustrated

  BUT: *The New Yorker* [The article is part of the proper name.]

▶ **45c**   Using nouns with prepositions

Some of the complex forms of prepositions in English are determined by their use with nouns. Nouns that follow prepositions are called **objects of prepositions** (see 7a-8 and 8b-1); this grouping forms a modifying **prepositional phrase** (7d-1). The distinctive function of such modifying phrases often determines which preposition to choose in an English sentence.

▶**I**   Using the preposition *of* to show possession

The preposition *of* is often widely used to show possession as an alternative to the possessive case form (*I hear a man's voice. I hear the voice of a man*). It is also widely used to show possession for many nouns that do not usually take a possessive form. For example, many inanimate nouns, as well as some nouns naming a large group of people (*crowd, mob, company*) or a location (*place, center*), are not typically used with a possessive case form, and are likely to show possession with the preposition *of.*

Faulty   I washed the *car's hood.*
Correct   I washed the *hood of her car.*

Faulty   *The Information Center's* location is unknown.
Correct   The location *of the Information Center* is unknown.

The preposition *of* is not used with proper nouns.

Faulty   I washed the *car of Luisa.*
Correct   I washed *Luisa's car.*

▶**2 Using prepositions in phrases with nouns or pronouns**

The distinctive function of a modifying prepositional phrase often determines which preposition to choose in an English sentence. Here are a few typical functions for prepositional phrases, with distinctive prepositions in use.

Function	Preposition	Example/Explanation
Passive voice (9g)	*by* the cook	He was insulted *by* the cook.
	with a snowball	I was hit *with* a snowball.
Time expressions	*on* January 1	use for specific dates
	on Sundays	use for specific days
	in January	use for months
	in 1984	use for years
	in spring	use for seasons
	at noon, *at* 5 P.M.	use for specific times
	by noon, *by* 5 P.M.	use to indicate *before* a specific hour
	by April 15	use to indicate *before* a specific date
Locations	*at* 301 South Street	use for an address
	in the house	
	on the floor	
Directions	*onto* the floor	
	beside the library	
	through the window	
	into the air	

For information on verbs with prepositions, see 46f; for information on adjectives with prepositions, see 47b.

▶ **EXERCISE I**

Complete the following sentences with *a, an, the,* or *some,* or write *X* for no article.

1. Please pass me _____ butter. I usually eat _____ bread with lunch.
2. Today we watched _____ policeman arguing with _____ driver. _____ driver didn't understand _____ English.
3. You need _____ furniture. You should buy _____ chair and borrow _____ round green table in my house.

Choose the correct form.

4. He admired (Sam's motorcycle/the motorcycle of Sam), which stood in the (driveway's center/center of the driveway).
5. Meet me (on/in/at) March 15 (on/at) the theater (on/in/at) six o'clock.

46

Using English Verbs

Distinguishing different types of verbs and verb constructions

http://vweb1.hiway.co.uk/ei/
intro.html
The English Institute's Preliminary
Grammar Book *has an extensive discussion with examples of English verbs,
aimed at second-language speakers.*

A verb, the main word in the predicate of an English sentence, asserts the action undertaken by the subject or else the condition in which the subject exists. The four types of verbs include transitive verbs (which take direct objects), intransitive verbs (which do not take direct objects), linking verbs, and helping or auxiliary verbs (which show tense or mood). Although only transitive verbs can show passive voice, most verbs can show various tenses and mood. (See Chapter 9 for a discussion of verb usage.)

▶ **1**   **Transitive and intransitive verbs work differently.**

A **transitive verb** can take an object. Examples of transitive verbs include *throw* and *take*.

| subject | verb | object | | subject | verb | object |
| He | throws | a pass. | | They | took | the ball. |

Because transitive verbs can take an object, most of them can operate in both the active and passive voices.[1] The active and the passive forms of the verb may be similar in meaning, but the emphasis changes with the rearrangement of the subject and object, as well as with changes in the verb form (to the past participle with *be*).

subject	verb	object		subject	verb	modifiers
Workers in Ohio	make	Hondas.		Hondas	are made	(by workers) in Ohio.
	active voice				passive voice	

Notice how the active-voice object *Hondas* in the first sentence becomes the passive-voice subject in the second. In a passive-voice sentence the original performer of the action (*workers* in the example) is not emphasized and may even be omitted. (See 9g on the uses of passive constructions.)

---

[1]**Exceptions:** Transitive verbs *have, get, want, like,* and *hate* are seldom used in passive voice.

By contrast, an **intransitive verb** never takes an object and can never be used in the passive voice. Examples of intransitive verbs include *smile* and *go*.

subject   verb   subject verb
The politician smiled.   He went into the crowd.

▶**2 Linking verbs are used in distinctive patterns.**

Linking verbs, the most common example of which is *be*, serve in sentences as "equals signs" to link a subject with an equivalent noun or adjective. Some other linking verbs are *appear, become,* and *seem.* (See 11d for a full list and description of linking verbs; see also 7b, Pattern 5.)

Things *seem* unsettled.

Shall I *become* a doctor?

Expletives

Linking verbs also serve in a distinctive English construction that uses changed word order with an **expletive** word, *there* or *it.* Expletives are used only with linking verbs, as in these sentences.

It *is* important to leave now.   It *appears* unnecessary to do that.

There *seems* to be a problem.   It *seems* important.

There and *it* form "dummy subjects" or filler words that occupy the position of the subject in a normal sentence; the true subject is elsewhere in the sentence, and the verb agrees with the true subject (see 10a-8).

Expletive in subject position	**True subject**
There is a cat in that tree.	*A cat* is in that tree.
There are some cats in the tree.	*Some cats* are in the tree.
It is convenient to use the train.	*To use the train* is convenient.

The expletive *it* also has a unique role in expressing length of time with *take* followed by an infinitive.

It takes an hour to get home by car.   *It took* us forever.

Expletive constructions are important in and useful for several other expressions, including time, distance, or weather.

It is three o'clock and it's raining.   It's a long way home from here.

Expletives are often used to form subject complements, sometimes with an infinitive, as well as to make short or emphatic statements.

It is fun to ride a sleigh.   It is a tale of great sorrow.   There were no survivors.

However, in complex and formal English sentences, the "dummy subject" expletive becomes an unnecessary word obscuring the true subject. The expletive also encourages using linking verbs instead of more direct, active verbs—transitive or intransitive verbs. To eliminate wordiness and promote the clear, direct style that is preferred in English academic prose, try to avoid expletives; revise sentences to restore normal word order (see 17a-3).

▶3 Verbs in the active versus the passive voice

Verbs using the **active voice** emphasize the actor of a sentence as the subject. (See section 9g.)

Brenda *scores* the winning goal.　Tom *plays* the violin.

When a transitive verb occurs in the **passive voice,** the sentence reverses its order: the verb converts to a past participle with an auxiliary, the original subject may be expressed in a phrase with *by,* and the original object of the sentence is moved to the front of the new sentence and is emphasized (see 9g):

The winning goal *is scored* by Brenda.　The violin *is played* by Tom.

In a further transformation of the active-voice sentence, the original actor/subject can be made to disappear entirely by omitting the prepositional phrase.

The winning goal *is scored.*　The violin *is played.*

The many uses and disadvantages of the passive voice are shown in detail in sections 9g-1 and 9g-2, as well as 16b-3 and 17b-1.

▶46b　Changing verb forms

Verb forms express *tense,* an indication of when an action or state of being occurs. The three basic tenses in English are the past, the present, and the future. (See 9a and 9b for a discussion of the forms of English verbs, and 9e-1, 2 for a basic discussion of tenses.) Section 9e presents a useful "time line" chart of English verb tenses and verb forms that express time relationships.

▶1　Not all verbs use progressive tense forms.

Each of the three basic tenses has a progressive form, made up of *be* and the present participle (the *-ing* form of the verb). The progressive tense emphasizes the *process* of doing whatever action the verb asserts. The tense is indicated by a form of *be:* present progressive (I *am going*), past progressive (I *was going*), past perfect progressive (I *had been going*), future progressive (I *will be going*). For examples, see 9e and 9f.

Certain verbs are generally *not* used in the progressive form; others have a progressive use only for process-oriented or ongoing meanings of the verb.

Words that are rarely seen in a progressive form

- **Think** (in the sense of "believe"): "I think not."

  Exception: The progressive form can be used for a process of considering something.

  Faulty　I *am thinking* it is wrong.
  Correct　I *am thinking* about changing jobs. [considering]

- **Believe, understand, recognize, realize, remember:** "You believe it."

Exception: The last four can sometimes use the progressive form if a process of recognition or recollection is meant: "He is slowly realizing the truth." "He is gradually remembering what happened."

- **Belong, possess, own, want, need:** "We want some." "We once owned it."
- **Have:** "You have what you need."

   Exception: The progressive form can be used in the sense of "experiencing."

Faulty	Maria *is having* a car.
Correct	Mary *is having* a baby. [experiencing childbirth]
	Maria *is having* success in her project.

- **Be, exist, seem:** "This seems acceptable."

   Exception: The progressive form is used only with an abstract emphasis on a process of "being" or "seeming": "Just existing from day to day is enough."

- **Smell, sound,** and **taste** as intransitive verbs, as in "It smells good"; "It sounds funny"; "It tastes bad."
- **Appear** in the sense of "seem": "It appeared to be the right time."

   Exception: Sometimes the progressive form is used in the sense of presenting itself/oneself over a time period. "She's appearing nightly as the star actress."

- **See:** "I can never see why you do it."

   Exception: The progressive form is used in the sense of interviewing someone or witnessing or experiencing something.

   | Faulty | I *am seeing* an airplane now. |
   | Revised | I *am seeing* a new patient. [interviewing] |

- **Surprise, hate, love, like:** "It surprises me"; "I hate lima beans."

2 Using the perfect forms

The perfect tense is made up of *have* and the past participle (the *-ed* form of the verb). The form of *have* indicates the tense: present perfect (*has* worked), past perfect (*had* worked), and future perfect (*will have* worked). (See 9e and 9f; also 9b, irregular past participles.)

Sometimes students confuse the use of the simple past with the use of the present perfect. The present perfect is used when an action or state of being that began in the past continues to the present; it is also used to express an action or state of being that happened at an indefinite time in the past.

| Present perfect | Linda has worked in Mexico since 1987. |
| Present perfect | Ann has worked in Mexico. [The time is unspecified.] |

By contrast, the simple past is used when an action or state of being began *and ended* in the past.

| Simple past | Linda worked in Mexico last year. [She no longer works there.] |

Since or *for* with perfect tenses in prepositional phrases of time

A phrase with *since* requires using the present perfect (*has worked*) or past perfect tenses (*had worked*); it indicates action beginning at *a single point in time* and still continuing at the time shown by the verb tense.

> She [has/had worked] *since* noon
> *since* July
> *since* 1991
> *since* the end of the school year
> *since* the last storm
> *since* the baby was born

A time phrase with *since* cannot have a noun object that shows plural time; *since* phrases must indicate a single point in time.

Faulty He lived here since three months.
I am here since May.

Revised He has lived here *for* three months.
I have been here since May.

Also, a time phrase with *since* cannot modify a simple past tense or any present tense.

Faulty He worked here since six months.
Revised He *had worked* here since February.

The perfect tenses can have a time modifier with a prepositional phrase formed either with *since* or *for*.

> He has worked since noon.
> He had worked for a month.

A modifying phrase with *for* indicates action *through a duration of time*.

> He [has/had worked] *for* three hours
> *for* a month and a half
> *for* two years
> *for* a few weeks

When a phrase uses a plural noun, thus showing duration of time, the plural signals that the preposition in the modifier must be *for*, not *since*.

Faulty I had worked on it since many years.
Revised I had worked on it for many years.

▶3 **Using the varied forms of English future tenses**

The following list shows different ways of expressing the future.

Verb form	*Explanation*
She *will call* us soon. She *is going to* call us soon.	These examples have the same meaning.
The movie *arrives* in town tomorrow. The next bus *leaves* in five minutes. The bus *is leaving* very soon.	The simple present and the present progressive are used to express definite future plans, as from a schedule.

Your flight *is taking off* at 6:55.
The doctor *is operating* at once.
I *am calling* them right now.

The present progressive is sometimes used to make strong statements about the future.

Hurry! The movie *is about to* begin.
Finish up! The bell *is about to* ring.

The "near" future is expressed by some form of *be* plus *about to* and a verb.

It's cold. *I'm going to* get a sweater.
It's cold. *I'll lend* you a sweater.

"Going to" suggests a plan.
"Will" suggests a willingness.

In choosing forms of future tenses, be alert to time expressions such as "soon," "five minutes," or "tomorrow" as context clues to events that will require use of future forms. Verbs expressing thoughts about future actions, such as *intend* and *hope*, are not used in any future tense, and the verb *plan* uses a future tense only in the idiomatic *plan on* (to make or follow a plan).

Faulty   I will intend to meet my friends tomorrow.

Revised   I intend to meet my friends tomorrow.
I plan to attend college.

See 46b-5 for guidelines on expressing future time in conditional sentences.

▶**4 Using verb tenses in sentences with a sequence of actions**

In complex sentences that have more than one verb, it is important to adjust the sequence of verb tenses to avoid confusion. See the discussion on verb tense combinations in 9f.

Verb tenses with reported speech

Reported speech, or indirect discourse, is very different from directly quoted speech, which gives the exact verb tense of the original.

Direct speech   Ellie said, "He is taking a picture of my boat."

Indirectly quoted speech may occasionally be reported immediately.

Reported speech   Ellie just said [that] he is taking a picture of her boat.

Some kinds of reported speech can be summarized with verbs such as *tell, ask, remind,* and *urge,* followed by an infinitive:

Reported speech   Ellie asked him to take a picture of her boat.

Most often, however, reported speech has occurred sometime before the time of the main verb reporting it. In English, the indirect quotation then requires changes in verb tense and pronouns.

Reported speech   She said [that] he had taken a picture of her boat.

In this situation, the reported speech itself takes the form of a *that* noun clause (although the word *that* is often omitted); its verb tense shifts to past tense, following the guidelines shown in 9f-1 for tense sequences. See also the Critical Decision box at 16d for a chart of verb forms needed to express direct speech versus reported speech. Punctuation for quotations is discussed at 28a-1.

Changing Verb Forms   **755**

5 Using verb tenses in conditional and subjunctive sentences

Conditional sentences talk about situations that are either possible in the future or else unreal (contrary to fact) in the present or past. Conditional sentences typically contain the conjunction *if* or a related conditional term (*unless, provided that, only if, (only) after, (only) when*, etc.). The following are guidelines for using verb forms in conditional sentences.

Possible or real statements about the future

Use the present tense to express the condition in possible statements about the future; in the same sentence, use the future to express the result of that condition.

	conditional + present future	(*will* + base form)
Real statement	If I *have* enough money,	I *will go* next week.
	When I *get* enough money,	I *will go*.

[Meaning: The speaker may have enough money.]

Unreal conditional statements about the future

Use the past subjunctive form (which looks like a past tense) with sentences that make "unreal" conditional statements about the future; in the same sentence, use the past form of a modal auxiliary (usually *would, could,* or *might*) to express an unreal result of that stated condition.

	If + past	past form of modal (*would*)
Unreal statement	If you *found* the money,	you *would go* next week.

[Meaning: The speaker now is fairly sure you will not have the money.]

Unreal conditional statements about the past

Use the subjunctive with appropriate perfect tense verb forms with sentences that make unreal conditional statements about the past. Use the past perfect tense for the unreal statement about the past. In the same sentence, use the past form of the modal auxiliary plus the present perfect to express the unreal result.

	If + past perfect (*had made*)	past modal + present perfect (*would*) (*have gone*)
Unreal statement	If I *had made* money,	I *would have gone* last week.

[Meaning: At that time the speaker did not have the money.]

For more on the subjunctive, see 9h-1; for more on modal auxiliaries, see 46d.

6 Expressing a wish or suggestion for a hypothetical event

In stating a wish in the present that might hypothetically occur, use the *past subjunctive* (which looks like the past tense) in the clause expressing the wish. (The object of the wish takes the form of a *that* clause, although the word *that* is often omitted.)

present	[that]	past subjunctive (like past tense)
He *wishes*	[that]	she *had* a holiday.
I *wish*	[that]	I *were* on vacation.

The auxiliaries *would* and *could* (which have the same form in the present and past tenses) are often used to express the object of a wish.

present	[that]	*would/could* + base form
I *wish*	[that]	she *would stay*.
We *wish*	[that]	we *could take* a vacation day.

In stating a wish made in the past or present for something that hypothetically might have occurred in the past, use the past perfect in the *that* clause. (The verb *wish* may be expressed either in the past or in the present tense.)

present OR past	[that]	past perfect *[had worked]*
I wished	[that]	I *had* not *worked* yesterday.
I wish	[that]	it *had been* a holiday.

See 9h-4 for guidelines on using the subjunctive mood with *that* clauses.

Expressing a recommendation, suggestion, or urgent request

In stating a recommendation, suggestion, or urgent request, use the *present subjunctive*—the base form of the verb (*be, do*)—in the *that* clause (see 9h).

present	[that]	present subjunctive = base form
We *suggest*	[that]	he *find* the money.
We *advise*	[that]	you *be* there on time.

(See 9h-4 for comments on the subjunctive in this form.)

▶ **EXERCISE I**

Circle the appropriate verb form.

1. Sam insisted that she (wants/wanted) something to drink.
2. For some reason it (smelled/was smelling) very strange.
3. Many years ago I (heard/have heard) an unusual story.
4. Perhaps if you (had wanted/would have wanted) the job, you (would have gotten/had gotten) to the interview on time.
5. She wishes that she (could do/can do) a good job.

▶ **46c** **Changing word order with verbs**

▶**I** **Invert the subject and all or part of the verb to form questions.**

The subject and verb are inverted from normal order to form questions. The following patterns are used with the verb *be*, with modal auxiliaries, with progressive forms, and with perfect forms.

	Normal Statement Form	Question Form
Be	He *is* sick today.	*Is he* sick today?
Modals	She *can* help us.	*Can she* help us?
Progressive	They *are* studying here.	*Are they* studying here?
Perfect	It *has* made this sound before.	*Has it* made this sound before?

Questions (and negatives) with the auxiliary *do/does*

Verbs other than those shown above use the auxiliary verbs *do/does* to form questions, and also to form negatives with *not*. In this form, when the auxiliary verb *do/does* is added, the verb changes to the base form (the dictionary form). Use this pattern for the simple present and simple past:

Question Form / Negative Form: Do + Base Form

Statement	He *gets on* this bus.
Question	*Does* he *get on* this bus?
Negative	He *does not get on* this bus.
Avoid	Does he *gets on* this bus? [Needs a base form.]

Statement	She *finishes* at noon.
Question	*Does* she *finish* at noon?
Negative	She *does not finish*.
Avoid	Does she *finishes* at noon? [Needs a base form.]

Statement	It *ran* better yesterday.
Question	*Did* it *run* better yesterday?
Negative	It *did not run* better.
Avoid	Did it *ran* better yesterday? [Needs a base form.]

Statement	They *arrived* at noon.
Question	When *did* they *arrive?*
Negative	They *did not arrive*.
Avoid	When do they *arrived?* [Needs a base form.]

For more on auxiliary verbs, see the listings in 9c and in 46d.

▶**2 Invert the subject and verb in some emphatic statements.**

The question form is also used with auxiliaries or expletives in some emphatic statements that begin with adverbs such as *never, rarely,* and *hardly,* producing a negative meaning.

Normal	**Emphatic**
There is never an easy answer.	Never *is there* an easy answer.
They have rarely come to check.	Rarely *have they* come to check.

▶**46d** Using the helping verbs: Auxiliaries and modal auxiliaries

▶**I Auxiliary verbs, or helping verbs, are part of basic grammar.**

The basic auxiliary verbs (*be, will, have, do*) are used to show tense, to form questions, to show emphasis, and to show negation.

To show tense, or aspect (*be, will, have*): He is driving. She has driven.

To form questions (*do/does*): Do they drive? Why do you drive?

To show negation (*do + not*): I do not drive.

To show emphasis (*do/does*): She does drive sometimes.

▶2 Use modal auxiliaries for a wide range of meanings.

Modal auxiliaries include *can, could, may, might, should, would,* and *must,* as well as the four modals that always appear with the particle *to: ought to, have to, able to,* and *have got to.* The base form of the verb (the dictionary form) is always used with a modal auxiliary, whether the time reference is to the future, present, or past. For a past time reference, use the modal plus the past perfect (*have* + the past participle).

Meaning Expressed	Present Time or Past Time	Modal + Past Perfect
ability and permission	She can drive. She could drive.	She could have driven.
possibility	She may drive. She might drive.	She might have driven.
advisability	She should drive. She ought to drive. She had better drive.	She should have driven. She ought to have driven.
necessity	She must drive. She has to drive.	She had to drive.
negative necessity versus prohibition*	She does not have to drive. [she need not] She must not drive. [she is not allowed]	

*Note that the two negatives above have very different meanings.

Some idiomatic expressions with modals

Some other idiomatic expressions with modals are expressed in the following list.

Example	**Meaning**
I *would rather* drive than fly.	I prefer driving to flying.
We *would talk* for hours.	We always talked for hours then.
She has car keys, so she *must* drive.	[must = probably does]
Shall we dance again?	I'm inviting you to dance again.
Would you mind turning the heat up?	[would you mind = would you object to]
Do you mind turning it off?	Please turn it off.

 46e   Choosing gerunds and infinitives with verbs

There are three types of verbals: infinitives, gerunds, and participles (see 7a-4).

▶1 Using infinitives and gerunds as nouns

Use an infinitive or a gerund to function either as a subject or as an object.

As subjects *To be one of the leaders here* is not really what I want.
His being one of the leaders here is unacceptable.

As objects I don't really want *to be one of the leaders here.*
I don't accept *his being one of the leaders here.*

Note: The possessive case is used with gerunds; see 8c-2. (See 7a-4 and 7d-2, 3 for basic definitions and examples of verbals. See 47a-1 for participles that function as modifiers, and 46b-1 for participles in the progressive form of English verbs.)

▶2 Learning idiomatic uses of verb/verbal sequences

Sometimes it is difficult to determine which verbs are followed by a gerund, which are followed by an infinitive, and which can be followed by either verbal. This usage is idiomatic and must be memorized; there are no rules to govern these forms. Note in the following examples that verb tense does not affect a verbal.

Verb + Gerund	Verb + Infinitive	Verb + Either Verbal
enjoy	**want**	**begin**
I enjoy swimming.	I want to swim now.	Today I begin swimming.
		Today I begin to swim.
go	**agree**	**continue**
I went swimming.	I agreed to swim.	I continued swimming.
		I continued to swim.
enjoy + gerund	want + infinitive	begin + either verbal
go + gerund	agree + infinitive	continue + either verbal
finish + gerund	decide + infinitive	like + either verbal
recommend + gerund	need + infinitive	prefer + either verbal
risk + gerund	plan + infinitive	start + either verbal
suggest + gerund	seem + infinitive	love + either verbal
consider + gerund	expect + infinitive	hate + either verbal
postpone + gerund	fall + infinitive	can't bear + either verbal
practice + gerund	pretend + infinitive	can't stand + either verbal

Note: There is no difference in meaning between *I begin to swim* and *I begin swimming.* However, sentences with other verbs differ in meaning depending on whether a gerund or an infinitive follows the verb. This difference in meaning is a function of certain verbs. See the following examples.

Example	Meaning
I always remember *to lock* the car.	I always remember to do this.
I remember *locking* the car.	I remember that I did this.
They stop *to drink* some water.	They stopped in order to drink.
They stopped *drinking* water.	They didn't drink anymore.

Information on idiomatic usage is provided in ESL dictionaries such as the *Longman Dictionary of American English: Your Complete Guide to American English*, 1997.

▶ **EXERCISE 2**

Circle the appropriate verb form.

1. I am certain that you (have to/might) walk to town.
2. They all need (doing/to do) some daily exercise.
3. You might consider (walking/to walk) to town.
4. Doesn't she (get/gets) angry sometimes?
5. We can postpone (doing/to do) the hard work till later.

▶ **46f** Using two- and three-word verbs, or phrasal verbs, with particles

Phrasal verbs consist of a verb and a *particle*. Note that a particle can be one or more prepositions (off, up, with) or an adverb (away, back). English has many phrasal verbs, often built on verbs that have one basic meaning in their simple one-word form, but different meanings when particles are added.

The coach *called off* the game because of the storm.
He *left out* some important details.

The meaning of a phrasal verb is idiomatic; that is, the words as a group have a different meaning from each of the words separately. Most of these varied meanings are found in a standard English dictionary. Here are some examples of sentences with two-word and three-word verbs.

I *got ready* for work.
She didn't go to the party because she didn't *feel up to* it.
The doctor told him to *cut down on* red meat.
They *did without* a television for a few years.

▶ **I** Some phrasal verbs are separable.

With separable phrasal verbs, a noun object either can separate a verb and particle or follow the particle.

| | noun object | | noun object |

Correct   I *made out* <u>a check</u> to the IRS.   I *made* <u>a check</u> *out* to the IRS.

However, a pronoun object always separates the verb and the particle. A pronoun never follows the particle.

pronoun object

Faulty   I *made out* <u>it</u> to the IRS.
Revised   I *made* <u>it</u> *out* to the IRS.

Other separable phrasal verbs include the following:

call off	hand out	prevent from
check out	leave in, out	set up
divide up	look up [research]	sign on, up
find out	pick up	start over, up

fill in	put over	take on
fit in	[present	throw out
give back, up	deceptively]	turn on, off,
hang out, up	put up to [promote]	up, down
[suspend:	put back	wake up
trans.]	put off	write down

2 Some phrasal verbs are nonseparable.

With nonseparable phrasal verbs, a noun or pronoun object always follows the particle. For these verbs it is not possible to separate the verb and its particle with a noun or pronoun object.

	noun object		pronoun object
Faulty	I ran Mary into.	**Faulty**	I ran her into.
Revised	I ran into Mary.	**Revised**	I ran into her.

Other nonseparable phrasal verbs include the following:

bump into	call on	do without
get into	get over	get through
keep on	keep up with	hang out [= stay]
refer to	see about	

Several verbs in their basic form are intransitive, but can become transitive phrasal verbs when a nonseparable prepositional particle is added to them.

Intransitive   The politician *smiled* sheepishly, then quickly *apologized.*

Transitive   He *smiled at* me sheepishly, then *apologized* quickly *for* being late.

Other examples of this kind of verb include the following:

complain about	laugh at	participate in
feel up to	look at, into	run into
insist on	object to	walk around, down, up, into, etc.

Note: An adverb, but not a noun or pronoun, may separate the verb from its particle.

He *apologized* quickly *for* being late.

The following are nonseparable two-word verbs that are intransitive, but that can be made transitive if still another particle is added to them:

run around with	*get ready* for	*get by* with
get away with	*drop out* of	*look out* for
read up on		

3 Some phrasal verbs can be either separable or nonseparable.

Some phrasal verbs can be either separable or nonseparable. The meaning of a phrasal verb will change, depending on whether or not the phrase is separated by an object. Note the difference in meaning that appears with the placement of the object in the similar verbs below.

Using English Verbs

Examples	Meaning
I *saw through* it. [nonsep.]	I found it transparent.
I *saw* it *through*. [sep.]	I persisted.
She *looked over* the wall. [nonsep.]	She looked over the top of it.
She *looked* the wall *over*. [sep.]	She examined or studied it.
I *turned on* him. [nonsep.]	I turned to attack him.
I *turned* it *on*. [sep.]	I flipped a switch.
I *turned* him *on*. [sep.]	I aroused his passion.
They *talked to* us. [nonsep.]	They spoke to us.
They *talked* us *into* staying. [sep.]	They convinced us to stay.

Note: Standard dictionaries usually list verbs with the meanings of most particles (indicating whether or not they are transitive), but they usually do not indicate whether a phrasal verb is separable or nonseparable. However, this information is provided in ESL dictionaries such as the *Longman Dictionary of American English: Your Complete Guide to American English*, 1997.

▶ **EXERCISE 3**

Circle the appropriate verb form.

1. Can you (fit in it/fit it in) to your busy schedule?
2. If you (call on her/call her on), she may not be home.
3. We may want to (wake up her/wake her up) early today.
4. I forgot to tell you something; I (left out it/left it out) of my note yesterday.
5. Will you (set up him/set him up) to do the job?

47

Using Modifiers and Connectors in English Sentences

Modifiers expand sentences in a variety of ways. The two types of modifiers are adjectives and adverbs, as well as phrases and clauses that function as adjectives or adverbs. There are two types of adverbs, descriptive and conjunctive. For basic discussions of the types of modifiers, how they function, and how they are placed or located in sentences, see 7a-5 and 6, and 7c. (For more on adjectives, see 11a-1 and 11e. For more on descriptive adverbs, see 11e and f. For more on conjunctive adverbs, see 19a-3.)

▶ 47a   Using single-word adjectives and nouns as modifiers of nouns

A modifier of a noun must be placed as close to the noun modified as possible (11a-1; 15a). Single-word adjectives are normally placed before a noun or after a linking verb.

Before a noun   The *bored student* slept through the *boring lecture*.
After a linking verb   Jack *is bored*. The lecture he heard *was boring*.

▶ I   Using the present and past participle forms of verbs as adjectives

The present participle and the past participle forms of verbs are often used as single-word adjectives. The choice of form has an important impact on meaning. In the following examples, notice that these forms can be very different—almost opposite—in meaning.

Past participle	Meaning
a tired student	The student is tired.
damaged buildings	The buildings are damaged.
a frightened passenger	The passenger is frightened.
excited tourists	The tourists are excited.
an accredited school	The school is accredited.

Present participle	Meaning
a tiring lecture	The lecture causes a feeling of being tired.
a damaging explosion	The explosion caused the damage.
a frightening storm	The storm causes the fright.
an exciting tour	The tour caused excitement.
an accrediting board	This group gives accrediting status.

▶2 Using nouns as modifiers

When two nouns are combined in sequence, the last is considered to be the noun modified; the first is the modifier. (This follows the pattern for single-word adjectives mentioned earlier.) The importance of sequence is evident in the following examples, where the same nouns are combined in different order to produce different meanings.

Modifier	+ Noun modified	Meaning
a car	company	a company whose business involves cars
a company	car	a car provided to someone by the business
a light	truck	a small truck
a truck	light	a light attached to a truck
a game	parlor	a place where indoor games are played
a parlor	game	a type of game, such as chess, played indoors

When more than two nouns are combined in sequence, it is increasingly difficult to determine which noun is modified and which is a modifier; see 47f-2. For this reason, it is best to avoid overusing nouns as modifiers (see 11g).

▶ **47b** Using adjectival modifiers with linking verbs and prepositions

Adjectives and past-participle adjectives in sentences with linking verbs are often followed by a modifying prepositional phrase.

We are *ready*. We are *ready for* the next phase of training.
Jenny seems an *involved* person. She is *involved with* a boyfriend.

The preposition to be used in such phrases is determined by the adjective or participle adjective. With each such adjective, the choice of preposition is idiomatic, not logical; therefore, adjective/preposition combinations must be memorized. Sometimes the same adjective will change its meaning with different prepositions, as in this example.

Jenny was *involved in* planning from the start. Meanwhile, she was *involved with* a new boyfriend.

Past-participle adjective examples include the following:

excited about	acquainted with	divorced from
composed of	opposed to	scared of/by
involved in	interested in	cautioned to/against
exhausted from	done with	angry at/with

Single-word adjective examples include the following:

absent from	afraid of	mad at
bad for	clear to	sure of
crazy about	familiar with	cruel to
excited about	capable of	accustomed to
guilty of	responsible for	

Note: Standard dictionaries may not indicate which preposition is typically used with a given adjective. However, this information is provided in ESL dictionaries such as the *Longman Dictionary of American English: Your Complete Guide to American English*, 1997.

▶ **47c**   Positioning adverbial modifiers

▶ **1**   Observe typical locations for adverbs in English sentences.

Adverbs have typical or standard locations in English sentences, although these patterns can be varied for special emphasis. Adverbs are typically located immediately before a verb.

Faulty   She finishes cheerfully her homework.

Revised   She cheerfully finishes her homework.

Emphatic She finishes her homework—cheerfully.

Common adverbs expressing frequency or probability typically come after the verb *be* and helping verbs. In questions, such adverbs can come after the subject.

> He was frequently at the gym on Fridays.
> She may often discuss politics.
> Does she often come here?

However, when sentences are inverted for negatives, these adverbs are usually placed before the helping verb.

Faulty   They don't frequently talk. It doesn't sometimes matter.

Revised   They frequently don't talk. It sometimes doesn't matter.

▶ **2**   Limiting modifiers cannot move without changing meaning.

Although many adverbs can be located at a number of different places in a sentence without changing the meaning, positioning is quite critical with certain **limiting modifiers** such as *only, almost, just, nearly, even, simply* (see 15b).

No change in meaning	Significant change in meaning
Generally it rains a lot in April.	*Only* Leonid sings those songs.
It *generally* rains a lot in April.	Leonid *only* sings those songs.
It rains a lot in April, *generally*.	Leonid sings *only* those songs.
	[OR sings those songs *only*.]

See 15a–g more on positioning modifiers. See also 46c-2 for inverted word order with adverbs—such as *rarely, never, seldom*—located at the beginning of a sentence.

▶ **47d** Using phrases and clauses to modify nouns and pronouns

See the guidelines for modifier placement in 15a–h.

▶ I Positioning adjective phrases and clauses

Unlike single-word adjective modifiers (which are placed before a noun and after a linking verb; 47a), clauses and most phrases functioning as adjectives must immediately *follow* the noun or pronoun they modify in order to avoid confusion with adverbial modifiers in the sentence.

Faulty	I brought the tire to the garage *with the puncture.*
	I brought the tire to the garage *that had a puncture.*
	[The modifier next to *garage* is very confusing.]
Revised	I brought the tire *with the puncture* to the garage.
	I brought the tire *that had a puncture* to the garage.

If two or more adjective phrases or clauses modify the same noun, typical patterns of sequence operate, as shown in 47f-1. (See 25d-1–3 for rules on punctuating adjective clauses.)

▶ 2 Avoid adding unnecessary pronouns after adjective clauses.

The subject in an English sentence can be stated only once; pronouns in the sentence refer to the subject (or to other nouns) but they do not repeat it. When a lengthy adjective clause follows the subject as a modifier, it is important not to repeat the subject with an unnecessary pronoun before the verb.

Faulty	The *person* who works in office #382 *she* decides. [The subject is repeated with an unnecessary pronoun.]
Revised	The person who works in office #382 decides.

This error is likely to occur because of a failure to observe the steps in forming a dependent clause. Here is the process for forming an adjective clause, using *who*, *which*, or *that* to replace the noun or pronoun of the dependent clause:

Two sentences	The person decides. *She* works in office #382.
Transform to a clause	[*she* = *who*] *who* works in office #382
Place the clause	The person *who works in office #382* decides.

The correct form for the relative pronouns *who* or *whom* in a dependent clause is discussed in 8f-2.

▶ 3 Use the relative pronoun *whose* for a clause showing possession.

An adjective clause is often constructed using the relative pronoun *whose* to show possession by the person or animate thing modified. (See 45c-1 on possession.) Students sometimes omit a step in transforming a separate possessive statement into an adjective clause with *whose.*

Faulty	The person whom her office was locked called security.
Revised	The person whose office was locked called security.

Here is the pattern for transforming a sentence showing possession to a relative clause showing possession, using *whose* to replace the possessive noun or pronoun.

Two sentences	The person called security. *Her* office was locked.
Replace possessive subject with *whose*	*whose office was locked* [Her = *whose*]
Place the clause	The person *whose* <u>office was locked</u> called security.

The same process is used for a clause showing possession of a thing.

Two sentences	The government made a protest. *Its* ambassador was insulted.
Transform: Replace with *whose*	[*its* = *whose*] ambassador was insulted
Place the clause	The government *whose* <u>ambassador was insulted</u> made a protest.

▶ 47e Combining phrases and clauses with connecting words

As writers combine phrases and clauses, they choose between two basic relation-ships: a coordinate or a subordinate connection. Elements that have a *coordinate* connection emphasize a balance or equality between elements. (See 19a for a dis-cussion of coordinate relationships.) Elements can also have a subordinate or de-pendent connection that emphasizes that the elements are unequal, with one having a dependent link to another. (See 7e and 19b for a discussion of subordi-nate relationships.)

Phrases and clauses are often logically linked with connecting words, **con-junctions** and **conjunctive adverbs,** that require careful consideration of the kind of connection students wish to establish.

▶ 1 Choose the right connecting word for coordinate structures.

Connecting words for a coordinate, or balanced, relationship include **coordinat-ing conjunctions** (*and, but, or, nor, so, for, yet*), **correlative conjunctions** (*either/or, neither/nor, both/and, not only/but, whether/or, not only/but also*), and many **conjunc-tive adverbs** (*however, nevertheless, accordingly, also, besides, afterward, then, indeed, otherwise*). These words show relationships of contrast, consequence, sequence, and emphasis; they are discussed in 19a-1–3.

After deciding on the desired relationship among sentence parts, select a *single set of connecting words*. Avoid a mixture of words that may cancel out the meaning.

Mixed	They were *both* competitive, *but however* they were well matched. [The mixed connecting words show similarity and contrast at the same time.]
Balanced	They were *both* competitive, *and* they were well matched. They were competitive; *however,* they were well matched.

See 25a-1 and 25f-1 for appropriate rules on punctuation.

> **2** Choose the subordinating conjunction that establishes the desired dependent relationship.

Subordinating conjunctions establish different relationships, including conditional relationships and relationships of contrast, cause and effect, time and place, purpose, and outcome (see Chapter 19). In your writing, choose a single coordinating conjunction, and avoid combinations that are contradictory or confusing.

Mixed *Because* she was sick, *so* she went to the clinic. [A relation of cause and effect is confusingly combined with one of purpose or outcome.]

Clear *Because* she was sick, she went to the clinic. [cause/effect]
She was sick, *so* she went to the clinic. [outcome]

See 19b for a full discussion on establishing clear subordinate relationships among sentence parts. See 25a-1 and 25f-1 for rules on punctuation.

> **47f** Arranging cumulative modifiers

> **1** Observing typical order of cumulative adjectives

Single-word adjective modifiers are placed close to a noun, immediately before a noun, or after a linking verb (47a).

Cumulative adjectives are groups of adjectives that modify the same noun. There is a typical order of modifiers and cumulative adjectives in an English sentence. A major disruption of typical order can be confusing.

Faulty a beach French gorgeous tent   red light my small bulb

Revised a gorgeous French beach tent   my small red light bulb

Although some stylistic variations from typical order in the location of cumulative adjectives are possible for emphasis, typical locations in an English sentence provide a very strong normal pattern. Here are some guidelines.

Possessives precede numbers. Ordinal numbers follow cardinal numbers.

Jill's first car   my first nine drafts

The typical order of descriptive adjectives is shown below:

(1)	(2)	(3)	(4)	(5)	(6)	(7)	(8)
Opinion	Size	Shape	Condition	Age	Color	Origin	Noun
ugly		round			green		fenders
	huge		muddy				spots
lovely				old	red	Turkish	slippers
comfortable			sunny				room

Arranging Cumulative Modifiers

2 Arranging cumulative phrases, clauses, or noun modifiers[1]

A single phrase or clause functioning as an adjective immediately follows the noun or pronoun it modifies to avoid confusion with any adverbial phrases in the same sentence (47b).

When accumulated adjective phrases or clauses modify the same noun, their flexible emphasis creates an extremely varied sequence, especially for issues of opinion. In a neutral context some of the same typical sequences may be observed as for single-word adjectives (above), except that the modifying phrases follow the noun.

I found *spots* that are *huge* and that are also very *muddy*.

We saw that the *rooms* were very *narrow* and yet they seemed *bright*.

When two adverbial phrases or clauses are accumulated, place phrases typically precede time phrases.

Not typical   They lived in the 1970s in Japan.

Typical   They lived in Japan in the 1970s.

Two-word modifiers of nouns

Three nouns are often combined, with the first two forming a two-word modifier for the last noun. When this happens, nouns fall into a typical arrangement somewhat comparable with that of adjectives.

Not typical   a file steel cabinet

Typical   a steel file cabinet

The sequence of two nouns to modify a third noun may be classified and arranged in this sequence.

Material, Number, or Location	Origin, Purpose, or Type	Noun Modified
chapter	review	questions
two-word	noun	modifier
slate	roofing	tile
steel	file	cabinet

However, the categories of meaning for nouns are less clear than for adjectives and the opportunity for confusion is much greater. Students are therefore advised to avoid accumulating noun modifiers beyond this limit, and to rewrite combinations as phrases and clauses (see 11g).

EXERCISE I

Circle the correct form.

1. The girls thought the ride was (excited/exciting) and they were (interested/interesting) in the things they saw.

[1]We owe this discussion on order of modifiers to Jean Praninskas, *Rapid Review of English Grammar* (Englewood Cliffs, NJ: Prentice-Hall, 1975).

2. These gang members seemed capable (of/in) any kind of violence and were cruel (at/to) their enemies.

3. Luisa (walks usually/usually walks) to her studio (even when/when even) she feels tired.

4. The famous preacher (he spoke/who spoke) at our meeting was inspiring.

5. I have lost my (yellow beautiful/beautiful yellow) umbrella with the (large Japanese/Japanese large) designs.

APPENDIX **A**

Manuscript Form
and Preparation

B efore readers register a word of your writing, they form an impression based on your paper's appearance. If you are committed enough to a paper to have revised it several times, surely you will want to give it a crisp appearance. A clean, well-prepared, typed manuscript is a sign of an attentive attitude taken toward all the stages of writing. Careful manuscript preparation implicitly shows respect for your readers, who will certainly appreciate any efforts to make their work easier.

Style guides in the disciplines recommend slightly different conventions for preparing manuscripts, and you should consult the specialized guides listed in 38f, 39e, and 40e when writing in the humanities, social sciences, and sciences. Consult your professor as well. The recommendations here follow the guide commonly used in the humanities, the *MLA [Modern Language Association] Handbook for Writers of Research Papers*, 5th ed.

▶ **A1**   Paper and binding

Prepare your work on plain white, twenty-pound paper that measures 8-1/2 × 11 inches. For economy's sake, you might consider buying a ream (500 sheets) if you are typing the manuscript or are preparing it on a laser printer. If you are working with a dot matrix printer, buy a box of 500 or 1,000 sheets of fanfold paper. Unless your instructor advises otherwise, avoid onion skin or erasable paper, both of which will easily smudge. (For ease of preparation, though, you might type your work on erasable paper and submit a photocopy, which will not smudge.) Make a copy of your final paper to keep for your files, and submit the original to your instructor. In binding pages, affix a single paper clip to the upper lefthand corner. To ease your reader's handling of your paper, do *not* place multiple staples along the left margin, and avoid plastic folders unless otherwise directed.

▶ **A2**   Page layout

Whether you adopt conventions for page layout suggested by the *MLA Handbook* or by other style guides, maintain consistent margins and spacing. Your paper's first

772

page, subsequent pages, and reference list page(s) should be designed according to standard practice in a discipline.

Margins and line spacing

Type on one side of a page, double-spacing all text (including footnotes and endnotes). Maintain double-spacing between paragraphs and between lines of text and any displayed quotations. Leave a one-inch margin on the top and bottom of a page and a one-inch margin on both sides of a page. If you are working on a computer, set the margins as well as the running head (your last name and a page number) automatically. With each new paragraph, indent five spaces (on a computer, press the Tab key). For displayed quotations (see 28a-4), indent ten spaces and maintain that indentation for the length of the quotation.

Design of first page

Following the MLA format, you do not need to prepare a separate title page for your research papers. (This convention differs in the sciences and social sciences. See the box on page 664 as well as the example research paper on page 689.) Observe the spacing of headings and title in the following example.

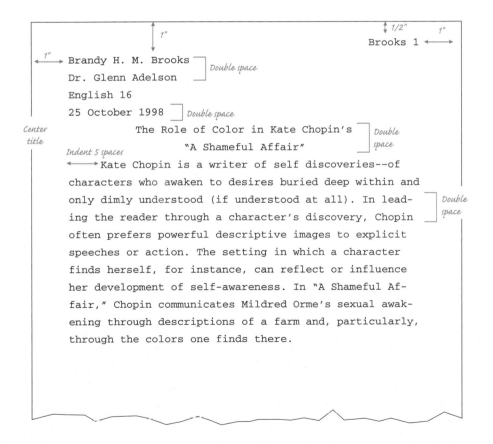

Design of subsequent pages

Observe the position of the running head and the first line of text on a paper's second or subsequent page.

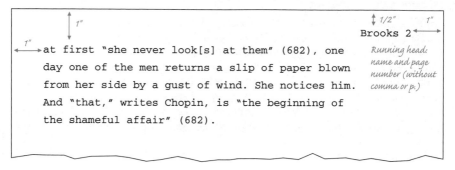

Design of "Works Cited" page

Observe the position of the running head, the title "Works Cited," and the indentation of the reference entry's second line.

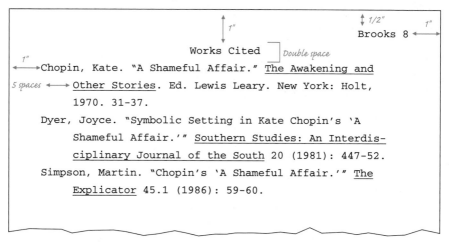

▶ A3   Text preparation

Printing a manuscript on a word processor

Print on one side of the page and, if possible, use a laser printer. If none is available, use a dot matrix printer with a fresh enough ribbon that readers will have no trouble reading your text. Keep the right-hand edge of your text ragged, or *un-*justified. If your dot matrix machine is printing a light page, you may be able to improve the product by photocopying the page with the photocopier adjusted to a darker than normal setting.

COMPUTER TIPS

Widows and Orphans

When your word processor paginates a final draft for you, a page or paragraph may break in an awkward spot, leaving either a *widow*—one word alone on a line at the end of a paragraph—or an *orphan*—one short line alone at the top of a page or column. For aesthetic reasons, you should avoid these awkward breaks. Many word processors have an option that will automatically eliminate widows and orphans. If your program does not have this option, then you may have to rewrite a sentence or paragraph to eliminate them yourself.

Printing a manuscript on a typewriter

Type on one side of a page with standard typewriter fonts. Avoid typefaces giving the appearance of script, since these are difficult to read. Use a fresh ribbon with black ink.

Handwriting a manuscript

Very few instructors accept handwritten papers. If yours does, use lined, white 8-1/2 × 11 inch paper. Do not use spiral-bound notebook paper with its ragged edges. Write neatly and legibly in pen, on one side of the page, using dark blue or black ink. Consult your instructor, who may ask you to skip every other line to allow room for editorial comments.

▶ A4 Alterations

In a final review of your paper, when you are working away from your typewriter or word processor, you may find it necessary to make minor changes to your text— perhaps to correct a typographical error or to improve your wording. Make corrections *neatly*. When striking out a word, do so with a single line. Use a caret (^) to mark an insertion in the text, and write your correction or addition above the line you are altering. If time permits and you have worked on a word processor, enter the changes into your file and reprint the affected pages. Retype or reprint a page when you make three or more handwritten corrections on it. If your typewriter or computer keyboard lacks a particular symbol or mark that you need, handwrite that symbol on the page.

```
                                                    nonetheless
For reasons Mildred does not yet understand but that^compel her,
she must be near Fred Evelyn.
```

A5 Punctuation and spacing

Observe the following standard conventions for spacing before and after marks of punctuation.

One space before

> beginning parenthesis or bracket
>
> beginning quotation mark
>
> period in a series denoting an omission—see ellipses, 29e

No space before (except as noted)

comma	question mark	semicolon
period[1]	apostrophe	end quotation mark
exclamation point	colon	hyphen or dash

No space after (except as noted)

> hyphen[2] or dash
>
> beginning parenthesis or bracket
>
> apostrophe[3]

One space after (except as noted)

> comma
>
> semicolon
>
> colon[4]
>
> apostrophe denoting the possessive form of a plural
>
> end parenthesis or bracket that does not end a sentence
>
> end quotation within a sentence
>
> period in a series denoting an omission—see ellipses, 29e
>
> period marking an abbreviated name or an initial

Two spaces after the following marks when they conclude a sentence

period	closing quotation
question mark	end parenthesis or bracket
exclamation	

Exceptions (as noted above)

[1]Unless the period occurs in a series denoting omission—see 29e.

[2]Unless the hyphen denotes one in a pair or series of delayed adjectives, as in *a first-, second-, or third-place finish.*

[3]Unless the apostrophe denotes the possessive form of a plural, as in *boys'*, in which case skip one space.

[4]Unless the colon denotes a ratio, as in *3:2.*

Glossary of Usage

This glossary is intended to provide definitions and descriptions of selected word usages current in formal academic writing. In consulting this kind of glossary, writers should be prepared to make informed decisions about the meaning and the level of diction that is most appropriate to their writing project.

Many entries in this glossary consist of commonly confused homonyms—words that are pronounced almost alike but have different meanings and spellings. A comprehensive listing of often-confused homonyms appears in 23a-1 in the spelling chapter.

a, an   Use *a* when the article precedes a noun beginning with a consonant. For example, *At last we found a hotel.* Use *an* when the article precedes a word beginning with a vowel or an unpronounced *h*. *It was an honor to receive an invitation.* (See 7a.)

accept, except   Use *accept* when your meaning is "to receive." Use *except* when you mean an exception, as in *He invited everyone except Thuan.* You can also use *except* as a verb that means "to leave out," as in *The report excepted the two episodes of misconduct.*

adverse, averse   Use *averse* when you mean a person's feelings of opposition. Use *adverse* when you refer to a thing that stands in opposition or is opposed to someone or something, as in *I was not averse to taking the roofing job, but the adverse circumstances of a tight deadline and bad weather almost kept me from it.*

advice, advise   Use *advice* as a noun meaning "a recommendation," as in *Longfellow gave excellent military advice.* Use *advise* as a verb meaning "to recommend," as in *Many counselors advise students to declare a double major.*

affect, effect   If your sentence requires a verb meaning "to have an influence on," use *affect.* If your sentence requires a noun meaning "result," use *effect.* *Effect* can also be a verb, however. Use *effect* as a verb when you mean "to make happen," as in *He was able to effect a change in how the city council viewed the benefits of recycling.*

aggravate, irritate   In formal writing, use *aggravate* when you mean "to make worse," as in *The smoke aggravated his cough.* Use *irritate* when you mean "to bother," as in *He became irritated when the drunken driver said the accident was not her fault.*

ain't   Do not use *ain't* in formal writing. Use *is not*, *are not*, or *am not* instead.

all ready, already   Use *all ready* when you mean "prepared" as in *He was all ready for an expedition to Antarctica.* Use *already* when you mean "by this time," as in *The ushers at Symphony Hall will not seat you if the concert has already started.*

all right   Do not use *alright.* It is simply a misspelling.

all together, altogether   Use *all together* when you mean "as a group" or "in unison," as in *Once we got the family all together, we could discuss the estate.* Use *altogether* when you mean "entirely," as in *Some of the stories about Poe's addictions and personal habits are not altogether correct.* (See 23a.)

allude, elude   Use *allude* when you mean "to refer indirectly to." Use *elude* when you mean "to avoid or escape."

allusion, illusion   Use *allusion* when you mean "an indirect reference," as in *The children did not understand the allusion to Roman mythology.* Use *illusion* when you mean "false or misleading belief or appearance," as in *Smith labored under the illusion that he was a great artist.*

a lot   Do not use *a lot* in formal writing. Use a more specific modifier instead. When you use *a lot* in other contexts, remember that it is always two words.

among, between   Use *between* when you are expressing a relationship involving two people or things, as in *There was general agreement between Robb and Jackson on that issue.* Use *among* when you are expressing a relationship involving three or more separable people or things, as in *He failed to detect a link among the blood cholesterol levels, the red blood cell counts, and the T-cell production rates.*

amongst   Do not use *amongst* in formal writing. Instead, use *among.*

amount, number   Use *amount* when you refer to a quantity of something that cannot be counted, as in *The amount of effort put into finding the cure for AIDS is beyond calculation.* Use *number* when you refer to something that can be counted, as in *The number of people who want to run the Boston Marathon increases yearly.*

an, and   Use *an* when the article precedes a noun beginning with a vowel or an unpronounced *h.* Use *and* when your sentence requires a conjunction that means "in addition to."

and etc.   Avoid using *etc.* in formal writing. When you must use *etc.* in nonformal writing, do not use *and. Et cetera* means "and so forth"; therefore, *and etc.* is redundant.

and/or   Use *and* or *or,* or explain your ideas by writing them out fully. But avoid *and/or,* which is usually too ambiguous to meet the demands of formal writing.

anxious, eager   Use *anxious* when you mean "worried" or "nervous." Use *eager* when you mean "excited or enthusiastic about the possibility of doing something."

anybody, any body; anyone, any one   Use *anybody* and *anyone* when the sense of your sentence requires an indefinite pronoun. Use *any body* and *any one* when the words *body* and *one* are modified by *any,* as in *The teacher was careful not to favor any one student* and *Any body of knowledge is subject to change.*

any more, anymore Use *any more* to mean "no more," as in *I don't want any more of those plums.* Use *anymore* as an adverb meaning "now," as in *He doesn't work here anymore.*

anyplace Do not use *anyplace* in formal writing. Use *anywhere* instead.

anyways, anywheres Do not use *anyways* and *anywheres* in formal writing; use *anyway* and *anywhere* instead.

apt, likely, liable Use *apt* when you mean "having a tendency to," as in *Khrushchev was apt to lose his temper in public.* Use *likely* when you mean "probably going to," as in *We will likely hear from the Senator by Friday.* Use *liable* when you mean "in danger of," as in *People who jog long distances over concrete surfaces are liable to sustain knee injuries.* Also use *liable* when you are referring to legal responsibility, as in *The driver who was at fault was liable for the damages.*

as, like Use *as* either as a preposition or as a conjunction, but use *like* as a preposition only. If your sentence requires a preposition, use *as* when you are making an exact equivalence, as in *Edison was known as the wizard of Menlo Park.* Use *like* when you are referring to likeness, resemblance, or similarity, as in *Like Roosevelt, Reagan was able to make his constituency feel optimism.*

as, than When you are making a comparison, you can follow both *as* and *than* with a subjective- or objective-case pronoun, depending on meaning. For example, *We trusted O'Keeffe more than him [we trusted Smith]* and *We trusted O'Keeffe more than he [Jones trusted O'Keeffe]. O'Keeffe was as talented as he [was talented]* and *We found O'Keeffe as trustworthy as [we found] him.* (See 8g.)

as to Do not use *as to* in formal writing. Rewrite a sentence such as *The president was questioned as to his recent decisions in the Middle East* to read *The president was questioned about his recent decisions in the Middle East.*

assure, ensure, insure Use *assure* when you mean "to promise" as in *He assured his mother that he would return early.* Use *ensure* when you mean "to make certain," as in *Taking a prep course does not ensure success in the SATs.* Use *insure* when you mean "to make certain" in a legal or financial sense, as in *He insured his boat against theft and vandalism.*

at Do not use *at* in a question formed with *where.* For example, rewrite a sentence such as *Where is the class at?* to read *Where is the class?*

a while, awhile Use *awhile* when your sentence requires an adverb, as in *He swam awhile.* If you are not modifying a verb, but rather want a noun with an article, use *a while,* as in *I have not seen you in a while.*

bad, badly Use *bad* as an adjective, as in *Bad pitching changed the complexion of the game.* Use *badly* as an adverb, as in *The refugees badly needed food and shelter.* Use *bad* to follow linking verbs that involve appearance or feeling, as in *She felt bad about missing the party.* (See 11d.)

being as, being that Do not use either *being as* or *being that* to mean "because" in formal writing. Use *because* instead.

beside, besides   Use *beside* as a preposition meaning "next to." Use *besides* as an adverb meaning "also" or "in addition to" as in *Besides, I needed to lose the weight.* Use *besides* as an adjective meaning "except" or "in addition to," as in *Rosa Parks seemed to have nothing besides courage to support her.*

better, had better; best, had best   Do not use *better, had better, best,* and *had best* for *should* in formal writing. Use *ought* or *should* instead.

between, among   See *among, between.*

breath, breathe   Use *breath* as a noun; use *breathe* as a verb.

bring, take   Use *bring* when you are referring to movement from a farther place to a nearer one, as in *The astronauts were asked to bring back rock samples.* Use *take* for all other types of movement.

broke   Use *broke* only as the past tense, as in *He broke the Ming vase.* Do not use *broke* as the past participle; for example, instead of writing *The priceless vase was broke as a result of careless handling,* write *The priceless vase was broken as a result of careless handling.*

bunch   Use *bunch* to refer to "a group or cluster of things growing together." Do not use *bunch* to refer to people or a group of items in formal writing.

burst, bust   Use *burst* when you mean "to fly apart suddenly," as in *The pomegranate burst open.* (Notice that the example sentence doesn't say *bursted;* there is no such form of the verb.) (See 9b.)

but however, but yet   When you use *however* and *yet,* do not precede them with *but* in formal writing. The *but* is redundant.

but that, but what   When you use *that* and *what,* do not precede them with *but* in formal writing. The *but* is unnecessary.

calculate, figure, reckon   If your sentence requires a word that means "imagine," use *imagine.* Do not use *calculate, figure,* or *reckon,* which are colloquial substitutes for "imagine."

can, may   Use *can* when you are writing about the ability to do something, as in *He can jump six feet.* Use *may* when you are referring to permission, as in *He may rejoin the team when the period of probation is over.*

can't, couldn't   Do not use these contractions in formal writing. Use *cannot* and *could not* instead.

can't hardly, can't scarcely   See *not but, not hardly, not scarcely.*

can't help but   Use *can't help* by itself; the *but* is redundant.

censor, censure   Use *censor* when you mean editing or removing from the public eye on the basis of morality. Use *censure* when you mean "to give a formal or official scolding or verbal punishment."

center around   Do not use *center around* in formal writing. Instead, use *center on.*

chose, choose   Use the verb *choose* in the present tense for the first and second person and for the future tense, as in *They choose [or will choose] their teams carefully.* Use *chose* for the past tense, as in *The presidential candidate chose a distinguished running mate.*

compare to, compare with   Use *compare to* to note similarities between things, as in *He compared the Chinese wine vessel to the Etruscan wine cup.* Use *compare with* to note similarities and contrasts, as in *When comparing market-driven economies with socialist economies, social scientists find a wide range of difference in the standard of living of individuals.*

complement, compliment   Use *complement* when you mean "something that completes," as in *The wine was the perfect complement for the elegant meal.* Use *compliment* when you mean "praise," as in *The administrator savored the compliment on her organizational skills.*

conscience, conscious   Use *conscience* when your sentence requires a noun meaning "a sense of right or wrong." Use *conscious* as an adjective to mean "aware of" or "awake."

consensus of opinion   Do not use *consensus of opinion* in formal writing. Use *consensus* instead to avoid redundancy.

continual, continuous   Use *continual* when you mean "constantly recurring," as in *Continual thunderstorms ruined their vacation days at the beach.* Use *continuous* when you mean "unceasing," as in *The continuous sound of a heartbeat, unceasing and increasing in volume, haunted the narrator.*

could of, would of, should of, might of, may of, must of   In formal writing, avoid combining modal auxiliaries (*could, would, should, might, may,* and *must*) with *of.* Instead, write *could have, would have, should have, might have, may have,* and *must have.*

couple, couple of   Do not use *couple* or *couple of* to mean "a few" in formal writing. Instead, write *a few.*

criteria   Use *criteria* when you want a plural word referring to more than one standard of judgment. Use *criterion* when you are referring to only one standard of judgment.

data   Use *data* when you are referring to more than one fact, statistic, or other means of support for a conclusion. When you are referring to a single fact, use the word *datum* in formal writing, or use *fact, figure,* or another term that is specific to the single means of support.

different from, different than   Use *different from* when an object or phrase follows, as in *Braque's style is different from Picasso's.* Use *different than* when a clause follows, as in *Smith's position on the deficit was <u>different</u> when he was seeking the presidency <u>than</u> it was when he was president.*

differ from, differ with   Use *differ from* when you are referring to unlike things, as in *Subsequent results of experiments in cold fusion differed radically from results first* *obtained in Utah.* Use *differ with* to mean "disagree," as in *One expert might differ with another on a point of usage.*

discreet, discrete   Use *discreet* to mean "respectfully reserved," as in *He was always discreet when he entered the synagogue.* Use *discrete* to mean "separate" or "distinct," as in *The essay was a discrete part of the examination and could be answered as a take-home assignment.*

disinterested, uninterested   Use *disinterested* to mean "impartial," as in *An umpire should always be disinterested in which team wins.* Use *uninterested* to mean "bored" or "not interested."

doesn't, don't   Do not use *doesn't* and *don't* in formal writing; instead, use *does not* and *do not.* In other contexts, use *don't* with the first and second person singular, as in *I don't smoke* and with the third person plural, as in *They don't smoke.* Use *doesn't* with the third person singular, as in *He doesn't ride the subway.*

done   Use *done* when your sentence requires the past participle; do not use done as the simple past. For example, rewrite a sentence such as *Van Gogh done the painting at Arles* to read *Van Gogh did the painting at Arles.*

due to, due to the fact that   Use *due to* to mean "because" only when it follows a form of the verb *be*, as in *The sensation of a leg falling asleep is due to pooling of the blood in the veins.* Do not use *due to* as a preposition, however. Also, do not use *due to the fact that* in formal writing because it is wordy. (See 17a.)

eager, anxious   See *anxious, eager.*

effect, affect   See *affect, effect.*

elicit, illicit   Use *elicit* to mean "to draw out," as in *The social worker finally elicited a response from the child.* Use *illicit* to mean "illegal," as in *Illicit transactions on the black market fuel an underground Soviet economy.* (See 23a.)

emigrate, immigrate, migrate   Use *emigrate* to mean "to move away from one's country." Use *immigrate* to mean "to move to another country." Use *migrate* to mean "to move to another place on a temporary basis."

ensure, assure, insure   See *assure, ensure, insure.*

enthused, enthusiastic   Use *enthusiastic* when you mean "excited about" or "showing enthusiasm." Do not use *enthused* in formal writing.

especially, specially   Use *especially* when you mean "particularly," as in *Maria Mitchell was especially talented as a mathematician.* Use *specially* when you mean "for a specific reason," as in *The drug was intended specially for the treatment of rheumatism.*

et al., etc.   Do not use *et al.* and *etc.* interchangeably. *Et al.* is generally used in references and bibliographies and is Latin for "and others." *Et cetera* is Latin for "and so forth." Like all abbreviations, *et al.* and *etc.* are generally not used in formal writing, except that *et al.* is acceptable in the context of a citation to a source.

etc.   Do not use *etc.* in formal writing. Use *and so forth* instead. Or, preferably, be as specific as necessary to eliminate the phrase.

everybody, every body Use *everybody* when you mean "everyone." Use *every body* when you are using *body* as a distinct word modified by *every*, as in *Is every body of water in Canada contaminated by acid rain?*

every day, everyday Use *everyday* when your sentence requires an adjective meaning "common" or "daily," as in *Availability of water was an everyday problem in ancient Egypt*. Use *every day* when you are using the word *day* and modifying it with the adjective *every*, as in *Enrico went to the art gallery every day*.

everywheres Do not use *everywheres* in formal writing. Use *everywhere* instead.

except, accept See *accept, except*.

except for the fact that In formal writing prefer the less wordy *except that*.

explicit, implicit Use *explicit* when you mean "stated outright," as in *The Supreme Court rules on issues that are not explicit in the Constitution*. Use *implicit* when you mean "implied," as in *Her respect for the constitution was implicit in her remarks*.

farther, further Use *farther* when you are referring to distance, as in *He was able to run farther after eating carbohydrates*. Use *further* when you are referring to something that cannot be measured, such as *Further negotiations are needed between the central government and the people of Azerbaijan*.

fewer, less Use *fewer* when you are referring to items that can be counted, as in *There are fewer savings accounts at the branch office this year*. Use *less* when you are referring to things that cannot be counted, as in *I have less confidence in the administration today than I did a year ago*. (See 11e.)

figure See *calculate, figure, reckon*.

fixing to Do not use *fixing to* in formal writing. Use *intend to* instead.

former, latter Use *former* and *latter* only when you are referring to two things. In that case, the former is the first thing, and the latter is the second. If you are referring to more than two things, use *first* for the first and *last* for the last.

get Do not overuse *get* in formal writing. Prefer more precise words. For example, instead of *get better*, write *improve*; instead of *get*, write *receive, catch,* or *become*; instead of *get done*, write *finish* or *end*.

gone, went Use *gone* when your sentence requires the past participle of *to go*, as in *They had gone there several times*. Use *went* when your sentence requires the past tense of *to go*, as in *They went to the theater Friday*.

good and Do not use *good and* in formal writing. Use *very* or, preferably, a more precise modifier instead.

good, well Use *good* as an adjective, as in *Astaire gave a good performance, but not one of his best*. Use *well* as an adverb, as in *He danced well*. You can also use *well* as an adjective when you refer to good health, as in *She felt well* or *She is well today*. (See 11d.)

got, have; has/have got to Do not use *got* in place of *have* in formal writing. For example, rewrite a sentence such as *I got to lose weight* to read *I have to [or I must] lose weight*.

had better, better; had best, best   See *better, had better.*

had ought   Do not use *had ought* in formal writing. Use *ought* by itself instead.

half   When you refer to half of something in formal writing, use *a half* or *one-half,* but do not use *a half a.* For example, rewrite a sentence such as *He had a half a sandwich for dinner* to read *He had a half sandwich for dinner.*

hanged, hung   Use *hanged* for the action of hanging a person, as in *The innocent man was hanged by an angry mob.* Use *hung* for all other meanings, such as *The clothes were hung on the line* and *The chandelier hung from a golden rope.* (See 9b.)

he, she; he/she; his, her; his/her; him, her; him/her   When you are using a pronoun to refer back to a noun that could be either masculine or feminine, you might use *he or she* in order to avoid language that is now considered sexist. For example, instead of writing *A doctor must be constantly alert; he cannot make a single mistake* to refer generally to doctors, you could write *A doctor must be constantly alert; he or she cannot make a single mistake.* Or you could recast the sentence in the plural to avoid this problem: *Doctors must be constantly alert; they cannot make a single mistake.* (See 10c and 21g for specific strategies on avoiding gender-offensive pronoun references.)

herself, himself, myself, yourself   Use pronouns ending in *-self* when the pronouns refer to a noun that they intensify, as in *The teacher himself could not pass the test.* Do not use pronouns ending in *-self* to take the place of subjective- or objective-case pronouns. Instead of writing, for example, *Joan and myself are good friends,* write *Joan and I are good friends.* (See 7a.)

himself   See *herself, himself, myself, yourself.*

his/her   See *he/she.*

hisself   Do not use *hisself* in formal writing. In a context such as *He hisself organized the picnic,* recast the sentence to read *He himself organized the picnic.*

hopefully   Use *hopefully* when you mean "with hope," as in *Relatives watched hopefully as the first miners emerged after the fire.* Avoid using *hopefully* as a modifier for an entire clause or to convey any other meaning. For example, avoid *Hopefully, a cure for leukemia is not far away.*

hung, hanged   See *hanged, hung.*

if, whether   Use *if* to begin a subordinate clause when a stated or implied result follows, as in *If the court rules against the cigarette manufacturers, [then] thousands of lawsuits could follow.* Use *whether* when you are expressing an alternative, as in *Economists do not know whether the dollar will rebound or fall against the strength of the yen.*

illicit, elicit   See *elicit, illicit.*

illusion, allusion   See *allusion, illusion.*

immigrate   See *emigrate, immigrate, migrate.*

impact   Use *impact* when you are referring to a forceful collision, as in *The impact of the cars was so great that one was flattened.* Do not use *impact* as a verb meaning "to have an effect on." Instead of writing *Each of us can positively impact waste reduction efforts,* write *Each of us can reduce waste.*

implicit, explicit   See *explicit, implicit.*

imply, infer   Use *imply* when you mean "to suggest without directly stating," as in *The doctor implied that being overweight was the main cause of my problem.* Use *infer* when you mean "to find the meaning of something," as in *I inferred from her lecture that drinking more than two cups of coffee a day was a health risk.*

in, into   Use *in* when you are referring to location or condition. Use *into* to refer to a change in location, such as *The famous portrait shows a man going into a palace.* In formal writing, do not use *into* for "interested in." For example, avoid a statement such as *I am into repairing engines.*

incredible, incredulous   Use *incredible* to mean "unbelievable," as in *Some of Houdini's exploits seem incredible to those who did not witness them.* Use *incredulous* to mean "unbelieving," as in *Many inlanders were incredulous when they heard tales of white people capturing men, women, and children who lived on the coast.*

individual, person, party   Use *individual* when you are referring to a single person and when your purpose is to stress that the person is unique, as in *Curie was a tireless and brilliant individual.* Use *party* when you mean a group, as in *The party of eight at the next table disturbed our conversation and ruined our evening.* The word *party* is also correctly used in legal documents referring to a single person. Use *person* for other meanings.

infer, imply   See *imply, infer.*

in regards to   Do not use *in regards to* in formal writing. Generally, you can substitute *about* for *in regards to.*

inside of, outside of   Use *inside* and *outside,* without *of,* when you are referring to location, as in *The roller blades were stored inside the garage.* In formal writing, do not use *inside of* to replace *within* in an expression of time. For example, avoid a sentence such as *I'll have that report inside of an hour.*

insure, assure, ensure   See *assure, ensure, insure.*

irregardless, regardless   Do not use *irregardless.* Use *regardless* instead.

is when, is where   Do not use *is when* and *is where* when you are defining something. Instead of writing *Dinner time is when my family relaxes,* write *At dinner time, my family relaxes.*

its, it's   Use *its* when your sentence requires a possessive pronoun, as in *Its leaves are actually long, slender blades.* (See 8c-1 and 27a-2.) Use *it's* only when you mean "it is." (See 23a.)

-ize   Do not use the suffix *-ize* to turn a noun into a verb in formal writing. For example, instead of writing *He is finalizing his draft,* write *He is finishing his draft* or *He is working on his final draft.*

kind, sort, type Do not precede the singular words *kind, sort,* and *type* with the plural word *these.* Use *this* instead. Also, prefer more specific words than *kind, sort,* and *type.* (See 17a.)

kind of, sort of Do not use these phrases as adjectives in formal writing. Instead, use *rather* or *somewhat.*

later, latter Use *later* when you refer to time, as in *I will go to the concert later.* Use *latter* when you refer to the second of two things, as in *The latter of the two dates is better for my schedule.* (See also *former, latter.*)

latter, former See *former, latter.*

lay, lie Use *lay* when you mean "to put" or "to place," as in *She lays the present on the table.* Use *lie* when you mean "recline," as in *She lies awake at night,* or when you mean "is situated," as in *The city lies between a desert and a mountain range.* Also, remember that *lay* is a transitive verb that takes a direct object. (See 9d.)

learn, teach Do not use *learn* to mean "teach." For example, rewrite a sentence such as *Ms. Chin learned us Algebra* to read *Ms. Chin taught us Algebra.*

leave, let Use *leave* to mean "depart." Use *let* to mean "allow." You can use either *leave* or *let* when the word is followed by *alone,* as in *Leave her alone* or *Let him alone.*

less, fewer See *fewer, less.*

liable See *apt, liable, likely.*

lie, lay See *lay, lie.*

like, as See *as, like.*

like, such as Use *like* to make a comparison, as in *Verbena is like ageratum in size and color.* Use *such as* when you are giving examples, as in *Many small flowers, such as verbena, ageratum, and alyssum, can be combined to create decorative borders and edgings.*

likely See *apt, liable, likely.*

lose, loose Use *lose* as a verb meaning "to misplace" or "to fail to win." Use *loose* as an adjective meaning "not tight" or "unfastened." You can also use *loose* as a verb meaning "to let loose," as in *They loosed the enraged bull when the matador entered the ring.* (See 23a.)

lots, lots of Do not use *lots* or *lots of* in formal writing. Use *many, very many, much,* or choose a more precise word instead.

man, mankind Do not use *man* and *mankind* to refer to all people in general. Instead, consider using *people, men and women, humans,* or *humankind.* (See 21g.)

may be, maybe Use *maybe* to mean "perhaps." Use *may be* as a verb (or auxiliary verb), as in *William may be visiting tomorrow.* (See 23a.)

may, can See *can, may.*

may of See *could of, would of, should of, might of, may of, must of.*

media   Use a plural verb with *media*, as in *The media are often credited with helping the consumer win cases against large companies. Medium* is the singular form.

might of   See *could of, would of, should of, might of, may of, must of.*

migrate   See *emigrate, immigrate, migrate.*

moral, morale   Use *moral* when you mean "an object lesson" or "knowing right from wrong." *What is the moral to the story?* Use *morale* when you mean "outlook" or "attitude." *The team's morale was high.* (See 23a.)

Ms.   Use *Ms.* to refer to a woman when a title is required and when you either know that she prefers this title or you do not know her marital status. An invented title, *Ms.* was intended to address the issue of discrimination or judgment based on marital status. In research writing, use last names alone, without any title, as in *Jenkins recommends.* In this case, do not use a title for either a man or a woman.

must of   See *could of, would of, should of, might of, may of, must of.*

myself   See *herself, himself, myself, yourself.*

nor, or   Use *nor* and *or* to suggest a choice. Use *nor* when the choice is negative; use *or* when the choice is positive. (See 7f.)

not but, not hardly, not scarcely   Do not use *not* to precede *hardly, scarcely,* and *but* in formal writing. Because *but, hardly,* and *scarcely* already carry the meaning of a negative, it is not necessary or correct to add another negative.

nothing like, nowhere near   Do not use *nothing like* and *nowhere near* in formal writing. Instead, use *not nearly.*

nowheres   Do not use *nowheres* in formal writing. Use *nowhere* instead.

number, amount   See *amount, number.*

off of   Do not use *off of* in formal writing. Use *off* or *from* alone instead, as in *She jumped off the bridge* or *He leaped from the rooftop.*

Ok, okay, O.K.   Do not use *Ok, okay,* or *O.K.* in formal writing as a substitute for *acceptable.*

on account of   Do not use this as a substitute for *because.* Use *because* instead.

on, upon   Use *on* instead of *upon* in formal writing.

or, nor   See *nor, or.*

outside of, inside of   See *inside of, outside of.*

party, individual, person   See *individual, person, party.*

people, persons   Use *people* to refer to a general group, as in *The people will make their voices heard.* Use *persons* to refer to a (usually small) collection of individuals, as in *The persons we interviewed were nearly unanimous in their opinion.*

per   Do not use *per* in formal writing. For example, instead of writing *The package was sent per your instructions,* it is better to write *The package was sent according to* *your instructions. Per* is acceptable in technical writing or when used with data and prices, as in *Charging $75 per hour, the consultant earned a handsome salary.*

percent (per cent), percentage Use *percent* (or *per cent*) with a specific number. Use *percentage* with specific descriptive words and phrases, such as *A small percentage of the group did not eat meat.* Do not use *percentage* as a substitute for *part*; for example, rewrite a sentence such as *A percentage of my diet consists of complex carbohydrates* to read *Part of my diet consists of complex carbohydrates.*

person, party, individual See *individual, person, party.*

plenty Do not use *plenty* as a substitute for *quite* or *very.* For example, instead of writing *The Confederate troops were plenty hungry during the winter of 1864,* write *The Confederate troops were hungry [or starving] during the winter of 1864.*

plus Avoid using *plus* as a conjunction joining independent clauses or as a conjunctive adverb. For example, rewrite *Picasso used color in a new way plus he experimented with shape; plus, he brought new meaning to ideas about abstract painting* to read *Picasso used color in a new way and he experimented with shape; moreover, he brought new meaning to ideas about abstract painting.* It is acceptable to use *plus* when you need an expression meaning "in addition to," as in *The costs of day care, plus the costs of feeding and clothing the child, weighed heavily on the single parent's budget.*

practicable, practical Use *practicable* when you mean "capable of putting into practice," as in *Although it seemed logical, the plan for saving the zoo was very expensive and turned out not to be practicable.* Use *practical* when you mean "sensible," as in *Lincoln was a practical young man who studied hard, paid his debts, and dealt with people honestly.*

precede, proceed Use *precede* when you mean "come before," as in *The opening remarks precede the speech.* Use *proceed* when you mean "go forward," as in *The motorists proceeded with caution.*

pretty Do not use *pretty,* as in *pretty close,* to mean "somewhat" or "quite" in formal writing. Use *somewhat, rather,* or *quite* instead.

previous to, prior to Avoid these wordy expressions. Use *before* instead.

principal, principle Use *principal* when you refer to a school administrator or an amount of money. Use *principle* when you are referring to a law, conviction, or fundamental truth. You can also use *principal* as an adjective meaning "major" or "most important," as in *The principal players in the decision were Sue Marks and Tom Cohen.*

quotation, quote Use *quotation* when your sentence requires a noun, as in *The quotation from Nobel laureate Joseph Goldstein was used to lend credence to the theory.* Use *quote* when your sentence requires a verb, as in *She asked Goldstein whether she could quote him.*

raise, rise Use *raise* when you mean "to lift." Use *rise* when you mean "to get up." To help you understand the difference, remember that *raise* is transitive and takes a direct object; *rise* is intransitive. (See 9d.)

rarely ever   Do not use *rarely ever* in formal writing. Use *rarely* or *hardly ever* instead.

real, really   Use *real* as an adjective and use *really* as an adverb.

reason is because   Do not use *reason is because* in formal writing. Rewrite your sentence to say, for example, *The real reason that the bomb was dropped was to end the war quickly* or *The bomb was dropped because Truman wanted to prevent Soviet influence in the Far Eastern settlement.*

reckon   See *calculate, figure, reckon.*

regarding, in regard to, with regard to   In formal writing that is not legal in nature, use *about* or *concerning* instead of these terms.

regardless, irregardless   See *irregardless, regardless.*

respectfully, respectively   Use *respectfully* when you mean "with respect," as in *He respectfully submitted his grievances.* Use *respectively* when you mean "in the given order," as in *The chief of police, the director of the department of public works, and the director of parks and recreation, respectively, submitted their ideas for budget cuts.*

right   Do not use *right* as an intensifier in formal writing. For example, instead of writing that *The farmer was right tired after milking the cows,* write *The farmer was tired [or exhausted] after milking the cows.*

rise, raise   See *raise, rise.*

seen   Do not use *seen* without an auxiliary such as *have, has,* or *had.* For example, rewrite a sentence such as *I seen the film* to read *I have seen the film.*

set, sit   Use *set* when you mean "to place." *Set* is a transitive verb that requires an object, as in *I set the book on the table.* Do not use *set* to mean "to sit" in formal writing. (See 9d.)

shall, will   Use *shall* instead of *will* for questions that contain the first person in extremely formal writing, as in *Shall we attend the meeting?* In all other cases, use *will.*

should of   See *could of, would of, should of, might of, may of, must of.*

should, would   Use *should* when you are referring to an obligation or a condition, as in *The governor's mansion should be restored.* Use *would* when you are referring to a wish, as in *I would like to see it repainted in its original colors.*

sit, set   See *set, sit.*

so   Do not use *so* in formal writing to mean "very" or "extremely," as in *He is so entertaining.* Use *very, extremely,* or, preferably, a more specific intensifier instead. Or follow *so* with an explanation preceded by *that,* as in *The reaction to the Freedom Riders was so violent that Robert F. Kennedy ordered a military escort.*

some   Do not use *some* to mean either "remarkable" or "somewhat" in formal writing. For example, rewrite a sentence such as *Babe Ruth was some hitter* to read *Babe Ruth was a remarkable hitter,* or use another more precise adjective to modify *hitter.* Also, rewrite a sentence such as *Wright's mother worried some about the kinds of building blocks her young child used* to read *Wright's mother worried a bit [or was somewhat worried about] the kinds of building blocks her young child used.*

somebody, some body; someone, some one   Use the indefinite pronouns *somebody* and *someone* when referring to a person, such as *There is someone I admire.* Use *some body* and *some one* when the adjective *some* modifies the noun *body* or *one,* as in *We will find the answer in some body of information.*

sometime, sometimes, some time   Use *sometime* when you mean "an indefinite, later time." Use *sometimes* when you mean "occasionally" or "from time to time." Use *some time* when *some* functions as an adjective modifying *time,* as in *His eyes required some time to adjust to the darkened room.*

sort   See *kind, sort, type.*

specially, especially   See *especially, specially.*

stationary, stationery   Use *stationary* to mean "standing still." Use *stationery* to mean "writing paper."

such   Do not use *such* to mean "very" or "extremely" unless *such* is followed by *that.* For example, rewrite a sentence such as *It had such boring lyrics* to read *It had extremely boring lyrics* or *It had <u>such</u> boring lyrics* that *I almost fell asleep half way through the song.*

such as, like   See *like, such as.*

supposed to, used to   Do not use *suppose to* or *use to* in formal writing. Use *supposed to* or *used to* instead.

sure and, sure to; try and, try to   Do not use *sure and* and *try and* in formal writing. Instead, use *sure to* and *try to.* For example, rewrite the sentence *Be sure and bring your computer* to read *Be sure to bring your computer.*

sure, surely   Use *surely* instead of *sure* when your sentence requires an adverb. For example, rewrite a sentence such as *Robert Fulton was sure a genius* to read *Robert Fulton was surely [or certainly] a genius.*

take, bring   See *bring, take.*

than, as   See *as, than.*

than, then   Use *than* when you mean "as compared with," as in *The violin is smaller than the cello.* Use *then* when you are stating a sequence of events, as in *First, he learned how to play the violin. Then he learned to play the cello.* Also use *then* when you mean "at that time" or "therefore." (See 23a.)

that there   See *this here, these here, that there, them there.*

that, which   Use *that* or *which* in an essential (or restrictive) clause, or a clause that is necessary to the meaning of the sentence, as in *This is the book that explains Locke's philosophy.* Use *which* in a nonessential (nonrestrictive) clause, or one that is not necessary to the meaning of the sentence, as in *My library just acquired Smith's book on Locke, which is not always easy to find.* (See 14e.)

their, there, they're   Use *their* as a possessive pronoun, as in *Their father prevented William and Henry James from being under the control of any one teacher for more than a year.* (See 8c-1.) Use *there* to refer to a place, as the opposite of *here.* Use *they're* to mean "they are." (See 27a-2.)

theirselves   Do not use *theirselves* in formal writing. Rewrite a sentence such as *They treated theirselves to ice cream* to read *They treated themselves to ice cream.*

them there   See *this here, these here, that there, them there.*

then, than   See *than, then.*

these here   See *this here, these here, that there, them there.*

these kind   See *kind, sort, type.*

this here, these here, that there, them there   Do not use *this here, these here, that there,* and *them there* in formal writing. Use *this, that, these,* and *those* instead.

thru   Do not use *thru* in formal writing. Use *through* instead.

thusly   Do not use *thusly* in formal writing. Use *thus* instead. (*Thus,* which is already an adverb, does not need an *-ly* ending.)

till, until, 'til   Do not use *'til* or *till* in formal writing. Prefer *until.*

to, too, two   Use *to* as a preposition meaning "toward"; use *too* to mean "also" or "excessively"; and use *two* as a number. (See 23a.)

toward, towards   Use *toward* instead of *towards* in formal writing. *Towards* is the British form.

try and, try to   See *sure and, sure to; try and, try to.*

type of   Do not use *type* in formal writing when you mean "type of." For example, rewrite a sentence such as *He is an anxious type person* to read *He is an anxious type of person.* (See also *kind, sort, type.*)

uninterested, disinterested   See *disinterested, uninterested.*

unique   Do not modify *unique* in formal writing. Because *unique* is an absolute, you should not write, for example, *most unique* or *very unique.*

until   See *till, until, 'til; until* is the preferred form in formal writing.

use, utilize   When you need a word that means "use," prefer *use. Utilize* is a less direct choice with the same meaning. (See 17a.)

used to   See *supposed to, used to.*

very   Avoid using *very* as an intensifier. Sometimes you will want to replace more than one word in order to eliminate *very.* For example, in the sentence *It was a very nice painting,* you could substitute more precise language, such as *It was a colorful [or provocative or highly abstract] painting.* (See 17a.)

Glossary of Usage   **791**

wait for, wait on   Unless you are referring to waiting on tables, use *wait for* instead of *wait on* in formal writing. For example, rewrite *We grew tired as we waited on Sarah* to read *We grew tired as we waited for Sarah.*

ways   Do not use *ways* in formal writing to mean "way." Use *way* instead.

well, good   See *good, well.*

where at   See *at.*

whether, if   See *if, whether.*

which, that   See *that, which.*

which, who   Use *which* when you are referring to things. Use *who* when you are referring to people.

who, whom   Use *who* when a sentence requires a subject pronoun, as in *Who can answer this question?* Use *whom* when a sentence requires an object pronoun, as in *Whom did you invite?* (See 8f.)

who's, whose   Do not use *who's* in formal writing. Use *who is* instead. (See 27a-2.) Use *whose* to show possession, as in *Whose computer did you use?* (See 8f.)

will, shall   See *shall, will.*

-wise   Do not attach the suffix *-wise* to nouns or adjectives to turn them into adverbs in formal writing. For example, instead of writing *I am not doing well gradewise,* you could recast the sentence to read *My grades are falling* or *My grades are low.*

would of   See *could of, would of, should of, might of, may of, must of.*

would, should   See *should, would.*

your, you're   Do not use *you're* in formal writing. Use *you are* instead. (See 27a-2.) Use *your* to show possession, as in *Your CD player is broken.* (See 8f.)

yourself   See *herself, himself, myself, yourself.*

Glossary of Terms:
Grammar and Composition

abbreviation   The shortened form of a word, usually followed by a period.

absolute phrase   See *phrase.*

abstract expression   An expression that refers to broad categories or ideas (*evil, friendship, love*).

abstract noun   See *noun.*

acronym   The uppercase, pronounceable abbreviation of a proper noun—a person, organization, government agency, or country. Periods are not used with acronyms (*ARCO, WAVES*). (See 31c.)

active voice   See *voice.*

adjective   A word that modifies or describes a noun, pronoun, or group of words functioning as a noun. Adjectives answer the questions: which, what kind, and how many. A single-word adjective is usually placed before the word it modifies. Pure adjectives are not derived from other words. (See 7a-5; Chapter 11.)

adjective clause   See *clause.*

adjective forms   Adjectives change form to express comparative relationships. The **positive form** of an adjective is its base form. The **comparative form** is used to express a relationship between two elements. The **superlative form** is used to express a relationship between three or more elements. Most single-syllable adjectives and many two-syllable adjectives show comparisons with the suffix *-er* (tall*er*) and superlatives with the suffix *-est* (tall*est*). Adjectives of three or more syllables change to the comparative and superlative forms with the words *more* and *most*, respectively (*more beautiful, most beautiful*). Negative comparisons are formed by placing the words *less* and *least* before the positive form (*less interesting, least interesting*). (See 11e.)

adverb   A word that modifies a verb, an adjective, another adverb, or an entire sentence. Adverbs describe, define, or otherwise limit the words they modify, answering the questions when, how, where, how often, to what extent, and to what degree. Adverbs (as words, phrases, or clauses) can appear in different places in a sentence, depending on the rhythm the writer wants to achieve. Most adverbs are formed by adding the suffix -*ly* to an adjective. (See 7a-6; Chapter 11.)

adverb clause   See *clause.*

adverb forms   The change of form that adverbs undergo to express comparative relationships. The **positive form** of an adverb is its base form. The **comparative form** is used to express a relationship between two elements. The **superlative form** is used to express a relationship among three or more elements. Most single-syllable adverbs show comparisons with the suffix -*er* (*nearer*) and superlatives with the suffix -*est* (*nearest*). Adverbs of two or more syllables change to comparative and superlative forms with *more* and *most*, respectively (*more beautifully, most beautifully*). Negative comparisons are formed by placing the words *less* and *least* before the positive form (*less strangely, least strangely*). (See 11e.)

adverbial conjunctions   See *conjunctive adverbs.*

agreement   The grammatical relationship between a subject and a verb, and a pronoun and its antecedent. If one element in these pairs is changed, the other must also be changed. Subjects and verbs must agree in number and person; pronouns and antecedents must agree in number, person, and gender. (See Chapter 10.)

analogy   A figure of speech that makes a comparison between two apparently unrelated people, objects, conditions, or events in order to clarify a process or a difficult concept. The unknown entity is explained in terms of the more familiar entity. (See 5e-7; 6d-1; 21f-1.)

analysis   A close, careful reading of a text in which parts are studied to determine how the text as a whole functions. In a written analysis, in most instances, the author is obliged to support his or her interpretation with direct evidence from a text. (See 38c-1.)

antecedent   A noun (or occasionally a pronoun) that a pronoun refers to and renames. A pronoun and its antecedent must agree in number, person, and gender. (See 10b; Chapter 14.)

antonym   A word whose denotation (dictionary meaning) is opposite that of another word.

apostrophe   A punctuation mark used to show possession, mark the omission of letters or numbers, and mark plural forms. (See Chapter 27.)

appositive   A word or phrase that describes, identifies, or renames a noun in a sentence. (See 8e-2.)

appositive phrase   See *phrase.*

article   The words *a, an,* or *the.* The **indefinite article,** *a* or *an,* introduces a generalized noun. *A* appears before nouns beginning with a consonant; *an* is placed before nouns beginning with a vowel or an unpronounced *h.* The **definite article,** *the,* denotes a specific noun. Also called *determiners.*

assumption   A core belief, often unstated, that shapes the way people perceive the world. (See 1g.)

audience   The person or people who will be reading a piece of writing. Writing that takes a particular audience's needs and experience into consideration is most effective.

auxiliary verb   The verbs *be, will, can, have, do, shall,* and *may,* combined with the base form of another verb, or its present or past participle. Such auxiliary verbs are used to establish tense, mood, and voice in a sentence. Also called *helping verbs.* (See 7a-3; 9c.)

base form   The infinitive form of a verb (*to be, to go*) from which all changes are made. Also called the *dictionary form.*

bibliography   The list of sources used in writing a paper. An **annotated bibliography** is a fully annotated working bibliography in manuscript form. A **working bibliography** includes all of the sources located in researching a paper. A **final bibliography** consists of only those sources used in the actual writing of a paper. In Modern Language Association (MLA) format, the bibliography is titled *Works Cited;* in American Psychological Association (APA) format, it is called *References;* and in Council of Biology Editors (CBE) format, it is called *Cited References.* (See 35d; Chapter 37.)

brackets   Punctuation marks used to clarify or insert remarks into quoted material. (See 29d.)

brainstorming   A technique of idea generation in which the writer quickly jots down words or phrases related to a broad subject. When the time limit (five or ten minutes) is reached, related items are grouped; groupings with the greatest number of items indicate potential topics for composition. (See 3b-2.)

buzzwords   Vague, often abstract expressions that sound as if they have meaning, but do not contribute anything of substance to a sentence. (See 17a-4.)

case   The change in form of a noun or pronoun, depending on its function in a sentence. The three cases are the subjective, objective, and possessive forms. Nouns and indefinite pronouns take all three cases, but change form only when they show possession (with the addition of an apostrophe and *s*). Pronouns change form in all three cases. The **subjective case** is used when a pronoun functions as a subject, subject complement, or as an appositive that renames a subject. The **objective case** is used when a pronoun functions as the object of a preposition, as the object or indirect object of a verb, as the object of a verbal, or as the subject of an infinitive. The **possessive case** of a noun or pronoun indicates possession or ownership. (See Chapter 8.)

chronological arrangement   A method of organizing a paper in which the writing begins at one point in time and proceeds in sequence, forward or backward, to some other point. (See 5d-1.)

clause   A grouping of words that has a subject and a predicate. An **independent clause** (or *main clause*) is a core statement that can stand alone as a sentence. A **dependent clause** (or *subordinate clause*) cannot stand alone as a sentence; it is joined to an independent clause by either a subordinating conjunction or a relative pronoun. There are four types of dependent clauses. **Adverb clauses** begin with subordinating conjunctions (*when, because, although*) and modify verbs, adjectives, and other adverbs. **Adjective clauses** begin with relative pronouns (*which, that, who, whom, whose*) and modify nouns or pronouns. **Noun clauses** are introduced by pronouns (*which, whichever, who, whoever, whom, whomever, whose*) and the words *how, when, why, where, whether,* and *whatever* and function as subjects, objects, complements, or appositives. **Elliptical clauses** have an omitted word or words (often relative pronouns or the logically parallel second parts of comparisons), but the sense of the sentence remains clear. (See 7e; 16e.)

cliché   A trite expression that has lost its impact. (See 21f-3.)

coherence   The clarity of the relationship between one unit of meaning and another. (See 4b-2.)

collective noun   See *noun.*

colloquial   Informal, conversational language. (See 21e-3.)

colon   A punctuation mark (:) generally used to make an announcement. In formal writing, the colon follows only a complete independent clause and introduces a word, phrase, sentence, or group of sentences. (See 29a.)

comma   A punctuation mark (,) used to signal that some element, some word or cluster of related words, is being set off from a main clause for a reason. (See Chapter 25.)

comma splice   The incorrect use of a comma to mark the boundary between two independent clauses. (See Chapter 13; 25f-1.)

common noun   See *noun.*

comparative form   See *adjective forms, adverb forms.*

complement   A word or group of words that completes the meaning of a subject or direct object by renaming it or describing it. A **subject complement** follows a linking verb and can be a noun, pronoun, adjective, or group of words substituting for an adjective or noun. An **object complement** typically follows verbs such as *appoint, call, choose, make,* and *show* and can be a noun, adjective, or group of words substituting for a noun or adjective.

complete predicate   See *predicate.*

complete subject   See *subject.*

complex sentence   See *sentence.*

compound adjective   Two or more words that are combined to modify a given noun. Often, when a compound adjective precedes a noun it is hyphenated to prevent misreading; when it follows the noun it modifies, it does not need hyphenation. (See 32a-1; 32a-3.)

compound-complex sentence   See *sentence.*

compound noun   Two or more words that are combined to function as a single noun. Hyphens are used when the first word of the compound could be read alone as a noun (*cross-reference*). (See 32a-2.)

compound predicate   Two or more verbs and their objects and modifiers that are joined with a coordinating conjunction to form a single predicate.

compound sentence   See *sentence.*

compound subject   Two or more nouns or pronouns and their modifiers that function as a single subject.

compound verb   Two or more verbs that are combined to function as a single verb. Hyphens are used when the first word of the compound could be read alone as a verb (*shrink-wrap*). (See 32a-2.)

compound words   Nouns, adjectives, or prepositions created when two or more words are brought together to form a distinctive meaning and to function grammatically as a single word. (See 32a.)

concrete expression   A vivid, detailed expression (*a throbbing headache*).

concrete noun   See *noun.*

conjunction   A word that joins sentence elements or entire sentences by establishing a coordinate or equal relationship among combined parts, or by establishing a subordinate or unequal relationship. **Coordinating conjunctions** (*and, but, or, nor, for, so, yet*) join complete sentences or parallel elements from two or more sentences into a single sentence and express specific logical relationships between these elements. **Correlative conjunctions** (*both/and, neither/nor, either/or, not only/ but also*) are pairs of coordinating conjunctions that place extra emphasis on the relationship between the parts of the coordinated construction. The parts of the sentence joined by correlative conjunctions must be grammatically parallel. **Subordinating conjunctions** (*when, while, although, because, if, since, whereas*) connect dependent clauses to independent clauses. (See 7a-9; 18b; 19a-1, 2.)

conjunctive adverb   An adverb (such as *however, therefore, consequently, otherwise,* or *indeed*) used to create a compound sentence in which the independent clauses that are joined share a logically balanced emphasis. Also called *adverbial conjunction.* (See 7a-9; 19a-3; 26b.)

connotation   The implications, associations, and nuances of a word's meaning. (See 21a.)

coordinate adjectives   Two or more adjectives in a series, whose order can be reversed without affecting the meaning of the noun being modified. Coordinate adjectives are linked by a comma or by a coordinating conjunction (*an intelligent, engaging speaker*). (See 25c-2.)

coordinating conjunction   See *conjunction.*

coordination   The combining of sentence elements by the use of coordinating and correlative conjunctions and conjunctive adverbs. Elements in a coordinate relationship share equal grammatical status and equal emphasis. (See 19a; 20b-1.)

correlative conjunction   See *conjunction.*

count noun   See *noun.*

cues   Words and phrases that remind readers as they move from sentence to sentence (1) that they continue to read about the same topic and (2) that ideas are unfolding logically. Four types of cues are pronouns, repetition, parallel structures, and transitions. (See 5d-2.)

cut   To delete sentences because they are off the point or because they give too much attention to a subordinate point. (See 4b-3.)

dangling modifier   A word, phrase, or clause whose referent in a sentence is not clearly apparent. (See 15h.)

dash   A punctuation mark (—) used to set off and give emphasis to brief or lengthy modifiers, appositives, repeating structures, and interruptions in dialogue. (See 29b.)

dead metaphor   A metaphor that has been used so much it has become an ordinary word.

declarative sentence   See *sentence.*

demonstrative pronoun   See *pronoun.*

denotation   The dictionary meaning of a word. (See 21a.)

dependent clause   See *clause.* Also called *subordinate clause.*

descriptive adverb   An adverb used to describe individual words within a sentence. (Poverty *almost* always can be eliminated at a higher cost to the rich.)

determiner   See *article.*

dialect   Expressions specific to certain social or ethnic groups as well as regional groups within a country. (See 21e-2.)

diction   A writer's choice of words. (See Chapter 21.)

dictionary form   See *base form.*

direct discourse   The exact re-creation, using quotation marks, of words spoken or written by a person. Also called *direct quotation.* (See 28a-1.)

direct object   See *object.*

direct quotation   See *direct discourse.*

documentation   The credit given to sources used in a paper, including the author, title of the work, city, name of publisher, and date of publication. There are different systems of documentation for various disciplines; three frequently used systems include the Modern Language Association (MLA), American Psychological Association (APA), and the Council of Biology Editors (CBE) systems of documentation. (See Chapter 37.)

double comparative   An incorrect method of showing the comparative form of an adverb or adjective by adding both the suffix *-er* to the word and placing the word *more* before the adverb or adjective. Only one form should be used. (See 11f.)

double negative   An incorrect method of negation in which two negative modifiers are used in the same sentence. Only one negative should be used. (See 11f.)

double superlative   An incorrect method of showing the superlative form of an adverb or adjective by adding both the suffix -*est* to the word and placing the word *most* before the adverb or adjective. Only one form should be used. (See 11f.)

drafting   The stage in the composition process in which the writer generates the first form of a paper from a working thesis or outline. (See 3e; 36e.)

editing   The stage in the composition process in which the writer examines and, if necessary, alters the work's style, grammar, punctuation, and word choice. (See 4c-1; 36f.)

ellipses   Punctuation marks (. . .) consisting of three spaced periods that indicate the writer has deleted either words or entire sentences from a passage being quoted. (See 29e.)

elliptical clause   See *clause*.

elliptical construction   A shortened sentence in which certain words have been omitted deliberately in order to streamline communication. (See 16g.)

essential modifier   A word, phrase, or clause that provides information crucial for identifying a noun; this type of modifier appears in its sentence without commas. The relative pronoun *that* is used only in essential clauses (*who* or *which* may also be used). Also called a *restrictive modifier*. (See 14e-2; 25d-1.)

etymology   The study of the history of words. (See 22d.)

euphemism   A polite rewording of a term that the writer feels will offend readers.

euphony   The pleasing sound produced by certain word combinations.

evaluation   A judgment of the effectiveness and reliability of a text in which the writer discusses the extent of his or her disagreement with an author.

exclamation point   A punctuation mark (!) used to indicate an emphatic statement or command. (See 24c.)

exclamatory sentence   See *sentence*.

expletive   A word that fills the space left in a sentence that has been rearranged. The words *it* and *there* are expletives (filler words without meaning of their own) when used with the verb *be* in sentences with a delayed subject.

fact   Any statement that can be verified.

faulty parallelism   An error in a sentence where elements that should be grammatically equivalent are not. Faulty parallelism is indicated in a sentence when the use of a coordinating conjunction makes part of the sentence sound out of place or illogical. (See 18a.)

faulty predication   An error in a sentence indicated when the predicate part of a sentence does not logically complete its subject. Faulty predication often involves a form of the linking verb *be*.

figure of speech A carefully controlled comparison that intensifies meaning. See *simile, analogy,* and *metaphor.*

final thesis See *thesis.*

first person See *person.*

formal English The acknowledged standard of correct English. (See 21e.)

formal register The writing of professional and academic worlds. Formal writing is precise and concise, avoids colloquial expressions, is thorough in content, and is highly structured. (See 3a-4.)

freewriting A technique of idea generation in which the writer chooses a broad area of interest and writes for a predetermined amount of time or in a prescribed number of pages, without pausing to organize or analyze thoughts. In *focused freewriting,* the same process is followed, but a specific topic is prescribed. (See 3b-3.)

fused sentence The joining of two independent clauses without a coordinate conjunction or proper punctuation. Also called a *run-on sentence.* (See Chapter 13.)

gender The labeling of nouns or pronouns as masculine, feminine, or neuter.

gerund The *-ing* form of a verb without its helping verbs; gerunds function as nouns.

gerund phrase See *phrase.*

historical present tense The present tense form used when referring to actions in an already existing work (a book, a movie). (See 9e-1.)

homonyms Words that sound alike or are pronounced alike but that have different spellings and meanings. (See 23a-1.)

hyphen A punctuation mark (-) used to join compound words and to divide words at the end of lines.

hypothesis A carefully stated prediction.

idiom A grouping of words, one of which is usually a preposition, whose meaning may or may not be apparent based solely on simple dictionary definitions. The grammar of idioms is often a matter of customary usage and is often difficult to explain. (See 21b-2.)

imperative mood See *mood.*

imperative sentence See *sentence.*

incomplete sentence A sentence that lacks certain important elements—a word, subject, or predicate.

indefinite pronoun See *pronoun.*

independent clause See *clause.*

indicative mood See *mood.*

indirect discourse   The inexact quotation of the spoken or written words of a person. Indirect discourse inserts the writer's voice into the quotation. Also called *indirect quotation*. (See 28a-1.)

indirect object   See *object*.

indirect question   A restatement of a question asked by someone else. An indirect question uses a period as punctuation, not a question mark.

indirect quotation   See *indirect discourse*.

infinitive   The base form of a verb, which is often preceded by the word *to*. Also called the *dictionary form*.

infinitive phrase   See *phrase*.

informal register   The more colloquial, casual writing of personal correspondence and journals. (See 3a-4.)

intensive pronoun   See *pronoun*.

interjection   An emphatic word or phrase. When it stands alone, an interjection is frequently followed by an exclamation point. As part of a sentence, an interjection is usually set off by commas. (See 7a-10.)

interrogative pronoun   See *pronoun*.

interrogative sentence   See *sentence*.

intransitive verb   See *verb*.

irregular verb   A verb that changes its root spelling to show the past tense and form the past participle, as opposed to adding *-d* or *-ed*.

jargon   The in-group language of professionals, who may use acronyms and other linguistic devices to take short-cuts when speaking with colleagues. (See 21e-4.)

limiting modifier   A word that restricts the meaning of another word placed directly after it (*only, almost, just, nearly, even, simply*).

linking verb   See *verb*.

list   A displayed series of items that are logically similar or comparable and are expressed in grammatically parallel form.

logical arrangement   A method of organizing a paper in which the topic is divided into its constituent parts, and the parts are discussed one at a time in an order that will make sense to readers. (See 5d-1.)

main clause   See *clause*.

mapping   A visual method of idea generation. The topic (word or phrase) is circled and from the circle are drawn spokes labeled with the "journalist's questions" (*who, what, where, when, how, why*). The answer to each question is then queried with the journalist's questions again. This method groups and subordinates ideas, thus assisting in generating main ideas and supporting information. (See 3b-7.)

mass noun   See *noun*.

metaphor   A figure of speech that illustrates or intensifies something relatively unknown by comparing it with something familiar. (See 21f-1.)

misplaced modifier   A word, phrase, or clause whose position confuses the meaning of a sentence. A misplaced modifier is not placed next to the word(s) it is meant to modify. (See 15a.)

mixed construction   A confused sentence structure that begins with a certain grammatical pattern and then abruptly changes direction with another grammatical pattern.

mixed metaphor   An illogical comparison of two elements. (See 21f-2.)

modal auxiliary   A verb that is paired with the base form of a verb to express urgency, obligation, likelihood, or possibility (*can, could, may, might, must, ought to, should, would*). (See 9c-1.)

modifier   An adjective or adverb, in the form of a single word, phrase, or clause, that adds descriptive information to a noun or verb. A single-word adjective is often positioned directly before the noun it modifies. Adverbs can be shifted to any part of a sentence. Depending on its location, an adverb will change the meaning or rhythm of a sentence, so care must be taken to ensure that an adverb modifies the word intended. (See 7c.)

mood   The form of a verb that indicates the writer's attitude about an action. The **indicative mood** expresses facts, opinions, or questions. The **imperative mood** expresses commands. The **subjunctive mood** expresses a recommendation, a wish, a requirement, or a statement contrary to fact. (See 9h.)

nonessential modifier   A word, phrase, or clause that provides information that is not essential for defining a word. Commas are used to set the clause apart from the sentence in which it appears. The relative pronouns *who* and *which* may be used in nonessential clauses. Also called *nonrestrictive modifier*. (See 14e-2; 25d-2.)

nonrestrictive modifier   See *nonessential modifier*.

noun   A noun names a person, place, thing, or idea. Nouns change their form to show number; the plural is usually formed by adding -*s* or -*es*. Possession is indicated with the addition of an apostrophe and usually an *s*. **Proper nouns,** which are capitalized, name particular persons, places, or things. **Common nouns** refer to general persons, places, or things. **Mass nouns** denote items that cannot be counted. **Count nouns** denote items that can be counted. **Concrete nouns** name tangible objects. **Abstract nouns** name intangible ideas, emotions, or qualities. **Animate** versus **inanimate nouns** differ according to whether they name something alive. **Collective nouns** are singular in form and have either a singular or plural sense, depending on the meaning of the sentence. (See 7a-2; 10a-5.)

noun clause   See *clause*.

noun phrase   See *phrase*.

number   A change in the form of a noun, pronoun, or verb that indicates whether it is singular or plural. (See 16a.)

object A noun, pronoun, or group of words substituting for a noun that receives the action of a transitive verb (**direct object**); is indirectly affected by the action of a transitive verb (**indirect object**); or follows a preposition (**object of a preposition**). (See 7b.)

object complement See *complement.*

objective case See *case.*

object of a preposition See *object.*

opinion A statement of interpretation and judgment.

outline A logically parallel list with further subdivision and subsections under individual items in the list. (See 18e-2.)

paragraph A group of related sentences organized by a single, controlling idea. (See Chapter 5.)

parallel case An argument that develops a relationship between directly related people, objects, events, or conditions.

parallelism The use of grammatically equivalent words, phrases, and sentences to achieve coherence and balance in writing. (See 5d-2; Chapter 18.)

paraphrase A restatement of a passage of text. The structure of a paraphrase reflects the structure of the source passage. (See 35f-2.)

parentheses Punctuation marks used to enclose and set off nonessential dates, words, phrases, or whole sentences that provide examples, comments, and other supporting information. (See 29c.)

participial phrase See *phrase.*

participle A verb form. The **present participle** (the *-ing* form) functions as a main verb of a sentence and shows continuing action when paired with *be;* functions as an adjective when paired with a noun or pronoun (*the loving parent*); and functions as a noun when used as a gerund (*studying takes time*). (See *gerund.*) The **past participle** (the past tense *-d, -ed, -n,* or *-en* forms) functions as the main verb of a sentence when paired with *have* (*I have studied for days*); forms a passive construction when paired with *be* (*The rock was thrown*); and functions as an adjective when paired with a noun or pronoun (*the contented cow*).

parts of speech The categories into which words are grouped according to their grammatical function in a sentence: nouns, verbs, verbals, adjectives, adverbs, pronouns, prepositions, conjunctions, interjections, and expletives. (See glossary entries for each category and 7a-2–11.)

passive voice See *voice.*

past participle See *participle.*

past tense See *tense.*

period A punctuation mark (.) that denotes a complete stop—the end of a sentence. (See 24a.)

person   The form of a pronoun or a noun that identifies whether the subject of a sentence is the person speaking (the **first person**); the person spoken to (the **second person**); or the person spoken about (the **third person**). (See 16a.)

personal pronoun   See *pronoun.*

phrase   A grouping of words that lacks a subject and predicate and cannot stand alone as a sentence. **Verbal phrases** consist of infinitive phrases, gerund phrases, and participial phrases—all of which are built on verb forms not functioning as verbs in a sentence, along with associated words (objects and modifiers). **Infinitive phrases** consist of the infinitive form, often preceded by *to;* they function as adjectives, adverbs, or nouns. **Gerund phrases** consist of the *-ing* form of a verb and function as nouns—as subjects, objects, or complements. **Participial phrases** consist of the present or past participle of a verb and function as adjectives. **Verb phrases** consist of the combination of an auxiliary and the base form, or present or past participle, of a verb. **Noun phrases** consist of a noun accompanied by all of its modifying words. A noun phrase may be quite lengthy, but it always functions as a single noun—as a subject, object, or complement. **Absolute phrases** consist of a subject and an incomplete predicate; they modify entire sentences, not individual words. **Appositive phrases** rename or further identify nouns and are placed directly beside the nouns they refer to. (See 7d; 12c; 29a-4; 29b-1.) **Prepositional phrases** consist of a preposition combined with a noun (called an *object*), which functions in a sentence as a modifier, such as an adjective or adverb.

plagiarism   A conscious attempt to pass off the ideas or the words of another as one's own. (See 35h.)

plot summary   A brief description of characters and events that provides readers context enough to follow a discussion. Plot summaries are written in the historical present tense.

popular register   The writing typical of most general-interest magazines. The language is more conversational than formal writing, but all conventions of grammar, usage, spelling, and punctuation are adhered to. (See 3a-4.)

positive form   See *adjective forms, adverb forms.*

possession   Nouns and pronouns indicate ownership, possession, or attachment with a change in case form. Nouns indicate possession with the addition of an apostrophe and usually an *s.* (See 7a-2.)

possessive case   See *case.*

predicate   A verb and other words associated with it that state the action undertaken by a subject or the condition in which the subject exists. A **simple predicate** consists of the verb and its auxiliaries. A **complete predicate** consists of the simple predicate and its modifiers and objects. A **compound predicate** consists of two verbs and their associated words which are joined with a coordinating conjunction and share the same subject. (See 7a-1.)

prefix   A group of letters joined to the beginning of a root word to form a new, derived word. Prefixes indicate number, size, status or condition, negation, and relations in time and space. (See 22d-2; 23c.)

preposition   A word (*in, at, of, for, on, by, above, under*) that links a noun, pronoun, or word group substituting for a noun to other words in a sentence—to nouns, pronouns, verbs, or adjectives. (See 7a-8.)

prepositional phrase   See *phrase.*

present participle   See *participle.*

primary source   An original document or artifact that may be referred to in a paper, such as a story, letter, or autobiography.

principal parts   The forms of a verb built from the infinitive, from which the tenses are formed: past tense, present participle, and past participle.

pronoun   A word that takes on the meaning of and substitutes for a noun (referred to as the pronoun's *antecedent*). Pronouns show number (singular or plural) and change case depending on their function in a sentence. **Personal pronouns** (*I, me, you, us, his, hers*) refer to people or things. **Relative pronouns** (*who, which, that*) introduce dependent clauses that usually function as adjectives. The pronouns *who, which,* and *that* rename and refer to the nouns they follow. **Demonstrative pronouns** (*this, that, these, those*) point to the nouns they replace. **Interrogative pronouns** (*who, which, what, whose*) form questions. **Intensive pronouns** (*herself, themselves*) are formed with the suffix *-self* or *-selves* to repeat and emphasize a noun or pronoun. **Reflexive pronouns** (*herself, ourselves*) are formed with the suffix *-self* or *-selves* and rename or reflect back to a preceding noun or pronoun. **Indefinite pronouns** (*one, anybody*) refer to general or nonspecific persons or things. **Reciprocal pronouns** (*one another, each other*) refer to the separate parts of a plural noun. (See 7a-7; Chapter 8; Chapter 14.)

proofreading   The final stage in the composition process in which the writer rereads the final paper to identify and correct misspelled words; words (often prepositions) omitted from sentences; words that have been doubled; punctuation that may have been forgotten; and homonyms. (See 4c-2.)

proper noun   See *noun.*

quotation   See *direct discourse.*

quotation marks   These marks (" ") denote the exact reproduction of words written or spoken by someone else.

reciprocal pronoun   See *pronoun.*

redundant phrase   An expression that repeats a message unnecessarily.

reflexive pronoun   See *pronoun.*

regionalism   An expression whose meaning is specific to certain areas of the country. Use of such expressions is inappropriate in formal writing. (See 21e-2.)

register   The level of language or tone used in a paper. (See *formal register, informal register, popular register.*)

regular verbs   Verbs that change form in predictable ways, taking the suffix *-ed* to show the past tense and the past participle.

relative pronoun   See *pronoun*.

restrictive modifier   See *essential modifier*.

revision   A stage in the composition process in which the writer examines the first draft to clarify the purpose or thesis; rewrites to achieve unity and coherence; and adjusts to achieve balance by expanding, condensing, or cutting material. (See Chapter 4; 36f.)

root word   The base form of a word that contains its core meaning. Suffixes and prefixes are added to a root word to form additional words.

run-on sentence   See *fused sentence*.

-*s* form   The form of a verb that occurs with third-person, singular subjects when an action is in the present. This form (created by adding *-s* or *-es* to a verb) is used with the personal pronoun *he*, *she*, or *it*; with any noun that can be replaced by these pronouns; and with a number of indefinite pronouns (e.g., *something* or *no one*), which are often considered singular.

second person   See *person*.

secondary source   The work of scholars who have interpreted the writings of others.

section   A grouping of paragraphs that constitutes part of the larger document. (See 5a-1.)

section thesis   See *thesis*.

semicolon   A punctuation mark (;) used to denote a partial separation between independent elements. (See Chapter 26.)

sentence   A fully expressed thought consisting of a complete subject and a complete predicate. A sentence begins with a capital letter and ends with a period, question mark, or exclamation point. The four functional types of sentences include declarative, interrogative, exclamatory, and imperative sentences. A **declarative sentence** makes a statement or assertion about a subject. An **interrogative sentence** poses a question and is formed either by inverting a sentence's usual word order or by preceding the sentence with a word such as *who, which, when, where,* or *how*. An **exclamatory sentence** is used as a direct expression of a speaker's or writer's strong emotion. An **imperative sentence** expresses a command. The four structural types of sentences are simple, compound, complex, and compound-complex sentences. A **simple sentence** has a single subject and a single predicate. A **compound sentence** has two subjects and two predicates. A **complex sentence** has an independent clause and one or more dependent clauses. A **compound-complex sentence** has at least two independent clauses and one subordinate, dependent clause.

sentence fragment   A partial sentence punctuated as if it were a complete sentence, with an uppercase letter at its beginning and a period, question mark, or exclamation point at its end. A sentence fragment lacks either a subject or a predicate, and sometimes both. It can also be a dependent clause that has not been joined to an independent clause.

sexism   In writing, the use of inappropriate gender-specific words (*a biologist in his lab*) that creates biased or inaccurate characterizations linked with a male or female reference. (See 21g.)

simile   A figure of speech in which two different things, one usually familiar, the other not, are explicitly compared. The properties of the known thing help to define the unknown thing. Similes often use the words *like* or *as* to set up the comparison. (See 21f-1.)

simple future tense   See *tense*.

simple past tense   See *tense*.

simple predicate   See *predicate*.

simple present tense   See *tense*.

simple sentence   See *sentence*.

simple subject   See *subject*.

slang   The informal language peculiar to a culture or subculture; inappropriate for formal writing.

slash   A punctuation mark (/) used to separate lines of poetry run in with the text of a sentence; to show choice, as in *either/or*; and to note division in fractions or formulas. (See 29f.)

spatial arrangement   A method of organizing a paper in which the subjects are described according to their relative positions; for example, for a photograph, the foreground, middle ground, and background might be described. (See 5d-1.)

split infinitive   The insertion of an adverbial modifier between the two parts of an infinitive—the word *to* and the base form—which can disrupt the intended meaning (*to* successfully *attempt*). (See 15f.)

squinting modifier   A word, phrase, or clause that ambiguously appears to modify two words in a sentence—both the word preceding and following it.

subject   A noun, pronoun, or group of words substituting for a noun, that engages in the main action of a sentence or is described by the sentence. A **simple subject** consists of a single noun or pronoun. A **complete subject** consists of a simple subject and its modifiers. A **compound subject** consists of a multiple subject created by using the coordinating conjunction *and*.

subject complement   See *complement*.

subjective case   See *case*.

subjunctive mood   See *mood*.

subordinate clause   See *clause, dependent clause*.

subordinating conjunction   See *conjunction*.

subordination   A method for linking words, phrases, or clauses that is used to give more emphasis to one idea than to another in a sentence. The words in a dependent (subordinate) clause cannot stand alone as a sentence. (See 19b.)

suffix   A group of letters joined to the end of a root word. Suffixes change the grammatical function of words and can be used to indicate tense.

summary   A brief, objective account of the main ideas of a source passage.

superlative form   See *adjective forms, adverb forms.*

synonym   A word that has approximately the same denotation (dictionary meaning) as another word.

synthesis   A presentation that draws together material from several sources. (See 2d.)

tag question   A brief question attached to a statement, set off by a comma. Tag questions consist of a helping verb, a pronoun, and frequently the word *not* (*He won the match, didn't he?*). (See 25e-5.)

tense   The change in form of a verb that shows when an action has occurred or when a subject exists in a certain state of being. Tenses are marked by verb endings and auxiliary verbs. (See 9e, f; 16b-1.) The **simple present tense** indicates an action taking place at the writer's present time. The verb's base form is used for singular or plural first- and second-person subjects, as well as for plural third-person subjects (*I go, you go, they go*). The verb for a third-person singular subject ends with the suffix *-s* (*she goes*). The **simple past tense** indicates an action completed at a definite time in the past. Regular verbs form this tense by adding *-d* or *-ed* to the base form. The **simple future tense** indicates an action or state of being that will begin in the future. All other tenses build on these basic tenses by using auxiliaries. See Chapter 9 for more information on the present, past, and future perfect tenses; the present, past, and future progressive tenses; and the perfect progressive tenses.

thesis   A general statement about a topic that crystallizes the main purpose of a writing and suggests its main parts. A **section thesis** explicitly announces the point to be addressed in a section and either directly or indirectly suggests what will be discussed relating to this point. (See 5a-2.) A **working thesis** is a statement that should prove to be a reasonably accurate summary of what will be written. A **final thesis** is an accurate, one-sentence summary of a work that will appear in the final draft. (See 3d; 33e; 36a.)

third person   See *person.*

tone   The expression of a writer's attitude toward the subject or audience. Tone is determined by word choice and quality of description, verb selection, sentence structure, and sentence mood and voice. The tone of a piece changes depending on the audience. (See 3a-4; 16c.)

topic   The subject of a piece of writing. (See 3a.)

topical development   The expansion of statements about a topic announced in the opening sentence of a paragraph. After its opening announcement, the topic is divided into two or three parts, each of which is developed at a different location in the paragraph. (See 5e.)

topic sentence   A paragraph's central, controlling idea. (See 5c.)

transition   A word, sentence, or paragraph devoted to building a smooth, logical relationship between ideas in a sentence, between sentences, between paragraphs, or between whole sections of an essay. (Phrases include *for example, on the other hand, in addition.*) (See 4b-2; 5d-3; 20c-1.)

transitive verb   See *verb*.

usage   The prevailing, customary conditions describing how, where, and when a word is normally used in speech and writing. Usage labels in a dictionary, such as *colloquial, slang, archaic,* and *dialect*, indicate special restrictions on the conditions for using a particular meaning or form of a word.

verb   The main word in the predicate of a sentence expressing an action or occurrence or establishing a state of being. Verbs change form to demonstrate tense, number, mood, and voice. **Transitive verbs** (*kick, buy*) transfer the action from an actor—the subject of the sentence—to a direct object—a person, place, or thing receiving that action. **Intransitive verbs** (*laugh, sing, smile*) show action that is limited to the subject; there is no direct object that is acted upon. (*The rock fell.*) The same verb can be transitive in one sentence and intransitive in another. (*She runs a good business. She runs every day.*) **Linking verbs** (*is, feel, appear, seem*) allow the word or words following the verb to complete the meaning of the subject. (*Joan is a lawyer.*) (See 7a-3; Chapter 9.)

verb phrase   See *phrase*.

verbal   A verb form that functions in a sentence as an adjective, an adverb, or a noun. Verbals include infinitives, participles, and gerunds. (See *infinitive, participle, gerund;* 7a-4; 7d-2.)

verbal phrase   See *phrase*.

voice   The form of a transitive verb in a sentence that shows whether emphasis is given to the actor or to the object acted upon. **Active-voice** sentences emphasize the doer of an action. **Passive-voice** sentences emphasize the object acted upon or deemphasize an unknown subject. In passive-voice sentences the words are rearranged so that the object occupies the first position. This construction requires the use of a form of the verb *be* and the preposition *by*. (*The house was designed by Frank Lloyd Wright.*)

working thesis   See *thesis*.

References and Works Cited

Chapter 1: Works Cited

All works cited in this chapter are listed in the "Works Cited" section of the student paper by Lou Cassetta in 4e.

Brunner, Cornelia, and Dorothy Bennett. "Technology Perceptions by Gender." *Education Digest* Feb. 1998.

Hamm, Steve. "Why Women Are So Invisible in Silicon Valley." *Business Week* 25 Aug. 1997.

Munk, Nina, and Suzanne Oliver. "Women of the Valley: Success Stories." *Forbes* 30 Dec. 1996.

Chapter 3: Work Cited

Rubens, Philip, ed. *Scientific and Technical Writing: A Manual of Style.* New York: Henry Holt, 1992. 15–16.

Chapter 5: References

The illustrative paragraphs in this chapter are attributed in the text as they occur; they are drawn from the following sources:

Bergom, Mike. *Technology, Jazz, and History.* Reprinted by permission of the author.

Capraro, Anthony F., III. "The Interview." *Barron's Profiles of American Colleges.* 19th ed. Hauppage, NY: Barron's Educational Services, 1992.

Carson, Rachel. *Silent Spring.* Boston: Houghton, 1962. 39, 105, 136.

Cheever, Daniel S., Jr. "Higher and Higher Ed." *Boston Sunday Globe* 26 April 1992: 73, 75.

Cornish, Roger, and Violet Ketels. Introduction. *Landmarks of Modern British Drama: The Plays of the Sixties.* Vol. 1. New York: Methuen, 1985: vii–xxxv.

Curtis, Helena. *Biology.* 2nd ed. New York: Worth, 1975. 47.

Dennis, Jerry. "Mates for Life." *Wildlife Conservation* May/June 1993: 70–71, 82.

Fagan, Brian M. *Archaeology: A Brief Introduction.* 3rd ed. Glenview: Scott, 1988. 37–38.

Gould, Stephen Jay. "Sex, Drugs, Disasters." *The Winchester Reader.* Ed. Donald McQuade and Robert Atwan. Boston: Bedford, 1991. 816.

"Update on Alzheimer's Disease—Part 1." *Harvard Mental Health Letter* 11.8 (Feb. 1995): 1–2.

Homsy, George. "From Kings to Caddies in Edinburgh—an Offbeat Tour of the City's History." *Boston Sunday Globe* 15 Oct. 1995: B:14 +.

Jones, Rachel L. "What's Wrong with Black English." *Newsweek,* "My Turn," 27 Dec. 1982: 7. Rpt. in *Effective Argument.* Ed. J. Karl Nicholas and James R. Nicholl. Boston: Allyn and Bacon, 1991. 157, 159.

Keller, Helen. *The Story of My Life.* New York: Doubleday, 1954. 35–37.

Kozol, Jonathan. "Distancing the Homeless." *The Winchester Reader.* Ed. Donald McQuade and Robert Atwan. Boston: Bedford, 1991. 175.

Lefton, Lester. "Aging." *Psychology.* 4th ed. Boston: Allyn & Bacon, 1991. 363.

Neuman, Susan B. "A Different Understanding of the Relation Between Media." *Literacy in the Television Age: The Myth of the TV Effect.* Ablex Publishing Corporation, 1991. 194–96.

Pelletier, Michele L. "The Volunteer Army: A Good Idea." Reprinted by permission of the author.

Raymo, Chet. "To Light the Fire of Science, Start with Some Fantasy and Wonder." *Boston Globe* 21 Dec. 1992, Science Musings. 36.

Rybczynski, Witold. "Downsizing Cities." *Atlantic Monthly* Oct. 1995: 36+.

Shaheen, Jack. *In Search of the Arab*. Bowling Green, OH: Bowling Green State UP, 1984. 7.

Sugarman, Josh. "The NRA Is Right." *Washington Monthly* June 1987: 11–15.

Shushan, Ronnie, and Don Wright. *Desktop Publishing by Design*. 3rd ed. Redmond, WA: Microsoft Press, 1994.

Tschopp, Alison. "Advertising to Children Should Not Be Banned." Reprinted by permission of the author.

Van Biema, David. "Crime: Murder on the Sunset Limited." *Time Magazine Online*. America Online. 8 Oct. 1995.

Watts, James, and Allen F. Davis, eds. *Your Family in Modern American History*. 2nd ed. New York: Knopf, 1978. Rpt. in *Writing and Reading Across the Curriculum*. Ed. Laurence Behrens and Leonard Rosen. Boston: Little, Brown, 1982. 136.

Wigginton, Eliot. "Furnaces." *Foxfire 5*. New York: Doubleday, 1979. 77–79.

Winn, Marie. "Television and Addiction." *The Plug-in Drug*. Rev. ed., New York: Viking Penguin, 1977, 1985. 23–25.

Yale Daily News Company. *The Insider's Guide to the Colleges, 1994*. New York: St. Martin's Press, 1994. 8–10.

Chapter 6: Works Cited

Berger, Arthur Asa. "Sex as Symbol in Fashion Advertising." *Media Analysis Techniques* (Vol 10, The Sage COMMTEXT Series), 1982. Rpt. in *Reading Culture*. Ed. Diana George and John Trimbur. New York: HarperCollins, 1992. 257.

Carson, Rachel L. "The Obligation to Endure." *Silent Spring*. Rpt. in *The Shape of this Century*. Ed. Diana Wyllie Rigden and Susan S. Waugh. New York: Harcourt, 1990. 393.

de la Croix, Horst, Richard D. Tansey, and Diane Kirkpatrick. *Gardner's Art through the Ages*. 9th ed. New York: Harcourt, Brace, Jovanovich, 1970.

Healy, Bernardine. "Quotable" column. *The Chronicle of Higher Education* 25 Mar. 1992: B-5.

Jones, Beau Fly, Annemarie Sullivan Palincsar, Donna Sederburg Ogle, and Eileen Glynn Carr. *Strategic Thinking and Learning: Cognitive Instruction in the Content Areas*. Alexandia: ASCD, 1987. 22–23.

McMillan, Victoria. *Writing Papers in the Biological Sciences* New York: St. Martins, 1988. 1–2.

Morais, Richard C. "Saga of Fire and Ice." *Forbes* 23 Oct. 1995: 162+.

Morris, Betsy. "Executive Women Confront Midlife Crisis." *Fortune* 18 Sept. 1995: 60+.

Quindlen, Anna. "A City's Needy." *New York Times* 30 Nov. 1986.

Tuchman, Barbara. "On Our Birthday—America as Idea." *Newsweek* 12 July 1976.

Turbak, Gary. "60 Billion Pounds of Trouble." *American Legion Magazine* Nov. 1989. Rpt. in *Effective Argument*. Ed. J. Karl Nicholas and James R. Nicholl. Boston: Allyn and Bacon, 1991. 135–136.

Weigel, George. "Are Human Rights Still Universal?" *Commentary* 99.2 (Feb. 1995).

West, Cornel. "Why I'm Marching on Washington." *The New York Times Large Type Weekly* 16 Oct. 1995: 20–21.

Chapter 7: References

Sharpe, Lora. "The Right Track." *Boston Sunday Globe*. Special Section "Careers 95" 15 Oct. 1995: 2.

Strauss, Bob. "Rebirth of the Cool." *Boston Sunday Globe*. "Arts Etc." 15 Oct. 1995: 63.

Varma, Devendra P. "The Vampire in Legend, Lore and Literature." *The Vampire in Literature*. Ed. Margaret L. Carter. Ann Arbor: UMI Research Press, 1989. 13–29.

Chapter 8: References

Weinstein, Miriam. "Presenting . . . the Past." *Boston Globe Magazine* 29 Oct. 1995: 26–34.

Chapter 9: References

Carr, Jay. " 'Scarlet' Woman" *Boston Sunday Globe*. "Arts, Etc." 8 Oct. 1995: B:21–22.

Fabricant, Florence. "Cradle of an Empire." *New York Times* 22 Oct. 1995: 5:16 +.

Johnston, David Cay. "Building a Better 401 (k)." *New York Times*. "Money & Business" 22 Oct. 1995: 3:1+.

Pedersen, Laura. " My TV, Your VCR: How to Avoid a House Divided." *New York Times* 22 Oct. 1995. 3:10.

Tschihart-Sanford, Linda, and Mary Ellen Donovan. *Women and Self-Esteem*. New York: Penguin, 1985.

Weisberg, Richard. *When Lawyers Write*. Boston: Little, Brown, 1987. 61–63.

Chapter 10: References

Berman, Kenneth. " So You Think O.J. Got Away with Murder." *Boston Sunday Globe* 8 Oct. 1995: A:32.

Publication Manual of the American Psychological Association. 4th ed. Washington, D.C. American Psychological Association, 1994. 47–48.

Winter, Douglas E. *Stephen King: The Art of Darkness*. New York: Signet, 1986.

Chapter 11: References

Wilks, Brian. *The Brontës*. London: The Hamlyn Publishing Group, 1975.

Chapter 12: References

Hansen, Arlen J. "The Imagination Gap." *Newsweek* 25 Jul. 1977: 9.

Leo, John. " A Good Word for Bad Words." *Time* 14 Dec. 1981: 77.

Mueller, John. " From Two-Step to Goose Step." Rev. of *Keeping Together in Time: Dance and Drill in Human History* by William H. McNeill. *New York Times Book Review* 22 Oct. 1995: 22.

Powers, John. "Bitespeak." *Boston Globe Magazine* 15 July 1990: 17–40.

Saltus, Richard. "Getting Organized." *Boston Globe* "Your Health" Special Section. 15 Oct. 1995: 1+.

Chapter 13: References

Miller, Margo. "At Forest Hills Cemetery, the *Gothic* Aesthetic Prevails." *Boston Globe* 26 Oct. 1995: A:1, 6.

Scarry, Elaine. *Resisting Representation*. New York: Oxford UP, 1994.

Wood, Christopher. *The Pre-Raphaelites*. New York: Viking, 1981.

Chapter 14: References

Carruth, Gordon. *The American Encyclopedia of American Facts and Dates*. 9th ed. New York: HarperCollins, 1993. 417.

Flamsteed, Sam. "Where Giants Come from." *Discover* Nov. 1995: 82+.

Pendick, David. "Tornado Troopers." *Earth* Oct. 1995: 40–49.

Tannen, Deborah. "The Power of Talk." *Harvard Business Review* Sept.–Oct. 1995: 138–48.

Chapter 15: References

Drexler, Madeline. "Record Collecting." *Boston Globe Magazine* 29 Oct. 1995: 8–9.

Greenwald, John. "The Battle to Revive the Unions." *Time* 30 Oct. 1995: 64–66.

Langreth, Robert. "Hypermusic!" *Popular Science* Oct. 1995: 61–64.

Chapter 16: References

Bevington, David. *Medieval Drama*. Boston: Houghton Mifflin Company, 1975.

Bratton, Lorna. "The Great Escape." *Boston Sunday Globe* 29 Oct. 1995: B:15+.

Hardaway, Francine. "Foul Play: Sports Metaphors as Public Doublespeak." *College English* 38.1 (Sept. 1976): 78–82.

Roddy, Joseph. *"Marat/Sade* Stuns Playgoers with Sanity from the Asylum." *Look* 22 Feb. 1966: 107–10.

Chapter 17: References
Auerbach, Jon."The Doctor Is On Line." *Boston Sunday Globe* 5 Nov. 1995: 1+.

Chapter 19: References
Anon. *Creepy Crawlies.* New York: Sterling Publishing Co., 1991.
Bassett, Richard. "Transylvania." *A Guide to Central Europe.* New York: Viking, 1987. 116–25.
Centofanti. M. "Mummified HIV: It's Still Dangerous." *Science News* 28 Oct. 1995: 276.
Luciano, Lani. "Cut College Costs in Half—Or More." *Money* Oct. 1995: 135.
Moers, Ellen. *Literary Women.* New York: Anchor/ Doubleday, 1977. 145–46.
Preston-Matham, Rod and Ken. *Spiders of the World.* New York: Blandford P., Ltd., 1984.
Sagan, Carl. *Cosmos.* New York: Random House, 1980. 39.
Smith, Dennis. "The Triangle Fire: New York, 1911." *Dennis Smith's History of Fire Fighting in America.* New York: Dial Press, 1978. 122–25.
Weier, T. Elliot, Ralph Stocking, and Michael G. Barbour. *Botany: Introduction to Plant Biology.* 5th ed. New York: John Wiley & Sons, 1974.
Zeiller, Warren. "Amazonian and West African Manatees." *Introducing the Manatee.* Gainesville: UP of Florida, 1992. 104–05.
Zweig, Stefan. *Marie Antoinette.* New York: Atrium P, Ltd., 1984. 13.

Chapter 20: References
Burton, Elizabeth. *The Pageant of Early Tudor England.* New York: Charles Scribner's Sons, 1976.
Celoria, Francis. *Archeology.* New York: Grosset & Dunlap, 1973.
Coogan, Tim Pat. *The IRA.* Niwot, CO: Roberts Rinehart, Publisher, 1994. 4.
Larsen, Ronald J. *The Puerto Ricans in America.* Minneapolis: Lerner Publications Co. 1989. 19–22.
Snow, Edward Rowe. *Unsolved Mysteries of Sea and Shore.* New York: Dodd, Mead & Co., 1963. 139–41.
Virch, Claus. *Francisco Goya.* New York: McGraw-Hill. 1967.

Chapter 21: References
Dembner, Alice. "Silber's Number One Job: Reading Skills." *Boston Sunday Globe* 5 Nov. 1995: 33–34.
Group for the Advancement of Psychiatry. *The Educated Woman.* New York: Charles Scribner's Sons, 1975. 103.
Mullin, Walter. "Professor Researches Public TV." *The Daily Pennsylvanian* 26 Oct. 1982.
Nilsen, Alleen Pace, et. al. *Sexism and Language.* Urbana, IL: National Council of Teachers of English, 1977. 172.

Chapter 24: References
Marcus, Geoffrey. *The Maiden Voyage.* New York: Viking Press, 1969. 148–49.
Quittel, Frances. *Fire Power.* Berkeley: Ten Speed Press, 1994. 44–45.

Chapter 25: References
Carnes, Mark C. "Hollywood History." *American Heritage* Sept. 1995: 76–84.
Green, Jonathan. *Greatest Criminals of All Time.* New York: Stein & Day, 1982. 193.
Lagerfeld, Steven. "What Main Street Can Learn from the Mall." *Atlantic Monthly* Nov. 95: 110–20.
de Lange, Nicholas. *Atlas of the Jewish World.* New York: Facts on File. 1984: 107+.
Vogel, Shawna. "Has Global Warming Begun?" *Earth* Dec. 1995: 25–34.

Chapter 26: References

Shreeve, James. "The Brain that Misplaced Its Body." *Discover* May 1995: 82–90.
Ullman, James Ramsey. *Americans on Everest*. Philadelphia: J. Lippincott Co., 1964. 6–7.
Woodward, Kenneth L. "Do We Need Satan?" *Newsweek* 13 Nov. 1995: 63–64.

Chapter 27: References

Woodcock, Joanne. *The Ultimate Windows 95 Book*. Redmond, WA: Microsoft Press, 1995.

Chapter 30: References

American Chemical Society. *The ACS Style Guide: A Manual for Authors and Editors*. Washington, D.C.: ACS, 1986. 11.
Cohen, Hennig, and Tristam P. Coffin, Eds. "Washing the Tombs on All Saints' Day." *The Folklore of American Holidays* 31.3 [Original Source: Wayne State University Folklore Archive, 196.]

Chapter 31: References

Dixon, Pam, and Sylvia Tiersten. *Be Your Own Headhunter Online*. New York: Random House, 1995.
Associated Press. "UK Brewer Bass to Offer Home Delivery Service." *Boston Sunday Globe* 12 Nov. 1995: A:125.

Chapter 34: Works Cited

Bergman, Michael. "Guide to Effective Searching on the Internet." The WebTools Company, P.O. Box 312, Vermillion, SD 57069.
Gresham, Keith. "Surfing with a Purpose." *Educom Review* 33.5 (Sept. 1998): 22–29.
Riddle, Prentice. Webmaster at Rice University.

Chapter 35: Work Cited

Morreal, John. *Taking Laughter Seriously*. Albany: State University of New York, 1983. 106.

Chapter 38: Works Cited

Chopin, Kate. "A Shameful Affair," *The Awakening and Other Stories* Ed. Lewis Leary. Rpt. New York: Harcourt Brace, 1979.
Fichtelberg, Joseph. "The Complex Image: Text and Reader in the *Autobiography* of Benjamin Franklin." *Early American Literature* 23.2 (1988): 206.
Frankel, Charles. "Why the Humanities?" *The Humanist as Citizen*. Ed. John Agresto and Peter Riesenberg. Chapel Hill: N. Carolina UP, 1981.
Franklin, Benjamin. *The Autobiography and Other Writings*. New York: Penguin, 1987.
Ketchem, Ralph. "Benjamin Franklin." *Encyclopedia of Philosophy*. Rpt. 1972 ed.
O'Reilly, Kevin. "Teaching Critical Thinking in High School History." *Social Education* Apr. 1985: 281.
Rieke, Richard D., and Malcolm O. Sillars. *Argumentation and the Decision Making Process*. 2nd ed. Glenview: Scott, 1984.
Stratton, Joanna L. *Pioneer Women*. New York: Touchstone, 1981.
Toulmin, Stephen, Richard Rieke, and Allan Janik. *An Introduction to Reasoning*. New York: Macmillan, 1979.
Trilling, Lionel. "The Greatness of *Huckleberry Finn*." *Adventures of Huckleberry Finn*. By Samuel Langhorn Clemens. Ed. Sculley Bradley, et al. 2nd ed. Norton Critical Edition. New York: Norton, 1977.
Van Doren, Carl. *Benjamin Franklin*. New York: Viking, 1938.
Wittgenstein, Ludwig. *Philosophical Investigations*. 3rd ed. Trans. G.E.M. Anscombe. New York: Macmillan, 1968.

Chapter 39: Works Cited

Braybrooke, David. *Philosophy of Social Science*. Prentice-Hall Foundations of Philosophy Series. Englewood Cliffs: Prentice, 1987.

Bromley, D. B. *The Case-study Method in Psychology and Related Disciplines*. Chichester, Great Britain: John Wiley, 1986.

Otis, Laura P. "Factors Influencing the Willingness to Taste Unusual Foods." *Psychological Reports* 54 (1984): 739–45.

Richlin-Klonsky, Judith, and Ellen Strenski, coordinators and eds. *A Guide to Writing Sociology Papers*. New York: St. Martin's, 1986.

Rieke, Richard D., and Malcolm O. Sillars. *Argumentation and the Decision Making Process*. 2nd ed. Glenview: Scott, 1984.

Rollinson, Paul A. "The Story of Edward: The Everyday Geography of Elderly Single Room Occupancy (SRO) Hotel Tenants." *Journal of Contemporary Ethnography* 19 (1990): 188–206.

Skinner, B. F. "Two Types of Conditioned Reflex and a Pseudo-type." *The Journal of General Psychology* 12 (1935): 66–77. Rpt. in B.F. Skinner, *Cumulative Record: A Selection of Papers*. 3rd ed. New York: Appleton, 1972, 479.

———. "How to Teach Animals." *Scientific American* 185 (1951): 26–29. Rpt. in B.F. Skinner, *Cumulative Record: A Selection of Papers*. 3rd ed. New York: Appleton, 1972, 539.

Solomon, Paul R. *A Student's Guide to Research Report Writing in Psychology*. Glenview: Scott, 1985.

Spencer, Herbert. *The Study of Sociology*. Ann Arbor: U of Michigan P, 1961.

Chapter 40: Works Cited

AIP [American Institute of Physics] Style Manual. 4th ed. New York: AIP, 1990.

American Association for the Advancement of Science. *Project 2061: Science for All Americans*. Washington: AAAS, 1989.

CBE [Council of Biology Editors] Style Manual. 5th ed. Bethesda: CBE, 1983.

Day, Robert. *How to Write and Publish a Scientific Paper*. 3rd ed. Phoenix: Oryx Press, 1988.

Gould, Stephen Jay. *Hen's Teeth and Horse's Toes: Further Reflections on Natural History*. New York: Norton, 1983.

Thuesen, Ingolf, and Jan Engberg. "Recovery and Analysis of Human Genetic Material from Mummified Tissue and Bone." *Journal of Archaeological Science* 17 (1990): 679–89.

Toulmin, Stephen, Richard Rieke, and Allan Janik. *An Introduction to Reasoning*. New York: Macmillan, 1979.

Woodruff, David S., and Stephen Jay Gould, "Fifty Years of Interspecific Hybridization: Genetics and Morphometrics of a Controlled Experiment on the Land Snail *Cerion* in the Florida Keys." *Evolution* 41 (1987): 1026.

Credits:

Index

Adverb(s), 169–170, 239–241, 242–247,
793–794
  adjectives distinguished from, 237
  comparative and superlative forms of,
    244–247, 793
    double comparison, superlatives,
      and negatives and, 245–247, 798
  conjunctive. *See* Conjunctive adverbs
  descriptive, 170, 798
  identifying, 239
  irregular, 244
  modifying adverbs or adjectives with,
    241
  modifying nouns with, 175
  modifying verbs and verbals with, 241
  positioning, 175–176, 240, 766
  positive form of, 793
Adverb clauses, 795–796
  dependent, 179
    subordinating conjunctions to form,
      329–330
  mixed constructions with, 296–297
Adverb forms, 794
Adverbial conjunctions. *See* Conjunctive
  adverbs
adverse, averse, 777
Advice. *See also* Peer editing
  giving, 98
  receiving, 97
advice, advise, 777
affect, effect, 777
afterward. See Conjunctive adverbs
Afterwords, CMS documentation system
  for, 611
aggravate, irritate, 777
Agreement, 793. *See also* Pronoun
  reference; Subject–verb
  agreement
ain't, 777
Aircraft, italics for names of, 462
all. See Indefinite pronouns
all ready, already, 778
all right, 778
all together, altogether, 778
allude, elude, 778
allusion, illusion, 778
-ally, rules for adding, 382
a lot, 778
already, all ready, 778
Alterations, on manuscripts, 775
altogether, all together, 778

The American Heritage Dictionary, 364
American Psychological Association. *See*
  APA in-text citation format; APA
  reference list format
American spellings, 378–379
among, between, 778, 780
amongst, 778
amount, number, 778
an, a, 166, 746, 777
Analogies, 356, 793
  argument from, 152–153
  paragraph development and, 125
Analyses, 793
  in humanities, 628–629
  writing. *See* Critical thinking and
    writing, writing analyses
an, and, 778
and. See also Coordinating conjunctions
  compound antecedents linked by,
    agreement with pronoun,
    231–232
  compound subjects linked by, subject–
    verb agreement and, 225
and, an, 778
and, or, 778
and etc., 778
Animate nouns, 166, 802
Annotated bibliographies, 538–539, 795
Anonymous FTP, 511
Anonymous works, MLA documentation
  format for, 583
Antecedents, 793
  of pronouns, 170, 230–231
    agreement with pronoun. *See*
      Pronoun–antecedent agreement;
      Pronoun reference
    agreement with verb, 229
Anthologies
  APA reference list format for, 603
  CMS documentation system for, 611
  selections from, MLA "Works Cited"
    format for, 586–587
Anthropology, Web resources on, 674
Antithesis. *See* Contrast
Antonyms, 793
anxious, eager, 778
any. See Indefinite pronouns
anybody, any body, 778
any more, anymore, 779
anyone, any one, 778
anyplace, 779

Argumentative theses (claims),
    (continued)
  developing support for, 149–157
    appealing to authority and, 154–155
    appealing to emotion and, 155–157
    appealing to logic and, 150–154
  in humanities, 622–625, 639–641
  in sciences, 679–680
  in social sciences, 655–657
Articles (documents)
  online
    APA reference list format for, 607
    MLA "Works Cited" format for,
      595
  scientific, reading, 682–683
Articles (parts of speech), 166, 746–748,
    793
  definite, 166, 747, 793
  indefinite, 166, 746, 777, 793
Art works
  MLA "Works Cited" list format for,
    592
  visual, italics for titles of, 462
as if, subjunctive mood with, 220
as, like, 779
Assumptions, 793
  distinguishing one's own from
    author's, 20–21
assure, ensure, insure, 779
as, than, 779
as though, subjunctive mood with, 220
as to, 779
Astronomy, Web resources on, 697
Asynchronous communication,
    507–508
at, 779
Attributions
  dashes to set off, 443–444
  to introduce quotations, 544–545
Audiences, 795
  analyzing, 56–58
  defining, 55–56
  diction and, 354
  reconsidering during early revision,
    92
  unspecified, writing for, 55
  visual design of documents and,
    715–716
Author(s)
  assumptions of, distinguishing one's
    own assumptions from, 20–21

citation of. *See* APA in-text citation
    format; APA reference list
    format; CBE "Cited References"
    list; CBE in-text citation format;
    CMS documentation system;
    Documentation; MLA in-text
    citation format; MLA "Works
    Cited" list
  clarifying relationships among, in
    writing syntheses, 47
  definitions of, distinguishing one's
    own definitions from, 21
Authorities
  appeals to, 154–155
  expert opinions in arguments and, 164
  referring readers to, 154–155
  as source of ideas for research papers,
    485
Auxiliary (helping) verbs, 167, 203–205,
    758–759, 795
  modal, 204, 759, 802
  nonstandard, revising, 204
averse, adverse, 777
a while, awhile, 779
Awkward diction, 348–350

bad, badly, 243, 779
Balance, focusing papers through, 94–95
Base form of verbs, 795. *See also*
    Infinitive(s)
be
  limiting use of, 309–310
  principal parts of, 201
  pronouns following, case of, 185,
    186
  subject–verb agreement and, 223
being as, being that, 779
beside, besides, 780
best, had best, 780
better, had better, 780
between, among, 778, 780
Biased language, 357–359
  sexist, 357–538
    correcting, 233–236
Biblical citations, colons in, 440
Bibliographic Index, 493–494
Bibliographies, 795
  abbreviations in, 467
  annotated, 538–539, 795
  of books, 500
  final, 795

as research sources, for research
 papers, 491
trade, 500
working. *See* Working bibliographies
Binding, 772–773
Biology, Web resources on, 698
Block format, for letters, 729
Block quotations, 430–431, 546
 in-text citations documenting,
 580–581
Body, of business letter, 727
Boldfacing
 to emphasize words, 333
 visual design of documents and, 718
Book(s)
 bibliographies of, 500
 citation of. *See* APA in-text citation
 format; APA reference list
 format; CBE "Cited References"
 list; CBE in-text citation format;
 CMS documentation system;
 Documentation; MLA in-text
 citation format; MLA "Works
 Cited" list
 reading scientific textbooks and, 683
 titles of. *See* Title(s) (of works)
Bookmarks, for URLs, 494
Book review(s), in humanities, 629–630
Book Review Digest, 500
Book review indexes, as research
 sources, for research papers,
 493
Boolean logic, for Internet searches,
 523–524
both. See also Indefinite pronouns
 verb agreement with, 227
both/and. See Correlative conjunctions
Boxes, visual design of documents and,
 718
Brackets, 447–448, 795
 to distinguish parentheses within
 parentheses, 448
 to insert words into quoted material,
 447–448
Brainstorming, 795
 to generate ideas and information,
 60–61
Brand name objects, capitalization of,
 458
breath, breathe, 780
bring, take, 780

British spellings, 378–379
Broadcast shows, italics for titles of, 462
broke, 780
Browsing, 510
bunch, 780
burst, bust, 780
Business writing, 725–739
 letters, 726–732
 of application, 730–732
 of complaint, 730
 of inquiry, 728–729
 standard formats for, 726
 standard information in, 726–728
 standard spacing for, 726
 memoranda, 738–739
 process of, 725
 résumés, 732–737
 online, 735–737
bust, burst, 780
but. See Coordinating conjunctions
but however; but yet, 780
but that, but what, 780
but yet, but however, 780
Buzzwords, 795
 eliminating, 304–305

calculate, figure, reckon, 780
can, may, 780
Canadian spellings, 378–379
can't, couldn't, 780
can't hardly, can't scarcely, 780
can't help but, 780
Capitalization, 453–459
 to emphasize words, 333
 of first letter of first word in
 sentences, 453–455
 of first word in every line of poetry,
 456
 of proper nouns, 456–459
 of titles of works, 455
Carriage returns, with computers, 514
Case, 170, 795. *See also* Objective case;
 Possessive case; Pronoun(s), case
 of; Subjective case
Case studies, in social sciences, writing,
 664–665
Categorizing, of ideas and information,
 65–68
Causation, argument from, 150–151
Cause and effect, paragraph
 development and, 125–126

CBE "Cited References" list, 612–613, 614–618
  books in
    by compilers or editors, 616
    by corporate authors, 616
    by individual or multiple authors, 615–616
  dissertations and theses in, 616–617
  electronic sources in, 618
  listing books in, 615–617
  periodicals in, 617–618
    journals, 617
    newspaper and magazine articles, 617–618
CBE in-text citation format, 612, 613–614
  citation-sequence system and, 614
  name-year system and, 613–614
CD-ROMs, 494–495
  APA reference list format for, 606
  MLA "Works Cited" list format for, 597–598
-cede, -ceed, rules for adding, 382
censor, censure, 780
center around, 780
Charts
  MLA "Works Cited" list format for, 593
  visual design of documents and, 722–723
Chemistry, Web resources on, 698
The Chicago Manual of Style. See CMS documentation system
chose, choose, 781
Chronological arrangement, 111–112, 795
Citation format software, 580
Citation indexes, as research sources, for research papers, 492
Citation of sources. *See* APA in-text citation format; APA reference list format; CBE "Cited References" list; CBE in-text citation format; CMS documentation system; Documentation; MLA in-text citation format; MLA "Works Cited" list
Citation-sequence system, of CBE, 614, 615–618

Claims, argumentative. *See* Argumentative theses (claims)
Classification, paragraph development and, 122–123
Clauses, 795–796
  adjective. *See* Adjective clauses
  adverb. *See* Adverb clauses
  combining with phrases, 768–769
  dependent. *See* Dependent (subordinate) clauses
  eliminating wordiness from, 303–304
  elliptical, 796
  functioning as nouns, sentence length and, 341
  functioning as subjects, agreement with verb, 230
  introductory. *See* Introductory clauses
  linking
    with commas and coordinating conjunctions, 262
    with semicolons, 262–263
    with semicolons and conjunctive adverbs, 264
    with subordinating conjunctions or constructions, 264–265
  modifying
    altering sentence rhythm with, 342–344
    with relative pronouns, punctuating, 402
    sentence length and, 340–341
  noun, 796
    dependent, 180
  parallel, 316–317
  positioning, 343–344
  repetition of, for emphasis, 334
  separating subject and verb, agreement and, 224–225
  transitional. *See* Transitions
Clichés, 357, 796
Closing, in business letters, 727
CMS documentation system, 608–612
  for citing books, 610–611
    with corporate authors, 610
    editions subsequent to first, 611
    introductions, prefaces, forewords, and afterwords and, 611
    with multiple authors, 610
    multivolume works, 610
    two sources cited in one note, 611

for citing periodicals, 611
  daily newspapers, 611
  journals with continuous pagination
    through annual volumes, 611
  monthly magazines, 611
  weekly magazines, 611
for computer software, 612
for dissertation abstracts, 611
for first and subsequent references,
  609–610
for government documents, 612
for Internet sources, 612
Coherence, 796
  focusing papers through, 93–94
  of paragraphs, 107, 111–119
    parallelism to enhance, 320–321
  transitions to highlight, 115–118
Collaborative writing, drafting and,
  81–82
Collective nouns, 166, 802
  pronoun–antecedent agreement and,
    233
  subject–verb agreement and, 227
Colloquial language, 353, 796
  quotation marks with, 436
Colons, 438–441, 796
  to announce important statements or
    questions, 438–439
  in Biblical citations, 440
  in bibliographic citations, 440
  capitalization of first word of sentence
    following, 455
  for emphasis, 333
  to introduce lists, 417, 438
  to introduce quotations, 439
  misuse in independent clauses, 438
  quotation marks with, 431
  after salutations in formal letters,
    440
  to separate titles from subtitles or
    subsidiary material, 440
  separating independent clauses with,
    261–262
  to set off appositives, summaries, or
    explanations, 439–440
  in times, 440
Comma(s), 393–412, 796
  common errors with, 396–397
  before coordinating conjunctions to
    join independent clauses,
    396–397, 398

after introductory clauses,
  subordinate, 417
after introductory words or word
  groups, 393–394, 396
to join two sentences, 396
linking clauses with coordinating
  conjunctions and, 262, 265
to mark mild exclamations, 392
to mark omissions of words, 405
in names, titles, dates, numbers, and
  addresses, 406–407
between paired *more/less*
  constructions, 405–406
to prevent misreading, 407–408
with quotation marks, 405, 410–411
quotation marks with, 431
to separate items in series, 397,
  398–399
to set off concluding words or word
  groups, 394–395, 396
to set off expressions of direct address,
  405
to set off nonessential elements, 397,
  400–402
to set off parenthetical or repeating
  elements, 402–404
to set off tag questions, 406
to set off *yes/no* remarks and mild
  exclamations, 406
Commands, mild, periods to mark ends
  of, 387
Comma splices, 408–409, 796
  correcting, 259, 261–266
  identifying, 259, 260, 261
Comments, parentheses to set off, 445
Commercial databases, 505
Common nouns, 166, 802
Company names, singular verbs with,
  230
Comparative forms
  of adjectives, 244–247, 793
    double, 245–246
  of adverbs, 244–247
    double, 245–246
compare to, compare with, 781
Comparisons
  consistent, complete, and clear, 301
  paragraph development and, 123–125
  parallelism for, 319–320
  pronoun case in second part of,
    193–195

Compass points, capitalization of, 457
Complaint, letters of, 730
Complement(s), 796
    object, 796
    subject, 242, 796
        pronouns as, possessive, 188
    of verbs, modifiers splitting verb from, 285–286
complement, compliment, 781
Complete predicates, 804
Complete subjects, 181, 329, 807
Complex sentences, 181, 329, 806
    tense sequence in, 213
compliment, complement, 781
Compound adjectives, 796
    series of, hanging hyphens in, 474–475
Compound antecedents, agreement with pronoun, 231–232
Compound-complex sentences, 181–182, 806
Compound nouns, 459, 796
    hyphens in, 474
Compound predicates, 797, 804
    as sentence fragments, 256
Compound sentences, 181, 806
Compound subjects, 797, 807
    pronoun case in, 189
    subject–verb agreement and, 225–226
Compound verbs, 797
    hyphens in, 474
Compound words, 797. *See also specific types of compound words, i.e.*
    Compound adjectives
    hyphens in, 473–475
    plurals of, rules for, 385
Computers. *See also* Internet; Web *entries*
    carriage returns, linefeeds, and formatting problems with, 514
    cutting versus deleting material and, 558
    drafting on, 55, 79
    note taking on, 31
    online sharing of materials using, 96
    resources available through, 491
    saving earlier versions of paper on, 93
    saving frequently and, 127
Computer software
    APA reference list format for, 606
    citation format software, 580
    CMS documentation system for, 612

dashes using, 443
electronic thesauri, 363
grammar checkers, 238
indenting paragraphs using, 122
MLA "Works Cited" list format for, 592–593, 597
for printing manuscript, 774–775
smart quotes and, 429
spelling checkers, 378
The Concise Oxford Dictionary of Current English, 364
Concluding paragraphs, 129–131
Concluding remarks, emphatic, dashes to set off, 442
Concrete expressions, 797
Concrete nouns, 166, 802
Conjunctions, 172–173, 797. *See also*
    Conjunctive adverbs;
    Coordinating conjunctions;
    Correlative conjunctions;
    Subordinating conjunctions
Conjunctive adverbs, 170, 173
    to emphasize equal ideas, 325–327
    linking clauses with semicolons and, 264, 265, 414–415
    to link phrases and clauses, 768–769
Connotation, 347–348, 797
conscience, conscious, 781
consensus of opinion, 781
Consonants, rules for doubling with suffixes, 382–383
Context, setting issues in, or critical thinking, 7–8
Contextual clues, 372
continual, continuous, 781
Contractions
    apostrophes in, 185, 421, 424–425
        with *be*, 185
    lack of hyphenation of, 477
Contrast. *See also* Comparisons
    paragraph development and, 123–125
    parallelism for, 319–320
Coordinate adjectives, 399, 797
Coordinating conjunctions, 173, 797
    to emphasize equal ideas, 323–325
    linking clauses with commas and, 262, 265, 396–397, 398, 768
    to link phrases, 768
    parallel words, phrases, and clauses with, 312–317

semicolons before, to join
  independent clauses, 416
Coordination, 323–329, 797. *See also*
    Coordinate adjectives;
    Coordinating conjunctions
  to emphasize equal ideas, 323–329
    conjunctive adverbs for, 325–327
    coordinating conjunctions for,
      323–325
    correlative conjunctions for, 325
  illogical or excessive, 327
  sentence length and, 339–340
Corporate abbreviations, 466
Corporate authors
  APA documentation format for, 601,
    603
  CBE documentation format for, 616
  CMS documentation system for, 610
  MLA documentation format for,
    582
Correlative conjunctions, 173, 797
  to emphasize equal ideas, 325
  to link phrases and clauses, 768
  parallelism with, 317–319
Council of Biology Editors. *See* CBE
    "Cited References" list; CBE
    in-text citation format
could, eliminating with subjunctive
    mood, 220–221
couldn't, can't, 780
could of, 781
Count nouns, 166, 744, 802
couple, couple of, 781
criteria, 781
Critical thinking and reading
  challenging and being challenged by
    sources in, 4–5
  forming and supporting opinions in,
    8
  reading to evaluate, 17–25, 637–638
    setting goals for, 17–19
    sources and, 536
    techniques for, 19–25
  reading to respond, 14–17, 631–637
    setting goals for, 15–16
    sources and, 535
    techniques for, 16–17
  reading to synthesize, 25–28
    setting goals for, 25
    sources and, 536
    techniques for, 25–28

reading to understand, 9–14
  setting goals for, 9–12
  sources and, 535
  techniques for, 12–14
  setting issues in broader context and,
    7–8
  similarities and differences in, 1–4,
    6
Critical thinking and writing, 29–49
  cumulative layers of writing and, 29
  forms of writing and, 29
  writing analyses, 42–45
    setting goals for, 42–43
    techniques for, 43–45
  writing evaluations, 34–41
    setting goals for, 34
    techniques for, 34–41
  writing summaries, 30–33
    setting goals for, 30
    techniques for, 30–33
  writing syntheses, 45–49
    setting goals for, 46
    techniques for, 46–49
Cross-referencing
  in reading to synthesize, 26
  in writing syntheses, 47
Cues, 798
  for coherence, 113
Cuts, 798

Dangling modifiers, 288–289, 798
Dashes, 441–444, 798
  computer-generated, 443
  for emphasis, 333
  to express interruption in dialogue,
    443
  to set off attributions following
    epigrams, 443–444
  to set off introductory series from
    summary or explanatory remark,
    443
  to set off nonessential elements,
    441–442
  to set off significant repeating
    structures and emphatic
    concluding elements, 442
data, 781
Databases
  commercial, 505
  online, MLA "Works Cited" format
    for, 596

Dates
    abbreviating, 464
    in business letters, 726
    commas with, 406–407
    parentheses to set off, 445
Days, capitalization of names of, 458
Dead metaphors, 798
Declarative sentences, 181, 806
Deductive arrangement, for arguments,
    158–160
Definite article, 166, 747, 793
Definitions
    distinguishing one's own from
        author's, 21
    of key words in claims, 145
    paragraph development and, 122
    of terms in arguments, 161–162
    of topic, 52
Demonstrative pronouns, 171, 805
Denotation, 347, 798
Dependent (subordinate) clauses,
    179–180, 329, 795
    adjective, 180
    adverb, 179
    converting to independent clauses,
        252
    joining to new sentences, 252–253
    noun, 180
    relative pronouns in
        as objects, 192
        as subjects, 192
    set off as sentences, 252–253
    verb of, agreement with pronoun
        antecedent, 229
Description, paragraph development
    and, 120–121
Descriptive adverbs, 170, 798
Determiners. *See* Articles (parts of
    speech)
Development, of paragraphs, 107,
    120–126
Diagrams, visual design of documents
    and, 723
Dialects, 352, 798
Dialogue
    dashes to express interruptions in, 443
    quotation marks in, 434–435
Diction, 347–360
    abstract and specific language and,
        351
    audience and, 354

awkward, 348–350
biased, dehumanizing language and,
    357–359
denotation and connotation and,
    347–348
euphemistic and pretentious language
    and, 359–360
euphony and, 350
figures of speech and, 355–357
formal English as academic standard
    and, 352–355
general and specific language and, 350
idioms and, 348–349
writing directly and, 349
Dictionaries, 361–367
    abridged, 364–365
    entries in, 362–363
    in humanities, 650
    MLA "Works Cited" format for, 586
    of origins/etymologies, 366
    of regionalisms and foreign terms,
        367
    as research sources for research
        papers, 492
    in sciences, 696
    of slang and idioms, 367
    in social sciences, 673
    of synonyms, 366
    unabridged, 365–366
    of usage, 366
    for vocabulary building, 372
Dictionary form of verbs. *See*
    Infinitive(s)
Differences, searching for and
    questioning, 1–3, 4, 6
different from, different than, 781
differ from, differ with, 781–782
Direct address, commas to set off
    expressions of, 405
Direct discourse, 294–295, 798
    lengthy, display of, 430–431
    short, quotation marks to set off,
        428–429
Direct objects, 174, 803
    verbs taking, 205–206
Disciplines. *See also* Humanities;
    Sciences; Social sciences
    conventions for use of abbreviations
        in, 467–468
    discipline-appropriate vocabularies
        and, 373–374

strategies for writing arguments in, 483

Discourse
  direct, 294–295, 798
    lengthy, display of, 430–431
    short, quotation marks to sct off, 428–429
  indirect, 294–295, 801
  shifts in, 294–295
discreet, discrete, 782
Discussion lists, 507–508
Discussion section, in social sciences, 664
Discussion section of lab reports, in sciences, 686
disinterested, uninterested, 782
Diskettes, MLA "Works Cited" list format for, 597–598
Displayed quotations, 430–431, 546
  in-text citations documenting, 580–581
Dissertations
  abstracts of, CMS documentation system for, 611
  APA reference list format for, 603
  CBE "Cited References" list format for, 616–617
  unpublished, MLA "Works Cited" list format for, 588
Division
  paragraph development and, 122–123
  slashes to indicate, 452
Documentation, 560–561, 575–618, 798.
  See also APA in-text citation format; APA reference list format; CBE "Cited References" list; CBE in-text citation format; CMS documentation system; MLA in-text citation format; MLA "Works Cited" list
  formats for, 575
do/does forming questions with, 758
doesn't, don't, 782
Domain name system, 517
done, 782
don't, doesn't, 782
Double comparatives/superlatives, 245–246, 798
Double negatives, 246–247, 799
Downloading, 510

Drafting, 799. *See also* Writing as a process, drafting
due to, due to the fact that, 782

-e, final, rules for keeping or dropping with suffixes, 380–381
eager, anxious, 778
Economics, Web resources on, 674
Edited books
  APA reference list format for, 603
  CMS documentation system for, 611
  selections from, MLA "Works Cited" format for, 586–587
Editing, 95, 799. *See also* Revision
  peer, 97–98, 560
Editorials
  MLA "Works Cited" format for, 590
  online, MLA "Works Cited" format for, 595–596
Education, Web resources on, 675
effect, affect, 777
either/or. See Correlative conjunctions
Electronic resources, 504–531. *See also*
  Computer *entries*; Internet; Web *entries*
  anonymous FTP and, 511
  asynchronous communication and, 507–508
  discussion lists, 507–508
  e-mail, 505–506
  synchronous communication and, 508–509
  Usenet newsgroups, 506–507
  World Wide Web, 509–511
Electronic sources, 494–495. *See also*
  CD-ROMs; Computers; Internet; Online services; Web *entries*
  citation of. *See* APA in-text citation format; APA reference list format; CBE "Cited References" list; CBE in-text citation format; CMS documentation system; Documentation; MLA in-text citation format; MLA "Works Cited" list
  commercial databases, 505
  documenting. *See* APA reference list format; MLA "Works Cited" list
  page locations for, 583–584
elicit, illicit, 782

Ellipses, 448–451, 799
  to indicate omission of whole
    sentences or parts of sentences,
    450–451
  to indicate omissions at end of
    sentence, 450
  to indicate omissions in middle of
    sentence, 449
  to indicate words omitted from
    middle of sentence, 449
  to show pauses and interruptions,
    451
Elliptical clauses, 796
Elliptical constructions, 299–300, 799
elude, allude, 778
E-mail, 505–506
emigrate, immigrate, migrate, 782
Emotion, appeals to, 155–157
Emphasis
  contrasts for, 334
  coordination for. *See* Coordination
  dashes for, 441–444
  exclamation points for, 391
  inverted word order for, 758
  italics for, 460
  passive constructions for, 218–219
  punctuation, capitalization, and
    highlighting for, 333
  quotation marks for, 435–436
  repetition for, 334
  specialized sentences for, 334–335
  subordination for. *See* Subordination
Encyclopedias
  in humanities, 649–650
  MLA "Works Cited" format for,
    586
  as research sources for research
    papers, 490–491
  in sciences, 696
  in social sciences, 673
End punctuation. *See* Exclamation
    marks; Period(s); Question marks
English language
  American, British, and Canadian
    spellings and, 378–379
  dialects in, 352
  formal, 800
    as academic standard, 352–355
  idioms in. *See* Idioms
  nonstandard. *See* Nonstandard usage,
    revising

  as second language. *See* ESL (English
    as a second language)
  slang in. *See* Slang
enough. See Indefinite pronouns
ensure, insure, assure, 779
Entertainment, writing for, 54–55
enthused, enthusiastic, 782
Envelopes, for business letters, 728
Environmental studies, Web resources
    on, 698
-es ending, rules for adding to plurals,
    384
-es form of verbs, subject–verb
    agreement and. *See* Subject–verb
    agreement
ESL (English as a Second Language),
    743–771
  connecting words and, 768–769
  modifier use and, 764–768, 769–770
  noun use and, 743–749
    articles and, 746–748
    classes of nouns and, 743–746
    prepositions and, 748–749
  verb use and, 750–763
    changing verb forms and, 752–757
    gerunds and infinitives and,
      759–761
    helping (auxiliary) verbs and,
      758–759
    phrasal verbs and, 761–763
    types of verbs and verb
      constructions and, 750–752
    word order and, 757–758
especially, specially, 782
Essay(s)
  unpublished, MLA "Works Cited"
    format for, 588
  writing of, as foundation for research
    writing, 480–481
Essay exams, 740–742
  importance of verbs in questions in,
    741–742
  strategy for taking, 740–741
Essential elements, 400–401
  misuse of commas to set off, 409
Essential modifiers, 276, 799
et al., 782
etc., 782
Etymologies, 367, 799
  dictionaries of, 366
Euphemisms, 359, 799

Fused (run-on) sentences, 258–266, 800
correcting, 259, 261–266
identifying, 259, 260
Future tenses, 210–211, 213, 754–755, 808

Gender, 800
Ms. and, 787
sexist language and, 357–358
renaming indefinite pronouns with gender-appropriate pronouns and, 233–236
Generalization, argument from, 150
General language, 350–351
Generating ideas and information, 58–65
brainstorming for, 60–61
freewriting for, 61–62
journal writing for, 63
"many parts" strategy for, 63–64
mapping for, 64
reading for, 59–60
for research papers, 484–485
instructors and other authorities as sources of, 485
research log for, 484–485
Gerund(s), 168, 177, 200, 800
functioning as nouns, 759–760
possessive nouns or pronouns before, 188
Gerund phrases, 804
as sentence fragments, 254
get, 783
gone, went, 783
good, well, 242–243, 783
good and, 783
got, have, 783
Government publications
APA reference list format for, 605
CMS documentation system for, 612
MLA "Works Cited" list format for, 591
as research sources for research papers, 493
Grammar checkers, 238
Graph(s)
MLA "Works Cited" list format for, 593
visual design of documents and, 722–723

Graphic material, visual design of, 721–723
diagrams and images, 723
elements and their functions and, 721
tables, charts, and graphs, 721–723
Greek words, plurals of, 386
Groups of people, capitalization of names of, 456
Guides to the literature, as research sources, for research papers, 492

had best, best, 780
had better, better, 780
had ought, 784
half, 784
Handbooks, as research sources for research papers, 492
Handwriting manuscripts, 775
hanged, hung, 784
Hanging hyphens, in series of compound adjectives, 474–475
has got to, 783
have
limiting use of, 309–310
in past tense with modal auxiliaries, 204
have, got, 783
have got to, 783
he, she, 784
Headings, visual design of documents and, 719–720
Helping (auxiliary) verbs, 167, 203–205, 758–759, 795
modal, 204, 759, 802
nonstandard, revising, 204
here, as adverb, subject–verb agreement and, 228
her, him, 784
her/him, 784
her, his, 784
her/his, 784
herself, 784
he/she, 784
Highlighting, visual design of documents and, 718
him, her, 784
him/her, 784
himself, 784
his, her, 784
his/her, 784
hisself, 784

many. See Indefinite pronouns

"Many parts" strategy, to generate ideas and information, 63–64

Map(s), MLA "Works Cited" list format for, 593

Mapping, 801–802
to generate ideas and information, 64

Margins
for manuscripts, 773
visual design of documents and, 718

Mass nouns, 166, 744–745, 802

Materials section, of lab reports in sciences, 684, 686

may, can, 780

may be, maybe, 786

may of, 781

media, 787

Memoranda, 738–739

Memorization, of spellings, 377–378

Merriam Webster's Collegiate Dictionary, 365

Metaphors, 356–357, 802
dead, 798
mixed, 356
worn out, 357

Methods section of lab reports
in sciences, 684, 686
in social sciences, 663–664

might of, 781

migrate, emigrate, immigrate, 782

Misplaced modifiers, 278–288, 802
clear reference to words modified and, 278–281
describing two elements simultaneously, 282–283
limiting modifiers and, 281–282
splitting parts of infinitives, 286–287
splitting subject and verb, 280, 284
splitting verb and object or complement, 285–286
splitting verb phrases, 287–288
squinting modifiers and, 282–283

Misreading
commas to prevent, 407–408
hyphenation to avoid, 474, 475

Mixed constructions, 296–297, 802
clear, grammatical relations between sentence parts and, 296–297
consistent relations between subjects and predicates and, 297–298

Mixed metaphors, 356

MLA in-text citation format, 576–577, 578–584
corporate authors and, 582
distinguishing authors with same last name and, 582
documenting block quotations and, 580–581
of electronic sources, 583–584
of literary works, 582–583
of material quoted in sources, 583
multiple authors and, 581
of multivolume works, 582
naming authors in parenthetical references and, 580
naming authors in text and, 580
of two or more sources in single reference, 582
of two or more sources with same authorship, 581

MLA "Works Cited" list, 576–578, 585–593
abstracts of articles in, 591
books in, 585–588
corporate authors, 587
dictionaries and encyclopedias, 586
editions subsequent to first, 588
introductions, prefaces, forewards, and afterwords of, 588
with multiple authors, 586
reprinted or reissued books, 586
selections from edited books or anthologies, 586–587
in series, 588
signaling unknown publication information and, 587–588
with single author, 586
translations, 587
two or more books by same author, 587
electronic sources in, 592–598
CD-ROMs and diskettes, 598
computer software, 592–593
online, 593–598
films or videotapes in, 591–592
government publications in, 591
interviews that have been broadcast, taped, or published in, 592
live performances and lectures in, 592
periodicals in, 588–590
separately issued maps, characters, or graphs in, 593

Paraphrasing, 541, 803
  weaving paraphrases into paragraphs
    and, 546–548
Parentheses, 444–446, 803
  brackets to distinguish parentheses
    within, 448
  to emphasize words, 333
  period with, 388
  punctuation with, 446
  question marks with, to indicate doubt
    about accuracy of information,
    390
  to set off acronyms, 445
  to set off dates, 445
  to set off nonessential information,
    444–445
  to set off numbers or letters marking
    items in series, 445–446
  to set off translations of non-English
    words, 445
Parenthetical elements
  capitalization of, 454
  commas to set off, 402–403
Parenthetical in-text citations, 575. *See
  also* APA in-text citation format;
  CBE in-text citation format;
  CMS documentation system;
  MLA in-text citation format
Participial phrases, 177, 804
  as sentence fragments, 254
Participles, 168, 803. *See also* Past
  participles; Present participles
  verb tense of, 215
Particles, 761
Particular objects, capitalization of,
  458
Parts of speech, 803
party, individual, person, 785
Passive voice, 216–219, 752
  dangling modifiers and, 288–289
  shifts in voice and, 293
Past participles, 168, 803
  of regular verbs, 197
Past subjunctive mood, 219
Past tenses, 168, 198, 210, 212, 808
  of regular verbs, 197
Pauses, ellipses to indicate, 451
Peer editing, 97–98, 560
people, persons, 787
per, 787
percent (per cent), percentage, 788

Perfect tenses, 198, 209, 210, 211, 212,
  213, 753–754
Period(s), 387–389, 803
  in abbreviations, 388
  to mark ends of mild exclamations,
    392
  to mark ends of statements or mild
    commands, 387
  with parentheses, 388
  with quotation marks, 388
  quotation marks with, 431
  separating independent clauses with,
    261–262
Periodical(s)
  citation of. *See* APA in-text citation
    format; APA reference list
    format; CBE "Cited References"
    list; CBE in-text citation system;
    CMS documentation system;
    Documentation; MLA in-text
    citation format; MLA "Works
    Cited" list
  italics for names of, 462
Periodical indexes, 496–498
  in humanities, 650–651
  in sciences, 696–697
  in social sciences, 673–674
Periodic sentences, 335
Person, 290, 804
  agreement in. *See* Subject–verb
    agreement
  shifts in, 290
person, party, individual, 785
Personal pronouns, 170, 183, 185, 805
  lack of apostrophes in, 420–421
persons, people, 787
Persuasive writing, 54
Philosophical studies, claims and
    evidence in, 624–625
Philosophy, Web resources on, 652
Phrasal verbs, 761–763
Phrases, 804
  absolute, 177–178, 804
    as sentence fragments, 255
  adjective, 767
    positioning, 770
  appositive, 804. *See also* Appositive(s)
  attributive, to introduce quotations,
    544–545
  combining with clauses, 768–769
  eliminating wordiness from, 303–304

Preposition(s), 171–172, 805
 adjectives with linking verbs and,
  765–766
 common, 172
 objects of, 748–749, 803
  pronoun case and, 189–190
  relative pronouns as, 192
 in parallel constructions, 300
Prepositional phrases, 171, 176, 749,
  804
 mixed constructions with, 297
 as sentence fragments, 255
Present participles, 168, 803
 functions of, 200
Present subjunctive mood, 219
Present tenses, 208, 212, 800, 808
 to introduce quotations, 545–546
Pretentious language, 359–360
pretty, 788
Previewing, in reading to understand,
  13
Primary sources, 533–535, 625, 805
principal, principle, 788
Principal parts of verbs, 168, 805
 of irregular verbs, 200–203
 of regular verbs, 196–197
Print sources. *See* Library research
proceed, precede, 788
Processes, paragraph development and,
  121–122
Programs. *See* Computer software
Progressive tenses, 209, 210, 211, 212,
  213, 752–753
Pronoun(s), 170–171, 805
 antecedents of, 170
  agreement with pronouns. *See*
   Pronoun–antecedent agreement;
   Pronoun reference
  agreement with verb, 229
 case of, 170, 183–195
  in comparisons, 193–195
  in compound constructions,
   189–190
  errors with, 184–185
  or personal pronouns following *and*,
   185
  for pronouns paired with nouns,
   190–191
  of relative pronouns, 191–193
 for coherence, 113–114
 demonstrative, 171, 805

gender-appropriate, pronoun–
  antecedent agreement and,
  233–236
 indefinite. *See* Indefinite pronouns
 intensive, 171, 805
 interrogative, 171, 805
 as objects, 186
 personal, 170, 183, 185, 805
  lack of apostrophes in, 420–421
 reciprocal, 171, 805
 reflexive, 784, 805
 relative. *See* Relative pronouns
Pronoun–antecedent agreement,
  231–236
 gender-appropriate pronouns and,
  233–236
 in number, 231–233
Pronoun reference, 267–277
 clear reference and, 267–268, 269
 common errors with, 269–270
 with *it*, 274
 keeping pronouns close to antecedents
  and, 268, 269–270, 271
 with relative pronouns, 270, 274–277
 shifts in, 270
 stating antecedents clearly and,
  271–274
Proofreading, 95–96, 805
Proper nouns, 166, 802
 adjectives formed from, 457–458
 capitalization of, 456–459
Psychology, Web resources on, 675–676
Publication information
 dates, for online sources, 593
 unknown, signaling in MLA
  documentation format, 587–588
Punctuation. *See also specific punctuation
  marks*
 to emphasize words, 333
 of manuscripts, 776
Purpose. *See also* Entertainment, writing
  for; Expressive writing; Informative writing; Persuasive writing
 analyzing, 56–58
 identifying, 53–55
 reconsidering during early revision,
  90–91

Qualitative studies, in social sciences
 reading, 660–663
 writing, 664–665

Rebuttals, to arguments, 157–158
Reciprocal pronouns, 171, 805
reckon, calculate, figure, 780
Recursive process, writing as, 51
Redundancy, 805
  eliminating, 305
Reference lists. *See* APA reference list
    format; CBE "Cited References"
    list; MLA "Works Cited" list
Reference materials. *See also*
    Dictionaries; Encyclopedias
  in humanities, 649–652
  in sciences, 695–698
  in social sciences, 672–676
  URLs for. *See* Internet, URLs for
    researching on
Reflexive pronouns, 784, 805
regarding, in regard to, with regard to, 789
regardless, irregardless, 785
Region(s), capitalization of, 457
Regionalisms, 352, 805
  dictionaries of, 367
Register, 57, 805
  formal, 57, 800
  informal, 57, 801
  popular, 57, 804
Regular verbs, 199, 805
  principal parts of, 196–197
Relative pronouns, 170, 805
  beginning modifying clauses
    interrupting or ending sentences,
    402
  case of, 191–193
  to form dependent adjective clauses,
    330–331
  pronoun reference and, 270, 272–273,
    274, 276
Religions
  capitalization of, 456
  Web resources on, 652
Religious titles, capitalization of, 456
Repeating elements
  commas to set off, 403–404
  dashes to set off, 442
  as sentence fragments, 256
Repetition, for coherence, 114
Research, 478–503. *See also* Library
    research; Research papers;
    Sources
  focused, print sources for. *See* Library
    research

interviews for, 501–502, 503
  personal interest in, 478–480
  preliminary, 490–495
    electronic sources for, 494–495
    print sources for, 490–494
  surveys for, 502–503
  systematic approach for, 486–488
    beginning, 486
    ending, 486–488
    refining thinking and, 486
Research papers, 553–574
  determining scope of, 481–482
  documenting sources in. *See*
    Documentation
  essay writing as foundation for
    writing, 480–481
  final thesis for, 559–560
  generating ideas for, 484–485
    instructors and other authorities as
      sources and, 485
    research log for, 484–485
  in humanities, 630
  plagiarism in. *See* Plagiarism
  plan for writing, 554–555
  research questions for
    answering, 489
    key, identifying, 482–483
  revising, 559–560
  sample, 561–574
  in social sciences, writing, 665–666
  strategies for writing arguments in
    different disciplines and, 483
  supporting ideas in, 556
  voice for, 556–557
  working thesis for. *See* Working
    theses, for research papers
  writing drafts of, 557–559
    skeleton, 558–559
    starting in the middle and,
      559
respectfully, respectively, 789
Responding, reading for. *See* Critical
    thinking and reading, reading to
    respond
Restrictive elements, 400–401
  misuse of commas to set off, 409
Results section of lab reports
  in sciences, 686
  in social sciences, 664
Résumés, 733–737
  online, 735–737

incomplete, 299–302, 800
  comparisons and, 301
  elliptical constructions and,
    299–300
interrogative, 181, 806. *See also*
  Question(s)
length of, 337–342
  emphasis and, 335
  tracking, 337, 338
  varying, 337–338, 339–342
marking boundaries between, 258
parts of, 165–174
periodic, 335
predicates of. *See* Predicates (of
  sentences); Verb(s)
punctuation of. *See* Punctuation;
  specific punctuation marks
repeating material, combining, 303
rhythm of, 342–346
  disruption of, 344
  modifying phrases and clauses to
    alter, 342–344
  varying sentence types and, 344–345
simple, 181, 806
subjects of. *See* Subject(s) (of
  sentences)
topic. *See* Topic sentences
Sentence fragments, 248–257, 806
  checking for, 248–252
  dependent clauses set off as sentences
    and, 252–253
  intentional use of, 257
  phrases set off as sentences and,
    253–256
  repeating structures or compound
    predicates set off as sentences
    and, 256–257
Sequence. *See also* Word order
  of arguments, inductive and deductive
    arrangements for, 158–160
  of cumulative modifiers, 769–770
  paragraph development and, 107,
    120–126
  of sentences
    chronological, 111–112, 795
    by importance, 112–113
    logical, 801
    spatial, 111, 807
  of tenses, 211–216, 292, 755
  of verbs and verbals, idiomatic,
    760–761

Series
  commas between items in, 397,
    398–399
  of complete statements or questions,
    capitalization of, 454
  of compound adjectives, hanging
    hyphens in, 474–475
  misuse of commas in, 409–410
  numbers in, parentheses to set off,
    445–446
  semicolons to separate items in,
    416
Series (of books), in MLA "Works
  Cited" list, 588
set, sit, 206, 207, 789
Sexist language, 357–358, 807
  renaming indefinite pronouns with
    gender-appropriate pronouns
    and, 233–236
-s form of verbs, 197, 806
  subject–verb agreement and. *See*
    Subject–verb agreement
shall, will, 789
she, he, 784
she/he, 784
Shifts, 290–296
  consistent use of direct or indirect
    discourse and, 294–296
  in person and number, 290–291
  in tense, mood, and voice,
    291–293
  in tone, 293–294
Ships, italics for names of, 462
should, would, 789
should of, 781
Sign, argument from, 151–152
Similarities, searching for and
  questioning, 1–4
Similes, 355–356, 807
Simple predicates, 165, 804
Simple sentences, 181, 806
Simple subjects, 165, 807
Simple tenses
  future, 808
  past, 210, 212, 808
  present, 208, 212, 808
sit, set, 206, 789
Site maps, for Web sites, 701–703
Slang, 352, 807
  dictionaries of, 367
  quotation marks with, 436

Strong verbs, 307–311
    revising nouns derived from verbs
        and, 310
Style guides
    for humanities, 649
    for sciences, 695 696
    for social sciences, 672–673
Subject(s) (of sentences), 165, 807
    agreement with verbs. *See* Subject–
        verb agreement
    clear, grammatical relations between
        predicates and, 297–298
    commas between verbs and, 410
    complete, 181, 329
    compound, 797, 807
        pronoun case in, 189
        subject–verb agreement and,
            225–226
    modifiers splitting verbs and, 284
    phrase and clauses functioning as,
        agreement with verb, 230
    pronouns as, 183, 186
        possessive, 188
    relative pronouns as, 192
    simple, 165, 807
Subject complements, 242, 796
    pronouns as, possessive, 188
Subject directories, for Internet, 513,
    516–517
Subjective case, 170, 795
    pronouns in, 183, 184, 186
Subject–verb agreement, 222–230
    with collective nouns, 227
    common errors in, 223
    compound subjects and, 223, 225–226
    with indefinite pronouns, 226–227
    with inverted word order, 228–229
    of linking verbs, 228
    with nouns plural in form but singular
        in sense, 227–228
    of phrases and clauses functioning as
        subjects, 230
    phrases or clauses separating subject
        and verb and, 223, 224–225
    revising nonstandard verb and noun
        forms to observe -*s* and -*es*
        endings and, 224
    of titled works, key words used as
        terms, and companies, 230
    "tradeoff" technique and, 224
    of verbs in dependent clauses, 229

Subjunctive mood, 199, 219–221,
    292–293, 802
    past, 219
    present, 219
Subordinate clauses. *See* Dependent
    (subordinate) clauses
Subordinating conjunctions, 173, 797
    to form dependent adverb clauses,
        329–330
    inappropriate and ambiguous use of,
        331
    linking clauses with, 264–265, 769
    linking phrases with, 769
Subordination, 329–333, 807. *See also*
        Dependent (subordinate) clauses;
        Subordinating conjunctions
    to emphasize a main idea, 329–333
        dependent adjective clauses and,
            330–331
        dependent adverb clauses and,
            329–330
        excessive subordination and, 332
        illogical subordination and,
            331–332
        inappropriate and ambiguous use of
            subordinating conjunctions and,
            331
such, 790
such as, like, 786
Suffixes, 370–371, 808
    hyphenation of compound modifiers
        with, 474
    hyphenation of compounds formed
        by, 475
    spelling with, 380–383
Summaries, 808
    colons to set off, 439
    plot, 804
    weaving into paragraphs, 546–548
    writing. *See* Critical thinking and
        writing, writing summaries
Summarizing sources, 540–541
Superlative forms
    of adjectives and adverbs, 244–247
    of adverbs, 793
Superlative forms, of adjectives and
        adverbs, 793
    double, 245–246, 799
supposed to, 790
sure, surely, 790
sure and, sure to, 790

Surveys, for focused research, 502–503
Symbols, apostrophes to mark plurals of, 426
Synchronous communications, 508–509
  MLA "Works Cited" format for, 596
Synonyms, 808
  dictionaries of, 366
  for Internet queries, 520–521
Syntheses, 808
  reading for. *See* Critical thinking and reading; Critical thinking and reading, reading to synthesize
  writing. *See* Critical thinking and writing

Tables, visual design of documents and, 721–722
Tag questions, 808
  commas to set off, 406
take, bring, 780
teach, learn, 786
Technical language, 360
Television programs
  APA reference list format for, 605
  MLA "Works Cited" list format for, 592
Tenses, 208–216, 808
  common errors in use of, 198–199
  in conditional and subjunctive sentences, 756
  expressing wishes or suggestions for hypothetical events and, 756–757
  future, 210–211, 213, 754–755, 808
  past, 168, 198, 210, 212, 808
  perfect, 198, 209, 210, 211, 212, 213, 753–754
  present, 208, 212, 800, 808
    to introduce quotations, 545–546
  progressive, 209, 210, 211, 212, 213, 752–753
  in scientific writing, 680
  sequence of, 211–216, 292, 755
  shifts in, 198–199, 291–292
Textbooks, scientific, reading, 683
than, as, 779
than, then, 790
that. See also Relative pronouns
  dependent clauses introduced by, adjective, 330–331
  pronoun reference and, 270, 272–273, 274, 276

to signal sentence relationships, 299–300
  subjunctive mood with, 221
that, which, 790
that there, 791
the, 166, 747, 793
the fact that, 296
their, there, they're, 791
theirselves, 791
them there, 791
then, than, 790
there, as adverb, subject–verb agreement and, 228
there, they're, their, 791
there is, sentences beginning with, 304
there were, sentences beginning with, 304
Thesauri
  electronic, 363
  for vocabulary building, 373
these here, 791
Theses, 68–77, 106, 808. *See also* Main ideas; Topic(s)
  ambitions for paper and, 70–73
  argumentative. *See* Argumentative theses (claims)
  basing on relationship to be clarified, 70
  final, 68, 808
    for research papers, 559–560
  focusing on subject of, 69–70
  identifying significant parts of, 74
  section, 106, 808
  working. *See* Working theses
Theses (dissertations). *See* Dissertations
they, pronoun reference and, 273
they're, their, there, 791
this, pronoun reference and, 270, 272–273
this here, 791
thusly, 791
'til, till, until, 791
Time(s). *See also* Dates; Tenses
  adapting writing process to, for essay exams, 741
  arranging sentences by, 111–112
  colons in, 440
Title(s) (of people)
  abbreviating, 463–464
  capitalization of, 458
  commas with, 406

848   Index

Verb(s), *(continued)*
  complements of, objects of, modifiers
    splitting verb from, 285–286
  compound, 797
    hyphens in, 474
  in essay questions, importance of,
    741–742
  helping. *See* Auxiliary (helping) verbs
  intransitive, 167, 199, 205–207, 751,
    809
  irregular, 199, 200–203, 801
  linking. *See* Linking verbs
  modifiers splitting from object or
    complement, 285–286
  modifiers splitting subjects and, 284
  mood of. *See* Mood; Subjunctive
    mood
  nonstandard forms of, revising, 200
  objects of. *See* Direct objects;
    Object(s), of verbs; Transitive
    verbs
  phrasal, 761–763
  principal parts of, 168, 805
    of irregular verbs, 200–203
    of regular verbs, 196–197
  regular, 196–197, 199, 806
  strong, 307–311, 805
  tenses of. *See* Tenses
  transitive, 167, 199, 205–207, 750, 809
  voice and. *See* Voice
  word order with, 757–758
Verbal(s), 168–169. *See also* Gerund(s);
    Infinitive(s); Participial phrases;
    Participles; Past participles;
    Present participles
  pronouns as objects of, 187
Verbal phrases, 804
  as sentence fragments, 254
Verb phrases, 203, 804
  modifiers splitting, 287–288
very, 791
Videotapes
  APA reference list format for, 605
  MLA "Works Cited" list format for,
    591–592
Viewpoint. *See* Point of view
Visual art, italics for titles of, 462
Visual design of documents, 715–724
  audiences and, 715–716
  for graphic material, 721–723
    diagrams and images, 723

elements and their functions and,
  721
  tables, charts, and graphs,
    721–723
  newsletters, 723–724
  for text
    boldface, italics, and boxes and,
      718
    headings and, 719–720
    itemized lists and, 720
    margins and, 718
    overall format and heading
      structure and, 718–719
    typeface and, 716–717
    type size and, 717–718
    white space and, 720
Vocabulary building, 367–374
  collecting words for, 373
  contextual clues and dictionaries for,
    372–373
  of discipline-appropriate vocabularies,
    373–374
  prefixes and, 369–370
  root words and, 368–369
  suffixes and, 370–371
  thesaurus for, 373
Voice, 216–219, 752, 809
  active, 216–217, 218–219, 752
    shifts in voice and, 293
    strong verbs and, 307–309
  passive, 216–219, 752
    dangling modifiers and, 288–289
    shifts in voice and, 293
  for research paper, 556–557
  shifts in, 291–292, 293

wait for, wait on, 792
ways, 792
Web documents, 699–714
  content planning, 701
  design and production process and,
    703
  HTML and, 706–709
  hyperlinks and, 709–710
  images in, 710–712
  launching, 713–714
  page design for, 712–713
  site maps for, 701–703
  storyboards and, 703–705
Web pages, 510
  evaluating, 526–528

Working theses, *(continued)*
  refining, 553–554
  for research papers, 489–490
    answering research question and,
      489
    as statement to be proven,
      489–490
"Works Cited" list. *See* MLA "Works
  Cited" list
World Wide Web, 509–511. *See also*
  Web *entries*
would, eliminating with subjunctive
  mood, 220–221
would, should, 789
would of, 781
Writer's block, beating, 78–79
Writing
  business. *See* Business writing
  direct, 349
  of essay exams, 740–742
    importance of verbs in questions
      and, 741–742
    strategy for, 740–741
  of essays, as foundation for research
    writing, 480–481
  in humanities. *See* Humanities;
    Literary works, writing
    about
  personal interest and, 479–480
  of research papers. *See* Research
    papers
  in sciences. *See* Sciences
  in social sciences. *See* Social
    sciences
  for Web. *See* Web documents

Writing as a process
  about poetry, 640
  in business environment, 725
  drafting, 77–86, 799
    beating writer's block and, 78–79
    collaborative writing and, 81–82
    on computer, 55
    computer for, 79
    example of, 82–86
    identifying problems mid-draft and,
      81
    of research papers, 557–559
    sketches and outlines for, 79–80
  freewriting and, 61–62, 800
  overview of, 50
  purpose and. *See* Purpose
  recursive nature of, 51
  revising. *See* Revision
  theses in. *See* Theses; Working theses
  topic and. *See* Topic(s)
  writing single sections and, 80

-y
  final, rules for keeping or dropping
    with suffixes, 381
  rule for plurals of words ending in,
    384
Year(s), apostrophes to mark plurals of,
  426
Yearbooks, as research sources, for
  research papers, 492
yes/no remarks, commas to set off, 406
you, pronoun reference and, 273
your, you're, 792
yourself, 784

REVISION SYMBOLS

The symbols below indicate a need to make revisions in the areas designated. Boldface numbers and letters refer to handbook sections.

ab	abbreviation **31 a–e**	ref	unclear pronoun reference **14**
ad	form of adjective/adverb **7c, 11**	rep	unnecessary repetition **17a**
agr	agreement **10**	sp	spelling error **23**
awk	awkward diction or construction **7b, 15, 21**	shift	inconsistent, shifted construction **16**
ca	case form **8**	sub	sentence subordination **7e–f, 19b**
cap	capitalization **30a–d**	t	verb tense error **9e–f**
coh	coherence **4b, 5d**	trans	transition needed **5a, 5d, 5f**
coord	coordination **7f, 18a, 19a**	var	sentence variety needed **19, 20**
cs	comma splice **13**	vb	verb form error **9, 17b**
d	diction, word choice **21, 22**	w	wordy **17a**
dm	dangling modifier **15h**	ww	wrong word; word choice **10c, 21, 22**
dev	development needed **3, 4, 18d**	//	faulty parallelism **18**
emph	emphasis needed **19, 20**	˄ ? !	end punctuation **24**
frag	sentence fragment **7b, 12**	:	colon **29a**
fs	fused sentence **13**	˅	apostrophe **27**
hyph	hyphen **32**	—	dash **29b**
inc	incomplete construction **7b, 16g–h**	( )	parentheses **29c**
ital	italics **30e–g**	[ ]	brackets **29d**
k	awkward diction or construction **7b, 11g, 15, 21**	. . .	ellipsis **29e**
lc	lowercase letter **30a–d**	/	slash **29f**
log	logic **6, 38a, 39a, 40a**	;	semicolon **26**
mm	misplaced modifier **7d, 15**	" "	quotation marks **28**
ms	manuscript form **36h, Appx. A**	˄	comma **25**
mix	mixed construction **16e–f**	⊂	close up
no ¶	no paragraph needed **5**	˄	insert a missing element
num	number **31f–h**	ℰ	delete
¶	paragraph **5**	⊔⊓	transpose order
¶ dev	paragraph development needed **5**		

SPOTLIGHT ON COMMON ERRORS

I. FORMS OF NOUNS AND PRONOUNS See the SPOTLIGHT (page 184), Chapter 8.

Apostrophes can show possession or contraction. Never use an apostrophe with a possessive pronoun.

Faulty Forms	*Revised*
The scarf is *Chris*. It is *her's.*	The scarf is *Chris's*. It is *hers.*
Give the dog *it's* collar.	Give the dog *its* collar.
Its a difficult thing.	*It's* [it is] a difficult thing.

Choose a pronoun's form depending on its use. For pronouns connected by *and,* or with forms of the verb *be (is/are/was/were),* decide which forms to use *(I/he/she/they* OR *me/him/her/them).*

Faulty Forms	*Revised*
This is *him.* It was *me.* Is that *her?*	This is *he.* It was *I.* Is that *she?*
The ball landed between *she* and *I.*	The ball landed between *her* and *me.*
Her and *me* practice daily.	*She* and *I* practice daily.

II. VERBS See the SPOTLIGHT (page 198), Chapter 9.

Keep verb tenses consistent when describing two closely connected events.

Inconsistent	*Revised*
She *liked* the work. Still, she *keeps* to herself.	She *likes* the work. Still, she *keeps* to herself.

(a) Choose the right verb forms with an *if* clause expressing an unreal or hypothetical condition.
(b) Decide on which of these verb forms to use: *sit* or *set, lie* or *lay, rise* or *raise.*

Faulty Verb Form	*Revised*
(a) If it *would be* any colder, the pipes *would* freeze.	(a) If it *were* any colder, the pipes *would* freeze.
(b) *Lie* the books here. Then *lay* down.	(b) *Lay* the books here. Then *lie* down.

III. AGREEMENT See the SPOTLIGHT (page 223), Chapter 10.

Match subjects with verbs. Make sure both are either singular or plural.

Not in Agreement	*Revised*
The *reason* she wins *are* her friends.	The *reason* she wins *is* her friends.

Match pronouns with the words they refer to. (a) Words joined by *and* require a plural pronoun and verb. (b) For words joined by *or/nor,* match the pronoun and verb to the nearer word.

Not in Agreement	*Revised*
(a) My friends **and** Sue *likes her* pizza hot.	(a) My friends **and** Sue *like their* pizza hot.
(b) Neither her friends **nor** Sue *like their* pizza cold.	(b) Neither her friends **nor** Sue *likes her* pizza cold.

IV. SENTENCE STRUCTURE: FRAGMENTS See SPOTLIGHT (page 249), Chapter 12.

Recognize sentence boundaries. Mark where sentences should end, usually with a period (or sometimes with a semicolon). Avoid a FRAGMENT—a word group that will not stand alone with a full subject and predicate. See the test for fragments in Chapter 12.

Faulty	*Revised*
If our cousins arrive today. [Fragment]	Our cousins may arrive today.

V. SENTENCE STRUCTURE: BOUNDARIES See the SPOTLIGHT (page 259), Chapter 13.

Recognize boundaries. (a) Avoid a FUSED SENTENCE: two sentences with no connecting word or punctuation. (b) Avoid a COMMA SPLICE: two sentences with only a comma between them.

Faulty	*Revised*
(a) He's here now later he'll go to Iowa. [Fused]	He's here now. Later he'll go to Iowa.
(b) He's here now, later he'll go to Iowa. [Splice]	He's here now; later he'll go to Iowa.